Internet & World Wide Web

How to Program

FOURTH EDITION

Deitel® Ser

How To Program Series

Internet & World Wide Web How to Program, 4/E

Java How to Program, 7/E

C++ How to Program, 6/E

C How to Program, 5/E

Visual Basic® 2005 How to Program, 3/E

Visual C#® 2005 How to Program, 2/E

Small Java™ How to Program, 6/E

Small C++ How to Program, 5/E

Advanced Java™ 2 Platform How to Program

XML How to Program

Visual C++® .NET How to Program

Perl How to Program

Python How to Program

Simply Series

Simply C++: An Application-Driven Tutorial Approach

Simply C#: An Application-Driven Tutorial Approach

Simply Java™ Programming: An Application-Driven Tutorial Approach

Simply Visual Basic® 2005, 2/E: An Application-Driven Tutorial Approach

ies Page

SafariX Web Books

www.deitel.com/books/SafariX.html

C++ How to Program, 5/E & 6/E

Java How to Program, 6/E & 7/E

Simply C++: An Application-Driven Tutorial Approach

Simply Visual Basic 2005: An Application-Driven Tutorial Approach, 2/E

Small C++ How to Program, 5/E

Small Java How to Program, 6/E

Visual Basic 2005 How to Program, 3/E

Visual C# 2005 How to Program, 2/E

To follow the Deitel publishing program, please register for the free *Deitel® Buzz Online* e-mail newsletter at:

`www.deitel.com/newsletter/subscribe.html`

To communicate with the authors, send e-mail to:

`deitel@deitel.com`

For information on corporate on-site seminars offered by Deitel & Associates, Inc. worldwide, visit:

`www.deitel.com/training/`

or write to

`deitel@deitel.com`

For continuing updates on Prentice Hall/Deitel publications visit:

```
www.deitel.com
www.prenhall.com/deitel
www.InformIT.com/deitel
```

Check out our Resource Centers for valuable web resources that will help you master C++, other important programming languages, software and Web 2.0 topics:

`www.deitel.com/ResourceCenters.html`

Library of Congress Cataloging-in-Publication Data
On file

Vice President and Editorial Director, ECS: ***Marcia J. Horton***
Associate Editor: ***Carole Snyder***
Supervisor/Editorial Assistant: ***Dolores Mars***
Director of Team-Based Project Management: ***Vince O'Brien***
Senior Managing Editor: ***Scott Disanno***
Managing Editor: ***Robert Engelhardt***
Production Editor: ***Marta Samsel***
A/V Production Editor: ***Greg Dulles***
Art Studio: ***Artworks, York, PA***
Art Director: ***Kristine Carney***
Cover Design: ***Abbey S. Deitel, Harvey M. Deitel, Francesco Santalucia, Kristine Carney***
Interior Design: ***Harvey M. Deitel, Kristine Carney***
Manufacturing Manager: ***Alexis Heydt-Long***
Manufacturing Buyer: ***Lisa McDowell***
Director of Marketing: ***Margaret Waples***

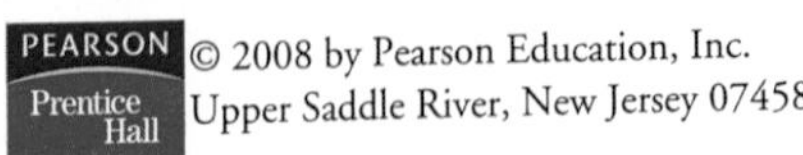

Upper Saddle River, New Jersey 07458

Printed in the United States of America

10 9 8 7 6 5 4 3 2 1

ISBN 0-13-175242-1

Pearson Education Ltd., *London*
Pearson Education Australia Pty. Ltd., *Sydney*
Pearson Education Singapore, Pte. Ltd.
Pearson Education North Asia Ltd., *Hong Kong*
Pearson Education Canada, Inc., *Toronto*
Pearson Educación de Mexico, S.A. de C.V.
Pearson Education–Japan, *Tokyo*
Pearson Education Malaysia, Pte. Ltd.
Pearson Education, Inc., *Upper Saddle River, New Jersey*

Internet & World Wide Web
HOW TO PROGRAM

FOURTH EDITION

P. J. Deitel

Deitel & Associates, Inc.

H. M. Deitel

Deitel & Associates, Inc.

Upper Saddle River, New Jersey 07458

Trademarks

DEITEL, the double-thumbs-up bug and DIVE INTO are registered trademarks of Deitel & Associates, Inc.

Adobe, Dreamweaver, Flex and Flash are either registered trademarks or trademarks of Adobe Systems, Inc.

Apache is a trademark of The Apache Software Foundation.

CSS, DOM, XHTML and XML are registered trademarks of the World Wide Web Consortium.

Del.icio.us and Flickr are trademarks of Yahoo! Inc.

Digg is a trademark of Digg Inc.

Firefox is a registered trademark of the Mozilla Foundation.

Google is a trademark of Google, Inc.

JavaScript, Java and all Java-based marks are trademarks or registered trademarks of Sun Microsystems, Inc. in the United States and other countries.

Microsoft, Internet Explorer, Silverlight and the Windows logo are either registered trademarks or trademarks of Microsoft Corporation in the United States and/or other countries.

MySpace is a registered trademark of MySpace.com.

UNIX is a registered trademark of The Open Group.

Ruby on Rails is a trademark of David Heinemeier Hansson.

MySQL is a registered trademark of MySQL AB.

Second Life is a registered trademark of Linden Research, Inc.

Skype is a trademark of eBay, Inc.

Web 2.0 is a service mark of CMP Media.

Wikipedia is a registered trademark of WikiMedia.

Throughout this book, trademarks are used. Rather than put a trademark symbol in every occurrence of a trademarked name, we state that we are using the names in an editorial fashion only and to the benefit of the trademark owner, with no intention of infringement of the trademark.

To Tim O'Reilly and John Battelle:

For your extraordinary efforts in bringing Web 2.0 to the world through the annual Web 2.0 Summit conference and so much more.

Paul and Harvey Deitel

Deitel Resource Centers

Our Resource Centers focus on the vast amounts of free content available online. Start your search here for resources, downloads, tutorials, documentation, books, e-books, journals, articles, blogs, RSS feeds and more on many of today's hottest programming and technology topics. For the most up-to-date list of our Resource Centers, visit:

`www.deitel.com/ResourceCenters.html`

Let us know what other Resource Centers you'd like to see! Also, please register for the free *Deitel® Buzz Online* e-mail newsletter at:

`www.deitel.com/newsletter/subscribe.html`

Programming
.NET
.NET 3.0
Adobe Flex
Ajax
Apex On-Demand Programming Language
ASP.NET
ASP.NET Ajax
C
C#
C++
C++ Boost Libraries
C++ Game Programming
Code Search Engines and Code Sites
Computer Game Programming
CSS 2.1
Dojo Toolkit
Flash 9
Flex
Java
Java Certification and Assessment Testing
Java Design Patterns
Java EE 5
Java SE 6
JavaFX
JavaScript
JSON
OpenGL
Perl
PHP
Programming Projects
Python
Ruby
Ruby on Rails
Silverlight
Visual Basic
Visual C++
Web Services
Web3D Technologies
XHTML
XML

Software
Apache
DotNetNuke (DNN)
Eclipse
Firefox
Flash CS3 (Flash 9)
Internet Explorer 7
Linux
MySQL
Open Source
Search Engines
Web Servers
Wikis
Windows Vista

Microsoft
.NET
.NET 3.0
ASP.NET
ASP.NET Ajax
C#
DotNetNuke (DNN)
Internet Explorer 7
Silverlight
Visual Basic
Visual C++
Windows Vista

Java
Java
Java Certification and Assessment Testing
Java Design Patterns
Java EE 5
Java SE 6
JavaFX

Web 2.0 and Internet Business
Affiliate Programs
Alert Services
Attention Economy
Blogging
Building Web Communities
Community-Generated Content
Google Adsense
Google Analytics
Google Base
Google Services
Google Video
Google Web Toolkit
Internet Advertising
Internet Business Initiative
Internet Public Relations
Internet Video
Joost
Link Building
Location-Based Services
Mashups
Microformats
Podcasting
Recommender Systems
RSS
Search Engine Optimization
Search Engines
Selling Digital Content
Skype
Social Media
Social Networking
Software as a Service (SaaS)
Virtual Worlds
Web 2.0
Web 3.0
Web Analytics
Website Monetization
Widgets
Wikis

Internet Business
Affiliate Programs
Google Adsense
Google Analytics
Google Services
Internet Advertising
Internet Business Initiative
Internet Public Relations
Link Building
Podcasting
Search Engine Optimization
Sitemaps
Web Analytics
Website Monetization

Open Source
Apache
DotNetNuke (DNN)
Eclipse
Firefox
Linux
MySQL
Open Source
Perl
PHP
Python
Ruby
Ruby on Rails

Other Topics
Computer Games
Computing Jobs
Gadgets and Gizmos
Sudoku

Contents

Preface

Science and technology and the various forms of art,
all unite humanity in a single and interconnected system.
—Zhores Aleksandrovich Medvede

Welcome to Internet and web programming and *Internet & World Wide Web How to Program, Fourth Edition*! At Deitel & Associates, we write programming language textbooks and professional books for Prentice Hall, deliver corporate training worldwide and develop Web 2.0 Internet businesses. The book has been substantially reworked to reflect today's Web 2.0 Rich Internet Application-development methodologies. We have significantly tuned each of the chapters and added new chapters on some of the latest technologies.

New and Updated Features

Here's a list of updates we've made to the fourth edition of *Internet & World Wide Web How to Program*:

- Substantially reworked to reflect today's Web 2.0 Rich Internet Application-development methodologies.
- Coverage of the two leading web browsers—Internet Explorer 7 and Firefox 2. All client-side applications in the book run correctly on both browsers.
- New focus on Web 2.0 technologies and concepts.
- New chapter on Web 2.0 and Internet Business (reviewed by leaders in the Web 2.0 community).
- New focus on building Rich Internet Applications with the interactivity of desktop applications.
- New chapter on building Ajax-enabled web applications, with applications that demonstrate partial-page updates and type-ahead capabilities.
- New chapter on Adobe Flex—a Rich Internet Application framework for creating scalable, cross-platform, multimedia-rich applications for delivery within the enterprise or across the Internet.
- New chapter on Microsoft Silverlight (a competitor to Adobe Flash and Flex)—a cross-browser and cross-platform plug-in for delivering .NET-based Rich Internet Applications that include audio, video and animations over the web.
- New chapter on rapid applications development of database-driven web applications with Ruby on Rails; also, discusses developing Ajax applications with the included Prototype and Script.aculo.us libraries.
- Updated chapter on Adobe Dreamweaver CS3 (Creative Suite 3), including new sections on CSS integration and the Ajax-enabled Spry framework.

- Updated chapters on Adobe Flash CS3, including a chapter on building a computer game.
- Significantly enhanced treatments of XHTML DOM manipulation and JavaScript events.
- Significantly enhanced treatment of XML DOM manipulation with JavaScript.
- New chapter on building SOAP-based web services with Java and REST-based web services with ASP.NET (using Visual Basic).
- Upgraded and enhanced the PHP chapter to PHP 5.
- Updated ASP.NET 1.1 coverage to ASP.NET 2.0, featuring ASP.NET Ajax.
- New JavaServer Faces (JSF) coverage emphasizing building Ajax-enabled JSF applications (replaces Servlets and JavaServer Pages).
- Client-side case studies that enable students to interact with preimplemented server-side applications and web services that we host at `test.deitel.com`.
- Several new and updated case studies including Deitel Cover Viewer (JavaScript/DOM), Address Book (Ajax), Cannon Game (Flash), Weather/Yahoo! Maps Mashup (Flex), Movie Player (Silverlight), Mailing List (PHP/MySQL), Message Forum and Flickr Photo Viewer (Ruby on Rails), Guest Book and Secure Books Database (ASP.NET), Address Book with Google Maps (JavaServer Faces) and Blackjack (JAX-WS web services).
- The Perl 5 and Python chapters from the previous edition of this book are posted in PDF form at `www.deitel.com/books/iw3htp4/`.

All of this has been carefully reviewed by distinguished academics and industry developers.

We believe that this book and its support materials will provide students and professionals with an informative, interesting, challenging and entertaining Internet and web programming educational experience. The book includes a suite of ancillary materials that help instructors maximize their students' learning experience.

If you have questions as you read this book, send an e-mail to `deitel@deitel.com`—we'll respond promptly. For updates on the book and the status of all supporting software, and for the latest news on Deitel publications and services, visit `www.deitel.com`. Sign up at `www.deitel.com/newsletter/subscribe.html` for the free *Deitel® Buzz Online* e-mail newsletter and check out `www.deitel.com/ResourceCenters.html` for our growing list of Internet and web programming, Internet business, Web 2.0 and related Resource Centers. Each week we announce our latest Resource Centers in the newsletter. Please let us know of other Resource Centers you'd like to see.

Dependency Chart

Figure 1 illustrates the dependencies that exist between chapters in the book. An arrow pointing into a chapter indicates that the chapter depends on the content of the chapter from which the arrow points. For example, Chapter 28, Web Services, depends on both Chapters 25 and 27. We recommend that you study all of a given chapter's dependencies before studying that chapter, though other orders are certainly possible. Some of the dependencies apply only to sections of chapters, so we advise readers to browse the material before designing a course of study. We've also commented on some additional dependen-

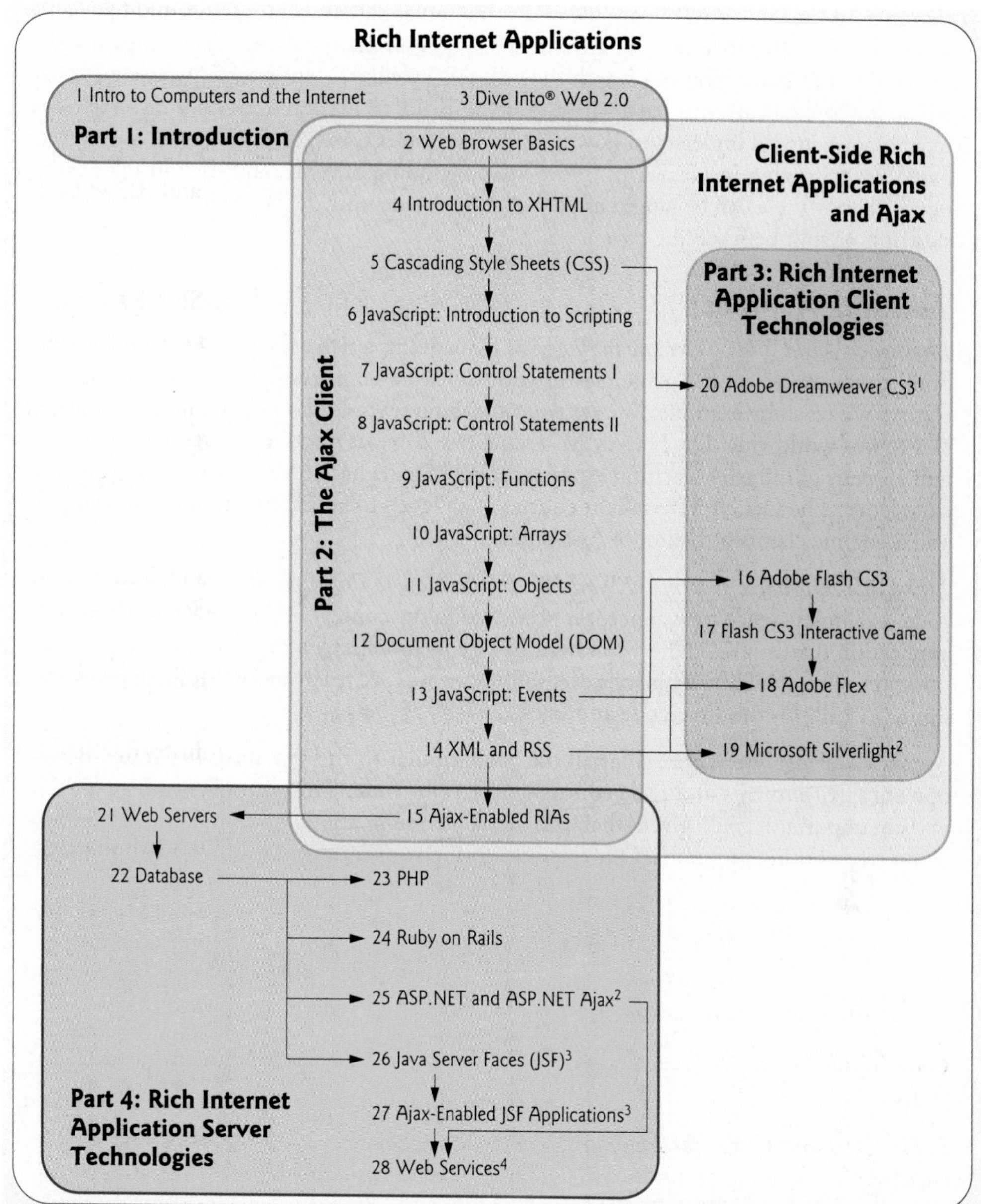

1. Section 20.9 requires a basic understanding of Ajax concepts (Chapter 15). Section 20.8 uses JavaScript events (Chapter 13).
2. Sections 19.8–19.10 and Chapter 25 require knowledge of Visual Basic and .NET.
3. Chapters 26–27 require knowledge of Java Standard Edition 6.
4. Sections 28.2–28.8 require Chapters 26–27. Section 28.9 requires Chapter 25.

Fig. 1 | *Internet & World Wide Web How to Program, 4/e* chapter dependency chart.

cies in the diagram's footnotes. This book is widely used in courses that teach pure client-side web programming, courses that teach pure server-side web programming, and courses that mix and match some client-side and some server-side web programming. Curricula for courses in web programming are still evolving, and many syllabi exist to organize the material in this book. You can search the web for "syllabus," "Internet," "web" and "Deitel" to find syllabi currently used with this book. Readers interested in studying server-side technologies should understand how to build web pages using XHTML, CSS and object-based programming in JavaScript. Note the positioning of XML and Ajax in the dependency chart—these can be taught as part of a client-side unit, at the beginning of a server-side unit or split between the two.

Teaching Approach

Internet & World Wide Web How to Program, 4/e contains a rich collection of examples. The book concentrates on the principles of good software engineering and stresses program clarity. We teach by example. We are educators who teach leading-edge topics in industry classrooms worldwide. Dr. Harvey M. Deitel has 20 years of college teaching experience and 18 years of industry teaching experience. Paul Deitel has 16 years of industry teaching experience. The Deitels have taught courses at all levels to government, industry, military and academic clients of Deitel & Associates.

Live-Code Approach. *Internet & World Wide Web How to Program, 4/e* is loaded with "live-code" examples—each new concept is presented in the context of a complete working web application that is immediately followed by one or more screen captures showing the application's functionality. This style exemplifies the way we teach and write about programming; we call this the "live-code approach."

Syntax Coloring. We syntax color all the code, similar to the way most integrated-development environments and code editors syntax color code. This improves code readability—an important goal, given that this book contains about 18,000 lines of code in complete, working programs. Our syntax-coloring conventions are as follows:

```
comments appear in green
keywords appear in dark blue
PHP, Ruby, ASP.NET and JSP delimiters, and errors appear in red
constants and literal values appear in light blue
all other code appears in black
```

Code Highlighting. We place gray rectangles around the key code segments in each program.

Using Fonts and Colors for Emphasis. We place the key terms and the index's page reference for each defining occurrence in **bold blue** text for easier reference. We emphasize on-screen components in the **bold Helvetica** font (e.g., the **File** menu) and emphasize program text in the `Lucida` font (e.g., `int x = 5`).

Web Access. All of the source-code examples for *Internet & World Wide Web How to Program, 4/e* are available for download from:

```
www.deitel.com/books/iw3htp4/
```

Site registration is quick, easy and free. Download all the examples, then run each program as you read the corresponding text discussions. Making changes to the examples and seeing the effects of those changes is a great way to enhance your Internet and web programming learning experience.

Objectives. Each chapter begins with a statement of objectives. This lets you know what to expect and gives you an opportunity to determine if you have met the objectives after reading the chapter.

Quotations. The learning objectives are followed by quotations. Some are humorous; some are philosophical; others offer interesting insights. We hope that you enjoy relating the quotations to the chapter material.

Outline. The chapter outline helps you approach the material in a top-down fashion, so you can anticipate what is to come and set a comfortable learning pace.

Illustrations/Figures. Abundant charts, tables, line drawings, programs and program output are included.

Programming Tips. We include programming tips to help you focus on important aspects of program development. These tips and practices represent the best we have gleaned from a combined six decades of programming and teaching experience. One of our students—a mathematics major—told us that she feels this approach is like the highlighting of axioms, theorems and corollaries in mathematics books—it provides a basis on which to build good software.

Good Programming Practices

Good Programming Practices *call attention to techniques that will help you produce programs that are clearer, more understandable and more maintainable.*

Common Programming Errors

Students tend to make certain kinds of errors frequently. Pointing out these Common Programming Errors *reduces the likelihood that you'll make the same mistakes.*

Error-Prevention Tips

These tips contain suggestions for exposing bugs and removing them from your programs; many describe aspects of programming that prevent bugs from getting into programs in the first place.

Performance Tips

Students like to "turbo charge" their programs. These tips highlight opportunities for making your programs run faster or minimizing the amount of memory that they occupy.

Portability Tips

We include Portability Tips *to help you write code that will run on a variety of platforms and to explain how to achieve a high degree of portability.*

Software Engineering Observations

The Software Engineering Observations *highlight architectural and design issues that affect the construction of software systems, especially large-scale systems.*

Wrap-Up Section. Each chapter ends with a brief "wrap-up" section that recaps the chapter content and transitions to the next chapter.

Summary Bullets. Each chapter ends with additional pedagogic features. We present a thorough, bulleted-list-style summary of the chapter, section by section.

Terminology. We include an alphabetized list of the important terms defined in each chapter. Each term also appears in the index, with its defining occurrence highlighted with a **bold, blue** page number.

Self-Review Exercises and Answers. Extensive self-review exercises and answers are included for self-study.

Exercises. Each chapter concludes with a substantial set of exercises, including simple recall of important terminology and concepts; writing individual statements; writing complete functions and scripts; and writing major term projects. The large number of exercises enables instructors to tailor their courses to the unique needs of their students and to vary course assignments each semester. Instructors can use these exercises to form homework assignments, short quizzes, major examinations and term projects. See our Programming Projects Resource Center (`www.deitel.com/ProgrammingProjects/`) for many additional exercise and project possibilities.

[*NOTE:* **Please do not write to us requesting access to the Prentice Hall Instructor's Resource Center. Access is limited strictly to college instructors teaching from the book. Instructors may obtain access only through their Pearson representatives.**]

Thousands of Index Entries. We have included an extensive index which is especially useful when you use the book as a reference.

"Double Indexing" of Live-Code Examples. For every source-code program in the book, we index the figure caption both alphabetically and as a subindex item under "Examples." This makes it easier to find examples using particular features.

Bibliography. An extensive bibliography of books, articles and online documentation is included to encourage further reading.

Student Resources Included with *Internet & World Wide Web How to Program, 4/e*

Many Internet and web development tools are available. We wrote *Internet & World Wide Web How to Program, 4/e* using Internet Explorer 7, Firefox 2 and other free-for-download software. Additional resources and software downloads are available in our Internet and Web programming related Resource Centers:

```
www.deitel.com/resourcecenters.html/
```

and at the website for this book:

```
www.deitel.com/books/iw3htp4/
```

Instructor Resources for *Internet & World Wide Web How to Program, 4/e*

Internet & World Wide Web How to Program, 4/e has extensive instructor resources. The Prentice Hall *Instructor's Resource Center* contains the *Solutions Manual* with solutions to the end-of-chapter exercises, a *Test Item File* of multiple-choice questions (approximately two per book section) and PowerPoint® slides containing all the code and figures in the text, plus bulleted items that summarize the key points in the text. Instructors can customize the slides. If you are not already a registered faculty member, contact your Pearson representative or visit `vig.prenhall.com/replocator/`.

Deitel® Buzz Online Free E-mail Newsletter

Each week, the *Deitel® Buzz Online* newsletter announces our latest Resource Center(s) and includes commentary on industry trends and developments, links to free articles and resources from our published books and upcoming publications, product-release schedules, errata, challenges, anecdotes, information on our corporate instructor-led training courses and more. It's also a good way for you to keep posted about issues related to *Internet & World Wide Web How to Program, 4/e*. To subscribe, visit

`www.deitel.com/newsletter/subscribe.html`

The Deitel Online Resource Centers

Our website, `www.deitel.com`, provides Resource Centers on various topics including programming languages, software, Web 2.0, Internet business and open source projects (Fig. 2). The Resource Centers have evolved out of the research we do to support our books and business endeavors. We've found many exceptional resources including tutorials, documentation, software downloads, articles, blogs, podcasts, videos, code samples, books, e-books and more. Most of them are free. In the spirit of Web 2.0, we share these resources with the worldwide community. The Deitel Resource Centers are a starting point for your own research. We help you wade through the vast amount of content on the Internet by providing links to the most valuable resources. Each week we announce our latest Resource Centers in the *Deitel® Buzz Online* (`www.deitel.com/newsletter/subscribe.html`).

Acknowledgments

It is a great pleasure to acknowledge the efforts of many people whose names may not appear on the cover, but whose hard work, cooperation, friendship and understanding were crucial to the production of the book. Many people at Deitel & Associates, Inc. devoted long hours to this project—thanks especially to Abbey Deitel and Barbara Deitel.

We'd also like to thank the participants in our Honors Internship program who contributed to this publication—Andrew Faden, a computer engineering major at Northeastern University; Scott Wehrwein, a computer science major at Middlebury College; Ilana Segall, a mathematical and computational science major at Stanford University; Mark Kagan, a computer science, economics and math major at Brandeis University; Jennifer Fredholm, an English and computer science major at New York University; Jessica Henkel, a psychology major and business minor at Northeastern University; and Kyle Banks, a computer science and business major at Northeastern University.

We are fortunate to have worked on this project with the talented and dedicated team of publishing professionals at Prentice Hall. We appreciate the extraordinary efforts of Marcia Horton, Editorial Director of Prentice Hall's Engineering and Computer Science Division. Carole Snyder and Dolores Mars did a remarkable job recruiting the book's large review team and managing the review process. Francesco Santalucia (an independent artist)

Deitel Resource Centers

Web 2.0 and Internet Business
Affiliate Programs
Alert Services
Attention Economy
Blogging
Building Web Communities
Community-Generated Content
Google Adsense
Google Analytics
Google Base
Google Services
Google Video
Google Web Toolkit
Internet Advertising
Internet Business Initiative
Internet Public Relations
Internet Video
Joost
Link Building
Location-Based Services
Mashups
Microformats
Podcasting
Recommender Systems
RSS
Search Engine Optimization
Selling Digital Content
Sitemaps
Skype
Social Media
Social Networking
Software as a Service (SaaS)
Virtual Worlds
Web 2.0
Web 3.0
Web Analytics
Website Monetization
Widgets

Open Source and LAMP Stack
Apache
DotNetNuke (DNN)
Eclipse
Firefox
Linux
MySQL
Open Source
Perl
PHP
Python
Ruby
Ruby on Rails

Software
Apache
DotNetNuke (DNN)
Eclipse
Firefox
Flash CS3 (Flash 9)
Internet Explorer 7
Linux
MySQL
Open Source
Search Engines
Web Servers
Wikis
Windows Vista

Programming
.NET
.NET 3.0
Adobe Flex
Ajax
Apex On-Demand Programming Language
ASP.NET
ASP.NET Ajax
C
C#
C++
C++ Boost Libraries
C++ Game Programming
Code Search Engines and Code Sites
Computer Game Programming
CSS 2.1
Dojo
Flash 9
Java
Java Certification and Assessment Testing
Java Design Patterns
Java EE 5
Java SE 6
JavaFX
JavaScript
JSON
OpenGL
Perl
PHP
Programming Projects
Python
Ruby
Ruby on Rails
Silverlight
Visual Basic
Visual C++
Web Services
Web 3D Technologies
XHTML
XML

Java
Java
Java Certification and Assessment Testing
Java Design Patterns
Java EE 5
Java SE 6
JavaFX

Microsoft
.NET
.NET 3.0
ASP.NET
ASP.NET Ajax
C#
DotNetNuke (DNN)
Internet Explorer 7
Silverlight
Visual Basic
Visual C++
Windows Vista

Other Topics
Computer Games
Computing Jobs
Gadgets and Gizmos
Sudoku

Fig. 2 | Deitel Resource Centers `www.deitel.com/resourcecenters.html`

and Kristine Carney of Prentice Hall did a wonderful job designing the book's cover; we provided the concept, and they made it happen. Vince O'Brien, Scott Disanno, Bob Engelhardt and Marta Samsel did a marvelous job managing the book's production.

We wish to acknowledge the efforts of our reviewers. Adhering to a tight time schedule, they scrutinized the text and the programs, providing countless suggestions for improving the accuracy and completeness of the presentation.

We sincerely appreciate the efforts of our third edition post-publication reviewers and our fourth edition reviewers:

Internet & World Wide Web How to Program, 4/e Reviewers

Roland Bouman (MySQL AB), Chris Bowen (Microsoft), Peter Brandano (KoolConnect Technologies, Inc.), Matt Chotin (Adobe), Chris Cornutt (PHPDeveloper.org), Phil Costa (Adobe), Umachitra Damodaran (Sun Microsystems), Vadiraj Deshpande (Sun Microsystems), Justin Erenkrantz (The Apache Software Foundation), Christopher Finke (Netscape), Jesse James Garrett (Adaptive Path), Mike Harsh (Microsoft), Kevin Henrikson (Zimbra.com), Tim Heuer (Microsoft), Molly E. Holtzschlag (W3C), Ralph Hooper (University of Alabama, Tuscaloosa), John Hrvatin (Microsoft), Johnvey Hwang (Splunk, Inc.), Joe Kromer (New Perspective and the Pittsburgh Adobe Flash Users Group), Eric Lawrence (Microsoft), Pete LePage (Microsoft), Billy B. L. Lim (Illinois State University), Shobana Mahadevan (Sun Microsystems), Patrick Mineault (Freelance Flash Programmer), Anand Narayanaswamy (Microsoft), Tim O'Reilly (O'Reilly Media, Inc.), John Peterson (Insync and V.I.O., Inc.), Jennifer Powers (University of Albany), Robin Schumacher (MySQL AB), José Antonio González Seco (Parlamento de Andalucia), Dr. George Semeczko (Royal & SunAlliance Insurance Canada), Steven Shaffer (Penn State University), Karen Tegtmeyer (Model Technologies, Inc.), Paul Vencill (MITRE), Raymond Wen (Microsoft), Eric M. Wendelin (Auto-trol Technology Corporation), Raymond F. Wisman (Indiana University) and Daniel Zappala (Brigham Young University).

Internet & World Wide Web How to Program, 3/e Reviewers

Americ Azevedo (University of California at Berkeley), Tim Buntel (Macromedia, Inc.), Sylvia Candelaria de Ram (Cognizor, LLC; HumanMarkup.org), Wesley J. Chun (CyberWeb Consulting), Marita Ellixson (Eglin AFB), Jay Glynn (American General AIG), James Greenwood (Poulternet), Timothy Greer (Middle Tennessee State University), James Huddleston (Independent Consultant), Lynn Kyle (Yahoo!, Inc.), Dan Livingston (Independent Consultant), Oge Marques (Florida Atlantic University), Mark Merkow (American Express Technologies), Dan Moore (Independent Consultant), George Semeczko (Royal & Sun Alliance Insurance Canada), Deborah Shapiro (Cittone Institutes), Matt Smith (Institute of Technology at Blanchardstown), Narayana Rao Surapaneni (Patni Computer Systems Limited), Stephanie Tauber (Tufts University), Yateen Thakkar (Syntel India, Ltd.), Cynthia Waddell (International Center for Disability Resources on the Internet), Loran Walker (Lawrence Technological University) and Alnisa White (ILL Designs).

Well, there you have it! Welcome to the exciting world of Internet and web programming in a Web 2.0 world. We hope you enjoy this look at contemporary computer programming. Good luck! As you read the book, we would sincerely appreciate your comments, criticisms, corrections and suggestions for improving the text. Please address all correspondence to:

```
deitel@deitel.com
```

We'll respond promptly, and post corrections and clarifications at:

```
www.deitel.com/books/iw3htp4/
```

We hope you enjoy reading *Internet & World Wide Web How to Program, Fourth Edition* as much as we enjoyed writing it!

Paul J. Deitel
Dr. Harvey M. Deitel
Maynard, Massachusetts
August 2007

About the Authors

Paul J. Deitel, CEO and Chief Technical Officer of Deitel & Associates, Inc., is a graduate of MIT's Sloan School of Management, where he studied Information Technology. He holds the Java Certified Programmer and Java Certified Developer certifications, and has been designated by Sun Microsystems as a Java Champion. Through Deitel & Associates, Inc., he has delivered Java, C, C++, C# and Visual Basic courses to industry clients, including IBM, Sun Microsystems, Dell, Lucent Technologies, Fidelity, NASA at the Kennedy Space Center, the National Severe Storm Laboratory, White Sands Missile Range, Rogue Wave Software, Boeing, Stratus, Cambridge Technology Partners, Open Environment Corporation, One Wave, Hyperion Software, Adra Systems, Entergy, CableData Systems, Nortel Networks, Puma, iRobot, Invensys and many more. He has also lectured on Java and C++ for the Boston Chapter of the Association for Computing Machinery. He and his father, Dr. Harvey M. Deitel, are the world's best-selling programming language textbook authors.

Dr. Harvey M. Deitel, Chairman and Chief Strategy Officer of Deitel & Associates, Inc., has 45 years of academic and industry experience in the computer field. Dr. Deitel earned B.S. and M.S. degrees from MIT and a Ph.D. from Boston University. He has 20 years of college teaching experience, including earning tenure and serving as the Chairman of the Computer Science Department at Boston College before founding Deitel & Associates, Inc., with his son, Paul J. Deitel. He and Paul are the co-authors of several dozen books and multimedia packages and they are writing many more. With translations published in Japanese, German, Russian, Spanish, Traditional Chinese, Simplified Chinese, Korean, French, Polish, Italian, Portuguese, Greek, Urdu and Turkish, the Deitels' texts have earned international recognition. Dr. Deitel has delivered hundreds of professional seminars to major corporations, academic institutions, government organizations and the military.

About Deitel & Associates, Inc.

Deitel & Associates, Inc., is an internationally recognized corporate training and content-creation organization specializing in computer programming languages, Internet and web software technology, object technology education and Internet business development through its Web 2.0 Internet Business Initiative. The company provides instructor-led courses on major programming languages and platforms, such as C++, Java, Advanced Java, C, C#, Visual C++, Visual Basic, XML, object technology and Internet and web programming. The founders of Deitel & Associates, Inc., are Dr. Harvey M. Deitel and Paul J. Deitel. The company's clients include many of the world's largest companies, government agencies, branches of the military, and academic institutions. Through its 31-year publishing partnership with Prentice Hall, Deitel & Associates, Inc. publishes leading-edge programming textbooks, professional books, interactive multimedia *Cyber Classrooms, Complete Training Courses,* Web-based training courses, online and offline video courses, and e-content for the popular course management systems WebCT, Blackboard and Pearson's CourseCompass. Deitel & Associates, Inc., and the authors can be reached via e-mail at:

```
deitel@deitel.com
```

To learn more about Deitel & Associates, Inc., its publications and its worldwide *Dive Into*® Series Corporate Training curriculum, visit:

```
www.deitel.com
```

and subscribe to the free *Deitel*® *Buzz Online* e-mail newsletter at:

```
www.deitel.com/newsletter/subscribe.html
```

Check out the growing list of online Deitel Resource Centers at:

```
www.deitel.com/resourcecenters.html
```

Individuals wishing to purchase Deitel publications can do so through:

```
www.deitel.com/books/index.html
```

Bulk orders by corporations, the government, the military and academic institutions should be placed directly with Prentice Hall. For more information, visit

```
www.prenhall.com/mischtm/support.html#order
```

Before You Begin

Please follow these instructions to download the book's examples and ensure you have a current web browser before you begin using this book.

Downloading the *Internet & World Wide Web How to Program, 4/e* Source Code

The source code in *Internet & World Wide Web How To Program, 4/e* can be downloaded as a ZIP archive file from `www.deitel.com/books/iw3htp4/`. After you register and log in, click the link for the examples under **Download Code Examples and Other Premium Content for Registered Users**. Extract the example files to your hard disk using a ZIP file extractor program, such as WinZip (`www.winzip.com`). On Windows, we suggest that you extract the files to a folder such as `C:\iw3htp4_examples`. On Mac OS X and Linux, we suggest that you extract the files to a folder named `iw3htp4_examples` in your home folder. [*Note:* If you are working in a computer lab, ask your instructor where you can save the example code.]

Web Browsers Used in This Book

We've tested every example in this book using Mozilla's Firefox 2 and Microsoft's Internet Explorer 7 web browsers. Before you begin, ensure that you have one or both of these browsers installed on your computer. Internet Explorer 7 is available only for Microsoft Windows operating systems. If you are a Windows user and do not have Internet Explorer 7, you can get download it from `www.update.microsoft.com` using Microsoft's Windows Update service. Firefox 2 is available for most platforms. You can download Firefox 2 from `www.firefox.com`.

Many of the book's examples *will not work* in Internet Explorer 6. Though the examples in this book may run on other web browsers, such as Opera (`www.opera.com`) or Apple's Safari (`www.apple.com/safari/`), we have not tested the examples on these or any other browsers.

You are now ready to begin your web programming studies with *Internet & World Wide Web How to Program, 4/e*. We hope you enjoy the book! If you have any questions, please feel free to email us at `deitel@deitel.com`. We'll respond promptly.

1

PART

Introduction

The renaissance of interest in the web that we call Web 2.0 has reached the mainstream.

—Tim O'Reilly

1

Introduction to Computers and the Internet

The renaissance of interest in the web that we call Web 2.0 has reached the mainstream.
—Tim O'Reilly

Billions of queries stream across the servers of these Internet services—the aggregate thoughtstream of humankind, online.
—John Battelle, *The Search*

People are using the web to build things they have not built or written or drawn or communicated anywhere else.
—Tim Berners-Lee

Some people take what we contribute and extend it and contribute it back [to Ruby on Rails]. That's really the basic open source success story.
—David Heinemeier Hansson, interviewed by Chris Karr at www.Chicagoist.com

OBJECTIVES

In this chapter you will learn:

- Basic computing concepts.
- The different types of programming languages.
- The evolution of the Internet and the World Wide Web.
- What Web 2.0 is and why it's having such an impact among Internet-based and traditional businesses.
- What Rich Internet Applications (RIAs) are and the key software technologies used to build RIAs.

Outline

1.1 Introduction

Welcome to Internet and World Wide Web programming and Web 2.0! And welcome to a walkthrough of the Web 2.0 phenomenon from the technical, business and social perspectives. We've worked hard to create what we hope you'll find to be an informative, entertaining and challenging learning experience. As you read this book, you may want to refer to `www.deitel.com` for updates and additional information.

The technologies you'll learn in this book are fun for novices, and simultaneously are appropriate for experienced professionals who build substantial information systems. *Internet & World Wide Web How to Program, Fourth Edition*, is designed to be an effective learning tool for each of these audiences. How can one book appeal to both groups? The answer is that the core of this book emphasizes achieving program clarity through the proven techniques of structured programming, object-based programming and object-oriented programming. Beginners will learn programming the right way from the beginning. Experienced programmers will find "industrial-strength" code examples. We have attempted to write in a clear and straightforward manner using best practices.

Perhaps most important, the book presents hundreds of working examples and shows the outputs produced when these examples are rendered in browsers or run on computers. We present all concepts in the context of complete working programs. We call this the "live-code approach." These examples are available for download from our website, `www.deitel.com/books/iw3htp4/`.

The early chapters introduce computer fundamentals, the Internet and the web. We show how to use software for browsing the web. We present a carefully paced introduction to "client-side" web programming, using the popular JavaScript language and the closely related technologies of XHTML (Extensible HyperText Markup Language), CSS (Cascading Style Sheets) and the DOM (Document Object Model). We often refer to "programming" as scripting—for reasons that will soon become clear. Novices will find that the material in the JavaScript chapters presents a solid foundation for the deeper treatment of scripting in the Adobe Flash, Adobe Flex, Microsoft Silverlight, PHP and Ruby on Rails chapters later in the book. Experienced programmers will read the early chapters quickly and find the treatment of scripting in the later chapters to be rigorous and challenging.

Most people are familiar with the exciting things that computers can do. Using this textbook, you'll learn how to command computers to perform specific tasks. **Software** (i.e., the instructions you write to command the computer to perform **actions** and make **decisions**) controls computers (often referred to as **hardware**). JavaScript and PHP are among today's most popular software development languages for web-based applications.

Computer use is increasing in almost every field of endeavor. In an era of steadily rising costs, computing costs have been decreasing dramatically because of rapid developments in both hardware and software technologies. Computers that filled large rooms and cost millions of dollars just two decades ago can now be inscribed on the surfaces of silicon chips smaller than fingernails, costing perhaps a few dollars each. Silicon is one of the most abundant materials on earth—it is an ingredient in common sand. Silicon-chip technology has made computing so economical that more than a billion general-purpose computers worldwide are now helping people in business, industry, government, education and in their personal lives. And billions more computers are embedded in cell phones, appliances, automobiles, security systems, game systems and so much more.

Through the early 1990s most students in introductory programming courses learned only the methodology called structured programming. As you study the various scripting languages in this book, you'll learn both structured programming and the newer methodology called object-based programming. After this, you'll be well prepared to study today's popular full-scale programming languages such as C++, Java, C# and Visual Basic .NET and to learn the even more powerful programming methodology of object-oriented programming. We believe that object-oriented programming will be the key programming methodology for at least several decades.

Today's users are accustomed to applications with rich graphical user interfaces (GUIs), such as those used on Apple's Mac OS X systems, Microsoft Windows systems, various Linux systems and more. Users want applications that employ the multimedia capabilities of graphics, images, animation, audio and video. They want applications that can run on the Internet and the web and communicate with other applications. Users want to apply database technologies for storing and manipulating their business and personal data. They want applications that are not limited to the desktop or even to some local computer network, but that can integrate Internet and web components, and remote databases. Programmers want to use all these capabilities in a truly portable manner so that applications will run without modification on a variety of **platforms** (i.e., different types of computers running different operating systems).

In this book, we present a number of powerful software technologies that will enable you to build these kinds of systems. Early in the book we concentrate on using technologies such as the Extensible HyperText Markup Language (XHTML), JavaScript, CSS, Flash, Flex, Silverlight, Dreamweaver and Extensible Markup Language (XML) to build the portions of web-based applications that reside on the **client side** (i.e., the portions of applications that typically run in your web browsers such as Mozilla's Firefox 2 or

Microsoft's Internet Explorer 7). Later in the book we concentrate on using technologies such as web servers, databases (integrated collections of data), PHP, Ruby on Rails, ASP.NET, ASP.NET Ajax and JavaServer Faces (JSF) to build the server side of web-based applications. These portions of applications typically run on "heavy-duty" computer systems on which organizations' business-critical websites reside. By mastering the technologies in this book, you'll be able to build substantial web-based, client/server, database-intensive, "multitier" applications. We begin with a discussion of computer hardware and software fundamentals. If you are generally familiar with computers, the Internet and the web, you may want to skip some or all of this chapter.

To keep up to date with Internet and web programming developments, and the latest information on *Internet & World Wide Web How to Program, 4/e*, at Deitel & Associates, please register for our free e-mail newsletter, *the Deitel® Buzz Online,* at

```
www.deitel.com/newsletter/subscribe.html
```

Please check out our growing list of Internet and web programming, and Internet business Resource Centers at

```
www.deitel.com/resourcecenters.html
```

Each week, we announce our latest Resource Centers in the newsletter. Figure 2 in the Preface includes a complete list of Deitel Resource Centers at the time of this writing. The Resource Centers include links to, and descriptions of, key tutorials, demos, free software tools, articles, e-books, white papers, videos, podcasts, blogs, RSS feeds and more that will help you deepen your knowledge of most of the subjects we discuss in this book.

Errata and updates for the book are posted at

```
www.deitel.com/books/iw3htp4/
```

You're embarking on a challenging and rewarding path. As you proceed, if you have any questions, please send e-mail to

```
deitel@deitel.com
```

We'll respond promptly. We hope that you'll enjoy learning with *Internet & World Wide Web How to Program, Fourth Edition.*

Architecture of Internet & World Wide Web How to Program, 4/e

This book focuses on Web 2.0 and Rich Internet Application (RIA) development. Our goal is to develop webtop applications that have the responsiveness, look and feel of traditional desktop applications. In the interim since the previous edition of this book, Deitel has evolved into a development organization, while maintaining its focus on programming languages textbook and professional book authoring, and corporate training. We're building the infrastructure for the Internet businesses we're designing and developing as part of our Web 2.0 Internet Business Initiative. This edition has been enhanced with discussions of many practical issues we've encountered in developing that infrastructure.

Figure 1.1 shows the architecture of *Internet & World Wide Web How to Program, 4/e.* The book is divided into several parts. The first part, Chapters 1–3, provides an introduction to the Internet and the web, web browsers and Web 2.0. These chapters provide a foundation for understanding Web 2.0 and Rich Internet Application development. Chapter 1 introduces hardware, software, communications and Web 2.0 topics. If you are

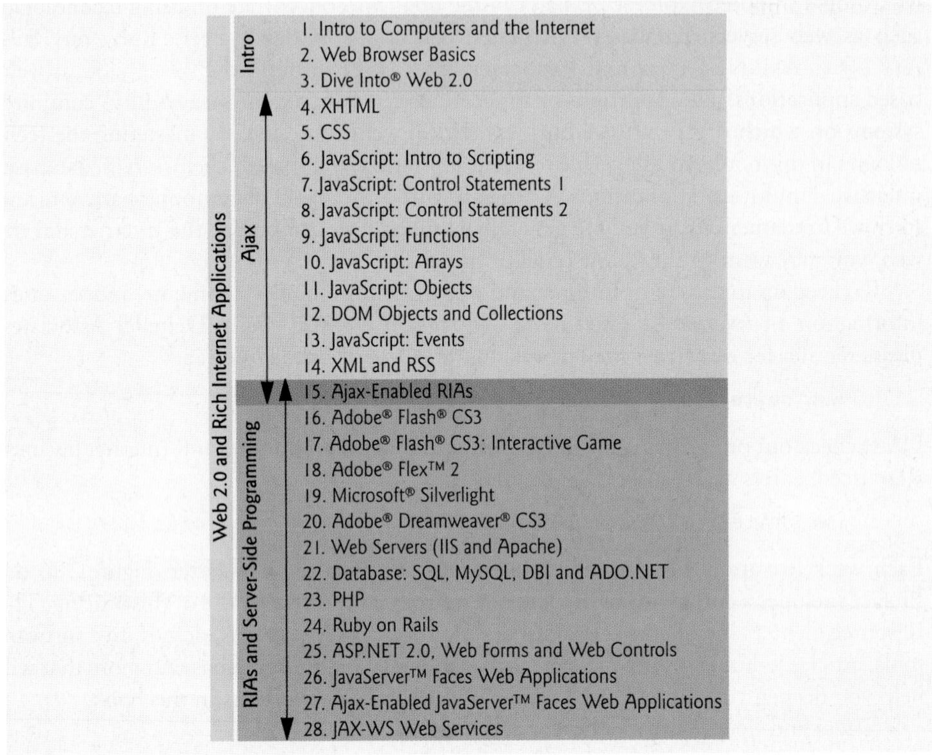

Web 2.0 and Rich Internet Applications
Intro
Ajax
RIAs and Server-Side Programming
1. Intro to Computers and the Internet
2. Web Browser Basics
3. Dive Into® Web 2.0
4. XHTML
5. CSS
6. JavaScript: Intro to Scripting
7. JavaScript: Control Statements 1
8. JavaScript: Control Statements 2
9. JavaScript: Functions
10. JavaScript: Arrays
11. JavaScript: Objects
12. DOM Objects and Collections
13. JavaScript: Events
14. XML and RSS
15. Ajax-Enabled RIAs
16. Adobe® Flash® CS3
17. Adobe® Flash® CS3: Interactive Game
18. Adobe® Flex™ 2
19. Microsoft® Silverlight
20. Adobe® Dreamweaver® CS3
21. Web Servers (IIS and Apache)
22. Database: SQL, MySQL, DBI and ADO.NET
23. PHP
24. Ruby on Rails
25. ASP.NET 2.0, Web Forms and Web Controls
26. JavaServer™ Faces Web Applications
27. Ajax-Enabled JavaServer™ Faces Web Applications
28. JAX-WS Web Services

Fig. 1.1 | Architecture of *Internet & World Wide Web How to Program, 4/e*.

a serious web developer, you'll want to test your web applications across many browsers and platforms. The examples for this book target Microsoft's Internet Explorer 7 (IE7) and Mozilla's Firefox 2 (FF2) browsers, each of which is introduced in Chapter 2. The examples execute correctly in both browsers. Many of the examples will also work in other browsers such as Opera and Safari. Many of the examples will not work on earlier browsers. Microsoft Windows users should upgrade to IE7 and install FF2; readers with other operating systems should install Firefox 2. Web browsers—a crucial component of web applications—are free, as are most of the software technologies we present in this book. Chapter 3 discusses Web 2.0 from technical, business and social perspectives.

The second part of the book, Chapters 4–15, presents a 12-chapter treatment of Ajax component technologies that concludes with Chapter 15's treatment of Ajax development. Ajax is not a new technology—we've been writing about all but one of its component technologies since the first edition of this book in 1999, and many of the technologies existed before that. However, Ajax is one of the key technologies of Web 2.0 and RIAs. Several later chapters in the book demonstrate technologies that encapsulate Ajax functionality to help make it operate across a wide variety of browsers and browser versions.

The third part of the book, Chapters 15–28, focuses on both the client and server sides of the GUI and graphical part of RIA development. Here we cover client-side technologies such as Adobe Flash, Adobe Flex and Microsoft Silverlight that use, or can be combined with, Ajax or Ajax-like capabilities to develop RIAs. Each of these technologies also can consume web services. Next, we present the server side of web application development with discussions of web servers (IIS and Apache), databases, several server-side scripting languages such as PHP and Ruby on Rails, and several server-side frameworks such as ASP.NET 2.0 and JavaServer Faces. We complete our server-side discussion with a chapter on building web services.

You may have noticed that Chapter 15, Ajax-Enabled Rich Internet Applications, overlaps the second and third parts of the book. Chapter 15 serves as a bridge from "raw" Ajax development to sophisticated RIA development.

1.2 What Is a Computer?

A computer is a device that can perform computations and make logical decisions billions of times faster than human beings can. For example, many of today's personal computers can perform several billion additions per second. A person could operate a desk calculator for an entire lifetime and still not complete as many calculations as a powerful personal computer can perform in one second! (Points to ponder: How would you know whether the person added the numbers correctly? How would you know whether the computer added the numbers correctly?) Today's fastest supercomputers can perform trillions of additions per second!

Computers process data under the control of sets of instructions called computer programs. These programs guide the computer through orderly sets of actions specified by people called computer programmers.

A computer consists of various devices referred to as hardware (e.g., the keyboard, screen, mouse, hard disk, memory, DVD drives and processing units). The programs that run on a computer are referred to as software. Hardware costs have been declining dramatically in recent years, to the point that personal computers have become a commodity. In this book, you'll learn proven methods that are reducing software development costs—object-oriented programming and object-oriented design.

1.3 Computer Organization

Regardless of differences in physical appearance, virtually every computer may be envisioned as divided into six logical units or sections:

1. Input unit. This is the "receiving" section of the computer. It obtains information (data and computer programs) from input devices and places this information at the disposal of the other units for processing. Most information is entered into computers through keyboards and mouse devices. Information also can be entered in many other ways, including by speaking to your computer, scanning images, uploading digital photos and videos, and receiving information from a network, such as the Internet.
2. Output unit. This is the "shipping" section of the computer. It takes information that the computer has processed and places it on various output devices to make the information available for use outside the computer. Most information output from computers today is displayed on screens, printed on paper or used to control other devices. Computers also can output their information to networks, such as the Internet.

3. Memory unit. This is the rapid-access, relatively low-capacity "warehouse" section of the computer. It stores computer programs while they are being executed. It retains information that has been entered through the input unit, so that it will be immediately available for processing when needed. The memory unit also retains processed information until it can be placed on output devices by the output unit. Information in the memory unit is typically lost when the computer's power is turned off. The memory unit is often called either memory or primary memory.
4. Arithmetic and logic unit (ALU). This is the "manufacturing" section of the computer. It is responsible for performing calculations, such as addition, subtraction, multiplication and division. It contains the decision mechanisms that allow the computer, for example, to compare two items from the memory unit to determine whether they are equal, or if one is larger than the other.
5. Central processing unit (CPU). This is the computer's "administrative" section. It coordinates and supervises the other sections' operations. The CPU tells the input unit when information should be read into the memory unit, tells the ALU when information from the memory unit should be used in calculations and tells the output unit when to send information from the memory unit to certain output devices. Many of today's computers have multiple CPUs and, hence, can perform many operations simultaneously—such computers are called multiprocessors.
6. Secondary storage unit. This is the computer's long-term, high-capacity "warehousing" section. Programs or data not actively being used by the other units normally are placed on secondary storage devices, such as your hard drive, until they are needed, possibly hours, days, months or even years later. Information in secondary storage takes much longer to access than information in primary memory, but the cost per unit of secondary storage is much less than that of primary memory. Other secondary storage devices include CDs and DVDs, which can hold hundreds of millions and billions of characters, respectively.

1.4 Machine Languages, Assembly Languages and High-Level Languages

Programmers write instructions in various programming languages, some directly understandable by computers and others requiring intermediate translation steps. Hundreds of computer languages are in use today. These may be divided into three general types:

1. Machine languages
2. Assembly languages
3. High-level languages

Any computer can directly understand only its own machine language. Machine language is the "natural language" of a computer and as such is defined by its hardware design. [*Note:* Machine language is often referred to as object code. This term predates "object-oriented programming." These two uses of "object" are unrelated.] Machine languages generally consist of strings of numbers (ultimately reduced to 1s and 0s) that instruct computers to perform their most elementary operations one at a time. Machine languages are machine dependent (i.e., a particular machine language can be used on only one type of computer). Such languages are cumbersome for humans, as illustrated by the following section of an early machine-language program that adds overtime pay to base pay and stores the result in gross pay:

```
+1300042774
+1400593419
+1200274027
```

Machine-language programming was simply too slow, tedious and error prone for most programmers. Instead of using the strings of numbers that computers could directly understand, programmers began using English-like abbreviations to represent elementary operations. These abbreviations formed the basis of assembly languages. Translator programs called assemblers were developed to convert early assembly-language programs to machine language at computer speeds. The following section of an assembly-language program also adds overtime pay to base pay and stores the result in gross pay:

```
load    basepay
add     overpay
store   grosspay
```

Although such code is clearer to humans, it is incomprehensible to computers until translated to machine language.

Computer usage increased rapidly with the advent of assembly languages, but programmers still had to use many instructions to accomplish even the simplest tasks. To speed the programming process, high-level languages were developed in which single statements could be written to accomplish substantial tasks. Translator programs called compilers convert high-level language programs into machine language. High-level languages allow programmers to write instructions that look almost like everyday English and contain commonly used mathematical notations. A payroll program written in a high-level language might contain a statement such as

```
grossPay = basePay + overTimePay;
```

From your standpoint, obviously, high-level languages are preferable to machine and assembly language. C, C++, Microsoft's .NET languages (e.g., Visual Basic, Visual C++ and Visual C#) and Java are among the most widely used high-level programming languages. All of the Internet and web application development languages that you'll learn in this book are high-level languages.

The process of compiling a high-level language program into machine language can take a considerable amount of computer time. Interpreter programs were developed to execute high-level language programs directly, although much more slowly. In this book, we study several key programming languages, including JavaScript, ActionScript, PHP and Ruby on Rails—each of these scripting languages is processed by interpreters. We also study markup languages such as XHTML and XML, which can be processed by interpreted scripting languages. You'll see that interpreters have played an especially important role in helping scripting languages and markup languages achieve their goal of portability across a variety of platforms.

Performance Tip 1.1

Interpreters have an advantage over compilers in scripting. An interpreted program can begin executing as soon as it is downloaded to the client's machine, without the need to be compiled before it can execute. On the downside, scripts generally run much slower than compiled code.

Portability Tip 1.1

Interpreted languages are more portable than compiled languages. Interpreters can be implemented for each platform on which the interpreted languages need to execute.

Software Engineering Observation 1.1

Interpreted languages are more dynamic than compiled languages. For example, server-side applications can generate code in response to user interactions, and that code can then be interpreted in a browser.

1.5 History of the Internet and World Wide Web

In the late 1960s, one of the authors (HMD) was a graduate student at MIT. His research at MIT's Project MAC (now the Laboratory for Computer Science—the home of the World Wide Web Consortium) was funded by ARPA—the Advanced Research Projects Agency of the Department of Defense. ARPA sponsored a conference at which several dozen ARPA-funded graduate students were brought together at the University of Illinois at Urbana-Champaign to meet and share ideas. During this conference, ARPA rolled out the blueprints for networking the main computer systems of about a dozen ARPA-funded universities and research institutions. They were to be connected with communications lines operating at a then-stunning 56 Kbps (i.e., 56,000 bits per second)—this at a time when most people (of the few who could) were connecting over telephone lines to computers at a rate of 110 bits per second. There was great excitement at the conference. Researchers at Harvard talked about communicating with the Univac 1108 "supercomputer" at the University of Utah to handle calculations related to their computer graphics research. Many other intriguing possibilities were raised. Academic research about to take a giant leap forward. Shortly after this conference, ARPA proceeded to implement the ARPANET, which eventually evolved into today's Internet.

Things worked out differently from what was originally planned. Rather than enabling researchers to share each other's computers, it rapidly became clear that enabling researchers to communicate quickly and easily via what became known as electronic mail (e-mail, for short) was the key early benefit of the ARPANET. This is true even today on the Internet, as e-mail facilitates communications of all kinds among a billion people worldwide.

One of the primary goals for ARPANET was to allow multiple users to send and receive information simultaneously over the same communications paths (e.g., phone lines). The network operated with a technique called packet switching, in which digital data was sent in small bundles called packets. The packets contained address, error-control and sequencing information. The address information allowed packets to be routed to their destinations. The sequencing information helped in reassembling the packets—which, because of complex routing mechanisms, could actually arrive out of order—into their original order for presentation to the recipient. Packets from different senders were intermixed on the same lines. This packet-switching technique greatly reduced transmission costs, as compared with the cost of dedicated communications lines.

The network was designed to operate without centralized control. If a portion of the network failed, the remaining working portions would still route packets from senders to receivers over alternative paths for reliability.

The protocol for communicating over the ARPANET became known as TCP—the Transmission Control Protocol. TCP ensured that messages were properly routed from sender to receiver and that they arrived intact.

As the Internet evolved, organizations worldwide were implementing their own networks for both intraorganization (i.e., within the organization) and interorganization (i.e., between organizations) communications. A wide variety of networking hardware and software appeared. One challenge was to get these different networks to communicate. ARPA accomplished this with the development of IP—the Internet Protocol, truly creating a "network of networks," the current architecture of the Internet. The combined set of protocols is now commonly called TCP/IP.

Initially, Internet use was limited to universities and research institutions; then the military began using the Internet. Eventually, the government decided to allow access to the Internet for commercial purposes. Initially, there was resentment in the research and military communities—these groups were concerned that response times would become poor as "the Net" became saturated with users.

In fact, the exact opposite has occurred. Businesses rapidly realized that they could tune their operations and offer new and better services to their clients, so they started spending vast amounts of money to develop and enhance the Internet. This generated fierce competition among communications carriers and hardware and software suppliers to meet this demand. The result is that bandwidth (i.e., the information-carrying capacity) on the Internet has increased tremendously and costs have decreased significantly.

The World Wide Web allows computer users to locate and view multimedia-based documents on almost any subject over the Internet. Though the Internet was developed decades ago, the web is a relatively recent creation. In 1989, Tim Berners-Lee of CERN (the European Organization for Nuclear Research) began to develop a technology for sharing information via hyperlinked text documents. Berners-Lee called his invention the HyperText Markup Language (HTML). He also wrote communication protocols to form the backbone of his new information system, which he called the World Wide Web. In particular, he wrote the Hypertext Transfer Protocol (HTTP)—a communications protocol used to send information over the web. Web use exploded with the availability in 1993 of the Mosaic browser, which featured a user-friendly graphical interface. Marc Andreessen, whose team at NCSA developed Mosaic, went on to found Netscape, the company that many people credit with initiating the explosive Internet economy of the late 1990s.

In the past, most computer applications ran on computers that were not connected to one another, whereas today's applications can be written to communicate among the world's computers. The Internet mixes computing and communications technologies. It makes our work easier. It makes information instantly and conveniently accessible worldwide. It enables individuals and small businesses to get worldwide exposure. It is changing the way business is done. People can search for the best prices on virtually any product or service. Special-interest communities can stay in touch with one another. Researchers can be made instantly aware of the latest breakthroughs. The Internet and the web are surely among humankind's most profound creations.

1.6 World Wide Web Consortium (W3C)

In October 1994, Tim Berners-Lee founded an organization—called the World Wide Web Consortium (W3C)—devoted to developing nonproprietary, interoperable technologies for the World Wide Web. One of the W3C's primary goals is to make the web universally accessible—regardless of ability, language or culture. The W3C home page (www.w3.org) provides extensive resources on Internet and web technologies.

The W3C is also a standardization organization. Web technologies standardized by the W3C are called Recommendations. W3C Recommendations include the Extensible HyperText Markup Language (XHTML), Cascading Style Sheets (CSS), HyperText Markup Language (HTML—now considered a "legacy" technology) and the Extensible Markup Language (XML). A recommendation is not an actual software product, but a document that specifies a technology's role, syntax rules and so forth.

1.7 Web 2.0

In 2003 there was a noticeable shift in how people and businesses were using the web and developing web-based applications. The term Web 2.0 was coined by Dale Dougherty of O'Reilly® Media[1] in 2003 to describe this trend. Although it became a major media buzzword, few people really know what Web 2.0 means. Generally, Web 2.0 companies use the web as a platform to create collaborative, community-based sites (e.g., social networking sites, blogs, wikis, etc.).

Web 1.0 (the state of the web through the 1990s and early 2000s) was focused on a relatively small number of companies and advertisers producing content for users to access (some people called it the "brochure web"). Web 2.0 *involves* the user—not only is the content often created by the users, but users help organize it, share it, remix it, critique it, update it, etc. One way to look at Web 1.0 is as a *lecture*, a small number of professors informing a large audience of students. In comparison, Web 2.0 is a *conversation*, with everyone having the opportunity to speak and share views.

Web 2.0 is providing new opportunities and connecting people and content in unique ways. Web 2.0 embraces an architecture of participation—a design that encourages user interaction and community contributions. You, the user, are the most important aspect of Web 2.0—so important, in fact, that in 2006, *TIME Magazine*'s "Person of the Year" was "you."[2] The article recognized the social phenomenon of Web 2.0—the shift away from a powerful few to an empowered many. Several popular blogs now compete with traditional media powerhouses, and many Web 2.0 companies are built almost entirely on user-generated content. For websites like MySpace®, Facebook®, Flickr™, YouTube, eBay® and Wikipedia®, users create the content, while the companies provide the platforms. These companies *trust their users*—without such trust, users cannot make significant contributions to the sites.

The architecture of participation has influenced software development as well. Open source software is available for anyone to use and modify with few or no restrictions. Using collective intelligence—the concept that a large diverse group of people will create smart ideas—communities collaborate to develop software that many people believe is better and more robust than proprietary software. Rich Internet Applications (RIAs) are being devel-

1. O'Reilly, T. "What is Web 2.0: Design Patterns and Business Models for the Next Generation of Software." September 2005 <http://www.oreillynet.com/pub/a/oreilly/tim/news/2005/09/30/what-is-web-20.html?page=1>.
2. Grossman, L. "TIME's Person of the Year: You." *TIME*, December 2006 <http://www.time.com/time/magazine/article/0,9171,1569514,00.html>.

oped using technologies (such as Ajax) that have the look and feel of desktop software, enhancing a user's overall experience. Software as a Service (SaaS)—software that runs on a server instead of a local computer—has also gained prominence because of sophisticated new technologies and increased broadband Internet access.

Search engines, including Google™, Yahoo!®, MSN®, Ask™, and many more, have become essential to sorting through the massive amount of content on the web. Social bookmarking sites such as del.icio.us and Ma.gnolia allow users to share their favorite sites with others. Social media sites such as Digg™, Spotplex™ and Netscape® enable the community to decide which news articles are the most significant. The way we find the information on these sites is also changing—people are tagging (i.e., labeling) web content by subject or keyword in a way that helps anyone locate information more effectively.

Web services have emerged and, in the process, have inspired the creation of many Web 2.0 businesses. Web services allow you to incorporate functionality from existing applications and websites into your own web applications quickly and easily. For example, using Amazon Web Services™, you can create a specialty bookstore and earn revenues through the Amazon Associates Program; or, using Google™ Maps web services with eBay web services, you can build location-based "mashup" applications to find auction items in certain geographical areas. Web services, inexpensive computers, abundant high-speed Internet access, open source software and many other elements have inspired new, exciting, lightweight business models that people can launch with only a small investment. Some types of websites with rich and robust functionality that might have required hundreds of thousands or even millions of dollars to build in the 1990s can now be built for nominal amounts of money.

In the future, we'll see computers learn to understand the meaning of the data on the web—the beginnings of the Semantic Web are already appearing. Continual improvements in hardware, software and communications technologies will enable exciting new types of applications.

These topics and more are covered in a detailed walkthrough in Chapter 3, Dive Into® Web 2.0. The chapter highlights the major characteristics and technologies of Web 2.0, providing examples of popular Web 2.0 companies and Web 2.0 Internet business and monetization models. You'll learn about user-generated content, blogging, content networks, social networking, location-based services and more. In Chapters 4–28, you'll learn key software technologies for building web-based applications in general, and Ajax-enabled, web-based Rich Internet Applications in particular. See our Web 2.0 Resource Center at `www.deitel.com/web2.0/` for more information.

1.8 Personal, Distributed and Client/Server Computing

In 1977, Apple Computer popularized personal computing. Computers became so economical that people could buy them for their own personal or business use. In 1981, IBM, the world's largest computer vendor, introduced the IBM Personal Computer. This quickly legitimized personal computing in business, industry and government organizations, where IBM mainframes were heavily used.

These computers were for the most part "stand-alone" units—people transported disks back and forth between them to share information (this was often called "sneakernet"). Although early personal computers were not powerful enough to timeshare several users, these machines could be linked together in computer networks, sometimes over telephone lines and sometimes in local area networks (LANs) within an organization. This led to the phenomenon of distributed computing, in which an organization's computing, instead of being performed only at some central computer installation, is distributed over networks to the sites where the organization's work is performed. Personal computers were powerful enough to handle the computing requirements of individual users as well as the basic communications tasks of passing information between computers electronically.

Today's personal computers are as powerful as the million-dollar machines of just a few decades ago. The most powerful desktop machines—called workstations—provide individual users with enormous capabilities. Information is shared easily across computer networks, where computers called servers (file servers, database servers, web servers, etc.) offer data storage and other capabilities that may be used by client computers distributed throughout the network, hence the term client/server computing. Today's popular operating systems, such as UNIX, Linux, Mac OS X and Microsoft's Windows-based systems, provide the kinds of capabilities discussed in this section.

1.9 Hardware Trends

The Internet community thrives on the continuing stream of dramatic improvements in hardware, software and communications technologies. In general, people expect to pay at least a little more for most products and services every year. The opposite generally has been the case in the computer and communications industries, especially with regard to the hardware costs of supporting these technologies. For many decades, and with no change expected in the foreseeable future, hardware costs have fallen rapidly. This is a phenomenon of technology. Moore's Law states that the power of hardware doubles every two years, while the price remains essentially the same.[3] Significant improvements also have occurred in the communications field, especially in recent years, with the enormous demand for communications bandwidth attracting tremendous competition, forcing communications bandwidth to increase and prices to decline. We know of no other fields in which technology moves so quickly and costs fall so rapidly.

When computer use exploded in the 1960s and 1970s, there was talk of the huge improvements in human productivity that computing and communications would bring about. However, these productivity improvements did not immediately materialize. Organizations were spending vast sums on computers and distributing them to their workforces, but without immediate productivity gains. On the hardware side, it was the invention of microprocessor chip technology and its wide deployment in the late 1970s and 1980s which laid the groundwork for significant productivity improvements in the 1990s. On the software side, productivity improvements are now coming from object technology, which we use throughout this book.

Recently, hardware has been moving toward mobile, wireless technology. Small handheld devices are now more powerful than early 1970s supercomputers. Portability is now a major focus for the computer industry. Wireless data-transfer speeds have become so fast that many Internet users' primary web access is through wireless networks. The next few years will see dramatic advances in wireless capabilities for personal users and businesses.

---

3. Moore, G. "Cramming More Components onto Integrated Circuits." *Electronics*, April 1965 `<ftp://download.intel.com/museum/Moores_Law/Articles-Press_Releases/Gordon_Moore_1965_Article.pdf>`.

1.10 Key Software Trend: Object Technology

One of the authors, HMD, remembers the great frustration felt in the 1960s by software development organizations, especially those working on large-scale projects. During his undergraduate years, he had the privilege of working summers at a leading computer vendor on the teams developing timesharing, virtual-memory operating systems. This was a great experience for a college student. But, in the summer of 1967, reality set in when the company "decommitted" from producing as a commercial product the particular system on which hundreds of people had been working for many years. It was difficult to get this thing called software right—software is "complex stuff."

Improvements to software technology did emerge, with the benefits of structured programming (and the related disciplines of structured systems analysis and design) being realized in the 1970s. Not until the technology of object-oriented programming became widely used in the 1990s, though, did software developers feel they had the necessary tools for making major strides in the software development process.

What are objects and why are they special? Actually, object technology is a packaging scheme that helps us create meaningful software units. These can be large and are highly focused on particular applications areas. There are date objects, time objects, paycheck objects, invoice objects, audio objects, video objects, file objects, record objects and so on. In fact, almost any noun can be reasonably represented as an object.

We live in a world of objects. Just look around you. There are cars, planes, people, animals, buildings, traffic lights, elevators and the like. Before object-oriented languages appeared, procedural programming languages (such as Fortran, COBOL, Pascal, BASIC and C) were focused on actions (verbs) rather than on things or objects (nouns). Programmers living in a world of objects programmed primarily using verbs. This made it awkward to write programs. Now, with the availability of popular object-oriented languages, such as C++, Java, Visual Basic and C#, programmers continue to live in an object-oriented world *and* can program in an object-oriented manner. This is a more natural process than procedural programming and has resulted in significant productivity gains.

A key problem with procedural programming is that the program units do not effectively mirror real-world entities, so these units are not particularly reusable. It's not unusual for programmers to "start fresh" on each new project and have to write similar software "from scratch." This wastes time and money, as people repeatedly "reinvent the wheel." With object technology, the software entities created (called classes), if properly designed, tend to be reusable on future projects. Using libraries of reusable componentry can greatly reduce effort required to implement certain kinds of systems (compared to the effort that would be required to reinvent these capabilities on new projects).

Software Engineering Observation 1.2

Extensive class libraries of reusable software components are available on the Internet. Many of these libraries are free.

Software Engineering Observation 1.3

Some organizations report that the key benefit object-oriented programming gives them is not software that is reusable but, rather, software that is more understandable, better organized and easier to maintain, modify and debug. This can be significant, because perhaps as much as 80 percent of software cost is associated not with the original efforts to develop the software, but with the continued evolution and maintenance of that software throughout its lifetime.

1.11 JavaScript: Object-Based Scripting for the Web

JavaScript is an object-based scripting language with strong support for proper software engineering techniques. Students learn to create and manipulate objects from the start in JavaScript. JavaScript is available free in today's popular web browsers.

Does JavaScript provide the solid foundation of programming principles typically taught in first programming courses—a portion of the intended audience for this book? We think so.

The JavaScript chapters of the book are more than just an introduction to the language. They also present an introduction to computer programming fundamentals, including control structures, functions, arrays, recursion, strings and objects. Experienced programmers will read Chapters 6–13 quickly and master JavaScript by reading our live-code examples and by examining the corresponding screenshots. Beginners will learn computer programming in these carefully paced chapters by reading the code explanations and completing the many exercises.

JavaScript is a powerful scripting language. Experienced programmers sometimes take pride in creating strange, contorted, convoluted JavaScript code. This kind of coding makes programs more difficult to read, test and debug. This book is also geared for novice programmers; for all readers we stress program clarity.

Good Programming Practice 1.1

Write your programs in a simple and straightforward manner. This is sometimes referred to as KIS ("keep it simple"). One key aspect of keeping it simple is another interpretation of KIS—"keep it small." Do not "stretch" the language by trying bizarre uses.

You'll see that JavaScript is a portable scripting language and that programs written in JavaScript can run in many web browsers. Actually, portability is an elusive goal.

Portability Tip 1.2

Although it is easier to write portable programs in JavaScript than in many other programming languages, differences among interpreters and browsers make portability difficult to achieve. Simply writing programs in JavaScript does not guarantee portability. Programmers occasionally need to research platform variations and write their code accordingly.

Portability Tip 1.3

When writing JavaScript programs, you need to deal directly with cross-browser portability issues. Such issues are hidden by JavaScript libraries (e.g., Dojo, Prototype, Script.aculo.us and ASP.NET Ajax) which provide powerful, ready-to-use capabilities that simplify JavaScript coding by making it cross-browser compatible.

Error-Prevention Tip 1.1

Always test your JavaScript programs on all systems and in all web browsers for which they are intended.

Good Programming Practice 1.2

Read the documentation for the JavaScript version you are using to access JavaScript's rich collection of features.

Error-Prevention Tip 1.2

Your computer and JavaScript interpreter are good teachers. If you are not sure how a feature works, even after studying the documentation, experiment and see what happens. Study each error or warning message and adjust the code accordingly.

JavaScript was created by Netscape, the company that created the first widely successful web browser. Both Netscape and Microsoft have been instrumental in the standardization of JavaScript by ECMA International (formerly the European Computer Manufacturers Association) as ECMAScript. In Chapters 16–17, we discuss Adobe Flash, which uses another scripting language named ActionScript. ActionScript and JavaScript are converging in the next version of the JavaScript standard (JavaScript 2/ECMA Script version 4) currently under development by ECMA. This will result in a universal client scripting language, greatly simplifying web application development.

1.12 Browser Portability

Ensuring a consistent look and feel on client-side browsers is one of the great challenges of developing web-based applications. Currently, a standard does not exist to which software developers must adhere when creating web browsers. Although browsers share a common set of features, each browser might render pages differently. Browsers are available in many versions and on many different platforms (Microsoft Windows, Apple Macintosh, Linux, UNIX, etc.). Vendors add features to each new version that sometimes result in cross-platform incompatibility issues. Clearly it is difficult to develop web pages that render correctly on all versions of each browser. In this book we develop web applications that execute on both the Internet Explorer 7 and Firefox 2 browsers.

Portability Tip 1.4

The web is populated with many different browsers, which makes it difficult for authors and web application developers to create universal solutions. The W3C is working toward the goal of a universal client-side platform.

1.13 C, C++ and Java

C

The C language was developed by Dennis Ritchie at Bell Laboratories. C was implemented in 1972. C initially became known as the development language of the UNIX operating system. Today, virtually all new major operating systems are written in C and/or C++.

C++

Bjarne Stroustrup developed C++, an extension of C, in the early 1980s. C++ provides a number of features that "spruce up" the C language, but more importantly, it provides capabilities for object-oriented programming. C++ is a hybrid language: It is possible to program in either a C-like style (procedural programming), in which the focus is on actions, or an object-oriented style, in which the focus is on objects, or both. C and C++ have influenced many subsequent programming languages, such as Java, C#, JavaScript and PHP, each of which has a syntax similar to C and C++.

Java

Microprocessors are having a profound impact in intelligent consumer electronic devices. Recognizing this, Sun Microsystems in 1991 funded an internal corporate research project code-named Green to provide software for these devices. The project resulted in the development of a C++-based language that its creator, James Gosling, called Oak after an oak tree outside his window at Sun. It was later discovered that there already was a computer language called Oak. When a group of Sun people visited a local coffee shop, the name Java was suggested and it stuck.

The Green project ran into some difficulties. The marketplace for intelligent consumer electronic devices did not develop in the early 1990s as quickly as Sun had anticipated. The project was in danger of being canceled. By sheer good fortune, the World Wide Web exploded in popularity in 1993, and Sun saw the immediate potential of using Java to add dynamic content (e.g., interactivity, animations and the like) to web pages. This breathed new life into the project.

Sun formally announced Java at an industry conference in May 1995. Java garnered the attention of the business community because of the phenomenal interest in the web. Java is now used to develop large-scale enterprise applications, to enhance the functionality of web servers (the computers that provide the content we see in our web browsers), to provide applications for consumer devices (e.g., cell phones, pagers and personal digital assistants) and for many other purposes.

1.14 BASIC, Visual Basic, Visual C++, C# and .NET

The BASIC (Beginner's All-purpose Symbolic Instruction Code) programming language was developed in the mid-1960s at Dartmouth College as a means of writing simple programs. BASIC's primary purpose was to familiarize novices with programming techniques. Microsoft's Visual Basic language, introduced in the early 1990s to simplify the development of Microsoft Windows applications, has become one of the most popular programming languages in the world.

Microsoft's latest development tools are part of its corporatewide strategy for integrating the Internet and the web into computer applications. This strategy is implemented in Microsoft's .NET platform, which provides the capabilities developers need to create computer applications that can execute on computers distributed across the Internet. Microsoft's three primary programming languages are Visual Basic (based on the original BASIC), Visual C++ (based on C++) and Visual C# (a relatively new language based on C++ and Java that was developed expressly for the .NET platform). Developers using .NET can write software components in the language they are most familiar with, then form applications by combining those components with others written in any .NET language.

1.15 Software Technologies

In this section, we discuss some software engineering topics and buzzwords that you'll hear in the software development community. We've created Resource Centers on most of these topics, with many more on the way.

Agile Software Development is a set of methodologies that try to get software implemented quickly with fewer resources than previous methodologies. Check out the Agile Alliance (`www.agilealliance.org`) and the Agile Manifesto (`www.agilemanifesto.org`).

Refactoring involves reworking code to make it clearer and easier to maintain while preserving its functionality. It's widely employed with agile development methodologies. Many refactoring tools are available to do major portions of the reworking automatically.

Design patterns are proven architectures for constructing flexible and maintainable object-oriented software. The field of design patterns tries to enumerate those recurring patterns, encouraging software designers to reuse them to develop better-quality software with less time, money and effort.

Game programming. The computer game business is larger than the first-run movie business. College courses and even majors are now devoted to the sophisticated software techniques used in game programming. Chapter 17 discusses building interactive games with Adobe Flash CS3. Also check out our Resource Centers on Game Programming, C++ Game Programming and Programming Projects.

Open source software is developed in a way unlike the proprietary development that dominated software's early years and remains strong today. With open source development, individuals and companies contribute their efforts in developing, maintaining and evolving software in exchange for the right to use that software for their own purposes, typically at no charge. Open source code generally gets scrutinized by a much larger audience than proprietary software, so bugs may be removed faster. Open source also encourages more innovation. Sun recently open sourced Java. Some organizations you'll hear a lot about in the open source community are the Eclipse Foundation (the Eclipse IDE is popular for C++ and Java software development), the Mozilla Foundation (the creators of the Firefox browser), the Apache Software Foundation (the creators of the Apache web server) and SourceForge (which provides the tools for managing open source projects and currently has over 150,000 open source projects under development).

Linux is an open source operating system and one of the greatest successes of the open source movement. Apache is the most popular open source web server. MySQL (see Chapters 22–24) is an open source database management system. PHP (see Chapter 23) is the most popular open source server-side "scripting" language for developing Internet-based applications. LAMP is an acronym for the set of open source technologies that many developers used to build web applications—it stands for Linux, Apache, MySQL and PHP (or Perl or Python—two other scripting languages used for similar purposes).

Ruby on Rails (see Chapter 24) combines the scripting language Ruby with the Rails web application framework developed by the company 37Signals. Their book, *Getting Real*, is a must read for today's web application developers; read it free at `gettingreal.37signals.com/toc.php`. Many Ruby on Rails developers have reported significant productivity gains over using other languages when developing database-intensive web applications.

Software has generally been viewed as a product; most software still is offered this way. If you want to run an application, you buy a software package from a software vendor. You then install that software on your computer and run it as needed. As new versions of the software appear, you upgrade your software, often at significant expense. This process can become cumbersome for organizations with tens of thousands of systems that must be maintained on a diverse array of computer equipment. With Software as a Service (SaaS), the software runs on servers elsewhere on the Internet. When those servers are updated, all clients worldwide see the new capabilities; no local installation is needed. You access the service through a browser—these are quite portable, so you can run the same applications on different kinds of computers from anywhere in the world. Salesforce.com, Google, Microsoft and 37Signals all offer SaaS.

1.16 Notes about *Internet & World Wide Web How to Program, 4/e*

In 1995, we saw an explosion of interest in the Internet and the World Wide Web. We immersed ourselves in these technologies, and a clear picture started to emerge in our minds of the next direction to take in writing textbooks for introductory programming courses. Electronic commerce, or e-commerce, as it is typically called, began to dominate the business, financial and computer industry news. This was a reconceptualization of the way business should be conducted. We still wanted to teach programming principles, but we felt compelled to do it in the context of the technologies that businesses and organizations need to create Internet-based and web-based applications. With this realization, the first edition of *Internet & World Wide Web How to Program* was born and published in December of 1999.

Internet & World Wide Web How to Program, Fourth Edition teaches programming languages and programming language principles. In addition, we focus on the broad range of technologies that will help you build real-world Internet-based and web-based applications that interact with other applications and with databases. These capabilities allow you to develop the kinds of enterprise-level, distributed applications popular in industry today.

You'll learn computer programming and basic principles of computer science and information technology. You also will learn proven software development methods—top-down stepwise-refinement, functionalization and object-based programming. Our primary programming language is JavaScript, a compact language that is especially designed for developing Internet- and web-based applications. Chapters 6–13 present a rich discussion of JavaScript and its capabilities, including dozens of complete examples followed by screen images that illustrate typical program inputs and outputs.

After you learn programming principles from the detailed JavaScript discussions, we present condensed treatments of four other popular Internet/web programming languages for building the server side of Internet- and web-based client/server applications. Chapter 23 introduces the popular PHP scripting language. Chapter 24 introduces Ruby, the scripting language used with the Ruby on Rails framework for rapid development of database-driven web applications. In Chapter 25, we discuss ASP.NET 2.0—Microsoft's technology for server-side scripting. ASP.NET pages can be written in Visual Basic and C#; we code ASP.NET pages using Visual Basic. In Chapters 26–27, we discuss JavaServer Faces, which uses the Java programming language. Finally, in Chapter 28, we discuss web services (using examples in both Java and ASP.NET).

1.17 Web Resources

`www.deitel.com/`

Check this site frequently for updates, corrections and additional resources for all Deitel & Associates, Inc., publications.

`www.deitel.com/resourcecenters.html`

Check out the complete list of Deitel Resource Centers, including numerous programming, open source, Web 2.0 and Internet business topics.

`netforbeginners.about.com`
The About.com *Internet for Beginners* guide provides valuable resources for further exploration of the history and workings of the Internet and the web.

`www.learnthenet.com/english/index.html`
Learn the Net is a website containing a complete overview of the Internet, the web and the underlying technologies. The site contains much information appropriate for novices.

`www.w3.org`
The World Wide Web Consortium (W3C) website offers a comprehensive description of web technologies. For each Internet technology with which the W3C is involved, the site provides a description of the technology, its benefits to web designers, the history of the technology and the future goals of the W3C in developing the technology.

Summary

Section 1.1 Introduction

- In an era of steadily rising costs, computing costs have been decreasing dramatically because of rapid developments in both hardware and software technologies.
- Technologies such as Extensible HyperText Markup Language (XHTML), JavaScript, Flash, Flex, Dreamweaver and Extensible Markup Language (XML) are used to build the portions of web-based applications that reside on the client side (i.e., the portions of applications that typically run on web browsers such as Firefox or Microsoft's Internet Explorer).
- Technologies such as web servers, databases, ASP.NET, PHP, Ruby on Rails and JavaServer Faces are used to build the server side of web-based applications. These parts of applications typically run on "heavy-duty" computer systems on which organizations' business-critical websites reside.

Section 1.2 What Is a Computer?

- A computer is a device capable of performing computations and making logical decisions at speeds billions of times faster than human beings can.
- A computer processes data under the control of sets of instructions called computer programs, which guide it through orderly sets of actions specified by computer programmers.
- The various devices that comprise a computer system are referred to as hardware.
- The computer programs that run on a computer are referred to as software.

Section 1.3 Computer Organization

- The input unit is the "receiving" section of the computer. It obtains information from input devices and places it at the disposal of the other units for processing.
- The output unit is the "shipping" section of the computer. It takes information processed by the computer and places it on output devices to make it available for use outside the computer.
- The memory unit is the rapid-access, relatively low-capacity "warehouse" section of the computer. It retains information that has been entered through the input unit, making it immediately available for processing when needed, and retains information that has already been processed until it can be placed on output devices by the output unit.
- The arithmetic and logic unit (ALU) is the "manufacturing" section of the computer. It is responsible for performing calculations and making decisions.
- The central processing unit (CPU) is the "administrative" section of the computer. It coordinates and supervises the operation of the other sections.

- The secondary storage unit is the long-term, high-capacity "warehousing" section of the computer. Programs or data not being used by the other units are normally placed on secondary storage devices (e.g., disks) until they are needed, possibly hours, days, months or even years later.

Section 1.4 Machine Languages, Assembly Languages and High-Level Languages

- Any computer can directly understand only its own machine language, which generally consists of strings of numbers ultimately reduced to 1s and 0s that instruct the computer to perform its most elementary operations.
- English-like abbreviations form the basis of assembly languages. Translator programs called assemblers convert assembly-language programs to machine language.
- Compilers translate high-level language programs into machine-language programs. High-level languages contain English words and conventional mathematical notations.
- Interpreter programs directly execute high-level language programs, eliminating the need to compile them into machine language.

Section 1.5 History of the Internet and World Wide Web

- In the late 1960s, ARPA, the Advanced Research Projects Agency of the U.S. Department of Defense rolled out the blueprints for networking the main computer systems of about a dozen ARPA-funded universities and research institutions. ARPA then proceeded to implement the ARPANET, the predecessor to today's Internet.
- The World Wide Web allows computer users to locate and view multimedia-based documents (i.e., documents with text, graphics, animations, audios or videos) on almost any subject.
- In 1989, Tim Berners-Lee of CERN began to develop the World Wide Web and several communication protocols that form the backbone of the web.
- Web use exploded with the availability in 1993 of the Mosaic browser, which featured a user-friendly graphical interface. Marc Andreessen, whose team at NCSA developed Mosaic, went on to found Netscape, the company that many people credit with initiating the explosive Internet economy of the late 1990s.

Section 1.6 World Wide Web Consortium (W3C)

- In October 1994, Tim Berners-Lee founded the World Wide Web Consortium (W3C)—an organization devoted to developing nonproprietary, interoperable technologies for the web.

Section 1.7 Web 2.0

- Web 2.0 companies use the web as a platform to create collaborative, community-based sites (e.g., social networking sites, blogs, wikis, etc.).
- Web 1.0 (the state of the web through the 1990s and early 2000s) was focused on a relatively small number of companies and advertisers producing content for users to access.
- Web 2.0 embraces an architecture of participation—a design that encourages user interaction and community contributions.
- Using the collective intelligence—the concept that a large diverse group of people will create smart ideas—communities collaborate to develop open source software that many people believe is better and more robust than proprietary software.
- Rich Internet Applications (RIAs) are being developed using technologies (such as Ajax) that have the look and feel of desktop software, enhancing a user's overall experience.
- Web services, inexpensive computers, abundant high-speed Internet access, open source software and many other elements have inspired new, exciting, lightweight business models that people can launch with only a small investment.

Section 1.8 Personal, Distributed and Client/Server Computing

- Apple Computer popularized personal computing.
- IBM's Personal Computer quickly legitimized personal computing in business, industry and government organizations, where IBM mainframes were heavily used.
- Although early personal computers were not powerful enough to timeshare several users, these machines could be linked together in computer networks, sometimes over telephone lines and sometimes in local area networks (LANs) within an organization. This led to the phenomenon of distributed computing.
- Today's personal computers are as powerful as the million-dollar machines of just a few decades ago, and information is shared easily across computer networks.

Section 1.9 Hardware Trends

- Moore's Law states that the power of hardware doubles every two years, while the price remains essentially the same.

Section 1.10 Key Software Trend: Object Technology

- Objects are essentially reusable software components that model real-world items.
- Not until object-oriented programming became widely used in the 1990s did software developers feel they had the tools to make major strides in the software development process.
- Object technology is a packaging scheme that helps us create meaningful software units.
- A key problem with procedural programming is that the program units do not effectively mirror real-world entities, so these units are not particularly reusable.
- With object technology, the software entities created (called classes), if properly designed, tend to be reusable on future projects. Using libraries of reusable componentry can greatly reduce effort required to implement certain kinds of systems.
- Some organizations report that the key benefit object-oriented programming gives them is the production of software which is more understandable, better organized and easier to maintain, modify and debug.

Section 1.11 JavaScript: Object-Based Scripting for the Web

- JavaScript is an object-based scripting language with strong support for proper software engineering techniques.
- JavaScript was created by Netscape. Both Netscape and Microsoft have been instrumental in the standardization of JavaScript by ECMA International as ECMAScript.

Section 1.12 Browser Portability

- Ensuring a consistent look and feel on client-side browsers is one of the great challenges of developing web-based applications.

Section 1.13 C, C++ and Java

- C initially became known as the development language of the UNIX operating system. Today, virtually all new major operating systems are written in C and/or C++.
- C++ provides a number of features that "spruce up" the C language, but more importantly, it provides capabilities for object-oriented programming.
- Java is used to create dynamic and interactive content for web pages, develop enterprise applications, enhance web-server functionality, provide applications for consumer devices and more.

Section 1.14 BASIC, Visual Basic, Visual C++, C# and .NET

- The BASIC programming language was developed in the mid-1960s at Dartmouth College. Its primary purpose was to familiarize novices with programming techniques.
- Microsoft's Visual Basic was introduced in the early 1990s to simplify the process of developing Microsoft Windows applications.
- Microsoft has a corporatewide strategy for integrating the Internet and the web into computer applications. This strategy is implemented in Microsoft's .NET platform.
- The .NET platform's three primary programming languages are Visual Basic, Visual C++ and Visual C#.
- .NET developers can write software components in their preferred language, then form applications by combining those components with components written in any .NET language.

Section 1.15 Software Technologies

- Agile Software Development is a set of methodologies that try to get software implemented quickly with fewer resources than previous methodologies.
- Refactoring involves reworking code to make it clearer and easier to maintain while preserving its functionality.
- Design patterns are proven architectures for constructing flexible and maintainable object-oriented software.
- Open source development allows individuals and companies to contribute their efforts in developing, maintaining and evolving software in exchange for the right to use that software for their own purposes, typically at no charge.
- With Software as a Service (SaaS), the software runs on servers elsewhere on the Internet, rather than on the desktop.

Terminology

actions
Agile Software Development
architecture of participation
arithmetic and logic unit (ALU)
ARPANET
assemblers
assembly language
bandwidth
BASIC
C
C++
central processing unit (CPU)
class
client side
client/server computing
collective intelligence
compilers
computer
computer program
computer programmer
CSS
Dale Dougherty
data
data structure
decision
design pattern
distributed computing
DOM (Document Object Model)
dynamic content
electronic commerce (e-commerce)
electronic mail (e-mail)
function
game programming
hardware
high-level languages
HTML (HyperText Markup Language)
HTTP (Hypertext Transfer Protocol)
input device
input unit
Internet
interpreter
IP (Internet Protocol)

Java
JavaScript
LAMP
library
lightweight business models
Linux
local area networks (LANs)
logical unit
machine dependent
machine language
memory
memory unit
method
Moore's Law
multiprocessor
MySQL
.NET platform
O'Reilly Media
object code
object-based programming
object-oriented programming
open source software
output devices
output unit
packet
packet switching
personal computer
PHP
platform
primary memory
refactoring
Ruby on Rails
scripting
scripting language
secondary storage unit
server side
server
software
Software as a Service (SaaS)
structured programming
structured systems analysis and design
supercomputer
tagging
TCP (Transmission Control Protocol)
TCP/IP
translation
translator program
Visual Basic
Visual C#
Visual C++
Web 1.0
Web 2.0
workstation
World Wide Web
World Wide Web Consortium (W3C)
XHTML (Extensible HyperText Markup Language)
XML (Extensible Markup Language)

Self-Review Exercises

1.1 Fill in the blanks in each of the following:

a) The company that popularized personal computing was _______.
b) The computer that made personal computing legitimate in business and industry was the _______.
c) Computers process data under the control of sets of instructions called computer _______.
d) The six key logical units of the computer are the _______, _______, _______, _______, _______ and the _______.
e) The three classes of languages discussed in the chapter are _______, _______, and _______.
f) The programs that translate high-level language programs into machine language are called _______.
g) _______, or labeling content, is another key part of the collaborative theme of Web 2.0.
h) With Internet applications, the desktop evolves to the _______.
i) _______ involves reworking code to make it clearer and easier to maintain while preserving its functionality.
j) With _______ development, individuals and companies contribute their efforts in developing, maintaining and evolving software in exchange for the right to use that software for their own purposes, typically at no charge.

k) The _______ was the predecessor to the Internet.
l) The information-carrying capacity of a communications medium like the Internet is called _______.
m) The acronym TCP/IP stands for _______.

1.2 Fill in the blanks in each of the following statements.
a) The _______ allows computer users to locate and view multimedia-based documents on almost any subject over the Internet.
b) _______ founded an organization—called the World Wide Web Consortium (W3C)—devoted to developing nonproprietary, interoperable technologies for the World Wide Web.
c) _______ are reusable software components that model items in the real world.
d) In a typical client/server relationship, the _______ requests that some action be performed and the _______ performs the action and responds.

Answers to Self-Review Exercises

1.1 a) Apple. b) IBM Personal Computer. c) programs. d) input unit, output unit, memory unit, arithmetic and logic unit, central processing unit, secondary storage unit. e) machine languages, assembly languages and high-level languages. f) compilers. g) Tagging. h) webtop. i) Refactoring. j) open source. k) ARPANET. l) bandwidth. m) Transmission Control Protocol/Internet Protocol.

1.2 a) World Wide Web. b) Tim Berners-Lee. c) Objects. d) client, server.

Exercises

1.3 Categorize each of the following items as either hardware or software:
a) CPU
b) ALU
c) input unit
d) an editor program

1.4 Fill in the blanks in each of the following statements:
a) Which logical unit of the computer receives information from outside the computer for use by the computer? _______.
b) The process of instructing the computer to solve specific problems is called _______.
c) What type of computer language uses English-like abbreviations for machine-language instructions? _______.
d) Which logical unit of the computer sends information that has already been processed by the computer to various devices so that the information may be used outside the computer? _______.
e) Which logical units of the computer retain information? _______.
f) Which logical unit of the computer performs calculations? _______.
g) Which logical unit of the computer makes logical decisions? _______.
h) The level of computer language most convenient for you to write programs quickly and easily is _______.
i) The only language that a computer directly understands is called that computer's _______.
j) Which logical unit of the computer coordinates the activities of all the other logical units? _______.

k) Some organizations report that the key benefit _______ gives them is the production of software which is more understandable, better organized and easier to maintain, modify and debug.
l) Web 2.0 embraces an _______—a design that encourages user interaction and community contributions.
m) _______ is the concept that a large diverse group of people will create smart ideas.

1.5 Fill in the blanks in each of the following statements (based on Section 1.15, Software Technologies):
a) The open source database management system used in LAMP development is _______.
b) A key advantage of Software as a Service (SaaS) is _______.
c) _______ are proven architectures for constructing flexible and maintainable object-oriented software.
d) _______ is the most popular open source server-side "scripting" language for developing Internet-based applications.

1.6 What is the relationship between JavaScript and ECMAScript?

1.7 In this chapter, we discussed a few popular Web 2.0 businesses including MySpace, Flickr, YouTube and Wikipedia. Indentify a Web 2.0 business and describe why it fits the Web 2.0 business model.

2

Web Browser Basics: Internet Explorer and Firefox

Give us the tools, and we will finish the job.
—Sir Winston Churchill

We must learn to explore all the options and possibilities that confront us in a complex and rapidly changing world.
—J. William Fulbright

OBJECTIVES

In this chapter you will learn:

- To understand the Microsoft Internet Explorer 7 (IE7) and Mozilla Firefox 2 (FF2) web browsers' capabilities.
- To use IE7 and FF2 to search the information available on the World Wide Web.
- To customize a browser according to your own needs and preferences.
- To understand the differences among various browsers.

Outline

2.1 Introduction to the Internet Explorer 7 and Firefox 2 Web Browsers

The Internet is an essential medium for communicating and interacting with people worldwide. The need to publish and share information has fueled the rapid growth of the web. Web browsers are software programs that allow users to access the web's rich content. Whether for business or personal use, millions of people use web browsers to access the tremendous amount of information available on the web and to share or exchange this content with other users. The www portion of the Internet, which we encounter often in this chapter, is made up of hyperlinked documents written in XHTML and rich media.

Popular web browsers at the time of publication are Microsoft's *Internet Explorer*, Mozilla's *Firefox*, Apple's *Safari* and Opera Software's *Opera*. This chapter focuses on the features of Internet Explorer (IE7) and Firefox 2 (FF2), which are the most widely used of these browsers. All examples in this book are supported by both IE7 and FF2.

2.2 Connecting to the Internet

A computer alone is not enough to access the Internet. In addition to web browser software, the computer needs specific hardware and a connection to an Internet Service Provider to view web pages. This section describes the components that enable Internet access.

First, a computer must have a modem or network card. A modem is hardware that enables a computer to connect to a network via phone lines. A modem converts data to audio tones and transmits the data over phone lines. A network card, also called a network interface card (NIC), is hardware that allows a computer to connect to the Internet through a network or a high-speed Internet connection, such as a local area network (LAN), cable modem or Digital Subscriber Line (DSL).

After ensuring that a computer has a modem or a network card (most computers come with one or both of these), the next step is to register with an Internet Service Provider (ISP). Computers connect to an ISP using a modem and phone line, or via a NIC using a LAN, DSL or cable modem. The ISP connects computers to the Internet. Most college and university campuses offer network connections, and many communities now offer wireless access. If a network connection is not available, then popular commercial ISPs, such as AOL (www.aol.com), Comcast (www.comcast.net), Earthlink (www.earthlink.net), Verizon (www.verizon.com), Microsoft Network (www.msn.com) and NetZero (www.netzero.net) are alternatives.

Bandwidth and cost are two considerations when deciding which commercial ISP service to use. Bandwidth refers to the amount of data that can be transferred through a communications medium in a fixed amount of time. Different ISPs offer different types of high-speed connections, called broadband connections—which include DSL, cable modem and Integrated Services Digital Network (ISDN)—and slower dial-up connections. Each connection type has a different bandwidth and cost to users.

Broadband is a category of high-bandwidth Internet service that is most often provided to home users by cable television and telephone companies. DSL is a broadband service that allows computers to be connected at all times to the Internet over existing phone lines, without interfering with telephone services. DSL requires a special modem provided by the ISP. Like DSL, cable modems enable the computer to be connected to the Internet at all times. Cable modems transmit data over the cables that bring television to homes and businesses. Unlike DSL, the bandwidth is shared by many users. This sharing can reduce the bandwidth available to each person when many use the system simultaneously. ISDN provides Internet service over either digital or standard telephone lines. ISDN requires specialized hardware, called a terminal adapter (TA), which is usually obtained from the ISP.

Dial-up service uses an existing telephone line. If a computer is connected to the Internet, the user usually cannot receive voice calls during this time. If the voice calls do connect, the Internet connection is interrupted. To prevent this, users may choose to install an extra phone line dedicated to Internet service.

Fiber optics are replacing traditional metal cables in many computer networks due to their greater bandwidth and mechanical advantages that provide a better signal. Though their popularity is currently limited by the high cost of materials and installation, consistent improvements in the industry will allow fiber optic cables to become a key element of the communications industry in the near future.

Once a computer is connected to a network, the user must choose a web browser for navigating the Internet. Internet Explorer is preinstalled on all Windows machines, and your version can be updated at www.microsoft.com/ie. Firefox can be downloaded at www.mozilla.com/firefox, and can be installed on many different operating systems. When installing this browser, select **Custom** when prompted for a setup type, and ensure that the **DOM Inspector** option is selected in the next screen. Doing so will ensure that you have additional Firefox functionality that we discuss in Chapter 12.

2.3 Internet Explorer 7 and Firefox 2 Features

A web browser is software that allows the user to view certain types of Internet files in an interactive environment. Figure 2.1 shows the Deitel Home Page using Internet Explorer 7 web browser, and Fig. 2.2 uses Firefox 2. The URL (Uniform Resource Locator) http://www.deitel.com is found in the **Address** bar in IE7, and the **Location** bar in FF2. The URL specifies the address (i.e., location) of the web page displayed in the browser window. Each web page on the Internet is associated with a unique URL. URLs usually begin with http://, which stands for Hypertext Transfer Protocol (HTTP), the standard protocol (or set of communication rules) for transferring web documents over the Internet. URLs of websites that handle private information, such as credit card numbers, often

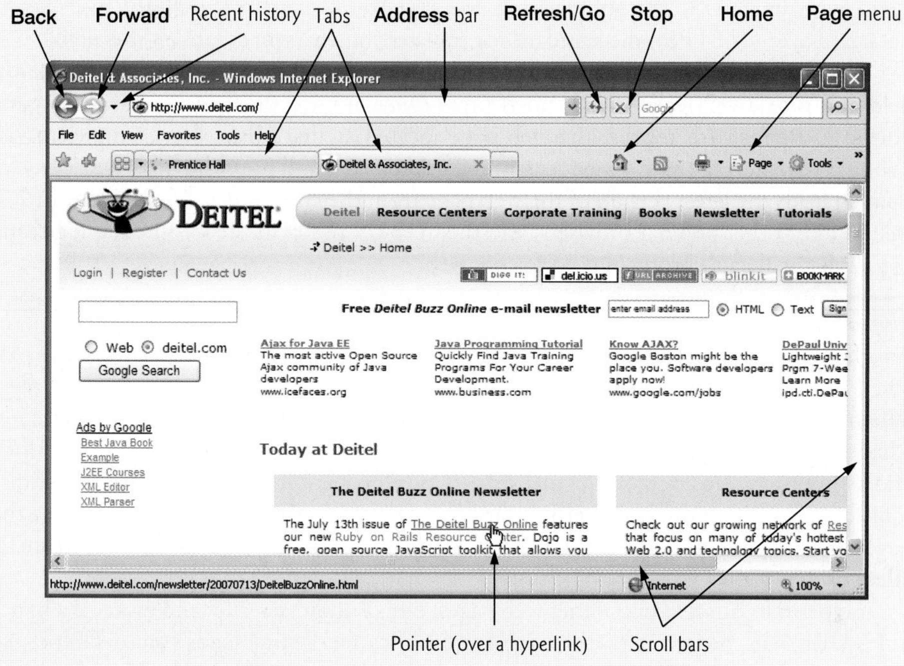

Fig. 2.1 | Deitel® website in Internet Explorer 7.

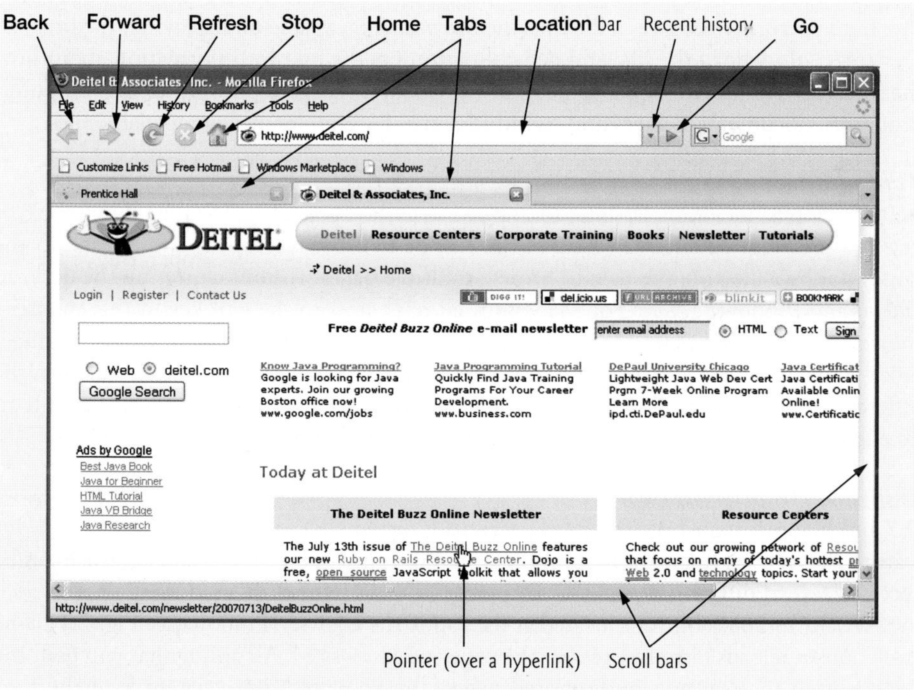

Fig. 2.2 | Deitel® website in Firefox 2.

begin with `https://`, the abbreviation for Hypertext Transfer Protocol over Secure Sockets Layer (HTTPS), the standard for transferring encrypted data on the web.

There are several techniques for navigating between URLs. You can click the **Address** field and type a web page's URL, then press *Enter* or click **Go** (in IE7, this is the same button as **Refresh**) to request the web page located at that URL. For example, to visit Yahoo!'s website, type `www.yahoo.com` in the **Address** bar and press the *Enter* key. Clicking **Refresh** loads the latest version of the web page from the current website. IE7 and FF2, as well as most other popular browsers, add the `http://` prefix to the website name because HTTP is the default protocol used for the web.

Hyperlinks

Another way to navigate the web is via visual elements on web pages called hyperlinks that, when clicked, load a specified web document. Both images and text may be hyperlinked. When the mouse pointer hovers over a hyperlink, the default arrow pointer changes into a hand with the index finger pointing upward. Often hyperlinked text appears underlined and as in different color from regular text in a web page. Originally used as a publishing tool for scientific research, hyperlinks are widely used to reference sources, or sites that have more information on a particular topic. The paths created by hyperlinking create the effect of the "web."

Hyperlinks can reference other web pages, e-mail addresses, files and more. If a hyperlink's URL is in the form `mailto:`*emailAddress*, clicking the link loads your default e-mail program and opens a message window addressed to the specified e-mail address. Note that these hyperlinks are generally displayed on the screen as just the e-mail address or the recipient's name.

If a hyperlink references a file that the browser is incapable of displaying, the browser prepares to download the file, and generally prompts the user for information about how the file should be stored. When a file is downloaded, it is copied onto the user's computer. Programs, documents, images and sound files are all examples of downloadable files.

Tabbed Browsing

Many browsers, including IE7 and FF2, provide tabbed browsing. Holding down the *Ctrl* key and pressing the letter *T* while in the IE7 or FF2 browser opens another tab in the same window, allowing the user to browse multiple pages without cluttering the desktop with many windows. [*Note:* For Mac users, all references to the *Ctrl* key in this chapter's shortcuts should be replaced with the *Command* key.] Also, pressing *Ctrl* while clicking a link will open the requested page in a new tab. Clicking on the tabs switches between the different pages in the browser, and web pages are then accessed normally. Using tabs is an excellent way to keep the browser organized when viewing multiple pages at once.

Using the History Feature

IE7 and FF2 maintain a **History** list of previously visited URLs in chronological order. This feature allows users to return to recently visited websites easily. The history feature can be accessed several different ways. The simplest and most frequently used method is to click the **Forward** and **Back** buttons located at the top of the browser window (see Fig. 2.1). The **Back** button reloads into the browser the page you last visited. Assuming that you used the **Back** button to view previously visited pages, the **Forward** button would load the next URL from the history into the browser. The keyboard shortcut for **Forward** is *<Alt>* and the *Right Arrow* key or just *Shift* and *Backspace*, and the shortcut for **Back** is <*Alt*> and the *Left Arrow* key or simply *Backspace*.

In IE7, the user can view the last and next nine web pages visited and the current page by clicking the down arrows immediately to the right of the **Forward** button; the user can then request one of the recently viewed pages by clicking the title of the page in the drop-down list. In FF2, there are separate menus to the right of both the **Forward** and the **Back** buttons. Each displays the previous and following fifteen pages in the history, respectively. Note that these methods only display history results from the browser's current **session**, which is the period when the browser remains open. In IE7 and FF2, there is a menu to the right of the address bar which displays a longer but more basic history of visited sites (it does not include any URLs accessed through hyperlinks), including websites that were visited in previous sessions. Another way to display sites from a previous session is to use **History**.

Selecting **History** from the down-arrow menu in IE7, or clicking the **History** menu, then the **Show In Sidebar** option in FF2, divides the browser window into two sections: the **History** window (on the left) and the content window (Figs. 2.3–2.4). In IE7, clicking the yellow star icon in the upper left of the window, then selecting the **History** option, displays a similar menu. By default, the **History** window lists the URLs visited in the past twenty days in IE7 and nine days in FF2.

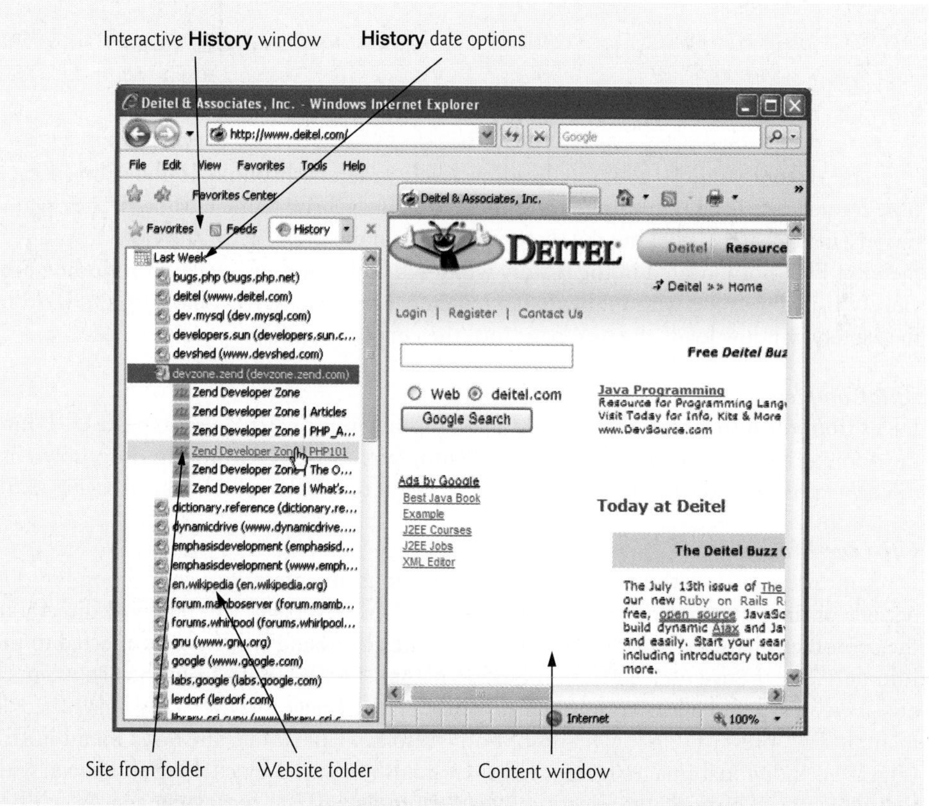

Fig. 2.3 | The **History** menu in Internet Explorer 7.

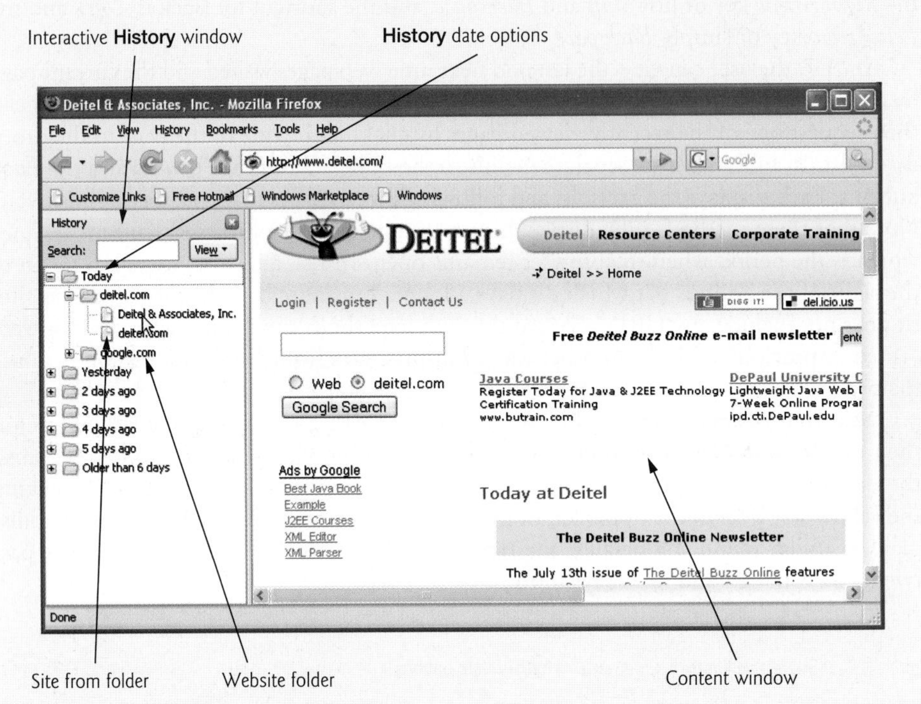

Fig. 2.4 | The **History** menu in Firefox 2.

The **History** window contains heading levels ordered chronologically. Within each time frame (e.g., **Today**) headings are alphabetized by website name (although the organization can be changed clicking the **History** drop-down menu in IE7 or the **View** drop-down menu of FF2, both located in the **History** window). This window is useful for finding previously visited websites without having to remember the exact URL. Selecting a URL from the **History** window loads the web page into the content window.

AutoComplete

URLs from the history can be displayed in a drop-down list when a user types a URL into the **Address** bar. This feature is called AutoComplete. Any URL from this drop-down list can be selected with the mouse to load the web page at that URL into the browser (Fig. 2.5).

Off-Line Browsing

For some users, such as those with dial-up connections, maintaining a connection for long periods of time may not be practical. For this reason, web pages can be saved directly to the computer's hard drive for off-line browsing (i.e., browsing while not connected to the Internet). Select **Save As...** in IE7, or **Save Page As...** in FF2, both from the **File** menu to save a web page and all its components, including the images. [*Note:* To display the **File** menu in IE7, press the *Alt* key.] This option is also available under the **Page** menu in IE7 (Fig. 2.1). Individual images from a website can also be saved by clicking the image with the right mouse button and selecting **Save Picture As...** (IE7) **or Save Image As...** (FF2) from the displayed context menu (Fig. 2.6).

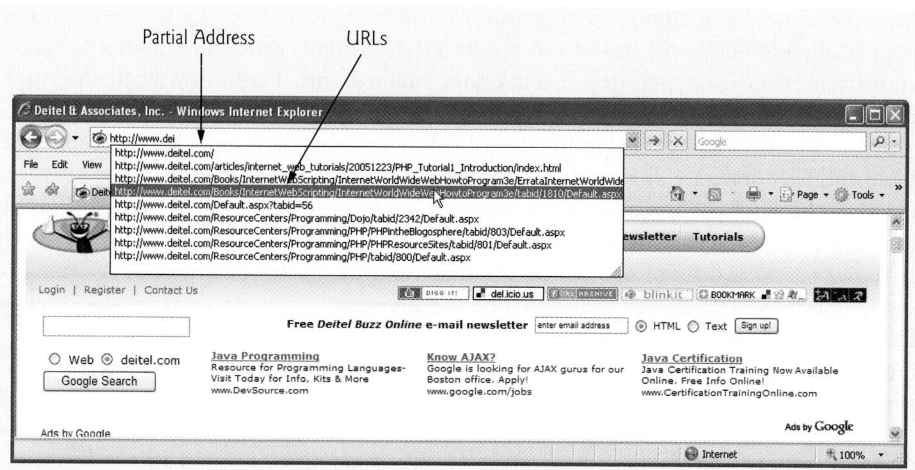

Fig. 2.5 | AutoComplete suggests possible URLs when given a partial address.

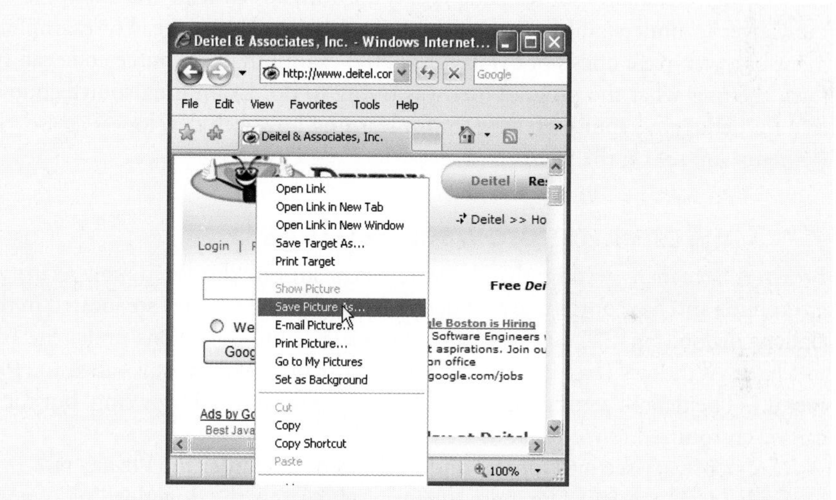

Fig. 2.6 | Saving a picture from a website.

Downloads

As mentioned earlier, files from the Internet may be copied to a computer's hard drive by a process called downloading. This section discusses the types of documents commonly downloaded from the Internet and techniques for downloading them. [*Note:* You should always be cautious when downloading files from the Internet, as they may contain viruses. Only download from sites that you trust.]

Some common Internet downloads are applications (i.e., software that performs specific functions, such as word processing), plug-ins and extensions. Plug-ins are specialized pieces of software that help the browser support additional content types. An example of an IE7 and FF2 plug-in is the Acrobat Reader from Adobe, Inc. (`www.adobe.com/products/acrobat/readstep2.html`), which allows users to view PDF (Portable Document Format) documents that otherwise cannot be rendered by the browser. Another popular plug-in allows the browser to render Flash content, which adds audio, video and animation effects to a website. To view sites enabled with Flash, download the Adobe Flash Player plug-in at `www.adobe.com/products/flashplayer`. Microsoft's rich media plug-in, Silverlight, is available for download at `silverlight.net/GetStarted`. (Both Flash and Silverlight are discussed in much greater depth in Chapters 16, 17 and 19). Normally the browser prompts the user to download a plug-in when one is needed. Plug-ins may also be downloaded from CNET (`www.download.com`). This site has a large, searchable index and database of many plug-in programs available for download.

Extensions are add-ons that enhance the preexisting functionality of the browser. Examples of extensions include blog editors, universal uploaders and various translation dictionaries and tools. Many IE7 add-ons can be found at `www.ieaddons.com`, and FF2 add-ons can be browsed and downloaded at `https://addons.mozilla.org`.

Viewing Source Code

Clicking on the **View** menu followed by the **Source** option in IE7 and **Page Source** in FF2 allows you to view the source code, or the original code written to create the web page you are viewing. Generally, source code is easy for humans to read and interpret, and allows the viewer to understand how the programmer created the page. For example, if an element of a web page does not display properly, examining the source code can help to inform the user what the programmer was trying to do. Examining source code is a useful tool for debugging your own code, or for learning how web developers create some of the elements you see on the web.

2.4 Customizing Browser Settings

Browsers have many settings that determine how sites are displayed, how security measures are applied and how outputs are rendered. Most of these settings are located in the **Internet Options** dialog (Fig. 2.7) in the **Tools** menu of IE7, and in **Options** under the **Tools** menu in FF2 in Windows (Fig. 2.8) [*Note:* For Firefox on a Mac, this is called the **Preferences** menu.]. The default settings are usually adequate for normal browsing, but these settings can be customized to suit each user's preferences.

Some privacy settings for IE7 and FF2 can be set under the **Privacy** tab. In IE7 there are six levels of privacy. The most lenient level permits the downloading of cookies (text files that are placed on the computer by websites to retain or gather information about the user); the most strict level blocks all cookies from all websites and constantly updates a report to the user about browsing privacy. Using this level may prevent certain websites from working correctly. In FF2 the **Privacy** tab displays options about how data is remembered in the system and when cookies should be accepted.

Security options for both browsers can be found under the **Security** tab. The browsers' options are significantly different, but both allow you to specify how much information you want to hide from unfamiliar sites, as well as how much of the site's content you would like to block from your own computer. Both browsers allow you to distinguish between trusted sites and the rest of the web, and to browse safe sites with lower security settings.

A personal home page can be specified under the **General** tab in IE7 and **Main** in FF2. The home page is the web page that loads when the browser is first opened and appears when the **Home** button at the top of the browser window is clicked (Figs. 2.1–2.2).

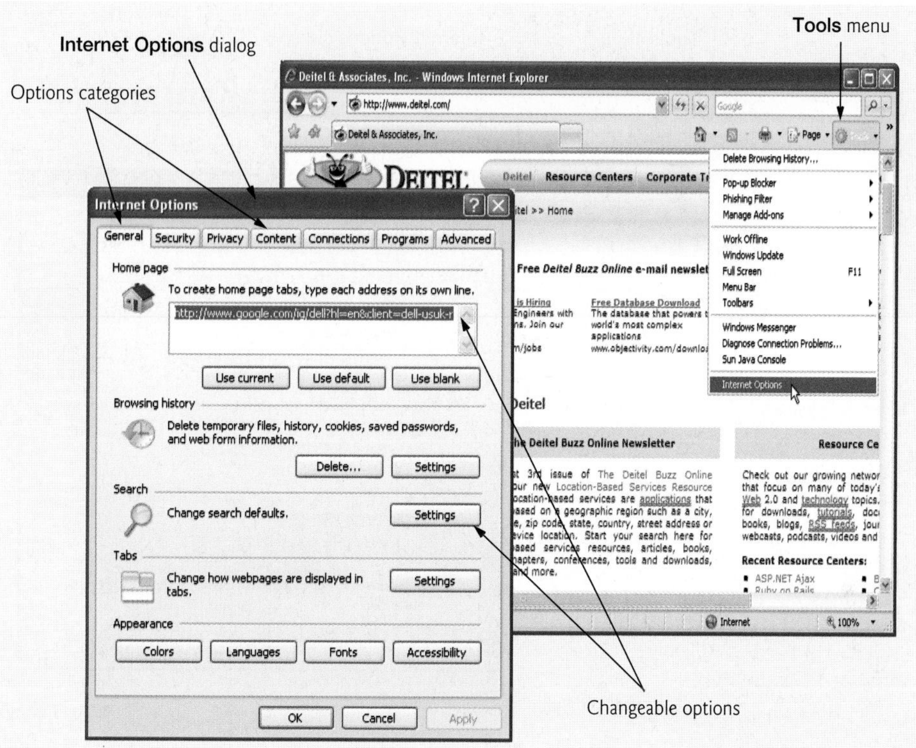

Fig. 2.7 | **Internet Options** in Internet Explorer 7.

History options also may be adjusted in this category. By clicking the **Settings** button in the **Browsing history** section of the **General** tab in IE7, or the **Network** option in the **Advanced** tab of FF2, the amount of disk space to be reserved for the web page cache can be set. The cache is an area of temporary storage that a browser designates for saving web pages for rapid future access. When a page is viewed that has been visited recently, IE7 and FF2 check whether they already have some elements on that page (such as images) saved in the cache, to reduce download time. Having a large cache can considerably speed up web browsing, whereas having a small cache saves disk space. Caching can sometimes cause problems, because Internet Explorer and Firefox do not always check to ensure that a cached page is the same as the latest version residing on the web server. Holding down the *Ctrl* key and pressing *F5* in either browser, or pressing *Ctrl*, *Shift* and *R* in FF2, remedies this problem by forcing the browser to retrieve the latest version of the web page from the website. Once the **Internet Options** are set, click **OK** in both browsers.

2.5 Searching the Internet

The Internet provides a wealth of information on virtually any topic. The sheer volume of information on the web can make it difficult for users to find specific information. To help users locate information, many websites provide search engines that explore the Internet and maintain searchable records containing information about website content. This section explains how search engines work and discusses two types of search engines.

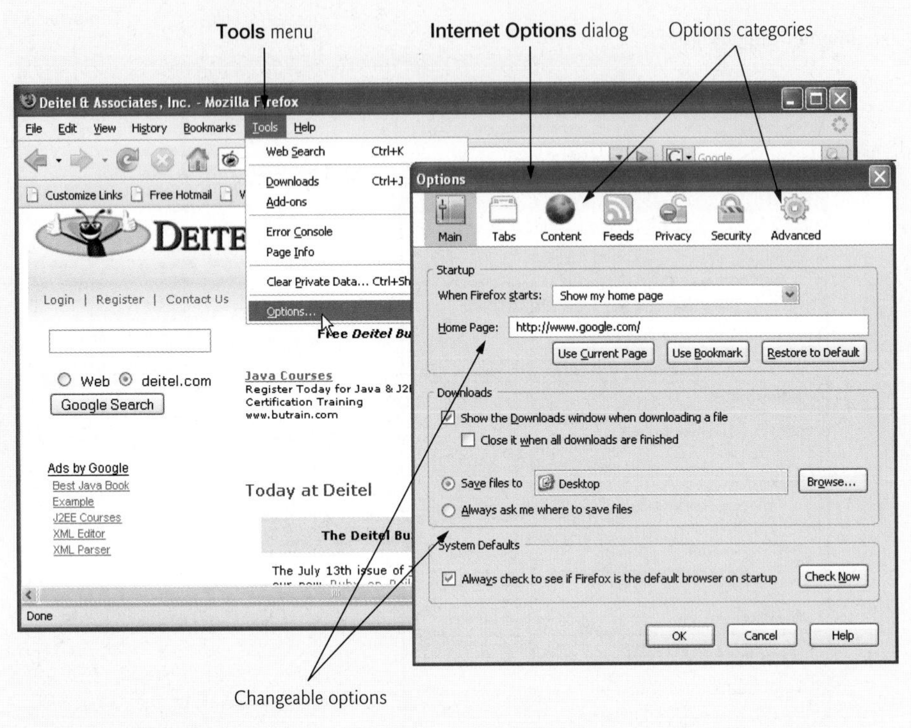

Fig. 2.8 | **Options** in Firefox 2.

Search engines such as Google (www.google.com), Yahoo! (www.yahoo.com), MSN (www.msn.com), AltaVista (www.altavista.com) and Ask.com (www.ask.com) store information in data repositories called databases that facilitate quick information retrieval. When the user enters a word or phrase, the search engine returns a list of hyperlinks to sites that satisfy the search criteria. Each search engine site has different criteria for narrowing searches, such as publishing date, language and relevance. Using multiple search engines may provide the best results in finding the desired content quickly. Sites such as MetaCrawler (www.metacrawler.com) use metasearch engines, which do not maintain databases. Instead, they send the search criteria to other search engines and aggregate the results. Many web browsers, including IE7 and FF2 (Figs. 2.9–2.10.), have a built-in search box placed in the window that can be used to browse the web. In both browsers, the user can choose which search engine to use by clicking the down-arrow menu (Fig. 2.9–2.10).

Search engines can also be used to help resolve programming errors. There are many websites that contain documentation about specific functions, how to use them correctly and related common errors. Putting a function name or error message into a search engine can often help a programmer discover where a mistake may have been made in the code. Also, websites such as www.thescripts.com allow users to post specific programming questions that can be answered by other programmers. Other websites like this one, as well as communities for specific languages, can be found using search engines.

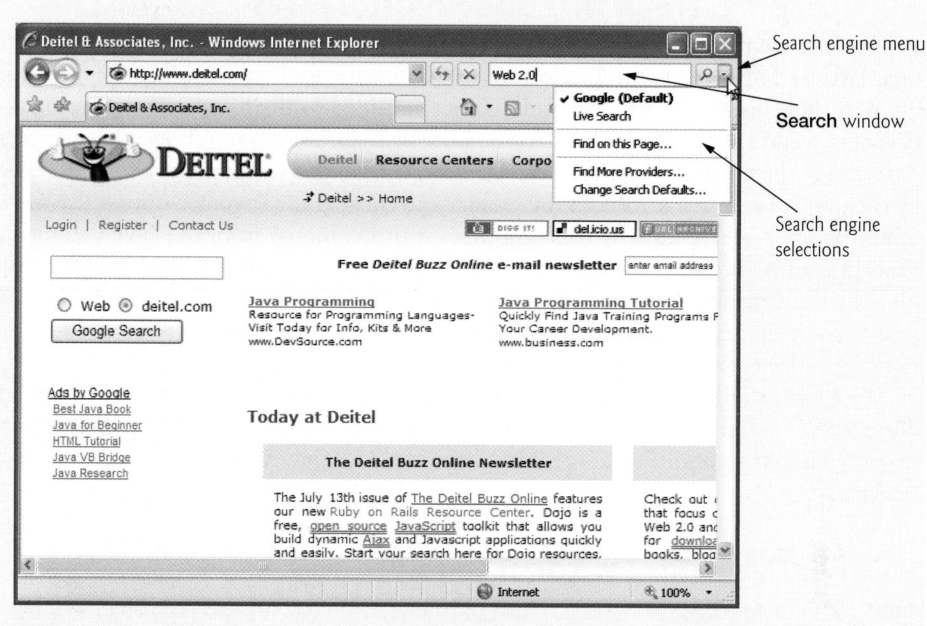

Fig. 2.9 | Searching the Internet with Internet Explorer 7.

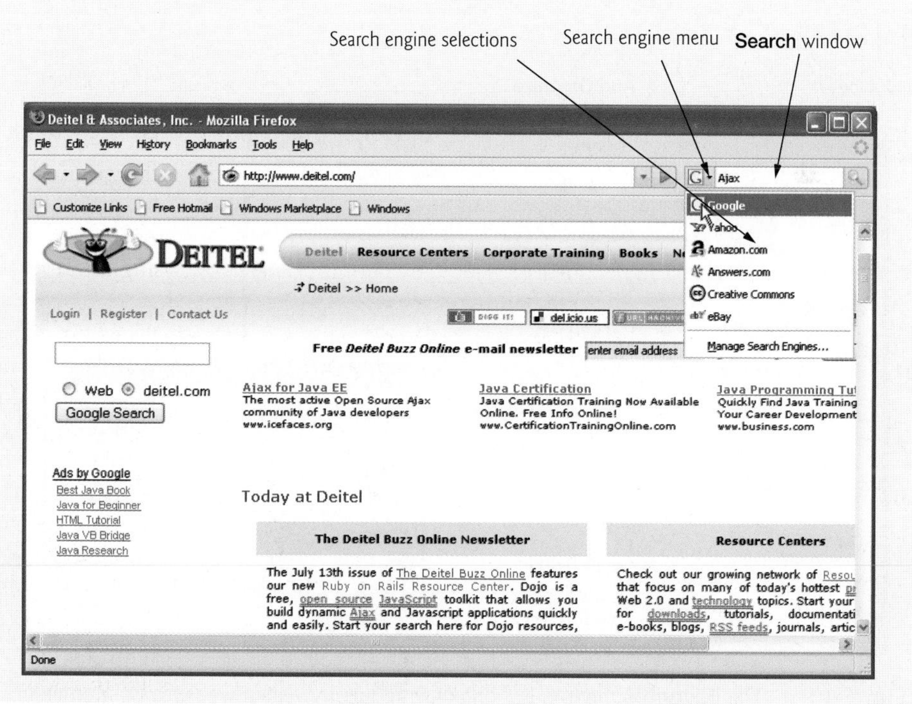

Fig. 2.10 | Searching the Internet with Firefox 2.

2.6 Keeping Track of Your Favorite Sites

As users browse the web, they often visit certain sites repeatedly and may want to record their URL and title. IE7 provides a feature called favorites for bookmarking (keeping track of) such sites (Fig. 2.11). Any page's URL can be added to the list of favorites using the **Favorites** menu's **Add to Favorites...** command, or by pressing the yellow star and green plus icon in the upper left corner of the window. A **Favorites** window can also be accessed by clicking the yellow star icon on the toolbar and clicking the **Favorites** option. Favorites can be accessed at any time by selecting them with the mouse from the **Favorites** menu. Favorites can be categorized and grouped into folders in the **Organize Favorites** dialog (displayed when **Organize Favorites...** is selected from the **Favorites** menu). These folders appear as submenus in the **Favorites** menu. The **Organize Favorites** dialog also allows users to rename, delete and move favorites between folders.

FF2 has a similar feature called bookmarks, which can be added with the **Bookmark This Page...** option in the **Bookmark** menu and used the same way that **Favorites** are described in this section (Fig. 2.12). Most browsers have their own version of **Favorites** or **Bookmarks.**

2.7 File Transfer Protocol (FTP)

The File Transfer Protocol (FTP) is a set of rules by which computers transfer data, especially large files, over the Internet. An FTP site's URL begins with `ftp://` rather than `http://`, and can also be accessed either with the web browser or software that supports FTP. Filezilla is a popular, open source FTP client for Windows that functions outside a

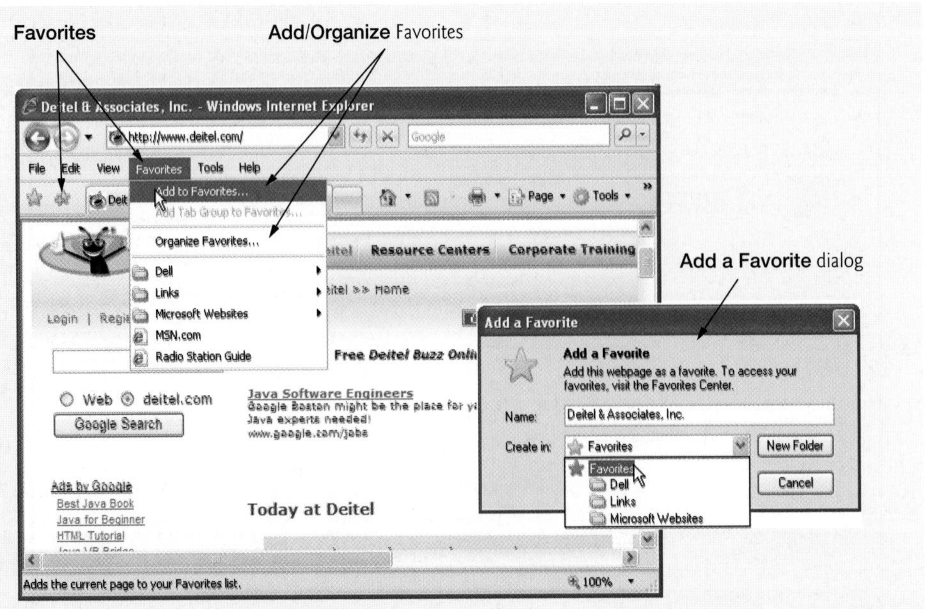

Fig. 2.11 | The **Favorites** menu helps organize frequently visited websites in Internet Explorer 7.

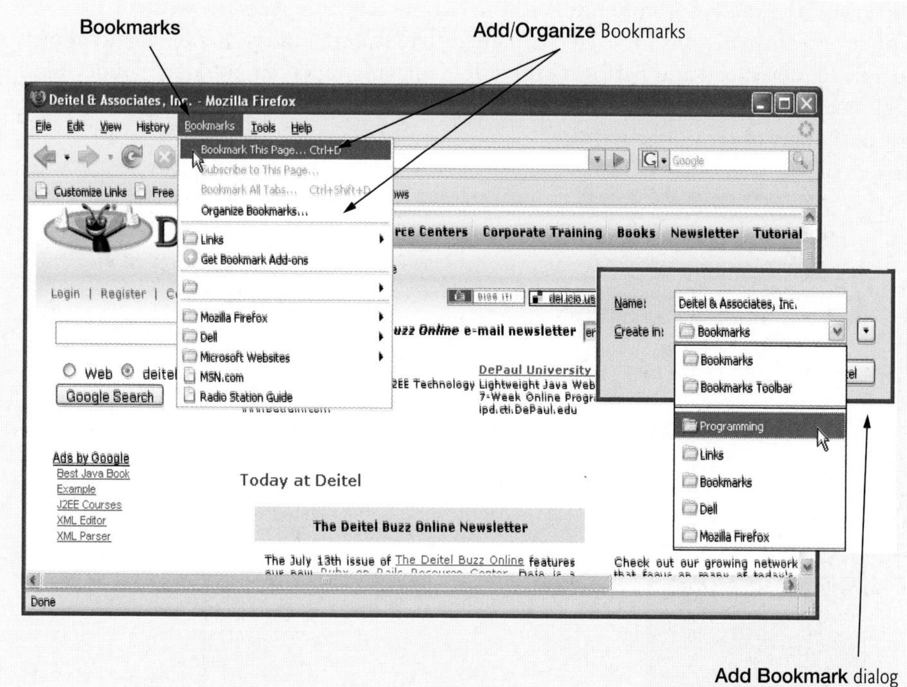

Fig. 2.12 | The **Bookmarks** menu helps organize frequently visited websites in Firefox 2.

web browser. It can be downloaded for free from `http://filezilla.sourceforge.net`. FF2 also has an extension, FireFTP, that adds the functionality of an FTP client to the browser. This add-on is available at `http://fireftp.mozdev.org`.

When your browser is pointed to an FTP site, the contents of the specified site directory appear in the window, and can be browsed as though they were files on the local computer. Files are downloaded by clicking their icons and following the browser's download instructions, or by dragging the file or folder with the mouse onto the desktop or into another directory. Windows users may copy and paste the URL into the address bar of the **My Computer** window, called the Windows Explorer (Fig. 2.13), which has a particularly straightforward interface for FTP. Windows Explorer can be accessed from the **Start** menu, or by clicking the **Page** menu, then selecting **Open FTP Site in Windows Explorer** in IE7.

When accessing an FTP site, the user may or may not be prompted for login information. Many FTP sites allow anonymous FTP access, where any user is permitted to view and download files. If login is required, the username is set by default to *anonymous*, and the user either is prompted for an e-mail address or should put an e-mail address in the password field. The browser sends the user's e-mail address and name to the website for tracking and information purposes. Other FTP sites contain directories with restricted access—only users with authorized usernames and passwords are permitted to access such directories. When a user is trying to enter a restricted-access FTP directory, a **Log On As** dialog like the one in Fig. 2.13 is displayed, prompting the user for login information.

Transferring a file from the local machine to another location on the Internet is called uploading and can be accomplished using the FTP protocol. Files can be transferred from the local machine (your computer) to the remote machine (server), with an FTP client. The specific instructions for each client are different, but almost all FTP clients allow you to upload, download and perform other file-managing tasks on your data. Understanding FTP is especially important for web developers, since uploading files to a web server is a necessary part of creating a website.

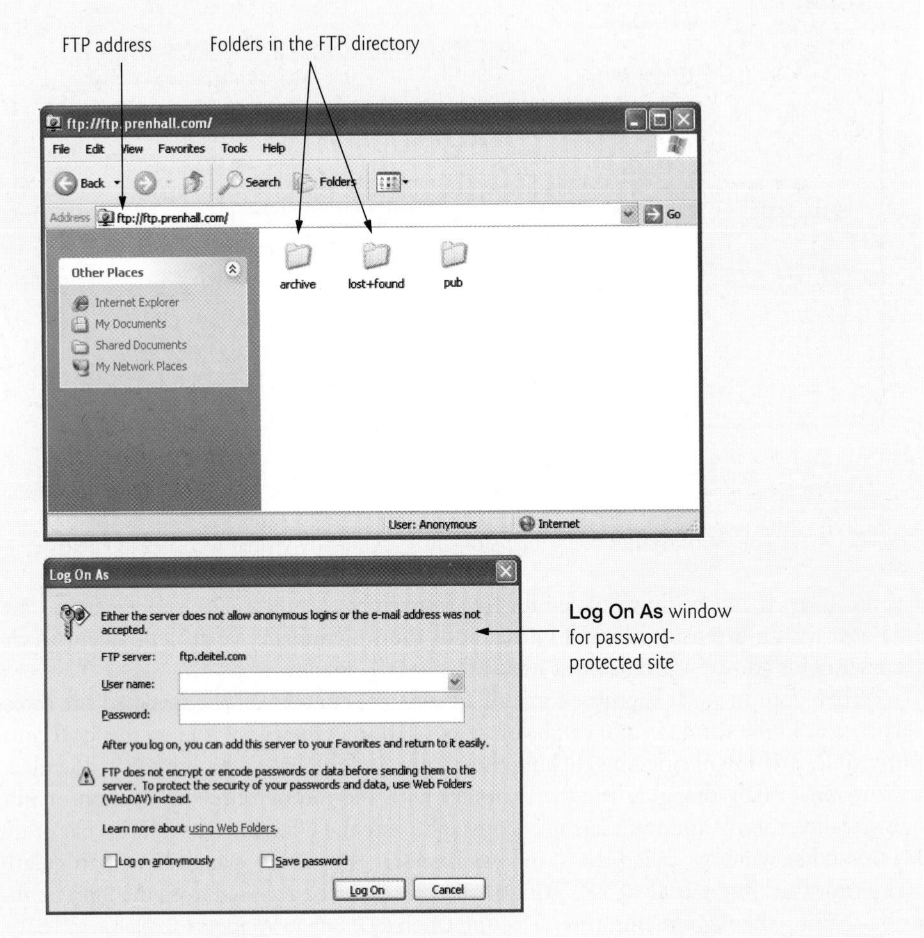

Fig. 2.13 | FTP site access.

2.8 Online Help

Web browsers are complex pieces of software with rich functionality. Although browser designers make every effort to produce user-friendly software, users still need time to familiarize themselves with each web browser and its particular features. Answers to frequently asked questions about using the web browser are included with FF2 and IE7, as well as most other browsers. This information is accessible through the built-in help feature available in the **Help** menu (Figs. 2.14–2.15).

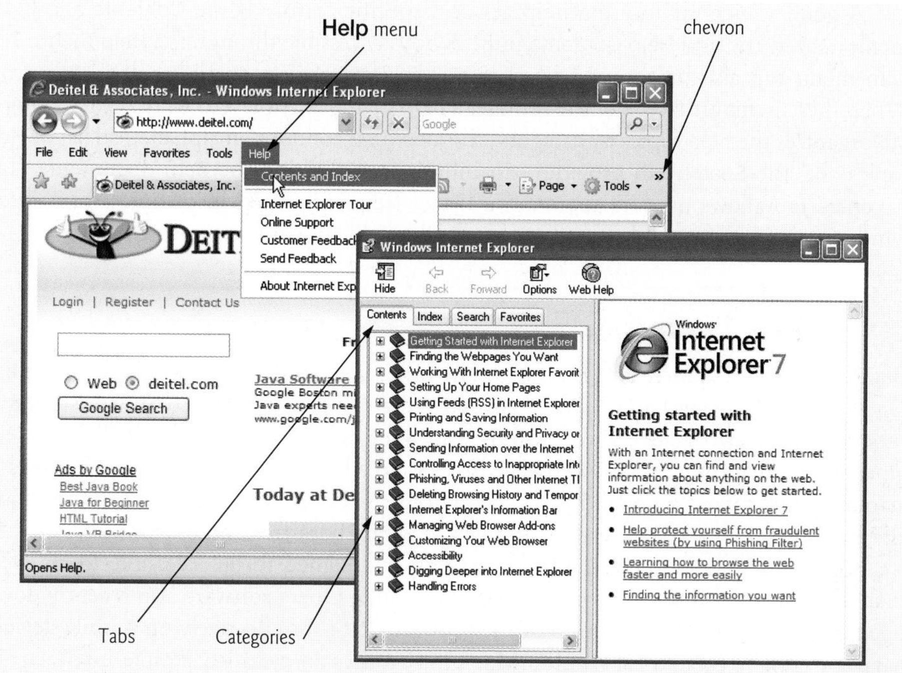

Fig. 2.14 | Internet Explorer 7 **Help** dialog.

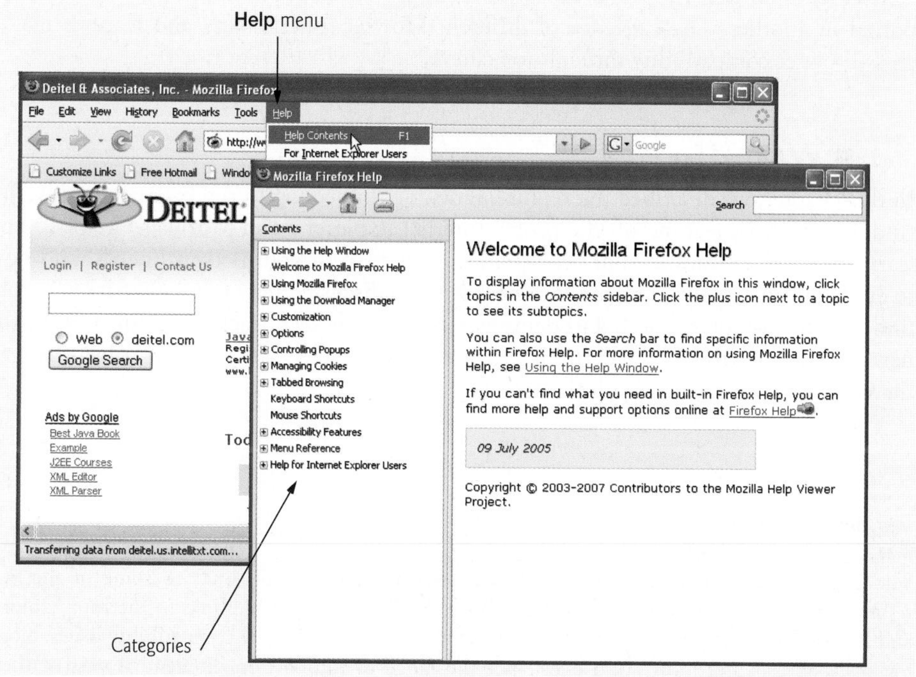

Fig. 2.15 | Firefox 2 **Help** dialog.

A good source for locating help about a specific feature is the **Contents and Index** menu item in IE7 and **Help Contents** in FF2, both accessible through the **Help** menu. IE's help menu can also be accessed by clicking the **Help** option on the toolbar's chevron. When these items are selected, the browser's help dialog is displayed. In IE7, the **Contents** tab organizes the help topics by category, the **Index** tab contains an alphabetical list of **Help** topics and the **Search** tab provides capabilities for searching the help documents. The **Favorites** tab allows users to maintain a list of frequently used help topics. FF2's **Help** window provides a search box and an expandable table of contents for browsing.

2.9 Other Web Browsers

Besides Internet Explorer and Firefox, many other web browsers are available, including *Opera* (`www.opera.com`) and *Safari* (`www.apple.com/safari`). All these browsers differ in functionality, performance and features. Also, they employ different HTML layout engines, which determine how a web page displays in a browser. Firefox 2 uses Gecko as its layout engine, Safari uses a modified version of the KHTML layout engine and Opera and IE7 have their own engines. Gecko and KHTML are both free and open source.

Opera, as well as IE7 and FF2, is a browser designed to be accessible to all users, including those with visual or mobility impairments. Opera software also recently developed a lightweight "Mini" version of the browser that runs effectively on mobile devices. Safari, originally created for Apple's Mac OS, features an elegantly simple interface and impressive speed, especially when executing JavaScript (discussed in Chapters 6–11). Because browsers use different HTML layout engines, they may display the same web page differently. Additionally, some capabilities supported in one browser may not be supported in another. The existence of different browser functionality and features makes cross-browser compatibility difficult to achieve.

2.10 Wrap-Up

In this chapter, we described the requirements for connecting to the Internet, and we introduced the basic features of Microsoft's Internet Explorer 7 and Mozilla's Firefox 2. You learned how to customize your browsing experience to fit your personal needs, and how to exchange data safely using the Internet. We also discussed how to use search engines to find information on the web and demonstrated how to keep track of useful sites. In the next chapter, we discuss the defining characteristics of Web 2.0 and how it has changed the way that users interact with the Internet.

2.11 Web Resources

`www.deitel.com/ie7`
`www.deitel.com/firefox`

The Deitel Internet Explorer and Firefox Resource Centers contain links to some of the best resources about these browsers on the web. There you'll find categorized links to Internet Explorer and Firefox downloads and add-ons, keyboard shortcuts, glossaries, code compatibility issues, blogs, forums, podcasts and more. Also check out the range of tutorials on different aspects of these browsers.

Summary

Section 2.1 Introduction to the Internet Explorer 7 and Firefox 2 Web Browsers

- Web browsers are software programs that allow users to access the web's rich multimedia content.
- The two most popular web browsers are Microsoft's *Internet Explorer* and Mozilla's *Firefox*.

Section 2.2 Connecting to the Internet

- A computer alone is not enough to access the Internet. In addition to web browser software, the computer needs specific hardware and a connection to an Internet Service Provider.
- A modem enables a computer to connect to the Internet. A modem converts data to audio tones and transmits the data over phone lines. A network card, also called a network interface card (NIC), allows a computer to connect to the Internet through a network or a high-speed Internet connection, such as a LAN, cable modem or a Digital Subscriber Line (DSL).
- Bandwidth refers to the amount of data that can be transferred through a communications medium in a fixed amount of time. Different ISPs offer different types of high-speed connections, called broadband connections.
- Broadband is a category of high-bandwidth Internet service that is most often provided by cable television and telephone companies to home users.
- DSL is a broadband service that allows computers to be connected at all times to the Internet over existing phone lines, without interfering with voice services.
- Cable modems enable the computer to be connected to the Internet at all times. Cable modems transmit data over the cables that bring television to homes and businesses.
- ISDN provides Internet service over either digital or standard telephone lines. ISDN requires specialized hardware, called a terminal adapter (TA), which is usually obtained from the ISP.
- Fiber optics are a cable alternative that provide greater bandwidth and a better signal, but their popularity is limited by high cost.

Section 2.3 Internet Explorer 7 and Firefox 2 Features

- A URL is the address of a web page. Each web page is associated with a unique URL. URLs usually begin with `http://`, which stands for Hypertext Transfer Protocol (HTTP), the industry standard protocol for transferring web documents over the Internet.
- URLs of websites that handle private information, such as credit card numbers, often begin with `https://`, the abbreviation for Hypertext Transfer Protocol over Secure Sockets Layer (HTTPS), the standard for transferring encrypted data over the Internet.
- Several techniques are available for navigating between different URLs. A user can click the **Address** field and type a web page's URL. The user can then press *Enter* or click **Go** to request the web page located at that URL.
- Another way to navigate the web is via visual elements on web pages called hyperlinks that, when clicked, load a specified web document. Both images and text serve as hyperlinks.
- Hyperlinks can reference other web pages, e-mail addresses and files. If a hyperlink is a `mailto:`*e-mailaddress*, clicking the link loads your default e-mail program and opens a message window addressed to the specified recipient's e-mail address.
- Tabbed browsing allows you to browse multiple pages without cluttering the desktop with many windows.
- When a file is downloaded, it is copied onto the user's computer. Programs, documents, images and sound files are all downloadable files.

- IE7 and FF2 maintain a list of previously visited URLs in chronological order, called the history.
- The **History** window contains heading levels ordered chronologically. Within each time frame headings are alphabetized by site directory name. This window is useful for finding previously visited sites without having to remember the exact URL.
- URLs from the history are displayed in a drop-down list when a user types a URL into the **Address** bar. This feature is called AutoComplete. Any URL from this drop-down list can be selected with the mouse to load the web page at that URL into the browser.
- Web pages can be saved directly to the computer's hard drive for off-line browsing. Select **Save As...** (IE7) or **Save Page As...** (FF2) from the **File** menu at the top of the browser window to save a web page and all its components.
- Individual images from a website can be saved by clicking the image with the right mouse button and selecting **Save Picture As...** (IE7) or **Save Image As...** (FF2) from the displayed context menu.
- Plug-ins are specialized pieces of software that enable the browser to support additional types of content. Normally the browser prompts the user to download a plug-in when a plug-in is needed.
- Extensions enhance the preexisting functionality of the browser.
- Clicking the **View** menu followed by the **Source** option in IE7 or **Page Source** in FF2 allows you to view the source code, or the original code written to create the web page you are viewing.

Section 2.4 Customizing Browser Settings

- IE7 and FF2 have many settings that determine how sites are displayed, how security measures are applied and how outputs are rendered. Many of these can be accessed through the **Tools** menu, then **Internet Options** in IE7, or **Options** in FF2.
- The privacy level for IE7 can be set under the **Privacy** tab of the **Internet Options** dialog. There are six levels of privacy. The most lenient level permits downloading and cookies; the strictest level renders a constant flow of alerts and alarms about browsing security and might prevent certain websites from working correctly.
- Privacy settings for FF2 can be found under the **Privacy** tab of **Options**, which displays options about how data is remembered in the system and when cookies should be accepted.
- Other security options can be found for both browsers under the **Security** tab.
- A personal home page can be specified under the **General** tab of the **Internet Options** dialog in IE7, and **Main** under **Options** in FF2. The home page is the web page that loads when the browser is first opened and appears when the **Home** button at the top of the browser window is clicked.
- History and cache options may be adjusted in the **General** tab of the **Internet Options** dialog by clicking the **Settings...** button in IE7, and the cache can be adjusted in the **Network** option in the **Advanced** tab of FF2. The amount of disk space to be reserved for web-page cache can be set here.

Section 2.5 Searching the Internet

- Search engines explore the Internet and maintain searchable records containing information about websites.
- Metasearch engines do not maintain databases. Instead, they send the search criteria to other search engines and aggregate the results. IE7 and FF2 have built-in search boxes next to the **Address** bar with several different search engines which can be selected by the user.
- Search engines are helpful tools for finding solutions to programming problems.

Section 2.6 Keeping Track of Your Favorite Sites

- As users browse the web, they often visit certain sites repeatedly. Internet Explorer 7 provides a feature called **Favorites** for bookmarking such sites, and Firefox 2 has a similar tool called **Book-**

marks. Sites can be remembered and organized under the **Favorites** menu in IE7 and the **Bookmarks** menu in FF2.

Section 2.7 File Transfer Protocol (FTP)

- FTP (file transfer protocol) is an older protocol for transferring information, especially large files, over the Internet. An FTP site's URL begins with `ftp://` rather than `http://`, and can be accessed through the browser or by any software that supports FTP.
- FTP sites with anonymous access allow any user access. Many FTP sites have restricted access; only users with authorized usernames and passwords are permitted to access such sites.
- Transferring a file from the local machine to another location on the Internet is called uploading and can be accomplished using the FTP protocol.

Section 2.8 Online Help

- The **Help** menu in the browsers allows the user to search or browse for answers to common questions and solutions to problems with the software.

Section 2.9 Other Web Browsers

- Many other browsers are available for download, each with its own set of features and advantages. Two of these browsers are Opera and Safari.

Terminology

Address bar
Adobe Acrobat Reader
Adobe Flash Player
anonymous FTP
applications
AutoComplete
Back button
bandwidth
bookmark
broadband connection
cable modem
cache
context menu
cookie
database
dial-up connection
Digital Subscriber Line (DSL)
download
extensions
Favorites
fiber optics
file transfer
File Transfer Protocol (FTP)
Filezilla
Firefox 2 (FF2)
Flash Content
Forward button
Gecko
Help menu
History
home page
HTML layout engine
hyperlink
Hypertext Transfer Protocol (HTTP)
Hypertext Transfer Protocol over Secure Sockets Layer (HTTPS)
Integrated Services Digital Network (ISDN)
Internet Explorer 7 (IE7)
Internet Options
Internet Service Provider (ISP)
metasearch engine
modem
Mozilla Firefox
network
network card
network interface card (NIC)
off-line browsing
Opera
plug-in
Portable Document Format (PDF)
Privacy
restricted access
Safari
Search
search engine
security level
session
sharing

Silverlight
source code
terminal adaptor (TA)
Uniform Resource Locator (URL)
uploading
web browser
web editor
Windows Internet Explorer

Self-Review Exercises

2.1 Fill in the blanks in each of the following statements:

a) The two most popular web browsers are _______ and _______.
b) A browser is used to view files on the _______.
c) The location of a file on the Internet is called its _______.
d) The element in a web page that, when clicked, causes a new web page to load is called a(n) _______; when your mouse passes over this element, the mouse pointer changes into a(n) _______ in IE7 and FF2.
e) IE7 and FF2 keep of a list of visited URLs called the _______.
f) You can save an image from a web page by right clicking the image and selecting _______ in IE7 or _______ in FF2.
g) The feature of IE7 and FF2 that provides options for completing URLs is called _______.
h) The feature that enables the user to save URLs of frequently visited sites is called _______ in IE7 or _______ in FF2.

2.2 State whether each of the following is *true* or *false*. If the statement is *false*, explain why.

a) Fiber optics cables have a better signal than traditional metal cables, but an inferior bandwidth.
b) It is not possible to view web pages when not connected to the Internet.
c) Search engines can be used to help resolve programming errors.
d) The cache is an area on the hard drive that is used for saving web pages for rapid future access.
e) FTP is a popular Internet mechanism by which files are uploaded and downloaded.
f) You can access any FTP site by logging in with the user name `anonymous`.

Answers to Self-Review Exercises

2.1 a) Internet Explorer, Firefox. b) Internet and the web. c) URL. d) hyperlink, hand. e) history. f) **Save Picture As...**, **Save Image As...** g) AutoComplete. h) **Favorites**, **Bookmarks**.

2.2 a) False. Fiber optic cables have a greater bandwidth than metal ones. b) False. Web pages saved to the hard drive can be viewed using off-line browsing. c) True. d) True. e) True. f) False. Many FTP sites are restricted and do not admit the general public.

Exercises

2.3 Spell out the following acronyms, and include a brief description of each:

a) HTTP
b) FTP
c) URL
d) DSL
e) PDF
f) ISP

2.4 Use your browser's FTP capability to access `ftp.cdrom.com` and `ftp.deitel.com`. Observe what happens in both cases, and, if the site can be accessed, list the directory output.

2.5 Go to `www.ieaddons.com` and browse the various extensions and plug-ins that can be installed into Internet Explorer. Choose one to install, and observe what capabilities are added as you browse the Internet.

2.6 Go to `addons.mozilla.org` and browse the various extensions and plug-ins that can be installed into Firefox. Choose one to install, and observe what capabilities are added as you browse the Internet.

2.7 Download and install the Opera (`www.opera.com`) and Safari (`www.apple.com/safari`) web browsers. Go to your favorite websites and try to observe any differences in speed, appearance and functionality.

3

Dive Into® Web 2.0

Network effects from user contributions are the key to market dominance in the Web 2.0 era.
—Tim O'Reilly

Link by link, click by click, search is building possibly the most lasting, ponderous, and significant cultural artifact in the history of humankind: the Database of Intentions.
—John Battelle, *The Search*

Web 2.0 is a massive social experiment…this is an opportunity to build a new kind of international understanding…citizen to citizen, person to person.
—Lev Grossman, *TIME*

One of the powerful things about networking technology like the Internet or the Web or the Semantic Web…is that the things we've just done with them far surpass the imagination of the people who invented them.
—Tim Berners-Lee, interviewed by Peter Moon, *IDG Now*

OBJECTIVES

In this chapter you will learn:

- The defining characteristics of Web 2.0.
- Why search is fundamental to Web 2.0.
- How Web 2.0 empowers the individual.
- The importance of collective intelligence and network effects.
- The significance and growth of blogging.
- Social networking, social media and social bookmarking.
- How tagging leads to folksonomies.
- How web services enable new applications to be quickly and easily "mashed up" from existing applications.
- Web 2.0 technologies.
- Web 2.0 Internet business and monetization models.
- The emerging Semantic Web (the "web of meaning").

Outline

[Note: *Chapter 3, Dive Into® Web 2.0, is also available as a free, frequently updated HTML-based e-book at* `http://www.deitel.com/freeWeb20ebook/`. *It is also available as a downloadable, fully-formatted PDF for a small fee. Check this site for the latest hyperlink-rich version. Many of the topics in this chapter are supplemented by extensive Resource Centers at* `http://www.deitel.com/resourcecenters.html`. *The e-book and the PDF link to the Resource Centers and other web resources for further study.*]

3.1 Introduction

Chapter 1 presented basic computing concepts and the roles of several key technologies in developing distributed client/server applications for the Internet and the web. Chapter 2 discussed the capabilities of web browsers and how to use the latest versions of the two most popular browsers, Internet Explorer 7 and Firefox 2. Chapter 3 introduces the principles, applications, technologies, companies, business models and monetization strategies of Web 2.0.

When the Mosaic browser was introduced in 1993, the web exploded in popularity. It continued to experience tremendous growth throughout the 1990s—a period referred to as the "dot-com bubble"; that bubble burst in 2001. In 2003 there was a noticeable shift in how people and businesses were using the web and developing web-based applications.

The term Web 2.0—coined by Dale Dougherty of O'Reilly® Media[1] in 2003 to describe this trend—became a major media buzzword, but few people really know what it means. Generally, Web 2.0 companies use the web as a platform to create collaborative, community-based sites (e.g., social networking sites, blogs, wikis, etc.). Web 2.0 was popularized by the annual O'Reilly Media Web 2.0 Summit (launched in 2004), in Tim O'Reilly's defining article on Web 2.0 entitled, "What is Web 2.0: Design Patterns and Business Models for the Next Generation of Software,"[2] and in John Musser and Tim O'Reilly's for-sale report, "Web 2.0 Principles and Best Practices."[3]

The growth of Web 2.0 can be attributed to some key factors. First, hardware keeps getting cheaper and faster, with memory capacities and speeds increasing at a rapid rate. Moore's Law states that the power of hardware doubles every two years, while the price remains essentially the same.[4] This allows for development of applications with high demands that would have been previously unthinkable. Second, broadband Internet use has exploded—a Pew Internet study in March 2006 found 42% of American adults had high-speed Internet in their homes. Of the 35% of Internet users who had posted content online, 73% had broadband Internet.[5] The abundance of digital media online would never have been possible without high-speed Internet. Third, the availability of abundant open source software (see Section 3.11) has resulted in cheaper (and often free) customizable software options. This makes it easier to start new Web 2.0 companies and greatly decreases the cost of failure. Fourth, unlike in Web 1.0 (the state of the web through the 1990s and early 2000s), there are many easy-to-employ models available to monetize Web 2.0 businesses—immediately generating (modest amounts of) revenue allows for more stable growth of new companies.

Our information on the companies in this chapter comes from common knowledge, the company websites and the footnoted books and articles.

3.2 What Is Web 2.0?

In a sense, this entire chapter defines Web 2.0, but let's begin with a brief, one-section discussion. Web 1.0 was focused on a relatively small number of companies and advertisers producing content for users to access—some people called the web at the time the "brochure web." Web 2.0 *involves* the user—not only is the content often created by users, but users help organize it, share it, remix it, critique it, update it, etc. One way to look at Web 1.0 is as a *lecture*, a small number of professors informing a large audience of students. In comparison, Web 2.0 is a *conversation*, with everyone having the opportunity to speak and share views.

---

1. O'Reilly, T. "What is Web 2.0: Design Patterns and Business Models for the Next Generation of Software." September 2005 <http://www.oreillynet.com/pub/a/oreilly/tim/news/2005/09/30/what-is-web-20.html>.
2. O'Reilly, T. "What is Web 2.0: Design Patterns and Business Models for the Next Generation of Software." September 2005 <http://www.oreillynet.com/pub/a/oreilly/tim/news/2005/09/30/what-is-web-20.html>.
3. Musser, J. and T. O'Reilly. *Web 2.0 Principles and Best Practices.* O'Reilly Media, Inc., 2006.
4. Moore, G. "Cramming More Components onto Integrated Circuits." *Electronics*, April 1965 <ftp://download.intel.com/museum/Moores_Law/Articles-Press_Releases/Gordon_Moore_1965_Article.pdf>.
5. Horrigan, J. B. "Home Broadband Adoption 2006." *Pew Internet & American Life Project*, May 2006 <http://www.pewinternet.org/pdfs/PIP_Broadband_trends2006.pdf>.

Web 2.0 embraces an architecture of participation—a design that encourages user interaction and community contributions.[6] You, the user, are the most important aspect of Web 2.0—so important, in fact, that in 2006, *TIME Magazine*'s "Person of the Year" was "you."[7] The article recognized the social phenomenon of Web 2.0—the shift away from a powerful few to an empowered many.

> *"We can't be device centric...we must be user centric."*
> —Bill Gates, MIX06 conference[8]

Many Web 2.0 companies are built almost entirely on user-generated content and harnessing collective intelligence. The significance is not just in having user-generated content, but in how it is used. Google—the leading search engine and Internet advertising company—sends its users to user-generated websites by considering what users collectively have valued in the past. For websites like MySpace®, Flickr™, YouTube and Wikipedia®, users create the content, while the sites provide the platforms. These companies *trust their users*—without such trust, users cannot make significant contributions to the sites.

> *"A platform beats an application every time."*
> —Tim O'Reilly[9]

The architecture of participation is seen in software development as well. Open source software is available for anyone to use and modify with few or no restrictions—this has played a major role in Web 2.0 development. Harnessing collective intelligence,[10] communities collaborate to develop software that many people believe is better than proprietary software.

You, the user, are not only contributing content and developing open source software, but you are also directing how media is delivered, and deciding which news and information outlets you trust. Many popular blogs now compete with traditional media powerhouses. Social bookmarking sites such as del.icio.us and Ma.gnolia allow users to recommend their favorite sites to others. Social media sites such as Digg™ or Reddit enable the community to decide which news articles are the most significant. You are also changing the way we find the information on these sites by tagging (i.e., labeling) web content by subject or keyword in a way that helps anyone locate information more effectively. This is just one of the ways Web 2.0 helps users identify new meaning in already existing content. RSS feeds (Chapter 14, XML and RSS) enable you to receive new information as it is updated—pushing the content right to your desktop.

---

6. O'Reilly, T. "What is Web 2.0: Design Patterns and Business Models for the Next Generation of Software." September 2005 <http://www.oreillynet.com/pub/a/oreilly/tim/news/2005/09/30/what-is-web-20.html>.
7. Grossman, L. "TIME's Person of the Year: You." *TIME*, December 2006 <http://www.time.com/time/magazine/article/0,9171,1569514,00.html>.
8. "Bill Gates: Microsoft MIX06 Conference." *Microsoft*, March 2006 <http://www.microsoft.com/presspass/exec/billg/speeches/2006/03-20MIX.mspx>.
9. O'Reilly, T. "What is Web 2.0: Design Patterns and Business Models for the Next Generation of Software." September 2005 <http://www.oreillynet.com/pub/a/oreilly/tim/news/2005/09/30/what-is-web-20.html>.
10. O'Reilly, T. "What is Web 2.0: Design Patterns and Business Models for the Next Generation of Software." September 2005 <http://www.oreillynet.com/pub/a/oreilly/tim/news/2005/09/30/what-is-web-20.html>.

The rise of social networks has changed the way we interact and network. MySpace—the largest social network—has rapidly become the world's most popular website. Other popular social networking sites include Facebook, Bebo, LinkedIn, and Second Life—a 3D virtual world where you interact with others via your online persona called an avatar.

Many Web 2.0 businesses leverage the Long Tail.[11] Coined by Chris Anderson in an article in the October 2004 *WIRED* magazine, the Long Tail refers to the economic model in which the market for non-hits (typically large numbers of low-volume items) could be significant and sometimes even greater than the market for big hits (typically small numbers of high-volume items).[12] So an online company like Netflix—which has a catalog of over 80,000 movie titles for rent—typically rents a large volume of less popular movies in addition to the substantial business it does renting hits. A local movie store has limited shelf space and serves a small, local population; it cannot afford the space to carry the Long Tail movies in every store. However, Netflix serves millions of people and does not have the physical constraints of stores; it can keep a small inventory of many Long Tail movies to serve its entire customer base. The opportunity to leverage the Long Tail is made possible by the relative ease of running a Web 2.0 Internet business and is fueled by the social effects of Web 2.0 that increase exposure for lesser-known products.

In this chapter, we introduce some of the key technologies used to create Web 2.0 applications. Many of these technologies are discussed in detail in the programming chapters of *Internet & World Wide Web How to Program, 4/e*. You'll learn web development technologies, such as Ajax (Chapter 15); its component technologies, including XHTML (Chapter 4), Cascading Style Sheets (CSS, Chapter 5), JavaScript (Chapters 6–11), the Document Object Model (DOM, Chapter 12), XML (Chapter 14) and the `XMLHttpRequest` object (Chapter 15); and the popular Ajax toolkits—Dojo (Chapter 15) and Script.aculo.us (Chapter 24).

You'll learn how to build Rich Internet Applications (RIAs)—web applications that offer the responsiveness and rich GUI features of desktop applications. We discuss key tools for building RIAs, including Adobe's Flex (Chapter 18), Microsoft's Silverlight (Chapter 19), ASP.NET Ajax (Chapter 25) and Sun's JavaServer Faces (Chapters 26–27). We present web development tools such as Adobe's Dreamweaver and its Ajax-enabling capabilities (Chapter 20). We also discuss other popular development technologies including JSON (Chapter 15), the web servers IIS and Apache (Chapter 21), MySQL (Chapter 22), PHP (Chapter 23), and ASP.NET (Chapter 25).

We discuss the emergence of web services (Chapter 28), which allow you to incorporate functionality from existing applications into your own applications quickly and easily. For example, using Amazon Web Services™, you can create a specialty bookstore and earn revenues through the Amazon Associates program; or using Google™ Maps web services with eBay web services, you can build location-based mashup applications to find auction items in certain geographical areas. Web services, inexpensive computers, abundant high-speed Internet access, open source software and many other elements have inspired new, exciting lightweight business models that people can launch with only a small investment. Some websites with robust functionality that might have required hundreds of thousands

---

11. Anderson, C. *The Long Tail: Why the Future of Business Is Selling Less of More.* Hyperion, 2006.
12. Anderson, C. "The Long Tail." *WIRED*, October 2004 `<http://www.wired.com/wired/archive/12.10/tail.html>`.

or even millions of dollars to build in the 1990s can now be built for nominal amounts of money.

Section 3.17 overviews key Web 2.0 business models, many of which are also explained in greater depth throughout the chapter. Fig. 3.1 includes a list of Web 2.0-related conferences. Some have a technology focus, while others have a business focus.

Web 2.0 and related conferences	
AdTech	Microsoft MIX
Affiliate Marketing Summit	Microsoft Tech Ed
AjaxWorld Expo	MySQL Conference and Expo
All Things Digital	Open Source (OSCON)
Always On	RailsConf
Blog Business Summit	Search Engine Strategies
eBay Live	Tools of Change for Publishing
Emerging Technology	Ubuntu Live
Emerging Telephony	Web 2.0 Expo
Future of Online Advertising	Web 2.0 Summit
JavaOne	Where 2.0

Fig. 3.1 | Web 2.0 and related conferences.

3.3 Search

"Google's mission is to organize the world's information and make it universally accessible and useful."

—Google[13]

In Web 2.0, the saying "content is king" remains a prevailing theme. With seemingly endless content available online, the findability of content becomes key. Search engines are the primary tools people use to find information on the web. Today, you perform searches with keywords, but the future of web search will use natural language (see, for example, Powerset.com). Currently, when you enter a keyword or phrase, the search engine finds matching web pages and shows you a search engine results page (SERP) with recommended web pages listed and sorted by relevance. People-assisted search engines have also emerged, such as Mahalo, which pays people to develop search results.[14] The popularity of vertical search engines—ones that focus on a specific topic or industry—is on the rise, though traffic to these search engines is still far behind the major (more generalized) search engines.

Traffic to the major search engines is growing rapidly—according to a recent comScore (a web analytics company) report, Americans conducted 8 billion search queries in June 2007, up 26% from the previous year. In the same report, the comScore analysis of

13. "Company Overview." *Google* <http://www.google.com/intl/en/corporate/index.html>.
14. "Mahalo Greenhouse FAQ." *Mahalo* <http://greenhouse.mahalo.com/Mahalo_Greenhouse_FAQ>.

U.S. market share across the most popular search engines reported Google at the top with 49.5% of the U.S. search market, followed by Yahoo! with 25.1%, Microsoft with 13.2%, Ask with 5.0% and Time Warner Network with 4.2%.[15]

John Battelle's book *The Search: How Google and Its Rivals Rewrote the Rules of Business and Transformed Our Culture* provides an extensive history of search engines and presents strong arguments for the importance of search in almost every aspect of our personal and business lives. John Battelle's *Searchblog* discusses search and technology issues (`http://battellemedia.com`).

Attention Economy

> *"Telecommunications bandwidth is not a problem, but human bandwidth is."*
> —Thomas Davenport and John Beck, *The Attention Economy*[16]

The abundant amounts of information being produced and people's limited free time has led to an attention economy. More content is available than users can sort through on their own, especially given the demands on their time, such as responsibilities to children, parents, friends, employers, etc. *The Attention Economy*, by Thomas Davenport and John Beck, begins with the familiar story of a man whose attention is constantly demanded by work and family. The authors explain that the constant flow of information in today's world causes attention to continually be diverted.

Though it used to be difficult to obtain diverse content, there are now seemingly endless options competing for an audience's attention. As a result, search engines have gained popularity by helping users quickly find and filter the information they want.[17]

Google Search

Google is the leading search and online advertising company, founded by Larry Page and Sergey Brin while they were Ph.D. students at Stanford University. Google is so popular that its name has been added to the Oxford English Dictionary—the verb "Google" means to find something on the Internet using the Google search engine. ("google" with a lowercase "g" is a cricket term, whereas "googol" or 10^{100} is the mathematical term Google was named after.)[18]

Google's success in search is largely based on its PageRank™ algorithm (patented by Stanford University and Larry Page) and its unique infrastructure of servers that uses linked PCs to achieve faster responses and increased scalability at lower costs.[19] Estimates on the number of Google servers range from hundreds of thousands to over one million.[20] The PageRank algorithm considers the number of links into a web page and the quality of

---

15. "comScore Releases June U.S. Search Engine Rankings." *CNNMoney*, 16 July 2007 `<http://money.cnn.com/news/newsfeeds/articles/prnewswire/AQM17916072007-1.htm>`.
16. Davenport, T. and J. Beck. *The Attention Economy: Understanding the New Currency of Business.* Harvard Business School Press, 2002, p.2.
17. Thompson, C. "Media in the Age of the Swarm." *cbc.ca* `<http://www.cbc.ca/10th/columns/media_thompson.html>`.
18. Brin, S. and L. Page. "The Anatomy of a Large-Scale Hypertextual Web Search Engine." `<http://infolab.stanford.edu/~backrub/google.html>`.
19. "Technology Overview." *Google* `<http://www.google.com/corporate/tech.html>`.
20. "Google: One Million and Counting." *Pandia Search Engine News*, 2 July 2007 `<http://www.pandia.com/sew/481-gartner.html>`.

the linking sites (among other factors) to determine the importance of the page. Each inbound link is a vote saying that site is valuable to someone else; however, votes are given different weights depending on the "voter" site's own value. So, two pages could have the same PageRank even if one has numerous links in from other pages and the other has fewer links in but from pages with higher PageRank. Google search also considers all of the content on the page, its fonts, its headers and the content of neighboring pages.[21] Sites with the highest PageRank will appear at the top of the search results.

In addition to its regular search engine, Google offers specialty search engines for images, news, videos, blogs and more. Using Google web services, you can build Google Maps and other Google services into your applications (see Section 3.13, Web Services, Mashups, Widgets and Gadgets).

AdWords, Google's pay-per-click (PPC) contextual advertising program (launched in 2000), is the company's main source of revenue. AdWords ads appear next to search results on the Google site (and are related to the search query). Advertisers write their own ads, which are unobtrusive and uniform in appearance—each ad consists of a headline, limited text and a URL. Advertisers bid on search keywords related to their ads and pay based on the number of users who click on the ads.

AdSense is Google's advertising program for publishers (sites like `http://www.deitel.com` that offer content), inspired by Susan Wojcicki, the vice president of product management. (In 1998, Wojcicki rented a spare room in her house to Larry Page and Sergey Brin where they founded Google.)[22] AdSense is a fundamental and popular form of website monetization, particularly for Web 2.0 startup companies. Google text ads (as well as banner and rich-media ads) are placed on participating sites with related content. Click-through rates on contextual ads are often higher than on non-contextual ads because the ads reach people expressing interest in a related topic. As a result, contextual pay-per-click ads generally pay a higher eCPM (effective cost per thousand impressions).

Yahoo!

Yahoo! was started in 1994 by Jerry Yang and David Filo (also Stanford Ph.D. students) as a web directory rather than a search engine. The original site, "Jerry and David's Guide to the World Wide Web," consisted of their favorite websites manually added to a categorized directory.[23] As the web grew, maintaining the directory structure became increasingly difficult, and a search capability was created for better access to the data. Focusing more on search, Yahoo! also expanded into other areas, becoming a popular provider of e-mail, user groups and more. In 2003, Yahoo! acquired Overture (now Yahoo! Search Marketing), which was the first search engine to offer sponsored search results successfully.[24]

MSN

MSN search was created in 1998, a year after Google was launched.[25] Over the past few years, Microsoft has made search engine technology development a top priority.[26] Mi-

21. "Technology Overview." *Google* `<http://www.google.com/corporate/tech.html>`.
22. Graham, J. "The House that Helped Build Google." *USA TODAY*, 5 July 2007, 1B.
23. "Company History." *Yahoo!* `<http://yhoo.client.shareholder.com/press/history.cfm>`.
24. Mills, E. "Google Rises at Yahoo's Expense." *CNET*, 23 April 2007 `<http://news.com.com/Google+rises+at+Yahoos+expense/2100-1038_3-6178164.html>`.
25. Underwood, L. "A Brief History of Search Engines." *Web Ref* `<http://www.webreference.com/authoring/search_history/>`.

crosoft search query volume and its search market share grew rapidly in June 2007; analysis companies comScore and Compete attribute this boost largely to MSN's Live Search club, a program introduced in May 2007 to reward users of Live Search.[27, 28] MSN's Live Search includes a new search engine, index and crawler.[29] It allows you to search the web, performing specialized searches (news, images, or local listings) or MSN content searches.[30] Another approach that Microsoft is taking to increase its search market share is buying vertical search sites such as MedStory, a health search engine. [31] Microsoft is also looking to gain market share in the contextual advertising market through Microsoft adCenter (similar to Google AdWords and Yahoo! Search Marketing).

Ask

Ask (formally known as AskJeeves.com) is owned by InterActiveCorp (IAC), which also owns Ticketmaster®, Match.com®, LendingTree.com®, RealEstate.com® and many other Internet properties. In June 2007, Ask launched a new search site, which includes a new design with a simple homepage default, customizable backgrounds, new video search (powered by Blinkx) and the ability to view video previews and listen to music clips. The search results are based on the searcher's location—Ask will report relevant local businesses and events. Searching for movies, for example, will show local show times.

Vertical Search

Vertical search engines are specialists (focusing on specific topics) in comparison to generalists (e.g., Google and Yahoo!).[32] Vertical search engines enable you to search for resources in a specific area, with the goal of providing you with a smaller number of more relevant results. Popular vertical search engines include travel sites (such as Kayak or Expedia), real-estate sites (such as Zillow or Trulia), job search sites (such as Indeed or Monster) and shopping search engines (such as Shopzilla and MySimon).

Location-Based Search

Location-based search (offered by most major search engines as well as some smaller specialized ones) uses geographic information about the searcher to provide more relevant search results. For example, search engines can ask the user for a ZIP code or estimate the user's general location based on IP address. The engine can then use this information to give higher priority to search results physically located near the user. This is particularly useful when searching for businesses such as restaurants or car services. (See Section 3.14 for more information on location-based services.)

---

26. Olson, S. "MSN Launches Revamped Search Engine." *CNET,* 30 June 2004 <http://news.com.com/MSN+launches+revamped+search+engine/2100-1032_3-5254083.html>.
27. "comScore Releases June U.S. Search Engine Rankings." *CNNMoney,* 16 July 2007 <http://money.cnn.com/news/newsfeeds/articles/prnewswire/AQM17916072007-1.htm>.
28. Sullivan, D. "Compete: Microsoft Gaining Searches; Live Search Club Giveaway Working?" *Search Engine Land,* 10 July 2007 <http://searchengineland.com/070710-105603.php>.
29. "MSN Live Search: About Us." *MSN* <http://search.msn.com/docs/default.aspx>.
30. "Web Search: How to use MSN Search." *MSN* <http://search.msn.com/docs/help.aspx?t=SEARCH_CONC_WhatsNewWithMSNSearch.htm>.
31. "Vertical Search-Engines: Know Your Subject." *Economist.com,* 12 July 2007 <http://www.economist.com/business/displaystory.cfm?story_id=9478224>.
32. "Vertical Search-Engines: Know Your Subject." *Economist.com,* 12 July 2007 <http://www.economist.com/business/displaystory.cfm?story_id=9478224>.

Creating Customized Search Engines

Rollyo—a build-your-own customized search engine website—allows you to explore, create and personalize search engines ("searchrolls") created by others. This helps you narrow your search to sites you already trust.[33] Other custom search sites include Gigablast and Google Custom Search Engine.

Search Engine Optimization (SEO)

Search Engine Optimization (SEO) is the process of designing and tuning your website to maximize your findability and improve your rankings in organic (non-paid) search engine results. To maximize traffic, you need to take into consideration how search engines work when you design your website. There are two ways of employing SEO. The first, white hat SEO, refers to methods that are approved by search engines, do not attempt to deceive the search engines, and produce quality, long-term results. Top white hat techniques for SEO include: offering quality content, using proper metadata and effective keywords, and having inbound links from relevant high-quality pages.[34] Black hat methods are used to deceive search engines. Although they may result in temporary improvement in search engine results, these tactics could get your site banned by the search engines. A "Googlebomb" (or link bomb) is an example of a black hat method—it attempts to trick the Google algorithm into promoting a certain page (generally for humorous reasons).[35]

Link Building

Link building is the process of increasing search engine rankings and traffic by generating inbound links to a particular website. Search engine algorithms regard each link as a vote for the destination website's content, so sites with the greatest link popularity (or number of high-quality inbound links) appear highest on search engine result pages (SERPs). The three most practiced methods of building links include reciprocal linking, link baiting and natural linking. Reciprocal linking is an exchange in which two related websites link to each other, increasing the link popularity of both sites and adding value for site users. Link baiting involves creating attention-grabbing web content specifically for viral (exponentially increasing) exposure through social media and social bookmarking websites. Natural linking is the process of building one-way inbound links by optimizing website content and user experience without the explicit solicitation of a backlink. Search algorithms are continuously updated to prevent black hat SEOs from deceiving search engines with automated linking software and links from directories or other low-quality websites. One-way links from websites with strong, related pages are given greater weight than reciprocal links, links from sites with unrelated content or links from sites with low PageRank.

Search Engine Marketing (SEM)

Search Engine Marketing (SEM) is the method of promoting your website to increase traffic and search results by raising the site's visibility on search engine results pages. Danny Sullivan (founder of Search Engine Watch and, more recently, Search Engine Land) introduced the term "Search Engine Marketing" in 2001 to include SEO, manag-

---

33. "About Rollyo." *Rollyo* `<http://www.rollyo.com/about.html>`.
34. Wilding, R. "Top 5 Black Hat and White Hat Search Engines Optimisation Techniques."*PushON* `<http://www.pushon.co.uk/articles/top5-black-hat-white-hat-seo.htm>`.
35. Calore, M. "Remembering the First Google Bomb." *Compiler (WIRED blog)*, 26 January 2007 `<http://blog.wired.com/monkeybites/2007/01/earlier_today_m.html>`.

ing paid listings, developing online marketing strategies and submitting sites to directories.[36] SEO is the most popular form of search engine marketing, which continues to take away business from other marketing channels (especially offline sources). According to the Search Engine Marketing Professional Organization's annual State of Search Engine Marketing survey, North American advertisers spent $9.4 billion on search engine marketing in 2006, a 62% increase over 2005 spending.[37]

Search Engine Watch and Search Engine Land

Search Engine Watch is a search engine marketing resource site. It includes articles, tutorials, conferences and more. The site, launched in 1997 by Danny Sullivan, was inspired by his 1996 release of "A Webmaster's Guide To Search Engines." Search Engine Watch incorporates Web 2.0 features (blogging and forums in addition to expert columnist articles). Other Search Engine Watch departments include search engine submission tips, web searching tips, popular search engines and search engine resources (numerous topics related to search engines). Danny Sullivan served as Search Engine Watch's editor-in-chief until November 2006, when he left the site and became the editor-in-chief for Search Engine Land. The site provides news and information on the major search engines—Google, Yahoo!, and Microsoft—as well as search engine marketing and searching issues. The site also informs users of upcoming related conferences and webcasts.

Search Engine Strategies Conferences

Search Engine Strategies is a global conference series focused on search engine advertising (including current SEO and SEM issues). Search Engine Strategies (hosted by Search Engine Watch) offers event information given by the top experts in the field as well as representatives from search engine companies.[38] Because traffic and advertising are so important to most Web 2.0 businesses, understanding the search process and making sure your site is easily found is vital.

Discovery

Rather than the traditional use of search engines (searching with a topic in mind), discovery refers to finding new content you would not have otherwise sought out. For example, Yahoo!'s original directory design allowed users to browse categories, and discover new interesting sites. StumbleUpon, a social bookmarking site, addresses discovery with its recommendation system that helps you discover and share websites based on your interests. Content networks also direct users to web content they would not necessarily have looked for otherwise.

3.4 Content Networks

Content networks are websites or collections of websites that provide information in various forms (such as articles, wikis, blogs, etc.). These provide another way of filtering the vast amounts of information on the Internet, by allowing users to go to a trusted site that

36. Sullivan, D. "Congratulations! You're a Search Engine Marketer!" *Search Engine Watch*, 5 November 2005 <http://searchenginewatch.com/showPage.html?page=2164351>.
37. Sherman, C. "The State of Search Engine Marketing 2006." *Search Engine Land*, 8 February 2007 <http://searchengineland.com/070208-095009.php>.
38. *Search Engine Strategies: Conference & Expos*, 2007 <http://www.searchenginestrategies.com>.

has already sorted through many sources to find the best content or has provided its own content. Figure 3.2 shows some examples of content networks.

Content networks

About.com—Acquired by the *New York Times,* About is a collection of information on a wide variety of topics. About was founded in 1996 and provides over 500 guides written by topic experts. The guides include new content as well as links to other websites.

b5media—A blog network with over 200 blogs related to travel, entertainment, technology and more.

Corante—A blog network authored by leading commentators in technology, business, law, science, and culture.

Deitel—Deitel Resource Centers (currently about 80 sites and growing rapidly) include links to, and descriptions of, key tutorials, demos, free software tools, articles, e-books, whitepapers, videos, podcasts, blogs, RSS feeds and more. Resource Centers are grouped into major topic areas, including Web 2.0, Internet business, programming languages, software development and open source. See Fig. 2 in the Preface for a complete list of Resource Centers.

eHow—eHow claims over 35,000 articles explaining "how to do just about everything." The articles are written by members, and the site also features a section of "how to" videos.

Gawker Media—A blog network that includes 14 blogs, such as Gizmodo, Gawker, Valleywag and Lifehacker. The blogs cover a range of topics including technology, gossip and more.

HowStuffWorks—HowStuffWorks offers articles explaining "how the world actually works." Articles are written by freelance writers, and experts from *Consumer Guide* and *Mobil Travel Guide.*

LifeTips—LifeTips provides short articles on both work and general life issues from hundreds of writers. Tips are voted on by readers (who can also mark their favorites for easy access).

9rules—A blog network with a wide range of blog topics. The site also includes social networking aspects.

Suite101—Suite101 offers thousands of articles on a variety of topics written by freelance writers. In addition to the articles, the site also provides discussion areas and free courses.

Weblogs, Inc.—A blog network of 90 blogs, including Engadget, Autoblog and Joystiq. Users can apply to write for one of the blogs (and get paid) or suggest topics for potential new blogs.

Fig. 3.2 | Content networks.

3.5 User-Generated Content

User-generated content has been the key to success for many of today's leading Web 2.0 companies, such as Amazon, eBay and Monster. The community adds value to these sites, which, in many cases, are almost entirely built on user-generated content. For example, eBay (an online auction site) relies on the community to buy and sell auction items, and Monster (a job search engine) connects job seekers with employers and recruiters.

User-generated content includes explicitly generated content such as articles, home videos and photos. It can also include implicitly generated content—information that is gathered from the users' actions online. For example, every product you buy from Amazon and every video you watch on YouTube provides these sites with valuable information about your interests. Companies like Amazon have developed massive databases of anonymous user data to understand how users interact with their site. For example, Amazon uses your purchase history and compares it to purchases made by other users with similar interests to make personalized recommendations (e.g., "customers who bought this item also bought..."). Implicitly generated content is often considered hidden content. For example, web links and tags are hidden content; every site you link to from your own site or bookmark on a social bookmarking site could be considered a vote for that site's importance. Search engines such as Google (which uses the PageRank algorithm) use the number and quality of these links to a site to determine the importance of a site in search results.

Collective Intelligence

Collective intelligence is the concept that collaboration can result in smart ideas. Working together, users combine their knowledge for everyone's benefit.

The first chapter of *Wikinomics*, by Don Tapscott and Anthony D. Williams, tells the Goldcorp story. Inspired by the community efforts in Linux, the CEO of Goldcorp released to the public proprietary geological information about the company's land. Goldcorp offered cash rewards to people who could use this information to help the company locate gold on the land. The community helped his company find 8 million ounces of gold, catapulting Goldcorp from $100 million in stock equity to $9 billion.[39] Goldcorp reaped amazing benefits by sharing information and encouraging community participation.

User-generated content is significant to Web 2.0 companies because of the innovative ways companies are harnessing collective intelligence. We've already discussed Google's PageRank (Section 3.3), which is a product of collective intelligence. Amazon's and Last.fm's personalized recommendations also result from collective intelligence, as algorithms evaluate user preferences to provide you with a better experience by helping you discover new products or music preferred by other people with similar interests. Wesabe is a web community where members share their decisions about money and savings—the site uses the collective financial experiences of the community to create recommendations.[40] Reputation systems (used by companies like eBay) also use collective intelligence to build trust between buyers and sellers by sharing user feedback with the community. Social bookmarking sites (Section 3.10), and social media sites (like Digg and Flickr) use collective intelligence to promote popular material, making it easier for others to find.

Wikis

Wikis, websites that allow users to edit existing content and add new information, are prime examples of user-generated content and collective intelligence. The most popular wiki is Wikipedia, a community-generated encyclopedia with articles available in over 200 languages. Wikipedia trusts its users to follow certain rules, such as not deleting accurate information and not adding biased information, while allowing community members to enforce the rules. The result has been a wealth of information growing much faster than could otherwise be produced. In 2005, an experiment comparing 42 entries from Wikipedia and *Britannica* (a popular printed traditional encyclopedia) showed only slightly

---

39. Tapscott, D. and A.D. Williams. *Wikinomics: How Mass Collaboration Changes Everything*. Portfolio Hardcover, 2006.
40. "FAQ." *Wesabe* <http://www.wesabe.com/page/faq>.

more inaccuracies in the Wikipedia articles.[41] The Wikipedia entries were promptly corrected, though, whereas errors in *Britannica* entries cannot be corrected until the book's next printing and will remain in already printed copies.

Wikipedia, Wikia (a site for specialized wiki communities about popular television shows, games, literature, shopping and more) and many other wikis use MediaWiki open source software (originally developed for Wikipedia). The software can be downloaded from MediaWiki's website (`www.mediawiki.org`), where you can also find descriptions, tutorials, suggestions and more to help navigate the software. Wikis are also used by many companies to provide product information, support and community resources. SocialText, the first wiki company, provides corporate wiki services. Many companies have found that using wikis for project collaboration reduces e-mails and phone calls between employees, while allowing the ability to closely track a project's changes.[42]

Collaborative Filtering

Though collaboration can result in a wealth of knowledge, some users might submit false or faulty information. For example, Wikipedia has experienced instances of people deliberately adding false information to entries. While moderation (monitoring of content by staff) is sometimes necessary, it is time consuming and costly. Many Web 2.0 companies rely on the community to help police their sites. This collaborative filtering lets users promote valuable material and flag offensive or inappropriate material. Users have the power to choose for themselves what is important. Examples of sites using collaborative filtering include Digg, a news site where users rate the stories (see Section 3.8), and social bookmarking sites such as del.icio.us, where users can easily find popular sites (see Section 3.10). Customer reviews on Amazon products also employ collaborative filtering—readers vote on the usefulness of each review (helping other readers to find the best reviews).

Craigslist

Craigslist, founded by Craig Newmark, is a popular classified ads website that has radically changed the classified advertising market. Newspapers have experienced a decline in classified ad sales,[43] as revenues from help-wanted ads on Craigslist climbed to $50 million in 2006.[44] Most ad postings on Craigslist are free, and it's easy for anyone to post ads. The site has gained popularity because of its job and housing postings. In 2005, a documentary, "24 Hours on Craigslist," showed the diverse postings that occur on the site in a single day.[45] Craigslist is built on user content, leveraging the Long Tail by connecting the unique (often unusual) needs of its users. The site also uses collaborative filtering—users are encouraged to flag inappropriate postings.

---

41. Cauchi, S. "Online Encyclopedias Put to the Test." *The Age*, 15 December 2005 `<http://www.theage.com.au/news/national/online-encyclopedias-put-to-the-test/2005/12/14/1134500913345.html>`.
42. "SocialText is the Enterprise Wiki Trusted Most by Global 2000 Corporations." *SocialText* `<http://www.socialtext.com/products/overview>`.
43. Steel, E. "Newspapers' Ad Sales Show Accelerating Drop." *The Wall Street Journal*, 18 July 2007, A4.
44. "Leading Indicators." *FORTUNE*, 13 November 2006, p.40.
45. "24 Hours on Craigslist."`<http://24hoursoncraigslist.com/>`.

Wisdom of Crowds

Wisdom of crowds (from the book of the same title written by James Surowiecki) is similar to collective intelligence—it suggests that a large diverse group of people (that does not necessarily include experts) can be smarter than a small group of specialists. The key difference between collective intelligence and the wisdom of crowds is that the latter is not meant to be a collaborative process—part of forming a reliable crowd is making sure people don't influence each other.[46] For example, Surowiecki describes how calculating the average of all submissions in a guessing contest (e.g., guessing the number of jelly beans in a jar) often results in nearly the correct answer, even though most individual estimates are incorrect and vary considerably. When the U.S. submarine *Scorpion* sank in 1968, the Navy asked various experts to work individually assessing what might have happened; their collective answers were then analyzed to determine the accurate location of the submarine.[47] Practical everyday applications of the wisdom of crowds can be seen in sites employing collaborative filtering.

3.6 Blogging

> *"The blog is the best relationship generator you've ever seen."*
> —Robert Scoble, blogger[48]

History of Blogging

Blogs are websites consisting of entries listed in reverse chronological order. They have existed since the mid-1990s; however, interest in blogging has grown exponentially in recent years because of easy-to-use blogging software and increasingly economical Internet access. The term "blog" evolved from weblog, a regularly updated list of interesting websites. These blogs consisted of short postings, in reverse chronological order, that contained links to other web pages and short commentaries or reactions. Blogging has since taken on a looser structure—some blogs still follow the traditional format of links and small amounts of text, while others consist of essays, sometimes not containing any links. Blogs can also now incorporate media, such as music or videos. Many people are familiar with personal journal blogs, like those on Xanga or LiveJournal. These sites include social networking features and are particularly popular with teenage bloggers, who often write about their day-to-day lives for friends.

Blogging has become a major social phenomenon, empowering users to participate in, rather than just view, the web. In July 2006 most bloggers, or blog authors, had not had a personal website before starting their blog.[49] The increased availability of user-friendly blogging software has allowed blogging to become accessible to more mainstream Internet users.

---

46. Jenkins, H. "Collective Intelligence vs. The Wisdom of Crowds." *Confessions of an Aca-Fan*, 27 November 2006 `<http://www.henryjenkins.org/2006/11/collective_intelligence_vs_the.html>`.
47. Surowiecki, J. *The Wisdom of Crowds*. Anchor, 2005.
48. Kirkpatrick, D. "Why There's No Escaping the Blog." *FORTUNE*, 10 January 2005 `<http://money.cnn.com/magazines/fortune/fortune_archive/2005/01/10/8230982/index.htm>`.
49. Lenhart, A. and S. Fox. "Bloggers: A Portrait of the Internet's New Storytellers." *Pew Internet & American Life Project*, July 2006 `<http://www.pewinternet.org/pdfs/PIP%20Bloggers%20Report%20July%2019%202006.pdf>`.

Blog Components

Reader comments create an interactive experience, allowing readers to react to blog entries. According to a Pew Internet study, 87% of blogs allow reader comments.[50] Successful bloggers pay attention to their readers and respond, often sparking interesting discussions and debates. However, allowing comments increases the possibility of spam (including irrelevant comments, inappropriate language and link spam—where a user tries to increase an irrelevant site's number of inbound links). By some estimates, over 90% of blog comments are spam.[51]

Permalinks provide blog readers with a way of linking to specific blog entries. Each blog post has a unique URL referring to that single post. Links stay relevant even after the blog entry moves off the homepage and into the archive.

Trackbacks tell bloggers who is linking to their posts. This enhances Internet content by making linking two-way. The blogger provides a trackback link, and sites that use the link are added to a list on the blog entry. For an example of a trackbacks section, visit `http://www.techcrunch.com/2006/08/08/web-20-the-24-minute-documentary/`. This is a permalink to a post on TechCrunch, a popular Internet technology blog, that features a Web 2.0 video from 2006.

A blogroll is a list of the blogger's favorite blogs. Though not all blogs feature a blogroll, it is common for the main page of a blog to contain links to several other blogs. For example, LiveJournal automatically incorporates a blogroll (consisting of users the blogger has marked as friends) into a user's profile page.

Blogging and Journalism

> *"Freedom of the press is guaranteed only to those who own one."*
>
> —A.J. Liebling[52]

Blogging has encouraged citizen journalism, allowing anyone to be a journalist. Blogs have become a significant news resource, drawing traffic away from the mainstream media. Some argue that this form of "participatory journalism" holds less biases than mainstream media, or at least makes these biases clear and provides many different views. This democratization of media allows a larger group to take part in journalism.[53] Traditional journalists had previously been able to create a representative democracy (much like the political system of the United States) by speaking for the masses. However, blogging gives a voice to everyone with a computer and Internet access, creating a more direct democracy.

Many bloggers are recognized as members of the media. Just as television and radio increased the speed of news delivery over that of newspapers, blogs have become a fast and in-depth (and often "unwashed") news medium. The mass media is embracing blogging; many TV news anchors suggest that viewers read their blogs after the show, and many newspaper websites feature blogs by reporters.

---

50. Lenhart, A. and S. Fox. "Bloggers: A Portrait of the Internet's New Storytellers." *Pew Internet & American Life Project*, July 2006 `<http://www.pewinternet.org/pdfs/PIP%20Bloggers%20Report%20July%2019%202006.pdf>`.
51. *Akismet*, 10 August 2007 `<http://akismet.com/stats/>`.
52. "A.J. Liebling Quotes." *ThinkExist.com Quotations* `<http://thinkexist.com/quotation/freedom_of_the_press_is_guaranteed_only_to_those/220714.html>`.
53. Bowman, S. and C. Willis. "We Media." July 2003 `<http://www.hypergene.net/wemedia/download/we_media.pdf>`.

Though journalism is a large part of the blogging phenomenon, according to a Pew Internet study only one-third of bloggers consider their blogs a form of journalism. Eighty-four percent of bloggers consider it a hobby, and only 10% spend more than ten hours a week blogging.[54] Posting new content and responding to reader comments requires a substantial time commitment.

Growth of Blogging

The number of blogs has been doubling about twice a year.[55] However, there is also a large number of abandoned blogs. A Caslon Analytics study found that "66.0% of surveyed blogs had not been updated in two months."[56]

Companies are reaching out to the blogosphere, or blogging community, to keep in touch with consumer opinions. Many CEOs and top executives from large companies such as Sun Microsystems, Marriott International and General Motors are now regular bloggers. This helps build consumer trust and loyalty. The NewPR Wiki lists over 250 CEOs and upper-management bloggers.[57]

Increased use of mobile devices has also lead to moblogging, or mobile blogging, as bloggers no longer need to be at their computer to update their blogs. Similarly, vlogging, or video blogging, has gained popularity. Rocketboom, for example, posts a three-minute video every day covering news and Internet stories.

Blogging and RSS Feeds

Many popular blogs provide RSS and Atom feeds to let readers know when new content is posted. Feeds, offered through blogging software or sites such as Feedburner (acquired by Google in 2007), help bloggers track and maintain a steady readership. The feeds (containing an entire post or just a selection with a link) can be automatically syndicated via the web and aggregated on a website or application designated by the user. Some sites (like Feedburner) provide an e-mail option, forwarding the day's posts to subscribers. While the use of feeds is certainly growing, a Pew Internet study in July 2006 reported that only 18% of bloggers provide RSS feeds.[58] (See "RSS and Atom" in Section 3.15.)

Blogging Software

Bloggers now have many options for building blogs. Online hosted blog software options include WordPress (which also offers server software), TypePad and Blogger. Blog server software programs include Movable Type and Textpattern. These require users to have their own web server; however, they also allow for more customization. Some word pro-

---

54. Lenhart, A. and S. Fox. "Bloggers: A Portrait of the Internet's New Storytellers." *Pew Internet & American Life Project,* July 2006 <http://www.pewinternet.org/pdfs/PIP%20Bloggers%20Report%20July%2019%202006.pdf>.
55. Walsh, B. *Clear Blogging: How People Are Changing the World and How You Can Join Them.* Apress, 2007.
56. "Blog Statistics and Demographics." *Caslon Analytics.* March 2007 <http://www.caslon.com.au/weblogprofile1.htm>.
57. "CEO Blog List." *NewPR Wiki* <http://www.thenewpr.com/wiki/pmwiki.php/Resources/CEOBlogsList?pagename=Resources.CEOBlogsList>.
58. Lenhart, A. and S. Fox. "Bloggers: A Portrait of the Internet's New Storytellers." *Pew Internet & American Life Project,* July 2006 <http://www.pewinternet.org/pdfs/PIP%20Bloggers%20Report%20July%2019%202006.pdf>.

cessors (such as Microsoft Word 2007) also offer blog publishing features or are compatible with blog posting extensions.

Blog Networks

Blog networks are collections of blogs, often with several editors. Popular blog networks include Corante, Weblogs, Inc., 9rules, b5media and Gawker Media. Many of these networks, with multiple bloggers and daily postings, draw significant traffic and a broad audience. Blog networks help bloggers build reputations and loyal readers. Some social networking sites like MySpace and Facebook also enable blogging to a private network of friends.

Blog Search Engines

Blog search engines, such as Technorati and Google Blog Search, monitor the blogosphere's constant changes. When dealing with blogs, search results cannot be based strictly on traditional factors such as reputations built over time (since the blogosphere is so dynamic). Technorati, which tracked over 93 million blogs in July 2007, addresses the unique needs of what they call the "World Live Web." Google Blog Search adjusts Google's search algorithms to specifically address the blogosphere. Other blog search engines include Feedster, IceRocket and Blogdigger.

3.7 Social Networking

Social networking sites, which allow users to keep track of their existing interpersonal relationships and form new ones, are experiencing extraordinary growth in Web 2.0. According to the "Hitwise US Consumer Generated Media Report," in September 2006 "one in every 20 Internet visits went to one of the top 20 social networks." A large portion of the traffic on shopping sites (and other Web 2.0 sites) comes from social networking websites such as MySpace.[59]

Network Effects

> *"What distinguished 2.0 is the design of systems that harness network effects—a broader way of saying community—to get better the more people use them."*
>
> —Tim O'Reilly[60]

The term network effects refers to the increased value of a network as its number of users grows. Metcalfe's Law states that the value of the network is proportional to the square of the number of users.[61] Consider, for example, eBay—the more buyers and sellers that use the site, the more valuable the site becomes to its users. Google's AdSense advertising program also increases in value as the number of participating advertisers and publishers grows and ads can be better matched to site content (see Section 3.3). Social networking sites also rely heavily on network effects, often attracting users only if their friends are on the site.

A key part of building a successful network and creating an architecture of participation is setting the user preferences to default to share content so users will automatically

59. Prescott, L. "Hitwise US Consumer Generated Media Report." *Hitwise,* February 2007.
60. Heiss, J. "Open Possibilities at the First CommunityOne Conference." *JavaOne,* 7 May 2007 `<http://java.sun.com/javaone/sf/2007/articles/comm1_post.jsp>`.
61. "Metcalf's Law." `<http://www-ec.njit.edu/~robertso/infosci/metcalf.html>`.

contribute to the value of the network.[62] Most users do not think about sharing capabilities, let alone care to alter their preferences. If companies do not enable sharing automatically, few users will take the time to share their data. *Providing the option to disable sharing is an important privacy feature.*

Network effects also make it difficult (though not impossible) to break into markets already claimed by successful companies. User content often loses value when moved into a new network. For example, a photo's tags (created by the community) on Flickr are lost if the photo is taken to a different site. Competitors must then find a unique way of convincing users that it's worth the switch.

Friendster

Friendster was an early leader in social networking. Within a year of Friendster's founding in 2002, Google offered to buy the site (Friendster rejected the offer). Created as a dating site, Friendster experienced a boom in popularity that quickly overwhelmed its servers. Friendster's popularity declined as new sites like MySpace emerged.[63] Though Friendster has not been able to keep pace with competing social networking sites, it still claims over 45 million members worldwide. It was granted a patent in 2006 on a key part of social networking, specifically how networks of friends are developed (i.e., identifying mutual friends and degrees of separation).[64]

MySpace

MySpace is the most popular social networking site. Hitwise reported it as the top website in May 2007 based on market share (beating Google by 1.5%).[65] Self-defined as "an online community that lets you meet your friends' friends," MySpace allows you to build a network of friends and identify mutual friends. Each user's page can contain general info, pictures, blog entries, a message board and more. Customization options, such as changing the background or adding music, give users an easy way to create their own unique web page. The site also features a private messaging system and special sections for film, music, videos, classifieds, etc.

MySpace plays an important role in the music scene, and even companies and politicians are creating accounts. MySpace reaches a younger audience than most conventional media outlets. Some political candidates have used MySpace to reach out to young voters and find new volunteers. Though candidates risk embarrassing connections (to inappropriate accounts) on these sites, they have often found the benefits to be worth it.[66] Businesses can also create profiles, which then become a form of free advertising. News Corp, which acquired MySpace in 2005 for $580 million, recognizes its benefits for local busi-

---

62. O'Reilly, T. "What is Web 2.0: Design Patterns and Business Models for the Next Generation of Software." September 2005 `<http://www.oreillynet.com/pub/a/oreilly/tim/news/2005/09/30/what-is-web-20.html>`.
63. Rivlin, G. "Wallflower at the Web Party." *New York Times*, 15 October 2006 <http://www.nytimes.com/2006/10/15/business/yourmoney/15friend.html>.
64. Kirkpatrick, M. "Friendster Awarded Patent on Social Networking." *TechCrunch*, 7 July 2006 <http://www.techcrunch.com/2006/07/07/friendster-awarded-patent-on-social-networking/>.
65. "Top 20 Websites." *Hitwise*, May 2007. <http://hitwise.com/datacenter/rankings.php>.
66. Jesdanun, A. "Candidates Seek Youths at MySpace." *ABC News*, 17 August 2006 <http://abcnews.go.com/Technology/wireStory?id=2325325&page=1>.

nesses that want to gain exposure.[67] Though many consider social networking sites to be more popular with teenagers and young adults, the largest user group on MySpace (and other large social networking sites) consists of 35–54 year olds.[68]

Facebook

Hitwise named Facebook the "preferred network among college students. Because Facebook was closed to non-students, students felt safer than on MySpace, and Facebook became nearly a social necessity for students seeking to connect with peers."[69] In July 2007, Facebook held an 85% market share of four-year U.S. universities and had over 31 million users.[70] Though Facebook has since allowed users without an `.edu` e-mail address to join, this elitism and idea of increased privacy drew a large enough crowd to compete with MySpace. A user can set privacy levels for networks or even individuals, but Facebook users (as well as users of other social networking sites) are warned about possible repercussions from information they post.

> *"Remember, unless you're prepared to attach something in your profile to a resume or scholarship application, don't post it."*
>
> —Facebook[71]

The site has added many features over the past few years, including photo albums where you can tag your friends in pictures, recently updated profiles lists, events, groups, a marketplace for classified ads, and user status updates. In May 2007, the site introduced third-party applications that can be integrated directly into Facebook. Not all feature implementations have gone smoothly, though. In Fall 2006, Facebook experienced resistance from users concerned over privacy issues when it added a "News Feed" feature, which lists updates of friends' Facebook activities in real time.[72] Facebook increased privacy options in response, quieting most complaints.

LinkedIn

In June 2007, LinkedIn claimed a membership of "11 million experienced professionals." The business-oriented social networking site allows users to stay in touch with professional contacts, network with new contacts, check references, and find a job or a potential employee. Its low-key design and feature implementations keep the site unobtrusive.[73] Because of its older, more mature audience, privacy concerns are more prevalent—some users worry that their professional contacts will be abused by other users or even their employers

---

67. "Businesses Find MySpace is a Place to Reach Youth." *Trend Watching*, 11 July 2006 <http://www.trendwatching.com/about/inmedia/articles/youniversal_branding/businesses_find_myspace_is_a_p.html>.
68. Arrington, M. "Bear Stearns: Yahoo Must Form A Social Networking Strategy." *TechCrunch*, 3 August 2007 <http://www.techcrunch.com/2007/08/03/bear-stearns-yahoo-must-form-a-social-networking-strategy>.
69. Prescott, L. "Hitwise US Consumer Generated Media Report." *Hitwise,* February 2007.
70. "Facebook Statistics." *Facebook*, 17 July 2007 <http://static.ak.facebook.com/press/facebook_statist ics.pdf?11:44617>.
71. "Customer Support." *Facebook* <http://www.facebook.com/help.php?tab=safety>.
72. Schmidt, T. S. "Inside the Backlash Against Facebook." *TIME*, 6 September 2006 <http://www.time.com/time/nation/article/0,8599,1532225,00.html>.
73. Copeland, M. "The Missing Link." *CNNMoney.com*, 28 February 2007 <http://money.cnn.com/magazines/business2/business2_archive/2006/12/01/8394967/index.htm>.

for marketing reasons.[74] However, the site has gained popularity as a convenient way of networking. Members can find other professionals through their mutual acquaintances and get introductions.

LinkedIn monetizes the site through advertising, premium accounts for power users (mostly recruiters), and groups for companies and organizations. Because of the growing size of its network, LinkedIn maintains a strong hold on the professional market.[75]

Xing

Xing is a professional networking site based out of Germany. Xing is most popular in Europe and offers its services across many countries, industries, and languages—an important factor, given today's globalization of organizations. With its discovery capability and management tools, Xing helps members find professionals, search for job opportunities and locate other business prospects. In April 2007, Xing reached 2 million users.[76] Xing has also been acquiring other social networks in an attempt to increase its global reach.

Second Life

Second Life, developed by Linden Labs, is a 3D virtual world with millions of inhabitants. Users create avatars, digital representations of themselves that they can use to meet other users with similar interests, conduct business, participate in group activities, take classes and more. Some users have created profitable businesses or continued their real-life professions in the virtual world. For example, lawyers have used Second Life to meet new clients (often software developers wanting to discuss patent laws).[77] Many large corporations, such as IBM and Hewlett-Packard, have created Second Life presences to connect with customers, hold meetings and even recruit and interview new hires.[78, 79]

Users can create objects and add scripts (to animate the objects) in the virtual world. Because Second Life allows users to maintain rights to whatever they create, a dynamic marketplace has emerged that does millions of dollars in transactions monthly—the site has its own exchange, the LindeX.[80] Not only does this create monetization opportunities for users (one woman claims to have earned over $1 million in Second Life assets[81]), but Second Life earns revenue from premium accounts, purchases of virtual land and more.

Gaia Online

Gaia Online is a popular teen virtual world. This online community allows teens to play games, make friends and express their creativity. Similar to Second Life, Gaia has its own marketplace where members can earn Gaia Gold for various actions they perform on the

---

74. "The CEO's Guide to Social Networks." *BusinessWeek*, 11 September 2006 <http://businessweek.com/mediacenter/qt/podcasts/guide_to_tech/guidetotech_09_11_06.mp3>.
75. Copeland, M. "The Missing Link." *CNNMoney.com*, 28 February 2007 <http://money.cnn.com/magazines/business2/business2_archive/2006/12/01/8394967/index.htm>.
76. "Xing Reaches 2 Million Users." Mashable, <http://mashable.com/2007/04/16/xing/>.
77. "Second Life Lawyer." *Business 2.0*, May 2007, p.86.
78. Athavely, A. "A Job Interview You Don't Have to Show Up For." *The Wall Street Journal Online*, 20 June 2007 <http://online.wsj.com/article/SB118229876637841321.html>.
79. Bulkeley, W. "Playing Well With Others." *The Wall Street Journal Online*, 18 June 2007 <http://online.wsj.com/article/SB118194536298737221.html>.
80. "What is Second Life." <http://secondlife.com/whatis>.
81. Lawson, S. "Second Life Creates a Millionaire." *IDG News*, 30 November 2006 <http://www.itworld.com/App/4201/061130secondlife/>.

site (e.g., playing games or posting), and use their earnings at the virtual stores or for creating their own shops. Nearly 300,000 members login daily and about 2 million unique visitors login to Gaia every month.[82]

Mobile Social Networking

Many social networking sites have found innovative ways of connecting people through the Internet and their mobile devices (such as cell phones and PDAs). Mobile users can send instant messages, check e-mail, and post content to the web from Internet-enabled mobile devices. The new Apple iPhone further realizes the dream of having the Internet in your pocket by allowing the full Internet (not a simplified mobile one) to be accessed wherever wireless Internet access is available.

Google's Dodgeball.com provides users with mobile access to a network of friends in many cities. GPS chips in mobile devices allow Dodgeball users to update their location and be notified of nearby friends or "crushes." Dodgeball also provides an easy way of sending messages to groups of friends to plan get-togethers. (See Section 3.14, Location-Based Services.)

Other sites such as Twitter provide similar services, accessible by text message, IM or a web client. Twitter users can message groups of friends at once and automatically receive their friends' updates on a cell phone or through a chat window. The site is considered to be a microblogging service (since users are limited to a small number of characters for each update). Twitter offers a web services API, which allows developers to integrate Twitter into other applications. (See Section 3.13, Web Services, Mashups, Widgets and Gadgets, for more information on web services APIs.)

3.8 Social Media

Social media refers to any media shared online (e.g., videos, music, photos, news, etc.). Hitwise reported that "increased broadband penetration, combined with the rise of consumer generated content and the proliferation of webcams and cell phone and home video cameras have firmly entrenched online video viewing into the habits of entertainment seekers in the United States."[83]

YouTube

YouTube, launched in late 2005, is the leading Internet video site. In true Web 2.0 fashion, the entire site is based on user-generated content. Users upload videos, and rate and comment on videos posted by other users. YouTube's Quick Capture Flash software makes it easy to upload content directly from a webcam. Users can browse videos by category, tag, or by following "related video" links. Highly rated videos are featured on YouTube's homepage. While many professionals and film students post content on the site, the most popular submissions are often simple spoofs or home videos. Because of the viral network effects of YouTube, these amateur videos can quickly gain worldwide attention.

Users can subscribe to other users' content, share videos with friends by e-mail, or embed videos directly into their blogs or other websites. YouTube addresses privacy and

82. "About Us." *Gaia Online*, <http://www.gaiaonline.com/info/about.php?>.
83. Prescott, L. "Hitwise US Consumer Generated Media Report." *Hitwise*, February 2007.

spam concerns by allowing users to set videos as "public" or "private" and flag inappropriate material for review by YouTube's staff.

Less than a year after its official launch, YouTube was acquired by Google (which had its own less popular Google Video site) for $1.65 billion. Less than six months after the acquisition, Viacom sued YouTube for $1 billion for copyright infringement.[84] The Digital Millennium Copyright Act of 1998 protects companies from prosecution due to user actions if they work in "good faith" to remove offending content.[85] However, interpretations of this act vary, and it has become a point of contention for many companies. YouTube is developing a mechanism that automatically detects copyrighted material. Currently, illegal content is removed from the site manually.

Internet TV

Many mass-media companies now offer full-length episodes of popular television shows on their websites to tap into the increasingly popular Internet television market. The average American watches 4.5 hours of television a day, not including Internet television.[86] Sites, such as Joost, Veoh and MobiTV, have emerged as a new way of watching television. Joost, for example, uses semantic technologies to help users find programs that interest them. (See Section 3.18, Future of the Web.)

Limited by copyright issues, Internet TV sites must make deals with mainstream networks to offer their content online. Viacom made a deal with Joost, allowing the site to include some shows from networks such as MTV, VH1 and Comedy Central.[87] As users take back the power to choose what they watch and when, networks may find themselves making more deals with Internet TV companies. As technologies continue to improve, Internet TV has the potential to radically change the television industry. Already, smaller content creators are able to gain access to worldwide audiences. In late June 2007, MySpace joined the market with its MySpaceTV. With MySpace's enormous membership, it could rapidly become a direct competitor to YouTube and Internet TV websites.

Internet TV allows advertisers to target their markets more precisely than with broadcast television. Advertisers can use demographic information, such as location, gender and age, to serve appropriate ads.

Digg

Digg features news, videos and podcasts, all posted and rated by users. It has gained popularity by allowing users to "digg" or "bury" posts and user comments. Valuable sites, marked by large numbers of diggs, are moved to the Digg front page where other users can easily find them. Formulas were adjusted to make sure the "wisdom of crowds" was not being hijacked by users trying to promote their own posts.[88] Sites that are "dugg" and fea-

---

84. Mills, E. "Copyright Quagmire for Google and YouTube." *ZDNet*, 14 March 2007 <http://news.zdnet.com/2100-9588_22-6167281.html>.
85. "Conference Report Filed in House." *Library of Congress*, 8 October 1998 <http://thomas.loc.gov/cgi-bin/bdquery/z?d105:HR02281:@@@D&summ2=m&>.
86. Colvin, G. "TV Is Dying? Long Live TV!" *FORTUNE*, 5 February 2007, p.43.
87. O'Hear, S. "Viacom to Partner with Joost." *ZDNet*, 20 February 2007 <http://blogs.zdnet.com/social/?p=96>.
88. Maney, K. "Techies Hot on Concept of 'Wisdom of Crowds,' But It Has Some Pitfalls." *USA Today*, 12 September 2006 <http://www.usatoday.com/tech/columnist/kevinmaney/2006-09-12-wisdom-of-crowds_x.htm>.

tured on the homepage typically experience a traffic surge. Bloggers can add Digg buttons to their sites, making it easy for readers to "digg" their posts.

Digg uses collaborative filtering to help reduce spam by "burying" it (users can vote against posts they don't like). Users can also set the threshold of diggs to automatically filter out content with low ratings. The site was criticized for removing popular posts of HD DVD security cracks (on the advice of lawyers); however, Kevin Rose (Digg's founder) decided to support the crowds and "deal with whatever the consequences might be."[89] Digg has additional social networking capabilities; users can view their friends' Digg activities and the Diggs of other users with similar interests. Some Digg-like sites include Netscape, Reddit and Newsvine.

Last.fm

Last.fm is an Internet radio website that uses Web 2.0 concepts to make music recommendations and build communities. The site provides open source desktop software that can be integrated into most popular music players. Its scrobbling feature tracks the music users listen to so that Last.fm can provide users with personalized recommendations. A streamable radio with "discovery mode" and a network of like-minded listeners help users find new music. Groups and an events section add social value. The site also offers tagging and wiki pages for artists and record labels.

Digital Rights Management (DRM)

Digital Rights Management (DRM) systems add software to media files to prevent them from being misused, but these systems restrict compatibility with many media players. Companies want to protect their digital products from illegal distribution; however, users want unrestricted access to media they've purchased.

iTunes, Apple's music store, has been criticized for restricting users' access to their own music by allowing only up to five computers to be authorized to play any given file. However, Apple's Steve Jobs advocated a DRM-free music world in February 2007, arguing the greater risk for piracy is in DRM-free CDs, which make up the majority of music sales.[90] CDs remain DRM-free because many CD players are not compatible with DRM systems. In June 2007, Amazon offered DRM-free downloads from more than 12,000 record labels, and both iTunes and Amazon sell DRM-free music from EMI (one of the four major record companies).[91]

Podcasting

Podcasting was popularized by Apple's iPod portable media player. A podcast is a digital audio file (e.g., an .mp3) that often takes on the characteristics of a radio talk show (though without live callers).[92] Much as blogging has made journalism accessible to everyone, pod-

---

89. Hefflinger, M. "Digg Users Revolt Over Deleted Posts of HD DVD Security Hack." *digitalmediawire*, 2 May 2007 `<http://www.dmwmedia.com/news/2007/05/02/digg-users-revolt-over-deleted-posts-of-hd-dvd-security-hack>`.
90. Jobs, S. "Thoughts on Music." 6 February 2007 `<http://www.apple.com/hotnews/thoughtsonmusic/>`.
91. "Amazon.com to Launch DRM-Free MP3 Music Download Store with Songs and Albums from EMI Music and More Than 12,000 Other Labels." 16 May 2007 `<http://phx.corporate-ir.net/phoenix.zhtml?c=176060&p=irol-newsArticle&ID=1003003>`.
92. Torrone, P. "What Is Podcasting?" *O'Reilly Media*, 20 July 2005 `<http://digitalmedia.oreilly.com/2005/07/20/WhatIsPodcasting.html>`.

casting has introduced a more democratic form of radio broadcasting. Podcasts are easily created with audio software and can be played on a computer or portable media player. The files are posted online at individual websites or distributed via programs like Apple's iTunes. Listeners can often subscribe to podcasts via RSS feeds. Forrester Research predicted 12 million households will be regularly subscribing to podcasts by 2010.[93]

3.9 Tagging

History of Tagging

Tagging, or labeling content, is part of the collaborative nature of Web 2.0. A tag is any user-generated word or phrase that helps organize web content and label it in a more human way. Though standard sets of labels allow users to mark content in a general way, tagging items with self-chosen labels creates a stronger identification of the content. In an interview by the Pew Internet & American Life Project, David Weinberger (author of *Everything is Miscellaneous*) said:

> *"Maybe the most interesting thing about tagging is that we now have millions and millions of people who are saying, in public, what they think pages and images are about."*
>
> —David Weinberger

As part of the same December 2006 report, 28% of Internet users had reportedly "tagged" content online.[94]

Tag Clouds

Tag Clouds are visual displays of tags weighted by popularity. Many Web 2.0 sites include a graphical representation of popular tags (the popularity of the tag marked by the size of its text). There are many ways of forming tag clouds—terms often appear in alphabetical order. However, tag clouds show only how the majority (or the crowd) thinks and disregard many individual unique points of view.[95] Figure 3.3 is an example of a "text cloud" that we created manually from the major terms in this chapter. (To build your own text cloud try ArtViper's TextTagCloud tool at `http://www.artviper.net/texttagcloud/`.)

Folksonomies

Folksonomies are classifications based on tags. The term is generally attributed to Thomas Vander Wal, who combined the words "taxonomy" and "folk" to create a new term for this Internet phenomenon.[96] Folksonomies are formed on sites such as Flickr, Technorati and del.icio.us. Users can search content by tags, which identify content in different (and sometimes more meaningful) ways than traditional keywords used by search engines.

An example of Web 2.0's reach outside of traditional technology fields can be seen in the steve.museum project, an experiment in tagging and folksonomies regarding museum

93. D'Agostino, D. "Security in the World of Web 2.0." *Innovations*, Winter 2006, p.15.
94. Rainie, L. "Tagging." *Pew Internet & American Life Project*, 31 January 2007. <`http://www.pewinternet.org/pdfs/PIP_Tagging.pdf`>.
95. Rainie, L. "Tagging." *Pew Internet & American Life Project*, 31 January 2007. <`http://www.pewinternet.org/pdfs/PIP_Tagging.pdf`>.
96. Vander Wal, T. "Folksonomy Coinage and Definition." *Vanderwal.net*, 2 February 2007 <`http://www.vanderwal.net/folksonomy.html`>.

37Signals℠ AdSense™ AdWords™ affiliate programs agile development Ajax Amazon® Mechanical Turk Amazon® Web Services™ APIs architecture of participation Attention Economy blog search engines blogging blogosphere broadband Internet citizen journalism collaborative filtering collective intelligence contextual advertising Craigslist® Creative Commons℠ default to share Deitel® del.icio.us™ democratization of media Digg™ Digital Millenium Copyright Act Dojo DotNetNuke™ DRM eBay® Facebook® Federated Media℠ Feedburner™ findability Firefox® 2 Flash® Flex™ Flickr™ folksonomies *Getting Real* globalization Google Maps™ Google™ Google™ Gears GPS housingmaps.com Internet advertising Internet business models Internet Explorer® 7 Internet TV Internet video iPhone™ iTunes® JavaServer™ Faces Joost™ JSON Last.fm® lightweight business models link popularity LinkedIn® location-based services mashups Metcalf's Law microformats Microsoft® adCenter moblogging monetization Moore's Law Mozilla® MSN® MySpace® MySQL® network effects O'Reilly® Media ontologies open source outsourcing permalinks perpetual beta PHPNuke podcasting premium content ProgrammableWeb.com℠ RDF recommender systems remixing reputation systems REST RIAs RSS/Atom Ruby on Rails™ Salesforce.com® Script.aculo.us search Search Engine Marketing (SEM) Search Engine Optimization (SEO) Second Life® Semantic Web Silverlight™ Skype™ social bookmarking social media social networking Software as a Service (SaaS) tag clouds tagging TechCrunch Technorati™ The Long Tail *TIME* Person of the Year trackbacks trust Twitter user-generated content vertical search virtual worlds vlogging VoIP Web 2.0 Web 2.0 Internet Business Initiative Web 2.0 Summit Web 3.0 web as a platform web services web-scale computing webtop widgets and gadgets *Wikinomics* Wikipedia® wikis wisdom of crowds XML® Yahoo!® Yahoo!® Publisher Network Yahoo!® Search Marketing YouTube

Fig. 3.3 | Text cloud of major Web 2.0 terms from this chapter.

collections. In 2005, The Metropolitan Museum of Art and the Guggenheim Museum organized a retreat to plan the project.[97] In 2007 they posted various collections of art online and asked the community for help tagging them.

Flickr

Flickr—a popular photo-sharing site—was launched in February 2004 and acquired by Yahoo! in 2005. The Flickr development team was originally working on "The Game

97. Chun, S., R. Cherry, D. Hiwiller, J. Trant and B. Wyman. "Steve.museum: An Ongoing Experiment in Social Tagging, Folksonomy, and Museums." *Archives & Museum Informatics*, 1 March 2006 <http://www.archimuse.com/mw2006/papers/wyman/wyman.html>.

Neverending"—a multiplayer Flash game based on IM (instant message) and chat interfaces.[98] However, the team listened to its users and developed real-time photo sharing (Flickr Live) and more traditional web pages where users could view uploaded pictures. The Game Neverending and Flickr Live were later retired as the popularity of photo sharing and commenting on the web pages grew.[99]

Flickr is a key content-tagging site. Intended as a way of organizing personal photo collections, tagging on the site gained popularity as the community became interested in "a global view of the tagscape" (how other people are tagging photos).[100] Users can search for photos by meaningful tags. The tags also encourage loyalty to the site, since the tags are lost if photos are moved to another site.

Technorati

Technorati, a social media search engine, uses tags to find relevant blogs and other forms of social media. To become searchable by Technorati, bloggers can add tags to their posts with a simple line of HTML or use the automated category system offered by some blogging software packages.[101] Technorati tag searches return results from the blogosphere, YouTube videos and Flickr photos. Technorati features a tag cloud on its homepage and a "where's the fire" section to promote the most popular tags and search results.

3.10 Social Bookmarking

Social bookmarking sites let you share your Internet bookmarks (e.g., your favorite websites, blogs, and articles) through a website. Users can access these bookmarks from any computer and discover new sites by searching popular bookmarks and tags. Some of the most popular social bookmarking sites are del.icio.us, Ma.gnolia, Blue Dot, StumbleUpon, Simpy and Furl.

del.icio.us

del.icio.us, a self-described "collection of favorites," reported its two-millionth user registration in March 2007.[102] Users can add a bookmark by going to the site or by using the del.icio.us downloadable browser buttons. Some sites post clickable badges—a button provided by del.icio.us to "save this page"—that make it easy for users to bookmark the site using del.icio.us.

del.icio.us is a great example of a Web 2.0 company that uses tagging, social networking and user-generated content. When bookmarking a website, users can add notes and tags to describe the site. These tags are searchable and help organize sites, making it easier for users to find the content they want based on what other users have recommended (by bookmarking). Users can also add descriptions to tags, which can help clear up what

---

98. Schonfeld, E. "The Flickrization of Yahoo!" *CNN Money.com*, 1 December 2005 <http://money.cnn.com/magazines/business2/business2_archive/2005/12/01/8364623/>.
99. Garrett, J.J. "An Interview with Flickr's Eric Costello." *Adaptive Path*, 4 August 2005 <http://www.adaptivepath.com/publications/essays/archives/000519.php>.
100. Garrett, J.J. "An Interview with Flickr's Eric Costello." *Adaptive Path*, 4 August 2005 <http://www.adaptivepath.com/publications/essays/archives/000519.php>.
101. "Using Technorati Tags." *Technorati* <http://support.technorati.com/support/siteguide/tags>.
102. "That was Fast." del.icio.us blog, 29 March 2007 <http://blog.del.icio.us/blog/2007/03/that_was_fast.html>.

a certain tag might mean to different people. Thus, searching for content on del.icio.us is based on collaborative filtering rather than search engine algorithms. The site also offers a fully searchable podcasting section.

Third parties can use the del.icio.us web services API to build tools and incorporate social bookmarking functionality into their applications (see Section 3.13, Web Services, Mashups, Widgets and Gadgets). For example, Adobe Illustrator uses the del.icio.us technology to organize bookmarks in the program's documentation.[103]

Ma.gnolia

> *"If searching was the first day of the web, people helping each other find what they want must be the second."*
>
> —Ma.gnolia[104]

Ma.gnolia is another social bookmarking site offering tagging and convenient bookmark accessibility through the site. Bookmarked pages are saved (when possible) so users need not worry about losing content if a page goes offline. The site also provides browser buttons (bookmarklets) for posting sites to Ma.gnolia, and a "roots" feature, which lets you see what other users have said about a site while surfing the Internet. Ma.gnolia encourages social networking through user groups and a private messaging feature. To deal with spam, Ma.gnolia trusts handpicked moderators, called "gardeners."[105]

3.11 Software Development

A key to Web 2.0 software development is to KIS (keep it simple; keep it small). At the 2006 Emerging Technology Conference, Rael Dornfest (now CEO of the company "values of n" and former O'Reilly CTO) explained, "great businesses will be built on giving you less."[106] This is particularly important given the "attention economy" (too much information, too little time)—the theme of the 2006 conference.

The Webtop

The web has now become an application, development, delivery, and execution platform. The webtop, or web desktop, allows you to run web applications in a desktop-like environment in a web browser. Using the web as a platform is part of a movement toward operating-system–independent applications. The removal of OS barriers allows the potential audience for any single product to become larger. An example of a popular webtop is the Laszlo Webtop (built on the OpenLaszlo framework), which runs applications written in OpenLaszlo as well as those written in other frameworks using XML requests.[107] Exam-

---

103. "Know How Adobe and del.icio.us Work Together?" del.icio.us blog, 30 May 2007 <http://blog.del.icio.us/blog/2007/05/knowhow_adobe_a.html>.
104. "About Ma.gnolia." <http://ma.gnolia.com/about>.
105. "Gardeners." Ma.gnolia Community Wiki, 29 March 2007 <http://wiki.ma.gnolia.com/Gardeners>.
106. Farber, D. "ETech: Attenuation, Web 2.0 and spimes." *ZDNet*, 7 March 2006 <http://blogs.zdnet.com/BTL/?p=2667>.
107. "The RIA Desktop in a Browser." *LaszloSystems* <http://www.laszlosystems.com/software/webtop>.

ples of Laszlo Webtop applications can be seen at http://www.laszlosystems.com/showcase/samples. Other webtops include eyeOS and StartForce.

Software as a Service (SaaS)

Software as a Service (SaaS), application software that runs on a web server rather than being installed on the client computer, has gained popularity, particularly with businesses. It provides many benefits, including fewer demands on internal IT departments, increased accessibility for out-of-the-office use, and an easy way to maintain software on a large scale.[108] Instead of being installed on the local machine, software is installed on the provider's web server and accessed by customers "as a service" over the Internet. Updates applied on the server impact every computer. This change from local to server machine makes it easier for large corporations to keep software updates uniform throughout the organization. Most Google software is offered as SaaS. Microsoft now offers SaaS products, Windows Live and Office Live.

Collaborating on projects with co-workers across the world is easier, since information is stored on a web server instead of on a single desktop. 37Signals has developed several SaaS products, including Basecamp (a product management and collaboration tool), Campfire (a group chat tool), Backpack (a personal organization tool), Ta-da (a "to-do" list tool), Highrise (a customer relations tool), and Writeboard (a collaborative word-processing tool). Salesforce.com, which specializes in Customer Relationship Management (CRM) software, is a key SaaS company—they provide popular business applications for sales, marketing, customer support, analytics and more.

Perpetual Beta and Agile Development

Due to the increased use of web applications there has been a shift away from the traditional software release cycle. Historically, companies would spend months or even years developing major new software releases. Because releases came so infrequently, each one had to go through extensive testing and beta periods to create a "final" release each time. There is now a greater focus on agile software development, which refers to development of fewer features at a time with more frequent releases. This "perpetual beta" of frequent smaller releases is made possible by using the web as a platform.[109] A new CD cannot be distributed to all customers every day; however, updates to web servers delivering the application can be easily made.

37Signals' *Getting Real*, an e-book that discusses agile techniques for building web applications, warns against the temptation to overuse "betas." The Internet is a dynamic medium—there will always be flaws and possible upgrades. Companies must decide how long it's really necessary to remain in a beta period, before it becomes just an excuse for a weak application. *Getting Real*, comprised of 91 short essays and numerous quotes and anecdotes, is a must read, providing an informative, insightful and entertaining walk through the software development process. The e-book can be read for free on their site or downloaded as a PDF for a fee.[110]

---

108. Peiris, M. "The Pros and Cons of Hosted Software." *SmartBiz*, March 2006 <http://www.smartbiz.com/article/articleview/1118/1/42>.
109. O'Reilly, T. "What is Web 2.0: Design Patterns and Business Models for the Next Generation of Software." September 2005 <http://www.oreillynet.com/pub/a/oreilly/tim/news/2005/09/30/what-is-web-20.html>.
110. 37Signals. *Getting Real.* 2006 <http://gettingreal.37signals.com>.

Open Source

The open source movement continues to gain momentum. The idea behind it is not new (it was popularized in 1998 with O'Reilly's Freeware Open Source Summit, now known as OSCON).[111] Historically, programs had been distributed by sharing the source code, before selling compiled programs became the norm. Though open source software is not always free, the source code is available (under license) to developers, who can customize it to meet their unique needs.

> *"Business-technology managers know all too well the adage about open source: It's free, as in a free puppy. The work and expense start once you get it home."*
>
> —Larry Greenemeier, *InformationWeek*[112]

Using open source projects, such as the popular Linux operating systems Red Hat or Ubuntu, may require more work and technical knowledge than using the Microsoft Windows or Apple Macintosh operating systems. However, advanced users are able to customize the software to fit their needs. Benefits to using an open source program include the possibility of reduced cost (if you have the skills to work with it) and the worldwide support networks where users help each other. Because the source code is available to everyone, users can look to the community for bug fixes and plug-ins (program extensions that add functionality), instead of waiting for the software vendor to address each issue. The Ubuntu forums, for example, contain a wealth of information created by users helping other users. In addition to the free support that springs up around open source projects, businesses have been built from developing project extensions and consulting. IBM invested $1 billion in Linux in 2001.

> *"Linux can do for business applications what the Internet did for networking and communications."*
>
> —Louis Gerstner, former CEO of IBM[113]

At `http://www.SourceForge.net` over 150,000 open source projects are under development. Other sites with open source downloads include freshmeat.net and Tucows. The popular Firefox web browser from the Mozilla Foundation, the Apache web server from the Apache Software Foundation, and the MySQL database system are all open source. DotNetNuke and PHPNuke offer open source frameworks for developing rich Internet portals, making it easy and economical to develop sophisticated websites. (`http://www.deitel.com` is a DotNetNuke site.)

Licensing: GNU Licenses and Creative Commons

Open source project licenses vary—many projects use the GNU General Public License (GPL), which allows redistribution of the project provided the source code is included and the copyright information is left intact. The Free Software Foundation provides other versions as well, including the GNU Lesser General Public License and the GNU Free Doc-

111. Van Rossum, G. "Open Source Summit Trip Report." *Linux Gazette*, 10 April 1998 <`http://linuxgazette.net/issue28/rossum.html`>.
112. Greenemeier, L. "Open-Source Exuberance." *InformationWeek*, 11 July 2005 <`http://www.informationweek.com/story/showArticle.jhtml?articleID=165700923`>.
113. Wilcox, J. "IBM to Spend $1 Billion on Linux in 2001." *CNET*, 12 December 2000 <`http://news.com.com/IBM+to+spend+1+billion+on+Linux+in+2001/2100-1001_3-249750.html`>.

umentation License. The Open Source Initiative also lists over 50 licenses available to open source software developers, including the BSD license and the MIT license.[114]

Creative Commons (`creativecommons.org`) deals with licensing issues for all types of digital media. The organization offers a variety of options to support remixing (extending existing content), commercial issues and attribution. By allowing users access to general licenses through Creative Commons or the Free Software Foundation, developers can worry less about the complicated issues of licensing and instead focus on developing.

3.12 Rich Internet Applications (RIAs)

Rich Internet Applications (RIAs) are web applications that offer the responsiveness, "rich" features and functionality approaching that of desktop applications. Early Internet applications supported only a basic HTML graphical user interface (GUI). Though they could serve simple functions, these applications did not have the look or feel of a desktop application. The relatively slow Internet connections these applications relied on led to the term "World Wide Wait." RIAs are a result of today's more advanced technologies that allow greater responsiveness and advanced GUIs.

Ajax

The term Ajax (Asynchronous JavaScript and XML) was coined by Adaptive Path's Jesse James Garrett in February 2005. Ajax (see Chapter 15, Ajax-Enabled Rich Internet Applications) allows partial page updates—meaning updates of individual pieces of a web page without having to reload the entire page. This creates a more responsive GUI, allowing users to continue interacting with the page as the server processes requests.

The technologies that make up Ajax—XHTML, CSS, JavaScript, the DOM, XML, and the `XMLHttpRequest` object—are not new. In fact, in the 1990s, Netscape used asynchronous page updates in LiveScript, which evolved into JavaScript. However, the popularity of Ajax has dramatically increased since its naming. Ajax performs a vital role in Web 2.0, particularly in building webtop applications and enhancing the user's overall experience. The following toolkits and frameworks (environments with standard components that make development faster and easier) provide libraries and tools for convenient Ajax-enabled application development.

Dojo

Dojo is an open source JavaScript toolkit—it is a library, not a framework. Dojo development began in late 2004.[115] Dojo helps standardize JavaScript by providing a variety of packages for cross-browser compatibility, rich GUI controls, event handling and more. (See the Dojo section in Chapter 15.)

Flex

Adobe Flex (see Chapter 18) is an RIA framework that allows you to build scalable, cross-platform, multimedia-rich applications that can be delivered over the Internet. It uses the Flash Player 9 runtime environment, which is installed on over 97% of computers, allow-

---

114. Tiemann, M. "Licenses by Name." *Open Source Initiative*, 18 September 2006 <`http://www.opensource.org/licenses/alphabetical`>.
115. "History." *The Dojo Toolkit*, 10 April 2007 <`http://dojotoolkit.org/book/dojo-book-0-9/introduction/history`>.

ing for almost universal compatibility.[116] Flash Player 9 is backed by ActionScript 3, Adobe's object-oriented scripting language—this uses an asynchronous programming model, which allows for partial page updates similar to Ajax. Flash CS3 (the development tool for creating Flash movies) is discussed in Chapters 16–17.

Silverlight

Microsoft's **Silverlight** (see Chapter 19), formerly known as Windows Presentation Foundation Everywhere (WPF/E) and released in May 2007, is Microsoft's new competitor to Flex and Flash. Silverlight 1.1 uses a compact version of the .NET framework. Silverlight applications have user interfaces built in Extensible Application Markup Language (XAML)—Microsoft's XML-based format for describing user interfaces. The new framework allows quick and easy development of RIAs and is designed to run on major browsers and operating systems.[117] **Moonlight**, an open source version of Silverlight for Linux operating systems, is being developed.

JavaFX

JavaFX is Sun Microsystems' counterpart to Flex and Silverlight, also designed for building Rich Internet Applications. It consists of the JavaFX Script and JavaFX Mobile (for mobile devices). The JavaFX Script, which takes advantage of the fact Java is installed on most computers, will be available under open source licences (see `https://openjfx.dev.java.net/`).[118]

Ruby on Rails

Ruby on Rails (see Chapter 24), developed by 37Signals' David Heinemeier Hansson, is an open source framework based on the Ruby scripting language that allows you to build database-intensive applications quickly, easily, and with less code. Ruby on Rails was designed to build 37Signals' Basecamp (a project management and collaboration tool) and other SaaS products.

Script.aculo.us

The **Script.aculo.us** library for creating "eye candy" effects is built on the Prototype JavaScript framework. Prototype encapsulates the DOM (Document Object Model, Chapter 12) and provides cross-browser processing capabilities.[119] Script.aculo.us uses this framework and adds capabilities for rich user interfaces. Its core effects include opacity, scale, morph, move, highlight and parallel (for combining multiple effects).[120] Script.aculo.us is used on many popular websites and is incorporated into other frameworks (such as Ruby on Rails). We discuss Script.aculo.us and present examples in Chapter 24, Ruby on Rails.

---

116. "Adobe Flex 2." *Adobe* <http://www.adobe.com/products/flex/whitepapers/pdfs/flex2wp_technicaloverview.pdf>.
117. Cubrilovic, N. "Silverlight: The Web Just Got Richer." *TechCrunch*, 30 April 2007 <http://www.techcrunch.com/2007/04/30/silverlight-the-web-just-got-richer>.
118. "Sun Radically Simplifies Content Authoring—Previews JavaFX Script." *Sun Microsystems*, 8 May 2007 <http://www.sun.com/aboutsun/pr/2007-05/sunflash.20070508.2.xml>.
119. "Prototype Tips and Tutorials." *Prototype JavaScript* <http://prototypejs.org/learn>.
120. "Core Effects." *Script.aculo.us Wiki* <http://wiki.script.aculo.us/scriptaculous/show/CoreEffects>.

JavaServer Faces

JavaServer Faces (JSF) is a Java-based web application framework. JSF separates design elements from business logic and provides a set of user-interface components (JSF components) that make developing RIAs simple. One of the Java BluePrints projects provides additional resources and libraries for building Ajax-enabled applications. We build RIAs with JSF in Chapters 26–27.

ASP.NET Ajax

ASP.NET Ajax (Chapter 25) is an extension of the .NET framework for creating Ajax-enabled applications. It includes an open source Ajax Control Toolkit for implementing asynchronous functionality. ASP.NET Ajax is easily used in Microsoft Visual Web Developer or Microsoft Visual Studio to quickly create Rich Internet Applications.

Adobe Integrated Runtime and Google Gears

Though web application use has been increasing, many feel these programs cannot truly compete with desktop applications until the "Offline Problem" (not being able to access web applications and data when not connected to the Internet) has been solved.[121] Businesses can lose valuable time and money when Internet issues occur such as a slow or broken Internet connection.

Adobe released its Adobe Integrated Runtime (AIR; previously called Apollo) in beta form in June 2007. AIR allows users to run Flex web applications on their desktops even when they are *not* connected to the Internet, thus allowing users to remain efficient when they are unable to access the Internet or when an SaaS application server goes down. Users can continue their work and synchronize it with the servers again later.

Google Gears, also in beta, is a similar product, allowing use of web applications while offline. Google Gears was created out of a Google engineer's 20% project, inspired by wanting to use Google Reader on a bus with "flaky" Internet access.[122] (Google engineers devote 20% of their time to projects other than their usual work and 10% of their time to projects that are "truly new.")[123] Dojo Offline (using the Dojo library) is built on top of Google Gears, creating an easy-to-use interface for using web applications offline.[124]

3.13 Web Services, Mashups, Widgets and Gadgets

> *"Design for 'hackability' and remixability."*
>
> —Tim O'Reilly[125]

Instead of reinventing the wheel with every new project, developers can use existing companies' web services to create feature-rich applications. Incorporating web services into new programs allows people to develop new applications quickly.

---

121. Berlind, D. "Google Gears Vies to be De Facto Tech for Offline Web Apps." *ZDNet*, 31 May 2007 `<http://blogs.zdnet.com/Berlind/?p=504>`.
122. Mills, E. "Google Gears Churns Toward Microsoft." *CNET*, 31 May 2007 `<http://news.com.com/2100-1012_3-6187942.html>`.
123. "The 70 Percent Solution." *Business 2.0*, 28 November 2005 `<http://money.cnn.com/2005/11/28/news/newsmakers/schmidt_biz20_1205/>`.
124. "The Dojo Offline Toolkit." *The Dojo Toolkit* `<http://dojotoolkit.org/offline>`.
125. O'Reilly, T. "What is Web 2.0: Design Patterns and Business Models for the Next Generation of Software." September 2005 `<http://www.oreillynet.com/pub/a/oreilly/tim/news/2005/09/30/what-is-web-20.html>`.

APIs

APIs (Application Programming Interfaces) provide applications with access to external services and databases. For example, a traditional programming API, like the Sun's Java API, allows programmers to use already-written methods and functions in their programs. Web services APIs are now offered by some websites as ways of sharing some of their functionality and information across the Internet.

Unique databases are central to Web 2.0; "data is the next Intel Inside."[126] Whether data is obtained from a proprietary source or collected over time from users, much of a site's value is in its databases. Many major Web 2.0 companies (e.g., eBay, Amazon, Google, Yahoo! and Flickr) provide APIs to encourage use of their services and data in the development of mashups, widgets and gadgets.

Mashups

Mashups combine content or functionality from existing web services, websites and RSS feeds to serve a new purpose. For example, Housingmaps.com is a mashup of Google Maps and real-estate listings from Craigslist. Mashups with maps are particularly popular, as are mashups using RSS feeds (see "RSS and Atom" in Section 3.15) created by using services such as Yahoo! Pipes™—a tool that enables you to aggregate and manipulate many data sources.

Using APIs can save time and money (some great mashups have been built in an afternoon); however, the mashup is then reliant on one or more third parties. If the API provider experiences downtime, the mashup will be unavailable as well (unless the mashup is programmed to avoid sites that are down). Always check the "terms of service" for using each company's web services. Many API providers charge usage fees based on the mashup's number of calls made to the server. Some sites require you to ask permission before using their APIs for commercial purposes, and others (e.g., Google) require that mashups based on their web services be free. Also, while mashups add value to data, there is always the question of who owns the data, and thus who should profit from the mashup.

Figure 3.4 lists some popular mashups. The site Programmable Web catalogs APIs and mashups and offers a "Mashup Matrix" (`http://www.programmableweb.com/matrix`) detailing which APIs have been combined to form each mashup. As more companies offer APIs, the only limitation on mashups (and the businesses built on them) is the developer's creativity. More complex mashups, using programs like Google Earth and Second Life, could be coming soon.[127]

Mashup	Combines
`http://www.housingmaps.com`	Google Maps and Craigslist real-estate listings to create a map marked with available housing listings.

Fig. 3.4 | Mashup examples. (Part 1 of 2.)

126. O'Reilly, T. "What is Web 2.0: Design Patterns and Business Models for the Next Generation of Software." September 2005 <`http://www.oreillynet.com/pub/a/oreilly/tim/news/2005/09/30/what-is-web-20.html`>.

127. Roush, W. "Second Earth." *Technology Review*, July/August 2007, p.38.

Mashup	Combines
`http://www.chicagocrime.org`	Google Maps and crime data from Citizen ICAM to create a map of Chicago marked with crime locations.
`http://www.feedmashr.com`	RSS feeds from Digg, ClipMarks, the *New York Times*, del.icio.us, Reddit and Slashdot to create a listing of the most popular stories from all sources.
`http://www.secretprices.com`	Amazon, Epinions.com and Shopping.com to create a comparison shopping site.
`http://paul.kedrosky.com/publicloos/`	Google Maps and Bathroom Diaries to create a map of San Francisco marked with the locations of public restrooms.

Fig. 3.4 | Mashup examples. (Part 2 of 2.)

Widgets and Gadgets

Widgets, also referred to as gadgets, are mini applications designed to run either as stand-alone applications or as add-on features in web pages. *Newsweek* called 2007 the "Year of the Widget" because of the huge increase in popularity of these applications.[128] Widgets can be used to personalize your Internet experience by displaying real-time weather conditions, aggregating RSS feeds, viewing maps, receiving event reminders, providing easy access to search engines and more. The availability of web services, APIs and various tools makes it easy even for beginner programmers to develop widgets. There are many catalogs of widgets online—one of the most all-inclusive is Widgipedia, which provides an extensive catalog of widgets and gadgets for a variety of platforms.

Amazon Web Services

Amazon is a leading provider of web services. The site provides historical pricing data and E-Commerce Services (ECS), which enable companies to use Amazon's systems to sell their own products. Amazon also offers hardware and communications infrastructure web services that are particularly popular with companies, providing economical web-scale computing. Amazon's Elastic Compute Cloud (EC2), Simple Storage Service (S3) and Simple Queue Service (SQS) enable businesses to pay for only the processing or storage space needed during any given period. This makes it possible for companies to save money (by not having to buy and maintain new hardware, software and communications equipment) while still being able to scale their storage and computing power to handle traffic surges (or reduce loss when the site's popularity declines). This is extremely significant in the Internet world, where a site's traffic can explode or crash overnight.

---

128. Braiker, B. "Tech: Welcome, Year of the Widget." *Newsweek*, 30 December 2006 `<http://www.msnbc.msn.com/id/16329739/site/newsweek/>`.

Amazon also provides "artificial artificial intelligence" with its unique Mechanical Turk. This web service allows applications to call on people to perform tasks (such as identifying pictures) that are easier for humans to do than computers. People can sign up to become part of the Mechanical Turk web service and bid on jobs (called Human Intelligence Tasks or HITs). This creates a competitive market, driving down developer costs, creating opportunities for people worldwide and allowing more applications to become feasible.

REST (Representational State Transfer)-Based Web Services

Representational State Transfer (REST) (originally proposed in Roy Thomas Fielding's doctoral dissertation[129]) refers to an architectural style for implementing web services. Though REST is not a standard, RESTful web services are implemented using web standards. Each operation in a RESTful web service is easily identified by a unique URL. So, when the server receives a request, it immediately knows what operation to perform. Such web services can be used in a program or directly from a web browser. In some cases, the results of a particular operation may be cached locally by the browser. This can make subsequent requests for the same operation faster by loading the result directly from the browser's cache.[130] Amazon's S3 is RESTful, and many other Web 2.0 web services provide RESTful interfaces.[131]

RESTful web services are alternatives to those implemented with SOAP (Simple Object Access Protocol). (We discuss both REST-based and SOAP-based web services in Chapter 28, Web Services.) With SOAP-based web services, the request and response are hidden (in entities known as a SOAP "envelopes"). SOAP requests must be deciphered as they are received at the server to determine the operation to perform and the arguments required to perform that operation. Similarly, the responses are encoded and deciphered on the client to obtain the result of the operation. SOAP does not currently provide a mechanism for caching results.

3.14 Location-Based Services

Location-Based Services (LBS) are applications that take your geographic location (city, state, location of your mobile device, etc.) into consideration. While the term generally refers to services accessed on mobile devices using the Global Positioning System (GPS), it can also be used to describe web applications that take your location into account. Search engines including Yahoo! Local and Google Maps use localization to provide you with geographically relevant content. Local search is particularly useful when you want to find a nearby business (e.g., plumbers, taxis, etc.). Location-based services are becoming increasingly popular in Web 2.0 applications. Conferences related to LBS include O'Reilly's Where 2.0 and the Location Intelligence Conference.

Global Positioning System (GPS)

The Global Positioning System (GPS), developed by the United States Department of Defense, uses numerous satellites that send signals to a GPS receiver to determine its exact

129. Fielding, R. T. "Architectural Styles and the Design of Network-Based Software Architectures." <http://www.ics.uci.edu/~fielding/pubs/dissertation/top.htm>.
130. Costello, R. "REST Tutorial." *xFront,* 26 June 2002 <http://www.xfront.com/REST.html>.
131. Richardson, L. and S. Ruby. *RESTful Web Services.* O'Reilly, 2007.

location. (A Russian system called GLONASS also exists, and a new system named Galileo is under development in Europe.) In the 1980s, the US Department of Defense opened GPS for civilian use to encourage satellite technology development.[132] Numerous location-based services are now available using GPS technology, such as GPS mapping devices used in cars or on mobile devices. GPS is also being used for safety. The US Federal Communications Commission (FCC) now requires wireless carriers to provide the locations of wireless customers calling 911 so emergency services can find them faster. To meet this requirement, wireless carriers have developed GPS-enabled cell phones.[133] These phones also provide premium services, such as driving directions and local information. The Disney Family Locator service uses GPS-enabled phones to help parents keep track of their children (as long as the child is carrying the special cell phone).[134]

Mapping Services

Google Maps is one of the most popular mapping applications available online. You can use Google Maps to locate businesses in your area, get driving directions and live traffic information, create custom maps with images and more. You can even get the information by using your mobile device. Google's local search allows you to locate a business in a geographic area and get its address, phone number, driving directions and even user reviews. Google Earth provides satellite images of virtually any location on the planet. In some areas, you can even get a panoramic view of a neighborhood at street level. You can use the Google Maps API to add mapping capabilities to your websites and web applications.

MapQuest, owned by AOL, provides similar mapping services. Use it to get directions and maps on your desktop or mobile device. The MapQuest OpenAPI allows you to add location-based services to your web applications. Additional mapping services include Yahoo! Local Maps and MSN Live Search. Both services offer maps, driving directions, traffic information and local search.

Companies such as NAVTEQ and Tele Atlas provide digital map data for in-vehicle and portable navigation devices, websites, location-based services and more. Developers building commercial location-based services can license the robust mapping products from these companies to build richly functional web applications.

GeoRSS and Geotagging

GeoRSS, based on the RSS standards, is a set of standards for representing geographical information in a feed. Location and geographical information in a GeoRSS feed can be used in GPS devices, mapping applications and other location-based services. For example, a blog post about a vacation could map the locations mentioned.[135]

Geotagging can be used to add location information (longitude, latitude, etc.) to websites, images, RSS feeds, videos and more. Websites can often determine a user's location by their IP address. Geotagging a website provides the user with location information about the site.[136] Geographic information can be used to add value to search results. Geotagging

---

132. Schiller, J. and A. Voisard. *Location-Based Services.* Morgan Kaufmann, 2004.
133. Malykhina, E. "Nokia Wants Your Cell Phone To Tell You Where You Are." *InformationWeek*, 9 October 2006 <http://www.informationweek.com/showArticle.jhtml?articleID=193105219>.
134. Magid, L. "Global Positioning by Cellphone." *New York Times*, 19 July 2007, C7.
135. "GeoRSS: Geographically Encoded Objects for RSS Feeds." *GeoRSS* <http://georss.org/>.
136. Turner, A. "Geotagging Web Pages and RSS Feeds." *Linux Journal*, 11 January 2005 <http://interactive.linuxjournal.com/node/8025>.

could also be mashed up with existing visualization systems, such as Google Earth or MSN Virtual Earth, which provide advanced satellite images for anywhere on the planet.

3.15 XML, RSS, Atom, JSON and VoIP

For more information on any of the following technologies, visit the corresponding Resource Centers at `http://www.deitel.com/resourcecenters.html` (see Fig. 2 in the Preface for a complete list of Deitel Resource Centers).

XML

XML (Extensible Markup Language, Chapter 14), developed in 1996 by the World Wide Web Consortium (W3C), is a markup language that allows you to label data based on its meaning. XML describes data in a way that is meaningful to both humans and computers.

XML documents are text files with a `.xml` extension; they can be created in text editors. These documents can reference a Document Type Definition (DTD) or a schema, which defines the structure for the document. This allows the information in the document to be verified by validating parsers, meaning they will check to make sure that no elements are missing (e.g., a last-name element in a document listing full names) and that the elements occur in the proper order. This makes XML data more reliable than data prepared with some other data-describing options. XML also can be used to create customized markup languages (e.g., XHTML for web content, CML for chemistry, MathML for mathematical content and formulas, and XBRL for financial data)—these are referred to as XML vocabularies. XHTML is described in Chapter 4, Introduction to XHTML. Chapter 14, XML and RSS, presents several examples that use MathML to render mathematical expressions.

RSS and Atom

Sites that offer RSS (Chapter 14) and Atom feeds can maintain an "open connection" with their readers. Users no longer have to regularly visit sites for updates—by subscribing to a site's feed, users receive updates as new information is posted to the site. The difference between RSS and Atom is subtle and unimportant to most users—many tools support both formats. Versions of RSS (an XML-based web content syndication format) have existed since the late 1990s; Atom dates to 2003.

Most major web browsers support RSS and Atom feeds, and many aggregators (or feed readers) are available to help users organize their subscriptions. Feedburner (acquired by Google) is used by many blogs to provide their readers with new posts by e-mail. This service also helps bloggers get a better idea of the size of their audience (by allowing them to see the number of subscribers).

JSON

JavaScript Object Notation (JSON) was developed in 1999 as an alternative to XML. JSON (discussed in Chapter 15, Ajax-Enabled Rich Internet Applications) is a text-based data interchange format used to represent JavaScript objects as strings and transmit them over a network. It is commonly used in Ajax applications. JSON text is easy to produce and read—it is also faster to parse (or extract) than XML.

VoIP

Voice over Internet Protocol (VoIP) is the technology used to make free or inexpensive phone calls over the Internet. Some businesses and individuals have switched completely to VoIP and eliminated traditional phone lines to cut costs. There are many VoIP services, such as Vonage, Packet8 or Lingo; Skype is the most popular. Acquired by eBay to integrate buyer and seller voice communication into auctions,[137] Skype offers free and fee-based services (such as calling non-Skype phones). VoIP is an enabling technology that can be layered into Web 2.0 companies and websites.

3.16 Web 2.0 Monetization Models

"The advertising model has come along; we underestimated how big that would be."
—Bill Gates, MIX06

Many Web 1.0 businesses discovered that popularity ("eyeballs") was not the same as financial success. Web 2.0 companies are paying more attention to monetizing their traffic. Starting an Internet business is cheaper than ever, and the cost of failure is lower. Anyone can start earning modest amounts of money almost immediately, using the monetization models described in Fig. 3.5.

Web 2.0 monetization is heavily reliant on advertising. Using Google's AdSense contextual advertising program is one of the fastest and most popular ways of monetizing a new Internet business. For more information see Deitel's Google AdSense and Website Monetization Resource Centers at `http://www.deitel.com/resourcecenters.html`.

Web 2.0 monetization models

affiliate network—A business (such as Commission Junction and LinkShare) that connects web publishers with cost-per-action affiliate programs. See affiliate program.

affiliate program—A deal offered by a company to share a portion of the revenues earned from traffic coming from web publisher websites. Affiliates provide text and image ads to post on the publishers' sites. If a user clicks through to the affiliate site and takes a specified action (e.g., makes a purchase, fills out a registration form, etc.) the publisher is paid a portion of the revenue or a flat fee. Companies offering affiliate programs include Amazon (the Amazon Associates program), Indeed, ClickBank, eBay and thousands more.

banner ad—An ad that consists of an image, often placed at the top of a page.

blog advertising—Advertising specifically designed for display on blog sites. Companies include Federated Media and Blogads.

contextual advertising—Advertising that is targeted to the content on a web page. Contextual ad programs include Google AdSense, Yahoo! Publisher Network, Vibrant Media, Kontera and Tribal Fusion.

cost-per-action (CPA)—Advertising that is billed to the advertiser per user action (e.g., purchasing a product or filling out a mortgage application). Companies include Amazon and Indeed. See also performance-based advertising.

Fig. 3.5 | Web 2.0 monetization models. (Part 1 of 2.)

137. Broache, A. "eBay to Nab Skype for $2.6 Billion." *CNET,* 12 September 2005 `<http://news.com.com/eBay+to+nab+Skype+for+2.6+billion/2100-1030_3-5860055.html>`.

Web 2.0 monetization models

cost-per-click (CPC)—Advertising that is billed by user click. The web publisher receives revenue each time a user clicks an ad on the publisher's site, regardless of whether the user makes a subsequent purchase. Companies include Google AdSense and Yahoo! Publisher Network.

cost-per-thousand impressions (CPM)—Advertising (usually banner advertising) that is billed per thousand impressions, regardless of whether the user clicks on the ad. Companies include DoubleClick, ValueClick and many more.

e-commerce—Selling products and/or services directly through a website. Companies include Amazon, Dell, CafePress.com and thousands more.

interstitial ad—An ad that plays between page loads. Companies include Tribal Fusion, DoubleClick, and many more.

in-text contextual advertising—Advertising that is marked by double-underlined keywords or phrases in the content of a web page. When a reader hovers the mouse cursor over a double-underlined word or phrase, a text ad pops up. By clicking on an ad, readers are taken to the advertiser's page. Companies providing in-text contextual advertising include Vibrant Media, Text Link Ads, Kontera and Tribal Fusion.

lead generation—Leads are generated when a visitor fills out an inquiry form so that a salesperson can follow through and potentially convert the lead to a sale. Lead generation is a subset of cost-per-action advertising. See cost-per-action (CPA).

paid blog post—A blog post (often a product review) that an advertiser pays a blogger to write. Some argue the ethics of this practice, and bloggers are encouraged to disclose that they are being paid for the posts. Companies that match bloggers and advertisers include PayPerPost, SponsoredReviews and ReviewMe.

performance-based advertising—Advertising that pays based on user action, such as making a purchase, filling out a registration form, etc. These are also often part of affiliate programs such as Amazon and ClickBank. See cost-per-action (CPA).

premium content—Content on a website that is available for an extra fee (e.g., e-books, articles, etc.). Companies that offer premium content include *The Wall Street Journal Online* and Search Engine Watch.

RSS ad—An ad included in RSS feeds. Companies include Feedster, Feedburner and Yahoo! Search Marketing.

tagging for profit—A site that buys inbound links or tags from other sites to help increase traffic, and thus increase potential advertising revenue. High-traffic sites can sell tags or links to other websites for a profit. (Caution: Search engines may lower the ranking of sites with paid links.) An example is 1000tags.com.

virtual worlds monetization—Selling products, premium services, virtual land and more in an online virtual world website. Virtual worlds include Second Life, IMVU, Habbo, Gaia Online and There.

Fig. 3.5 | Web 2.0 monetization models. (Part 2 of 2.)

3.17 Web 2.0 Business Models

The technologies and collaborative nature of Web 2.0 have opened up new business models. Some of these would not have been feasible even ten years ago, but because of Moore's Law they are not only possible but thriving. At the moment, there is no foreseeable end to the advancements attributed to Moore's Law, so fantastic ideas that are impossible today may become possible within just a few years. Figure 3.6 outlines many popular Internet business models and lists some companies that use each one. In just about every case, there are many more companies using that business model.

Web 2.0 business models

advertising exchange—An online marketplace where web publishers can sell their advertising inventory (ad space) to advertisers. Companies include DoubleClick Advertising Exchange and Right Media Exchange.

affiliate network—A business that connects web publishers with cost-per-action affiliate programs, which are a form of cost-per-action advertising. Companies include Commission Junction and LinkShare. (See Fig. 3.5 for more information on affiliate programs.)

blog—A website with a series of posts in reverse chronological order. Many blogs attract significant traffic and monetize with advertising and affiliate programs. Popular blogs include BoingBoing, Gizmodo, TechCrunch, John Battelle's Searchblog, Problogger and Scobleizer.

blog search engine—A search engine devoted to the blogosphere. Companies include Technorati, Feedster, IceRocket and Google Blog Search.

blog network—A collection of blogs with multiple editors. Popular blog networks include Corante, 9rules, Gawker Media and Weblogs, Inc.

buying and selling domain names—A company purchases domain names with the intent of selling them in the future as Internet real estate becomes more valuable. Companies include Afternic.com and GreatDomains.

competitive intelligence—A company that analyzes Internet usage for use by client websites. Companies include Hitwise and Compete, Inc.

content network—A site (or collection of sites) that provides content including articles, wikis, blogs and more. Companies include About.com, Deitel, LifeTips and Suite101.

discovery—A site that introduces users to valuable content they would not have looked for otherwise. Sites include StumbleUpon, Aggregate Knowledge, MOG and Deitel.

domain registrar—A site that sells domain names. Companies include Register.com, GoDaddy and Network Solutions.

encyclopedia and reference source—An online reference encyclopedia, dictionary, thesaurus, etc. Sites include Wikipedia, Reference.com and Citizendium.

feed aggregator—An application that combines RSS or Atom feeds so the user can view all subscriptions in a single location. Applications include NetNewsWire, Google Reader and Bloglines.

file sharing—An application where users can share files, music, software and more. Companies include BitTorrent, LimeWire, Kazaa, AllPeers and Shareaza.

infrastructure for distributing open source projects—A site that hosts collaborative open source software projects. Sites include SourceForge, freshmeat.net and Tucows.

Internet and web conference organizer—A company that organizes conferences on Internet and web topics. Companies include O'Reilly Media, CMP and Jupiter.

Internet radio—A site that distributes music and radio shows over the Internet. Companies include Last.fm and Pandora.

Internet TV—A site that distributes television shows (or allows you to distribute your own shows) over the Internet. Companies include Joost and Brightcove.

Internet video—A video sharing site where users upload and share content. Companies include YouTube and Yahoo! Video.

Fig. 3.6 | Web 2.0 business models. (Part 1 of 4.)

Web 2.0 business models

job boards and job search—A site that connects job seekers with employers and/or job search engines. Job boards include Monster, CareerBuilder and Dice. Job search engines include Indeed, Jobster and SimplyHired.

mashup—A combination of two or more existing web services and feeds to create a new application. For example, `http://www.housingmaps.com` combines real estate listings from Craigslist with Google Maps so you can view the listings on a map. For a list of popular mashups, see `http://www.programmableweb.com/popular`.

massively multiplayer online game—An online role playing or strategy game where Internet users interact with one another. Games include World of Warcraft, Guild Wars and Lineage.

mobile social networking—A social network oriented towards mobile devices (such as cell phones). Companies include Twitter, Dodgeball and MocoSpace.

music distribution site—An online music site where you can purchase electronic versions (e.g., `.mp3`) of single songs or entire albums. Companies include iTunes, Rhapsody and Amie Street.

online advertising—An online advertising company that offers contextual advertising, banner advertising, in-text contextual advertising and more. Companies include Google, Yahoo!, Microsoft, DoubleClick, Vibrant Media, Tribal Fusion, Kontera, Quigo, ValueClick, Federated Media and many more.

online auction—A marketplace where visitors bid for products (and services) over the Internet. Companies include eBay, Overstock.com and Amazon Auctions.

online classifieds—A classifieds "advertising" site where users can post jobs, real-estate listings, personal ads, etc. Companies include Craigslist, Yahoo! Classifieds and Google Base.

online survey site—A site that offers survey services to other companies. A popular example is Survey Monkey.

open source—Software that is available (under license) for anyone to use and modify with few or no restrictions. Many Web 2.0 companies use open source software to power their sites and offer open source products and content. Companies include the Free Software Foundation, Apache, Mozilla, Zend and many more.

outsourcing marketplaces—An online marketplace where contractors and freelancers can connect with potential clients for short-term work. Companies include Elance and Guru.com.

payments—A site that handles secure payments for e-commerce sites. Companies include PayPal and Google Checkout.

people-assisted search—A search engine or search-driven content site that is filtered and organized by people to provide users with more relevant search results. Companies include Mahalo and Deitel.

personalized start page—A site that allows you to customize a start page with weather, news, etc. Companies include Netvibes, iGoogle, Pageflakes and Protopage.

photo sharing site—A site where users can post and share their photos with other users. Companies include Flickr and Photobucket.

real estate—A site that offers online real estate listings and information. Companies include Redfin, Trulia and Zillow.

recommender system—A system that collects data using collaborative filtering systems to determine users' tastes and interests. Sites can gather information about your personal interests, compare you to other users with similar interests and make recommendations. Popular examples of sites using recommender systems include Pandora, Netflix, CleverSet, ChoiceStream, MyStrands, StumbleUpon, Last.fm, and MovieLens.

Fig. 3.6 | Web 2.0 business models. (Part 2 of 4.)

Web 2.0 business models

reputation system—A system used by businesses like eBay and Amazon to encourage trust. For example, after each eBay transaction, the buyer and the seller can each leave positive or negative comments about the other party.

search engine—The primary tool people use to find information on the web. Companies include Google, Yahoo!, MSN, Ask and many more.

selling digital content—An e-commerce site that sells digital media (e.g., e-books). Companies include ClickBank, Blish, Lulu and more.

social bookmarking site—A site that allows users to share their bookmarks with others. Users bookmark their favorites sites, articles, blogs and more, and tag them by keyword. Companies include del.icio.us, Ma.gnolia and Blue Dot.

social media site—A site that allows digital media (text, photos, videos, music, etc.) to be shared online. Companies include Digg, YouTube, Flickr, Reddit, Wikipedia and more.

social networking site—A site that helps users organize their existing relationships and establish new ones. Companies include MySpace, Facebook, Bebo, LinkedIn, Second Life, Gaia Online and more.

Software as a Service (SaaS)—Software that runs on a web server rather than being installed on a local client computer. By modifying the version of the software on the server, a company can simultaneously update all users to the latest version. SaaS applications include Salesforce.com, Microsoft Office Live, Microsoft Windows Live, Zoho Office Suite and many Google and 37Signals products.

subscription site—A site that offers member-only areas and premium content (additional content for a fee). Examples include Safari Books Online and the *Wall Street Journal*.

travel site—An online travel resource site that allows you to find and book hotels, air travel, rental cars and more. Companies include Expedia, Travelocity and Orbitz.

vertical search engine—A search engine that allows you to focus your search on a narrow topic. For example, travel search engines include Yahoo! Fare Finder, SideStep and Kayak; source-code search engines include Krugle and Koders.

virtual world—A social networking site (or program) where users create an avatar (their online image and persona) that they use to meet other users with similar interests, conduct business, participate in group activities, take classes and more. Companies include Second Life, Habbo, Gaia Online and There.

Voice over Internet Protocol (VoIP) site—A site that offers inexpensive or free telephone services over the Internet. Companies include Skype, Packet8, Lingo and Vonage.

Web 2.0 software—Software designed to build Web 2.0 sites and applications (e.g., blogging software). Companies include Six Apart, 37Signals, Adobe and Microsoft.

web analytics—Software (desktop and SaaS) and companies that analyze Internet traffic, demographics, navigation and more. Companies include Alexa, WebTrends, ClickTracks, Google Analytics and WebSideStory.

web and mobile messaging—A service that allows you to chat with your contacts from various Internet messaging services (AIM, Yahoo! Messenger, MSN Messenger, Google Talk). Companies include Meebo and eBuddy.

web conferencing—An application that enables users to collaborate remotely. This often includes chat, VoIP and desktop sharing. Companies include WebEx, GoToMeeting and DimDim (open source).

Fig. 3.6 | Web 2.0 business models. (Part 3 of 4.)

Web 2.0 business models	
webmail—A web-based e-mail system that allows you to send and receive e-mail using a standard browser. Popular webmail services include Google gmail, .Mac, Yahoo! Mail and MSN Hotmail.	**wiki**—A site that offers collaborative, editable documents online. Companies include Wikipedia, Wikia and SocialText.

Fig. 3.6 | Web 2.0 business models. (Part 4 of 4.)

3.18 Future of the Web

> *"Web 2.0 will make the cover of* Time *magazine, and thus its moment in the sun will have passed. However, the story that drives Web 2.0 will only strengthen, and folks will cast about for the next best name for the phenomenon."*
>
> —John Battelle[138]

> *"We're a long way from the full realization of the potential of intelligent systems, and there will no doubt be a tipping point where the systems get smart enough that we'll be ready to say, 'this is qualitatively different. Let's call it Web 3.0.'"*
>
> —Tim O'Reilly[139]

The XHTML coding on websites defines their structure and layout, specifying colors, fonts, sizes, use of bold and italic, paragraphs, tables and the like, but *not* specifying the *meaning* of the data on the page. Web 1.0 servers sent mostly static web pages coded in HTML or XHTML to browsers that rendered the pages on the screen. Web 2.0 applications are more dynamic, generally enabling significant interaction between the user (the client) and the computer (the server), and among communities of users.

Computers have a hard time deciphering meaning from XHTML content. The web today involves *users'* interpretations of what pages and images mean, but the future entails a shift from XHTML to a more sophisticated system based on XML, enabling *computers* to better understand meaning.

Web 2.0 companies use "data mining" to extract as much meaning as they can from XHTML-encoded pages. For example, Google's AdSense contextual advertising program does a remarkable job placing relevant ads next to content based on some interpretation of the meaning of that content. XHTML-encoded content does not explicitly convey meaning, but XML-encoded content does. So if we can encode in XML (and derivative technologies) much or all of the content on the web, we'll take a great leap forward towards realizing the Semantic Web.

It is unlikely that web developers and users will directly encode all web content in XML—it's simply too tedious and probably too complex for most web designers. Rather, the XML encoding will occur naturally as a by-product of using various content creation tools. For example, to submit a resume on a website, there may be a tool that enables the

---

138. Battelle, John. "2006 Predictions, How Did I Do?" *John Battelle Searchblog*, <`http://battellemedia.com/archives/003216.php`>.

139. O'Reilly, Tim. "Web 3.0 Maybe when we get there." *O'Reilly Radar*, 13 November 2006 <`http://radar.oreilly.com/archives/2006/11/web_30_maybe_wh.html`>.

user to fill out a form (with first name, last name, phone number, career goal, etc.). When the resume is submitted, the tool could create a computer readable microformat that could easily be found and read by applications that process resumes. Such tools might help a company find qualified potential employees, or help a job seeker who wants to write a resume find resumes of people with similar qualifications).

Tagging and Folksonomies

Tagging and folksonomies are early hints of a "web of meaning." Without tagging, searching for a picture on Flickr would be like searching for a needle in a giant haystack. Flickr's tagging system allows users to subjectively tag pictures with meaning, making photos findable by search engines. Tagging is a "loose" classification system, quite different, for example, from using the Dewey Decimal System for cataloging books, which follows a rigid taxonomy system, limiting your choices to a set of predetermined categories. Tagging is a more "democratic" labeling system that allows people, for example, to associate whatever meanings they choose with a picture (e.g. who is in the picture, where it was taken, what is going on, the colors, the mood, etc.).

Semantic Web

> *"People keep asking what Web 3.0 is. I think maybe when you've got an overlay of scalable vector graphics—everything rippling and folding and looking misty—on Web 2.0 and access to a semantic Web integrated across a huge space of data, you'll have access to an unbelievable data resource."*
>
> —Tim Berners-Lee[140]

> *"The Holy Grail for developers of the semantic Web is to build a system that can give a reasonable and complete response to a simple question like: I'm looking for a warm place to vacation and I have a budget of $3,000. Oh, and I have an 11-year-old child... Under Web 3.0, the same search would ideally call up a complete vacation package that was planned as meticulously as if it had been assembled by a human travel agent."*
>
> —John Markoff[141]

Many people consider the Semantic Web to be the next generation in web development, one that helps to realize the full potential of the web. This is Tim Berners-Lee's original vision of the web, also known as the "web of meaning."[142] Though Web 2.0 applications are finding meaning in content, the Semantic Web will attempt to make those meanings clear to computers as well as humans. It will be a web able to answer complex and subtle questions.

Realization of the Semantic Web depends heavily on XML and XML-based technologies (see Chapter 14), which help make web content more understandable to computers. Currently, computers "understand" data on basic levels, but are progressing to find mean-

---

140. Shannon, V. "A 'More Revolutionary' Web." May 2006 <http://www.iht.com/articles/2006/05/23/business/web.php>.

141. Markoff, John. "Entrepreneurs See a Web Guided by Common Sense." The New York Times, November 2006 <http://www.nytimes.com/2006/11/12/business/12web.html?ex=1320987600&en=254d697964cedc62&ei=5088>.

142. Berners-Lee, T. *Weaving the Web.* Harper-Collins, 2000.

ingful connections and links between data points. The emerging Semantic Web technologies highlight new relationships among web data. Some experiments that emphasize this are Flickr and FOAF (Friend of a Friend), a research project that "is creating a Web of machine-readable pages describing people, the links between them and the things they create and do."[143] Programming in both instances involves links between databases—ultimately allowing users to share, transfer, and use each other's information (photos, blogs, etc.).[144]

Preparations for the Semantic Web have been going on for years. XML is already widely used in both online and offline applications, but still only a minute portion of the web is coded in XML or derivative technologies. Many companies, including Zepheira, an information management company, and Joost, an Internet TV provider, already use semantic technologies in working with data. Deterring Semantic Web development are concerns about the consequences of false information and the abuse of data. Since the Semantic Web will rely on computers having greater access to information and will yield a deeper understanding of its significance, some people worry about the potentially increased consequences of security breaches. The Policy Aware Web Project is an early attempt at developing standards to encourage data sharing by providing access policies that can sufficiently protect individuals' privacy concerns.[145]

Microformats

> *"We need microformats that people agree on."*
> — Bill Gates, MIX06 conference[146]

Some people look at the web and see lots of "loose" information. Others see logical aggregates, such as business cards, resumes, events and so forth. Microformats are standard formats for representing information aggregates that can be understood by computers, enabling better search results and new types of applications. The key is for developers to use standard microformats, rather than developing customized, non-standard data aggregations. Microformat standards encourage sites to similarly organize their information, thus increasing interoperability. For example, if you want to create an event or an events calendar, you could use the hCalendar microformat. Some other microformats are adr for address information, hresume for resumes, and xfolk for collections of bookmarks.[147]

Resource Description Framework (RDF)

The Resource Description Framework (RDF), developed by the World Wide Web Consortium (W3C), is based on XML and used to describe content in a way that is understood by computers. RDF helps connect isolated databases across the web with consistent semantics.[148] The structure of any expression in RDF is a collection of triples.[149] RDF triples consist of two pieces of information (subject and object) and a linking fact (predicate).

143. Friend of a Friend Project homepage. `<http://www.foaf-project.org/>`.
144. Shannon, Victoria. "A 'More Revolutionary' Web." *International Herald Tribune.* May 24 2006 `<http://www.iht.com/articles/2006/05/23/business/web.php>`.
145. Weitzner, D., J. Hendler, T. Berners-Lee, and D. Connolly. "Creating a Policy-Aware Web: Discretionary, Rule-based Access for the World Wide Web." October 2004 `<http://www.w3.org/2004/09/Policy-Aware-Web-acl.pdf>`.
146. "Bill Gates: Microsoft MIX06 Conference." *Microsoft,* March 2006.
147. "Microformats Wiki." *microformats.org* `<http://microformats.org/wiki/Main_Page>`.

Let's create a simple RDF triple. "Chapter 3, Dive Into® Web 2.0" is the title of this document and one property (the document's subject) that we'll use in our RDF triple. Another property of this chapter is "Deitel" as the author. So the sentence "Chapter 3, Dive Into® Web 2.0 is written by Deitel" is an RDF triple, containing two properties and a linking fact ("is written by").

DBpedia.org is currently transferring content into RDF from Wikipedia, one of the largest and most popular resources of online information. Using SPARQL (SPARQL Protocol and RDF Query Language), DBpedia.org is converting data from Wikipedia entries into RDF triples. In June 2007, they claimed to have over 91 million triples—this will allow the information (from Wikipedia) to be accessed by more advanced search queries.[150]

Ontologies

Ontologies are ways of organizing and describing related items, and are used to represent semantics. This is another means of cataloging Internet content in a way that can be understood by computers.[151] RDF is designed for formatting ontologies. OWL (Web Ontology Language), also designed for formatting ontologies in XML, extends beyond the basic semantics of RDF ontologies to enable even deeper machine understanding of content.[152]

Closing Comment

This book will get you up to speed on Web 2.0 applications development. Building a "web of meaning" will ultimately open a floodgate of opportunities for web developers and entrepreneurs to write new applications, create new kinds of businesses, etc. We don't know exactly what the "web of meaning" will look like, but it's starting to take shape. If it helps accomplish what many leaders in the web community believe is possible, the future of the web will be exciting indeed.

3.19 Wrap-Up

In this chapter, you learned how Web 2.0 embraces an architecture of participation, encouraging user interaction and community contributions. User-generated content is the key to success for many leading Web 2.0 companies. Harnessing collective intelligence can result in smart ideas. Collaborative filtering lets users promote valuable content, and flag offensive or inappropriate material. The wisdom of crowds suggests that a large diverse group of people can be smarter than a small group of specialists.

We presented several popular Web 2.0 business models. You learned how you, the user, are deciding which news and information outlets you trust, enabling popular blogs and social media networks to compete with traditional media powerhouses. People are using social networks to interact and network, personally and professionally. We discussed

---

148. Miller, E. "An Introduction to the Resource Description Framework." *D-Lib Magazine*, May 1998 <http://dlib.org/dlib/may98/miller/05miller.html>.
149. "Resource Description Framework (RDF) Concepts and Abstract Sytax." *w3.org* <http://www.w3.org/TR/rdf-concepts/#section-Concepts>.
150. *DBPedia.org*. <http://dbpedia.org/docs/>.
151. Heflin, J. "OWL Web Ontology Language Use Cases and Requirements." *W3C*, 10 February 2004 <http://www.w3.org/TR/webont-req/>.
152. "Introduction to OWL." *W3Schools* <http://www.w3schools.com/rdf/rdf_owl.asp>.

popular social bookmarking sites that let you share your favorite websites, blogs, and articles with other users.

You learned about the Long Tail economic model and how Web 2.0 Internet businesses are increasing exposure for lesser-known products in a way that traditional businesses cannot. Web 2.0 companies are monetizing their content with advertising, affiliate programs and more.

We discussed how the explosion of content combined with people's increasing demands on time has led to an attention economy, increasing the importance of search engines used to find content online. SEO, link building and SEM can help you maximize your website's findability and improve search engine results. Many Web 2.0 sites enable discovery, pointing you to valuable new content that you might not have otherwise sought. Tagging and folksonomies help you locate content on the web more effectively, especially content that computers have a hard time identifying, such as photos and videos. Search engines are using localization to provide you with geographically relevant content.

You learned how Software as a Service (SaaS) applications offer companies (and users) many benefits, including fewer demands on internal IT departments, increased accessibility for out-of-the-office use, an easy way to maintain software across a diversity of platforms on a large scale and more. Rich Internet Applications offer responsiveness, "rich" features and functionality similar to desktop applications. Web services are used to create feature-rich mashup applications, combining content or functionality from existing web services, websites and RSS feeds. Many people believe that the Semantic Web—the "web of meaning"—will be the next generation of the web, enabling exciting new kinds of applications.

This chapter concludes our introduction to computers, the Internet, browsers and Web 2.0. The remainder of the book is devoted to building web applications—you'll learn how to program the client side and the server side, including interacting with databases. We'll focus on building Ajax-enabled Rich Internet Applications. We begin in Chapter 4 by discussing how to use XHTML (the Extensible HyperText Markup Language) to create web pages to be rendered by web browsers. You'll use XHTML to incorporate images into your web pages, add internal linking for page navigation, create forms for collecting information from a user, create tables and more.

3.20 Where to Go for More Web 2.0 Information

Figure 3.4 lists some popular resources for Web 2.0 news and analysis.

Resource	Description
TechCrunch `http://www.techcrunch.com/`	Edited by Michael Arrington, this blog is the leading Web 2.0 news resource that profiles innovative and important Internet companies and products.
Mashable `http://www.mashable.com/`	A social networking news blog, edited by Pete Cashmore. The site includes sections devoted to MySpace, YouTube, Bebo, Facebook and Xanga.

Fig. 3.7 | Web 2.0 news, analysis, technology and business resources. (Part 1 of 2.)

Resource	Description
ReadWriteWeb `http://www.readwriteweb.com/`	Edited by Richard MacManus, this blog provides web technology news, reviews and analysis.
GigaOM `http://www.gigaom.com/`	Technology news and analysis blog, edited by Om Malik—founder of GigaOmniMedia and a former writer for Business 2.0, Red Herring and Forbes.com.
Dion Hinchcliffe's Web 2.0 Blog `http://web2.socialcomputingmagazine.com/`	Web 2.0 news and analysis blog by Dion Hinchcliffe, Editor-in-Chief of *Social Computing* Magazine.
Matt Cutts' Blog `http://www.mattcutts.com/blog/`	Matt Cutts, a software engineer at Google, blogs about gadgets, Google and SEO.
O'Reilly Radar `http://radar.oreilly.com/`	O'Reilly Media's blog about Web 2.0, open source, emerging technology and more.
SearchEngineLand `http://www.searchengineland.com/`	Search engine news blog, edited by Danny Sullivan—a leading search engine expert.
SearchEngineWatch `http://searchenginewatch.com/`	News and analysis of the search engine industry. Includes blogs, tutorials, forums and more.
Deitel Resource Centers `http://www.deitel.com/resourcecenters.html` (See Fig. 2 in the Preface for a list of Resource Centers.)	Numerous Web 2.0 technology and Internet business Resource Centers that include links to, and descriptions of tutorials, demos, free software tools, articles, e-books, whitepapers, videos, podcasts, blogs, RSS feeds and more.

Fig. 3.7 | Web 2.0 news, analysis, technology and business resources. (Part 2 of 2.)

3.21 Web 2.0 Bibliography

General Web 2.0

Anderson, C. *The Long Tail: Why the Future of Business Is Selling Less of More.* Hyperion, 2006.

Anderson, C. "The Long Tail." *WIRED*, October 2004 <`http://www.wired.com/wired/archive/12.10/tail.html`>.

Battelle, J. *The Search: How Google and Its Rivals Rewrote the Rules of Business and Transformed Our Culture.* Portfolio, 2005.

"Bill Gates: Microsoft MIX06 Conference." *Microsoft*, March 2006 <`http://www.microsoft.com/presspass/exec/billg/speeches/2006/03-20MIX.mspx`>.

Brin, S. and L. Page. "The Anatomy of a Large-Scale Hypertextual Web Search Engine." <`http://infolab.stanford.edu/~backrub/google.html`>.

Farber, D. "ETech: Attenuation, Web 2.0 and spimes." *ZDNet*, March 2006 <`http://blogs.zdnet.com/BTL/?p=2667`>.

Graham, P. "Web 2.0." November 2005 <`http://www.paulgraham.com/web20.html`>.

Grossman, L. "*TIME*'s Person of the Year: You." *TIME*, December 2006 <http://www.time.com/time/magazine/article/0,9171,1569514,00.html>.

Hinchcliffe, D. "The State of Web 2.0." April 2006 <http://web2.socialcomputingmagazine.com/the_state_of_web_20.htm>.

Horrigan, J. B. "Home Broadband Adoption 2006." *Pew Internet & American Life Project*, May 2006 <http://www.pewinternet.org/pdfs/PIP_Broadband_trends2006.pdf>.

Madden, M. and S. Fox. "Riding the Waves of 'Web 2.0.'" *Pew Internet & American Life Project*, October 2006 <http://www.pewinternet.org/pdfs/PIP_Web_2.0.pdf>.

Miller, P. "Thinking About This Web 2.0 Thing." August 2005 <http://paulmiller.typepad.com/thinking_about_the_future/2005/08/thinking_about_.html>.

Moore, G. "Cramming More Components onto Integrated Circuits." *Electronics*, April 1965 <http://ftp://download.intel.com/museum/Moores_Law/Articles-Press_Releases/Gordon_Moore_1965_Article.pdf>.

Musser, J. and T. O'Reilly. *Web 2.0 Principles and Best Practices*. O'Reilly Media, Inc., 2006.

O'Reilly, T. "Web 2.0: Compact Definition?" October 2005 <http://radar.oreilly.com/archives/2005/10/web_20_compact_definition.html>.

O'Reilly, T. "What is Web 2.0: Design Patterns and Business Models for the Next Generation of Software." September 2005 <http://www.oreillynet.com/pub/a/oreilly/tim/news/2005/09/30/what-is-web-20.html>.

"Tim O'Reilly's seven principles of web 2.0 make a lot more sense if you change the order." *Open Gardens*, April 2006 <http://opengardensblog.futuretext.com/archives/2006/04/tim_o_reillys_s.html>.

Search

"About Rollyo." *Rollyo* <http://www.rollyo.com/about.html>.

"About Us." *Microsoft adCenter Labs* <http://adlab.msn.com/AboutUs.aspx>.

Brin, S. and L. Page. "The Anatomy of a Large-Scale Hypertextual Web Search Engine." <http://infolab.stanford.edu/~backrub/google.html>.

Calore, M. "Remembering the First Google Bomb." *Compiler (WIRED blog)*, 26 January 2007 <http://blog.wired.com/monkeybites/2007/01/earlier_today_m.html>.

"Company History." *Yahoo!* <http://yhoo.client.shareholder.com/press/history.cfm>.

"Company Overview." *Google* <http://www.google.com/intl/en/corporate/index.html>.

"comScore Search Rankings." *CNN*, 16 July 2007 <http://money.cnn.com/news/newsfeeds/articles/prnewswire/AQM17916072007-1.htm>.

Davenport, T. and J. Beck. *The Attention Economy: Understanding the New Currency of Business*. Harvard Business School Press, 2002.

"Google: One Million and Counting." *Pandia Search Engine News*, 2 July 2007 <http://www.pandia.com/sew/481-gartner.html>.

"Mahalo FAQ." *Mahalo* <http://www.mahalo.com/Mahalo_FAQ>.

"Microsoft Digital Advertising Solutions." *Microsoft*. <http://advertising.microsoft.com/advertising-online>.

Mills, E. "Google Rises at Yahoo's expense." *CNET*, 23 April 2007 <http://news.com.com/Google+rises+at+Yahoos+expense/2100-1038_3-6178164.html>.

Morville, P. *Ambient Findability: What We Find Changes Who We Become*. O'Reilly Media Inc., 2005.

"MSN Live Search: About Us." *MSN* <http://search.msn.com/docs/default.aspx?FORM=HLHP2>.

Olson, S. "MSN Launches Revamped Search Engine." *CNET,* 30 June 2004 <http://news.com.com/MSN+launches+revamped+search+engine/2100-1032_3-5254083.html>.

Search Engine Strategies: Conference & Expos, 2007 <http://www.searchenginestrategies.com>.

Sherman, C. "The State of Search Engine Marketing 2006." *Search Engine Land*, 8 February 2007 <http://searchengineland.com/070208-095009.php>.

Sullivan, D. "Congratulations! You're a Search Engine Marketer!" *Search Engine Watch*, 5 November 2005 <http://searchenginewatch.com/showPage.html?page=2164351>.

"Technology Overview." *Google* <http://www.google.com/corporate/tech.html>.

Thompson, C. "Media in the Age of the Swarm." *cbc.ca* <http://www.cbc.ca/10th/columns/media_thompson.html>.

Underwood, L. "A Brief History of Search Engines." *Web Ref.* <http://www.webreference.com/authoring/search_history/>.

"Vertical Search-Engines: Know Your Subject." *Economist.com*, 12 July 2007 <http://www.economist.com/business/displaystory.cfm?story_id=9478224>.

"Web Search: How to use MSN Search." *MSN* <http://search.msn.com/docs/help.aspx?t=SEARCH_CONC_WhatsNewWithMSNSearch.htm#2D>.

Wilding, R. "Top 5 Black Hat and White Hat Search Engines Optimisation Techniques." *PushON* <http://www.pushon.co.uk/articles/top5-black-hat-white-hat-seo.htm>.

User-Generated Content

Cauchi, S. "Online Encyclopedias Put to the Test." *The Age*, December 2005 <http://www.theage.com/au/news/national/online-encyclopedias-put-to-the-test/2005/12/14/1134500913345.html>.

"Leading Indicators." *FORTUNE*, 13 November 2006, p.40.

Maney, K. "Techies Hot on Concept of 'Wisdom of Crowds,' But It Has Some Pitfalls." *USA Today*, September 2006 <http://www.usatoday.com/tech/columnist/kevinmaney/2006-09-12-wisdom-of-crowds_x.htm>.

O'Reilly, T. "The Architecture of Participation." June 2004 <http://oreillynet.com/lpt/a/5994>.

Seigenthaler, J. "A False Wikipedia 'Biography.'" *USA Today*, November 2005 <http://www.usatoday.com/news/opinion/editorials/2005-11-29-wikipedia-edit_x.htm>.

"SocialText is the Enterprise Wiki Trusted Most by Global 2000 Corporations." *SocialText* <http://www.socialtext.com/products/overview>.

Steel, E. "Newspapers' Ad Sales Show Accelerating Drop." *The Wall Street Journal*, 18 July 2007, A4.

Surowiecki, J. *The Wisdom of Crowds*. Anchor, 2005.

Tapscott, D. and A. D. Williams. *Wikinomics: How Mass Collaboration Changes Everything*. Portfolio Hardcover, 2006.

Vara, V. "Wikis at Work." *The Wall Street Journal*, 18 June 2007, R11.

Blogging

Akismet <http://http://akismet.com/stats/>.

"Blog Statistics and Demographics." *Caslon Analytics*, March 2007 <http://www.caslon.comau/weblogprofile1.htm>.

Blood, R. "Weblogs: A History and Perspective." *Rebecca's Pocket*, September 2000 <http://www.rebeccablood.net/essays/weblog_history.html>.

Bowman, S. and C. Willis. "We Media." July 2003 <http://www.hypergene.net/wemedia/download/we_media.pdf>.

"CEO Blog List." *NewPR Wiki* <http://www.thenewpr.com/wiki/pmwiki.php/Resources/CEOBlogsList?pagename=Resources.CEOBlogsList>.

Kirkpatrick, D. "Why There's No Escaping the Blog." *FORTUNE*, 10 January 2005 <http://money.cnn.com/magazines/fortune/fortune_archive/2005/01/10/8230982/index.htm>.

Lenhart, A. and S. Fox. "Bloggers: A Portrait of the Internet's New Storytellers." *Pew Internet & American Life Project*, July 2006 <http://www.pewinternet.org/pdfs/PIP%20Bloggers%20Report%20July%2019%202006.pdf>.

Thompson, C. "A Timeline of the History of Blogging." *New York Magazine*, February 2006 <http://nymag.com/news/media/15971/>.

Walsh, B. *Clear Blogging: How People Are Changing the World and How You Can Join Them.* APress, 2007.

Social Networking

Arrington, M. "Bear Stearns: Yahoo Must Form A Social Networking Strategy." *TechCrunch*, 3 August 2007 <http://www.techcrunch.com/2007/08/03/bear-stearns-yahoo-must-form-a-social-networking-strategy>.

Athavely, A. "A Job Interview You Don't Have to Show Up For." *The Wall Street Journal Online*, June 2007 <http://online.wsj.com/article/SB118229876637841321.html?mod=tff_main_tff_top>.

Baker, S. "IBM on Second Life: More than PR." *BusinessWeek*, 15 November 2006 <http://www.businessweek.com/the_thread/blogspotting/archives/2006/11/ibm_on_second_l.html>.

Bulkeley, W. "Playing Well With Others." *The Wall Street Journal Online*, 18 June 2007 <http://online.wsj.com/article/SB118194536298737221.html>.

"Businesses Find MySpace is a Place to Reach Youth." *Trend Watching*, July 2006 <http://www.trendwatching.com/about/inmedia/articles/youniversal_branding/businesses_find_myspace_is_a_p.html>.

Copeland, M. "The Missing Link." *CNNMoney.com*, February 2007 <http://money.cnn.com/magazines/business2/business2_archive/2006/12/01/8394967/index.htm>.

"Customer Support." *Facebook* <http://www.facebook.com/help.php?tab=safety>.

"Facebook Statistics." *Facebook*, 17 July 2007 <http://static.ak.facebook.com/press/facebook_statistics.pdf?11:44617>.

Jesdanun, A. "Candidates Seek Youths at MySpace." *ABC News*, August 2006 <http://abcnews.go.com/Technology/wireStory?id=2325325&page=1>.

Kirkpatrick, M. "Friendster Awarded Patent on Social Networking." *TechCrunch*, July 2006 <http://www.techcrunch.com/2006/07/07/friendster-awarded-patent-on-social-networking/>.

Lawson, S. "Second Life Creates a Millionaire." *IDG News*, 30 November 2006 <http://www.itworld.com/App/4201/061130secondlife/>.

"Metcalf's Law." <http://www-ec.njit.edu/~robertso/infosci/metcalf.html>.

Prescott, L. "Hitwise US Consumer Generated Media Report." *Hitwise,* February 2007.

Rivlin, G. "Wallflower at the Web Party." *New York Times*, October 2006 <http://www.nytimes.com/2006/10/15/business/yourmoney/15friend.html>.

"Second Life Lawyer." *Business 2.0*, May 2007, p.86.

"The CEO's Guide to Social Networks." *BusinessWeek*, September 2006 <http://businessweek.com/mediacenter/qt/podcasts/guide_to_tech/guidetotech_09_11_06.mp3>.

"Top 20 Websites." *Hitwise*, May 2007 <http://hitwise.com/datacenter/rankings.php>.

"What is Second Life." <http://secondlife.com/whatis>.

Social Media

"Amazon.com to Launch DRM-Free MP3 Music Download Store with Songs and Albums from EMI Music and More Than 12,000 Other Labels." May 2007 <http://phx.corporate-ir.net/phoenix.zhtml?c=176060&p=irol-newsArticle&ID=1003003>.

Colvin, G. "TV Is Dying? Long Live TV!" *FORTUNE*, 5 February 2007, p.43.

"Conference Report Filed in House." *Library of Congress*, 8 October 1998 <http://thomas.loc.gov/cgi-bin/bdquery/z?d105:HR02281:@@@D&summ2=m&>.

D'Agostino, D. "Security in the World of Web 2.0." *Innovations*, Winter 2006, p.15.

Hefflinger, M. "Digg Users Revolt Over Deleted Posts of HD DVD Security Hack." *digitalmediawire*, 2 May 2007 <http://www.dmwmedia.com/news/2007/05/02/digg-users-revolt-over-deleted-posts-of-hd-dvd-security-hack>.

Jobs, S. "Thoughts on Music." February 2007 <http://www.apple.com/hotnews/thoughtsonmusic>.

"Leading Indicators." *FORTUNE*, 13 November 2006, p.40.

Maney, K. "Techies Hot on Concept of 'Wisdom of Crowds,' but it has some pitfalls." *USA Today*, September 2006 <http://www.usatoday.com/tech/columnist/kevinmaney/2006-09-12-wisdom-of-crowds_x.htm>.

Mills, E. "Copyright Quagmire for Google and YouTube." *ZDNet*, March 2007 <http://news.zdnet.com/2100-9588_22-6167281.html>.

O'Hear, S. "Viacom to Partner with Joost." *ZDNet*, 20 February 2007 <http://blogs.zdnet.com/social/?p=96>.

Prescott, L. "Hitwise US Consumer Generated Media Report." *Hitwise*, February 2007.

Steel, E. "Newspapers' Ad Sales Show Accelerating Drop." *The Wall Street Journal*, 18 July 2007, A4.

Smith E. and K. Delaney. "Vivendi's Universal Sues Two Web Sites Over Video Sharing." *The Wall Street Journal*, 18 October 2006, B3.

Torrone, P. "What Is Podcasting?" *O'Reilly Media*, 20 July 2005 <http://digitalmedia.oreilly.com/2005/07/20/WhatIsPodcasting.html>.

Tagging

Chun, S., R. Cherry, D. Hiwiller, J. Trant and B. Wyman. "Steve.museum: An Ongoing Experiment in Social Tagging, Folksonomy, and Museums." *Archives & Museum Informatics*, March 2006 <http://www.archimuse.com/mw2006/papers/wyman/wyman.html>.

Garrett, J. J. "An Interview with Flickr's Eric Costello." *Adaptive Path*, August 2005 <http://www.adaptivepath.com/publications/essays/archives/000519.php>.

Masters, C. "Programming Provocateurs." *TIME*, 19 March 2007, p. 84.

Mayfield, R. "Buy Side Publishing." *Ross Mayfield's Weblog*, April 2006 <http://ross.typepad.com/blog/2006/04/buy_side_publis.html>.

Rainie, L. "Tagging." *Pew Internet & American Life Project*, December 2006 <http://www.pewinternet.org/pdfs/PIP_Tagging.pdf>.

Schonfeld, E. "The Flickrization of Yahoo!" *CNN Money.com*, December 2005 <http://money.cnn.com/magazines/business2/business2_archive/2005/12/01/8364623/>.

"Using Technorati Tags." *Technorati* <http://support.technorati.com/support/siteguide/tags>.

Vander Wal, T. "Folksonomy Coinage and Definition." *Vanderwal.net*, February 2007 <http://www.vanderwal.net/folksonomy.html>.

Social Bookmarking

"About Ma.gnolia" <http://ma.gnolia.com/about>.

"Gardeners." *Ma.gnolia Community Wiki*, March 2007 <http://wiki.ma.gnolia.com/Gardeners>.

"Know How Adobe and del.icio.us Work Together?" *del.icio.us blog*, May 2007 <http://blog.del.icio.us/blog/2007/05/knowhow_adobe_a.html>.

"That was Fast." *del.icio.us blog*, March 2007 <http://blog.del.icio.us/blog/2007/03/that_was_fast.html>.

Software Development

37Signals. *Getting Real*, 2006 <http://gettingreal.37signals.com>.

Fallows, D. "China's Online Population Explosion." *Pew Internet & American Life Project*, July 2007 <http://www.pewinternet.org/pdfs/China_Internet_July_2007.pdf>.

Farber, D. "ETech: Attenuation, Web 2.0 and Spimes." *ZDNet*, March 2006 <http://blogs.zdnet.com/BTL/?p=2667>.

Greenemeier, L. "Open-Source Exuberance." *InformationWeek*, July 2005 <http://www.informationweek.com/story/showArticle.jhtml?articleID=165700923>.

Peiris, M. "The Pros and Cons of Hosted Software." *SmartBiz*, March 2006 <http://www.smartbiz.com/article/articleview/1118/1/42>.

Pink, D. H. "Why the World Is Flat." *Wired*, May 2005 <http://http://www.wired.com/wired/archive/13.05/friedman.html>.

Tapscott, D. and A. D. Williams. *Wikinomics: How Mass Collaboration Changes Everything*. Portfolio Hardcover, 2006.

"The RIA Desktop in a Browser." *LaszloSystems* <http://www.laszlosystems.com/software/webtop>.

Tiemann, M. "Licenses by Name." *Open Source Initiative*, 18 September 2006 <http://www.opensource.org/licenses/alphabetical>.

Van Rossum, G. "Open Source Summit Trip Report." *Linux Gazette*, 10 April 1998 <http://linuxgazette.net/issue28/rossum.html>.

Wilcox, J. "IBM to Spend $1 Billion on Linux in 2001." *CNET*, January 2002 <http://news.com.com/IBM+to+spend+1+billion+on+Linux+in+2001/2100-1001_3-249750.html>.

Rich Internet Applications

"Adobe Flex 2." *Adobe* <http://www.adobe.com/products/flex/whitepapers/pdfs/flex2wp_technicaloverview.pdf>.

Berlind, D. "Google Gears Vies to be De Facto Tech for Offline Web Apps." *ZDNet*, 31 May 2007 <http://blogs.zdnet.com/Berlind/?p=504>.

"Core Effects." *Script.aculo.us Wiki* <http://wiki.script.aculo.us/scriptaculous/show/CoreEffects>.

Cubrilovic, N. “Silverlight: The Web Just Got Richer.” *TechCrunch*, April 2007 <http://www.techcrunch.com/2007/04/30/silverlight-the-web-just-got-richer>.

Mills, E. “Google Gears Churns Toward Microsoft.” *CNET*, 31 May 2007 <http://news.com.com/2100-1012_3-6187942.html>.

“Prototype Tips and Tutorials.” *Prototype JavaScript* <http://prototypejs.org/learn>.

“Sun Radically Simplifies Content Authoring—Previews JavaFX Script.” *Sun Microsystems*, 8 May 2007 <http://www.sun.com/aboutsun/pr/2007-05/sunflash.20070508.2.xml>.

Taft, E. “Google Gears Allows Offline Web Development.” *eWeek*, 30 May 2007 <http://www.eweek.com/article2/0,1895,2139083,00.asp>.

“The 70 Percent Solution.” *Business 2.0*, 28 November 2005 <http://money.cnn.com/2005/11/28/news/newsmakers/schmidt_biz20_1205/>.

“The Dojo Offline Toolkit.” *The Dojo Toolkit* <http://dojotoolkit.org/offline>.

Web Services and Mashups

Amazon Web Services <http://aws.amazon.com>.

Braiker, B. “Tech: Welcome, Year of the Widget.” *Newsweek*, December 2006 <http://www.msnbc.msn.com/id/16329739/site/newsweek/>.

Costello, R. “REST Tutorial.” *xFront*, June 2002 <http://www.xfront.com/REST.html>.

Fielding, R. T. “Architectural Styles and the Design of Network-Based Software Architectures.” <http://www.ics.uci.edu/~fielding/pubs/dissertation/top.htm>.

Richardson, L. and S. Ruby. *RESTful Web Services*. O’Reilly, 2007.

Roush, W. “Second Earth.” *Technology Review*, July/August 2007, p.38.

Location-Based Services

Magid, L. “Global Positioning by Cellphone.” *New York Times*, 19 July 2007, C7.

Malykhina, E. “Nokia Wants Your Cell Phone To Tell You Where You Are.” *InformationWeek*, 9 October 2006 <http://www.informationweek.com/showArticle.jhtml?articleID=193105219>.

Schiller, J. and A. Voisard. *Location-Based Services*. Morgan Kaufmann, 2004.

XML, RSS, Atom, JSON and VoIP

Broache, A. “eBay to Nab Skype for $2.6 billion.” *CNET*, 12 September 2005 <http://news.com.com/eBay+to+nab+Skype+for+2.6+billion/2100-1030_3-5860055.html>.

“Introducing JSON” <http://www.json.org>.

Internet Business

Anderson, C. *The Long Tail: Why the Future of Business Is Selling Less of More*. Hyperion, 2006.

Copeland, M. “The Missing Link.” *CNNMoney.com*, February 2007 <http://money.cnn.com/magazines/business2/business2_archive/2006/12/01/8394967/index.htm>.

Deutschman, A. “Inside the Mind of Jeff Bezos.” *Fast Company*, August 2004 <http://www.fastcompany.com/magazine/85/bezos_1.html>.

Graham, J. “The House that Helped Build Google.” *USA TODAY*, 5 July 2007, 1B.

Helft, M. “eBay Spawns a Marketplace for the Bizarre.” *CNN*, 20 September 1999 <http://www.cnn.com/TECH/computing/9909/20/ebay.side.show.idg/>.

Newman, A. A. “Google to Expand Program, Giving Newspapers a Lift.” *New York Times*, 18 July 2007, C8.

O'Connell, P. "Pierre Omidyar on 'Connecting People.'" *BusinessWeek*, 20 June 2005 `<http://www.businessweek.com/magazine/content/05_25/b3938900.htm>`.

Second Life `<http://www.secondlife.com/whatis/economy.php>`.

Semantic Web

Berners-Lee, T. *Weaving the Web*. Harper-Collins, 2000.

"Bill Gates: Microsoft MIX06 Conference." *Microsoft*, March 2006 `<http://www.microsoft.com/presspass/exec/billg/speeches/2006/03-20MIX.mspx>`.

Copeland, M. V. "Weaving The [Semantic] Web." *Business 2.0*, July 2007, p.89-93.

Heflin, J. "OWL Web Ontology Language Use Cases and Requirements." *W3C*, 10 February 2004 `<http://www.w3.org/TR/webont-req/>`.

"Introduction to OWL." *W3Schools* `<http://www.w3schools.com/rdf/rdf_owl.asp>`.

"Microformats FAQs for RDF fans." *Microformat.org Wiki* `<http://microformats.org/wiki/faqs-for-RDF>`.

"Microformats Wiki." *microformats.org* `<http://microformats.org/wiki/Main_Page>`.

Miller, E. "An Introduction to the Resource Description Framework." *D-Lib Magazine*, May 1998 `<http://dlib.org/dlib/may98/miller/05miller.html>`.

Rapoza, J. "Semantic Web Technology Gains Steam." *eWEEK*, June 2007 `<http://etech.eweek.com/content/web_technology/semantic_web_technology_gains_steam.html>`.

Rapoza, J. "SPARQL Will Make the Web Shine." *eWEEK*, May 2006 `<http://www.eweek.com/article2/0,1759,1965980,00.asp>`.

Rapoza, J. "Weaving the Semantic Web." *eWEEK*, May 2007 `<http://etech.eweek.com/content/web_technology/spinning_the_semantic_web.html>`.

Tauberer, J. "What Is RDF?" *xml.com*, July 2006 `<http://www.xml.com/pub/a/2001/01/24/rdf.html>`.

Weitzner, D., J. Hendler, T. Berners-Lee, and D. Connolly. "Creating a Policy-Aware Web: Discretionary, Rule-based Access for the World Wide Web." October 2004 `<http://www.w3.org/2004/09/Policy-Aware-Web-acl.pdf>`.

3.22 Web 2.0 Glossary

Adaptive Path—A strategy and design consulting company that helps companies build products that improve the users' experiences. Founder Jesse James Garrett coined the term Ajax and is a major proponent of the technology.

Adobe Integrated Runtime (AIR)—Allows offline access to web applications (i.e., when an Internet connection is not available).

AdSense—Google's search advertising program for web publishers. This is a fundamental and popular form of monetization, particularly for Web 2.0 startup companies.

AdWords—Google's search advertising program for advertisers.

affiliate network—A company (see Commission Junction and LinkShare) that connects web publishers with cost-per-action affiliate programs. (See affiliate program.)

affiliate program—A program that allows publishers to post text and image ads on their sites. If a user clicks through to the affiliate site and takes a specified action (e.g., makes a purchase, fills out a registration form, etc.) the publisher is paid a portion of the sale or a flat fee.

agile software development—A process that focuses on developing small pieces and upgrades to a program quickly and continuously throughout the life cycle of the product.

Amazon—An online retailer and web services provider. The Amazon Associates affiliate program allows web publishers to monetize their sites by recommending Amazon products.

Apache—An open source software foundation, responsible for the Apache Web Server and many other open source products.

API (Application Programming Interface)—An interface called by a program. Web services are often referred to as APIs and are accessible over the Internet.

Apple—A leading computer company, responsible for Macintosh computers, the iPod, iTunes and the iPhone.

architecture of participation—A design that encourages user interaction, where the community contributes content and/or participates in the design and development process. Creating websites that encourage participation is a key part of Web 2.0.

Ajax (Asynchronous JavaScript and XML)—Allows pieces of a web page to be refreshed separately, while the user continues to work on the page. Ajax improves the user's experience by making webtop applications approach the responsiveness of desktop applications.

Atom—Used for web feeds; similar to RSS.

attention economy—The result of the abundant amounts of information being produced and people's limited free time. More content is available than users can sort through on their own.

avatar—A person's digital representation in a 3D world such as Second Life.

Basecamp—An SaaS project management and collaboration tool from 37Signals.

Blinkx—A video search engine with over 12 million hours of video indexed (which makes the content searchable).

blog—A website consisting of posts in reverse chronological order. For common blog components see: blogroll, permalink, reader comment, and trackback.

blog search engine—A search engine devoted to the blogosphere. Some of the top blog search engines include Technorati, Feedster, IceRocket and Google Blog Search.

Blogger—A popular blogging platform now owned by Google.

blogger—The author of a blog.

blogging—The act of writing a blog.

blog network—A collection of blogs with multiple editors. Popular blog networks include Corante, 9rules, Gawker and Weblogs, Inc.

blogosphere—The blogging community. In mid 2007 there were over 90 million blogs.

blogroll—A list of links to a blogger's favorite blogs.

broadband Internet—High-speed Internet, often offered by cable companies and satellite companies.

collaborative filtering—The act of working together to promote valuable content and remove spam or offensive content.

collective intelligence—The idea that collaboration and competition among large groups results in grand and intelligent ideas.

Commission Junction—A popular affiliate network with member advertisers including eBay, Best Buy, Hewlett-Packard and hundreds more.

community-generated content—Content (writing, videos, etc.) that is created by Internet users.

contextual advertising—Advertising that is targeted to web page content. Because these ads are relevant to the nearby content, contextual ads often enhance the value of that content and generate higher clickthrough rates.

Corante—A blog network whose blogs are written by leading commentators in their field. Categories include law, policy, business, management, media, the Internet, technology and science.

cost-per-action (CPA)—Advertising that is billed by user action (e.g., purchasing a product or filling out a form).

cost-per-click (CPC)—Advertising that is billed by user click. The publisher receives revenue each time the user clicks an ad on the publisher's site, regardless of whether the user makes a subsequent purchase.

cost-per-thousand impressions (CPM)—Advertising that is billed per thousand impressions, regardless of whether the user clicks the ad or makes a subsequent purchase.

Craigslist—A popular classifieds and social networking website that fits the Web 2.0 lightweight business model. The company has few employees and all of the content is user generated. Craigslist was originally free; however, it is now transitioning to charging for certain services such as real-estate and job postings. A portion of the company is owned by eBay.

DBPedia.org—A website working on converting Wikipedia articles into RDF triples. This is a step toward the Semantic Web.

Deitel—A content-creation, corporate training and Web 2.0 business development organization. Deitel has a rapidly growing content network (currently about 80 Resource Centers) specializing in topic categories, including Web 2.0, Internet business, programming languages, software development and more.

del.icio.us—A social bookmarking site.

Digg—A social media site where users submit news stories and the community votes on the stories. The most popular stories are featured on the site's front page.

Digital Rights Management (DRM)—Technology used to prevent piracy and misuse of digital media. Several high-profile executives, including Apple CEO Steve Jobs, have recently started an anti-DRM movement.

discovery—The future of search; the idea of introducing users to valuable content they might not have looked for otherwise. For example, social bookmarking sites and Deitel Resource Centers suggest valuable resources.

Dodgeball.com—A social networking site designed for use on mobile devices, owned by Google. Allows users to locate friends and "crushes" who are nearby so they can meet up.

DotNetNuke—An open source web application framework based on Microsoft's .NET framework. DotNetNuke allows users to build dynamic websites quickly and easily. For more information, visit the DotNetNuke Resource Center (`http://www.deitel.com/ResourceCenters/Software/DotNetNukeDNN/tabid/1217/Default.aspx`).

DoubleClick—An Internet advertising company acquired by Google in 2007 for $3.1 billion. Their advertising exchange connects advertisers with online publishers.

Dougherty, Dale—Coined the term "Web 2.0."

eBay—The leading online auction site.

Extensible Markup Language (XML)—A widely supported open (i.e., nonproprietary) technology for electronic data exchange and storage, which is fundamental to Web 2.0 and the Semantic Web. It can be used to create other markup languages to describe data in a structured manner.

Facebook—A social networking site. Though it is now open to the public, Facebook was originally designed for and is especially popular with college students.

Federated Media—A company that connects bloggers with advertisers. Founded by John Battelle, the chair for the annual Web 2.0 Summit Conference, and the author of *The Search: How Google and Its Rivals Rewrote the Rules of Business and Transformed Our Culture.*

Feedburner—Provides RSS feeds for blogs, feed monetization, podcast tracking and more. Acquired by Google.

Firefox—Open source web browser (based on the Netscape Navigator browser introduced in 1994) developed by the Mozilla Foundation. For more information, visit the Firefox Resource Center (`http://www.deitel.com/ResourceCenters/Software/Firefox/tabid/1213/Default .aspx`).

Flex—A Rich Internet Application (RIA) framework developed by Adobe. For more information, visit the Flex Resource Center (`http://www.deitel.com/ResourceCenters/Programming/AdobeFlex/tabid/1682/Default.aspx`).

Flickr—A photo-sharing website often credited as one of the best examples of tagging content.

folksonomy—A classification based on tagging content. Users tag the web content (web pages, photos, etc.), making it easier to find the content online. Folksonomies are formed on sites such as Flickr, Technorati and del.icio.us. Users can search tags for content that is identified in different (and sometimes more meaningful) ways than by traditional search engines.

Friendster—A social networking site; an early leader in the category of social networking. In 2006, Friendster was awarded a patent for a method and tool called the "Web of Friends," which gathers descriptive and relationship information for users in the network. The combined data is used to show all of the social relationships connecting two users in the social network. It also allows users to find people connected to their friends, their friends' friends, etc.

Garrett, Jesse James—Coined the term "Ajax" and founded Adaptive Path.

Gawker Media—A blog network that includes Gawker.com (New York City gossip), Gizmodo.com (technology and gadgets) and more.

Google—A Web 2.0 search and online advertising company founded by Larry Page and Sergey Brin when they were Ph.D. students at Stanford University. It is the most widely used search engine, commanding almost 50% market share. In addition to its regular search engine, Google offers specialty search engines for images, news, videos, blogs and more. Google provides web services that allow you to build Google Maps and other Google services into your applications.

Google Gears—An open source web browser extension that enables developers to provide offline usage of their web applications. The program can easily be resynchronized when an Internet connection becomes available.

Google Maps—Google's mapping web service, hugely popular in mashups.

Hitwise—An Internet competitive intelligence service provider. Hitwise collects and sells usage information from over one million websites in numerous industries. Clients use the information to find market share, keyword, web traffic flow and demographic data.

housingmaps.com—A mashup of Google Maps and Craigslist apartment and real-estate listings; often credited as being the first mashup.

IceRocket—A blog search engine.

Intel—The computer hardware company that creates the processors that power most of the world's computers.

interstitial ad—Ad that plays between page loads.

in-text contextual advertising—Advertising that is marked by double-underlined keywords in the content of a web page. When a reader hovers the mouse over a double-underlined word, a text ad pops up. By clicking on the ad, the reader is taken to the advertiser's page. Companies providing in-text contextual advertising include Vibrant Media, Kontera, Text Link Ads and Tribal Fusion.

iPhone—Apple's mobile phone, released June 2007. The iPhone is designed to run a full version of the Internet.

iPod—Apple's portable media player.

iTunes—Apple's online music and video store; designed to sync with the iPod.

John Battelle's Searchblog—A blog in which John Battelle discusses search, media, technology, and more. (See Federated Media.)

JSON (JavaScript Object Notation)—A text-based data interchange format used to represent data structures and objects, and transmit them over a network. JSON is most often used with JavaScript in Ajax applications, but it can also be used with other programming languages.

Joost—An Internet TV company using semantic technologies to provide high-quality video with time shifting (recording for later viewing) and social networking capabilities. Joost allows advertisers to target their markets precisely. Advertisers can use demographic information such as location, gender, age, and more, to serve appropriate ads and to get a better return on investment from their advertising campaigns.

Last.fm—A popular social music website that uses the wisdom of crowds to recommend music to its users. The Last.fm Audioscrobbler music engine automatically sends the name of every song the user plays to the server. It then uses the information to recommend songs and artists, connect users with similar tastes and more.

Laszlo Webtop—A desktop-like environment for running web applications built on the OpenLaszlo framework.

lead generation—A monetization model for many sites that send traffic to another site and typically collect a fee when the visitor fills out an inquiry form so a salesperson can follow through and potentially convert the lead into a sale.

lightweight business model—A plan that allows a company to start quickly and with little capital investment. This is facilitated by powerful yet economical computers, the wide availability of inexpensive broadband Internet, robust open source software offerings, and well-developed, easy-to-employ monetization models—especially advertising and affiliate programs.

link baiting—Attracting other sites to link to your site, but without specifically asking for links. Providing quality content is considered the best form of link baiting.

link building—Using various methods to encourage other sites to link to your site. It is widely believed that increasing the number of inbound links to your site will encourage search engines to send you more traffic.

LinkedIn—A social networking site for business professionals. It can be used to stay in touch with professional contacts or make new contacts in your extended network.

LinkShare—A popular affiliate network with over 600 member companies (including American Express, Office Depot and Walmart).

Livejournal—A website where you can create your own blog.

Long Tail—Coined by Chris Anderson in an article in the October 2004 *WIRED* magazine (`http://www.wired.com/wired/archive/12.10/tail.html`). Refers to the continuous sales of numerous items with low sales volume that can add up to a significant part of a company's total sales. Amazon and Netflix are classic Long Tail companies.

mashup—A combination of two or more existing web services, RSS feeds or other sources of data to create a new application. For example, `http://www.housingmaps.com` combines real estate listings from Craigslist with Google Maps so you can view the listings on a map. For a list of popular mashups, see `http://www.programmableweb.com/popular`.

Mechanical Turk—Amazon's "artificial artificial intelligence," which uses people in a web service to perform tasks that are difficult for computers to perform, such as identifying the subject of a picture and transcribing dictation recordings. Users can post a HIT (Human Intelligence Task). Anyone interested in completing the task can submit a response. If the response is approved by the person who posted the HIT, the responder is paid a predetermined fee for each task completed. The key is that the human task is interwoven with the execution of the web service, creating applications that mix computing power with human intelligence accessed worldwide.

MediaWiki—Open source software written originally for Wikipedia and now used by many popular wikis.

Metcalfe's Law—The value of a network is proportional to the square of the number of its users. Metcalfe's Law was authored by Robert Metcalfe, the creator of Ethernet. (See also network effects.)

microformat—A common standard for identifying information in a way that can be understood by computers. Some current microformats include adr (for address information), hresume (for resumes and CVs), and xfolk (for collections of bookmarks). See `http://microformats.org` for more information.

mobile technology—Devices such as cell phones and PDAs. An increasing number now offer web access, which has opened up new web application possibilities. (See also iPhone.)

moblogging—Blogging from mobile devices.

moderation—Monitoring and censoring inappropriate content and comments in blog or forum postings. The potential need for moderation is a drawback to allowing user-generated content.

monetization—Generating money through your website (e.g., using contextual advertising, affiliate programs, e-commerce and other revenue-generating models).

Moonlight—An open source version of Microsoft's Silverlight for Linux operating systems.

Movable Type—A blogging software package from the company Six Apart that is installed on the blogger's server.

Mozilla Foundation—Creates and maintains open source software including the Mozilla Firefox web browser and the Mozilla Thunderbird e-mail client.

MySpace—The most popular social networking site, and the most popular site on the Internet.

network effects—The increased value of a network as its number of users grows. For example, as the number of people with Internet connections grows worldwide, the value and benefit to all users of the Internet grows (individuals can communicate with more people, companies can reach more customers, etc.). (See Metcalfe's Law.)

9Rules—A blog network.

ontology—A way of organizing and relating things. Ontologies are a key technology in the Semantic Web.

open source software—Software that is available for anyone to use and modify with few or no restrictions. Users can modify source code to meet their unique needs, or collaborate with others to enhance the software. Many Web 2.0 companies use open source software to power their sites, and offer open source products and content.

O'Reilly Media—The company that introduced and promoted the term Web 2.0 (coined by company executive Dale Dougherty). O'Reilly Media publishes technology books and websites, and hosts several conferences, including the Web 2.0 Summit, Web 2.0 Expo, OSCON™ (the Open Source Convention), Emerging Technology, Emerging Telephony, Where 2.0, RailsConf, MySQL, Ubuntu Live and more. See the O'Reilly Radar (`http://radar.oreilly.com/`) to keep up-to-date on emerging technology trends.

outsourcing—A company's hiring of independent contractors or other companies to perform various tasks. Outsourcing is often cheaper for the company.

performance-based advertising—Advertising that pays based on user actions, such as making a purchase, filling out a registration form, etc. (See also cost-per-action.)

permalink—A URL that links to a specific blog entry instead of the blog's homepage. Links stay relevant even after the blog entry moves off the home page and into the archive.

perpetual beta—The idea of continually releasing new features even if they aren't "final." This allows software companies to constantly fix bugs and improve the software by getting continuous feedback from real users.

Pew Internet & American Life Project—A non-profit Internet research company. The project is funded by the Pew Charitable Trusts, which has also initiated other research and cultural projects.

PHPNuke—An open source content-management system and web publishing tool based on PHP and MySQL.

podcast—A media file designed for syndicated distribution online. It can be played on a personal computer or mobile media player (such as an iPod or MP3 player).

Policy Aware Web Project—A site devoted to developing policies regarding Internet data. This is an attempt to deal with Semantic Web security concerns.

premium content—Website content that is available for a fee (e.g., e-books, articles, etc.). It is a way for publishers to monetize their sites. Sites offering premium content typically offer free content as well.

Problogger—A blog about blogging. It teaches bloggers how to monetize their sites with Google AdSense and other programs.

Programmable Web—A website with extensive directories of web services APIs and mashups.

publisher—See "web publisher."

RDF (Resource Description Framework)—An XML-based language used to describe content attributes such as the page title, author, etc.

RDF triples—Composed of two pieces of information and a linking fact. They are used to help computers understand data, a vital part of the Semantic Web.

reader comment—Feedback left by readers on a blog.

recommender systems—Systems that collect data using collaborative filtering to determine users' tastes and interests as they search the Internet. For example, Amazon's "customers who bought this item also bought..."

Red Hat—A popular version of the Linux operating system. The company is a leader in the open source movement.

remixing—Combining existing applications and/or content into something new; this is fundamental to Web 2.0.

reputation systems—Systems used by businesses like eBay and Amazon to encourage trust. For example, after each eBay transaction, the buyer and the seller can each leave positive or negative comments about the other party.

REST (Representational State Transfer)—A simple alternative to SOAP for implementing web services. Many developers prefer REST-based web services to SOAP-based web services for their simplicity, their ability to be cached and more. Amazon offers some REST-based web services. (See also SOAP.)

Rich Internet Applications (RIAs)—Web applications that have the responsiveness and the rich GUI normally associated with desktop applications. Related technologies for building RIAs include Ajax, Dojo, Silverlight, Flex and more.

RSS—An XML-based web-content syndication format. Syndicated RSS feeds are used to publish frequently updated content such as news, blog entries, podcasts, and more. Some RSS feeds include the full text, but most contain only a portion of the document, encouraging the reader to visit the content site.

Ruby on Rails—An open source, web application development scripting language and framework that increases the speed at which you can create typical database-driven web applications.

Salesforce.com—An SaaS company that specializes in Customer Relationship Management (CRM) software; a leader in the SaaS movement.

scrobbling—Last.fm's music tracking and analysis feature that provides you with recommendations based on the music you listen to through the site or on your iPod. (See also recommender systems.)

search engine marketing (SEM)—Promoting your website to increase traffic and search results. This includes paid search, online advertising and more.

search engine optimization (SEO)—Designing your website to maximize your findability and improve your rankings in organic search engine results.

search engine result page (SERP)—The page shown to a user by a search engine with a listing of web pages matching the search query sorted by relevance.

SearchEngineLand.com—Danny Sullivan's search engine news blog.

SearchEngineWatch.com—A search engine marketing resource site. Includes articles, tutorials, conferences and more.

Second Life—A 3D virtual world social networking program developed by Linden Labs. Users create an avatar (their online image and persona) that they use to meet other users with similar interests, conduct business, participate in group activities, take classes and more.

Semantic Web—The "web of meaning." What some believe will be the next evolution of the web in which web content can be read and understood by software applications.

Silverlight—A Rich Internet Application (RIA) framework developed by Microsoft; competes with Adobe Flash and Flex.

Six Apart—The company responsible for several blogging software applications and websites, including Movable Type, TypePad and Vox.

Skype—The most popular VoIP company. Users can place free calls to other Skype users around the world over their Internet connection. They also offer fee-based services that allow you to call non-Skype phone numbers. Skype was purchased by eBay in 2005 for $2.6 billion. Its founders recently launched Joost (an Internet TV site).

SOAP (Simple Object Access Protocol)—A protocol for exchanging XML-based information over a network. SOAP is used as a messaging framework in web services.

social bookmarking—The act of sharing your bookmarks with others through a website such as del.icio.us or Ma.gnolia. Users bookmark their favorites sites, articles, blogs and more, and tag them by keyword.

social media—Any media (e.g., photos, videos, music, etc.) shared online. Social media sites, such as Digg, YouTube and Flickr, often include features for user comments, collaborative filtering and tagging.

social networking—Sites designed to organize users' existing relationships and help users establish new ones. Popular social networking sites include MySpace, Facebook, LinkedIn, Second Life and more.

SocialText—The first wiki company; provides wiki services to corporations. (See also wiki.)

Software as a Service (SaaS)—Software that runs on a web server. It does not need to be installed on your local computer, and companies can instantly update all users to the latest version. Salesforce.com, Google, 37Signals and Microsoft all have extensive SaaS offerings.

spam—Junk e-mail messages, blog comments and forum postings.

SPARQL Protocol and RDF Query Language (SPARQL)—An RDF query language for the Semantic Web.

tag—An author- and/or user-submitted label for web content used to classify it by subject or keyword. For example, a picture of the Statue of Liberty posted on Flickr might be tagged with "newyorkcity," "statueofliberty," "usa," etc. Users can search for content on a site by tags. For examples of tag usage, see Technorati and Flickr.

tag cloud—A weighted list of content tags on a website. A tag cloud is usually in alphabetical order, with the most popular tags often appearing in a larger or bold font. Each tag links to a page where you'll find all of the content on that site that has been "tagged" (by publishers and/or users) with that term. Tag clouds are used by many Web 2.0 companies, including Technorati, Flickr, del.icio.us and more.

tagging—The act of adding tags to content.

tagscape—The tagging "landscape"; the patterns and trends that are seen in tagging and tag clouds.

TechCrunch—A popular Internet technology blog that focuses on the companies, products, people and events of Web 2.0.

Technorati—A popular blog search engine that uses tagging.

37Signals—The company that developed Ruby on Rails (`http://www.deitel.com/ResourceCenters/Programming/Ruby/tabid/715/Default.aspx`) and many SaaS applications, including Basecamp.

trackback—A method for web content authors to request notification when a website links to their content (articles, blog postings, etc.). It is a great way for authors to track links into their sites, measure the viral effects of their work, find related sites and more.

Twitter—A mobile web service that enables users to message groups of friends at once and automatically receive their friends' updates on a cell phone or through a chat window.

Ubuntu—A popular distribution of the Linux operating system.

user-generated content—Content that is created by users. User-generated content is central to Web 2.0.

ValueClick—An Internet advertising company.

vlogging—Video blogging.

VoIP (Voice over Internet Protocol)—Voice services over the Internet; used to build telephone services. The leading VoIP company is Skype, which offers free phone service among Skype users worldwide.

Vonage—A VoIP company. They provide broadband Internet telephone services that can be used with a standard phone (with adapter).

Web 1.0—The Internet experience previous to Web 2.0, focusing more on static content. Some people called it the "brochure web."

Web 2.0—A term coined by Dale Dougherty of O'Reilly Media in 2003. It refers to the current state of the web, which has a strong emphasis on user participation and community. Web 2.0 sites include social networking, wikis, blogging, social media, tagging, collaborative filtering, and more.

web as a platform—Instead of viewing the operating system as the application platform and building "Windows-based applications" or "Linux-based applications," developers now build "web-based applications."

web of meaning—Another name for the "Semantic Web."

Web Ontology Language (OWL)—A key Semantic Web technology, used for organizing data.

web publisher—A site that offers content. Advertisers place ads on web publisher sites.

web-scale computing—Refers to the ability to scale memory and processing power according to need, by using web-based processing power and memory, often provided by other companies. Amazon offers web-scale computing through web services such as Simple Storage Service (S3) and Elastic Compute Cloud (EC2).

web service—A service provided online that can be called by another program across the Internet.

Weblogsinc—A blog network.

webtop—A desktoplike environment (such as Laszlo Webtop) for running web applications in a web browser.

wiki—A collaborative, editable document online. The best known example of a wiki is Wikipedia, which has quickly become a leading web resource for virtually any topic.

Wikia—A site offering specialized wiki communities about popular television shows, games, literature, shopping and more.

Wikipedia—A community-generated encyclopedia using wiki technology.

wisdom of crowds—The concept that a large diverse group of individuals that does not necessarily include experts can provide more accurate answers than a small group of specialists working together.

WordPress—Popular blogging software.

World Wide Web Consortium (W3C)—An organization that develops web standards.

Xanga—A popular personal blogging site that includes community features.

XML (Extensible Markup Language)—A markup language developed in 1996 by the World Wide Web Consortium (W3C) that allows you to label data based on its meaning.

XML vocabularies—Customized XML-based markup languages, such as XHTML for web content, CML for chemistry, MathML for mathematical content and formulas, and XBRL for financial data.

Yahoo! Pipes—A mashup tool that enables you to aggregate and manipulate many data sources.

Yahoo! Publisher Network—Yahoo's contextual advertising program for publishers. This is a fundamental and popular form of monetization, particularly for Web 2.0 startup companies.

Yahoo! Search Marketing—Yahoo!'s advertising program for advertisers.

YouTube—An Internet video sharing site that has created a huge social phenomenon. Users upload and share videos. The company was bought by Google in 2006 for $1.65 billion.

Zepheira—A company that provides Semantic Web knowledge management and enterprise data integration products and services.

Self-Review Exercises

3.1 Fill in the blanks in each of the following statements:

a) ________ content refers to (legally) taking someone else's existing content and adding to it or changing it in some way.

b) The term Web 2.0 was coined by ________ of O'Reilly® Media in 2003.

c) ________ are user-generated labels used to categorize content.

d) The major Ajax technologies are ________, ________, ________, ________, ________ and ________.

e) ________ are webtop applications that have responsiveness and functionality approaching that of desktop applications.

f) Amazon's hardware and communications infrastructure web services are examples of ________. They enable businesses to pay for only the processing or storage space needed during any given period.

g) The increased value of a network as its number of users grows is referred to as ________.

h) Two popular RIA frameworks are Adobe's ________ and Microsoft's ________.

3.2 State whether each of the following is *true* or *false*. If *false*, explain why.

a) Tagging is for personal organization of content only.

b) The user is at the center of Web 2.0.

c) Location-based services always use GPS.

d) Open source software is often called "free" because it does not cost money.

e) Google's PageRank is determined by the number of page views a website receives.

Answers to Self-Review Exercises

3.1 a) Remixing.

b) Dale Dougherty

c) Tags.

d) XHTML, CSS, JavaScript, the DOM, XML, the `XMLHttpRequest` object.

e) Rich Internet Applications (RIAs).

f) web-scale computing.

g) network effects (an aspect of Metcalfe's Law).

h) Flex, Silverlight.

3.2 a) False. User-generated tags are used by many websites to categorize content so that it is easily searchable by other users.

b) True.

c) False. Location-based services often use GPS; however, they often use other information to determine your location, such as your IP address.

d) False. Open source software is free in terms of allowing access to the source code. It is not necessarily free of cost.

e) False. The PageRank algorithm considers the number of links into a web page and the quality of the linking sites (among other factors) to determine the importance of the page. Google search also considers all of the content on the page, its fonts, its headers and the content of neighboring pages.

Exercises

3.3 Fill in the blanks in each of the following statements:

a) ________ is an example of an agile development process.

b) The ________ is a design that encourages user interaction and community contributions.
c) Ruby on Rails was developed by ________.
d) ________ systems add software to digital media to prevent piracy.
e) ________are attempts at consistent naming conventions.
f) Wikis rely on the ________.

3.4 State whether each of the following is *true* or *false*. If *false*, explain why.
a) Advertising is the most common Web 2.0 monetization model.
b) Collaborative filtering is used by search engines.
c) XML is an executable language.
d) Most bloggers provide RSS feeds.
e) Holding people's attention is difficult in today's society.

3.5 Define each of the following terms:
a) collective intelligence.
b) folksonomy.
c) permalink.
d) tag cloud.
e) web service.
f) monetization.

3.6 List some of the key factors that have attributed to the growth of Web 2.0.

3.7 Discuss some of the methods you can use to increase the findability of your website.

3.8 In Section 3.3 we discussed how many Web 2.0 sites are enabling discovery—helping you find new content you would not have otherwise sought out. Pick three Web 2.0 sites and describe how they are enabling you to discover new content through their sites.

3.9 Consider a picture of the Eiffel Tower. List 10 words you might use to tag this picture on a photosharing site such as Flickr so that others searching the site will find it.

2 PART

The Ajax Client

... the challenges are for the designers of these applications: to forget what we think we know about the limitations of the web, and begin to imagine a wider, richer range of possibilities. It's going to be fun.

—Jesse James Garrett

4

Introduction to XHTML

To read between the lines was easier than to follow the text.

—Henry James

High thoughts must have high language.

—Aristophanes

Yea, from the table of my memory
I'll wipe away all trivial fond records.

—William Shakespeare

He had a wonderful talent for packing thought close, and rendering it portable.

—Thomas Babington Macaulay

OBJECTIVES

In this chapter you will learn:

- To understand important components of XHTML documents.
- To use XHTML to create web pages.
- To add images to web pages.
- To create and use hyperlinks to navigate web pages.
- To mark up lists of information.
- To create tables with rows and columns of data and control table formatting.
- To create and use forms to get user input.
- To make web pages accessible to search engines using <meta> tags.

4.1 Introduction

Welcome to the world of opportunity created by the World Wide Web. The Internet is almost four decades old, but it wasn't until the web's growth in popularity in the 1990s and the recent start of the Web 2.0 era that the explosion of opportunity we are experiencing began. Exciting new developments occur almost daily—the pace of innovation is unprecedented. In this chapter, you'll develop your own web pages. As the book proceeds, you'll create increasingly appealing and powerful web pages. Later in the book, you'll learn how to create complete web-based applications with databases and user interfaces.

This chapter begins unlocking the power of web-based application development with XHTML—the Extensible HyperText Markup Language. Later in the chapter, we introduce more sophisticated XHTML techniques such as internal linking for easier page navigation, forms for collecting information from a web-page visitor and tables, which are particularly useful for structuring information from databases (i.e., software that stores structured sets of data). In the next chapter, we discuss a technology called Cascading Style Sheets™ (CSS), a technology that makes web pages more visually appealing.

Unlike procedural programming languages such as C, C++, or Java, XHTML is a markup language that specifies the format of the text that is displayed in a web browser such as Microsoft's Internet Explorer or Mozilla Firefox.

One key issue when using XHTML is the separation of the presentation of a document (i.e., the document's appearance when rendered by a browser) from the structure of the document's information. XHTML is based on HTML (HyperText Markup Language)—a legacy technology of the World Wide Web Consortium (W3C). In HTML, it was common to specify both the document's structure and its formatting. Formatting might specify where the browser placed an element in a web page or the fonts and colors used to display an element. The XHTML 1.0 Strict recommendation (the version of

XHTML that we use in this book) allows only a document's structure to appear in a valid XHTML document, and not its formatting. Normally, such formatting is specified with Cascading Style Sheets (Chapter 5). All our examples in this chapter are based upon the XHTML 1.0 Strict Recommendation.

4.2 Editing XHTML

In this chapter, we write XHTML in its source-code form. We create XHTML documents by typing them in a text editor (e.g., Notepad, TextEdit, vi, emacs) and saving them with either an `.html` or an `.htm` filename extension.

Good Programming Practice 4.1

Assign filenames to documents that describe their functionality. This practice can help you identify documents faster. It also helps people who want to link to a page, by giving them an easy-to-remember name. For example, if you are writing an XHTML document that contains product information, you might want to call it `products.html`.

Computers called web servers running specialized software store XHTML documents. Clients (e.g., web browsers) request specific resources such as the XHTML documents from web servers. For example, typing `www.deitel.com/books/downloads.html` into a web browser's address field requests `downloads.html` from the `books` directory on the web server running at `www.deitel.com`. We discuss web servers in detail in Chapter 21. For now, we simply place the XHTML documents on our computer and render them by opening them locally with a web browser such as Internet Explorer or Firefox.

4.3 First XHTML Example

This chapter presents XHTML markup and provides screen captures that show how a browser renders (i.e., displays) the XHTML. You can download the examples from `www.deitel.com/books/iw3htp4`. Every XHTML document we show has line numbers for the reader's convenience—these line numbers are not part of the XHTML documents. As you read this book, open each XHTML document in your web browser so you can view and interact with it as it was originally intended.

Figure 4.1 is an XHTML document named `main.html`. This first example displays the message "Welcome to XHTML!" in the browser. The key line in the program is line 13, which tells the browser to display "Welcome to XHTML!" Now let us consider each line of the program.

Lines 1–3 are required in XHTML documents to conform with proper XHTML syntax. For now, copy and paste these lines into each XHTML document you create. The meaning of these lines is discussed in detail in Chapter 14.

Lines 5–6 are XHTML comments. XHTML document creators insert comments to improve markup readability and describe the content of a document. Comments also help other people read and understand an XHTML document's markup and content. Comments do not cause the browser to perform any action when the user loads the XHTML document into the web browser to view it. XHTML comments always start with `<!--` and end with `-->`. Each of our XHTML examples includes comments that specify the figure number and filename and provide a brief description of the example's purpose. Subsequent examples include comments in the markup, especially to highlight new features.

```
1  <?xml version = "1.0" encoding = "utf-8"?>
2  <!DOCTYPE html PUBLIC "-//W3C//DTD XHTML 1.0 Strict//EN"
3     "http://www.w3.org/TR/xhtml1/DTD/xhtml1-strict.dtd">
4
5  <!-- Fig. 4.1: main.html -->
6  <!-- First XHTML example. -->
7  <html xmlns = "http://www.w3.org/1999/xhtml">
8     <head>
9        <title>Welcome</title>
10    </head>
11
12    <body>
13       <p>Welcome to XHTML!</p>
14    </body>
15 </html>
```

Title bar shows contents of `title` element

Welcome - Windows Internet Explorer

C:\examples\ch04\main.html

Welcome to XHTML!

Fig. 4.1 | First XHTML example.

Good Programming Practice 4.2

Place comments throughout your markup. Comments help other programmers understand the markup, assist in debugging and list useful information that you do not want the browser to render. Comments also help you understand your own markup when you revisit a document to modify or update it in the future.

XHTML markup contains text that represents the content of a document and elements that specify a document's structure. Some important elements of an XHTML document are the `html` element, the `head` element and the `body` element. The `html` element encloses the head section (represented by the `head` element) and the body section (represented by the `body` element). The head section contains information about the XHTML document, such as its title. The head section also can contain special document formatting instructions called style sheets and client-side programs called scripts for creating dynamic web pages. (We introduce style sheets in Chapter 5 and scripting with JavaScript in Chapter 6.) The body section contains the page's content that the browser displays when the user visits the web page.

XHTML documents delimit an element with start and end tags. A start tag consists of the element name in angle brackets (e.g., `<html>`). An end tag consists of the element name preceded by a forward slash (/) in angle brackets (e.g., `</html>`). In this example, lines 7 and 15 define the start and end of the `html` element. Note that the end tag in line 15 has the same name as the start tag, but is preceded by a / inside the angle brackets. Many start tags have attributes that provide additional information about an element. Browsers can use this additional information to determine how to process the element.

Each attribute has a name and a value separated by an equals sign (=). Line 7 specifies a required attribute (xmlns) and value (http://www.w3.org/1999/xhtml) for the html element in an XHTML document. For now, simply copy and paste the html element start tag in line 7 into your XHTML documents. We discuss the details of the xmlns attribute in Chapter 14.

Common Programming Error 4.1

Not enclosing attribute values in either single or double quotes is a syntax error. However, some web browsers may still render the element correctly.

Common Programming Error 4.2

Using uppercase letters in an XHTML element or attribute name is a syntax error. However, some web browsers may still render the element correctly.

An XHTML document divides the html element into two sections—head and body. Lines 8–10 define the web page's head section with a head element. Line 9 specifies a title element. This is called a nested element because it is enclosed in the head element's start and end tags. The head element is also a nested element because it is enclosed in the html element's start and end tags. The title element describes the web page. Titles usually appear in the title bar at the top of the browser window, in the browser tab that the page is displayed on, and also as the text identifying a page when users add the page to their list of **Favorites** or **Bookmarks** that enables them to return to their favorite sites. Search engines (i.e., sites that allow users to search the web) also use the title for indexing purposes.

Good Programming Practice 4.3

Indenting nested elements emphasizes a document's structure and promotes readability.

Common Programming Error 4.3

XHTML does not permit tags to overlap—a nested element's end tag must appear in the document before the enclosing element's end tag. For example, the nested XHTML tags <head><title>hello</head></title> *cause a syntax error, because the enclosing* head *element's ending* </head> *tag appears before the nested* title *element's ending* </title> *tag.*

Good Programming Practice 4.4

Use a consistent title*-naming convention for all pages on a site. For example, if a site is named "Bailey's Website," then the* title *of the contact page might be "Bailey's Website - Contact." This practice can help users better understand the website's structure.*

Line 12 begins the document's body element. The body section of an XHTML document specifies the document's content, which may include text and elements.

Some elements, such as the paragraph element (denoted with <p> and </p>) in line 13, mark up text for display in a browser. All the text placed between the <p> and </p> tags forms one paragraph. When the browser renders a paragraph, a blank line usually precedes and follows paragraph text.

This document ends with two end tags (lines 14–15). These tags close the body and html elements, respectively. The </html> tag in an XHTML document informs the browser that the XHTML markup is complete.

To open an XHTML example from this chapter, open the folder where you saved the book's examples, browse to the ch04 folder and double click the file to open it in your default web browser. At this point your browser window should appear similar to the sample screen capture shown in Fig. 4.1. (Note that we resized the browser window to save space in the book.)

4.4 W3C XHTML Validation Service

Programming web-based applications can be complex, and XHTML documents must be written correctly to ensure that browsers process them properly. To promote correctly written documents, the World Wide Web Consortium (W3C) provides a **validation service** (`validator.w3.org`) for checking a document's syntax. Documents can be validated by providing a URL that specifies the file's location, by uploading a file to `validator.w3.org/file-upload.html` or by pasting code directly into a text area. Uploading a file copies the file from the user's computer to another computer on the Internet. The W3C's web page indicates that the service name is **MarkUp Validation Service** and that the validation service is able to validate the syntax of XHTML documents. All the XHTML examples in this book have been validated successfully using `validator.w3.org`.

By clicking **Choose...**, users can select files on their own computers for upload. After selecting a file, clicking the **Check** button uploads and validates the file. If a document contains syntax errors, the validation service displays error messages describing the errors.

Error-Prevention Tip 4.1

Most current browsers attempt to render XHTML documents even if they are invalid. This often leads to unexpected and possibly undesirable results. Use a validation service, such as the W3C ***MarkUp Validation Service****, to confirm that an XHTML document is syntactically correct.*

4.5 Headings

Some text in an XHTML document may be more important than other text. For example, the text in this section is considered more important than a footnote. XHTML provides six **headings**, called **heading elements**, for specifying the relative importance of information. Figure 4.2 demonstrates these elements (`h1` through `h6`). Heading element `h1` (line 13) is considered the most significant heading and is typically rendered in a larger font than the other five headings (lines 14–18). Each successive heading element (i.e., `h2`, `h3`, etc.) is typically rendered in a progressively smaller font.

Portability Tip 4.1

The text size used to display each heading element can vary significantly between browsers. In Chapter 5, we discuss how to control the text size and other text properties.

Look-and-Feel Observation 4.1

Placing a heading at the top of every XHTML page helps viewers understand the purpose of each page.

Look-and-Feel Observation 4.2

Use larger headings to emphasize more important sections of a web page.

```
<?xml version = "1.0" encoding = "utf-8"?>
<!DOCTYPE html PUBLIC "-//W3C//DTD XHTML 1.0 Strict//EN"
   "http://www.w3.org/TR/xhtml1/DTD/xhtml1-strict.dtd">

<!-- Fig. 4.2: heading.html -->
<!-- Heading elements h1 through h6. -->
<html xmlns = "http://www.w3.org/1999/xhtml">
   <head>
      <title>Headings</title>
   </head>

   <body>
      <h1>Level 1 Heading</h1>
      <h2>Level 2 heading</h2>
      <h3>Level 3 heading</h3>
      <h4>Level 4 heading</h4>
      <h5>Level 5 heading</h5>
      <h6>Level 6 heading</h6>
   </body>
</html>
```

Fig. 4.2 | Heading elements `h1` through `h6`.

4.6 Linking

One of the most important XHTML features is the hyperlink, which references (or links to) other resources, such as XHTML documents and images. When a user clicks a hyperlink, the browser tries to execute an action associated with it (e.g., navigate to a URL, open an e-mail client, etc.). In XHTML, both text and images can act as hyperlinks. Web browsers typically underline text hyperlinks and color their text blue by default, so that users can distinguish hyperlinks from plain text. In Fig. 4.3, we create text hyperlinks to four different websites.

Line 14 introduces the `strong` element, which indicates that its contents has high importance. Browsers typically display such text in a bold font.

Links are created using the `a` (anchor) element. Line 17 defines a hyperlink to the URL assigned to attribute `href`, which specifies the location of a linked resource, such as

```
<?xml version = "1.0" encoding = "utf-8"?>
<!DOCTYPE html PUBLIC "-//W3C//DTD XHTML 1.0 Strict//EN"
   "http://www.w3.org/TR/xhtml1/DTD/xhtml1-strict.dtd">

<!-- Fig. 4.3: links.html -->
<!-- Linking to other web pages. -->
<html xmlns = "http://www.w3.org/1999/xhtml">
   <head>
      <title>Links</title>
   </head>

   <body>
      <h1>Here are my favorite sites</h1>
      <p><strong>Click a name to go to that page.</strong></p>

      <!-- Create four text hyperlinks -->
      <p><a href = "http://www.deitel.com">Deitel</a></p>
      <p><a href = "http://www.prenhall.com">Prentice Hall</a></p>
      <p><a href = "http://www.yahoo.com">Yahoo!</a></p>
      <p><a href = "http://www.usatoday.com">USA Today</a></p>
   </body>
</html>
```

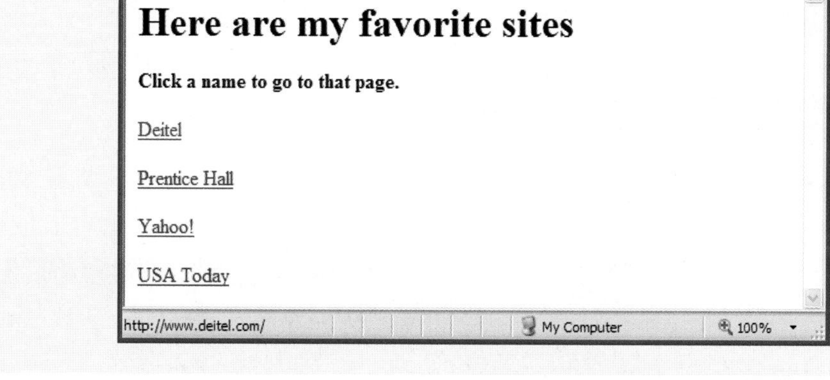

Fig. 4.3 | Linking to other web pages.

a web page, a file or an e-mail address. This particular anchor element links the text `Deitel` to a web page located at `http://www.deitel.com`. When a URL does not indicate a specific document on the website, the web server returns a default web page. This page is often called `index.html`; however, most web servers can be configured to use any file as the default web page for the site. If the web server cannot locate a requested document, it returns an error indication to the web browser, and the browser displays a web page containing an error message to the user.

Hyperlinking to an E-Mail Address

Anchors can link to e-mail addresses using a `mailto:` URL. When someone clicks this type of anchored link, most browsers launch the default e-mail program (e.g., Microsoft Outlook or Mozilla Thunderbird) to enable the user to write an e-mail message to the linked address. Figure 4.4 demonstrates this type of anchor. Lines 15–17 contain an e-mail link. The form of an e-mail anchor is `<a href = "mailto:`*emailAddress*`">...</a>`. In this case, we link to the e-mail address `deitel@deitel.com`.

```
1  <?xml version = "1.0" encoding = "utf-8"?>
2  <!DOCTYPE html PUBLIC "-//W3C//DTD XHTML 1.0 Strict//EN"
3     "http://www.w3.org/TR/xhtml1/DTD/xhtml1-strict.dtd">
4
5  <!-- Fig. 4.4: contact.html -->
6  <!-- Linking to an e-mail address. -->
7  <html xmlns = "http://www.w3.org/1999/xhtml">
8     <head>
9        <title>Contact Page</title>
10    </head>
11
12    <body>
13       <p>
14          My email address is
15          <a href = "mailto:deitel@deitel.com">
16             deitel@deitel.com
17          </a>
18          . Click the address and your default email client
19           will open an e-mail message and address it to me.
20       </p>
21    </body>
22 </html>
```

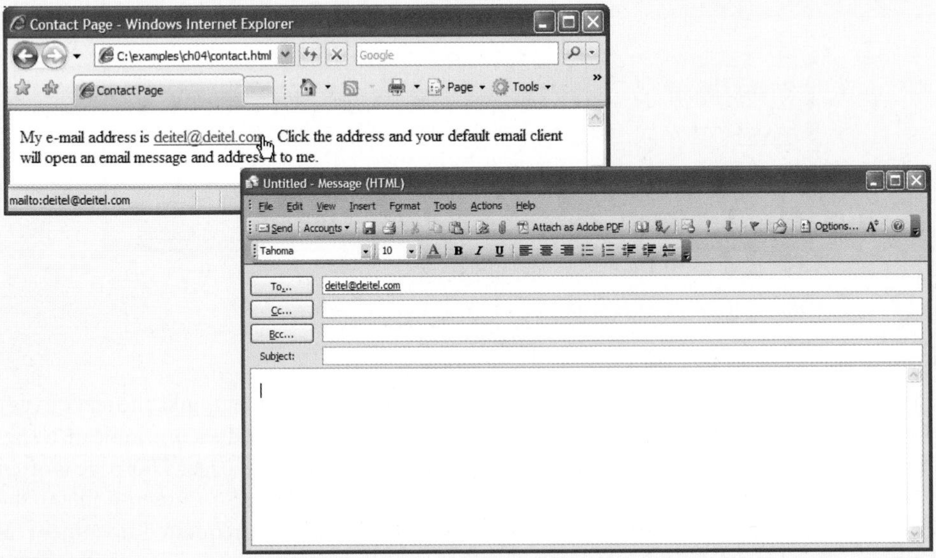

Fig. 4.4 | Linking to an e-mail address.

4.7 Images

The examples discussed so far demonstrate how to mark up documents that contain only text. However, most web pages contain both text and images. In fact, images are an equally important, if not essential, part of web-page design. The three most popular image formats used by web developers are Graphics Interchange Format (GIF), Joint Photographic Experts Group (JPEG) and Portable Network Graphics (PNG) images. Users can create images using specialized software, such as Adobe Photoshop Elements (`www.adobe.com`), G.I.M.P. (`http://www.gimp.org`) and Inkscape (`http://www.inkscape.org`). Images may also be acquired from various websites. Figure 4.5 demonstrates how to incorporate images into web pages.

Lines 14–15 use an **`img` element** to insert an image in the document. The image file's location is specified with the `img` element's **`src` attribute**. This image is located in the same directory as the XHTML document, so only the image's filename is required. Optional attributes **`width`** and **`height`** specify the image's width and height, respectively. You can scale an image by increasing or decreasing the values of the image `width` and `height` attributes. If these attributes are omitted, the browser uses the image's actual width and height. Images are measured in **pixels** ("picture elements"), which represent dots of color on the screen. Any image-editing program will have a feature that displays the dimensions, in pixels, of an image. The image in Fig. 4.5 is `92` pixels wide and `120` pixels high.

Good Programming Practice 4.5

Always include the `width` and the `height` of an image inside the `<img>` tag. When the browser loads the XHTML file, it will know immediately from these attributes how much screen space to provide for the image and will lay out the page properly, even before it downloads the image.

Performance Tip 4.1

Including the `width` and `height` attributes in an `<img>` tag can result in the browser's loading and rendering pages faster.

Common Programming Error 4.4

Entering new dimensions for an image that change its inherent width-to-height ratio distorts the appearance of the image. For example, if your image is 200 pixels wide and 100 pixels high, you should ensure that any new dimensions have a 2:1 width-to-height ratio.

```
1  <?xml version = "1.0" encoding = "utf-8"?>
2  <!DOCTYPE html PUBLIC "-//W3C//DTD XHTML 1.0 Strict//EN"
3     "http://www.w3.org/TR/xhtml1/DTD/xhtml1-strict.dtd">
4
5  <!-- Fig. 4.5: picture.html -->
6  <!-- Images in XHTML files. -->
7  <html xmlns = "http://www.w3.org/1999/xhtml">
8     <head>
9        <title>Images</title>
10    </head>
11
```

Fig. 4.5 | Images in XHTML files. (Part 1 of 2.)

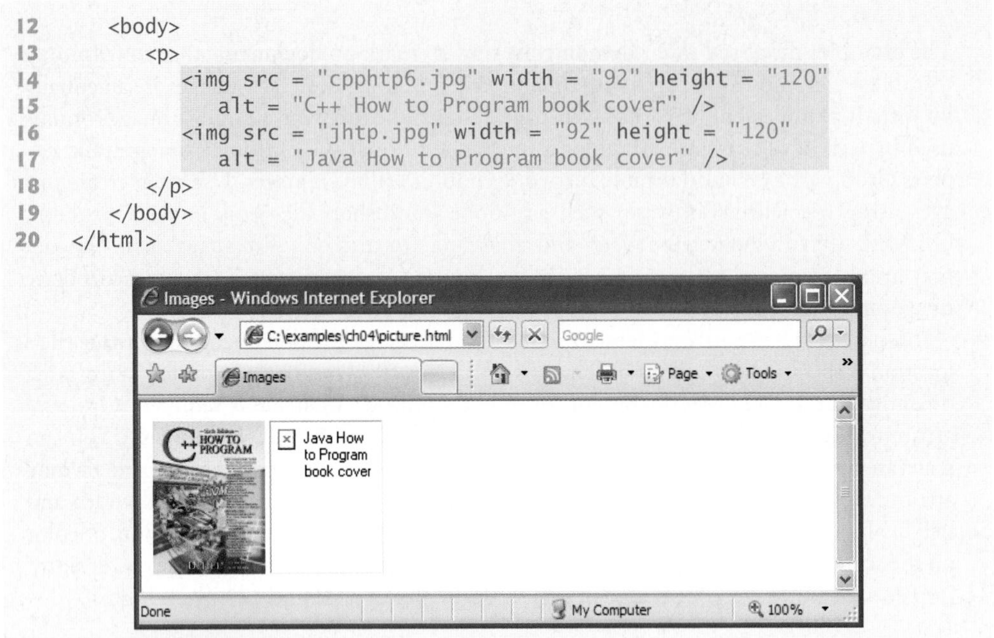

```
12     <body>
13        <p>
14           <img src = "cpphtp6.jpg" width = "92" height = "120"
15              alt = "C++ How to Program book cover" />
16           <img src = "jhtp.jpg" width = "92" height = "120"
17              alt = "Java How to Program book cover" />
18        </p>
19     </body>
20  </html>
```


Fig. 4.5 | Images in XHTML files. (Part 2 of 2.)

Every `img` element in an XHTML document must have an `alt` attribute. If a browser cannot render an image, the browser displays the `alt` attribute's value. A browser may not be able to render an image for several reasons. It may not support images—as is the case with a text-based browser (i.e., a browser that can display only text)—or the client may have disabled image viewing to reduce download time. Figure 4.5 shows Internet Explorer 7 rendering a red `x` symbol and displaying the `alt` attribute's value, signifying that the image (`jhtp.jpg`) cannot be found.

The `alt` attribute helps you create accessible web pages for users with disabilities, especially those with vision impairments who use text-based browsers. Specialized software called a speech synthesizer can "speak" the `alt` attribute's value so that a user with a visual impairment knows what the browser is displaying.

Some XHTML elements (called empty elements) contain only attributes and do not mark up text (i.e., text is not placed between the start and end tags). Empty elements (e.g., `img`) must be terminated, either by using the forward slash character (/) inside the closing right angle bracket (>) of the start tag or by explicitly including the end tag. When using the forward slash character, we add a space before it to improve readability (as shown at the ends of lines 15 and 17). Rather than using the forward slash character, lines 16–17 could be written with a closing `</img>` tag as follows:

```
<img src = "jhtp.jpg" width = "92" height = "120"
   alt = "Java How to Program book cover"></img>
```

Using Images as Hyperlinks

By using images as hyperlinks, web developers can create graphical web pages that link to other resources. In Fig. 4.6, we create six different image hyperlinks.

```
<?xml version = "1.0" encoding = "utf-8"?>
<!DOCTYPE html PUBLIC "-//W3C//DTD XHTML 1.0 Strict//EN"
   "http://www.w3.org/TR/xhtml1/DTD/xhtml1-strict.dtd">

<!-- Fig. 4.6: nav.html -->
<!-- Images as link anchors. -->
<html xmlns = "http://www.w3.org/1999/xhtml">
   <head>
      <title>Navigation Bar</title>
   </head>

   <body>
      <p>
         <a href = "links.html">
            <img src = "buttons/links.jpg" width = "65"
               height = "50" alt = "Links Page" />
         </a>

         <a href = "list.html">
            <img src = "buttons/list.jpg" width = "65"
               height = "50" alt = "List Example Page" />
         </a>

         <a href = "contact.html">
            <img src = "buttons/contact.jpg" width = "65"
               height = "50" alt = "Contact Page" />
         </a>

         <a href = "table1.html">
            <img src = "buttons/table.jpg" width = "65"
               height = "50" alt = "Table Page" />
         </a>

         <a href = "form.html">
            <img src = "buttons/form.jpg" width = "65"
               height = "50" alt = "Feedback Form" />
         </a>
      </p>
   </body>
</html>
```

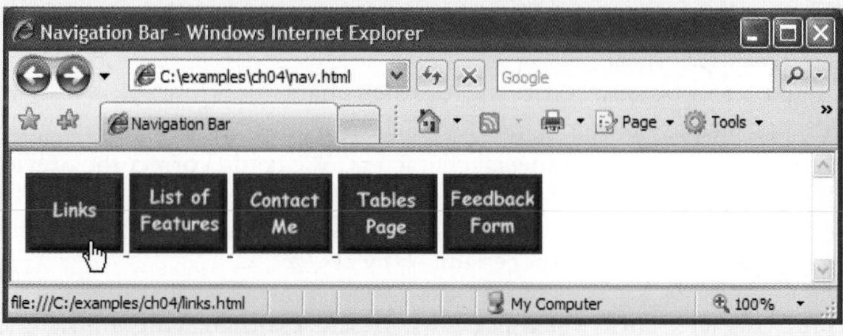

Fig. 4.6 | Images as link anchors. (Part 1 of 2.)

Fig. 4.6 | Images as link anchors. (Part 2 of 2.)

Lines 14–17 create an **image hyperlink** by nesting an `img` element in an anchor (`a`) element. The value of the `img` element's `src` attribute value specifies that this image (`links.jpg`) resides in a directory named `buttons`. The `buttons` directory and the XHTML document are in the same directory. Images from other web documents also can be referenced by setting the `src` attribute to the name and location of the image. Note that if you're hosting a publicly available web page that uses an image from another site, you should get permission to use the image and host a copy of image on your own website. If you refer to an image on another website, the browser has to request the image resource from the other site's server. Clicking an image hyperlink takes a user to the web page specified by the surrounding anchor element's `href` attribute. Notice that when the mouse hovers over a link of any kind, the URL that the link points to is displayed in the status bar at the bottom of the browser window.

4.8 Special Characters and Horizontal Rules

When marking up text, certain characters or symbols (e.g., <) may be difficult to embed directly into an XHTML document. Some keyboards do not provide these symbols, or the presence of these symbols may cause syntax errors. For example, the markup

```
<p>if x < 10 then increment x by 1</p>
```

results in a syntax error because it uses the less-than character (<), which is reserved for start tags and end tags such as `<p>` and `</p>`. XHTML provides **character entity references** (in the form `&`*code*`;`) for representing special characters. We could correct the previous line by writing

```
<p>if x &lt; 10 then increment x by 1</p>
```

which uses the character entity reference `<` for the less-than symbol (<).

Figure 4.7 demonstrates how to use special characters in an XHTML document. For a list of special characters, see Appendix A, XHTML Special Characters.

Lines 24–25 contain other special characters, which can be expressed as either character entity references (coded using word abbreviations such as `&` for ampersand and `©` for copyright) or **numeric character references**—decimal or **hexadecimal (hex)** values representing special characters. For example, the `&` character is represented in decimal and hexadecimal notation as `&` and `&`, respectively. Hexadecimal numbers are base 16 numbers—digits in a hexadecimal number have values from 0 to 15 (a total of 16 different values). The letters A–F represent the hexadecimal digits corresponding to decimal values 10–15. Thus in hexadecimal notation we can have numbers like 876 consisting solely of decimal-like digits, numbers like DA19F consisting of digits and letters, and numbers like DCB consisting solely of letters. We discuss hexadecimal numbers in detail in Appendix E, Number Systems.

```
1  <?xml version = "1.0" encoding = "utf-8"?>
2  <!DOCTYPE html PUBLIC "-//W3C//DTD XHTML 1.0 Strict//EN"
3     "http://www.w3.org/TR/xhtml1/DTD/xhtml1-strict.dtd">
4
5  <!-- Fig. 4.7: contact2.html -->
6  <!-- Inserting special characters. -->
7  <html xmlns = "http://www.w3.org/1999/xhtml">
8     <head>
9        <title>Contact Page</title>
10    </head>
11
12    <body>
13       <p>
14          Click
15          <a href = "mailto:deitel@deitel.com">here</a>
16          to open an email message addressed to
17          deitel@deitel.com.
18       </p>
19
20       <hr /> <!-- inserts a horizontal rule -->
21
22       <!-- special characters are entered -->
23       <!-- using the form &code; -->
24       <p>All information on this site is <strong>&copy;
25          Deitel &amp; Associates, Inc. 2007.</strong></p>
26
27       <!-- to strike through text use <del> tags -->
28       <!-- to subscript text use <sub> tags -->
29       <!-- to superscript text use <sup> tags -->
30       <!-- these tags are nested inside other tags -->
31       <p><del>You may download 3.14 x 10<sup>2</sup>
32          characters worth of information from this site.</del>
33          Only <sub>one</sub> download per hour is permitted.</p>
34       <p><em>Note: &lt; &frac14; of the information
35          presented here is updated daily.</em></p>
36    </body>
37 </html>
```

Fig. 4.7 | Inserting special characters. (Part 1 of 2.)

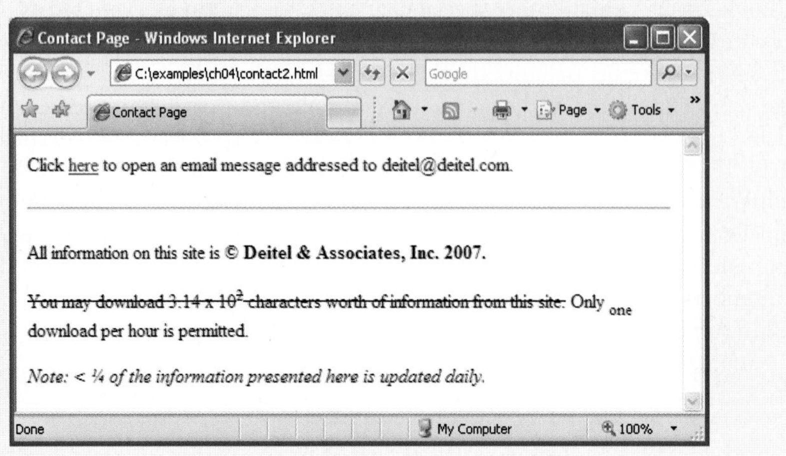

Fig. 4.7 | Inserting special characters. (Part 2 of 2.)

In lines 31–33, we introduce four new elements. Most browsers render the `del` element as strike-through text. With this format users can easily indicate document revisions. To superscript text (i.e., raise text above the baseline and decreased font size) or subscript text (i.e., lower text below the baseline and decreased font size), use the `sup` or `sub` element, respectively. The paragraph in lines 34–35 contains an `em` element, which indicates that its contents should be emphasized. Browsers usually render `em` elements in an italic font. We also use character entity reference `<` for a less-than sign and `¼` for the fraction 1/4 (line 34).

In addition to special characters, this document introduces a horizontal rule, indicated by the `<hr />` tag in line 22. Most browsers render a horizontal rule as a horizontal line with a blank line above and below it.

4.9 Lists

Up to this point, we have presented basic XHTML elements and attributes for linking to resources, creating headings, using special characters and incorporating images. In this section, we discuss how to organize information on a web page using lists. In the next section, we introduce another feature for organizing information, called a table. Figure 4.8 displays text in an unordered list (i.e., a list that does not order its items by letter or number). The unordered list element `ul` creates a list in which each item begins with a bullet symbol (called a disc). Each entry in an unordered list (element `ul` in line 17) is an `li` (list item) element (lines 19–22). Most web browsers render each `li` element on a new line with a bullet symbol indented from the beginning of the line.

```
1  <?xml version = "1.0" encoding = "utf-8"?>
2  <!DOCTYPE html PUBLIC "-//W3C//DTD XHTML 1.0 Strict//EN"
3     "http://www.w3.org/TR/xhtml1/DTD/xhtml1-strict.dtd">
4
```

Fig. 4.8 | Unordered list containing hyperlinks. (Part 1 of 2.)

```
<!-- Fig. 4.8: links2.html -->
<!-- Unordered list containing hyperlinks. -->
<html xmlns = "http://www.w3.org/1999/xhtml">
   <head>
      <title>Links</title>
   </head>

   <body>
      <h1>Here are my favorite sites</h1>
      <p><strong>Click on a name to go to that page.</strong></p>

      <!-- create an unordered list -->
      <ul>
         <!-- add four list items -->
         <li><a href = "http://www.deitel.com">Deitel</a></li>
         <li><a href = "http://www.w3.org">W3C</a></li>
         <li><a href = "http://www.yahoo.com">Yahoo!</a></li>
         <li><a href = "http://www.cnn.com">CNN</a></li>
        </ul>
   </body>
</html>
```

Fig. 4.8 | Unordered list containing hyperlinks. (Part 2 of 2.)

Nested Lists

Lists may be nested to represent hierarchical relationships, as in an outline format. Figure 4.9 demonstrates nested lists and ordered lists. The ordered list element `ol` creates a list in which each item begins with a number.

A web browser indents each nested list to indicate a hierarchical relationship. The first ordered list begins at line 30. Items in an ordered list are enumerated one, two, three and so on. Nested ordered lists are enumerated in the same manner. The items in the outermost unordered list (line 16) are preceded by discs. List items nested inside the unordered list of line 16 are preceded by circular bullets. Although not demonstrated in this example, subsequent nested list items are preceded by square bullets.

```
<?xml version = "1.0" encoding = "utf-8"?>
<!DOCTYPE html PUBLIC "-//W3C//DTD XHTML 1.0 Strict//EN"
   "http://www.w3.org/TR/xhtml1/DTD/xhtml1-strict.dtd">

<!-- Fig. 4.9: list.html -->
<!-- Nested and ordered lists. -->
<html xmlns = "http://www.w3.org/1999/xhtml">
   <head>
      <title>Lists</title>
   </head>

   <body>
      <h1>The Best Features of the Internet</h1>

      <!-- create an unordered list -->
      <ul>
         <li>You can meet new people from countries around
            the world.</li>
         <li>
            You have access to new media as it becomes public:

            <!-- this starts a nested list, which uses a -->
            <!-- modified bullet. The list ends when you -->
            <!-- close the <ul> tag. -->
            <ul>
               <li>New games</li>
               <li>New applications

                  <!-- nested ordered list -->
                  <ol>
                     <li>For business</li>
                     <li>For pleasure</li>
                  </ol>
               </li> <!-- ends line 27 new applications li -->

               <li>Around the clock news</li>
               <li>Search engines</li>
               <li>Shopping</li>
               <li>Programming

                  <!-- another nested ordered list -->
                  <ol>
                     <li>XML</li>
                     <li>Java</li>
                     <li>XHTML</li>
                     <li>Scripts</li>
                     <li>New languages</li>
                  </ol>
               </li> <!-- ends programming li of line 39 -->
            </ul> <!-- ends the nested list of line 25 -->
         </li>

```

Fig. 4.9 | Nested and ordered lists. (Part 1 of 2.)

```
            <li>Links</li>
            <li>Keeping in touch with old friends</li>
            <li>It is the technology of the future!</li>
         </ul> <!-- ends the unordered list of line 16 -->
      </body>
   </html>
```

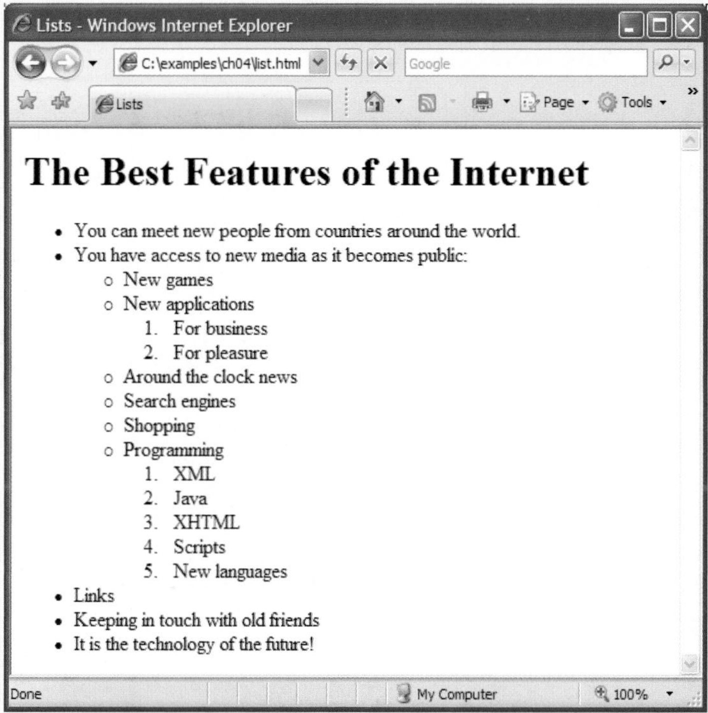

Fig. 4.9 | Nested and ordered lists. (Part 2 of 2.)

4.10 Tables

Tables are frequently used to organize data into rows and columns. Our first example (Fig. 4.10) creates a table with six rows and two columns to display price information for fruit.

Tables are defined with the `table` element (lines 15–62). Lines 15–17 specify the start tag for a `table` element that has several attributes. The `border` attribute specifies the table's border width in pixels. To create a table without a border, set `border` to `"0"`. This example assigns attribute `width` the value `"40%"` to set the table's width to 40 percent of the browser's width. A developer can also set attribute `width` to a specified number of pixels. Try resizing the browser window to see how the width of the window affects the width of the table.

As its name implies, attribute `summary` (lines 16–17) describes the table's contents. Speech devices use this attribute to make the table more accessible to users with visual impairments. The `caption` element (line 21) describes the table's content and helps text-

```
<?xml version = "1.0" encoding = "utf-8"?>
<!DOCTYPE html PUBLIC "-//W3C//DTD XHTML 1.0 Strict//EN"
   "http://www.w3.org/TR/xhtml1/DTD/xhtml1-strict.dtd">

<!-- Fig. 4.10: table1.html -->
<!-- Creating a basic table. -->
<html xmlns = "http://www.w3.org/1999/xhtml">
   <head>
      <title>A simple XHTML table</title>
   </head>

   <body>

      <!-- the <table> tag opens a table -->
      <table border = "1" width = "40%"
         summary = "This table provides information about
            the price of fruit">

         <!-- the <caption> tag summarizes the table's -->
         <!-- contents (this helps the visually impaired) -->
         <caption><strong>Price of Fruit</strong></caption>

         <!-- the <thead> section appears first in the table -->
         <!-- it formats the table header area -->
         <thead>
            <tr> <!-- <tr> inserts a table row -->
               <th>Fruit</th> <!-- insert a heading cell -->
               <th>Price</th>
            </tr>
         </thead>

         <!-- the <tfoot> section appears last in the table -->
         <!-- it formats the table footer -->
         <tfoot>
            <tr>
               <th>Total</th>
               <th>$3.75</th>
            </tr>
         </tfoot>

         <!-- all table content is enclosed -->
         <!-- within the <tbody> -->
         <tbody>
            <tr>
               <td>Apple</td> <!-- insert a data cell -->
               <td>$0.25</td>
            </tr>
            <tr>
               <td>Orange</td>
               <td>$0.50</td>
            </tr>
            <tr>
               <td>Banana</td>
```

Fig. 4.10 | Creating a basic table. (Part 1 of 2.)

```
54                  <td>$1.00</td>
55               </tr>
56               <tr>
57                  <td>Pineapple</td>
58                  <td>$2.00</td>
59               </tr>
60            </tbody>
61         </table>
62
63      </body>
64   </html>
```

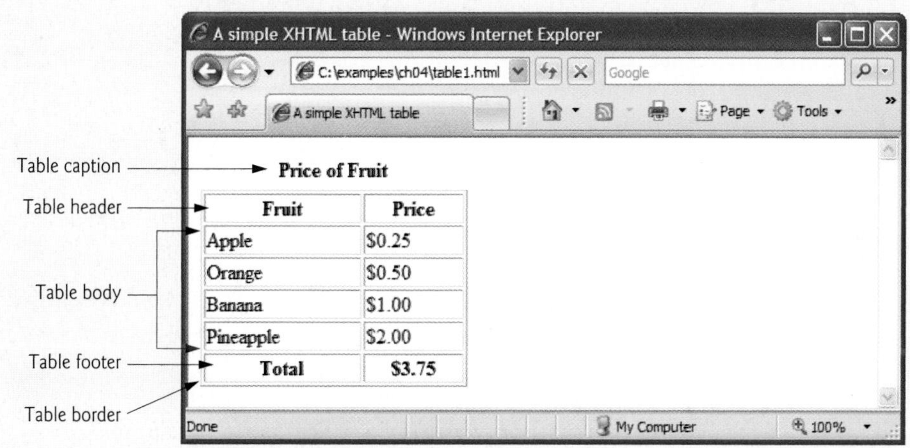

Fig. 4.10 | Creating a basic table. (Part 2 of 2.)

based browsers interpret the table data. Text inside the `<caption>` tag is rendered above the table by most browsers. Attribute `summary` and element `caption` are two of the many XHTML features that make web pages more accessible to users with disabilities.

A table has three distinct sections—**head**, **body** and **foot**. The head section (or header cell) is defined with a **`thead`** element (lines 25–30), which contains header information such as column names. Each **`tr`** element (lines 26–29) defines an individual **table row**. The columns in the head section are defined with **`th`** elements. Most browsers center text formatted by `th` (table header column) elements and display them in bold. Table header elements are nested inside table row elements (lines 27–28).

The body section, or **table body**, contains the table's primary data. The table body (lines 43–60) is defined in a **`tbody`** element. In the body, each `tr` element specifies one row. **Data cells** contain individual pieces of data and are defined with **`td`** (**table data**) elements in each row.

The foot section (lines 34–39) is defined with a **`tfoot`** (table foot) element. The text placed in the footer commonly includes calculation results and footnotes. Like other sections, the foot section can contain table rows, and each row can contain cells. As in the head section, cells in the foot section are created using `th` elements, instead of the `td` elements used in the table body. Note that the table foot section must be above the body section in the code, but the table foot displays at the bottom of the table.

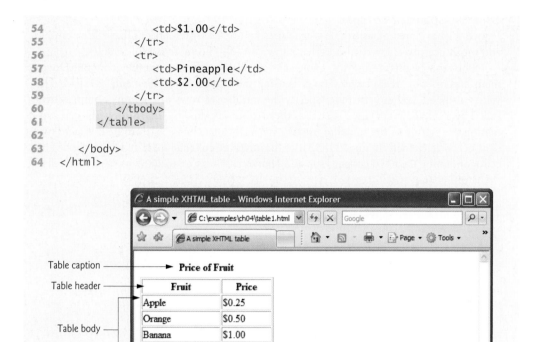

Using **rowspan** *and* **colspan**

Figure 4.10 explored a basic table's structure. Figure 4.11 presents another table example and introduces two new attributes that allow you to build more complex tables.

The table begins in line 15. Table cells are sized to fit the data they contain. Document authors can create larger data cells using the attributes **rowspan** and **colspan**. The values assigned to these attributes specify the number of rows or columns occupied by a cell. The `th` element at lines 23–26 uses the attribute `rowspan = "2"` to allow the cell containing the picture of the camel to use two vertically adjacent cells (thus the cell *spans* two rows). The `th` element in lines 29–32 uses the attribute `colspan = "4"` to widen the header cell (containing `Camelid comparison` and `Approximate as of 6/2007`) to span four cells.

```
1  <?xml version = "1.0" encoding = "utf-8"?>
2  <!DOCTYPE html PUBLIC "-//W3C//DTD XHTML 1.0 Strict//EN"
3     "http://www.w3.org/TR/xhtml1/DTD/xhtml1-strict.dtd">
4
5  <!-- Fig. 4.11: table2.html -->
6  <!-- Complex XHTML table. -->
7  <html xmlns = "http://www.w3.org/1999/xhtml">
8     <head>
9        <title>Tables</title>
10    </head>
11
12    <body>
13       <h1>Table Example Page</h1>
14
15       <table border = "1">
16          <caption>Here is a more complex sample table.</caption>
17
18          <thead>
19             <!-- rowspans and colspans merge the specified -->
20             <!-- number of cells vertically or horizontally -->
21             <tr>
22                <!-- merge two rows -->
23                <th rowspan = "2">
24                   <img src = "camel.gif" width = "205"
25                      height = "167" alt = "Picture of a camel" />
26                </th>
27
28                <!-- merge four columns -->
29                <th colspan = "4">
30                   <h1>Camelid comparison</h1>
31                   <p>Approximate as of 6/2007</p>
32                </th>
33             </tr>
34             <tr>
35                <th># of Humps</th>
36                <th>Indigenous region</th>
37                <th>Spits?</th>
38                <th>Produces Wool?</th>
39             </tr>
40          </thead>
```

Fig. 4.11 | Complex XHTML table. (Part 1 of 2.)

```
         <tbody>
            <tr>
               <th>Camels (bactrian)</th>
               <td>2</td>
               <td>Africa/Asia</td>
               <td>Yes</td>
               <td>Yes</td>
            </tr>
            <tr>
               <th>Llamas</th>
               <td>1</td>
               <td>Andes Mountains</td>
               <td>Yes</td>
               <td>Yes</td>
            </tr>
         </tbody>
      </table>
   </body>
</html>
```

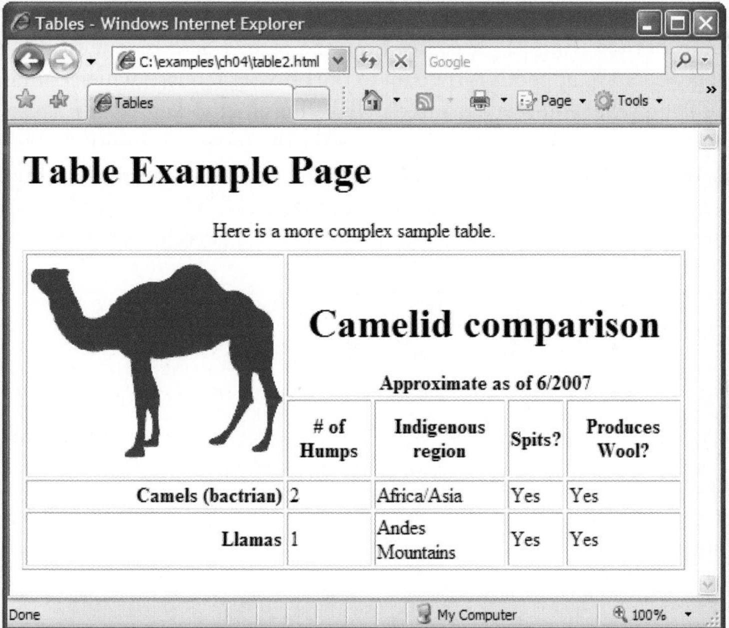

Fig. 4.11 | Complex XHTML table. (Part 2 of 2.)

4.11 Forms

When browsing websites, users often need to provide such information as search keywords, e-mail addresses and zip codes. XHTML provides a mechanism, called a form, for collecting data from a user.

Data that users enter on a web page is normally sent to a web server that provides access to a site's resources (e.g., XHTML documents, images). These resources are located either on the same machine as the web server or on a machine that the web server can access through the network. When a browser requests a web page or file that is located on a server, the server processes the request and returns the requested resource. A request contains the name and path of the desired resource and the method of communication (called a **protocol**). XHTML documents use the Hypertext Transfer Protocol (HTTP).

Figure 4.12 is a simple form that sends data to the web server, which passes the form data to a program. The program processes the data received from the web server and typically returns information to the web server. The web server then sends the information as an XHTML document to the web browser. We discuss web servers in Chapter 21. [*Note:* This example demonstrates client-side functionality. If the form is submitted (by clicking **Submit**), nothing will happen, because we don't yet know how to process the form data. In later chapters, we present the server-side programming (e.g., in ASP.NET, JavaServer Faces, and PHP) necessary to process information entered into a form.]

Forms can contain visual and nonvisual components. Visual components include clickable buttons and other graphical user interface components with which users interact. Nonvisual components, called **hidden inputs**, store any data that you specify, such as e-mail addresses and XHTML document filenames that act as links. The form is defined in lines 21–46 by a **`form`** element.

Attribute **`method`** (line 21) specifies how the form's data is sent to the web server. Using `method = "post"` appends form data to the browser request, which contains the protocol (HTTP) and the requested resource's URL. This method of passing data to the server is transparent—the user doesn't see the data after the form is submitted. The other possible value, `method = "get"`, appends the form data directly to the end of the URL of the script, where it is visible in the browser's **Address** field. The *post* and *get* methods for sending form data are discussed in detail in Chapter 21, Web Servers (IIS and Apache).

```
1  <?xml version = "1.0" encoding = "utf-8"?>
2  <!DOCTYPE html PUBLIC "-//W3C//DTD XHTML 1.0 Strict//EN"
3     "http://www.w3.org/TR/xhtml1/DTD/xhtml1-strict.dtd">
4
5  <!-- Fig. 4.12: form.html -->
6  <!-- Form with hidden fields and a text box. -->
7  <html xmlns = "http://www.w3.org/1999/xhtml">
8     <head>
9        <title>Forms</title>
10    </head>
11
12    <body>
13       <h1>Feedback Form</h1>
14
15       <p>Please fill out this form to help
16          us improve our site.</p>
17
18       <!-- this tag starts the form, gives the -->
19       <!-- method of sending information and the -->
20       <!-- location of form script -->
21       <form method = "post" action = "">
22          <p>
```

Fig. 4.12 | Form with hidden fields and a text box. (Part 1 of 2.)

```
23             <!-- hidden inputs contain non-visual -->
24             <!-- information -->
25             <input type = "hidden" name = "recipient"
26                value = "deitel@deitel.com" />
27             <input type = "hidden" name = "subject"
28                value = "Feedback Form" />
29             <input type = "hidden" name = "redirect"
30                value = "main.html" />
31          </p>
32
33          <!-- <input type = "text"> inserts a text box -->
34          <p><label>Name:
35                <input name = "name" type = "text" size = "25"
36                   maxlength = "30" />
37             </label></p>
38
39          <p>
40             <!-- input types "submit" and "reset" insert -->
41             <!-- buttons for submitting and clearing the -->
42             <!-- form's contents -->
43             <input type = "submit" value = "Submit" />
44             <input type = "reset" value = "Clear" />
45          </p>
46       </form>
47    </body>
48 </html>
```

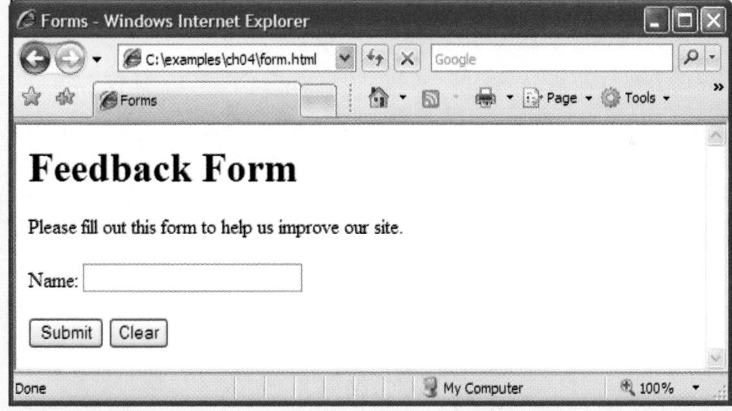

Fig. 4.12 | Form with hidden fields and a text box. (Part 2 of 2.)

The **action** attribute in the `<form>` tag in line 21 specifies the URL of a script on the web server that will be invoked to process the form's data. Since we haven't introduced server-side programming yet, we leave this attribute empty for now.

Lines 25–44 define six **input** elements that specify data to provide to the script that processes the form (also called the **form handler**). There are several types of input elements. An input's type is determined by its **type attribute**. This form uses a `text` input, a `submit` input, a `reset` input and three `hidden` inputs.

The **text** input in lines 35–36 inserts a **text box** in the form. Users can type data in text boxes. The `label` element (lines 34–37) provides users with information about the `input` element's purpose. The `input` element's **size** attribute specifies the number of characters visible in the text box. Optional attribute **maxlength** limits the number of characters input into the text box—in this case, the user is not permitted to type more than 30 characters.

Look-and-Feel Observation 4.3

Include a `label` element for each form element to help users determine the purpose of each form element.

Two `input` elements in lines 43–44 create two buttons. The **submit** `input` element is a button. When the `submit` button is pressed, the user is sent to the location specified in the `form`'s `action` attribute. The **value** attribute sets the text displayed on the button. The **reset** `input` element allows a user to reset all `form` elements to their default values. The `value` attribute of the `reset` `input` element sets the text displayed on the button (the default value is **Reset** if you omit the `value` attribute).

The three `input` elements in lines 25–30 have the `type` attribute `hidden`, which allows you to send form data that is not input by a user. The three hidden inputs are an e-mail address to which the data will be sent, the e-mail's subject line and a URL for the browser to open after submission of the form. Two other `input` attributes are **name**, which identifies the `input` element, and **value**, which provides the value that will be sent (or posted) to the web server.

Good Programming Practice 4.6

Place hidden `input` elements at the beginning of a form, immediately after the opening `<form>` tag. This placement allows document authors to locate hidden `input` elements quickly.

Additional Form Elements

In the previous example, you saw basic elements of XHTML forms. Now that you know the general structure of a form, we introduce elements and attributes for creating more complex forms. Figure 4.13 contains a form that solicits user feedback about a website.

```
<?xml version = "1.0" encoding = "utf-8"?>
<!DOCTYPE html PUBLIC "-//W3C//DTD XHTML 1.0 Strict//EN"
   "http://www.w3.org/TR/xhtml11/DTD/xhtml11-strict.dtd">

<!-- Fig. 4.13: form2.html -->
<!-- Form using a variety of components. -->
<html xmlns = "http://www.w3.org/1999/xhtml">
   <head>
      <title>More Forms</title>
   </head>

   <body>
      <h1>Feedback Form</h1>
```

Fig. 4.13 | Form using a variety of components. (Part 1 of 4.)

```
      <p>Please fill out this form to help
         us improve our site.</p>

      <form method = "post" action = "">
         <p>
            <input type = "hidden" name = "recipient"
               value = "deitel@deitel.com" />
            <input type = "hidden" name = "subject"
               value = "Feedback Form" />
            <input type = "hidden" name = "redirect"
               value = "main.html" />
         </p>

         <p><label>Name:
               <input name = "name" type = "text" size = "25" />
            </label></p>

         <!-- <textarea> creates a multiline textbox -->
         <p><label>Comments:<br />
            <textarea name = "comments"
                rows = "4" cols = "36">Enter comments here.</textarea>
         </label></p>

         <!-- <input type = "password"> inserts a -->
         <!-- textbox whose display is masked with -->
         <!-- asterisk characters -->
         <p><label>E-mail Address:
            <input name = "email" type = "password" size = "25" />
         </label></p>

         <p>
            <strong>Things you liked:</strong><br />

            <label>Site design
               <input name = "thingsliked" type = "checkbox"
                  value = "Design" /></label>
            <label>Links
               <input name = "thingsliked" type = "checkbox"
                  value = "Links" /></label>
            <label>Ease of use
               <input name = "thingsliked" type = "checkbox"
                  value = "Ease" /></label>
            <label>Images
               <input name = "thingsliked" type = "checkbox"
                  value = "Images" /></label>
            <label>Source code
               <input name = "thingsliked" type = "checkbox"
                  value = "Code" /></label>
         </p>

         <!-- <input type = "radio" /> creates a radio -->
         <!-- button. The difference between radio buttons -->
```

Fig. 4.13 | Form using a variety of components. (Part 2 of 4.)

```
         <!-- and checkboxes is that only one radio button -->
         <!-- in a group can be selected. -->
         <p>
            <strong>How did you get to our site?:</strong><br />

            <label>Search engine
               <input name = "howtosite" type = "radio"
                  value = "search engine" checked = "checked" /></label>
            <label>Links from another site
               <input name = "howtosite" type = "radio"
                  value = "link" /></label>
            <label>Deitel.com Website
               <input name = "howtosite" type = "radio"
                  value = "deitel.com" /></label>
            <label>Reference in a book
               <input name = "howtosite" type = "radio"
                  value = "book" /></label>
            <label>Other
               <input name = "howtosite" type = "radio"
                  value = "other" /></label>
         </p>

         <p>
            <label>Rate our site:

                <!-- the <select> tag presents a drop-down -->
                <!-- list with choices indicated by the -->
                <!-- <option> tags -->
               <select name = "rating">
                  <option selected = "selected">Amazing</option>
                  <option>10</option>
                  <option>9</option>
                  <option>8</option>
                  <option>7</option>
                  <option>6</option>
                  <option>5</option>
                  <option>4</option>
                  <option>3</option>
                  <option>2</option>
                  <option>1</option>
                  <option>Awful</option>
               </select>
            </label>
         </p>

         <p>
            <input type = "submit" value = "Submit" />
            <input type = "reset" value = "Clear" />
         </p>
      </form>
   </body>
</html>
```

Fig. 4.13 | Form using a variety of components. (Part 3 of 4.)

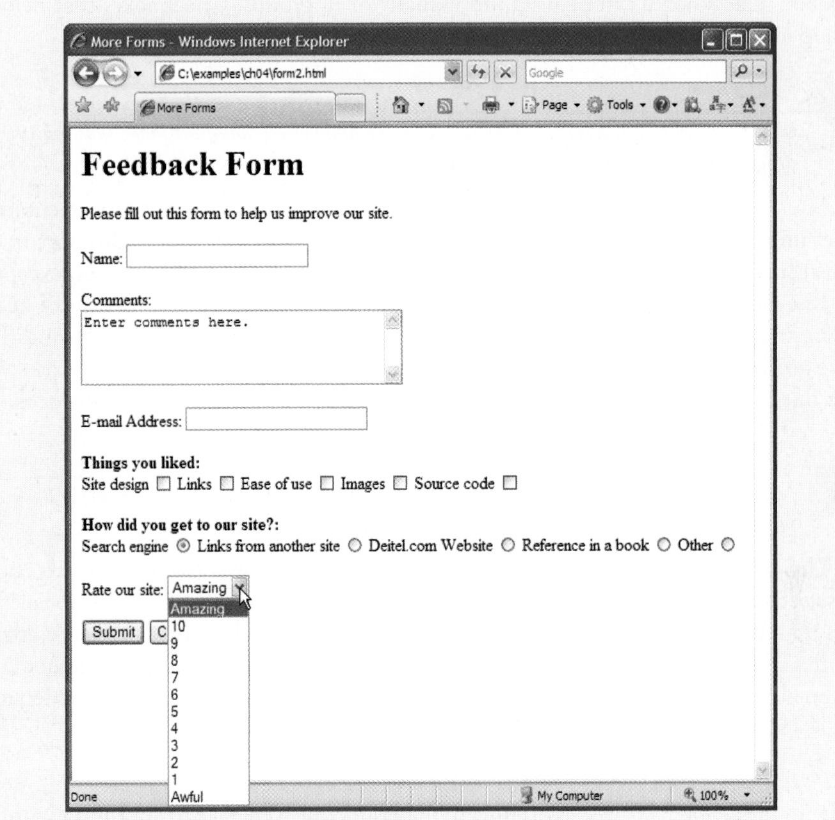

Fig. 4.13 | Form using a variety of components. (Part 4 of 4.)

In line 32, we introduce the **br** element, which most browsers render as a =**line break**. Any markup or text following a `br` element is rendered on the next line. Like the `img` element, `br` is an example of an empty element terminated with a forward slash. We add a space before the forward slash to enhance readability.

The **`textarea`** element (lines 33–34) inserts a multiline text box, called a **text area**, into the form. The number of rows is specified with the **`rows`** attribute, and the number of columns (i.e., characters per line) is specified with the **`cols`** attribute. In this example, the `textarea` is four rows high and 36 characters wide. To display default text in the text area, place the text between the `<textarea>` and `</textarea>` tags. Default text can be specified in other `input` types, such as text boxes, by using the `value` attribute.

The **`password`** input in line 41 inserts a password box with the specified `size` (maximum number of characters allowed). A password box allows users to enter sensitive information, such as credit card numbers and passwords, by "masking" the information input with asterisks (*). The actual value input is sent to the web server, not the characters that mask the input.

Lines 47–61 introduce the **checkbox** `form` element. Checkboxes enable users to select from a set of options. When a user selects a checkbox, a check mark appears in the checkbox. Otherwise, the checkbox remains empty. Each **`"checkbox"`** `input` creates a new checkbox. Checkboxes can be used individually or in groups. Checkboxes that belong to a group are assigned the same `name` (in this case, `"thingsliked"`).

Common Programming Error 4.5

When your `form` has several checkboxes with the same `name`, you must make sure that they have different `values`, or the scripts running on the web server will not be able to distinguish them.

After the checkboxes, we present two more ways to allow the user to make choices. In this example, we introduce two new `input` types. The first type is the radio button (lines 71–85) specified with type `"radio"`. Radio buttons are similar to checkboxes, except that only one radio button in a group of radio buttons may be selected at any time. The radio buttons in a group all have the same `name` attributes and are distinguished by their different `value` attributes. The attribute–value pair `checked = "checked"` (line 73) indicates which radio button, if any, is selected initially. The `checked` attribute also applies to checkboxes.

Common Programming Error 4.6

Not setting the `name` attributes of the radio buttons in a form to the same name is a logic error because it lets the user select all of them at the same time.

The `select` element (lines 94–107) provides a drop-down list from which the user can select an item. The `name` attribute identifies the drop-down list. The `option` elements (lines 95–106) add items to the drop-down list. The `option` element's `selected` attribute specifies which item initially is displayed as the selected item in the `select` element. If no `option` element is marked as `selected`, the browser selects the first `option` by default.

4.12 Internal Linking

Earlier in the chapter, we discussed how to hyperlink one web page to another. Figure 4.14 introduces internal linking—a mechanism that enables the user to jump between locations in the same document. Internal linking is useful for long documents that contain many sections. Clicking an internal link enables users to find a section without scrolling through the entire document.

Line 14 contains a tag with the `id` attribute (set to `"features"`) for an internal hyperlink. To link to a tag with this attribute inside the same web page, the `href` attribute of an anchor element includes the `id` attribute value preceded by a pound sign (as in `#features`). Line 56 contains a hyperlink with the `id features` as its target. Selecting this hyperlink in a web browser scrolls the browser window to the `h1` tag in line 14. Note that you may have to resize your browser to a small window and scroll down before clicking the link to see the browser scroll to the `h1` element.

```
1  <?xml version = "1.0" encoding = "utf-8"?>
2  <!DOCTYPE html PUBLIC "-//W3C//DTD XHTML 1.0 Strict//EN"
3     "http://www.w3.org/TR/xhtml1/DTD/xhtml1-strict.dtd">
4
5  <!-- Fig. 4.14: internal.html -->
6  <!-- Internal hyperlinks to make pages more navigable. -->
7  <html xmlns = "http://www.w3.org/1999/xhtml">
```

Fig. 4.14 | Internal hyperlinks to make pages more navigable. (Part 1 of 3.)

```
   <head>
      <title>Internal Links</title>
   </head>

   <body>
      <!-- id attribute creates an internal hyperlink destination -->
      <h1 id = "features">The Best Features of the Internet</h1>

      <!-- an internal link's address is "#id" -->
      <p><a href = "#bugs">Go to <em>Favorite Bugs</em></a></p>

      <ul>
         <li>You can meet people from countries
            around the world.</li>
         <li>You have access to new media as it becomes public:
            <ul>
               <li>New games</li>
               <li>New applications
                  <ul>
                     <li>For Business</li>
                     <li>For Pleasure</li>
                  </ul>
               </li>

               <li>Around the clock news</li>
               <li>Search Engines</li>
               <li>Shopping</li>
               <li>Programming
                  <ul>
                     <li>XHTML</li>
                     <li>Java</li>
                     <li>Dynamic HTML</li>
                     <li>Scripts</li>
                     <li>New languages</li>
                  </ul>
               </li>
            </ul>
         </li>

         <li>Links</li>
         <li>Keeping in touch with old friends</li>
         <li>It is the technology of the future!</li>
      </ul>

      <!-- id attribute creates an internal hyperlink destination -->
      <h1 id = "bugs">My 3 Favorite Bugs</h1>
      <p>
         <!-- internal hyperlink to features -->
         <a href = "#features">Go to <em>Favorite Features</em></a>
      </p>
      <ol>
         <li>Fire Fly</li>
         <li>Gal Ant</li>
```

Fig. 4.14 | Internal hyperlinks to make pages more navigable. (Part 2 of 3.)

```
            <li>Roman Tic</li>
         </ol>
      </body>
   </html>
```

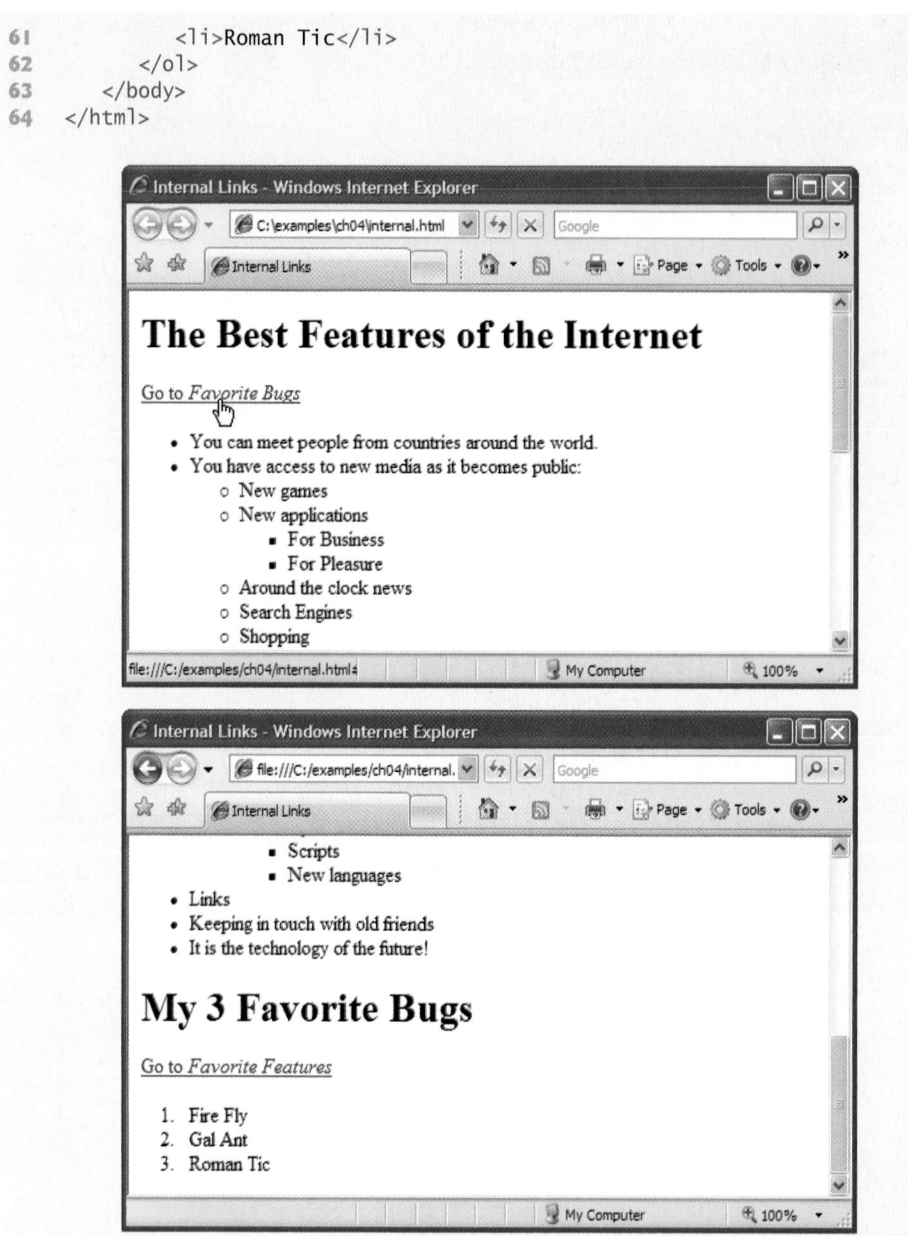

Fig. 4.14 | Internal hyperlinks to make pages more navigable. (Part 3 of 3.)

Look-and-Feel Observation 4.4

Internal hyperlinks are useful in XHTML documents that contain large amounts of information. Internal links to different parts of the page make it easier for users to navigate the page—they do not have to scroll to find the section they want.

Although not demonstrated in this example, a hyperlink can specify an internal link in another document by specifying the document name followed by a pound sign and the id value, as in:

href = "*filename*.html#*id*"

For example, to link to a tag with the id attribute called booklist in books.html, href is assigned "books.html#booklist". You can also send the browser to an internal link on another website by appending the pound sign and id value of an element to any URL, as in:

href = "*URL*/filename.html#*id*"

4.13 meta Elements

Search engines help people find websites. They usually catalog sites by following links from page to page (often known as spidering or crawling) and saving identification and classification information for each page. One way that search engines catalog pages is by reading the content in each page's meta elements, which specify information about a document.

Two important attributes of the meta element are name, which identifies the type of meta element, and content, which provides the information search engines use to catalog pages. Figure 4.15 introduces the meta element.

```
<?xml version = "1.0" encoding = "utf-8"?>
<!DOCTYPE html PUBLIC "-//W3C//DTD XHTML 1.0 Strict//EN"
   "http://www.w3.org/TR/xhtml1/DTD/xhtml1-strict.dtd">

<!-- Fig. 4.15: meta.html -->
<!-- meta elements provide keywords and a description of a page. -->
<html xmlns = "http://www.w3.org/1999/xhtml">
   <head>
      <title>Welcome</title>

      <!-- <meta> tags provide search engines with -->
      <!-- information used to catalog a site -->
      <meta name = "keywords" content = "web page, design,
         XHTML, tutorial, personal, help, index, form,
         contact, feedback, list, links, deitel" />
      <meta name = "description" content = "This website will
         help you learn the basics of XHTML and web page design
         through the use of interactive examples and
         instruction." />
   </head>
   <body>
      <h1>Welcome to Our Website!</h1>

      <p>We have designed this site to teach about the wonders
      of <strong><em>XHTML</em></strong>. <em>XHTML</em> is
      better equipped than <em>HTML</em> to represent complex
      data on the Internet. <em>XHTML</em> takes advantage of
      XML's strict syntax to ensure well-formedness. Soon you
```

Fig. 4.15 | meta elements provide keywords and a description of a page. (Part 1 of 2.)

```
29          will know about many of the great features of
30          <em>XHTML.</em></p>
31
32          <p>Have Fun With the Site!</p>
33       </body>
34    </html>
```

Fig. 4.15 | `meta` elements provide keywords and a description of a page. (Part 2 of 2.)

Lines 13–15 demonstrate a `"keywords"` `meta` element. The `content` attribute of such a `meta` element provides search engines with a list of words that describe a page. These words are compared with words in search requests. Thus, including `meta` elements and their `content` information can draw more viewers to your site.

Lines 16–19 demonstrate a `"description"` `meta` element. The `content` attribute of such a `meta` element provides a three- to four-line description of a site, written in sentence form. Search engines also use this description to catalog your site and sometimes display this information as part of the search results. Note that this use of the `meta` element is one of many methods of search engine optimization (SEO). For more information on SEO, visit Deitel's SEO Resource Center at `www.deitel.com/searchengineoptimization`.

Software Engineering Observation 4.1

`meta` elements are not visible to users and must be placed inside the `head` section of your XHTML document. If `meta` elements are not placed in this section, they will not be read by search engines.

4.14 Wrap-Up

This chapter introduced XHTML and explored many of its features. We discussed the basics of XHTML as well as marking up information in tables, creating forms for gathering user input, linking to sections in the same document and using `<meta>` tags. In Chapter 5, we build on the XHTML introduced in this chapter by discussing how to make web pages more visually appealing with Cascading Style Sheets.

4.15 Web Resources

www.deitel.com/xhtml

Visit our online XHTML Resource Center for links to some of the best XHTML information on the web. There you'll find categorized links to introductions, tutorials, books, blogs, forums, sample chapters, and more. Also check out links about XHTML 2, the upcoming version of the XHTML standard.

Summary

Section 4.1 Introduction

- XHTML (Extensible HyperText Markup Language) is a markup language for creating web pages.
- XHTML is based on HTML (HyperText Markup Language)—a legacy technology of the World Wide Web Consortium (W3C).
- XHTML 1.0 allows only a document's content and structure to appear in a valid XHTML document, and not its formatting.
- Formatting is specified with Cascading Style Sheets

Section 4.2 Editing XHTML

- A machine that runs a specialized piece of software called a web server stores XHTML documents.

Section 4.3 First XHTML Example

- In XHTML, text is marked up with elements delimited by tags that are names contained in pairs of angle brackets. Some elements may contain attributes that provide additional information about the element.
- Every XHTML document contains a start <html> tag and an end </html> tag.
- Comments in XHTML always begin with <!-- and end with -->. The browser ignores all text inside a comment.
- Every XHTML document contains a head element, which generally contains information, such as a title, and a body element, which contains the page content. Information in the head element generally is not rendered in the display window but may be made available to the user through other means.
- The title element names a web page. The title usually appears in the colored bar (called the title bar) at the top of the browser window and also appears as the text identifying a page when users add your page to their list of **Favorites** or **Bookmarks**.
- The body of an XHTML document is the area in which the document's content is placed. The content may include text and tags.
- All text placed between the <p> and </p> tags forms one paragraph.

Section 4.4 W3C XHTML Validation Service

- XHTML documents that are syntactically correct are guaranteed to render properly. XHTML documents that contain syntax errors may not display properly.
- Validation services (e.g., validator.w3.org) ensure that an XHTML document is syntactically correct.

Section 4.5 Headings

- XHTML provides six headings (`h1` through `h6`) for specifying the relative importance of information. Heading element `h1` is considered the most significant heading and is rendered in a larger font than the other five headings. Each successive heading element (i.e., `h2`, `h3`, etc.) is rendered in a progressively smaller font.

Section 4.6 Linking

- Web browsers typically underline text hyperlinks and color them blue by default.
- The `strong` element typically causes the browser to render text in a bold font.
- Users can insert links with the a (anchor) element. The most important attribute for the a element is `href`, which specifies the resource (e.g., page, file, e-mail address) being linked.
- Anchors can link to an e-mail address using a `mailto:` URL. When someone clicks this type of anchored link, most browsers launch the default e-mail program (e.g., Outlook Express) to initiate an e-mail message addressed to the linked address.

Section 4.7 Images

- The `img` element's `src` attribute specifies an image's location. In a valid XHTML document every `img` element must have an `alt` attribute, which contains text that is displayed if the client cannot render the image.
- The `alt` attribute makes web pages more accessible to users with disabilities, especially those with vision impairments.
- Some XHTML elements are empty elements that contain only attributes and do not mark up text. Empty elements (e.g., `img`) must be terminated, either by using the forward slash character (`/`) or by explicitly writing an end tag.

Section 4.8 Special Characters and Horizontal Rules

- XHTML provides special characters or entity references (in the form `&`*code*`;`) for representing characters that cannot be rendered otherwise.
- Special character codes can be either word abbreviations or numbers, decimal or hexadecimal.
- Most browsers render a horizontal rule, indicated by the `<hr />` tag, as a horizontal line. The `hr` element also inserts a line break above and below the horizontal line.

Section 4.9 Lists

- The unordered list element `ul` creates a list in which each item in the list begins with a bullet symbol (called a disc). Each entry in an unordered list is an `li` (list item) element. Most web browsers render these elements with a line break and a bullet symbol at the beginning of the line.
- The ordered list element `ol` creates a list in which each item begins with a number.
- Lists may be nested to represent hierarchical data relationships.

Section 4.10 Tables

- XHTML tables are used to mark up tabular data. The `table` element defines an XHTML table.
- Element `summary` summarizes the table's contents and is used by speech devices to make the table more accessible to users with visual impairments.
- Element `caption` describe's the table's content. The text inside the `<caption>` tag is rendered above the table in most browsers.
- A table can be split into three distinct sections: head (`thead`), body (`tbody`) and foot (`tfoot`). The head section contains such information as table titles and column headers. The table body contains the primary table data. The table foot contains such information as footnotes.

- Element `tr`, or table row, defines individual table rows. Element `th` defines a header cell. Other data in a row is defined with `td`, or table data, elements.
- You can merge data cells with the `rowspan` and `colspan` attributes. The values assigned to these attributes specify the number of rows or columns occupied by the cell. These attributes can be placed inside any data cell or table header cell.

Section 4.11 Forms

- XHTML provides forms for collecting information from users. Forms contain visual components, such as buttons, that users interact with. Forms may also contain nonvisual components, called hidden inputs, which are used to store any data that needs to be sent to the server, but is not entered by the user.
- A form begins with the `form` element. Attribute `method` specifies how the form's data is sent to the web server.
- The `action` attribute of the `form` element specifies the script to which the `form` data will be sent.
- The `"text"` input inserts a text box into the form. Text boxes allow the user to input data.
- The `input` element's `size` attribute specifies the number of characters visible in the `input` element. Optional attribute `maxlength` limits the number of characters input into a text box.
- The `"submit"` input submits the data entered in the form to the web server for processing. Most web browsers create a button that submits the form data when clicked. The `"reset"` input allows a user to reset all `form` elements to their default values.
- The `textarea` element inserts a multiline text box, called a text area, into a form. The number of rows in the text area is specified with the `rows` attribute, and the number of columns (i.e., characters per line) is specified with the `cols` attribute.
- The `"password"` input inserts a password box into a form. A password box allows users to enter sensitive information, such as credit card numbers and passwords, by "masking" the information input with another character. Asterisks are usually the masking character used for password boxes. The actual value input is sent to the web server, not the asterisks that mask the input.
- The checkbox input allows the user to make a selection. When the checkbox is selected, a check mark appears in the checkbox. Otherwise, the checkbox is empty. Checkboxes can be used individually and in groups. Checkboxes that are part of the same group have the same `name`.
- The `br` element causes most browsers to render a line break. Any markup or text following a `br` element is rendered on the next line.
- A radio button is similar in function and use to a checkbox, except that only one radio button in a group can be selected at any time. All radio buttons in a group have the same `name` attribute but different `value` attributes.
- The `select` input provides a drop-down list of items. The `name` attribute identifies the drop-down list. The `option` element adds items to the drop-down list.

Section 4.12 Internal Linking

- The a tag can be used to link to another section of the same document by specifying the element's `id` as the link's `href`.
- To link internally to an element with its id attribute set, use the syntax *#id*.

Section 4.13 `meta` Elements

- One way that search engines catalog pages is by reading the `meta` element's contents. Two important attributes of the `meta` element are `name`, which identifies the type of `meta` element, and `content`, which provides information a search engine uses to catalog a page.

- The content attribute of a keywords meta element provides search engines with a list of words that describe a page. These words are compared with words in search requests.
- The content attribute of a description meta element provides a three- to four-line description of a site, written in sentence form. Search engines also use this description to catalog your site and sometimes display this information as part of the search results.

Terminology

<!--...--> (XHTML comment)
a element (<a>...</a>)
accessible web pages
action attribute (form)
alt attribute (img)
& (& special character)
anchor
angle brackets (< >)
attribute
body element
border attribute (table)
br element (line break)
browser request
caption element
Cascading Syle Sheets (CSS)
character entity reference
checkbox
checked attribute (input)
cols attribute (textarea)
colspan attribute (th, td)
comment in XHTML
© (© special character)
data cells
database
debugging
del element
element
em element
e-mail anchor
empty element
end tag
Extensible HyperText Markup Language (XHTML)
form
form element
form handler
get request type
head element
header cell
heading
h1 through h6 (heading elements)
height attribute (img)
hexadecimal code
hidden input element
hr element (horizontal rule)
href attribute (a)
.htm (XHTML filename extension)
<html> tag
.html (XHTML filename extension)
hyperlink
img element
input element
internal linking
level of nesting
li element (list item)
line break
link
linked document
list item
< (< special character)
mailto: URL
markup language
maxlength attribute (input)
meta element
method attribute (form)
name attribute
nested list
nested tag
numeric character reference
ol element (ordered list)
option element
p element (paragraph)
password box
pixel
post request type
presentation of a document
protocol
radio input
reset input
resources
rows attribute (textarea)
rowspan attribute (th, tr)
script
select element
selected attribute (option)
size attribute (input)

source code
special character
speech synthesizer
`src` attribute (`img`)
start tag
`strong` element
`sub` element
`submit` input
subscript
superscript
`table` element
tag
`tbody` element
`td` element
text editor
text-based browser
textarea
`textarea` element
`tfoot` element (table foot)
`thead` element (table head)
`title` element
`tr` element (table row)
`type` attribute (`input`)
`ul` element (unordered list)
valid document
validation service
`value` attribute (`input`)
value of an attribute
web page
web server
`width` attribute (`img`)
World Wide Web (WWW)
World Wide Web Consortium (W3C)
XHTML (Extensible HyperText Markup Language)
XHTML comment
XHTML document
XHTML form
XHTML markup
XHTML tag
XML declaration
`xmlns` attribute

Self-Review Exercises

4.1 State whether each of the following is *true* or *false*. If *false*, explain why.

a) An ordered list cannot be nested inside an unordered list.
b) XHTML is an acronym for XML HTML.
c) Element `br` represents a line break.
d) Hyperlinks are denoted by `link` elements.
e) The width of all data cells in a table must be the same.
f) You are limited to a maximum of 100 internal links per page.

4.2 Fill in the blanks in each of the following:

a) The _________ element inserts a horizontal rule.
b) A superscript is marked up using element _________ and a subscript is marked up using element _________.
c) The least important heading element is _________ and the most important heading element is _________.
d) Element _________ marks up an unordered list.
e) Element _________ marks up a paragraph.
f) The _________ attribute in an `input` element inserts a button that, when clicked, clears the contents of the form.
g) The _________ element marks up a table row.
h) _________ are usually used as masking characters in a password box.

Answers to Self-Review Exercises

4.1 a) False. An ordered list can be nested inside an unordered list and vice versa. b) False. XHTML is an acronym for Extensible HyperText Markup Language. c) True. d) False. Hyperlinks are denoted by a elements. e) False. You can specify the width of any column, either in pixels or as a percentage of the table width. f) False. You can have an unlimited number of internal links.

4.2 a) `hr`. b) `sup`, `sub`. c) `h6`, `h1`. d) `ul`. e) `p`. f) `type = "reset"`. g) `tr`. h) Asterisks.

Exercises

4.3 Use XHTML to create a document that contains the following text:

```
Internet and World Wide Web How to Program: Fourth Edition
Welcome to the world of Internet programming. We have provided
topical coverage for many Internet-related topics.
```

Use `h1` for the title (the first line of text), `p` for text (the second and third lines of text) and `sub` for each word that begins with a capital letter (except the title). Insert a horizontal rule between the `h1` element and the `p` element. Open your new document in a web browser to view the marked-up document.

4.4 Why is the following markup invalid?

```
<p>Here is some text...
<hr />
<p>And some more text...</p>
```

4.5 Why is the following markup invalid?

```
<p>Here is some text...<br>
And some more text...</p>
```

4.6 An image named `deitel.gif` is 200 pixels wide and 150 pixels high. Write an XHTML statement using the `width` and `height` attributes of the `img` element to perform each of the following transformations:

a) Increase the size of the image by 100 percent.
b) Increase the size of the image by 50 percent.
c) Change the width-to-height ratio to 2:1, keeping the `width` attained in part (a).

4.7 Create a link to each of the following:

a) The file `index.html`, located in the `files` directory.
b) The file `index.html`, located in the `text` subdirectory of the `files` directory.
c) The file `index.html`, located in the `other` directory in your parent directory. [*Hint:* `..` signifies parent directory.]
d) The President's e-mail address (`president@whitehouse.gov`).
e) The file named `README` in the `pub` directory of `ftp.cdrom.com`. [*Hint:* Use `ftp://`.]

4.8 Create an XHTML document containing three ordered lists: ice cream, soft serve and frozen yogurt. Each ordered list should contain a nested, unordered list of your favorite flavors. Provide a minimum of three flavors in each unordered list.

4.9 Create an XHTML document that uses an image as an e-mail link. Use attribute `alt` to provide a description of the image and link.

4.10 Create an XHTML document that contains links to your favorite websites. Your page should contain the heading "My Favorite Web Sites."

4.11 Create an XHTML document that contains an unordered list with links to all the examples presented in this chapter. [*Hint:* Place all the chapter examples in one directory.]

4.12 Identify each of the following as either an element or an attribute:

a) `html`
b) `width`
c) `href`
d) `br`
e) `h3`
f) `a`
g) `src`

4.13 State which of the following statements are *true* and which are *false*. If *false*, explain why.

a) A valid XHTML document can contain uppercase letters in element names.
b) Tags need not be closed in a valid XHTML document.
c) XHTML documents can have the file extension `.htm`.
d) Valid XHTML documents can contain tags that overlap.
e) `&less;` is the character entity reference for the less-than (<) character.
f) In a valid XHTML document, `<li>` can be nested inside either `<ol>` or `<ul>` tags.

4.14 Fill in the blanks in each of the following:

a) XHTML comments begin with `<!--` and end with ________.
b) In XHTML, attribute values must be enclosed in ________.
c) ________ is the character entity reference for an ampersand.
d) Element ________ can be used to bold text.

4.15 Categorize each of the following as an element or an attribute:

a) `width`
b) `td`
c) `th`
d) `name`
e) `select`
f) `type`

4.16 Create the XHTML markup that produces the table shown in Fig. 4.16. Use `<em>` and `<strong>` tags as necessary. The image (`camel.gif`) is included in the Chapter 4 examples directory that can be downloaded from `http://www.deitel.com/books/iw3htp4/`.

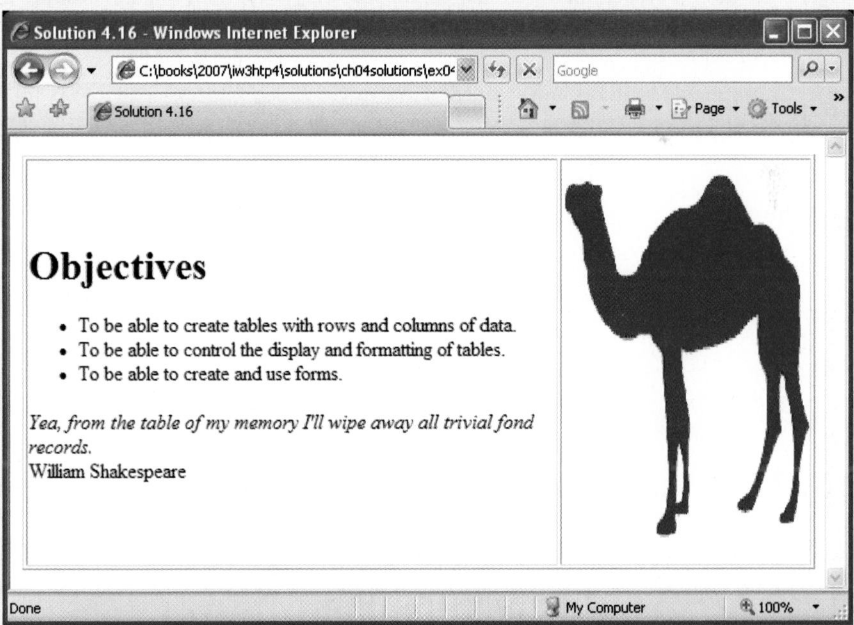

Fig. 4.16 | XHTML table for Exercise 4.16.

4.17 Write an XHTML document that produces the table shown in Fig. 4.17.

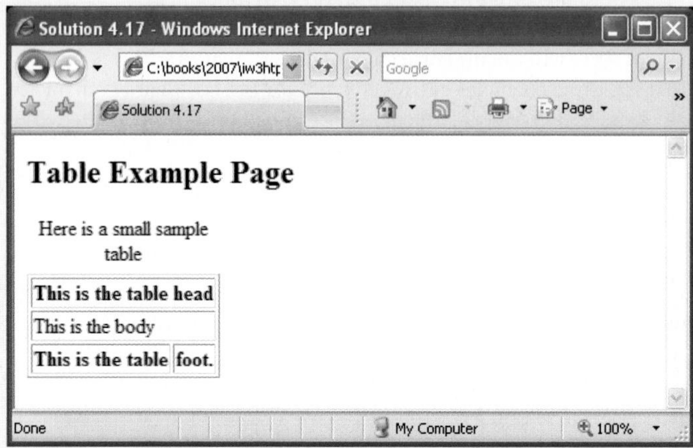

Fig. 4.17 | XHTML table for Exercise 4.17.

4.18 A local university has asked you to create an XHTML document that allows prospective students to provide feedback about their campus visit. Your XHTML document should contain a form with text boxes for a name, address and e-mail. Provide checkboxes that allow prospective students to indicate what they liked most about the campus. The checkboxes should include: students, location, campus, atmosphere, dorm rooms and sports. Also, provide radio buttons that ask the prospective students how they became interested in the university. Options should include: friends, television, Internet and other. In addition, provide a text area for additional comments, a submit button and a reset button.

4.19 Create an XHTML document titled "How to Get Good Grades." Use `<meta>` tags to include a series of keywords that describe your document.

5

Cascading Style Sheets™ (CSS)

Fashions fade, style is eternal.
—Yves Saint Laurent

A style does not go out of style as long as it adapts itself to its period. When there is an incompatibility between the style and a certain state of mind, it is never the style that triumphs.
—Coco Chanel

How liberating to work in the margins, outside a central perception.
—Don DeLillo

I've gradually risen from lower-class background to lower-class foreground.
—Marvin Cohen

OBJECTIVES

In this chapter you will learn:

- To control the appearance of a website by creating style sheets.
- To use a style sheet to give all the pages of a website the same look and feel.
- To use the `class` attribute to apply styles.
- To specify the precise font, size, color and other properties of displayed text.
- To specify element backgrounds and colors.
- To understand the box model and how to control margins, borders and padding.
- To use style sheets to separate presentation from content.

Outline

5.1 Introduction

In Chapter 4, we introduced the Extensible HyperText Markup Language (XHTML) for marking up information to be rendered in a browser. In this chapter, we shift our focus to formatting and presenting information. To do this, we use a W3C technology called Cascading Style Sheets™ (CSS) that allows document authors to specify the presentation of elements on a web page (e.g., fonts, spacing, colors) separately from the structure of the document (section headers, body text, links, etc.). This separation of structure from presentation simplifies maintaining and modifying a web page.

XHTML was designed to specify the content and structure of a document. Though it has some attributes that control presentation, it is better not to mix presentation with content. If a website's presentation is determined entirely by a style sheet, a web designer can simply swap in a new style sheet to completely change the appearance of the site. CSS provides a way to apply style outside of XHTML, allowing the XHTML to dictate the content while the CSS dictates how it's presented.

As with XHTML, the W3C provides a CSS code validator located at `jigsaw.w3.org/css-validator/`. It is a good idea to validate all CSS code with this tool to make sure that your code is correct and works on as many browsers as possible.

CSS is a large topic. As such, we can introduce only the basic knowledge of CSS that you'll need to understand the examples and exercises in the rest of the book. For more CSS references and resources, check out our CSS Resource Center at `www.deitel.com/css21`.

The W3C's CSS specification is currently in its second major version, with a third in development. The current versions of most major browsers support much of the functionality in CSS 2. This allows programmers to make full use of its features. In this chapter, we introduce CSS, demonstrate some of the features introduced in CSS 2 and discuss some of the upcoming CSS 3 features. As you read this book, open each XHTML document in your web browser so you can view and interact with it in a web browser, as it was originally intended.

Remember that the examples in this book have been tested in Internet Explorer 7 and Firefox 2. The latest versions of many other browsers (e.g., Safari, Opera, Konqueror) should render this chapter's examples properly, but we have not tested them. Some examples in this chapter *will not work* in older browsers, such as Internet Explorer 6 and earlier. Make sure you have either Internet Explorer 7 (Windows only) or Firefox 2 (available for all major platforms) installed before running the examples in this chapter.

5.2 Inline Styles

You can declare document styles in several ways. This section presents inline styles that declare an individual element's format using the XHTML attribute **style**. Inline styles override any other styles applied using the techniques we discuss later in the chapter. Figure 5.1 applies inline styles to p elements to alter their font size and color.

Good Programming Practice 5.1

Inline styles do not truly separate presentation from content. To apply similar styles to multiple elements, use embedded style sheets or external style sheets, introduced later in this chapter.

The first inline style declaration appears in line 17. Attribute style specifies an element's style. Each CSS property (**font-size** in this case) is followed by a colon and a value. In line 17, we declare this particular p element to use 20-point font size.

```
1  <?xml version = "1.0" encoding = "utf-8"?>
2  <!DOCTYPE html PUBLIC "-//W3C//DTD XHTML 1.0 Strict//EN"
3     "http://www.w3.org/TR/xhtml1/DTD/xhtml1-strict.dtd">
4
5  <!-- Fig. 5.1: inline.html -->
6  <!-- Using inline styles -->
7  <html xmlns = "http://www.w3.org/1999/xhtml">
8     <head>
9        <title>Inline Styles</title>
10    </head>
11    <body>
12       <p>This text does not have any style applied to it.</p>
13
14       <!-- The style attribute allows you to declare -->
15       <!-- inline styles. Separate multiple style properties -->
16       <!-- with a semicolon. -->
17       <p style = "font-size: 20pt">This text has the
18          <em>font-size</em> style applied to it, making it 20pt.
19       </p>
20
21       <p style = "font-size: 20pt; color: #6666ff">
22       This text has the <em>font-size</em> and
23       <em>color</em> styles applied to it, making it
24       20pt. and light blue.</p>
25    </body>
26 </html>
```

Fig. 5.1 | Using inline styles. (Part 1 of 2.)

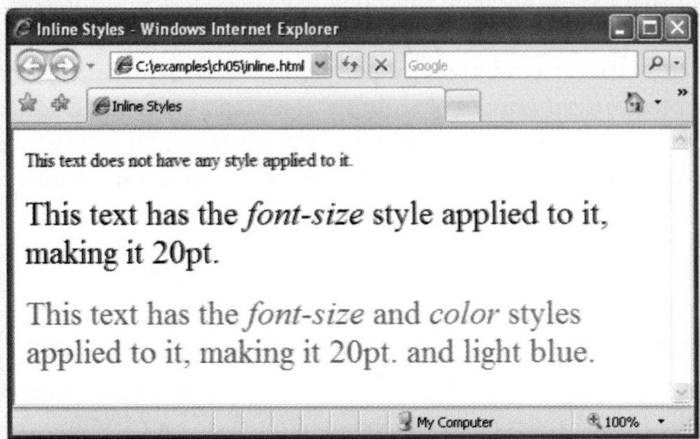

Fig. 5.1 | Using inline styles. (Part 2 of 2.)

Line 21 specifies the two properties, `font-size` and **`color`**, separated by a semicolon. In this line, we set the given paragraph's `color` to light blue, using the hexadecimal code `#6666ff`. Color names may be used in place of hexadecimal codes. We provide a list of hexadecimal color codes and color names in Appendix B, XHTML Colors.

5.3 Embedded Style Sheets

A second technique for using style sheets is **embedded style sheets**. Embedded style sheets enable a you to embed an entire CSS document in an XHTML document's `head` section. To achieve this separation between the CSS code and the XHTML that it styles, we will use **CSS selectors**. Figure 5.2 creates an embedded style sheet containing four styles.

```
<?xml version = "1.0" encoding = "utf-8"?>
<!DOCTYPE html PUBLIC "-//W3C//DTD XHTML 1.0 Strict//EN"
   "http://www.w3.org/TR/xhtml1/DTD/xhtml1-strict.dtd">

<!-- Fig. 5.2: embedded.html -->
<!-- Embedded style sheets. -->
<html xmlns = "http://www.w3.org/1999/xhtml">
   <head>
      <title>Style Sheets</title>

      <!-- this begins the style sheet section -->
      <style type = "text/css">
         em       { font-weight: bold;
                    color: black }
         h1       { font-family: tahoma, helvetica, sans-serif }
         p        { font-size: 12pt;
                    font-family: arial, sans-serif }
         .special { color: #6666ff }
      </style>
   </head>
```

Fig. 5.2 | Embedded style sheets. (Part 1 of 2.)

```
21     <body>
22        <!-- this class attribute applies the .special style -->
23        <h1 class = "special">Deitel &amp; Associates, Inc.</h1>
24
25        <p>Deitel &amp; Associates, Inc. is an internationally
26        recognized corporate training and publishing organization
27        specializing in programming languages, Internet/World
28        Wide Web technology and object technology education.
29        The company provides courses on Java, C++, Visual Basic,
30        C#, C, Internet and World Wide Web programming, Object
31        Technology, and more.</p>
32
33        <h1>Clients</h1>
34        <p class = "special"> The company's clients include many
35        <em>Fortune 1000 companies</em>, government agencies,
36        branches of the military and business organizations.
37        Through its publishing partnership with Prentice Hall,
38        Deitel &amp; Associates, Inc. publishes leading-edge
39        programming textbooks, professional books, interactive
40        web-based multimedia Cyber Classrooms, satellite
41        courses and World Wide Web courses.</p>
42     </body>
43  </html>
```

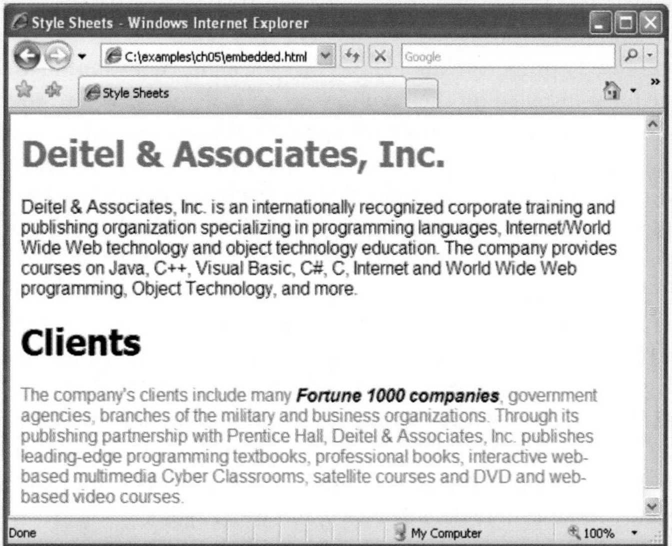

Fig. 5.2 | Embedded style sheets. (Part 2 of 2.)

The `style` element (lines 12–19) defines the embedded style sheet. Styles placed in the `head` apply to matching elements wherever they appear in the entire document. The `style` element's `type` attribute specifies the **Multipurpose Internet Mail Extensions (MIME) type** that describes a file's content. CSS documents use the MIME type `text/css`. Other MIME types include `image/gif` (for GIF images), `text/javascript` (for the JavaScript scripting language, which we discuss in Chapters 6–11), and more.

The body of the style sheet (lines 13–18) declares the CSS rules for the style sheet. A CSS selector determines which elements will be styled according to a rule. Our first rule begins with the selector em (line 13) to select all em elements in the document. The font-weight property in line 13 specifies the "boldness" of text. Possible values are bold, normal (the default), bolder (bolder than bold text) and lighter (lighter than normal text). Boldness also can be specified with multiples of 100, from 100 to 900 (e.g., 100, 200, ..., 900). Text specified as normal is equivalent to 400, and bold text is equivalent to 700. However, many systems do not have fonts that can scale with this level of precision, so using the values from 100 to 900 might not display the desired effect.

In this example, all em elements will be displayed in a bold font. We also apply styles to all h1 (line 15) and p (lines 16–17) elements. The body of each rule is enclosed in curly braces ({ and }).

Line 18 uses a new kind of selector to declare a style class named special. Style classes define styles that can be applied to any element. In this example, we declare class special, which sets color to blue. We can apply this style to any element type, whereas the other rules in this style sheet apply only to specific element types defined in the style sheet (i.e., em, h1 or p). Style-class declarations are preceded by a period. We will discuss how to apply a style class momentarily.

CSS rules in embedded style sheets use the same syntax as inline styles; the property name is followed by a colon (:) and the value of the property. Multiple properties are separated by semicolons (;). In the rule for em elements, the color property specifies the color of the text, and property font-weight makes the font bold.

The font-family property (line 15) specifies the name of the font to use. Not all users have the same fonts installed on their computers, so CSS allows you to specify a comma-separated list of fonts to use for a particular style. The browser attempts to use the fonts in the order they appear in the list. It's advisable to end a font list with a generic font family name in case the other fonts are not installed on the user's computer. In this example, if the tahoma font is not found on the system, the browser will look for the helvetica font. If neither is found, the browser will display its default sans-serif font. Other generic font families include serif (e.g., times new roman, Georgia), cursive (e.g., script), fantasy (e.g., critter) and monospace (e.g., courier, fixedsys).

The font-size property (line 16) specifies a 12-point font. Other possible measurements in addition to pt (point) are introduced later in the chapter. Relative values— xx-small, x-small, small, smaller, medium, large, larger, x-large and xx-large—also can be used. Generally, relative values for font-size are preferred over point sizes because an author does not know the specific measurements of the display for each client. Relative font-size values permit more flexible viewing of web pages.

For example, a user may wish to view a web page on a handheld device with a small screen. Specifying an 18-point font size in a style sheet will prevent such a user from seeing more than one or two characters at a time. However, if a relative font size is specified, such as large or larger, the actual size is determined by the browser that displays the font. Using relative sizes also makes pages more accessible to users with disabilities. Users with impaired vision, for example, may configure their browser to use a larger default font, upon which all relative sizes are based. Text that the author specifies to be smaller than the main text still displays in a smaller size font, yet it is clearly visible to each user. Accessibility is an important consideration—in 1998, congress passed the Section 508 Amendment to the Rehabilitation Act of 1973, mandating that websites of government agencies are required to be accessible to disabled users.

Line 23 uses the XHTML attribute `class` in an `h1` element to apply a style class—in this case class `special` (declared with the `.special` selector in the style sheet on line 18). When the browser renders the `h1` element, note that the text appears on screen with the properties of both an `h1` element (`arial` or `sans-serif` font defined in line 17) and the `.special` style class applied (the color `#6666ff` defined in line 18). Also notice that the browser still applies its own default style to the `h1` element—the header is still displayed in a large font size. Similarly, all `em` elements will still be italicized by the browser, but they will also be bold as a result of our style rule.

The formatting for the `p` element and the `.special` class is applied to the text in lines 34–41. In many cases, the styles applied to an element (the parent or ancestor element) also apply to the element's nested elements (child or descendant elements). The `em` element nested in the `p` element in line 35 inherits the style from the `p` element (namely, the 12-point font size in line 16) but retains its italic style. In other words, styles defined for the paragraph and not defined for the em element is applied to the em element. Because multiple values of one property can be set or inherited on the same element, they must be reduced to one style per element before being rendered. We discuss the rules for resolving these conflicts in the next section.

5.4 Conflicting Styles

Styles may be defined by a user, an author or a user agent (e.g., a web browser). A user is a person viewing your web page, you are the author—the person who writes the document—and the user agent is the program used to render and display the document. Styles "cascade," or flow together, such that the ultimate appearance of elements on a page results from combining styles defined in several ways. Styles defined by the user take precedence over styles defined by the user agent, and styles defined by authors take precedence over styles defined by the user.

Most styles defined for parent elements are also inherited by child (nested) elements. While it makes sense to inherit most styles, such as font properties, there are certain properties that we don't want to be inherited. Consider for example the `background-image` property, which allows the programmer to set an image as the background of an element. If the `body` element is assigned a background image, we don't want the same image to be in the background of every element in the body of our page. Instead, the `background-image` property of all child elements retains its default value of `none`. In this section, we discuss the rules for resolving conflicts between styles defined for elements and styles inherited from parent and ancestor elements.

Figure 5.2 presented an example of inheritance in which a child `em` element inherited the `font-size` property from its parent `p` element. However, in Fig. 5.2, the child `em` element had a `color` property that conflicted with (i.e., had a different value than) the `color` property of its parent `p` element. Properties defined for child and descendant elements have a greater specificity than properties defined for parent and ancestor elements. Conflicts are resolved in favor of properties with a higher specificity. In other words, the styles explicitly defined for a child element are more specific than the styles defined for the child's parent element; therefore, the child's styles take precedence. Figure 5.3 illustrates examples of inheritance and specificity.

Line 12 applies property `text-decoration` to all `a` elements whose `class` attribute is set to `nodec`. The `text-decoration` property applies **decorations** to text in an element. By default, browsers underline the text of an `a` (anchor) element. Here, we set the `text-decoration` property to `none` to indicate that the browser should not underline hyperlinks. Other possible values for `text-decoration` include `overline`, `line-through`, `underline` and `blink`. [*Note:* `blink` is not supported by Internet Explorer.] The `.nodec` appended to `a` is a more specific class selector; this style will apply only to `a` (anchor) elements that specify `nodec` in their `class` attribute.

```
1  <?xml version = "1.0" encoding = "utf-8"?>
2  <!DOCTYPE html PUBLIC "-//W3C//DTD XHTML 1.0 Strict//EN"
3     "http://www.w3.org/TR/xhtml1/DTD/xhtml1-strict.dtd">
4
5  <!-- Fig. 5.3: advanced.html -->
6  <!-- Inheritance in style sheets. -->
7  <html xmlns = "http://www.w3.org/1999/xhtml">
8     <head>
9        <title>More Styles</title>
10       <style type = "text/css">
11          body     { font-family: arial, helvetica, sans-serif }
12          a.nodec  { text-decoration: none }
13          a:hover  { text-decoration: underline }
14          li em    { font-weight: bold }
15          h1, em   { text-decoration: underline }
16          ul       { margin-left: 20px }
17          ul ul    { font-size: .8em }
18       </style>
19    </head>
20    <body>
21       <h1>Shopping list for Monday:</h1>
22
23       <ul>
24          <li>Milk</li>
25          <li>Bread
26             <ul>
27                <li>White bread</li>
28                <li>Rye bread</li>
29                <li>Whole wheat bread</li>
30             </ul>
31          </li>
32          <li>Rice</li>
33          <li>Potatoes</li>
34          <li>Pizza <em>with mushrooms</em></li>
35       </ul>
36
37       <p><em>Go to the</em>
38          <a class = "nodec" href = "http://www.deitel.com">
39             Grocery store</a>
40       </p>
41    </body>
42 </html>
```

Fig. 5.3 | Inheritance in style sheets. (Part 1 of 2.)

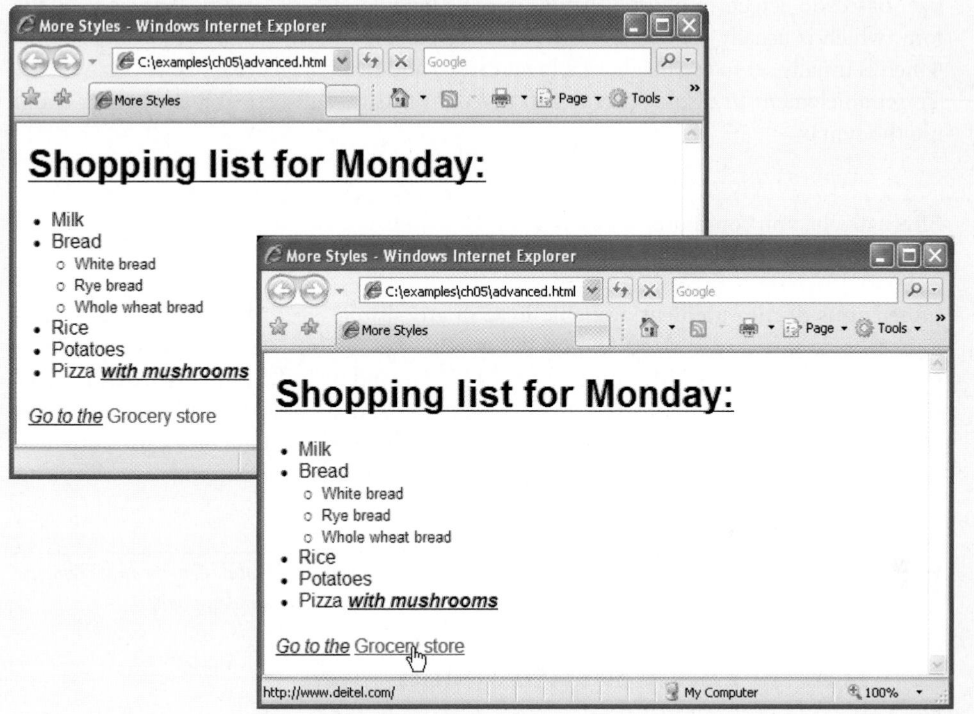

Fig. 5.3 | Inheritance in style sheets. (Part 2 of 2.)

Portability Tip 5.1

To ensure that your style sheets work in various web browsers, test them on all the client web browsers that will render documents using your styles, as well as using the W3C CSS Validator.

Line 13 specifies a style for `hover`, which is a **pseudoclass**. Pseudoclasses give the author access to content not specifically declared in the document. The **`hover` pseudoclass** is activated dynamically when the user moves the mouse cursor over an element. Note that pseudoclasses are separated by a colon (with no surrounding spaces) from the name of the element to which they are applied.

Common Programming Error 5.1

Including a space before or after the colon separating a pseudoclass from the name of the element to which it is applied is an error that prevents the pseudoclass from being applied properly.

Line 14 causes all `em` elements that are children of `li` elements to be bold. In the screen output of Fig. 5.3, note that Go to the (contained in an `em` element in line 37) does not appear bold, because the `em` element is not in an `li` element. However, the `em` element containing with mushrooms (line 34) is nested in an `li` element; therefore, it is formatted in bold. The syntax for applying rules to multiple elements is similar. In line 15, we separate the selectors with a comma to apply an underline style rule to all `h1` and all `em` elements.

Line 16 assigns a left margin of 20 pixels to all `ul` elements. We will discuss the `margin` properties in detail in Section 5.9. A pixel is a **relative-length measurement**—it varies in size, based on screen resolution. Other relative lengths include em (the *M*-height of the font, which is usually set to the height of an uppercase *M*), ex (the *x*-height of the font, which is usually set to the height of a lowercase *x*) and percentages (e.g., `font-size: 50%`). To set an element to display text at 150 percent of its default text size, the author could use the syntax

```
font-size: 1.5em
```

Alternatively, you could use

```
font-size: 150%
```

Other units of measurement available in CSS are absolute-length measurements—i.e., units that do not vary in size based on the system. These units are in (inches), cm (centimeters), mm (millimeters), pt (points; 1 pt = 1/72 in) and pc (picas; 1 pc = 12 pt). Line 17 specifies that all nested unordered lists (`ul` elements that are descendants of `ul` elements) are to have font size `.8em`. [*Note:* When setting a style property that takes a measurement (e.g. `font-size`, `margin-left`), no units are necessary if the value is zero.]

Good Programming Practice 5.2

Whenever possible, use relative-length measurements. If you use absolute-length measurements, your document may not be readable on some client browsers (e.g., wireless phones).

5.5 Linking External Style Sheets

Style sheets are a convenient way to create a document with a uniform theme. With external style sheets (i.e., separate documents that contain only CSS rules), you can provide a uniform look and feel to an entire website. Different pages on a site can all use the same style sheet. When changes to the styles are required, the author needs to modify only a single CSS file to make style changes across the entire website. Note that while embedded style sheets separate content from presentation, both are still contained in a single file, preventing a web designer and a content author from working in parallel. External style sheets solve this problem by separating the content and style into separate files.

Software Engineering Observation 5.1

Always use an external style sheet when developing a website with multiple pages. External style sheets separate content from presentation, allowing for more consistent look-and-feel, more efficient development, and better performance.

Figure 5.4 presents an external style sheet. Lines 1–2 are CSS comments. Like XHTML comments, CSS comments describe the content of a CSS document. Comments may be placed in any type of CSS code (i.e., inline styles, embedded style sheets and external style sheets) and always start with /* and end with */. Text between these delimiters is ignored by the browser.

```
1  /* Fig. 5.4: styles.css */
2  /* External stylesheet */
3
```

Fig. 5.4 | External style sheet. (Part 1 of 2.)

```
body     { font-family: arial, helvetica, sans-serif }

a.nodec  { text-decoration: none }

a:hover  { text-decoration: underline }

li em    { font-weight: bold }

h1, em   { text-decoration: underline }

ul       { margin-left: 20px }

ul ul    { font-size: .8em; }
```

Fig. 5.4 | External style sheet. (Part 2 of 2.)

Figure 5.5 contains an XHTML document that references the external style sheet in Fig. 5.4. Lines 10–11 (Fig. 5.5) show a `link` element that uses the `rel` attribute to specify a **relationship** between the current document and another document. In this case, we declare the linked document to be a `stylesheet` for this document. The `type` attribute specifies the MIME type of the related document as `text/css`. The `href` attribute provides the URL for the document containing the style sheet. In this case, `styles.css` is in the same directory as `external.html`.

```
1  <?xml version = "1.0" encoding = "utf-8"?>
2  <!DOCTYPE html PUBLIC "-//W3C//DTD XHTML 1.0 Strict//EN"
3     "http://www.w3.org/TR/xhtml1/DTD/xhtml1-strict.dtd">
4
5  <!-- Fig. 5.6: external.html -->
6  <!-- Linking an external style sheet. -->
7  <html xmlns = "http://www.w3.org/1999/xhtml">
8     <head>
9        <title>Linking External Style Sheets</title>
10       <link rel = "stylesheet" type = "text/css"
11          href = "styles.css" />
12    </head>
13    <body>
14       <h1>Shopping list for <em>Monday</em>:</h1>
15
16       <ul>
17          <li>Milk</li>
18          <li>Bread
19             <ul>
20                <li>White bread</li>
21                <li>Rye bread</li>
22                <li>Whole wheat bread</li>
23             </ul>
24          </li>
25          <li>Rice</li>
26          <li>Potatoes</li>
```

Fig. 5.5 | Linking an external style sheet. (Part 1 of 2.)

```
            <li>Pizza <em>with mushrooms</em></li>
         </ul>

         <p><em>Go to the</em>
            <a class = "nodec" href = "http://www.deitel.com">
               Grocery store</a>
         </p>
      </body>
   </html>
```

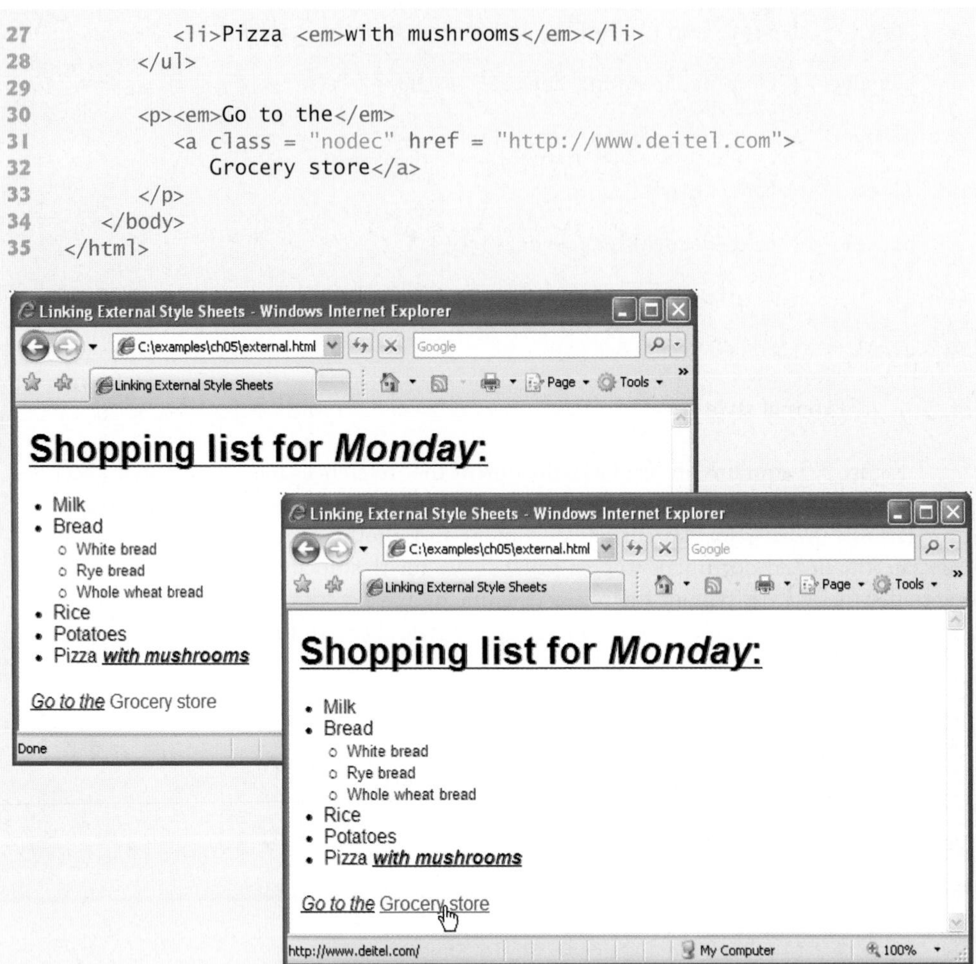

Fig. 5.5 | Linking an external style sheet. (Part 2 of 2.)

Software Engineering Observation 5.2

External style sheets are reusable. Creating them once and reusing them reduces programming effort.

Performance Tip 5.1

Reusing external style sheets reduces load time and bandwidth usage on a server, since the style sheet can be downloaded once, stored by the web browser, and applied to all pages on a website.

5.6 Positioning Elements

Before CSS, controlling the positioning of elements in an XHTML document was difficult—the browser determined positioning. CSS introduced the `position` property and a capability called **absolute positioning**, which gives authors greater control over how document elements are displayed. Figure 5.6 demonstrates absolute positioning.

```
<?xml version = "1.0" encoding = "utf-8"?>
<!DOCTYPE html PUBLIC "-//W3C//DTD XHTML 1.0 Strict//EN"
   "http://www.w3.org/TR/xhtml1/DTD/xhtml1-strict.dtd">

<!-- Fig. 5.6: positioning.html -->
<!-- Absolute positioning of elements. -->
<html xmlns = "http://www.w3.org/1999/xhtml">
   <head>
      <title>Absolute Positioning</title>
      <style type = "text/css">
         .bgimg   { position: absolute;
                    top: 0px;
                    left: 0px;
                    z-index: 1 }
         .fgimg   { position: absolute;
                    top: 25px;
                    left: 100px;
                    z-index: 2 }
         .text    { position: absolute;
                    top: 25px;
                    left: 100px;
                    z-index: 3;
                    font-size: 20pt;
                    font-family: tahoma, geneva, sans-serif }
      </style>
   </head>
   <body>
      <p><img src = "bgimg.gif" class = "bgimg"
         alt = "First positioned image" /></p>

      <p><img src = "fgimg.gif" class = "fgimg"
         alt = "Second positioned image" /></p>

      <p class = "text">Positioned Text</p>
   </body>
</html>
```

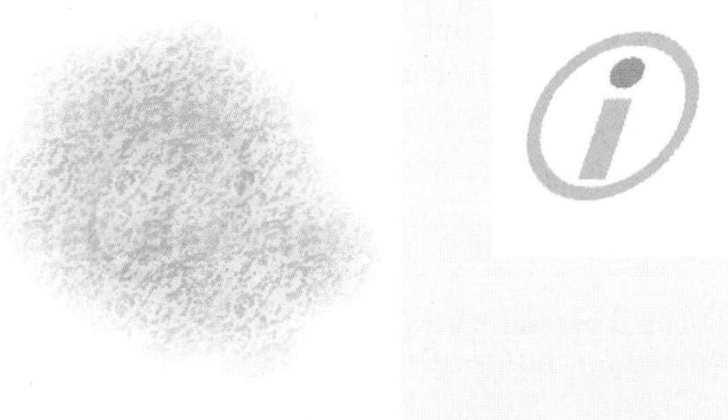

Fig. 5.6 | Absolute positioning of elements. (Part 1 of 2.)

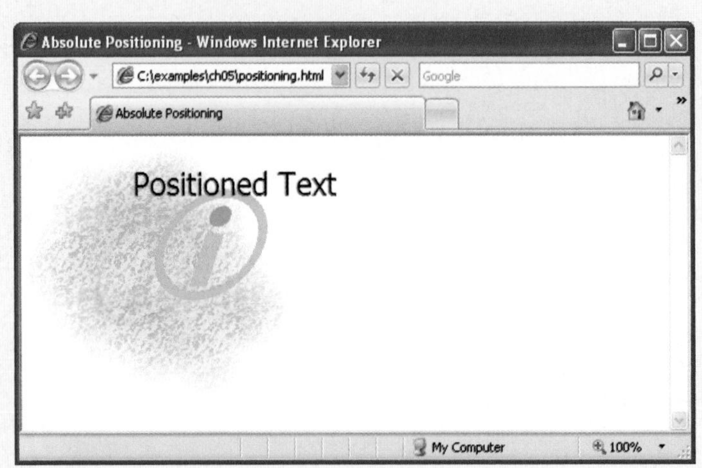

Fig. 5.6 | Absolute positioning of elements. (Part 2 of 2.)

Normally, elements are positioned on the page in the order that they appear in the XHTML document. Lines 11–14 define a style called `bgimg` for the first `img` element (`i.gif`) on the page. Specifying an element's `position` as `absolute` removes the element from the normal flow of elements on the page, instead positioning it according to the distance from the `top`, `left`, `right` or `bottom` margins of its containing block-level element (i.e., an element such as `body` or `p`). Here, we position the element to be `0` pixels away from both the `top` and `left` margins of its containing element. In line 28, this style is applied to the image, which is contained in a `p` element.

The `z-index` property allows you to layer overlapping elements properly. Elements that have higher `z-index` values are displayed in front of elements with lower `z-index` values. In this example, `i.gif` has the lowest `z-index` (`1`), so it displays in the background. The `.fgimg` CSS rule in lines 15–18 gives the circle image (`circle.gif`, in lines 31–32) a `z-index` of 2, so it displays in front of `i.gif`. The `p` element in line 34 (`Positioned Text`) is given a `z-index` of 3 in line 22, so it displays in front of the other two. If you do not specify a `z-index` or if elements have the same `z-index` value, the elements are placed from background to foreground in the order they are encountered in the document.

Absolute positioning is not the only way to specify page layout. Figure 5.7 demonstrates relative positioning, in which elements are positioned relative to other elements.

```
<?xml version = "1.0" encoding = "utf-8"?>
<!DOCTYPE html PUBLIC "-//W3C//DTD XHTML 1.0 Strict//EN"
   "http://www.w3.org/TR/xhtml1/DTD/xhtml1-strict.dtd">

<!-- Fig. 5.7: positioning2.html -->
<!-- Relative positioning of elements. -->
<html xmlns = "http://www.w3.org/1999/xhtml">
   <head>
      <title>Relative Positioning</title>
```

Fig. 5.7 | Relative positioning of elements. (Part 1 of 2.)

```
10        <style type = "text/css">
11           p            { font-size: 1.3em;
12                          font-family: verdana, arial, sans-serif }
13           span         { color: red;
14                          font-size: .6em;
15                          height: 1em }
16           .super       { position: relative;
17                          top: -1ex }
18           .sub         { position: relative;
19                          bottom: -1ex }
20           .shiftleft   { position: relative;
21                          left: -1ex }
22           .shiftright  { position: relative;
23                          right: -1ex }
24        </style>
25     </head>
26     <body>
27        <p>The text at the end of this sentence
28        <span class = "super">is in superscript</span>.</p>
29
30        <p>The text at the end of this sentence
31        <span class = "sub">is in subscript</span>.</p>
32
33        <p>The text at the end of this sentence
34        <span class = "shiftleft">is shifted left</span>.</p>
35
36        <p>The text at the end of this sentence
37        <span class = "shiftright">is shifted right</span>.</p>
38     </body>
39  </html>
```

Fig. 5.7 | Relative positioning of elements. (Part 2 of 2.)

Setting the `position` property to `relative`, as in class `super` (lines 16–17), lays out the element on the page and offsets it by the specified `top`, `bottom`, `left` or `right` value. Unlike absolute positioning, relative positioning keeps elements in the general flow of elements on the page, so positioning is relative to other elements in the flow. Recall that ex (line 17) is the *x*-height of a font, a relative-length measurement typically equal to the height of a lowercase *x*.

Common Programming Error 5.2

Because relative positioning keeps elements in the flow of text in your documents, be careful to avoid unintentionally overlapping text.

Inline and Block-Level Elements

We introduce the `span` element in line 28. Lines 13–15 define the CSS rule for all `span` elements. The `height` of the `span` determines how much vertical space the span will occupy. The `font-size` determines the size of the text inside the `span`.

Element `span` is a grouping element—it does not apply any inherent formatting to its contents. Its primary purpose is to apply CSS rules or `id` attributes to a section of text. Element `span` is an inline-level element—it applies formatting to text without changing the flow of the document. Examples of inline elements include `span`, `img`, `a`, `em` and `strong`. The `div` element is also a grouping element, but it is a block-level element. This means it is displayed on its own line and has a virtual box around it. Examples of block-level elements include `div`, `p` and heading elements (`h1` through `h6`). We'll discuss inline and block-level elements in more detail in Section 5.9.

5.7 Backgrounds

CSS provides control over the background of block-level elements. CSS can set a background color or add background images to XHTML elements. Figure 5.8 adds a corporate logo to the bottom-right corner of the document. This logo stays fixed in the corner even when the user scrolls up or down the screen.

```
<?xml version = "1.0" encoding = "utf-8"?>
<!DOCTYPE html PUBLIC "-//W3C//DTD XHTML 1.0 Strict//EN"
   "http://www.w3.org/TR/xhtml1/DTD/xhtml1-strict.dtd">

<!-- Fig. 5.8: background.html -->
<!-- Adding background images and indentation. -->
<html xmlns = "http://www.w3.org/1999/xhtml">
   <head>
      <title>Background Images</title>
      <style type = "text/css">
         body  { background-image: url(logo.gif);
                 background-position: bottom right;
                 background-repeat: no-repeat;
                 background-attachment: fixed;
                 background-color: #eeeeee }
         p     { font-size: 18pt;
                 color: #1144AA;
                 text-indent: 1em;
                 font-family: arial, sans-serif; }
         .dark { font-weight: bold }
      </style>
   </head>
```

Fig. 5.8 | Adding background images and indentation. (Part 1 of 2.)

```
23     <body>
24        <p>
25        This example uses the background-image,
26        background-position and background-attachment
27        styles to place the <span class = "dark">Deitel
28        &amp; Associates, Inc.</span> logo in the bottom,
29        right corner of the page. Notice how the logo
30        stays in the proper position when you resize the
31        browser window. The background-color fills in where
32        there is no image.
33        </p>
34     </body>
35  </html>
```

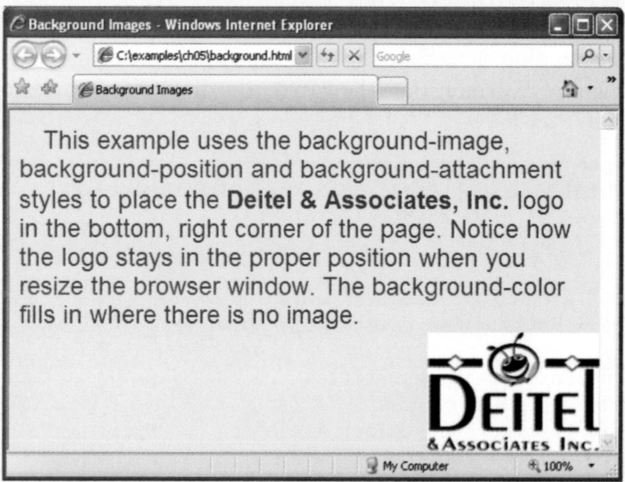

Fig. 5.8 | Adding background images and indentation. (Part 2 of 2.)

The **`background-image`** property (line 11) specifies the image URL for the image `logo.gif` in the format `url(`*fileLocation*`)`. You can also set the **`background-color`** property in case the image is not found (and to fill in where the image does not cover).

The **`background-position`** property (line 12) places the image on the page. The keywords `top`, `bottom`, `center`, `left` and `right` are used individually or in combination for vertical and horizontal positioning. An image can be positioned using lengths by specifying the horizontal length followed by the vertical length. For example, to position the image as horizontally centered (positioned at 50 percent of the distance across the screen) and 30 pixels from the top, use

```
background-position: 50% 30px;
```

The **`background-repeat`** property (line 13) controls background image **tiling**, which places multiple copies of the image next to each other to fill the background. Here, we set the tiling to `no-repeat` to display only one copy of the background image. Other values include `repeat` (the default) to tile the image vertically and horizontally, `repeat-x` to tile the image only horizontally or `repeat-y` to tile the image only vertically.

The final property setting, **`background-attachment: fixed`** (line 14), fixes the image in the position specified by **`background-position`**. Scrolling the browser window will not move the image from its position. The default value, `scroll`, moves the image as the user scrolls through the document.

Line 18 uses the **`text-indent`** property to indent the first line of text in the element by a specified amount, in this case `1em`. An author might use this property to create a web page that reads more like a novel, in which the first line of every paragraph is indented.

Another CSS property that formats text is the **`font-style`** property, which allows the developer to set text to `none`, `italic` or `oblique` (`oblique` is simply more slanted than italic—the browser will default to `italic` if the system or font does not support oblique text).

5.8 Element Dimensions

In addition to positioning elements, CSS rules can specify the actual dimensions of each page element. Figure 5.9 demonstrates how to set the dimensions of elements.

```
<?xml version = "1.0" encoding = "utf-8"?>
<!DOCTYPE html PUBLIC "-//W3C//DTD XHTML 1.0 Strict//EN"
   "http://www.w3.org/TR/xhtml1/DTD/xhtml1-strict.dtd">

<!-- Fig. 5.9: width.html -->
<!-- Element dimensions and text alignment. -->
<html xmlns = "http://www.w3.org/1999/xhtml">
   <head>
      <title>Box Dimensions</title>
      <style type = "text/css">
         div { background-color: #aaccff;
               margin-bottom: .5em;
               font-family: arial, helvetica, sans-serif }
      </style>
   </head>
   <body>
      <div style = "width: 20%">Here is some
      text that goes in a box which is
      set to stretch across twenty percent
      of the width of the screen.</div>

      <div style = "width: 80%; text-align: center">
      Here is some CENTERED text that goes in a box
      which is set to stretch across eighty percent of
      the width of the screen.</div>

      <div style = "width: 20%; height: 150px; overflow: scroll">
      This box is only twenty percent of
      the width and has a fixed height.
      What do we do if it overflows? Set the
      overflow property to scroll!</div>
   </body>
</html>
```

Fig. 5.9 | Element dimensions and text alignment. (Part 1 of 2.)

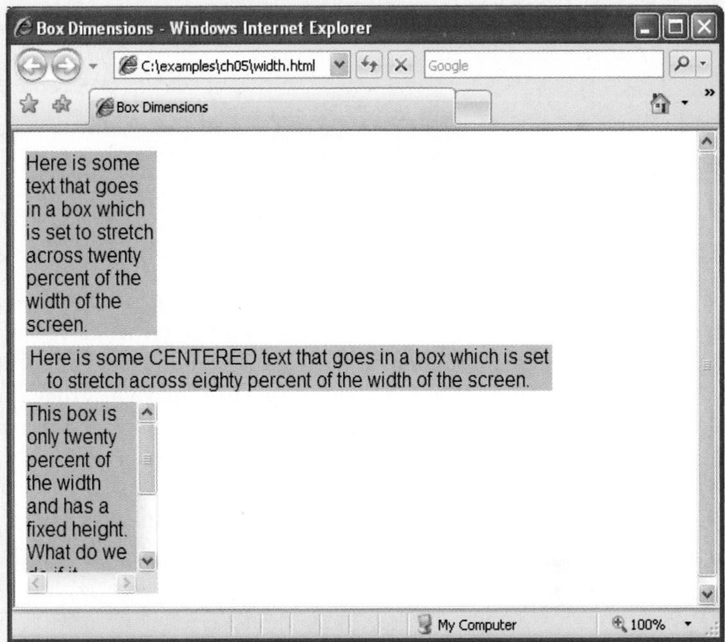

Fig. 5.9 | Element dimensions and text alignment. (Part 2 of 2.)

The inline style in line 17 illustrates how to set the **width** of an element on screen; here, we indicate that the `div` element should occupy 20 percent of the screen width. The height of an element can be set similarly, using the **height** property. The `height` and `width` values also can be specified as relative or absolute lengths. For example,

```
width: 10em
```

sets the element's width to 10 times the font size. Most elements are left aligned by default; however, this alignment can be altered to position the element elsewhere. Line 22 sets text in the element to be `center` aligned; other values for the **text-align** property include `left` and `right`.

In the third `div`, we specify a percentage height and a pixel width. One problem with setting both dimensions of an element is that the content inside the element can exceed the set boundaries, in which case the element is simply made large enough for all the content to fit. However, in line 27, we set the **overflow** property to `scroll`, a setting that adds scroll bars if the text overflows the boundaries.

5.9 Box Model and Text Flow

All block-level XHTML elements have a virtual box drawn around them based on what is known as the **box model**. When the browser renders elements using the box model, the content of each element is surrounded by **padding**, a **border** and a **margin** (Fig. 5.10).

CSS controls the border using three properties: **border-width**, **border-color** and **border-style**. We illustrate these three properties in Fig. 5.11.

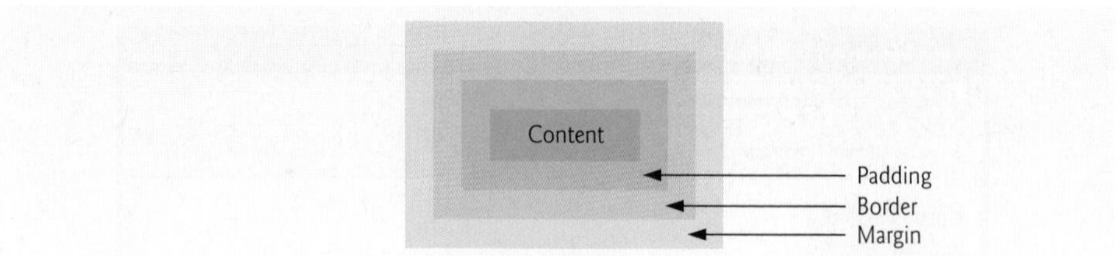

Fig. 5.10 | Box model for block-level elements.

Property `border-width` may be set to any valid CSS length (e.g., `em`, `ex`, `px`, etc.) or to the predefined value of `thin`, `medium` or `thick`. The **`border-color` property** sets the color. [*Note:* This property has different meanings for different style borders.] The `border-style` options are `none`, `hidden`, `dotted`, `dashed`, `solid`, `double`, `groove`, `ridge`, `inset` and `outset`. Borders `groove` and `ridge` have opposite effects, as do `inset` and `outset`. When border-style is set to none, no border is rendered.

```
<?xml version = "1.0" encoding = "utf-8"?>
<!DOCTYPE html PUBLIC "-//W3C//DTD XHTML 1.0 Strict//EN"
   "http://www.w3.org/TR/xhtml1/DTD/xhtml1-strict.dtd">

<!-- Fig. 5.11: borders.html -->
<!-- Borders of block-level elements. -->
<html xmlns = "http://www.w3.org/1999/xhtml">
   <head>
      <title>Borders</title>
      <style type = "text/css">
         div     { text-align: center;
                   width: 50%;
                   position: relative;
                   left: 25%;
                   border-width: 4px }
         .medium { border-width: medium }
         .thin   { border-width: thin }
         .solid  { border-style: solid }
         .double { border-style: double }
         .groove { border-style: groove }
         .inset  { border-style: inset }
         .outset { border-style: outset }
         .dashed { border-style: dashed }
         .red    { border-color: red }
         .blue   { border-color: blue }
      </style>
   </head>
   <body>
      <div class = "solid">Solid border</div><hr />
      <div class = "double">Double border</div><hr />
      <div class = "groove">Groove border</div><hr />
      <div class = "inset">Inset border</div><hr />
      <div class = "dashed">Dashed border</div><hr />
```

Fig. 5.11 | Borders of block-level elements. (Part 1 of 2.)

```
34         <div class = "thin red solid">Thin Red Solid border</div><hr />
35         <div class = "medium blue outset">Medium Blue Outset border</div
36      </body>
37   </html>
```

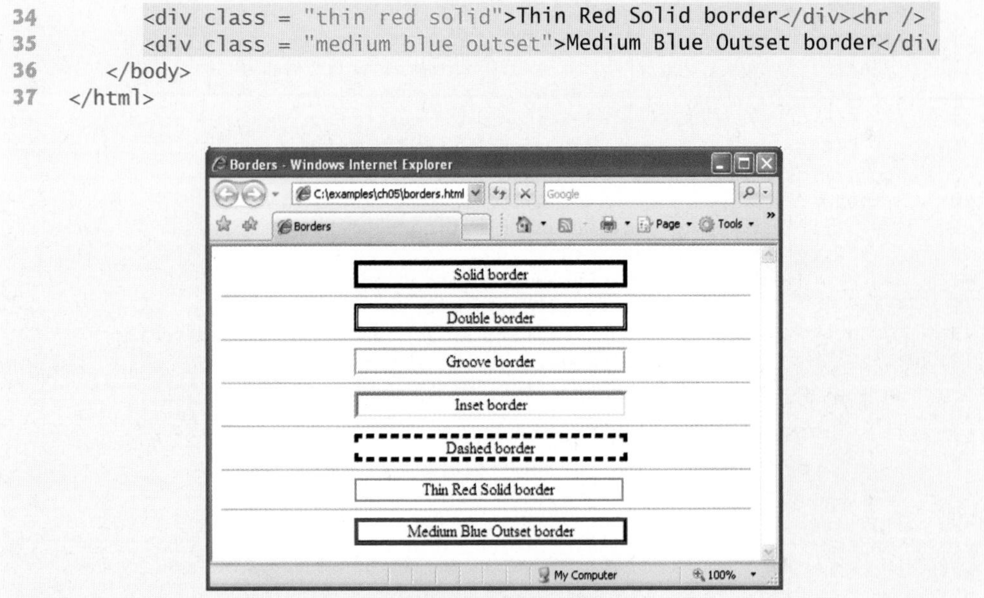

Fig. 5.11 | Borders of block-level elements. (Part 2 of 2.)

Each border property may be set for an individual side of the box (e.g., `border-top-style` or `border-left-color`). Note that we assign more than one class to an XHTML element by separating multiple class names with spaces, as shown in lines 36–37.

As we have seen with absolute positioning, it is possible to remove elements from the normal flow of text. **Floating** allows you to move an element to one side of the screen; other content in the document then flows around the floated element. Figure 5.12 demonstrates how floats and the box model can be used to control the layout of an entire page.

Looking at the XHTML code, we can see that the general structure of this document consists of a header and two main sections. Each section contains a subheading and a paragraph of text.

Block-level elements (such as `div`s) render with a line break before and after their content, so the header and two sections will render vertically one on top of another. In the absence of our styles, the subheading `div`s would also stack vertically on top of the text in the `p` tags. However, in line 24 we set the `float` property to `right` in the class `floated`, which is applied to the subheadings. This causes each subheading `div` to float to the right edge of its containing element, while the paragraph of text will flow around it.

Line 17 assigns a margin of `.5em` to all paragraph tags. The **`margin` property** sets the space between the outside of the border and all other content on the page. In line 21, we assign `.2em` of padding to the floated `div`s. The **`padding` property** determines the distance between the content inside an element and the inside of the element's border. Margins for individual sides of an element can be specified (lines 22–23) by using the properties **`margin-top`**, **`margin-right`**, **`margin-left`** and **`margin-bottom`**. Padding can be specified in the same way, using **`padding-top`**, **`padding-right`**, **`padding-left`** and **`padding-bottom`**. To see the effects of margins and padding, try putting the margin and padding properties inside comments and observing the difference.

```
<?xml version = "1.0" encoding = "utf-8"?>
<!DOCTYPE html PUBLIC "-//W3C//DTD XHTML 1.0 Strict//EN"
   "http://www.w3.org/TR/xhtml1/DTD/xhtml1-strict.dtd">

<!-- Fig. 5.12: floating.html -->
<!-- Floating elements. -->
<html xmlns = "http://www.w3.org/1999/xhtml">
   <head>
      <title>Flowing Text Around Floating Elements</title>
      <style type = "text/css">
         div.heading { background-color: #bbddff;
                       text-align: center;
                       font-family: arial, helvetica, sans-serif;
                       padding: .2em }
         p           { text-align: justify;
                       font-family: verdana, geneva, sans-serif;
                       margin: .5em }
         div.floated { background-color: #eeeeee;
                       font-size: 1.5em;
                       font-family: arial, helvetica, sans-serif;
                       padding: .2em;
                       margin-left: .5em;
                       margin-bottom: .5em;
                       float: right;
                       text-align: right;
                       width: 50% }
         div.section { border: 1px solid #bbddff }
      </style>
   </head>
   <body>
      <div class = "heading"><img src = "deitel.png" alt = "Deitel" />
         </div>
      <div class = "section">
         <div class = "floated">Corporate Training and Publishing</div>
         <p>Deitel &amp; Associates, Inc. is an internationally
         recognized corporate training and publishing organization
         specializing in programming languages, Internet/World
         Wide Web technology and object technology education.
         The company provides courses on Java, C++, Visual Basic, C#,
         C, Internet and web programming, Object
         Technology, and more.</p>
      </div>
      <div class = "section">
         <div class = "floated">Leading-Edge Programming Textbooks</div>
         <p>Through its publishing
         partnership with Prentice Hall, Deitel &amp; Associates,
         Inc. publishes leading-edge programming textbooks,
         professional books, interactive CD-ROM-based multimedia
         Cyber Classrooms, satellite courses and DVD and web-based
         video courses.</p>
      </div>
   </body>
</html>
```

Fig. 5.12 | Floating elements. (Part 1 of 2.)

Fig. 5.12 | Floating elements. (Part 2 of 2.)

In line 27, we assign a border to the `section` boxes using a shorthand declaration of the border properties. CSS allows shorthand assignments of borders to allow you to define all three border properties in one line. The syntax for this shorthand is `border: <width> <style> <color>`. Our border is one pixel thick, `solid`, and the same color as the `background-color` property of the heading `div` (line 11). This allows the border to blend with the header and makes the page appear as one box with a line dividing its sections.

5.10 Media Types

CSS media types allow a programmer to decide what a page should look like depending on the kind of media being used to display the page. The most common media type for a web page is the `screen` media type, which is a standard computer screen. Other media types in CSS 2 include `handheld`, `braille`, `aural` and `print`. The `handheld` medium is designed for mobile Internet devices, while `braille` is for machines that can read or print web pages in braille. `aural` styles allow the programmer to give a speech-synthesizing web browser more information about the content of the web page. This allows the browser to present a web page in a sensible manner to a visually impaired person. The `print` media type affects a web page's appearance when it is printed. For a complete list of CSS media types, see `http://www.w3.org/TR/REC-CSS2/media.html#media-types`.

Media types allow a programmer to decide how a page should be presented on any one of these media without affecting the others. Figure 5.13 gives a simple example that applies one set of styles when the document is viewed on the screen, and another when the document is printed. To see the difference, look at the screen captures below the paragraph or use the **Print Preview** feature in Internet Explorer or Firefox.

In line 11, we begin a block of styles that applies to all media types, declared by `@media all` and enclosed in curly braces (`{` and `}`). In lines 13–18, we define some styles for all media types. Lines 20–27 set styles to be applied only when the page is printed, beginning with the declaration `@media print` and enclosed in curly braces.

The styles we applied for all media types look nice on a screen but would not look good on a printed page. A colored background would use a lot of ink, and a black-and-white printer may print a page that's hard to read because there isn't enough contrast

```
1  <?xml version = "1.0" encoding = "utf-8"?>
2  <!DOCTYPE html PUBLIC "-//W3C//DTD XHTML 1.0 Strict//EN"
3     "http://www.w3.org/TR/xhtml1/DTD/xhtml1-strict.dtd">
4  
5  <!-- Fig. 5.13: mediatypes.html -->
6  <!-- CSS media types. -->
7  <html xmlns = "http://www.w3.org/1999/xhtml">
8     <head>
9        <title>Media Types</title>
10       <style type = "text/css">
11          @media all
12          {
13             body  { background-color: #4488aa }
14             h1    { font-family: verdana, helvetica, sans-serif;
15                     color: #aaffcc }
16             p     { font-size: 12pt;
17                     color: white;
18                     font-family: arial, sans-serif }
19          } /* end @media all declaration. */
20          @media print
21          {
22             body  { background-color: white }
23             h1    { color: #008844}
24             p     { font-size: 14pt;
25                     color: #4488aa;
26                     font-family: "times new roman", times, serif }
27          } /* end @media print declaration. */
28       </style>
29    </head>
30    <body>
31       <h1>CSS Media Types Example</h1>
32 
33       <p>
34       This example uses CSS media types to vary how the page
35       appears in print and how it appears on any other media.
36       This text will appear one font on the screen and a
37       different font on paper or in a print preview. To see
38       the difference in Internet Explorer, go to the Print
39       menu and select Print Preview. In Firefox, select Print
40       Preview from the File menu.
41       </p>
42    </body>
43 </html>
```

Fig. 5.13 | CSS media types. (Part 1 of 2.)

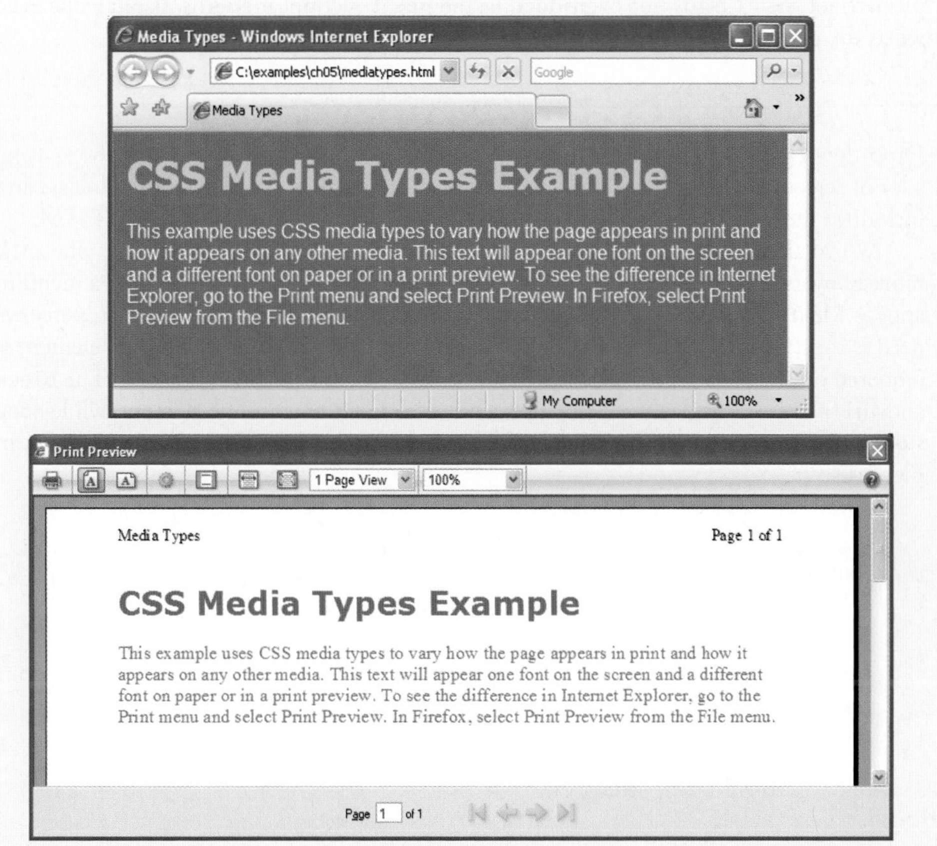

Fig. 5.13 | CSS media types. (Part 2 of 2.)

between the colors. Also, `sans-serif` fonts like `arial`, `helvetica`, and `geneva` are easier to read on a screen, while `serif` fonts like `times new roman` are easier to read on paper.

Look-and-Feel Observation 5.1

Pages with dark background colors and light text use a lot of ink and may be difficult to read when printed, especially on a black-and white-printer. Use the `print` *media type to avoid this.*

Look-and-Feel Observation 5.2

In general, sans-serif fonts look better on a screen, while serif fonts look better on paper. The `print` *media type allows your web page to display sans-serif font on a screen and change to a serif font when it is printed.*

To solve these problems, we apply specific styles for the `print` media type. We change the `background-color` of the `body`, the `color` of the `h1` tag, and the `font-size`, `color`, and `font-family` of the `p` tag to be more suited for printing and viewing on paper. Notice that most of these styles conflict with the declarations in the section for all media types. Since the `print` media type has higher specificity than `all` media types, the `print` styles override the styles for all media types when the page is printed. Since the `font-family` property of the `h1` tag is not overridden in the `print` section, it retains its old value even when the page is printed.

5.11 Building a CSS Drop-Down Menu

Drop-down menus are a good way to provide navigation links on a website without using a lot of screen space. In this section, we take a second look at the `:hover` pseudoclass and introduce the `display` property to create a drop-down menu using CSS and XHTML.

We've already seen the `:hover` pseudoclass used to change a link's style when the mouse hovers over it. We will use this feature in a more advanced way to cause a menu to appear when the mouse hovers over a menu button. The other important property we need is the **`display`** property. This allows a programmer to decide whether an element is rendered on the page or not. Possible values include `block`, `inline` and `none`. The `block` and `inline` values display the element as a block element or an inline element, while `none` stops the element from being rendered. The code for the drop-down menu is shown in Fig. 5.14.

```
<?xml version = "1.0" encoding = "utf-8"?>
<!DOCTYPE html PUBLIC "-//W3C//DTD XHTML 1.0 Strict//EN"
   "http://www.w3.org/TR/xhtml1/DTD/xhtml1-strict.dtd">

<!-- Fig. 5.14: dropdown.html -->
<!-- CSS drop-down menu. -->
<html xmlns = "http://www.w3.org/1999/xhtml">
   <head>
      <title>
         Drop-Down Menu
      </title>
      <style type = "text/css">
         body              { font-family: arial, sans-serif }
         div.menu          { font-weight: bold;
                             color: white;
                             border: 2px solid #225599;
                             text-align: center;
                             width: 10em;
                             background-color: #225599 }
         div.menu:hover a  { display: block }
         div.menu a        { display: none;
                             border-top: 2px solid #225599;
                             background-color: white;
                             width: 10em;
                             text-decoration: none;
                             color: black }
         div.menu a:hover  { background-color: #dfeeff }
      </style>
   </head>
   <body>
      <div class = "menu">Menu
         <a href = "#">Home</a>
         <a href = "#">News</a>
```

Fig. 5.14 | CSS drop-down menu. (Part 1 of 2.)

```
34             <a href = "#">Articles</a>
35             <a href = "#">Blog</a>
36             <a href = "#">Contact</a>
37          </div>
38       </body>
39    </html>
```

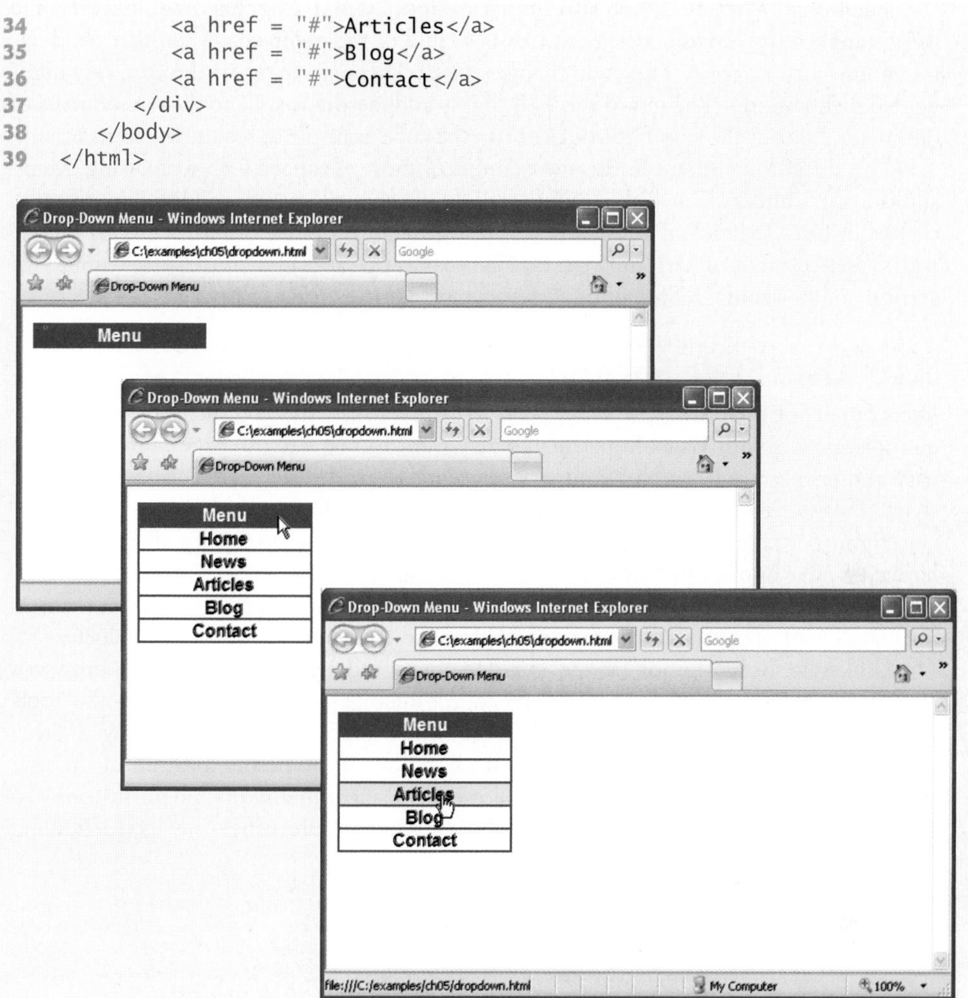

Fig. 5.14 | CSS drop-down menu. (Part 2 of 2.)

First let's look at the XHTML code. In lines 31–37, a `div` of class `menu` has the text "Menu" and five links inside it. This is our drop-down menu. The behavior we want is as follows: the text that says "Menu" should be the only thing visible on the page, unless the mouse is over the menu `div`. When the mouse cursor hovers over the menu `div`, we want the links to appear below the menu for the user to choose from.

To see how we get this functionality, let's look at the CSS code. There are two lines that give us the drop-down functionality. Line 21 selects all the links inside the menu `div` and sets their `display` value to `none`. This instructs the browser not to render the links. The other important style is in line 20. The selectors in this line are similar to those in line 21, except that this line selects only the `a` (anchor) elements that are children of a menu `div` that has the mouse over it. The `display: block` in this line means that when the mouse is over the menu `div`, the links inside it will be displayed as block-level elements.

The selectors in line 27 are also similar to lines 20 and 21. This time, however, the style is applied only to any a element that is a child of the menu div when that child has the mouse cursor over it. This style changes the background-color of the currently highlighted menu option. The rest of the CSS simply adds aesthetic style to the components of our menu. Look at the screen captures or run the code example to see the menu in action.

This drop-down menu is just one example of more advanced CSS formatting. Many additional resources are available online for CSS navigation menus and lists. Specifically, check out List-o-Matic, an automatic CSS list generator located at www.accessify.com/tools-and-wizards/developer-tools/list-o-matic/ and Dynamic Drive's library of vertical and horizontal CSS menus at www.dynamicdrive.com/style/.

5.12 User Style Sheets

Users can define their own user style sheets to format pages based on their preferences. For example, people with visual impairments may want to increase the page's text size. Web page authors need to be careful not to inadvertently override user preferences with defined styles. This section discusses possible conflicts between author styles and user styles.

Figure 5.15 contains an author style. The font-size is set to 9pt for all <p> tags that have class note applied to them.

User style sheets are external style sheets. Figure 5.16 shows a user style sheet that sets the body's font-size to 20pt, color to yellow and background-color to #000080.

User style sheets are not linked to a document; rather, they are set in the browser's options. To add a user style sheet in IE7, select **Internet Options...**, located in the **Tools** menu. In the **Internet Options** dialog (Fig. 5.17) that appears, click **Accessibility...**, check the **Format documents using my style sheet** checkbox, and type the location of the user style sheet. Internet Explorer 7 applies the user style sheet to any document it loads. To add a user style sheet in Firefox, find your Firefox profile using the instructions at

```
<?xml version = "1.0" encoding = "utf-8"?>
<!DOCTYPE html PUBLIC "-//W3C//DTD XHTML 1.0 Strict//EN"
   "http://www.w3.org/TR/xhtml1/DTD/xhtml1-strict.dtd">

<!-- Fig. 5.15: user_absolute.html -->
<!-- pt measurement for text size. -->
<html xmlns = "http://www.w3.org/1999/xhtml">
   <head>
      <title>User Styles</title>
      <style type = "text/css">
         .note { font-size: 9pt }
      </style>
   </head>
   <body>
      <p>Thanks for visiting my website. I hope you enjoy it.
      </p><p class = "note">Please Note: This site will be
      moving soon. Please check periodically for updates.</p>
   </body>
</html>
```

Fig. 5.15 | pt measurement for text size. (Part 1 of 2.)

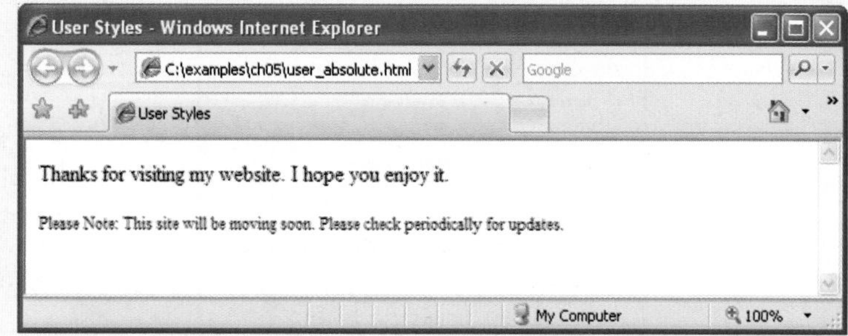

Fig. 5.15 | `pt` measurement for text size. (Part 2 of 2.)

```
/* Fig. 5.16: userstyles.css */
/* A user stylesheet */
body       { font-size: 20pt;
             color: yellow;
             background-color: #000080 }
```

Fig. 5.16 | User style sheet.

`www.mozilla.org/support/firefox/profile#locate` and place a style sheet called `userContent.css` in the `chrome` subdirectory.

The web page from Fig. 5.15 is displayed in Fig. 5.18, with the user style sheet from Fig. 5.16 applied.

In this example, if users define their own `font-size` in a user style sheet, the author style has a higher precedence and overrides the user style. The `9pt` font specified in the author style sheet overrides the `20pt` font specified in the user style sheet. This small font

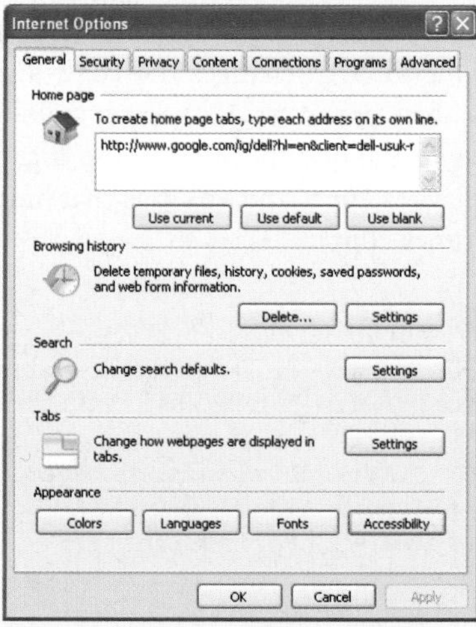

Fig. 5.17 | User style sheet in Internet Explorer 7. (Part 1 of 2.)

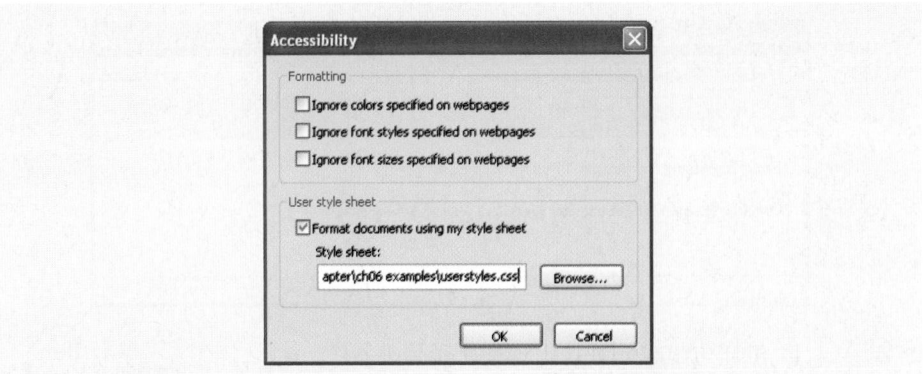

Fig. 5.17 | User style sheet in Internet Explorer 7. (Part 2 of 2.)

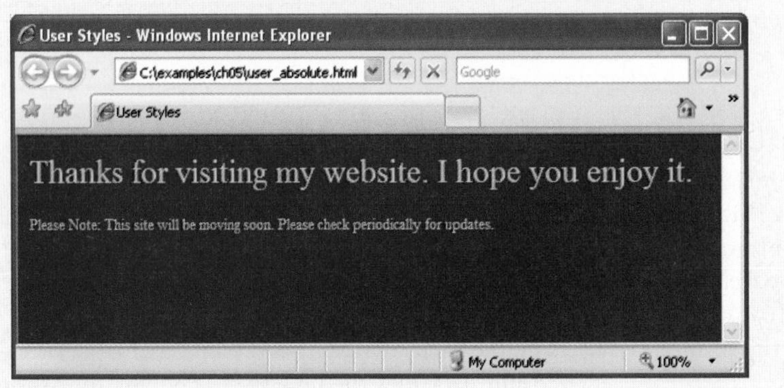

Fig. 5.18 | User style sheet applied with `pt` measurement.

may make pages difficult to read, especially for individuals with visual impairments. You can avoid this problem by using relative measurements (e.g., `em` or `ex`) instead of absolute measurements, such as `pt`. Figure 5.19 changes the `font-size` property to use a relative measurement (line 11) that does not override the user style set in Fig. 5.16. Instead, the font size displayed is relative to the one specified in the user style sheet. In this case, text enclosed in the <p> tag displays as `20pt`, and <p> tags that have class `note` applied to them are displayed in `15pt` (`.75` times `20pt`).

```
1  <?xml version = "1.0" encoding = "utf-8"?>
2  <!DOCTYPE html PUBLIC "-//W3C//DTD XHTML 1.0 Strict//EN"
3     "http://www.w3.org/TR/xhtml1/DTD/xhtml1-strict.dtd">
4
5  <!-- Fig. 5.19: user_relative.html -->
6  <!-- em measurement for text size. -->
7  <html xmlns = "http://www.w3.org/1999/xhtml">
8     <head>
9        <title>User Styles</title>
```

Fig. 5.19 | `em` measurement for text size. (Part 1 of 2.)

```
      <style type = "text/css">
         .note { font-size: .75em }
      </style>
   </head>
   <body>
      <p>Thanks for visiting my website. I hope you enjoy it.
      </p><p class = "note">Please Note: This site will be
      moving soon. Please check periodically for updates.</p>
   </body>
</html>
```

Fig. 5.19 | em measurement for text size. (Part 2 of 2.)

Figure 5.20 displays the web page from Fig. 5.19 with the user style sheet from Fig. 5.16 applied. Note that the second line of text displayed is larger than the same line of text in Fig. 5.18.

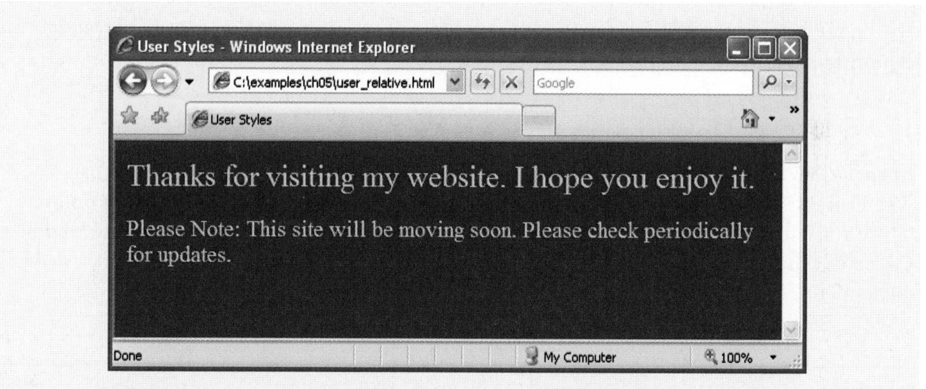

Fig. 5.20 | User style sheet applied with em measurement.

5.13 CSS 3

The W3C is currently developing CSS 3 and some browsers are beginning to implement some of the new features that will be in the CSS 3 specification. We discuss a few of the upcoming features that will most likely be included in CSS 3.

CSS 3 will allow for more advanced control of borders. In addition to the `border-style`, `border-color`, and `border-width` properties, you will be able to set multiple border colors, use images for borders, add shadows to boxes, and create borders with rounded corners.

Background images will be more versatile in CSS 3, allowing the programmer to set the size of a background image, specify an offset to determine where in the element the image should be positioned, and use multiple background images in one element. There will also be properties to set shadow effects on text and more options for text overflow when the text is too long to fit in its containing element.

Additional features will include resizable boxes, enhanced selectors, multicolumn layouts, and more developed speech (aural) styles. The Web Resources section points you to the Deitel CSS Resource Center, where you can find links to the latest information on the development and features of CSS 3.

5.14 Wrap-Up

In this chapter we introduced Cascading Style Sheets, a technology that allows us to create flexibility in formatting XHTML documents. We learned how to define styles inline, using embedded style sheets, and linking to external style sheets. We learned that external style sheets achieve true separation of content and presentation by putting each in its own file. We discussed how style sheets "cascade" to resolve conflicting style property definitions. We used absolute and relative positioning, background images and colors, and set the dimensions of XHTML elements.

We also learned about the box model and how to use borders, padding, and margins, as well as how to float elements to one side of the page. We provided examples of a web page with separate styles for the `print` media type, a drop-down menu using the `display` property, and learned more about accessibility and user styles.

XHTML and CSS are the basic technologies behind web pages. In the next chapter, we begin our treatment of JavaScript, which allows us to make more interactive and dynamic pages.

5.15 Web Resources

`http://www.deitel.com/css21`

The Deitel CSS Resource Center contains links to some of the best CSS information on the web. There you'll find categorized links to tutorials, references, code examples, demos, videos, and more. Check out the demos section for more advanced examples of layouts, menus, and other web page components.

Summary

Section 5.2 Inline Styles

- The inline style allows you to declare a style for an individual element by using the `style` attribute in the element's start tag.
- Each CSS property is followed by a colon and the value of the attribute. Multiple property declarations are separated by a semicolon.
- The `color` property sets text color. Color names and hexadecimal codes may be used as the value.

Section 5.3 Embedded Style Sheets

- Styles that are placed in a `style` element use selectors to apply style elements throughout the entire document.
- `style` element attribute `type` specifies the MIME type (the specific encoding format) of the style sheet. Style sheets use `text/css`.
- Each rule body in a style sheet begins and ends with a curly brace (`{` and `}`).
- The `font-weight` property specifies the "boldness" of text. Possible values are `bold`, `normal` (the default), `bolder` (bolder than bold text) and `lighter` (lighter than `normal` text).
- Boldness also can be specified with multiples of 100, from 100 to 900 (e.g., `100`, `200`, …, `900`). Text specified as `normal` is equivalent to `400`, and `bold` text is equivalent to `700`.
- Style-class declarations are preceded by a period and are applied to elements of the specific class. The `class` attribute applies a style class to an element.
- The CSS rules in a style sheet use the same format as inline styles: The property is followed by a colon (`:`) and the value of that property. Multiple properties are separated by semicolons (`;`).
- The `background-color` attribute specifies the background color of the element.
- The `font-family` attribute names a specific font that should be displayed. Generic font families allow authors to specify a type of font instead of a specific font, in case a browser does not support a specific font. The `font-size` property specifies the size used to render the font.

Section 5.4 Conflicting Styles

- Most styles are inherited from parent elements. Styles defined for children have higher specificity and take precedence over the parent's styles.
- Pseudoclasses give the author access to content not specifically declared in the document. The `hover` pseudoclass is activated when the user moves the mouse cursor over an element.
- The `text-decoration` property applies decorations to text in an element, such as `underline`, `overline`, `line-through` and `blink`.
- To apply rules to multiple elements, separate the elements with commas in the style sheet.
- To apply rules to only a certain type of element that is a child of another type, separate the element names with spaces.
- A pixel is a relative-length measurement: It varies in size based on screen resolution. Other relative lengths are `em`, `ex` and percentages.
- The other units of measurement available in CSS are absolute-length measurements—that is, units that do not vary in size. These units can be `in` (inches), `cm` (centimeters), `mm` (millimeters), `pt` (points; 1 `pt` = 1/72 `in`) or `pc` (picas; 1 `pc` = 12 `pt`).

Section 5.5 Linking External Style Sheets

- External linking of style sheets can create a uniform look for a website; separate pages can all use the same styles. Modifying a single style-sheet file makes changes to styles across an entire website.
- `link`'s `rel` attribute specifies a relationship between two documents. For style sheets, the `rel` attribute declares the linked document to be a `stylesheet` for the document. The `type` attribute specifies the MIME type of the related document as `text/css`. The `href` attribute provides the URL for the document containing the style sheet.

Section 5.6 Positioning Elements

- The CSS `position` property allows absolute positioning, which provides greater control over where on a page elements reside. Specifying an element's `position` as `absolute` removes it from the normal flow of elements on the page and positions it according to distance from the `top`, `left`, `right` or `bottom` margin of its parent element.

- The `z-index` property allows a developer to layer overlapping elements. Elements that have higher `z-index` values are displayed in front of elements with lower `z-index` values.
- Unlike absolute positioning, relative positioning keeps elements in the general flow on the page and offsets them by the specified `top`, `left`, `right` or `bottom` value.
- Element `span` is a grouping element—it does not apply any inherent formatting to its contents. Its primary purpose is to apply CSS rules or `id` attributes to a section of text.
- `span` is an inline-level element—it applies formatting to text without changing the flow of the document. Examples of inline elements include `span`, `img`, `a`, `em` and `strong`.
- The div element is also a grouping element, but it is a block-level element. This means it is displayed on its own line and has a virtual box around it. Examples of block-level elements include `div`, `p` and heading elements (`h1` through `h6`).

Section 5.7 Backgrounds

- Property background-image specifies the URL of the image, in the format url(fileLocation). The property background-position places the image on the page using the values top, bottom, center, left and right individually or in combination for vertical and horizontal positioning. You can also position by using lengths.
- The background-repeat property controls the tiling of the background image. Setting the tiling to no-repeat displays one copy of the background image on screen. The background-repeat property can be set to repeat (the default) to tile the image vertically and horizontally, to repeat-x to tile the image only horizontally or to repeat-y to tile the image only vertically.
- The property setting background-attachment: fixed fixes the image in the position specified by background-position. Scrolling the browser window will not move the image from its set position. The default value, scroll, moves the image as the user scrolls the window.
- The text-indent property indents the first line of text in the element by the specified amount.
- The font-style property allows you to set text to none, italic or oblique (oblique will default to italic if the system does not have a separate font file for oblique text, which is normally the case).

Section 5.8 Element Dimensions

- The dimensions of elements on a page can be set with CSS by using properties height and width.
- Text in an element can be centered using text-align; other values for the text-align property are left and right.
- One problem with setting both vertical and horizontal dimensions of an element is that the content inside the element might sometimes exceed the set boundaries, in which case the element must be made large enough for all the content to fit. However, a developer can set the overflow property to scroll; this setting adds scroll bars if the text overflows the boundaries set for it.

Section 5.9 Box Model and Text Flow

- The `border-width` property may be set to any of the CSS lengths or to the predefined value of `thin`, `medium` or `thick`.
- The `border-styles` available are `none`, `hidden`, `dotted`, `dashed`, `solid`, `double`, `groove`, `ridge`, `inset` and `outset`.
- The `border-color` property sets the color used for the border.
- The `class` attribute allows more than one class to be assigned to an XHTML element by separating each class name from the next with a space.

- Browsers normally place text and elements on screen in the order in which they appear in the XHTML file. Elements can be removed from the normal flow of text. Floating allows you to move an element to one side of the screen; other content in the document will then flow around the floated element.
- CSS uses a box model to render elements on screen. The content of each element is surrounded by padding, a border and margins. The properties of this box are easily adjusted.
- The `margin` property determines the distance between the element's edge and any outside text.
- Margins for individual sides of an element can be specified by using `margin-top`, `margin-right`, `margin-left` and `margin-bottom`.
- The `padding` property determines the distance between the content inside an element and the edge of the element. Padding also can be set for each side of the box by using `padding-top`, `padding-right`, `padding-left` and `padding-bottom`.

Section 5.10 Media Types

- CSS media types allow a programmer to decide what a page should look like depending on the kind of media being used to display the page. The most common media type for a web page is the `screen` media type, which is a standard computer screen.
- A block of styles that applies to all media types is declared by `@media all` and enclosed in curly braces. To create a block of styles that apply to a single media type such as `print`, use `@media print` and enclose the style rules in curly braces.
- Other media types in CSS 2 include `handheld`, `braille`, `aural` and `print`. The `handheld` medium is designed for mobile Internet devices, while `braille` is for machines that can read or print web pages in braille. `aural` styles allow the programmer to give a speech-synthesizing web browser more information about the content of the web page. The `print` media type affects a web page's appearance when it is printed.

Section 5.11 Building a CSS Drop-Down Menu

- The `:hover` pseudoclass is used to apply styles to an element when the mouse cursor is over it.
- The `display` property allows a programmer to decide if an element is displayed as a `block` element, `inline` element, or is not rendered at all (`none`).

Section 5.12 User Style Sheets

- Users can define their own user style sheets to format pages based on their preferences.
- Absolute font size measurements override user style sheets, while relative font sizes will yield to a user-defined style.

Section 5.13 CSS 3

- While CSS 2 is the current W3C Recommendation, CSS 3 is in development, and some browsers are beginning to implement some of the new features that will be in the CSS 3 specification.
- CSS 3 will introduce new features related to borders, backgrounds, text effects, layout, and more.

Terminology

absolute positioning
absolute-length measurement
ancestor element
`arial` font
`aural` media type
author style
`background-attachment` property
`background-color` property
`background-image` property
`background-position` property
`background-repeat` property
`blink` text decoration

block-level element
border
border-color property
border-style property
border-width property
box model
braille media type
Cascading Style Sheets (CSS)
class attribute
cm (centimeter)
colon (:)
color property
CSS 2
CSS 3
CSS comment
CSS property
CSS rule
CSS selector
cursive generic font family
dashed border style
descendant element
display property
div element
dotted border style
double border style
em (*M*-height of font)
embedded style sheet
ex (*x*-height of font)
external style sheets
float property
floated element
font-family property
font-size property
font-style property
font-weight property
generic font family
groove border style
grouping element
handheld media type
height property
hidden border style
in (inch)
inheritance
inline-level element
inline style
inset border style
large relative font size
larger relative font size
left property value
line-through text decoration
link element
linking to an external style sheet
margin property
margin-bottom property
margin-left property
margin-right property
margin-top property
media types
medium relative border width
medium relative font size
MIME (Multipurpose Internet Mail Extensions) type
mm (millimeter)
monospace font
none border style
outset border style
overflow property
overline text decoration
padding property
parent element
pc (pica)
position property
print media type
pseudoclass
pt (point)
rel attribute (link)
relative positioning
relative-length measurement
repeat property value
ridge border style
right property value
sans-serif generic font family
screen media type
scroll property value
selector
separation of structure from content
serif generic font family
small relative font size
smaller relative font size
solid border style
span element
specificity
style
style attribute
style class
style in header section of document
text flow
text/css MIME type
text-align property
text-decoration property

text-indent property
thick border width
thin border width
user agent
user style sheet
width property
x-large relative font size
x-small relative font size
xx-large relative font size
xx-small relative font size
z-index property

Self-Review Exercises

5.1 Assume that the size of the base font on a system is 12 points.
a) How big is a 36-point font in ems?
b) How big is a 9-point font in ems?
c) How big is a 24-point font in picas?
d) How big is a 12-point font in inches?
e) How big is a 1-inch font in picas?

5.2 Fill in the blanks in the following statements:
a) Using the _______ element allows authors to use external style sheets in their pages.
b) To apply a CSS rule to more than one element at a time, separate the element names with a(n) _______.
c) Pixels are a(n) _______-length measurement unit.
d) The _______ pseudoclass is activated when the user moves the mouse cursor over the specified element.
e) Setting the overflow property to _______ provides a mechanism for containing inner content without compromising specified box dimensions.
f) _______ is a generic inline element that applies no inherent formatting and _______ is a generic block-level element that applies no inherent formatting.
g) Setting property background-repeat to _______ tiles the specified background-image vertically.
h) To begin a block of styles that applies to only the print media type, you use the declaration _______ print, followed by an opening curly brace ({).
i) The _______ property allows you to indent the first line of text in an element.
j) The three components of the box model are the _______, _______ and _______.

Answers to Self-Review Exercises

5.1 a) 3 ems. b) 0.75 ems. c) 2 picas. d) 1/6 inch. e) 6 picas.

5.2 a) link. b) comma. c) relative. d) hover. e) scroll. f) span, div. g) repeat-y. h) @media. i) text-indent. j) padding, border, margin.

Exercises

5.3 Write a CSS rule that makes all text 1.5 times larger than the base font of the system and colors the text red.

5.4 Write a CSS rule that places a background image halfway down the page, tiling it horizontally. The image should remain in place when the user scrolls up or down.

5.5 Write a CSS rule that gives all h1 and h2 elements a padding of 0.5 ems, a dashed border style and a margin of 0.5 ems.

5.6 Write a CSS rule that changes the color of all elements containing attribute class = "greenMove" to green and shifts them down 25 pixels and right 15 pixels.

5.7 Make a layout template that contains a header and two columns. Use `div`s for the each layout component, and use `float` to line up the columns side by side. Give each component a border and/or a background color so you can see where your `div`s are.

5.8 Add an embedded style sheet to the XHTML document in Fig. 4.5. The style sheet should contain a rule that displays `h1` elements in blue. In addition, create a rule that displays all links in blue without underlining them. When the mouse hovers over a link, change the link's background color to yellow.

5.9 Make a navigation button using a `div` with a link inside it. Give it a border, background, and text color, and make them change when the user hovers the mouse over the button. Use an external style sheet. Make sure your style sheet validates at `http://jigsaw.w3.org/css-validator/`. Note that some warnings may be unavoidable, but your CSS should have no errors.

6

JavaScript: Introduction to Scripting

Comment is free, but facts are sacred.
—C. P. Scott

The creditor hath a better memory than the debtor.
—James Howell

When faced with a decision, I always ask, "What would be the most fun?"
—Peggy Walker

Equality, in a social sense, may be divided into that of condition and that of rights.
—James Fenimore Cooper

OBJECTIVES

In this chapter you will learn:

- To write simple JavaScript programs.
- To use input and output statements.
- Basic memory concepts.
- To use arithmetic operators.
- The precedence of arithmetic operators.
- To write decision-making statements.
- To use relational and equality operators.

Outline

6.1 Introduction

In the first five chapters, we introduced the Internet and Web, web browsers, Web 2.0, XHTML and Cascading Style Sheets (CSS). In this chapter, we begin our introduction to the JavaScript[1] scripting language, which facilitates a disciplined approach to designing computer programs that enhance the functionality and appearance of web pages.[2]

In Chapters 6–11, we present a detailed discussion of JavaScript—the *de facto* standard client-side scripting language for web-based applications due to its highly portable nature. Our treatment of JavaScript serves two purposes—it introduces client-side scripting (used in Chapters 6–13), which makes web pages more dynamic and interactive, and it provides the programming foundation for the more complex server-side scripting presented later in the book.

We now introduce JavaScript programming and present examples that illustrate several important features of JavaScript. Each example is carefully analyzed one line at a time. In Chapters 7–8, we present a detailed treatment of program development and program control in JavaScript.

Before you can run code examples with JavaScript on your computer, you may need to change your browser's security settings. By default, Internet Explorer 7 prevents scripts on your local computer from running, displaying a yellow warning bar at the top of the window instead. To allow scripts to run in files on your computer, select **Internet Options** from the **Tools** menu. Click the **Advanced** tab and scroll down to the **Security** section of

1. Many people confuse the scripting language JavaScript with the programming language Java (from Sun Microsystems, Inc.). Java is a full-fledged object-oriented programming language. It can be used to develop applications that execute on a range of devices—from the smallest devices (such as cell phones and PDAs) to supercomputers. Java is popular for developing large-scale distributed enterprise applications and web applications. JavaScript is a browser-based scripting language developed by Netscape and implemented in all major browsers.
2. JavaScript was originally created by Netscape. Both Netscape and Microsoft have been instrumental in the standardization of JavaScript by ECMA International as ECMAScript. Detailed information about the current ECMAScript standard can be found at `www.ecma-international.org/publications/standards/ECMA-262.htm`.

the **Settings** list. Check the box labeled **Allow active content to run in files on My Computer** (Fig. 6.1). Click **OK** and restart Internet Explorer. XHTML documents on your own computer that contain JavaScript code will now run properly. Firefox has JavaScript enabled by default.

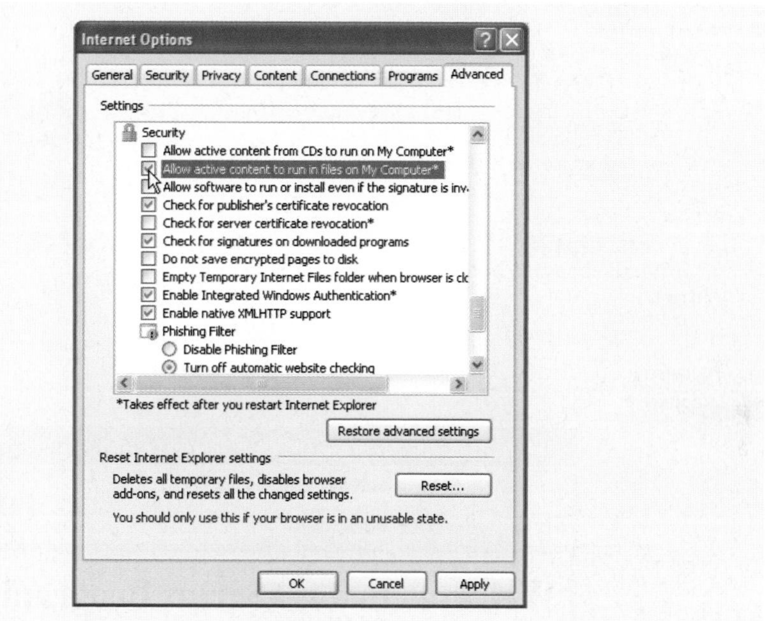

Fig. 6.1 | Enabling JavaScript in Internet Explorer 7

6.2 Simple Program: Displaying a Line of Text in a Web Page

JavaScript uses notations that may appear strange to nonprogrammers. We begin by considering a simple **script** (or **program**) that displays the text `"Welcome to JavaScript Programming!"` in the body of an XHTML document. All major web browsers contain **JavaScript interpreters**, which process the commands written in JavaScript. The JavaScript code and its output in Internet Explorer are shown in Fig. 6.2.

This program illustrates several important JavaScript features. We consider each line of the XHTML document and script in detail. As in the preceding chapters, we have given each XHTML document line numbers for the reader's convenience; the line numbers are not part of the XHTML document or of the JavaScript programs. Lines 12–13 do the "real work" of the script, namely, displaying the phrase `Welcome to JavaScript Programming!` in the web page.

Line 8 indicates the beginning of the `<head>` section of the XHTML document. For the moment, the JavaScript code we write will appear in the `<head>` section. The browser interprets the contents of the `<head>` section first, so the JavaScript programs we write there execute before the `<body>` of the XHTML document displays. In later chapters on JavaScript and in the chapters on dynamic HTML, we illustrate **inline scripting**, in which JavaScript code is written in the `<body>` of an XHTML document.

```
1  <?xml version = "1.0" encoding = "utf-8"?>
2  <!DOCTYPE html PUBLIC "-//W3C//DTD XHTML 1.0 Strict//EN"
3     "http://www.w3.org/TR/xhtml1/DTD/xhtml1-strict.dtd">
4
5  <!-- Fig. 6.2: welcome.html -->
6  <!-- Displaying a line of text. -->
7  <html xmlns = "http://www.w3.org/1999/xhtml">
8     <head>
9        <title>A First Program in JavaScript</title>
10       <script type = "text/javascript">
11          <!--
12          document.writeln(
13             "<h1>Welcome to JavaScript Programming!</h1>" );
14          // -->
15       </script>
16    </head><body></body>
17 </html>
```

Title of the XHTML document

Location and name of the loaded XHTML document

Script result

Fig. 6.2 | Displaying a line of text.

Line 10 uses the `<script>` tag to indicate to the browser that the text which follows is part of a script. The `type` attribute specifies the type of file as well as the scripting language used in the script—in this case, a `text` file written in `javascript`. Both Internet Explorer and Firefox use JavaScript as the default scripting language.

Line 11 contains the XHTML opening comment tag `<!--`. Some older web browsers do not support scripting. In such browsers, the actual text of a script often will display in the web page. To prevent this from happening, many script programmers enclose the script code in an XHTML comment, so that browsers that do not support scripts will simply ignore the script. The syntax used is as follows:

```
<script type = "text/javascript">
   <!--
   script code here
   // -->
</script>
```

When a browser that does not support scripts encounters the preceding code, it ignores the `<script>` and `</script>` tags and the script code in the XHTML comment. Browsers that do support scripting will interpret the JavaScript code as expected. [*Note:* Some browsers require the JavaScript single-line comment // (see Section 6.4 for an explanation) before the ending XHTML comment delimiter (-->) to interpret the script properly. The opening HTML comment tag (<!--) also serves as a single line comment delimiter in JavaScript, therefore it does not need to be commented.]

Portability Tip 6.1

Some browsers do not support the `<script>...</script>` *tags. If your document is to be rendered with such browsers, enclose the script code between these tags in an XHTML comment, so that the script text does not get displayed as part of the web page. The closing comment tag of the XHTML comment (-->) is preceded by a JavaScript comment (//) to prevent the browser from trying to interpret the XHTML comment as a JavaScript statement.*

Lines 12–13 instruct the browser's JavaScript interpreter to perform an action, namely, to display in the web page the string of characters contained between the double quotation (") marks. A string is sometimes called a character string, a message or a string literal. We refer to characters between double quotation marks as strings. Individual white-space characters between words in a string are not ignored by the browser. However, if consecutive spaces appear in a string, browsers condense them to a single space. Also, in most cases, browsers ignore leading white-space characters (i.e., white space at the beginning of a string).

Software Engineering Observation 6.1

Strings in JavaScript can be enclosed in either double quotation marks (") or single quotation marks (').

Lines 12–13 use the browser's `document` object, which represents the XHTML document the browser is currently displaying. The `document` object allows you to specify text to display in the XHTML document. The browser contains a complete set of objects that allow script programmers to access and manipulate every element of an XHTML document. In the next several chapters, we overview some of these objects as we discuss the Document Object Model (DOM).

An object resides in the computer's memory and contains information used by the script. The term object normally implies that attributes (data) and behaviors (methods) are associated with the object. The object's methods use the attributes to perform useful actions for the client of the object (i.e., the script that calls the methods). A method may require additional information (arguments) to perform its action; this information is enclosed in parentheses after the name of the method in the script. In lines 12–13, we call the `document` object's `writeln` method to write a line of XHTML markup in the XHTML document. The parentheses following the method name `writeln` contain the one argument that method `writeln` requires (in this case, the string of XHTML that the browser is to display). Method `writeln` instructs the browser to display the argument string. If the string contains XHTML elements, the browser interprets these elements and renders them on the screen. In this example, the browser displays the phrase `Welcome to JavaScript Programming!` as an `h1`-level XHTML heading, because the phrase is enclosed in an `h1` element.

The code elements in lines 12–13, including `document.writeln`, its argument in the parentheses (the string) and the semicolon (`;`), together are called a statement. Every statement ends with a semicolon (also known as the **statement terminator**), although this practice is not required by JavaScript. Line 15 indicates the end of the script.

Good Programming Practice 6.1

Always include a semicolon at the end of a statement to terminate the statement. This notation clarifies where one statement ends and the next statement begins.

Common Programming Error 6.1

Forgetting the ending `</script>` tag for a script may prevent the browser from interpreting the script properly and may prevent the XHTML document from loading properly.

The `</head>` tag in line 16 indicates the end of the `<head>` section. Also in line 16, the tags `<body>` and `</body>` specify that this XHTML document has an empty body. Line 17 indicates the end of this XHTML document.

We are now ready to view our XHTML document in a web browser—open it in Internet Explorer or Firefox. If the script contains no syntax errors, it should produce the output shown in Fig. 6.2.

Common Programming Error 6.2

JavaScript is case sensitive. Not using the proper uppercase and lowercase letters is a syntax error. *A syntax error occurs when the script interpreter cannot recognize a statement. The interpreter normally issues an error message to help you locate and fix the incorrect statement. Syntax errors are violations of the rules of the programming language. The interpreter notifies you of a syntax error when it attempts to execute the statement containing the error. The JavaScript interpreter in Internet Explorer reports all syntax errors by indicating in a separate popup window that a* "runtime error" *has occurred (i.e., a problem occurred while the interpreter was running the script). [*Note: *To enable this feature in IE7, select* **Internet Options...** *from the* **Tools** *menu. In the* **Internet Options** *dialog that appears, select the* **Advanced** *tab and click the checkbox labelled* **Display a notification about every script error** *under the* **Browsing** *category. Firefox has an error console that reports JavaScript errors and warnings. It is accessible by choosing* **Error Console** *from the* **Tools** *menu.]*

Error-Prevention Tip 6.1

When the interpreter reports a syntax error, sometimes the error is not on the line number indicated by the error message. First, check the line for which the error was reported. If that line does not contain errors, check the preceding several lines in the script.

6.3 Modifying Our First Program

This section continues our introduction to JavaScript programming with two examples that modify the example in Fig. 6.2.

Displaying a Line of Colored Text

A script can display `Welcome to JavaScript Programming!` several ways. Figure 6.3 uses two JavaScript statements to produce one line of text in the XHTML document. This example also displays the text in a different color, using the CSS `color` property.

Most of this XHTML document is identical to Fig. 6.2, so we concentrate only on lines 12–14 of Fig. 6.3, which display one line of text in the XHTML document. The first statement uses `document` method **`write`** to display a string. Unlike `writeln`, `write` does

```
1  <?xml version = "1.0" encoding = "utf-8"?>
2  <!DOCTYPE html PUBLIC "-//W3C//DTD XHTML 1.0 Strict//EN"
3     "http://www.w3.org/TR/xhtml1/DTD/xhtml1-strict.dtd">
4
5  <!-- Fig. 6.3: welcome2.html -->
6  <!-- Printing one line with multiple statements. -->
7  <html xmlns = "http://www.w3.org/1999/xhtml">
8     <head>
9        <title>Printing a Line with Multiple Statements</title>
10       <script type = "text/javascript">
11          <!--
12          document.write( "<h1 style = \"color: magenta\">" );
13          document.write( "Welcome to JavaScript " +
14             "Programming!</h1>" );
15          // -->
16       </script>
17    </head><body></body>
18 </html>
```

Fig. 6.3 | Printing one line with separate statements.

not position the output cursor in the XHTML document at the beginning of the next line after writing its argument. [*Note:* The output cursor keeps track of where the next character appears in the XHTML document, not where the next character appears in the web page as rendered by the browser.] The next character written in the XHTML document appears immediately after the last character written with `write`. Thus, when lines 13–14 execute, the first character written, "`W`," appears immediately after the last character displayed with `write` (the > character inside the right double quote in line 12). Each `write` or `writeln` statement resumes writing characters where the last `write` or `writeln` statement stopped writing characters. So, after a `writeln` statement, the next output appears on the beginning of the next line. In effect, the two statements in lines 12–14 result in one line of XHTML text. Remember that statements in JavaScript are separated by semicolons (`;`). Therefore, lines 13–14 represent only one complete statement. JavaScript allows large statements to be split over many lines. However, you cannot split a statement in the middle of a string. The + operator (called the "concatenation operator" when used in this manner) in line 13 joins two strings together and is explained in more detail later in this chapter.

Common Programming Error 6.3

Splitting a statement in the middle of a string is a syntax error.

Note that the characters \" (in line 12) are not displayed in the browser. The backslash (\) in a string is an escape character. It indicates that a "special" character is to be used in the string. When a backslash is encountered in a string of characters, the next character is combined with the backslash to form an escape sequence. The escape sequence \" is the double-quote character, which causes a double-quote character to be inserted into the string. We use this escape sequence to insert double quotes around the attribute value for style without terminating the string. Note that we could also have used single quotes for the attribute value, as in document.write("<h1 style = 'color: magenta'>");, because the single quotes do not terminate a double-quoted string. We discuss escape sequences in greater detail momentarily.

It is important to note that the preceding discussion has nothing to do with the actual rendering of the XHTML text. Remember that the browser does not create a new line of text unless the browser window is too narrow for the text being rendered or the browser encounters an XHTML element that explicitly starts a new line—for example, <br/> to start a new line or <p> to start a new paragraph.

Common Programming Error 6.4

Many people confuse the writing of XHTML text with the rendering of XHTML text. Writing XHTML text creates the XHTML that will be rendered by the browser for presentation to the user.

Displaying Multiple Lines of Text

In the next example, we demonstrate that a single statement can cause the browser to display multiple lines by using line-break XHTML tags (<br/>) throughout the string of XHTML text in a write or writeln method call. Figure 6.4 demonstrates the use of line-break XHTML tags. Lines 12–13 produce three separate lines of text when the browser renders the XHTML document.

```
1  <?xml version = "1.0" encoding = "utf-8"?>
2  <!DOCTYPE html PUBLIC "-//W3C//DTD XHTML 1.0 Strict//EN"
3     "http://www.w3.org/TR/xhtml1/DTD/xhtml1-strict.dtd">
4
5  <!-- Fig. 6.4: welcome3.html -->
6  <!-- Printing on multiple lines with a single statement. -->
7  <html xmlns = "http://www.w3.org/1999/xhtml">
8     <head>
9        <title>Printing Multiple Lines</title>
10       <script type = "text/javascript">
11          <!--
12          document.writeln( "<h1>Welcome to<br />JavaScript" +
13             "<br />Programming!</h1>" );
14          // -->
15       </script>
16    </head><body></body>
17 </html>
```

Fig. 6.4 | Printing on multiple lines with a single statement. (Part 1 of 2.)

Fig. 6.4 | Printing on multiple lines with a single statement. (Part 2 of 2.)

Displaying Text in an Alert Dialog

The first several programs in this chapter display text in the XHTML document. Sometimes it is useful to display information in windows called **dialogs** (or **dialog boxes**) that "pop up" on the screen to grab the user's attention. Dialogs typically display important messages to users browsing the web page. JavaScript allows you easily to display a dialog box containing a message. The program in Fig. 6.5 displays `Welcome to JavaScript Programming!` as three lines in a predefined dialog called an **`alert` dialog**.

```
<?xml version = "1.0" encoding = "utf-8"?>
<!DOCTYPE html PUBLIC "-//W3C//DTD XHTML 1.0 Strict//EN"
   "http://www.w3.org/TR/xhtml1/DTD/xhtml1-strict.dtd">

<!-- Fig. 6.5: welcome4.html -->
<!-- Alert dialog displaying multiple lines. -->
<html xmlns = "http://www.w3.org/1999/xhtml">
   <head>
      <title>Printing Multiple Lines in a Dialog Box</title>
      <script type = "text/javascript">
         <!--
            window.alert( "Welcome to\nJavaScript\nProgramming!" );
         // -->
      </script>
   </head>
   <body>
      <p>Click Refresh (or Reload) to run this script again.</p>
   </body>
</html>
```

Title bar

Windows Internet Explorer

Welcome to
JavaScript
Programming!

OK

The dialog is automatically sized to accommodate the string.

The **OK** button allows the user to dismiss (or hide) the dialog.

Mouse cursor

Fig. 6.5 | Alert dialog displaying multiple lines. (Part 1 of 2.)

Fig. 6.5 | Alert dialog displaying multiple lines. (Part 2 of 2.)

Line 12 in the script uses the browser's **window** object to display an alert dialog. The argument to the `window` object's **alert** method is the string to display. Executing the preceding statement displays the dialog shown in the first window of Fig. 6.5. The **title bar** of the dialog contains the string **Windows Internet Explorer** to indicate that the browser is presenting a message to the user. The dialog provides an **OK** button that allows the user to **dismiss** (i.e., **close**) the dialog by clicking the button. To dismiss the dialog, position the **mouse cursor** (also called the **mouse pointer**) over the **OK** button and click the mouse. Firefox's alert dialog looks similar, but the title bar contains the text **[JavaScript Application]**.

Common Programming Error 6.5

Dialogs display plain text; they do not render XHTML. Therefore, specifying XHTML elements as part of a string to be displayed in a dialog results in the actual characters of the tags being displayed.

Note that the `alert` dialog contains three lines of plain text. Normally, a dialog displays the characters in a string exactly as they appear between the double quotes. Note, however, that the dialog does not display the characters `\n`. The escape sequence `\n` is the **newline character**. In a dialog, the newline character causes the **cursor** (i.e., the current screen position indicator) to move to the beginning of the next line in the dialog. Some other common escape sequences are listed in Fig. 6.6. The `\n`, `\t` and `\r` escape sequences in the table do not affect XHTML rendering unless they are in a **pre element** (this element displays the text between its tags in a fixed-width font exactly as it is formatted between the tags, including leading white-space characters and consecutive white-space characters). The other escape sequences result in characters that will be displayed in plain text dialogs and in XHTML.

Escape sequence	Description
`\n`	New line. Position the screen cursor at the beginning of the next line.
`\t`	Horizontal tab. Move the screen cursor to the next tab stop.

Fig. 6.6 | Some common escape sequences. (Part 1 of 2.)

Escape sequence	Description
`\r`	Carriage return. Position the screen cursor to the beginning of the current line; do not advance to the next line. Any characters output after the carriage return overwrite the characters previously output on that line.
`\\`	Backslash. Used to represent a backslash character in a string.
`\"`	Double quote. Used to represent a double-quote character in a string contained in double quotes. For example, `window.alert( "\"in quotes\"" );` displays `"in quotes"` in an `alert` dialog.
`\'`	Single quote. Used to represent a single-quote character in a string. For example, `window.alert( '\'in quotes\'' );` displays `'in quotes'` in an `alert` dialog.

Fig. 6.6 | Some common escape sequences. (Part 2 of 2.)

Common Programming Error 6.6

XHTML elements in an alert dialog's message are not interpreted as XHTML. This means that using `<br />`, for example, to create a line break in an alert box is an error. The string `<br/>` will simply be included in your message.

6.4 Obtaining User Input with prompt Dialogs

Scripting gives you the ability to generate part or all of a web page's content at the time it is shown to the user. A script can adapt the content based on input from the user or other variables, such as the time of day or the type of browser used by the client. Such web pages are said to be **dynamic**, as opposed to static, since their content has the ability to change. The next two subsections use scripts to demonstrate dynamic web pages.

6.4.1 Dynamic Welcome Page

Our next script builds on prior scripts to create a dynamic welcome page that obtains the user's name, then displays it on the page. The script uses another predefined dialog box from the `window` object—a **prompt** dialog—which allows the user to input a value that the script can use. The program asks the user to input a name, then displays the name in the XHTML document. Figure 6.7 presents the script and sample output. [*Note:* In later JavaScript chapters, we obtain input via GUI components in XHTML forms, as introduced in Chapter 4.]

Line 12 is a **declaration** that contains the JavaScript **keyword** `var`. Keywords are words that have special meaning in JavaScript. The keyword **var** at the beginning of the statement indicates that the word `name` is a **variable**. A variable is a location in the computer's memory where a value can be stored for use by a program. All variables have a name, type and value, and should be declared with a `var` statement before they are used in

```
<?xml version = "1.0" encoding = "utf-8"?>
<!DOCTYPE html PUBLIC "-//W3C//DTD XHTML 1.0 Strict//EN"
   "http://www.w3.org/TR/xhtml1/DTD/xhtml1-strict.dtd">

<!-- Fig. 6.7: welcome5.html -->
<!-- Prompt box used on a welcome screen. -->
<html xmlns = "http://www.w3.org/1999/xhtml">
   <head>
      <title>Using Prompt and Alert Boxes</title>
      <script type = "text/javascript">
         <!--
         var name; // string entered by the user

         // read the name from the prompt box as a string
         name = window.prompt( "Please enter your name" );

         document.writeln( "<h1>Hello, " + name +
            ", welcome to JavaScript programming!</h1>" );
         // -->
      </script>
   </head>
   <body>
      <p>Click Refresh (or Reload) to run this script again.</p>
   </body>
</html>
```

Fig. 6.7 | Prompt box used on a welcome screen.

a program. Although using var to declare variables is not required, we will see in Chapter 9, JavaScript: Functions, that var sometimes ensures proper behavior of a script.

The name of a variable can be any valid **identifier**. An identifier is a series of characters consisting of letters, digits, underscores (_) and dollar signs ($) that does not begin with a digit and is not a reserved JavaScript keyword. [*Note:* A complete list of keywords can be found in Fig. 7.2.] Identifiers may not contain spaces. Some valid identifiers are `Welcome`, `$value`, `_value`, `m_inputField1` and `button7`. The name `7button` is not a valid identifier, because it begins with a digit, and the name `input field` is not valid, because it contains a space. Remember that JavaScript is case sensitive—uppercase and lowercase letters are considered to be different characters, so `name`, `Name` and `NAME` are different identifiers.

Good Programming Practice 6.2

Choosing meaningful variable names helps a script to be "self-documenting" (i.e., easy to understand by simply reading the script, rather than having to read manuals or extended comments).

Good Programming Practice 6.3

By convention, variable-name identifiers begin with a lowercase first letter. Each subsequent word should begin with a capital first letter. For example, identifier `itemPrice` *has a capital* `P` *in its second word,* `Price`*.*

Common Programming Error 6.7

Splitting a statement in the middle of an identifier is a syntax error.

Declarations end with a semicolon (`;`) and can be split over several lines with each variable in the declaration separated by a comma—known as a comma-separated list of variable names. Several variables may be declared either in one declaration or in multiple declarations.

Programmers often indicate the purpose of each variable in the program by placing a JavaScript comment at the end of each line in the declaration. In line 12, a single-line comment that begins with the characters `//` states the purpose of the variable in the script. This form of comment is called a single-line comment because it terminates at the end of the line in which it appears. A `//` comment can begin at any position in a line of JavaScript code and continues until the end of the line. Comments do not cause the browser to perform any action when the script is interpreted; rather, comments are ignored by the JavaScript interpreter.

Good Programming Practice 6.4

Some programmers prefer to declare each variable on a separate line. This format allows for easy insertion of a descriptive comment next to each declaration. This is a widely followed professional coding standard.

Another comment notation facilitates the writing of multiline comments. For example,

```
/* This is a multiline
   comment. It can be
   split over many lines. */
```

is a multiline comment spread over several lines. Such comments begin with the delimiter `/*` and end with the delimiter `*/`. All text between the delimiters of the comment is ignored by the interpreter.

Common Programming Error 6.8

Forgetting one of the delimiters of a multiline comment is a syntax error.

Common Programming Error 6.9

Nesting multiline comments (i.e., placing a multiline comment between the delimiters of another multiline comment) is a syntax error.

JavaScript adopted comments delimited with `/*` and `*/` from the C programming language and single-line comments delimited with `//` from the C++ programming language. JavaScript programmers generally prefer C++-style single-line comments over C-style comments. Throughout this book, we use C++-style single-line comments.

Line 14 is a comment indicating the purpose of the statement in the next line. Line 15 calls the `window` object's `prompt` method, which displays the dialog in Fig. 6.8. The dialog allows the user to enter a string representing the user's name.

The argument to `prompt` specifies a message telling the user what to type in the text field. This message is called a **prompt** because it directs the user to take a specific action. An optional second argument, separated from the first by a comma, may specify the default string displayed in the text field; our code does not supply a second argument. In this case, Internet Explorer displays the default value `undefined`, while Firefox and most other browsers leave the text field empty. The user types characters in the text field, then clicks the **OK** button to submit the string to the program. We normally receive input from a user through a GUI component such as the `prompt` dialog, as in this program, or through an XHTML form GUI component, as we will see in later chapters.

The user can type anything in the text field of the `prompt` dialog. For this program, whatever the user enters is considered the name. If the user clicks the **Cancel** button, no string value is sent to the program. Instead, the `prompt` dialog submits the value **`null`**, a JavaScript keyword signifying that a variable has no value. Note that `null` is not a string literal, but rather a predefined term indicating the absence of value. Writing a `null` value to the document, however, displays the word `null` in the web page.

The statement in line 15 **assigns** the value returned by the `window` object's `prompt` method (a string containing the characters typed by the user—or the default value or `null` if the **Cancel** button is clicked) to variable `name` by using the **assignment operator**, `=`. The statement is read as, "`name` gets the value returned by `window.prompt( "Please enter your name" )`." The `=` operator is called a **binary operator** because it has two **operands**—`name` and the result of the expression `window.prompt( "Please enter your name" )`. This entire statement is called an **assignment statement** because it assigns a value to a variable. The expression to the right of the assignment operator is always evaluated first.

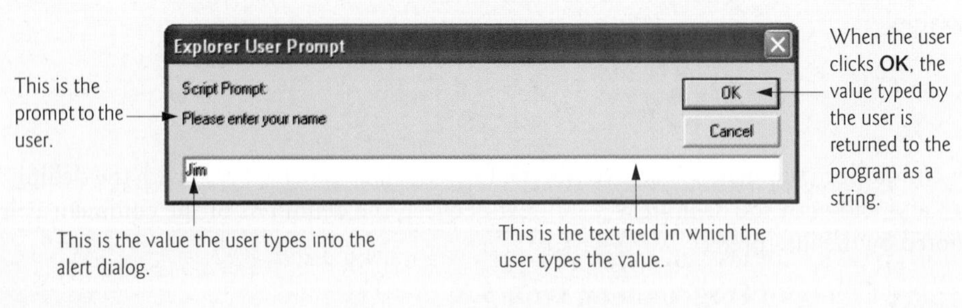
Explorer User Prompt
Script Prompt:
Please enter your name
OK
Cancel
Jim
This is the prompt to the user.
When the user clicks OK, the value typed by the user is returned to the program as a string.
This is the value the user types into the alert dialog.
This is the text field in which the user types the value.

Fig. 6.8 | Prompt dialog displayed by the `window` object's `prompt` method.

Good Programming Practice 6.5

Place spaces on either side of a binary operator. This format makes the operator stand out and makes the program more readable.

Lines 17–18 use document.writeln to display the new welcome message. The expression inside the parentheses uses the operator + to "add" a string (the literal "<h1>Hello, "), the variable name (the string that the user entered in line 15) and another string (the literal ", welcome to JavaScript programming!</h1>"). JavaScript has a version of the + operator for string concatenation that enables a string and a value of another data type (including another string) to be combined. The result of this operation is a new (and normally longer) string. If we assume that name contains the string literal "Jim", the expression evaluates as follows: JavaScript determines that the two operands of the first + operator (the string "<h1>Hello, " and the value of variable name) are both strings, then concatenates the two into one string. Next, JavaScript determines that the two operands of the second + operator (the result of the first concatenation operation, the string "<h1>Hello, Jim", and the string ", welcome to JavaScript programming!</h1>") are both strings and concatenates the two. This results in the string "<h1>Hello, Jim, welcome to JavaScript programming!</h1>". The browser renders this string as part of the XHTML document. Note that the space between Hello, and Jim is part of the string "<h1>Hello, ".

As we'll illustrate later, the + operator used for string concatenation can convert other variable types to strings if necessary. Because string concatenation occurs between two strings, JavaScript must convert other variable types to strings before it can proceed with the operation. For example, if a variable age has an integer value equal to 21, then the expression "my age is " + age evaluates to the string "my age is 21". JavaScript converts the value of age to a string and concatenates it with the existing string literal "my age is ".

After the browser interprets the <head> section of the XHTML document (which contains the JavaScript), it then interprets the <body> of the XHTML document (lines 22–24) and renders the XHTML. Notice that the XHTML page is not rendered until the prompt is dismissed because the prompt pauses execution in the head, before the body is processed. If you click your browser's **Refresh** (Internet Explorer) or **Reload** (Firefox) button after entering a name, the browser will reload the XHTML document, so that you can execute the script again and change the name. [*Note:* In some cases, it may be necessary to hold down the *Shift* key while clicking the **Refresh** or **Reload** button, to ensure that the XHTML document reloads properly. Browsers often save a recent copy of a page in memory, and holding the *Shift* key forces the browser to download the most recent version of a page.]

6.4.2 Adding Integers

Our next script illustrates another use of prompt dialogs to obtain input from the user. Figure 6.9 inputs two integers (whole numbers, such as 7, –11, 0 and 31914) typed by a user at the keyboard, computes the sum of the values and displays the result.

Lines 12–16 declare the variables firstNumber, secondNumber, number1, number2 and sum. Single-line comments state the purpose of each of these variables. Line 19 employs a prompt dialog to allow the user to enter a string representing the first of the two

```
<?xml version = "1.0" encoding = "utf-8"?>
<!DOCTYPE html PUBLIC "-//W3C//DTD XHTML 1.0 Strict//EN"
   "http://www.w3.org/TR/xhtml1/DTD/xhtml1-strict.dtd">

<!-- Fig. 6.9: addition.html -->
<!-- Addition script. -->
<html xmlns = "http://www.w3.org/1999/xhtml">
   <head>
      <title>An Addition Program</title>
      <script type = "text/javascript">
         <!--
         var firstNumber; // first string entered by user
         var secondNumber; // second string entered by user
         var number1; // first number to add
         var number2; // second number to add
         var sum; // sum of number1 and number2

         // read in first number from user as a string
         firstNumber = window.prompt( "Enter first integer" );

         // read in second number from user as a string
         secondNumber = window.prompt( "Enter second integer" );

         // convert numbers from strings to integers
         number1 = parseInt( firstNumber );
         number2 = parseInt( secondNumber );

         sum = number1 + number2; // add the numbers

         // display the results
         document.writeln( "<h1>The sum is " + sum + "</h1>" );
         // -->
      </script>
   </head>
   <body>
      <p>Click Refresh (or Reload) to run the script again</p>
   </body>
</html>
```

Explorer User Prompt
Script Prompt:
Enter first integer
OK
Cancel
45

Explorer User Prompt
Script Prompt:
Enter second integer
OK
Cancel
72

Fig. 6.9 | Addition script. (Part 1 of 2.)

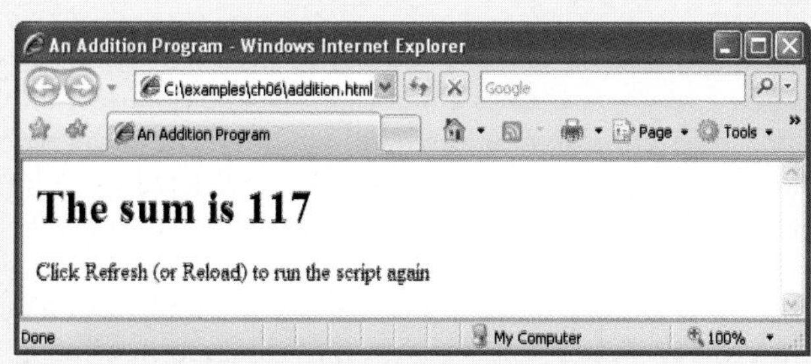

Fig. 6.9 | Addition script. (Part 2 of 2.)

integers that will be added. The script assigns the first value entered by the user to the variable `firstNumber`. Line 22 displays a `prompt` dialog to obtain the second number to add and assign this value to the variable `secondNumber`.

As in the preceding example, the user can type anything in the `prompt` dialog. For this program, if the user either types a noninteger value or clicks the **Cancel** button, a logic error will occur, and the sum of the two values will appear in the XHTML document as NaN (meaning not a number). A logic error is caused by syntactically correct code that produces an undesired result. In Chapter 11, JavaScript: Objects, we discuss the `Number` object and its methods that can determine whether a value is not a number.

Recall that a `prompt` dialog returns to the program as a string the value typed by the user. Lines 25–26 convert the two strings input by the user to integer values that can be used in a calculation. Function `parseInt` converts its string argument to an integer. Line 25 assigns to the variable `number1` the integer that function `parseInt` returns. Line 26 assigns an integer value to variable `number2` in a similar manner. Any subsequent references to `number1` and `number2` in the program use these integer values. [*Note:* We refer to `parseInt` as a function rather than a method because we do not precede the function call with an object name (such as `document` or `window`) and a dot (`.`). The term method means that the function belongs to a particular object. For example, method `writeln` belongs to the `document` object and method `prompt` belongs to the `window` object.]

Line 28 calculates the sum of the variables `number1` and `number2` using the addition operator, `+`, and assigns the result to variable `sum` by using the assignment operator, `=`. Notice that the `+` operator can perform both addition and string concatenation. In this case, the `+` operator performs addition, because both operands contain integers. After line 28 performs this calculation, line 31 uses `document.writeln` to display the result of the addition on the web page. Lines 33 and 34 close the `script` and `head` elements, respectively. Lines 35–37 render the `body` of XHTML document. Use your browser's **Refresh** or **Reload** button to reload the XHTML document and run the script again.

Common Programming Error 6.10

Confusing the + operator used for string concatenation with the + operator used for addition often leads to undesired results. For example, if integer variable `y` *has the value* `5`*, the expression* `"y + 2 = " + y + 2` *results in* `"y + 2 = 52"`*, not* `"y + 2 = 7"`*, because first the value of* `y` *(i.e.,* `5`*) is concatenated with the string* `"y + 2 = "`*, then the value* `2` *is concatenated with the new, larger string* `"y + 2 = 5"`*. The expression* `"y + 2 = " + (y + 2)` *produces the string* `"y + 2 = 7"` *because the parentheses ensure that* `y + 2` *is executed mathematically before it is conveted to a string.*

6.5 Memory Concepts

Variable names such as number1, number2 and sum actually correspond to **locations** in the computer's memory. Every variable has a **name**, a **type** and a **value**.

In the addition program in Fig. 6.9, when line 25 executes, the string firstNumber (previously entered by the user in a prompt dialog) is converted to an integer and placed into a memory location to which the name number1 has been assigned by the interpreter. Suppose the user entered the string 45 as the value for firstNumber. The program converts firstNumber to an integer, and the computer places the integer value 45 into location number1, as shown in Fig. 6.10. Whenever a value is placed in a memory location, the value replaces the previous value in that location. The previous value is lost.

Suppose that the user enters 72 as the second integer. When line 26 executes, the program converts secondNumber to an integer and places that integer value, 72, into location number2; then the memory appears as shown in Fig. 6.11.

Once the program has obtained values for number1 and number2, it adds the values and places the sum into variable sum. The statement

```
sum = number1 + number2;
```

performs the addition and also replaces sum's previous value. After sum is calculated, the memory appears as shown in Fig. 6.12. Note that the values of number1 and number2 appear exactly as they did before they were used in the calculation of sum. These values were used, but not destroyed, when the computer performed the calculation—when a value is read from a memory location, the process is nondestructive.

number1	45

Fig. 6.10 | Memory location showing the name and value of variable number1.

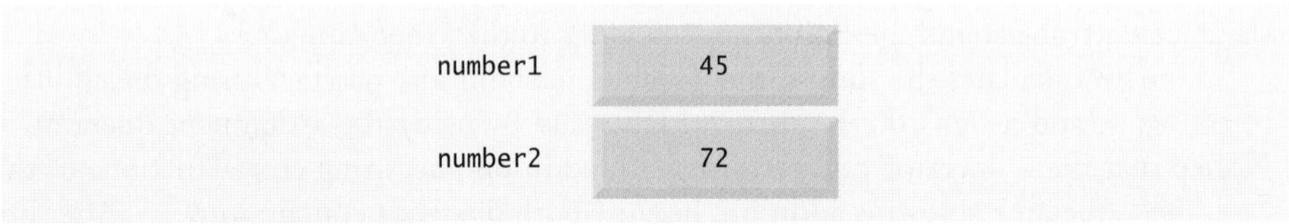

number1	45
number2	72

Fig. 6.11 | Memory locations after inputting values for variables number1 and number2.

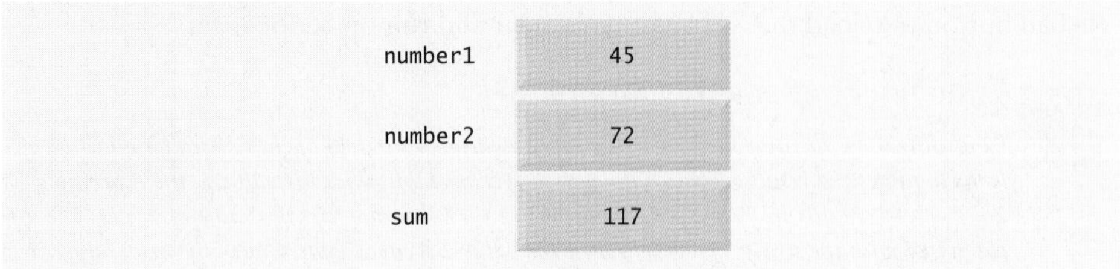

number1	45
number2	72
sum	117

Fig. 6.12 | Memory locations after calculating the sum of number1 and number2.

Data Types in JavaScript

Unlike its predecessor languages C, C++ and Java, JavaScript does not require variables to have a declared type before they can be used in a program. A variable in JavaScript can contain a value of any data type, and in many situations JavaScript automatically converts between values of different types for you. For this reason, JavaScript is referred to as a loosely typed language. When a variable is declared in JavaScript, but is not given a value, the variable has an undefined value. Attempting to use the value of such a variable is normally a logic error.

When variables are declared, they are not assigned values unless specified by the programmer. Assigning the value `null` to a variable indicates that it does not contain a value.

6.6 Arithmetic

Many scripts perform arithmetic calculations. Figure 6.13 summarizes the arithmetic operators. Note the use of various special symbols not used in algebra. The asterisk (`*`) indicates multiplication; the percent sign (`%`) is the remainder operator, which will be discussed shortly. The arithmetic operators in Fig. 6.13 are binary operators, because each operates on two operands. For example, the expression `sum + value` contains the binary operator `+` and the two operands `sum` and `value`.

JavaScript provides the remainder operator, `%`, which yields the remainder after division. [*Note:* The `%` operator is known as the modulus operator in some programming languages.] The expression `x % y` yields the remainder after `x` is divided by `y`. Thus, `17 % 5` yields `2` (i.e., 17 divided by 5 is 3, with a remainder of 2), and `7.4 % 3.1` yields `1.2`. In later chapters, we consider applications of the remainder operator, such as determining whether one number is a multiple of another. There is no arithmetic operator for exponentiation in JavaScript. (Chapter 8, JavaScript: Control Statements II, shows how to perform exponentiation in JavaScript using the `Math` object's `pow` method.)

Arithmetic expressions in JavaScript must be written in straight-line form to facilitate entering programs into the computer. Thus, expressions such as "`a` divided by `b`" must be written as `a / b`, so that all constants, variables and operators appear in a straight line. The following algebraic notation is generally not acceptable to computers:

$$\frac{a}{b}$$

JavaScript operation	Arithmetic operator	Algebraic expression	JavaScript expression
Addition	`+`	$f + 7$	`f + 7`
Subtraction	`-`	$p - c$	`p - c`
Multiplication	`*`	bm	`b * m`
Division	`/`	x / y or $\frac{x}{y}$ or $x \div y$	`x / y`
Remainder	`%`	$r \bmod s$	`r % s`

Fig. 6.13 | Arithmetic operators.

Parentheses are used to group expressions in the same manner as in algebraic expressions. For example, to multiply a times the quantity b + c we write:

```
a * ( b + c )
```

JavaScript applies the operators in arithmetic expressions in a precise sequence determined by the following rules of operator precedence, which are generally the same as those followed in algebra:

1. Multiplication, division and remainder operations are applied first. If an expression contains several multiplication, division and remainder operations, operators are applied from left to right. Multiplication, division and remainder operations are said to have the same level of precedence.
2. Addition and subtraction operations are applied next. If an expression contains several addition and subtraction operations, operators are applied from left to right. Addition and subtraction operations have the same level of precedence.

The rules of operator precedence enable JavaScript to apply operators in the correct order. When we say that operators are applied from left to right, we are referring to the associativity of the operators—the order in which operators of equal priority are evaluated. We will see that some operators associate from right to left. Figure 6.14 summarizes the rules of operator precedence. The table in Fig. 6.14 will be expanded as additional JavaScript operators are introduced. A complete precedence chart is included in Appendix C.

Now, in light of the rules of operator precedence, let us consider several algebraic expressions. Each example lists an algebraic expression and the equivalent JavaScript expression.

The following is an example of an arithmetic mean (average) of five terms:

Algebra: $$m = \frac{a + b + c + d + e}{5}$$

JavaScript: `m = ( a + b + c + d + e ) / 5;`

The parentheses are required to group the addition operators, because division has higher precedence than addition. The entire quantity (a + b + c + d + e) is to be divided by 5. If the parentheses are erroneously omitted, we obtain a + b + c + d + e / 5, which evaluates as

$$a + b + c + d + \frac{e}{5}$$

and would not lead to the correct answer.

Operator(s)	Operation(s)	Order of evaluation (precedence)
*, / or %	Multiplication Division Remainder	Evaluated first. If there are several such operations, they are evaluated from left to right.
+ or -	Addition Subtraction	Evaluated last. If there are several such operations, they are evaluated from left to right.

Fig. 6.14 | Precedence of arithmetic operators.

The following is an example of the equation of a straight line:

Algebra: $y = mx + b$

JavaScript: `y = m * x + b;`

No parentheses are required. The multiplication operator is applied first, because multiplication has a higher precedence than addition. The assignment occurs last, because it has a lower precedence than multiplication and addition.

The following example contains remainder (%), multiplication, division, addition and subtraction operations:

Algebra: $z = pr\%q + w/x - y$

Java:

```
z = p * r % q + w / x - y;
  6   1   2   4   3   5
```

The circled numbers under the statement indicate the order in which JavaScript applies the operators. The multiplication, remainder and division operations are evaluated first in left-to-right order (i.e., they associate from left to right), because they have higher precedence than addition and subtraction. The addition and subtraction operations are evaluated next. These operations are also applied from left to right.

To develop a better understanding of the rules of operator precedence, consider the evaluation of a second-degree polynomial ($y = ax^2 + bx + c$):

```
y = a * x * x + b * x + c;
  6   1   2   4   3   5
```

The circled numbers indicate the order in which JavaScript applies the operators.

Suppose that `a`, `b`, `c` and `x` are initialized as follows: `a = 2`, `b = 3`, `c = 7` and `x = 5`. Figure 6.15 illustrates the order in which the operators are applied in the preceding second-degree polynomial.

As in algebra, it is acceptable to use unnecessary parentheses in an expression to make the expression clearer. These are also called redundant parentheses. For example, the preceding second-degree polynomial might be parenthesized as follows:

```
y = ( a * x * x ) + ( b * x ) + c;
```

Good Programming Practice 6.6

Using parentheses for complex arithmetic expressions, even when the parentheses are not necessary, can make the arithmetic expressions easier to read.

6.7 Decision Making: Equality and Relational Operators

This section introduces a version of JavaScript's `if` statement that allows a program to make a decision based on the truth or falsity of a condition. If the condition is met (i.e., the condition is true), the statement in the body of the `if` statement is executed. If the condition is not met (i.e., the condition is false), the statement in the body of the `if` state-

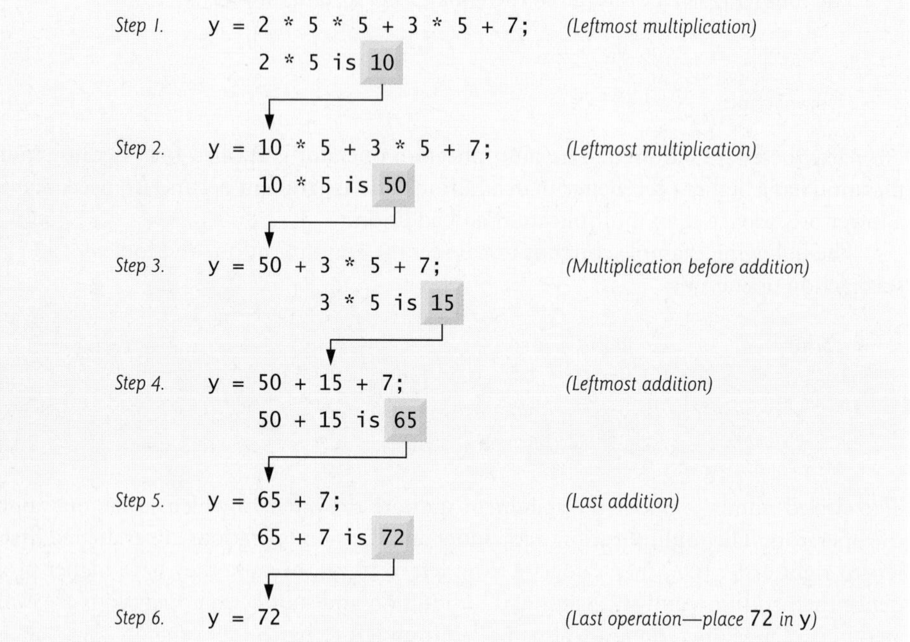

Step 1. y = 2 * 5 * 5 + 3 * 5 + 7; (Leftmost multiplication)
2 * 5 is 10
Step 2. y = 10 * 5 + 3 * 5 + 7; (Leftmost multiplication)
10 * 5 is 50
Step 3. y = 50 + 3 * 5 + 7; (Multiplication before addition)
3 * 5 is 15
Step 4. y = 50 + 15 + 7; (Leftmost addition)
50 + 15 is 65
Step 5. y = 65 + 7; (Last addition)
65 + 7 is 72
Step 6. y = 72 (Last operation—place 72 in y)

Fig. 6.15 | Order in which a second-degree polynomial is evaluated.

ment is not executed. We will see an example shortly. [*Note:* Other versions of the `if` statement are introduced in Chapter 7, JavaScript: Control Statements I.]

Conditions in `if` statements can be formed by using the **equality operators** and **relational operators** summarized in Fig. 6.16. The relational operators all have the same level

Standard algebraic equality operator or relational operator	JavaScript equality or relational operator	Sample JavaScript condition	Meaning of JavaScript condition
Equality operators			
=	`==`	`x == y`	x is equal to y
≠	`!=`	`x != y`	x is not equal to y
Relational operators			
>	`>`	`x > y`	x is greater than y
<	`<`	`x < y`	x is less than y
≥	`>=`	`x >= y`	x is greater than or equal to y
≤	`<=`	`x <= y`	x is less than or equal to y

Fig. 6.16 | Equality and relational operators.

of precedence and associate from left to right. The equality operators both have the same level of precedence, which is lower than the precedence of the relational operators. The equality operators also associate from left to right.

Common Programming Error 6.11

It is a syntax error if the operators ==, !=, >= *and* <= *contain spaces between their symbols, as in* = =, ! =, > = *and* < =, *respectively.*

Common Programming Error 6.12

Reversing the operators !=, >= *and* <=, *as in* =!, => *and* =<, *respectively, is a syntax error.*

Common Programming Error 6.13

Confusing the equality operator, ==, *with the assignment operator,* =, *is a logic error. The equality operator should be read as "is equal to," and the assignment operator should be read as "gets" or "gets the value of." Some people prefer to read the equality operator as "double equals" or "equals equals."*

The script in Fig. 6.17 uses four `if` statements to display a time-sensitive greeting on a welcome page. The script obtains the local time from the user's computer and converts it from 24-hour clock format (0–23) to a 12-hour clock format (0–11). Using this value, the script displays an appropriate greeting for the current time of day. The script and sample output are shown in Fig. 6.17.

Lines 12–14 declare the variables used in the script. Remember that variables may be declared in one declaration or in multiple declarations. If more than one variable is declared in a single declaration (as in this example), the names are separated by commas (,). This list of names is referred to as a comma-separated list. Once again, note the comment at the end of each line, indicating the purpose of each variable in the program. Also note that some of the variables are assigned a value in the declaration—JavaScript allows you to assign a value to a variable when the variable is declared.

```
1  <?xml version = "1.0" encoding = "utf-8"?>
2  <!DOCTYPE html PUBLIC "-//W3C//DTD XHTML 1.0 Strict//EN"
3     "http://www.w3.org/TR/xhtml1/DTD/xhtml1-strict.dtd">
4
5  <!-- Fig. 6.17: welcome6.html -->
6  <!-- Using equality and relational operators. -->
7  <html xmlns = "http://www.w3.org/1999/xhtml">
8     <head>
9        <title>Using Relational Operators</title>
10       <script type = "text/javascript">
11          <!--
12          var name; // string entered by the user
13          var now = new Date();       // current date and time
14          var hour = now.getHours(); // current hour (0-23)
15
16          // read the name from the prompt box as a string
17          name = window.prompt( "Please enter your name" );
```

Fig. 6.17 | Using equality and relational operators. (Part 1 of 2.)

```
18
19          // determine whether it is morning
20          if ( hour < 12 )
21             document.write( "<h1>Good Morning, " );
22
23          // determine whether the time is PM
24          if ( hour >= 12 )
25          {
26             // convert to a 12-hour clock
27             hour = hour - 12;
28
29             // determine whether it is before 6 PM
30             if ( hour < 6 )
31                document.write( "<h1>Good Afternoon, " );
32
33             // determine whether it is after 6 PM
34             if ( hour >= 6 )
35                document.write( "<h1>Good Evening, " );
36          } // end if
37
38          document.writeln( name +
39             ", welcome to JavaScript programming!</h1>" );
40          // -->
41       </script>
42    </head>
43    <body>
44       <p>Click Refresh (or Reload) to run this script again.</p>
45    </body>
46 </html>
```

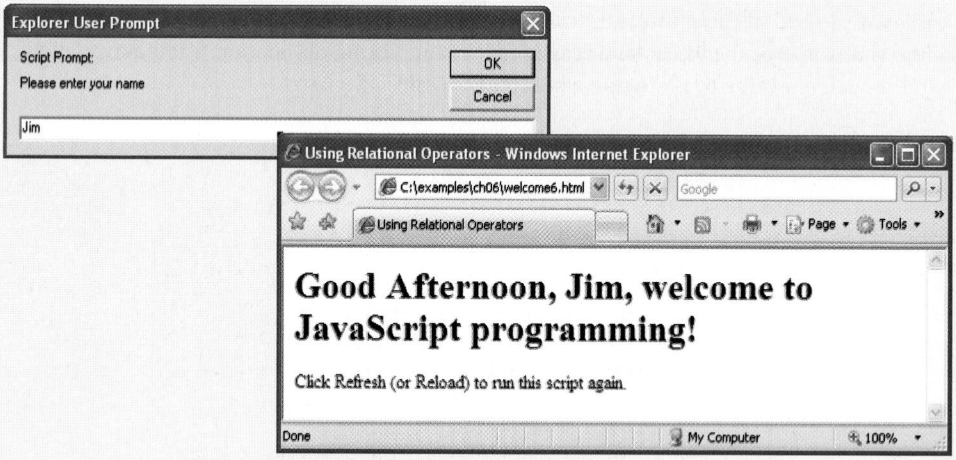

Fig. 6.17 | Using equality and relational operators. (Part 2 of 2.)

Line 13 sets the variable now to a new **Date object**, which contains information about the current local time. In Section 6.2, we introduced the document object, an object that encapsulates data pertaining to the current web page. Programmers may choose to use other objects to perform specific tasks or obtain particular pieces of information. Here, we use JavaScript's built-in `Date` object to acquire the current local time. We create a new instance of an object by using the **new** operator followed by the type of the object, `Date`, and a pair of parentheses. Some objects require that arguments be placed in the parentheses to specify details about the object to be created. In this case, we leave the parentheses empty to create a default `Date` object containing information about the current date and time. After line 13 executes, the variable `now` refers to the new `Date` object. [*Note:* We did not need to use the `new` operator when we used the `document` and `window` objects because these objects always are created by the browser.] Line 14 sets the variable `hour` to an integer equal to the current hour (in a 24-hour clock format) returned by the `Date` object's `getHours` method. Chapter 11 presents a more detailed discussion of the `Date` object's attributes and methods, and of objects in general. As in the preceding example, the script uses `window.prompt` to allow the user to enter a name to display as part of the greeting (line 17).

To display the correct time-sensitive greeting, the script must determine whether the user is visiting the page during the morning, afternoon or evening. The first `if` statement (lines 20–21) compares the value of variable `hour` with `12`. If `hour` is less than `12`, then the user is visiting the page during the morning, and the statement at line 21 outputs the string `"Good morning"`. If this condition is not met, line 21 is not executed. Line 24 determines whether `hour` is greater than or equal to `12`. If `hour` is greater than or equal to `12`, then the user is visiting the page in either the afternoon or the evening. Lines 25–36 execute to determine the appropriate greeting. If `hour` is less than `12`, then the JavaScript interpreter does not execute these lines and continues to line 38.

The brace `{` in line 25 begins a block of statements (lines 27–35) that are all executed together if `hour` is greater than or equal to `12`—to execute multiple statements inside an `if` construct, enclose them in curly braces. Line 27 subtracts `12` from `hour`, converting the current hour from a 24-hour clock format (0–23) to a 12-hour clock format (0–11). The `if` statement (line 30) determines whether `hour` is now less than `6`. If it is, then the time is between noon and 6 PM, and line 31 outputs the beginning of an XHTML `h1` element (`"<h1>Good Afternoon, "`). If `hour` is greater than or equal to `6`, the time is between 6 PM and midnight, and the script outputs the greeting `"Good Evening"` (lines 34–35). The brace `}` in line 36 ends the block of statements associated with the `if` statement in line 24. Note that `if` statements can be **nested**, i.e., one `if` statement can be placed inside another `if` statement. The `if` statements that determine whether the user is visiting the page in the afternoon or the evening (lines 30–31 and lines 34–35) execute only if the script has already established that `hour` is greater than or equal to `12` (line 24). If the script has already determined the current time of day to be morning, these additional comparisons are not performed. (Chapter 7, JavaScript: Control Statements I, presents a more in-depth discussion of blocks and nested `if` statements.) Finally, lines 38–39 output the rest of the XHTML `h1` element (the remaining part of the greeting), which does not depend on the time of day.

Good Programming Practice 6.7

Include comments after the closing curly brace of control statements (such as `if` statements) to indicate where the statements end, as in line 36 of Fig. 6.17.

Note the indentation of the `if` statements throughout the program. Such indentation enhances program readability.

Good Programming Practice 6.8

Indent the statement in the body of an `if` statement to make the body of the statement stand out and to enhance program readability.

Good Programming Practice 6.9

Place only one statement per line in a program. This enhances program readability.

Common Programming Error 6.14

Forgetting the left and/or right parentheses for the condition in an `if` statement is a syntax error. The parentheses are required.

Note that there is no semicolon (`;`) at the end of the first line of each `if` statement. Including such a semicolon would result in a logic error at execution time. For example,

```
if ( hour < 12 ) ;
   document.write( "<h1>Good Morning, " );
```

would actually be interpreted by JavaScript erroneously as

```
if ( hour < 12 )
   ;

document.write( "<h1>Good Morning, " );
```

where the semicolon on the line by itself—called the **empty statement**—is the statement to execute if the condition in the `if` statement is true. When the empty statement executes, no task is performed in the program. The program then continues with the next statement, which executes regardless of whether the condition is true or false. In this example, `"<h1>Good Morning, "` would be printed regardless of the time of day.

Common Programming Error 6.15

Placing a semicolon immediately after the right parenthesis of the condition in an `if` statement is normally a logic error. The semicolon would cause the body of the `if` statement to be empty, so the `if` statement itself would perform no action, regardless of whether its condition was true. Worse yet, the intended body statement of the `if` statement would now become a statement in sequence after the `if` statement and would always be executed.

Common Programming Error 6.16

Leaving out a condition in a series of `if` statements is normally a logic error. For instance, checking if `hour` is greater than `12` or less than `12`, but not if `hour` is equal to `12`, would mean that the script takes no action when `hour` is equal to `12`. Always be sure to handle every possible condition.

Note the use of spacing in lines 38–39 of Fig. 6.17. Remember that white-space characters, such as tabs, newlines and spaces, are normally ignored by the browser. So, statements may be split over several lines and may be spaced according to the programmer's preferences without affecting the meaning of a program. However, it is incorrect to split identifiers and string literals. Ideally, statements should be kept small, but it is not always possible to do so.

Good Programming Practice 6.10

A lengthy statement may be spread over several lines. If a single statement must be split across lines, choose breaking points that make sense, such as after a comma in a comma-separated list or after an operator in a lengthy expression. If a statement is split across two or more lines, indent all subsequent lines.

The chart in Fig. 6.18 shows the precedence of the operators introduced in this chapter. The operators are shown from top to bottom in decreasing order of precedence. Note that all of these operators, with the exception of the assignment operator, `=`, associate from left to right. Addition is left associative, so an expression like `x + y + z` is evaluated as if it had been written as `(x + y) + z`. The assignment operator, `=`, associates from right to left, so an expression like `x = y = 0` is evaluated as if it had been written as `x = (y = 0)`, which first assigns the value `0` to variable `y`, then assigns the result of that assignment, `0`, to `x`.

Good Programming Practice 6.11

Refer to the operator precedence chart when writing expressions containing many operators. Confirm that the operations are performed in the order in which you expect them to be performed. If you are uncertain about the order of evaluation in a complex expression, use parentheses to force the order, exactly as you would do in algebraic expressions. Be sure to observe that some operators, such as assignment (=), associate from right to left rather than from left to right.

Operators	Associativity	Type
`*` `/` `%`	left to right	multiplicative
`+` `-`	left to right	additive
`<` `<=` `>` `>=`	left to right	relational
`==` `!=`	left to right	equality
`=`	right to left	assignment

Fig. 6.18 | Precedence and associativity of the operators discussed so far.

6.8 Wrap-Up

We've introduced many important features of JavaScript, including how to display data, how to input data from the keyboard, how to perform calculations and how to make decisions. We also discussed the basics of memory and how variables are stored in a computer. In Chapter 7, we introduce structured programming. You will become more familiar with indentation techniques. We will study how to specify and vary the order in which statements are executed; this order is called the flow of control.

6.9 Web Resources

`www.deitel.com/javascript`

The Deitel JavaScript Resource Center contains links to some of the best JavaScript resources on the web. There you'll find categorized links to JavaScript tools, code generators, forums, books, libraries, frameworks and more. Also check out the tutorials for all skill levels, from introductory to advanced.

Summary

Section 6.1 Introduction

- The JavaScript language facilitates a disciplined approach to the design of computer programs that enhance web pages.

Section 6.2 Simple Program: Displaying a Line of Text in a Web Page

- The spacing displayed by a browser in a web page is determined by the XHTML elements used to format the page.
- Often, JavaScripts appear in the <head> section of the XHTML document.
- The browser interprets the contents of the <head> section first.
- The <script> tag indicates to the browser that the text that follows is part of a script. Attribute type specifies the scripting language used in the script—such as text/javascript.
- A string of characters can be contained between double (") or single (') quotation marks.
- A string is sometimes called a character string, a message or a string literal.
- The browser's document object represents the XHTML document currently being displayed in the browser. The document object allows a script programmer to specify XHTML text to be displayed in the XHTML document.
- The browser contains a complete set of objects that allow script programmers to access and manipulate every element of an XHTML document.
- An object resides in the computer's memory and contains information used by the script. The term object normally implies that attributes (data) and behaviors (methods) are associated with the object. The object's methods use the attributes' data to perform useful actions for the client of the object—the script that calls the methods.
- The document object's writeln method writes a line of XHTML text in the XHTML document.
- The parentheses following the name of a method contain the arguments that the method requires to perform its task (or its action).
- Using writeln to write a line of XHTML text into a document does not guarantee that a corresponding line of text will appear in the XHTML document. The text displayed is dependent on the contents of the string written, which is subsequently rendered by the browser. The browser will interpret the XHTML elements as it normally does to render the final text in the document.
- Every statement should end with a semicolon (also known as the statement terminator), although none is required by JavaScript.
- JavaScript is case sensitive. Not using the proper uppercase and lowercase letters is a syntax error.

Section 6.3 Modifying Our First Program

- Sometimes it is useful to display information in windows called dialogs that "pop up" on the screen to grab the user's attention. Dialogs are typically used to display important messages to the user browsing the web page. The browser's window object uses method alert to display an alert dialog. Method alert requires as its argument the string to be displayed.
- When a backslash is encountered in a string of characters, the next character is combined with the backslash to form an escape sequence. The escape sequence \n is the newline character. It causes the cursor in the XHTML document to move to the beginning of the next line.

Section 6.4 Obtaining User Input with **prompt** *Dialogs*

- Keywords are words with special meaning in JavaScript.

- The keyword var is used to declare the names of variables. A variable is a location in the computer's memory where a value can be stored for use by a program. All variables have a name, type and value, and should be declared with a var statement before they are used in a program.
- A variable name can be any valid identifier consisting of letters, digits, underscores (_) and dollar signs ($) that does not begin with a digit and is not a reserved JavaScript keyword.
- Declarations end with a semicolon (;) and can be split over several lines, with each variable in the declaration separated by a comma (forming a comma-separated list of variable names). Several variables may be declared in one declaration or in multiple declarations.
- Programmers often indicate the purpose of a variable in the program by placing a JavaScript comment at the end of the variable's declaration. A single-line comment begins with the characters / / and terminates at the end of the line. Comments do not cause the browser to perform any action when the script is interpreted; rather, comments are ignored by the JavaScript interpreter.
- Multiline comments begin with delimiter /* and end with delimiter */. All text between the delimiters of the comment is ignored by the interpreter.
- The window object's prompt method displays a dialog into which the user can type a value. The first argument is a message (called a prompt) that directs the user to take a specific action. The optional second argument is the default string to display in the text field.
- A variable is assigned a value with an assignment statement, using the assignment operator, =. The = operator is called a binary operator, because it has two operands.
- The null keyword signifies that a variable has no value. Note that null is not a string literal, but rather a predefined term indicating the absence of value. Writing a null value to the document, however, displays the word "null".
- Function parseInt converts its string argument to an integer.
- JavaScript has a version of the + operator for string concatenation that enables a string and a value of another data type (including another string) to be concatenated.

Section 6.5 Memory Concepts

- Variable names correspond to locations in the computer's memory. Every variable has a name, a type and a value.
- When a value is placed in a memory location, the value replaces the previous value in that location. When a value is read out of a memory location, the process is nondestructive.
- JavaScript does not require variables to have a type before they can be used in a program. A variable in JavaScript can contain a value of any data type, and in many situations, JavaScript automatically converts between values of different types for you. For this reason, JavaScript is referred to as a loosely typed language.
- When a variable is declared in JavaScript, but is not given a value, it has an undefined value. Attempting to use the value of such a variable is normally a logic error.
- When variables are declared, they are not assigned default values, unless specified otherwise by the programmer. To indicate that a variable does not contain a value, you can assign the value null to it.

Section 6.6 Arithmetic

- The basic arithmetic operators (+, -, *, /, and %) are binary operators, because they each operate on two operands.
- Parentheses can be used to group expressions as in algebra.
- Operators in arithmetic expressions are applied in a precise sequence determined by the rules of operator precedence.

- When we say that operators are applied from left to right, we are referring to the associativity of the operators. Some operators associate from right to left.

Section 6.7 Decision Making: Equality and Relational Operators
- JavaScript's `if` statement allows a program to make a decision based on the truth or falsity of a condition. If the condition is met (i.e., the condition is true), the statement in the body of the `if` statement is executed. If the condition is not met (i.e., the condition is false), the statement in the body of the `if` statement is not executed.
- Conditions in `if` statements can be formed by using the equality operators and relational operators.

Terminology

`\"` double-quote escape sequence
`\\` backslash escape sequence
`\'` single quote escape sequence
`\n` newline escape sequence
`\r` carriage return escape sequence
`\t` tab escape sequence
action
addition operator (+)
`alert` dialog
`alert` method of the `window` object
argument to a method
arithmetic expression in straight-line form
arithmetic operator
assignment
assignment operator (=)
assignment statement
associativity of operators
attribute
backslash (\) escape character
behavior
binary operator
case sensitive
character string
client of an object
comma-separated list
comment
condition
cursor
data
data type
`Date` object
decision making
declaration
dialog
division operator (/)
`document` object
double quotation (") marks
ECMAScript standard
empty statement
equality operators
error message
escape sequence
false
function
identifier
`if` statement
inline scripting
integer
interpreter
JavaScript
JavaScript interpreter
keyword
level of precedence
literal
location in the computer's memory
logic error
loosely typed language
meaningful variable name
method
mouse cursor
multiline comment (/* and */)
multiplication operator (*)
name of a variable
`NaN` (not a number)
nested `if` statements
`new` operator
newline character (`\n`)
`null`
object
operand
operator associativity
operator precedence
parentheses
`parseInt` function
perform an action
`pre` element

program
prompt
prompt dialog
prompt method of the window object
redundant parentheses
relational operator
remainder after division
remainder operator (%)
rules of operator precedence
runtime error
script
script element
scripting language
semicolon (;) statement terminator
single quotation (') mark
single-line comment (//)
statement
straight-line form
string
string concatenation
string concatenation operator (+)
string literal
string of characters
subtraction operator (-)
syntax error
text field
title bar of a dialog
true
type attribute of the <script> tag
type of a variable
undefined
value of a variable
var keyword
variable
violation of the language rules
white-space character
whole number
window object
write method of the document object
writeln method of the document object

Self-Review Exercises

6.1 Fill in the blanks in each of the following statements:

a) _______ begins a single-line comment.
b) Every statement should end with a(n) _______.
c) The _______ statement is used to make decisions.
d) _______, _______, _______ and _______ are known as white space.
e) The _______ object displays alert dialogs and prompt dialogs.
f) _______ are words that are reserved for use by JavaScript.
g) Methods _______ and _______ of the _______ object write XHTML text into an XHTML document.

6.2 State whether each of the following is *true* or *false*. If *false*, explain why.

a) Comments cause the computer to print the text after the // on the screen when the program is executed.
b) JavaScript considers the variables number and NuMbEr to be identical.
c) The remainder operator (%) can be used only with numeric operands.
d) The arithmetic operators *, /, %, + and - all have the same level of precedence.
e) Method parseInt converts an integer to a string.

6.3 Write JavaScript statements to accomplish each of the following tasks:

a) Declare variables c, thisIsAVariable, q76354 and number.
b) Display a dialog asking the user to enter an integer. Show a default value of 0 in the text field.
c) Convert a string to an integer, and store the converted value in variable age. Assume that the string is stored in stringValue.
d) If the variable number is not equal to 7, display "The variable number is not equal to 7" in a message dialog.
e) Output a line of XHTML text that will display the message "This is a JavaScript program" on one line in the XHTML document.

f) Output a line of XHTML text that will display the message "This is a JavaScript program" on two lines in the XHTML document. Use only one statement.

6.4 Identify and correct the errors in each of the following statements:

a)
```
if ( c < 7 );
   window.alert( "c is less than 7" );
```
b)
```
if ( c => 7 )
   window.alert( "c is equal to or greater than 7" );
```

6.5 Write a statement (or comment) to accomplish each of the following tasks:

a) State that a program will calculate the product of three integers [*Hint:* Use text that helps to document a program.]
b) Declare the variables `x`, `y`, `z` and `result`.
c) Declare the variables `xVal`, `yVal` and `zVal`.
d) Prompt the user to enter the first value, read the value from the user and store it in the variable `xVal`.
e) Prompt the user to enter the second value, read the value from the user and store it in the variable `yVal`.
f) Prompt the user to enter the third value, read the value from the user and store it in the variable `zVal`.
g) Convert `xVal` to an integer, and store the result in the variable `x`.
h) Convert `yVal` to an integer, and store the result in the variable `y`.
i) Convert `zVal` to an integer, and store the result in the variable `z`.
j) Compute the product of the three integers contained in variables `x`, `y` and `z`, and assign the result to the variable `result`.
k) Write a line of XHTML text containing the string "`The product is` " followed by the value of the variable `result`.

6.6 Using the statements you wrote in Exercise 6.5, write a complete program that calculates and prints the product of three integers.

Answers to Self-Review Exercises

6.1 a) `//`. b) Semicolon (`;`). c) `if`. d) Space characters, newline characters and tab characters. e) `window`. f) Keywords. g) `write`, `writeln`, `document`.

6.2 a) False. Comments do not cause any action to be performed when the program is executed. They are used to document programs and improve their readability. b) False. JavaScript is case sensitive, so these variables are distinct. c) True. d) False. The operators `*`, `/` and `%` are on the same level of precedence, and the operators `+` and `-` are on a lower level of precedence. e) False. Function `parseInt` converts a string to an integer value.

6.3

a) `var c, thisIsAVariable, q76354, number;`
b) `value = window.prompt( "Enter an integer", "0" );`
c) `var age = parseInt( stringValue );`
d)
```
if ( number != 7 )
   window.alert( "The variable number is not equal to 7" );
```
e) `document.writeln( "This is a JavaScript program" );`
f) `document.writeln( "This is a<br />JavaScript program" );`

6.4 a) Error: There should not be a semicolon after the right parenthesis of the condition in the `if` statement.
Correction: Remove the semicolon after the right parenthesis. [*Note:* The result of this error is that the output statement is executed whether or not the condition in the `if`

statement is true. The semicolon after the right parenthesis is considered an empty statement—a statement that does nothing.]

b) Error: The relational operator => is incorrect.
Correction: Change => to >=.

6.5

a) `// Calculate the product of three integers`
b) `var x, y, z, result;`
c) `var xVal, yVal, zVal;`
d) `xVal = window.prompt( "Enter first integer:", "0" );`
e) `yVal = window.prompt( "Enter second integer:", "0" );`
f) `zVal = window.prompt( "Enter third integer:", "0" );`
g) `x = parseInt( xVal );`
h) `y = parseInt( yVal );`
i) `z = parseInt( zVal );`
j) `result = x * y * z;`
k) `document.writeln( "<h1>The product is " + result + "</h1>" );`

6.6 The program is as follows:

```
<?xml version = "1.0" encoding = "utf-8"?>
<!DOCTYPE html PUBLIC "-//W3C//DTD XHTML 1.0 Strict//EN"
   "http://www.w3.org/TR/xhtml1/DTD/xhtml1-strict.dtd">

<!-- Exercise 6.6: product.html -->
<html xmlns = "http://www.w3.org/1999/xhtml">
   <head>
      <title>Product of Three Integers</title>
      <script type = "text/javascript">
         <!--
         // Calculate the product of three integers
         var x, y, z, result;
         var xVal, yVal, zVal;

         xVal = window.prompt( "Enter first integer:", "0" );
         yVal = window.prompt( "Enter second integer:", "0" );
         zVal = window.prompt( "Enter third integer:", "0" );

         x = parseInt( xVal );
         y = parseInt( yVal );
         z = parseInt( zVal );

         result = x * y * z;
         document.writeln( "<h1>The product is " +
            result + "<h1>" );
         // -->
      </script>
   </head><body></body>
</html>
```

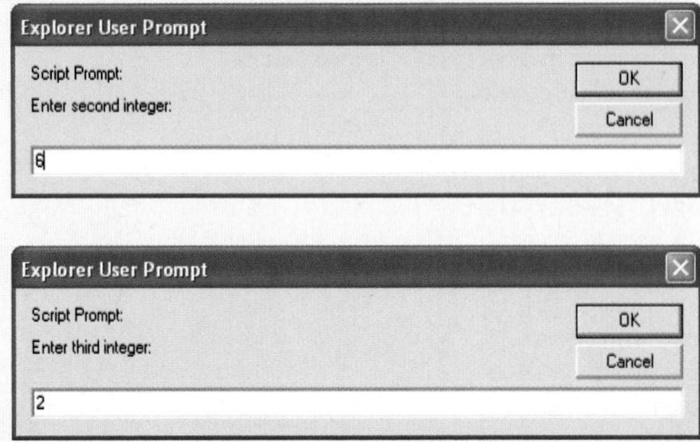

Exercises

6.7 Fill in the blanks in each of the following statements:

a) _______ are used to document a program and improve its readability.

b) A dialog capable of receiving input from the user is displayed with method _______ of object _______.

c) A JavaScript statement that makes a decision is the _______ statement.

d) Calculations are normally performed by _______ operators.

e) A dialog capable of showing a message to the user is displayed with method _______ of object _______.

6.8 Write JavaScript statements that accomplish each of the following tasks:

a) Display the message `"Enter two numbers"` using the `window` object.

b) Assign the product of variables `b` and `c` to variable `a`.

c) State that a program performs a sample payroll calculation.

6.9 State whether each of the following is *true* or *false*. If *false*, explain why.

a) JavaScript operators are evaluated from left to right.

b) The following are all valid variable names: `_under_bar_`, `m928134`, `t5`, `j7`, `her_sales$`, `his_$account_total`, `a`, `b$`, `c`, `z`, `z2`.

c) A valid JavaScript arithmetic expression with no parentheses is evaluated from left to right.

d) The following are all invalid variable names: `3g`, `87`, `67h2`, `h22`, `2h`.

6.10 Fill in the blanks in each of the following statements:

a) What arithmetic operations have the same precedence as multiplication? ________.
b) When parentheses are nested, which set of parentheses is evaluated first in an arithmetic expression? ________.
c) A location in the computer's memory that may contain different values at various times throughout the execution of a program is called a ________.

6.11 What displays in the message dialog when each of the given JavaScript statements is performed? Assume that `x = 2` and `y = 3`.

a) `window.alert( "x = " + x );`
b) `window.alert( "The value of x + x is " + ( x + x ) );`
c) `window.alert( "x =" );`
d) `window.alert( ( x + y ) + " = " + ( y + x ) );`

6.12 Which of the following JavaScript statements contain variables whose values are destroyed (i.e., changed or replaced)?

a) `p = i + j + k + 7;`
b) `window.alert( "variables whose values are destroyed" );`
c) `window.alert( "a = 5" );`
d) `stringVal = window.prompt( "Enter string:" );`

6.13 Given $y = ax^3 + 7$, which of the following are correct JavaScript statements for this equation?

a) `y = a * x * x * x + 7;`
b) `y = a * x * x * (x + 7);`
c) `y = (a * x) * x * (x + 7);`
d) `y = (a * x) * x * x + 7;`
e) `y = a * (x * x * x) + 7;`
f) `y = a * x * (x * x + 7);`

6.14 State the order of evaluation of the operators in each of the following JavaScript statements, and show the value of `x` after each statement is performed.

a) `x = 7 + 3 * 6 / 2 - 1;`
b) `x = 2 % 2 + 2 * 2 - 2 / 2;`
c) `x = ( 3 * 9 * ( 3 + ( 9 * 3 / ( 3 ) ) ) );`

6.15 Write a script that displays the numbers 1 to 4 on the same line, with each pair of adjacent numbers separated by one space. Write the program using the following methods:

a) Using one `document.writeln` statement.
b) Using four `document.write` statements.

6.16 Write a script that asks the user to enter two numbers, obtains the two numbers from the user and outputs text that displays the sum, product, difference and quotient of the two numbers. Use the techniques shown in Fig. 6.9.

6.17 Write a script that asks the user to enter two integers, obtains the numbers from the user and outputs text that displays the larger number followed by the words "`is larger`" in an alert dialog. If the numbers are equal, output XHTML text that displays the message "`These numbers are equal`." Use the techniques shown in Fig. 6.17.

6.18 Write a script that takes three integers from the user and displays the sum, average, product, smallest and largest of the numbers in an `alert` dialog.

6.19 Write a script that gets from the user the radius of a circle and outputs XHTML text that displays the circle's diameter, circumference and area. Use the constant value 3.14159 for π. Use the GUI techniques shown in Fig. 6.9. [*Note:* You may also use the predefined constant `Math.PI` for the value of π. This constant is more precise than the value 3.14159. The `Math` object is defined by Java-

Script and provides many common mathematical capabilities.] Use the following formulas (*r* is the radius): *diameter* = $2r$, *circumference* = $2\pi r$, *area* = πr^2.

6.20 Write a script that outputs XHTML text that displays in the XHTML document a rectangle, an oval, an arrow and a diamond using asterisks (*), as follows [*Note:* Use the `<pre>` and `</pre>` tags to specify that the asterisks should be displayed using a fixed-width font]:

```
*********          ***              *               *
*       *        *     *           ***             * *
*       *       *       *         *****           *   *
*       *       *       *           *            *     *
*       *       *       *           *           *       *
*       *       *       *           *            *     *
*       *       *       *           *             *   *
*       *        *     *            *              * *
*********          ***              *               *
```

6.21 Modify the program you created in Exercise 6.20 by removing the `<pre>` and `</pre>` tags. Does the program display the shapes exactly as in Exercise 6.20?

6.22 What does the following code print?

```
document.writeln( "*\n**\n***\n****\n*****" );
```

6.23 What does the following code print?

```
document.writeln( "*" );
document.writeln( "***" );
document.writeln( "*****" );
document.writeln( "****" );
document.writeln( "**" );
```

6.24 What does the following code print?

```
document.write( "*<br />" );
document.write( "***<br />" );
document.write( "*****<br />" );
document.write( "****<br />" );
document.writeln( "**" );
```

6.25 What does the following code print?

```
document.write( "*<br />" );
document.writeln( "***" );
document.writeln( "*****" );
document.write( "****<br />" );
document.writeln( "**" );
```

6.26 Write a script that reads five integers and determines and outputs XHTML text that displays the largest and smallest integers in the group. Use only the programming techniques you learned in this chapter.

6.27 Write a script that reads an integer and determines and outputs XHTML text that displays whether it is odd or even. [*Hint:* Use the remainder operator. An even number is a multiple of 2. Any multiple of 2 leaves a remainder of zero when divided by 2.]

6.28 Write a script that reads in two integers and determines and outputs XHTML text that displays whether the first is a multiple of the second. [*Hint*: Use the remainder operator.]

6.29 Write a script that outputs XHTML text that displays in the XHTML document a checkerboard pattern, as follows:

6.30 Write a script that inputs five numbers and determines and outputs XHTML text that displays the number of negative numbers input, the number of positive numbers input and the number of zeros input.

6.31 Write a script that calculates the squares and cubes of the numbers from 0 to 10 and outputs XHTML text that displays the resulting values in an XHTML table format, as follows:

number	square	cube
0	0	0
1	1	1
2	4	8
3	9	27
4	16	64
5	25	125
6	36	216
7	49	343
8	64	512
9	81	729
10	100	1000

[*Note:* This program does not require any input from the user.]

7

JavaScript: Control Statements I

Let's all move one place on.
—Lewis Carroll

The wheel is come full circle.
—William Shakespeare

How many apples fell on Newton's head before he took the hint!
—Robert Frost

OBJECTIVES

In this chapter you will learn:

- Basic problem-solving techniques.
- To develop algorithms through the process of top-down, stepwise refinement.
- To use the `if` and `if...else` selection statements to choose among alternative actions.
- To use the `while` repetition statement to execute statements in a script repeatedly.
- Counter-controlled repetition and sentinel-controlled repetition.
- To use the increment, decrement and assignment operators.

Outline

7.1 Introduction

Before writing a script to solve a problem, it is essential to have a thorough understanding of the problem and a carefully planned approach to solving the problem. When writing a script, it is equally essential to understand the types of building blocks that are available and to employ proven program-construction principles. In this chapter and in Chapter 8, we discuss these issues in our presentation of the theory and principles of structured programming. The techniques you will learn here are applicable to most high-level languages, including JavaScript.

7.2 Algorithms

Any computable problem can be solved by executing a series of actions in a specific order. A procedure for solving a problem in terms of

1. the actions to be executed, and
2. the order in which the actions are to be executed

is called an algorithm. The following example demonstrates that correctly specifying the order in which the actions are to execute is important.

Consider the "rise-and-shine algorithm" followed by one junior executive for getting out of bed and going to work: (1) get out of bed, (2) take off pajamas, (3) take a shower, (4) get dressed, (5) eat breakfast, (6) carpool to work. This routine gets the executive to work well prepared to make critical decisions. Suppose, however, that the same steps are performed in a slightly different order: (1) get out of bed, (2) take off pajamas, (3) get dressed, (4) take a shower, (5) eat breakfast, (6) carpool to work. In this case, our junior executive shows up for work soaking wet. Specifying the order in which statements are to be executed in a computer program is called program control. In this chapter and Chapter 8, we investigate the program-control capabilities of JavaScript.

7.3 Pseudocode

Pseudocode is an artificial and informal language that helps programmers develop algorithms. The pseudocode we present here is useful for developing algorithms that will be converted to structured portions of JavaScript programs. Pseudocode is similar to everyday English; it is convenient and user friendly, although it is not an actual computer programming language.

Software Engineering Observation 7.1

Pseudocode is often used to "think out" a program during the program-design process. Then the pseudocode program is converted to a programming language such as JavaScript.

The style of pseudocode we present consists purely of characters, so that programmers may conveniently type pseudocode in an editor program. The computer can produce a fresh printed copy of a pseudocode program on demand. Carefully prepared pseudocode may easily be converted to a corresponding JavaScript program. This process is done in many cases simply by replacing pseudocode statements with their JavaScript equivalents. In this chapter, we give several examples of pseudocode.

Pseudocode normally describes only executable statements—the actions that are performed when the program is converted from pseudocode to JavaScript and is run. Declarations are not executable statements. For example, the declaration

```
var value1;
```

instructs the JavaScript interpreter to reserve space in memory for the variable `value1`. This declaration does not cause any action—such as input, output or a calculation—to occur when the script executes. Some programmers choose to list variables and mention the purpose of each variable at the beginning of a pseudocode program.

7.4 Control Structures

Normally, statements in a program execute one after the other in the order in which they are written. This process is called sequential execution. Various JavaScript statements we will soon discuss enable the programmer to specify that the next statement to execute may not be the next one in sequence. This is known as transfer of control.

During the 1960s, it became clear that the indiscriminate use of transfers of control was the root of much difficulty experienced by software development groups. The finger of blame was pointed at the goto statement, which allowed the programmer to specify a transfer of control to one of a wide range of possible destinations in a program. The notion of so-called structured programming became almost synonymous with "goto elimination." JavaScript does not have a `goto` statement.

The research of Bohm and Jacopini demonstrated that programs could be written without `goto` statements.[1] The challenge of the era for programmers was to shift their styles to "`goto`-less programming." It was not until the 1970s that programmers started taking structured programming seriously. The results were impressive, as software development groups reported reduced development times, more frequent on-time delivery of

1. Bohm, C., and G. Jacopini, "Flow Diagrams, Turing Machines, and Languages with Only Two Formation Rules," *Communications of the ACM*, Vol. 9, No. 5, May 1966, pp. 336–371.

systems and more frequent within-budget completion of software projects. The key to these successes is that structured programs are clearer, easier to debug and modify and more likely to be bug free in the first place.

Bohm and Jacopini's work demonstrated that all programs could be written in terms of only three control structures, namely the sequence structure, the selection structure and the repetition structure. The sequence structure is built into JavaScript. Unless directed otherwise, the computer executes JavaScript statements one after the other in the order in which they are written (i.e., in sequence). The flowchart segment of Fig. 7.1 illustrates a typical sequence structure in which two calculations are performed in order.

A flowchart is a graphical representation of an algorithm or of a portion of an algorithm. Flowcharts are drawn using certain special-purpose symbols, such as rectangles, diamonds, ovals and small circles; these symbols are connected by arrows called flowlines, which indicate the order in which the actions of the algorithm execute.

Like pseudocode, flowcharts often are useful for developing and representing algorithms, although pseudocode is strongly preferred by many programmers. Flowcharts show clearly how control structures operate; that is all we use them for in this text. Carefully compare the pseudocode and flowchart representations of each control structure.

Consider the flowchart segment for the sequence structure on the left side of Fig. 7.1. We use the rectangle symbol (or action symbol) to indicate any type of action, including a calculation or an input/output operation. The flowlines in the figure indicate the order in which the actions are performed—the first action adds `grade` to `total`, then the second action adds `1` to `counter`. JavaScript allows us to have as many actions as we want in a sequence structure. Anywhere a single action may be placed, as we will soon see, we may place several actions in sequence.

In a flowchart that represents a *complete* algorithm, an oval symbol containing the word "Begin" is the first symbol used; an oval symbol containing the word "End" indicates where the algorithm ends. In a flowchart that shows only a portion of an algorithm, as in Fig. 7.1, the oval symbols are omitted in favor of using small circle symbols, also called connector symbols.

Perhaps the most important flowcharting symbol is the diamond symbol, also called the decision symbol, which indicates that a decision is to be made. We discuss the diamond symbol in the next section.

JavaScript provides three types of selection structures; we discuss each in this chapter and in Chapter 8. The `if` selection statement performs (selects) an action if a condition is true or skips the action if the condition is false. The `if...else` selection statement per-

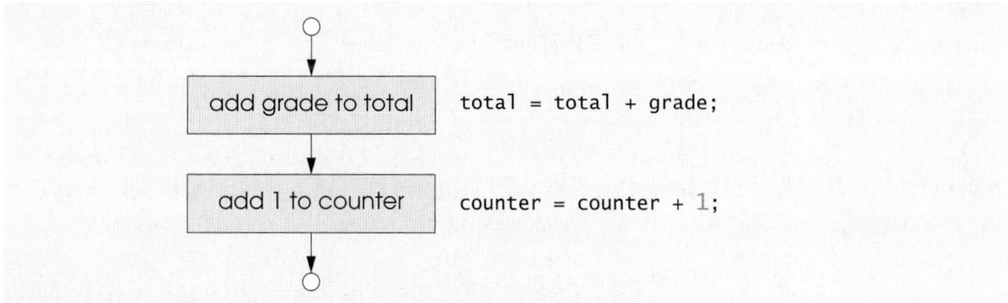

Fig. 7.1 | Flowcharting JavaScript's sequence structure.

forms an action if a condition is true and performs a different action if the condition is false. The `switch` selection statement (Chapter 8) performs one of many different actions, depending on the value of an expression.

The `if` statement is called a **single-selection structure** because it selects or ignores a single action (or, as we will soon see, a single group of actions). The `if...else` statement is a **double-selection structure** because it selects between two different actions (or groups of actions). The `switch` statement is a **multiple-selection structure** because it selects among many different actions (or groups of actions).

JavaScript provides four repetition structure types, namely `while`, `do...while`, `for` and `for...in`. (`do...while` and `for` are covered in Chapter 8; `for...in` is covered in Chapter 10.) Each of the words `if`, `else`, `switch`, `while`, `do`, `for` and `in` is a JavaScript **keyword**. These words are reserved by the language to implement various features, such as JavaScript's control structures. Keywords cannot be used as identifiers (e.g., for variable names). A complete list of JavaScript keywords is shown in Fig. 7.2.

Common Programming Error 7.1

Using a keyword as an identifier is a syntax error.

As we have shown, JavaScript has only eight control structures: sequence, three types of selection and four types of repetition. A program is formed by combining control structures as necessary to implement the program's algorithm. As with the sequence structure in Fig. 7.1, we will see that each control structure is flowcharted with two small circle symbols, one at the entry point to the control structure and one at the exit point.

JavaScript keywords				
`break`	`case`	`catch`	`continue`	`default`
`delete`	`do`	`else`	`false`	`finally`
`for`	`function`	`if`	`in`	`instanceof`
`new`	`null`	`return`	`switch`	`this`
`throw`	`true`	`try`	`typeof`	`var`
`void`	`while`	`with`		
Keywords that are reserved but not used by JavaScript				
`abstract`	`boolean`	`byte`	`char`	`class`
`const`	`debugger`	`double`	`enum`	`export`
`extends`	`final`	`float`	`goto`	`implements`
`import`	`int`	`interface`	`long`	`native`
`package`	`private`	`protected`	`public`	`short`
`static`	`super`	`synchronized`	`throws`	`transient`
`volatile`				

Fig. 7.2 | JavaScript keywords.

Single-entry/single-exit control structures make it easy to build programs; the control structures are attached to one another by connecting the exit point of one to the entry point of the next. This process is similar to the way in which a child stacks building blocks, so we call it control-structure stacking. We will learn that there is only one other way in which control structures may be connected—control-structure nesting. Thus, algorithms in JavaScript programs are constructed from only eight different types of control structures combined in only two ways.

7.5 `if` Selection Statement

A selection structure is used to choose among alternative courses of action in a program. For example, suppose that the passing grade on an examination is 60 (out of 100). Then the pseudocode statement

If student's grade is greater than or equal to 60
    Print "Passed"

determines whether the condition "student's grade is greater than or equal to 60" is true or false. If the condition is true, then "Passed" is printed, and the next pseudocode statement in order is "performed" (remember that pseudocode is not a real programming language). If the condition is false, the print statement is ignored, and the next pseudocode statement in order is performed.

Note that the second line of this selection structure is indented. Such indentation is optional but is highly recommended, because it emphasizes the inherent structure of structured programs. The JavaScript interpreter ignores white-space characters—blanks, tabs and newlines used for indentation and vertical spacing. Programmers insert these white-space characters to enhance program clarity.

Good Programming Practice 7.1

Consistently applying reasonable indentation conventions throughout your programs improves program readability. We suggest a fixed-size tab of about 1/4 inch or three spaces per indent.

The preceding pseudocode *If* statement can be written in JavaScript as

```
if ( studentGrade >= 60 )
   document.writeln( "Passed" );
```

Note that the JavaScript code corresponds closely to the pseudocode. This similarity is the reason that pseudocode is a useful program-development tool. The statement in the body of the `if` statement outputs the character string `"Passed"` in the XHTML document.

The flowchart in Fig. 7.3 illustrates the single-selection `if` statement. This flowchart contains what is perhaps the most important flowcharting symbol—the diamond symbol (or decision symbol), which indicates that a decision is to be made. The decision symbol contains an expression, such as a condition, that can be either true or false. The decision symbol has two flowlines emerging from it. One indicates the path to follow in the program when the expression in the symbol is true; the other indicates the path to follow in the program when the expression is false. A decision can be made on any expression that evaluates to a value of JavaScript's boolean type (i.e., any expression that evaluates to `true` or `false`—also known as a boolean expression).

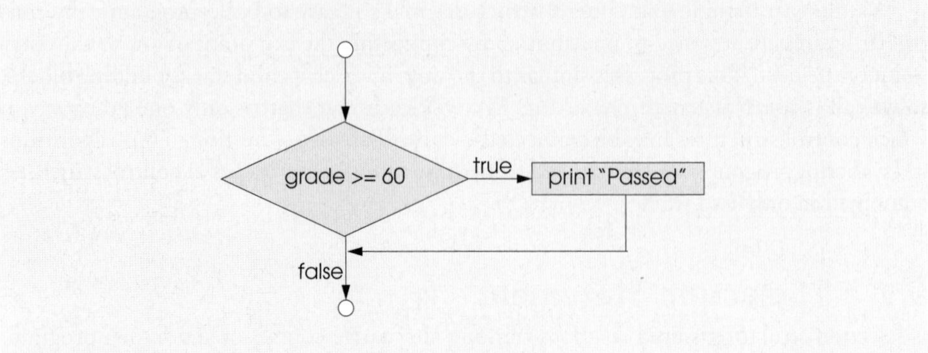

Fig. 7.3 | Flowcharting the single-selection `if` statement.

Software Engineering Observation 7.2

In JavaScript, any nonzero numeric value in a condition evaluates to `true`*, and 0 evaluates to* `false`*. For strings, any string containing one or more characters evaluates to* `true`*, and the empty string (the string containing no characters, represented as* `""`*) evaluates to* `false`*. Also, a variable that has been declared with* `var` *but has not been assigned a value evaluates to* `false`*.*

Note that the `if` statement is a single-entry/single-exit control structure. We will soon learn that the flowcharts for the remaining control structures also contain (besides small circle symbols and flowlines) only rectangle symbols, to indicate the actions to be performed, and diamond symbols, to indicate decisions to be made. This type of flowchart represents the **action/decision model of programming**.

We can envision eight bins, each containing only the control structures of one of the eight types. These control structures are empty. Nothing is written in the rectangles or in the diamonds. The programmer's task, then, is to assemble a program from as many of each type of control structure as the algorithm demands, combining them in only two possible ways (stacking or nesting), then filling in the actions and decisions in a manner appropriate for the algorithm. We will discuss the variety of ways in which actions and decisions may be written.

7.6 `if...else` Selection Statement

The `if` selection statement performs an indicated action only when the condition evaluates to `true`; otherwise, the action is skipped. The **`if...else` selection** statement allows the programmer to specify that a different action is to be performed when the condition is true than when the condition is false. For example, the pseudocode statement

If student's grade is greater than or equal to 60
    Print "Passed"
Else
    Print "Failed"

prints `Passed` if the student's grade is greater than or equal to 60 and prints `Failed` if the student's grade is less than 60. In either case, after printing occurs, the next pseudocode statement in sequence (i.e., the next statement after the whole `if...else` structure) is performed. Note that the body of the *Else* part of the structure is also indented.

Good Programming Practice 7.2

Indent both body statements of an `if...else` *statement.*

The indentation convention you choose should be applied carefully throughout your programs (both in pseudocode and in JavaScript). It is difficult to read programs that do not use uniform spacing conventions.

The preceding pseudocode *If...Else* statement may be written in JavaScript as

```
if ( studentGrade >= 60 )
   document.writeln( "Passed" );
else
   document.writeln( "Failed" );
```

The flowchart shown in Fig. 7.4 illustrates the `if...else` selection statement's flow of control. Once again, note that the only symbols in the flowchart (besides small circles and arrows) are rectangles (for actions) and a diamond (for a decision). We continue to emphasize this action/decision model of computing. Imagine again a deep bin containing as many empty double-selection structures as might be needed to build a JavaScript algorithm. The programmer's job is to assemble the selection structures (by stacking and nesting) with other control structures required by the algorithm and to fill in the empty rectangles and empty diamonds with actions and decisions appropriate to the algorithm's implementation.

JavaScript provides an operator, called the conditional operator (`?:`), that is closely related to the `if...else` statement. The operator `?:` is JavaScript's only ternary operator—it takes three operands. The operands together with the `?:` form a conditional expression. The first operand is a boolean expression, the second is the value for the conditional expression if the expression evaluates to `true` and the third is the value for the conditional expression if the expression evaluates to `false`. For example, consider the following statement

```
document.writeln( studentGrade >= 60 ? "Passed" : "Failed" );
```

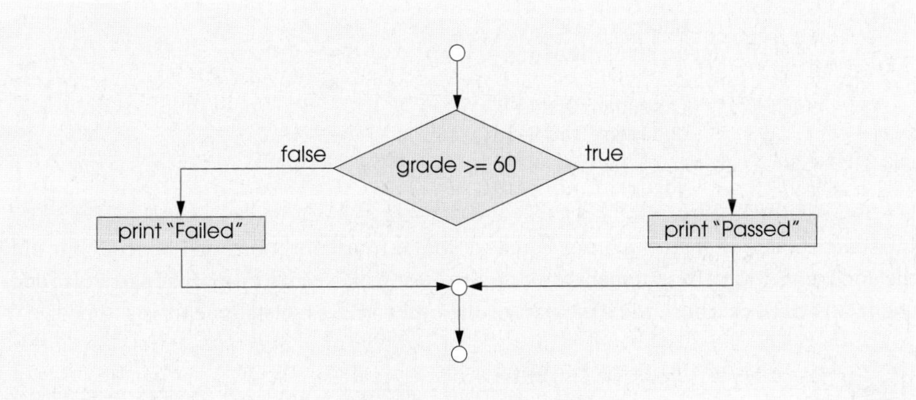

Fig. 7.4 | Flowcharting the double-selection `if...else` statement.

contains a conditional expression that evaluates to the string `"Passed"` if the condition `studentGrade >= 60` is true and evaluates to the string `"Failed"` if the condition is false. Thus, this statement with the conditional operator performs essentially the same operation as the preceding `if...else` statement. The precedence of the conditional operator is low, so the entire conditional expression is normally placed in parentheses to ensure that it evaluates correctly.

Nested `if...else` statements test for multiple cases by placing `if...else` statements inside `if...else` statements. For example, the following pseudocode statement indicates that the program should print `A` for exam grades greater than or equal to 90, `B` for grades in the range 80 to 89, `C` for grades in the range 70 to 79, `D` for grades in the range 60 to 69 and `F` for all other grades:

```
If student's grade is greater than or equal to 90
    Print "A"
Else
    If student's grade is greater than or equal to 80
        Print "B"
    Else
        If student's grade is greater than or equal to 70
            Print "C"
        Else
            If student's grade is greater than or equal to 60
                Print "D"
            Else
                Print "F"
```

This pseudocode may be written in JavaScript as

```
if ( studentGrade >= 90 )
   document.writeln( "A" );
else
   if ( studentGrade >= 80 )
      document.writeln( "B" );
   else
      if ( studentGrade >= 70 )
         document.writeln( "C" );
      else
         if ( studentGrade >= 60 )
            document.writeln( "D" );
         else
            document.writeln( "F" );
```

If `studentGrade` is greater than or equal to 90, all four conditions will be true, but only the `document.writeln` statement after the first test will execute. After that particular `document.writeln` executes, the `else` part of the outer `if...else` statements is skipped.

Good Programming Practice 7.3

If there are several levels of indentation, each level should be indented the same additional amount of space.

Most JavaScript programmers prefer to write the preceding `if` structure as

```
if ( grade >= 90 )
   document.writeln( "A" );
else if ( grade >= 80 )
   document.writeln( "B" );
else if ( grade >= 70 )
   document.writeln( "C" );
else if ( grade >= 60 )
   document.writeln( "D" );
else
   document.writeln( "F" );
```

The two forms are equivalent. The latter form is popular because it avoids the deep indentation of the code to the right. Such deep indentation often leaves little room on a line, forcing lines to be split and decreasing program readability.

It is important to note that the JavaScript interpreter always associates an `else` with the previous `if`, unless told to do otherwise by the placement of braces (`{}`). This situation is referred to as the dangling-else problem. For example,

```
if ( x > 5 )
   if ( y > 5 )
      document.writeln( "x and y are > 5" );
else
   document.writeln( "x is <= 5" );
```

appears to indicate with its indentation that if `x` is greater than `5`, the `if` structure in its body determines whether `y` is also greater than `5`. If so, the body of the nested `if` structure outputs the string `"x and y are > 5"`. Otherwise, it *appears* that if `x` is not greater than `5`, the `else` part of the `if...else` structure outputs the string `"x is <= 5"`.

Beware! The preceding nested `if` statement does not execute as it appears. The interpreter actually interprets the preceding statement as

```
if ( x > 5 )
   if ( y > 5 )
      document.writeln( "x and y are > 5" );
   else
      document.writeln( "x is <= 5" );
```

in which the body of the first `if` statement is a nested `if...else` statement. This statement tests whether `x` is greater than `5`. If so, execution continues by testing whether `y` is also greater than `5`. If the second condition is true, the proper string—`"x and y are > 5"`—is displayed. However, if the second condition is false, the string `"x is <= 5"` is displayed, even though we know that `x` is greater than `5`.

To force the preceding nested `if` statement to execute as it was intended originally, it must be written as follows:

```
if ( x > 5 )
{
   if ( y > 5 )
      document.writeln( "x and y are > 5" );
}
else
   document.writeln( "x is <= 5" );
```

The braces ({}) indicate to the interpreter that the second `if` statement is in the body of the first `if` statement and that the `else` is matched with the first `if` statement. In Exercises 7.21 and 7.22, you will investigate the dangling-else problem further.

The `if` selection statement expects only one statement in its body. To include several statements in an `if` statement's body, enclose the statements in braces ({ and }). This can also be done in the else section of an `if...else` statement. A set of statements contained within a pair of braces is called a block.

Software Engineering Observation 7.3

A block can be placed anywhere in a program that a single statement can be placed.

Software Engineering Observation 7.4

Unlike individual statements, a block does not end with a semicolon. However, each statement within the braces of a block should end with a semicolon.

The following example includes a block in the `else` part of an `if...else` statement:

```
if ( grade >= 60 )
   document.writeln( "Passed" );
else
{
   document.writeln( "Failed<br />" );
   document.writeln( "You must take this course again." );
}
```

In this case, if `grade` is less than 60, the program executes both statements in the body of the `else` and prints

```
Failed.
You must take this course again.
```

Note the braces surrounding the two statements in the `else` clause. These braces are important. Without them, the statement

```
document.writeln( "You must take this course again." );
```

would be outside the body of the `else` part of the `if` and would execute regardless of whether the grade is less than 60.

Common Programming Error 7.2

Forgetting one or both of the braces that delimit a block can lead to syntax errors or logic errors.

Syntax errors (e.g., when one brace in a block is left out of the program) are caught by the interpreter when it attempts to interpret the code containing the syntax error. A logic error (e.g., the one caused when both braces around a block are left out of the program) also has its effect at execution time. A fatal logic error causes a program to fail and terminate prematurely. A nonfatal logic error allows a program to continue executing, but the program produces incorrect results.

Good Programming Practice 7.4

Some programmers prefer to type the beginning and ending braces of blocks before typing the individual statements within the braces. This helps avoid omitting one or both of the braces.

Software Engineering Observation 7.5

Just as a block can be placed anywhere a single statement can be placed, it is also possible to have no statement at all (the empty statement) in such places. The empty statement is represented by placing a semicolon (;) where a statement would normally be.

Common Programming Error 7.3

Placing a semicolon after the condition in an `if` structure leads to a logic error in single-selection `if` structures and a syntax error in double-selection `if` structures (if the `if` part contains a non-empty body statement).

7.7 while Repetition Statement

A repetition structure (also known as a **loop**) allows the programmer to specify that a script is to repeat an action while some condition remains true. The pseudocode statement

> *While there are more items on my shopping list*
> *Purchase next item and cross it off my list*

describes the repetition that occurs during a shopping trip. The condition "there are more items on my shopping list" may be true or false. If it's true, then the action "Purchase next item and cross it off my list" is performed. This action is performed repeatedly while the condition remains true. The statement(s) contained in the *While* repetition structure constitute its body. The body of a loop such as the *While* structure may be a single statement or a block. Eventually, the condition becomes false (i.e., when the last item on the shopping list has been purchased and crossed off the list). At this point, the repetition terminates, and the first pseudocode statement after the repetition structure executes.

Common Programming Error 7.4

*If the body of a `while` statement never causes the while statement's condition to become true, a logic error occurs. Normally, such a repetition structure will never terminate—an error called an **infinite loop**. Both Internet Explorer and Firefox show a dialog allowing the user to terminate a script that contains an infinite loop.*

Common Programming Error 7.5

Remember that JavaScript is a case-sensitive language. In code, spelling the keyword `while` with an uppercase `W`, as in `While`, is a syntax error. All of JavaScript's reserved keywords, such as `while`, `if` and `else`, contain only lowercase letters.

As an example of a `while` statement, consider a program segment designed to find the first power of 2 larger than 1000. Variable `product` begins with the value 2. The statement is as follows:

```
var product = 2;

while ( product <= 1000 )
   product = 2 * product;
```

When the `while` statement finishes executing, `product` contains the result 1024. The flowchart in Fig. 7.5 illustrates the flow of control of the preceding `while` repetition statement. Once again, note that (besides small circles and arrows) the flowchart contains only a rectangle symbol and a diamond symbol.

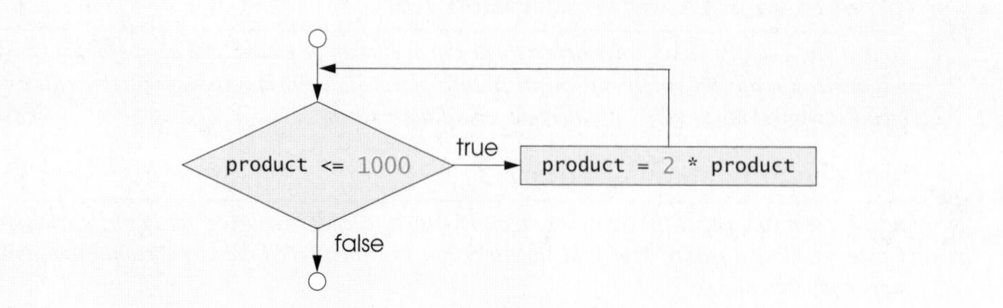

Fig. 7.5 | Flowcharting the `while` repetition statement.

When the script enters the `while` statement, `product` is 2. The script repeatedly multiplies variable `product` by 2, so `product` takes on the values 4, 8, 16, 32, 64, 128, 256, 512 and 1024 successively. When `product` becomes 1024, the condition `product <= 1000` in the `while` statement becomes `false`. This terminates the repetition, with 1024 as `product`'s final value. Execution continues with the next statement after the `while` statement. [*Note:* If a `while` statement's condition is initially `false`, the body statement(s) will never execute.]

The flowchart clearly shows the repetition. The flowline emerging from the rectangle wraps back to the decision, which the script tests each time through the loop until the decision eventually becomes false. At this point, the `while` statement exits, and control passes to the next statement in the program.

7.8 Formulating Algorithms: Counter-Controlled Repetition

To illustrate how to develop algorithms, we solve several variations of a class-averaging problem. Consider the following problem statement:

> *A class of ten students took a quiz. The grades (integers in the range 0 to 100) for this quiz are available to you. Determine the class average on the quiz.*

The class average is equal to the sum of the grades divided by the number of students (10 in this case). The algorithm for solving this problem on a computer must input each of the grades, perform the averaging calculation and display the result.

Let us use pseudocode to list the actions to execute and specify the order in which the actions should execute. We use counter-controlled repetition to input the grades one at a time. This technique uses a variable called a counter to control the number of times a set of statements executes. In this example, repetition terminates when the counter exceeds 10. In this section, we present a pseudocode algorithm (Fig. 7.6) and the corresponding program (Fig. 7.7). In the next section, we show how to develop pseudocode algorithms. Counter-controlled repetition often is called definite repetition, because the number of repetitions is known before the loop begins executing.

Note the references in the algorithm to a total and a counter. A total is a variable in which a script accumulates the sum of a series of values. A counter is a variable a script uses to count—in this case, to count the number of grades entered. Variables that store totals should normally be initialized to zero before they are used in a program.

```
Set total to zero
Set grade counter to one

While grade counter is less than or equal to ten
    Input the next grade
    Add the grade into the total
    Add one to the grade counter

Set the class average to the total divided by ten
Print the class average
```

Fig. 7.6 | Pseudocode algorithm that uses counter-controlled repetition to solve the class-average problem.

```
<?xml version = "1.0" encoding = "utf-8"?>
<!DOCTYPE html PUBLIC "-//W3C//DTD XHTML 1.0 Strict//EN"
   "http://www.w3.org/TR/xhtml1/DTD/xhtml1-strict.dtd">

<!-- Fig. 7.7: average.html -->
<!-- Counter-controlled repetition to calculate a class average. -->
<html xmlns = "http://www.w3.org/1999/xhtml">
   <head>
      <title>Class Average Program</title>
      <script type = "text/javascript">
         <!--
         var total; // sum of grades
         var gradeCounter; // number of grades entered
         var grade; // grade typed by user (as a string)
         var gradeValue; // grade value (converted to integer)
         var average; // average of all grades

         // Initialization Phase
         total = 0; // clear total
         gradeCounter = 1; // prepare to loop

         // Processing Phase
         while ( gradeCounter <= 10 ) // loop 10 times
         {

            // prompt for input and read grade from user
            grade = window.prompt( "Enter integer grade:", "0" );

            // convert grade from a string to an integer
            gradeValue = parseInt( grade );

            // add gradeValue to total
            total = total + gradeValue;

```

Fig. 7.7 | Counter-controlled repetition to calculate a class average. (Part 1 of 2.)

```
35             // add 1 to gradeCounter
36             gradeCounter = gradeCounter + 1;
37          } // end while
38
39          // Termination Phase
40          average = total / 10; // calculate the average
41
42          // display average of exam grades
43          document.writeln(
44             "<h1>Class average is " + average + "</h1>" );
45          // -->
46       </script>
47    </head>
48    <body>
49       <p>Click Refresh (or Reload) to run the script again<p>
50    </body>
51 </html>
```

This dialog is displayed 10 times. User input is 100, 88, 93, 55, 68, 77, 83, 95, 73 and 62.

Fig. 7.7 | Counter-controlled repetition to calculate a class average. (Part 2 of 2.)

Lines 12–16 declare variables `total`, `gradeCounter`, `grade`, `gradeValue`, `average`. The variable `grade` will store the string the user types into the `prompt` dialog. The variable `gradeValue` will store the integer value of the `grade` the user enters into the `prompt` dialog.

Lines 19–20 are assignment statements that initialize `total` to `0` and `gradeCounter` to `1`. Note that variables `total` and `gradeCounter` are initialized before they are used in a calculation.

Common Programming Error 7.6

Not initializing a variable that will be used in a calculation results in a logic error that produces the value `NaN—Not a Number`. You must initialize the variable before it is used in a calculation.

Line 23 indicates that the `while` statement continues iterating while the value of `gradeCounter` is less than or equal to 10. Line 27 corresponds to the pseudocode statement "*Input the next grade.*" The statement displays a `prompt` dialog with the prompt `"Enter integer grade:"` on the screen.

After the user enters the `grade`, line 30 converts it from a string to an integer. We must convert the string to an integer in this example; otherwise, the addition statement in line 33 will be a string-concatenation statement rather than a numeric sum.

Next, the program updates the `total` with the new `gradeValue` entered by the user. Line 33 adds `gradeValue` to the previous value of `total` and assigns the result to `total`. This statement seems a bit strange, because it does not follow the rules of algebra. Keep in mind that JavaScript operator precedence evaluates the addition (+) operation before the assignment (=) operation. The value of the expression on the right side of the assignment operator always replaces the value of the variable on the left side of the assignment operator.

The program now is ready to increment the variable `gradeCounter` to indicate that a grade has been processed and to read the next grade from the user. Line 36 adds `1` to `gradeCounter`, so the condition in the `while` statement will eventually become `false` and terminate the loop. After this statement executes, the program continues by testing the condition in the `while` statement in line 23. If the condition is still true, the statements in lines 27–36 repeat. Otherwise the program continues execution with the first statement in sequence after the body of the loop (i.e., line 40).

Line 40 assigns the results of the average calculation to variable `average`. Lines 43–44 write a line of XHTML text in the document that displays the string `"Class average is "` followed by the value of variable `average` as an `<h1>` element in the browser.

Execute the script in a web browser by double clicking the XHTML document (from Windows Explorer). This script parses any user input as an integer. In the sample program execution in Fig. 7.7, the sum of the values entered (100, 88, 93, 55, 68, 77, 83, 95, 73 and 62) is 794. Although the treats all input as integers, the averaging calculation in the program does not produce an integer. Rather, the calculation produces a **floating-point number** (i.e., a number containing a decimal point). The average of the 10 integers input by the user in this example is 79.4.

Software Engineering Observation 7.6

If the string passed to `parseInt` contains a floating-point numeric value, `parseInt` simply truncates the floating-point part. For example, the string "27.95" results in the integer 27, and the string "–123.45" results in the integer –123. If the string passed to `parseInt` is not a numeric value, `parseInt` returns `NaN` (not a number).

JavaScript actually represents all numbers as floating-point numbers in memory. Floating-point numbers often develop through division, as shown in this example. When we divide 10 by 3, the result is 3.3333333…, with the sequence of 3's repeating infinitely. The computer allocates only a fixed amount of space to hold such a value, so the stored floating-point value can be only an approximation. Although floating-point numbers are not always 100 percent precise, they have numerous applications. For example, when we speak of a "normal" body temperature of 98.6, we do not need to be precise to a large number of digits. When we view the temperature on a thermometer and read it as 98.6, it may actually be 98.5999473210643. The point here is that few applications require high-precision floating-point values, so calling this number simply 98.6 is fine for most applications.

Common Programming Error 7.7

Using floating-point numbers in a manner that assumes they are represented precisely can lead to incorrect results. Real numbers are represented only approximately by computers. For example, no fixed-size floating-point representation of π can ever be precise, because π is a transcendental number whose value cannot be expressed as digits in a finite amount of space.

7.9 Formulating Algorithms: Sentinel-Controlled Repetition

Let us generalize the class-average problem. Consider the following problem:

> *Develop a class-averaging program that will process an arbitrary number of grades each time the program is run.*

In the first class-average example, the number of grades (10) was known in advance. In this example, no indication is given of how many grades the user will enter. The program must process an arbitrary number of grades. How can the program determine when to stop the input of grades? How will it know when to calculate and display the class average?

One way to solve this problem is to use a special value called a sentinel value (also called a signal value, a dummy value or a flag value) to indicate the end of data entry. The user types in grades until all legitimate grades have been entered. Then the user types the sentinel value to indicate that the last grade has been entered. Sentinel-controlled repetition is often called indefinite repetition, because the number of repetitions is not known before the loop begins executing.

Clearly, one must choose a sentinel value that cannot be confused with an acceptable input value. –1 is an acceptable sentinel value for this problem because grades on a quiz are normally nonnegative integers from 0 to 100. Thus, an execution of the class-average program might process a stream of inputs such as 95, 96, 75, 74, 89 and –1. The program would compute and print the class average for the grades 95, 96, 75, 74 and 89 (–1 is the sentinel value, so it should not enter into the average calculation).

Common Programming Error 7.8

Choosing a sentinel value that is also a legitimate data value results in a logic error and may prevent a sentinel-controlled loop from terminating properly.

We approach the class-average program with a technique called top-down, stepwise refinement, a technique that is essential to the development of well-structured algorithms. We begin with a pseudocode representation of the top:

> *Determine the class average for the quiz*

The top is a single statement that conveys the program's overall purpose. As such, the top is, in effect, a complete representation of a program. Unfortunately, the top rarely conveys sufficient detail from which to write the JavaScript algorithm. Therefore we must begin a refinement process. First, we divide the top into a series of smaller tasks and list them in the order in which they need to be performed, creating the following first refinement:

Initialize variables
Input, sum up and count the quiz grades
Calculate and print the class average

Here, only the sequence structure is used; the steps listed are to be executed in order, one after the other.

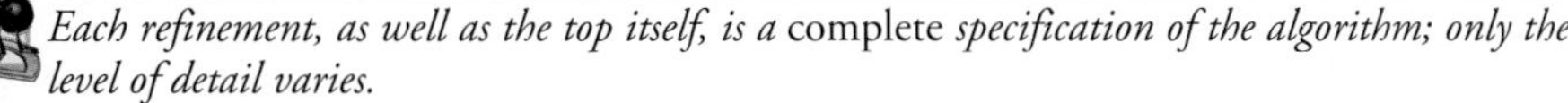

Software Engineering Observation 7.7

Each refinement, as well as the top itself, is a complete *specification of the algorithm; only the level of detail varies.*

To proceed to the next level of refinement (the **second refinement**), we commit to specific variables. We need a running total of the numbers, a count of how many numbers have been processed, a variable to receive the string representation of each grade as it is input, a variable to store the value of the grade after it is converted to an integer and a variable to hold the calculated average. The pseudocode statement

Initialize variables

may be refined as follows:

Initialize total to zero
Initialize gradeCounter to zero

Note that only the variables *total* and *gradeCounter* are initialized before they are used; the variables *average*, *grade* and *gradeValue* (for the calculated average, the user input and the integer representation of the *grade*, respectively) need not be initialized, because their values are determined as they are calculated or input.

The pseudocode statement

Input, sum up and count the quiz grades

requires a repetition structure (a loop) that successively inputs each grade. We do not know in advance how many grades are to be processed, so we will use sentinel-controlled repetition. The user will enter legitimate grades, one at a time. After entering the last legitimate grade, the user will enter the sentinel value. The program will test for the sentinel value after the user enters each grade and will terminate the loop when the sentinel value is encountered. The second refinement of the preceding pseudocode statement is then

```
Input the first grade (possibly the sentinel)
While the user has not as yet entered the sentinel
    Add this grade into the running total
    Add one to the grade counter
    Input the next grade (possibly the sentinel)
```

Note that in pseudocode, we do not use braces around the pseudocode that forms the body of the *While* structure. We simply indent the pseudocode under the *While*, to show that it belongs to the body of the *While*. Remember, pseudocode is only an informal program-development aid.

The pseudocode statement

Calculate and print the class average

may be refined as follows:

If the counter is not equal to zero
Set the average to the total divided by the counter
Print the average
Else
Print "No grades were entered"

Note that we are testing for the possibility of division by zero—a logic error that, if undetected, would cause the program to produce invalid output. The complete second refinement of the pseudocode algorithm for the class-average problem is shown in Fig. 7.8.

Error-Prevention Tip 7.1

When performing division by an expression whose value could be zero, explicitly test for this case, and handle it appropriately in your program (e.g., by printing an error message) rather than allowing the division by zero to occur.

Good Programming Practice 7.5

Include completely blank lines in pseudocode programs to make the pseudocode more readable. The blank lines separate pseudocode control structures and separate the program phases.

Software Engineering Observation 7.8

Many algorithms can be divided logically into three phases: an initialization phase that initializes the program variables, a processing phase that inputs data values and adjusts program variables accordingly, and a termination phase that calculates and prints the results.

The pseudocode algorithm in Fig. 7.8 solves the more general class-averaging problem. This algorithm was developed after only two refinements. Sometimes more refinements are necessary.

```
Initialize total to zero
Initialize gradeCounter to zero

Input the first grade (possibly the sentinel)
While the user has not as yet entered the sentinel
    Add this grade into the running total
    Add one to the grade counter
    Input the next grade (possibly the sentinel)

If the counter is not equal to zero
    Set the average to the total divided by the counter
    Print the average
Else
    Print "No grades were entered"
```

Fig. 7.8 | Sentinel-controlled repetition to solve the class-average problem.

Software Engineering Observation 7.9

The programmer terminates the top-down, stepwise refinement process after specifying the pseudocode algorithm in sufficient detail for the programmer to convert the pseudocode to a JavaScript program. Then, implementing the JavaScript program will normally be straightforward.

Good Programming Practice 7.6

When converting a pseudocode program to JavaScript, keep the pseudocode in the JavaScript program as comments.

Software Engineering Observation 7.10

Experience has shown that the most difficult part of solving a problem on a computer is developing the algorithm for the solution. Once a correct algorithm is specified, the process of producing a working JavaScript program from the algorithm is normally straightforward.

Software Engineering Observation 7.11

Many experienced programmers write programs without ever using program-development tools like pseudocode. As they see it, their ultimate goal is to solve the problem on a computer, and writing pseudocode merely delays the production of final outputs. Although this approach may work for simple and familiar problems, it can lead to serious errors in large, complex projects.

Figure 7.9 shows the JavaScript program and a sample execution. Although each grade is an integer, the averaging calculation is likely to produce a number with a decimal point (a real number).

In this example, we see that control structures may be stacked on top of one another (in sequence) just as a child stacks building blocks. The `while` statement (lines 31–45) is followed immediately by an `if...else` statement (lines 48–57) in sequence. Much of the code in this program is identical to the code in Fig. 7.7, so we concentrate in this example on the new features.

Line 21 initializes `gradeCounter` to `0`, because no grades have been entered yet. Remember that the program uses sentinel-controlled repetition. To keep an accurate record of the number of grades entered, the script increments `gradeCounter` only after processing a valid grade value.

```
1  <?xml version = "1.0" encoding = "utf-8"?>
2  <!DOCTYPE html PUBLIC "-//W3C//DTD XHTML 1.0 Strict//EN"
3     "http://www.w3.org/TR/xhtml1/DTD/xhtml1-strict.dtd">
4
5  <!-- Fig. 7.9: average2.html -->
6  <!-- Sentinel-controlled repetition to calculate a class average. -->
7  <html xmlns = "http://www.w3.org/1999/xhtml">
8     <head>
9        <title>Class Average Program: Sentinel-controlled Repetition</title>
10
11       <script type = "text/javascript">
12          <!--
```

Fig. 7.9 | Sentinel-controlled repetition to calculate a class average. (Part 1 of 3.)

```
         var total; // sum of grades
         var gradeCounter; // number of grades entered
         var grade; // grade typed by user (as a string)
         var gradeValue; // grade value (converted to integer)
         var average; // average of all grades

         // Initialization phase
         total = 0; // clear total
         gradeCounter = 0; // prepare to loop

         // Processing phase
         // prompt for input and read grade from user
         grade = window.prompt(
              "Enter Integer Grade, -1 to Quit:", "0" );

         // convert grade from a string to an integer
         gradeValue = parseInt( grade );

         while ( gradeValue != -1 )
         {
            // add gradeValue to total
            total = total + gradeValue;

            // add 1 to gradeCounter
            gradeCounter = gradeCounter + 1;

            // prompt for input and read grade from user
            grade = window.prompt(
               "Enter Integer Grade, -1 to Quit:", "0" );

            // convert grade from a string to an integer
            gradeValue = parseInt( grade );
         } // end while

         // Termination phase
         if ( gradeCounter != 0 )
         {
            average = total / gradeCounter;

            // display average of exam grades
            document.writeln(
               "<h1>Class average is " + average + "</h1>" );
         } // end if
         else
            document.writeln( "<p>No grades were entered</p>" );
         // -->
      </script>
   </head>
   <body>
      <p>Click Refresh (or Reload) to run the script again</p>
   </body>
</html>
```

Fig. 7.9 | Sentinel-controlled repetition to calculate a class average. (Part 2 of 3.)

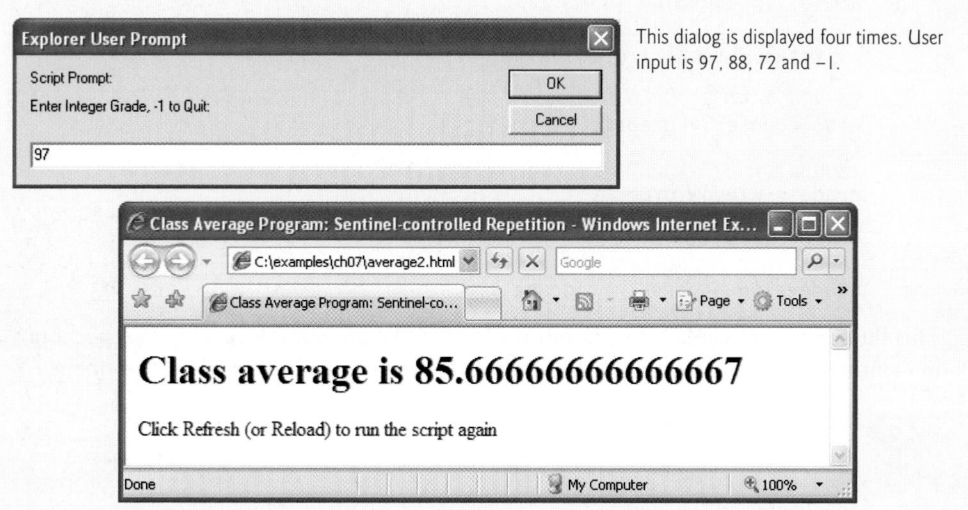

Fig. 7.9 | Sentinel-controlled repetition to calculate a class average. (Part 3 of 3.)

Note the difference in program logic for sentinel-controlled repetition as compared with the counter-controlled repetition in Fig. 7.7. In counter-controlled repetition, we read a value from the user during each iteration of the `while` statement's body for the specified number of iterations. In sentinel-controlled repetition, we read one value (lines 25–26) and convert it to an integer (line 29) before the program reaches the `while` statement. The script uses this value to determine whether the program's flow of control should enter the body of the `while` statement. If the `while` statement's condition is `false` (i.e., the user typed the sentinel as the first grade), the script ignores the body of the `while` statement (i.e., no grades were entered). If the condition is `true`, the body begins execution and processes the value entered by the user (i.e., adds the value to the `total` in line 34). After processing the value, the script increments `gradeCounter` by 1 (line 37), inputs the next `grade` from the user (lines 40–41) and converts the `grade` to an integer (line 44), before the end of the `while` statement's body. When the script reaches the closing right brace (`}`) of the body in line 45, execution continues with the next test of the condition of the `while` statement (line 31), using the new value just entered by the user to determine whether the `while` statement's body should execute again. Note that the next value always is input from the user immediately before the script evaluates the condition of the `while` statement. This order allows us to determine whether the value just entered by the user is the sentinel value *before* processing it (i.e., adding it to the `total`). If the value entered is the sentinel value, the `while` statement terminates and the script does not add the value to the `total`.

Good Programming Practice 7.7

In a sentinel-controlled loop, the prompts requesting data entry should explicitly remind the user what the sentinel value is.

Note the block in the `while` loop in Fig. 7.9 (lines 32–45). Without the braces, the last three statements in the body of the loop would fall outside of the loop, causing the computer to interpret the code incorrectly, as follows:

```
while ( gradeValue != -1 )
   // add gradeValue to total
   total = total + gradeValue;

// add 1 to gradeCounter
gradeCounter = gradeCounter + 1;

// prompt for input and read grade from user
grade = window.prompt(
   "Enter Integer Grade, -1 to Quit:", "0" );

// convert grade from a string to an integer
gradeValue = parseInt( grade );
```

This interpretation would cause an infinite loop in the program if the user does not input the sentinel `-1` as the first input value in lines 25–26 (i.e., before the `while` statement).

Common Programming Error 7.9

Omitting the braces that delineate a block can lead to logic errors such as infinite loops.

7.10 Formulating Algorithms: Nested Control Statements

Let us work through another complete problem. We once again formulate the algorithm using pseudocode and top-down, stepwise refinement, and write a corresponding JavaScript program.

Consider the following problem statement:

> *A college offers a course that prepares students for the state licensing exam for real estate brokers. Last year, several of the students who completed this course took the licensing exam. Naturally, the college wants to know how well its students performed. You have been asked to write a program to summarize the results. You have been given a list of these 10 students. Next to each name is written a 1 if the student passed the exam and a 2 if the student failed.*
>
> *Your program should analyze the results of the exam as follows:*
>
> 1. *Input each test result (i.e., a 1 or a 2). Display the message "Enter result" on the screen each time the program requests another test result.*
> 2. *Count the number of test results of each type.*
> 3. *Display a summary of the test results indicating the number of students who passed and the number of students who failed.*
> 4. *If more than eight students passed the exam, print the message "Raise tuition."*

After reading the problem statement carefully, we make the following observations about the problem:

1. The program must process test results for 10 students. A counter-controlled loop will be used.
2. Each test result is a number—either a 1 or a 2. Each time the program reads a test result, the program must determine whether the number is a 1 or a 2. We test for a 1 in our algorithm. If the number is not a 1, we assume that it is a 2. (An exercise at the end of the chapter considers the consequences of this assumption.)

3. Two counters are used to keep track of the exam results—one to count the number of students who passed the exam and one to count the number of students who failed the exam.

After the program processes all the results, it must decide whether more than eight students passed the exam. Let us proceed with top-down, stepwise refinement. We begin with a pseudocode representation of the top:

Analyze exam results and decide whether tuition should be raised

Once again, it is important to emphasize that the top is a complete representation of the program, but that several refinements are necessary before the pseudocode can be evolved naturally into a JavaScript program. Our first refinement is as follows:

Initialize variables
Input the ten exam grades and count passes and failures
Print a summary of the exam results and decide whether tuition should be raised

Here, too, even though we have a complete representation of the entire program, further refinement is necessary. We now commit to specific variables. Counters are needed to record the passes and failures; a counter will be used to control the looping process, and a variable is needed to store the user input. The pseudocode statement

Initialize variables

may be refined as follows:

Initialize passes to zero
Initialize failures to zero
Initialize student to one

Note that only the counters for the number of passes, the number of failures and the number of students are initialized. The pseudocode statement

Input the ten quiz grades and count passes and failures

requires a loop that successively inputs the result of each exam. Here, it is known in advance that there are precisely 10 exam results, so counter-controlled looping is appropriate. Inside the loop (i.e., *nested* within the loop), a double-selection structure will determine whether each exam result is a pass or a failure and will increment the appropriate counter accordingly. The refinement of the preceding pseudocode statement is then

```
While student counter is less than or equal to ten
    Input the next exam result

    If the student passed
        Add one to passes
    Else
        Add one to failures

    Add one to student counter
```

Note the use of blank lines to set off the *If...Else* control structure to improve program readability. The pseudocode statement

Print a summary of the exam results and decide whether tuition should be raised

may be refined as follows:

Print the number of passes
Print the number of failures
If more than eight students passed
    Print "Raise tuition"

The complete second refinement appears in Fig. 7.10. Note that blank lines are also used to set off the *While* statement for program readability.

This pseudocode is now refined sufficiently for conversion to JavaScript. The JavaScript program and two sample executions are shown in Fig. 7.11.

```
Initialize passes to zero
Initialize failures to zero
Initialize student to one

While student counter is less than or equal to ten
    Input the next exam result

    If the student passed
        Add one to passes
    Else
        Add one to failures

    Add one to student counter

Print the number of passes
Print the number of failures
If more than eight students passed
    Print "Raise tuition"
```

Fig. 7.10 | Examination-results problem pseudocode.

```
<?xml version = "1.0" encoding = "utf-8"?>
<!DOCTYPE html PUBLIC "-//W3C//DTD XHTML 1.0 Strict//EN"
   "http://www.w3.org/TR/xhtml1/DTD/xhtml1-strict.dtd">

<!-- Fig. 7.11: analysis.html -->
<!-- Examination-results calculation. -->
<html xmlns = "http://www.w3.org/1999/xhtml">
   <head>
      <title>Analysis of Examination Results</title>
      <script type = "text/javascript">
         <!--
         // initializing variables in declarations
         var passes = 0; // number of passes
         var failures = 0; // number of failures
         var student = 1; // student counter
         var result; // one exam result

```

Fig. 7.11 | Examination-results calculation. (Part 1 of 3.)

```
      // process 10 students; counter-controlled loop
      while ( student <= 10 )
      {
         result = window.prompt( "Enter result (1=pass,2=fail)", "0" );

         if ( result == "1" )
            passes = passes + 1;
         else
            failures = failures + 1;

         student = student + 1;
      } // end while

      // termination phase
      document.writeln( "<h1>Examination Results</h1>" );
      document.writeln(
         "Passed: " + passes + "<br />Failed: " + failures );

      if ( passes > 8 )
         document.writeln( "<br />Raise Tuition" );
      // -->
    </script>
  </head>
  <body>
    <p>Click Refresh (or Reload) to run the script again</p>
  </body>
</html>
```

This dialog is displayed 10 times. User input is 1, 2, 1, 1, 1, 1, 1, 1, 1 and 1.

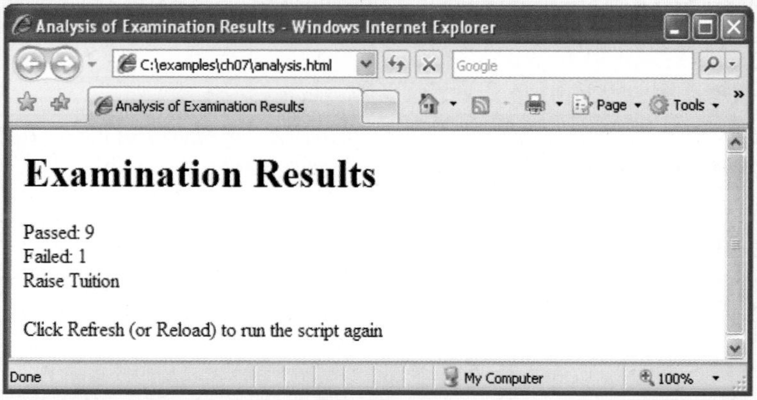

Fig. 7.11 | Examination-results calculation. (Part 2 of 3.)

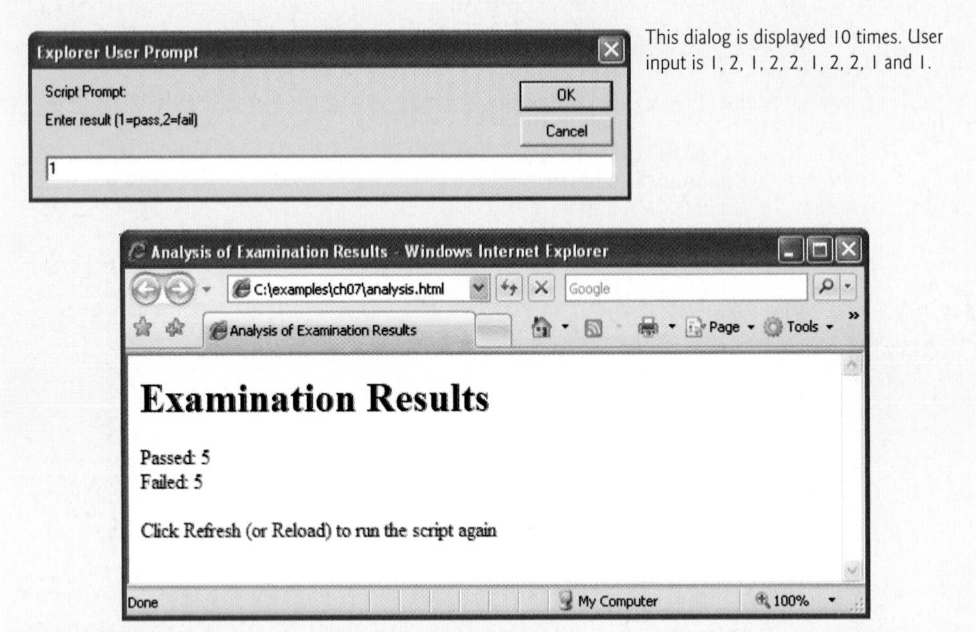

Fig. 7.11 | Examination-results calculation. (Part 3 of 3.)

Lines 13–16 declare the variables used to process the examination results. Note that JavaScript allows variable initialization to be incorporated into declarations (`passes` is assigned `0`, `failures` is assigned `0` and `student` is assigned `1`). Some programs may require reinitialization at the beginning of each repetition; such reinitialization would normally occur in assignment statements.

The processing of the exam results occurs in the `while` statement in lines 19–29. Note that the `if...else` statement in lines 23–26 in the loop tests only whether the exam result was 1; it assumes that all other exam results are 2. Normally, you should validate the values input by the user (i.e., determine whether the values are correct). In the exercises, we ask you to modify this example to validate the input values to ensure that they are either 1 or 2.

Good Programming Practice 7.8

When inputting values from the user, validate the input to ensure that it is correct. If an input value is incorrect, prompt the user to input the value again.

7.11 Assignment Operators

JavaScript provides several assignment operators (called **compound assignment operators**) for abbreviating assignment expressions. For example, the statement

```
c = c + 3;
```

can be abbreviated with the **addition assignment operator**, `+=`, as

```
c += 3;
```

The += operator adds the value of the expression on the right of the operator to the value of the variable on the left of the operator and stores the result in the variable on the left of the operator. Any statement of the form

variable = *variable operator expression*;

where *operator* is one of the binary operators +, -, *, / or % (or others we will discuss later in the text), can be written in the form

variable operator = *expression*;

Thus, the assignment c += 3 adds 3 to c. Figure 7.12 shows the arithmetic assignment operators, sample expressions using these operators and explanations of the meaning of the operators.

Performance Tip 7.1

Programmers can write programs that execute a bit faster when the arithmetic assignment operators are used, because the variable on the left side of the assignment does not have to be evaluated twice.

Performance Tip 7.2

Many of the performance tips we mention in this text result in only nominal improvements, so the reader may be tempted to ignore them. Significant performance improvement often is realized when a supposedly nominal improvement is placed in a loop that may repeat a large number of times.

Assignment operator	Initial value of variable	Sample expression	Explanation	Assigns
+=	c = 3	c += 7	c = c + 7	10 to c
-=	d = 5	d -= 4	d = d - 4	1 to d
*=	e = 4	e *= 5	e = e * 5	20 to e
/=	f = 6	f /= 3	f = f / 3	2 to f
%=	g = 12	g %= 9	g = g % 9	3 to g

Fig. 7.12 | Arithmetic assignment operators.

7.12 Increment and Decrement Operators

JavaScript provides the unary increment operator (++) and decrement operator (--) (summarized in Fig. 7.13). If a variable c is incremented by 1, the increment operator, ++, can be used rather than the expression c = c + 1 or c += 1. If an increment or decrement operator is placed before a variable, it is referred to as the preincrement or predecrement operator, respectively. If an increment or decrement operator is placed after a variable, it is referred to as the postincrement or postdecrement operator, respectively.

Operator	Example	Called	Explanation
++	++a	preincrement	Increment a by 1, then use the new value of a in the expression in which a resides.
++	a++	postincrement	Use the current value of a in the expression in which a resides, then increment a by 1.
--	--b	predecrement	Decrement b by 1, then use the new value of b in the expression in which b resides.
--	b--	postdecrement	Use the current value of b in the expression in which b resides, then decrement b by 1.

Fig. 7.13 | Increment and decrement operators.

Error-Prevention Tip 7.2

The predecrement and postdecrement JavaScript operators cause the W3C XHTML Validator to incorrectly report errors. The validator attempts to interpret the decrement operator as part of an XHTML comment tag (<!-- or -->). You can avoid this problem by using the subtraction assignment operator (-=) to subtract one from a variable. Note that the validator may report many more (nonexistent) errors once it improperly parses the decrement operator.

Preincrementing (or predecrementing) a variable causes the program to increment (decrement) the variable by 1, then use the new value of the variable in the expression in which it appears. Postincrementing (postdecrementing) the variable causes the program to use the current value of the variable in the expression in which it appears, then increment (decrement) the variable by 1.

The script in Fig. 7.14 demonstrates the difference between the preincrementing version and the postincrementing version of the ++ increment operator. Postincrementing the variable c causes it to be incremented after it is used in the `document.writeln` method call (line 18). Preincrementing the variable c causes it to be incremented before it is used in the `document.writeln` method call (line 25). The program displays the value of c before and after the ++ operator is used. The decrement operator (--) works similarly.

```
1  <?xml version = "1.0" encoding = "utf-8"?>
2  <!DOCTYPE html PUBLIC "-//W3C//DTD XHTML 1.0 Strict//EN"
3     "http://www.w3.org/TR/xhtml1/DTD/xhtml1-strict.dtd">
4
5  <!-- Fig. 7.14: increment.html -->
6  <!-- Preincrementing and Postincrementing. -->
7  <html xmlns = "http://www.w3.org/1999/xhtml">
8     <head>
9        <title>Preincrementing and Postincrementing</title>
10       <script type = "text/javascript">
11          <!--
12          var c;
```

Fig. 7.14 | Preincrementing and postincrementing. (Part 1 of 2.)

```

         c = 5;
         document.writeln( "<h3>Postincrementing</h3>" );
         document.writeln( c ); // prints 5
         // prints 5 then increments
         document.writeln( "<br />" + c++ );
         document.writeln( "<br />" + c ); // prints 6

         c = 5;
         document.writeln( "<h3>Preincrementing</h3>" );
         document.writeln( c ); // prints 5
         // increments then prints 6
         document.writeln( "<br />" + ++c );
         document.writeln( "<br />" + c ); // prints 6
         // -->
      </script>
   </head><body></body>
</html>
```

Fig. 7.14 | Preincrementing and postincrementing. (Part 2 of 2.)

Good Programming Practice 7.9

For readability, unary operators should be placed next to their operands, with no intervening spaces.

The three assignment statements in Fig. 7.11 (lines 24, 26 and 28, respectively),

```
passes = passes + 1;
failures = failures + 1;
student = student + 1;
```

can be written more concisely with assignment operators as

```
passes += 1;
failures += 1;
student += 1;
```

with preincrement operators as

```
++passes;
++failures;
++student;
```

or with postincrement operators as

```
passes++;
failures++;
student++;
```

It is important to note here that when incrementing or decrementing a variable in a statement by itself, the preincrement and postincrement forms have the same effect, and the predecrement and postdecrement forms have the same effect. It is only when a variable appears in the context of a larger expression that preincrementing the variable and post-incrementing the variable have different effects. Predecrementing and postdecrementing behave similarly.

Common Programming Error 7.10

Attempting to use the increment or decrement operator on an expression other than a left-hand-side expression*—commonly called an* lvalue*—is a syntax error. A left-hand-side expression is a variable or expression that can appear on the left side of an assignment operation. For example, writing* `++(x + 1)` *is a syntax error, because* `(x + 1)` *is not a left-hand-side expression.*

Figure 7.15 lists the precedence and associativity of the operators introduced to this point. The operators are shown top to bottom in decreasing order of precedence. The second column describes the associativity of the operators at each level of precedence. Notice that the conditional operator (`?:`), the unary operators increment (`++`) and decrement (`--`) and the assignment operators `=`, `+=`, `-=`, `*=`, `/=` and `%=` associate from right to left. All other operators in the operator precedence table (Fig. 7.15) associate from left to right. The third column names the groups of operators.

Operator	Associativity	Type
`++ --`	right to left	unary
`* / %`	left to right	multiplicative
`+ -`	left to right	additive
`< <= > >=`	left to right	relational
`== !=`	left to right	equality
`?:`	right to left	conditional
`= += -= *= /= %=`	right to left	assignment

Fig. 7.15 | Precedence and associativity of the operators discussed so far.

7.13 Wrap-Up

In this chapter, we introduced the concept of algorithms, and explained how to introduce structure into your programs. We used pseudocode and flowcharts to represent algorithms and demonstrated how to translate them into control structures, which form the basis of all programs. We explored selection and repetition statements, and how to integrate them to make decisions and repeat statements in your code. We also introduced assignment, increment and decrement operators, as well as different types of errors that can result from incorrect implementation of control statements.

7.14 Web Resources

`www.deitel.com/javascript/`

The Deitel JavaScript Resource Center contains links to some of the best JavaScript resources on the web. There you'll find categorized links to JavaScript tools, code generators, forums, books, libraries, frameworks and more. Also check out the tutorials for all skill levels, from introductory to advanced. Be sure to visit the related Resource Centers on XHTML (`www.deitel.com/xhtml/`) and CSS 2.1 (`www.deitel.com/css21/`).

Summary

Section 7.2 Algorithms

- Any computable problem can be solved by executing a series of actions in a specific order.
- A procedure for solving a problem in terms of the actions to execute and the order in which the actions are to execute is called an algorithm.
- Specifying the order in which statements are to be executed in a computer program is called program control.

Section 7.3 Pseudocode

- Pseudocode is an artificial and informal language that helps programmers develop algorithms.
- Carefully prepared pseudocode may be converted easily to a corresponding JavaScript program.
- Pseudocode normally describes only executable statements—the actions that are performed when the program is converted from pseudocode to JavaScript and executed.

Section 7.4 Control Structures

- Normally, statements in a program execute one after the other, in the order in which they are written. This process is called sequential execution.
- Various JavaScript statements enable the programmer to specify that the next statement to be executed may be other than the next one in sequence. This process is called transfer of control.
- All programs can be written in terms of only three control structures, namely, the sequence structure, the selection structure and the repetition structure.
- A flowchart is a graphical representation of an algorithm or of a portion of an algorithm. Flowcharts are drawn using certain special-purpose symbols, such as rectangles, diamonds, ovals and small circles; these symbols are connected by arrows called flowlines, which indicate the order in which the actions of the algorithm execute.
- JavaScript provides three selection structures. The `if` statement either performs (selects) an action if a condition is true or skips the action if the condition is false. The `if...else` statement performs an action if a condition is true and performs a different action if the condition is false.

The `switch` statement performs one of many different actions, depending on the value of an expression.

- JavaScript provides four repetition statements, namely, `while`, `do...while`, `for` and `for...in`.
- Keywords cannot be used as identifiers (e.g., for variable names).
- Single-entry/single-exit control structures make it easy to build programs. Control structures are attached to one another by connecting the exit point of one control structure to the entry point of the next. This procedure is called control-structure stacking. There is only one other way control structures may be connected: control-structure nesting.

Section 7.5 `if` Selection Statement

- The JavaScript interpreter ignores white-space characters: blanks, tabs and newlines used for indentation and vertical spacing. Programmers insert white-space characters to enhance program clarity.
- A decision can be made on any expression that evaluates to a value of JavaScript's boolean type (i.e., any expression that evaluates to `true` or `false`).
- The indentation convention you choose should be carefully applied throughout your programs. It is difficult to read programs that do not use uniform spacing conventions.

Section 7.6 `if...else` Selection Statement

- The conditional operator (`?:`) is closely related to the `if...else` statement. Operator `?:` is JavaScript's only ternary operator—it takes three operands. The operands together with the `?:` operator form a conditional expression. The first operand is a boolean expression, the second is the value for the conditional expression if the boolean expression evaluates to true and the third is the value for the conditional expression if the boolean expression evaluates to false.
- Nested `if...else` statements test for multiple cases by placing `if...else` statements inside other `if...else` structures.
- The JavaScript interpreter always associates an `else` with the previous `if`, unless told to do otherwise by the placement of braces (`{}`).
- The `if` selection statement expects only one statement in its body. To include several statements in the body of an `if` statement, enclose the statements in braces (`{` and `}`). A set of statements contained within a pair of braces is called a block.
- A logic error has its effect at execution time. A fatal logic error causes a program to fail and terminate prematurely. A nonfatal logic error allows a program to continue executing, but the program produces incorrect results.

Section 7.7 `while` Repetition Statement

- The `while` repetition structure allows the programmer to specify that an action is to be repeated while some condition remains true.

Section 7.8 Formulating Algorithms: Counter-Controlled Repetition

- Counter-controlled repetition is often called definite repetition, because the number of repetitions is known before the loop begins executing.
- Uninitialized variables used in mathematical calculations result in logic errors and produce the value `NaN` (not a number).
- JavaScript represents all numbers as floating-point numbers in memory. Floating-point numbers often develop through division. The computer allocates only a fixed amount of space to hold such a value, so the stored floating-point value can only be an approximation.

Section 7.9 Formulating Algorithms: Sentinel-Controlled Repetition

- In sentinel-controlled repetition, a special value called a sentinel value (also called a signal value, a dummy value or a flag value) indicates the end of data entry. Sentinel-controlled repetition often is called indefinite repetition, because the number of repetitions is not known in advance.
- It is necessary to choose a sentinel value that cannot be confused with an acceptable input value.

Section 7.10 Formulating Algorithms: Nested Control Statements.

- Top-down, stepwise refinement is a technique essential to the development of well-structured algorithms. The top is a single statement that conveys the overall purpose of the program. As such, the top is, in effect, a complete representation of a program. The stepwise refinement process divides the top into a series of smaller tasks. The programmer terminates the top-down, stepwise refinement process when the pseudocode algorithm is specified in sufficient detail for the programmer to be able to convert the pseudocode to a JavaScript program.

Section 7.11 Assignment Operators

- JavaScript provides the arithmetic assignment operators `+=`, `-=`, `*=`, `/=` and `%=`, which abbreviate certain common types of expressions.

Section 7.12 Increment and Decrement Operators

- The increment operator, `++`, and the decrement operator, `--`, increment or decrement a variable by 1, respectively. If the operator is prefixed to the variable, the variable is incremented or decremented by 1, then used in its expression. If the operator is postfixed to the variable, the variable is used in its expression, then incremented or decremented by 1.

Terminology

`--` operator
`?:` operator
`++` operator
action symbol
action/decision model
algorithm
arithmetic assignment operators:
    `+=`, `-=`, `*=`, `/=` and `%=`
arrow
block
body of a loop
boolean expression
braces (`{}`)
compound assignment operator
conditional expression
conditional operator (`?:`)
connector symbol
control structure
control-structure nesting
control-structure stacking
counter
counter-controlled repetition
dangling-else problem
decision symbol
decrement operator (`--`)
definite repetition
diamond symbol
division by zero
double-selection structure
dummy value
empty statement (`;`)
fatal logic error
first refinement
flag value
floating-point number
flowchart
flowlines
`goto` elimination
`goto` statement
`if` selection statement
`if...else` selection statement
increment operator (`++`)
indefinite repetition
infinite loop
initialization
initialization phase
keyword
left-hand-side expression
logic error
loop

loop-continuation condition
lvalue
multiple-selection structure
NaN (not a number)
nested control structures
nonfatal logic error
`null`
oval symbol
postdecrement operator
postincrement operator
predecrement operator
preincrement operator
procedure
processing phase
program control
pseudocode
rectangle symbol
repetition
repetition structure
second refinement
selection
selection structure
sentinel value
sentinel-controlled repetition
sequence structure
sequential execution
signal value
single-entry/single-exit control structure
single-selection structure
small circle symbol
stacked control structures
statement
structured programming
syntax error
terminate a loop
termination phase
ternary operator
top
top-down, stepwise refinement
transfer of control
unary operator
`while` repetition statement
white-space character

Self-Review Exercises

7.1 Fill in the blanks in each of the following statements:

a) All programs can be written in terms of three types of control structures: _______, _______ and _______.
b) The _______ double-selection statement is used to execute one action when a condition is true and another action when that condition is false.
c) Repeating a set of instructions a specific number of times is called _______ repetition.
d) When it is not known in advance how many times a set of statements will be repeated, a(n) _______ (or a(n) _______, _______ or _______) value can be used to terminate the repetition.

7.2 Write four JavaScript statements that each add 1 to variable `x`, which contains a number.

7.3 Write JavaScript statements to accomplish each of the following tasks:

a) Assign the sum of `x` and `y` to `z`, and increment the value of `x` by 1 after the calculation. Use only one statement.
b) Test whether the value of the variable `count` is greater than 10. If it is, print `"Count is greater than 10"`.
c) Decrement the variable `x` by 1, then subtract it from the variable `total`. Use only one statement.
d) Calculate the remainder after `q` is divided by `divisor`, and assign the result to `q`. Write this statement in two different ways.

7.4 Write a JavaScript statement to accomplish each of the following tasks:

a) Declare variables `sum` and `x`.
b) Assign `1` to variable `x`.
c) Assign `0` to variable `sum`.
d) Add variable `x` to variable `sum`, and assign the result to variable `sum`.
e) Print `"The sum is: "`, followed by the value of variable `sum`.

7.5 Combine the statements that you wrote in Exercise 7.4 into a JavaScript program that calculates and prints the sum of the integers from 1 to 10. Use the `while` statement to loop through the calculation and increment statements. The loop should terminate when the value of `x` becomes 11.

7.6 Determine the value of each variable after the calculation is performed. Assume that, when each statement begins executing, all variables have the integer value 5.

a) `product *= x++;`
b) `quotient /= ++x;`

7.7 Identify and correct the errors in each of the following segments of code:

a)
```
while ( c <= 5 ) {
   product *= c;
   ++c;
```
b)
```
if ( gender == 1 )
   document.writeln( "Woman" );
else;
   document.writeln( "Man" );
```

7.8 What is wrong with the following `while` repetition statement?

```
while ( z >= 0 )
   sum += z;
```

Answers to Self-Review Exercises

7.1 a) Sequence, selection and repetition. b) `if...else`. c) Counter-controlled (or definite). d) Sentinel, signal, flag or dummy.

7.2
```
x = x + 1;
x += 1;
++x;
x++;
```

7.3
a) `z = x++ + y;`
b)
```
if ( count > 10 )
   document.writeln( "Count is greater than 10" );
```
c) `total -= --x;`
d) `q %= divisor;`
`q = q % divisor;`

7.4
a) `var sum, x;`
b) `x = 1;`
c) `sum = 0;`
d) `sum += x;` or `sum = sum + x;`
e) `document.writeln( "The sum is: " + sum );`

7.5 The solution is as follows:

```
<?xml version = "1.0" encoding = "utf-8"?>
<!DOCTYPE html PUBLIC "-//W3C//DTD XHTML 1.0 Strict//EN"
   "http://www.w3.org/TR/xhtml11/DTD/xhtml11-strict.dtd">

<!-- Exercise 7.5: ex07_05.html -->
<html xmlns = "http://www.w3.org/1999/xhtml">
   <head><title>Sum the Integers from 1 to 10</title>
      <script type = "text/javascript">
         <!--
```

```
         var sum; // stores the total
          var x; // counter control variable

         x = 1;
         sum = 0;

         while ( x <= 10 )
         {
            sum += x;
            ++x;
         } // end while

         document.writeln( "The sum is: " + sum );
         // -->
      </script>
   </head><body></body>
</html>
```

7.6 a) `product = 25, x = 6;`
b) `quotient = 0.833333..., x = 6;`

7.7 a) Error: Missing the closing right brace of the `while` body.
Correction: Add closing right brace after the statement `++c;`.

```
<?xml version = "1.0" encoding = "utf-8"?>
<!DOCTYPE html PUBLIC "-//W3C//DTD XHTML 1.0 Strict//EN"
   "http://www.w3.org/TR/xhtml1/DTD/xhtml1-strict.dtd">

<!-- Exercise 7.7a: ex07_07a.html -->
<html xmlns = "http://www.w3.org/1999/xhtml">
   <head>
      <title>Finding Code Errors</title>
      <script type = "text/javascript">
         <!--
         var c;
         var product;

         c = 1;
         product = 1;

         while ( c <= 5 )
         {
            product *= c;
            ++c;
         } // end while

         document.writeln( "The product is: " + product );
```

```
            // -->
        </script>
    </head><body></body>
</html>
```

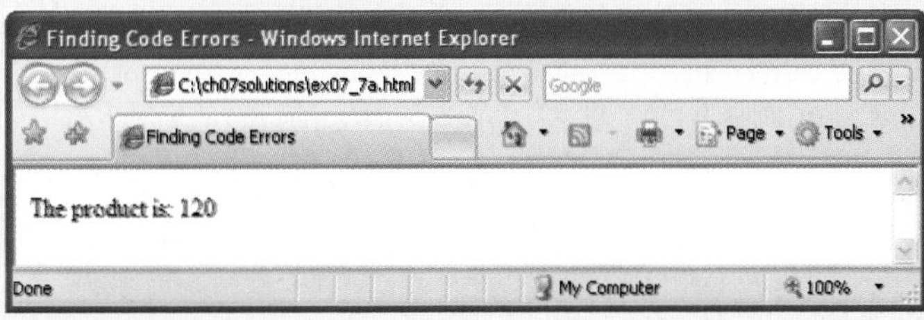

b) Error: The semicolon after `else` results in a logic error. The second output statement will always be executed.
Correction: Remove the semicolon after `else`.

```
<?xml version = "1.0" encoding = "utf-8"?>
<!DOCTYPE html PUBLIC "-//W3C//DTD XHTML 1.0 Strict//EN"
   "http://www.w3.org/TR/xhtml1/DTD/xhtml1-strict.dtd">

<!-- Exercise 7.7b: ex07_07b.html -->
<html xmlns = "http://www.w3.org/1999/xhtml">
   <head>
      <title>Finding Code Errors</title>
      <script type = "text/javascript">
         <!--
         var gender;
         gender = window.prompt( "Enter gender"
               + "(1=Woman,2=Man)", "1" );

         if ( gender == 1 )
            document.writeln( "Woman" );
         else
            document.writeln( "Man" );
         // -->
      </script>
   </head><body></body>
</html>
```

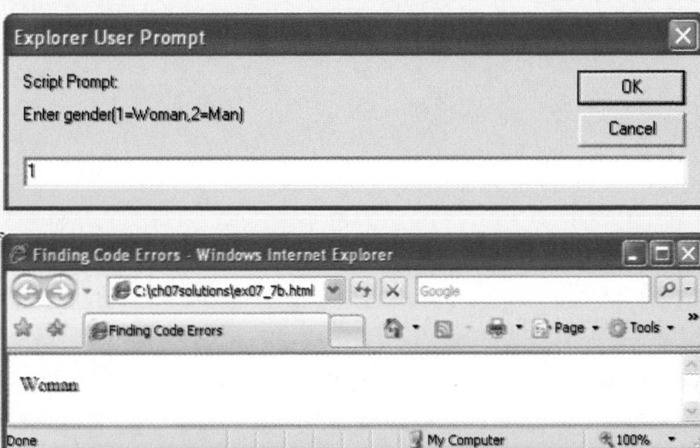

7.8 The value of the variable `z` is never changed in the body of the `while` statement. Therefore, if the loop-continuation condition `( z >= 0 )` is true, an infinite loop is created. To prevent the creation of the infinite loop, `z` must be decremented so that it eventually becomes less than 0.

Exercises

7.9 Identify and correct the errors in each of the following segments of code [*Note:* There may be more than one error in each piece of code]:

a)
```
if ( age >= 65 );
   document.writeln( "Age greater than or equal to 65" );
else
   document.writeln( "Age is less than 65" );
```

b)
```
var x = 1, total;
while ( x <= 10 )
{
   total += x;
   ++x;
}
```

c)
```
var x = 1;
var total = 0;
While ( x <= 100 )
   total += x;
   ++x;
```

d)
```
var y = 5;
while ( y > 0 )
{
   document.writeln( y );
   ++y;
```

7.10 What does the following program print?

```
<?xml version = "1.0" encoding = "utf-8"?>
<!DOCTYPE html PUBLIC "-//W3C//DTD XHTML 1.0 Strict//EN"
   "http://www.w3.org/TR/xhtml1/DTD/xhtml1-strict.dtd">

<!-- Exercise 7.10: ex07_10.html -->
<html xmlns="http://www.w3.org/1999/xhtml">
   <head><title>Mystery Script</title>
      <script type = "text/javascript">
         <!--
         var y;
         var x = 1;
         var total = 0;

         while ( x <= 10 )
         {
            y = x * x;
            document.writeln( y + "<br />" );
            total += y;
            ++x;
         } // end while

         document.writeln( "<br />Total is " + total );
         // -->
```

```
        </script>
    </head><body></body>
</html>
```

For Exercises 7.11–7.14, perform each of the following steps:

a) Read the problem statement.
b) Formulate the algorithm using pseudocode and top-down, stepwise refinement.
c) Write a JavaScript program.
d) Test, debug and execute the JavaScript program.
e) Process three complete sets of data.

7.11 Drivers are concerned with the mileage obtained by their automobiles. One driver has kept track of several tankfuls of gasoline by recording the number of miles driven and the number of gallons used for each tankful. Develop a JavaScript program that will take as input the miles driven and gallons used (both as integers) for each tankful. The program should calculate and output XHTML text that displays the number of miles per gallon obtained for each tankful and prints the combined number of miles per gallon obtained for all tankfuls up to this point. Use `prompt` dialogs to obtain the data from the user.

7.12 Develop a JavaScript program that will determine whether a department-store customer has exceeded the credit limit on a charge account. For each customer, the following facts are available:

a) Account number
b) Balance at the beginning of the month
c) Total of all items charged by this customer this month
d) Total of all credits applied to this customer's account this month
e) Allowed credit limit

The program should input each of these facts from a `prompt` dialog as an integer, calculate the new balance (= *beginning balance + charges – credits*), display the new balance and determine whether the new balance exceeds the customer's credit limit. For customers whose credit limit is exceeded, the program should output XHTML text that displays the message "Credit limit exceeded."

7.13 A large company pays its salespeople on a commission basis. The salespeople receive $200 per week, plus 9 percent of their gross sales for that week. For example, a salesperson who sells $5000 worth of merchandise in a week receives $200 plus 9 percent of $5000, or a total of $650. You have been supplied with a list of the items sold by each salesperson. The values of these items are as follows:

Item	Value
1	239.99
2	129.75
3	99.95
4	350.89

Develop a program that inputs one salesperson's items sold for last week, calculates the salesperson's earnings and outputs XHTML text that displays the salesperson's earnings.

7.14 Develop a JavaScript program that will determine the gross pay for each of three employees. The company pays "straight time" for the first 40 hours worked by each employee and pays "time and a half" for all hours worked in excess of 40 hours. You are given a list of the employees of the company, the number of hours each employee worked last week and the hourly rate of each employee. Your program should input this information for each employee, determine the employee's gross pay and output XHTML text that displays the employee's gross pay. Use `prompt` dialogs to input the data.

7.15 The process of finding the largest value (i.e., the maximum of a group of values) is used frequently in computer applications. For example, a program that determines the winner of a sales contest would input the number of units sold by each salesperson. The salesperson who sells the most units wins the contest. Write a pseudocode program and then a JavaScript program that inputs a series of 10 single-digit numbers as characters, determines the largest of the numbers and outputs a message that displays the largest number. Your program should use three variables as follows:

a) `counter`: A counter to count to 10 (i.e., to keep track of how many numbers have been input and to determine when all 10 numbers have been processed);
b) `number`: The current digit input to the program;
c) `largest`: The largest number found so far.

7.16 Write a JavaScript program that uses looping to print the following table of values. Output the results in an XHTML table. Use CSS to center the data in each column.

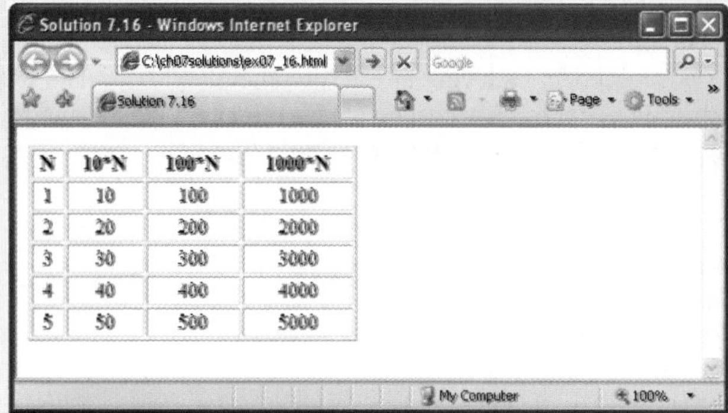

N	10*N	100*N	1000*N
1	10	100	1000
2	20	200	2000
3	30	300	3000
4	40	400	4000
5	50	500	5000

7.17 Using an approach similar to that in Exercise 7.15, find the *two* largest values among the 10 digits entered. [*Note:* You may input each number only once.]

7.18 Modify the program in Fig. 7.11 to validate its inputs. For every value input, if the value entered is other than 1 or 2, keep looping until the user enters a correct value.

7.19 What does the following program print?

```
<?xml version = "1.0" encoding = "utf-8"?>
<!DOCTYPE html PUBLIC "-//W3C//DTD XHTML 1.0 Strict//EN"
   "http://www.w3.org/TR/xhtml1/DTD/xhtml1-strict.dtd">

<!-- Exercise 7.19: ex07_19.html -->
<html xmlns = "http://www.w3.org/1999/xhtml">
   <head><title>Mystery Script</title>
      <script type = "text/javascript">
         <!--
         var count = 1;

         while ( count <= 10 )
         {
            document.writeln(
               count % 2 == 1 ? "****<br />" : "++++++++<br />" );
            ++count;
         } // end while
         // -->
      </script>
   </head><body></body>
</html>
```

7.20 What does the following program print?

```
<?xml version = "1.0" encoding = "utf-8"?>
<!DOCTYPE html PUBLIC "-//W3C//DTD XHTML 1.0 Strict//EN"
   "http://www.w3.org/TR/xhtml1/DTD/xhtml1-strict.dtd">

<!-- Exercise 7.20: ex07_20.html -->
<html xmlns = "http://www.w3.org/1999/xhtml">
   <head><title>Mystery Script</title>
      <script type = "text/javascript">
         <!--
         var row = 10;
         var column;

         while ( row >= 1 )
         {
            column = 1;

            while ( column <= 10 )
            {
               document.write( row % 2 == 1 ? "<" : ">" );
               ++column;
            } // end while

            --row;
            document.writeln( "<br />" );
         } // end while
         // -->
      </script>
   </head><body></body>
</html>
```

7.21 (*Dangling-Else Problem*) Determine the output for each of the given segments of code when `x` is `9` and `y` is `11`, and when `x` is `11` and `y` is `9`. Note that the interpreter ignores the indentation in a JavaScript program. Also, the JavaScript interpreter always associates an `else` with the previous `if`, unless told to do otherwise by the placement of braces (`{}`). You may not be sure at first glance which `if` an `else` matches. This situation is referred to as the "dangling-else" problem. We have eliminated the indentation from the given code to make the problem more challenging. [*Hint:* Apply the indentation conventions you have learned.]

a)
```
if ( x < 10 )
if ( y > 10 )
document.writeln( "*****<br />" );
else
document.writeln( "#####<br />" );
document.writeln( "$$$$$<br />" );
```

b)
```
if ( x < 10 )
{
if ( y > 10 )
document.writeln( "*****<br />" );
}
else
{
document.writeln( "#####<br />" );
document.writeln( "$$$$$<br />" );
}
```

7.22 *(Another Dangling-Else Problem)* Modify the given code to produce the output shown in each part of this problem. Use proper indentation techniques. You may not make any changes other than inserting braces, changing the code indentation and inserting blank lines. The interpreter ignores indentation in JavaScript. We have eliminated the indentation from the given code to make the problem more challenging. [*Note:* It is possible that no modification is necessary for some of the segments of code.]

```
if ( y == 8 )
if ( x == 5 )
document.writeln( "@@@@@<br />" );
else
document.writeln( "#####<br />" );
document.writeln( "$$$$$<br />" );
document.writeln( "&&&&&<br />" );
```

a) Assuming that `x = 5` and `y = 8`, the following output is produced:

```
@@@@@
$$$$$
&&&&&
```

b) Assuming that `x = 5` and `y = 8`, the following output is produced:

```
@@@@@
```

c) Assuming that `x = 5` and `y = 8`, the following output is produced:

```
@@@@@
&&&&&
```

d) Assuming that `x = 5` and `y = 7`, the following output is produced [*Note:* The last three output statements after the `else` statements are all part of a block]:

```
#####
$$$$$
&&&&&
```

7.23 Write a script that reads in the size of the side of a square and outputs XHTML text that displays a hollow square of that size constructed of asterisks. Use a `prompt` dialog to read the size from the user. Your program should work for squares of all side sizes between 1 and 20.

7.24 A palindrome is a number or a text phrase that reads the same backward and forward. For example, each of the following five-digit integers is a palindrome: 12321, 55555, 45554 and 11611. Write a script that reads in a five-digit integer and determines whether it is a palindrome. If the number is not five digits long, display an `alert` dialog indicating the problem to the user. Allow the user to enter a new value after dismissing the `alert` dialog. [*Hint:* It is possible to do this exercise with the techniques learned in this chapter. You will need to use both division and remainder operations to "pick off" each digit.]

7.25 Write a script that outputs XHTML text that displays the following checkerboard pattern:

```
* * * * * * * *
 * * * * * * * *
* * * * * * * *
 * * * * * * * *
* * * * * * * *
 * * * * * * * *
* * * * * * * *
 * * * * * * * *
```

Your program may use only three output statements to display the pattern, one of the form

```
document.write( "* " );
```

one of the form

```
document.write( " " );
```

and one of the form

```
document.writeln(); //writes a newline character
```

You may use XHTML tags (e.g., <pre>) for alignment purposes. [*Hint:* Repetition structures are required in this exercise.]

7.26 Write a script that outputs XHTML text that keeps displaying in the browser window the multiples of the integer 2, namely 2, 4, 8, 16, 32, 64, etc. Your loop should *not terminate* (i.e., you should create an infinite loop). What happens when you run this program?

7.27 A company wants to transmit data over the telephone, but it is concerned that its phones may be tapped. All of its data is transmitted as four-digit integers. It has asked you to write a program that will encrypt its data so that the data may be transmitted more securely. Your script should read a four-digit integer entered by the user in a `prompt` dialog and encrypt it as follows: Replace each digit by *(the sum of that digit plus 7) modulus 10.* Then swap the first digit with the third, and swap the second digit with the fourth. Then output XHTML text that displays the encrypted integer.

7.28 Write a program that inputs an encrypted four-digit integer (from Exercise 7.27) and decrypts it to form the original number.

8

JavaScript: Control Statements II

Not everything that can be counted counts, and not every thing that counts can be counted.
—Albert Einstein

Who can control his fate?
—William Shakespeare

The used key is always bright.
—Benjamin Franklin

Intelligence ... is the faculty of making artificial objects, especially tools to make tools.
—Henri Bergson

Every advantage in the past is judged in the light of the final issue.
—Demosthenes

OBJECTIVES

In this chapter you will learn:

- The essentials of counter-controlled repetition
- To use the `for` and `do...while` repetition statements to execute statements in a program repeatedly.
- To perform multiple selection using the `switch` selection statement.
- To use the `break` and `continue` program-control statements
- To use the logical operators.

8.1 Introduction

Chapter 7 began our introduction to the types of building blocks that are available for problem solving and used them to employ proven program-construction principles. In this chapter, we continue our presentation of the theory and principles of structured programming by introducing JavaScript's remaining control statements (with the exception of `for...in`, which is presented in Chapter 10). As in Chapter 7, the JavaScript techniques you will learn here are applicable to most high-level languages. In later chapters, you'll see that control structures are helpful in manipulating objects.

8.2 Essentials of Counter-Controlled Repetition

Counter-controlled repetition requires:

1. The *name* of a control variable (or loop counter).
2. The *initial value* of the control variable.
3. The *increment* (or *decrement*) by which the control variable is modified each time through the loop (also known as *each iteration of the loop*).
4. The condition that tests for the *final value* of the control variable to determine whether looping should continue.

To see the four elements of counter-controlled repetition, consider the simple script shown in Fig. 8.1, which displays lines of XHTML text that illustrate the seven different font sizes supported by XHTML. The declaration in line 12 *names* the control variable (`counter`), reserves space for it in memory and sets it to an *initial value* of `1`. The declaration and initialization of `counter` could also have been accomplished by the following declaration and assignment statement:

```
var counter; // declare counter
counter = 1; // initialize counter to 1
```

Lines 16–18 in the `while` statement write a paragraph element consisting of the string "`XHTML font size`" concatenated with the control variable `counter`'s value, which repre-

```
<?xml version = "1.0" encoding = "utf-8"?>
<!DOCTYPE html PUBLIC "-//W3C//DTD XHTML 1.0 Strict//EN"
   "http://www.w3.org/TR/xhtml1/DTD/xhtml1-strict.dtd">

<!-- Fig. 8.1: WhileCounter.html -->
<!-- Counter-controlled repetition. -->
<html xmlns = "http://www.w3.org/1999/xhtml">
   <head>
      <title>Counter-Controlled Repetition</title>
      <script type = "text/javascript">
         <!--
         var counter = 1; // initialization

         while ( counter <= 7 ) // repetition condition
         {
            document.writeln( "<p style = \"font-size: " +
               counter + "ex\">XHTML font size " + counter +
               "ex</p>" );
            ++counter; // increment
         } //end while
         // -->
      </script>
   </head><body></body>
</html>
```

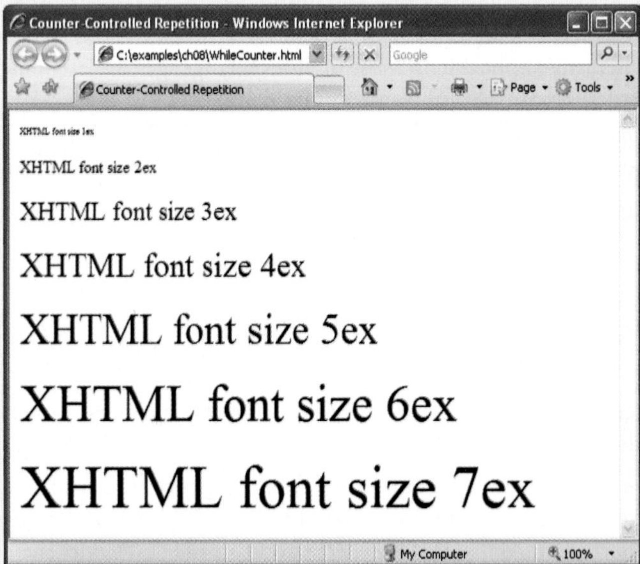

Fig. 8.1 | Counter-controlled repetition.

sents the font size. An inline CSS `style` attribute sets the `font-size` property to the value of `counter` concatenated to `ex`. Note the use of the escape sequence `\"`, which is placed around attribute `style`'s value. Because the double-quote character delimits the beginning and end of a string literal in JavaScript, it cannot be used in the contents of the string unless it is preceded by a \ to create the escape sequence \". For example, if `counter` is 5, the preceding statement produces the markup

```
<p style = "font-size: 5ex">XHTML font size 5ex</p>
```

XHTML allows either single quotes (') or double quotes (") to be placed around the value specified for an attribute. JavaScript allows single quotes to be placed in a string literal. Thus, we could have placed single quotes around the `font-size` property to produce equivalent XHTML output without the use of escape sequences.

Common Programming Error 8.1

Placing a double-quote (") character inside a string literal that is delimited by double quotes causes a runtime error when the script is interpreted. To be displayed as part of a string literal, a double-quote (") character must be preceded by a \ to form the escape sequence \".

Line 19 in the `while` statement *increments* the control variable by 1 for each iteration of the loop (i.e., each time the body of the loop is performed). The loop-continuation condition (line 14) in the `while` statement tests whether the value of the control variable is less than or equal to `7` (the *final value* for which the condition is `true`). Note that the body of this `while` statement executes even when the control variable is `7`. The loop terminates when the control variable exceeds `7` (i.e., `counter` becomes `8`).

Good Programming Practice 8.1

Use integer values to control loop counting.

Good Programming Practice 8.2

Indent the statements in the body of each control structure.

Good Programming Practice 8.3

Put a blank line before and after each control structure, to make it stand out in the program.

Good Programming Practice 8.4

Too many levels of nesting can make a program difficult to understand. As a general rule, try to avoid using more than three levels of nesting.

Good Programming Practice 8.5

Vertical spacing above and below control structures and indentation of the bodies of control structures in the headers of the control structure give programs a two-dimensional appearance that enhances readability.

8.3 for Repetition Statement

The `for` repetition statement handles all the details of counter-controlled repetition. Figure 8.2 illustrates the power of the `for` statement by reimplementing the script of Fig. 8.1.

When the `for` statement begins executing (line 15), the control variable `counter` is declared and is initialized to `1` (i.e., the first statement of the `for` statement declares the control variable's *name* and provides the control variable's *initial value*). Next, the loop-

```
1  <?xml version = "1.0" encoding = "utf-8"?>
2  <!DOCTYPE html PUBLIC "-//W3C//DTD XHTML 1.0 Strict//EN"
3     "http://www.w3.org/TR/xhtml1/DTD/xhtml1-strict.dtd">
4  
5  <!-- Fig. 8.2: ForCounter.html -->
6  <!-- Counter-controlled repetition with the for statement. -->
7  <html xmlns = "http://www.w3.org/1999/xhtml">
8     <head>
9        <title>Counter-Controlled Repetition</title>
10       <script type = "text/javascript">
11          <!--
12          // Initialization, repetition condition and
13          // incrementing are all included in the for
14          // statement header.
15          for ( var counter = 1; counter <= 7; ++counter )
16             document.writeln( "<p style = \"font-size: " +
17                counter + "ex\">XHTML font size " + counter +
18                "ex</p>" );
19          // -->
20       </script>
21    </head><body></body>
22 </html>
```

Fig. 8.2 | Counter-controlled repetition with the `for` statement.

continuation condition, `counter <= 7`, is checked. The condition contains the *final value* (7) of the control variable. The initial value of `counter` is 1. Therefore, the condition is satisfied (i.e., `true`), so the body statement (lines 16–18) writes a paragraph element in the XHTML document. Then, variable `counter` is incremented in the expression `++counter` and the loop continues execution with the loop-continuation test. The control variable is now equal to 2, so the final value is not exceeded and the program performs the body statement again (i.e., performs the next iteration of the loop). This process continues until the control variable counter becomes 8, at which point the loop-continuation test fails and the repetition terminates.

The program continues by performing the first statement after the for statement. (In this case, the script terminates, because the interpreter reaches the end of the script.)

Figure 8.3 takes a closer look at the for statement at line 15 of Fig. 8.2. The for statement's first line (including the keyword for and everything in parentheses after for) is often called the **for statement header**. Note that the for statement "does it all"—it specifies each of the items needed for counter-controlled repetition with a control variable. Remember that a block is a group of statements enclosed in curly braces that can be placed anywhere that a single statement can be placed, so you can use a block to put multiple statements into the body of a for statement.

Note that Fig. 8.3 uses the loop-continuation condition counter <= 7. If you incorrectly write counter < 7, the loop will execute only six times. This is an example of the common logic error called an **off-by-one error**.

Common Programming Error 8.2

Using an incorrect relational operator or an incorrect final value of a loop counter in the condition of a while*,* for *or* do...while *statement can cause an off-by-one error or an infinite loop.*

Good Programming Practice 8.6

Using the final value in the condition of a while *or* for *statement and using the* <= *relational operator will help avoid off-by-one errors. For a loop used to print the values 1 to 10, for example, the initial value of* counter *should be* 1*, and the loop-continuation condition should be* counter <= 10 *rather than* counter < 10 *(which is an off-by-one error) or* counter < 11 *(which is correct). Many programmers, however, prefer so-called* **zero-based counting***, in which, to count 10 times through the loop,* counter *would be initialized to zero and the loop-continuation test would be* counter < 10*.*

The general format of the for statement is

for (*initialization*; *loopContinuationTest*; *increment*)
    statements

where the *initialization* expression names the loop's control variable and provides its initial value, *loopContinuationTest* is the expression that tests the loop-continuation condition (containing the final value of the control variable for which the condition is true), and

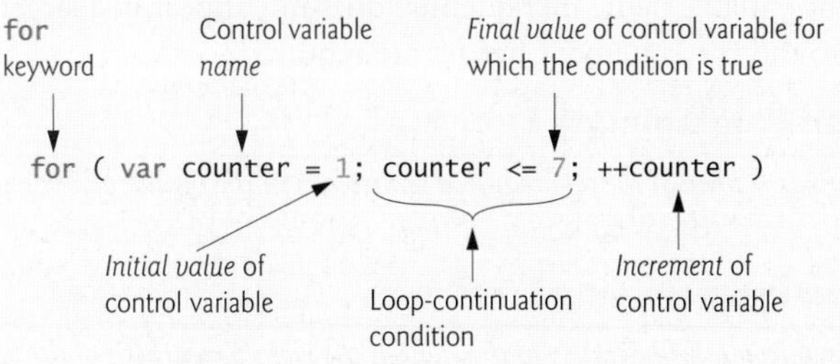

Fig. 8.3 | for statement header components.

increment is an expression that increments the control variable. The for statement can be represented by an equivalent while statement, with *initialization*, *loopContinuationTest* and *increment* placed as follows:

```
initialization;

while ( loopContinuationTest )
{
   statements
   increment;
}
```

In Section 8.7 we discuss an exception to this rule.

If the *initialization* expression in the for statement's header is the first definition of the control variable, the control variable can still be used after the for statement in the script. The part of a script in which a variable name can be used is known as the variable's **scope**. Scope is discussed in detail in Chapter 9, JavaScript: Functions.

Good Programming Practice 8.7

Place only expressions involving the control variable in the initialization and increment sections of a for *statement. Manipulations of other variables should appear either before the loop (if they execute only once, like initialization statements) or in the loop body (if they execute once per iteration of the loop, like incrementing or decrementing statements).*

The three expressions in the for statement are optional. If *loopContinuationTest* is omitted, JavaScript assumes that the loop-continuation condition is true, thus creating an infinite loop. One might omit the *initialization* expression if the control variable is initialized before the loop. One might omit the *increment* expression if the increment is calculated by statements in the body of the for statement or if no increment is needed. The increment expression in the for statement acts like a stand-alone statement at the end of the body of the for statement. Therefore, the expressions

```
counter = counter + 1
counter += 1
++counter
counter++
```

are all equivalent in the incrementing portion of the for statement. Many programmers prefer the form counter++. This is because the incrementing of the control variable occurs after the body of the loop is executed, and therefore the postincrementing form seems more natural. Preincrementing and postincrementing both have the same effect in our example, because the variable being incremented does not appear in a larger expression. The two semicolons in the for statement header are required.

Common Programming Error 8.3

Using commas instead of the two required semicolons in the header of a for *statement is a syntax error.*

Common Programming Error 8.4

Placing a semicolon immediately to the right of the right parenthesis of the header of a for *statement makes the body of that* for *statement an empty statement. This code is normally a logic error.*

The initialization, loop-continuation condition and increment portions of a for statement can contain arithmetic expressions. For example, assume that x = 2 and y = 10. If x and y are not modified in the body of the loop, then the statement

```
for ( var j = x; j <= 4 * x * y; j += y / x )
```

is equivalent to the statement

```
for ( var j = 2; j <= 80; j += 5 )
```

The "increment" of a for statement may be negative, in which case it is really a decrement and the loop actually counts downward.

If the loop-continuation condition initially is false, the for statement's body is not performed. Instead, execution proceeds with the statement following the for statement.

The control variable frequently is printed or used in calculations in the body of a for statement, but it does not have to be. Other times, the control variable is used for controlling repetition but never mentioned in the body of the for statement.

Error-Prevention Tip 8.1

Although the value of the control variable can be changed in the body of a for *statement, avoid changing it, because doing so can lead to subtle errors.*

The for statement is flowcharted much like the while statement. For example, Fig. 8.4 shows the flowchart of the for statement

```
for ( var counter = 1; counter <= 7; ++counter )
   document.writeln( "<p style = \"font-size: " +
      counter + "ex\">XHTML font size " + counter +
      "ex</p>" );
```

This flowchart makes it clear that the initialization occurs only once and that incrementing occurs *after* each execution of the body statement. Note that, besides small circles and arrows, the flowchart contains only rectangle symbols and a diamond symbol.

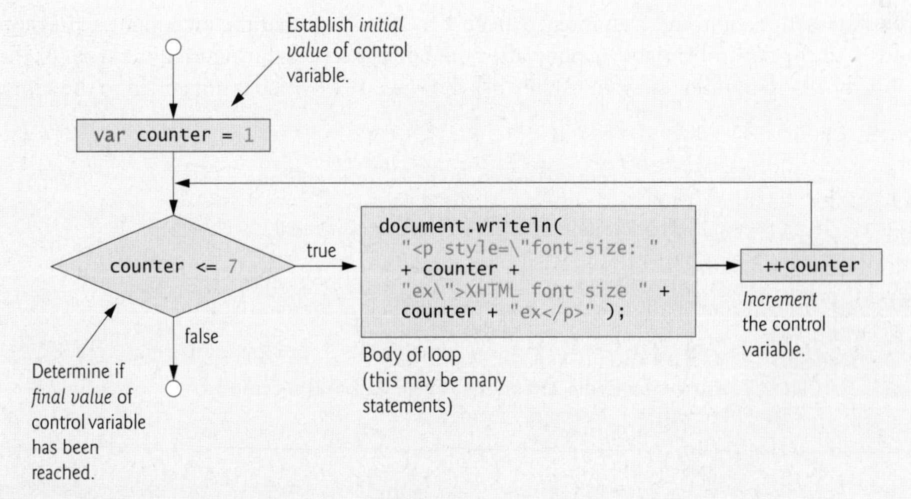

Fig. 8.4 | for repetition statement flowchart.

8.4 Examples Using the for Statement

The examples in this section show methods of varying the control variable in a `for` statement. In each case, we write the appropriate `for` header. Note the change in the relational operator for loops that decrement the control variable.

a) Vary the control variable from `1` to `100` in increments of `1`.

```
for ( var i = 1; i <= 100; ++i )
```

b) Vary the control variable from `100` to `1` in increments of `-1` (i.e., decrements of `1`).

```
for ( var i = 100; i >= 1; --i )
```

c) Vary the control variable from `7` to `77` in steps of `7`.

```
for ( var i = 7; i <= 77; i += 7 )
```

d) Vary the control variable from `20` to `2` in steps of `-2`.

```
for ( var i = 20; i >= 2; i -= 2 )
```

e) Vary the control variable over the following sequence of values: `2`, `5`, `8`, `11`, `14`, `17`, `20`.

```
for ( var j = 2; j <= 20; j += 3 )
```

f) Vary the control variable over the following sequence of values: `99`, `88`, `77`, `66`, `55`, `44`, `33`, `22`, `11`, `0`.

```
for ( var j = 99; j >= 0; j -= 11 )
```

Common Programming Error 8.5

Not using the proper relational operator in the loop-continuation condition of a loop that counts downward (e.g., using `i <= 1` *in a loop that counts down to 1) is usually a logic error that will yield incorrect results when the program runs.*

The next two scripts demonstrate the `for` repetition statement. Figure 8.5 uses the `for` statement to sum the even integers from `2` to `100`. Note that the increment expression adds `2` to the control variable `number` after the body executes during each iteration of the loop. The loop terminates when `number` has the value `102` (which is not added to the sum).

```
<?xml version = "1.0" encoding = "utf-8"?>
<!DOCTYPE html PUBLIC "-//W3C//DTD XHTML 1.0 Strict//EN"
   "http://www.w3.org/TR/xhtml1/DTD/xhtml1-strict.dtd">

<!-- Fig. 8.5: Sum.html -->
<!-- Summation with the for repetition structure. -->
<html xmlns = "http://www.w3.org/1999/xhtml">
   <head>
      <title>Sum the Even Integers from 2 to 100</title>
      <script type = "text/javascript">
         <!--
         var sum = 0;
```

Fig. 8.5 | Summation with the `for` repetition structure. (Part 1 of 2.)

```
      for ( var number = 2; number <= 100; number += 2 )
         sum += number;

      document.writeln( "The sum of the even integers " +
         "from 2 to 100 is " + sum );
      // -->
    </script>
  </head><body></body>
</html>
```

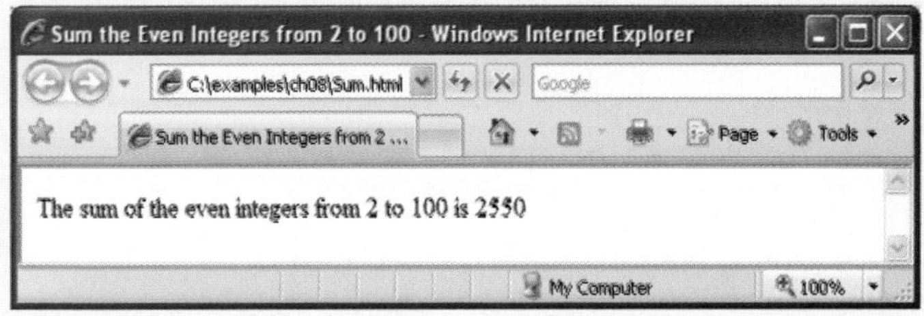

Fig. 8.5 | Summation with the for repetition structure. (Part 2 of 2.)

Note that the body of the for statement in Fig. 8.5 actually could be merged into the rightmost (increment) portion of the for header by using a comma, as follows:

```
for ( var number = 2; number <= 100; sum += number, number += 2)
   ;
```

Similarly, the initialization sum = 0 could be merged into the initialization section of the for statement.

Good Programming Practice 8.8

Although statements preceding a for *statement and in the body of a* for *statement can often be merged into the* for *header, avoid doing so, because it makes the program more difficult to read.*

Good Programming Practice 8.9

For clarity, limit the size of control-statement headers to a single line, if possible.

The next example computes compound interest (compounded yearly) using the for statement. Consider the following problem statement:

> *A person invests $1000.00 in a savings account yielding 5 percent interest. Assuming that all the interest is left on deposit, calculate and print the amount of money in the account at the end of each year for 10 years. Use the following formula to determine the amounts:*
>
> $a = p\,(1 + r)^{n}$
>
> *where*
>
> p is the original amount invested (i.e., the principal)
> r is the annual interest rate
> n is the number of years
> a is the amount on deposit at the end of the nth year.

This problem involves a loop that performs the indicated calculation for each of the 10 years the money remains on deposit. Figure 8.6 presents the solution to this problem, displaying the results in a table.

Lines 16–18 declare three variables and initialize `principal` to `1000.0` and `rate` to `.05`. Lines 20–21 write an XHTML <table> tag, and lines 22–23 write the `caption` that summarizes the table's content. Lines 24–25 create the table's header section (<thead>), a

```
1  <?xml version = "1.0" encoding = "utf-8"?>
2  <!DOCTYPE html PUBLIC "-//W3C//DTD XHTML 1.0 Strict//EN"
3     "http://www.w3.org/TR/xhtml1/DTD/xhtml1-strict.dtd">
4
5  <!-- Fig. 8.6: Interest.html -->
6  <!-- Compound interest calculation with a for loop. -->
7  <html xmlns = "http://www.w3.org/1999/xhtml">
8     <head>
9        <title>Calculating Compound Interest</title>
10       <style type = "text/css">
11          table { width: 100% }
12          th    { text-align: left }
13       </style>
14       <script type = "text/javascript">
15          <!--
16          var amount; // current amount of money
17          var principal = 1000.0; // principal amount
18          var rate = .05; // interest rate
19
20          document.writeln(
21             "<table border = \"1\">" ); // begin the table
22          document.writeln(
23             "<caption>Calculating Compound Interest</caption>" );
24          document.writeln(
25             "<thead><tr><th>Year</th>" ); // year column heading
26          document.writeln(
27             "<th>Amount on deposit</th>" ); // amount column heading
28          document.writeln( "</tr></thead><tbody>" );
29
30          // output a table row for each year
31          for ( var year = 1; year <= 10; ++year )
32          {
33             amount = principal * Math.pow( 1.0 + rate, year );
34             document.writeln( "<tr><td>" + year +
35                "</td><td>" + amount.toFixed(2) +
36                "</td></tr>" );
37          } //end for
38
39          document.writeln( "</tbody></table>" );
40          // -->
41       </script>
42    </head><body></body>
43 </html>
```

Fig. 8.6 | Compound interest calculation with a `for` loop. (Part 1 of 2.)

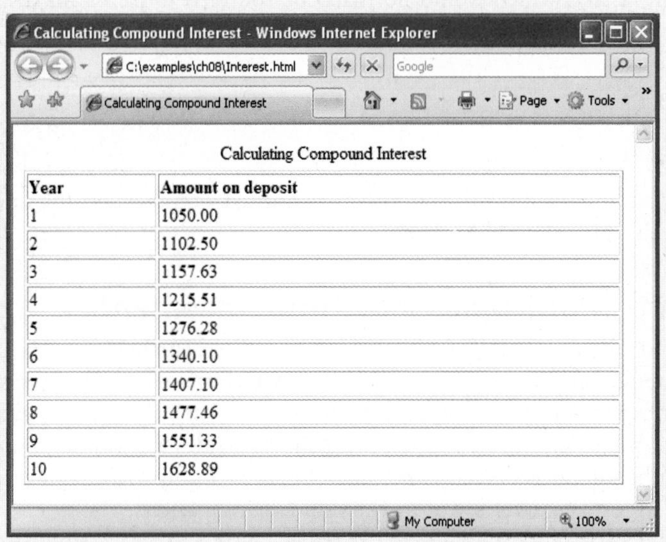

Year	Amount on deposit
1	1050.00
2	1102.50
3	1157.63
4	1215.51
5	1276.28
6	1340.10
7	1407.10
8	1477.46
9	1551.33
10	1628.89

Fig. 8.6 | Compound interest calculation with a `for` loop. (Part 2 of 2.)

row (`<tr>`) and a column heading (`<th>`) containing "`Year`." Lines 26–28 create a table heading for "`Amount on deposit`" and write the closing `</tr>` and `</thead>` tags.

The `for` statement (lines 31–37) executes its body 10 times, incrementing control variable `year` from 1 to 10 (note that `year` represents *n* in the problem statement). JavaScript does not include an exponentiation operator. Instead, we use the `Math` object's `pow` method for this purpose. `Math.pow(x, y)` calculates the value of `x` raised to the `y`th power. Method `Math.pow` takes two numbers as arguments and returns the result.

Line 33 performs the calculation using the formula given in the problem statement. Lines 34–36 write a line of XHTML markup that creates another row in the table. The first column is the current `year` value. The second column displays the value of `amount`. Line 39 writes the closing `</tbody>` and `</table>` tags after the loop terminates.

Line 35 introduces the **`Number` object** and its **`toFixed` method**. The variable `amount` contains a numerical value, so JavaScript represents it as a `Number` object. The `toFixed` method of a `Number` object formats the value by rounding it to the specified number of decimal places. On line 35, `amount.toFixed(2)` outputs the value of amount with two decimal places.

Variables `amount`, `principal` and `rate` represent numbers in this script. Remember that JavaScript represents all numbers as floating-point numbers. This feature is convenient in this example, because we are dealing with fractional parts of dollars and need a type that allows decimal points in its values.

Unfortunately, floating-point numbers can cause trouble. Here is a simple example of what can go wrong when using floating-point numbers to represent dollar amounts (assuming that dollar amounts are displayed with two digits to the right of the decimal point): Two dollar amounts stored in the machine could be 14.234 (which would normally be rounded to 14.23 for display purposes) and 18.673 (which would normally be rounded to 18.67 for display purposes). When these amounts are added, they produce the internal sum 32.907, which would normally be rounded to 32.91 for display purposes. Thus your printout could appear as

```
  14.23
+ 18.67
-------
  32.91
```

but a person adding the individual numbers as printed would expect the sum to be 32.90. You have been warned!

8.5 switch Multiple-Selection Statement

Previously, we discussed the `if` single-selection statement and the `if...else` double-selection statement. Occasionally, an algorithm will contain a series of decisions in which a variable or expression is tested separately for each of the values it may assume, and different actions are taken for each value. JavaScript provides the `switch` multiple-selection statement to handle such decision making. The script in Fig. 8.7 demonstrates three different CSS list formats determined by the value the user enters.

Line 12 in the script declares the variable `choice`. This variable stores the user's choice, which determines what type of XHTML list to display. Lines 13–14 declare variables `startTag` and `endTag`, which will store the XHTML tags that will be used to create the list element. Line 15 declares variable `validInput` and initializes it to `true`. The script uses this variable to determine whether the user made a valid choice (indicated by the value of `true`). If a choice is invalid, the script sets `validInput` to `false`. Line 16 declares variable `listType`, which will store an `h1` element indicating the list type. This heading appears before the list in the XHTML document.

Lines 18–19 prompt the user to enter a `1` to display a numbered list, a `2` to display a lettered list and a `3` to display a list with roman numerals. Lines 21–40 define a **`switch` statement** that assigns to the variables `startTag`, `endTag` and `listType` values based on the value input by the user in the `prompt` dialog. We create these different lists using the CSS property **`list-style-type`**, which allows us to set the numbering system for the list. Possible values include `decimal` (numbers—the default), `lower-roman` (lowercase Roman numerals), `upper-roman` (uppercase Roman numerals), `lower-alpha` (lowercase letters), `upper-alpha` (uppercase letters), and several others.

The `switch` statement consists of a series of **case labels** and an optional **`default` case**. When the flow of control reaches the `switch` statement, the script evaluates the **controlling expression** (`choice` in this example) in the parentheses following keyword `switch`. The value of this expression is compared with the value in each of the `case` labels, starting with the first `case` label. Assume that the user entered `2`. Remember that the value typed

```
1  <?xml version = "1.0" encoding = "utf-8"?>
2  <!DOCTYPE html PUBLIC "-//W3C//DTD XHTML 1.0 Strict//EN"
3     "http://www.w3.org/TR/xhtml1/DTD/xhtml1-strict.dtd">
4
5  <!-- Fig. 8.7: SwitchTest.html -->
6  <!-- Using the switch multiple-selection statement. -->
```

Fig. 8.7 | Using the `switch` multiple-selection statement. (Part 1 of 4.)

```
<html xmlns = "http://www.w3.org/1999/xhtml">
   <head>
      <title>Switching between XHTML List Formats</title>
      <script type = "text/javascript">
         <!--
         var choice; // user's choice
         var startTag; // starting list item tag
         var endTag; // ending list item tag
         var validInput = true; // indicates if input is valid
         var listType; // type of list as a string

         choice = window.prompt( "Select a list style:\n" +
            "1 (numbered), 2 (lettered), 3 (roman)", "1" );

         switch ( choice )
         {
            case "1":
               startTag = "<ol>";
               endTag = "</ol>";
               listType = "<h1>Numbered List</h1>";
               break;
            case "2":
               startTag = "<ol style = \"list-style-type: upper-alpha\">";
               endTag = "</ol>";
               listType = "<h1>Lettered List</h1>";
               break;
            case "3":
               startTag = "<ol style = \"list-style-type: upper-roman\">";
               endTag = "</ol>";
               listType = "<h1>Roman Numbered List</h1>";
               break;
            default:
               validInput = false;
         } //end switch

         if ( validInput == true )
         {
            document.writeln( listType + startTag );

            for ( var i = 1; i <= 3; ++i )
               document.writeln( "<li>List item " + i + "</li>" );

            document.writeln( endTag );
         } //end if
         else
            document.writeln( "Invalid choice: " + choice );
         // -->
      </script>
   </head>
   <body>
      <p>Click Refresh (or Reload) to run the script again</p>
   </body>
</html>
```

Fig. 8.7 | Using the switch multiple-selection statement. (Part 2 of 4.)

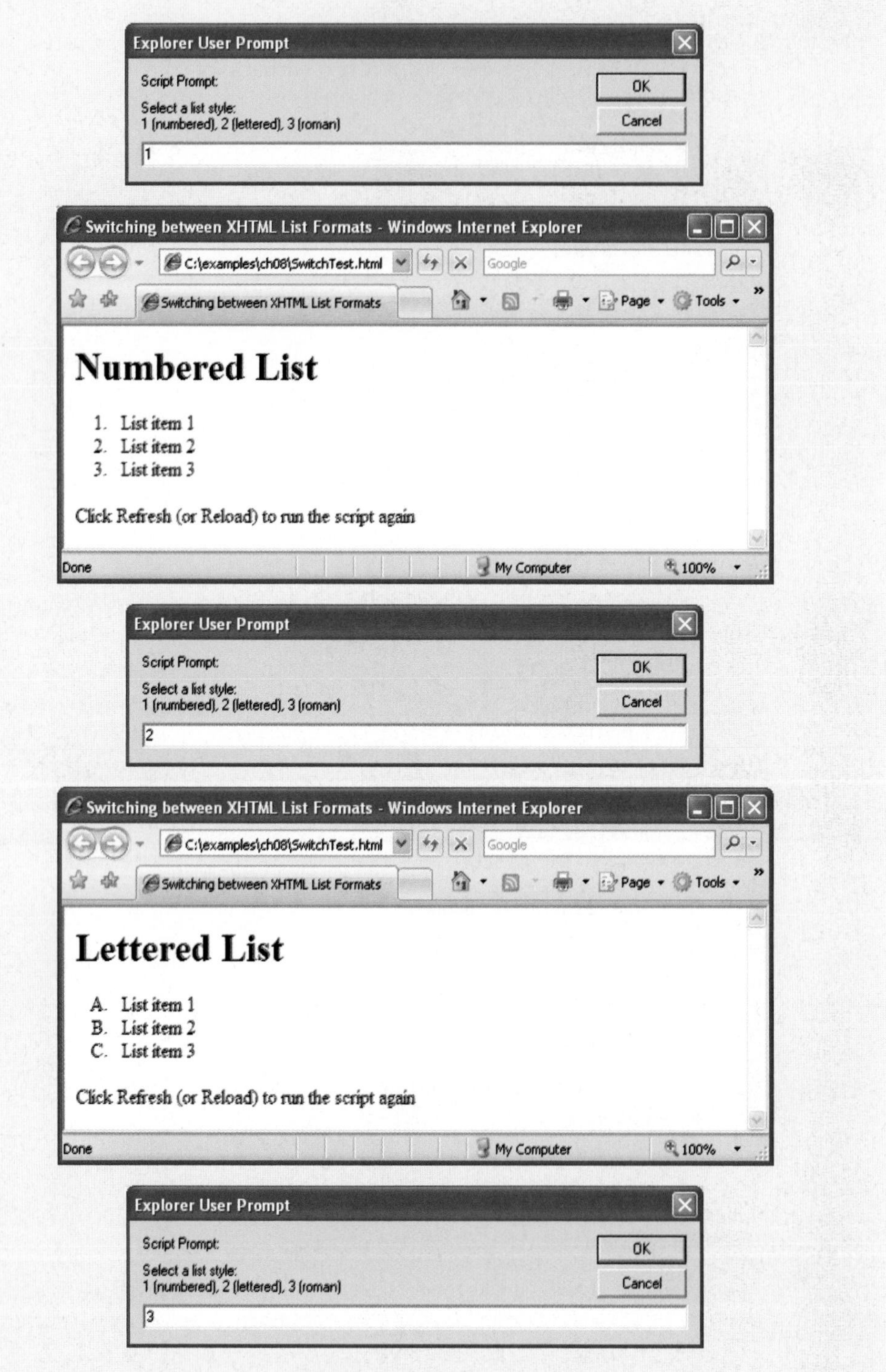

Fig. 8.7 | Using the `switch` multiple-selection statement. (Part 3 of 4.)

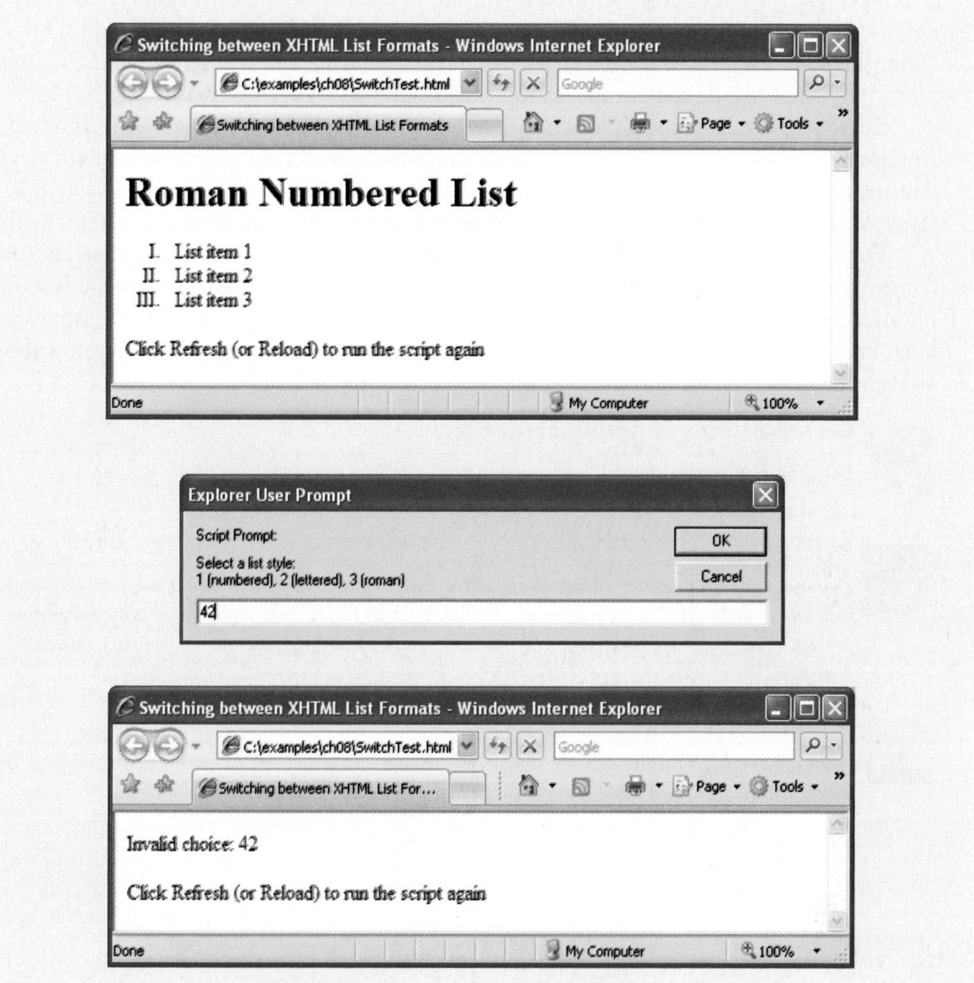

Fig. 8.7 | Using the `switch` multiple-selection statement. (Part 4 of 4.)

by the user in a `prompt` dialog is returned as a string. So, the string `2` is compared to the string in each `case` in the `switch` statement. If a match occurs (`case "2":`), the statements for that `case` execute. For the string `2` (lines 29–32), we set `startTag` to an opening `ol` tag with the style property `list-style-type` set to `upper-alpha`, set `endTag` to `"</ol>"` to indicate the end of an ordered list and set `listType` to `"<h1>Lettered List</h1>"`. If no match occurs between the controlling expression's value and a `case` label, the `default` case executes and sets variable `validInput` to `false`.

The `break` statement in line 32 causes program control to proceed with the first statement after the `switch` statement. The `break` statement is used because the `case`s in a `switch` statement would otherwise run together. If `break` is not used anywhere in a `switch` statement, then each time a match occurs in the statement, the statements for all the remaining `case`s execute.

Next, the flow of control continues with the `if` statement in line 42, which tests variable `validInput` to determine whether its value is `true`. If so, lines 44–49 write the `listType`, the `startTag`, three list items (`<li>`) and the `endTag`. Otherwise, the script writes text in the XHTML document indicating that an invalid choice was made (line 52).

Each `case` can have multiple actions (statements). The `switch` statement is different from others in that braces are not required around multiple actions in a `case` of a `switch`. The general `switch` statement (i.e., using a `break` in each `case`) is flowcharted in Fig. 8.8. [*Note:* As an exercise, flowchart the general `switch` statement without `break` statements.]

The flowchart makes it clear that each `break` statement at the end of a `case` causes control to exit from the `switch` statement immediately. The `break` statement is not required for the last `case` in the `switch` statement (or the `default` case, when it appears last), because program control automatically continues with the next statement after the `switch` statement.

Common Programming Error 8.6

Forgetting a `break` *statement when one is needed in a* `switch` *statement is a logic error.*

Software Engineering Observation 8.1

Provide a `default` *case in* `switch` *statements. Cases not explicitly tested in a* `switch` *statement without a* `default` *case are ignored. Including a* `default` *case focuses the programmer on processing exceptional conditions. However, there are situations in which no* `default` *processing is needed.*

Good Programming Practice 8.10

Although the `case` *clauses and the* `default` *case clause in a* `switch` *statement can occur in any order, it is clearer (and more common) to place the* `default` *clause last.*

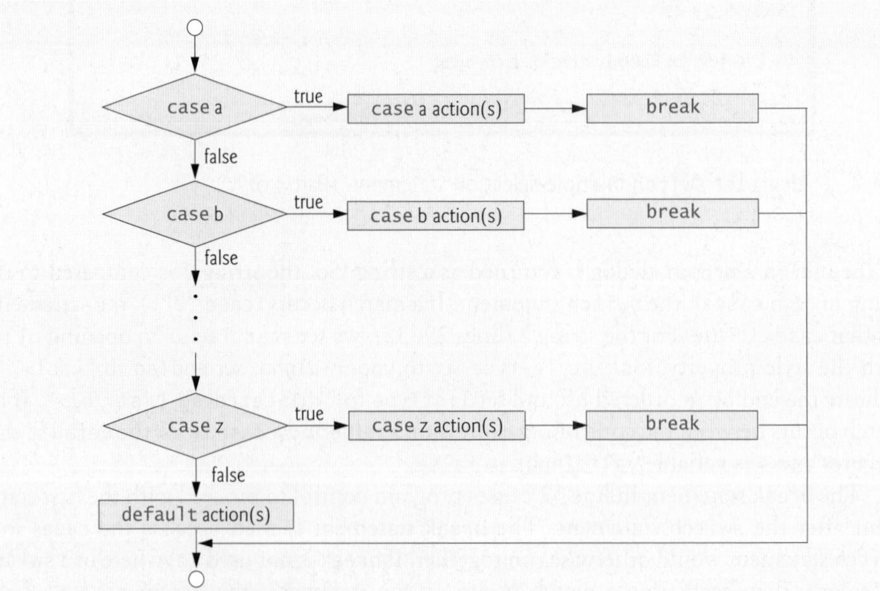

Fig. 8.8 | `switch` multiple-selection statement.

Good Programming Practice 8.11

In a `switch` statement, when the `default` clause is listed last, the `break` for that `case` statement is not required. Some programmers include this `break` for clarity and for symmetry with other `case`s.

Note that having several `case` labels listed together (e.g., `case 1: case 2:` with no statements between the cases) simply means that the same set of actions is to occur for each case. Again, note that, besides small circles and arrows, the flowchart contains only rectangle symbols and diamond symbols.

8.6 do...while Repetition Statement

The **`do...while` repetition statement** is similar to the `while` statement. In the `while` statement, the loop-continuation test occurs at the beginning of the loop, before the body of the loop executes. The `do...while` statement tests the loop-continuation condition *after* the loop body executes—therefore, *the loop body always executes at least once.* When a `do...while` terminates, execution continues with the statement after the `while` clause. Note that it is not necessary to use braces in a `do...while` statement if there is only one statement in the body. However, the braces usually are included, to avoid confusion between the `while` and `do...while` statements. For example,

```
while ( condition )
```

normally is regarded as the header to a `while` statement. A `do...while` statement with no braces around a single-statement body appears as

```
do
   statement
while ( condition );
```

which can be confusing. The last line—`while(` *condition* `);`—may be misinterpreted by the reader as a `while` statement containing an empty statement (the semicolon by itself). Thus, to avoid confusion, the `do...while` statement with a one-statement body is often written as follows:

```
do
{
   statement
} while ( condition );
```

Good Programming Practice 8.12

Some programmers always include braces in a `do...while` statement even if they are not necessary. This helps eliminate ambiguity between the `while` statement and the `do...while` statement containing a one-statement body.

Common Programming Error 8.7

Infinite loops are caused when the loop-continuation condition never becomes `false` in a `while`, `for` or `do...while` statement. To prevent this, make sure that there is not a semicolon immediately after the header of a `while` or `for` statement. In a counter-controlled loop, make sure that the control variable is incremented (or decremented) in the body of the loop. In a sentinel-controlled loop, make sure that the sentinel value is eventually input.

The script in Fig. 8.9 uses a do...while statement to display each of the six different XHTML heading types (h1 through h6). Line 12 declares control variable counter and initializes it to 1. Upon entering the do...while statement, lines 15–17 write a line of XHTML text in the document. The value of control variable counter is used to create the starting and ending header tags (e.g., <h1> and </h1>) and to create the line of text to display (e.g., This is an h1 level head). Line 18 increments the counter before the loop-continuation test occurs at the bottom of the loop.

The do...while flowchart in Fig. 8.10 makes it clear that the loop-continuation test does not occur until the action executes at least once.

```
1  <?xml version = "1.0" encoding = "utf-8"?>
2  <!DOCTYPE html PUBLIC "-//W3C//DTD XHTML 1.0 Strict//EN"
3     "http://www.w3.org/TR/xhtml1/DTD/xhtml1-strict.dtd">
4
5  <!-- Fig. 8.9: DoWhileTest.html -->
6  <!-- Using the do...while repetition statement. -->
7  <html xmlns = "http://www.w3.org/1999/xhtml">
8     <head>
9        <title>Using the do...while Repetition Statement</title>
10       <script type = "text/javascript">
11          <!--
12          var counter = 1;
13
14          do {
15             document.writeln( "<h" + counter + ">This is " +
16                "an h" + counter + " level head" + "</h" +
17                counter + ">" );
18             ++counter;
19          } while ( counter <= 6 );
20          // -->
21       </script>
22
23    </head><body></body>
24 </html>
```

Fig. 8.9 | Using the do...while repetition statement.

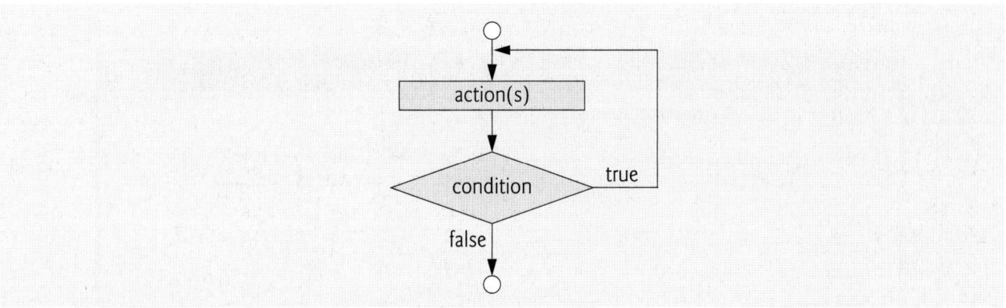

Fig. 8.10 | do...while repetition statement flowchart.

8.7 break and continue Statements

The **break** and **continue statements** alter the flow of control. The `break` statement, when executed in a `while`, `for`, `do...while` or `switch` statement, causes immediate exit from the statement. Execution continues with the first statement after the structure. The `break` statement is commonly used to escape early from a loop or to skip the remainder of a `switch` statement (as in Fig. 8.7). Figure 8.11 demonstrates the `break` statement in a `for` repetition statement.

During each iteration of the `for` statement in lines 14–20, the script writes the value of count in the XHTML document. When the `if` statement in line 16 detects that count

```
1  <?xml version = "1.0" encoding = "utf-8"?>
2  <!DOCTYPE html PUBLIC "-//W3C//DTD XHTML 1.0 Strict//EN"
3     "http://www.w3.org/TR/xhtml1/DTD/xhtml1-strict.dtd">
4
5  <!-- Fig. 8.11: BreakTest.html -->
6  <!-- Using the break statement in a for statement. -->
7  <html xmlns = "http://www.w3.org/1999/xhtml">
8     <head>
9        <title>
10          Using the break Statement in a for Statement
11       </title>
12       <script type = "text/javascript">
13          <!--
14          for ( var count = 1; count <= 10; ++count )
15          {
16             if ( count == 5 )
17                break; // break loop only if count == 5
18
19             document.writeln( "Count is: " + count + "<br />" );
20          } //end for
21
22          document.writeln(
23             "Broke out of loop at count = " + count );
24          // -->
25       </script>
26    </head><body></body>
27 </html>
```

Fig. 8.11 | Using the break statement in a for statement. (Part 1 of 2.)

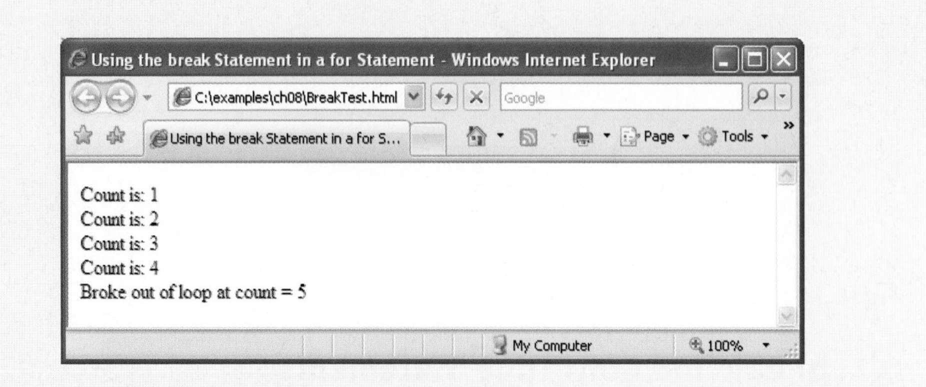

Fig. 8.11 | Using the `break` statement in a `for` statement. (Part 2 of 2.)

is `5`, the `break` in line 17 executes. This statement terminates the `for` statement, and the program proceeds to line 22 (the next statement in sequence immediately after the `for` statement), where the script writes the value of `count` when the loop terminated (i.e., `5`). The loop executes line 19 only four times.

The `continue` statement, when executed in a `while`, `for` or `do...while` statement, skips the remaining statements in the body of the statement and proceeds with the next iteration of the loop. In `while` and `do...while` statements, the loop-continuation test evaluates immediately after the `continue` statement executes. In `for` statements, the increment expression executes, then the loop-continuation test evaluates. This is the one case in which `for` and `while` differ. Improper placement of `continue` before the increment in a `while` may result in an infinite loop.

Figure 8.12 uses `continue` in a `for` statement to skip the `document.writeln` statement in line 20 when the `if` statement in line 17 determines that the value of `count` is `5`. When the `continue` statement executes, the script skips the remainder of the `for` statement's body. Program control continues with the increment of the `for` statement's control variable, followed by the loop-continuation test to determine whether the loop should continue executing.

Software Engineering Observation 8.2

Some programmers feel that `break` *and* `continue` *violate structured programming. They do not use* `break` *and* `continue`*, because the effects of these statements can be achieved by structured programming techniques.*

Performance Tip 8.1

The `break` *and* `continue` *statements, when used properly, perform faster than the corresponding structured techniques.*

Software Engineering Observation 8.3

There is a tension between achieving quality software engineering and achieving the best-performing software. Often, one of these goals is achieved at the expense of the other. For all but the most performance-intensive situations, the following rule of thumb should be followed: First make your code simple, readable and correct; then make it fast and small, but only if necessary.

```
<?xml version = "1.0" encoding = "utf-8"?>
<!DOCTYPE html PUBLIC "-//W3C//DTD XHTML 1.0 Strict//EN"
   "http://www.w3.org/TR/xhtml1/DTD/xhtml1-strict.dtd">

<!-- Fig. 8.12: ContinueTest.html -->
<!-- Using the continue statement in a for statement. -->
<html xmlns = "http://www.w3.org/1999/xhtml">
   <head>
      <title>
         Using the continue Statement in a for Statement
      </title>

      <script type = "text/javascript">
         <!--
         for ( var count = 1; count <= 10; ++count )
         {
            if ( count == 5 )
               continue; // skip remaining loop code only if count == 5

            document.writeln( "Count is: " + count + "<br />" );
         } //end for

         document.writeln( "Used continue to skip printing 5" );
         // -->
      </script>

   </head><body></body>
</html>
```

Using the continue Statement in a for Statement - Windows Internet Explorer

Count is: 1
Count is: 2
Count is: 3
Count is: 4
Count is: 6
Count is: 7
Count is: 8
Count is: 9
Count is: 10
Used continue to skip printing 5

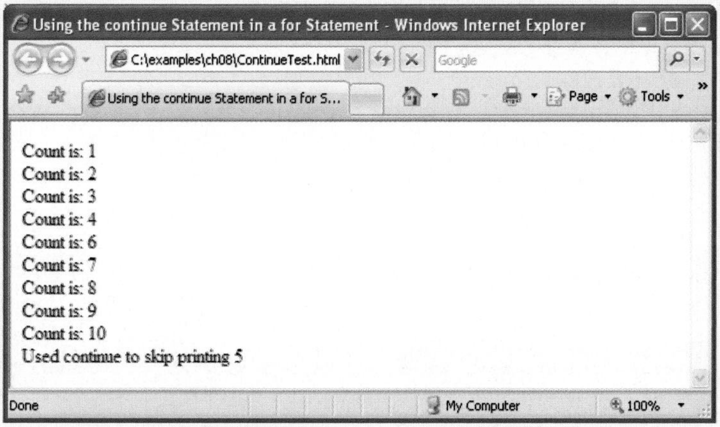

Fig. 8.12 | Using the `continue` statement in a `for` statement.

8.8 Labeled break and continue Statements

The `break` statement can break out of an immediately enclosing `while`, `for`, `do…while` or `switch` statement. To break out of a nested set of structures, you can use the **labeled break statement**. This statement, when executed in a `while`, `for`, `do…while` or `switch` statement, causes immediate exit from that statement and any number of enclosing repetition statements; program execution resumes with the first statement after the enclosing labeled statement (a statement preceded by a label). The labeled statement can be a block (a set of statements enclosed in curly braces, `{}`). Labeled `break` statements commonly are used to terminate nested looping structures containing `while`, `for`, `do...while` or `switch` statements. Figure 8.13 demonstrates the labeled `break` statement in a nested `for` statement.

```
<?xml version = "1.0" encoding = "utf-8"?>
<!DOCTYPE html PUBLIC "-//W3C//DTD XHTML 1.0 Strict//EN"
   "http://www.w3.org/TR/xhtml1/DTD/xhtml1-strict.dtd">

<!-- Fig. 8.13: BreakLabelTest.html -->
<!-- Labeled break statement in a nested for statement. -->
<html xmlns = "http://www.w3.org/1999/xhtml">
   <head>
      <title>Using the break Statement with a Label</title>
      <script type = "text/javascript">
         <!--
         stop: { // labeled block
            for ( var row = 1; row <= 10; ++row )
            {
               for ( var column = 1; column <= 5 ; ++column )
               {
                  if ( row == 5 )
                     break stop; // jump to end of stop block

                  document.write( "* " );
               } //end for

               document.writeln( "<br />" );
            } //end for

            // the following line is skipped
            document.writeln( "This line should not print" );
         } // end block labeled stop

         document.writeln( "End of script" );
         // -->
      </script>
   </head><body></body>
</html>
```

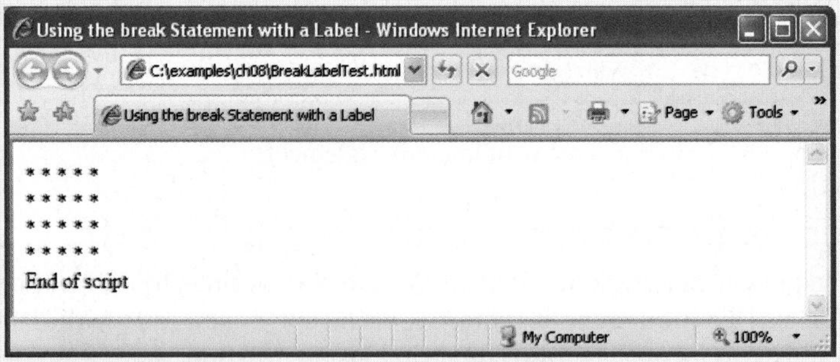

```
Using the break Statement with a Label - Windows Internet Explorer
C:\examples\ch08\BreakLabelTest.html
* * * * *
* * * * *
* * * * *
* * * * *
End of script
My Computer    100%
```

Fig. 8.13 | Labeled `break` statement in a nested `for` statement.

The labeled block (lines 12–28) begins with a label (an identifier followed by a colon). Here, we use the label `stop:`. The block is enclosed between the braces at the end of line 12 and in line 28, and includes both the nested `for` statement starting in line 13 and the `document.writeln` statement in line 27. When the `if` statement in line 17 detects that `row` is equal to `5`, the statement in line 18 executes. This statement terminates both the `for` statement in line 15 and its enclosing `for` statement in line 13, and the program proceeds to the statement in line 30 (the first statement in sequence after the labeled block). The inner `for` statement executes its body only four times. Note that the `document.writeln` statement in line 27 never executes, because it is included in the labeled block and the outer `for` statement never completes.

The `continue` statement proceeds with the next iteration (repetition) of the immediately enclosing `while`, `for` or `do...while` statement. The **labeled `continue` statement**, when executed in a repetition statement (`while`, `for` or `do...while`), skips the remaining statements in the structure's body and any number of enclosing repetition statements, then proceeds with the next iteration of the enclosing **labeled repetition statement** (a repetition statement preceded by a label). In labeled `while` and `do...while` statements, the loop-continuation test evaluates immediately after the `continue` statement executes. In a labeled `for` statement, the increment expression executes, then the loop-continuation test evaluates. Figure 8.14 uses the labeled `continue` statement in a nested `for` statement to cause execution to continue with the next iteration of the outer `for` statement.

```
<?xml version = "1.0" encoding = "utf-8"?>
<!DOCTYPE html PUBLIC "-//W3C//DTD XHTML 1.0 Strict//EN"
   "http://www.w3.org/TR/xhtml1/DTD/xhtml1-strict.dtd">

<!-- Fig. 8.14: ContinueLabelTest.html -->
<!-- Labeled continue statement in a nested for statement. -->
<html xmlns = "http://www.w3.org/1999/xhtml">
   <head>
      <title>Using the continue Statement with a Label</title>
      <script type = "text/javascript">
         <!--
         nextRow: // target label of continue statement
            for ( var row = 1; row <= 5; ++row )
            {
               document.writeln( "<br />" );

               for ( var column = 1; column <= 10; ++column )
               {
                  if ( column > row )
                     continue nextRow; // next iteration of labeled loop

                  document.write( "* " );
               } //end for
            } //end for
         // -->
      </script>
   </head><body></body>
</html>
```

Fig. 8.14 | Labeled `continue` statement in a nested `for` statement. (Part 1 of 2.)

Fig. 8.14 | Labeled `continue` statement in a nested `for` statement. (Part 2 of 2.)

The labeled `for` statement (lines 13–24) starts with the `nextRow` label in line 12. When the `if` statement in line 19 in the inner `for` statement detects that `column` is greater than `row`, line 20 executes and program control continues with the increment of the control variable of the outer `for` statement. Even though the inner `for` statement counts from 1 to 10, the number of * characters output on a row never exceeds the value of `row`.

8.9 Logical Operators

So far, we have studied only such simple conditions as `count <= 10`, `total > 1000` and `number != sentinelValue`. These conditions were expressed in terms of the relational operators >, <, >= and <=, and in terms of the equality operators == and `!=`. Each decision tested one condition. To make a decision based on multiple conditions, we performed these tests in separate statements or in nested `if` or `if...else` statements.

JavaScript provides logical operators that can be used to form more complex conditions by combining simple conditions. The logical operators are `&&` (logical AND), `||` (logical OR) and `!` (logical NOT, also called logical negation). We consider examples of each of these operators.

Suppose that, at some point in a program, we wish to ensure that two conditions are *both* `true` before we choose a certain path of execution. In this case, we can use the logical && operator, as follows:

```
if ( gender == 1 && age >= 65 )
   ++seniorFemales;
```

This `if` statement contains two simple conditions. The condition `gender == 1` might be evaluated to determine, for example, whether a person is a female. The condition `age >= 65` is evaluated to determine whether a person is a senior citizen. The `if` statement then considers the combined condition

```
gender == 1 && age >= 65
```

This condition is `true` *if and only if* both of the simple conditions are `true`. Finally, if this combined condition is indeed `true`, the count of `seniorFemales` is incremented by `1`. If either or both of the simple conditions are `false`, the program skips the incrementing and proceeds to the statement following the `if` statement. The preceding combined condition can be made more readable by adding redundant parentheses:

```
( gender == 1 ) && ( age >= 65 )
```

The table in Fig. 8.15 summarizes the && operator. The table shows all four possible combinations of `false` and `true` values for *expression1* and *expression2*. Such tables are often called **truth tables**. JavaScript evaluates to `false` or `true` all expressions that include relational operators, equality operators and/or logical operators.

Now let us consider the || (logical OR) operator. Suppose we wish to ensure that either *or* both of two conditions are `true` before we choose a certain path of execution. In this case, we use the || operator, as in the following program segment:

```
if ( semesterAverage >= 90 || finalExam >= 90 )
   document.writeln( "Student grade is A" );
```

This statement also contains two simple conditions. The condition `semesterAverage >= 90` is evaluated to determine whether the student deserves an "A" in the course because of a solid performance throughout the semester. The condition `finalExam >= 90` is evaluated to determine whether the student deserves an "A" in the course because of an outstanding performance on the final exam. The `if` statement then considers the combined condition

```
semesterAverage >= 90 || finalExam >= 90
```

and awards the student an "A" if either or both of the simple conditions are `true`. Note that the message `"Student grade is A"` is *not* printed only when both of the simple conditions are `false`. Figure 8.16 is a truth table for the logical OR operator (||).

The && operator has a higher precedence than the || operator. Both operators associate from left to right. An expression containing && or || operators is evaluated only until truth or falsity is known. Thus, evaluation of the expression

```
gender == 1 && age >= 65
```

expression1	expression2	expression1 && expression2
false	false	false
false	true	false
true	false	false
true	true	true

Fig. 8.15 | Truth table for the && (logical AND) operator.

expression1	expression2	expression1 || expression2
false	false	false
false	true	true
true	false	true
true	true	true

Fig. 8.16 | Truth table for the || (logical OR) operator.

stops immediately if gender is not equal to 1 (i.e., the entire expression is false) and continues if gender is equal to 1 (i.e., the entire expression could still be true if the condition age >= 65 is true). Similarly, the || operator immediately returns true if the first operand is true. This performance feature for evaluation of logical AND and logical OR expressions is called short-circuit evaluation.

JavaScript provides the ! (logical negation) operator to enable a programmer to "reverse" the meaning of a condition (i.e., a true value becomes false, and a false value becomes true). Unlike the logical operators && and ||, which combine two conditions (i.e., they are binary operators), the logical negation operator has only a single condition as an operand (i.e., it is a unary operator). The logical negation operator is placed before a condition to choose a path of execution if the original condition (without the logical negation operator) is false, as in the following program segment:

```
if ( ! ( grade == sentinelValue ) )
   document.writeln( "The next grade is " + grade );
```

The parentheses around the condition grade == sentinelValue are needed, because the logical negation operator has a higher precedence than the equality operator. Figure 8.17 is a truth table for the logical negation operator.

In most cases, the programmer can avoid using logical negation by expressing the condition differently with an appropriate relational or equality operator. For example, the preceding statement may also be written as follows:

```
if ( grade != sentinelValue )
   document.writeln( "The next grade is " + grade );
```

The script in Fig. 8.18 demonstrates all the logical operators by producing their truth tables. The script produces an XHTML table containing the results.

expression	!expression
false	true
true	false

Fig. 8.17 | Truth table for operator ! (logical negation).

```
<?xml version = "1.0" encoding = "utf-8"?>
<!DOCTYPE html PUBLIC "-//W3C//DTD XHTML 1.0 Strict//EN"
   "http://www.w3.org/TR/xhtml1/DTD/xhtml1-strict.dtd">

<!-- Fig. 8.18: LogicalOperators.html -->
<!-- Demonstrating logical operators. -->
<html xmlns = "http://www.w3.org/1999/xhtml">
   <head>
      <title>Demonstrating the Logical Operators</title>
```

Fig. 8.18 | Demonstrating logical operators. (Part 1 of 2.)

```
      <style type = "text/css">
         table   { width: 100% }
         td.left { width: 25% }
      </style>
      <script type = "text/javascript">
         <!--
         document.writeln(
            "<table border = \"1\"" );
         document.writeln(
            "<caption>Demonstrating Logical " +
               "Operators</caption>" );
         document.writeln(
            "<tr><td class = \"left\">Logical AND (&&)</td>" +
            "<td>false && false: " + ( false && false ) +
            "<br />false && true: " + ( false && true ) +
            "<br />true && false: " + ( true && false ) +
            "<br />true && true: " + ( true && true ) +
            "</td></tr>" );
         document.writeln(
            "<tr><td class = \"left\">Logical OR (||)</td>" +
            "<td>false || false: " + ( false || false ) +
            "<br />false || true: " + ( false || true ) +
            "<br />true || false: " + ( true || false ) +
            "<br />true || true: " + ( true || true ) +
            "</td></tr>" );
         document.writeln(
            "<tr><td class = \"left\">Logical NOT (!)</td>" +
            "<td>!false: " + ( !false ) +
            "<br />!true: " + ( !true ) + "</td></tr>" );
         document.writeln( "</table>" );
         // -->
      </script>
   </head><body></body>
</html>
```

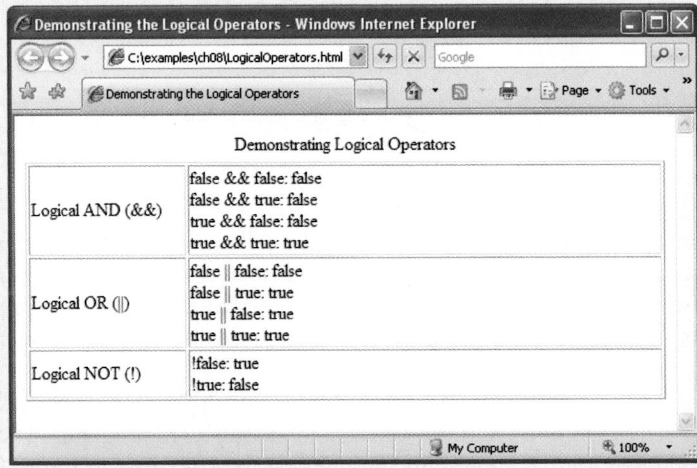

Fig. 8.18 | Demonstrating logical operators. (Part 2 of 2.)

In the output of Fig. 8.18, the strings "false" and "true" indicate false and true for the operands in each condition. The result of the condition is shown as true or false. Note that when you use the concatenation operator with a boolean value and a string, JavaScript automatically converts the boolean value to string "false" or "true". Lines 16–39 build an XHTML table containing the results.

An interesting feature of JavaScript is that most nonboolean values can be converted to a boolean true or false value. Nonzero numeric values are considered to be true. The numeric value zero is considered to be false. Any string that contains characters is considered to be true. The empty string (i.e., the string containing no characters) is considered to be false. The value null and variables that have been declared but not initialized are considered to be false. All objects (e.g., the browser's document and window objects and JavaScript's Math object) are considered to be true.

Figure 8.19 shows the precedence and associativity of the JavaScript operators introduced up to this point. The operators are shown top to bottom in decreasing order of precedence.

Operator	Associativity	Type
++ -- !	right to left	unary
* / %	left to right	multiplicative
+ -	left to right	additive
< <= > >=	left to right	relational
== !=	left to right	equality
&&	left to right	logical AND
||	left to right	logical OR
?:	right to left	conditional
= += -= *= /= %=	right to left	assignment

Fig. 8.19 | Precedence and associativity of the operators discussed so far.

8.10 Summary of Structured Programming

Just as architects design buildings by employing the collective wisdom of their profession, so should programmers design programs. Our field is younger than architecture, and our collective wisdom is considerably sparser. We have learned that structured programming produces programs that are easier to understand than unstructured programs, and thus are easier to test, debug, and modify.

Flowcharts reveal the structured nature of programs or the lack thereof. Connecting individual flowchart symbols arbitrarily can lead to unstructured programs. Therefore, the programming profession has chosen to combine flowchart symbols to form a limited set of control structures and to build structured programs by properly combining control structures in two simple ways.

For simplicity, only single-entry/single-exit control structures are used—that is, there is only one way to enter and one way to exit each control structure. Connecting control structures in sequence to form structured programs is simple: The exit point of one control structure is connected to the entry point of the next control structure (i.e., the control structures are simply placed one after another in a program). We have called this process control-structure stacking. The rules for forming structured programs also allow for control structures to be nested. Figure 8.20 summarizes JavaScript's control structures. Small circles are used in the figure to indicate the single entry point and the single exit point of each structure.

Figure 8.21 shows the rules for forming properly structured programs. The rules assume that the rectangle flowchart symbol may be used to indicate any action, including input/output. [*Note:* An oval flowchart symbol indicates the beginning and end of a process.]

Applying the rules in Fig. 8.21 always results in a structured flowchart with a neat, building-block-like appearance. For example, repeatedly applying Rule 2 to the simplest

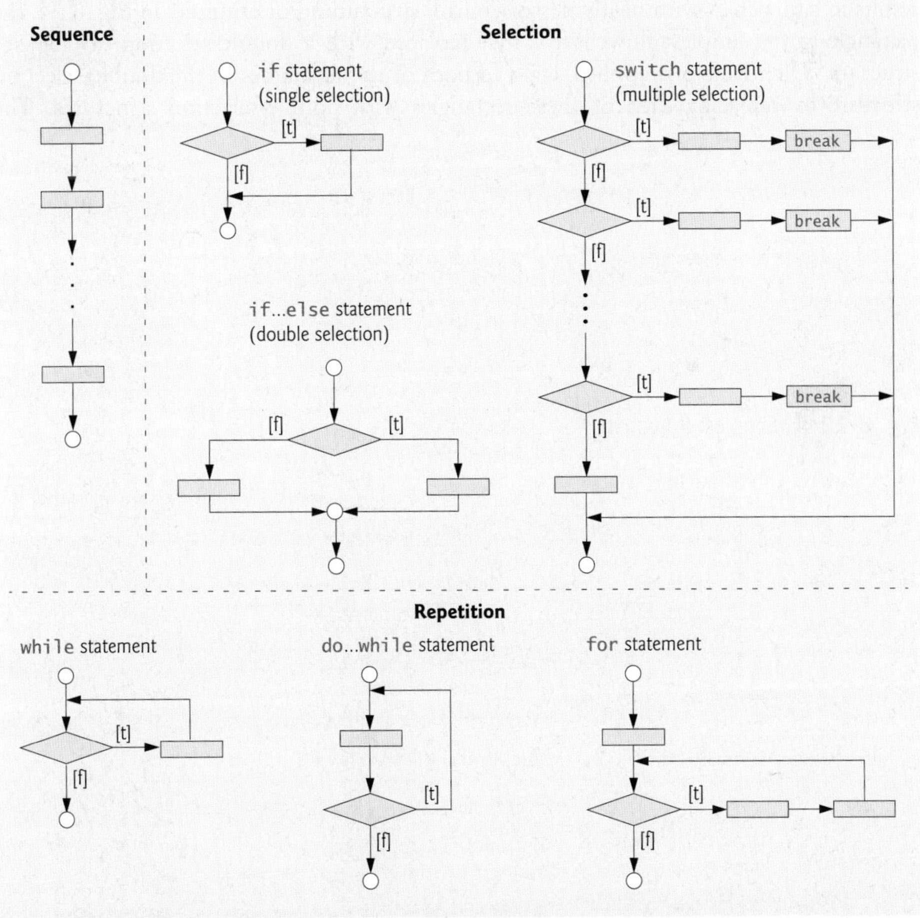

Fig. 8.20 | Single-entry/single-exit sequence, selection and repetition structures.

Rules for forming structured programs

1. Begin with the "simplest flowchart" (Fig. 8.22).
2. Any rectangle (action) can be replaced by two rectangles (actions) in sequence.
3. Any rectangle (action) can be replaced by any control structure (sequence, `if`, `if...else`, `switch`, `while`, `do...while` or `for`).
4. Rules 2 and 3 may be applied as often as necessary and in any order.

Fig. 8.21 | Forming rules for structured programs.

flowchart (Fig. 8.22) results in a structured flowchart containing many rectangles in sequence (Fig. 8.23). Note that Rule 2 generates a stack of control structures; so let us call Rule 2 the stacking rule.

Rule 3 is called the nesting rule. Repeatedly applying Rule 3 to the simplest flowchart results in a flowchart with neatly nested control structures. For example, in Fig. 8.24, the rectangle in the simplest flowchart is first replaced with a double-selection (`if...else`) structure. Then Rule 3 is applied again to both of the rectangles in the double-selection structure by replacing each of these rectangles with double-selection structures. The

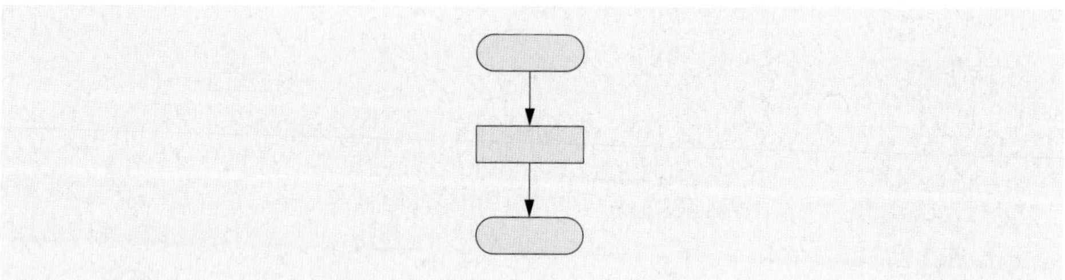

Fig. 8.22 | Simplest flowchart.

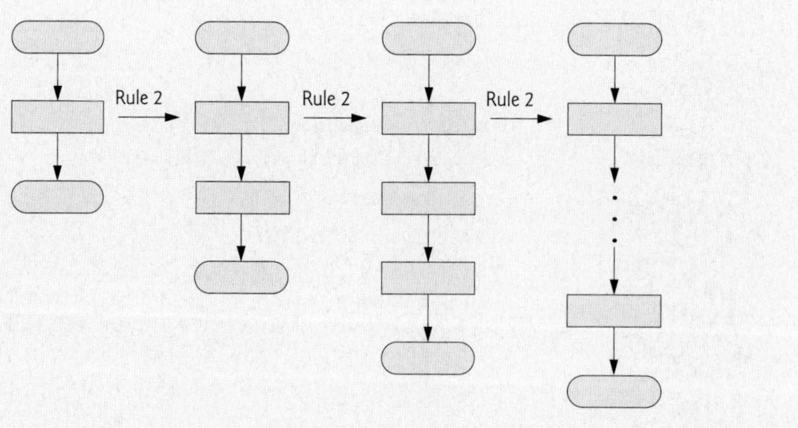

Fig. 8.23 | Repeatedly applying Rule 2 of Fig. 8.21 to the simplest flowchart.

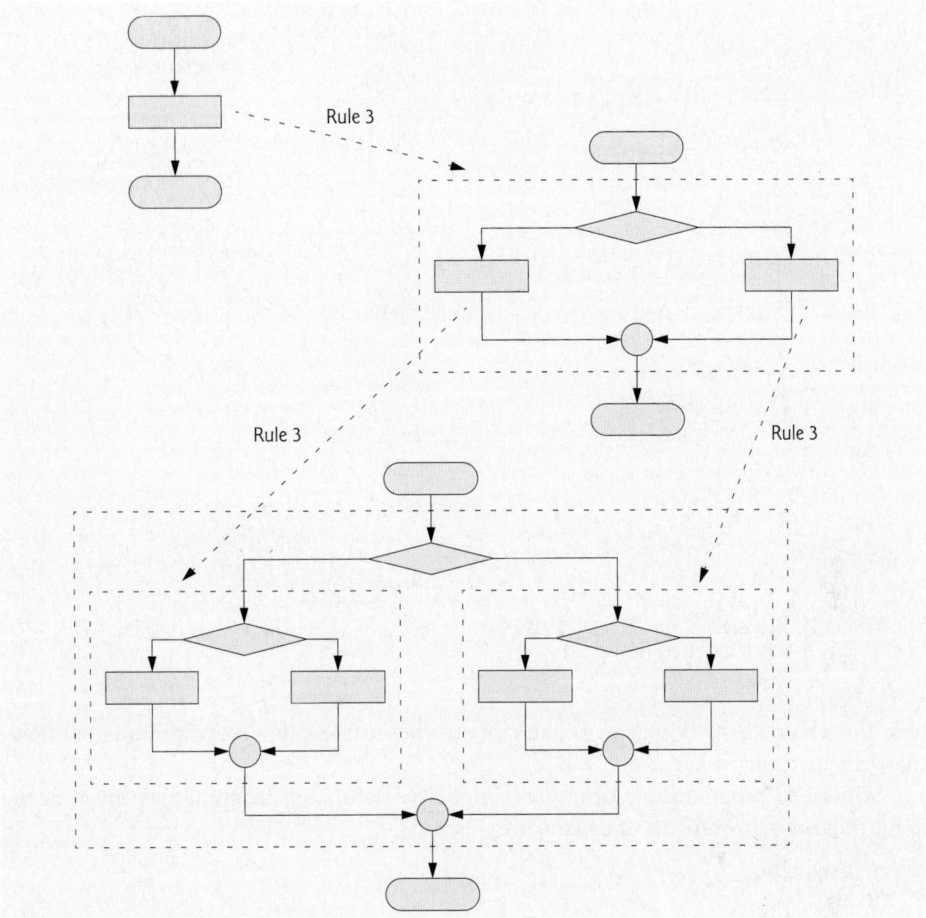

Fig. 8.24 | Applying Rule 3 of Fig. 8.21 to the simplest flowchart.

dashed box around each of the double-selection structures represents the rectangle in the original simplest flowchart that was replaced.

Rule 4 generates larger, more involved and more deeply nested structures. The flowcharts that emerge from applying the rules in Fig. 8.21 constitute the set of all possible structured flowcharts and thus the set of all possible structured programs.

The beauty of the structured approach is that we use only seven simple single-entry/single-exit pieces and assemble them in only two simple ways. Figure 8.25 shows the kinds of stacked building blocks that emerge from applying Rule 2 and the kinds of nested building blocks that emerge from applying Rule 3. The figure also shows the kind of overlapped building blocks that cannot appear in structured flowcharts (because of the elimination of the `goto` statement).

If the rules in Fig. 8.21 are followed, an unstructured flowchart (like the one in Fig. 8.26) cannot be created. If you are uncertain about whether a particular flowchart is structured, apply the rules of Fig. 8.21 in reverse to try to reduce the flowchart to the sim-

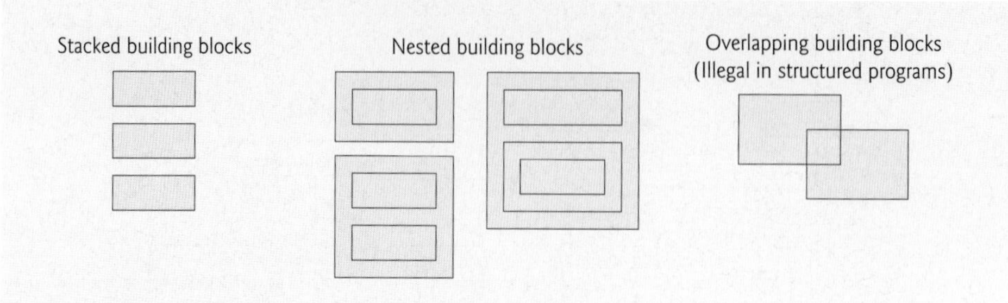

Fig. 8.25 | Stacked, nested and overlapped building blocks.

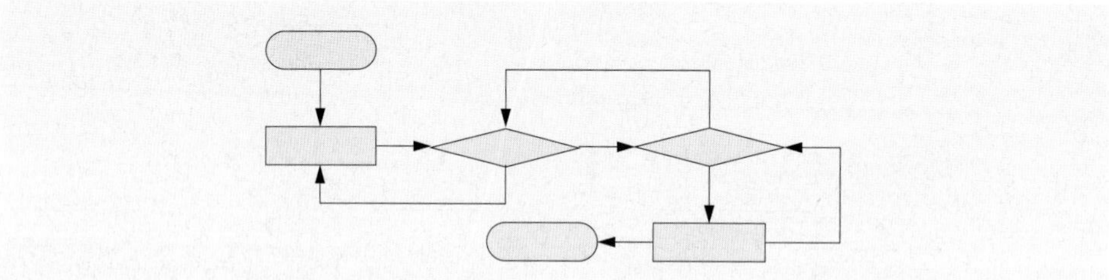

Fig. 8.26 | Unstructured flowchart.

plest flowchart. If the flowchart is reducible to the simplest flowchart, the original flowchart is structured; otherwise, it is not.

Structured programming promotes simplicity. Bohm and Jacopini have given us the result that only three forms of control are needed:

- sequence
- selection
- repetition

Sequence is trivial. Selection is implemented in one of three ways:

- `if` statement (single selection)
- `if...else` statement (double selection)
- `switch` statement (multiple selection)

In fact, it is straightforward to prove that the `if` statement is sufficient to provide any form of selection; everything that can be done with the `if...else` statement and the `switch` statement can be implemented by combining `if` statements (although perhaps not as smoothly).

Repetition is implemented in one of four ways:

- `while` statement
- `do...while` statement
- `for` statement
- `for...in` statement (discussed in Chapter 10)

It is straightforward to prove that the `while` statement is sufficient to provide any form of repetition. Everything that can be done with the `do...while` statement and the `for` statement can be done with the `while` statement (although perhaps not as elegantly).

Combining these results illustrates that any form of control ever needed in a JavaScript program can be expressed in terms of:

- sequence
- `if` statement (selection)
- `while` statement (repetition)

These control structures can be combined in only two ways—stacking and nesting. Indeed, structured programming promotes simplicity.

8.11 Wrap-Up

In this chapter, we discussed the composition of programs from control structures containing actions and decisions. We expanded the previous chapter's discussion on control structures, discussing the `for` statement, the `do...while` statement and the `switch` statement. We also saw how `break` and `continue` can be used to alter the flow of the program.

In Chapter 9, we introduce another program-structuring unit, called the function. You'll learn to compose large programs by combining functions that are composed of control structures. We will also discuss how functions promote software reusability.

8.12 Web Resources

`www.deitel.com/javascript/`

The Deitel JavaScript Resource Center contains links to some of the best JavaScript resources on the web. There you'll find categorized links to JavaScript tools, code generators, forums, books, libraries, frameworks and more. Also check out the tutorials for all skill levels, from introductory to advanced. Be sure to visit the related Resource Centers on XHTML (`www.deitel.com/xhtml/`) and CSS 2.1 (`www.deitel.com/css21/`).

Summary

Section 8.2 Essentials of Counter-Controlled Repetition

- Counter-controlled repetition requires: the *name* of a control variable, the *initial value* of the control variable, the *increment* (or *decrement*) by which the control variable is modified each time through the loop, and the condition that tests for the *final value* of the control variable to determine whether looping should continue.
- Because the double-quote character delimits the beginning and end of a string literal in JavaScript, it cannot be used in the contents of the string unless it is preceded by a \ to create the escape sequence \". XHTML allows either single quotes (') or double quotes (") to be placed around the value specified for an attribute. JavaScript allows single quotes to be placed in a string literal.

Section 8.3 `for` Repetition Statement

- The `for` statement "does it all"—it specifies each of the items needed for counter-controlled repetition with a control variable.

- You can use a block to put multiple statements into the body of a `for` construct.
- The for statement takes three expressions: an initialization, a condition and an expression.
- The increment expression in the `for` statement acts like a stand-alone statement at the end of the body of the `for` statement.
- Place only expressions involving the control variable in the initialization and increment sections of a `for` statement.
- The three expressions in the `for` statement are optional. The two semicolons in the `for` statement are required.
- The initialization, loop-continuation condition and increment portions of a `for` statement can contain arithmetic expressions.
- The part of a script in which a variable name can be used is known as the variable's scope.
- The "increment" of a `for` statement may be negative, in which case it is called a decrement and the loop actually counts downward.
- If the loop-continuation condition initially is `false`, the body of the `for` statement is not performed. Instead, execution proceeds with the statement following the `for` statement.

Section 8.4 Examples Using the `for` *Statement*

- JavaScript does not include an exponentiation operator. Instead, we use the `Math` object's `pow` method for this purpose. `Math.pow(x, y)` calculates the value of `x` raised to the `y`th power.
- Floating-point numbers can cause trouble as a result of rounding errors.

Section 8.5 `switch` *Multiple-Selection Statement*

- JavaScript provides the `switch` multiple-selection statement in which a variable or expression is tested separately for each of the values it may assume. Different actions are taken for each value.
- The CSS property `list-style-type` allows you to set the numbering system for the list. Possible values include `decimal` (numbers—the default), `lower-roman` (lowercase roman numerals), `upper-roman` (uppercase roman numerals), `lower-alpha` (lowercase letters), `upper-alpha` (uppercase letters), and several others.
- The `switch` statement consists of a series of case labels and an optional default case. When the flow of control reaches the `switch` statement, the script evaluates the controlling expression in the parentheses following keyword `switch`. The value of this expression is compared with the value in each of the `case` labels, starting with the first `case` label. If the comparison evaluates to `true`, the statements after the case label are executed in order until a `break` statement is reached.
- The `break` statement is used as the last statement in each `case` to exit the switch statement immediately.
- The `default` case allows you to specify a set of statements to execute if no other `case` is satisfied. This `case` is usually the last `case` in the `switch` statement.
- Each `case` can have multiple actions (statements). The `switch` statement is different from other statements in that braces are not required around multiple actions in a `case` of a `switch`.
- The `break` statement is not required for the last `case` in the `switch` statement because program control automatically continues with the next statement after the `switch` statement.
- Having several `case` labels listed together (e.g., `case 1: case 2:` with no statements between the cases) simply means that the same set of actions is to occur for each case.

Section 8.6 `do...while` *Repetition Statement*

- The `do...while` statement tests the loop-continuation condition *after* the loop body executes—therefore, *the loop body always executes at least once.*

Section 8.7 **break** *and* **continue** *Statements*

- The break statement, when executed in a while, for, do...while or switch statement, causes immediate exit from the statement. Execution continues with the first statement after the structure.
- The break statement is commonly used to escape early from a loop or to skip the remainder of a switch statement.
- The continue statement, when executed in a while, for or do...while statement, skips the remaining statements in the body of the statement and proceeds with the next iteration of the loop. In while and do...while statements, the loop-continuation test evaluates immediately after the continue statement executes. In for statements, the increment expression executes, then the loop-continuation test evaluates.

Section 8.8 Labeled **break** *and* **continue** *Statements*

- To break out of a nested control statement, you can use the labeled break statement. This statement, when executed in a while, for, do...while or switch statement, causes immediate exit from that statement and any number of enclosing repetition statements; program execution resumes with the first statement after the specified labeled statement (a statement preceded by a label).
- A labeled statement can be a block (a set of statements enclosed in curly braces, {}).
- Labeled break statements commonly are used to terminate nested looping structures containing while, for, do...while or switch statements.
- The labeled continue statement, when executed in a repetition statement (while, for or do...while), skips the remaining statements in the structure's body and any number of enclosing repetition statements, then proceeds with the next iteration of the specified labeled repetition statement (a repetition statement preceded by a label).
- In labeled while and do...while statements, the loop-continuation test evaluates immediately after the continue statement executes. In a labeled for statement, the increment expression executes, then the loop-continuation test evaluates.

Section 8.9 Logical Operators

- JavaScript provides logical operators that can be used to form more complex conditions by combining simple conditions. The logical operators are && (logical AND), || (logical OR) and ! (logical NOT, also called logical negation).
- The && operator is used to ensure that two conditions are *both* true before choosing a certain path of execution.
- JavaScript evaluates to false or true all expressions that include relational operators, equality operators and/or logical operators.
- The || (logical OR) operator is used to ensure that either *or* both of two conditions are true before choosing choose a certain path of execution.
- The && operator has a higher precedence than the || operator. Both operators associate from left to right.
- An expression containing && or || operators is evaluated only until truth or falsity is known. This is called short-circuit evaluation.
- JavaScript provides the ! (logical negation) operator to enable a programmer to "reverse" the meaning of a condition (i.e., a true value becomes false, and a false value becomes true).
- The logical negation operator has only a single condition as an operand (i.e., it is a unary operator). The logical negation operator is placed before a condition to evaluate to true if the original condition (without the logical negation operator) is false.
- The logical negation operator has a higher precedence than the equality operator.

- Most nonboolean values can be converted to a boolean `true` or `false` value. Nonzero numeric values are considered to be `true`. The numeric value zero is considered to be `false`. Any string that contains characters is considered to be `true`. The empty string (i.e., the string containing no characters) is considered to be `false`. The value `null` and variables that have been declared but not initialized are considered to be `false`. All objects (e.g., the browser's `document` and `window` objects and JavaScript's `Math` object) are considered to be `true`.

Terminology

`!` operator
`&&` operator
`||` operator
`break`
`case` label
`continue`
counter-controlled repetition
`default` case in `switch`
`do...while` repetition statement
`for` repetition statement
`for` statement header
infinite loop
labeled `break` statement
labeled block
labeled `continue` statement
labeled repetition statement
logical AND (`&&`)
logical negation (`!`)
logical operator
logical OR (`||`)
loop-continuation condition
`Math` object
multiple selection
nested control structure
nesting rule
`Number` object
off-by-one error
`pow` method of the `Math` object
repetition structure
scope
short-circuit evaluation
simple condition
single-entry/single-exit control structure
stacked control structure
stacking rule
`switch` selection statement
`toFixed` method
truth tables
`while` repetition statement
zero-based counting

Self-Review Exercises

8.1 State whether each of the following is *true* or *false*. If *false*, explain why.

a) The `default` case is required in the `switch` selection statement.
b) The `break` statement is required in the last case of a `switch` selection statement.
c) The expression `( x > y && a < b )` is true if either `x > y` is true or `a < b` is true.
d) An expression containing the `||` operator is true if either or both of its operands is true.

8.2 Write a JavaScript statement or a set of statements to accomplish each of the following tasks:

a) Sum the odd integers between 1 and 99. Use a `for` statement. Assume that the variables `sum` and `count` have been declared.
b) Calculate the value of `2.5` raised to the power of `3`. Use the `pow` method.
c) Print the integers from 1 to 20 by using a `while` loop and the counter variable `x`. Assume that the variable `x` has been declared, but not initialized. Print only five integers per line. [*Hint:* Use the calculation `x % 5`. When the value of this expression is `0`, use `document.write( "<br />" )` to output a line break in the XHTML document.]
d) Repeat Exercise 8.2 (c), but using a `for` statement.

8.3 Find the error in each of the following code segments, and explain how to correct it:

a)
```
x = 1;
while ( x <= 10 );
   ++x;
}
```

b)
```
for ( y = .1; y != 1.0; y += .1 )
   document.write( y + " " );
```
c)
```
switch ( n )
{
   case 1:
      document.writeln( "The number is 1" );
   case 2:
      document.writeln( "The number is 2" );
      break;
   default:
      document.writeln( "The number is not 1 or 2" );
      break;
}
```
d) The following code should print the values from 1 to 10:
```
n = 1;
while ( n < 10 )
   document.writeln( n++ );
```

Answers to Self-Review Exercises

8.1 a) False. The `default` case is optional. If no default action is needed, then there is no need for a `default` case. b) False. The `break` statement is used to exit the `switch` statement. The `break` statement is not required for the last case in a `switch` statement. c) False. Both of the relational expressions must be true in order for the entire expression to be true when using the `&&` operator. d) True.

8.2 a)
```
sum = 0;
for ( count = 1; count <= 99; count += 2 )
   sum += count;
```
b)
```
Math.pow( 2.5, 3 )
```
c)
```
x = 1;
while ( x <= 20 ) {
   document.write( x + " " );
   if ( x % 5 == 0 )
      document.write( "<br />" );
   ++x;
}
```
d)
```
for ( x = 1; x <= 20; x++ ) {
    document.write( x + " " );

   if ( x % 5 == 0 )
      document.write( "<br />" );
}
```
or
```
for ( x = 1; x <= 20; x++ )

   if ( x % 5 == 0 )
      document.write( x + "<br />" );
   else
      document.write( x + " " );
```

8.3 a) Error: The semicolon after the `while` header causes an infinite loop, and there is a missing left brace.
Correction: Replace the semicolon by a `{`, or remove both the `;` and the `}`.

b) Error: Using a floating-point number to control a `for` repetition statement may not work, because floating-point numbers are represented approximately by most computers.
Correction: Use an integer, and perform the proper calculation to get the values you desire:

```
for ( y = 1; y != 10; y++ )
   document.writeln( ( y / 10 ) + " " );
```

c) Error: Missing `break` statement in the statements for the first `case`.
Correction: Add a `break` statement at the end of the statements for the first `case`. Note that this missing statement is not necessarily an error if the programmer wants the statement of `case 2:` to execute every time the `case 1:` statement executes.

d) Error: Improper relational operator used in the `while` continuation condition.
Correction: Use `<=` rather than `<`, or change `10` to `11`.

Exercises

8.4 Find the error in each of the following segments of code. [*Note:* There may be more than one error.]

a)
```
For ( x = 100, x >= 1, x++ )
   document.writeln( x );
```

b) The following code should print whether integer value is odd or even:
```
switch ( value % 2 ) {
   case 0:
      document.writeln( "Even integer" );
   case 1:
      document.writeln( "Odd integer" );
}
```

c) The following code should output the odd integers from 19 to 1:
```
for ( x = 19; x >= 1; x += 2 )
   document.writeln( x );
```

d) The following code should output the even integers from 2 to 100:
```
counter = 2;
do {
   document.writeln( counter );
   counter += 2;
} While ( counter < 100 );
```

8.5 What does the following script do?

```
<?xml version = "1.0" encoding = "utf-8"?>
<!DOCTYPE html PUBLIC "-//W3C//DTD XHTML 1.0 Strict//EN"
   "http://www.w3.org/TR/xhtml1/DTD/xhtml1-strict.dtd">

<!-- Exercise 8.5: ex08_05.html -->
<html xmlns = "http://www.w3.org/1999/xhtml">
   <head><title>Mystery</title>
      <script type = "text/javascript">
         <!--
         document.writeln( "<table>" );

```

```
            for ( var i = 1; i <= 10; i++ )
            {
               document.writeln( "<tr>" );

               for ( var j = 1; j <= 5; j++ )
                  document.writeln( "<td>(" + i + ", " + j + ")</td>" );

               document.writeln( "</tr>" );
            } // end for

            document.writeln( "</table>" );
            -->
         </script>
      </head><body />
   </html>
```

8.6 Write a script that finds the smallest of several non-negative integers. Assume that the first value read specifies the number of values to be input from the user.

8.7 Write a script that calculates the product of the odd integers from 1 to 15 then outputs XHTML text that displays the results.

8.8 Modify the compound interest program in Fig. 8.6 to repeat its steps for interest rates of 5, 6, 7, 8, 9 and 10 percent. Use a for statement to vary the interest rate. Use a separate table for each rate.

8.9 Write a script that outputs XHTML to display the given patterns separately, one below the other. Use for statements to generate the patterns. All asterisks (*) should be printed by a single statement of the form document.write("*"); (this causes the asterisks to print side by side). A statement of the form document.writeln("<br />"); can be used to position to the next line. A statement of the form document.write(" "); can be used to display a space (needed for the last two patterns). There should be no other output statements in the program. [*Hint:* The last two patterns require that each line begin with an appropriate number of blanks. You may need to use the XHTML <pre></pre> tags.]

```
(a)               (b)              (c)               (d)
*                 **********       **********                 *
**                *********         *********                **
***               ********           ********               ***
****              *******             *******              ****
*****             ******               ******             *****
******            *****                 *****            ******
*******           ****                   ****           *******
********          ***                     ***          ********
*********         **                       **         *********
**********        *                         *        **********
```

8.10 One interesting application of computers is the drawing of graphs and bar charts (sometimes called histograms). Write a script that reads five numbers between 1 and 30. For each number read, output XHTML text that displays a line containing the same number of adjacent asterisks. For example, if your program reads the number 7, it should output XHTML text that displays *******.

8.11 (*"The Twelve Days of Christmas" Song*) Write a script that uses repetition and a switch structures to print the song "The Twelve Days of Christmas." You can find the words at the site

www.santas.net/twelvedaysofchristmas.htm

8.12 A mail-order house sells five different products whose retail prices are as follows: product 1, \$2.98; product 2, \$4.50; product 3, \$9.98; product 4, \$4.49; and product 5, \$6.87. Write a script that reads a series of pairs of numbers as follows:

a) Product number
b) Quantity sold for one day

Your program should use a `switch` statement to determine each product's retail price and should calculate and output XHTML that displays the total retail value of all the products sold last week. Use a `prompt` dialog to obtain the product number and quantity from the user. Use a sentinel-controlled loop to determine when the program should stop looping and display the final results.

8.13 Assume that `i = 1`, `j = 2`, `k = 3` and `m = 2`. What does each of the given statements print? Are the parentheses necessary in each case?

a) `document.writeln( i == 1 );`
b) `document.writeln( j == 3 );`
c) `document.writeln( i >= 1 && j < 4 );`
d) `document.writeln( m <= 99 && k < m );`
e) `document.writeln( j >= i || k == m );`
f) `document.writeln( k + m < j || 3 - j >= k );`
g) `document.writeln( !( k > m ) );`

8.14 Modify Exercise 8.9 to combine your code from the four separate triangles of asterisks into a single script that prints all four patterns side by side, making clever use of nested `for` statements.

```
*           **********  **********           *
**          *********    *********          **
***         ********      ********         ***
****        *******        *******        ****
*****       ******          ******       *****
******      *****            *****      ******
*******     ****              ****     *******
********    ***                ***    ********
*********   **                  **   *********
**********  *                    *  **********
```

8.15 *(De Morgan's Laws)* In this chapter, we have discussed the logical operators `&&`, `||` and `!`. De Morgan's Laws can sometimes make it more convenient for us to express a logical expression. These laws state that the expression `!(`*condition1* `&&` *condition2*`)` is logically equivalent to the expression `(!`*condition1* `||` `!`*condition2*`)`. Also, the expression `!(`*condition1* `||` *condition2*`)` is logically equivalent to the expression `(!`*condition1* `&&` `!`*condition2*`)`. Use De Morgan's Laws to write equivalent expressions for each of the following, then write a program to show that the original expression and the new expression are equivalent in each case:

a) `!( x < 5 ) && !( y >= 7 )`
b) `!( a == b ) || !( g != 5 )`
c) `!( ( x <= 8 ) && ( y > 4 ) )`
d) `!( ( i > 4 ) || ( j <= 6 ) )`

8.16 Write a script that prints the following diamond shape:

```
    *
   ***
  *****
 *******
*********
 *******
  *****
   ***
    *
```

You may use output statements that print a single asterisk (*), a single space or a single newline character. Maximize your use of repetition (with nested `for` statements), and minimize the number of output statements.

8.17 Modify the program you wrote in Exercise 8.16 to read an odd number in the range 1 to 19. This number specifies the number of rows in the diamond. Your program should then display a diamond of the appropriate size.

8.18 A criticism of the `break` statement and the `continue` statement is that each is unstructured. Actually, `break` statements and `continue` statements can always be replaced by structured statements, although coding the replacement can be awkward. Describe in general how you would remove any `break` statement from a loop in a program and replace it with some structured equivalent. [*Hint:* The `break` statement "jumps out of" a loop from the body of that loop. The other way to leave is by failing the loop-continuation test. Consider using in the loop-continuation test a second test that indicates "early exit because of a 'break' condition."] Use the technique you develop here to remove the `break` statement from the program in Fig. 8.11.

8.19 What does the following script do?

```
<?xml version = "1.0" encoding = "utf-8"?>
<!DOCTYPE html PUBLIC "-//W3C//DTD XHTML 1.0 Strict//EN"
   "http://www.w3.org/TR/xhtml1/DTD/xhtml1-strict.dtd">

<!-- Exercise 8.19: ex08_19.html -->
<html xmlns = "http://www.w3.org/1999/xhtml">
   <head><title>Mystery</title>
      <script type = "text/javascript">
         <!--
         for ( var i = 1; i <= 5; i++ )
         {
            for ( var j = 1; j <= 3; j++ )
            {
               for ( var k = 1; k <= 4; k++ )
                  document.write( "*" );
               document.writeln( "<br />" );
            } // end for
            document.writeln( "<br />" );
         } // end for
         // -->
      </script>
   </head><body></body>
</html>
```

8.20 Describe in general how you would remove any `continue` statement from a loop in a program and replace it with some structured equivalent. Use the technique you develop to remove the `continue` statement from the program in Fig. 8.12.

8.21 Given the following `switch` statement:

```
switch ( k )
{
   case 1:
      break;
   case 2:
   case 3:
      ++k;
      break;
```

```
    case 4:
       --k;
       break;
    default:
       k *= 3;
 } //end switch

 x = k;
```

What values are assigned to x when k has values of 1, 2, 3, 4 and 10?

9

JavaScript: Functions

Form ever follows function.
—Louis Sullivan

E pluribus unum.
(One composed of many.)
—Virgil

O! call back yesterday, bid time return.
—William Shakespeare

Call me Ishmael.
—Herman Melville

When you call me that, smile.
—Owen Wister

OBJECTIVES

In this chapter you will learn:

- To construct programs modularly from small pieces called functions.
- To create new functions.
- How to pass information between functions.
- Simulation techniques that use random number generation.
- How the visibility of identifiers is limited to specific regions of programs.

Outline

9.1 Introduction

Most computer programs that solve real-world problems are much larger than the programs presented in the first few chapters of this book. Experience has shown that the best way to develop and maintain a large program is to construct it from small, simple pieces, or modules. This technique is called divide and conquer. This chapter describes many key features of JavaScript that facilitate the design, implementation, operation and maintenance of large scripts.

9.2 Program Modules in JavaScript

Modules in JavaScript are called functions. JavaScript programs are written by combining new functions that the programmer writes with "prepackaged" functions and objects available in JavaScript. The prepackaged functions that belong to JavaScript objects (such as `Math.pow` and `Math.round`, introduced previously) are called methods. The term method implies that the function belongs to a particular object. We refer to functions that belong to a particular JavaScript object as methods; all others are referred to as functions.

JavaScript provides several objects that have a rich collection of methods for performing common mathematical calculations, string manipulations, date and time manipulations, and manipulations of collections of data called arrays. These objects make your job easier, because they provide many of the capabilities programmers frequently need. Some common predefined objects of JavaScript and their methods are discussed in Chapter 10, JavaScript: Arrays, and Chapter 11, JavaScript: Objects.

Good Programming Practice 9.1

Familiarize yourself with the rich collection of objects and methods provided by JavaScript.

Software Engineering Observation 9.1

Avoid reinventing the wheel. Use existing JavaScript objects, methods and functions instead of writing new ones. This reduces script-development time and helps avoid introducing errors.

Portability Tip 9.1

Using the methods built into JavaScript objects helps make scripts more portable.

You can write functions to define specific tasks that may be used at many points in a script. These functions are referred to as programmer-defined functions. The actual statements defining the function are written only once and are hidden from other functions.

A function is invoked (i.e., made to perform its designated task) by a function call. The function call specifies the function name and provides information (as arguments) that the called function needs to perform its task. A common analogy for this structure is the hierarchical form of management. A boss (the calling function, or caller) asks a worker (the called function) to perform a task and return (i.e., report back) the results when the task is done. The boss function does not know how the worker function performs its designated tasks. The worker may call other worker functions—the boss will be unaware of this. We'll soon see how this "hiding" of implementation details promotes good software engineering. Figure 9.1 shows the `boss` function communicating with several worker functions in a hierarchical manner. Note that `worker1` acts as a "boss" function to `worker4` and `worker5`, and `worker4` and `worker5` report back to `worker1`.

Functions are invoked by writing the name of the function, followed by a left parenthesis, followed by a comma-separated list of zero or more arguments, followed by a right parenthesis. For example, a programmer desiring to convert a string stored in variable `inputValue` to a floating-point number and add it to variable `total` might write

```
total += parseFloat( inputValue );
```

When this statement executes, JavaScript function **`parseFloat`** converts the string in the `inputValue` variable to a floating-point value and adds that value to `total`. Variable `inputValue` is function `parseFloat`'s argument. Function `parseFloat` takes a string representation of a floating-point number as an argument and returns the corresponding floating-point numeric value. Function arguments may be constants, variables or expressions.

Methods are called in the same way, but require the name of the object to which the method belongs and a dot preceding the method name. For example, we've already seen the syntax `document.writeln("Hi there.");`. This statement calls the `document` object's `writeln` method to output the text.

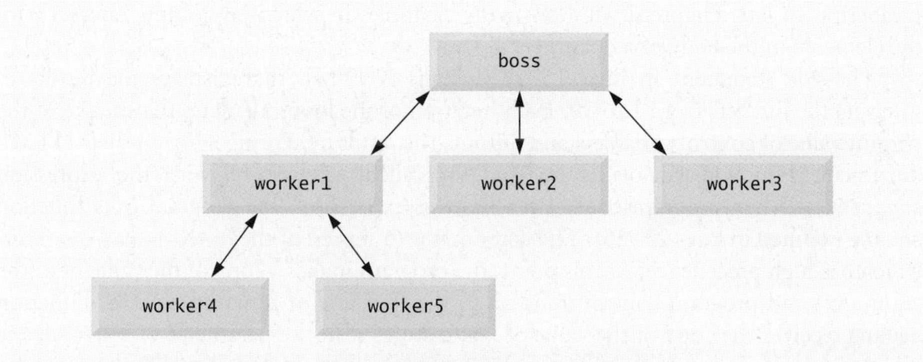

Fig. 9.1 | Hierarchical boss-function/worker-function relationship.

9.3 Programmer-Defined Functions

Functions allow you to modularize a program. All variables declared in function definitions are local variables—this means that they can be accessed only in the function in which they are defined. Most functions have a list of parameters that provide the means for communicating information between functions via function calls. A function's parameters are also considered to be local variables. When a function is called, the arguments in the function call are assigned to the corresponding parameters in the function definition.

There are several reasons for modularizing a program with functions. The divide-and-conquer approach makes program development more manageable. Another reason is software reusability (i.e., using existing functions as building blocks to create new programs). With good function naming and definition, programs can be created from standardized functions rather than built by using customized code. For example, we did not have to define how to convert strings to integers and floating-point numbers—JavaScript already provides function `parseInt` to convert a string to an integer and function `parseFloat` to convert a string to a floating-point number. A third reason is to avoid repeating code in a program. Code that is packaged as a function can be executed from several locations in a program by calling the function.

Software Engineering Observation 9.2

If a function's task cannot be expressed concisely, perhaps the function is performing too many different tasks. It is usually best to break such a function into several smaller functions.

9.4 Function Definitions

Each script we have presented thus far in the text has consisted of a series of statements and control structures in sequence. These scripts have been executed as the browser loads the web page and evaluates the `<head>` section of the page. We now consider how you can write your own customized functions and call them in a script.

Programmer-Defined Function `square`

Consider a script (Fig. 9.2) that uses a function `square` to calculate the squares of the integers from 1 to 10. [*Note:* We continue to show many examples in which the `body` element of the XHTML document is empty and the document is created directly by JavaScript. In later chapters, we show many examples in which JavaScripts interact with the elements in the `body` of a document.]

The `for` statement in lines 15–17 outputs XHTML that displays the results of squaring the integers from 1 to 10. Each iteration of the loop calculates the `square` of the current value of control variable `x` and outputs the result by writing a line in the XHTML document. Function `square` is invoked, or called, in line 17 with the expression `square(x)`. When program control reaches this expression, the program calls function `square` (defined in lines 23–26). The parentheses `()` represent the function-call operator, which has high precedence. At this point, the program makes a copy of the value of `x` (the argument) and program control transfers to the first line of function `square`. Function `square` receives the copy of the value of `x` and stores it in the parameter `y`. Then `square` calculates `y * y`. The result is passed back (returned) to the point in line 17 where `square` was invoked. Lines 16–17 concatenate `"The square of "`, the value of `x`, the string `" is "`,

```
<?xml version = "1.0" encoding = "utf-8"?>
<!DOCTYPE html PUBLIC "-//W3C//DTD XHTML 1.0 Strict//EN"
   "http://www.w3.org/TR/xhtml1/DTD/xhtml1-strict.dtd">

<!-- Fig. 9.2: SquareInt.html -->
<!-- Programmer-defined function square. -->
<html xmlns = "http://www.w3.org/1999/xhtml">
   <head>
      <title>A Programmer-Defined square Function</title>
      <script type = "text/javascript">
         <!--
         document.writeln( "<h1>Square the numbers from 1 to 10</h1>" );

         // square the numbers from 1 to 10
         for ( var x = 1; x <= 10; x++ )
            document.writeln( "The square of " + x + " is " +
               square( x ) + "<br />" );

         // The following square function definition is executed
         // only when the function is explicitly called.

         // square function definition
         function square( y )
         {
            return y * y;
         } // end function square
         // -->
      </script>
   </head><body></body>
</html>
```

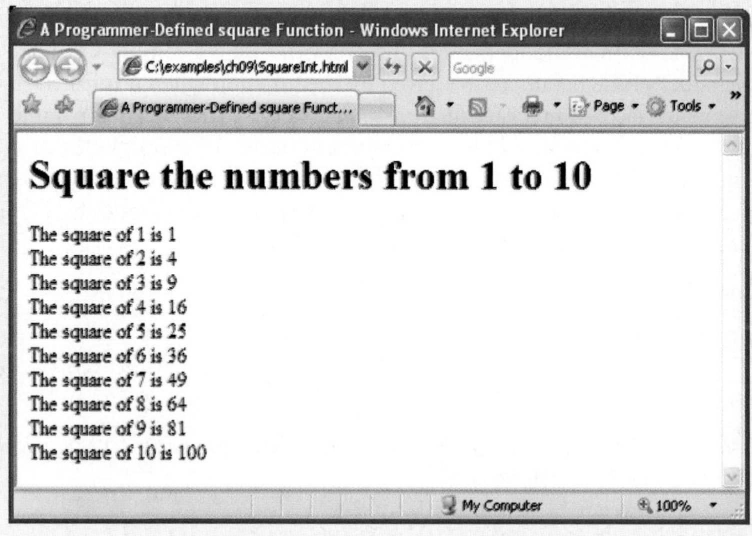

Fig. 9.2 | Programmer-defined function square.

the value returned by function `square` and a `<br />` tag and write that line of text in the XHTML document. This process is repeated 10 times.

The definition of function `square` (lines 23–26) shows that `square` expects a single parameter `y`. Function `square` uses this name in its body to manipulate the value passed to `square` from line 17. The return statement in `square` passes the result of the calculation `y * y` back to the calling function. Note that JavaScript keyword `var` is not used to declare variables in the parameter list of a function.

Common Programming Error 9.1

Using the JavaScript `var` *keyword to declare a variable in a function parameter list results in a JavaScript runtime error.*

In this example, function `square` follows the rest of the script. When the `for` statement terminates, program control does *not* flow sequentially into function `square`. A function must be called explicitly for the code in its body to execute. Thus, when the `for` statement terminates in this example, the script terminates.

Good Programming Practice 9.2

Place a blank line between function definitions to separate the functions and enhance program readability.

Software Engineering Observation 9.3

Statements that are enclosed in the body of a function definition are not executed by the JavaScript interpreter unless the function is invoked explicitly.

The format of a function definition is

```
function function-name( parameter-list )
{
   declarations and statements
}
```

The *function-name* is any valid identifier. The *parameter-list* is a comma-separated list containing the names of the parameters received by the function when it is called (remember that the arguments in the function call are assigned to the corresponding parameter in the function definition). There should be one argument in the function call for each parameter in the function definition. If a function does not receive any values, the *parameter-list* is empty (i.e., the function name is followed by an empty set of parentheses). The *declarations* and *statements* in braces form the function body.

Common Programming Error 9.2

Forgetting to return a value from a function that is supposed to return a value is a logic error.

Common Programming Error 9.3

Placing a semicolon after the right parenthesis enclosing the parameter list of a function definition results in a JavaScript runtime error.

Common Programming Error 9.4

Redefining a function parameter as a local variable in the function is a logic error.

Common Programming Error 9.5

Passing to a function an argument that is not compatible with the corresponding parameter's expected type is a logic error and may result in a JavaScript runtime error.

Good Programming Practice 9.3

Although it is not incorrect to do so, do not use the same name for an argument passed to a function and the corresponding parameter in the function definition. Using different names avoids ambiguity.

Software Engineering Observation 9.4

To promote software reusability, every function should be limited to performing a single, well-defined task, and the name of the function should express that task effectively. Such functions make programs easier to write, debug, maintain and modify.

Error-Prevention Tip 9.1

A small function that performs one task is easier to test and debug than a larger function that performs many tasks.

There are three ways to return control to the point at which a function was invoked. If the function does not return a result, control returns when the program reaches the function-ending right brace or by executing the statement

```
return;
```

If the function does return a result, the statement

```
return expression;
```

returns the value of *expression* to the caller. When a `return` statement is executed, control returns immediately to the point at which the function was invoked.

Programmer-Defined Function `maximum`

The script in our next example (Fig. 9.3) uses a programmer-defined function called `maximum` to determine and return the largest of three floating-point values.

The three floating-point values are input by the user via `prompt` dialogs (lines 12–14). Lines 16–18 use function `parseFloat` to convert the strings entered by the user to floating-point values. The statement in line 20 passes the three floating-point values to function `maximum` (defined in lines 28–31), which determines the largest floating-point value. This value is returned to line 20 by the `return` statement in function `maximum`. The value returned is assigned to variable `maxValue`. Lines 22–25 display the three floating-point values input by the user and the calculated `maxValue`.

Note the implementation of the function `maximum` (lines 28–31). The first line indicates that the function's name is `maximum` and that the function takes three parameters (`x`, `y` and `z`) to accomplish its task. Also, the body of the function contains the statement which returns the largest of the three floating-point values, using two calls to the `Math` object's `max` method. First, method `Math.max` is invoked with the values of variables `y` and `z` to determine the larger of the two values. Next, the value of variable `x` and the result of the first call to `Math.max` are passed to method `Math.max`. Finally, the result of the second call to `Math.max` is returned to the point at which `maximum` was invoked (i.e., line 20). Note

```
<?xml version = "1.0" encoding = "utf-8"?>
<!DOCTYPE html PUBLIC "-//W3C//DTD XHTML 1.0 Strict//EN"
   "http://www.w3.org/TR/xhtml1/DTD/xhtml1-strict.dtd">

<!-- Fig. 9.3: maximum.html -->
<!-- Programmer-Defined maximum function. -->
<html xmlns = "http://www.w3.org/1999/xhtml">
   <head>
      <title>Finding the Maximum of Three Values</title>
      <script type = "text/javascript">
         <!--
         var input1 = window.prompt( "Enter first number", "0" );
         var input2 = window.prompt( "Enter second number", "0" );
         var input3 = window.prompt( "Enter third number", "0" );

         var value1 = parseFloat( input1 );
         var value2 = parseFloat( input2 );
         var value3 = parseFloat( input3 );

         var maxValue = maximum( value1, value2, value3 );

         document.writeln( "First number: " + value1 +
            "<br />Second number: " + value2 +
            "<br />Third number: " + value3 +
            "<br />Maximum is: " + maxValue );

         // maximum function definition (called from line 20)
         function maximum( x, y, z )
         {
            return Math.max( x, Math.max( y, z ) );
         } // end function maximum
         // -->
      </script>
   </head>
   <body>
      <p>Click Refresh (or Reload) to run the script again</p>
   </body>
</html>
```

Fig. 9.3 | Programmer-defined `maximum` function. (Part 1 of 2.)

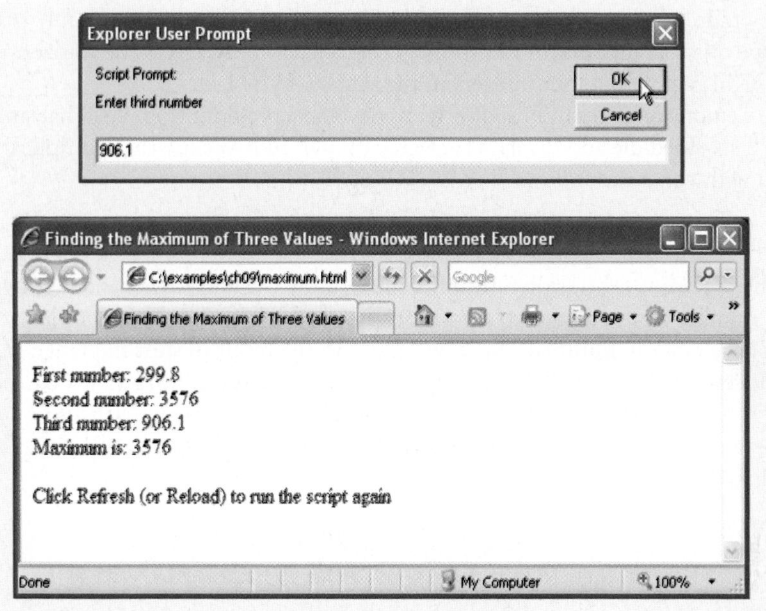

Fig. 9.3 | Programmer-defined `maximum` function. (Part 2 of 2.)

once again that the script terminates before sequentially reaching the definition of function `maximum`. The statement in the body of function `maximum` executes only when the function is invoked from line 20.

9.5 Random Number Generation

We now take a brief and, it is hoped, entertaining diversion into a popular programming application, namely simulation and game playing. In this section and the next, we develop a nicely structured game-playing program that includes multiple functions. The program uses most of the control structures we have studied.

There is something in the air of a gambling casino that invigorates people, from the high rollers at the plush mahogany-and-felt craps tables to the quarter poppers at the one-armed bandits. It is the **element of chance**, the possibility that luck will convert a pocketful of money into a mountain of wealth. The element of chance can be introduced through the `Math` object's **`random` method**. (Remember, we are calling `random` a method because it belongs to the `Math` object.)

Consider the following statement:

```
var randomValue = Math.random();
```

Method `random` generates a floating-point value from 0.0 up to, but not including, 1.0. If `random` truly produces values at random, then every value from 0.0 up to, but not including, 1.0 has an equal **chance** (or **probability**) of being chosen each time `random` is called.

The range of values produced directly by `random` is often different than what is needed in a specific application. For example, a program that simulates coin tossing might require only 0 for heads and 1 for tails. A program that simulates rolling a six-sided die would require random integers in the range from 1 to 6. A program that randomly predicts the next type of spaceship, out of four possibilities, that will fly across the horizon in a video game might require random integers in the range 0–3 or 1–4.

To demonstrate method random, let us develop a program (Fig. 9.4) that simulates 20 rolls of a six-sided die and displays the value of each roll. We use the multiplication operator (*) with random as follows:

```
Math.floor( 1 + Math.random() * 6 )
```

First, the preceding expression multiplies the result of a call to Math.random() by 6 to produce a number in the range 0.0 up to, but not including, 6.0. This is called scaling the range of the random numbers. Next, we add 1 to the result to shift the range of numbers to produce a number in the range 1.0 up to, but not including, 7.0. Finally, we use method **Math.floor** to *round* the result down to the closest integer not greater than the argument's value—for example, 1.75 is rounded to 1. Figure 9.4 confirms that the results are in the range 1 to 6.

```
<?xml version = "1.0" encoding = "utf-8"?>
<!DOCTYPE html PUBLIC "-//W3C//DTD XHTML 1.0 Strict//EN"
   "http://www.w3.org/TR/xhtml1/DTD/xhtml1-strict.dtd">

<!-- Fig. 9.4: RandomInt.html -->
<!-- Random integers, shifting and scaling. -->
<html xmlns = "http://www.w3.org/1999/xhtml">
   <head>
      <title>Shifted and Scaled Random Integers</title>
      <style type = "text/css">
         table { width: 50%;
                 border: 1px solid gray;
                 text-align: center }
      </style>
      <script type = "text/javascript">
         <!--
         var value;

         document.writeln( "<table>" );
         document.writeln( "<caption>Random Numbers</caption><tr>" );

         for ( var i = 1; i <= 20; i++ )
         {
            value = Math.floor( 1 + Math.random() * 6 );
            document.writeln( "<td>" + value + "</td>" );

            // start a new table row every 5 entries
            if ( i % 5 == 0 && i != 20 )
               document.writeln( "</tr><tr>" );
         } // end for

         document.writeln( "</tr></table>" );
```

Fig. 9.4 | Random integers, shifting and scaling. (Part 1 of 2.)

```
            // -->
        </script>
    </head>
    <body>
        <p>Click Refresh (or Reload) to run the script again</p>
    </body>
</html>
```

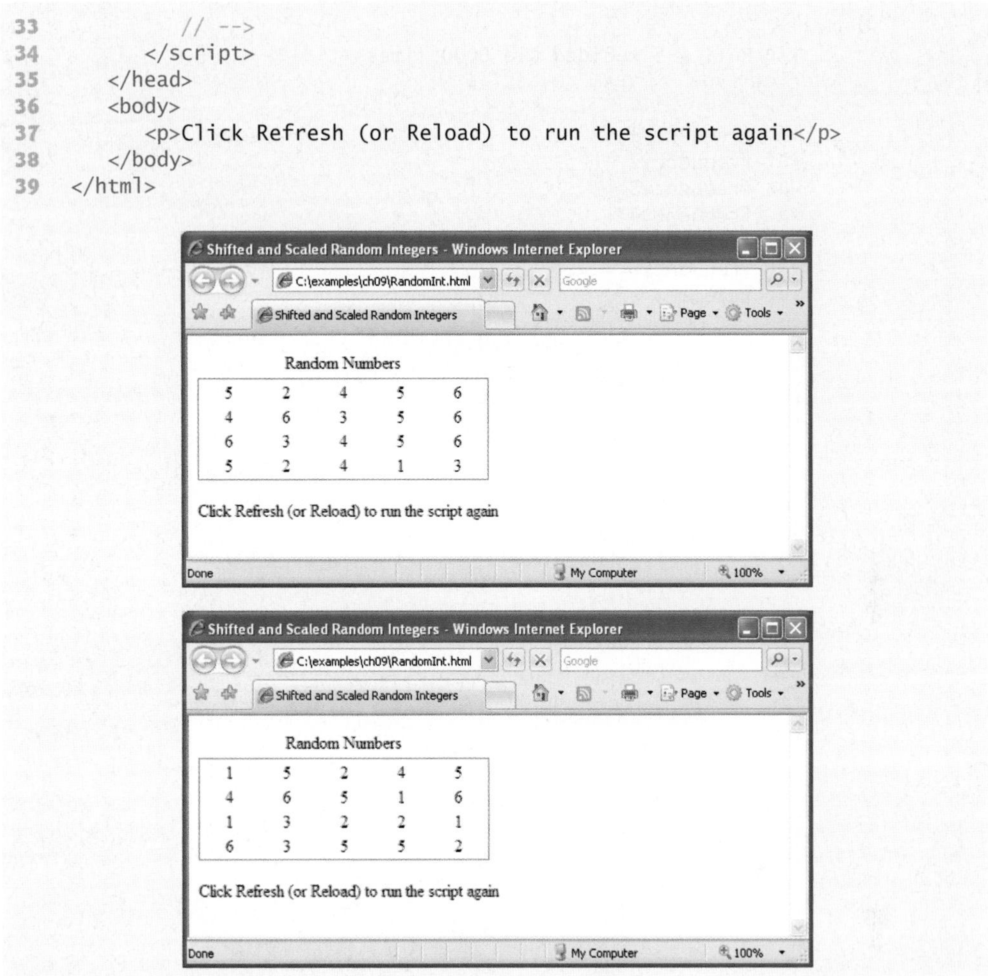

Fig. 9.4 | Random integers, shifting and scaling. (Part 2 of 2.)

To show that these numbers occur with approximately equal likelihood, let us simulate 6000 rolls of a die with the program in Fig. 9.5. Each integer from 1 to 6 should appear approximately 1000 times. Use your browser's **Refresh** (or **Reload**) button to execute the script again.

```
<?xml version = "1.0" encoding = "utf-8"?>
<!DOCTYPE html PUBLIC "-//W3C//DTD XHTML 1.0 Strict//EN"
   "http://www.w3.org/TR/xhtml1/DTD/xhtml1-strict.dtd">

<!-- Fig. 9.5: RollDie.html -->
<!-- Rolling a Six-Sided Die 6000 times. -->
<html xmlns = "http://www.w3.org/1999/xhtml">
```

Fig. 9.5 | Rolling a six-sided die 6000 times. (Part 1 of 3.)

```
   <head>
      <title>Roll a Six-Sided Die 6000 Times</title>
      <script type = "text/javascript">
         <!--
         var frequency1 = 0;
         var frequency2 = 0;
         var frequency3 = 0;
         var frequency4 = 0;
         var frequency5 = 0;
         var frequency6 = 0;
         var face;

         // roll die 6000 times and accumulate results
         for ( var roll = 1; roll <= 6000; roll++ )
         {
            face = Math.floor( 1 + Math.random() * 6 );

            switch ( face )
            {
               case 1:
                  ++frequency1;
                  break;
               case 2:
                  ++frequency2;
                  break;
               case 3:
                  ++frequency3;
                  break;
               case 4:
                  ++frequency4;
                  break;
               case 5:
                  ++frequency5;
                  break;
               case 6:
                  ++frequency6;
                  break;
            } // end switch
         } // end for

         document.writeln( "<table border = \"1\">" );
         document.writeln( "<thead><th>Face</th>" +
            "<th>Frequency</th></thead>" );
         document.writeln( "<tbody><tr><td>1</td><td>" +
            frequency1 + "</td></tr>" );
         document.writeln( "<tr><td>2</td><td>" + frequency2 +
            "</td></tr>" );
         document.writeln( "<tr><td>3</td><td>" + frequency3 +
            "</td></tr>" );
         document.writeln( "<tr><td>4</td><td>" + frequency4 +
            "</td></tr>" );
         document.writeln( "<tr><td>5</td><td>" + frequency5 +
            "</td></tr>" );
```

Fig. 9.5 | Rolling a six-sided die 6000 times. (Part 2 of 3.)

```
61              document.writeln( "<tr><td>6</td><td>" + frequency6 +
62                 "</td></tr></tbody></table>" );
63              // -->
64           </script>
65        </head>
66        <body>
67           <p>Click Refresh (or Reload) to run the script again</p>
68        </body>
69     </html>
```

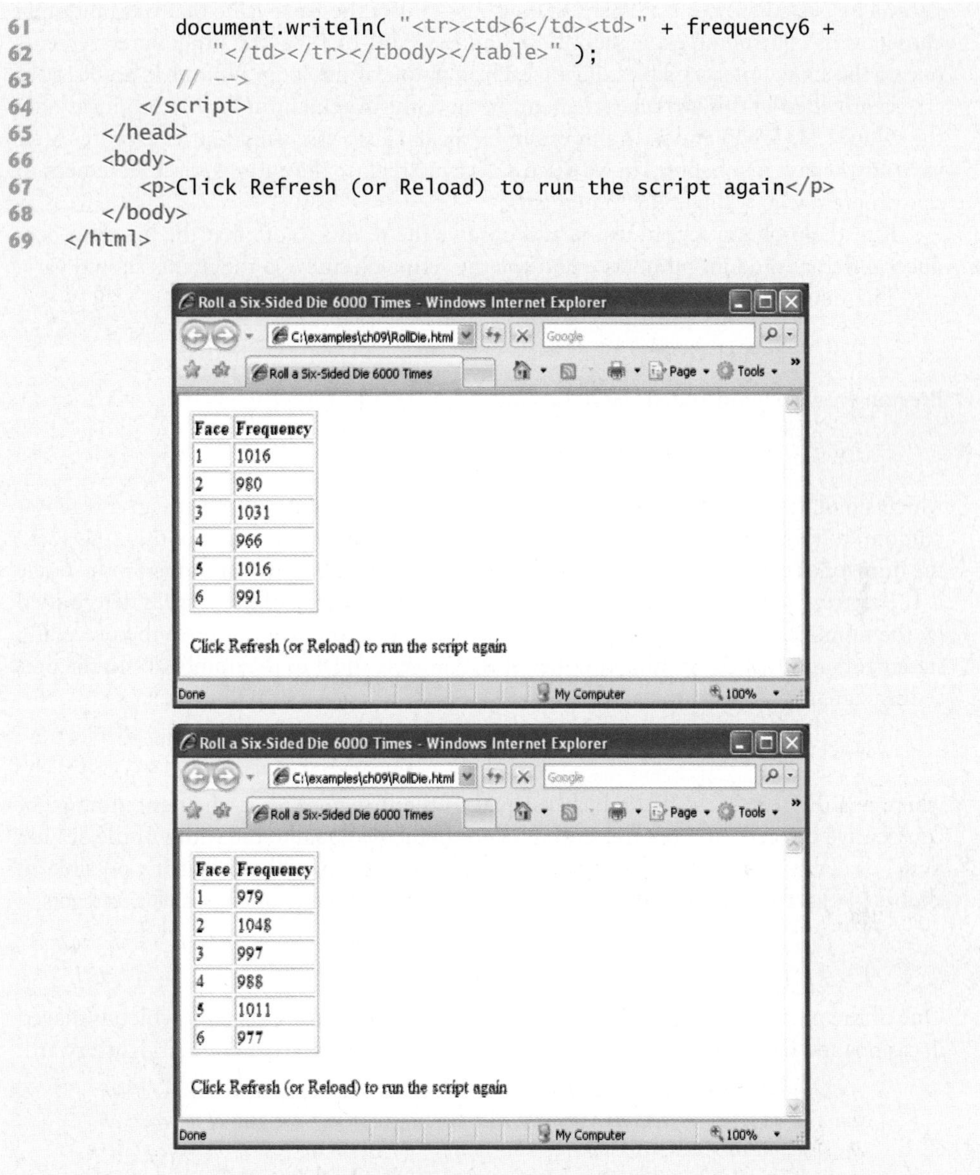

Fig. 9.5 | Rolling a six-sided die 6000 times. (Part 3 of 3.)

As the output of the program shows, we used `Math` method `random` and the scaling and shifting techniques of the previous example to simulate the rolling of a six-sided die. Note that we used nested control structures to determine the number of times each side of the six-sided die occurred. Lines 12–17 declare and initialize counter variables to keep track of the number of times each of the six die values appears. Line 18 declares a variable to store the face value of the die. The `for` statement in lines 21–46 iterates 6000 times. During each iteration of the loop, line 23 produces a value from 1 to 6, which is stored in face. The nested switch statement in lines 25–45 uses the face value that was randomly chosen as its controlling expression. Based on the value of face, the program increments one of the six counter variables during each iteration of the loop. Note that no default case is provided in this switch statement, because the statement in line 23 produces only the values 1, 2, 3, 4, 5 and 6. In this example, the default case would never execute. After we study Arrays in Chapter 10, we discuss a way to replace the entire switch statement in this program with a single-line statement.

Run the program several times, and observe the results. Note that the program produces different random numbers each time the script executes, so the results should vary.

The values returned by random are always in the range

```
0.0 ≤ Math.random() < 1.0
```

Previously, we demonstrated the statement

```
face = Math.floor( 1 + Math.random() * 6 );
```

which simulates the rolling of a six-sided die. This statement always assigns an integer (at random) to variable face, in the range 1 ≤ face ≤ 6. Note that the width of this range (i.e., the number of consecutive integers in the range) is 6, and the starting number in the range is 1. Referring to the preceding statement, we see that the width of the range is determined by the number used to scale random with the multiplication operator (6 in the preceding statement) and that the starting number of the range is equal to the number (1 in the preceding statement) added to Math.random() * 6. We can generalize this result as

```
face = Math.floor( a + Math.random() * b );
```

where a is the shifting value (which is equal to the first number in the desired range of consecutive integers) and b is the scaling factor (which is equal to the width of the desired range of consecutive integers). In this chapter's exercises, you'll see that it's possible to choose integers at random from sets of values other than ranges of consecutive integers.

9.6 Example: Game of Chance

One of the most popular games of chance is a dice game known as craps, which is played in casinos and back alleys throughout the world. The rules of the game are straightforward:

> *A player rolls two dice. Each die has six faces. These faces contain one, two, three, four, five and six spots, respectively. After the dice have come to rest, the sum of the spots on the two upward faces is calculated. If the sum is 7 or 11 on the first throw, the player wins. If the sum is 2, 3 or 12 on the first throw (called "craps"), the player loses (i.e., the "house" wins). If the sum is 4, 5, 6, 8, 9 or 10 on the first throw, that sum becomes the player's "point." To win, you must continue rolling the dice until you "make your point" (i.e., roll your point value). You lose by rolling a 7 before making the point.*

The script in Fig. 9.6 simulates the game of craps.

Note that the player must roll two dice on the first and all subsequent rolls. When you execute the script, click the **Roll Dice** button to play the game. A message below the **Roll Dice** button displays the status of the game after each roll.

Until now, all user interactions with scripts have been through either a prompt dialog (in which the user types an input value for the program) or an alert dialog (in which a message is displayed to the user, and the user can click **OK** to dismiss the dialog). Although these dialogs are valid ways to receive input from a user and to display messages, they are fairly limited in their capabilities. A `prompt` dialog can obtain only one value at a time from the user, and a message dialog can display only one message.

More frequently, multiple inputs are received from the user at once via an XHTML form (such as one in which the user enters name and address information) or to display many pieces of data at once (e.g., the values of the dice, the sum of the dice and the point in this example). To begin our introduction to more elaborate user interfaces, this program uses an XHTML form (discussed in Chapter 4) and a new graphical user interface concept—GUI event handling. This is our first example in which the JavaScript executes in response to the user's interaction with a GUI component in an XHTML form. This interaction causes an event. Scripts are often used to respond to events.

```
<?xml version = "1.0" encoding = "utf-8"?>
<!DOCTYPE html PUBLIC "-//W3C//DTD XHTML 1.0 Strict//EN"
   "http://www.w3.org/TR/xhtml1/DTD/xhtml1-strict.dtd">

<!-- Fig. 9.6: Craps.html -->
<!-- Craps game simulation. -->
<html xmlns = "http://www.w3.org/1999/xhtml">
   <head>
      <title>Program that Simulates the Game of Craps</title>
      <style type = "text/css">
         table   { text-align: right }
         body    { font-family: arial, sans-serif }
         div.red { color: red }
      </style>
      <script type = "text/javascript">
         <!--
         // variables used to test the state of the game
         var WON = 0;
         var LOST = 1;
         var CONTINUE_ROLLING = 2;

         // other variables used in program
         var firstRoll = true; // true if current roll is first
         var sumOfDice = 0; // sum of the dice
         var myPoint = 0; // point if no win/loss on first roll
         var gameStatus = CONTINUE_ROLLING; // game not over yet

         // process one roll of the dice
         function play()
         {
            // get the point field on the page
            var point = document.getElementById( "pointfield" );

            // get the status div on the page
            var statusDiv = document.getElementById( "status" );
            if ( firstRoll ) // first roll of the dice
            {
```

Fig. 9.6 | Craps game simulation. (Part 1 of 4.)

```
            sumOfDice = rollDice();

            switch ( sumOfDice )
            {
               case 7: case 11: // win on first roll
                  gameStatus = WON;
                  // clear point field
                  point.value = "";
                  break;
               case 2: case 3: case 12: // lose on first roll
                  gameStatus = LOST;
                  // clear point field
                  point.value = "";
                  break;
               default:                 // remember point
                  gameStatus = CONTINUE_ROLLING;
                  myPoint = sumOfDice;
                  point.value = myPoint;
                  firstRoll = false;
            } // end switch
         } // end if
         else
         {
            sumOfDice = rollDice();

            if ( sumOfDice == myPoint ) // win by making point
               gameStatus = WON;
            else
               if ( sumOfDice == 7 )    // lose by rolling 7
                  gameStatus = LOST;
         } // end else

         if ( gameStatus == CONTINUE_ROLLING )
            statusDiv.innerHTML = "Roll again";
         else
         {
            if ( gameStatus == WON )
               statusDiv.innerHTML = "Player wins. " +
                  "Click Roll Dice to play again.";
            else
               statusDiv.innerHTML = "Player loses. " +
                  "Click Roll Dice to play again.";

            firstRoll = true;
         } // end else
      } // end function play

      // roll the dice
      function rollDice()
      {
         var die1;
         var die2;
         var workSum;
```

Fig. 9.6 | Craps game simulation. (Part 2 of 4.)

```

            die1 = Math.floor( 1 + Math.random() * 6 );
            die2 = Math.floor( 1 + Math.random() * 6 );
            workSum = die1 + die2;

            document.getElementById( "die1field" ).value = die1;
            document.getElementById( "die2field" ).value = die2;
            document.getElementById( "sumfield" ).value = workSum;

            return workSum;
         } // end function rollDice
         // -->
      </script>
   </head>
   <body>
      <form action = "">
         <table>
         <caption>Craps</caption>
         <tr><td>Die 1</td>
            <td><input id = "die1field" type = "text" />
            </td></tr>
         <tr><td>Die 2</td>
            <td><input id = "die2field" type = "text" />
            </td></tr>
         <tr><td>Sum</td>
            <td><input id = "sumfield" type = "text" />
            </td></tr>
         <tr><td>Point</td>
            <td><input id = "pointfield" type = "text" />
            </td></tr>
         <tr><td /><td><input type = "button" value = "Roll Dice"
           onclick = "play()" /></td></tr>
         </table>
         <div id = "status" class = "red">
            Click the Roll Dice button to play</div>
      </form>
   </body>
</html>
```

Fig. 9.6 | Craps game simulation. (Part 3 of 4.)

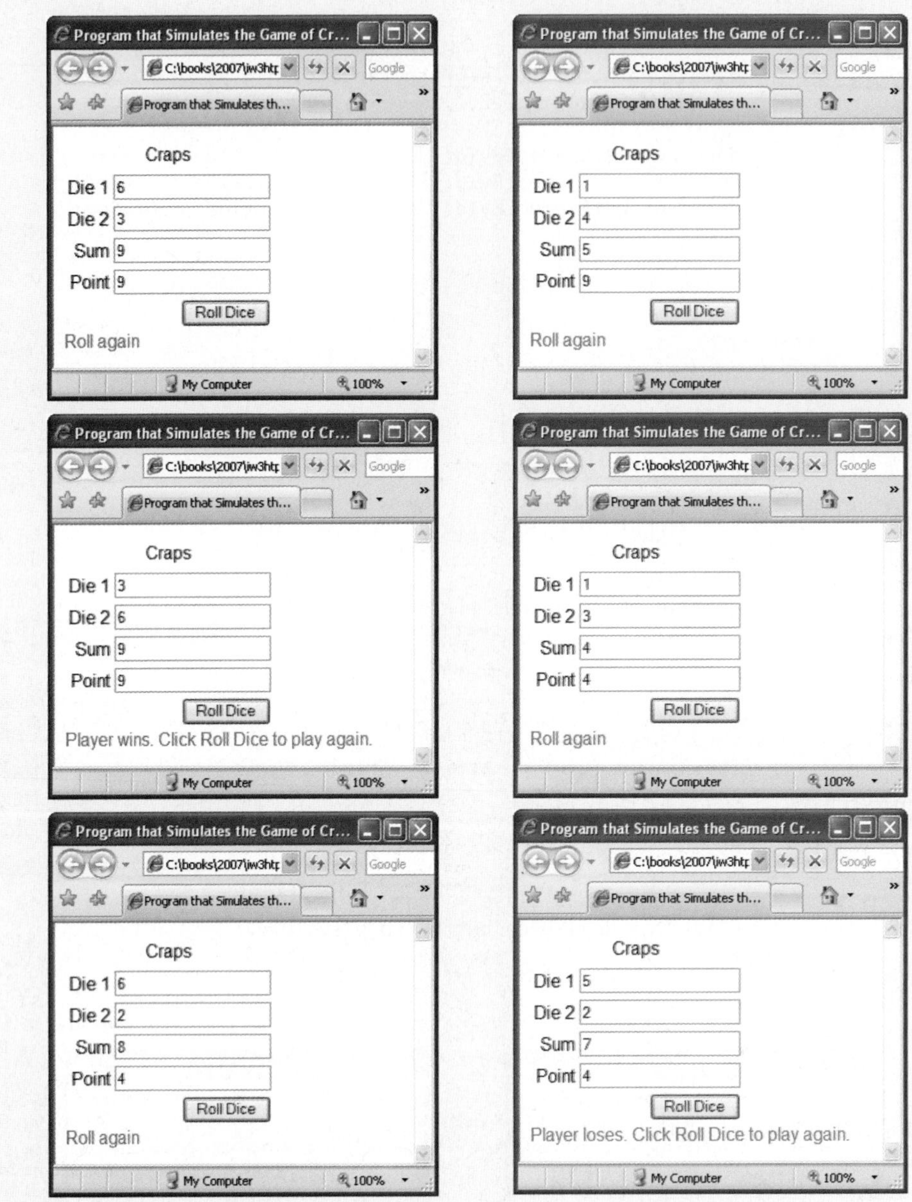

Fig. 9.6 | Craps game simulation. (Part 4 of 4.)

Before we discuss the script code, we discuss the body element (lines 105–126) of the XHTML document. The GUI components in this section are used extensively in the script.

Line 106 begins the definition of an XHTML `form` element. The XHTML standard requires that every `form` contain an `action` attribute, but because this form does not post its information to a web server, the empty string ("") is used.

In this example, we have decided to place the form's GUI components in an XHTML `table` element, so line 107 begins the definition of the XHTML table. Lines 109–120 create four table rows. Each row contains a left cell with a text label and an `input` element in the right cell.

Four `input` fields (lines 110, 113, 116 and 119) are created to display the value of the first die, the second die, the sum of the dice and the current point value, if any. Their `id` attributes are set to `die1field`, `die2field`, `sumfield`, and `pointfield`, respectively. The `id` attribute can be used to apply CSS styles and to enable script code to refer to an element in an XHTML document. Because the `id` attribute, if specified, must have a unique value, JavaScript can reliably refer to any single element via its `id` attribute. We see how this is done in a moment.

Lines 121–122 create a fifth row with an empty cell in the left column before the **Roll Dice** button. The button's `onclick` attribute indicates the action to take when the user of the XHTML document clicks the **Roll Dice** button. In this example, clicking the button causes a call to function `play`.

This style of programming is known as event-driven programming—the user interacts with a GUI component, the script is notified of the event and the script processes the event. The user's interaction with the GUI "drives" the program. The button click is known as the event. The function that is called when an event occurs is known as an event-handling function or event handler. When a GUI event occurs in a form, the browser calls the specified event-handling function. Before any event can be processed, each GUI component must know which event-handling function will be called when a particular event occurs. Most XHTML GUI components have several different event types. The event model is discussed in detail in Chapter 13, JavaScript: Events. By specifying `onclick = "play()"` for the **Roll Dice** button, we instruct the browser to listen for events (button-click events in particular). This registers the event handler for the GUI component, causing the browser to begin listening for the click event on the component. If no event handler is specified for the **Roll Dice** button, the script will not respond when the user presses the button.

Lines 123–125 end the `table` and `form` elements, respectively. After the table, a `div` element is created with an `id` attribute of `"status"`. This element will be updated by the script to display the result of each roll to the user. A style declaration in line 13 colors the text contained in this `div` red.

The game is reasonably involved. The player may win or lose on the first roll, or may win or lose on any subsequent roll. Lines 18–20 create variables that define the three game states—game won, game lost and continue rolling the dice. Unlike many other programming languages, JavaScript does not provide a mechanism to define a constant (i.e., a variable whose value cannot be modified). For this reason, we use all capital letters for these variable names, to indicate that we do not intend to modify their values and to make them stand out in the code—a common industry practice for genuine constants.

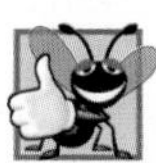

Good Programming Practice 9.4

Use only uppercase letters (with underscores between words) in the names of variables that should be used as constants. This format makes such variables stand out in a program.

Good Programming Practice 9.5

Use meaningfully named variables rather than literal values (such as 2) to make programs more readable.

Lines 23–26 declare several variables that are used throughout the script. Variable firstRoll indicates whether the next roll of the dice is the first roll in the current game. Variable sumOfDice maintains the sum of the dice from the last roll. Variable myPoint stores the point if the player does not win or lose on the first roll. Variable gameStatus keeps track of the current state of the game (WON, LOST or CONTINUE_ROLLING).

We define a function rollDice (lines 86–101) to roll the dice and to compute and display their sum. Function rollDice is defined once, but is called from two places in the program (lines 38 and 61). Function rollDice takes no arguments, so it has an empty parameter list. Function rollDice returns the sum of the two dice.

The user clicks the **Roll Dice** button to roll the dice. This action invokes function play (lines 29–83) of the script. Lines 32 and 35 create two new variables with objects representing elements in the XHTML document using the document object's **getElementById method**. The getElementById method, given an id as an argument, finds the XHTML element with a matching id attribute and returns a JavaScript object representing the element. Line 32 stores an object representing the pointfield input element (line 119) in the variable point. Line 35 gets an object representing the status div from line 124. In a moment, we show how you can use these objects to manipulate the XHTML document.

Function play checks the variable firstRoll (line 36) to determine whether it is true or false. If true, the roll is the first roll of the game. Line 38 calls rollDice, which picks two random values from 1 to 6, displays the value of the first die, the value of the second die and the sum of the dice in the first three text fields and returns the sum of the dice. (We discuss function rollDice in detail shortly.) After the first roll (if firstRoll is false), the nested switch statement in lines 40–57 determines whether the game is won or lost, or whether it should continue with another roll. After the first roll, if the game is not over, sumOfDice is saved in myPoint and displayed in the text field point in the XHTML form.

Note how the text field's value is changed in lines 45, 50 and 55. The object stored in the variable point allows access to the pointfield text field's contents. The expression point.value accesses the **value property** of the text field referred to by point. The value property specifies the text to display in the text field. To access this property, we specify the object representing the text field (point), followed by a **dot** (.) and the name of the property to access (value). This technique for accessing properties of an object (also used to access methods as in Math.pow) is called **dot notation**. We discuss using scripts to access elements in an XHTML page in more detail in Chapter 13.

The program proceeds to the nested if...else statement in lines 70–82, which uses the statusDiv variable to update the div that displays the game status. Using the object's **innerHTML property**, we set the text inside the div to reflect the most recent status. In lines 71, 75–76 and 78–79, we set the div's innerHTML to

```
Roll again.
```

if gameStatus is equal to CONTINUE_ROLLING, to

```
Player wins. Click Roll Dice to play again.
```

if gameStatus is equal to WON and to

```
Player loses. Click Roll Dice to play again.
```

if gameStatus is equal to LOST. If the game is won or lost, line 81 sets firstRoll to true to indicate that the next roll of the dice begins the next game.

The program then waits for the user to click the button **Roll Dice** again. Each time the user clicks **Roll Dice**, the program calls function `play`, which, in turn, calls the `rollDice` function to produce a new value for `sumOfDice`. If `sumOfDice` matches `myPoint`, `gameStatus` is set to `WON`, the `if...else` statement in lines 70–82 executes and the game is complete. If `sum` is equal to `7`, `gameStatus` is set to `LOST`, the `if...else` statement in lines 70–82 executes and the game is complete. Clicking the **Roll Dice** button starts a new game. The program updates the four text fields in the XHTML form with the new values of the dice and the sum on each roll, and updates the text field `point` each time a new game begins.

Function `rollDice` (lines 86–101) defines its own local variables `die1`, `die2` and `workSum` (lines 88–90). Because they are defined inside the `rollDice` function, these variables are accessible only inside that function. Lines 92–93 pick two random values in the range 1 to 6 and assign them to variables `die1` and `die2`, respectively. Lines 96–98 once again use the `document`'s `getElementById` method to find and update the correct `input` elements with the values of `die1`, `die2` and `workSum`. Note that the integer values are converted automatically to strings when they are assigned to each text field's `value` property. Line 100 returns the value of `workSum` for use in function `play`.

Software Engineering Observation 9.5

Variables that are declared inside the body of a function are known only in that function. If the same variable names are used elsewhere in the program, they will be entirely separate variables in memory.

Note the use of the various program-control mechanisms. The craps program uses two functions—`play` and `rollDice`—and the `switch`, `if...else` and nested `if` statements. Note also the use of multiple `case` labels in the `switch` statement to execute the same statements (lines 42 and 47). In the exercises at the end of this chapter, we investigate various interesting characteristics of the game of craps.

Error-Prevention Tip 9.2

Initializing variables when they are declared in functions helps avoid incorrect results and interpreter messages warning of uninitialized data.

9.7 Another Example: Random Image Generator

Web content that varies randomly adds dynamic, interesting effects to a page. In the next example, we build a random image generator, a script that displays a randomly selected image every time the page that contains the script is loaded.

For the script in Fig. 9.7 to function properly, the directory containing the file `RandomPicture.html` must also contain seven images with integer filenames (i.e., `1.gif`, `2.gif`, …, `7.gif`). The web page containing this script displays one of these seven images, selected at random, each time the page loads.

Lines 12–13 randomly select an image to display on a web page. This `document.write` statement creates an image tag in the web page with the `src` attribute set to a random integer from 1 to 7, concatenated with `".gif"`. Thus, the script dynamically sets the source of the image tag to the name of one of the image files in the current directory.

```
<?xml version = "1.0" encoding = "utf-8"?>
<!DOCTYPE html PUBLIC "-//W3C//DTD XHTML 1.0 Strict//EN"
   "http://www.w3.org/TR/xhtml1/DTD/xhtml1-strict.dtd">

<!-- Fig. 9.7: RandomPicture.html -->
<!-- Random image generation using Math.random. -->
<html xmlns = "http://www.w3.org/1999/xhtml">
   <head>
      <title>Random Image Generator</title>
      <script type = "text/javascript">
         <!--
         document.write ( "<img src = \"" +
            Math.floor( 1 + Math.random() * 7 ) + ".gif\" />" );
         // -->
      </script>
   </head>
   <body>
      <p>Click Refresh (or Reload) to run the script again</p>
   </body>
</html>
```

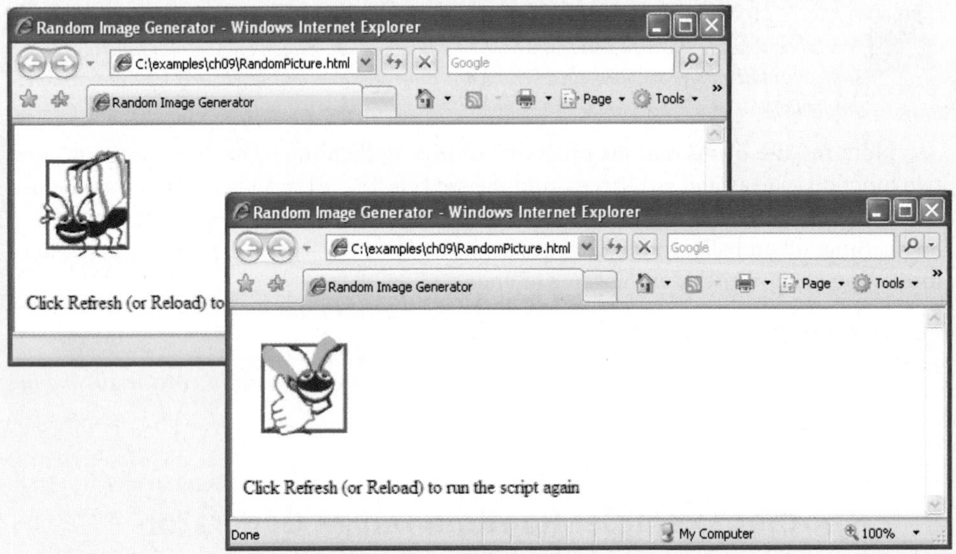

Fig. 9.7 | Random image generation using `Math.random`.

9.8 Scope Rules

Chapters 6–8 used identifiers for variable names. The attributes of variables include name, value and data type (e.g., string, number or boolean). We also use identifiers as names for user-defined functions. Each identifier in a program also has a scope.

The **scope** of an identifier for a variable or function is the portion of the program in which the identifier can be referenced. **Global variables** or **script-level variables** that are declared in the `head` element are accessible in any part of a script and are said to have **global scope**. Thus every function in the script can potentially use the variables.

Identifiers declared inside a function have function (or local) scope and can be used only in that function. Function scope begins with the opening left brace ({) of the function in which the identifier is declared and ends at the terminating right brace (}) of the function. Local variables of a function and function parameters have function scope. If a local variable in a function has the same name as a global variable, the global variable is "hidden" from the body of the function.

Good Programming Practice 9.6

Avoid local-variable names that hide global-variable names. This can be accomplished by simply avoiding the use of duplicate identifiers in a script.

The script in Fig. 9.8 demonstrates the scope rules that resolve conflicts between global variables and local variables of the same name. This example also demonstrates the `onload` event (line 52), which calls an event handler (`start`) when the <body> of the XHTML document is completely loaded into the browser window.

```
1  <?xml version = "1.0" encoding = "utf-8"?>
2  <!DOCTYPE html PUBLIC "-//W3C//DTD XHTML 1.0 Strict//EN"
3     "http://www.w3.org/TR/xhtml1/DTD/xhtml1-strict.dtd">
4
5  <!-- Fig. 9.8: scoping.html -->
6  <!-- Scoping example. -->
7  <html xmlns = "http://www.w3.org/1999/xhtml">
8     <head>
9        <title>A Scoping Example</title>
10       <script type = "text/javascript">
11          <!--
12          var x = 1; // global variable
13
14          function start()
15          {
16             var x = 5; // variable local to function start
17
18             document.writeln( "local x in start is " + x );
19
20             functionA(); // functionA has local x
21             functionB(); // functionB uses global variable x
22             functionA(); // functionA reinitializes local x
23             functionB(); // global variable x retains its value
24
25             document.writeln(
26                "<p>local x in start is " + x + "</p>" );
27          } // end function start
28
29          function functionA()
30          {
31             var x = 25; // initialized each time
32                         // functionA is called
33
34             document.writeln( "<p>local x in functionA is " +
35                x + " after entering functionA" );
```

Fig. 9.8 | Scoping example. (Part 1 of 2.)

```
36             ++x;
37             document.writeln( "<br />local x in functionA is " +
38                x + " before exiting functionA" + "</p>" );
39          } // end functionA
40
41          function functionB()
42          {
43             document.writeln( "<p>global variable x is " + x +
44                " on entering functionB" );
45             x *= 10;
46             document.writeln( "<br />global variable x is " +
47                x + " on exiting functionB" + "</p>" );
48          } // end functionB
49          // -->
50       </script>
51    </head>
52    <body onload = "start()"></body>
53 </html>
```

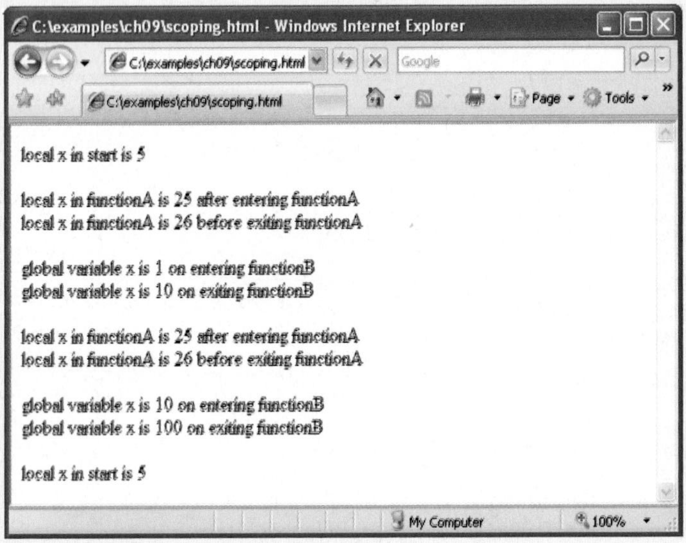

C:\examples\ch09\scoping.html - Windows Internet Explorer

local x in start is 5

local x in functionA is 25 after entering functionA
local x in functionA is 26 before exiting functionA

global variable x is 1 on entering functionB
global variable x is 10 on exiting functionB

local x in functionA is 25 after entering functionA
local x in functionA is 26 before exiting functionA

global variable x is 10 on entering functionB
global variable x is 100 on exiting functionB

local x in start is 5

Fig. 9.8 | Scoping example. (Part 2 of 2.)

Global variable `x` (line 12) is declared and initialized to 1. This global variable is hidden in any block (or function) that declares a variable named `x`. Function `start` (line 14–27) declares a local variable `x` (line 16) and initializes it to `5`. This variable is output in a line of XHTML text to show that the global variable `x` is hidden in `start`. The script defines two other functions—`functionA` and `functionB`—that each take no arguments and return nothing. Each function is called twice from function `start`.

Function `functionA` defines local variable `x` (line 31) and initializes it to `25`. When `functionA` is called, the variable is output in a line of XHTML text to show that the global variable `x` is hidden in `functionA`; then the variable is incremented and output in a line of XHTML text again before the function is exited. Each time this function is called, local variable `x` is re-created and initialized to `25`.

Function `functionB` does not declare any variables. Therefore, when it refers to variable `x`, the global variable `x` is used. When `functionB` is called, the global variable is output in a line of XHTML text, multiplied by `10` and output in a line of XHTML text again before the function is exited. The next time function `functionB` is called, the global variable has its modified value, `10`, which again gets multiplied by `10`, and `100` is output. Finally, the program outputs local variable `x` in `start` in a line of XHTML text again, to show that none of the function calls modified the value of `x` in `start`, because the functions all referred to variables in other scopes.

9.9 JavaScript Global Functions

JavaScript provides seven global functions. We have already used two of these functions—`parseInt` and `parseFloat`. The global functions are summarized in Fig. 9.9.

Actually, the global functions in Fig. 9.9 are all part of JavaScript's **`Global` object**. The `Global` object contains all the global variables in the script, all the user-defined functions in the script and all the functions listed in Fig. 9.9. Because global functions and user-defined functions are part of the `Global` object, some JavaScript programmers refer to these functions as methods. We use the term method only when referring to a function that is called for a particular object (e.g., `Math.random()`). As a JavaScript programmer, you do not need to use the `Global` object directly; JavaScript references it for you.

Global function	Description
`escape`	Takes a string argument and returns a string in which all spaces, punctuation, accent characters and any other character that is not in the ASCII character set (see Appendix D, ASCII Character Set) are encoded in a hexadecimal format (see Appendix E, Number Systems) that can be represented on all platforms.
`eval`	Takes a string argument representing JavaScript code to execute. The JavaScript interpreter evaluates the code and executes it when the `eval` function is called. This function allows JavaScript code to be stored as strings and executed dynamically. [*Note:* It is considered a serious security risk to use `eval` to process any data entered by a user because a malicious user could exploit this to run dangerous code.]
`isFinite`	Takes a numeric argument and returns `true` if the value of the argument is not `NaN`, `Number.POSITIVE_INFINITY` or `Number.NEGATIVE_INFINITY` (values that are not numbers or numbers outside the range that JavaScript supports)—otherwise, the function returns `false`.
`isNaN`	Takes a numeric argument and returns `true` if the value of the argument is not a number; otherwise, it returns `false`. The function is commonly used with the return value of `parseInt` or `parseFloat` to determine whether the result is a proper numeric value.

Fig. 9.9 | JavaScript global functions. (Part 1 of 2.)

Global function	Description
parseFloat	Takes a string argument and attempts to convert the beginning of the string into a floating-point value. If the conversion is unsuccessful, the function returns NaN; otherwise, it returns the converted value (e.g., `parseFloat( "abc123.45" )` returns NaN, and `parseFloat( "123.45abc" )` returns the value 123.45).
parseInt	Takes a string argument and attempts to convert the beginning of the string into an integer value. If the conversion is unsuccessful, the function returns NaN; otherwise, it returns the converted value (e.g., `parseInt( "abc123" )` returns NaN, and `parseInt( "123abc" )` returns the integer value 123). This function takes an optional second argument, from 2 to 36, specifying the **radix** (or **base**) of the number. Base 2 indicates that the first argument string is in **binary** format, base 8 indicates that the first argument string is in **octal** format and base 16 indicates that the first argument string is in **hexadecimal** format. See Appendix E, Number Systems, for more information on binary, octal and hexadecimal numbers.
unescape	Takes a string as its argument and returns a string in which all characters previously encoded with escape are decoded.

Fig. 9.9 | JavaScript global functions. (Part 2 of 2.)

9.10 Recursion

The programs we have discussed thus far are generally structured as functions that call one another in a disciplined, hierarchical manner. A **recursive function** is a function that calls *itself*, either directly, or indirectly through another function. **Recursion** is an important topic discussed at length in computer science courses. In this section, we present a simple example of recursion.

We consider recursion conceptually first; then we examine several programs containing recursive functions. Recursive problem-solving approaches have a number of elements in common. A recursive function is called to solve a problem. The function actually knows how to solve only the simplest case(s), or **base case(s)**. If the function is called with a base case, the function returns a result. If the function is called with a more complex problem, it divides the problem into two conceptual pieces—a piece that the function knows how to process (the base case) and a piece that the function does not know how to process. To make recursion feasible, the latter piece must resemble the original problem, but be a simpler or smaller version it. Because this new problem looks like the original problem, the function invokes (calls) a fresh copy of itself to go to work on the smaller problem; this invocation is referred to as a **recursive call**, or the **recursion step**. The recursion step also normally includes the keyword return, because its result will be combined with the portion of the problem the function knew how to solve to form a result that will be passed back to the original caller.

The recursion step executes while the original call to the function is still open (i.e., it has not finished executing). The recursion step can result in many more recursive calls as the function divides each new subproblem into two conceptual pieces. For the recursion eventually to terminate, each time the function calls itself with a simpler version of the original problem, the sequence of smaller and smaller problems must converge on the base case. At that point, the function recognizes the base case, returns a result to the previous copy of the function, and a sequence of returns ensues up the line until the original function call eventually returns the final result to the caller. This process sounds exotic when compared with the conventional problem solving we have performed to this point.

As an example of these concepts at work, let us write a recursive program to perform a popular mathematical calculation. The factorial of a nonnegative integer n, written $n!$ (and pronounced "n factorial"), is the product

$$n \cdot (n-1) \cdot (n-2) \cdot \ldots \cdot 1$$

where 1! is equal to 1 and 0! is defined as 1. For example, 5! is the product $5 \cdot 4 \cdot 3 \cdot 2 \cdot 1$, which is equal to 120.

The factorial of an integer (`number` in the following example) greater than or equal to zero can be calculated iteratively (nonrecursively) using a `for` statement, as follows:

```
var factorial = 1;

for ( var counter = number; counter >= 1; --counter )
   factorial *= counter;
```

A recursive definition of the factorial function is arrived at by observing the following relationship:

$$n! = n \cdot (n-1)!$$

For example, *5!* is clearly equal to 5 * 4!, as is shown by the following equations:

$$5! = 5 \cdot 4 \cdot 3 \cdot 2 \cdot 1$$
$$5! = 5 \cdot (4 \cdot 3 \cdot 2 \cdot 1)$$
$$5! = 5 \cdot (4!)$$

The evaluation of 5! would proceed as shown in Fig. 9.10. Figure 9.10 (a) shows how the succession of recursive calls proceeds until 1! is evaluated to be 1, which terminates the recursion. Figure 9.10 (b) shows the values returned from each recursive call to its caller until the final value is calculated and returned.

Figure 9.11 uses recursion to calculate and print the factorials of the integers 0 to 10. The recursive function `factorial` first tests (line 24) whether a terminating condition is `true`, i.e., whether `number` is less than or equal to 1. If so, `factorial` returns 1, no further recursion is necessary and the function returns. If `number` is greater than 1, line 27 expresses the problem as the product of `number` and the value returned by a recursive call to `factorial` evaluating the factorial of `number - 1`. Note that `factorial( number - 1 )` is a simpler problem than the original calculation, `factorial( number )`.

Function `factorial` (lines 22–28) receives as its argument the value for which to calculate the factorial. As can be seen in the screen capture in Fig. 9.11, factorial values become large quickly.

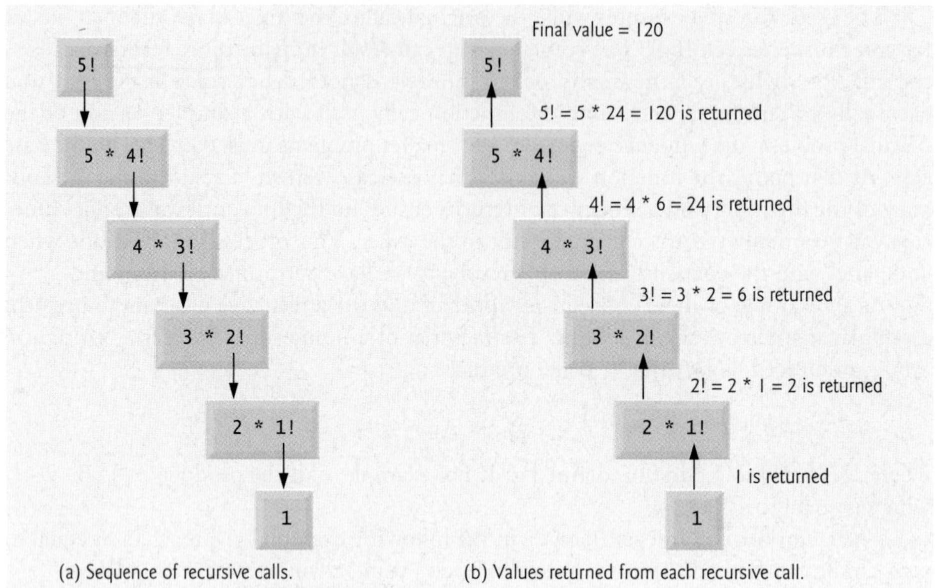

(a) Sequence of recursive calls. (b) Values returned from each recursive call.

Fig. 9.10 | Recursive evaluation of 5!.

```
<?xml version = "1.0" encoding = "utf-8"?>
<!DOCTYPE html PUBLIC "-//W3C//DTD XHTML 1.0 Strict//EN"
   "http://www.w3.org/TR/xhtml1/DTD/xhtml1-strict.dtd">

<!-- Fig. 9.11: FactorialTest.html -->
<!-- Factorial calculation with a recursive function. -->
<html xmlns = "http://www.w3.org/1999/xhtml">
   <head>
      <title>Recursive Factorial Function</title>
      <script type = "text/javascript">
      <!--
         document.writeln( "<h1>Factorials of 1 to 10</h1>" );
         document.writeln( "<table>" );

         for ( var i = 0; i <= 10; i++ )
            document.writeln( "<tr><td>" + i + "!</td><td>" +
               factorial( i ) + "</td></tr>" );

         document.writeln( "</table>" );

         // Recursive definition of function factorial
         function factorial( number )
         {
            if ( number <= 1 )  // base case
               return 1;
            else
               return number * factorial( number - 1 );
         } // end function factorial
```

Fig. 9.11 | Factorial calculation with a recursive function. (Part 1 of 2.)

```
        // -->
      </script>
   </head><body></body>
</html>
```

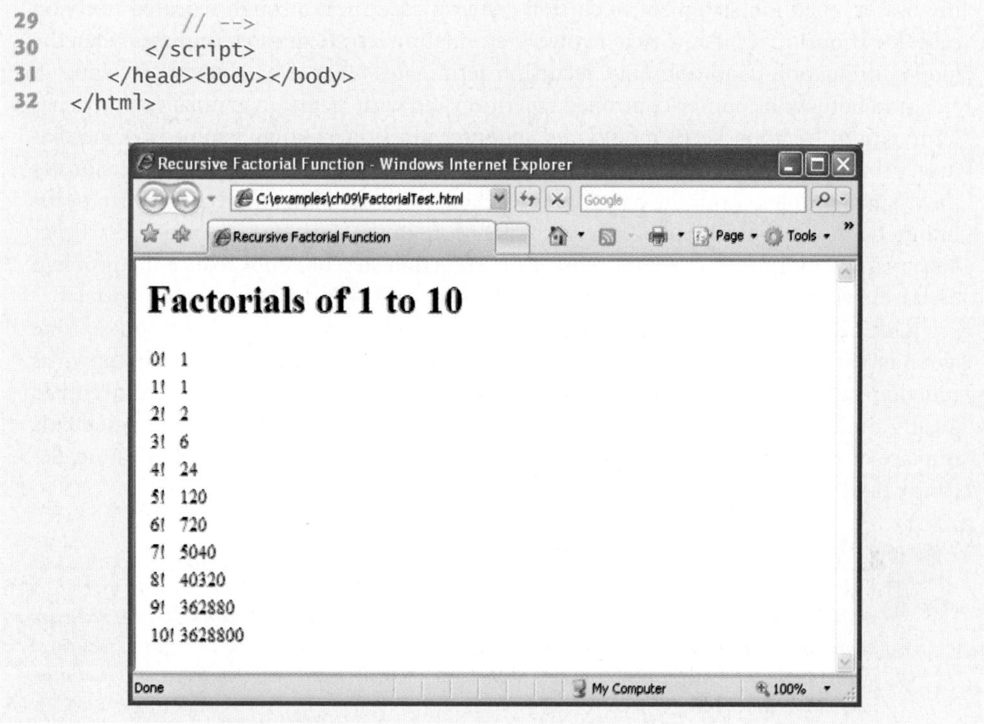

Fig. 9.11 | Factorial calculation with a recursive function. (Part 2 of 2.)

Common Programming Error 9.6

Forgetting to return a value from a recursive function when one is needed results in a logic error.

Common Programming Error 9.7

Omitting the base case and writing the recursion step incorrectly so that it does not converge on the base case are both errors that cause infinite recursion, eventually exhausting memory. This situation is analogous to the problem of an infinite loop in an iterative (nonrecursive) solution.

Error-Prevention Tip 9.3

Internet Explorer displays an error message when a script seems to be going into infinite recursion. Firefox simply terminates the script after detecting the problem. This allows the user of the web page to recover from a script that contains an infinite loop or infinite recursion.

9.11 Recursion vs. Iteration

In the preceding section, we studied a function that can easily be implemented either recursively or iteratively. In this section, we compare the two approaches and discuss why you might choose one approach over the other in a particular situation.

Both iteration and recursion are based on a control statement: Iteration uses a repetition statement (e.g., `for`, `while` or `do...while`); recursion uses a selection statement (e.g., `if`, `if...else` or `switch`). Both iteration and recursion involve repetition: Iteration explicitly uses a repetition statement; recursion achieves repetition through repeated function calls. Iteration and recursion each involve a termination test: Iteration terminates when the loop-continuation condition fails; recursion terminates when a base case is recognized. Iteration both with counter-controlled repetition and with recursion gradually approaches termination: Iteration keeps modifying a counter until the counter assumes a value that makes the loop-continuation condition fail; recursion keeps producing simpler versions of the original problem until the base case is reached. Both iteration and recursion can occur infinitely: An infinite loop occurs with iteration if the loop-continuation test never becomes false; infinite recursion occurs if the recursion step does not reduce the problem each time via a sequence that converges on the base case or if the base case is incorrect.

One negative aspect of recursion is that function calls require a certain amount of time and memory space not directly spent on executing program instructions. This is known as function-call overhead. Because recursion uses repeated function calls, this overhead greatly affects the performance of the operation. In many cases, using repetition statements in place of recursion is more efficient. However, some problems can be solved more elegantly (and more easily) with recursion.

Software Engineering Observation 9.6

Any problem that can be solved recursively can also be solved iteratively (nonrecursively). A recursive approach is normally chosen in preference to an iterative approach when the recursive approach more naturally mirrors the problem and results in a program that is easier to understand and debug. Another reason to choose a recursive solution is that an iterative solution may not be apparent.

Performance Tip 9.1

Avoid using recursion in performance-oriented situations. Recursive calls take time and consume additional memory.

Common Programming Error 9.8

Accidentally having a nonrecursive function call itself, either directly, or indirectly through another function, can cause infinite recursion.

In addition to the Factorial function examnple (Fig. 9.11), we also provide several recursion exercises—raising an integer to an integer power (Exercise 9.34), visualizing recursion (Exercise 9.35) and sum of two integers (Exercise 9.36). Also, Fig. 14.26 uses recursion to traverse an XML document tree.

9.12 Wrap-Up

This chapter introduced JavaScript functions, which allow you to modularize your programs. We showed how to call functions and methods and how to define your own functions that accomplish tasks. We also showed how parameters are used to pass data into a function, while return values are used to pass a result back to the caller. We discussed how to get a range of random numbers and built a craps game and a random image generator using these concepts. Finally, we introduced recursion, which provides an alternative method for solving problems that involve repetitive calculations. In the next chapter, we introduce arrays, which allow you to store lists of data in a single variable.

9.13 Web Resources

`www.deitel.com/javascript/`

The Deitel JavaScript Resource Center contains links to some of the best JavaScript resources on the web. There you'll find categorized links to JavaScript tools, code generators, forums, books, libraries, frameworks and more. Also check out the tutorials for all skill levels, from introductory to advanced. Be sure to visit the related Resource Centers on XHTML (`www.deitel.com/xhtml/`) and CSS 2.1 (`www.deitel.com/css21/`).

Summary

Section 9.1 Introduction

- The best way to develop and maintain a large program is to construct it from small, simple pieces, or modules. This technique is called divide and conquer.

Section 9.2 Program Modules in JavaScript

- JavaScript programs are written by combining new functions that the programmer writes with "prepackaged" functions and objects available in JavaScript.
- The term method implies that the function belongs to a particular object. We refer to functions that belong to a particular JavaScript object as methods; all others are referred to as functions.
- JavaScript provides several objects that have a rich collection of methods for performing common mathematical calculations, string manipulations, date and time manipulations, and manipulations of collections of data called arrays. These objects make your job easier, because they provide many of the capabilities programmers frequently need.
- Whenever possible, use existing JavaScript objects, methods and functions instead of writing new ones. This reduces script-development time and helps avoid introducing errors.
- You can define functions that perform specific tasks and use them at many points in a script. These functions are referred to as programmer-defined functions. The actual statements defining the function are written only once and are hidden from other functions.
- Functions are invoked by writing the name of the function, followed by a left parenthesis, followed by a comma-separated list of zero or more arguments, followed by a right parenthesis.
- Methods are called in the same way as functions, but require the name of the object to which the method belongs and a dot preceding the method name.
- Function (and method) arguments may be constants, variables or expressions.

Section 9.3 Programmer-Defined Functions

- All variables declared in function definitions are local variables—this means that they can be accessed only in the function in which they are defined.
- A function's parameters are considered to be local variables. When a function is called, the arguments in the call are assigned to the corresponding parameters in the function definition.
- Code that is packaged as a function can be executed from several locations in a program by calling the function.
- Each function should perform a single, well-defined task, and the name of the function should express that task effectively. This promotes software reusability.

Section 9.4 Function Definitions

- The return statement passes information from inside a function back to the point in the program where it was called.

- A function must be called explicitly for the code in its body to execute.
- The format of a function definition is

```
function function-name( parameter-list )
{
    declarations and statements
}
```

- There are three ways to return control to the point at which a function was invoked. If the function does not return a result, control returns when the program reaches the function-ending right brace or by executing the statement `return;`. If the function does return a result, the statement `return` *expression*; returns the value of *expression* to the caller.

Section 9.5 Random Number Generation

- Method `random` generates a floating-point value from 0.0 up to, but not including, 1.0.
- Random integers in a certain range can be generated by scaling and shifting the values returned by `random`, then using Math.floor to convert them to integers. The scaling factor determines the size of the range (i.e. a scaling factor of 4 means four possible integers). The shift number is added to the result to determine where the range begins (i.e. shifting the numbers by 3 would give numbers between 3 and 7.)

Section 9.6 Example: Game of Chance

- JavaScript can execute actions in response to the user's interaction with a GUI component in an XHTML form. This is referred to as GUI event handling
- An XHTML element's `onclick` attribute indicates the action to take when the user of the XHTML document clicks on the element.
- In event-driven programming, the user interacts with a GUI component, the script is notified of the event and the script processes the event. The user's interaction with the GUI "drives" the program. The function that is called when an event occurs is known as an event-handling function or event handler.
- The `getElementById` method, given an `id` as an argument, finds the XHTML element with a matching `id` attribute and returns a JavaScript object representing the element.
- The `value` property of a JavaScript object representing an XHTML text input element specifies the text to display in the text field.
- Using an XHTML container (e.g. `div`, `span`, `p`) object's `innerHTML` property, we can use a script to set the contents of the element.

Section 9.7 Another Example: Random Image Generator

- We can use random number generation to randomly select from a number of images in order to display a random image each time a page loads.

Section 9.8 Scope Rules

- Each identifier in a program has a scope. The scope of an identifier for a variable or function is the portion of the program in which the identifier can be referenced.
- Global variables or script-level variables (i.e., variables declared in the head element of the XHTML document) are accessible in any part of a script and are said to have global scope. Thus every function in the script can potentially use the variables.
- Identifiers declared inside a function have function (or local) scope and can be used only in that function. Function scope begins with the opening left brace ({) of the function in which the iden-

tifier is declared and ends at the terminating right brace (}) of the function. Local variables of a function and function parameters have function scope.

- If a local variable in a function has the same name as a global variable, the global variable is "hidden" from the body of the function.
- The `onload` property of the body element calls an event handler when the **body** of the XHTML document is completely loaded into the browser window.

Section 9.9 JavaScript Global Functions

- JavaScript provides seven global functions as part of a `Global` object. This object contains all the global variables in the script, all the user-defined functions in the script and all the built-in global functions functions listed in Fig. 9.9.
- You do not need to use the `Global` object directly; JavaScript uses it for you.

Section 9.10 Recursion

- A recursive function calls itself, either directly, or indirectly through another function.
- A recursive function knows how to solve only the simplest case, or base case. If the function is called with a base case, it returns a result. If the function is called with a more complex problem, it knows how to divide the problem into two conceptual pieces—a piece that the function knows how to process (the base case) and a simpler or smaller version of the original problem.
- The function invokes (calls) a fresh copy of itself to go to work on the smaller problem; this invocation is referred to as a recursive call, or the recursion step.
- The recursion step executes while the original call to the function is still open (i.e., it has not finished executing).
- For recursion eventually to terminate, each time the function calls itself with a simpler version of the original problem, the sequence of smaller and smaller problems must converge on the base case. At that point, the function recognizes the base case, returns a result to the previous copy of the function, and a sequence of returns ensues up the line until the original function call eventually returns the final result to the caller.

Section 9.11 Recursion vs. Iteration

- Both iteration and recursion involve repetition: Iteration explicitly uses a repetition statement; recursion achieves repetition through repeated function calls.
- Iteration and recursion each involve a termination test: Iteration terminates when the loop-continuation condition fails; recursion terminates when a base case is recognized.
- Iteration with counter-controlled repetition and recursion both gradually approach termination: Iteration keeps modifying a counter until the counter assumes a value that makes the loop-continuation condition fail; recursion keeps producing simpler versions of the original problem until the base case is reached.
- Recursion repeatedly invokes the mechanism and, consequently, the overhead of function calls. This effect can be expensive in terms of processor time and memory space.
- Some problems can be understood or solved more easily with recursion than with iteration.

Terminology

argument in a function call
base case
binary format
block
called function
caller
calling function
computer-assisted instruction (CAI)

constant
converge on the base case
copy of a value
divide and conquer
dot (.)
dot notation
element of chance
escape function
eval function
element of chance
event
event handler
event-handling function
event-driven programming
floor method of the Math object
function
function (local) scope
function argument
function body
function call
function definition
function name
function parameter
function-call operator ()
getElementById method of the document object
Global object
global scope
global variable
hexadecimal
innerHTML property
invoke a function
isFinite function
isNaN function
iterative solution
listen for events
local scope
local variable
max method of the Math object
method
modularize a program
module
object
octal
onclick event
onload event
parameter in a function definition
parseFloat function
parseInt function
programmer-defined function
probability
programmer-defined function
radix
random method of the Math object
random-number generation
recursion
recursive function
recursive step
registering an event handler
respond to an event
return statement
scaling
scaling factor
scope
script-level variable
shifting value
simulation
software engineering
software reusability
unescape function
value property of an XHTML text field

Self-Review Exercises

9.1 Fill in the blanks in each of the following statements:

a) Program modules in JavaScript are called ________.
b) A function is invoked using a(n) ________.
c) A variable known only inside the function in which it is defined is called a(n) ________.
d) The ________ statement in a called function can be used to pass the value of an expression back to the calling function.
e) The keyword ________ indicates the beginning of a function definition.

9.2 For the given program, state the scope (either global scope or function scope) of each of the following elements:

a) The variable x.
b) The variable y.
c) The function cube.
d) The function output.

```
<?xml version = "1.0" encoding = "utf-8"?>
<!DOCTYPE html PUBLIC "-//W3C//DTD XHTML 1.0 Transitional//EN"
   "http://www.w3.org/TR/xhtml1/DTD/xhtml1-transitional.dtd">

<!-- Exercise 9.2: cube.html -->
<html xmlns = "http://www.w3.org/1999/xhtml">
   <head>
      <title>Scoping</title>
      <script type = "text/javascript">
         <!--
         var x;

         function output()
         {
            for ( x = 1; x <= 10; x++ )
               document.writeln( cube( x ) + "<br />" );
         } // end function output

         function cube( y )
         {
            return y * y * y;
         } // end function cube
         // -->
   </script>
   </head><body onload = "output()"></body>
</html>
```

9.3 Fill in the blanks in each of the following statements:

a) Programmer-defined functions, global variables and JavaScript's global functions are all part of the _______ object.

b) Function _______ determines if its argument is or is not a number.

c) Function _______ takes a string argument and returns a string in which all spaces, punctuation, accent characters and any other character that is not in the ASCII character set are encoded in a hexadecimal format.

d) Function _______ takes a string argument representing JavaScript code to execute.

e) Function _______ takes a string as its argument and returns a string in which all characters that were previously encoded with `escape` are decoded.

9.4 Fill in the blanks in each of the following statements:

a) An identifier's _______ is the portion of the program in which the it can be used.

b) The three ways to return control from a called function to a caller are _______, _______ and _______.

c) The _______ function is used to produce random numbers.

d) Variables declared in a block or in a function's parameter list are of _______ scope.

9.5 Locate the error in each of the following program segments and explain how to correct it:

a)
```
method g()
{
   document.writeln( "Inside method g" );
}
```

b)
```
// This function should return the sum of its arguments
function sum( x, y )
{
   var result;
   result = x + y;
}
```

c)
```
function f( a );
{
   document.writeln( a );
}
```

9.6 Write a complete JavaScript program to prompt the user for the radius of a sphere, and call function `sphereVolume` to calculate and display the volume of the sphere. Use the statement

```
volume = ( 4.0 / 3.0 ) * Math.PI * Math.pow( radius, 3 );
```

to calculate the volume. The user should input the radius through an XHTML text field in a `<form>` and click an XHTML button to initiate the calculation.

Answers to Self-Review Exercises

9.1 a) functions. b) function call. c) local variable. d) `return`. e) `function`.

9.2 a) Global scope. b) Function scope. c) Global scope. d) Global scope.

9.3 a) `Global`. b) `isNaN`. c) `escape`. d) `eval`. e) `unescape`.

9.4 a) scope. b) `return;` or `return` *expression*`;` or encountering the closing right brace of a function. c) `Math.random`. d) local.

9.5
a) Error: `method` is not the keyword used to begin a function definition.
Correction: Change `method` to `function`.

b) Error: The function is supposed to return a value, but does not.
Correction: Either delete variable `result` and place the statement
```
return x + y;
```
in the function or add the following statement at the end of the function body:
```
return result;
```

c) Error: The semicolon after the right parenthesis that encloses the parameter list.
Correction: Delete the semicolon after the right parenthesis of the parameter list.

9.6 The solution below calculates the volume of a sphere using the radius entered by the user.

```
<?xml version = "1.0" encoding = "utf-8"?>
<!DOCTYPE html PUBLIC "-//W3C//DTD XHTML 1.0 Strict//EN"
   "http://www.w3.org/TR/xhtml1/DTD/xhtml1-strict.dtd">

<!-- Exercise 9.6: volume.html -->
<html xmlns = "http://www.w3.org/1999/xhtml">
   <head>
      <title>Calculating Sphere Volumes</title>
      <script type = "text/javascript">
         <!--
         function displayVolume()
         {
            var inputField = document.getElementById( "radiusField" );
            var radius = parseFloat( inputField.value );
            var answerField = document.getElementById( "answer" );
            answerField.value = sphereVolume( radius );
         } // end function displayVolume

         function sphereVolume( radius )
         {
            return ( 4.0 / 3.0 ) * Math.PI * Math.pow( radius, 3 );
         } // end function sphereVolume
         // -->
```

```
        </script>
    </head>
    <body>
        <form action = "">
            <div>
                <label>Radius:
                    <input id = "radiusField" type = "text" /></label>
                    <input type = "button" value = "Calculate"
                       onclick = "displayVolume()" />
                <br />
                <label>Answer:
                    <input id = "answer" type = "text" /></label>
            </div>
        </form>
    </body>
</html>
```

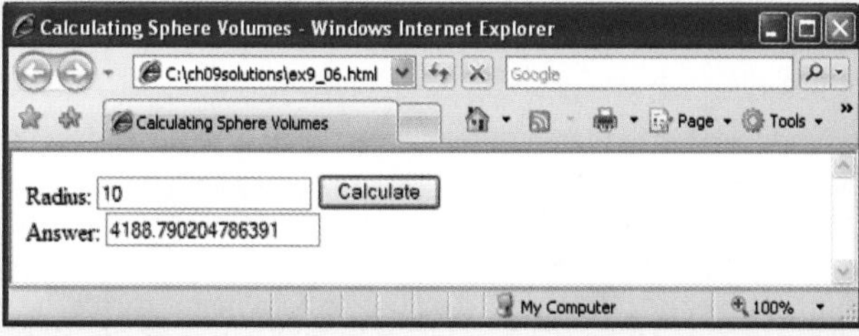

Exercises

9.7 Write a script that prompts the user for the radius of a circle, uses a function `circleArea` to calculate the area of the circle, and prints the area of the circle.

9.8 A parking garage charges a $2.00 minimum fee to park for up to three hours. The garage charges an additional $0.50 per hour for each hour *or part thereof* in excess of three hours. The maximum charge for any given 24-hour period is $10.00. Assume that no car parks for longer than 24 hours at a time. Write a script that calculates and displays the parking charges for each customer who parked a car in this garage yesterday. You should input from the user the hours parked for each customer. The program should display the charge for the current customer and should calculate and display the running total of yesterday's receipts. The program should use the function `calculateCharges` to determine the charge for each customer. Use a text input field to obtain the input from the user.

9.9 Write function `distance` that calculates the distance between two points ($x1$, $y1$) and ($x2$, $y2$). All numbers and return values should be floating-point values. Incorporate this function into a script that enables the user to enter the coordinates of the points through an XHTML form.

9.10 Answer each of the following questions:

a) What does it mean to choose numbers “at random”?
b) Why is the `Math.random` function useful for simulating games of chance?
c) Why is it often necessary to scale and/or shift the values produced by `Math.random`?
d) Why is computerized simulation of real-world situations a useful technique?

9.11 Write statements that assign random integers to the variable n in the following ranges:

a) $1 \le n \le 2$
b) $1 \le n \le 100$
c) $0 \le n \le 9$
d) $1000 \le n \le 1112$

e) $-1 \leq n \leq 1$
f) $-3 \leq n \leq 11$

9.12 For each of the following sets of integers, write a single statement that will print a number at random from the set:

a) 2, 4, 6, 8, 10.
b) 3, 5, 7, 9, 11.
c) 6, 10, 14, 18, 22.

9.13 Write a function `integerPower( base, exponent )` that returns the value of

$$base^{exponent}$$

For example, `integerPower( 3, 4 ) = 3 * 3 * 3 * 3`. Assume that `exponent` and `base` are integers. Function `integerPower` should use a `for` or `while` statement to control the calculation. Incorporate this function into a script that reads integer values from an XHTML form for `base` and `exponent` and performs the calculation with the `integerPower` function. The XHTML form should consist of two text fields and a button to initiate the calculation. The user should interact with the program by typing numbers in both text fields then clicking the button.

9.14 Write a function `multiple` that determines, for a pair of integers, whether the second integer is a multiple of the first. The function should take two integer arguments and return `true` if the second is a multiple of the first, and `false` otherwise. Incorporate this function into a script that inputs a series of pairs of integers (one pair at a time). The XHTML form should consist of two text fields and a button to initiate the calculation. The user should interact with the program by typing numbers in both text fields, then clicking the button.

9.15 Write a script that inputs integers (one at a time) and passes them one at a time to function `isEven`, which uses the modulus operator to determine whether an integer is even. The function should take an integer argument and return `true` if the integer is even and `false` otherwise. Use sentinel-controlled looping and a `prompt` dialog.

9.16 Write a function `squareOfAsterisks` that displays a solid square of asterisks whose side is specified in integer parameter `side`. For example, if `side` is `4`, the function displays

```
****
****
****
****
```

Incorporate this function into a script that reads an integer value for `side` from the user at the keyboard and performs the drawing with the `squareOfAsterisks` function.

9.17 Modify the script created in Exercise 9.16 to also prompt the user for a character which will be used to create the square. Thus, if `side` is `5` and `fillCharacter` is `#`, the function should print

```
#####
#####
#####
#####
#####
```

9.18 Write program segments that accomplish each of the following tasks:

a) Calculate the integer part of the quotient when integer `a` is divided by integer `b`.
b) Calculate the integer remainder when integer `a` is divided by integer `b`.
c) Use the program pieces developed in parts (a) and (b) to write a function `displayDigits` that receives an integer between `1` and `99999` and prints it as a series of digits, each pair of which is separated by two spaces. For example, the integer `4562` should be printed as

```
4  5  6  2
```

d) Incorporate the function developed in part (c) into a script that inputs an integer from a `prompt` dialog and invokes `displayDigits` by passing to the function the integer entered.

9.19 Implement the following functions:

a) Function `celsius` returns the Celsius equivalent of a Fahrenheit temperature, using the calculation

```
C = 5.0 / 9.0 * ( F - 32 );
```

b) Function `fahrenheit` returns the Fahrenheit equivalent of a Celsius temperature, using the calculation

```
F = 9.0 / 5.0 * C + 32;
```

c) Use these functions to write a script that enables the user to enter either a Fahrenheit or a Celsius temperature and displays the Celsius or Fahrenheit equivalent.

Your XHTML document should contain two buttons—one to initiate the conversion from Fahrenheit to Celsius and one to initiate the conversion from Celsius to Fahrenheit.

9.20 Write a function `minimum3` that returns the smallest of three floating-point numbers. Use the `Math.min` function to implement `minimum3`. Incorporate the function into a script that reads three values from the user and determines the smallest value.

9.21 An integer number is said to be a **perfect number** if its factors, including 1 (but not the number itself), sum to the number. For example, 6 is a perfect number, because 6 = 1 + 2 + 3. Write a function `perfect` that determines whether parameter `number` is a perfect number. Use this function in a script that determines and displays all the perfect numbers between 1 and 1000. Print the factors of each perfect number to confirm that the number is indeed perfect. Challenge the computing power of your computer by testing numbers much larger than 1000. Display the results in a `<textarea>`.

9.22 An integer is said to be **prime** if it is greater than 1 and divisible only by 1 and itself. For example, 2, 3, 5 and 7 are prime, but 4, 6, 8 and 9 are not.

a) Write a function that determines whether a number is prime.

b) Use this function in a script that determines and prints all the prime numbers between 1 and 10,000. How many of these 10,000 numbers do you really have to test before being sure that you have found all the primes? Display the results in a `<textarea>`.

c) Initially, you might think that $n/2$ is the upper limit for which you must test to see whether a number is prime, but you only need go as high as the square root of n. Why? Rewrite the program using the `Math.sqrt` method to calculate the square root, and run it both ways. Estimate the performance improvement.

9.23 Write a function that takes an integer value and returns the number with its digits reversed. For example, given the number 7631, the function should return 1367. Incorporate the function into a script that reads a value from the user. Display the result of the function in the status bar.

9.24 The **greatest common divisor** (GCD) of two integers is the largest integer that evenly divides each of the two numbers. Write a function `gcd` that returns the greatest common divisor of two integers. Incorporate the function into a script that reads two values from the user.

9.25 Write a function `qualityPoints` that inputs a student's average and returns 4 if the student's average is 90–100, 3 if the average is 80–89, 2 if the average is 70–79, 1 if the average is 60–69 and 0 if the average is lower than 60. Incorporate the function into a script that reads a value from the user.

9.26 Write a script that simulates coin tossing. Let the program toss the coin each time the user clicks the **Toss** button. Count the number of times each side of the coin appears. Display the results.

The program should call a separate function `flip` that takes no arguments and returns `false` for tails and `true` for heads. [*Note:* If the program realistically simulates the coin tossing, each side of the coin should appear approximately half the time.]

9.27 Computers are playing an increasing role in education. Write a program that will help an elementary-school student learn multiplication. Use `Math.random` to produce two positive one-digit integers. It should then display a question such as

```
How much is 6 times 7?
```

The student then types the answer into a text field. Your program checks the student's answer. If it is correct, display the string `"Very good!"` and generate a new question. If the answer is wrong, display the string `"No. Please try again."` and let the student try the same question again repeatedly until the student finally gets it right. A separate function should be used to generate each new question. This function should be called once when the script begins execution and each time the user answers the question correctly.

9.28 The use of computers in education is referred to as computer-assisted instruction (CAI). One problem that develops in CAI environments is student fatigue. This problem can be eliminated by varying the computer's dialogue to hold the student's attention. Modify the program in Exercise 9.27 to print one of a variety of comments for each correct answer and each incorrect answer. The set of responses for correct answers is as follows:

```
Very good!
Excellent!
Nice work!
Keep up the good work!
```

The set of responses for incorrect answers is as follows:

```
No. Please try again.
Wrong. Try once more.
Don't give up!
No. Keep trying.
```

Use random number generation to choose a number from 1 to 4 that will be used to select an appropriate response to each answer. Use a `switch` statement to issue the responses.

9.29 More sophisticated computer-assisted instruction systems monitor the student's performance over a period of time. The decision to begin a new topic is often based on the student's success with previous topics. Modify the program in Exercise 9.28 to count the number of correct and incorrect responses typed by the student. After the student answers 10 questions, your program should calculate the percentage of correct responses. If the percentage is lower than 75 percent, print `Please ask your instructor for extra help`, and reset the program so another student can try it.

9.30 Write a script that plays a "guess the number" game as follows: Your program chooses the number to be guessed by selecting a random integer in the range 1 to 1000. The script displays the prompt `Guess a number between 1 and 1000` next to a text field. The player types a first guess into the text field and clicks a button to submit the guess to the script. If the player's guess is incorrect, your program should display `Too high. Try again.` or `Too low. Try again.` to help the player "zero in" on the correct answer and should clear the text field so the user can enter the next guess. When the user enters the correct answer, display `Congratulations. You guessed the number!` and clear the text field so the user can play again. [*Note:* The guessing technique employed in this problem is similar to a binary search, which we discuss in Chapter 10, JavaScript: Arrays.]

9.31 Modify the program of Exercise 9.30 to count the number of guesses the player makes. If the number is 10 or fewer, display `Either you know the secret or you got lucky!` If the player guesses the number in 10 tries, display `Ahah! You know the secret!` If the player makes more than 10

guesses, display `You should be able to do better!` Why should it take no more than 10 guesses? Well, with each good guess, the player should be able to eliminate half of the numbers. Now show why any number 1 to 1000 can be guessed in 10 or fewer tries.

9.32 Exercises 9.27 through 9.29 developed a computer-assisted instruction program to teach an elementary-school student multiplication. This exercise suggests enhancements to that program.

a) Modify the program to allow the user to enter a grade-level capability. A grade level of 1 means to use only single-digit numbers in the problems, a grade level of 2 means to use numbers as large as two digits, and so on.

b) Modify the program to allow the user to pick the type of arithmetic problems he or she wishes to study. An option of 1 means addition problems only, 2 means subtraction problems only, 3 means multiplication problems only, 4 means division problems only and 5 means to intermix randomly problems of all these types.

9.33 Modify the craps program in Fig. 9.6 to allow wagering. Initialize variable `bankBalance` to 1000 dollars. Prompt the player to enter a `wager`. Check that the `wager` is less than or equal to `bankBalance` and, if not, have the user reenter `wager` until a valid `wager` is entered. After a valid `wager` is entered, run one game of craps. If the player wins, increase `bankBalance` by `wager`, and print the new `bankBalance`. If the player loses, decrease `bankBalance` by `wager`, print the new `bankBalance`, check whether `bankBalance` has become zero and, if so, print the message `Sorry. You busted!` As the game progresses, print various messages to create some chatter, such as `Oh, you're going for broke, huh?` or `Aw c'mon, take a chance!` or `You're up big. Now's the time to cash in your chips!`. Implement the chatter as a separate function that randomly chooses the string to display.

9.34 Write a recursive function `power( base, exponent )` that, when invoked, returns

$$base^{exponent}$$

for example, `power( 3, 4 ) = 3 * 3 * 3 * 3`. Assume that `exponent` is an integer greater than or equal to 1. The recursion step would use the relationship

$$base^{exponent} = base \cdot base^{exponent-1}$$

and the terminating condition occurs when `exponent` is equal to `1`, because

$$base^{1} = base$$

Incorporate this function into a script that enables the user to enter the `base` and `exponent`.

9.35 *(Visualizing Recursion)* It is interesting to watch recursion in action. Modify the factorial function in Fig. 9.11 to display its local variable and recursive-call parameter. For each recursive call, display the outputs on a separate line and add a level of indentation. Do your utmost to make the outputs clear, interesting and meaningful. Your goal here is to design and implement an output format that helps a person understand recursion better. You may want to add such display capabilities to the many other recursion examples and exercises throughout the text.

9.36 What does the following function do?

```
// Parameter b must be a positive
// integer to prevent infinite recursion
function mystery( a, b )
{
   if ( b == 1 )
      return a;
   else
      return a + mystery( a, b - 1 );
}
```

10

JavaScript: Arrays

With sobs and tears he sorted out
Those of the largest size . . .
—Lewis Carroll

Attempt the end, and never stand to doubt;
Nothing's so hard, but search will find it out.
—Robert Herrick

Now go, write it before them in a table,
and note it in a book.
—Isaiah 30:8

'Tis in my memory lock'd,
And you yourself shall keep the key of it.
—William Shakespeare

OBJECTIVES

In this chapter you will learn:

- To use arrays to store lists and tables of values.
- To declare an array, initialize an array and refer to individual elements of an array.
- To pass arrays to functions.
- To search and sort an array.
- To declare and manipulate multidimensional arrays.

Outline

10.1 Introduction

This chapter serves as an introduction to the important topic of data structures. Arrays are data structures consisting of related data items (sometimes called collections of data items). JavaScript arrays are "dynamic" entities in that they can change size after they are created. Many of the techniques demonstrated in this chapter are used frequently in Chapters 12–13 as we introduce the collections that allow a script programmer to manipulate every element of an XHTML document dynamically.

10.2 Arrays

An array is a group of memory locations that all have the same name and normally are of the same type (although this attribute is not required in JavaScript). To refer to a particular location or element in the array, we specify the name of the array and the position number of the particular element in the array.

Figure 10.1 shows an array of integer values named `c`. This array contains 12 elements. Any one of these elements may be referred to by giving the name of the array followed by the position number of the element in square brackets (`[]`). The first element in every array is the zeroth element. Thus, the first element of array `c` is referred to as `c[0]`, the second element of array `c` is referred to as `c[1]`, the seventh element of array `c` is referred to as `c[6]` and, in general, the *i*th element of array `c` is referred to as `c[i-1]`. Array names follow the same conventions as other identifiers.

The position number in square brackets is called a subscript (or an index). A subscript must be an integer or an integer expression. If a program uses an expression as a subscript, then the expression is evaluated to determine the value of the subscript. For example, if we assume that variable `a` is equal to `5` and that variable `b` is equal to `6`, then the statement

```
c[ a + b ] += 2;
```

adds 2 to array element `c[ 11 ]`. Note that a subscripted array name is a left-hand-side expression—it can be used on the left side of an assignment to place a new value into an array

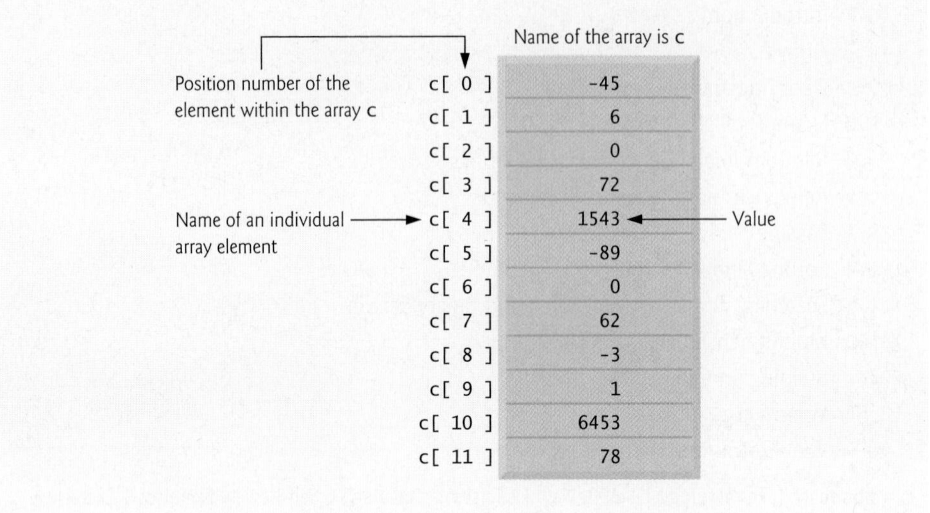

Fig. 10.1 | Array with 12 elements.

element. It can also be used on the right side of an assignment to assign its value to another left-hand side expression.

Let us examine array c in Fig. 10.1 more closely. The array's name is c. The length of array c is 12 and can be found using by the following expression:

```
c.length
```

Every array in JavaScript knows its own length. The array's 12 elements are referred to as c[0], c[1], c[2], ..., c[11]. The value of c[0] is -45, the value of c[1] is 6, the value of c[2] is 0, the value of c[7] is 62 and the value of c[11] is 78. To calculate the sum of the values contained in the first three elements of array c and store the result in variable sum, we would write

```
sum = c[ 0 ] + c[ 1 ] + c[ 2 ];
```

To divide the value of the seventh element of array c by 2 and assign the result to the variable x, we would write

```
x = c[ 6 ] / 2;
```

Common Programming Error 10.1

It is important to note the difference between the "seventh element of the array" and "array element seven." Because array subscripts begin at 0, the seventh element of the array has a subscript of 6, while array element seven has a subscript of 7 and is actually the eighth element of the array. This confusion is a source of "off-by-one" errors.

The brackets that enclose the array subscript are a JavaScript operator. Brackets have the same level of precedence as parentheses. The chart in Fig. 10.2 shows the precedence and associativity of the operators introduced so far in the text. They are shown from top to bottom in decreasing order of precedence, alongside their associativity and type.

Operators	Associativity	Type
() [] .	left to right	highest
++ -- !	right to left	unary
* / %	left to right	multiplicative
+ -	left to right	additive
< <= > >=	left to right	relational
== !=	left to right	equality
&&	left to right	logical AND
||	left to right	logical OR
?:	right to left	conditional
= += -= *= /= %=	right to left	assignment

Fig. 10.2 | Precedence and associativity of the operators discussed so far.

10.3 Declaring and Allocating Arrays

Arrays occupy space in memory. Actually, an array in JavaScript is an **Array object**. The programmer uses **operator new** to allocate dynamically (request memory for) the number of elements required by each array. Operator new creates an object as the program executes by obtaining enough memory to store an object of the type specified to the right of new. The process of creating new objects is also known as **creating an instance** or **instantiating an object**, and operator new is known as the **dynamic memory allocation operator**. Arrays are allocated with new because arrays are considered to be objects, and all objects must be created with new. To allocate 12 elements for integer array c, use the statement

```
var c = new Array( 12 );
```

The preceding statement can also be performed in two steps, as follows:

```
var c; // declares the array
c = new Array( 12 ); // allocates the array
```

When arrays are allocated, the elements are not initialized—they have the value undefined.

Common Programming Error 10.2

Assuming that the elements of an array are initialized when the array is allocated may result in logic errors.

10.4 Examples Using Arrays

This section presents several examples of creating and manipulating arrays.

Creating and Initializing Arrays

The script in Fig. 10.3 uses operator new to allocate an Array of five elements and an empty array. The script demonstrates initializing an Array of existing elements and also shows that an `Array` can grow dynamically to accommodate new elements. The `Array`'s values are displayed in XHTML tables.

Line 17 creates `Array n1` as an array of five elements. Line 18 creates `Array n2` as an empty array. Lines 21–22 use a `for` statement to initialize the elements of `n1` to their sub-

```
1  <?xml version = "1.0" encoding = "utf-8"?>
2  <!DOCTYPE html PUBLIC "-//W3C//DTD XHTML 1.0 Strict//EN"
3     "http://www.w3.org/TR/xhtml1/DTD/xhtml1-strict.dtd">
4
5  <!-- Fig. 10.3: InitArray.html -->
6  <!-- Initializing the elements of an array. -->
7  <html xmlns = "http://www.w3.org/1999/xhtml">
8     <head>
9        <title>Initializing an Array</title>
10       <style type = "text/css">
11          table { width: 10em }
12          th    { text-align: left }
13       </style>
14       <script type = "text/javascript">
15          <!--
16          // create (declare) two new arrays
17          var n1 = new Array( 5 ); // allocate five-element Array
18          var n2 = new Array(); // allocate empty Array
19
20          // assign values to each element of Array n1
21          for ( var i = 0; i < n1.length; ++i )
22             n1[ i ] = i;
23
24          // create and initialize five elements in Array n2
25          for ( i = 0; i < 5; ++i )
26             n2[ i ] = i;
27
28          outputArray( "Array n1:", n1 );
29          outputArray( "Array n2:", n2 );
30
31          // output the heading followed by a two-column table
32          // containing subscripts and elements of "theArray"
33          function outputArray( heading, theArray )
34          {
35             document.writeln( "<h2>" + heading + "</h2>" );
36             document.writeln( "<table border = \"1\"" );
37             document.writeln( "<thead><th>Subscript</th>" +
38                "<th>Value</th></thead><tbody>" );
39
40             // output the subscript and value of each array element
41             for ( var i = 0; i < theArray.length; i++ )
42                document.writeln( "<tr><td>" + i + "</td><td>" +
43                   theArray[ i ] + "</td></tr>" );
44
45             document.writeln( "</tbody></table>" );
46          } // end function outputArray
47          // -->
```

Fig. 10.3 | Initializing the elements of an array. (Part 1 of 2.)

```
48        </script>
49      </head><body></body>
50  </html>
```

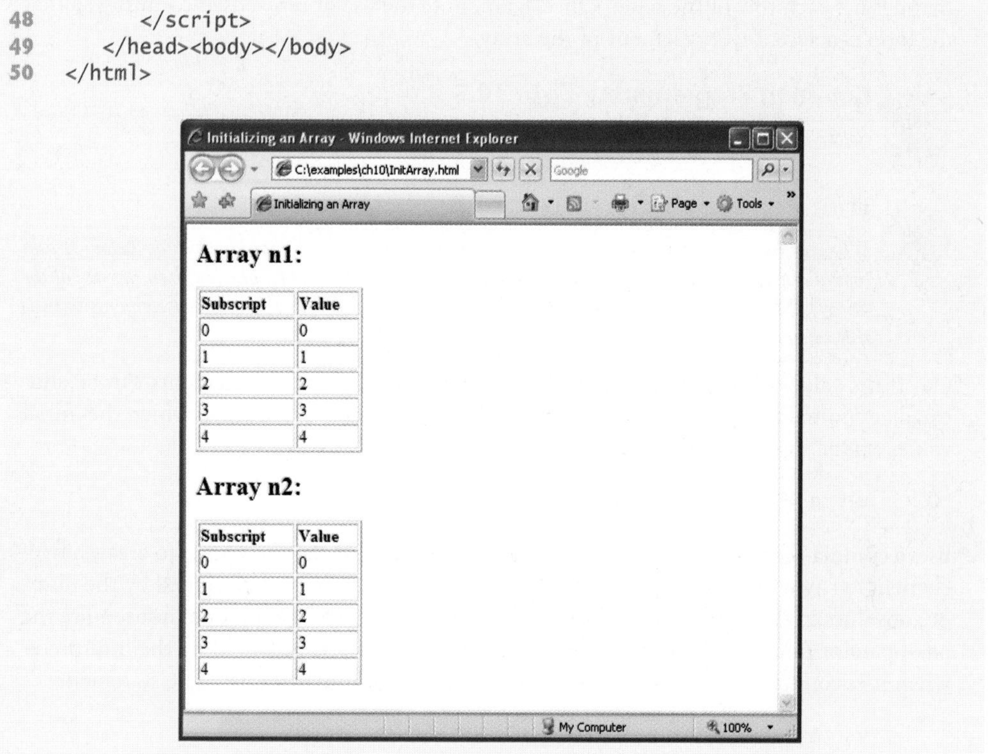

Fig. 10.3 | Initializing the elements of an array. (Part 2 of 2.)

script numbers (0 to 4). Note also the use of zero-based counting (remember, array subscripts start at 0) so that the loop can access every element of the array. Note too the use of the expression `n1.length` in the condition for the `for` statement to determine the length of the array. In this example, the length of the array is 5, so the loop continues executing as long as the value of control variable `i` is less than `5`. For a five-element array, the subscript values are 0 through 4, so using the less than operator, <, guarantees that the loop does not attempt to access an element beyond the end of the array. Zero-based counting is usually used to iterate through arrays.

Lines 25–26 use a `for` statement to add five elements to the `Array n2` and initialize each element to its subscript number (0 to 4). Note that `Array n2` grows dynamically to accommodate the values assigned to each element of the array.

Software Engineering Observation 10.1

JavaScript automatically reallocates an `Array` *when a value is assigned to an element that is outside the bounds of the original* `Array`*. Elements between the last element of the original* `Array` *and the new element have undefined values.*

Lines 28–29 invoke function `outputArray` (defined in lines 33–46) to display the contents of each array in an XHTML table. Function `outputArray` receives two arguments—a string to be output before the XHTML table that displays the contents of the array and the array to output. Lines 41–43 use a `for` statement to output XHTML text that defines each row of the table. Once again, note the use of zero-based counting so that the loop can access every element of the array.

Common Programming Error 10.3

Referring to an element outside the `Array` bounds is normally a logic error.

Error-Prevention Tip 10.1

When using subscripts to loop through an `Array`, the subscript should never go below 0 and should always be less than the number of elements in the `Array` (i.e., one less than the size of the `Array`). Make sure that the loop-terminating condition prevents the access of elements outside this range.

If the values of an `Array`'s elements are known in advance, the elements can be allocated and initialized in the declaration of the array. There are two ways in which the initial values can be specified. The statement

```
var n = [ 10, 20, 30, 40, 50 ];
```

uses a comma-separated **initializer list** enclosed in square brackets (`[` and `]`) to create a five-element `Array` with subscripts of `0`, `1`, `2`, `3` and `4`. The array size is determined by the number of values in the initializer list. Note that the preceding declaration does not require the `new` operator to create the `Array` object—this functionality is provided by the interpreter when it encounters an array declaration that includes an initializer list. The statement

```
var n = new Array( 10, 20, 30, 40, 50 );
```

also creates a five-element array with subscripts of `0`, `1`, `2`, `3` and `4`. In this case, the initial values of the array elements are specified as arguments in the parentheses following `new Array`. The size of the array is determined by the number of values in parentheses. It is also possible to reserve a space in an `Array` for a value to be specified later by using a comma as a **place holder** in the initializer list. For example, the statement

```
var n = [ 10, 20, , 40, 50 ];
```

creates a five-element array with no value specified for the third element (`n[ 2 ]`).

Initializing Arrays with Initializer Lists

The script in Fig. 10.4 creates three `Array` objects to demonstrate initializing arrays with initializer lists (lines 18–20) and displays each array in an XHTML table using the same function `outputArray` discussed in Fig. 10.3. Note that when `Array integers2` is displayed in the web page, the elements with subscripts 1 and 2 (the second and third elements of the array) appear in the web page as `undefined`. These are the two elements for which we did not supply values in the declaration in line 20 in the script.

Summing the Elements of an Array with `for` and `for...in`

The script in Fig. 10.5 sums the values contained in `theArray`, the 10-element integer array declared, allocated and initialized in line 13. The statement in line 19 in the body of the first `for` statement does the totaling. Note that the values supplied as initializers for array `theArray` could be read into the program using an XHTML form.

In this example, we introduce JavaScript's **`for...in` statement**, which enables a script to perform a task for each element in an array (or, as we will see in Chapters 12–13, for each element in a collection). This process is also known as **iterating over the elements of an array**. Lines 25-26 show the syntax of a `for...in` statement. Inside the parentheses, we declare the `element` variable used to select each element in the object to the right of key-

```
1  <?xml version = "1.0" encoding = "utf-8"?>
2  <!DOCTYPE html PUBLIC "-//W3C//DTD XHTML 1.0 Strict//EN"
3     "http://www.w3.org/TR/xhtml1/DTD/xhtml1-strict.dtd">
4
5  <!-- Fig. 10.4: InitArray2.html -->
6  <!-- Declaring and initializing arrays. -->
7  <html xmlns = "http://www.w3.org/1999/xhtml">
8     <head>
9        <title>Initializing an Array with a Declaration</title>
10       <style type = "text/css">
11          table { width: 15em }
12          th    { text-align: left }
13       </style>
14       <script type = "text/javascript">
15          <!--
16          // Initializer list specifies the number of elements and
17          // a value for each element.
18          var colors = new Array( "cyan", "magenta","yellow", "black" );
19          var integers1 = [ 2, 4, 6, 8 ];
20          var integers2 = [ 2, , , 8 ];
21
22          outputArray( "Array colors contains", colors );
23          outputArray( "Array integers1 contains", integers1 );
24          outputArray( "Array integers2 contains", integers2 );
25
26          // output the heading followed by a two-column table
27          // containing the subscripts and elements of theArray
28          function outputArray( heading, theArray )
29          {
30             document.writeln( "<h2>" + heading + "</h2>" );
31             document.writeln( "<table border = \"1\"" );
32             document.writeln( "<thead><th>Subscript</th>" +
33                "<th>Value</th></thead><tbody>" );
34
35             // output the subscript and value of each array element
36             for ( var i = 0; i < theArray.length; i++ )
37                document.writeln( "<tr><td>" + i + "</td><td>" +
38                   theArray[ i ] + "</td></tr>" );
39
40             document.writeln( "</tbody></table>" );
41          } // end function outputArray
42          // -->
43       </script>
44    </head><body></body>
45 </html>
```

Fig. 10.4 | Declaring and initializing arrays. (Part 1 of 2.)

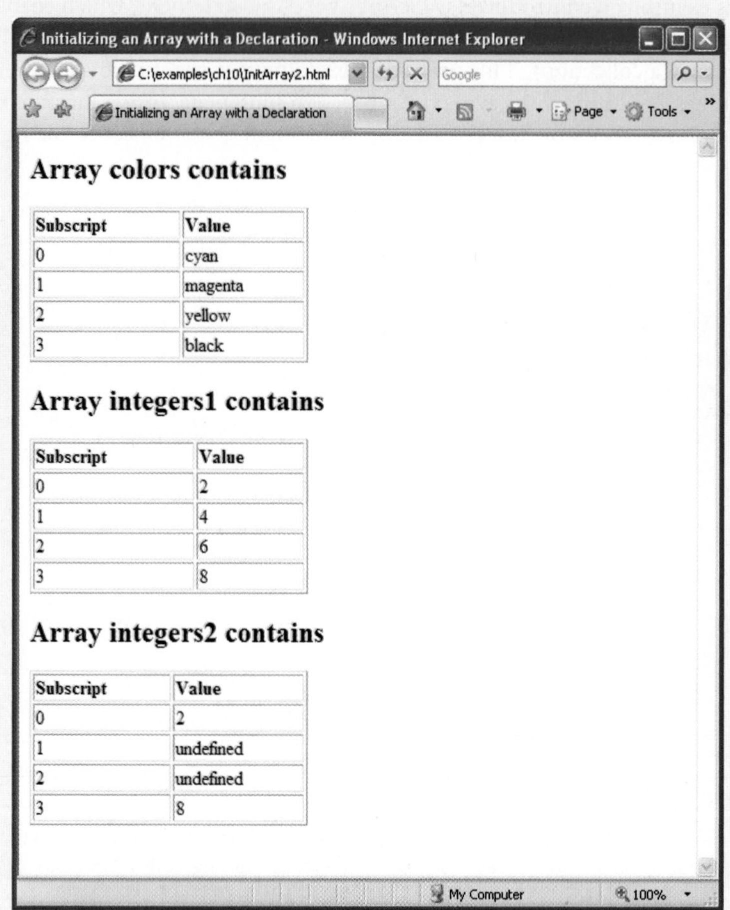

Fig. 10.4 | Declaring and initializing arrays. (Part 2 of 2.)

```
<?xml version = "1.0" encoding = "utf-8"?>
<!DOCTYPE html PUBLIC "-//W3C//DTD XHTML 1.0 Strict//EN"
   "http://www.w3.org/TR/xhtml1/DTD/xhtml1-strict.dtd">

<!-- Fig. 10.5: SumArray.html -->
<!-- Summing elements of an array. -->
<html xmlns = "http://www.w3.org/1999/xhtml">
   <head>
      <title>Sum the Elements of an Array</title>

      <script type = "text/javascript">
         <!--
         var theArray = [ 1, 2, 3, 4, 5, 6, 7, 8, 9, 10 ];
         var total1 = 0, total2 = 0;

```

Fig. 10.5 | Summing elements of an array. (Part 1 of 2.)

```
         // iterates through the elements of the array in order and adds
         // each element's value to total1
         for ( var i = 0; i < theArray.length; i++ )
            total1 += theArray[ i ];

         document.writeln( "Total using subscripts: " + total1 );

         // iterates through the elements of the array using a for... in
         // statement to add each element's value to total2
         for ( var element in theArray )
            total2 += theArray[ element ];

         document.writeln( "<br />Total using for...in: " + total2 );
         // -->
      </script>
   </head><body></body>
</html>
```

Fig. 10.5 | Summing elements of an array. (Part 2 of 2.)

word `in` (`theArray` in this case). When using `for...in`, JavaScript automatically determines the number of elements in the array. As the JavaScript interpreter iterates over `theArray`'s elements, variable `element` is assigned a value that can be used as a subscript for `theArray`. In the case of an `Array`, the value assigned is a subscript in the range from `0` up to, but not including, `theArray.length`. Each value is added to `total2` to produce the sum of the elements in the array.

Error-Prevention Tip 10.2

When iterating over all the elements of an `Array`*, use a* `for...in` *statement to ensure that you manipulate only the existing elements of the* `Array`*. Note that a* `for...in` *statement skips any undefined elements in the array.*

Using the Elements of an Array as Counters

In Chapter 9, we indicated that there is a more elegant way to implement the dice-rolling program in Fig. 9.5. The program rolled a single six-sided die 6000 times and used a `switch` statement to total the number of times each value was rolled. An array version of this script is shown in Fig. 10.6. The `switch` statement in Fig. 9.5 is replaced by line 24 of this program. This line uses the random `face` value as the subscript for the array `frequency` to determine which element to increment during each iteration of the loop. Because the random number calculation in line 23 produces numbers from 1 to 6 (the values for a six-sided die), the `frequency` array must be large enough to allow subscript values of 1 to 6. The smallest number of elements required for an array to have these subscript values is seven elements (subscript values from 0 to 6). In this program, we ignore element 0 of array `frequency` and use only the elements that correspond to values on the sides of a die. Also, lines 32–34 of this program use a loop to generate the table that was written one line at a time in Fig. 9.5. Because we can loop through array `frequency` to help produce the output, we do not have to enumerate each XHTML table row as we did in Fig. 9.5.

```
1  <?xml version = "1.0" encoding = "utf-8"?>
2  <!DOCTYPE html PUBLIC "-//W3C//DTD XHTML 1.0 Strict//EN"
3     "http://www.w3.org/TR/xhtml1/DTD/xhtml1-strict.dtd">
4
5  <!-- Fig. 10.6: RollDie.html -->
6  <!-- Dice-rolling program using an array instead of a switch. -->
7  <html xmlns = "http://www.w3.org/1999/xhtml">
8     <head>
9        <title>Roll a Six-Sided Die 6000 Times</title>
10       <style type = "text/css">
11          table { width: 15em }
12          th    { text-align: left }
13       </style>
14       <script type = "text/javascript">
15          <!--
16          var face;
17          var frequency = [ , 0, 0, 0, 0, 0, 0 ]; // leave frequency[0]
18                                                   // uninitialized
19
20          // summarize results
21          for ( var roll = 1; roll <= 6000; ++roll )
22          {
23             face = Math.floor( 1 + Math.random() * 6 );
24             ++frequency[ face ];
25          } // end for
26
27          document.writeln( "<table border = \"1\"><thead>" );
28          document.writeln( "<th>Face</th>" +
29             "<th>Frequency</th></thead><tbody>" );
30
31          // generate entire table of frequencies for each face
32          for ( face = 1; face < frequency.length; ++face )
33             document.writeln( "<tr><td>" + face + "</td><td>" +
34                frequency[ face ] + "</td></tr>" );
35
36          document.writeln( "</tbody></table>" );
37          // -->
38       </script>
39    </head>
40    <body>
41       <p>Click Refresh (or Reload) to run the script again</p>
42    </body>
43 </html>
```

Fig. 10.6 | Dice-rolling program using an array instead of a `switch`. (Part 1 of 2.)

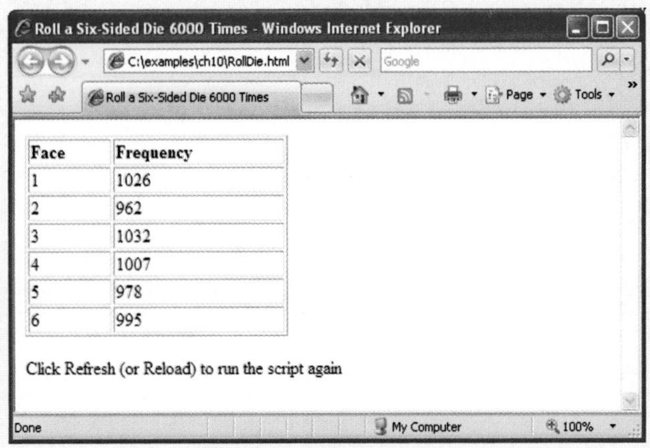

Fig. 10.6 | Dice-rolling program using an array instead of a `switch`. (Part 2 of 2.)

10.5 Random Image Generator Using Arrays

In Chapter 9, we created a random image generator that required image files to be named `1.gif`, `2.gif`, …, `7.gif`. In this example (Fig. 10.7), we create a more elegant random image generator that does not require the image filenames to be integers. This version of the random image generator uses an array `pictures` to store the names of the image files as strings. The script generates a random integer and uses it as a subscript into the `pictures` array. The script outputs an XHTML `img` element whose `src` attribute contains the image filename located in the randomly selected position in the `pictures` array.

```
<?xml version = "1.0" encoding = "utf-8"?>
<!DOCTYPE html PUBLIC "-//W3C//DTD XHTML 1.0 Strict//EN"
   "http://www.w3.org/TR/xhtml1/DTD/xhtml1-strict.dtd">

<!-- Fig. 10.7: RandomPicture2.html -->
<!-- Random image generation using arrays. -->
<html xmlns = "http://www.w3.org/1999/xhtml">
   <head>
      <title>Random Image Generator</title>
      <style type = "text/css">
         table { width: 15em }
         th    { text-align: left }
      </style>
      <script type = "text/javascript">
         <!--
         var pictures =
            [ "CPE", "EPT", "GPP", "GUI", "PERF", "PORT", "SEO" ];

         // pick a random image from the pictures array and displays by
         // creating an img tag and appending the src attribute to the
         // filename
```

Fig. 10.7 | Random image generation using arrays. (Part 1 of 2.)

```
22             document.write ( "<img src = \"" +
23                pictures[ Math.floor( Math.random() * 7 ) ] + ".gif\" />" );
24             // -->
25          </script>
26       </head>
27       <body>
28          <p>Click Refresh (or Reload) to run the script again</p>
29       </body>
30    </html>
```

Fig. 10.7 | Random image generation using arrays. (Part 2 of 2.)

The script declares the array `pictures` in lines 16–17 and initializes it with the names of seven image files. Lines 22–23 create the `img` tag that displays the random image on the web page. Line 22 opens the `img` tag and begins the `src` attribute. Line 23 generates a random integer from 0 to 6 as an index into the `pictures` array, the result of which is a randomly selected image filename. The expression

```
pictures[ Math.floor( Math.random() * 7 ) ]
```

evaluates to a string from the `pictures` array, which then is written to the document (line 23). Line 23 completes the `img` tag with the extension of the image file (`.gif`).

10.6 References and Reference Parameters

Two ways to pass arguments to functions (or methods) in many programming languages are pass-by-value and pass-by-reference. When an argument is passed to a function by value, a *copy* of the argument's value is made and is passed to the called function. In JavaScript, numbers, boolean values and strings are passed to functions by value.

With pass-by-reference, the caller gives the called function direct access to the caller's data and allows it to modify the data if it so chooses. This procedure is accomplished by passing to the called function the actual location in memory (also called the address) where the data resides. Pass-by-reference can improve performance because it can eliminate the overhead of copying large amounts of data, but it can weaken security because the called function can access the caller's data. In JavaScript, all objects (and thus all `Arrays`) are passed to functions by reference.

Error-Prevention Tip 10.3

With pass-by-value, changes to the copy of the called function do not affect the original variable's value in the calling function. This prevents the accidental side effects that so greatly hinder the development of correct and reliable software systems.

Software Engineering Observation 10.2

Unlike some other languages, JavaScript does not allow the programmer to choose whether to pass each argument by value or by reference. Numbers, boolean values and strings are passed by value. Objects are passed to functions by reference. When a function receives a reference to an object, the function can manipulate the object directly.

Software Engineering Observation 10.3

When returning information from a function via a `return` *statement, numbers and boolean values are always returned by value (i.e., a copy is returned), and objects are always returned by reference (i.e., a reference to the object is returned). Note that, in the pass-by-reference case, it is not necessary to return the new value, since the object is already modified.*

To pass a reference to an object into a function, simply specify the reference name in the function call. Normally, the reference name is the identifier that the program uses to manipulate the object. Mentioning the reference by its parameter name in the body of the called function actually refers to the original object in memory, and the original object can be accessed directly by the called function.

`Array`s are objects in JavaScript, so `Array`s are passed to a function by reference—a called function can access the elements of the caller's original `Array`s. The name of an array actually is a reference to an object that contains the array elements and the `length` variable, which indicates the number of elements in the array. In the next section, we demonstrate pass-by-value and pass-by-reference, using arrays.

10.7 Passing Arrays to Functions

To pass an array argument to a function, specify the name of the array (a reference to the array) without brackets. For example, if array `hourlyTemperatures` has been declared as

```
var hourlyTemperatures = new Array( 24 );
```

then the function call

```
modifyArray( hourlyTemperatures );
```

passes array `hourlyTemperatures` to function `modifyArray`. As stated in Section 10.2, every array object in JavaScript knows its own size (via the `length` attribute). Thus, when we pass an array object into a function, we do not pass the size of the array separately as an argument. Figure 10.3 illustrated this concept when we passed `Array`s `n1` and `n2` to function `outputArray` to display each `Array`'s contents.

Although entire arrays are passed by reference, *individual numeric and boolean array elements* are passed *by value* exactly as simple numeric and boolean variables are passed (the objects referred to by individual elements of an `Array` of objects are still passed by reference). Such simple single pieces of data are called **scalars**, or **scalar quantities**. To pass an array element to a function, use the subscripted name of the element as an argument in the function call.

```
<?xml version = "1.0" encoding = "utf-8"?>
<!DOCTYPE html PUBLIC "-//W3C//DTD XHTML 1.0 Strict//EN"
   "http://www.w3.org/TR/xhtml1/DTD/xhtml1-strict.dtd">

<!-- Fig. 10.8: PassArray.html -->
<!-- Passing arrays and individual array elements to functions. -->
<html xmlns = "http://www.w3.org/1999/xhtml">
   <head>
      <title>Passing arrays and individual array
         elements to functions</title>
      <script type = "text/javascript">
         <!--
         var a = [ 1, 2, 3, 4, 5 ];

         document.writeln( "<h2>Effects of passing entire " +
            "array by reference</h2>" );
         outputArray( "Original array: ", a );

         modifyArray( a );  // array a passed by reference

         outputArray( "Modified array: ", a );

         document.writeln( "<h2>Effects of passing array " +
            "element by value</h2>" +
            "a[3] before modifyElement: " + a[ 3 ] );

         modifyElement( a[ 3 ] ); // array element a[3] passed by value

         document.writeln( "<br />a[3] after modifyElement: " + a[ 3 ] );

         // outputs heading followed by the contents of "theArray"
         function outputArray( heading, theArray )
         {
            document.writeln(
               heading + theArray.join( " " ) + "<br />" );
         } // end function outputArray

         // function that modifies the elements of an array
         function modifyArray( theArray )
         {
            for ( var j in theArray )
               theArray[ j ] *= 2;
         } // end function modifyArray

         // function that modifies the value passed
         function modifyElement( e )
         {
            e *= 2; // scales element e only for the duration of the
                    // function
            document.writeln( "<br />value in modifyElement: " + e );
         } // end function modifyElement
         // -->
      </script>
```

Fig. 10.8 | Passing arrays and individual array elements to functions. (Part 1 of 2.)

```
54      </head><body></body>
55   </html>
```

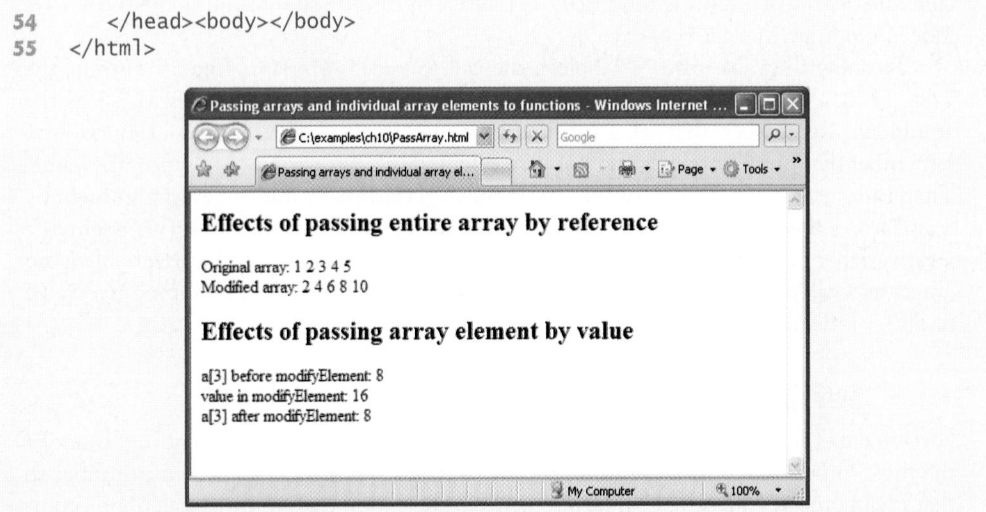

Fig. 10.8 | Passing arrays and individual array elements to functions. (Part 2 of 2.)

For a function to receive an `Array` through a function call, the function's parameter list must specify a parameter that will refer to the `Array` in the body of the function. Unlike other programming languages, JavaScript does not provide a special syntax for this purpose. JavaScript simply requires that the identifier for the `Array` be specified in the parameter list. For example, the function header for function `modifyArray` might be written as

```
function modifyArray( b )
```

indicating that `modifyArray` expects to receive a parameter named `b` (the argument supplied in the calling function must be an `Array`). Arrays are passed by reference, and therefore when the called function uses the array name `b`, it refers to the actual array in the caller (array `hourlyTemperatures` in the preceding call). The script in Fig. 10.8 demonstrates the difference between passing an entire array and passing an array element.

Software Engineering Observation 10.4

JavaScript does not check the number of arguments or types of arguments that are passed to a function. It is possible to pass any number of values to a function. JavaScript will attempt to perform conversions when the values are used.

The statement in line 17 invokes function `outputArray` to display the contents of array `a` before it is modified. Function `outputArray` (defined in lines 32–36) receives a string to output and the array to output. The statement in lines 34–35 uses `Array` method `join` to create a string containing all the elements in `theArray`. Method `join` takes as its argument a string containing the separator that should be used to separate the elements of the array in the string that is returned. If the argument is not specified, the empty string is used as the separator.

Line 19 invokes function `modifyArray` (lines 39–43) and passes it array `a`. The `modifyArray` function multiplies each element by 2. To illustrate that array `a`'s elements were modified, the statement in line 21 invokes function `outputArray` again to display the contents of array a after it is modified. As the screen capture shows, the elements of a are indeed modified by modifyArray.

To show the value of a[3] before the call to modifyElement, line 25 outputs the value of a[3]. Line 27 invokes modifyElement (lines 46–51) and passes a[3] as the argument. Remember that a[3] actually is one integer value in the array a. Also remember that numeric values and boolean values are always passed to functions by value. Therefore, a copy of a[3] is passed. Function modifyElement multiplies its argument by 2 and stores the result in its parameter e. The parameter of function modifyElement is a local variable in that function, so when the function terminates, the local variable is no longer accessible. Thus, when control is returned to the main script, the unmodified value of a[3] is displayed by the statement in line 29.

10.8 Sorting Arrays

Sorting data (putting data in a particular order, such as ascending or descending) is one of the most important computing functions. A bank sorts all checks by account number so that it can prepare individual bank statements at the end of each month. Telephone companies sort their lists of accounts by last name and, within that, by first name, to make it easy to find phone numbers. Virtually every organization must sort some data—in many cases, massive amounts of data. Sorting data is an intriguing problem that has attracted some of the most intense research efforts in the field of computer science.

The Array object in JavaScript has a built-in method **sort** for sorting arrays. Figure 10.9 demonstrates the Array object's sort method.

```
<?xml version = "1.0" encoding = "utf-8"?>
<!DOCTYPE html PUBLIC "-//W3C//DTD XHTML 1.0 Strict//EN"
   "http://www.w3.org/TR/xhtml1/DTD/xhtml1-strict.dtd">

<!-- Fig. 10.9: Sort.html -->
<!-- Sorting an array with sort. -->
<html xmlns = "http://www.w3.org/1999/xhtml">
   <head>
      <title>Sorting an Array with Array Method sort</title>
      <script type = "text/javascript">
         <!--
         var a = [ 10, 1, 9, 2, 8, 3, 7, 4, 6, 5 ];

         document.writeln( "<h1>Sorting an Array</h1>" );
         outputArray( "Data items in original order: ", a );
         a.sort( compareIntegers );  // sort the array
         outputArray( "Data items in ascending order: ", a );

         // output the heading followed by the contents of theArray
         function outputArray( heading, theArray )
         {
            document.writeln( "<p>" + heading +
               theArray.join( " " ) + "</p>" );
         } // end function outputArray
```

Fig. 10.9 | Sorting an array with sort. (Part 1 of 2.)

```
25
26             // comparison function for use with sort
27             function compareIntegers( value1, value2 )
28             {
29                return parseInt( value1 ) - parseInt( value2 );
30             } // end function compareIntegers
31             // -->
32          </script>
33       </head><body></body>
34    </html>
```

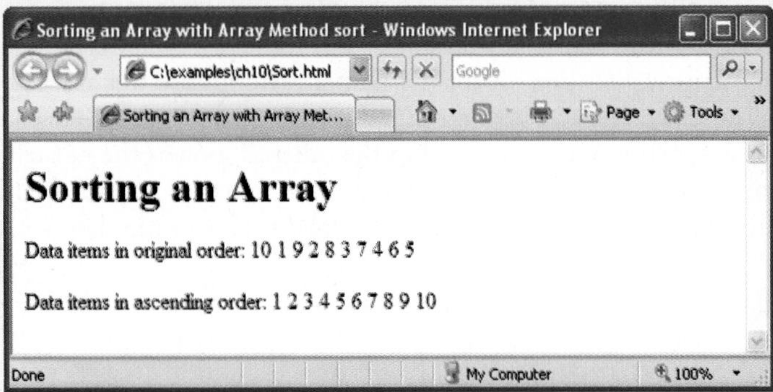

Fig. 10.9 | Sorting an array with `sort`. (Part 2 of 2.)

By default, `Array` method `sort` (with no arguments) uses string comparisons to determine the sorting order of the `Array` elements. The strings are compared by the ASCII values of their characters. [*Note:* String comparison is discussed in more detail in Chapter 11, JavaScript: Objects.] In this example, we'd like to sort an array of integers.

Method `sort` takes as its optional argument the name of a function (called the **comparator function**) that compares its two arguments and returns one of the following:

- a negative value if the first argument is less than the second argument
- zero if the arguments are equal, or
- a positive value if the first argument is greater than the second argument

This example uses function `compareIntegers` (defined in lines 27–30) as the comparator function for method `sort`. It calculates the difference between the integer values of its two arguments (function `parseInt` ensures that the arguments are handled properly as integers). If the first argument is less than the second argument, the difference will be a negative value. If the arguments are equal, the difference will be zero. If the first argument is greater than the second argument, the difference will be a positive value.

Line 16 invokes `Array` object `a`'s `sort` method and passes function `compareIntegers` as an argument. Method `sort` receives function `compareIntegers` as an argument, then uses the function to compare elements of the `Array` `a` to determine their sorting order.

Software Engineering Observation 10.5

Functions in JavaScript are considered to be data. Therefore, functions can be assigned to variables, stored in `Arrays` and passed to functions just like other data types.

10.9 Searching Arrays: Linear Search and Binary Search

Often, a programmer will be working with large amounts of data stored in arrays. It may be necessary to determine whether an array contains a value that matches a certain key value. The process of locating a particular element value in an array is called searching. In this section we discuss two searching techniques—the simple linear search technique (Fig. 10.10) and the more efficient binary search technique (Fig. 10.11).

Searching an Array with Linear Search

The script in Fig. 10.10 performs a linear search on an array. Function `linearSearch` (defined in lines 42–50) uses a `for` statement containing an `if` statement to compare each element of an array with a search key (lines 45–47). If the search key is found, the function returns the subscript value (line 47) of the element to indicate the exact position of the search key in the array. [*Note:* The loop (lines 45–47) in the `linearSearch` function terminates, and the function returns control to the caller as soon as the `return` statement in its body executes.] If the search key is not found, the function returns a value of `-1`. The function returns the value `-1` because it is not a valid subscript number.

```
1  <?xml version = "1.0" encoding = "utf-8"?>
2  <!DOCTYPE html PUBLIC "-//W3C//DTD XHTML 1.0 Strict//EN"
3     "http://www.w3.org/TR/xhtml1/DTD/xhtml1-strict.dtd">
4
5  <!-- Fig. 10.10: LinearSearch.html -->
6  <!-- Linear search of an array. -->
7  <html xmlns = "http://www.w3.org/1999/xhtml">
8     <head>
9        <title>Linear Search of an Array</title>
10       <script type = "text/javascript">
11          <!--
12          var a = new Array( 100 );  // create an Array
13
14          // fill Array with even integer values from 0 to 198
15          for ( var i = 0; i < a.length; ++i )
16             a[ i ] = 2 * i;
17
18          // function called when "Search" button is pressed
19          function buttonPressed()
20          {
21             // get the input text field
22             var inputVal = document.getElementById( "inputVal" );
23
24             // get the result text field
25             var result = document.getElementById( "result" );
26
27             // get the search key from the input text field
28             var searchKey = inputVal.value;
29
30             // Array a is passed to linearSearch even though it
31             // is a global variable. Normally an array will
32             // be passed to a method for searching.
```

Fig. 10.10 | Linear search of an array. (Part 1 of 2.)

```
            var element = linearSearch( a, parseInt( searchKey ) );

            if ( element != -1 )
               result.value = "Found value in element " + element;
            else
               result.value = "Value not found";
         } // end function buttonPressed

         // Search "theArray" for the specified "key" value
         function linearSearch( theArray, key )
         {
            // iterates through each element of the array in order
            for ( var n = 0; n < theArray.length; ++n )
               if ( theArray[ n ] == key )
                  return n;

            return -1;
         } // end function linearSearch
         // -->
      </script>
   </head>

   <body>
      <form action = "">
         <p>Enter integer search key<br />
         <input id = "inputVal" type = "text" />
         <input type = "button" value = "Search"
                onclick = "buttonPressed()" /><br /></p>
         <p>Result<br />
         <input id = "result" type = "text" size = "30" /></p>
      </form>
   </body>
</html>
```

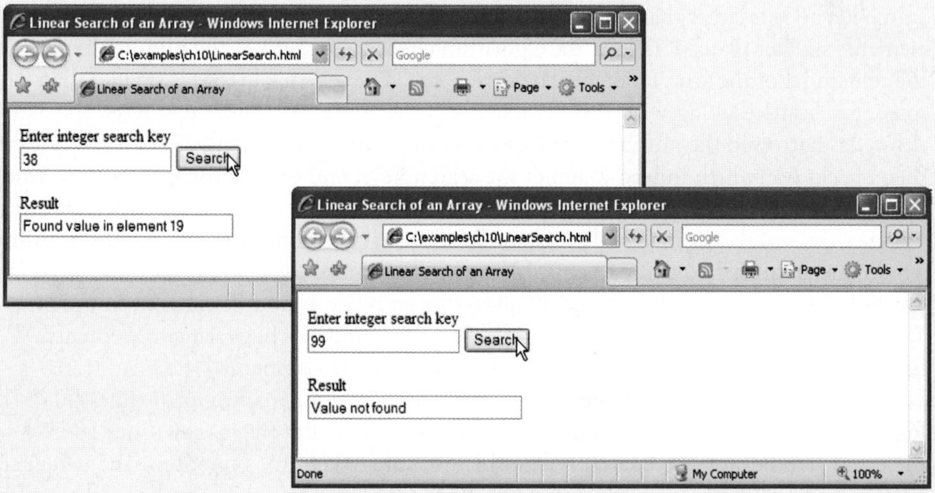

Fig. 10.10 | Linear search of an array. (Part 2 of 2.)

If the array being searched is not in any particular order, the value is just as likely to be found in the first element as the last. On average, therefore, the program will have to compare the search key with half the elements of the array.

The program contains a 100-element array (defined in line 12) filled with the even integers from 0 to 198. The user types the search key in a text field (defined in the XHTML form in lines 56–63) and clicks the **Search** button to start the search. [*Note:* The array is passed to `linearSearch` even though the array is a global script variable. We do this because arrays are normally passed to functions for searching.]

Searching an Array with Binary Search

The linear search method works well for small arrays or for unsorted arrays. However, for large arrays, linear searching is inefficient. The **binary search algorithm** is more efficient, but it requires that the array be sorted. The first iteration of this algorithm tests the middle element in the array. If this matches the search key, the algorithm ends. Assuming the array is sorted in ascending order, then if the search key is less than the middle element, it cannot match any element in the second half of the array and the algorithm continues with only the first half of the array (i.e., the first element up to, but not including, the middle element). If the search key is greater than the middle element, it cannot match any element in the first half of the array and the algorithm continues with only the second half of the array (i.e., the element after the middle element through the last element). Each iteration tests the middle value of the remaining portion of the array. If the search key does not match the element, the algorithm eliminates half of the remaining elements. The algorithm ends by either finding an element that matches the search key or reducing the subarray to zero size.

As an example consider the sorted 15-element array

```
2  3  5  10  27  30  34  51  56  65  77  81  82  93  99
```

and a search key of 65. A program implementing the binary search algorithm would first check whether 51 is the search key (because 51 is the middle element of the array). The search key (65) is larger than 51, so 51 is discarded along with the first half of the array (all elements smaller than 51.) Next, the algorithm checks whether 81 (the middle element of the remainder of the array) matches the search key. The search key (65) is smaller than 81, so 81 is discarded along with the elements larger than 81. After just two tests, the algorithm has narrowed the number of values to check to three (56, 65 and 77). The algorithm then checks 65 (which indeed matches the search key), and returns the index of the array element containing 65. This algorithm required just three comparisons to determine whether the search key matched an element of the array. Using a linear search algorithm would have required 10 comparisons. [*Note:* In this example, we have chosen to use an array with 15 elements so that there will always be an obvious middle element in the array. With an even number of elements, the middle of the array lies between two elements. We implement the algorithm to choose the lower of those two elements.]

Figure 10.11 presents the iterative version of function `binarySearch` (lines 40–64). Function `binarySearch` is called from line 31 of function `buttonPressed` (lines 18–37)—the event handler for the **Search** button in the XHTML form. Function `binarySearch` receives two arguments—an array called `theArray` (the array to search) and `key` (the search key). The array is passed to `binarySearch` even though the array is a global variable. Once again, we do this because an array is normally passed to a function for searching. If `key` matches the `middle` element of a subarray (line 55), `middle` (the subscript of the current element) is returned, to indicate that the value was found and the search is complete. If `key` does not match the `middle` element of a subarray, the `low` subscript or the `high` subscript (both declared in the function) is adjusted, so that a smaller subarray can be searched. If `key` is less than the middle element (line 57), the `high` subscript is set to `middle - 1` and the search is continued on the elements from `low` to `middle - 1`. If `key` is greater than the middle element (line 59), the `low` subscript is set to `middle + 1` and the search is continued on the elements from `middle + 1` to `high`. These comparisons are performed by the nested `if...else` statement in lines 55–60.

```
1  <?xml version = "1.0" encoding = "utf-8"?>
2  <!DOCTYPE html PUBLIC "-//W3C//DTD XHTML 1.0 Strict//EN"
3     "http://www.w3.org/TR/xhtml1/DTD/xhtml1-strict.dtd">
4  
5  <!-- Fig. 10.11: BinarySearch.html -->
6  <!-- Binary search of an array. -->
7  <html xmlns = "http://www.w3.org/1999/xhtml">
8     <head>
9        <title>Binary Search</title>
10       <script type = "text/javascript">
11          <!--
12          var a = new Array( 15 );
13 
14          for ( var i = 0; i < a.length; ++i )
15             a[ i ] = 2 * i;
16 
17          // function called when "Search" button is pressed
18          function buttonPressed()
19          {
20             var inputVal = document.getElementById( "inputVal" );
21             var result = document.getElementById( "result" );
22             var searchKey = inputVal.value;
23 
24             result.value = "Portions of array searched\n";
25 
26             // Array a is passed to binarySearch even though it
27             // is a global variable. This is done because
28             // normally an array is passed to a method
29             // for searching.
30             var element =
31                binarySearch( a, parseInt( searchKey ) );
32 
33             if ( element != -1 )
34                result.value += "\nFound value in element " + element;
35             else
36                result.value += "\nValue not found";
37          } // end function buttonPressed
38 
```

Fig. 10.11 | Binary search of an array. (Part 1 of 3.)

```
         // binary search function
         function binarySearch( theArray, key )
         {
            var low = 0; // low subscript
            var high = theArray.length - 1; // high subscript
            var middle; // middle subscript

            while ( low <= high ) {
               middle = ( low + high ) / 2;

               // The following line is used to display the
               // part of theArray currently being manipulated
               // during each iteration of the binary
               // search loop.
               buildOutput( theArray, low, middle, high );

               if ( key == theArray[ middle ] )  // match
                  return middle;
               else if ( key < theArray[ middle ] )
                  high = middle - 1; // search low end of array
               else
                  low = middle + 1; // search high end of array
            } // end while

            return -1;   // searchKey not found
         } // end function binarySearch

         // Build one row of output showing the current
         // part of the array being processed.
         function buildOutput( theArray, low, mid, high )
         {
            var result = document.getElementById( "result" );

            for ( var i = 0; i < theArray.length; i++ )
            {
               if ( i < low || i > high )
                  result.value += "    ";
               else if ( i == mid ) // mark middle element in output
                  result.value += theArray[ i ] +
                     ( theArray[ i ] < 10 ? "*  " : "* " );
               else
                  result.value += theArray[ i ] +
                     ( theArray[ i ] < 10 ? "   " : "  " );
            } // end for

            result.value += "\n";
         } // end function buildOutput
         // -->
      </script>
   </head>

```

Fig. 10.11 | Binary search of an array. (Part 2 of 3.)

```
   <body>
      <form action = "">
         <p>Enter integer search key<br />
         <input id = "inputVal" type = "text" />
         <input type = "button" value = "Search"
            onclick = "buttonPressed()" /><br /></p>
         <p>Result<br />
         <textarea id = "result" rows = "7" cols = "60">
         </textarea></p>
      </form>
   </body>
</html>
```

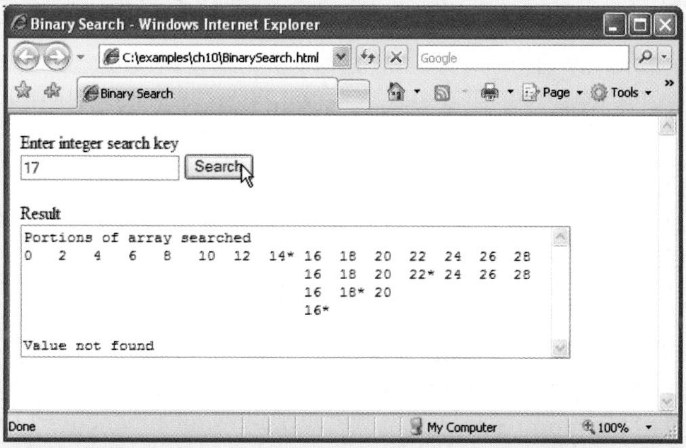

Binary Search - Windows Internet Explorer
C:\examples\ch10\BinarySearch.html
Binary Search
Enter integer search key
17
Search
Result
Portions of array searched
0 2 4 6 8 10 12 14* 16 18 20 22 24 26 28
16 18 20 22* 24 26 28
16 18* 20
16*
Value not found
Done
My Computer
100%

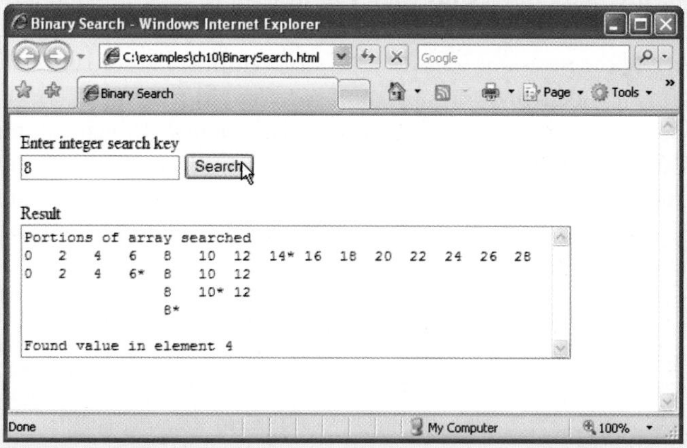

Binary Search - Windows Internet Explorer
C:\examples\ch10\BinarySearch.html
Binary Search
Enter integer search key
8
Search
Result
Portions of array searched
0 2 4 6 8 10 12 14* 16 18 20 22 24 26 28
0 2 4 6* 8 10 12
8 10* 12
8*
Found value in element 4
Done
My Computer
100%

Fig. 10.11 | Binary search of an array. (Part 3 of 3.)

In a worst-case scenario, searching an array of 1023 elements will take only 10 comparisons using a binary search. Repeatedly dividing 1024 by 2 (because after each comparison we are able to eliminate half of the array) yields the values 512, 256, 128, 64, 32, 16, 8, 4, 2 and 1. The number 1024 (2^{10}) is divided by 2 only ten times to get the value 1. Dividing by 2 is equivalent to one comparison in the binary search algorithm. An array of about one million elements takes a maximum of 20 comparisons to find the key. An array of about one billion elements takes a maximum of 30 comparisons to find the key. When searching a sorted array, this is a tremendous increase in performance over the linear search that required comparing the search key to an average of half the elements in the array. For a one-billion-element array, this is the difference between an average of 500 million comparisons and a maximum of 30 comparisons! The maximum number of comparisons needed for the binary search of any sorted array is the exponent of the first power of 2 greater than the number of elements in the array.

Our program uses a 15-element array (defined at line 12). The first power of 2 greater than the number of elements is 16 (2^4), so `binarySearch` requires at most four comparisons to find the `key`. To illustrate this, line 53 calls method `buildOutput` (declared in lines 68–85) to output each subarray during the binary search process. Method `buildOutput` marks the middle element in each subarray with an asterisk (*) to indicate the element with which the `key` is compared. No matter what search key is entered, each search in this example results in a maximum of four lines of output—one per comparison.

10.10 Multidimensional Arrays

Multidimensional arrays with two subscripts are often used to represent tables of values consisting of information arranged in **rows** and **columns**. To identify a particular table element, we must specify the two subscripts; by convention, the first identifies the element's row, and the second identifies the element's column. Arrays that require two subscripts to identify a particular element are called **two-dimensional arrays**.

Multidimensional arrays can have more than two dimensions. JavaScript does not support multidimensional arrays directly, but does allow the programmer to specify arrays whose elements are also arrays, thus achieving the same effect. When an array contains one-dimensional arrays as its elements, we can imagine these one-dimensional arrays as rows of a table, and the positions in these arrays as columns. Figure 10.12 illustrates a two-dimensional array named a that contains three rows and four columns (i.e., a three-by-four array—three one-dimensional arrays, each with 4 elements). In general, an array with *m* rows and *n* columns is called an ***m*-by-*n* array**.

Every element in array a is identified in Fig. 10.12 by an element name of the form `a[ i ][ j ]`; `a` is the name of the array, and `i` and `j` are the subscripts that uniquely identify

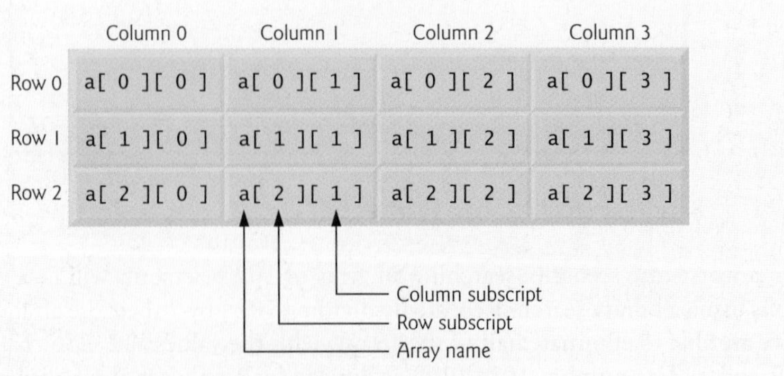

Fig. 10.12 | Two-dimensional array with three rows and four columns.

the row and column, respectively, of each element in a. Note that the names of the elements in the first row all have a first subscript of 0; the names of the elements in the fourth column all have a second subscript of 3.

Arrays of One-Dimensional Arrays

Multidimensional arrays can be initialized in declarations like a one-dimensional array. Array b with two rows and two columns could be declared and initialized with the statement

```
var b = [ [ 1, 2 ], [ 3, 4 ] ];
```

The values are grouped by row in square brackets. The array [1, 2] initializes element b[0], and the array [3, 4] initializes element b[1]. So 1 and 2 initialize b[0][0] and b[0][1], respectively. Similarly, 3 and 4 initialize b[1][0] and b[1][1], respectively. The interpreter determines the number of rows by counting the number of sub initializer lists—arrays nested within the outermost array. The interpreter determines the number of columns in each row by counting the number of values in the sub-array that initializes the row.

Two-Dimensional Arrays with Rows of Different Lengths

The rows of a two-dimensional array can vary in length. The declaration

```
var b = [ [ 1, 2 ], [ 3, 4, 5 ] ];
```

creates array b with row 0 containing two elements (1 and 2) and row 1 containing three elements (3, 4 and 5).

Creating Two-Dimensional Arrays with **new**

A multidimensional array in which each row has a different number of columns can be allocated dynamically, as follows:

```
var b;
b = new Array( 2 );        // allocate rows
b[ 0 ] = new Array( 5 );  // allocate columns for row 0
b[ 1 ] = new Array( 3 );  // allocate columns for row 1
```

The preceding code creates a two-dimensional array with two rows. Row 0 has five columns, and row 1 has three columns.

Two-Dimensional Array Example: Displaying Element Values

Figure 10.13 initializes two-dimensional arrays in declarations and uses nested for...in loops to traverse the arrays (i.e., manipulate every element of the array).

```
<?xml version = "1.0" encoding = "utf-8"?>
<!DOCTYPE html PUBLIC "-//W3C//DTD XHTML 1.0 Strict//EN"
   "http://www.w3.org/TR/xhtml1/DTD/xhtml1-strict.dtd">

<!-- Fig. 10.13: InitArray3.html -->
<!-- Initializing multidimensional arrays. -->
<html xmlns = "http://www.w3.org/1999/xhtml">
```

Fig. 10.13 | Initializing multidimensional arrays. (Part 1 of 2.)

```
   <head>
      <title>Initializing Multidimensional Arrays</title>
      <script type = "text/javascript">
         <!--
         var array1 = [ [ 1, 2, 3 ], // first row
                        [ 4, 5, 6 ] ]; // second row
         var array2 = [ [ 1, 2 ], // first row
                        [ 3 ], // second row
                        [ 4, 5, 6 ] ]; // third row

         outputArray( "Values in array1 by row", array1 );
         outputArray( "Values in array2 by row", array2 );

         function outputArray( heading, theArray )
         {
            document.writeln( "<h2>" + heading + "</h2><pre>" );

            // iterates through the set of one-dimensional arrays
            for ( var i in theArray )
            {
               // iterates through the elements of each one-dimensional
               // array
               for ( var j in theArray[ i ] )
                  document.write( theArray[ i ][ j ] + " " );

               document.writeln( "<br />" );
            } // end for

            document.writeln( "</pre>" );
         } // end function outputArray
         // -->
      </script>
   </head><body></body>
</html>
```

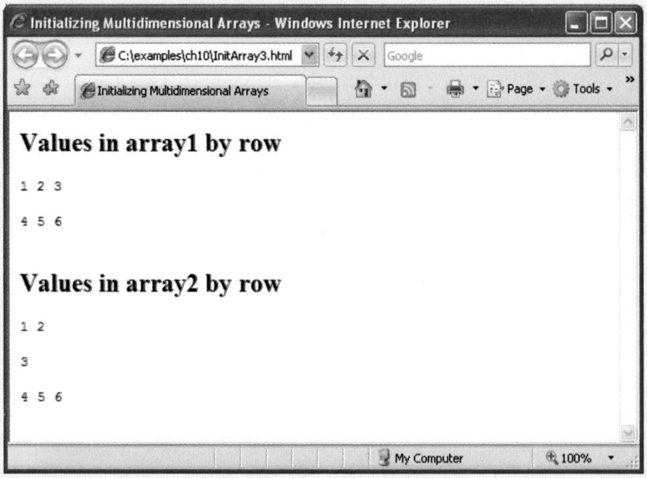

Fig. 10.13 | Initializing multidimensional arrays. (Part 2 of 2.)

The program declares two arrays in main script (in the XHTML head element). The declaration of array1 (lines 12–13 provides six initializers in two sublists. The first sublist initializes the first row of the array to the values 1, 2 and 3; the second sublist initializes the second row of the array to the values 4, 5 and 6. The declaration of array2 (lines 14–16) provides six initializers in three sublists. The sublist for the first row explicitly initializes the first row to have two elements, with values 1 and 2, respectively. The sublist for the second row initializes the second row to have one element, with value 3. The sublist for the third row initializes the third row to the values 4, 5 and 6.

The script calls function outputArray from lines 18–19 to display each array's elements in the web page. Function outputArray (lines 21–37) receives two arguments—a string heading to output before the array and the array to output (called theArray). Note the use of a nested for...in statement to output the rows of each two-dimensional array. The outer for...in statement iterates over the rows of the array. The inner for...in statement iterates over the columns of the current row being processed. The nested for...in statement in this example could have been written with for statements, as follows:

```
for ( var i = 0; i < theArray.length; ++i ) {

   for ( var j = 0; j < theArray[ i ].length; ++j )
      document.write( theArray[ i ][ j ] + " " );

   document.writeln( "<br />" );
}
```

In the outer for statement, the expression theArray.length determines the number of rows in the array. In the inner for statement, the expression theArray[i].length determines the number of columns in each row of the array. This condition enables the loop to determine, for each row, the exact number of columns.

Common Multidimensional-Array Manipulations with **for** *and* **for...in** *Statements*

Many common array manipulations use for or for...in repetition statements. For example, the following for statement sets all the elements in the third row of array a in Fig. 10.12 to zero:

```
for ( var col = 0; col < a[ 2 ].length; ++col )
   a[ 2 ][ col ] = 0;
```

We specified the *third* row; therefore, we know that the first subscript is always 2 (0 is the first row and 1 is the second row). The for loop varies only the second subscript (i.e., the column subscript). The preceding for statement is equivalent to the assignment statements

```
a[ 2 ][ 0 ] = 0;
a[ 2 ][ 1 ] = 0;
a[ 2 ][ 2 ] = 0;
a[ 2 ][ 3 ] = 0;
```

The following for...in statement is also equivalent to the preceding for statement:

```
for ( var col in a[ 2 ] )
   a[ 2 ][ col ] = 0;
```

The following nested for statement determines the total of all the elements in array a:

```
var total = 0;

for ( var row = 0; row < a.length; ++row )

   for ( var col = 0; col < a[ row ].length; ++col )
      total += a[ row ][ col ];
```

The for statement totals the elements of the array, one row at a time. The outer for statement begins by setting the row subscript to 0, so that the elements of the first row may be totaled by the inner for statement. The outer for statement then increments row to 1, so that the elements of the second row can be totaled. Then the outer for statement increments row to 2, so that the elements of the third row can be totaled. The result can be displayed when the nested for statement terminates. The preceding for statement is equivalent to the following for...in statement:

```
var total = 0;

for ( var row in a )

   for ( var col in a[ row ] )
      total += a[ row ][ col ];
```

10.11 Building an Online Quiz

Online quizzes and polls are popular web applications often used for educational purposes or just for fun. Web developers typically build quizzes using simple XHTML forms and process the results with JavaScript. Arrays allow a programmer to represent several possible answer choices in a single data structure. Figure 10.14 contains an online quiz consisting of one question. The quiz page contains one of the tip icons used throughout this book and an XHTML form in which the user identifies the type of tip the image represents by selecting one of four radio buttons. After the user selects one of the radio button choices and submits the form, the script determines whether the user selected the correct type of tip to match the mystery image. The JavaScript function that checks the user's answer combines several of the concepts from the current chapter and previous chapters in a concise and useful script.

Before we discuss the script code, we first discuss the body element (lines 25–48) of the XHTML document. The body's GUI components play an important role in the script.

Lines 26–47 define the form that presents the quiz to users. Line 26 begins the form element and specifies the onsubmit attribute to "checkAnswers()", indicating that the interpreter should execute the JavaScript function checkAnswers (lines 12–21) when the user submits the form (i.e., clicks the **Submit** button or presses *Enter*).

Line 29 adds the tip image to the page. Lines 32–42 display the radio buttons and corresponding labels that display possible answer choices. Lines 44–45 add the submit and reset buttons to the page.

We now examine the script used to check the answer submitted by the user. Lines 12–21 declare the function checkAnswers that contains all the JavaScript required to grade the quiz. The if...else statement in lines 17–20 determines whether the user answered the question correctly. The image that the user is asked to identify is the Error-Prevention Tip icon. Thus the correct answer to the quiz corresponds to the second radio button.

An XHTML form's elements can be accessed individually using `getElementById` or through the **`elements` property** of the containing `form` object. The `elements` property

```
<?xml version = "1.0" encoding = "utf-8"?>
<!DOCTYPE html PUBLIC "-//W3C//DTD XHTML 1.0 Strict//EN"
   "http://www.w3.org/TR/xhtml1/DTD/xhtml1-strict.dtd">

<!-- Fig. 10.14: quiz.html -->
<!-- Online quiz graded with JavaScript. -->
<html xmlns = "http://www.w3.org/1999/xhtml">
   <head>
      <title>Online Quiz</title>
      <script type = "text/JavaScript">
         <!--
         function checkAnswers()
         {
            var myQuiz = document.getElementById( "myQuiz" );

            // determine whether the answer is correct
            if ( myQuiz.elements[ 1 ].checked )
               alert( "Congratulations, your answer is correct" );
            else // if the answer is incorrect
               alert( "Your answer is incorrect. Please try again" );
         } // end function checkAnswers
         -->
      </script>
   </head>
   <body>
      <form id = "myQuiz" onsubmit = "checkAnswers()" action = "">
         <p>Select the name of the tip that goes with the
            image shown:<br />
            <img src="EPT.gif" alt="mystery tip"/>
            <br />

            <input type = "radio" name = "radiobutton" value = "CPE" />
            <label>Common Programming Error</label>

            <input type = "radio" name = "radiobutton" value = "EPT" />
            <label>Error-Prevention Tip</label>

            <input type = "radio" name = "radiobutton" value = "PERF" />
            <label>Performance Tip</label>

            <input type = "radio" name = "radiobutton" value = "PORT" />
            <label>Portability Tip</label><br />

            <input type = "submit" name = "submit" value = "Submit" />
            <input type = "reset" name = "reset" value = "Reset" />
         </p>
      </form>
   </body>
</html>
```

Fig. 10.14 | Online quiz graded with JavaScript. (Part 1 of 2.)

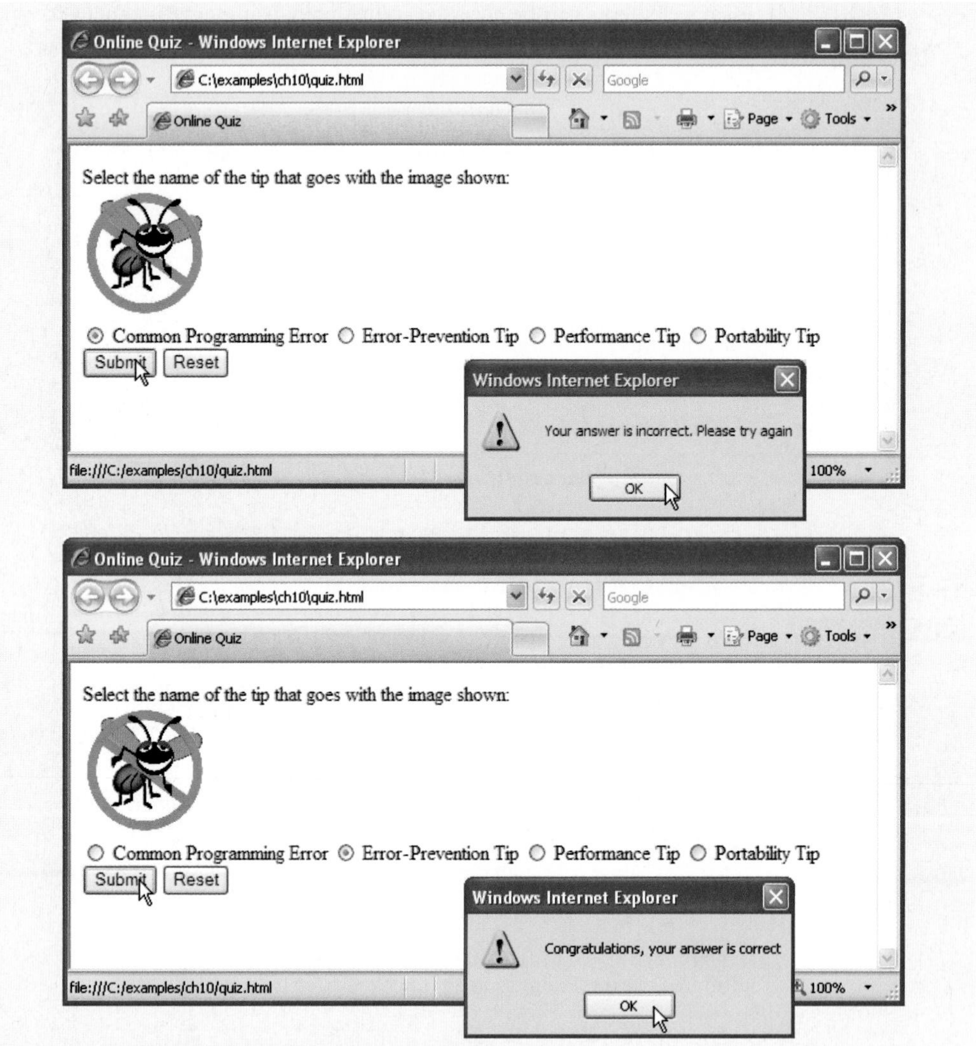

Fig. 10.14 | Online quiz graded with JavaScript. (Part 2 of 2.)

contains an array of all the `form`'s controls. The radio buttons are part of the XHTML form `myQuiz`, so we access the elements array in line 17 using dot notation (`myQuiz.elements[ 1 ]`). The array element `myQuiz.elements[ 1 ]` corresponds to the correct answer (i.e., the second radio button). Finally, line 17 determines whether the property **checked** of the second radio button is `true`. Property `checked` of a radio button is `true` when the radio button is selected, and it is `false` when the radio button is not selected. Recall that only one radio button may be selected at any given time. If property `myQuiz.elements[ 1 ].checked` is `true`, indicating that the correct answer is selected, the script alerts a congratulatory message. If property `checked` of the radio button is `false`, then the script alerts an alternate message (line 20).

10.12 Wrap-Up

In this chapter, we discussed how to store related data items into an array structure. After demonstrating the declaration and initialization of an array, we described how to access and manipulate individual elements of the array using subscripts. We then introduced the concept of an `Array` object, and learned that objects are passed to a method by reference instead of by value. We explored the sorting of arrays, and described two different methods of searching them. Finally, we discussed multidimensional arrays and how to use them to organize arrays in other arrays.

10.13 Web Resources

`www.deitel.com/javascript/`

The Deitel JavaScript Resource Center contains links to some of the best JavaScript resources on the web. There you'll find categorized links to JavaScript tools, code generators, forums, books, libraries, frameworks and more. Also check out the tutorials for all skill levels, from introductory to advanced. Be sure to visit the related Resource Centers on XHTML (`www.deitel.com/xhtml/`) and CSS 2.1 (`www.deitel.com/css21/`).

Summary

Section 10.1 Introduction

- Arrays are data structures consisting of related data items (sometimes called collections of data items).
- JavaScript arrays are "dynamic" entities in that they can change size after they are created.

Section 10.2 Arrays

- An array is a group of memory locations that all have the same name and normally are of the same type (although this attribute is not required in JavaScript).
- Each individual location is called an element. Any one of these elements may be referred to by giving the name of the array followed by the position number (an integer normally referred to as the subscript or index) of the element in square brackets (`[]`).
- The first element in every array is the zeroth element. In general, the *i*th element of array `c` is referred to as `c[i-1]`. Array names follow the same conventions as other identifiers.
- A subscripted array name is a left-hand-side expression—it can be used on the left side of an assignment to place a new value into an array element. It can also be used on the right side of an assignment operation to assign its value to another left-hand-side expression.
- Every array in JavaScript knows its own length, which it stores in its `length` attribute.

Section 10.3 Declaring and Allocating Arrays

- JavaScript arrays are represented by `Array` objects.
- The process of creating new objects using the new operator is known as creating an instance or instantiating an object, and operator `new` is known as the dynamic memory allocation operator.

Section 10.4 Examples Using Arrays

- Zero-based counting is usually used to iterate through arrays.

- JavaScript automatically reallocates an `Array` when a value is assigned to an element that is outside the bounds of the original `Array`. Elements between the last element of the original `Array` and the new element have undefined values.
- Arrays can be created using a comma-separated initializer list enclosed in square brackets (`[` and `]`). The array's size is determined by the number of values in the initializer list.
- The initial values of an array can also be specified as arguments in the parentheses following `new Array`. The size of the array is determined by the number of values in parentheses.
- JavaScript's `for...in` statement enables a script to perform a task for each element in an array. This process is known as iterating over the elements of an array.

Section 10.5 Random Image Generator Using Arrays

- We create a more elegant random image generator than the one in the previous chapter that does not require the image filenames to be integers by using a `pictures` array to store the names of the image files as strings and accessing the array using a randomized index.

Section 10.6 References and Reference Parameters

- Two ways to pass arguments to functions (or methods) in many programming languages are pass-by-value and pass-by-reference.
- When an argument is passed to a function by value, a *copy* of the argument's value is made and is passed to the called function.
- In JavaScript, numbers, boolean values and strings are passed to functions by value.
- With pass-by-reference, the caller gives the called function direct access to the caller's data and allows it to modify the data if it so chooses. Pass-by-reference can improve performance because it can eliminate the overhead of copying large amounts of data, but it can weaken security because the called function can access the caller's data.
- In JavaScript, all objects (and thus all `Array`s) are passed to functions by reference.
- `Array`s are objects in JavaScript, so `Array`s are passed to a function by reference—a called function can access the elements of the caller's original `Array`s. The name of an array is actually a reference to an object that contains the array elements and the `length` variable, which indicates the number of elements in the array.

Section 10.7 Passing Arrays to Functions

- To pass an array argument to a function, specify the name of the array (a reference to the array) without brackets.
- Although entire arrays are passed by reference, *individual numeric and boolean array elements* are passed *by value* exactly as simple numeric and boolean variables are passed. Such simple single pieces of data are called scalars, or scalar quantities. To pass an array element to a function, use the subscripted name of the element as an argument in the function call.
- The `join` method of an `Array` returns a string that contains all of the elements of an array, separated by the string supplied in the function's argument. If an argument is not specified, the empty string is used as the separator.

Section 10.8 Sorting Arrays

- Sorting data (putting data in a particular order, such as ascending or descending) is one of the most important computing functions.
- The `Array` object in JavaScript has a built-in method sort for sorting arrays.
- By default, `Array` method `sort` (with no arguments) uses string comparisons to determine the sorting order of the `Array` elements.

- Method `sort` takes as its optional argument the name of a function (called the comparator function) that compares its two arguments and returns a negative value, zero, or a positive value, if the first argument is less than, equal to, or greater than the second, respectively.
- Functions in JavaScript are considered to be data. Therefore, functions can be assigned to variables, stored in `Array`s and passed to functions just like other data types.

Section 10.9 Searching Arrays: Linear Search and Binary Search

- The linear search algorithm iterates through the elements of an array until it finds an element that matches a search key.
- If the array being searched is not in any particular order, it is just as likely that the value will be found in the first element as the last. On average, therefore, the program will have to compare the search key with half the elements of the array.
- The binary search algorithm is more efficient than the linear search algorithm, but it requires that the array be sorted.
- The binary search algorithm tests the middle element in the array and returns the index if it matches the search key. If not, it cuts the list in half, depending on whether the key is greater than or less than the middle element, and repeats the process on the remaining half of the sorted list. The algorithm ends by either finding an element that matches the search key or reducing the subarray to zero size.
- When searching a sorted array, the binary search provides a tremendous increase in performance over the linear search. For a one-billion-element array, this is the difference between an average of 500 million comparisons and a maximum of 30 comparisons.
- The maximum number of comparisons needed for the binary search of any sorted array is the exponent of the first power of 2 greater than the number of elements in the array.

Section 10.10 Multidimensional Arrays

- To identify a particular two-dimensional multidimensional array element, we must specify the two subscripts; by convention, the first identifies the element's row, and the second identifies the element's column.
- In general, an array with *m* rows and *n* columns is called an *m*-by-*n* array.
- Every element in a two-dimensional array is accessed using an element name of the form `a[ i ][ j ]`; `a` is the name of the array, and `i` and `j` are the subscripts that uniquely identify the row and column, respectively, of each element in `a`.
- Multidimensional arrays are maintained as arrays of arrays.

Section 10.11 Building an Online Quiz

- An XHTML form's elements can be accessed individually using `getElementById` or through the `elements` property of the containing `form` object. The `elements` property contains an array of all the `form`'s controls.
- Property `checked` of a radio button is `true` when the radio button is selected, and it is `false` when the radio button is not selected.

Terminology

`a[i]`
`a[i][j]`
address in memory
array data structure
array initializer list
`Array` object
binary search
bounds of an array

checked property of a radio button
collections of data items
column subscript
comma-separated initializer list
comparator function
creating an instance
data structure
declare an array
dynamic memory allocation operator (new)
element of an array
elements property of a form object
for...in repetition statement
index of an element
initialize an array
initializer
initializer list
instantiating an object
iterating over an array's elements
join method of an Array object
left-hand-side expression
length of an Array object
linear search of an array
location in an array
m-by-*n* array
multidimensional array
name of an array
new operator
off-by-one error
one-dimensional array
pass-by-reference
pass-by-value
passing arrays to functions
place holder in an initializer list (,)
position number of an element
reserve a space in an Array
row subscript
scalar quantities
separator
search key
searching an array
sort method of the Array object
sorting an array
square brackets []
subscript
table of values
tabular format
traverse an array
two-dimensional array
value of an element
zeroth element

Self-Review Exercises

10.1 Fill in the blanks in each of the following statements:

a) Lists and tables of values can be stored in _______.
b) The elements of an array are related by the fact that they normally have the same _______.
c) The number used to refer to a particular element of an array is called its _______.
d) The process of putting the elements of an array in order is called _______ the array.
e) Determining whether an array contains a certain key value is called _______ the array.
f) An array that uses two subscripts is referred to as a(n) _________ array.

10.2 State whether each of the following is *true* or *false*. If *false*, explain why.

a) An array can store many different types of values.
b) An array subscript should normally be a floating-point value.
c) An individual array element that is passed to a function and modified in it will contain the modified value when the called function completes execution.

10.3 Write JavaScript statements (regarding array fractions) to accomplish each of the following tasks:

a) Declare an array with 10 elements, and initialize the elements of the array to 0.
b) Refer to the fourth element of the array.
c) Refer to array element 4.
d) Assign the value 1.667 to array element 9.
e) Assign the value 3.333 to the seventh element of the array.
f) Sum all the elements of the array, using a for...in statement. Define variable x as a control variable for the loop.

10.4 Write JavaScript statements (regarding array `table`) to accomplish each of the following tasks:

a) Declare and create the array with three rows and three columns.
b) Display the number of elements.
c) Use a `for...in` statement to initialize each element of the array to the sum of its subscripts. Assume that the variables `x` and `y` are declared as control variables.

10.5 Find the error(s) in each of the following program segments, and correct them.

a)
```
var b = new Array( 10 );
for ( var i = 0; i <= b.length; ++i )
   b[ i ] = 1;
```
b)
```
var a = [ [ 1, 2 ], [ 3, 4 ] ];
a[ 1, 1 ] = 5;
```

Answers to Self-Review Exercises

10.1 a) arrays. b) type. c) subscript. d) sorting. e) searching. f) two-dimensional.

10.2 a) True. b). False. An array subscript must be an integer or an integer expression. c) False. Individual primitive-data-type elements are passed by value. If a reference to an array is passed, then modifications to the elements of the array are reflected in the original element of the array. Also, an individual element of an object type passed to a function is passed by reference, and changes to the object will be reflected in the original array element.

10.3
a) `var fractions = [ 0, 0, 0, 0, 0, 0, 0, 0, 0, 0 ];`
b) `fractions[ 3 ]`
c) `fractions[ 4 ]`
d) `fractions[ 9 ] = 1.667;`
e) `fractions[ 6 ] = 3.333;`
f)
```
var total = 0;
for ( var x in fractions )
   total += fractions[ x ];
```

10.4
a)
```
var table = new Array( new Array( 3 ), new Array( 3 ),
   new Array( 3 ) );
```
b)
```
document.write( "total: " + ( table.length * table[ 0 ].length ) );
```
c)
```
for ( var x in table )
   for ( var y in table[ x ] )
      table[ x ][ y ] = x + y;
```

10.5 a) Error: Referencing an array element outside the bounds of the array (`b[10]`). [*Note:* This error is actually a logic error, not a syntax error.] Correction: Change the `<=` operator to `<`. b) Error: The array subscripting is done incorrectly. Correction: Change the statement to `a[ 1 ][ 1 ] = 5;`.

Exercises

10.6 Fill in the blanks in each of the following statements:

a) JavaScript stores lists of values in ________.
b) The names of the four elements of array `p` are ________, ________, ________ and ________.
c) In a two-dimensional array, the first subscript identifies the ________ of an element, and the second subscript identifies the ________ of an element.
d) An *m*-by-*n* array contains ________ rows, ________ columns and ________ elements.
e) The name the element in row 3 and column 5 of array `d` is ________.

f) The name of the element in the third row and fifth column of array `d` is _______.

10.7 State whether each of the following is *true* or *false*. If *false*, explain why.

a) To refer to a particular location or element in an array, we specify the name of the array and the value of the element.
b) A variable declaration reserves space for an array.
c) To indicate that 100 locations should be reserved for integer array `p`, the programmer should write the declaration

```
p[ 100 ];
```

d) A JavaScript program that initializes the elements of a 15-element array to zero must contain at least one `for` statement.
e) A JavaScript program that totals the elements of a two-dimensional array must contain nested `for` statements.

10.8 Write JavaScript statements to accomplish each of the following tasks:

a) Display the value of the seventh element of array `f`.
b) Initialize each of the five elements of one-dimensional array `g` to `8`.
c) Total the elements of array `c`, which contains 100 numeric elements.
d) Copy 11-element array a into the first portion of array `b`, which contains 34 elements.
e) Determine and print the smallest and largest values contained in 99-element floating-point array `w`.

10.9 Consider a two-by-three array `t` that will store integers.

a) Write a statement that declares and creates array `t`.
b) How many rows does `t` have?
c) How many columns does `t` have?
d) How many elements does `t` have?
e) Write the names of all the elements in the second row of `t`.
f) Write the names of all the elements in the third column of `t`.
g) Write a single statement that sets the elements of `t` in row 1 and column 2 to zero.
h) Write a series of statements that initializes each element of `t` to zero. Do not use a repetition structure.
i) Write a nested `for` statement that initializes each element of `t` to zero.
j) Write a series of statements that determines and prints the smallest value in array `t`.
k) Write a statement that displays the elements of the first row of `t`.
l) Write a statement that totals the elements of the fourth column of `t`.
m) Write a series of statements that prints the array `t` in neat, tabular format. List the column subscripts as headings across the top, and list the row subscripts at the left of each row.

10.10 Use a one-dimensional array to solve the following problem: A company pays its salespeople on a commission basis. The salespeople receive $200 per week plus 9 percent of their gross sales for that week. For example, a salesperson who grosses $5000 in sales in a week receives $200 plus 9 percent of $5000, or a total of $650. Write a script (using an array of counters) that obtains the gross sales for each employee through an XHTML form and determines how many of the salespeople earned salaries in each of the following ranges (assume that each salesperson's salary is truncated to an integer amount):

a) $200–299
b) $300–399
c) $400–499
d) $500–599
e) $600–699
f) $700–799

g) $800–899
h) $900–999
i) $1000 and over

10.11 Write statements that perform the following operations for a one-dimensional array:
a) Set the 10 elements of array `counts` to zeros.
b) Add 1 to each of the 15 elements of array `bonus`.
c) Display the five values of array `bestScores`, separated by spaces.

10.12 Use a one-dimensional array to solve the following problem: Read in 20 numbers, each of which is between 10 and 100. As each number is read, print it only if it is not a duplicate of a number that has already been read. Provide for the "worst case," in which all 20 numbers are different. Use the smallest possible array to solve this problem.

10.13 Label the elements of three-by-five two-dimensional array `sales` to indicate the order in which they are set to zero by the following program segment:

```
for ( var row in sales )
   for ( var col in sales[ row ] )
      sales[ row ][ col ] = 0;
```

10.14 Write a script to simulate the rolling of two dice. The script should use `Math.random` to roll the first die and again to roll the second die. The sum of the two values should then be calculated. [*Note:* Since each die can show an integer value from 1 to 6, the sum of the values will vary from 2 to 12, with 7 being the most frequent sum, and 2 and 12 the least frequent sums. Figure 10.15 shows the 36 possible combinations of the two dice. Your program should roll the dice 36,000 times. Use a one-dimensional array to tally the numbers of times each possible sum appears. Display the results in an XHTML table. Also determine whether the totals are reasonable (e.g., there are six ways to roll a 7, so approximately 1/6 of all the rolls should be 7).]

10.15 Write a script that runs 1000 games of craps and answers the following questions:
a) How many games are won on the first roll, second roll, …, twentieth roll and after the twentieth roll?
b) How many games are lost on the first roll, second roll, …, twentieth roll and after the twentieth roll?
c) What are the chances of winning at craps? [*Note:* You should discover that craps is one of the fairest casino games. What do you suppose this means?]
d) What is the average length of a game of craps?
e) Do the chances of winning improve with the length of the game?

10.16 *(Airline Reservations System)* A small airline has just purchased a computer for its new automated reservations system. You have been asked to program the new system. You are to write a program to assign seats on each flight of the airline's only plane (capacity: 10 seats).

	1	2	3	4	5	6
1	2	3	4	5	6	7
2	3	4	5	6	7	8
3	4	5	6	7	8	9
4	5	6	7	8	9	10
5	6	7	8	9	10	11
6	7	8	9	10	11	12

Fig. 10.15 | Thirty-six possible outcomes of rolling two dice.

Your program should display the following menu of alternatives: `Please type 1 for "First Class"` and `Please type 2 for "Economy"`. If the person types `1`, your program should assign a seat in the first-class section (seats 1–5). If the person types `2`, your program should assign a seat in the economy section (seats 6–10). Your program should print a boarding pass indicating the person's seat number and whether it is in the first-class or economy section of the plane.

Use a one-dimensional array to represent the seating chart of the plane. Initialize all the elements of the array to `0` to indicate that all the seats are empty. As each seat is assigned, set the corresponding elements of the array to `1` to indicate that the seat is no longer available.

Your program should, of course, never assign a seat that has already been assigned. When the first-class section is full, your program should ask the person if it is acceptable to be placed in the economy section (and vice versa). If yes, then make the appropriate seat assignment. If no, then print the message `"Next flight leaves in 3 hours."`

10.17 Use a two-dimensional array to solve the following problem: A company has four salespeople (1 to 4) who sell five different products (1 to 5). Once a day, each salesperson passes in a slip for each different type of product actually sold. Each slip contains

a) the salesperson number,
b) the product number, and
c) the total dollar value of the product sold that day.

Thus, each salesperson passes in between zero and five sales slips per day. Assume that the information from all of the slips for last month is available. Write a script that will read all this information for last month's sales and summarize the total sales by salesperson by product. All totals should be stored in the two-dimensional array `sales`. After processing all the information for last month, display the results in an XHTML table format, with each of the columns representing a different salesperson and each of the rows representing a different product. Cross-total each row to get the total sales of each product for last month; cross-total each column to get the total sales by salesperson for last month. Your tabular printout should include these cross-totals to the right of the totaled rows and to the bottom of the totaled columns.

10.18 *(Turtle Graphics)* The Logo language, which is popular among young computer users, made the concept of turtle graphics famous. Imagine a mechanical turtle that walks around the room under the control of a JavaScript program. The turtle holds a pen in one of two positions, up or down. When the pen is down, the turtle traces out shapes as it moves; when the pen is up, the turtle moves about freely without writing anything. In this problem, you will simulate the operation of the turtle and create a computerized sketchpad as well.

Use a 20-by-20 array `floor` that is initialized to zeros. Read commands from an array that contains them. Keep track of the current position of the turtle at all times and of whether the pen is currently up or down. Assume that the turtle always starts at position (0, 0) of the floor, with its pen up. The set of turtle commands your script must process are as in Fig. 10.16.

Suppose that the turtle is somewhere near the center of the floor. The following "program" would draw and print a 12-by-12 square, then leave the pen in the up position:

```
2
5,12
3
5,12
3
5,12
3
5,12
1
6
9
```

Command	Meaning
1	Pen up
2	Pen down
3	Turn right
4	Turn left
5,10	Move forward 10 spaces (or a number other than 10)
6	Print the 20-by-20 array
9	End of data (sentinel)

Fig. 10.16 | Turtle graphics commands.

As the turtle moves with the pen down, set the appropriate elements of array `floor` to `1`s. When the `6` command (print) is given, display an asterisk or some other character of your choosing wherever there is a `1` in the array. Wherever there is a zero, display a blank. Write a script to implement the turtle-graphics capabilities discussed here. Write several turtle-graphics programs to draw interesting shapes. Add other commands to increase the power of your turtle-graphics language.

10.19 *(The Sieve of Eratosthenes)* A prime integer is an integer greater than 1 that is evenly divisible only by itself and 1. The Sieve of Eratosthenes is an algorithm for finding prime numbers. It operates as follows:

a) Create an array with all elements initialized to 1 (true). Array elements with prime subscripts will remain as 1. All other array elements will eventually be set to zero.
b) Set the first two elements to zero, since 0 and 1 are not prime. Starting with array subscript 2, every time an array element is found whose value is 1, loop through the remainder of the array and set to zero every element whose subscript is a multiple of the subscript for the element with value 1. For array subscript 2, all elements beyond 2 in the array that are multiples of 2 will be set to zero (subscripts 4, 6, 8, 10, etc.); for array subscript 3, all elements beyond 3 in the array that are multiples of 3 will be set to zero (subscripts 6, 9, 12, 15, etc.); and so on.

When this process is complete, the array elements that are still set to 1 indicate that the subscript is a prime number. These subscripts can then be printed. Write a script that uses an array of 1000 elements to determine and print the prime numbers between 1 and 999. Ignore element 0 of the array.

10.20 *(Simulation: The Tortoise and the Hare)* In this problem, you will re-create one of the truly great moments in history, namely the classic race of the tortoise and the hare. You will use random number generation to develop a simulation of this memorable event.

Our contenders begin the race at square 1 of 70 squares. Each square represents a possible position along the race course. The finish line is at square 70. The first contender to reach or pass square 70 is rewarded with a pail of fresh carrots and lettuce. The course weaves its way up the side of a slippery mountain, so occasionally the contenders lose ground.

There is a clock that ticks once per second. With each tick of the clock, your script should adjust the position of the animals according to the rules in Fig. 10.17.

Use variables to keep track of the positions of the animals (i.e., position numbers are 1–70). Start each animal at position 1 (i.e., the "starting gate"). If an animal slips left before square 1, move the animal back to square 1.

Animal	Move type	Percentage of the time	Actual move
Tortoise	Fast plod	50%	3 squares to the right
	Slip	20%	6 squares to the left
	Slow plod	30%	1 square to the right
Hare	Sleep	20%	No move at all
	Big hop	20%	9 squares to the right
	Big slip	10%	12 squares to the left
	Small hop	30%	1 square to the right
	Small slip	20%	2 squares to the left

Fig. 10.17 | Rules for adjusting the position of the tortoise and the hare.

Generate the percentages in Fig. 10.17 by producing a random integer i in the range $1 \leq i \leq 10$. For the tortoise, perform a "fast plod" when $1 \leq i \leq 5$, a "slip" when $6 \leq i \leq 7$ and a "slow plod" when $8 \leq i \leq 10$. Use a similar technique to move the hare.

Begin the race by printing

```
BANG !!!!!
AND THEY'RE OFF !!!!!
```

Then, for each tick of the clock (i.e., each repetition of a loop), print a 70-position line showing the letter `T` in the position of the tortoise and the letter `H` in the position of the hare. Occasionally, the contenders will land on the same square. In this case, the tortoise bites the hare, and your script should print `OUCH!!!` beginning at that position. All print positions other than the `T`, the `H` or the `OUCH!!!` (in case of a tie) should be blank.

After each line is printed, test whether either animal has reached or passed square 70. If so, print the winner, and terminate the simulation. If the tortoise wins, print `TORTOISE WINS!!! YAY!!!` If the hare wins, print `Hare wins. Yuck!` If both animals win on the same tick of the clock, you may want to favor the turtle (the "underdog"), or you may want to print `It's a tie`. If neither animal wins, perform the loop again to simulate the next tick of the clock. When you are ready to run your script, assemble a group of fans to watch the race. You'll be amazed at how involved your audience gets!

Later in the book, we introduce a number of Dynamic HTML capabilities, such as graphics, images, animation and sound. As you study those features, you might enjoy enhancing your tortoise-and-hare contest simulation.

My object all sublime
I shall achieve in time.
—W. S. Gilbert

Is it a world to hide virtues in?
—William Shakespeare

Good as it is to inherit a library, it is better to collect one.
—Augustine Birrell

A philosopher of imposing stature doesn't think in a vacuum. Even his most abstract ideas are, to some extent, conditioned by what is or is not known in the time when he lives.
—Alfred North Whitehead

JavaScript: Objects

OBJECTIVES

In this chapter you will learn:

- Object-based programming terminology and concepts.
- The concepts of encapsulation and data hiding.
- The value of object orientation.
- To use the JavaScript objects `Math`, `String`, `Date`, `Boolean` and `Number`.
- To use the browser's `document` and `window` objects.
- To use cookies.
- To represent objects simply using JSON.

Outline

11.1 Introduction

Most of the JavaScript programs we've demonstrated illustrate basic programming concepts. These programs provide you with the foundation you need to build powerful and complex scripts as part of your web pages. As you proceed beyond this chapter, you will use JavaScript to manipulate every element of an XHTML document from a script.

This chapter presents a more formal treatment of **objects**. We begin by giving a brief introduction to the concepts behind object-orientation. The remainder of the chapter overviews—and serves as a reference for—several of JavaScript's built-in objects and demonstrates many of their capabilities. We also provide a brief introduction to JSON, a means for creating JavaScript objects. In the chapters on the Document Object Model and Events that follow this chapter, you will be introduced to many objects provided by the browser that enable scripts to interact with the elements of an XHTML document.

11.2 Introduction to Object Technology

This section provides a general introduction to object orientation. The terminology and technologies discussed here support various chapters that come later in the book. Here, you'll learn that objects are a natural way of thinking about the world and about scripts that manipulate XHTML documents. In Chapters 6–10, we used built-in JavaScript objects—`Math` and `Array`—and objects provided by the web browser—`document` and `win-`

window—to perform tasks in our scripts. JavaScript uses objects to perform many tasks and therefore is referred to as an object-based programming language. As we have seen, JavaScript also uses constructs from the "conventional" structured programming methodology supported by many other programming languages. The first five JavaScript chapters concentrated on these conventional parts of JavaScript because they are important components of all JavaScript programs. Our goal here is to help you develop an object-oriented way of thinking. Many concepts in this book, including CSS, JavaScript, Ajax, Ruby on Rails, ASP.NET, and JavaServer Faces are based on at least some of the concepts introduced in this section.

Basic Object-Technology Concepts

We begin our introduction to object technology with some key terminology. Everywhere you look in the real world you see objects—people, animals, plants, cars, planes, buildings, computers, monitors and so on. Humans think in terms of objects. Telephones, houses, traffic lights, microwave ovens and water coolers are just a few more objects we see around us every day.

We sometimes divide objects into two categories: animate and inanimate. Animate objects are "alive" in some sense—they move around and do things. Inanimate objects do not move on their own. Objects of both types, however, have some things in common. They all have attributes (e.g., size, shape, color and weight), and they all exhibit behaviors (e.g., a ball rolls, bounces, inflates and deflates; a baby cries, sleeps, crawls, walks and blinks; a car accelerates, brakes and turns; a towel absorbs water). We'll study the kinds of attributes and behaviors that software objects have.

Humans learn about existing objects by studying their attributes and observing their behaviors. Different objects can have similar attributes and can exhibit similar behaviors. Comparisons can be made, for example, between babies and adults, and between humans and chimpanzees.

Object-oriented design (OOD) models software in terms similar to those that people use to describe real-world objects. It takes advantage of class relationships, where objects of a certain class, such as a class of vehicles, have the same characteristics—cars, trucks, little red wagons and roller skates have much in common. OOD takes advantage of inheritance relationships, where new classes of objects are derived by absorbing characteristics of existing classes and adding unique characteristics of their own. An object of class "convertible" certainly has the characteristics of the more general class "automobile," but more specifically, the roof goes up and down.

Object-oriented design provides a natural and intuitive way to view the software design process—namely, modeling objects by their attributes, behaviors and interrelationships just as we describe real-world objects. OOD also models communication between objects. Just as people send messages to one another (e.g., a sergeant commands a soldier to stand at attention), objects also communicate via messages. A bank account object may receive a message to decrease its balance by a certain amount because the customer has withdrawn that amount of money.

OOD encapsulates (i.e., wraps) attributes and operations (behaviors) into objects—an object's attributes and operations are intimately tied together. Objects have the property of information hiding. This means that objects may know how to communicate with one another across well-defined interfaces, but normally they are not allowed to know how other objects are implemented—implementation details are hidden within the objects themselves. We can drive a car effectively, for instance, without knowing the details of how engines, transmissions, brakes and exhaust systems work internally—as long as we know how to use the accelerator pedal, the brake pedal, the steering wheel and so on. Information hiding, as we'll see, is crucial to good software engineering.

Like the designers of an automobile, the designers of web browsers have defined a set of objects that encapsulate an XHTML document's elements and expose to a JavaScript programmer the attributes and behaviors that enable a JavaScript program to interact with (or script) those elements (objects). You'll soon see that the browser's `document` object contains attributes and behaviors that provide access to every element of an XHTML document. Similarly, JavaScript provides objects that encapsulate various capabilities in a script. For example, the JavaScript `Array` object provides attributes and behaviors that enable a script to manipulate a collection of data. The `Array` object's `length` property (attribute) contains the number of elements in the `Array`. The `Array` object's `sort` method (behavior) orders the elements of the `Array`.

Some programming languages—like Java, Visual Basic, C# and C++—are object oriented. Programming in such a language is called object-oriented programming (OOP), and it allows computer programmers to implement object-oriented designs as working software systems. Languages like C, on the other hand, are procedural, so programming tends to be action oriented. In procedural languages, the unit of programming is the function. In object-oriented languages, the unit of programming is the class from which objects are eventually instantiated (an OOP term for "created"). Classes contain functions that implement operations and data that comprises attributes.

Procedural programmers concentrate on writing functions. Programmers group actions that perform some common task into functions, and group functions to form programs. Data is certainly important in procedural languages, but the view is that data exists primarily in support of the actions that functions perform. The verbs in a system specification help a procedural programmer determine the set of functions that work together to implement the system.

Classes, Properties and Methods

Object-oriented programmers concentrate on creating their own user-defined types called classes. Each class contains data as well as the set of functions that manipulate that data and provide services to clients (i.e., other classes or functions that use the class). The data components of a class are called properties. For example, a bank account class might include an account number and a balance. The function components of a class are called methods. For example, a bank account class might include methods to make a deposit (increasing the balance), make a withdrawal (decreasing the balance) and inquire what the current balance is. You use built-in types (and other user-defined types) as the "building blocks" for constructing new user-defined types (classes). The nouns in a system specification help you determine the set of classes from which objects are created that work together to implement the system.

Classes are to objects as blueprints are to houses—a class is a "plan" for building an object of the class. Just as we can build many houses from one blueprint, we can instantiate (create) many objects from one class. You cannot cook meals in the kitchen of a blueprint; you can cook meals in the kitchen of a house. You cannot sleep in the bedroom of a blueprint; you can sleep in the bedroom of a house.

Classes can have relationships with other classes. For example, in an object-oriented design of a bank, the "bank teller" class needs to relate to other classes, such as the "customer" class, the "cash drawer" class, the "safe" class, and so on. These relationships are called **associations**.

Packaging software as classes makes it possible for future software systems to **reuse** the classes. Groups of related classes are often packaged as reusable **components**. Just as realtors often say that the three most important factors affecting the price of real estate are "location, location and location," some people in the software development community say that the three most important factors affecting the future of software development are "reuse, reuse and reuse.

Indeed, with object technology, you can build much of the new software you'll need by combining existing classes, just as automobile manufacturers combine interchangeable parts. Each new class you create will have the potential to become a valuable software asset that you and other programmers can reuse to speed and enhance the quality of future software development efforts. Now that we've introduced the terminology associated with object-orientation, you'll see it used in the upcoming discussions of some of JavaScript's objects.

11.3 Math Object

The Math object's methods allow you to perform many common mathematical calculations. As shown previously, an object's methods are called by writing the name of the object followed by a dot (.) and the name of the method. In parentheses following the method name is the argument (or a comma-separated list of arguments) to the method. For example, to calculate and display the square root of 900.0 you might write

```
document.writeln( Math.sqrt( 900.0 ) );
```

which calls method Math.sqrt to calculate the square root of the number contained in the parentheses (900.0), then outputs the result. The number 900.0 is the argument of the Math.sqrt method. The preceding statement would display 30.0. Some **Math** object methods are summarized in Fig. 11.1.

Method	Description	Examples
abs(x)	absolute value of x	abs(7.2) is 7.2 abs(0.0) is 0.0 abs(-5.6) is 5.6
ceil(x)	rounds x to the smallest integer not less than x	ceil(9.2) is 10.0 ceil(-9.8) is -9.0
cos(x)	trigonometric cosine of x (x in radians)	cos(0.0) is 1.0
exp(x)	exponential method e^x	exp(1.0) is 2.71828 exp(2.0) is 7.38906

Fig. 11.1 | Math object methods. (Part 1 of 2.)

Method	Description	Examples
`floor( x )`	rounds x to the largest integer not greater than x	`floor( 9.2 )` is `9.0` `floor( -9.8 )` is `-10.0`
`log( x )`	natural logarithm of x (base *e*)	`log( 2.718282 )` is `1.0` `log( 7.389056 )` is `2.0`
`max( x, y )`	larger value of x and y	`max( 2.3, 12.7 )` is `12.7` `max( -2.3, -12.7 )` is `-2.3`
`min( x, y )`	smaller value of x and y	`min( 2.3, 12.7 )` is `2.3` `min( -2.3, -12.7 )` is `-12.7`
`pow( x, y )`	x raised to power y (x^y)	`pow( 2.0, 7.0 )` is `128.0` `pow( 9.0, .5 )` is `3.0`
`round( x )`	rounds x to the closest integer	`round( 9.75 )` is `10` `round( 9.25 )` is `9`
`sin( x )`	trigonometric sine of x (x in radians)	`sin( 0.0 )` is `0.0`
`sqrt( x )`	square root of x	`sqrt( 900.0 )` is `30.0` `sqrt( 9.0 )` is `3.0`
`tan( x )`	trigonometric tangent of x (x in radians)	`tan( 0.0 )` is `0.0`

Fig. 11.1 | `Math` object methods. (Part 2 of 2.)

Common Programming Error 11.1

Forgetting to invoke a `Math` method by preceding the method name with the object name `Math` and a dot (.) is an error.

Software Engineering Observation 11.1

The primary difference between invoking a standalone function and invoking a method of an object is that an object name and a dot are not required to call a standalone function.

The `Math` object defines several commonly used mathematical constants, summarized in Fig. 11.2. [*Note:* By convention, the names of constants are written in all uppercase letters so they stand out in a program.]

Constant	Description	Value
`Math.E`	Base of a natural logarithm (*e*).	Approximately 2.718
`Math.LN2`	Natural logarithm of 2	Approximately 0.693
`Math.LN10`	Natural logarithm of 10	Approximately 2.302

Fig. 11.2 | Properties of the `Math` object. (Part 1 of 2.)

Constant	Description	Value
Math.LOG2E	Base 2 logarithm of *e*	Approximately 1.442
Math.LOG10E	Base 10 logarithm of *e*	Approximately 0.434
Math.PI	π—the ratio of a circle's circumference to its diameter	Approximately 3.141592653589793
Math.SQRT1_2	Square root of 0.5	Approximately 0.707
Math.SQRT2	Square root of 2.0	Approximately 1.414

Fig. 11.2 | Properties of the `Math` object. (Part 2 of 2.)

Good Programming Practice 11.1

Use the mathematical constants of the `Math` object rather than explicitly typing the numeric value of the constant.

11.4 String Object

In this section, we introduce JavaScript's string- and character-processing capabilities. The techniques discussed here are appropriate for processing names, addresses, telephone numbers, and similar items.

11.4.1 Fundamentals of Characters and Strings

Characters are the fundamental building blocks of JavaScript programs. Every program is composed of a sequence of characters grouped together meaningfully that is interpreted by the computer as a series of instructions used to accomplish a task.

A string is a series of characters treated as a single unit. A string may include letters, digits and various special characters, such as +, -, *, /, and $. JavaScript supports the set of characters called Unicode®, which represents a large portion of the world's languages. (We discuss Unicode in detail in Appendix F.) A string is an object of type `String`. String literals or string constants (often called anonymous `String` objects) are written as a sequence of characters in double quotation marks or single quotation marks, as follows:

```
"John Q. Doe"                    (a name)
'9999 Main Street'               (a street address)
"Waltham, Massachusetts"         (a city and state)
'(201) 555-1212'                 (a telephone number)
```

A `String` may be assigned to a variable in a declaration. The declaration

```
var color = "blue";
```

initializes variable `color` with the `String` object containing the string `"blue"`. `Strings` can be compared via the relational (<, <=, > and >=) and equality operators (== and !=). Strings are compared using the Unicode values of the corresponding characters. For example, the expression `"hello" < "Hello"` evaluates to false because lowercase letters have higher Unicode values.

11.4.2 Methods of the String Object

The `String` object encapsulates the attributes and behaviors of a string of characters. It provides many methods (behaviors) that accomplish useful tasks such as selecting characters from a string, combining strings (called **concatenation**), obtaining substrings of a string, searching for substrings within a string, tokenizing strings (i.e., splitting strings into individual words) and converting strings to all uppercase or lowercase letters. The `String` object also provides several methods that generate XHTML tags. Figure 11.3 summarizes many `String` methods. Figures 11.4–11.7 demonstrate some of these methods.

Method	Description
`charAt(` *index* `)`	Returns a string containing the character at the specified *index*. If there is no character at the *index*, `charAt` returns an empty string. The first character is located at *index* 0.
`charCodeAt(` *index* `)`	Returns the Unicode value of the character at the specified *index*, or `NaN` (not a number) if there is no character at that *index*.
`concat(` *string* `)`	Concatenates its argument to the end of the string that invokes the method. The string invoking this method is not modified; instead a new `String` is returned. This method is the same as adding two strings with the string-concatenation operator + (e.g., `s1.concat(s2)` is the same as `s1 + s2`).
`fromCharCode(` *value1*, *value2*, ...`)`	Converts a list of Unicode values into a string containing the corresponding characters.
`indexOf(` *substring*, *index* `)`	Searches for the first occurrence of *substring* starting from position *index* in the string that invokes the method. The method returns the starting index of *substring* in the source string or –1 if *substring* is not found. If the *index* argument is not provided, the method begins searching from index 0 in the source string.
`lastIndexOf(` *substring*, *index* `)`	Searches for the last occurrence of *substring* starting from position *index* and searching toward the beginning of the string that invokes the method. The method returns the starting index of *substring* in the source string or –1 if *substring* is not found. If the *index* argument is not provided, the method begins searching from the end of the source string.
`replace(` *searchString*, *replaceString* `)`	Searches for the substring *searchString*, and replaces the first occurrence with *replaceString* and returns the modified string, or the original string if no replacement was made.
`slice(` *start*, *end* `)`	Returns a string containing the portion of the string from index *start* through index *end*. If the *end* index is not specified, the method returns a string from the *start* index to the end of the source string. A negative *end* index specifies an offset from the end of the string, starting from a position one past the end of the last character (so –1 indicates the last character position in the string).

Fig. 11.3 | Some `String` object methods. (Part 1 of 2.)

Method	Description
`split( string )`	Splits the source string into an array of strings (tokens), where its *string* argument specifies the delimiter (i.e., the characters that indicate the end of each token in the source string).
`substr( start, length )`	Returns a string containing *length* characters starting from index *start* in the source string. If *length* is not specified, a string containing characters from *start* to the end of the source string is returned.
`substring( start, end )`	Returns a string containing the characters from index *start* up to but not including index *end* in the source string.
`toLowerCase()`	Returns a string in which all uppercase letters are converted to lowercase letters. Nonletter characters are not changed.
`toUpperCase()`	Returns a string in which all lowercase letters are converted to uppercase letters. Nonletter characters are not changed.
Methods that generate XHTML tags	
`anchor( name )`	Wraps the source string in an anchor element (`<a></a>`) with *name* as the anchor name.
`fixed()`	Wraps the source string in a `<tt></tt>` element (same as `<pre></pre>`).
`link( url )`	Wraps the source string in an anchor element (`<a></a>`) with *url* as the hyperlink location.
`strike()`	Wraps the source string in a `<strike></strike>` element.
`sub()`	Wraps the source string in a `<sub></sub>` element.
`sup()`	Wraps the source string in a `<sup></sup>` element.

Fig. 11.3 | Some `String` object methods. (Part 2 of 2.)

11.4.3 Character-Processing Methods

The script in Fig. 11.4 demonstrates some of the `String` object's character-processing methods, including **`charAt`** (returns the character at a specific position), **`charCodeAt`** (returns the Unicode value of the character at a specific position), **`fromCharCode`** (returns a string created from a series of Unicode values), **`toLowerCase`** (returns the lowercase version of a string) and **`toUpperCase`** (returns the uppercase version of a string).

```
<?xml version = "1.0" encoding = "utf-8"?>
<!DOCTYPE html PUBLIC "-//W3C//DTD XHTML 1.0 Strict//EN"
   "http://www.w3.org/TR/xhtml1/DTD/xhtml1-strict.dtd">

<!-- Fig. 11.4: CharacterProcessing.html -->
<!-- String methods charAt, charCodeAt, fromCharCode, toLowercase and
   toUpperCase. -->
```

Fig. 11.4 | String methods `charAt`, `charCodeAt`, `fromCharCode`, `toLowercase` and `toUpperCase`. (Part 1 of 2.)

```
8  <html xmlns = "http://www.w3.org/1999/xhtml">
9     <head>
10       <title>Character Processing Methods</title>
11       <script type = "text/javascript">
12          <!--
13          var s = "ZEBRA";
14          var s2 = "AbCdEfG";
15
16          document.writeln( "<p>Character at index 0 in '" +
17             s + "' is " + s.charAt( 0 ) );
18          document.writeln( "<br />Character code at index 0 in '"
19             + s + "' is " + s.charCodeAt( 0 ) + "</p>" );
20
21          document.writeln( "<p>'" +
22             String.fromCharCode( 87, 79, 82, 68 ) +
23             "' contains character codes 87, 79, 82 and 68</p>" )
24
25          document.writeln( "<p>'" + s2 + "' in lowercase is '" +
26             s2.toLowerCase() + "'" );
27          document.writeln( "<br />'" + s2 + "' in uppercase is '"
28             + s2.toUpperCase() + "'</p>" );
29          // -->
30       </script>
31    </head><body></body>
32 </html>
```

Character Processing Methods - Windows Internet Explorer

C:\examples\ch11\CharacterProcessing.html

Character at index 0 in 'ZEBRA' is Z
Character code at index 0 in 'ZEBRA' is 90

'WORD' contains character codes 87, 79, 82 and 68

'AbCdEfG' in lowercase is 'abcdefg'
'AbCdEfG' in uppercase is 'ABCDEFG'

Fig. 11.4 | String methods `charAt`, `charCodeAt`, `fromCharCode`, `toLowercase` and `toUpperCase`. (Part 2 of 2.)

Lines 16–17 display the first character in `String` `s` (`"ZEBRA"`) using `String` method `charAt`. Method **`charAt`** returns a string containing the character at the specified index (0 in this example). Indices for the characters in a string start at 0 (the first character) and go up to (but do not include) the string's `length` (i.e., if the string contains five characters, the indices are 0 through 4). If the index is outside the bounds of the string, the method returns an empty string.

Lines 18–19 display the character code for the first character in `String` `s` (`"ZEBRA"`) by calling `String` method `charCodeAt`. Method `charCodeAt` returns the Unicode value of the character at the specified index (0 in this example). If the index is outside the bounds of the string, the method returns NaN.

String method fromCharCode receives as its argument a comma-separated list of Unicode values and builds a string containing the character representation of those Unicode values. Lines 21–23 display the string "WORD", which consists of the character codes 87, 79, 82 and 68. Note that the String object calls method fromCharCode, rather than a specific String variable. Appendix D, ASCII Character Set, contains the character codes for the ASCII character set—a subset of the Unicode character set (Appendix F) that contains only Western characters.

The statements in lines 25–26 and 27–28 use String methods **toLowerCase** and **toUpperCase** to display versions of String s2 ("AbCdEfG") in all lowercase letters and all uppercase letters, respectively.

11.4.4 Searching Methods

Being able to search for a character or a sequence of characters in a string is often useful. For example, if you are creating your own word processor, you may want to provide a capability for searching through the document. The script in Fig. 11.5 demonstrates the String object methods **indexOf** and **lastIndexOf** that search for a specified substring in a string. All the searches in this example are performed on the global string letters (initialized in line 14 with "abcdefghijklmnopqrstuvwxyzabcdefghijklm" in the script).

The user types a substring in the XHTML form searchForm's inputVal text field and presses the **Search** button to search for the substring in letters. Clicking the **Search** button calls function buttonPressed (defined in lines 16–29) to respond to the onclick event and perform the searches. The results of each search are displayed in the appropriate text field of searchForm.

Lines 21–22 use String method indexOf to determine the location of the first occurrence in string letters of the string inputVal.value (i.e., the string the user typed in the

```
1  <?xml version = "1.0" encoding = "utf-8"?>
2  <!DOCTYPE html PUBLIC "-//W3C//DTD XHTML 1.0 Strict//EN"
3     "http://www.w3.org/TR/xhtml1/DTD/xhtml1-strict.dtd">
4
5  <!-- Fig. 11.5: SearchingStrings.html -->
6  <!-- String searching with indexOf and lastIndexOf. -->
7  <html xmlns = "http://www.w3.org/1999/xhtml">
8     <head>
9        <title>
10          Searching Strings with indexOf and lastIndexOf
11       </title>
12       <script type = "text/javascript">
13          <!--
14          var letters = "abcdefghijklmnopqrstuvwxyzabcdefghijklm";
15
16          function buttonPressed()
17          {
18             var searchForm = document.getElementById( "searchForm" );
19             var inputVal = document.getElementById( "inputVal" );
```

Fig. 11.5 | String searching with indexOf and lastIndexOf. (Part 1 of 3.)

```

            searchForm.elements[2].value =
               letters.indexOf( inputVal.value );
            searchForm.elements[3].value =
               letters.lastIndexOf( inputVal.value );
            searchForm.elements[4].value =
               letters.indexOf( inputVal.value, 12 );
            searchForm.elements[5].value =
               letters.lastIndexOf( inputVal.value, 12 );
         } // end function buttonPressed
         // -->
      </script>
   </head>
   <body>
      <form id = "searchForm" action = "">
         <h1>The string to search is:<br />
             abcdefghijklmnopqrstuvwxyzabcdefghijklm</h1>
         <p>Enter substring to search for
         <input id = "inputVal" type = "text" />
         <input id = "search" type = "button" value = "Search"
                onclick = "buttonPressed()" /><br /></p>

         <p>First occurrence located at index
         <input id = "first" type = "text" size = "5" />
         <br />Last occurrence located at index
         <input id = "last" type = "text" size = "5" />
         <br />First occurrence from index 12 located at index
         <input id = "first12" type = "text" size = "5" />
         <br />Last occurrence from index 12 located at index
         <input id = "last12" type = "text" size = "5" /></p>
      </form>
   </body>
</html>
```

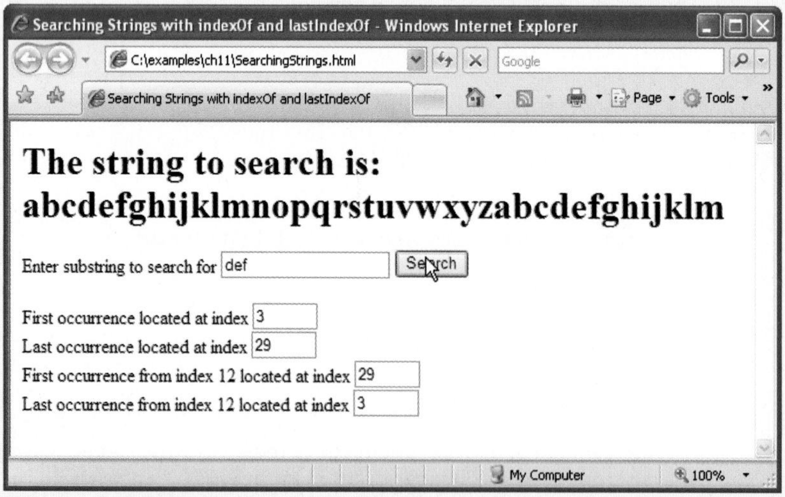

Fig. 11.5 | `String` searching with `indexOf` and `lastIndexOf`. (Part 2 of 3.)

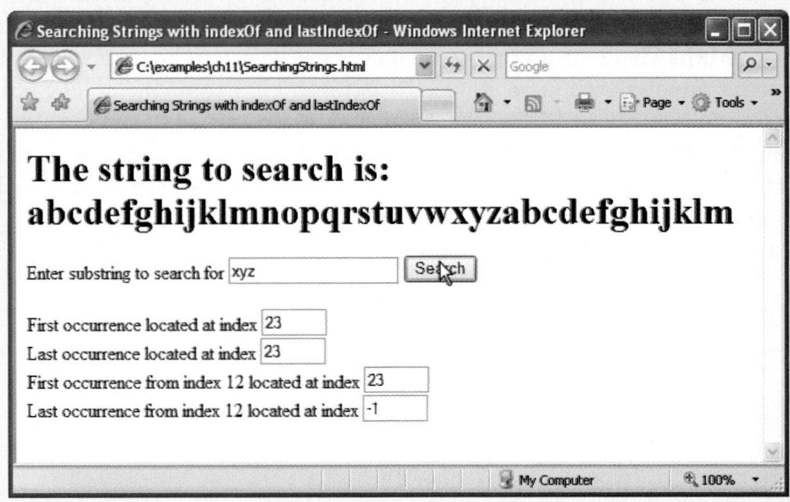

Fig. 11.5 | `String` searching with `indexOf` and `lastIndexOf`. (Part 3 of 3.)

`inputVal` text field). If the substring is found, the index at which the first occurrence of the substring begins is returned; otherwise, –1 is returned.

Lines 23–24 use `String` method `lastIndexOf` to determine the location of the last occurrence in `letters` of the string in `inputVal`. If the substring is found, the index at which the last occurrence of the substring begins is returned; otherwise, –1 is returned.

Lines 25–26 use `String` method `indexOf` to determine the location of the first occurrence in string `letters` of the string in the `inputVal` text field, starting from index `12` in `letters`. If the substring is found, the index at which the first occurrence of the substring (starting from index `12`) begins is returned; otherwise, –1 is returned.

Lines 27–28 use `String` method `lastIndexOf` to determine the location of the last occurrence in `letters` of the string in the `inputVal` text field, starting from index `12` in `letters` and moving toward the beginning of the input. If the substring is found, the index at which the first occurrence of the substring (if one appears before index `12`) begins is returned; otherwise, –1 is returned.

Software Engineering Observation 11.2

`String` methods `indexOf` and `lastIndexOf`, with their optional second argument (the starting index from which to search), are particularly useful for continuing a search through a large amount of text.

11.4.5 Splitting Strings and Obtaining Substrings

When you read a sentence, your mind breaks it into individual words, or **tokens**, each of which conveys meaning to you. The process of breaking a string into tokens is called **tokenization**. Interpreters also perform tokenization. They break up statements into such individual pieces as keywords, identifiers, operators and other elements of a programming language. Figure 11.6 demonstrates `String` method **`split`**, which breaks a string into its component tokens. Tokens are separated from one another by **delimiters**, typically white-space characters such as blanks, tabs, newlines and carriage returns. Other characters may also be used as delimiters to separate tokens. The XHTML document displays a form containing a text field where the user types a sentence to tokenize. The results of the tokenization process are displayed in an XHTML `textarea` GUI component. The script also demonstrates `String` method **`substring`**, which returns a portion of a string.

The user types a sentence into the text field with `id` `inputVal` text field and presses the **Split** button to tokenize the string. Function `splitButtonPressed` (lines 12–21) handles the button's `onclick` event.

```
1  <?xml version = "1.0" encoding = "utf-8"?>
2  <!DOCTYPE html PUBLIC "-//W3C//DTD XHTML 1.0 Strict//EN"
3     "http://www.w3.org/TR/xhtml1/DTD/xhtml1-strict.dtd">
4
5  <!-- Fig. 11.6: SplitAndSubString.html -->
6  <!-- String object methods split and substring. -->
7  <html xmlns = "http://www.w3.org/1999/xhtml">
8     <head>
9        <title>String Methods split and substring</title>
10       <script type = "text/javascript">
11          <!--
12          function splitButtonPressed()
13          {
14             var inputString = document.getElementById( "inputVal" ).value;
15             var tokens = inputString.split( " " );
16             document.getElementById( "output" ).value =
17                tokens.join( "\n" ) ;
18
19             document.getElementById( "outputSubstring" ).value =
20                inputString.substring( 0, 10 );
21          } // end function splitButtonPressed
22          // -->
23       </script>
24    </head>
25    <body>
26       <form action = "">
27          <p>Enter a sentence to split into words<br />
28          <input id = "inputVal" type = "text" size = "40" />
29          <input type = "button" value = "Split"
30             onclick = "splitButtonPressed()" /></p>
31
32          <p>The sentence split into words is<br />
33          <textarea id = "output" rows = "8" cols = "34">
34          </textarea></p>
35
36          <p>The first 10 characters of the input string are
37          <input id = "outputSubstring" type = "text"
38                size = "15" /></p>
39       </form>
40    </body>
41 </html>
```

Fig. 11.6 | `String` object methods `split` and `substring`. (Part 1 of 2.)

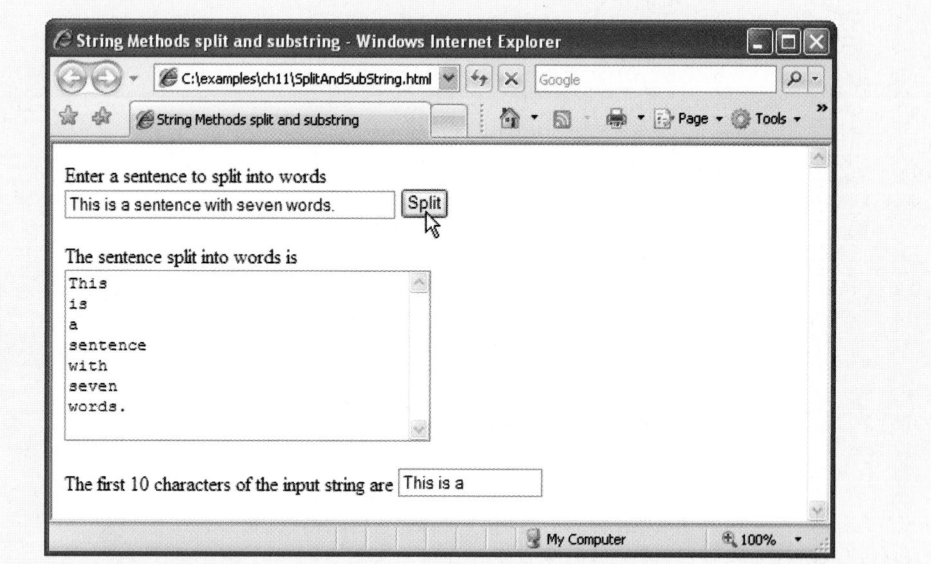

Fig. 11.6 | `String` object methods `split` and `substring`. (Part 2 of 2.)

Line 14 gets the value of the input field and stores it in variable `inputString`. Line 15 calls `String` method `split` to tokenize `inputString`. The argument to method `split` is the **delimiter string**—the string that determines the end of each token in the original string. In this example, the space character delimits the tokens. The delimiter string can contain multiple characters that should be used as delimiters. Method `split` returns an array of strings containing the tokens. Line 17 uses `Array` method `join` to combine the tokens in array `tokens` and separate each token with a newline character (`\n`). The resulting string is assigned to the `value` property of the XHTML form's `output` GUI component (an XHTML `textarea`).

Lines 19–20 use `String` method `substring` to obtain a string containing the first 10 characters of the string the user entered (still stored in `inputString`). The method returns the substring from the **starting index** (`0` in this example) up to but not including the **ending index** (`10` in this example). If the ending index is greater than the length of the string, the substring returned includes the characters from the starting index to the end of the original string.

11.4.6 XHTML Markup Methods

The script in Fig. 11.7 demonstrates the `String` object's methods that generate XHTML markup tags. When a `String` object invokes a markup method, the method wraps the `String`'s contents in the appropriate XHTML tag. These methods are particularly useful for generating XHTML dynamically during script processing.

Lines 12–17 define the strings that call each of the XHTML markup methods of the `String` object. Line 19 uses `String` method **`anchor`** to format the string in variable `anchorText` (`"This is an anchor"`) as

```
<a name = "top">This is an anchor</a>
```

```
<?xml version = "1.0" encoding = "utf-8"?>
<!DOCTYPE html PUBLIC "-//W3C//DTD XHTML 1.0 Strict//EN"
   "http://www.w3.org/TR/xhtml1/DTD/xhtml1-strict.dtd">

<!-- Fig. 11.7: MarkupMethods.html -->
<!-- String object XHTML markup methods. -->
<html xmlns = "http://www.w3.org/1999/xhtml">
   <head>
      <title>XHTML Markup Methods of the String Object</title>
      <script type = "text/javascript">
         <!--
         var anchorText = "This is an anchor";
         var fixedText = "This is monospaced text";
         var linkText = "Click here to go to anchorText";
         var strikeText = "This is strike out text";
         var subText = "subscript";
         var supText = "superscript";

         document.writeln( anchorText.anchor( "top" ) );
         document.writeln( "<br />" + fixedText.fixed() );
         document.writeln( "<br />" + strikeText.strike() );
         document.writeln(
            "<br />This is text with a " + subText.sub() );
         document.writeln(
            "<br />This is text with a " + supText.sup() );
         document.writeln( "<br />" + linkText.link( "#top" ) );
         // -->
      </script>
   </head><body></body>
</html>
```

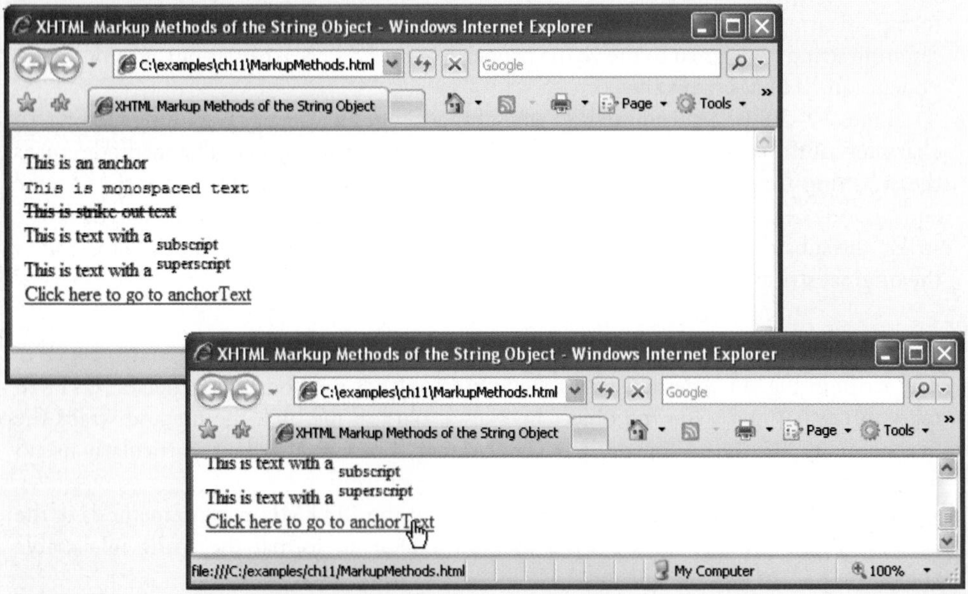

Fig. 11.7 | String object XHTML markup methods. (Part 1 of 2.)

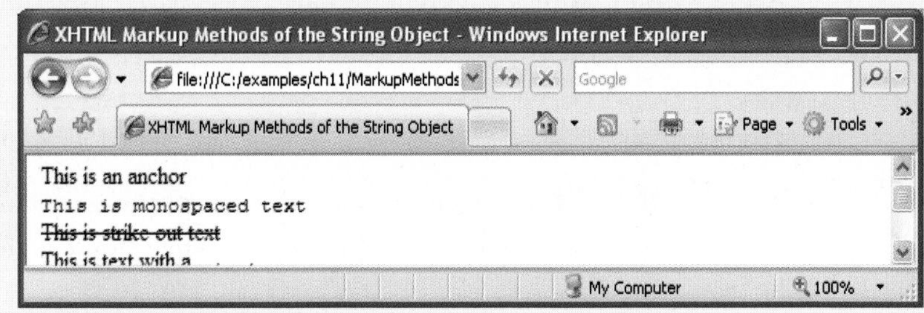

Fig. 11.7 | String object XHTML markup methods. (Part 2 of 2.)

The name of the anchor is the argument to the method. This anchor will be used later in the example as the target of a hyperlink.

Line 20 uses String method **fixed** to display text in a fixed-width font by formatting the string in variable fixedText ("This is monospaced text") as

```
<tt>This is monospaced text</tt>
```

Line 21 uses String method **strike** to display text with a line through it by formatting the string in variable strikeText ("This is strike out text") as

```
<strike>This is strike out text</strike>
```

Lines 22–23 use String method **sub** to display subscript text by formatting the string in variable subText ("subscript") as

```
<sub>subscript</sub>
```

Note that the resulting line in the XHTML document displays the word subscript smaller than the rest of the line and slightly below the line.

Lines 24–25 call String method **sup** to display superscript text by formatting the string in variable supText ("superscript") as

```
<sup>superscript</sup>
```

Note that the resulting line in the XHTML document displays the word superscript smaller than the rest of the line and slightly above the line.

Line 26 uses String method **link** to create a hyperlink by formatting the string in variable linkText ("Click here to go to anchorText") as

```
<a href = "#top">Click here to go to anchorText</a>
```

The target of the hyperlink (#top in this example) is the argument to the method and can be any URL. In this example, the hyperlink target is the anchor created in line 19. If you make your browser window short and scroll to the bottom of the web page, then click this link, the browser will reposition to the top of the web page.

11.5 Date Object

JavaScript's **Date** object provides methods for date and time manipulations. Date and time processing can be performed based on the computer's **local time zone** or based on World Time Standard's **Coordinated Universal Time** (abbreviated **UTC**)—formerly called

Greenwich Mean Time (GMT). Most methods of the `Date` object have a local time zone and a UTC version. The methods of the `Date` object are summarized in Fig. 11.8.

Method	Description
`getDate()` `getUTCDate()`	Returns a number from 1 to 31 representing the day of the month in local time or UTC.
`getDay()` `getUTCDay()`	Returns a number from 0 (Sunday) to 6 (Saturday) representing the day of the week in local time or UTC.
`getFullYear()` `getUTCFullYear()`	Returns the year as a four-digit number in local time or UTC.
`getHours()` `getUTCHours()`	Returns a number from 0 to 23 representing hours since midnight in local time or UTC.
`getMilliseconds()` `getUTCMilliSeconds()`	Returns a number from 0 to 999 representing the number of milliseconds in local time or UTC, respectively. The time is stored in hours, minutes, seconds and milliseconds.
`getMinutes()` `getUTCMinutes()`	Returns a number from 0 to 59 representing the minutes for the time in local time or UTC.
`getMonth()` `getUTCMonth()`	Returns a number from 0 (January) to 11 (December) representing the month in local time or UTC.
`getSeconds()` `getUTCSeconds()`	Returns a number from 0 to 59 representing the seconds for the time in local time or UTC.
`getTime()`	Returns the number of milliseconds between January 1, 1970, and the time in the `Date` object.
`getTimezoneOffset()`	Returns the difference in minutes between the current time on the local computer and UTC (Coordinated Universal Time).
`setDate(` *val* `)` `setUTCDate(` *val* `)`	Sets the day of the month (1 to 31) in local time or UTC.
`setFullYear(` *y*, *m*, *d* `)` `setUTCFullYear(` *y*, *m*, *d* `)`	Sets the year in local time or UTC. The second and third arguments representing the month and the date are optional. If an optional argument is not specified, the current value in the `Date` object is used.
`setHours(` *h*, *m*, *s*, *ms* `)` `setUTCHours(` *h*, *m*, *s*, *ms* `)`	Sets the hour in local time or UTC. The second, third and fourth arguments, representing the minutes, seconds and milliseconds, are optional. If an optional argument is not specified, the current value in the `Date` object is used.
`setMilliSeconds(` *ms* `)` `setUTCMilliseconds(` *ms* `)`	Sets the number of milliseconds in local time or UTC.

Fig. 11.8 | `Date` object methods. (Part 1 of 2.)

Method	Description
`setMinutes(` *m*, *s*, *ms* `)` `setUTCMinutes(` *m*, *s*, *ms* `)`	Sets the minute in local time or UTC. The second and third arguments, representing the seconds and milliseconds, are optional. If an optional argument is not specified, the current value in the `Date` object is used.
`setMonth(` *m*, *d* `)` `setUTCMonth(` *m*, *d* `)`	Sets the month in local time or UTC. The second argument, representing the date, is optional. If the optional argument is not specified, the current date value in the `Date` object is used.
`setSeconds(` *s*, *ms* `)` `setUTCSeconds(` *s*, *ms* `)`	Sets the second in local time or UTC. The second argument, representing the milliseconds, is optional. If this argument is not specified, the current millisecond value in the `Date` object is used.
`setTime(` *ms* `)`	Sets the time based on its argument—the number of elapsed milliseconds since January 1, 1970.
`toLocaleString()`	Returns a string representation of the date and time in a form specific to the computer's locale. For example, September 13, 2007, at 3:42:22 PM is represented as *09/13/07 15:47:22* in the United States and *13/09/07 15:47:22* in Europe.
`toUTCString()`	Returns a string representation of the date and time in the form: *15 Sep 2007 15:47:22 UTC*
`toString()`	Returns a string representation of the date and time in a form specific to the locale of the computer (*Mon Sep 17 15:47:22 EDT 2007* in the United States).
`valueOf()`	The time in number of milliseconds since midnight, January 1, 1970. (Same as `getTime`.)

Fig. 11.8 | `Date` object methods. (Part 2 of 2.)

The script of Fig. 11.9 demonstrates many of the local time zone methods in Fig. 11.8. Line 12 creates a new `Date` object. The `new` operator allocates the memory for the `Date` object. The empty parentheses indicate a call to the `Date` object's **constructor** with no arguments. A constructor is an initializer method for an object. Constructors are called automatically when an object is allocated with `new`. The `Date` constructor with no arguments initializes the `Date` object with the local computer's current date and time.

Software Engineering Observation 11.3

When an object is allocated with `new`*, the object's constructor is called automatically to initialize the object before it is used in the program.*

Lines 16–19 demonstrate the methods `toString`, `toLocaleString`, `toUTCString` and `valueOf`. Note that method `valueOf` returns a large integer value representing the total number of milliseconds between midnight, January 1, 1970, and the date and time stored in `Date` object `current`.

Lines 23–32 demonstrate the `Date` object's *get* methods for the local time zone. Note that method `getFullYear` returns the year as a four-digit number. Note as well that method `getTimeZoneOffset` returns the difference in minutes between the local time zone and UTC time (i.e., a difference of four hours in our time zone when this example was executed).

```
1  <?xml version = "1.0" encoding = "utf-8"?>
2  <!DOCTYPE html PUBLIC "-//W3C//DTD XHTML 1.0 Strict//EN"
3     "http://www.w3.org/TR/xhtml1/DTD/xhtml1-strict.dtd">
4
5  <!-- Fig. 11.9: DateTime.html -->
6  <!-- Date and time methods of the Date object. -->
7  <html xmlns = "http://www.w3.org/1999/xhtml">
8     <head>
9        <title>Date and Time Methods</title>
10       <script type = "text/javascript">
11          <!--
12          var current = new Date();
13
14          document.writeln(
15             "<h1>String representations and valueOf</h1>" );
16          document.writeln( "toString: " + current.toString() +
17             "<br />toLocaleString: " + current.toLocaleString() +
18             "<br />toUTCString: " + current.toUTCString() +
19             "<br />valueOf: " + current.valueOf() );
20
21          document.writeln(
22             "<h1>Get methods for local time zone</h1>" );
23          document.writeln( "getDate: " + current.getDate() +
24             "<br />getDay: " + current.getDay() +
25             "<br />getMonth: " + current.getMonth() +
26             "<br />getFullYear: " + current.getFullYear() +
27             "<br />getTime: " + current.getTime() +
28             "<br />getHours: " + current.getHours() +
29             "<br />getMinutes: " + current.getMinutes() +
30             "<br />getSeconds: " + current.getSeconds() +
31             "<br />getMilliseconds: " + current.getMilliseconds() +
32             "<br />getTimezoneOffset: " + current.getTimezoneOffset() );
33
34          document.writeln(
35             "<h1>Specifying arguments for a new Date</h1>" );
36          var anotherDate = new Date( 2007, 2, 18, 1, 5, 0, 0 );
37          document.writeln( "Date: " + anotherDate );
38
39          document.writeln( "<h1>Set methods for local time zone</h1>" );
40          anotherDate.setDate( 31 );
41          anotherDate.setMonth( 11 );
42          anotherDate.setFullYear( 2007 );
43          anotherDate.setHours( 23 );
44          anotherDate.setMinutes( 59 );
45          anotherDate.setSeconds( 59 );
46          document.writeln( "Modified date: " + anotherDate );
```

Fig. 11.9 | Date and time methods of the `Date` object. (Part 1 of 2.)

```
47            // -->
48         </script>
49      </head><body></body>
50   </html>
```

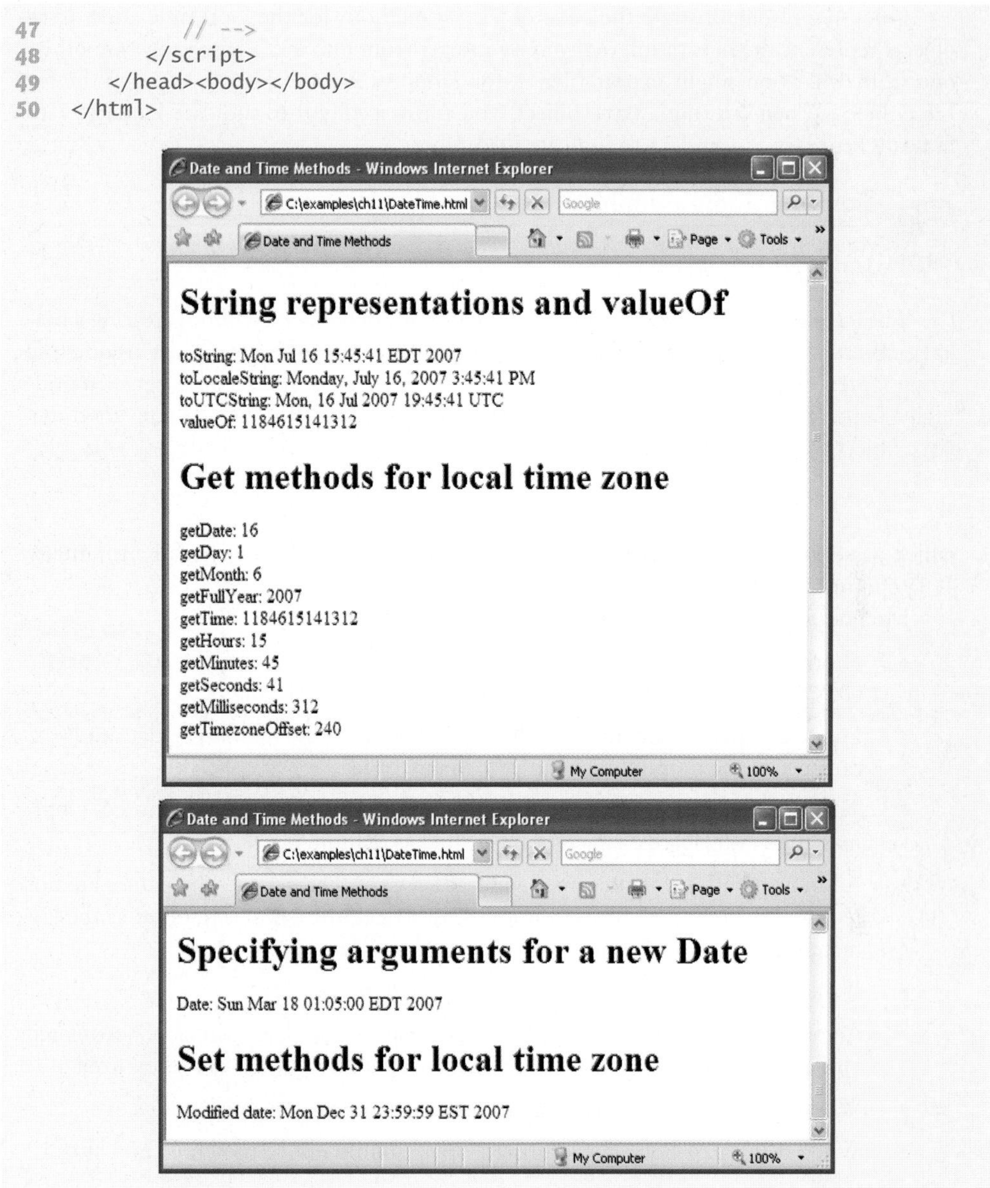

Fig. 11.9 | Date and time methods of the `Date` object. (Part 2 of 2.)

Line 36 demonstrates creating a new `Date` object and supplying arguments to the `Date` constructor for *year*, *month*, *date*, *hours*, *minutes*, *seconds* and *milliseconds*. Note that the *hours*, *minutes*, *seconds* and *milliseconds* arguments are all optional. If any one of these arguments is not specified, a zero is supplied in its place. For the *hours*, *minutes* and *seconds* arguments, if the argument to the right of any of these arguments is specified, it too must be specified (e.g., if the *minutes* argument is specified, the *hours* argument must be specified; if the *milliseconds* argument is specified, all the arguments must be specified).

Lines 40–45 demonstrate the `Date` object *set* methods for the local time zone. `Date` objects represent the month internally as an integer from 0 to 11. These values are off by one from what you might expect (i.e., 1 for January, 2 for February, …, and 12 for December). When creating a `Date` object, you must specify 0 to indicate January, 1 to indicate February, …, and 11 to indicate December.

Common Programming Error 11.2

Assuming that months are represented as numbers from 1 to 12 leads to off-by-one errors when you are processing `Dates`*.*

The `Date` object provides two other methods that can be called without creating a new `Date` object—**`Date.parse`** and **`Date.UTC`**. Method `Date.parse` receives as its argument a string representing a date and time, and returns the number of milliseconds between midnight, January 1, 1970, and the specified date and time. This value can be converted to a `Date` object with the statement

```
var theDate = new Date( numberOfMilliseconds );
```

which passes to the `Date` constructor the number of milliseconds since midnight, January 1, 1970, for the `Date` object.

Method `parse` converts the string using the following rules:

- Short dates can be specified in the form `MM-DD-YY`, `MM-DD-YYYY`, `MM/DD/YY` or `MM/DD/YYYY`. The month and day are not required to be two digits.
- Long dates that specify the complete month name (e.g., "January"), date and year can specify the month, date and year in any order.
- Text in parentheses within the string is treated as a comment and ignored. Commas and white-space characters are treated as delimiters.
- All month and day names must have at least two characters. The names are not required to be unique. If the names are identical, the name is resolved as the last match (e.g., "Ju" represents "July" rather than "June").
- If the name of the day of the week is supplied, it is ignored.
- All standard time zones (e.g., EST for Eastern Standard Time), Coordinated Universal Time (UTC) and Greenwich Mean Time (GMT) are recognized.
- When specifying hours, minutes and seconds, separate each by colons.
- When using a 24-hour-clock format, "PM" should not be used for times after 12 noon.

`Date` method `UTC` returns the number of milliseconds between midnight, January 1, 1970, and the date and time specified as its arguments. The arguments to the `UTC` method include the required *year*, *month* and *date*, and the optional *hours*, *minutes*, *seconds* and *milliseconds*. If any of the *hours*, *minutes*, *seconds* or *milliseconds* arguments is not specified, a zero is supplied in its place. For the *hours*, *minutes* and *seconds* arguments, if the argument to the right of any of these arguments in the argument list is specified, that argument must also be specified (e.g., if the *minutes* argument is specified, the *hours* argument must be specified; if the *milliseconds* argument is specified, all the arguments must be specified). As with the result of `Date.parse`, the result of `Date.UTC` can be converted to a `Date` object by creating a new `Date` object with the result of `Date.UTC` as its argument.

11.6 Boolean and Number Objects

JavaScript provides the `Boolean` and `Number` objects as object wrappers for boolean `true`/`false` values and numbers, respectively. These wrappers define methods and properties useful in manipulating boolean values and numbers. Wrappers provide added functionality for working with simple data types.

When a JavaScript program requires a boolean value, JavaScript automatically creates a `Boolean` object to store the value. JavaScript programmers can create `Boolean` objects explicitly with the statement

```
var b = new Boolean( booleanValue );
```

The constructor argument *booleanValue* specifies whether the value of the `Boolean` object should be `true` or `false`. If *booleanValue* is `false`, `0`, `null`, `Number.NaN` or an empty string (`""`), or if no argument is supplied, the new `Boolean` object contains `false`. Otherwise, the new `Boolean` object contains `true`. Figure 11.10 summarizes the methods of the `Boolean` object.

JavaScript automatically creates `Number` objects to store numeric values in a JavaScript program. JavaScript programmers can create a `Number` object with the statement

```
var n = new Number( numericValue );
```

The constructor argument *numericValue* is the number to store in the object. Although you can explicitly create `Number` objects, normally the JavaScript interpreter creates them as needed. Figure 11.11 summarizes the methods and properties of the `Number` object.

Method	Description
`toString()`	Returns the string `"true"` if the value of the `Boolean` object is true; otherwise, returns the string `"false"`.
`valueOf()`	Returns the value `true` if the `Boolean` object is `true`; otherwise, returns `false`.

Fig. 11.10 | `Boolean` object methods.

Method or property	Description
`toString(` *radix* `)`	Returns the string representation of the number. The optional *radix* argument (a number from 2 to 36) specifies the number's base. For example, radix 2 results in the binary representation of the number, 8 results in the octal representation, 10 results in the decimal representation and 16 results in the hexadecimal representation. See Appendix E, Number Systems, for a review of the binary, octal, decimal and hexadecimal number systems.

Fig. 11.11 | `Number` object methods and properties. (Part 1 of 2.)

Method or property	Description
`valueOf()`	Returns the numeric value.
`Number.MAX_VALUE`	This property represents the largest value that can be stored in a JavaScript program—approximately 1.79E+308.
`Number.MIN_VALUE`	This property represents the smallest value that can be stored in a JavaScript program—approximately 5.00E–324.
`Number.NaN`	This property represents *not a number*—a value returned from an arithmetic expression that does not result in a number (e.g., the expression `parseInt( "hello" )` cannot convert the string `"hello"` into a number, so `parseInt` would return `Number.NaN`. To determine whether a value is `NaN`, test the result with function `isNaN`, which returns `true` if the value is `NaN`; otherwise, it returns `false`.
`Number.NEGATIVE_INFINITY`	This property represents a value less than `-Number.MAX_VALUE`.
`Number.POSITIVE_INFINITY`	This property represents a value greater than `Number.MAX_VALUE`.

Fig. 11.11 | `Number` object methods and properties. (Part 2 of 2.)

11.7 document Object

The **`document`** object is used to manipulate the document that is currently visible in the browser window. The `document` object has many properties and methods, such as methods `document.write` and `document.writeln`, which have both been used in prior JavaScript examples. Figure 11.12 shows the methods and properties of the `document` objects that are used in this chapter. You can learn more about the properties and methods of the `document` object in our JavaScript Resource Center (`www.deitel.com/javascript`).

Method or property	Description
`getElementById(` *id* `)`	Returns the DOM node representing the XHTML element whose `id` attribute matches *id*.
`write(` *string* `)`	Writes the string to the XHTML document as XHTML code.
`writeln(` *string* `)`	Writes the string to the XHTML document as XHTML code and adds a newline character at the end.
`cookie`	A string containing the values of all the cookies stored on the user's computer for the current document. See Section 11.9, Using Cookies.
`lastModified`	The date and time that this document was last modified.

Fig. 11.12 | Important `document` object methods and properties.

11.8 window Object

The `window` object provides methods for manipulating browser windows. The following script shows many of the commonly used properties and methods of the `window` object and uses them to create a website that spans multiple browser windows. Figure 11.13 allows the user to create a new, fully customized browser window by completing an XHTML form and clicking the **Submit** button. The script also allows the user to add text to the new window and navigate the window to a different URL.

The script starts in line 10. Line 12 declares a variable to refer to the new window. We refer to the new window as the child window because it is created and controlled by the main, or parent, window in this script. Lines 14–50 define the `createChildWindow` function, which determines the features that have been selected by the user and creates a child window with those features (but does not add any content to the window). Lines 18–20 declare several variables to store the status of the checkboxes on the page. Lines 23–38 set each variable to `"yes"` or `"no"` based on whether the corresponding checkbox is checked or unchecked.

```
1  <?xml version = "1.0" encoding = "utf-8"?>
2  <!DOCTYPE html PUBLIC "-//W3C//DTD XHTML 1.0 Strict//EN"
3     "http://www.w3.org/TR/xhtml1/DTD/xhtml1-strict.dtd">
4
5  <!-- Fig. 11.13: window.html -->
6  <!-- Using the window object to create and modify child windows. -->
7  <html xmlns = "http://www.w3.org/1999/xhtml">
8  <head>
9  <title>Using the Window Object</title>
10 <script type = "text/javascript">
11    <!--
12    var childWindow; // variable to control the child window
13
14    function createChildWindow()
15    {
16       // these variables all contain either "yes" or "no"
17       // to enable or disable a feature in the child window
18       var toolBar;
19       var menuBar;
20       var scrollBars;
21
22       // determine whether the Tool Bar checkbox is checked
23       if ( document.getElementById( "toolBarCheckBox" ).checked )
24          toolBar = "yes";
25       else
26          toolBar = "no";
27
28       // determine whether the Menu Bar checkbox is checked
29       if ( document.getElementById( "menuBarCheckBox" ).checked )
30          menuBar = "yes";
31       else
32          menuBar = "no";
33
```

Fig. 11.13 | Using the `window` object to create and modify child windows. (Part 1 of 4.)

```
         // determine whether the Scroll Bar checkbox is checked
         if ( document.getElementById( "scrollBarsCheckBox" ).checked )
            scrollBars = "yes";
         else
            scrollBars = "no";

         //display window with selected features
         childWindow = window.open( "", "",
            ",toolbar = " + toolBar +
            ",menubar = " + menuBar +
            ",scrollbars = " + scrollBars );

         // disable buttons
         document.getElementById( "closeButton" ).disabled = false;
         document.getElementById( "modifyButton" ).disabled = false;
         document.getElementById( "setURLButton" ).disabled = false;
      } // end function createChildWindow

      // insert text from the textbox in the child window
      function modifyChildWindow()
      {
         if ( childWindow.closed )
            alert( "You attempted to interact with a closed window" );
         else
            childWindow.document.write(
               document.getElementById( "textForChild" ).value );
      } // end function modifyChildWindow

      // close the child window
      function closeChildWindow()
      {
         if ( childWindow.closed )
            alert( "You attempted to interact with a closed window" );
         else
            childWindow.close();

         document.getElementById( "closeButton" ).disabled = true;
         document.getElementById( "modifyButton" ).disabled = true;
         document.getElementById( "setURLButton" ).disabled = true;
      } // end function closeChildWindow

      // set the URL of the child window to the URL
      // in the parent window's myChildURL
      function setChildWindowURL()
      {
         if ( childWindow.closed )
            alert( "You attempted to interact with a closed window" );
         else
            childWindow.location =
               document.getElementById( "myChildURL" ).value;
      } // end function setChildWindowURL
      //-->
   </script>
```

Fig. 11.13 | Using the `window` object to create and modify child windows. (Part 2 of 4.)

```
   </head>
   <body>
      <h1>Hello, this is the main window</h1>
      <p>Please check the features to enable for the child window<br/>
      <input id = "toolBarCheckBox" type = "checkbox" value = ""
         checked = "checked" />
         <label>Tool Bar</label>
      <input id = "menuBarCheckBox" type = "checkbox" value = ""
         checked = "checked" />
         <label>Menu Bar</label>
      <input id = "scrollBarsCheckBox" type = "checkbox" value = ""
         checked = "checked" />
         <label>Scroll Bars</label></p>

      <p>Please enter the text that you would like to display
      in the child window<br/>
      <input id = "textForChild" type = "text"
         value = "<h1>Hello, I am a child window.</h1> " />
      <input id = "createButton" type = "button"
         value = "Create Child Window" onclick = "createChildWindow()" />
      <input id= "modifyButton" type = "button" value = "Modify Child Window"
         onclick = "modifyChildWindow()" disabled = "disabled" />
      <input id = "closeButton" type = "button" value = "Close Child Window"
         onclick = "closeChildWindow()" disabled = "disabled" /></p>

      <p>The other window's URL is: <br/>
      <input id = "myChildURL" type = "text" value = "./" />
      <input id = "setURLButton" type = "button" value = "Set Child URL"
         onclick = "setChildWindowURL()" disabled = "disabled" /></p>
   </body>
</html>
```

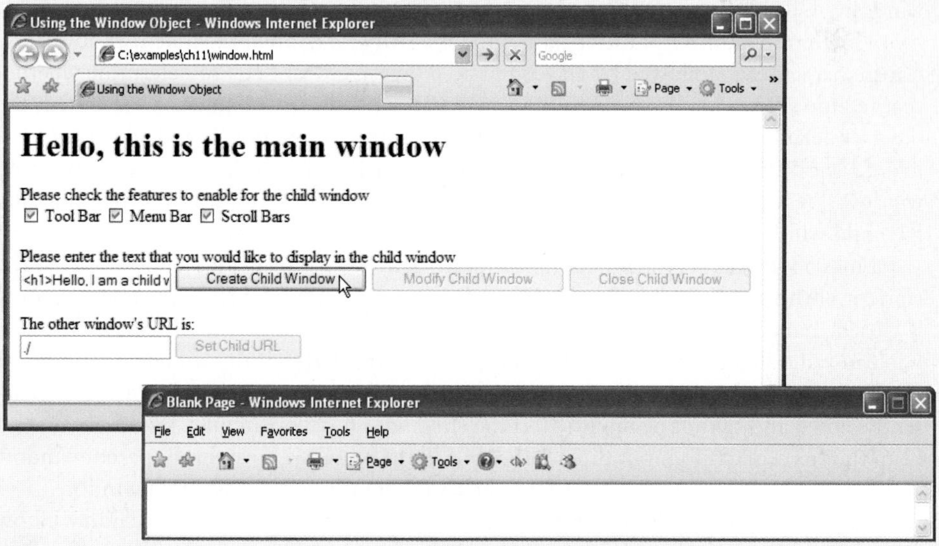

Fig. 11.13 | Using the window object to create and modify child windows. (Part 3 of 4.)

Fig. 11.13 | Using the `window` object to create and modify child windows. (Part 4 of 4.)

The statement in lines 41–44 uses the `window` object's `open` method to create the requested child window. Method `open` has three parameters. The first parameter is the URL of the page to open in the new window, and the second parameter is the name of the window. If you specify the `target` attribute of an `a` (anchor) element to correspond to the name of a window, the `href` of the link will be opened in the window. In our example, we pass `window.open` empty strings as the first two parameter values because we want the new window to open a blank page, and we use a different method to manipulate the child window's URL.

The third parameter of the `open` method is a string of comma-separated, all-lowercase feature names, each followed by an = sign and either `"yes"` or `"no"` to determine whether that feature should be displayed in the new window. If these parameters are omitted, the browser defaults to a new window containing an empty page, no title and all features visible. [*Note:* If your menu bar is normally hidden in IE7, it will not appear in the child window. Press the *Alt* key to display it.] Lines 47–49 enable the buttons for manipulating the child window—these are initially disabled when the page loads.

Lines 53–60 define the function `modifyChildWindow`, which adds a line of text to the content of the child window. In line 55, the script determines whether the child window is closed. Function `modifyChildWindow` uses property `childWindow.closed` to obtain a boolean value that is `true` if `childWindow` is closed and `false` if the window is still open. If the window is closed, an alert box is displayed notifying the user that the window is currently closed and cannot be modified. If the child window is open, lines 58–59 obtain text from the `textForChild` input (lines 103–104) in the XHTML form in the parent window and uses the child's `document.write` method to write this text to the child window.

Function `closeChildWindow` (lines 63–73) also determines whether the child window is closed before proceeding. If the child window is closed, the script displays an alert box telling the user that the window is already closed. If the child window is open, line 68 closes it using the `childWindow.close` method. Lines 70–72 disable the buttons that interact with the child window.

Look-and-Feel Observation 11.1

Popup windows should be used sparingly. Many users dislike websites that open additional windows, or that resize or reposition the browser. Some some users have popup blockers that will prevent new windows from opening.

Software Engineering Observation 11.4

`window.location` is a property that always contains a string representation of the URL displayed in the current window. Typically, web browsers will allow a script to retrieve the `window.location` property of another window only if the script belongs to the same website as the page in the other window.

Function `setChildWindowURL` (lines 77–84) copies the contents of the `myChildURL` text field to the `location` property of the child window. If the child window is open, lines 81–82 set property `location` of the child window to the string in the `myChildURL` textbox. This action changes the URL of the child window and is equivalent to typing a new URL into the window's address bar and clicking **Go** (or pressing *Enter*).

The script ends in line 86. Lines 88–116 contain the body of the XHTML document, comprising a form that contains checkboxes, buttons, textboxes and form field labels. The script uses the form elements defined in the body to obtain input from the user. Lines 106, 108, 110, and 115 specify the `onclick` attributes of XHTML buttons. Each button is set to call a corresponding JavaScript function when clicked.

Figure 11.14 contains a list of some commonly used methods and properties of the `window` object.

Method or property	Description
`open( url, name, options )`	Creates a new window with the URL of the window set to *url*, the name set to *name* to refer to it in the script, and the visible features set by the string passed in as *option.*
`prompt( prompt, default )`	Displays a dialog box asking the user for input. The text of the dialog is *prompt*, and the default value is set to *default.*
`close()`	Closes the current window and deletes its object from memory.
`focus()`	This method gives focus to the window (i.e., puts the window in the foreground, on top of any other open browser windows).
`blur()`	This method takes focus away from the window (i.e., puts the window in the background).
`window.document`	This property contains the `document` object representing the document currently inside the window.
`window.closed`	This property contains a boolean value that is set to true if the window is closed, and false if it is not.

Fig. 11.14 | Important `window` object methods and properties. (Part 1 of 2.)

Method or property	Description
`window.opener`	This property contains the `window` object of the window that opened the current window, if such a window exists.

Fig. 11.14 | Important `window` object methods and properties. (Part 2 of 2.)

11.9 Using Cookies

Cookies provide web developers with a tool for personalizing web pages. A cookie is a piece of data that is stored on the user's computer to maintain information about the client during and between browser sessions. A website may store a cookie on the client's computer to record user preferences or other information that the website can retrieve during the client's subsequent visits. For example, a website can retrieve the user's name from a cookie and use it to display a personalized greeting.

Microsoft Internet Explorer and Mozilla Firefox store cookies as small text files on the client's hard drive. When a user visits a website, the browser locates any cookies written by scripts on that site and makes them available to any scripts located on the site. Note that cookies may be accessed only by scripts belonging to the same website from which they originated (i.e., a cookie set by a script on `amazon.com` can be read only by other scripts on `amazon.com`).

Cookies are accessible in JavaScript through the `document` object's `cookie` property. JavaScript treats a cookie as a string of text. Any standard string function or method can manipulate a cookie. A cookie has the syntax "*identifier=value*," where *identifier* is any valid JavaScript variable identifier, and *value* is the value of the cookie variable. When multiple cookies exist for one website, *identifier-value* pairs are separated by semicolons in the `document.cookie` string.

Cookies differ from ordinary strings in that each cookie has an expiration date, after which the web browser deletes it. This date can be defined by setting the `expires` property in the cookie string. If a cookie's expiration date is not set, then the cookie expires by default after the user closes the browser window. A cookie can be deleted immediately by setting the `expires` property to a date and time in the past.

The assignment operator does not overwrite the entire list of cookies, but appends a cookie to the end of it. Thus, if we set two cookies

```
document.cookie = "name1=value1;";
document.cookie = "name2=value2;";
```

`document.cookie` will contain `"name1=value1; name2=value2"`.

Figure 11.15 uses a cookie to store the user's name and displays a personalized greeting. This example improves upon the functionality in the dynamic welcome page example of Fig. 6.17 by requiring the user to enter a name only during the first visit to the web page. On each subsequent visit, the script can display the user name that is stored in the cookie.

Line 10 begins the script. Lines 12–13 declare the variables needed to obtain the time, and line 14 declares the variable that stores the name of the user. Lines 16–27 contain the same `if...else` statement used in Fig. 6.17 to display a time-sensitive greeting.

Lines 30–66 contain the code used to manipulate the cookie. Line 30 determines whether a cookie exists on the client computer. The expression `document.cookie` evaluates to `true` if a cookie exists. If a cookie does not exist, then the script prompts the user to enter a name (line 45). The script creates a cookie containing the string `"name="`, followed by a copy of the user's name produced by the built-in JavaScript function **`escape`** (line 49). The function `escape` converts any non-alphanumeric characters, such as spaces

```
1  <?xml version = "1.0" encoding = "utf-8"?>
2  <!DOCTYPE html PUBLIC "-//W3C//DTD XHTML 1.0 Strict//EN"
3     "http://www.w3.org/TR/xhtml1/DTD/xhtml1-strict.dtd">
4
5  <!-- Fig. 11.15: cookie.html -->
6  <!-- Using cookies to store user identification data. -->
7  <html xmlns = "http://www.w3.org/1999/xhtml">
8     <head>
9        <title>Using Cookies</title>
10       <script type = "text/javascript">
11          <!--
12          var now = new Date(); // current date and time
13          var hour = now.getHours(); // current hour (0-23)
14          var name;
15
16          if ( hour < 12 ) // determine whether it is morning
17             document.write( "<h1>Good Morning, " );
18          else
19          {
20             hour = hour - 12; // convert from 24-hour clock to PM time
21
22             // determine whether it is afternoon or evening
23             if ( hour < 6 )
24                document.write( "<h1>Good Afternoon, " );
25             else
26                document.write( "<h1>Good Evening, " );
27          } // end else
28
29          // determine whether there is a cookie
30          if ( document.cookie )
31          {
32             // convert escape characters in the cookie string to their
33             // English notation
34             var myCookie = unescape( document.cookie );
35
36             // split the cookie into tokens using = as delimiter
37             var cookieTokens = myCookie.split( "=" );
38
39             // set name to the part of the cookie that follows the = sign
40             name = cookieTokens[ 1 ];
41          } // end if
42          else
43          {
44             // if there was no cookie, ask the user to input a name
45             name = window.prompt( "Please enter your name", "Paul" );
```

Fig. 11.15 | Using cookies to store user identification data. (Part 1 of 3.)

```

            // escape special characters in the name string
            // and add name to the cookie
            document.cookie = "name=" + escape( name );
         } // end else

         document.writeln(
            name + ", welcome to JavaScript programming!</h1>" );
         document.writeln( "<a href = 'javascript:wrongPerson()'> " +
            "Click here if you are not " + name + "</a>" );

         // reset the document's cookie if wrong person
         function wrongPerson()
         {
            // reset the cookie
            document.cookie= "name=null;" +
               " expires=Thu, 01-Jan-95 00:00:01 GMT";

            // reload the page to get a new name after removing the cookie
            location.reload();
         } // end function wrongPerson

         // -->
      </script>
   </head>
   <body>
      <p>Click Refresh (or Reload) to run the script again</p>
   </body>
</html>
```

Fig. 11.15 | Using cookies to store user identification data. (Part 2 of 3.)

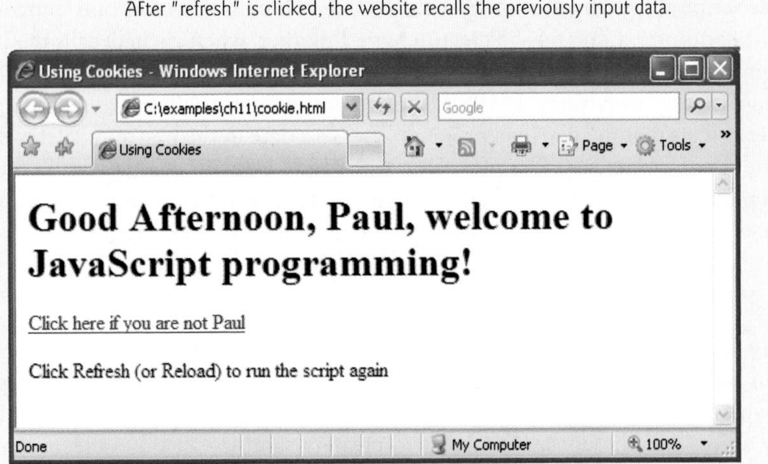
AFter "refresh" is clicked, the website recalls the previously input data.
Using Cookies - Windows Internet Explorer
C:\examples\ch11\cookie.html
Google
Using Cookies
Page
Tools
Good Afternoon, Paul, welcome to JavaScript programming!
Click here if you are not Paul
Click Refresh (or Reload) to run the script again
Done
My Computer
100%

Fig. 11.15 | Using cookies to store user identification data. (Part 3 of 3.)

and semicolons, in a string to their equivalent hexadecimal escape sequences of the form "%*XX*," where *XX* is the two-digit hexadecimal ASCII value of a special character. For example, if `name` contains the value `"David Green"`, the statement `escape( name )` evaluates to `"David%20Green"`, because the hexadecimal ASCII value of a blank space is `20`. It is a good idea to always escape cookie values before writing them to the client. This conversion prevents any special characters in the cookie from being misinterpreted as having a special meaning in the code, rather than being a character in a cookie value. For instance, a semicolon in a cookie value could be misinterpreted as a semicolon separating two adjacent *identifier-value* pairs. Applying the function **unescape** to cookies when they are read out of the `document.cookie` string converts the hexadecimal escape sequences back to English characters for display in a web page.

Good Programming Practice 11.2

Always store values in cookies with self-documenting identifiers. Do not forget to include the identifier followed by an = sign before the value being stored.

If a cookie exists (i.e., the user has been to the page before), then the script parses the user name out of the cookie string and stores it in a local variable. Parsing generally refers to the act of splitting a string into smaller, more useful components. Line 34 uses the JavaScript function `unescape` to replace all the escape sequences in the cookie with their equivalent English-language characters. The script stores the unescaped cookie value in the variable `myCookie` (line 34) and uses the JavaScript function `split` (line 37), introduced in Section 11.4.5, to break the cookie into identifier and value tokens. At this point in the script, `myCookie` contains a string of the form `"name=`*value*`"`. We call `split` on `myCookie` with = as the delimiter to obtain the `cookieTokens` array, with the first element equal to the name of the identifier and the second element equal to the value of the identifier. Line 40 assigns the value of the second element in the `cookieTokens` array (i.e., the actual value stored in the cookie) to the variable `name`. Lines 52–53 add the personalized greeting to the web page, using the user's name stored in the cookie.

The script allows the user to reset the cookie, which is useful in case someone new is using the computer. Lines 54–55 create a hyperlink that, when clicked, calls the JavaScript function `wrongPerson` (lines 58–66). Lines 61–62 set the cookie `name` to `null` and the `expires` property to January 1, 1995 (though any date in the past will suffice). Internet Explorer detects that the `expires` property is set to a date in the past and deletes the cookie from the user's computer. The next time this page loads, no cookie will be found. The **`reload`** method of the `location` object forces the page to refresh (line 65), and, unable to find an existing cookie, the script prompts the user to enter a new name.

11.10 Final JavaScript Example

The past few chapters have explored many JavaScript concepts and how they can be applied on the web. The next JavaScript example combines many of these concepts into a single web page. Figure 11.16 uses functions, cookies, arrays, loops, the `Date` object, the `window` object and the `document` object to create a sample welcome screen containing a personalized greeting, a short quiz, a random image and a random quotation. We have seen all of these concepts before, but this example illustrates how they work together on one web page.

```
<?xml version = "1.0" encoding = "utf-8"?>
<!DOCTYPE html PUBLIC "-//W3C//DTD XHTML 1.0 Strict//EN"
   "http://www.w3.org/TR/xhtml1/DTD/xhtml1-strict.dtd">

<!-- Fig. 11.16: final.html -->
<!-- Rich welcome page using several JavaScript concepts. -->
<html xmlns = "http://www.w3.org/1999/xhtml">
   <head>
      <title>Putting It All Together</title>
      <script type = "text/javascript">
         <!--
         var now = new Date(); // current date and time
         var hour = now.getHours(); // current hour

         // array with names of the images that will be randomly selected
         var pictures =
            [ "CPE", "EPT", "GPP", "GUI", "PERF", "PORT", "SEO" ];

         // array with the quotes that will be randomly selected
         var quotes = [ "Form ever follows function.<br/>" +
            " Louis Henri Sullivan", "E pluribus unum." +
            " (One composed of many.) <br/> Virgil", "Is it a" +
            " world to hide virtues in?<br/> William Shakespeare" ];

         // write the current date and time to the web page
         document.write( "<p>" + now.toLocaleString() + "<br/></p>" );

         // determine whether it is morning
         if ( hour < 12 )
            document.write( "<h2>Good Morning, " );
```

Fig. 11.16 | Rich welcome page using several JavaScript concepts. (Part 1 of 5.)

```
         else
         {
            hour = hour - 12; // convert from 24-hour clock to PM time

            // determine whether it is afternoon or evening
            if ( hour < 6 )
               document.write( "<h2>Good Afternoon, " );
            else
               document.write( "<h2>Good Evening, " );
         } // end else

         // determine whether there is a cookie
         if ( document.cookie )
         {
            // convert escape characters in the cookie string to their
            // English notation
            var myCookie = unescape( document.cookie );

            // split the cookie into tokens using = as delimiter
            var cookieTokens = myCookie.split( "=" );

            // set name to the part of the cookie that follows the = sign
            name = cookieTokens[ 1 ];
         } // end if
         else
         {
            // if there was no cookie, ask the user to input a name
            name = window.prompt( "Please enter your name", "Paul" );

            // escape special characters in the name string
            // and add name to the cookie
            document.cookie = "name =" + escape( name );
         } // end else

         // write the greeting to the page
         document.writeln(
            name + ", welcome to JavaScript programming!</h2>" );

         // write the link for deleting the cookie to the page
         document.writeln( "<a href = \"javascript:wrongPerson()\" > " +
            "Click here if you are not " + name + "</a><br/>" );

         // write the random image to the page
         document.write ( "<img src = \"" +
            pictures[ Math.floor( Math.random() * 7 ) ] +
            ".gif\" /> <br/>" );

         // write the random quote to the page
         document.write ( quotes[ Math.floor( Math.random() * 3 ) ] );

         // create a window with all the quotes in it
         function allQuotes()
         {
```

Fig. 11.16 | Rich welcome page using several JavaScript concepts. (Part 2 of 5.)

```
            // create the child window for the quotes
            var quoteWindow = window.open( "", "", "resizable=yes, " +
               "toolbar=no, menubar=no, status=no, location=no," +
               " scrollBars=yes" );
            quoteWindow.document.write( "<p>" )

            // loop through all quotes and write them in the new window
            for ( var i = 0; i < quotes.length; i++ )
               quoteWindow.document.write( ( i + 1 ) + ".) " +
                  quotes[ i ] + "<br/><br/>");

            // write a close link to the new window
            quoteWindow.document.write( "</p><br/><a href = " +
               "\"javascript:window.close()\">Close this window</a>" );
         } // end function allQuotes

         // reset the document's cookie if wrong person
         function wrongPerson()
         {
            // reset the cookie
            document.cookie= "name=null;" +
               " expires=Thu, 01-Jan-95 00:00:01 GMT";

            // reload the page to get a new name after removing the cookie
            location.reload();
         } // end function wrongPerson

         // open a new window with the quiz2.html file in it
         function openQuiz()
         {
            window.open( "quiz2.html", "", "toolbar = no, " +
               "menubar = no, scrollBars = no" );
         } // end function openQuiz
      // -->
      </script>
   </head>
   <body>
      <p><a href = "javascript:allQuotes()">View all quotes</a></p>

      <p id = "quizSpot">
         <a href = "javascript:openQuiz()">Please take our quiz</a></p>

      <script type = "text/javascript">
         // variable that gets the last modification date and time
         var modDate = new Date( document.lastModified );

         // write the last modified date and time to the page
         document.write ( "This page was last modified " +
            modDate.toLocaleString() );
      </script>
   </body>
</html>
```

Fig. 11.16 | Rich welcome page using several JavaScript concepts. (Part 3 of 5.)

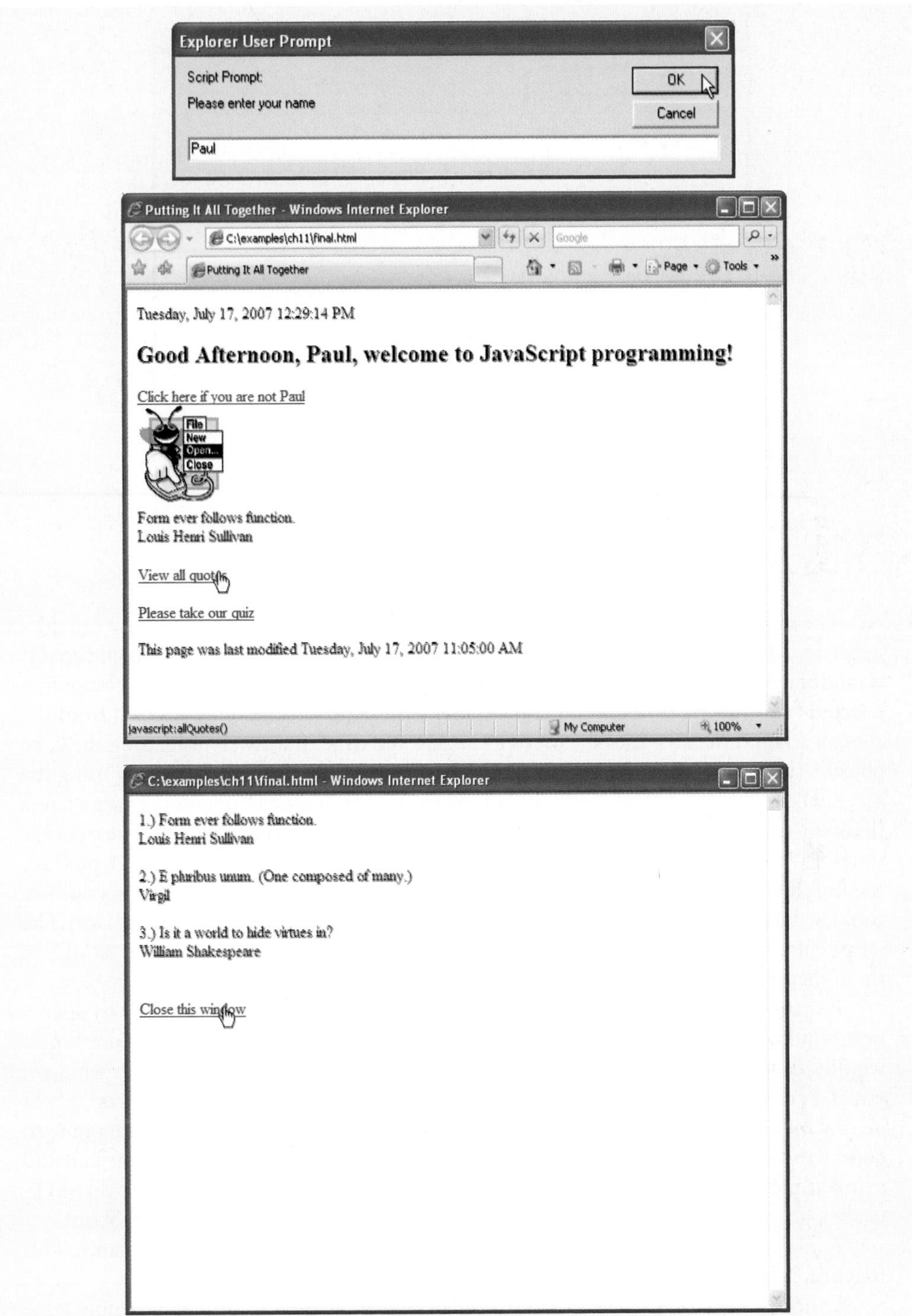

Fig. 11.16 | Rich welcome page using several JavaScript concepts. (Part 4 of 5.)

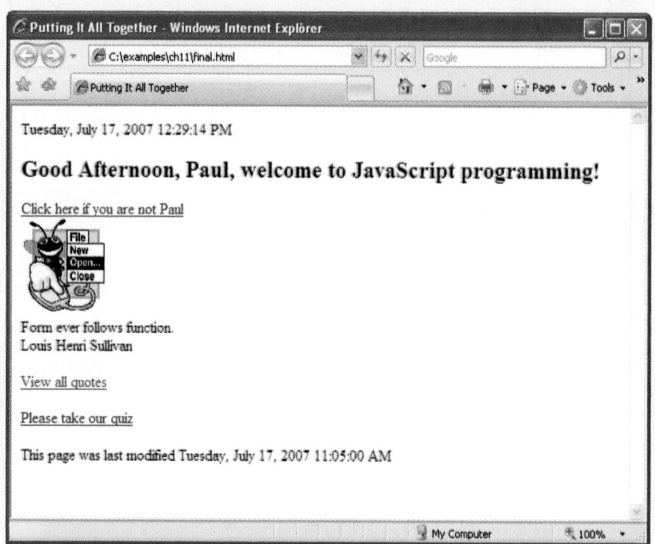

Fig. 11.16 | Rich welcome page using several JavaScript concepts. (Part 5 of 5.)

The script that builds most of this page starts in line 10. Lines 12–13 declare variables needed for determining the time of day. Lines 16–23 create two arrays from which content is randomly selected. This web page contains both an image (whose filename is randomly selected from the `pictures` array) and a quote (whose text is randomly selected from the `quotes` array). Line 26 writes the user's local date and time to the web page using the `Date` object's `toLocaleString` method. Lines 29–40 display a time-sensitive greeting using the same code as Fig. 6.17. The script either uses an existing cookie to obtain the user's name (lines 43–54) or prompts the user for a name, which the script then stores in a new cookie (lines 55–63). Lines 66–67 write the greeting to the web page, and lines 70–71 produce the link for resetting the cookie. This is the same code used in Fig. 11.15 to manipulate cookies. Lines 74–79 write the random image and random quote to the web page. The script chooses each by randomly selecting an index into each array. This code is similar to the code used in Fig. 10.7 to display a random image using an array.

Function `allQuotes` (lines 82–98) uses the `window` object and a `for` loop to open a new window containing all the quotes in the `quotes` array. Lines 85–87 create a new window called `quoteWindow`. The script does not assign a URL or a name to this window, but it does specify the window features to display. Line 88 opens a new paragraph in `quoteWindow`. A `for` loop (lines 91–93) traverses the quotes array and writes each quote to `quoteWindow`. Lines 96–97 close the paragraph in `quoteWindow`, insert a new line and add a link at the bottom of the page that allows the user to close the window. Note that `allQuotes` generates a web page and opens it in an entirely new window with JavaScript.

Function `wrongPerson` (lines 101–109) resets the cookie storing the user's name. This function is identical to function `wrongPerson` in Fig. 11.15.

Function `openQuiz` (lines 112–116) opens a new window to display a sample quiz. Using the `window.open` method, the script creates a new window containing `quiz2.html` (lines 114–115). We discuss `quiz2.html` later in this section.

The primary script ends in line 118, and the body of the XHTML document begins in line 120. Line 121 creates the link that calls function `allQuotes` when clicked. Lines 123–124 create a paragraph element containing the attribute `id = "quizSpot"`. This paragraph contains a link that calls function `openQuiz`.

Lines 126–133 contain a second script. This script appears in the XHTML document's `body` because it adds a dynamic footer to the page, which must appear after the static XHTML content contained in the first part of the `body`. This script creates another instance of the `Date` object, but the date is set to the last modified date and time of the XHTML document, rather than the current date and time (line 128). The script obtains the last modified date and time using property `document.lastModified`. Lines 131–132 add this information to the web page. Note that the last modified date and time appear at the bottom of the page, after the rest of the `body` content. If this script were in the `head` element, this information would be displayed before the entire `body` of the XHTML document. Lines 133–135 close the `script`, the `body` and the XHTML document.

The Quiz Page

The quiz used in this example is in a separate XHTML document named `quiz2.html` (Fig. 11.17). This document is similar to `quiz.html` in Fig. 10.14. The quiz in this example differs from the quiz in Fig. 10.14 in that it shows the result in the main window in the example, whereas the earlier quiz example alerts the result. After the **Submit** button in the quiz window is clicked, the main window changes to reflect that the quiz was taken, and the quiz window closes.

```
<?xml version = "1.0" encoding = "utf-8"?>
<!DOCTYPE html PUBLIC "-//W3C//DTD XHTML 1.0 Strict//EN"
   "http://www.w3.org/TR/xhtml1/DTD/xhtml1-strict.dtd">

<!-- Fig. 11.17: quiz2.html -->
<!-- Online quiz in a child window. -->
<html xmlns = "http://www.w3.org/1999/xhtml">
   <head>
      <title>Online Quiz</title>
      <script type = "text/JavaScript">
         <!--
         function checkAnswers()
         {
            // determine whether the answer is correct
            if ( document.getElementById( "myQuiz" ).elements[1].checked )
               window.opener.document.getElementById( "quizSpot" ).
                  innerHTML = "Congratulations, your answer is correct";
            else // if the answer is incorrect
               window.opener.document.getElementById( "quizSpot" ).
                  innerHTML = "Your answer is incorrect. " +
                  "Please try again <br /> <a href = " +
                  \"javascript:openQuiz()\">Please take our quiz</a>";

            window.opener.focus();
            window.close();
         } // end function checkAnswers
```

Fig. 11.17 | Online quiz in a child window. (Part 1 of 3.)

```
      //-->
      </script>
   </head>
   <body>
      <form id = "myQuiz" action = "javascript:checkAnswers()">
         <p>Select the name of the tip that goes with the
            image shown:<br />
            <img src = "EPT.gif" alt = "mystery tip"/>
            <br />

            <input type = "radio" name = "radiobutton" value = "CPE" />
            <label>Common Programming Error</label>

            <input type = "radio" name = "radiobutton" value = "EPT" />
            <label>Error-Prevention Tip</label>

            <input type = "radio" name = "radiobutton" value = "PERF" />
            <label>Performance Tip</label>

            <input type = "radio" name = "radiobutton" value = "PORT" />
            <label>Portability Tip</label><br />

            <input type = "submit" name = "Submit" value = "Submit" />
            <input type = "reset" name = "reset" value = "Reset" />
         </p>
      </form>
   </body>
</html>
```

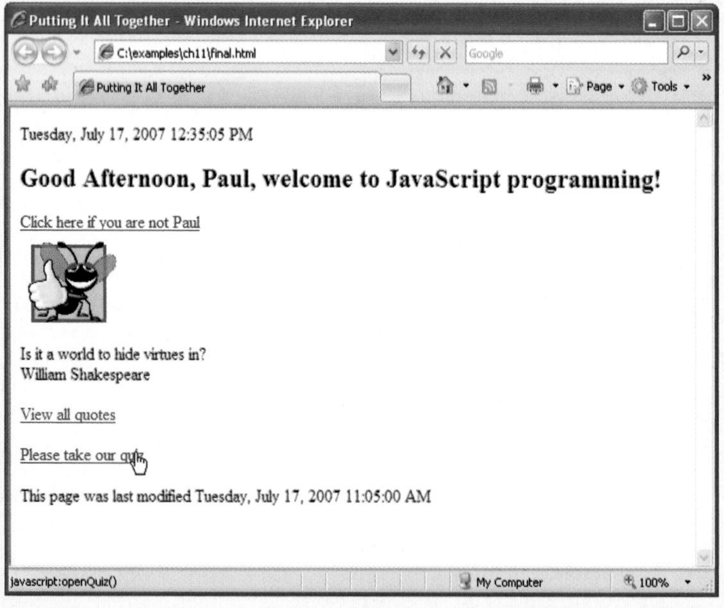

Fig. 11.17 | Online quiz in a child window. (Part 2 of 3.)

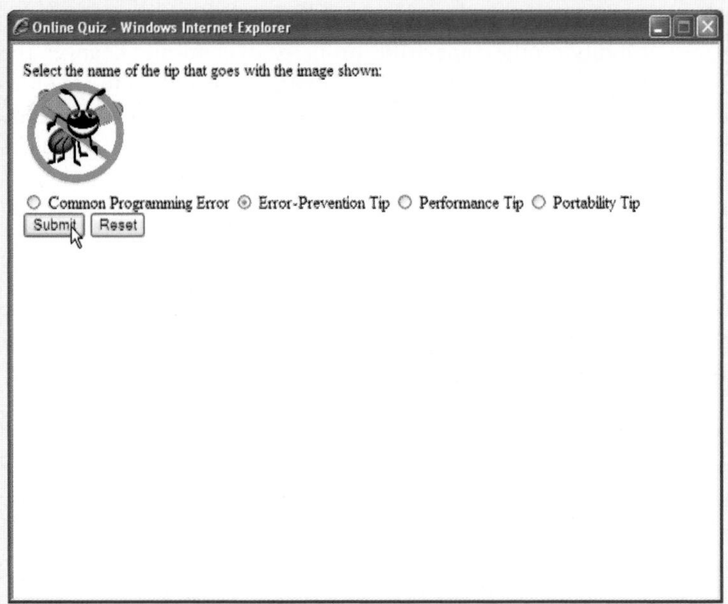

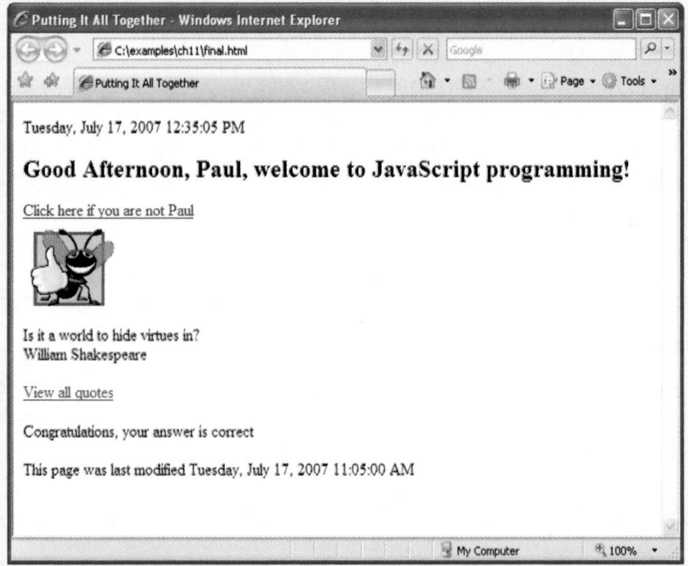

Fig. 11.17 | Online quiz in a child window. (Part 3 of 3.)

Lines 15–22 of this script check the user's answer and output the result to the main window. Lines 16–17 use `window.opener` to write to the main window. The property **window.opener** always contains a reference to the window that opened the current window, if such a window exists. Lines 16–17 write to property `window.opener.document.getElementById("quizSpot").innerHTML`. Recall that `quizSpot` is the `id` of the paragraph in the main window that contains the link to open the quiz. Property innerHTML refers to the HTML code inside the quizSpot paragraph (i.e., the code between <p> and </p>). Modifying the innerHTML property dynamically changes the XHTML code in the paragraph. Thus, when lines 16–17 execute, the link in the main window disappears, and the string "Congratulations, your answer is correct." appears. Lines 19–22 modify window.opener.document.getElementById("quizSpot").innerHTML. Lines 19–22 use the same technique to display "Your answer is incorrect. Please try again", followed by a link to try the quiz again.

After checking the quiz answer, the script gives focus to the main window (i.e., puts the main window in the foreground, on top of any other open browser windows), using the method focus of the main window's window object. The property window.opener references the main window, so window.opener.focus() (line 24) gives the main window focus, allowing the user to see the changes made to the text of the main window's quizSpot paragraph. Finally, the script closes the quiz window, using method window.close (line 25).

Lines 28–29 close the script and head elements of the XHTML document. Line 30 opens the body of the XHTML document. The body contains the form, image, text labels and radio buttons that comprise the quiz. Lines 52–54 close the form, the body and the XHTML document.

11.11 Using JSON to Represent Objects

In 1999, JSON (JavaScript Object Notation)—a simple way to represent JavaScript objects as strings—was introduced as an alternative to XML as a data-exchange technique. JSON has gained acclaim due to its simple format, making objects easy to read, create and parse. Each JSON object is represented as a list of property names and values contained in curly braces, in the following format:

```
{ propertyName1 : value1, propertyName2 : value2 }
```

Arrays are represented in JSON with square brackets in the following format:

```
[ value1, value2, value3 ]
```

Each value can be a string, a number, a JSON object, true, false or null. To appreciate the simplicity of JSON data, examine this representation of an array of address-book entries from Chapter 15:

```
[ { first: 'Cheryl', last: 'Black' },
  { first: 'James', last: 'Blue' },
  { first: 'Mike', last: 'Brown' },
  { first: 'Meg', last: 'Gold' } ]
```

JSON provides a straightforward way to manipulate objects in JavaScript, and many other programming languages now support this format. In addition to simplifying object creation, JSON allows programs to extract data easily and to efficiently transmit data across the Internet. JSON integrates especially well with Ajax applications, discussed in Chapter 15. See Section 15.7 for a more detailed discussion of JSON, as well as an Ajax-specific example. For more information on JSON, visit our JSON Resource Center at www.deitel.com/json.

11.12 Wrap-Up

This chapter provided an introduction to Object Technology, many of JavaScript's built-in objects, and a brief introduction to JSON, a simple way to represent new JavaScript objects. We introduced vocabulary and concepts integral to object-oriented and object-based programming. We took a closer look at some methods and properties of the `Math`, `Date`, `Boolean`, `Number`, `String`, `document`, and `window` objects. In the next chapter, we introduce the Document Object Model, a set of JavaScript objects that represent the elements in a web page that allows you to dynamically modify the page's content.

11.13 Web Resources

`www.deitel.com/javascript/`

The Deitel JavaScript Resource Center contains links to some of the best JavaScript resources on the web. There you'll find categorized links to JavaScript tools, code generators, forums, books, libraries, frameworks and more. Also check out the tutorials for all skill levels, from introductory to advanced. Be sure to visit the related Resource Centers on XHTML (`www.deitel.com/xhtml/`) and CSS 2.1 (`www.deitel.com/css21/`).

Summary

Section 11.1 Introduction

- The chapter describes several of JavaScript's built-in objects, which will serve as a basis for understanding browser objects in the chapters on Dynamic HTML.

Section 11.2 Introduction to Object Technology

- Objects are a natural way of thinking about the world and about scripts that manipulate XHTML documents.
- JavaScript uses objects to perform many tasks and therefore is referred to as an object-based programming language.
- Objects have attributes and exhibit behaviors.
- Object-oriented design (OOD) models software in terms similar to those that people use to describe real-world objects. It takes advantage of class relationships, where objects of a certain class, such as a class of vehicles, have the same characteristics.
- OOD takes advantage of inheritance relationships, where new classes of objects are derived by absorbing characteristics of existing classes and adding unique characteristics of their own.
- Object-oriented design provides a natural and intuitive way to view the software design process—namely, modeling objects by their attributes, behaviors and interrelationships just as we describe real-world objects.
- OOD also models communication between objects.
- OOD encapsulates attributes and operations (behaviors) into objects.
- Objects have the property of information hiding. This means that objects may know how to communicate with one another across well-defined interfaces, but normally they are not allowed to know how other objects are implemented—implementation details are hidden within the objects themselves.
- The designers of web browsers have defined a set of objects that encapsulate an XHTML document's elements and expose to a JavaScript programmer the attributes and behaviors that enable a JavaScript program to interact with (or script) those elements (objects).

- Some programming languages—like Java, Visual Basic, C# and C++—are object oriented. Programming in such a language is called object-oriented programming (OOP), and it allows computer programmers to implement object-oriented designs as working software systems.
- Languages like C are procedural, so programming tends to be action oriented.
- In procedural languages, the unit of programming is the function.
- In object-oriented languages, the unit of programming is the class from which objects are eventually instantiated. Classes contain functions that implement operations and data that implements attributes.
- Procedural programmers concentrate on writing functions. Programmers group actions that perform some common task into functions, and group functions to form programs.
- Object-oriented programmers concentrate on creating their own user-defined types called classes. Each class contains data as well as the set of functions that manipulate that data and provide services to clients.
- The data components of a class are called properties.
- The function components of a class are called methods.
- The nouns in a system specification help you determine the set of classes from which objects are created that work together to implement the system.
- Classes are to objects as blueprints are to houses.
- Classes can have relationships with other classes. These relationships are called associations.
- Packaging software as classes makes it possible for future software systems to reuse the classes. Groups of related classes are often packaged as reusable components.
- With object technology, you can build much of the new software you'll need by combining existing classes, just as automobile manufacturers combine interchangeable parts. Each new class you create will have the potential to become a valuable software asset that you and other programmers can reuse to speed and enhance the quality of future software development efforts.

Section 11.3 `Math` Object

- `Math` object methods allow you to perform many common mathematical calculations.
- An object's methods are called by writing the name of the object followed by a dot operator (`.`) and the name of the method. In parentheses following the method name is the argument (or a comma-separated list of arguments) to the method.

Section 11.4 `String` Object

- Characters are the fundamental building blocks of JavaScript programs. Every program is composed of a sequence of characters grouped together meaningfully that is interpreted by the computer as a series of instructions used to accomplish a task.
- A string is a series of characters treated as a single unit.
- A string may include letters, digits and various special characters, such as `+`, `-`, `*`, `/`, and `$`.
- JavaScript supports Unicode, which represents a large portion of the world's languages.
- String literals or string constants (often called anonymous `String` objects) are written as a sequence of characters in double quotation marks or single quotation marks.
- Combining strings is called concatenation.
- String method `charAt` returns the character at a specific index in a string. Indices for the characters in a string start at 0 (the first character) and go up to (but do not include) the string's `length` (i.e., if the string contains five characters, the indices are 0 through 4). If the index is outside the bounds of the string, the method returns an empty string.

- String method charCodeAt returns the Unicode value of the character at a specific index in a string. If the index is outside the bounds of the string, the method returns NaN. String method fromCharCode creates a string from a list of Unicode values.
- String method toLowerCase returns the lowercase version of a string. String method toUpperCase returns the uppercase version of a string.
- String method indexOf determines the location of the first occurrence of its argument in the string used to call the method. If the substring is found, the index at which the first occurrence of the substring begins is returned; otherwise, -1 is returned. This method receives an optional second argument specifying the index from which to begin the search.
- String method lastIndexOf determines the location of the last occurrence of its argument in the string used to call the method. If the substring is found, the index at which the last occurrence of the substring begins is returned; otherwise, -1 is returned. This method receives an optional second argument specifying the index from which to begin the search.
- The process of breaking a string into tokens is called tokenization. Tokens are separated from one another by delimiters, typically white-space characters such as blank, tab, newline and carriage return. Other characters may also be used as delimiters to separate tokens.
- String method split breaks a string into its component tokens. The argument to method split is the delimiter string—the string that determines the end of each token in the original string. Method split returns an array of strings containing the tokens.
- String method substring returns the substring from the starting index (its first argument) up to but not including the ending index (its second argument). If the ending index is greater than the length of the string, the substring returned includes the characters from the starting index to the end of the original string.
- String method anchor wraps the string that calls the method in XHTML element <a></a> with the name of the anchor supplied as the argument to the method.
- String method fixed displays text in a fixed-width font by wrapping the string that calls the method in a <tt></tt> XHTML element.
- String method strike displays struck-out text (i.e., text with a line through it) by wrapping the string that calls the method in a <strike></strike> XHTML element.
- String method sub displays subscript text by wrapping the string that calls the method in a XHTML element.
- String method sup displays superscript text by wrapping the string that calls the method in a XHTML element.
- String method link creates a hyperlink by wrapping the string that calls the method in XHTML element <a></a>. The target of the hyperlink (i.e, value of the href property) is the argument to the method and can be any URL.

Section 11.5 Date Object

- JavaScript's Date object provides methods for date and time manipulations.
- Date and time processing can be performed based either on the computer's local time zone or on World Time Standard's Coordinated Universal Time (abbreviated UTC)—formerly called Greenwich Mean Time (GMT).
- Most methods of the Date object have a local time zone and a UTC version.
- Date method parse receives as its argument a string representing a date and time and returns the number of milliseconds between midnight, January 1, 1970, and the specified date and time.

- Date method UTC returns the number of milliseconds between midnight, January 1, 1970, and the date and time specified as its arguments. The arguments to the UTC method include the required year, month and date, and the optional hours, minutes, seconds and milliseconds. If any of the hours, minutes, seconds or milliseconds arguments is not specified, a zero is supplied in its place. For the hours, minutes and seconds arguments, if the argument to the right of any of these arguments is specified, that argument must also be specified (e.g., if the minutes argument is specified, the hours argument must be specified; if the milliseconds argument is specified, all the arguments must be specified).

Section 11.6 `Boolean` *and* `Number` *Objects*

- JavaScript provides the Boolean and Number objects as object wrappers for boolean true/false values and numbers, respectively.
- When a boolean value is required in a JavaScript program, JavaScript automatically creates a Boolean object to store the value.
- JavaScript programmers can create Boolean objects explicitly with the statement

```
var b = new Boolean( booleanValue );
```

  The argument *booleanValue* specifies the value of the Boolean object (true or false). If *booleanValue* is false, 0, null, Number.NaN or the empty string (""), or if no argument is supplied, the new Boolean object contains false. Otherwise, the new Boolean object contains true.
- JavaScript automatically creates Number objects to store numeric values in a JavaScript program.
- JavaScript programmers can create a Number object with the statement

```
var n = new Number( numericValue );
```

  The argument *numericValue* is the number to store in the object. Although you can explicitly create Number objects, normally they are created when needed by the JavaScript interpreter.

Section 11.7 `document` *Object*

- JavaScript provides the document object for manipulating the document that is currently visible in the browser window.

Section 11.8 `window` *Object*

- JavaScript's window object provides methods for manipulating browser windows.

Section 11.9 Using Cookies

- A cookie is a piece of data that is stored on the user's computer to maintain information about the client during and between browser sessions.
- Cookies are accessible in JavaScript through the document object's cookie property.
- A cookie has the syntax "*identifier=value*," where *identifier* is any valid JavaScript variable identifier, and *value* is the value of the cookie variable. When multiple cookies exist for one website, *identifier-value* pairs are separated by semicolons in the document.cookie string.
- The expires property in a cookie string sets an expiration date, after which the web browser deletes the cookie. If a cookie's expiration date is not set, then the cookie expires by default after the user closes the browser window. A cookie can be deleted immediately by setting the expires property to a date and time in the past.
- The assignment operator does not overwrite the entire list of cookies, but appends a cookie to the end of it.

Section 11.10 Final JavaScript Example

- `window.opener` always contains a reference to the window that opened the current window.
- The property `innerHTML` refers to the HTML code inside the current paragraph element.
- Method `focus` puts the window it references on top of all the others.
- The `window` object's `close` method closes the browser window represented by the `window` object.

Section 11.11 Using JSON to Represent Objects

- JSON (JavaScript Object Notation) is a simple way to represent JavaScript objects as strings.
- JSON was introduced in 1999 as an alternative to XML for data exchange.
- Each JSON object is represented as a list of property names and values contained in curly braces, in the following format:

  `{ `*propertyName1*` : `*value1*`, `*propertyName2*` : `*value2*` }`
- Arrays are represented in JSON with square brackets in the following format:

  `[ `*value1*`, `*value2*`, `*value3*` ]`
- Values in JSON can be strings, numbers, JSON objects, `true`, `false` or `null`.

Terminology

`abs` method of `Math`
abstraction
action-oriented programming language
`anchor` method of `String`
anonymous `String` object
association
attribute (property)
behavior (method)
`blink` method of `String`
`Boolean` object
`ceil` method of `Math`
character
`charAt` method of `String`
`charCodeAt` method of `String`
class
`close` method of `window`
code reuse
components
`concat` method of `String`
cookie
Coordinated Universal Time (UTC)
`cos` method of `Math`
date
`Date` object
delimiter
`document` object
`E` property of `Math`
empty string
encapsulation
`escape` function
`exp` method of `Math`
`fixed` method of `String`
`floor` method of `Math`
`focus` method of `window`
`fromCharCode` method of `String`
`getDate` method of `Date`
`getDay` method of `Date`
`getFullYear` method of `Date`
`getHours` method of `Date`
`getMilliseconds` method of `Date`
`getMinutes` method of `Date`
`getMonth` method of `Date`
`getSeconds` method of `Date`
`getTime` method of `Date`
`getTimezoneOffset` method of `Date`
`getUTCDate` method of `Date`
`getUTCDay` method of `Date`
`getUTCFullYear` method of `Date`
`getUTCHours` method of `Date`
`getUTCMilliSeconds` method of `Date`
`getUTCMinutes` method of `Date`
`getUTCMonth` method of `Date`
`getUTCSeconds` method of `Date`
Greenwich Mean Time (GMT)
hexadecimal escape sequences
hiding
index in a string
`indexOf` method of `String`
information hiding
inheritance

innerHTML property
instantiation
interface
lastIndexOf method of String
link method of String
LN10 property of Math
LN2 property of Math
local time zone
log method of Math
LOG10E property of Math
LOG2E property of Math
Math object
max method of Math
MAX_SIZE property of Number
method
min method of Math
MIN_SIZE property of Number
NaN property of Number
NEGATIVE_INFINITY property of Number
Number object
object
object wrapper
object-based programming language
object-oriented design (OOD)
object-oriented programming (OOP)
open method of window
opener property of window
operation
parse method of Date
PI property of Math
POSITIVE_INFINITY property of Number
pow method of Math
property
round method of Math
search a string
sending a message to an object
setDate method of Date
setFullYear method of Date
setHours method of Date
setMilliSeconds method of Date
setMinutes method of Date
setMonth method of Date
setSeconds method of Date
setTime method of Date
setUTCDate method of Date
setUTCFullYear method of Date
setUTCHours method of Date
setUTCMilliseconds method of Date
setUTCMinutes method of Date
setUTCMonth method of Date
setUTCSeconds method of Date
sin method of Math
slice method of String
special characters
split method of String
sqrt method of Math
SQRT1_2 property of Math
SQRT2 property of Math
strike method of String
string
string constant
string literal
String object
sub method of String
substr method of String
substring
substring method of String
sup method of String
tan method of Math
time
token
tokenization
toLocaleString method of Date
toLowerCase method of String
toString method of Date
toString method of String
toUpperCase method of String
toUTCString method of Date
unescape function
Unicode
user-defined type
UTC (Coordinated Universal Time)
UTC method of Date
valueOf method of Boolean
valueOf method of Date
valueOf method of Number
valueOf method of String
well-defined interfaces
window object
wrap in XHTML tags

Self-Review Exercise

11.1 Fill in the blanks in each of the following statements:

a) Because JavaScript uses objects to perform many tasks, JavaScript is commonly referred to as a(n) ________.

b) All objects have _______ and exhibit _______.
c) The methods of the _______ object allow you to perform many common mathematical calculations.
d) Invoking (or calling) a method of an object is referred to as _______.
e) String literals or string constants are written as a sequence of characters in _______ or _______.
f) Indices for the characters in a string start at _______.
g) `String` methods _______ and _______ search for the first and last occurrences of a substring in a `String`, respectively.
h) The process of breaking a string into tokens is called _______.
i) `String` method _______ formats a `String` as a hyperlink.
j) Date and time processing can be performed based on the _______ or on World Time Standard's _______.
k) `Date` method _______ receives as its argument a string representing a date and time, and returns the number of milliseconds between midnight, January 1, 1970, and the specified date and time.

Answers to Self-Review Exercise

11.1 a) object-based programming language. b) attributes, behaviors. c) `Math`. d) sending a message to the object. e) double quotation marks, single quotation marks. f) 0. g) `indexOf`, `lastIndexOf`. h) tokenization. i) `link`. j) computer's local time zone, Coordinated Universal Time (UTC). k) `parse`.

Exercises

11.2 Create a web page that contains four XHTML buttons. Each button, when clicked, should cause an alert dialog to display a different time or date in relation to the current time. Create a `Now` button that alerts the current time and date and a `Yesterday` button that alerts the time and date 24 hours ago. The other two buttons should alert the time and date ten years ago and one week from today.

11.3 Write a script that tests as many of the `Math` library functions in Fig. 11.1 as you can. Exercise each of these functions by having your program display tables of return values for several argument values in an XHTML `textarea`.

11.4 `Math` method `floor` may be used to round a number to a specific decimal place. For example, the statement

```
y = Math.floor( x * 10 + .5 ) / 10;
```

rounds x to the tenths position (the first position to the right of the decimal point). The statement

```
y = Math.floor( x * 100 + .5 ) / 100;
```

rounds `x` to the hundredths position (i.e., the second position to the right of the decimal point). Write a script that defines four functions to round a number `x` in various ways:

a) `roundToInteger( number )`
b) `roundToTenths( number )`
c) `roundToHundredths( number )`
d) `roundToThousandths( number )`

For each value read, your program should display the original value, the number rounded to the nearest integer, the number rounded to the nearest tenth, the number rounded to the nearest hundredth and the number rounded to the nearest thousandth.

11.5 Modify the solution to Exercise 11.4 to use `Math` method `round` instead of method `floor`.

11.6 Write a script that uses relational and equality operators to compare two `String`s input by the user through an XHTML form. Output in an XHTML `textarea` whether the first string is less than, equal to or greater than the second.

11.7 Write a script that uses random number generation to create sentences. Use four arrays of strings called `article`, `noun`, `verb` and `preposition`. Create a sentence by selecting a word at random from each array in the following order: `article`, `noun`, `verb`, `preposition`, `article` and `noun`. As each word is picked, concatenate it to the previous words in the sentence. The words should be separated by spaces. When the final sentence is output, it should start with a capital letter and end with a period.

The arrays should be filled as follows: the `article` array should contain the articles `"the"`, `"a"`, `"one"`, `"some"` and `"any"`; the `noun` array should contain the nouns `"boy"`, `"girl"`, `"dog"`, `"town"` and `"car"`; the `verb` array should contain the verbs `"drove"`, `"jumped"`, `"ran"`, `"walked"` and `"skipped"`; the `preposition` array should contain the prepositions `"to"`, `"from"`, `"over"`, `"under"` and `"on"`.

The program should generate 20 sentences to form a short story and output the result to an XHTML `textarea`. The story should begin with a line reading `"Once upon a time..."` and end with a line reading `"THE END"`.

11.8 *(Limericks)* A limerick is a humorous five-line verse in which the first and second lines rhyme with the fifth, and the third line rhymes with the fourth. Using techniques similar to those developed in Exercise 11.7, write a script that produces random limericks. Polishing this program to produce good limericks is a challenging problem, but the result will be worth the effort!

11.9 *(Pig Latin)* Write a script that encodes English-language phrases in pig Latin. Pig Latin is a form of coded language often used for amusement. Many variations exist in the methods used to form pig Latin phrases. For simplicity, use the following algorithm:

To form a pig Latin phrase from an English-language phrase, tokenize the phrase into an array of words using `String` method `split`. To translate each English word into a pig Latin word, place the first letter of the English word at the end of the word and add the letters "ay." Thus the word "`jump`" becomes "`umpjay`," the word "`the`" becomes "`hetay`" and the word "`computer`" becomes "`omputercay`." Blanks between words remain as blanks. Assume the following: The English phrase consists of words separated by blanks, there are no punctuation marks and all words have two or more letters. Function `printLatinWord` should display each word. Each token (i.e., word in the sentence) is passed to method `printLatinWord` to print the pig Latin word. Enable the user to input the sentence through an XHTML form. Keep a running display of all the converted sentences in an XHTML `textarea`.

11.10 Write a script that inputs a telephone number as a string in the form `(555) 555-5555`. The script should use `String` method `split` to extract the area code as a token, the first three digits of the phone number as a token and the last four digits of the phone number as a token. Display the area code in one text field and the seven-digit phone number in another text field.

11.11 Write a script that inputs a line of text, tokenizes it with `String` method `split` and outputs the tokens in reverse order.

11.12 Write a script that inputs text from an XHTML form and outputs it in uppercase and lowercase letters.

11.13 Write a script that inputs several lines of text and a search character and uses `String` method `indexOf` to determine the number of occurrences of the character in the text.

11.14 Write a script based on the program in Exercise 11.13 that inputs several lines of text and uses `String` method `indexOf` to determine the total number of occurrences of each letter of the alphabet in the text. Uppercase and lowercase letters should be counted together. Store the totals for each letter in an array, and print the values in tabular format in an XHTML `textarea` after the totals have been determined.

11.15 Write a script that reads a series of strings and outputs in an XHTML `textarea` only those strings beginning with the character "`b`."

11.16 Write a script that reads a series of strings and outputs in an XHTML `textarea` only those strings ending with the characters "`ed`."

11.17 Write a script that inputs an integer code for a character and displays the corresponding character.

11.18 Modify your solution to Exercise 11.17 so that it generates all possible three-digit codes in the range 000 to 255 and attempts to display the corresponding characters. Display the results in an XHTML `textarea`.

11.19 Write your own version of the `String` method `indexOf` and use it in a script.

11.20 Write your own version of the `String` method `lastIndexOf` and use it in a script.

11.21 Write a program that reads a five-letter word from the user and produces all possible three-letter words that can be derived from the letters of the five-letter word. For example, the three-letter words produced from the word "bathe" include the commonly used words "ate," "bat," "bet," "tab," "hat," "the" and "tea." Output the results in an XHTML `textarea`.

11.22 *(Printing Dates in Various Formats)* Dates are printed in several common formats. Write a script that reads a date from an XHTML form and creates a `Date` object in which to store it. Then use the various methods of the `Date` object that convert `Date`s into strings to display the date in several formats.

Special Section: Challenging String-Manipulation Exercises

The preceding exercises are keyed to the text and designed to test the reader's understanding of fundamental string-manipulation concepts. This section includes a collection of intermediate and advanced string-manipulation exercises. The reader should find these problems challenging, yet entertaining. The problems vary considerably in difficulty. Some require an hour or two of program writing and implementation. Others are useful for lab assignments that might require two or three weeks of study and implementation. Some are challenging term projects.

11.23 *(Text Analysis)* The availability of computers with string-manipulation capabilities has resulted in some rather interesting approaches to analyzing the writings of great authors. Much attention has been focused on whether William Shakespeare really wrote the works attributed to him. Some scholars believe there is substantial evidence indicating that Christopher Marlowe actually penned these masterpieces. Researchers have used computers to find similarities in the writings of these two authors. This exercise examines three methods for analyzing texts with a computer.

a) Write a script that reads several lines of text from the keyboard and prints a table indicating the number of occurrences of each letter of the alphabet in the text. For example, the phrase

```
To be, or not to be: that is the question:
```

contains one "a," two "b's," no "c's," etc.

b) Write a script that reads several lines of text and prints a table indicating the number of one-letter words, two-letter words, three-letter words, etc., appearing in the text. For example, the phrase

```
Whether 'tis nobler in the mind to suffer
```

contains

Word length	Occurrences
1	0
2	2
3	1
4	2 (including 'tis)
5	0
6	2
7	1

c) Write a script that reads several lines of text and prints a table indicating the number of occurrences of each different word in the text. The first version of your program should include the words in the table in the same order in which they appear in the text. For example, the lines

```
To be, or not to be: that is the question:
Whether 'tis nobler in the mind to suffer
```

contain the word "to" three times, the word "be" twice, and the word "or" once. A more interesting (and useful) printout should then be attempted in which the words are sorted alphabetically.

11.24 *(Check Protection)* Computers are frequently employed in check-writing systems such as payroll and accounts payable applications. Many strange stories circulate regarding weekly paychecks being printed (by mistake) for amounts in excess of $1 million. Incorrect amounts are printed by computerized check-writing systems because of human error and/or machine failure. Systems designers build controls into their systems to prevent erroneous checks from being issued.

Another serious problem is the intentional alteration of a check amount by someone who intends to cash a check fraudulently. To prevent a dollar amount from being altered, most computerized check-writing systems employ a technique called *check protection.*

Checks designed for imprinting by computer contain a fixed number of spaces in which the computer may print an amount. Suppose a paycheck contains eight blank spaces in which the computer is supposed to print the amount of a weekly paycheck. If the amount is large, then all eight of those spaces will be filled, for example:

```
1,230.60 (check amount)
--------
12345678 (position numbers)
```

On the other hand, if the amount is less than $1000, then several of the spaces would ordinarily be left blank. For example,

```
   99.87
--------
12345678
```

contains three blank spaces. If a check is printed with blank spaces, it is easier for someone to alter the amount of the check. To prevent a check from being altered, many check-writing systems insert *leading asterisks* to protect the amount as follows:

```
***99.87
--------
12345678
```

Write a script that inputs a dollar amount to be printed on a check, then prints the amount in check-protected format with leading asterisks if necessary. Assume that nine spaces are available for printing the amount.

11.25 *(Writing the Word Equivalent of a Check Amount)* Continuing the discussion in the preceding exercise, we reiterate the importance of designing check-writing systems to prevent alteration of check amounts. One common security method requires that the check amount be written both in numbers and spelled out in words. Even if someone is able to alter the numerical amount of the check, it is extremely difficult to change the amount in words.

Many computerized check-writing systems do not print the amount of the check in words. Perhaps the main reason for this omission is the fact that most high-level languages used in commercial applications do not contain adequate string-manipulation features. Another reason is that the logic for writing word equivalents of check amounts is somewhat involved.

Write a script that inputs a numeric check amount and writes the word equivalent of the amount. For example, the amount 112.43 should be written as

```
ONE HUNDRED TWELVE and 43/100
```

11.26 *(Morse Code)* Perhaps the most famous of all coding schemes is the Morse code, developed by Samuel Morse in 1832 for use with the telegraph system. The Morse code assigns a series of dots and dashes to each letter of the alphabet, each digit and a few special characters (e.g., period, comma, colon and semicolon). In sound-oriented systems, the dot represents a short sound and the dash represents a long sound. Other representations of dots and dashes are used with light-oriented systems and signal-flag systems.

Separation between words is indicated by a space or, quite simply, by the absence of a dot or dash. In a sound-oriented system, a space is indicated by a short period of time during which no sound is transmitted. The international version of the Morse code appears in Fig. 11.18.

Write a script that reads an English-language phrase and encodes it in Morse code. Also write a program that reads a phrase in Morse code and converts the phrase into the English-language equivalent. Use one blank between each Morse-coded letter and three blanks between each Morse-coded word.

11.27 *(Metric Conversion Program)* Write a script that will assist the user with metric conversions. Your program should allow the user to specify the names of the units as strings (e.g., centimeters, liters, grams, for the metric system and inches, quarts, pounds, for the English system) and should respond to simple questions such as

```
"How many inches are in 2 meters?"
"How many liters are in 10 quarts?"
```

Your program should recognize invalid conversions. For example, the question

```
"How many feet in 5 kilograms?"
```

is not a meaningful question because `"feet"` is a unit of length whereas `"kilograms"` is a unit of mass.

11.28 *(Project: A Spell Checker)* Many popular word-processing software packages have built-in spell checkers.

In this project, you are asked to develop your own spell-checker utility. We make suggestions to help get you started. You should then consider adding more capabilities. Use a computerized dictionary (if you have access to one) as a source of words.

Why do we type so many words with incorrect spellings? In some cases, it is because we simply do not know the correct spelling, so we make a best guess. In some cases, it is because we transpose two letters (e.g., "defualt" instead of "default"). Sometimes we double-type a letter

Character	Code	Character	Code
A	.-	T	-
B	-...	U	..-
C	-.-.	V	...-
D	-..	W	.--
E	.	X	-..-
F	..-.	Y	-.--
G	--.	Z	--..
H	....		
I	..	*Digits*	
J	.---	1	.----
K	-.-	2	..---
L	.-..	3	...--
M	--	4	....-
N	-.	5	.....
O	---	6	-....
P	.--.	7	--...
Q	--.-	8	---..
R	.-.	9	----.
S	...	0	-----

Fig. 11.18 | Letters of the alphabet as expressed in international Morse code.

accidentally (e.g., "hanndy" instead of "handy"). Sometimes we type a nearby key instead of the one we intended (e.g., "biryhday" instead of "birthday"). And so on.

Design and implement a spell-checker application in JavaScript. Your program should maintain an array `wordList` of strings. Enable the user to enter these strings.

Your program should ask a user to enter a word. The program should then look up the word in the `wordList` array. If the word is present in the array, your program should print "`Word is spelled correctly.`"

If the word is not present in the array, your program should print "`word is not spelled correctly.`" Then your program should try to locate other words in `wordList` that might be the word the user intended to type. For example, you can try all possible single transpositions of adjacent letters to discover that the word "default" is a direct match to a word in `wordList`. Of course, this implies that your program will check all other single transpositions, such as "edfault," "dfeault," "deafult," "defalut" and "defautl." When you find a new word that matches one in `wordList`, print that word in a message, such as "`Did you mean "default?"`"

Implement other tests, such as replacing each double letter with a single letter and any other tests you can develop, to improve the value of your spell checker.

11.29 *(Project: Crossword Puzzle Generator)* Most people have worked a crossword puzzle, but few have ever attempted to generate one. Generating a crossword puzzle is suggested here as a string-manipulation project requiring substantial sophistication and effort.

There are many issues you must resolve to get even the simplest crossword puzzle generator program working. For example, how does one represent the grid of a crossword puzzle in the computer? Should one use a series of strings, or use double-subscripted arrays?

You need a source of words (i.e., a computerized dictionary) that can be directly referenced by the program. In what form should these words be stored to facilitate the complex manipulations required by the program?

The really ambitious reader will want to generate the clues portion of the puzzle, in which the brief hints for each across word and each down word are printed for the puzzle worker. Merely printing a version of the blank puzzle itself is not a simple problem.

12

Document Object Model (DOM): Objects and Collections

Our children may learn about heroes of the past. Our task is to make ourselves architects of the future.

—Jomo Mzee Kenyatta

Though leaves are many, the root is one.

—William Butler Yeats

The thing that impresses me most about America is the way parents obey their children.

—Duke of Windsor

Most of us become parents long before we have stopped being children.

—Mignon McLaughlin

To write it, it took three months; to conceive it three minutes; to collect the data in it—all my life.

—F. Scott Fitzgerald

Sibling rivalry is inevitable. The only sure way to avoid it is to have one child.

—Nancy Samalin

OBJECTIVES

In this chapter you will learn:

- How to use JavaScript and the W3C Document Object Model to create dynamic web pages.
- The concept of DOM nodes and DOM trees.
- How to traverse, edit and modify elements in an XHTML document.
- How to change CSS styles dynamically.
- To create JavaScript animations.

Outline

12.1 Introduction

In this chapter we introduce the Document Object Model (DOM). The DOM gives you access to all the elements on a web page. Inside the browser, the whole web page—paragraphs, forms, tables, etc.—is represented in an object hierarchy. Using JavaScript, you can create, modify and remove elements in the page dynamically.

Previously, both Internet Explorer and Netscape had different versions of Dynamic HTML, which provided similar functionality to the DOM. However, while they provided many of the same capabilities, these two models were incompatible with each other. In an effort to encourage cross-browser websites, the W3C created the standardized Document Object Model. Firefox 2, Internet Explorer 7, and most other major browsers implement *most* of the features of the W3C DOM.

This chapter begins by formally introducing the concept of DOM nodes and DOM trees. We then discuss properties and methods of DOM nodes and cover additional methods of the `document` object. We also discuss how to dynamically change style properties, which enables you to create many types of effects, such as user-defined background colors and animations. Then, we present a diagram of the extensive object hierarchy, with explanations of the various objects and properties, and we provide links to websites with further information on the topic.

Software Engineering Observation 12.1

With the DOM, XHTML elements can be treated as objects, and many attributes of XHTML elements can be treated as properties of those objects. Then, objects can be scripted (through their `id` *attributes) with JavaScript to achieve dynamic effects.*

12.2 Modeling a Document: DOM Nodes and Trees

As we saw in previous chapters, the `document`'s `getElementById` method is the simplest way to access a specific element in a page. In this section and the next, we discuss more thoroughly the objects returned by this method.

The `getElementById` method returns objects called DOM nodes. Every element in an XHTML page is modeled in the web browser by a DOM node. All the nodes in a document make up the page's DOM tree, which describes the relationships among elements. Nodes are related to each other through child-parent relationships. An XHTML element inside another element is said to be a child of the containing element. The containing element is known as the parent. A node may have multiple children, but only one parent. Nodes with the same parent node are referred to as siblings.

Some browsers have tools that allow you to see a visual representation of the DOM tree of a document. When installing Firefox, you can choose to install a tool called the DOM Inspector, which allows you to view the DOM tree of an XHTML document. To inspect a document, Firefox users can access the **DOM Inspector** from the **Tools** menu of Firefox. If the DOM inspector is not in the menu, run the Firefox installer and choose **Custom** in the **Setup Type** screen, making sure the **DOM Inspector** box is checked in the **Optional Components** window.

Microsoft provides a Developer Toolbar for Internet Explorer that allows you to inspect the DOM tree of a document. The toolbar can be downloaded from Microsoft at `go.microsoft.com/fwlink/?LinkId=92716`. Once the toolbar is installed, restart the browser, then click the » icon at the right of the toolbar and choose **IE Developer Toolbar** from the menu. Figure 12.1 shows an XHTML document and its DOM tree displayed in Firefox's DOM Inspector and in IE's Web Developer Toolbar.

The XHTML document contains a few simple elements. We explain the example based on the Firefox DOM Inspector—the IE Toolbar displays the document with only minor differences. A node can be expanded and collapsed using the **+** and **-** buttons next to the node's name. Figure 12.1(b) shows all the nodes in the document fully expanded. The document node (shown as **#document**) at the top of the tree is called the root node, because it has no parent. Below the document node, the **HTML** node is indented from the document node to signify that the **HTML** node is a child of the **#document** node. The **HTML** node represents the `html` element (lines 7–24).

The **HEAD** and **BODY** nodes are siblings, since they are both children of the **HTML** node. The **HEAD** contains two **#comment** nodes, representing lines 5–6. The **TITLE** node

```
1  <?xml version = "1.0" encoding = "utf-8"?>
2  <!DOCTYPE html PUBLIC "-//W3C//DTD XHTML 1.0 Strict//EN"
3     "http://www.w3.org/TR/xhtml1/DTD/xhtml1-strict.dtd">
4
5  <!-- Fig. 12.1: domtree.html -->
6  <!-- Demonstration of a document's DOM tree. -->
7  <html xmlns = "http://www.w3.org/1999/xhtml">
8     <head>
9        <title>DOM Tree Demonstration</title>
10    </head>
11    <body>
12       <h1>An XHTML Page</h1>
13       <p>This page contains some basic XHTML elements. We use the Firefox
14          DOM Inspector and the IE Developer Toolbar to view the DOM tree
15          of the document, which contains a DOM node for every element in
16          the document.</p>
17       <p>Here's a list:</p>
18       <ul>
19          <li>One</li>
20          <li>Two</li>
21          <li>Three</li>
22       </ul>
23    </body>
24 </html>
```

Fig. 12.1 | Demonstration of a document's DOM tree. (Part 1 of 3.)

a) The XHTML document is rendered in Firefox.

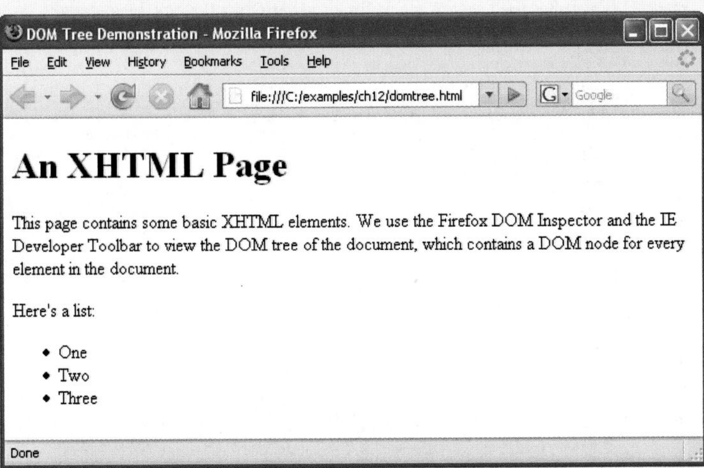

b) The Firefox DOM inspector displays the document tree in the left panel. The right panel shows information about the currently selected node.

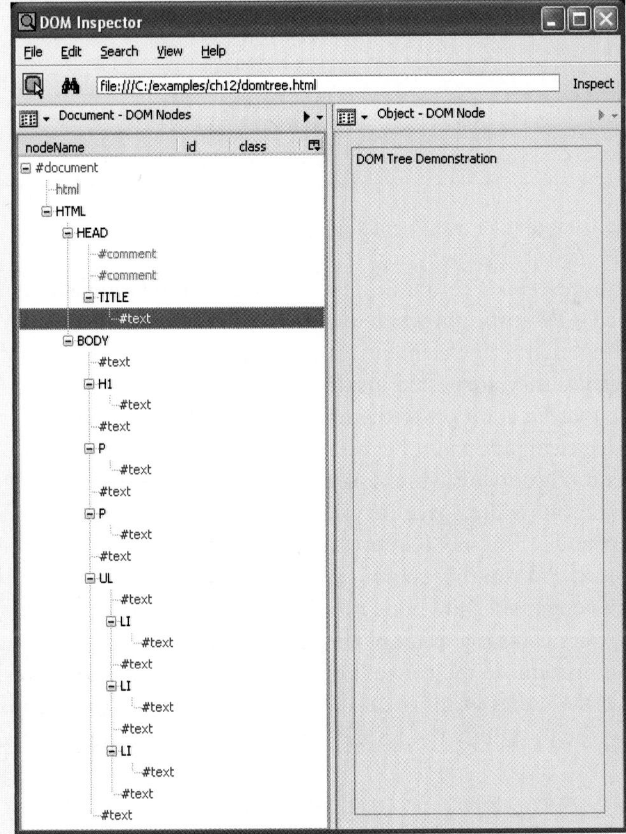

Fig. 12.1 | Demonstration of a document's DOM tree. (Part 2 of 3.)

c) The Internet Explorer Web Developer Toolbar displays much of the same information as the DOM inspector in Firefox in a panel at the bottom of the browser window.

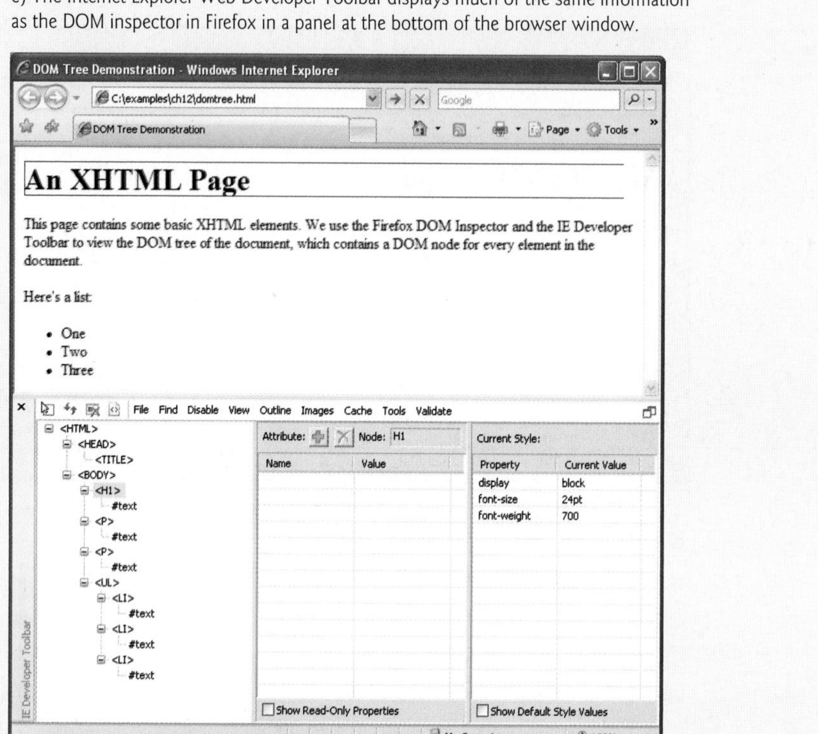

Fig. 12.1 | Demonstration of a document's DOM tree. (Part 3 of 3.)

has a child text node (**#text**) containing the text **DOM Tree Demonstration**, visible in the right pane of the DOM inspector when the text node is selected. The **BODY** node contains nodes representing each of the elements in the page. Note that the **LI** nodes are children of the **UL** node, since they are nested inside it.

Also, notice that, in addition to the text nodes representing the text inside the body, paragraphs and list elements, a number of other text nodes appear in the document. These text nodes contain nothing but white space. When Firefox parses an XHTML document into a DOM tree, the white space between sibling elements is interpreted as text and placed inside text nodes. Internet Explorer ignores white space and does not convert it into empty text nodes. If you run this example on your own computer, you will notice that the **BODY** node has a **#comment** child node not present above in both the Firefox and Internet Explorer DOM trees. This is a result of the copyright line at the end of the posted file.

This section introduced the concept of DOM nodes and DOM trees. The next section discusses DOM nodes in more detail, discussing methods and properties of DOM nodes that allow you to modify the DOM tree of a document using JavaScript.

12.3 Traversing and Modifying a DOM Tree

The DOM gives you access to the elements of a document, allowing you to modify the contents of a page dynamically using event-driven JavaScript. This section introduces properties and methods of all DOM nodes that enable you to traverse the DOM tree, modify nodes and create or delete content dynamically.

Figure 12.2 showcases some of the functionality of DOM nodes, as well as two additional methods of the `document` object. The program allows you to highlight, modify, insert and remove elements.

Lines 117–132 contain basic XHTML elements and content. Each element has an `id` attribute, which is also displayed at the beginning of the element in square brackets. For example, the `id` of the `h1` element in lines 117–118 is set to `bigheading`, and the heading text begins with `[bigheading]`. This allows the user to see the `id` of each element in the page. The body also contains an `h3` heading, several `p` elements, and an unordered list.

A `div` element (lines 133–162) contains the remainder of the XHTML `body`. Line 134 begins a `form` element, assigning the empty string to the required `action` attribute (because we're not submitting to a server) and returning `false` to the `onsubmit` attribute. When a `form`'s `onsubmit` handler returns `false`, the navigation to the address specified in the `action` attribute is aborted. This allows us to modify the page using JavaScript event handlers without reloading the original, unmodified XHTML.

```
1   <?xml version = "1.0" encoding = "utf-8"?>
2   <!DOCTYPE html PUBLIC "-//W3C//DTD XHTML 1.0 Strict//EN"
3      "http://www.w3.org/TR/xhtml1/DTD/xhtml1-strict.dtd">
4
5   <!-- Fig. 12.2: dom.html -->
6   <!-- Basic DOM functionality. -->
7   <html xmlns = "http://www.w3.org/1999/xhtml">
8      <head>
9         <title>Basic DOM Functionality</title>
10        <style type = "text/css">
11           h1, h3       { text-align: center;
12                          font-family: tahoma, geneva, sans-serif }
13           p            { margin-left: 5%;
14                          margin-right: 5%;
15                          font-family: arial, helvetica, sans-serif }
16           ul           { margin-left: 10% }
17           a            { text-decoration: none }
18           a:hover      { text-decoration: underline }
19           .nav         { width: 100%;
20                          border-top: 3px dashed blue;
21                          padding-top: 10px }
22           .highlighted { background-color: yellow }
23           .submit      { width: 120px }
24        </style>
25        <script type = "text/javascript">
26           <!--
27           var currentNode; // stores the currently highlighted node
28           var idcount = 0; // used to assign a unique id to new elements
29
30           // get and highlight an element by its id attribute
31           function byId()
32           {
```

Fig. 12.2 | Basic DOM functionality. (Part 1 of 8.)

```
            var id = document.getElementById( "gbi" ).value;
            var target = document.getElementById( id );

            if ( target )
               switchTo( target );
         } // end function byId

         // insert a paragraph element before the current element
         // using the insertBefore method
         function insert()
         {
            var newNode = createNewNode(
               document.getElementById( "ins" ).value );
            currentNode.parentNode.insertBefore( newNode, currentNode );
            switchTo( newNode );
         } // end function insert

         // append a paragraph node as the child of the current node
         function appendNode()
         {
            var newNode = createNewNode(
               document.getElementById( "append" ).value );
            currentNode.appendChild( newNode );
            switchTo( newNode );
         } // end function appendNode

         // replace the currently selected node with a paragraph node
         function replaceCurrent()
         {
            var newNode = createNewNode(
               document.getElementById( "replace" ).value );
            currentNode.parentNode.replaceChild( newNode, currentNode );
            switchTo( newNode );
         } // end function replaceCurrent

         // remove the current node
         function remove()
         {
            if ( currentNode.parentNode == document.body )
               alert( "Can't remove a top-level element." );
            else
            {
               var oldNode = currentNode;
               switchTo( oldNode.parentNode );
               currentNode.removeChild( oldNode );
            }
         } // end function remove

         // get and highlight the parent of the current node
         function parent()
         {
            var target = currentNode.parentNode;

```

Fig. 12.2 | Basic DOM functionality. (Part 2 of 8.)

```
            if ( target != document.body )
               switchTo( target );
            else
               alert( "No parent." );
         } // end function parent

         // helper function that returns a new paragraph node containing
         // a unique id and the given text
         function createNewNode( text )
         {
            var newNode = document.createElement( "p" );
            nodeId = "new" + idcount;
            ++idcount;
            newNode.id = nodeId;
            text = "[" + nodeId + "] " + text;
            newNode.appendChild(document.createTextNode( text ) );
            return newNode;
         } // end function createNewNode

         // helper function that switches to a new currentNode
         function switchTo( newNode )
         {
            currentNode.className = ""; // remove old highlighting
            currentNode = newNode;
            currentNode.className = "highlighted"; // highlight new node
            document.getElementById( "gbi" ).value = currentNode.id;
         } // end function switchTo
         // -->
      </script>
   </head>
   <body onload = "currentNode = document.getElementById( 'bigheading' )">
      <h1 id = "bigheading" class = "highlighted">
         [bigheading] DHTML Object Model</h1>
      <h3 id = "smallheading">[smallheading] Element Functionality</h3>
      <p id = "para1">[para1] The Document Object Model (DOM) allows for
         quick, dynamic access to all elements in an XHTML document for
         manipulation with JavaScript.</p>
      <p id = "para2">[para2] For more information, check out the
         "JavaScript and the DOM" section of Deitel's
         <a id = "link" href = "http://www.deitel.com/javascript">
            [link] JavaScript Resource Center.</a></p>
      <p id = "para3">[para3] The buttons below demonstrate:(list)</p>
      <ul id = "list">
         <li id = "item1">[item1] getElementById and parentNode</li>
         <li id = "item2">[item2] insertBefore and appendChild</li>
         <li id = "item3">[item3] replaceChild and removeChild </li>
      </ul>
      <div id = "nav" class = "nav">
         <form onsubmit = "return false" action = "">
            <table>
               <tr>
                  <td><input type = "text" id = "gbi"
                     value = "bigheading" /></td>
```

Fig. 12.2 | Basic DOM functionality. (Part 3 of 8.)

```
                  <td><input type = "submit" value = "Get By id"
                     onclick = "byId()" class = "submit" /></td>
               </tr><tr>
                  <td><input type = "text" id = "ins" /></td>
                  <td><input type = "submit" value = "Insert Before"
                     onclick = "insert()" class = "submit" /></td>
               </tr><tr>
                  <td><input type = "text" id = "append" /></td>
                  <td><input type = "submit" value = "Append Child"
                     onclick = "appendNode()" class = "submit" /></td>
               </tr><tr>
                  <td><input type = "text" id = "replace" /></td>
                  <td><input type = "submit" value = "Replace Current"
                     onclick = "replaceCurrent()" class = "submit" /></td>
               </tr><tr><td />
                  <td><input type = "submit" value = "Remove Current"
                     onclick = "remove()" class = "submit" /></td>
               </tr><tr><td />
                  <td><input type = "submit" value = "Get Parent"
                     onclick = "parent()" class = "submit" /></td>
               </tr>
            </table>
         </form>
      </div>
   </body>
</html>
```

a) This is the page when it first loads. It begins with the large heading highlighted.

Fig. 12.2 | Basic DOM functionality. (Part 4 of 8.)

b) This is the document after using the Get By id button to select para3.

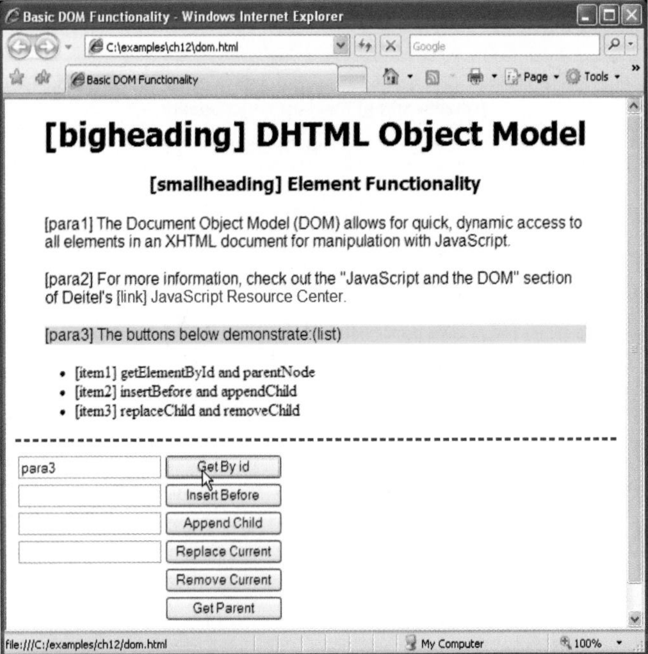

c) This is the document after inserting a new paragraph before the selected one.

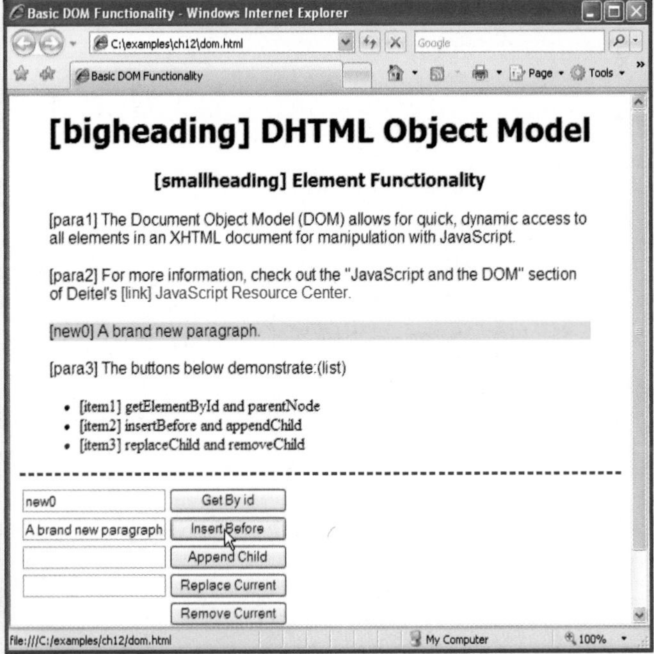

Fig. 12.2 | Basic DOM functionality. (Part 5 of 8.)

d) Using the Append Child button, a child paragraph is created.

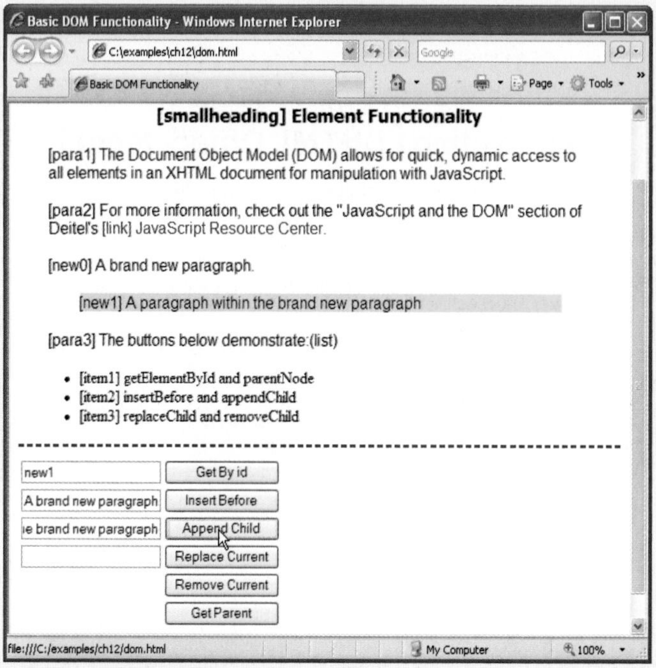

e) The selected paragraph is replaced with a new one.

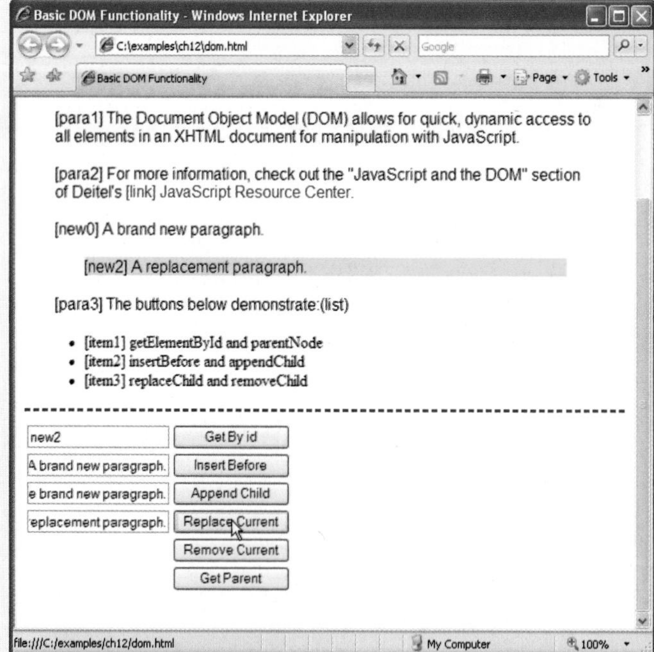

Fig. 12.2 | Basic DOM functionality. (Part 6 of 8.)

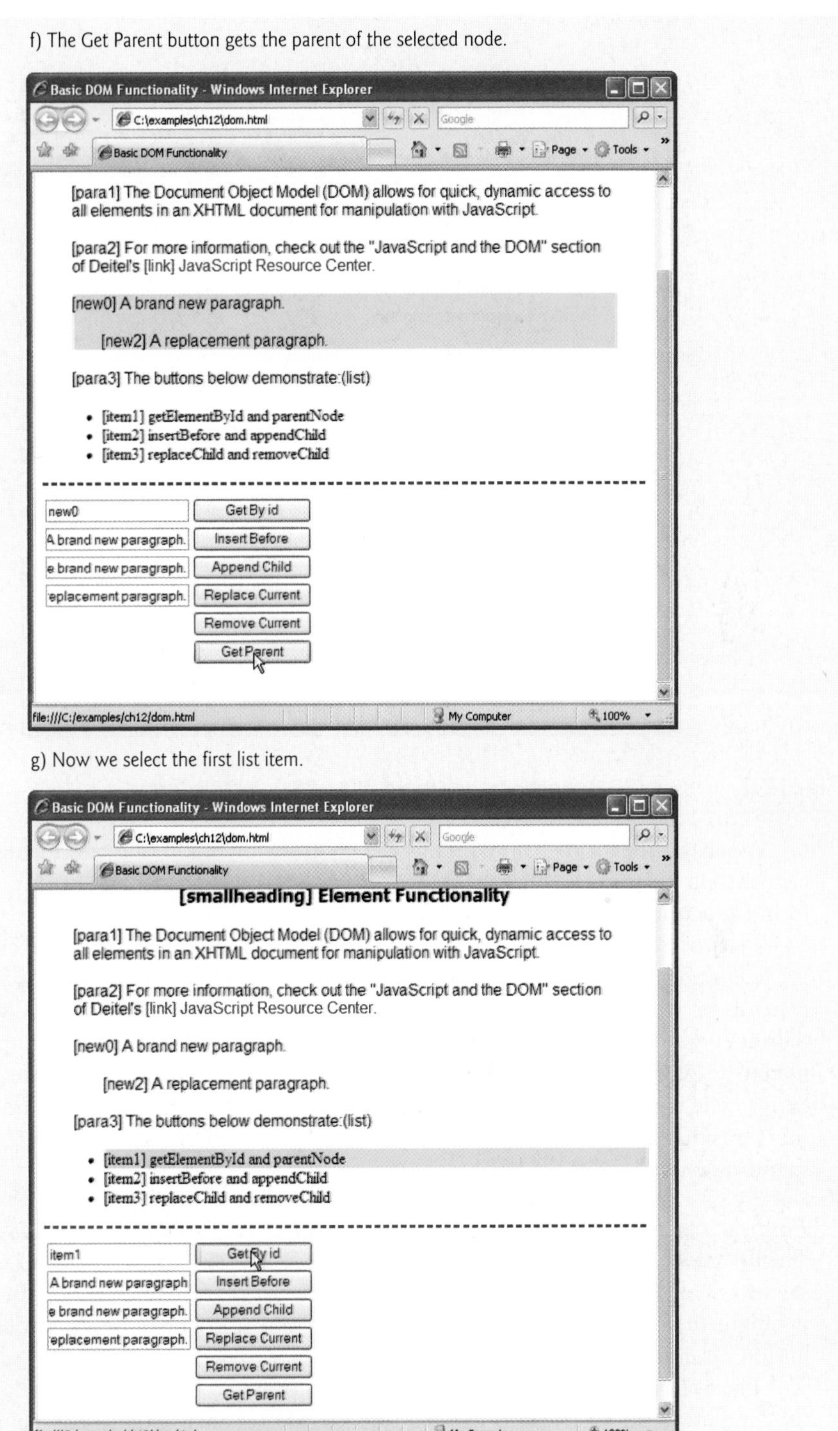

Fig. 12.2 | Basic DOM functionality. (Part 7 of 8.)

h) The Remove Current button removes the current node and selects its parent.

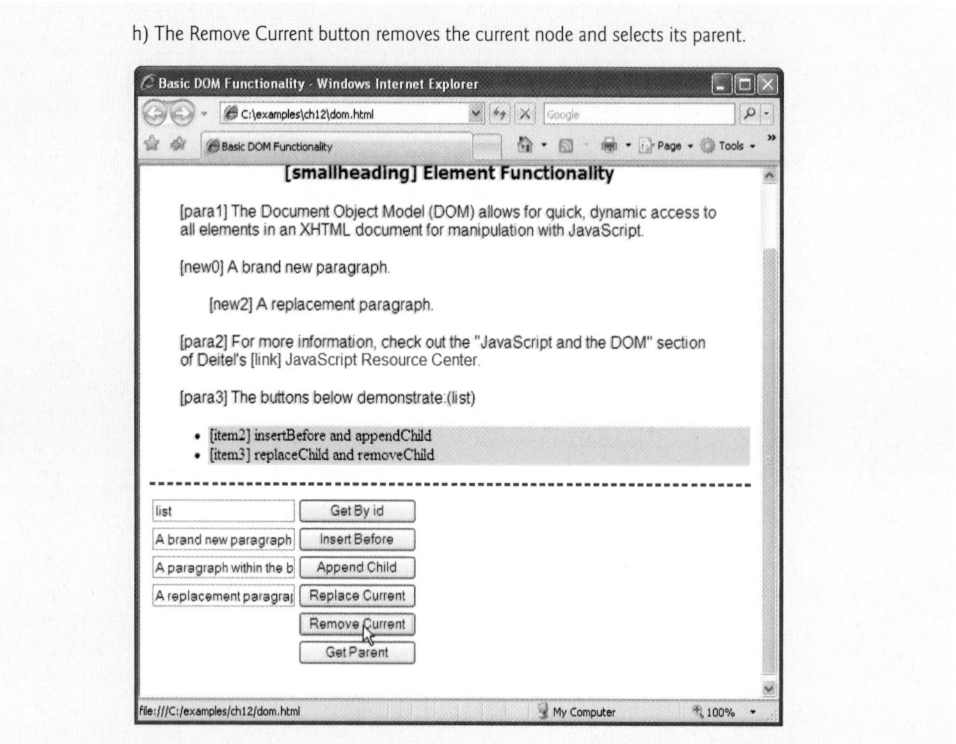

Fig. 12.2 | Basic DOM functionality. (Part 8 of 8.)

A `table` (lines 135–160) contains the controls for modifying and manipulating the elements on the page. Each of the six buttons calls its own event-handling function to perform the action described by its `value`.

The JavaScript code begins by declaring two variables. The variable `currentNode` (line 27) keeps track of the currently highlighted node, because the functionality of the buttons depends on which node is currently selected. The `body`'s `onload` attribute (line 116) initializes `currentNode` to the `h1` element with `id` `bigheading`. Variable `idcount` (line 28) is used to assign a unique `id` to any new elements that are created. The remainder of the JavaScript code contains event handling functions for the XHTML buttons and two helper functions that are called by the event handlers. We now discuss each button and its corresponding event handler in detail.

Finding and Highlighting an Element Using `getElementById` *and* `className`

The first row of the table (lines 136-141) allows the user to enter the `id` of an element into the text field (lines 137–138) and click the `Get By Id` button (lines 139–140) to find and highlight the element, as shown in Fig. 12.2(b) and (g). The `onclick` attribute sets the button's event handler to function `byId`.

The `byId` function is defined in lines 31–38. Line 33 uses `getElementById` to assign the contents of the text field to variable `id`. Line 34 uses `getElementById` again to find the element whose `id` attribute matches the contents of variable `id`, and assign it to variable `target`. If an element is found with the given `id`, `getElementById` returns an object representing that element. If no element is found, getElementById returns null. Line 36 checks whether target is an object—recall that any object used as a boolean expression is true, while null is false. If target evaluates to true, line 37 calls the switchTo function with target as its argument.

The switchTo function, defined in lines 106–112, is used throughout the program to highlight a new element in the page. The current element is given a yellow background using the style class highlighted, defined in line 22. Line 108 sets the current node's className property to the empty string. The className property allows you to change an XHTML element's class attribute. In this case, we clear the class attribute in order to remove the highlighted class from the currentNode before we highlight the new one.

Line 109 assigns the newNode object (passed into the function as a parameter) to variable currentNode. Line 110 adds the highlighted style class to the new currentNode using the className property.

Finally, line 111 uses the id property to assign the current node's id to the input field's value property. Just as className allows access to an element's class attribute, the id property controls an element's id attribute. While this isn't necessary when switchTo is called by byId, we will see shortly that other functions call switchTo. This line makes sure that the text field's value is consistent with the currently selected node's id. Having found the new element, removed the highlighting from the old element, updated the currentNode variable and highlighted the new element, the program has finished selecting a new node by a user-entered id.

Creating and Inserting Elements Using **insertBefore** *and* **appendChild**

The next two table rows allow the user to create a new element and insert it before the current node or as a child of the current node. The second row (lines 141–145) allows the user to enter text into the text field and click the Insert Before button. The text is placed in a new paragraph element, which is then inserted into the document before the currently selected element, as in Fig. 12.2(c). The button in lines 143–144 calls the insert function, defined in lines 42–48.

Lines 44–45 call the function createNewNode, passing it the value of the input field (whose id is ins) as an argument. Function createNewNode, defined in lines 94–103, creates a paragraph node containing the text passed to it. Line 96 creates a p element using the document object's createElement method. The createElement method creates a new DOM node, taking the tag name as an argument. Note that while createElement *creates* an element, it does not *insert* the element on the page.

Line 97 creates a unique id for the new element by concatenating "new" and the value of idcount before incrementing idcount in line 98. Line 99 assigns the id to the new element. Line 100 concatenates the element's id in square brackets to the beginning of text (the parameter containing the paragraph's text).

Line 101 introduces two new methods. The document's createTextNode method creates a node that can contain only text. Given a string argument, createTextNode inserts the string into the text node. In line 101, we create a new text node containing the contents of variable text. This new node is then used (still in line 101) as the argument to the appendChild method, which is called on the paragraph node. Method appendChild is called on a parent node to insert a child node (passed as an argument) after any existing children.

After the p element is created, line 102 returns the node to the calling function insert, where it is assigned to variable newNode in lines 44–45. Line 46 inserts the newly created node before the currently selected node. The **parentNode property** of any DOM node contains the node's parent. In line 46, we use the parentNode property of currentNode to get its parent.

We call the insertBefore method (line 46) on the parent with newNode and currentNode as its arguments to insert newNode as a child of the parent directly before currentNode. The general syntax of the **insertBefore method** is

```
parent.insertBefore( newChild, existingChild );
```

The method is called on a parent with the new child and an existing child as arguments. The node *newChild* is inserted as a child of *parent* directly before *existingChild.* Line 47 uses the switchTo function (discussed earlier in this section) to update the currentNode to the newly inserted node and highlight it in the XHTML page.

The third table row (lines 145–149) allows the user to append a new paragraph node as a child of the current element, demonstrated in Fig. 12.2(d). This features uses a similar procedure to the insertBefore functionality. Lines 53–54 in function appendNode create a new node, line 55 inserts it as a child of the current node, and line 56 uses switchTo to update currentNode and highlight the new node.

Replacing and Removing Elements Using **replaceChild** *and* **removeChild**

The next two table rows (lines 149–156) allow the user to replace the current element with a new p element or simply remove the current element. Lines 150–152 contain a text field and a button that replaces the currently highlighted element with a new paragraph node containing the text in the text field. This feature is demonstrated in Fig. 12.2(e).

The button in lines 151–152 calls function replaceCurrent, defined in lines 60–66. Lines 62–63 call createNewNode, in the same way as in insert and appendNode, getting the text from the correct input field. Line 64 gets the parent of currentNode, then calls the replaceChild method on the parent. The **replaceChild method** works as follows:

```
parent.replaceChild( newChild, oldChild );
```

The *parent*'s replaceChild method inserts *newChild* into its list of children in place of *oldChild.*

The Remove Current feature, shown in Fig. 12.2(h), removes the current element entirely and highlights the parent. No text field is required because a new element is not being created. The button in lines 154-155 calls the remove function, defined in lines 69–79. If the node's parent is the body element, line 72 alerts an error—the program does not allow the entire body element to be selected. Otherwise, lines 75–77 remove the current element. Line 75 stores the old currentNode in variable oldNode. We do this to maintain a reference to the node to be removed after we've changed the value of currentNode. Line 76 calls switchTo to highlight the parent node.

Line 77 uses the **removeChild method** to remove the oldNode (a child of the new currentNode) from its place in the XHTML document. In general,

```
parent.removeChild( child );
```

looks in *parent*'s list of children for *child* and removes it.

The final button (lines 157–158) selects and highlights the parent element of the currently highlighted element by calling the `parent` function, defined in lines 82–90. Function `parent` simply gets the parent node (line 84), makes sure it is not the `body` element, (line 86) and calls `switchTo` to highlight it (line 87). Line 89 alerts an error if the parent node is the `body` element. This feature is shown in Fig. 12.2(f).

This section introduced the basics of DOM tree traversal and manipulation. Next, we introduce the concept of collections, which give you access to multiple elements in a page.

12.4 DOM Collections

Included in the Document Object Model is the notion of **collections**, which are groups of related objects on a page. DOM collections are accessed as properties of DOM objects such as the `document` object or a DOM node. The document object has properties containing the **`images` collection**, **`links` collection**, **`forms` collection** and **`anchors` collection**. These collections contain all the elements of the corresponding type on the page. Figure 12.3 gives an example that uses the `links` collection to extract all of the links on a page and display them together at the bottom of the page.

```
<?xml version = "1.0" encoding = "utf-8"?>
<!DOCTYPE html PUBLIC "-//W3C//DTD XHTML 1.0 Strict//EN"
   "http://www.w3.org/TR/xhtml1/DTD/xhtml1-strict.dtd">

<!-- Fig. 12.3: collections.html -->
<!-- Using the links collection. -->
<html xmlns = "http://www.w3.org/1999/xhtml">
   <head>
      <title>Using Links Collection</title>
      <style type = "text/css">
         body           { font-family: arial, helvetica, sans-serif }
         h1             { font-family: tahoma, geneva, sans-serif;
                          text-align: center }
         p              { margin: 5% }
         p a            { color: #aa0000 }
         .links         { font-size: 14px;
                          text-align: justify;
                          margin-left: 10%;
                          margin-right: 10% }
         .link a        { text-decoration: none }
         .link a:hover { text-decoration: underline }
      </style>
      <script type = "text/javascript">
         <!--
         function processlinks()
         {
            var linkslist = document.links; // get the document's links
            var contents = "Links in this page:\n<br />| ";

            // concatenate each link to contents
            for ( var i = 0; i < linkslist.length; i++ )
            {
```

Fig. 12.3 | Using the `links` collection. (Part 1 of 2.)

```
               var currentLink = linkslist[ i ];
               contents += "<span class = 'link'>" +
                  currentLink.innerHTML.link( currentLink.href ) +
                  "</span> | ";
            } // end for

            document.getElementById( "links" ).innerHTML = contents;
         } // end function processlinks
         // -->
      </script>
   </head>
   <body onload = "processlinks()">
      <h1>Deitel Resource Centers</h1>
      <p><a href = "http://www.deitel.com/">Deitel's website</a> contains
         a rapidly growing
         <a href = "http://www.deitel.com/ResourceCenters.html">list of
         Resource Centers</a> on a wide range of topics. Many Resource
         centers related to topics covered in this book,
         <a href = "http://www.deitel.com/iw3htp4">Internet and World Wide
         Web How to Program, 4th Edition</a>. We have Resouce Centers on
         <a href = "http://www.deitel.com/Web2.0">Web 2.0</a>,
         <a href = "http://www.deitel.com/Firefox">Firefox</a> and
         <a href = "http://www.deitel.com/IE7">Internet Explorer 7</a>,
         <a href = "http://www.deitel.com/XHTML">XHTML</a>, and
         <a href = "http://www.deitel.com/JavaScript">JavaScript</a>.
         Watch the list of Deitel Resource Centers for related new
         Resource Centers.</p>
      <div id = "links" class = "links"></div>
   </body>
</html>
```

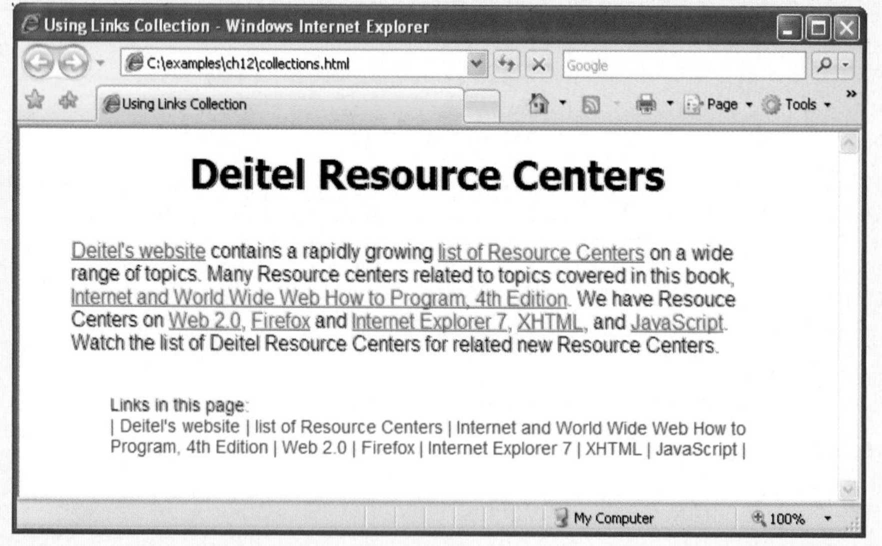

Fig. 12.3 | Using the `links` collection. (Part 2 of 2.)

The XHTML body contains a paragraph (lines 46–59) with links at various places in the text and an empty `div` (line 60) with `id` `links`. The `body`'s `onload` attribute specifies that the `processlinks` method is called when the `body` finishes loading.

Method `processlinks` declares variable `linkslist` (line 27) to store the `document`'s `links` collection, which is accessed as the `links` property of the `document` object. Line 28 creates the string (`contents`) that will contain all the document's links, to be inserted into the `links` `div` later. Line 31 begins a `for` statement to iterate through each link. To find the number of elements in the collection, we use the collection's **`length` property**.

Line 33 inside the `for` statement creates a variable (`currentlink`) that stores the current link. Note that we can access the collection stored in `linkslist` using indices in square brackets, just as we did with arrays. DOM collections are stored in objects which have only one property and two methods—the `length` property, the **`item` method** and the **`namedItem` method**. The `item` method—an alternative to the square bracketed indices—can be used to access specific elements in a collection by taking an index as an argument. The `namedItem` method takes a name as a parameter and finds the element in the collection, if any, whose `id` attribute or `name` attribute matches it.

Lines 34–36 add a `span` element to the `contents` string containing the current link. Recall that the `link` method of a string object returns the string as a link to the URL passed to the method. Line 35 uses the `link` method to create an `a` (anchor) element containing the proper text and `href` attribute.

Notice that variable `currentLink` (a DOM node representing an `a` element) has a specialized **`href` property** to refer to the link's `href` attribute. Many types of XHTML elements are represented by special types of nodes that extend the functionality of a basic DOM node. Line 39 inserts the contents into the empty `div` with `id` `"links"` (line 60) in order to show all the links on the page in one location.

Collections allow easy access to all elements of a single type in a page. This is useful for gathering elements into one place and for applying changes across an entire page. For example, the forms collection could be used to disable all form inputs after a submit button has been pressed to avoid multiple submissions while the next page loads. The next section discusses how to dynamically modify CSS styles using JavaScript and DOM nodes.

12.5 Dynamic Styles

An element's style can be changed dynamically. Often such a change is made in response to user events, which we discuss in Chapter 13. Such style changes can create many effects, including mouse hover effects, interactive menus, and animations. Figure 12.4 is a simple example that changes the `background-color` style property in response to user input.

```
<?xml version = "1.0" encoding = "utf-8"?>
<!DOCTYPE html PUBLIC "-//W3C//DTD XHTML 1.0 Strict//EN"
   "http://www.w3.org/TR/xhtml1/DTD/xhtml1-strict.dtd">

<!-- Fig. 12.4: dynamicstyle.html -->
<!-- Dynamic styles. -->
<html xmlns = "http://www.w3.org/1999/xhtml">
   <head>
```

Fig. 12.4 | Dynamic styles. (Part 1 of 2.)

```
9          <title>Dynamic Styles</title>
10         <script type = "text/javascript">
11            <!--
12            function start()
13            {
14               var inputColor = prompt( "Enter a color name for the " +
15                  "background of this page", "" );
16               document.body.style.backgroundColor = inputColor;
17            } // end function start
18            // -->
19         </script>
20      </head>
21      <body id = "body" onload = "start()">
22         <p>Welcome to our website!</p>
23      </body>
24   </html>
```

Fig. 12.4 | Dynamic styles. (Part 2 of 2.)

Function `start` (lines 12–17) `prompt`s the user to enter a color name, then sets the background color to that value. [*Note:* An error occurs if the value entered is not a valid color. See Appendix B, XHTML Colors, for further information.] We refer to the background color as `document.body.style.backgroundColor`—the **body property** of the `document` object refers to the `body` element. We then use the `style` property (a property of most XHTML elements) to set the `background-color` CSS property. This is referred to as `backgroundColor` in JavaScript—the hyphen is removed to avoid confusion with the subtraction (-) operator. This naming convention is consistent for most CSS properties. For example, `borderWidth` correlates to the `border-width` CSS property, and `fontFamily` correlates to the `font-family` CSS property. In general, CSS properties are accessed in the format *node*`.style.`*styleproperty*.

Figure 12.5 introduces the `setInterval` and `clearInterval` methods of the `window` object, combining them with dynamic styles to create animated effects. This example is a basic image viewer that allows you to select a Deitel book cover and view it in a larger size. When one of the thumbnail images on the right is clicked, the larger version grows from the top-left corner of the main image area.

The `body` (lines 66–85) contains two `div` elements, both floated `left` using styles defined in lines 14 and 17 in order to present them side by side. The left `div` contains the full-size image `iw3htp4.jpg`, the cover of this book, which appears when the page loads. The right `div` contains six thumbnail images which respond to the click event by calling the `display` method and passing it the filename of the corresponding full-size image.

The `display` function (lines 46–62) dynamically updates the image in the left `div` to the one corresponding to the user's click. Lines 48–49 prevent the rest of the function from executing if `interval` is defined (i.e., an animation is in progress.) Line 51 gets the left `div` by its `id`, `imgCover`. Line 52 creates a new `img` element. Lines 53–55 set its `id` to `imgCover`, set its `src` to the correct image file in the `fullsize` directory, and set its required `alt` attribute. Lines 56–59 do some additional initialization before beginning the animation in line 61. To create the growing animation effect, lines 57–58 set the image `width` and `height` to `0`. Line 59 replaces the current `bigImage` node with `newNode` (created in line 52), and line 60 sets `count`, the variable that controls the animation, to `0`.

Line 61 introduces the `window` object's **`setInterval` method**, which starts the animation. This method takes two parameters—a statement to execute repeatedly, and an integer specifying how often to execute it, in milliseconds. We use `setInterval` to call

```
1  <?xml version = "1.0" encoding = "utf-8"?>
2  <!DOCTYPE html PUBLIC "-//W3C//DTD XHTML 1.0 Strict//EN"
3     "http://www.w3.org/TR/xhtml1/DTD/xhtml1-strict.dtd">
4
5  <!-- Fig. 12.5: coverviewer.html -->
6  <!-- Dynamic styles used for animation. -->
7  <html xmlns = "http://www.w3.org/1999/xhtml">
8     <head>
9        <title>Deitel Book Cover Viewer</title>
10       <style type = "text/css">
11          .thumbs    { width: 192px;
12                       height: 370px;
13                       padding: 5px;
14                       float: left }
15          .mainimg   { width: 289px;
16                       padding: 5px;
17                       float: left }
18          .imgCover { height: 373px }
19          img        { border: 1px solid black }
20       </style>
21       <script type = "text/javascript">
22          <!--
23          var interval = null; // keeps track of the interval
24          var speed = 6; // determines the speed of the animation
25          var count = 0; // size of the image during the animation
26
27          // called repeatedly to animate the book cover
28          function run()
29          {
30             count += speed;
31
32             // stop the animation when the image is large enough
33             if ( count >= 375 )
34             {
```

Fig. 12.5 | Dynamic styles used for animation. (Part 1 of 4.)

```
               window.clearInterval( interval );
               interval = null;
            } // end if

            var bigImage = document.getElementById( "imgCover" );
            bigImage.style.width = .7656 * count + "px";
            bigImage.style.height = count + "px";
         } // end function run

         // inserts the proper image into the main image area and
         // begins the animation
         function display( imgfile )
         {
            if ( interval )
               return;

            var bigImage = document.getElementById( "imgCover" );
            var newNode = document.createElement( "img" );
            newNode.id = "imgCover";
            newNode.src = "fullsize/" + imgfile;
            newNode.alt = "Large image";
            newNode.className = "imgCover";
            newNode.style.width = "0px";
            newNode.style.height = "0px";
            bigImage.parentNode.replaceChild( newNode, bigImage );
            count = 0; // start the image at size 0
            interval = window.setInterval( "run()", 10 ); // animate
         } // end function display
         // -->
      </script>
   </head>
   <body>
      <div id = "mainimg" class = "mainimg">
         <img id = "imgCover" src = "fullsize/iw3htp4.jpg"
            alt = "Full cover image" class = "imgCover" />
      </div>
      <div id = "thumbs" class = "thumbs" >
         <img src = "thumbs/iw3htp4.jpg" alt = "iw3htp4"
            onclick = "display( 'iw3htp4.jpg' )" />
         <img src = "thumbs/chtp5.jpg" alt = "chtp5"
            onclick = "display( 'chtp5.jpg' )" />
         <img src = "thumbs/cpphtp6.jpg" alt = "cpphtp6"
            onclick = "display( 'cpphtp6.jpg' )" />
         <img src = "thumbs/jhtp7.jpg" alt = "jhtp7"
            onclick = "display( 'jhtp7.jpg' )" />
         <img src = "thumbs/vbhtp3.jpg" alt = "vbhtp3"
            onclick = "display( 'vbhtp3.jpg' )" />
         <img src = "thumbs/vcsharphtp2.jpg" alt = "vcsharphtp2"
            onclick = "display( 'vcsharphtp2.jpg' )" />
      </div>
   </body>
</html>
```

Fig. 12.5 | Dynamic styles used for animation. (Part 2 of 4.)

a) The cover viewer page loads with the cover of this book.

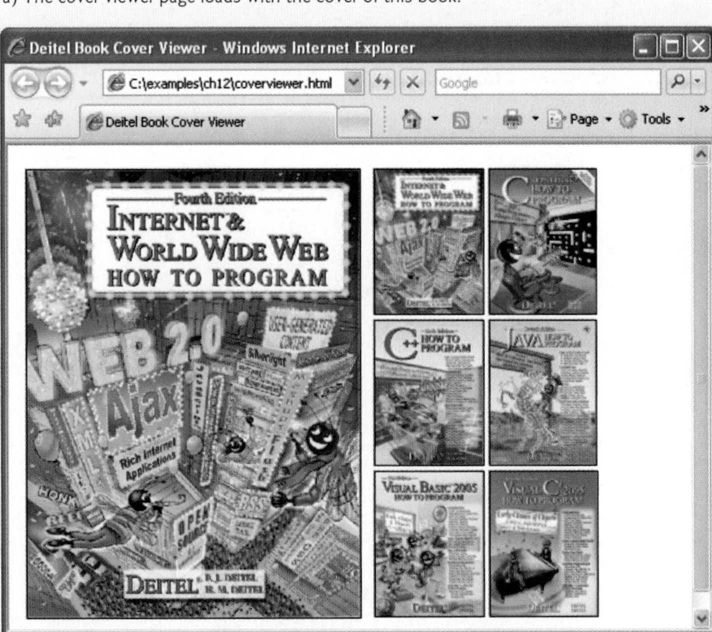

b) When the user clicks the thumbnail of C How to Program, the full-size image begins growing from the top-left corner of the window.

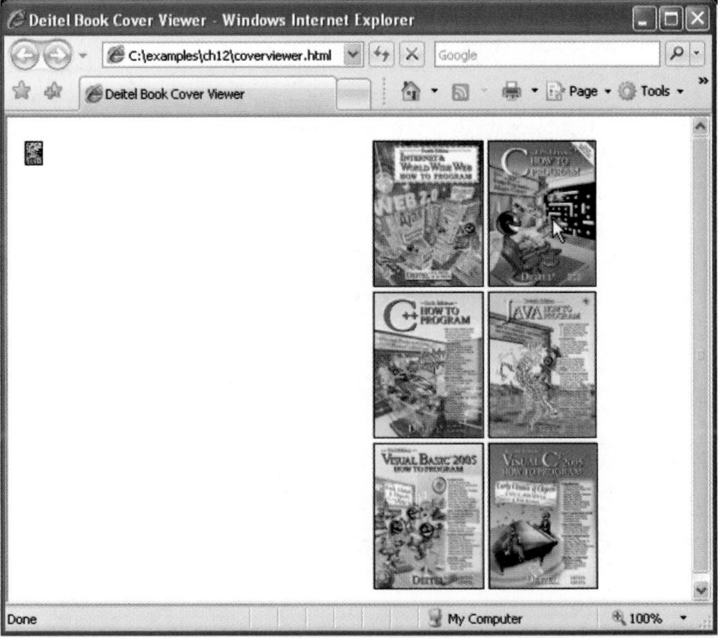

Fig. 12.5 | Dynamic styles used for animation. (Part 3 of 4.)

c) The cover continues to grow.

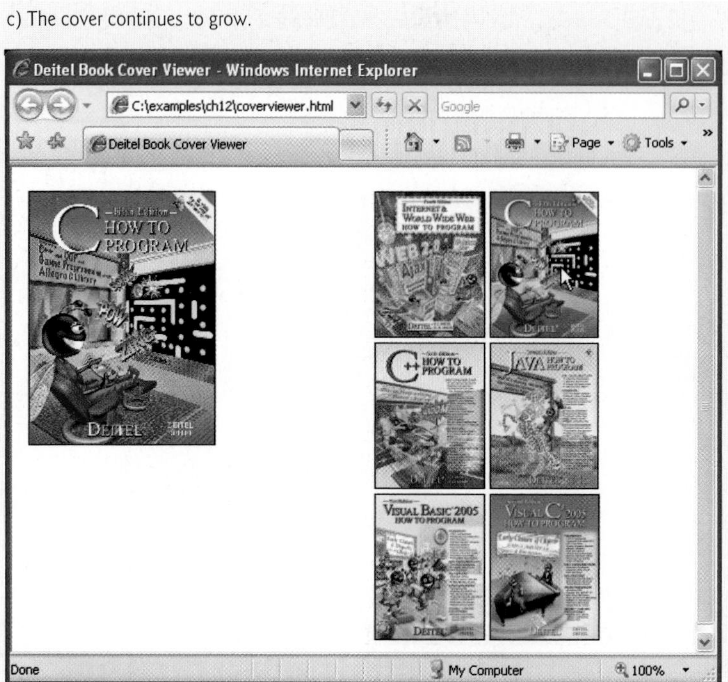

d) The animation finishes when the cover reaches its full size.

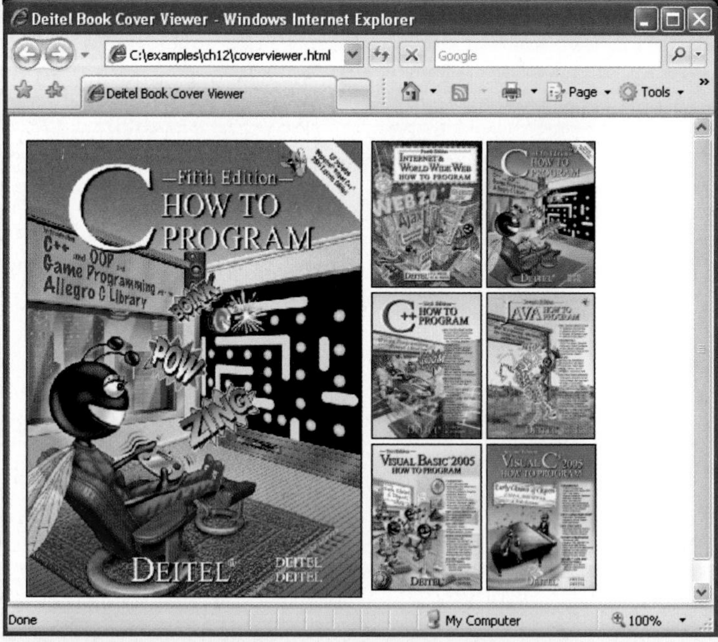

Fig. 12.5 | Dynamic styles used for animation. (Part 4 of 4.)

function run every 10 milliseconds. The setInterval method returns a unique identifier to keep track of that particular interval—we assign this identifier to the variable interval. We use this identifier to stop the animation when the image has finished growing.

The run function, defined in lines 28–42, increases the height of the image by the value of speed and updates its width accordingly to keep the aspect ratio consistent. Because the run function is called every 10 milliseconds, this increase happens repeatedly to create an animated growing effect. Line 30 adds the value of speed (declared and initialized to 6 in line 24) to count, which keeps track of the animation's progress and dictates the current size of the image. If the image has grown to its full height (375), line 35 uses the window's **clearInterval method** to stop the repetitive calls of the run method. We pass to clearInterval the interval identifier (stored in interval) that setInterval created in line 61. Although it seems unnecessary in this script, this identifier allows the script to keep track of multiple intervals running at the same time and to choose which interval to stop when calling clearInterval.

Line 39 gets the image and lines 40–41 set its width and height CSS properties. Note that line 40 multiplies count by a scaling factor of .7656 in order to keep the ratio of the image's dimensions consistent with the actual dimensions of the image. Run the code example and click on a thumbnail image to see the full animation effect.

This section demonstrated the concept of dynamically changing CSS styles using JavaScript and the DOM. We also discussed the basics of how to create scripted animations using setInterval and clearInterval.

12.6 Summary of the DOM Objects and Collections

As you have seen in the preceding sections, the objects and collections in the W3C DOM give you flexibility in manipulating the elements of a web page. We have shown how to access the objects in a page, how to access the objects in a collection, and how to change element styles dynamically.

The W3C DOM allows you to access every element in an XHTML document. Each element in a document is represented by a separate object. The diagram in Fig. 12.6 shows many of the important objects and collections provided by the W3C DOM. Figure 12.7 provides a brief description of each object and collection in Fig. 12.6.

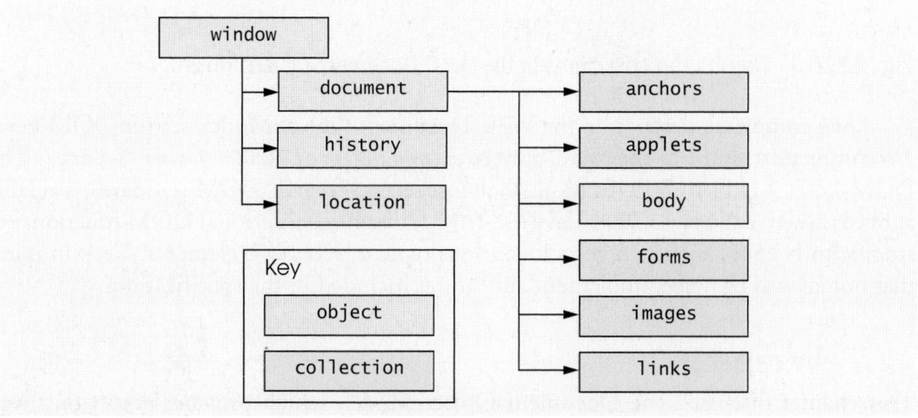

Fig. 12.6 | W3C Document Object Model.

Object or collection	Description
Objects	
`window`	Represents the browser window and provides access to the `document` object contained in the `window`. Also contains `history` and `location` objects.
`document`	Represents the XHTML document rendered in a `window`. The `document` object provides access to every element in the XHTML document and allows dynamic modification of the XHTML document. Contains several collections for accessing all elements of a given type.
`body`	Provides access to the `body` element of an XHTML document.
`history`	Keeps track of the sites visited by the browser user. The object provides a script programmer with the ability to move forward and backward through the visited sites.
`location`	Contains the URL of the rendered document. When this object is set to a new URL, the browser immediately navigates to the new location.
Collections	
`anchors`	Collection contains all the anchor elements (a) that have a `name` or `id` attribute. The elements appear in the collection in the order in which they were defined in the XHTML document.
`forms`	Contains all the `form` elements in the XHTML document. The elements appear in the collection in the order in which they were defined in the XHTML document.
`images`	Contains all the `img` elements in the XHTML document. The elements appear in the collection in the order in which they were defined in the XHTML document.
`links`	Contains all the anchor elements (a) with an `href` property. The elements appear in the collection in the order in which they were defined in the XHTML document.

Fig. 12.7 | Objects and collections in the W3C Document Object Model.

For a complete reference on the W3C Document Object Model, see the DOM Level 3 recommendation from the W3C at `http://www.w3.org/TR/DOM-Level-3-Core/`. The DOM Level 2 HTML Specification (the most recent HTML DOM standard), available at `http://www.w3.org/TR/DOM-Level-2-HTML/`, describes additional DOM functionality specific to HTML, such as objects for various types of XHTML elements. Keep in mind that not all web browsers implement all features included in the specification.

12.7 Wrap-Up

This chapter discussed the Document Object Model, which provides access to a web page's elements. We described the child-parent relationships that exist between a document's nodes, and provided visual representations of a DOM tree to illustrate how elements in a web page are related. We introduced several properties and methods that allow us to manipulate nodes, and described groups of related objects on a page, called collections. Finally, we discussed how to dynamically modify content in a web page, adding interactivity and animation to the existing site. In the next chapter, we discuss JavaScript events, which enable JavaScript programs to process user interactions with a web page.

12.8 Web Resources

`www.deitel.com/javascript/`

The Deitel JavaScript Resource Center contains links to some of the best JavaScript resources on the web. There you'll find categorized links to JavaScript tools, code generators, forums, books, libraries, frameworks, tutorials and more. Check out the section specifically dedicated to the Document Object Model. Be sure to visit the related Resource Centers on XHTML (`www.deitel.com/xhtml/`) and CSS 2.1 (`www.deitel.com/css21/`).

Summary

Section 12.1 Introduction

- The Document Object Model gives you access to all the elements on a web page. Using JavaScript, you can create, modify and remove elements in the page dynamically.

Section 12.2 Modeling a Document: DOM Nodes and Trees

- The `getElementById` method returns objects called DOM nodes. Every element in an XHTML page is modeled in the web browser by a DOM node.
- All the nodes in a document make up the page's DOM tree, which describes the relationships among elements.
- Nodes are related to each other through child-parent relationships. An XHTML element inside another element is said to be a child of the containing element. The containing element is known as the parent. A node may have multiple children, but only one parent. Nodes with the same parent node are referred to as siblings.
- Firefox's DOM Inspector and the IE Web Developer Toolbar allow you to see a visual representation of a document's DOM tree and information about each node.
- The document node in a DOM tree is called the root node, because it has no parent.

Section 12.3 Traversing and Modifying a DOM Tree

- The `className` property of a DOM node allows you to change an XHTML element's `class` attribute.
- The `id` property of a DOM node controls an element's `id` attribute.
- The `document` object's `createElement` method creates a new DOM node, taking the tag name as an argument. Note that while `createElement` *creates* an element, it does not *insert* the element on the page.
- The `document`'s `createTextNode` method creates a DOM node that can contain only text. Given a string argument, `createTextNode` inserts the string into the text node.
- Method `appendChild` is called on a parent node to insert a child node (passed as an argument) after any existing children.

- The `parentNode` property of any DOM node contains the node's parent.
- The `insertBefore` method is called on a parent with a new child and an existing child as arguments. The new child is inserted as a child of the parent directly before the existing child.
- The `replaceChild` method is called on a parent, taking a new child and an existing child as arguments. The method inserts the new child into its list of children in place of the existing child.
- The `removeChild` method is called on a parent with a child to be removed as an argument.

Section 12.4 DOM Collections

- Included in the Document Object Model is the notion of collections, which are groups of related objects on a page. DOM collections are accessed as properties of DOM objects such as the `document` object or a DOM node.
- The `document` object has properties containing the `images` collection, `links` collection, `forms` collection and `anchors` collection. These collections contain all the elements of the corresponding type on the page.
- To find the number of elements in the collection, use the collection's `length` property.
- To access items in a collection, use square brackets the same way you would with an array, or use the `item` method. The `item` method of a DOM collection is used to access specific elements in a collection, taking an index as an argument. The `namedItem` method takes a name as a parameter and finds the element in the collection, if any, whose `id` attribute or `name` attribute matches it.
- The `href` property of a DOM link node refers to the link's `href` attribute. Many types of XHTML elements are represented by special types of nodes that extend the functionality of a basic DOM node.
- Collections allow easy access to all elements of a single type in a page. This is useful for gathering elements into one place and for applying changes across an entire page.

Section 12.5 Dynamic Styles

- An element's style can be changed dynamically. Often such a change is made in response to user events, which are discussed in the next chapter. Such style changes can create many effects, including mouse hover effects, interactive menus, and animations.
- The `body` property of the `document` object refers to the `body` element in the XHTML page.
- The `style` property can access a CSS property in the format *node*`.style.`*styleproperty*.
- A CSS property with a hyphen (-), such as `background-color`, is referred to as `backgroundColor` in JavaScript, to avoid confusion with the subtraction (-) operator. Removing the hyphen and capitalizing the first letter of the following word is the convention for most CSS properties.
- The `setInterval` method of the `window` object repeatedly executes a statement on a certain interval. It takes two parameters—a statement to execute repeatedly, and an integer specifying how often to execute it, in milliseconds. The `setInterval` method returns a unique identifier to keep track of that particular interval.
- The `window` object's `clearInterval` method stops the repetitive calls of object's `setInterval` method. We pass to `clearInterval` the interval identifier that `setInterval` returned.

Section 12.6 Summary of the DOM Objects and Collections

- The objects and collections in the W3C DOM give you flexibility in manipulating the elements of a web page.
- The W3C DOM allows you to access every element in an XHTML document. Each element in a document is represented by a separate object.

- For a reference on the W3C Document Object Model, see the DOM Level 3 recommendation from the W3C at `http://www.w3.org/TR/DOM-Level-3-Core/`. The DOM Level 2 HTML Specification, available at `http://www.w3.org/TR/DOM-Level-2-HTML/`, describes additional DOM functionality specific to HTML, such as objects for various types of XHTML elements.
- Not all web browsers implement all features included in the DOM specification.

Terminology

`anchors` collection of the `document` object
`body` property of the `document` object
`appendChild` method of a DOM node
child
`className` property of a DOM node
`clearInterval` method of the `window` object
collection
`createElement` method of the `document` object
`createTextNode` method of the `document` object
`document` object
Document Object Model
DOM collection
DOM Inspector
DOM node
DOM tree
dynamic style
`forms` collection of the `document` object
`href` property of an a (anchor) node
Internet Explorer Web Developer Toolbar
`id` property of a DOM node
`images` collection
`innerHTML` property of a DOM node
`insertBefore` method of a DOM node
`item` method of a DOM collection
`length` property of a DOM collection
`links` collection of the `document` object
`namedItem` method of a DOM collection
object hierarchy
parent
`removeChild` method of a DOM node
`replaceChild` method of a DOM node
root node
`setInterval` method of the `window` object
sibling
`style` property of a DOM node
W3C Document Object Model

Self-Review Exercises

12.1 State whether each of the following is *true* or *false*. If *false*, explain why.

a) Every XHTML element in a page is represented by a DOM tree.
b) A text node cannot have child nodes.
c) The `document` node in a DOM tree cannot have child nodes.
d) You can change an element's style class dynamically with the `style` property.
e) The `createElement` method creates a new node and inserts it into the document.
f) The `setInterval` method calls a function repeatedly at a set time interval.
g) The `insertBefore` method is called on the document object, taking a new node and an existing one to insert the new one before.
h) The most recently started interval is stopped when the `clearInterval` method is called.
i) The collection `links` contains all the links in a document with specified `name` or `id` attributes.

12.2 Fill in the blanks for each of the following statements.

a) The _______ property refers to the text inside an element, including XHTML tags.
b) A document's DOM _______ represents all of the nodes in a document, as well as their relationships to each other.
c) The _______ property contains the number of elements in a collection.
d) The _______ method allows access to an individual element in a collection.
e) The _______ collection contains all the `img` elements on a page.
f) The _______ object contains information about the sites that a user previously visited.
g) CSS properties may be accessed using the _______ object.

Answers to Self-Review Exercises

12.1 a) False. Every element is represented by a DOM *node*. Each node is a member of the document's DOM tree. b) True. c) False. The `document` is the root node, therefore has no parent node. d) False. The style class is changed with the `className` property. e) False. The `createElement` method creates a node, but does not insert it into the DOM tree. f) True. g) False. `insertBefore` is called on the parent. h) False. `clearInterval` takes an interval identifier as an argument to determine which interval to end. i) False. The `links` collection contains all links in a document.

12.2 a) `innerHTML`. b) tree. c) `length`. d) `item`. e) `images`. f) `history`. g) `style`.

Exercises

12.3 Modify Fig. 12.3 to use a background color to highlight all the links in the page instead of displaying them in a box at the bottom.

12.4 Use the Firefox DOM Inspector or the IE Web Developer Toolbar to view the DOM tree of the document in Fig. 12.2. Look at the document tree of your favorite website. Notice the information these tools give you in the right panel(s) about an element when you click it.

12.5 Write a script that contains a button and a counter in a `div`. The button should increment the counter each time it is clicked.

12.6 Write a script that prints out the length of all the JavaScript collections on a page.

12.7 Create a web page in which users are allowed to select their favorite layout and formatting through the use of the `className` property.

12.8 *(15 Puzzle)* Write a web page that enables the user to play the game of 15. There is a 4-by-4 board (implemented as an XHTML table) for a total of 16 slots. One of the slots is empty. The other slots are occupied by 15 tiles, randomly numbered from 1 through 15. Any tile next to the currently empty slot can be moved into the currently empty slot by clicking on the tile. Your program should create the board with the tiles out of order. The user's goal is to arrange the tiles in sequential order row by row. Using the DOM and the `onclick` event, write a script that allows the user to swap the positions of the open position and an adjacent tile. [*Hint:* The `onclick` event should be specified for each table cell.]

12.9 Modify your solution to Exercise 12.8 to determine when the game is over, then prompt the user to determine whether to play again. If so, scramble the numbers using the `Math.random` method.

12.10 Modify your solution to Exercise 12.9 to use an image that is split into 16 equally sized pieces. Discard one of the pieces and randomly place the other 15 pieces in the XHTML table.

13

JavaScript: Events

The wisest prophets make sure of the event first.
—Horace Walpole

Do you think I can listen all day to such stuff?
—Lewis Carroll

The user should feel in control of the computer; not the other way around. This is achieved in applications that embody three qualities: responsiveness, permissiveness, and consistency.
—*Inside Macintosh, Volume 1*
Apple Computer, Inc., 1985

We are responsible for actions performed in response to circumstances for which we are not responsible.
—Allan Massie

OBJECTIVES

In this chapter you will learn:

- The concepts of events, event handlers and event bubbling.
- To create and register event handlers that respond to mouse and keyboard events.
- To use the `event` object to get information about an event.
- To recognize and respond to many common events.

Outline

13.1 Introduction

We've seen that XHTML pages can be controlled via scripting, and we've already used a few events to trigger scripts, such as the `onclick` and `onsubmit` events. This chapter goes into more detail on JavaScript events, which allow scripts to respond to user interactions and modify the page accordingly. Events allow scripts to respond to a user who is moving the mouse, entering form data or pressing keys. Events and event handling help make web applications more responsive, dynamic and interactive.

In this chapter, we discuss how to set up functions to react when an event fires (occurs). We give examples of event handling for nine common events, including mouse events and form-processing events. A the end of the chapter, we provide a table of the events covered in this chapter and other useful events.

13.2 Registering Event Handlers

Functions that handle events are called event handlers. Assigning an event handler to an event on a DOM node is called registering an event handler. Previously, we have registered event handlers using the inline model, treating events as attributes of XHTML elements (e.g., `<p onclick = "myfunction()">`). Another model, known as the traditional model, for registering event handlers is demonstrated alongside the inline model in Fig. 13.1.

In the earliest event-capable browsers, the inline model was the only way to handle events. Later, Netscape developed the traditional model and Internet Explorer adopted it. Since then, both Netscape and Microsoft have developed separate (incompatible)

```
<?xml version = "1.0" encoding = "utf-8"?>
<!DOCTYPE html PUBLIC "-//W3C//DTD XHTML 1.0 Strict//EN"
   "http://www.w3.org/TR/xhtml1/DTD/xhtml1-strict.dtd">

```

Fig. 13.1 | Event registration models. (Part 1 of 3.)

```
<!-- Fig. 13.1: registering.html -->
<!-- Event registration models. -->
<html xmlns = "http://www.w3.org/1999/xhtml">
   <head>
      <title>Event Registration Models</title>
      <style type = "text/css">
         div { padding: 5px;
               margin: 10px;
               border: 3px solid #0000BB;
               width: 12em }
      </style>
      <script type = "text/javascript">
         <!--
         // handle the onclick event regardless of how it was registered
         function handleEvent()
         {
            alert( "The event was successfully handled." );
         } // end function handleEvent

         // register the handler using the traditional model
         function registerHandler()
         {
            var traditional = document.getElementById( "traditional" );
            traditional.onclick = handleEvent;
         } // end function registerHandler
         // -->
      </script>
   </head>
   <body onload = "registerHandler()">
      <!-- The event handler is registered inline -->
      <div id = "inline" onclick = "handleEvent()">
         Inline registration model</div>

      <!-- The event handler is registered by function registerHandler -->
      <div id = "traditional">Traditional registration model</div>
   </body>
</html>
```

a) The user clicks the **div** for which the event handler was registered using the inline model.

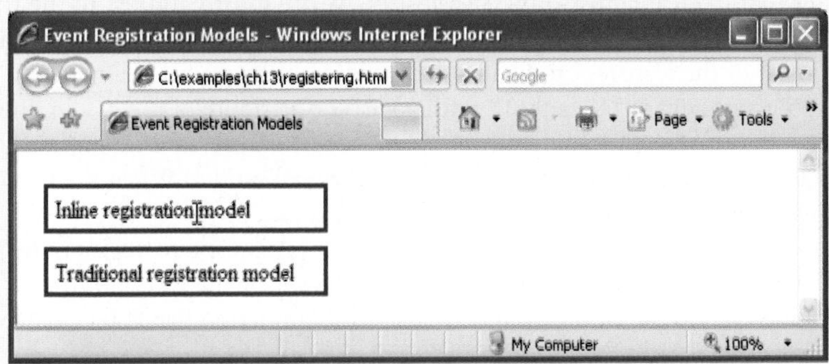

Fig. 13.1 | Event registration models. (Part 2 of 3.)

b) The event handler displays an alert dialog.

c) The user clicks the **div** for which the event handler was registered using the traditional model.

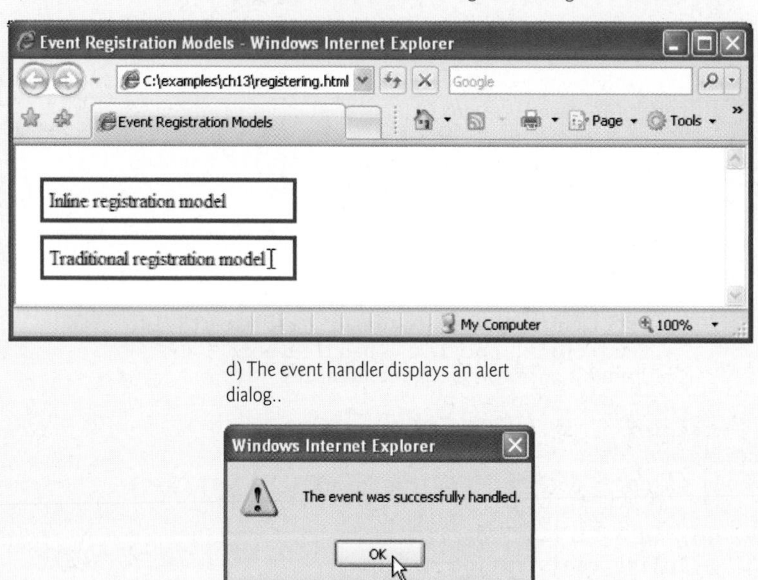

d) The event handler displays an alert dialog..

Fig. 13.1 | Event registration models. (Part 3 of 3.)

advanced event models with more functionality than either the inline or the traditional model. Netscape's advanced model was adapted by the W3C to create a DOM Events Specification. Most browsers support the W3C model, but Internet Explorer 7 does not. This means that to create cross-browser websites, we are mostly limited to the traditional and inline event models. While the advanced models provide more convenience and functionality, most of the features can be implemented with the traditional model.

Line 35 assigns `"handleEvent()"` to the `onclick` attribute of the `div` in lines 35–36. This is the inline model for event registration we've seen in previous examples. The `div` in line 39 is assigned an event handler using the traditional model. When the `body` element (lines 33–40) loads, the `registerHandler` function is called.

Function `registerHandler` (lines 25–29) uses JavaScript to register the function `handleEvent` as the event handler for the `onclick` event of the `div` with the `id` `"traditional"`. Line 27 gets the `div`, and line 28 assigns the function `handleEvent` to the `div`'s `onclick` property.

Notice that in line 28, we do not put `handleEvent` in quotes or include parentheses at the end of the function name, as we do in the inline model in line 35. In the inline model, the value of the XHTML attribute is a *JavaScript statement* to execute when the event occurs. The value of the `onclick` property of a DOM node is not an executable statement, but the name of a *function* to be called when the event occurs. Recall that JavaScript functions can be treated as data (i.e., passed into methods, assigned to variables, etc.).

Common Programming Error 13.1

Putting quotes around the function name when registering it using the inline model would assign a string to the `onclick` *property of the node—a string cannot be called.*

Common Programming Error 13.2

Putting parentheses after the function name when registering it using the inline model would call the function immediately and assign its return value to the `onclick` *property.*

Once the event handler is registered in line 28, the `div` in line 39 has the same behavior as the `div` in lines 35–36, because `handleEvent` (lines 19–22) is set to handle the `onclick` event for both `div`s. When either `div` is clicked, an alert will display `"The event was successfully handled."`

The traditional model allows us to register event handlers in JavaScript code. This has important implications for what we can do with JavaScript events. For example, traditional event-handler registration allows us to assign event handlers to many elements quickly and easily using repetition statements, instead of adding an inline event handler to each XHTML element. In the remaining examples in this chapter, we use both the inline and traditional registration models depending on which is more convenient.

13.3 Event `onload`

The `onload` event fires whenever an element finishes loading successfully (i.e., all its children are loaded). Frequently, this event is used in the `body` element to initiate a script after the page loads in the client's browser. Figure 13.2 uses the `onload` event for this purpose. The script called by the `onload` event updates a timer that indicates how many seconds have elapsed since the document was loaded.

```
<?xml version = "1.0" encoding = "utf-8"?>
<!DOCTYPE html PUBLIC "-//W3C//DTD XHTML 1.0 Strict//EN"
   "http://www.w3.org/TR/xhtml1/DTD/xhtml1-strict.dtd">

<!-- Fig. 13.2: onload.html -->
<!-- Demonstrating the onload event. -->
<html xmlns = "http://www.w3.org/1999/xhtml">
   <head>
      <title>onload Event</title>
      <script type = "text/javascript">
         <!--
         var seconds = 0;

         // called when the page loads to begin the timer
         function startTimer()
         {
```

Fig. 13.2 | Demonstrating the `onload` event. (Part 1 of 2.)

```
17            // 1000 milliseconds = 1 second
18            window.setInterval( "updateTime()", 1000 );
19         } // end function startTimer
20
21         // called every 1000 ms to update the timer
22         function updateTime()
23         {
24            ++seconds;
25            document.getElementById( "soFar" ).innerHTML = seconds;
26         } // end function updateTime
27         // -->
28      </script>
29   </head>
30   <body onload = "startTimer()">
31      <p>Seconds you have spent viewing this page so far:
32      <strong id = "soFar">0</strong></p>
33   </body>
34 </html>
```

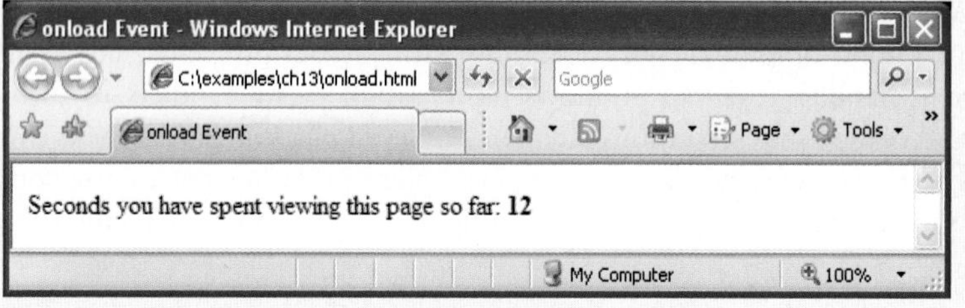

Fig. 13.2 | Demonstrating the `onload` event. (Part 2 of 2.)

Our use of the `onload` event occurs in line 30. After the `body` section loads, the browser triggers the `onload` event. This calls function `startTimer` (lines 15–19), which in turn uses method `window.setInterval` to specify that function `updateTime` (lines 22–26) should be called every `1000` milliseconds. The `updateTime` function increments variable `seconds` and updates the counter on the page.

Note that we could not have created this program without the onload event, because elements in the XHTML page cannot be accessed until the page has loaded. If a script in the `head` attempts to get a DOM node for an XHTML element in the `body`, `getElementById` returns `null` because the `body` has not yet loaded. Other uses of the `onload` event include opening a pop-up window once a page has loaded and triggering a script when an image or Java applet loads.

Common Programming Error 13.3

Trying to get an element in a page before the page has loaded is a common error. Avoid this by putting your script in a function using the `onload` event to call the function.

13.4 Event onmousemove, the event Object and this

This section introduces the `onmousemove` event, which fires repeatedly whenever the user moves the mouse over the web page. We also discuss the `event` object and the keyword this, which permit more advanced event-handling capabilities. Figure 13.3 uses onmousemove and this to create a simple drawing program that allows the user to draw inside a box in red or blue by holding down the *Shift* or *Ctrl* keys.

The XHTML body has a table with a tbody containing one row that gives the user instructions on how to use the program. The body's onload attribute (line 61) calls function createCanvas, which initializes the program by filling in the table.

The createCanvas function (lines 23–41) fills in the table with a grid of cells. The CSS rule in lines 14–15 sets the width and height of every td element to 4px. Line 11

```
1  <?xml version = "1.0" encoding = "utf-8"?>
2  <!DOCTYPE html PUBLIC "-//W3C//DTD XHTML 1.0 Strict//EN"
3     "http://www.w3.org/TR/xhtml1/DTD/xhtml1-strict.dtd">
4
5  <!-- Fig. 13.3: draw.html -->
6  <!-- A simple drawing program. -->
7  <html xmlns = "http://www.w3.org/1999/xhtml">
8     <head>
9        <title>Simple Drawing Program</title>
10       <style type = "text/css">
11          #canvas { width: 400px;
12                    border: 1px solid #999999;
13                    border-collapse: collapse }
14          td      { width: 4px;
15                    height: 4px }
16          th.key  { font-family: arial, helvetica, sans-serif;
17                    font-size: 12px;
18                    border-bottom: 1px solid #999999 }
19       </style>
20       <script type = "text/javascript">
21          <!--
22          //initialization function to insert cells into the table
23          function createCanvas ()
24          {
25             var side = 100;
26             var tbody = document.getElementById( "tablebody" );
27
28             for ( var i = 0; i < side; i++ )
29             {
30                var row = document.createElement( "tr" );
31
32                for ( var j = 0; j < side; j++ )
33                {
34                   var cell = document.createElement( "td" );
35                   cell.onmousemove = processMouseMove;
36                   row.appendChild( cell );
37                } // end for
38
39                tbody.appendChild( row );
40             } // end for
41          } // end function createCanvas
42
```

Fig. 13.3 | Simple drawing program. (Part 1 of 3.)

```
         // processes the onmousemove event
         function processMouseMove( e )
         {
            // get the event object from IE
            if ( !e )
               var e = window.event;

            // turn the cell blue if the Ctrl key is pressed
            if ( e.ctrlKey )
               this.style.backgroundColor = "blue";

            // turn the cell red if the Shift key is pressed
            if ( e.shiftKey )
               this.style.backgroundColor = "red";
         } // end function processMouseMove
         // -->
      </script>
   </head>
   <body onload = "createCanvas()">
      <table id = "canvas" class = "canvas"><tbody id = "tablebody">
      <tr><th class = "key" colspan = "100">Hold <tt>ctrl</tt>
         to draw blue. Hold <tt>shift</tt> to draw red.</th></tr>
      </tbody></table>
   </body>
</html>
```

a) The page loads and fills with white cells. With no keys held down, moving the mouse does not draw anything.

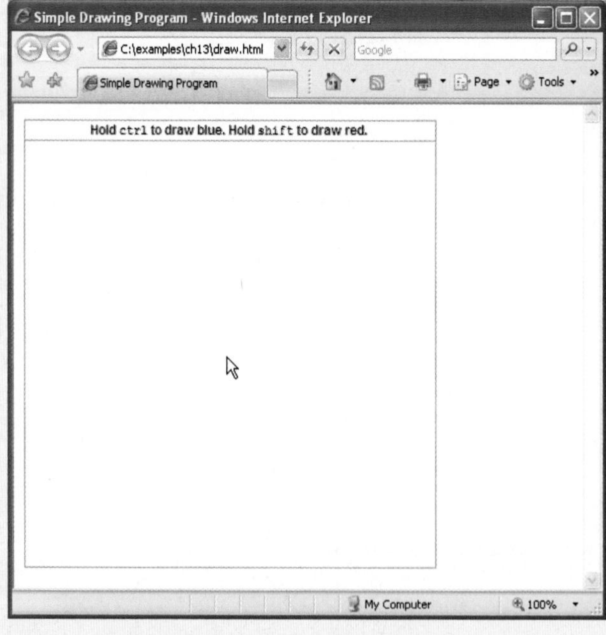

Fig. 13.3 | Simple drawing program. (Part 2 of 3.)

b) The user holds the *Ctrl* key and moves the mouse to draw a blue line.

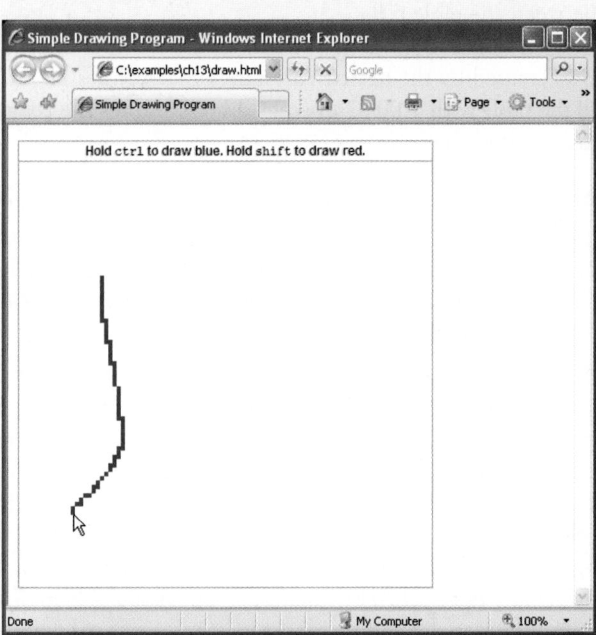

c) The user holds the *Shift* key and moves the mouse to draw a red line.

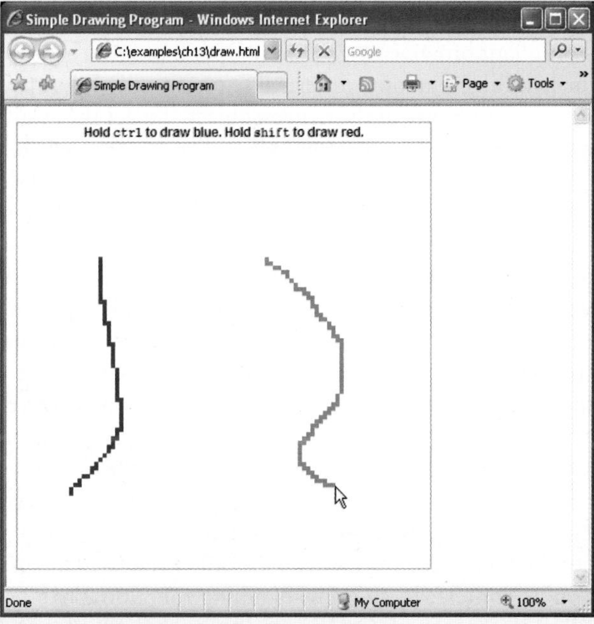

Fig. 13.3 | Simple drawing program. (Part 3 of 3.)

dictates that the table is 400px wide. Line 13 uses the border-collapse CSS property to eliminate space between the table cells.

Line 25 defines variable side, which determines the number of cells in each row and the number of rows created by the nested for statements in lines 28–40. We set side to 100 in order to fill the table with 10,000 4px cells. Line 26 stores the tbody element so that we can append rows to it as they are generated.

Common Programming Error 13.4

Although you can omit the tbody element in an XHTML table, without it you cannot append tr elements as children of a table using JavaScript. While Firefox treats appended rows as members of the table body, Internet Explorer will not render any table cells that are dynamically added to a table outside a thead, tbody or tfoot element.

The nested for statements in lines 28–40 fill the table with a 100 × 100 grid of cells. The outer loop creates each table row, while the inner loop creates each cell. The inner loop uses the createElement method to create a table cell, assigns function processMouseMove as the event handler for the cell's onmousemove event and appends the cell as a child of the row. The **onmousemove event** of an element fires whenever the user moves the mouse over that element.

At this point, the program is initialized and simply calls processMouseMove whenever the mouse moves over any table cell. The function processMouseMove (lines 44–57) colors the cell the mouse moves over, depending on the key that is pressed when the event occurs. Lines 44–48 get the **event object**, which stores information about the event that called the event-handling function.

Internet Explorer and Firefox do not implement the same event models, so we need to account for some differences in how the event object can be handled and used. Firefox and other W3C-compliant browsers (e.g., Safari, Opera) pass the event object as an argument to the event-handling function. Internet Explorer, on the other hand, stores the event object in the event property of the window object. To get the event object regardless of the browser, we use a two-step process. Function processMouseMove takes the parameter e in line 44 to get the event object from Firefox. Then, if e is undefined (i.e., if the client is Internet Explorer), we assign the object in window.event to e in line 48.

In addition to providing different ways to access the event object, Firefox and Internet Explorer also implement different functionality in the event object itself. However, there are several event properties that both browsers implement with the same name, and some that both browsers implement with different names. In this book, we use properties that are implemented in both event models, or we write our code to use the correct property depending on the browser—all of our code runs properly in IE7 and Firefox 2.

Once e contains the event object, we can use it to get information about the event. Lines 51–56 do the actual drawing. The event object's **ctrlKey property** contains a boolean which reflects whether the *Ctrl* key was pressed during the event. If ctrlKey is true, line 52 executes, changing the color of a table cell.

To determine which table cell to color, we introduce the **this keyword**. The meaning of this depends on its context. In an event-handling function, this refers to the DOM object on which the event occurred. Our function uses this to refer to the table cell over which the mouse moved. The this keyword allows us to use one event handler to apply a change to one of many DOM elements, depending on which one received the event.

Lines 51–52 change the background color of `this` table cell to blue if the *Ctrl* key is pressed during the event. Similarly, lines 55–56 color the cell red if the *Shift* key is pressed. To determine this, we use the **`shiftKey` property** of the event object. This simple function allows the user to draw inside the table on the page in red and blue. You'll add more functionality to this example in the exercises at the end of this chapter.

This example demonstrated the `ctrlKey` and `shiftKey` properties of the `event` object. Figure 13.4 provides a table of some important cross-browser properties of the `event` object.

This section introduced the event `onmousemove` and the keyword `this`. We also discussed more advanced event handling using the `event` object to get information about the event. The next section continues our introduction of events with the `onmouseover` and `onmouseout` events.

Property	Description
`altKey`	This value is `true` if the *Alt* key was pressed when the event fired.
`cancelBubble`	Set to `true` to prevent the event from bubbling. Defaults to `false`. (See Section 14.9, Event Bubbling.)
`clientX` and `clientY`	The coordinates of the mouse cursor inside the client area (i.e., the active area where the web page is displayed, excluding scrollbars, navigation buttons, etc.).
`ctrlKey`	This value is `true` if the *Ctrl* key was pressed when the event fired.
keyCode	The ASCII code of the key pressed in a keyboard event. See Appendix D for more information on the ASCII character set.
`screenX` and `screenY`	The coordinates of the mouse cursor on the screen coordinate system.
`shiftKey`	This value is `true` if the *Shift* key was pressed when the event fired.
`type`	The name of the event that fired, without the prefix `"on"`.

Fig. 13.4 | Some `event` object properties.

13.5 Rollovers with `onmouseover` and `onmouseout`

Two more events fired by mouse movements are `onmouseover` and `onmouseout`. When the mouse cursor moves into an element, an **`onmouseover` event** occurs for that element. When the cursor leaves the element, an **`onmouseout` event** occurs. Figure 13.5 uses these events to achieve a **rollover effect** that updates text when the mouse cursor moves over it. We also introduce a technique for creating rollover images.

```
<?xml version = "1.0" encoding = "utf-8"?>
<!DOCTYPE html PUBLIC "-//W3C//DTD XHTML 1.0 Strict//EN"
   "http://www.w3.org/TR/xhtml1/DTD/xhtml1-strict.dtd">

```

Fig. 13.5 | Events `onmouseover` and `onmouseout`. (Part 1 of 5.)

```
<!-- Fig. 13.5: onmouseoverout.html -->
<!-- Events onmouseover and onmouseout. -->
<html xmlns = "http://www.w3.org/1999/xhtml">
   <head>
      <title>Events onmouseover and onmouseout</title>
      <style type = "text/css">
         body  { background-color: wheat }
         table { border-style: groove;
                 text-align: center;
                 font-family: monospace;
                 font-weight: bold }
         td    { width: 6em }
      </style>
      <script type = "text/javascript">
         <!--
         image1 = new Image();
         image1.src = "heading1.gif";
         image2 = new Image();
         image2.src = "heading2.gif";

         function mouseOver( e )
         {
            if ( !e )
               var e = window.event;

            var target = getTarget( e );

            // swap the image when the mouse moves over it
            if ( target.id == "heading" )
            {
               target.src = image2.src;
               return;
            } // end if

            // if an element's id is defined, assign the id to its color
            // to turn hex code's text the corresponding color
            if ( target.id )
                target.style.color = target.id;
         } // end function mouseOver

         function mouseOut( e )
         {
            if ( !e )
               var e = window.event;

            var target = getTarget( e );

            // put the original image back when the mouse moves away
            if ( target.id == "heading" )
            {
               target.src = image1.src;
               return;
            } // end if
```

Fig. 13.5 | Events onmouseover and onmouseout. (Part 2 of 5.)

```

            // if an element's id is defined, assign id to innerHTML
            // to display the color name
            if ( target.id )
               target.innerHTML = target.id;
         } // end function mouseOut

         // return either e.srcElement or e.target, whichever exists
         function getTarget( e )
         {
            if ( e.srcElement )
               return e.srcElement;
            else
               return e.target;
         } // end function getTarget

         document.onmouseover = mouseOver;
         document.onmouseout = mouseOut;
         // -->
      </script>
   </head>
   <body>
      <img src = "heading1.gif" id = "heading" alt = "Heading Image" />
      <p>Can you tell a color from its hexadecimal RGB code
      value? Look at the hex code, guess its color. To see
      what color it corresponds to, move the mouse over the
      hex code. Moving the mouse out of the hex code's table
      cell will display the color name.</p>
      <table>
         <tr>
            <td id = "Black">#000000</td>
            <td id = "Blue">#0000FF</td>
            <td id = "Magenta">#FF00FF</td>
            <td id = "Gray">#808080</td>
         </tr>
         <tr>
            <td id = "Green">#008000</td>
            <td id = "Lime">#00FF00</td>
            <td id = "Maroon">#800000</td>
            <td id = "Navy">#000080</td>
         </tr>
         <tr>
            <td id = "Olive">#808000</td>
            <td id = "Purple">#800080</td>
            <td id = "Red">#FF0000</td>
            <td id = "Silver">#C0C0C0</td>
         </tr>
         <tr>
            <td id = "Cyan">#00FFFF</td>
            <td id = "Teal">#008080</td>
            <td id = "Yellow">#FFFF00</td>
            <td id = "White">#FFFFFF</td>
         </tr>
```

Fig. 13.5 | Events onmouseover and onmouseout. (Part 3 of 5.)

```
         </table>
      </body>
   </html>
```

a) The page loads with the blue heading image and all the hex codes in black.

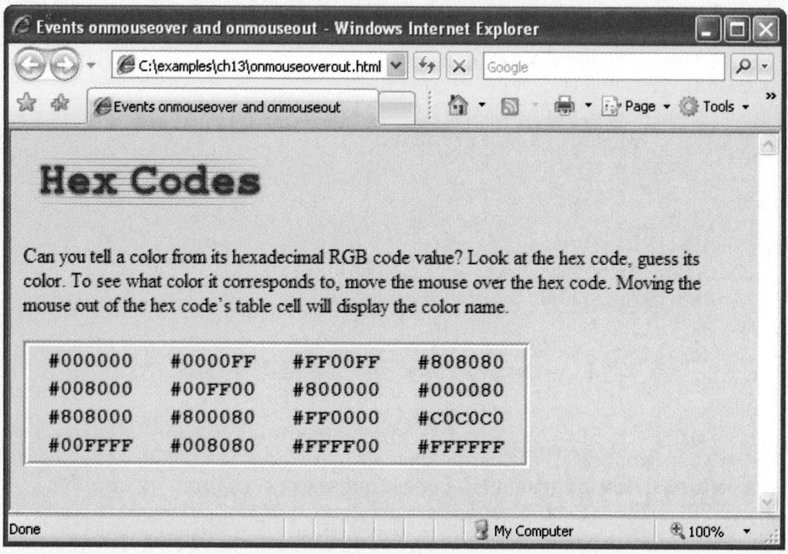

b) The heading image switches to an image with green text when the mouse rolls over it.

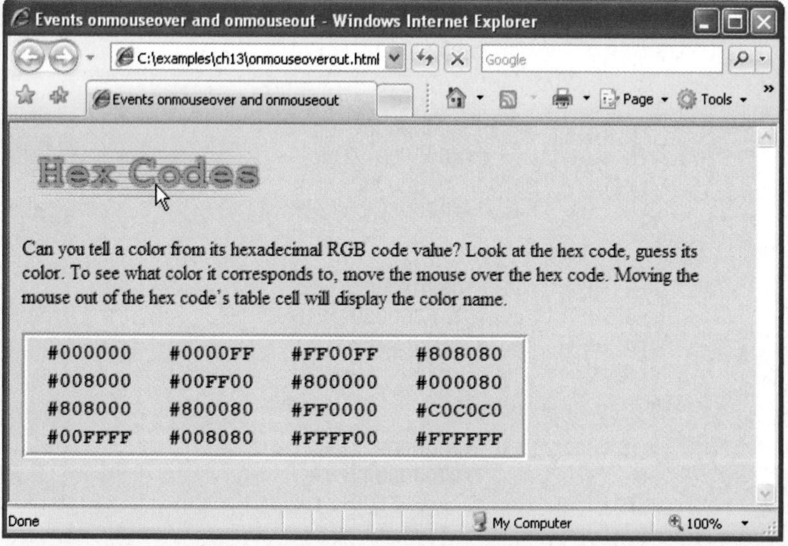

Fig. 13.5 | Events `onmouseover` and `onmouseout`. (Part 4 of 5.)

c) When mouse rolls over a hex code, the text color changes to the color represented by the hex code. Notice that the heading image has become blue again because the mouse is no longer over it.

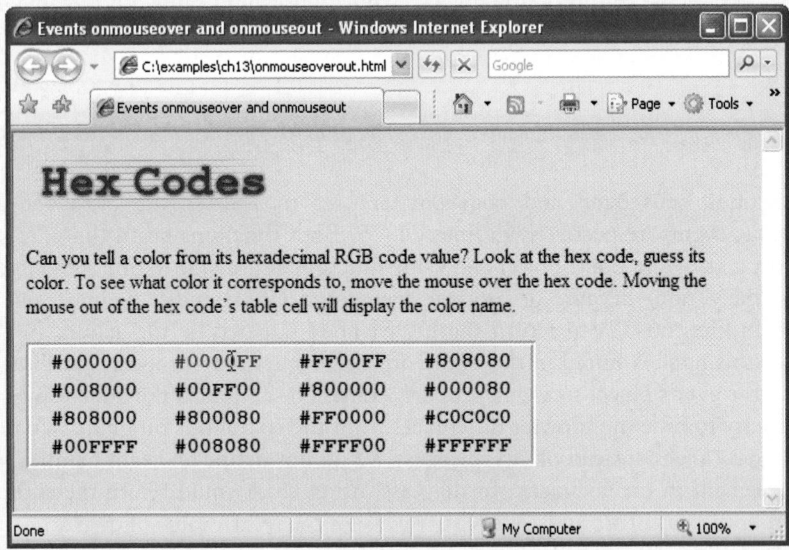

d) When the mouse leaves the hex code's table cell, the text changes to the name of the color.

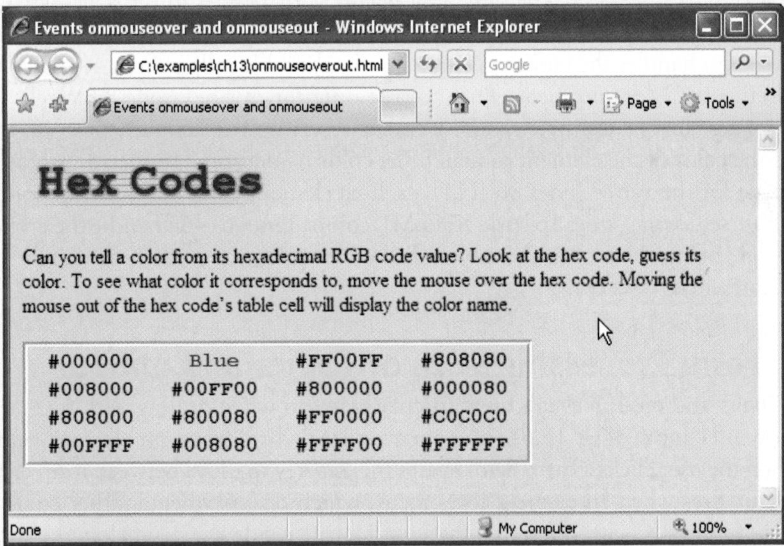

Fig. 13.5 | Events `onmouseover` and `onmouseout`. (Part 5 of 5.)

To create a rollover effect for the image in the heading, lines 20–23 create two new JavaScript `Image` objects—`image1` and `image2`. Image `image2` displays when the mouse hovers over the image. Image `image1` displays when the mouse is outside the image. The script sets the `src` properties of each `Image` in lines 21 and 23, respectively. Creating `Image` objects preloads the images (i.e., loads the images in advance), so the browser does not need to download the rollover image the first time the script displays the image. If the image is large or the connection is slow, downloading would cause a noticeable delay in the image update.

Performance Tip 13.1

Preloading images used in rollover effects prevents a delay the first time an image is displayed.

Functions `mouseOver` and `mouseOut` are set to process the `onmouseover` and `onmouseout` events, respectively, in lines 74–75. Both functions begin (lines 25–28 and 45–48) by getting the `event` object and using function `getTarget` to find the element that received the action. Because of browser event model differences, we need `getTarget` (defined in lines 66–72) to return the DOM node targeted by the action. In Internet Explorer, this node is stored in the `event` object's **`srcElement` property**. In Firefox, it is stored in the `event` object's **`target` property**. Lines 68–71 return the node using the correct property to hide the browser differences from the rest of our program. We must use function `getTarget` instead of `this` because we do not define an event handler for each specific element in the `document`. In this case, using `this` would return the entire document. In both `mouseOver` and `mouseOut`, we assign the return value of `getTarget` to variable `target` (lines 30 and 50).

Lines 33–37 in the `mouseOver` function handle the `onmouseover` event for the heading image by setting its `src` attribute (`target.src`) to the `src` property of the appropriate `Image` object (`image2.src`). The same task occurs with `image1` in the `mouseOut` function (lines 53–57).

The script handles the `onmouseover` event for the table cells in lines 41–42. This code tests whether an `id` is specified, which is true only for our hex code table cells and the heading image in this example. If the element receiving the action has an `id`, the code changes the color of the element to match the color name stored in the `id`. As you can see in the code for the `table` (lines 86–111), each `td` element containing a color code has an `id` attribute set to one of the 16 basic XHTML colors. Lines 61–62 handle the `onmouseout` event by changing the text in the table cell the mouse cursor just left to match the color that it represents.

13.6 Form Processing with `onfocus` and `onblur`

The `onfocus` and `onblur` events are particularly useful when dealing with form elements that allow user input (Fig. 13.6). The `onfocus` event fires when an element gains focus (i.e., when the user clicks a form field or uses the *Tab* key to move between form elements), and `onblur` fires when an element loses focus, which occurs when another control gains the focus. In lines 31–32, the script changes the text inside the `div` below the form (line 58) based on the `messageNum` passed to function `helpText` (lines 29–33). Each of the elements of the form, such as the `name` input in lines 40–41, passes a different value to the `helpText` function when it gains focus (and its `onfocus` event fires). These values are used as indices for `helpArray`, which is declared and initialized in lines 17–27 and stores help messages. When elements lose focus, they all pass the value `6` to `helpText` to clear the `tip` `div` (note that the empty string `""` is stored in the last element of the array).

```
<?xml version = "1.0" encoding = "utf-8"?>
<!DOCTYPE html PUBLIC "-//W3C//DTD XHTML 1.0 Strict//EN"
   "http://www.w3.org/TR/xhtml1/DTD/xhtml1-strict.dtd">

<!-- Fig. 13.6: onfocusblur.html -->
<!-- Demonstrating the onfocus and onblur events. -->
<html xmlns = "http://www.w3.org/1999/xhtml">
   <head>
      <title>A Form Using onfocus and onblur</title>
      <style type = "text/css">
         .tip { font-family: sans-serif;
                color: blue;
                font-size: 12px }
      </style>
      <script type = "text/javascript">
         <!--
         var helpArray =
            [ "Enter your name in this input box.", // element 0
              "Enter your e-mail address in this input box, " +
              "in the format user@domain.", // element 1
              "Check this box if you liked our site.", // element 2
              "In this box, enter any comments you would " +
              "like us to read.", // element 3
              "This button submits the form to the " +
              "server-side script.", // element 4
              "This button clears the form.", // element 5
              "" ]; // element 6

         function helpText( messageNum )
         {
            document.getElementById( "tip" ).innerHTML =
               helpArray[ messageNum ];
         } // end function helpText
         // -->
      </script>
   </head>
   <body>
      <form id = "myForm" action = "">
         <div>
         Name: <input type = "text" name = "name"
            onfocus = "helpText(0)" onblur = "helpText(6)" /><br />
         E-mail: <input type = "text" name = "e-mail"
            onfocus = "helpText(1)" onblur = "helpText(6)" /><br />
         Click here if you like this site
         <input type = "checkbox" name = "like" onfocus =
            "helpText(2)" onblur = "helpText(6)" /><br /><hr />

         Any comments?<br />
         <textarea name = "comments" rows = "5" cols = "45"
            onfocus = "helpText(3)" onblur = "helpText(6)"></textarea>
         <br />
         <input type = "submit" value = "Submit" onfocus =
            "helpText(4)" onblur = "helpText(6)" />
```

Fig. 13.6 | Demonstrating the onfocus and onblur events. (Part 1 of 2.)

```
            <input type = "reset" value = "Reset" onfocus =
               "helpText(5)" onblur = "helpText(6)" />
            </div>
         </form>
         <div id = "tip" class = "tip"></div>
      </body>
   </html>
```

a) The blue message at the bottom of the page instructs the user to enter an e-mail when the e-mail field has focus.

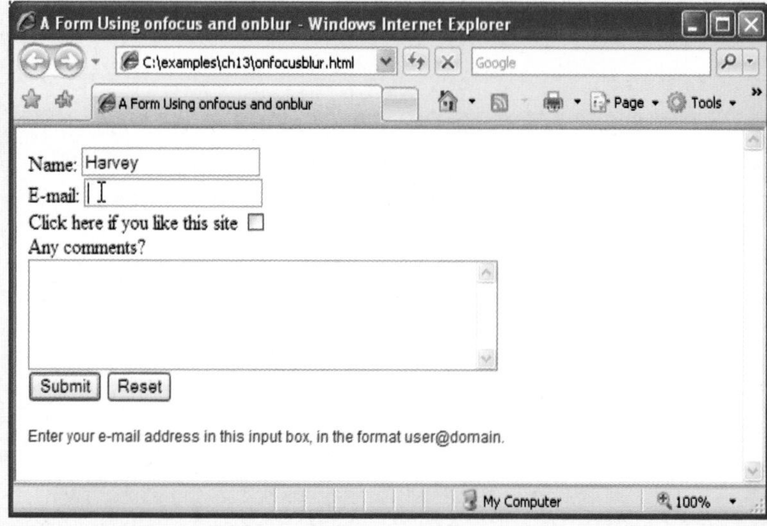

b) The message changes depending on which field has focus. Now it gives instructions for the comments box.

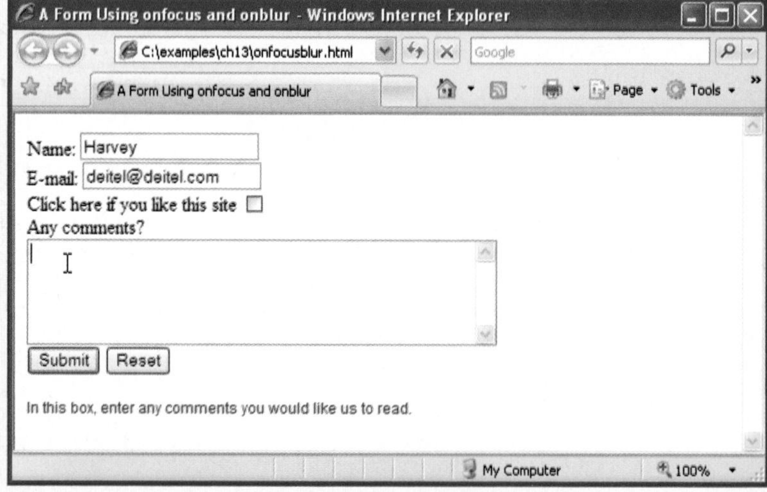

Fig. 13.6 | Demonstrating the `onfocus` and `onblur` events. (Part 2 of 2.)

13.7 More Form Processing with onsubmit and onreset

Two more useful events for processing forms are `onsubmit` and `onreset`. These events fire when a form is submitted or reset, respectively (Fig. 13.7). Function `registerEvents` (lines 35–46) registers the event handlers for the form after the body has loaded.

```
1  <?xml version = "1.0" encoding = "utf-8"?>
2  <!DOCTYPE html PUBLIC "-//W3C//DTD XHTML 1.0 Strict//EN"
3     "http://www.w3.org/TR/xhtml1/DTD/xhtml1-strict.dtd">
4
5  <!-- Fig. 13.7: onsubmitreset.html -->
6  <!-- Demonstrating the onsubmit and onreset events. -->
7  <html xmlns = "http://www.w3.org/1999/xhtml">
8     <head>
9        <title>A Form Using onsubmit and onreset</title>
10       <style type = "text/css">
11          .tip { font-family: sans-serif;
12                 color: blue;
13                 font-size: 12px }
14       </style>
15       <script type = "text/javascript">
16          <!--
17          var helpArray =
18             [ "Enter your name in this input box.",
19               "Enter your e-mail address in this input box, " +
20               "in the format user@domain.",
21               "Check this box if you liked our site.",
22               "In this box, enter any comments you would " +
23               "like us to read.",
24               "This button submits the form to the " +
25               "server-side script.",
26               "This button clears the form.",
27               "" ];
28
29          function helpText( messageNum )
30          {
31             document.getElementById( "tip" ).innerHTML =
32                helpArray[ messageNum ];
33          } // end function helpText
34
35          function registerEvents()
36          {
37             document.getElementById( "myForm" ).onsubmit = function()
38             {
39                return confirm( "Are you sure you want to submit?" );
40             } // end anonymous function
41
42             document.getElementById( "myForm" ).onreset = function()
43             {
44                return confirm( "Are you sure you want to reset?" );
45             } // end anonymous function
46          } // end function registerEvents
```

Fig. 13.7 | Demonstrating the `onsubmit` and `onreset` events. (Part 1 of 2.)

```
      // -->
      </script>
   </head>
   <body onload = "registerEvents()">
      <form id = "myForm" action = "">
         <div>
         Name: <input type = "text" name = "name"
            onfocus = "helpText(0)" onblur = "helpText(6)" /><br />
         E-mail: <input type = "text" name = "e-mail"
            onfocus = "helpText(1)" onblur = "helpText(6)" /><br />
         Click here if you like this site
         <input type = "checkbox" name = "like" onfocus =
            "helpText(2)" onblur = "helpText(6)" /><br /><hr />

         Any comments?<br />
         <textarea name = "comments" rows = "5" cols = "45"
            onfocus = "helpText(3)" onblur = "helpText(6)"></textarea>
         <br />
         <input type = "submit" value = "Submit" onfocus =
            "helpText(4)" onblur = "helpText(6)" />
         <input type = "reset" value = "Reset" onfocus =
            "helpText(5)" onblur = "helpText(6)" />
         </div>
      </form>
      <div id = "tip" class = "tip"></div>
   </body>
</html>
```

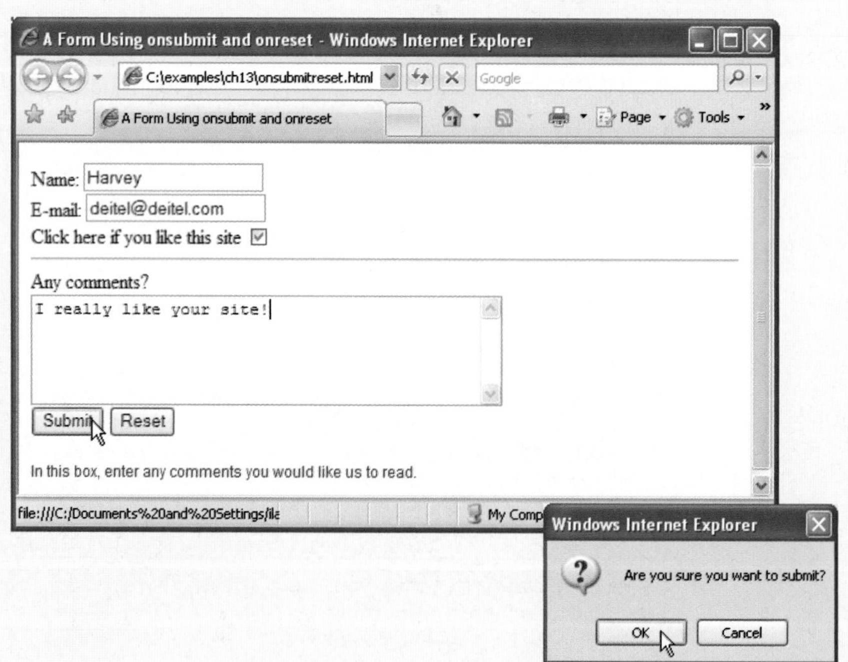

Fig. 13.7 | Demonstrating the `onsubmit` and `onreset` events. (Part 2 of 2.)

Lines 37–40 and 42–45 introduce several new concepts. Line 37 gets the `form` element ("`myForm`", lines 51–70), then lines 37–40 assign an anonymous function to its `onsubmit` property. An anonymous function is defined with no name—it is created in nearly the same way as any other function, but with no identifier after the keyword `function`. This notation is useful when creating a function for the sole purpose of assigning it to an event handler. We never call the function ourselves, so we don't need to give it a name, and it's more concise to create the function and register it as an event handler at the same time.

The anonymous function (lines 37–40) assigned to the `onsubmit` property of `myForm` executes in response to the user submitting the form (i.e., clicking the **Submit** button or pressing the *Enter* key). Line 39 introduces the `confirm` method of the window object. As with `alert`, we do not need to prefix the call with the object name `window` and the dot (`.`) operator. The confirm dialog asks the users a question, presenting them with an **OK** button and a **Cancel** button. If the user clicks **OK**, `confirm` returns `true`; otherwise, `confirm` returns `false`.

Our event handlers for the form's `onsubmit` and `onreset` events simply return the value of the `confirm` dialog, which asks the users if they are sure they want to submit or reset (lines 39 and 44, respectively). By returning either `true` or `false`, the event handlers dictate whether the default action for the event—in this case submitting or resetting the form—is taken. (Recall that we also returned `false` from some event-handling functions to prevent forms from submitting in Chapter 12.) Other default actions, such as following a hyperlink, can be prevented by returning `false` from an `onclick` event handler on the link. If an event handler returns `true` or does not return a value, the default action is taken once the event handler finishes executing.

13.8 Event Bubbling

Event bubbling is the process by which events fired in child elements "bubble" up to their parent elements. When an event is fired on an element, it is first delivered to the element's event handler (if any), then to the parent element's event handler (if any). This might result in event handling that was not intended. If you intend to handle an event in a child element alone, you should cancel the bubbling of the event in the child element's event-handling code by using the `cancelBubble` property of the `event` object, as shown in Fig. 13.8.

```
<?xml version = "1.0" encoding = "utf-8"?>
<!DOCTYPE html PUBLIC "-//W3C//DTD XHTML 1.0 Strict//EN"
   "http://www.w3.org/TR/xhtml1/DTD/xhtml1-strict.dtd">

<!-- Fig. 13.8: bubbling.html -->
<!-- Canceling event bubbling. -->
<html xmlns = "http://www.w3.org/1999/xhtml">
   <head>
      <title>Event Bubbling</title>
      <script type = "text/javascript">
         <!--
```

Fig. 13.8 | Canceling event bubbling. (Part 1 of 3.)

```
         function documentClick()
         {
            alert( "You clicked in the document." );
         } // end function documentClick

         function bubble( e )
         {
            if ( !e )
               var e = window.event;

            alert( "This will bubble." );
            e.cancelBubble = false;
         } // end function bubble

         function noBubble( e )
         {
            if ( !e )
               var e = window.event;

            alert( "This will not bubble." );
            e.cancelBubble = true;
         } // end function noBubble

         function registerEvents()
         {
            document.onclick = documentClick;
            document.getElementById( "bubble" ).onclick = bubble;
            document.getElementById( "noBubble" ).onclick = noBubble;
         } // end function registerEvents
         // -->
      </script>
   </head>
   <body onload = "registerEvents()">
      <p id = "bubble">Bubbling enabled.</p>
      <p id = "noBubble">Bubbling disabled.</p>
   </body>
</html>
```

a) The user clicks the first paragraph, for which bubbling is enabled.

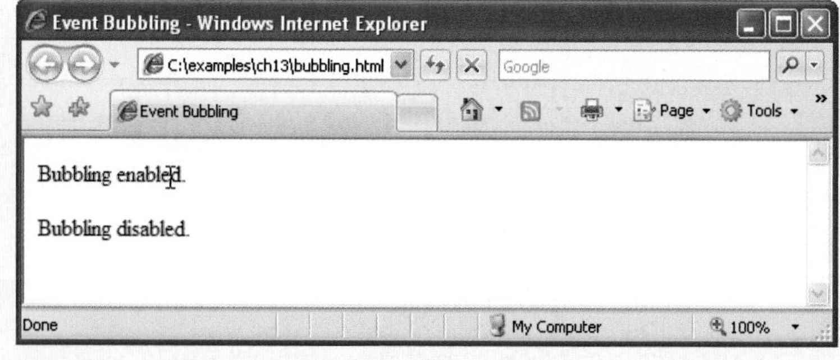

Fig. 13.8 | Canceling event bubbling. (Part 2 of 3.)

b) The paragraph's event handler causes an alert.

c) The document's event handler causes another alert, because the event bubbles up to the document.

d) The user clicks the second paragraph, for which bubbling is disabled.

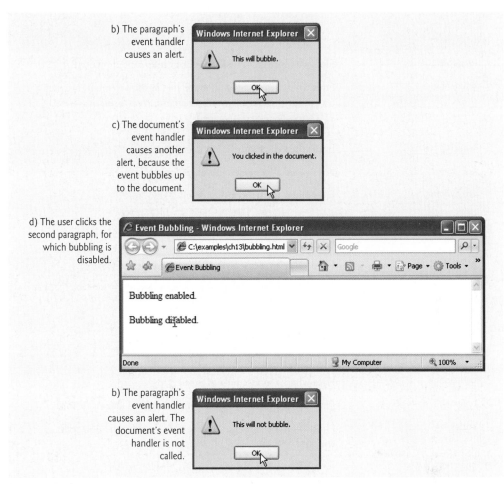

b) The paragraph's event handler causes an alert. The document's event handler is not called.

Fig. 13.8 | Canceling event bubbling. (Part 3 of 3.)

Clicking the first `p` element (line 45) triggers a call to `bubble`. Then, because line 37 registers the `document`'s `onclick` event, `documentClick` is also called. This occurs because the `onclick` event bubbles up to the `document`. This is probably not the desired result. Clicking the second `p` element (line 46) calls `noBubble`, which disables the event bubbling for this event by setting the `cancelBubble` property of the `event` object to `true`. [*Note:* The default value of `cancelBubble` is `false`, so the statement in line 23 is unnecessary.]

Common Programming Error 13.5

Forgetting to cancel event bubbling when necessary may cause unexpected results in your scripts.

13.9 More Events

The events we covered in this chapter are among the most commonly used. A list of some events supported by both Firefox and Internet Explorer is given with descriptions in Fig. 13.9.

Event	Description
`onabort`	Fires when image transfer has been interrupted by user.
`onchange`	Fires when a new choice is made in a `select` element, or when a text input is changed and the element loses focus.
`onclick`	Fires when the user clicks using the mouse.
`ondblclick`	Fires when the mouse is double clicked.
`onfocus`	Fires when a form element gains focus.
`onkeydown`	Fires when the user pushes down a key.
`onkeypress`	Fires when the user presses then releases a key.
`onkeyup`	Fires when the user releases a key.
`onload`	Fires when an element and all its children have loaded.
`onmousedown`	Fires when a mouse button is pressed down.
`onmousemove`	Fires when the mouse moves.
`onmouseout`	Fires when the mouse leaves an element.
`onmouseover`	Fires when the mouse enters an element.
`onmouseup`	Fires when a mouse button is released.
`onreset`	Fires when a form resets (i.e., the user clicks a reset button).
`onresize`	Fires when the size of an object changes (i.e., the user resizes a window or frame).
`onselect`	Fires when a text selection begins (applies to `input` or `textarea`).
`onsubmit`	Fires when a form is submitted.
`onunload`	Fires when a page is about to unload.

Fig. 13.9 | Cross-browser events.

13.10 Wrap-Up

This chapter introduced JavaScript events, which allow scripts to respond to user interactions and make web pages more dynamic. We described event handlers and how to register them to specific events on DOM nodes in the script. We introduced the event object and the keyword `this`, which allows us to use one event handler to apply a change to the recipient of an event. We discussed various events that fire from mouse actions, as well as the `onfocus`, `onblur`, `onsubmit` and `onreset` events. Finally, we learned about event bubbling, which can produce unexpected effects in scripts that use events. The next chapter introduces XML, an open technology used for data exchange.

13.11 Web Resources

`http://www.quirksmode.org/js/introevents.html`

An introduction and reference site for JavaScript events. Includes comprehensive information on history of events, the different event models, and making events work across multiple browsers.

`wsabstract.com/dhtmltutors/domevent1.shtml`

This *JavaScript Kit* tutorial introduces event handling and discusses the W3C DOM advanced event model.

`http://www.w3schools.com/jsref/jsref_events.asp`

The W3 School's JavaScript Event Reference site has a comprehensive list of JavaScript events, a description of their usage and their browser compatibilities.

`http://www.brainjar.com/dhtml/events/`

BrainJar.com's DOM Event Model site provides a comprehensive introduction to the DOM event model, and has example code to demonstrate several different ways of assigning and using events.

Summary

Section 13.1 Introduction

- JavaScript events allow scripts to respond to user interactions and modify the page accordingly.
- Events and event handling help make web applications more responsive, dynamic and interactive.

Section 13.2 Registering Event Handlers

- Functions that handle events are called event handlers. Assigning an event handler to an event on a DOM node is called registering an event handler.
- We discuss two models for registering event handlers. The inline model treats events as attributes of XHTML elements.
- To register events using the traditional model, we assign the name of the function to the event property of a DOM node.
- In the inline model, the value of the XHTML attribute is a *JavaScript statement* to be executed when the event occurs.
- In the traditional model, the value of the event property of a DOM node is the name of a *function* to be called when the event occurs.
- Traditional registration of event handlers allows us to quickly and easily assign event handlers to many elements using repetition statements, instead of adding an inline event handler to each XHTML element.

Section 13.3 Event `onload`

- The `onload` event fires whenever an element finishes loading successfully.
- If a script in the `head` attempts to get a DOM node for an XHTML element in the `body`, `getElementById` returns `null` because the `body` has not yet loaded.

Section 13.4 Event `onmousemove`, the `event` Object and `this`

- The `onmousemove` event fires whenever the user moves the mouse.
- The `event` object stores information about the event that called the event-handling function.
- The `event` object's `ctrlKey` property contains a boolean which reflects whether the *Ctrl* key was pressed during the event.

- The event object's shiftKey property reflects whether the *Shift* key was pressed during the event.
- In an event-handling function, this refers to the DOM object on which the event occurred.
- The this keyword allows us to use one event handler to apply a change to one of many DOM elements, depending on which one received the event.

Section 13.5 Rollovers with **onmouseover** *and* **onmouseout**

- When the mouse cursor enters an element, an onmouseover event occurs for that element. When the mouse cursor leaves the element, an onmouseout event occurs for that element.
- Creating an Image object and setting its src property preloads the image.
- The event object stores the node on which the action occurred. In Internet Explorer, this node is stored in the event object's srcElement property. In Firefox, it is stored in the event object's target property.

Section 13.6 Form Processing with **onfocus** *and* **onblur**

- The onfocus event fires when an element gains focus (i.e., when the user clicks a form field or uses the *Tab* key to move between form elements).
- onblur fires when an element loses focus, which occurs when another control gains the focus.

Section 13.7 More Form Processing with **onsubmit** *and* **onreset**

- The onsubmit and onreset events fire when a form is submitted or reset, respectively.
- An anonymous function is a function that is defined with no name—it is created in nearly the same way as any other function, but with no identifier after the keyword function.
- Anonymous functions are useful when creating a function for the sole purpose of assigning it to an event handler.
- The confirm method asks the users a question, presenting them with an OK button and a Cancel button. If the user clicks OK, confirm returns true; otherwise, confirm returns false.
- By returning either true or false, event handlers dictate whether the default action for the event is taken.
- If an event handler returns true or does not return a value, the default action is taken once the event handler finishes executing.

Section 13.8 Event Bubbling

- Event bubbling is the process whereby events fired in child elements "bubble" up to their parent elements. When an event is fired on an element, it is first delivered to the element's event handler (if any), then to the parent element's event handler (if any).
- If you intend to handle an event in a child element alone, you should cancel the bubbling of the event in the child element's event-handling code by using the cancelBubble property of the event object.

Terminology

altKey property of event object
anonymous function
cancelBubble property of event object
clientX property of event object
clientY property of event object
confirm method of window object
ctrlKey property of event object
default action for an event
event bubbling
event handler
event models
event object
event registration models
events in JavaScript

fire an event
inline model of event registration
keyboard event
`keyCode` property of an `event` object
mouse event
`onabort` event
`onblur` event
`onchange` event
`onclick` event
`ondblclick` event
`onfocus` event
`onkeydown` event
`onkeypress` event
`onkeyup` event
`onload` event
`onmousedown` event
`onmousemove` event
`onmouseout` event
`onmouseover` event
`onmouseup` event
`onreset` event
`onresize` event
`onselect` event
`onsubmit` event
`onunload` event
registering an event handler
return value of an event handler
rollover effect
`screenX` property of `event` object
`screenY` property of `event` object
`setInterval` method of `window` object
`shiftkey` property of `event` object
`srcElement` property of `event` object
Tab key to switch between fields on a form
`target` property of `event` object
`this` keyword
traditional model of event registration
trigger an event
`type` property of `event` object

Self-Review Exercises

13.1 Fill in the blanks in each of the following statements:

a) Event handlers can be registered in XHTML using the ______ model or in JavaScript using the ______ model.
b) The state of three keys can be retrieved by using the `event` object. These keys are ______, ______ and ______.
c) If a child element does not handle an event, ______ lets the event rise through the object hierarchy.
d) The ______ of an event-handling function specifies whether to perform the default action for the event.
e) In an event handler, the reference for the `id` of an element that fired an event is ______ in Firefox and ______ in Internet Explorer.
f) Three events that fire when the user clicks the mouse are ______, ______ and ______.

13.2 State whether each of the following is *true* or *false*. If the statement is *false*, explain why.

a) The `onload` event fires whenever an element starts loading.
b) The `onclick` event fires when the user clicks the mouse on an element.
c) The `onfocus` event fires when an element loses focus.
d) When using the rollover effect with images, it is a good practice to create `Image` objects that preload the desired images.
e) Returning `true` in an event handler on an a (anchor) element prevents the browser from following the link when the event handler finishes.

Answers to Self-Review Exercises

13.1 a) inline, traditional. b) *Ctrl*, *Alt* and *Shift*. c) event bubbling. d) return value. e) `event.target.id`, `event.srcElement.id`. f) `onclick`, `onmousedown`, `onmouseup`.

13.2 a) False. The `onload` event fires when an element *finishes* loading. b) True. c) False. It fires when an element gains focus. d) True. e) False. Returning `false` prevents the default action.

Exercises

13.3 Add an erase feature to the drawing program in Fig. 13.3. Try setting the background color of the table cell over which the mouse moved to `white` when the *Alt* key is pressed.

13.4 Add a button to your program from Exercise 13.3 to erase the entire drawing window.

13.5 You have a server-side script that cannot handle any ampersands (`&`) in the form data. Write a function that converts all ampersands in a form field to `" and "` when the field loses focus (`onblur`).

13.6 Write a function that responds to a click anywhere on the page by displaying an `alert` dialog. Display the event name if the user held *Shift* during the mouse click. Display the element name that triggered the event if the user held *Ctrl* during the mouse click.

13.7 Use CSS absolute positioning, `onmousedown`, `onmousemove`, `onmouseup` and the `clientX`/`clientY` properties of the `event` object to create a program that allows you to drag and drop an image. When the user clicks the image, it should follow the cursor until the mouse button is released.

13.8 Modify Exercise 13.7 to allow multiple images to be dragged and dropped in the same page.

14

XML and RSS

Knowing trees, I understand the meaning of patience. Knowing grass, I can appreciate persistence.
—Hal Borland

Like everything metaphysical, the harmony between thought and reality is to be found in the grammar of the language.
—Ludwig Wittgenstein

I played with an idea, and grew willful; tossed it into the air; transformed it; let it escape and recaptured it; made it iridescent with fancy, and winged it with paradox.
—Oscar Wilde

OBJECTIVES

In this chapter you will learn:

- To mark up data using XML.
- How XML namespaces help provide unique XML element and attribute names.
- To create DTDs and schemas for specifying and validating the structure of an XML document.
- To create and use simple XSL style sheets to render XML document data.
- To retrieve and manipulate XML data programmatically using JavaScript.
- RSS and how to programmatically apply an XSL transformation to an RSS document using JavaScript.

Outline

14.1 Introduction

The Extensible Markup Language (XML) was developed in 1996 by the World Wide Web Consortium's (W3C's) XML Working Group. XML is a widely supported open technology (i.e., nonproprietary technology) for describing data that has become the standard format for data exchanged between applications over the Internet.

Web applications use XML extensively and web browsers provide many XML-related capabilities. Sections 14.2–14.7 introduce XML and XML-related technologies—XML namespaces for providing unique XML element and attribute names, and Document Type Definitions (DTDs) and XML Schemas for validating XML documents. These sections support the use of XML in many subsequent chapters. Sections 14.8–14.9 present additional XML technologies and key JavaScript capabilities for loading and manipulating XML documents programmatically—this material is optional but is recommended if you plan to use XML in your own applications. Finally, Section 14.10 introduces RSS—an XML format used to syndicate simple website content—and shows how to format RSS elements using JavaScript and other technologies presented in this chapter.

14.2 XML Basics

XML permits document authors to create markup (i.e., a text-based notation for describing data) for virtually any type of information. This enables document authors to create entirely new markup languages for describing any type of data, such as mathematical formulas, software-configuration instructions, chemical molecular structures, music, news, recipes and financial reports. XML describes data in a way that both human beings and computers can understand.

Figure 14.1 is a simple XML document that describes information for a baseball player. We focus on lines 5–9 to introduce basic XML syntax. You will learn about the other elements of this document in Section 14.3.

```
1 <?xml version = "1.0"?>
2
3 <!-- Fig. 14.1: player.xml -->
4 <!-- Baseball player structured with XML -->
5 <player>
6    <firstName>John</firstName>
7    <lastName>Doe</lastName>
8    <battingAverage>0.375</battingAverage>
9 </player>
```

Fig. 14.1 | XML that describes a baseball player's information.

XML documents contain text that represents content (i.e., data), such as John (line 6 of Fig. 14.1), and elements that specify the document's structure, such as firstName (line 6 of Fig. 14.1). XML documents delimit elements with start tags and end tags. A start tag consists of the element name in angle brackets (e.g., <player> and <firstName> in lines 5 and 6, respectively). An end tag consists of the element name preceded by a forward slash (/) in angle brackets (e.g., </firstName> and </player> in lines 6 and 9, respectively). An element's start and end tags enclose text that represents a piece of data (e.g., the player's firstName—John—in line 6, which is enclosed by the <firstName> start tag and </firstName> end tag). Every XML document must have exactly one root element that contains all the other elements. In Fig. 14.1, the root element is player (lines 5–9).

XML-based markup languages—called XML vocabularies—provide a means for describing particular types of data in standardized, structured ways. Some XML vocabularies include XHTML (Extensible HyperText Markup Language), MathML (for mathematics), VoiceXML™ (for speech), CML (Chemical Markup Language—for chemistry), XBRL (Extensible Business Reporting Language—for financial data exchange) and others that we discuss in Section 14.7.

Massive amounts of data are currently stored on the Internet in many formats (e.g., databases, web pages, text files). Much of this data, especially that which is passed between systems, will soon take the form of XML. Organizations see XML as the future of data encoding. Information technology groups are planning ways to integrate XML into their systems. Industry groups are developing custom XML vocabularies for most major industries that will allow business applications to communicate in common languages. For example, many web services allow web-based applications to exchange data seamlessly through standard protocols based on XML. We discuss web services in Chapter 28.

The next generation of the web is being built on an XML foundation, enabling you to develop more sophisticated web-based applications. XML allows you to assign meaning to what would otherwise be random pieces of data. As a result, programs can "understand" the data they manipulate. For example, a web browser might view a street address in a simple web page as a string of characters without any real meaning. In an XML document, however, this data can be clearly identified (i.e., marked up) as an address. A program that uses the document can recognize this data as an address and provide links to a map of that location, driving directions from that location or other location-specific information. Likewise, an application can recognize names of people, dates, ISBN numbers and any other type of XML-encoded data. The application can then present users with other related information, providing a richer, more meaningful user experience.

Viewing and Modifying XML Documents

XML documents are highly portable. Viewing or modifying an XML document—which is a text file that usually ends with the `.xml` filename extension—does not require special software, although many software tools exist, and new ones are frequently released that make it more convenient to develop XML-based applications. Any text editor that supports ASCII/Unicode characters can open XML documents for viewing and editing. Also, most web browsers can display XML documents in a formatted manner that shows the XML's structure. Section 14.3 demonstrates this in Internet Explorer and Firefox. An important characteristic of XML is that it is both human and machine readable.

Processing XML Documents

Processing an XML document requires software called an XML parser (or XML processor). A parser makes the document's data available to applications. While reading an XML document's contents, a parser checks that the document follows the syntax rules specified by the W3C's XML Recommendation (`www.w3.org/XML`). XML syntax requires a single root element, a start tag and end tag for each element, and properly nested tags (i.e., the end tag for a nested element must appear before the end tag of the enclosing element). Furthermore, XML is case sensitive, so the proper capitalization must be used in elements. A document that conforms to this syntax is a well-formed XML document and is syntactically correct. We present fundamental XML syntax in Section 14.3. If an XML parser can process an XML document successfully, that XML document is well-formed. Parsers can provide access to XML-encoded data in well-formed documents only.

Often, XML parsers are built into software or available for download over the Internet. Some popular parsers include Microsoft XML Core Services (MSXML)—which is included with Internet Explorer, the Apache Software Foundation's Xerces (`xml.apache.org`) and the open-source Expat XML Parser (`expat.sourceforge.net`).

Validating XML Documents

An XML document can reference a Document Type Definition (DTD) or a schema that defines the proper structure of the XML document. When an XML document references a DTD or a schema, some parsers (called validating parsers) can read the DTD/schema and check that the XML document follows the structure defined by the DTD/schema. If the XML document conforms to the DTD/schema (i.e., the document has the appropriate structure), the XML document is valid. For example, if in Fig. 14.1 we were referencing a DTD that specified that a `player` element must have `firstName`, `lastName` and `battingAverage` elements, then omitting the `lastName` element (line 7 in Fig. 14.1) would invalidate the XML document `player.xml`. However, the XML document would still be well-formed, because it follows proper XML syntax (i.e., it has one root element, each element has a start tag and an end tag, and the elements are nested properly). By definition, a valid XML document is well-formed. Parsers that cannot check for document conformity against DTDs/schemas are nonvalidating parsers—they determine only whether an XML document is well-formed, not whether it is valid.

We discuss validation, DTDs and schemas, as well as the key differences between these two types of structural specifications, in Sections 14.5–14.6. For now, note that schemas are XML documents themselves, whereas DTDs are not. As you will learn in Section 14.6, this difference presents several advantages in using schemas over DTDs.

Software Engineering Observation 14.1

DTDs and schemas are essential for business-to-business (B2B) transactions and mission-critical systems. Validating XML documents ensures that disparate systems can manipulate data structured in standardized ways and prevents errors caused by missing or malformed data.

Formatting and Manipulating XML Documents

Most XML documents contain only data, not formatting instructions, so applications that process XML documents must decide how to manipulate or display the data. For example, a PDA (personal digital assistant) may render an XML document differently than a wireless phone or a desktop computer. You can use **Extensible Stylesheet Language (XSL)** to specify rendering instructions for different platforms. We discuss XSL in Section 14.8.

XML-processing programs can also search, sort and manipulate XML data using XSL. Some other XML-related technologies are XPath (XML Path Language—a language for accessing parts of an XML document), XSL-FO (XSL Formatting Objects—an XML vocabulary used to describe document formatting) and XSLT (XSL Transformations—a language for transforming XML documents into other documents). We present XSLT and XPath in Section 14.8.

14.3 Structuring Data

In this section and throughout this chapter, we create our own XML markup. XML allows you to describe data precisely in a well-structured format.

XML Markup for an Article

In Fig. 14.2, we present an XML document that marks up a simple article using XML. The line numbers shown are for reference only and are not part of the XML document.

This document begins with an **XML declaration** (line 1), which identifies the document as an XML document. The **`version` attribute** specifies the XML version to which the document conforms. The current XML standard is version `1.0`. Though the W3C released a version 1.1 specification in February 2004, this newer version is not yet widely supported. The W3C may continue to release new versions as XML evolves to meet the requirements of different fields.

```
1  <?xml version = "1.0"?>
2
3  <!-- Fig. 14.2: article.xml -->
4  <!-- Article structured with XML -->
5  <article>
6     <title>Simple XML</title>
7     <date>July 4, 2007</date>
8     <author>
9        <firstName>John</firstName>
10       <lastName>Doe</lastName>
11    </author>
12    <summary>XML is pretty easy.</summary>
13    <content>This chapter presents examples that use XML.</content>
14 </article>
```

Fig. 14.2 | XML used to mark up an article.

Portability Tip 14.1

Documents should include the XML declaration to identify the version of XML used. A document that lacks an XML declaration might be assumed to conform to the latest version of XML—when it does not, errors could result.

As in most markup languages, blank lines (line 2), white spaces and indentation help improve readability. Blank lines are normally ignored by XML parsers. XML comments (lines 3–4), which begin with `<!--` and end with `-->`, can be placed almost anywhere in an XML document and can span multiple lines. There must be exactly one end marker (`-->`) for each begin marker (`<!--`).

Common Programming Error 14.1

Placing any characters, including white space, before the XML declaration is an error.

Common Programming Error 14.2

In an XML document, each start tag must have a matching end tag; omitting either tag is an error. Soon, you will learn how such errors are detected.

Common Programming Error 14.3

XML is case sensitive. Using different cases for the start tag and end tag names for the same element is a syntax error.

In Fig. 14.2, `article` (lines 5–14) is the root element. The lines that precede the root element (lines 1–4) are the XML prolog. In an XML prolog, the XML declaration must appear before the comments and any other markup.

The elements we use in the example do not come from any specific markup language. Instead, we chose the element names and markup structure that best describe our particular data. You can invent elements to mark up your data. For example, element `title` (line 6) contains text that describes the article's title (e.g., `Simple XML`). Similarly, `date` (line 7), `author` (lines 8–11), `firstName` (line 9), `lastName` (line 10), `summary` (line 12) and `content` (line 13) contain text that describes the date, author, the author's first name, the author's last name, a summary and the content of the document, respectively. XML element names can be of any length and may contain letters, digits, underscores, hyphens and periods. However, they must begin with either a letter or an underscore, and they should not begin with "`xml`" in any combination of uppercase and lowercase letters (e.g., `XML`, `Xml`, `xMl`), as this is reserved for use in the XML standards.

Common Programming Error 14.4

Using a white-space character in an XML element name is an error.

Good Programming Practice 14.1

XML element names should be meaningful to humans and should not use abbreviations.

XML elements are nested to form hierarchies—with the root element at the top of the hierarchy. This allows document authors to create parent/child relationships between data. For example, elements `title`, `date`, `author`, `summary` and `content` are nested within `article`. Elements `firstName` and `lastName` are nested within `author`. We discuss the hierarchy of Fig. 14.2 later in this chapter (Fig. 14.25).

Common Programming Error 14.5

Nesting XML tags improperly is a syntax error. For example, `<x><y>hello</x></y>` *is an error, because the* `</y>` *tag must precede the* `</x>` *tag.*

Any element that contains other elements (e.g., `article` or `author`) is a container element. Container elements also are called parent elements. Elements nested inside a container element are child elements (or children) of that container element. If those child elements are at the same nesting level, they are siblings of one another.

Viewing an XML Document in Internet Explorer and Firefox

The XML document in Fig. 14.2 is simply a text file named `article.xml`. This document does not contain formatting information for the article. This is because XML is a technology for describing the structure of data. Formatting and displaying data from an XML document are application-specific issues. For example, when the user loads `article.xml` in Internet Explorer, MSXML (Microsoft XML Core Services) parses and displays the document's data. Firefox has a similar capability. Each browser has a built-in style sheet to format the data. Note that the resulting format of the data (Fig. 14.3) is similar to the format of the listing in Fig. 14.2. In Section 14.8, we show how to create style sheets to transform your XML data into various formats suitable for display.

Note the minus sign (–) and plus sign (+) in the screen shots of Fig. 14.3. Although these symbols are not part of the XML document, both browsers place them next to every container element. A minus sign indicates that the browser is displaying the container element's child elements. Clicking the minus sign next to an element collapses that element

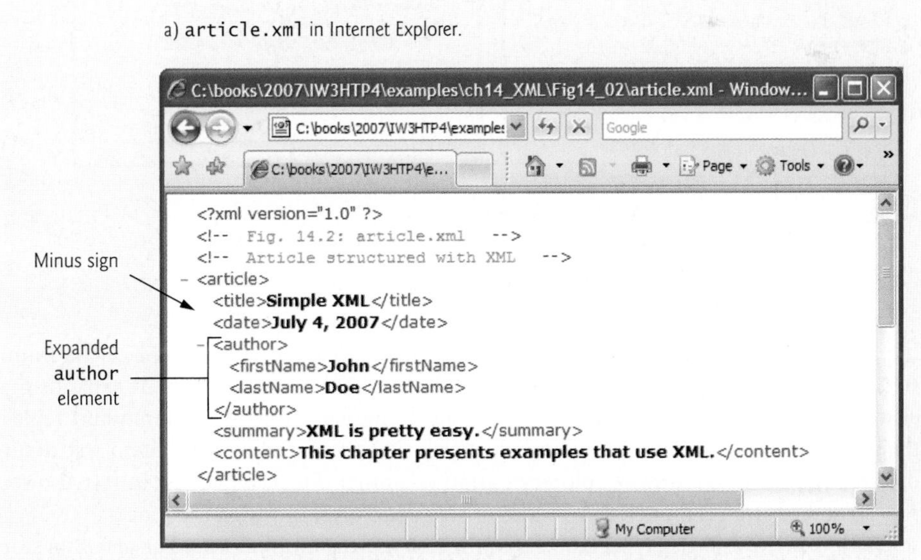

Fig. 14.3 | `article.xml` displayed by Internet Explorer 7 and Firefox 2. (Part 1 of 2.)

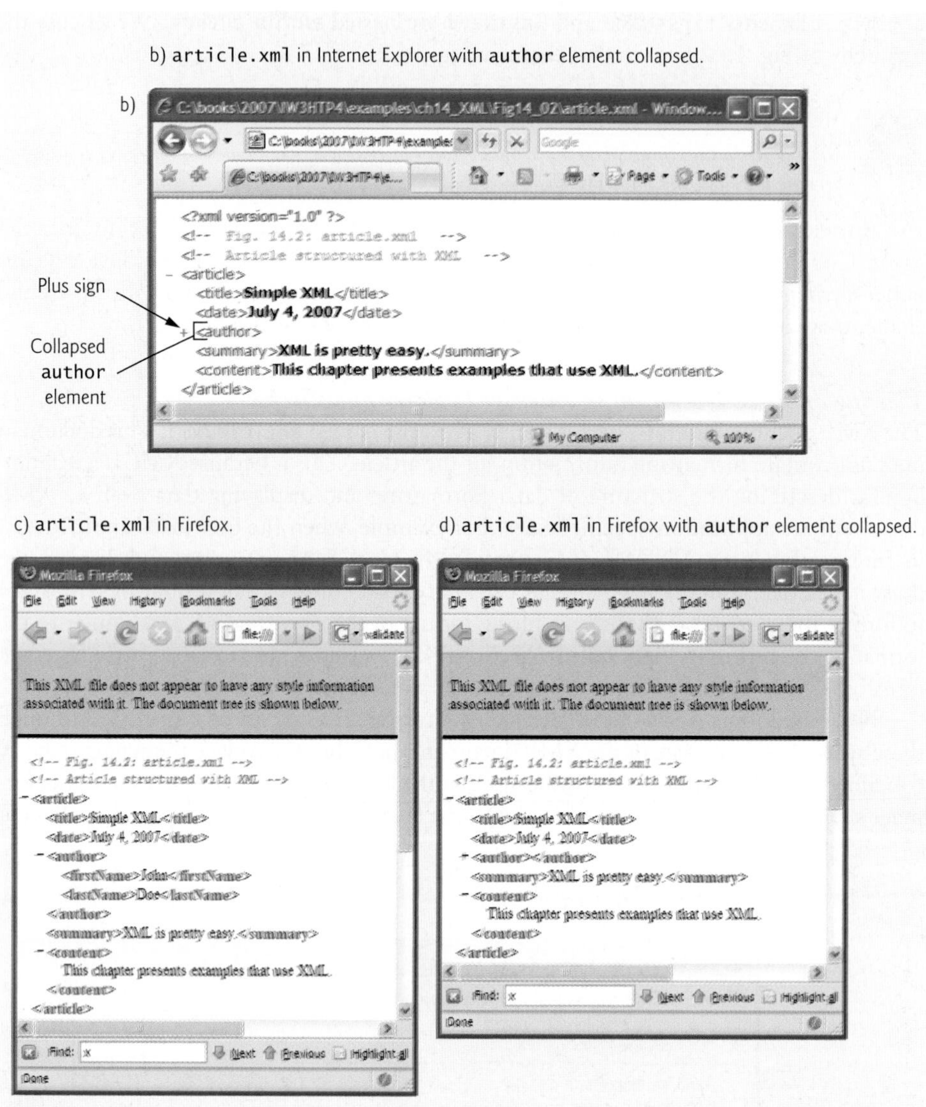

Fig. 14.3 | `article.xml` displayed by Internet Explorer 7 and Firefox 2. (Part 2 of 2.)

(i.e., causes the browser to hide the container element's children and replace the minus sign with a plus sign). Conversely, clicking the plus sign next to an element expands that element (i.e., causes the browser to display the container element's children and replace the plus sign with a minus sign). This behavior is similar to viewing the directory structure on your system in Windows Explorer or another similar directory viewer. In fact, a directory structure often is modeled as a series of tree structures, in which the **root** of a tree represents a disk drive (e.g., `C:`), and **nodes** in the tree represent directories. Parsers often store XML data as tree structures to facilitate efficient manipulation, as discussed in Section 14.9.

[*Note:* In Windows XP Service Pack 2 and Windows Vista, by default Internet Explorer displays all the XML elements in expanded view, and clicking the minus sign (Fig. 14.3(a)) does not do anything. To enable collapsing and expanding, right click the *Information Bar* that appears just below the **Address** field and select **Allow Blocked Content....** Then click **Yes** in the pop-up window that appears.]

XML Markup for a Business Letter

Now that you've seen a simple XML document, let's examine a more complex XML document that marks up a business letter (Fig. 14.4). Again, we begin the document with the XML declaration (line 1) that states the XML version to which the document conforms.

```
1  <?xml version = "1.0"?>
2
3  <!-- Fig. 14.4: letter.xml -->
4  <!-- Business letter marked up as XML -->
5  <!DOCTYPE letter SYSTEM "letter.dtd">
6
7  <letter>
8     <contact type = "sender">
9        <name>Jane Doe</name>
10       <address1>Box 12345</address1>
11       <address2>15 Any Ave.</address2>
12       <city>Othertown</city>
13       <state>Otherstate</state>
14       <zip>67890</zip>
15       <phone>555-4321</phone>
16       <flag gender = "F" />
17    </contact>
18
19    <contact type = "receiver">
20       <name>John Doe</name>
21       <address1>123 Main St.</address1>
22       <address2></address2>
23       <city>Anytown</city>
24       <state>Anystate</state>
25       <zip>12345</zip>
26       <phone>555-1234</phone>
27       <flag gender = "M" />
28    </contact>
29
30    <salutation>Dear Sir:</salutation>
31
32    <paragraph>It is our privilege to inform you about our new database
33       managed with XML. This new system allows you to reduce the
34       load on your inventory list server by having the client machine
35       perform the work of sorting and filtering the data.
36    </paragraph>
37
38    <paragraph>Please visit our website for availability and pricing.
39    </paragraph>
40
```

Fig. 14.4 | Business letter marked up as XML. (Part 1 of 2.)

```
41      <closing>Sincerely,</closing>
42      <signature>Ms. Jane Doe</signature>
43   </letter>
```

Fig. 14.4 | Business letter marked up as XML. (Part 2 of 2.)

Line 5 specifies that this XML document references a DTD. Recall from Section 14.2 that DTDs define the structure of the data for an XML document. For example, a DTD specifies the elements and parent/child relationships between elements permitted in an XML document.

Error-Prevention Tip 14.1

An XML document is not required to reference a DTD, but validating XML parsers can use a DTD to ensure that the document has the proper structure.

Portability Tip 14.2

Validating an XML document helps guarantee that independent developers will exchange data in a standardized form that conforms to the DTD.

The `DOCTYPE` reference (line 5) contains three items, the name of the root element that the DTD specifies (`letter`); the keyword `SYSTEM` (which denotes an external DTD—a DTD declared in a separate file, as opposed to a DTD declared locally in the same file); and the DTD's name and location (i.e., `letter.dtd` in the current directory; this could also be a fully qualified URL). DTD document filenames typically end with the `.dtd` extension. We discuss DTDs and `letter.dtd` in detail in Section 14.5.

Several tools (many of which are free) validate documents against DTDs (discussed in Section 14.5) and schemas (discussed in Section 14.6). Microsoft's XML Validator is available free of charge from the **Download sample** link at

```
msdn.microsoft.com/archive/en-us/samples/internet/
xml/xml_validator/default.asp
```

This validator can validate XML documents against both DTDs and schemas. To install it, run the downloaded executable file `xml_validator.exe` and follow the steps to complete the installation. Once the installation is successful, open the `validate_js.htm` file located in your XML Validator installation directory in IE to validate your XML documents. We installed the XML Validator at `C:\XMLValidator` (Fig. 14.5). The output (Fig. 14.6) shows the results of validating the document using Microsoft's XML Validator. You can click a node to expand it and see its contents. Visit `www.w3.org/XML/Schema` for a list of additional validation tools.

Root element `letter` (lines 7–43 of Fig. 14.4) contains the child elements `contact`, `contact`, `salutation`, `paragraph`, `paragraph`, `closing` and `signature`. Data can be placed between an elements' tags or as attributes—name/value pairs that appear within the angle brackets of an element's start tag. Elements can have any number of attributes (separated by spaces) in their start tags. The first `contact` element (lines 8–17) has an attribute named `type` with attribute value `"sender"`, which indicates that this `contact` element identifies the letter's sender. The second `contact` element (lines 19–28) has attribute `type` with value `"receiver"`, which indicates that this `contact` element identifies the letter's recipient. Like element names, attribute names are case sensitive, can be any

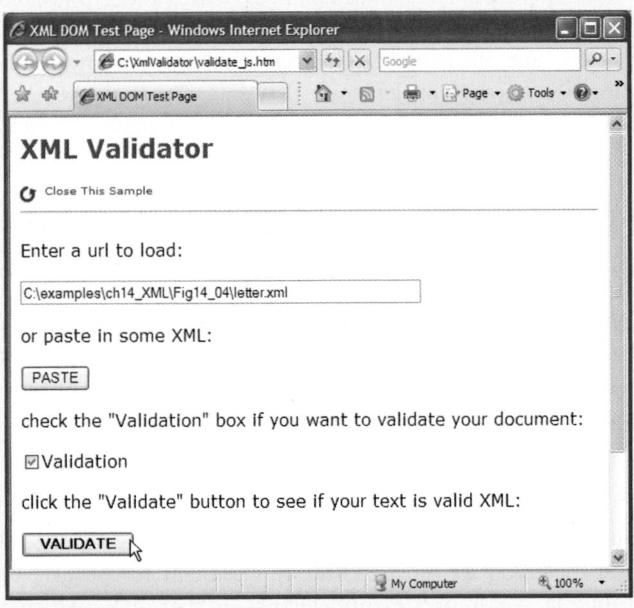

Fig. 14.5 | Validating an XML document with Microsoft's XML Validator.

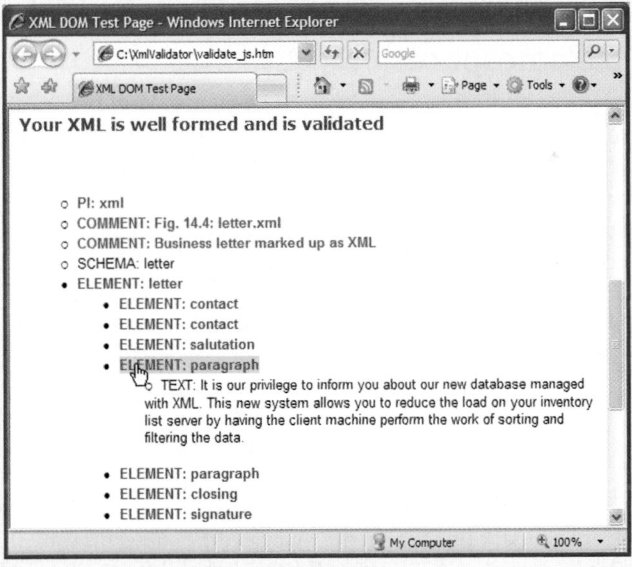

Fig. 14.6 | Validation result using Microsoft's XML Validator.

length, may contain letters, digits, underscores, hyphens and periods, and must begin with either a letter or an underscore character. A `contact` element stores various items of information about a contact, such as the contact's name (represented by element `name`), address (represented by elements address1, address2, city, state and zip), phone number (represented by element phone) and gender (represented by attribute gender of element flag). Element salutation (line 30) marks up the letter's salutation. Lines 32–39 mark up the letter's body using two paragraph elements. Elements closing (line 41) and signature (line 42) mark up the closing sentence and the author's "signature," respectively.

Common Programming Error 14.6

Failure to enclose attribute values in double ("") or single ('') quotes is a syntax error.

Line 16 introduces the empty element flag. An empty element is one that does not have any content. Instead, an empty element sometimes places data in attributes. Empty element flag has one attribute that indicates the gender of the contact (represented by the parent contact element). Document authors can close an empty element either by placing a slash immediately preceding the right angle bracket, as shown in line 16, or by explicitly writing an end tag, as in line 22

```
<address2></address2>
```

Note that the address2 element in line 22 is empty because there is no second part to this contact's address. However, we must include this element to conform to the structural rules specified in the XML document's DTD—letter.dtd (which we present in Section 14.5). This DTD specifies that each contact element must have an address2 child element (even if it is empty). In Section 14.5, you will learn how DTDs indicate required and optional elements.

14.4 XML Namespaces

XML allows document authors to create custom elements. This extensibility can result in naming collisions among elements in an XML document that each have the same name. For example, we may use the element book to mark up data about a Deitel publication. A stamp collector may use the element book to mark up data about a book of stamps. Using both of these elements in the same document could create a naming collision, making it difficult to determine which kind of data each element contains.

An XML namespace is a collection of element and attribute names. XML namespaces provide a means for document authors to unambiguously refer to elements with the same name (i.e., prevent collisions). For example,

```
<subject>Geometry</subject>
```

and

```
<subject>Cardiology</subject>
```

use element subject to mark up data. In the first case, the subject is something one studies in school, whereas in the second case, the subject is a field of medicine. Namespaces can differentiate these two subject elements—for example:

```
<highschool:subject>Geometry</highschool:subject>
```

and

```
<medicalschool:subject>Cardiology</medicalschool:subject>
```

Both `highschool` and `medicalschool` are **namespace prefixes**. A document author places a namespace prefix and colon (:) before an element name to specify the namespace to which that element belongs. Document authors can create their own namespace prefixes using virtually any name except the reserved namespace prefix `xml`. In the next subsections, we demonstrate how document authors ensure that namespaces are unique.

Common Programming Error 14.7

Attempting to create a namespace prefix named `xml` in any mixture of uppercase and lowercase letters is a syntax error—the `xml` namespace prefix is reserved for internal use by XML itself.

Differentiating Elements with Namespaces

Figure 14.7 demonstrates namespaces. In this document, namespaces differentiate two distinct elements—the `file` element related to a text file and the `file` document related to an image file.

```
<?xml version = "1.0"?>

<!-- Fig. 14.7: namespace.xml -->
<!-- Demonstrating namespaces -->
<text:directory
   xmlns:text = "urn:deitel:textInfo"
   xmlns:image = "urn:deitel:imageInfo">

   <text:file filename = "book.xml">
      <text:description>A book list</text:description>
   </text:file>

   <image:file filename = "funny.jpg">
      <image:description>A funny picture</image:description>
      <image:size width = "200" height = "100" />
   </image:file>
</text:directory>
```

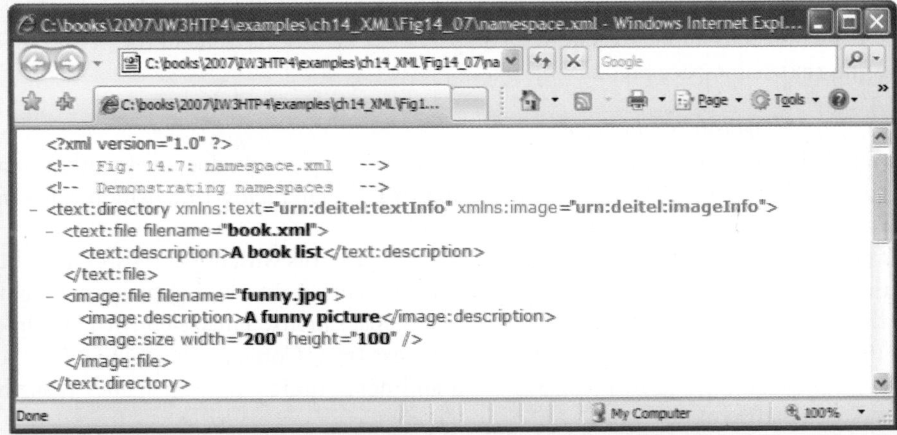

Fig. 14.7 | XML namespaces demonstration.

Lines 6–7 use the XML-namespace reserved attribute `xmlns` to create two namespace prefixes—`text` and `image`. Each namespace prefix is bound to a series of characters called a Uniform Resource Identifier (URI) that uniquely identifies the namespace. Document authors create their own namespace prefixes and URIs. A URI is a way to identifying a resource, typically on the Internet. Two popular types of URI are Uniform Resource Name (URN) and Uniform Resource Locator (URL).

To ensure that namespaces are unique, document authors must provide unique URIs. In this example, we use the text `urn:deitel:textInfo` and `urn:deitel:imageInfo` as URIs. These URIs employ the URN scheme frequently used to identify namespaces. Under this naming scheme, a URI begins with `"urn:"`, followed by a unique series of additional names separated by colons.

Another common practice is to use URLs, which specify the location of a file or a resource on the Internet. For example, `www.deitel.com` is the URL that identifies the home page of the Deitel & Associates website. Using URLs guarantees that the namespaces are unique because the domain names (e.g., `www.deitel.com`) are guaranteed to be unique. For example, lines 5–7 could be rewritten as

```
<text:directory
   xmlns:text = "http://www.deitel.com/xmlns-text"
   xmlns:image = "http://www.deitel.com/xmlns-image">
```

where URLs related to the `deitel.com` domain name serve as URIs to identify the `text` and `image` namespaces. The parser does not visit these URLs, nor do these URLs need to refer to actual web pages. They each simply represent a unique series of characters used to differentiate URI names. In fact, any string can represent a namespace. For example, our `image` namespace URI could be `hgjfkdlsa4556`, in which case our prefix assignment would be

```
xmlns:image = "hgjfkdlsa4556"
```

Lines 9–11 use the `text` namespace prefix for elements `file` and `description`. Note that the end tags must also specify the namespace prefix `text`. Lines 13–16 apply namespace prefix `image` to the elements `file`, `description` and `size`. Note that attributes do not require namespace prefixes (although they can have them), because each attribute is already part of an element that specifies the namespace prefix. For example, attribute `filename` (line 9) is implicitly part of namespace `text` because its element (i.e., `file`) specifies the `text` namespace prefix.

Specifying a Default Namespace

To eliminate the need to place namespace prefixes in each element, document authors may specify a default namespace for an element and its children. Figure 14.8 demonstrates using a default namespace (`urn:deitel:textInfo`) for element `directory`.

Line 5 defines a default namespace using attribute `xmlns` with no prefix specified, but with a URI as its value. Once we define this default namespace, child elements belonging to the namespace need not be qualified by a namespace prefix. Thus, element `file` (lines 8–10) is in the default namespace `urn:deitel:textInfo`. Compare this to lines 9–10 of Fig. 14.7, where we had to prefix the `file` and `description` element names with the namespace prefix `text`.

The default namespace applies to the `directory` element and all elements that are not qualified with a namespace prefix. However, we can use a namespace prefix to specify a

```
1  <?xml version = "1.0"?>
2
3  <!-- Fig. 14.8: defaultnamespace.xml -->
4  <!-- Using default namespaces -->
5  <directory xmlns = "urn:deitel:textInfo"
6     xmlns:image = "urn:deitel:imageInfo">
7
8     <file filename = "book.xml">
9        <description>A book list</description>
10    </file>
11
12    <image:file filename = "funny.jpg">
13       <image:description>A funny picture</image:description>
14       <image:size width = "200" height = "100" />
15    </image:file>
16 </directory>
```

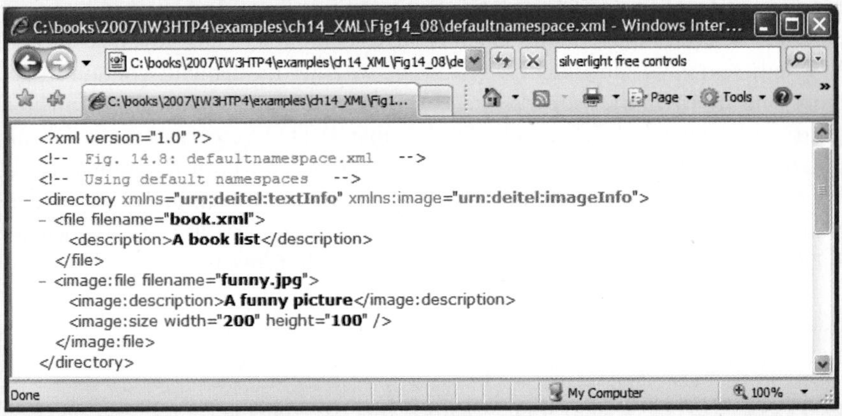

```
<?xml version="1.0" ?>
<!-- Fig. 14.8: defaultnamespace.xml -->
<!-- Using default namespaces -->
- <directory xmlns="urn:deitel:textInfo" xmlns:image="urn:deitel:imageInfo">
  - <file filename="book.xml">
      <description>A book list</description>
    </file>
  - <image:file filename="funny.jpg">
      <image:description>A funny picture</image:description>
      <image:size width="200" height="100" />
    </image:file>
  </directory>
```

Fig. 14.8 | Default namespace demonstration.

different namespace for a particular element. For example, the `file` element in lines 12–15 includes the `image` namespace prefix, indicating that this element is in the `urn:deitel:imageInfo` namespace, not the default namespace.

Namespaces in XML Vocabularies

XML-based languages, such as XML Schema (Section 14.6) and Extensible Stylesheet Language (XSL) (Section 14.8), often use namespaces to identify their elements. Each of these vocabularies defines special-purpose elements that are grouped in namespaces. These namespaces help prevent naming collisions between predefined elements and user-defined elements.

14.5 Document Type Definitions (DTDs)

Document Type Definitions (DTDs) are one of two main types of documents you can use to specify XML document structure. Section 14.6 presents W3C XML Schema documents, which provide an improved method of specifying XML document structure.

Software Engineering Observation 14.2

XML documents can have many different structures, and for this reason an application cannot be certain whether a particular document it receives is complete, ordered properly, and not missing data. DTDs and schemas (Section 14.6) solve this problem by providing an extensible way to describe XML document structure. Applications should use DTDs or schemas to confirm whether XML documents are valid.

Software Engineering Observation 14.3

*Many organizations and individuals are creating DTDs and schemas for a broad range of applications. These collections—called **repositories**—are available free for download from the web (e.g.,* `www.xml.org`, `www.oasis-open.org`*).*

Creating a Document Type Definition

Figure 14.4 presented a simple business letter marked up with XML. Recall that line 5 of `letter.xml` references a DTD—`letter.dtd` (Fig. 14.9). This DTD specifies the business letter's element types and attributes, and their relationships to one another.

A DTD describes the structure of an XML document and enables an XML parser to verify whether an XML document is valid (i.e., whether its elements contain the proper attributes and appear in the proper sequence). DTDs allow users to check document structure and to exchange data in a standardized format. A DTD expresses the set of rules for document structure using an EBNF (Extended Backus-Naur Form) grammar. DTDs are not themselves XML documents. [*Note:* EBNF grammars are commonly used to define programming languages. To learn more about EBNF grammars, visit `en.wikipedia.org/wiki/EBNF` or `www.garshol.priv.no/download/text/bnf.html`.]

```
<!-- Fig. 14.9: letter.dtd      -->
<!-- DTD document for letter.xml -->

<!ELEMENT letter ( contact+, salutation, paragraph+,
   closing, signature )>

<!ELEMENT contact ( name, address1, address2, city, state,
   zip, phone, flag )>
<!ATTLIST contact type CDATA #IMPLIED>

<!ELEMENT name ( #PCDATA )>
<!ELEMENT address1 ( #PCDATA )>
<!ELEMENT address2 ( #PCDATA )>
<!ELEMENT city ( #PCDATA )>
<!ELEMENT state ( #PCDATA )>
<!ELEMENT zip ( #PCDATA )>
<!ELEMENT phone ( #PCDATA )>
<!ELEMENT flag EMPTY>
<!ATTLIST flag gender (M | F) "M">

<!ELEMENT salutation ( #PCDATA )>
<!ELEMENT closing ( #PCDATA )>
<!ELEMENT paragraph ( #PCDATA )>
<!ELEMENT signature ( #PCDATA )>
```

Fig. 14.9 | Document Type Definition (DTD) for a business letter.

Common Programming Error 14.8

For documents validated with DTDs, any document that uses elements, attributes or nesting relationships not explicitly defined by a DTD is an invalid document.

Defining Elements in a DTD

The ELEMENT **element type declaration** in lines 4–5 defines the rules for element `letter`. In this case, `letter` contains one or more `contact` elements, one `salutation` element, one or more `paragraph` elements, one `closing` element and one `signature` element, in that sequence. The **plus sign (+) occurrence indicator** specifies that the DTD requires one or more occurrences of an element. Other occurence indicators include the **asterisk** (*), which indicates an optional element that can occur zero or more times, and the **question mark** (?), which indicates an optional element that can occur at most once (i.e., zero or one occurrence). If an element does not have an occurrence indicator, the DTD requires exactly one occurrence.

The `contact` element type declaration (lines 7–8) specifies that a `contact` element contains child elements `name`, `address1`, `address2`, `city`, `state`, `zip`, `phone` and `flag`—in that order. The DTD requires exactly one occurrence of each of these elements.

Defining Attributes in a DTD

Line 9 uses the ATTLIST **attribute-list declaration** to define an attribute named `type` for the `contact` element. Keyword `#IMPLIED` specifies that if the parser finds a `contact` element without a `type` attribute, the parser can choose an arbitrary value for the attribute or can ignore the attribute. Either way the document will still be valid (if the rest of the document is valid)—a missing `type` attribute will not invalidate the document. Other keywords that can be used in place of `#IMPLIED` in an `ATTLIST` declaration include `#REQUIRED` and `#FIXED`. Keyword `#REQUIRED` specifies that the attribute must be present in the element, and keyword `#FIXED` specifies that the attribute (if present) must have the given fixed value. For example,

```
<!ATTLIST address zip CDATA #FIXED "01757">
```

indicates that attribute `zip` (if present in element `address`) must have the value `01757` for the document to be valid. If the attribute is not present, then the parser, by default, uses the fixed value that the `ATTLIST` declaration specifies.

Character Data vs. Parsed Character Data

Keyword CDATA (line 9) specifies that attribute `type` contains **character data** (i.e., a string). A parser will pass such data to an application without modification.

Software Engineering Observation 14.4

DTD syntax cannot describe an element's or attribute's data type. For example, a DTD cannot specify that a particular element or attribute can contain only integer data.

Keyword #PCDATA (line 11) specifies that an element (e.g., `name`) may contain **parsed character data** (i.e., data that is processed by an XML parser). Elements with parsed character data cannot contain markup characters, such as less than (<), greater than (>) or ampersand (&). The document author should replace any markup character in a `#PCDATA` element with the character's corresponding **character entity reference**. For example, the character entity reference `<` should be used in place of the less-than symbol (<), and the character entity reference `>` should be used in place of the greater-than symbol (>). A document author who wishes to use a literal ampersand should use the entity reference `&` instead—parsed character data can contain ampersands (&) only for inserting entities. See Appendix A, XHTML Special Characters, for a list of other character entity references.

Common Programming Error 14.9

Using markup characters (e.g., <, > and &) in parsed character data is an error. Use character entity references (e.g., `<`*,* `>` *and* `&`*) instead.*

Defining Empty Elements in a DTD

Line 18 defines an empty element named `flag`. Keyword `EMPTY` specifies that the element does not contain any data between its start and end tags. Empty elements commonly describe data via attributes. For example, `flag`'s data appears in its `gender` attribute (line 19). Line 19 specifies that the `gender` attribute's value must be one of the enumerated values (`M` or `F`) enclosed in parentheses and delimited by a vertical bar (`|`) meaning "or." Note that line 19 also indicates that `gender` has a default value of `M`.

Well-Formed Documents vs. Valid Documents

In Section 14.3, we demonstrated how to use the Microsoft XML Validator to validate an XML document against its specified DTD. The validation revealed that the XML document `letter.xml` (Fig. 14.4) is well-formed and valid—it conforms to `letter.dtd` (Fig. 14.9). Recall that a well-formed document is syntactically correct (i.e., each start tag has a corresponding end tag, the document contains only one root element, etc.), and a valid document contains the proper elements with the proper attributes in the proper sequence. An XML document cannot be valid unless it is well-formed.

When a document fails to conform to a DTD or a schema, the Microsoft XML Validator displays an error message. For example, the DTD in Fig. 14.9 indicates that a `contact` element must contain the child element `name`. A document that omits this child element is still well-formed, but is not valid. In such a scenario, Microsoft XML Validator displays the error message shown in Fig. 14.10.

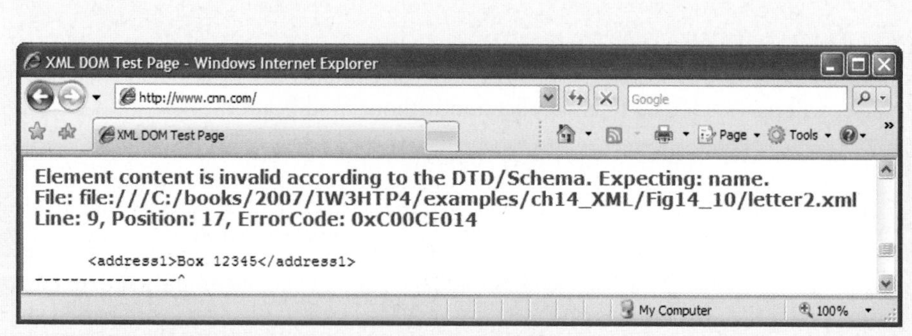

Fig. 14.10 | XML Validator displaying an error message.

14.6 W3C XML Schema Documents

In this section, we introduce schemas for specifying XML document structure and validating XML documents. Many developers in the XML community believe that DTDs are not flexible enough to meet today's programming needs. For example, DTDs lack a way of indicating what specific type of data (e.g., numeric, text) an element can contain, and DTDs are not themselves XML documents, forcing developers to learn multiple grammars and developers to create multiple types of parsers. These and other limitations have led to the development of schemas.

Unlike DTDs, schemas do not use EBNF grammar. Instead, schemas use XML syntax and are actually XML documents that programs can manipulate. Like DTDs, schemas are used by validating parsers to validate documents.

In this section, we focus on the W3C's XML Schema vocabulary (note the capital "S" in "Schema"). We use the term XML Schema in the rest of the chapter whenever we refer to W3C's XML Schema vocabulary. For the latest information on XML Schema, visit `www.w3.org/XML/Schema`. For tutorials on XML Schema concepts beyond what we present here, visit `www.w3schools.com/schema/default.asp`.

Recall that a DTD describes an XML document's structure, not the content of its elements. For example,

```
<quantity>5</quantity>
```

contains character data. If the document that contains element `quantity` references a DTD, an XML parser can validate the document to confirm that this element indeed does contain `PCDATA` content. However, the parser cannot validate that the content is numeric; DTDs do not provide this capability. So, unfortunately, the parser also considers

```
<quantity>hello</quantity>
```

to be valid. An application that uses the XML document containing this markup should test that the data in element `quantity` is numeric and take appropriate action if it is not.

XML Schema enables schema authors to specify that element `quantity`'s data must be numeric or, even more specifically, an integer. A parser validating the XML document against this schema can determine that `5` conforms and `hello` does not. An XML document that conforms to a schema document is schema valid, and one that does not conform is schema invalid. Schemas are XML documents and therefore must themselves be valid.

Validating Against an XML Schema Document

Figure 14.11 shows a schema-valid XML document named `book.xml`, and Fig. 14.12 shows the pertinent XML Schema document (`book.xsd`) that defines the structure for `book.xml`. By convention, schemas use the `.xsd` extension. We used an online XSD schema validator provided at

```
www.xmlforasp.net/SchemaValidator.aspx
```

to ensure that the XML document in Fig. 14.11 conforms to the schema in Fig. 14.12. To validate the schema document itself (i.e., `book.xsd`) and produce the output shown in Fig. 14.12, we used an online XSV (XML Schema Validator) provided by the W3C at

```
www.w3.org/2001/03/webdata/xsv
```

These tools are free and enforce the W3C's specifications regarding XML Schemas and schema validation.

```
<?xml version = "1.0"?>

<!-- Fig. 14.11: book.xml -->
<!-- Book list marked up as XML -->
<deitel:books xmlns:deitel = "http://www.deitel.com/booklist">
   <book>
      <title>Visual Basic 2005 How to Program, 3/e</title>
   </book>
   <book>
      <title>Visual C# 2005 How to Program, 2/e</title>
   </book>
   <book>
      <title>Java How to Program, 7/e</title>
   </book>
   <book>
      <title>C++ How to Program, 6/e</title>
   </book>
   <book>
      <title>Internet and World Wide Web How to Program, 4/e</title>
   </book>
</deitel:books>
```

Fig. 14.11 | Schema-valid XML document describing a list of books.

```
<?xml version = "1.0"?>

<!-- Fig. 14.12: book.xsd               -->
<!-- Simple W3C XML Schema document -->
<schema xmlns = "http://www.w3.org/2001/XMLSchema"
   xmlns:deitel = "http://www.deitel.com/booklist"
   targetNamespace = "http://www.deitel.com/booklist">

   <element name = "books" type = "deitel:BooksType"/>

   <complexType name = "BooksType">
      <sequence>
         <element name = "book" type = "deitel:SingleBookType"
            minOccurs = "1" maxOccurs = "unbounded"/>
      </sequence>
   </complexType>

   <complexType name = "SingleBookType">
      <sequence>
         <element name = "title" type = "string"/>
      </sequence>
   </complexType>
</schema>
```

Fig. 14.12 | XML Schema document for `book.xml`. (Part 1 of 2.)

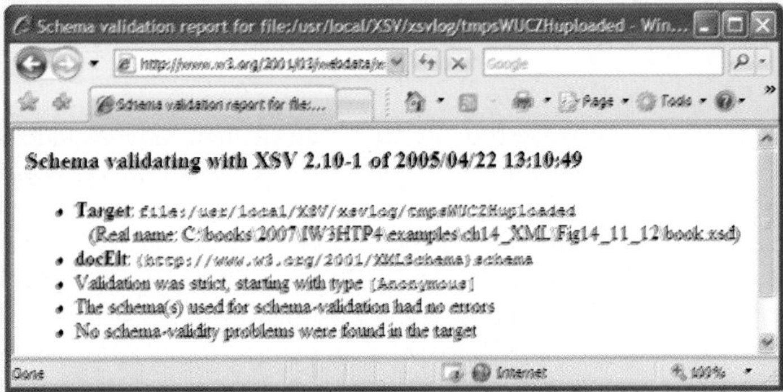

Fig. 14.12 | XML Schema document for `book.xml`. (Part 2 of 2.)

Figure 14.11 contains markup describing several Deitel books. The `books` element (line 5) has the namespace prefix `deitel`, indicating that the `books` element is a part of the `http://www.deitel.com/booklist` namespace.

Creating an XML Schema Document

Figure 14.12 presents the XML Schema document that specifies the structure of `book.xml` (Fig. 14.11). This document defines an XML-based language (i.e., a vocabulary) for writing XML documents about collections of books. The schema defines the elements, attributes and parent/child relationships that such a document can (or must) include. The schema also specifies the type of data that these elements and attributes may contain.

Root element **`schema`** (Fig. 14.12, lines 5–23) contains elements that define the structure of an XML document such as `book.xml`. Line 5 specifies as the default namespace the standard W3C XML Schema namespace URI—**`http://www.w3.org/2001/XMLSchema`**. This namespace contains predefined elements (e.g., root-element `schema`) that comprise the XML Schema vocabulary—the language used to write an XML Schema document.

Portability Tip 14.3

W3C XML Schema authors specify URI `http://www.w3.org/2001/XMLSchema` *when referring to the XML Schema namespace. This namespace contains predefined elements that comprise the XML Schema vocabulary. Specifying this URI ensures that validation tools correctly identify XML Schema elements and do not confuse them with those defined by document authors.*

Line 6 binds the URI `http://www.deitel.com/booklist` to namespace prefix `deitel`. As we discuss momentarily, the schema uses this namespace to differentiate names created by us from names that are part of the XML Schema namespace. Line 7 also specifies `http://www.deitel.com/booklist` as the **`targetNamespace`** of the schema. This attribute identifies the namespace of the XML vocabulary that this schema defines. Note that the `targetNamespace` of `book.xsd` is the same as the namespace referenced in line 5 of `book.xml` (Fig. 14.11). This is what "connects" the XML document with the schema that defines its structure. When an XML schema validator examines `book.xml` and `book.xsd`, it will recognize that `book.xml` uses elements and attributes from the `http://www.deitel.com/booklist` namespace. The validator also will recognize that this namespace is the namespace defined in `book.xsd` (i.e., the schema's `targetNamespace`).

Thus the validator knows where to look for the structural rules for the elements and attributes used in `book.xml`.

Defining an Element in XML Schema

In XML Schema, the `element` tag (line 9) defines an element to be included in an XML document that conforms to the schema. In other words, `element` specifies the actual *elements* that can be used to mark up data. Line 9 defines the `books` element, which we use as the root element in `book.xml` (Fig. 14.11). Attributes `name` and `type` specify the `element`'s name and type, respectively. An element's type indicates the data that the element may contain. Possible types include XML Schema-defined types (e.g., `string`, `double`) and user-defined types (e.g., `BooksType`, which is defined in lines 11–16). Figure 14.13 lists several of XML Schema's many built-in types. For a complete list of built-in types, see Section 3 of the specification found at `www.w3.org/TR/xmlschema-2`.

XML Schema type	Description	Ranges or structures	Examples
`string`	A character string		`"hello"`
`boolean`	True or false	`true`, `false`	`true`
`decimal`	A decimal numeral	`i` * (10^n), where `i` is an integer and `n` is an integer that is less than or equal to zero.	`5, -12, -45.78`
`float`	A floating-point number	`m` * (2^e), where `m` is an integer whose absolute value is less than 2^{24} and `e` is an integer in the range `-149` to `104`. Plus three additional numbers: positive infinity, negative infinity and not-a-number (`NaN`).	`0, 12, -109.375, NaN`
`double`	A floating-point number	`m` * (2^e), where `m` is an integer whose absolute value is less than 2^{53} and `e` is an integer in the range `-1075` to `970`. Plus three additional numbers: positive infinity, negative infinity and not-a-number (`NaN`).	`0, 12, -109.375, NaN`
`long`	A whole number	`-9223372036854775808` to `9223372036854775807`, inclusive.	`1234567890, -1234567890`
`int`	A whole number	`-2147483648` to `2147483647`, inclusive.	`1234567890, -1234567890`

Fig. 14.13 | Some XML Schema types. (Part 1 of 2.)

XML Schema type	Description	Ranges or structures	Examples
short	A whole number	-32768 to 32767, inclusive.	12, -345
date	A date consisting of a year, month and day	yyyy-mm with an optional dd and an optional time zone, where yyyy is four digits long and mm and dd are two digits long.	2005-05-10
time	A time consisting of hours, minutes and seconds	hh:mm:ss with an optional time zone, where hh, mm and ss are two digits long.	16:30:25-05:00

Fig. 14.13 | Some XML Schema types. (Part 2 of 2.)

In this example, books is defined as an element of type deitel:BooksType (line 9). BooksType is a user-defined type (lines 11–16) in the http://www.deitel.com/booklist namespace and therefore must have the namespace prefix deitel. It is not an existing XML Schema type.

Two categories of type exist in XML Schema—simple types and complex types. Simple and complex types differ only in that simple types cannot contain attributes or child elements and complex types can.

A user-defined type that contains attributes or child elements must be defined as a complex type. Lines 11–16 use element complexType to define BooksType as a complex type that has a child element named book. The sequence element (lines 12–15) allows you to specify the sequential order in which child elements must appear. The element (lines 13–14) nested within the complexType element indicates that a BooksType element (e.g., books) can contain child elements named book of type deitel:SingleBookType (defined in lines 18–22). Attribute minOccurs (line 14), with value 1, specifies that elements of type BooksType must contain a minimum of one book element. Attribute maxOccurs (line 14), with value unbounded, specifies that elements of type BooksType may have any number of book child elements.

Lines 18–22 define the complex type SingleBookType. An element of this type contains a child element named title. Line 20 defines element title to be of simple type string. Recall that elements of a simple type cannot contain attributes or child elements. The schema end tag (</schema>, line 23) declares the end of the XML Schema document.

A Closer Look at Types in XML Schema

Every element in XML Schema has a type. Types include the built-in types provided by XML Schema (Fig. 14.13) or user-defined types (e.g., SingleBookType in Fig. 14.12).

Every simple type defines a restriction on an XML Schema-defined type or a restriction on a user-defined type. Restrictions limit the possible values that an element can hold.

Complex types are divided into two groups—those with simple content and those with complex content. Both can contain attributes, but only complex content can contain child elements. Complex types with simple content must extend or restrict some other existing type. Complex types with complex content do not have this limitation. We demonstrate complex types with each kind of content in the next example.

The schema document in Fig. 14.14 creates both simple types and complex types. The XML document in Fig. 14.15 (`laptop.xml`) follows the structure defined in Fig. 14.14 to describe parts of a laptop computer. A document such as `laptop.xml` that conforms to a schema is known as an **XML instance document**—the document is an instance (i.e., example) of the schema.

Line 5 declares the default namespace to be the standard XML Schema namespace—any elements without a prefix are assumed to be in the XML Schema namespace. Line 6 binds the namespace prefix `computer` to the namespace `http://www.deitel.com/computer`. Line 7 identifies this namespace as the `targetNamespace`—the namespace being defined by the current XML Schema document.

To design the XML elements for describing laptop computers, we first create a simple type in lines 9–13 using the **`simpleType`** element. We name this `simpleType` `gigahertz`

```
1  <?xml version = "1.0"?>
2  <!-- Fig. 14.14: computer.xsd -->
3  <!-- W3C XML Schema document  -->
4
5  <schema xmlns = "http://www.w3.org/2001/XMLSchema"
6     xmlns:computer = "http://www.deitel.com/computer"
7     targetNamespace = "http://www.deitel.com/computer">
8
9     <simpleType name = "gigahertz">
10       <restriction base = "decimal">
11          <minInclusive value = "2.1"/>
12       </restriction>
13    </simpleType>
14
15    <complexType name = "CPU">
16       <simpleContent>
17          <extension base = "string">
18             <attribute name = "model" type = "string"/>
19          </extension>
20       </simpleContent>
21    </complexType>
22
23    <complexType name = "portable">
24       <all>
25          <element name = "processor" type = "computer:CPU"/>
26          <element name = "monitor" type = "int"/>
27          <element name = "CPUSpeed" type = "computer:gigahertz"/>
28          <element name = "RAM" type = "int"/>
29       </all>
30       <attribute name = "manufacturer" type = "string"/>
31    </complexType>
32
33    <element name = "laptop" type = "computer:portable"/>
34 </schema>
```

Fig. 14.14 | XML Schema document defining simple and complex types.

because it will be used to describe the clock speed of the processor in gigahertz. Simple types are restrictions of a type typically called a **base type**. For this `simpleType`, line 10 declares the base type as `decimal`, and we restrict the value to be at least `2.1` by using the **`minInclusive`** element in line 11.

Next, we declare a `complexType` named `CPU` that has **`simpleContent`** (lines 16–20). Remember that a complex type with simple content can have attributes but not child elements. Also recall that complex types with simple content must extend or restrict some XML Schema type or user-defined type. The **`extension`** element with attribute **`base`** (line 17) sets the base type to `string`. In this `complexType`, we extend the base type `string` with an attribute. The **`attribute`** element (line 18) gives the `complexType` an attribute of type `string` named `model`. Thus an element of type `CPU` must contain `string` text (because the base type is `string`) and may contain a `model` attribute that is also of type `string`.

Last, we define type `portable`, which is a `complexType` with complex content (lines 23–31). Such types are allowed to have child elements and attributes. The element **`all`** (lines 24–29) encloses elements that must each be included once in the corresponding XML instance document. These elements can be included in any order. This complex type holds four elements—`processor`, `monitor`, `CPUSpeed` and `RAM`. They are given types `CPU`, `int`, `gigahertz` and `int`, respectively. When using types `CPU` and `gigahertz`, we must include the namespace prefix `computer`, because these user-defined types are part of the `computer` namespace (`http://www.deitel.com/computer`)—the namespace defined in the current document (line 7). Also, `portable` contains an attribute defined in line 30. The `attribute` element indicates that elements of type `portable` contain an attribute of type `string` named `manufacturer`.

Line 33 declares the actual element that uses the three types defined in the schema. The element is called `laptop` and is of type `portable`. We must use the namespace prefix `computer` in front of `portable`.

We have now created an element named `laptop` that contains child elements `processor`, `monitor`, `CPUSpeed` and `RAM`, and an attribute `manufacturer`. Figure 14.15 uses the `laptop` element defined in the `computer.xsd` schema. Once again, we used an online XSD schema validator (`www.xmlforasp.net/SchemaValidator.aspx`) to ensure that this XML instance document adheres to the schema's structural rules.

Line 5 declares namespace prefix `computer`. The `laptop` element requires this prefix because it is part of the `http://www.deitel.com/computer` namespace. Line 6 sets the

```
1  <?xml version = "1.0"?>
2
3  <!-- Fig. 14.15: laptop.xml              -->
4  <!-- Laptop components marked up as XML -->
5  <computer:laptop xmlns:computer = "http://www.deitel.com/computer"
6     manufacturer = "IBM">
7
8     <processor model = "Centrino">Intel</processor>
9     <monitor>17</monitor>
10    <CPUSpeed>2.4</CPUSpeed>
11    <RAM>256</RAM>
12 </computer:laptop>
```

Fig. 14.15 | XML document using the `laptop` element defined in `computer.xsd`.

laptop's `manufacturer` attribute, and lines 8–11 use the elements defined in the schema to describe the laptop's characteristics.

This section introduced W3C XML Schema documents for defining the structure of XML documents, and we validated XML instance documents against schemas using an online XSD schema validator. Section 14.7 discusses several XML vocabularies and demonstrates the MathML vocabulary. Section 14.10 demonstrates the RSS vocabulary.

14.7 XML Vocabularies

XML allows authors to create their own tags to describe data precisely. People and organizations in various fields of study have created many different kinds of XML for structuring data. Some of these markup languages are: MathML (Mathematical Markup Language), Scalable Vector Graphics (SVG), Wireless Markup Language (WML), Extensible Business Reporting Language (XBRL), Extensible User Interface Language (XUL) and Product Data Markup Language (PDML). Two other examples of XML vocabularies are W3C XML Schema and the Extensible Stylesheet Language (XSL), which we discuss in Section 14.8. The following subsections describe MathML and other custom markup languages.

14.7.1 MathML™

Until recently, computers typically required specialized software packages such as TeX and LaTeX for displaying complex mathematical expressions. This section introduces MathML, which the W3C developed for describing mathematical notations and expressions. One application that can parse, render and edit MathML is the W3C's Amaya™ browser/editor, which can be downloaded from

```
www.w3.org/Amaya/User/BinDist.html
```

This page contains download links for several platforms. Amaya documentation and installation notes also are available at the W3C website. Firefox also can render MathML, but it requires additional fonts. Instructions for downloading and installing these fonts are available at `www.mozilla.org/projects/mathml/fonts/`. You can download a plug-in (`www.dessci.com/en/products/mathplayer/`) to render MathML in Internet Explorer .

MathML markup describes mathematical expressions for display. MathML is divided into two types of markup—content markup and presentation markup. Content markup provides tags that embody mathematical concepts. Content MathML allows programmers to write mathematical notation specific to different areas of mathematics. For instance, the multiplication symbol has one meaning in set theory and another meaning in linear algebra. Content MathML distinguishes between different uses of the same symbol. Programmers can take content MathML markup, discern mathematical context and evaluate the marked-up mathematical operations. Presentation MathML is directed toward formatting and displaying mathematical notation. We focus on Presentation MathML in the MathML examples.

Simple Equation in MathML

Figure 14.16 uses MathML to mark up a simple expression. For this example, we show the expression rendered in Firefox.

```
1  <?xml version="1.0" encoding="iso-8859-1"?>
2  <!DOCTYPE math PUBLIC "-//W3C//DTD MathML 2.0//EN"
3     "http://www.w3.org/TR/MathML2/dtd/mathml2.dtd">
4
5  <!-- Fig. 14.16: mathml1.mml -->
6  <!-- MathML equation. -->
7  <math xmlns="http://www.w3.org/1998/Math/MathML">
8     <mn>2</mn>
9     <mo>+</mo>
10    <mn>3</mn>
11    <mo>=</mo>
12    <mn>5</mn>
13 </math>
```

Fig. 14.16 | Expression marked up with MathML and displayed in the Firefox browser.

By convention, MathML files end with the `.mml` filename extension. A MathML document's root node is the `math` element, and its default namespace is `http://www.w3.org/1998/Math/MathML` (line 7). The **`mn` element** (line 8) marks up a number. The **`mo` element** (line 9) marks up an operator (e.g., +). Using this markup, we define the expression 2 + 3 = 5, which any MathML capable browser can display.

Algebraic Equation in MathML

Let's consider using MathML to mark up an algebraic equation containing exponents and arithmetic operators (Fig. 14.17). For this example, we again show the expression rendered in Firefox.

```
<?xml version="1.0" encoding="iso-8859-1"?>
<!DOCTYPE math PUBLIC "-//W3C//DTD MathML 2.0//EN"
   "http://www.w3.org/TR/MathML2/dtd/mathml2.dtd">

<!-- Fig. 14.17: mathml2.html -->
<!-- MathML algebraic equation. -->
<math xmlns="http://www.w3.org/1998/Math/MathML">
   <mn>3</mn>
   <mo>&InvisibleTimes;</mo>
   <msup>
      <mi>x</mi>
      <mn>2</mn>
   </msup>
```

Fig. 14.17 | Algebraic equation marked up with MathML and displayed in the Firefox browser. (Part 1 of 2.)

```
14       <mo>+</mo>
15       <mn>x</mn>
16       <mo>&minus;</mo>
17       <mfrac>
18          <mn>2</mn>
19          <mi>x</mi>
20       </mfrac>
21       <mo>=</mo>
22       <mn>0</mn>
23    </math>
```

Fig. 14.17 | Algebraic equation marked up with MathML and displayed in the Firefox browser. (Part 2 of 2.)

Line 9 uses **entity reference `⁢`** to indicate a multiplication operation without explicit **symbolic representation** (i.e., the multiplication symbol does not appear between the 3 and x). For exponentiation, lines 10–13 use the `msup` element, which represents a superscript. This **`msup` element** has two children—the expression to be superscripted (i.e., the base) and the superscript (i.e., the exponent). Correspondingly, the `msub` element represents a subscript. To display variables such as x, line 11 uses **identifier element `mi`**.

To display a fraction, lines 17–20 uses the **`mfrac` element**. Lines 18–19 specify the numerator and the denominator for the fraction. If either the numerator or the denominator contains more than one element, it must appear in an `mrow` element.

Calculus Expression in MathML

Figure 14.18 marks up a calculus expression that contains an integral symbol and a square-root symbol.

```
<?xml version="1.0" encoding="iso-8859-1"?>
<!DOCTYPE math PUBLIC "-//W3C//DTD MathML 2.0//EN"
   "http://www.w3.org/TR/MathML2/dtd/mathml2.dtd">

<!-- Fig. 14.18 mathml3.html -->
<!-- Calculus example using MathML -->
<math xmlns="http://www.w3.org/1998/Math/MathML">
   <mrow>
      <msubsup>
         <mo>&int;</mo>
```

Fig. 14.18 | Calculus expression marked up with MathML and displayed in the Amaya browser. [Courtesy of World Wide Web Consortium (W3C).] (Part 1 of 2.)

```
11             <mn>0</mn>
12             <mrow>
13                <mn>1</mn>
14                <mo>&minus;</mo>
15                <mi>y</mi>
16             </mrow>
17          </msubsup>
18          <msqrt>
19             <mn>4</mn>
20             <mo>&InvisibleTimes;</mo>
21             <msup>
22                <mi>x</mi>
23                <mn>2</mn>
24             </msup>
25             <mo>+</mo>
26             <mi>y</mi>
27          </msqrt>
28          <mo>&delta;</mo>
29          <mi>x</mi>
30       </mrow>
31    </math>
```

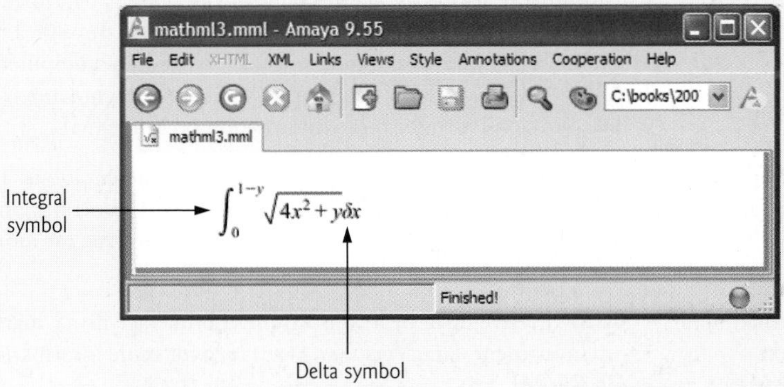

Integral symbol

Delta symbol

Fig. 14.18 | Calculus expression marked up with MathML and displayed in the Amaya browser. [Courtesy of World Wide Web Consortium (W3C).] (Part 2 of 2.)

Lines 8–30 group the entire expression in an **`mrow` element**, which is used to group elements that are positioned horizontally in an expression. The entity reference `∫` (line 10) represents the integral symbol, while the **`msubsup` element** (lines 9–17) specifies the subscript and superscript a base expression (e.g., the integral symbol). Element `mo` marks up the integral operator. The `msubsup` element requires three child elements—an operator (e.g., the integral entity, line 10), the subscript expression (line 11) and the superscript expression (lines 12–16). Element `mn` (line 11) marks up the number (i.e., `0`) that represents the subscript. Element `mrow` (lines 12–16) marks up the superscript expression (i.e., `1-`*y*).

Element **`msqrt`** (lines 18–27) represents a square-root expression. Line 28 introduces entity reference `δ` for representing a lowercase delta symbol. Delta is an operator, so line 28 places this entity in element `mo`. To see other operations and symbols in MathML, visit `www.w3.org/Math`.

14.7.2 Other Markup Languages

Literally hundreds of markup languages derive from XML. Every day developers find new uses for XML. Figure 14.20 summarizes a few of these markup languages. The website

```
www.service-architecture.com/xml/articles/index.html
```

provides a nice list of common XML vocabularies and descriptions.

Markup language	Description
Chemical Markup Language (CML)	Chemical Markup Language (CML) is an XML vocabulary for representing molecular and chemical information. Many previous methods for storing this type of information (e.g., special file types) inhibited document reuse. CML takes advantage of XML's portability to enable document authors to use and reuse molecular information without corrupting important data in the process.
VoiceXML™	The VoiceXML Forum founded by AT&T, IBM, Lucent and Motorola developed VoiceXML. It provides interactive voice communication between humans and computers through a telephone, PDA (personal digital assistant) or desktop computer. IBM's VoiceXML SDK can process VoiceXML documents. Visit `www.voicexml.org` for more information on VoiceXML.
Synchronous Multimedia Integration Language (SMIL™)	SMIL is an XML vocabulary for multimedia presentations. The W3C was the primary developer of SMIL, with contributions from some companies. Visit `www.w3.org/AudioVideo` for more on SMIL.
Research Information Exchange Markup Language (RIXML)	RIXML, developed by a consortium of brokerage firms, marks up investment data. Visit `www.rixml.org` for more information on RIXML.
Geography Markup Language (GML)	OpenGIS developed the Geography Markup Language to describe geographic information. Visit `www.opengis.org` for more information on GML.
Extensible User Interface Language (XUL)	The Mozilla Project created the Extensible User Interface Language for describing graphical user interfaces in a platform-independent way.

Fig. 14.19 | Various markup languages derived from XML.

14.8 Extensible Stylesheet Language and XSL Transformations

Extensible Stylesheet Language (XSL) documents specify how programs are to render XML document data. XSL is a group of three technologies—XSL-FO (XSL Formatting Objects), XPath (XML Path Language) and XSLT (XSL Transformations). XSL-FO is a vocabulary for specifying formatting, and XPath is a string-based language of expressions used by XML and many of its related technologies for effectively and efficiently locating structures and data (such as specific elements and attributes) in XML documents.

The third portion of XSL—XSL Transformations (XSLT)—is a technology for transforming XML documents into other documents—i.e., transforming the structure of the XML document data to another structure. XSLT provides elements that define rules for transforming one XML document to produce a different XML document. This is useful when you want to use data in multiple applications or on multiple platforms, each of which may be designed to work with documents written in a particular vocabulary. For example, XSLT allows you to convert a simple XML document to an XHTML document that presents the XML document's data (or a subset of the data) formatted for display in a web browser.

Transforming an XML document using XSLT involves two tree structures—the **source tree** (i.e., the XML document to be transformed) and the **result tree** (i.e., the XML document to be created). XPath is used to locate parts of the source-tree document that match **templates** defined in an **XSL style sheet**. When a match occurs (i.e., a node matches a template), the matching template executes and adds its result to the result tree. When there are no more matches, XSLT has transformed the source tree into the result tree. The XSLT does not analyze every node of the source tree; it selectively navigates the source tree using XPath's `select` and `match` attributes. For XSLT to function, the source tree must be properly structured. Schemas, DTDs and validating parsers can validate document structure before using XPath and XSLTs.

A Simple XSL Example

Figure 14.20 lists an XML document that describes various sports. The output shows the result of the transformation (specified in the XSLT template of Fig. 14.21) rendered by Internet Explorer.

To perform transformations, an XSLT processor is required. Popular XSLT processors include Microsoft's MSXML and the Apache Software Foundation's **Xalan 2** (`xml.apache.org`). The XML document in Fig. 14.20 is transformed into an XHTML document by MSXML when the document is loaded in Internet Explorer. MSXML is both an XML parser and an XSLT processor. Firefox also includes an XSLT processor.

```
<?xml version = "1.0"?>
<?xml-stylesheet type = "text/xsl" href = "sports.xsl"?>

<!-- Fig. 14.20: sports.xml -->
<!-- Sports Database -->

<sports>
   <game id = "783">
      <name>Cricket</name>

      <paragraph>
         More popular among commonwealth nations.
      </paragraph>
   </game>
```

Fig. 14.20 | XML document that describes various sports. (Part 1 of 2.)

```
15
16    <game id = "239">
17       <name>Baseball</name>
18
19       <paragraph>
20          More popular in America.
21       </paragraph>
22    </game>
23
24    <game id = "418">
25       <name>Soccer (Futbol)</name>
26
27       <paragraph>
28          Most popular sport in the world.
29       </paragraph>
30    </game>
31 </sports>
```

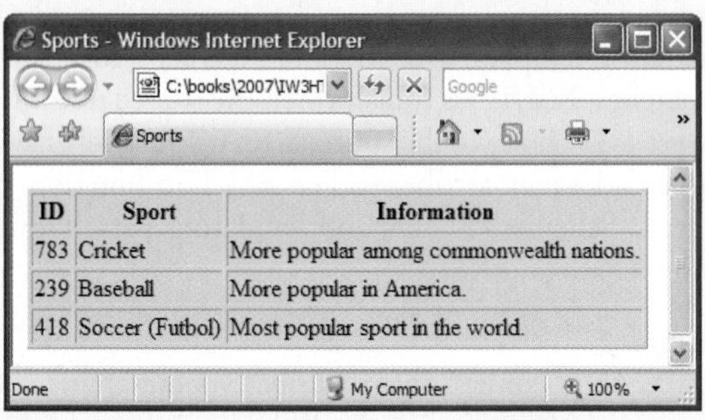

ID	Sport	Information
783	Cricket	More popular among commonwealth nations.
239	Baseball	More popular in America.
418	Soccer (Futbol)	Most popular sport in the world.

Fig. 14.20 | XML document that describes various sports. (Part 2 of 2.)

Line 2 (Fig. 14.20) is a processing instruction (PI) that references the XSL style sheet `sports.xsl` (Fig. 14.21). A processing instruction is embedded in an XML document and provides application-specific information to whichever XML processor the application uses. In this particular case, the processing instruction specifies the location of an XSLT document with which to transform the XML document. The <? and ?> (line 2, Fig. 14.20) delimit a processing instruction, which consists of a PI target (e.g., `xml-stylesheet`) and a PI value (e.g., `type = "text/xsl" href = "sports.xsl"`). The PI value's `type` attribute specifies that `sports.xsl` is a `text/xsl` file (i.e., a text file containing XSL content). The `href` attribute specifies the name and location of the style sheet to apply—in this case, `sports.xsl` in the current directory.

Software Engineering Observation 14.5

XSL enables document authors to separate data presentation (specified in XSL documents) from data description (specified in XML documents).

Common Programming Error 14.10

You will sometimes see the XML processing instruction `<?xml-stylesheet?>` written as `<?xml:stylesheet?>` with a colon rather than a dash. The version with a colon results in an XML parsing error in Firefox.

Figure 14.21 shows the XSL document for transforming the structured data of the XML document of Fig. 14.20 into an XHTML document for presentation. By convention, XSL documents have the filename extension `.xsl`.

Lines 6–7 begin the XSL style sheet with the **`stylesheet`** start tag. Attribute **`version`** specifies the XSLT version to which this document conforms. Line 7 binds namespace prefix `xsl` to the W3C's XSLT URI (i.e., `http://www.w3.org/1999/XSL/Transform`).

```
1  <?xml version = "1.0"?>
2  <!-- Fig. 14.21: sports.xsl -->
3  <!-- A simple XSLT transformation -->
4
5  <!-- reference XSL style sheet URI -->
6  <xsl-stylesheet version = "1.0"
7     xmlns:xsl = "http://www.w3.org/1999/XSL/Transform">
8
9     <xsl:output method = "html" omit-xml-declaration = "no"
10       doctype-system =
11          "http://www.w3c.org/TR/xhtml11/DTD/xhtml1-strict.dtd"
12       doctype-public = "-//W3C//DTD XHTML 1.0 Strict//EN"/>
13
14    <xsl:template match = "/"> <!-- match root element -->
15
16    <html xmlns = "http://www.w3.org/1999/xhtml">
17       <head>
18          <title>Sports</title>
19       </head>
20
21       <body>
22          <table border = "1" bgcolor = "wheat">
23             <thead>
24                <tr>
25                   <th>ID</th>
26                   <th>Sport</th>
27                   <th>Information</th>
28                </tr>
29             </thead>
30
31             <!-- insert each name and paragraph element value -->
32             <!-- into a table row. -->
33             <xsl:for-each select = "/sports/game">
34                <tr>
35                   <td><xsl:value-of select = "@id"/></td>
36                   <td><xsl:value-of select = "name"/></td>
37                   <td><xsl:value-of select = "paragraph"/></td>
38                </tr>
39             </xsl:for-each>
40          </table>
41       </body>
42    </html>
43
44    </xsl:template>
45 </xsl:stylesheet>
```

Fig. 14.21 | XSLT that creates elements and attributes in an XHTML document.

Lines 9–12 use element `xsl:output` to write an XHTML document type declaration (`DOCTYPE`) to the result tree (i.e., the XML document to be created). The `DOCTYPE` identifies XHTML as the type of the resulting document. Attribute `method` is assigned `"html"`, which indicates that HTML is being output to the result tree. Attribute `omit-xml-declaration` specifies whether the transformation should write the XML declaration to the result tree. In this case, we do not want to omit the XML declaration, so we assign to this attribute the value `"no"`. Attributes `doctype-system` and `doctype-public` write the `DOCTYPE` DTD information to the result tree.

XSLT uses templates (i.e., `xsl:template` elements) to describe how to transform particular nodes from the source tree to the result tree. A template is applied to nodes that are specified in the required `match` attribute. Line 14 uses the `match` attribute to select the document root (i.e., the conceptual part of the document that contains the root element and everything below it) of the XML source document (i.e., `sports.xml`). The XPath character `/` (a forward slash) always selects the document root. Recall that XPath is a string-based language used to locate parts of an XML document easily. In XPath, a leading forward slash specifies that we are using absolute addressing (i.e., we are starting from the root and defining paths down the source tree). In the XML document of Fig. 14.20, the child nodes of the document root are the two processing instruction nodes (lines 1–2), the two comment nodes (lines 4–5) and the `sports` element node (lines 7–31). The template in Fig. 14.21, line 14, matches a node (i.e., the root node), so the contents of the template are now added to the result tree.

The MSXML processor writes the XHTML in lines 16–29 (Fig. 14.21) to the result tree exactly as it appears in the XSL document. Now the result tree consists of the `DOCTYPE` definition and the XHTML code from lines 16–29. Lines 33–39 use element `xsl:for-each` to iterate through the source XML document, searching for `game` elements. Attribute `select` is an XPath expression that specifies the nodes (called the node set) on which the `xsl:for-each` operates. Again, the first forward slash means that we are using absolute addressing. The forward slash between `sports` and `game` indicates that `game` is a child node of `sports`. Thus, the `xsl:for-each` finds `game` nodes that are children of the `sports` node. The XML document `sports.xml` contains only one `sports` node, which is also the document root node. After finding the elements that match the selection criteria, the `xsl:for-each` processes each element with the code in lines 34–38 (these lines produce one row in a table each time they execute) and places the result of lines 34–38 in the result tree.

Line 35 uses element `value-of` to retrieve attribute `id`'s value and place it in a `td` element in the result tree. The XPath symbol `@` specifies that `id` is an attribute node of the context node `game`. Lines 36–37 place the `name` and `paragraph` element values in `td` elements and insert them in the result tree. When an XPath expression has no beginning forward slash, the expression uses relative addressing. Omitting the beginning forward slash tells the `xsl:value-of select` statements to search for `name` and `paragraph` elements that are children of the context node, not the root node. Due to the last XPath expression selection, the current context node is `game`, which indeed has an `id` attribute, a `name` child element and a `paragraph` child element.

Using XSLT to Sort and Format Data

Figure 14.22 presents an XML document (`sorting.xml`) that marks up information about a book. Note that several elements of the markup describing the book appear out of

```
1  <?xml version = "1.0"?>
2  <?xml-stylesheet type = "text/xsl" href = "sorting.xsl"?>
3
4  <!-- Fig. 14.22: sorting.xml -->
5  <!-- XML document containing book information -->
6  <book isbn = "999-99999-9-X">
7     <title>Deitel&apos;s XML Primer</title>
8
9     <author>
10       <firstName>Jane</firstName>
11       <lastName>Blue</lastName>
12    </author>
13
14    <chapters>
15       <frontMatter>
16          <preface pages = "2" />
17          <contents pages = "5" />
18          <illustrations pages = "4" />
19       </frontMatter>
20
21       <chapter number = "3" pages = "44">Advanced XML</chapter>
22       <chapter number = "2" pages = "35">Intermediate XML</chapter>
23       <appendix number = "B" pages = "26">Parsers and Tools</appendix>
24       <appendix number = "A" pages = "7">Entities</appendix>
25       <chapter number = "1" pages = "28">XML Fundamentals</chapter>
26    </chapters>
27
28    <media type = "CD" />
29 </book>
```

Fig. 14.22 | XML document containing book information.

order (e.g., the element describing Chapter 3 appears before the element describing Chapter 2). We arranged them this way purposely to demonstrate that the XSL style sheet referenced in line 2 (`sorting.xsl`) can sort the XML file's data for presentation purposes.

Figure 14.23 presents an XSL document (`sorting.xsl`) for transforming `sorting.xml` (Fig. 14.22) to XHTML. Recall that an XSL document navigates a source tree and builds a result tree. In this example, the source tree is XML, and the output tree is XHTML. Line 14 of Fig. 14.23 matches the root element of the document in Fig. 14.22. Line 15 outputs an `html` start tag to the result tree. In line 16, the `<xsl:apply-templates/>` element specifies that the XSLT processor is to apply the `xsl:templates` defined in this XSL document to the current node's (i.e., the document root's) children. The content from the applied templates is output in the `html` element that ends at line 17.

Lines 21–84 specify a template that matches element `book`. The template indicates how to format the information contained in `book` elements of `sorting.xml` (Fig. 14.22) as XHTML.

Lines 23–24 create the title for the XHTML document. We use the `book`'s ISBN (from attribute `isbn`) and the contents of element `title` to create the string that appears in the browser window's title bar (**ISBN 999-99999-9-X - Deitel's XML Primer**).

Line 28 creates a header element that contains the book's title. Lines 29–31 create a header element that contains the book's author. Because the context node (i.e., the current

```
<?xml version = "1.0"?>

<!-- Fig. 14.23: sorting.xsl -->
<!-- Transformation of book information into XHTML -->
<xsl:stylesheet version = "1.0"
   xmlns:xsl = "http://www.w3.org/1999/XSL/Transform">

   <!-- write XML declaration and DOCTYPE DTD information -->
   <xsl:output method = "html" omit-xml-declaration = "no"
      doctype-system = "http://www.w3.org/TR/xhtml11/DTD/xhtml11.dtd"
      doctype-public = "-//W3C//DTD XHTML 1.1//EN"/>

   <!-- match document root -->
   <xsl:template match = "/">
      <html xmlns = "http://www.w3.org/1999/xhtml">
         <xsl:apply-templates/>
      </html>
   </xsl:template>

   <!-- match book -->
   <xsl:template match = "book">
      <head>
         <title>ISBN <xsl:value-of select = "@isbn"/> -
            <xsl:value-of select = "title"/></title>
      </head>

      <body>
         <h1 style = "color: blue"><xsl:value-of select = "title"/></h1>
         <h2 style = "color: blue">by
            <xsl:value-of select = "author/lastName"/>,
            <xsl:value-of select = "author/firstName"/></h2>

         <table style = "border-style: groove; background-color: wheat">

            <xsl:for-each select = "chapters/frontMatter/*">
               <tr>
                  <td style = "text-align: right">
                     <xsl:value-of select = "name()"/>
                  </td>

                  <td>
                     ( <xsl:value-of select = "@pages"/> pages )
                  </td>
               </tr>
            </xsl:for-each>

            <xsl:for-each select = "chapters/chapter">
               <xsl:sort select = "@number" data-type = "number"
                    order = "ascending"/>
               <tr>
                  <td style = "text-align: right">
                     Chapter <xsl:value-of select = "@number"/>
                  </td>
```

Fig. 14.23 | XSL document that transforms `sorting.xml` into XHTML. (Part 1 of 2.)

```

                  <td>
                     <xsl:value-of select = "text()"/>
                     ( <xsl:value-of select = "@pages"/> pages )
                  </td>
               </tr>
            </xsl:for-each>

            <xsl:for-each select = "chapters/appendix">
               <xsl:sort select = "@number" data-type = "text"
                  order = "ascending"/>
               <tr>
                  <td style = "text-align: right">
                     Appendix <xsl:value-of select = "@number"/>
                  </td>

                  <td>
                     <xsl:value-of select = "text()"/>
                     ( <xsl:value-of select = "@pages"/> pages )
                  </td>
               </tr>
            </xsl:for-each>
         </table>

         <br /><p style = "color: blue">Pages:
            <xsl:variable name = "pagecount"
               select = "sum(chapters//*/@pages)"/>
            <xsl:value-of select = "$pagecount"/>
         <br />Media Type: <xsl:value-of select = "media/@type"/></p>
      </body>
   </xsl:template>
</xsl:stylesheet>
```

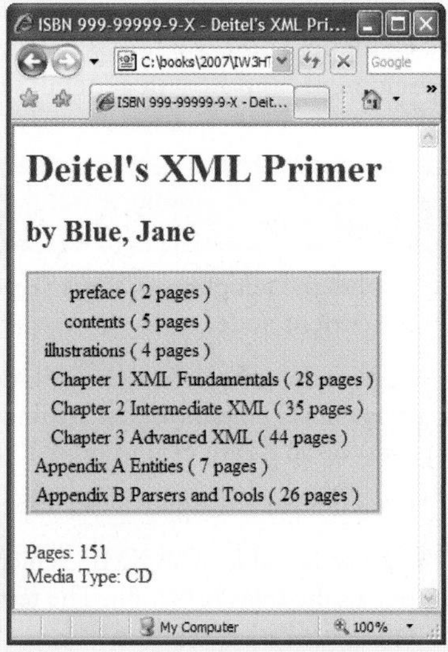

Fig. 14.23 | XSL document that transforms `sorting.xml` into XHTML. (Part 2 of 2.)

node being processed) is book, the XPath expression author/lastName selects the author's last name, and the expression author/firstName selects the author's first name.

Line 35 selects each element (indicated by an asterisk) that is a child of element frontMatter. Line 38 calls node-set function name to retrieve the current node's element name (e.g., preface). The current node is the context node specified in the xsl:for-each (line 35). Line 42 retrieves the value of the pages attribute of the current node.

Line 47 selects each chapter element. Lines 48–49 use element xsl:sort to sort chapters by number in ascending order. Attribute select selects the value of attribute number in context node chapter. Attribute data-type, with value "number", specifies a numeric sort, and attribute order, with value "ascending", specifies ascending order. Attribute data-type also accepts the value "text" (line 63), and attribute order also accepts the value "descending". Line 56 uses node-set function text to obtain the text between the chapter start and end tags (i.e., the name of the chapter). Line 57 retrieves the value of the pages attribute of the current node. Lines 62–75 perform similar tasks for each appendix.

Lines 79–80 use an XSL variable to store the value of the book's total page count and output the page count to the result tree. Attribute name specifies the variable's name (i.e., pagecount), and attribute select assigns a value to the variable. Function sum (line 80) totals the values for all page attribute values. The two slashes between chapters and * indicate a recursive descent—the MSXML processor will search for elements that contain an attribute named pages in all descendant nodes of chapters. The XPath expression

```
//*
```

selects all the nodes in an XML document. Line 81 retrieves the value of the newly created XSL variable pagecount by placing a dollar sign in front of its name.

Summary of XSL Style-Sheet Elements

This section's examples used several predefined XSL elements to perform various operations. Figure 14.24 lists these elements and several other commonly used XSL elements. For more information on these elements and XSL in general, see www.w3.org/Style/XSL.

Element	Description
<xsl:apply-templates>	Applies the templates of the XSL document to the children of the current node.
<xsl:apply-templates match = "*expression*">	Applies the templates of the XSL document to the children of *expression*. The value of the attribute match (i.e., *expression*) must be an XPath expression that specifies elements.
<xsl:template>	Contains rules to apply when a specified node is matched.
<xsl:value-of select = "*expression*">	Selects the value of an XML element and adds it to the output tree of the transformation. The required select attribute contains an XPath expression.

Fig. 14.24 | XSL style-sheet elements. (Part 1 of 2.)

Element	Description
`<xsl:for-each select = "expression">`	Applies a template to every node selected by the XPath specified by the `select` attribute.
`<xsl:sort select = "expression">`	Used as a child element of an `<xsl:apply-templates>` or `<xsl:for-each>` element. Sorts the nodes selected by the `<xsl:apply-template>` or `<xsl:for-each>` element so that the nodes are processed in sorted order.
`<xsl:output>`	Has various attributes to define the format (e.g., XML, XHTML), version (e.g., 1.0, 2.0), document type and media type of the output document. This tag is a top-level element—it can be used only as a child element of an `xml:stylesheet`.
`<xsl:copy>`	Adds the current node to the output tree.

Fig. 14.24 | XSL style-sheet elements. (Part 2 of 2.)

This section introduced Extensible Stylesheet Language (XSL) and showed how to create XSL transformations to convert XML documents from one format to another. We showed how to transform XML documents to XHTML documents for display in a web browser. Recall that these transformations are performed by MSXML, Internet Explorer's built-in XML parser and XSLT processor. In most business applications, XML documents are transferred between business partners and are transformed to other XML vocabularies programmatically. Section 14.9 discusses the XML Document Object Model (DOM) and demonstrates how to manupulate the DOM of an XML document using JavaScript.

14.9 Document Object Model (DOM)

Although an XML document is a text file, retrieving data from the document using traditional sequential file processing techniques is neither practical nor efficient, especially for adding and removing elements dynamically.

Upon successfully parsing a document, some XML parsers store document data as tree structures in memory. Figure 14.25 illustrates the tree structure for the root element of the document `article.xml` (Fig. 14.2). This hierarchical tree structure is called a Document Object Model (DOM) tree, and an XML parser that creates this type of structure is known as a DOM parser. Each element name (e.g., `article`, `date`, `firstName`) is represented by a node. A node that contains other nodes (called child nodes or children) is called a parent node (e.g., `author`). A parent node can have many children, but a child node can have only one parent node. Nodes that are peers (e.g., `firstName` and `lastName`) are called sibling nodes. A node's descendant nodes include its children, its children's children and so on. A node's ancestor nodes include its parent, its parent's parent and so on. Many of the XML DOM capabilities you'll see in this section are similar or identical to those of the XHTML DOM you learned in Chapter 12.

The DOM tree has a single root node, which contains all the other nodes in the document. For example, the root node of the DOM tree that represents `article.xml` contains a node for the XML declaration (line 1), two nodes for the comments (lines 3–4) and a node for the XML document's root element `article` (line 5).

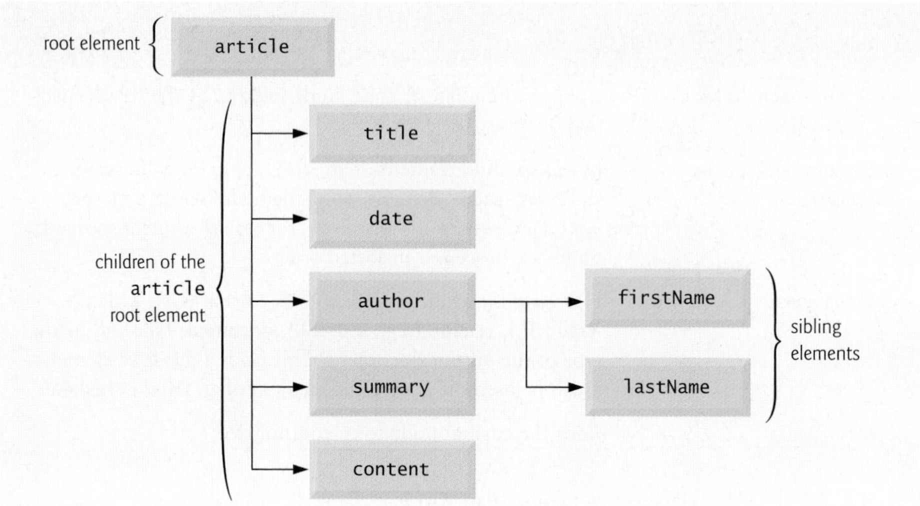

Fig. 14.25 | Tree structure for the document `article.xml` of Fig. 14.2.

To introduce document manipulation with the XML Document Object Model, we provide a scripting example (Fig. 14.26) that uses JavaScript and XML. This example loads the XML document `article.xml` (Fig. 14.2) and uses the XML DOM API to display the document's element names and values. The example also provides buttons that enable you to navigate the DOM structure. As you click each button, an appropriate part of the document is highlighted. All of this is done in a manner that enables the example to execute in both Internet Explorer 7 and Firefox 2. Figure 14.26 lists the JavaScript code that manipulates this XML document and displays its content in an XHTML page.

Overview of the **body** *Element*

Lines 203–217 create the XHTML document's `body`. When the body loads, its `onload` event calls our JavaScript function `loadXMLDocument` to load and display the contents of `article.xml` in the `div` at line 216 (`outputDiv`). Lines 204–215 define a form consisting of five buttons. When each button is pressed, it invokes one of our JavaScript functions to navigate `article.xml`'s DOM structure.

Global Script Variables

Lines 16–21 in the `script` element (lines 14–201) declare several variables used throughout the script. Variable `doc` references a DOM object representation of `article.xml`. Variable `outputHTML` stores the markup that will be placed in `outputDiv`. Variable `idCounter` is used to track the unique `id` attributes that we assign to each element in the `outputHTML` markup. These `id`s will be used to dynamically highlight parts of the document when the user clicks the buttons in the form. Variable `depth` determines the indentation level for the content in `article.xml`. We use this to structure the output using the nesting of the elements in `article.xml`. Variables `current` and `previous` track the current and previous nodes in `article.xml`'s DOM structure as the user navigates it.

```
<?xml version = "1.0" encoding = "utf-8"?>
<!DOCTYPE html PUBLIC "-//W3C//DTD XHTML 1.0 Strict//EN"
   "http://www.w3.org/TR/xhtml1/DTD/xhtml1-strict.dtd">

<!-- Fig. 14.26: XMLDOMTraversal.html -->
<!-- Traversing an XML document using the XML DOM. -->
<html xmlns = "http://www.w3.org/1999/xhtml">
<head>
   <title>Traversing an XML document using the XML DOM</title>
   <style type = "text/css">
      .highlighted { background-color: yellow }
      #outputDiv { font: 10pt "Lucida Console", monospace; }
   </style>
   <script type="text/javascript">
   <!--
   var doc; // variable to reference the XML document
   var outputHTML = ""; // stores text to output in outputDiv
   var idCounter = 1; // used to create div IDs
   var depth = -1; // tree depth is -1 to start
   var current = null; // represents the current node for traversals
   var previous = null; // represent prior node in traversals

   // load XML document based on whether the browser is IE7 or Firefox 2
   function loadXMLDocument( url )
   {
      if ( window.ActiveXObject ) // IE7
      {
         // create IE7-specific XML document object
         doc = new ActiveXObject( "Msxml2.DOMDocument.6.0" );
         doc.async = false; // specifies synchronous loading of XML doc
         doc.load( url ); // load the XML document specified by url
         buildHTML( doc.childNodes ); // display the nodes
         displayDoc();
      } // end if
      else if ( document.implementation &&
         document.implementation.createDocument ) // other browsers
      {
         // create XML document object
         doc = document.implementation.createDocument( "", "", null );
         doc.load( url ); // load the XML document specified by url
         doc.onload = function() // function to execute when doc loads
         {
            buildHTML( doc.childNodes ); // called by XML doc onload event
            displayDoc(); // display the HTML
         } // end XML document's onload event handler
      } // end else
      else // not supported
         alert( 'This script is not supported by your browser' );
   } // end function loadXMLDocument

   // traverse xmlDocument and build XHTML representation of its content
   function buildHTML( childList )
   {
```

Fig. 14.26 | Traversing an XML document using the XML DOM. (Part 1 of 8.)

```
      ++depth; // increase tab depth

      // display each node's content
      for ( var i = 0; i < childList.length; i++ )
      {
         switch ( childList[ i ].nodeType )
         {
            case 1: // Node.ELEMENT_NODE; value used for portability
               outputHTML += "<div id=\"id" + idCounter + "\">";
               spaceOutput( depth ); // insert spaces
               outputHTML += childList[ i ].nodeName; // show node's name
               ++idCounter; // increment the id counter

               // if current node has children, call buildHTML recursively
               if ( childList[ i ].childNodes.length != 0 )
                  buildHTML( childList[ i ].childNodes );

               outputHTML += "</div>";
               break;
            case 3: // Node.TEXT_NODE; value used for portability
            case 8: // Node.COMMENT_NODE; value used for portability
               // if nodeValue is not 3 or 6 spaces (Firefox issue),
               // include nodeValue in HTML
               if ( childList[ i ].nodeValue.indexOf( "   " ) == -1 &&
                  childList[ i ].nodeValue.indexOf( "      " ) == -1 )
               {
                  outputHTML += "<div id=\"id" + idCounter + "\">";
                  spaceOutput( depth ); // insert spaces
                  outputHTML += childList[ i ].nodeValue + "</div>";
                  ++idCounter; // increment the id counter
               } // end if
         } // end switch
      } // end for

      --depth; // decrease tab depth
   } // end function buildHTML

   // display the XML document and highlight the first child
   function displayDoc()
   {
      document.getElementById( "outputDiv" ).innerHTML = outputHTML;
      current = document.getElementById( 'id1' );
      setCurrentNodeStyle( current.id, true );
   } // end function displayDoc

   // insert non-breaking spaces for indentation
   function spaceOutput( number )
   {
      for ( var i = 0; i < number; i++ )
      {
         outputHTML += "   ";
      } // end for
   } // end function spaceOutput
```

Fig. 14.26 | Traversing an XML document using the XML DOM. (Part 2 of 8.)

```

      // highlight first child of current node
      function processFirstChild()
      {
         if ( current.childNodes.length == 1 && // only one child
            current.firstChild.nodeType == 3 )  // and it's a text node
         {
            alert( "There is no child node" );
         } // end if
         else if ( current.childNodes.length > 1 )
         {
            previous = current; // save currently highlighted node

            if ( current.firstChild.nodeType != 3 ) // if not text node
               current = current.firstChild; // get new current node
            else // if text node, use firstChild's nextSibling instead
               current = current.firstChild.nextSibling; // get first sibling

            setCurrentNodeStyle( previous.id, false ); // remove highlight
            setCurrentNodeStyle( current.id, true ); // add highlight
         } // end if
         else
            alert( "There is no child node" );
      } // end function processFirstChild

      // highlight next sibling of current node
      function processNextSibling()
      {
         if ( current.id != "outputDiv" && current.nextSibling )
         {
            previous = current; // save currently highlighted node
            current = current.nextSibling; // get new current node
            setCurrentNodeStyle( previous.id, false ); // remove highlight
            setCurrentNodeStyle( current.id, true ); // add highlight
         } // end if
         else
            alert( "There is no next sibling" );
      } // end function processNextSibling

      // highlight previous sibling of current node if it is not a text node
      function processPreviousSibling()
      {
         if ( current.id != "outputDiv" && current.previousSibling &&
            current.previousSibling.nodeType != 3 )
         {
            previous = current; // save currently highlighted node
            current = current.previousSibling; // get new current node
            setCurrentNodeStyle( previous.id, false ); // remove highlight
            setCurrentNodeStyle( current.id, true ); // add highlight
         } // end if
         else
            alert( "There is no previous sibling" );
      } // end function processPreviousSibling
```

Fig. 14.26 | Traversing an XML document using the XML DOM. (Part 3 of 8.)

```

    // highlight last child of current node
    function processLastChild()
    {
       if ( current.childNodes.length == 1 &&
          current.lastChild.nodeType == 3 )
       {
          alert( "There is no child node" );
       } // end if
       else if ( current.childNodes.length != 0 )
       {
          previous = current; // save currently highlighted node
          current = current.lastChild; // get new current node
          setCurrentNodeStyle( previous.id, false ); // remove highlight
          setCurrentNodeStyle( current.id, true ); // add highlight
       } // end if
       else
          alert( "There is no child node" );
    } // end function processLastChild

    // highlight parent of current node
    function processParentNode()
    {
       if ( current.parentNode.id != "body" )
       {
          previous = current; // save currently highlighted node
          current = current.parentNode; // get new current node
          setCurrentNodeStyle( previous.id, false ); // remove highlight
          setCurrentNodeStyle( current.id, true ); // add highlight
       } // end if
       else
          alert( "There is no parent node" );
    } // end function processParentNode

    // set style of node with specified id
    function setCurrentNodeStyle( id, highlight )
    {
       document.getElementById( id ).className =
          ( highlight ? "highlighted" : "" );
    } // end function setCurrentNodeStyle
    // -->
    </script>
 </head>
 <body id = "body" onload = "loadXMLDocument( 'article.xml' );">
    <form action = "" onsubmit = "return false;">
       <input type = "submit" value = "firstChild"
          onclick = "processFirstChild()"/>
       <input type = "submit" value = "nextSibling"
          onclick = "processNextSibling()"/>
       <input type = "submit" value = "previousSibling"
          onclick = "processPreviousSibling()"/>
       <input type = "submit" value = "lastChild"
          onclick = "processLastChild()"/>
```

Fig. 14.26 | Traversing an XML document using the XML DOM. (Part 4 of 8.)

```
      <input type = "submit" value = "parentNode"
         onclick = "processParentNode()"/>
   </form><br/>
   <div id = "outputDiv"></div>
</body>
</html>
```

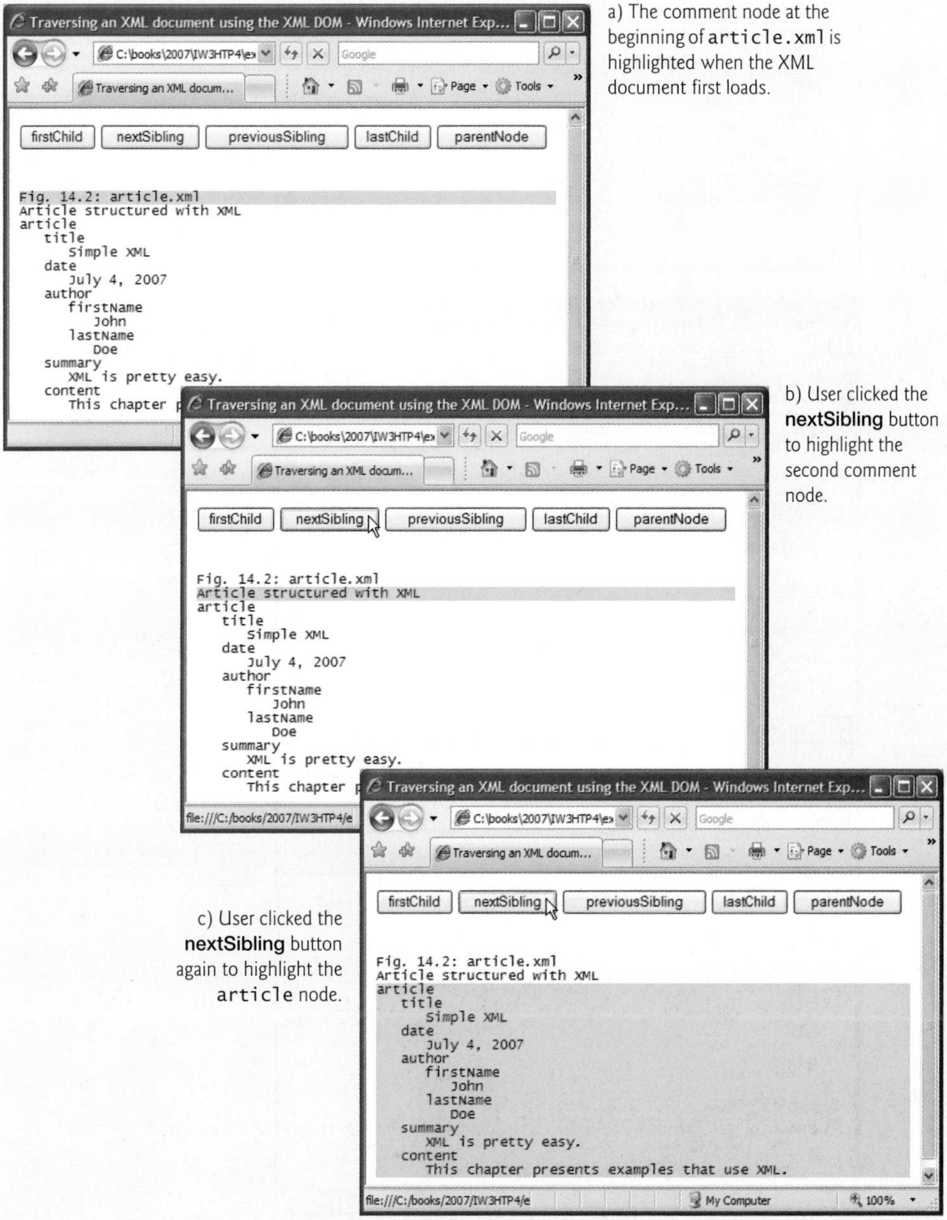

a) The comment node at the beginning of `article.xml` is highlighted when the XML document first loads.

b) User clicked the **nextSibling** button to highlight the second comment node.

c) User clicked the **nextSibling** button again to highlight the `article` node.

Fig. 14.26 | Traversing an XML document using the XML DOM. (Part 5 of 8.)

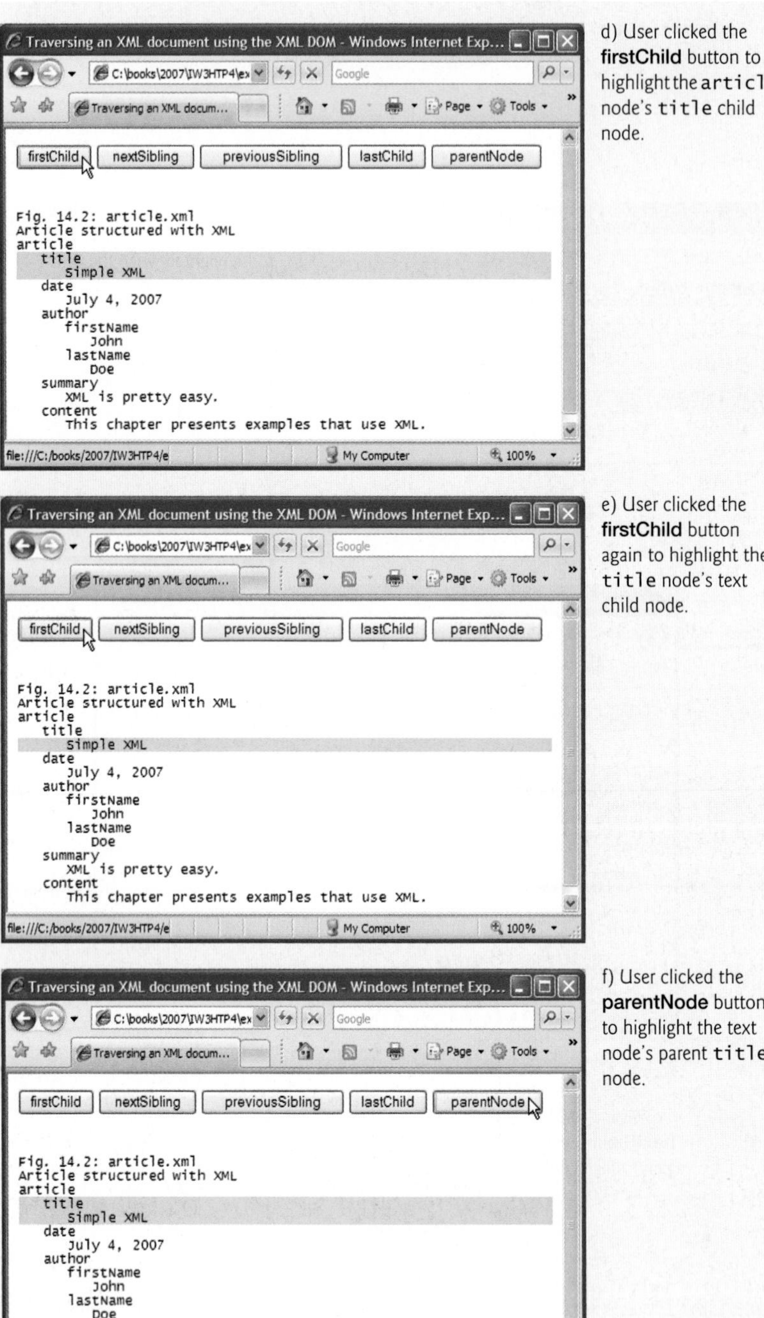

d) User clicked the **firstChild** button to highlight the `article` node's `title` child node.

e) User clicked the **firstChild** button again to highlight the `title` node's text child node.

f) User clicked the **parentNode** button to highlight the text node's parent `title` node.

Fig. 14.26 | Traversing an XML document using the XML DOM. (Part 6 of 8.)

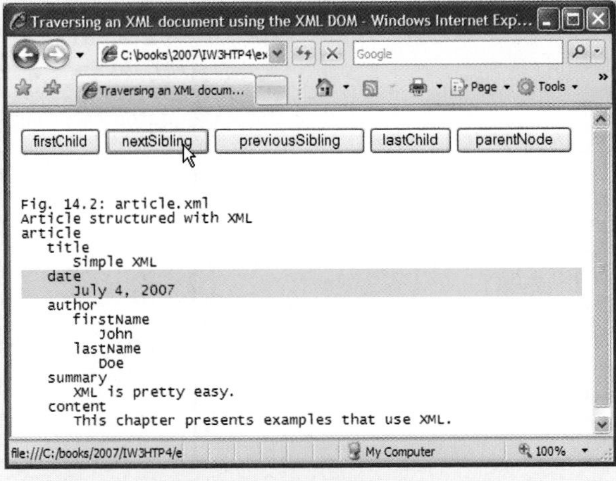

g) User clicked the **nextSibling** button to highlight the `title` node's `date` sibling node.

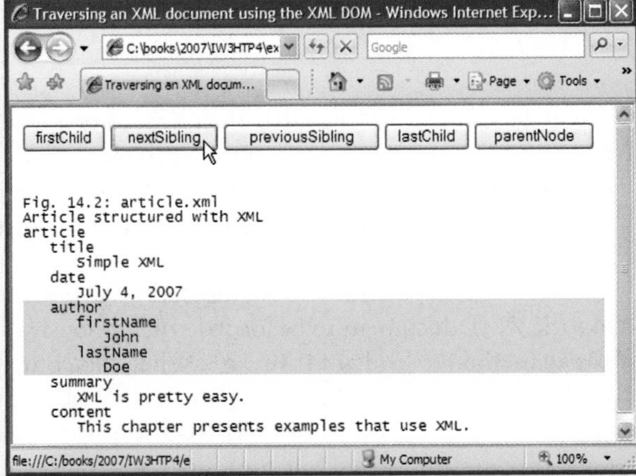

h) User clicked the **nextSibling** button to highlight the `date` node's `author` sibling node.

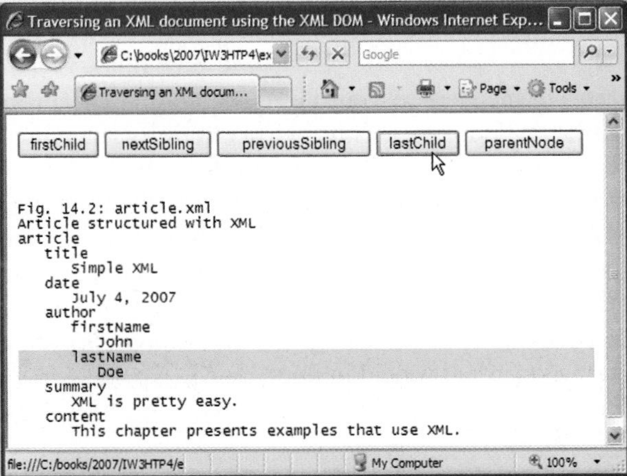

i) User clicked the **lastChild** button to highlight the `author` node's last child node (`lastName`).

Fig. 14.26 | Traversing an XML document using the XML DOM. (Part 7 of 8.)

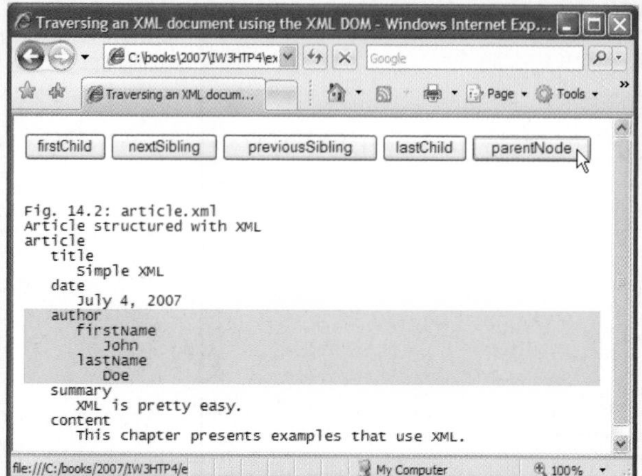

j) User clicked the **parentNode** button to highlight the `lastName` node's `author` parent node.

Fig. 14.26 | Traversing an XML document using the XML DOM. (Part 8 of 8.)

Function `loadXMLDocument`

Function `loadXMLDocument` (lines 24–49) receives the URL of an XML document to load, then loads the document based on whether the browser is Internet Explorer 7 (26–34) or Firefox 2 (lines 35–46)—the code for Firefox 2 works in several other browsers as well. Line 26 determines whether `window.ActiveXObject` exists. If so, this indicates that the browser is Internet Explorer. Line 29 creates a Microsoft `ActiveXObject` that loads Microsoft's MSXML parser, which provides capabilities for manipulating XML documents. Line 30 indicates that we'd like the XML document to be loaded synchronously, then line 31 uses the `ActiveXObject`'s `load` method to load `article.xml`. When this completes, we call our `buildHTML` method (defined in lines 52–89) to construct an XHTML representation of the XML document. The expression `doc.childNodes` is a list of the XML document's top-level nodes. Line 33 calls our `displayDoc` function (lines 92–97) to display the contents of `article.xml` in `outputDiv`.

If the browser is Firefox 2, then the `document` object's `implementation` property and the `implementation` property's `createDocument` method will exist (lines 35–36). In this case, line 39 uses the `createDocument` method to create an empty XML document object. If necessary, you can specify the XML document's namespace as the first argument and its root element as the second argument. We used empty strings for both in this example. According to the site `www.w3schools.com/xml/xml_parser.asp`, the third argument is not implemented yet, so it should always be `null`. Line 40 calls its `load` method to load `article.xml`. Firefox loads the XML document asynchronously, so you must use the XML document's `onload` property to specify a function to call (an anonymous function in this example) when the document finishes loading. When this event occurs, lines 43–44 call `buildHTML` and `displayDoc` just as we did in lines 32–33.

Common Programming Error 14.11

Attempting to process the contents of a dynamically loaded XML document in Firefox before the document's `onload` *event fires is a logic error. The document's contents are not available until the* `onload` *event fires.*

Function **buildHTML**

Function `buildHTML` (lines 52–89) is a recursive function that receives a list of nodes as an argument. Line 54 increments the `depth` for indentation purposes. Lines 57–86 iterate through the nodes in the list. The `switch` statement (lines 59–85) uses the current node's **`nodeType` property** to determine whether the current node is an element (line 61), a text node (i.e., the text content of an element; line 73) or a comment node (line 74). If it is an element, then we begin a new `div` element in our XHTML (line 62) and give it a unique `id`. Then function `spaceOutput` (defined in lines 100–106) appends **nonbreaking spaces** (` `)—i.e., spaces that the browser is not allowed to collapse or that can be used to keep words together—to indent the current element to the correct level. Line 64 appends the name of the current element using the node's **`nodeName` property**. If the current element has children, the length of the current node's `childNodes` list is nonzero and line 69 recursively calls `buildHTML` to append the current element's child nodes to the markup. When that recursive call completes, line 71 completes the `div` element that we started at line 62.

If the current element is a text node, lines 77–78 obtain the node's value with the **`nodeValue` property** and use the string method `indexOf` to determine whether the node's value starts with three or six spaces. Unfortunately, unlike MSMXL, Firefox's XML parser does not ignore the white space used for indentation in XML documents. Instead it creates text nodes containing just the space characters. The condition in lines 77–78 enables us to ignore these nodes in Firefox. If the node contains text, lines 80–82 append a new `div` to the markup and use the node's `nodeValue` property to insert that text in the `div`. Line 88 in `buildHTML` decrements the `depth` counter.

Portability Tip 14.4

Firefox's XML parser does not ignore white space used for indentation in XML documents. Instead, it creates text nodes containing the white-space characters.

Function **displayDoc**

In function `displayDoc` (lines 92–97), line 94 uses the DOM's `getElementById` method to obtain the `outputDiv` element and set its `innerHTML` property to the new markup generated by `buildHTML`. Then, line 95 sets variable `current` to refer to the `div` with `id 'id1'` in the new markup, and line 96 uses our `setCurrentNodeStyle` method (defined at lines 195–199) to highlight that `div`.

Functions **processFirstChild** *and* **processLastChild**

Function `processFirstChild` (lines 109–130) is invoked by the `onclick` event of the button at lines 205–206. If the `current` node has only one child and it's a text node (lines 111–112), line 114 displays an alert dialog indicating that there is no child node—we navigate only to nested XML elements in this example. If there are two or more children, line 118 stores the value of `current` in `previous`, and lines 120–123 set `current` to refer to its **`firstChild`** (if this child is not a text node) or its `firstChild`'s **`nextSibling`** (if the `firstChild` is a text node)—again, this is to ensure that we navigate only to nodes that represent XML elements. Then lines 125–126 unhighlight the `previous` node and highlight the new `current` node. Function `processLastChild` (lines 162–178) works similarly, using the `current` node's **`lastChild`** property.

Functions processNextSibling *and* processPreviousSibling

Function processNextSibling (lines 133–144) first ensures that the current node is not the outputDiv and that nextSibling exists. If so, lines 137–140 adjust the previous and current nodes accordingly and update their highlighting. Function processPrevious-Sibling (lines 147–159) works similarly, ensuring first that the current node is not the outputDiv, that previousSibling exists and that previousSibling is not a text node.

Function processParentNode

Function processParentNode (lines 181–192) first checks whether the current node's parentNode is the XHTML page's body. If not, lines 185–188 adjust the previous and current nodes accordingly and update their highlighting.

Common DOM Properties

The tables in Figs. 14.27–14.32 describe many common DOM properties and methods. Some of the key DOM objects are Node (a node in the tree), NodeList (an ordered set of Nodes), Document (the document), Element (an element node), Attr (an attribute node) and Text (a text node). There are many more objects, properties and methods than we can possibly list here. Our XML Resource Center (www.deitel.com/XML/) includes links to various DOM reference websites.

Property/Method	Description
nodeType	An integer representing the node type.
nodeName	The name of the node.
nodeValue	A string or null depending on the node type.
parentNode	The parent node.
childNodes	A NodeList (Fig. 14.28) with all the children of the node.
firstChild	The first child in the Node's NodeList.
lastChild	The last child in the Node's NodeList.
previousSibling	The node preceding this node; null if there is no such node.
nextSibling	The node following this node; null if there is no such node.
attributes	A collection of Attr objects (Fig. 14.31) containing the attributes for this node.
insertBefore	Inserts the node (passed as the first argument) before the existing node (passed as the second argument). If the new node is already in the tree, it is removed before insertion. The same behavior is true for other methods that add nodes.
replaceChild	Replaces the second argument node with the first argument node.
removeChild	Removes the child node passed to it.
appendChild	Appends the node it receives to the list of child nodes.

Fig. 14.27 | Common Node properties and methods.

Property/Method	Description
`item`	Method that receives an index number and returns the element node at that index. Indices range from 0 to *length* – 1. You can also access the nodes in a `NodeList` via array indexing.
`length`	The total number of nodes in the list.

Fig. 14.28 | `NodeList` property and method.

Property/Method	Description
`documentElement`	The root node of the document.
`createElement`	Creates and returns an element node with the specified tag name.
`createAttribute`	Creates and returns an `Attr` node (Fig. 14.31) with the specified name and value.
`createTextNode`	Creates and returns a text node that contains the specified text.
`getElementsByTagName`	Returns a `NodeList` of all the nodes in the subtree with the name specified as the first argument, ordered as they would be encountered in a preorder traversal. An optional second argument specifies either the direct child nodes (0) or any descendant (1).

Fig. 14.29 | `Document` properties and methods.

Property/Method	Description
`tagName`	The name of the element.
`getAttribute`	Returns the value of the specified attribute.
`setAttribute`	Changes the value of the attribute passed as the first argument to the value passed as the second argument.
`removeAttribute`	Removes the specified attribute.
`getAttributeNode`	Returns the specified attribute node.
`setAttributeNode`	Adds a new attribute node with the specified name.

Fig. 14.30 | `Element` property and methods.

Property	Description
`value`	The specified attribute's value.
`name`	The name of the attribute.

Fig. 14.31 | `Attr` properties.

Property	Description
`data`	The text contained in the node.
`length`	The number of characters contained in the node.

Fig. 14.32 | `Text` methods.

Locating Data in XML Documents with XPath

Although you can use XML DOM capabilities to navigate through and manipulate nodes, this is not the most efficient means of locating data in an XML document's DOM tree. A simpler way to locate nodes is to search for lists of nodes matching search criteria that are written as XPath expressions. Recall that XPath (XML Path Language) provides a syntax for locating specific nodes in XML documents effectively and efficiently. XPath is a string-based language of expressions used by XML and many of its related technologies (such as XSLT, discussed in Section 14.8).

Figure 14.33 enables the user to enter XPath expressions in an XHTML form. When the user clicks the **Get Matches** button, the script applies the XPath expression to the XML DOM and displays the matching nodes. Figure 14.34 shows the XML document `sports.xml` that we use in this example. [*Note:* The versions of `sports.xml` presented in Fig. 14.34 and Fig. 14.20 are nearly identical. In the current example, we do not want to apply an XSLT, so we omit the processing instruction found in line 2 of Fig. 14.20. We also removed extra blank lines to save space.]

```
<?xml version = "1.0" encoding = "utf-8"?>
<!DOCTYPE html PUBLIC "-//W3C//DTD XHTML 1.0 Strict//EN"
   "http://www.w3.org/TR/xhtml1/DTD/xhtml1-strict.dtd">

<!-- Fig. 14.33: xpath.html -->
<!-- Using XPath to locate nodes in an XML document. -->
<html xmlns = "http://www.w3.org/1999/xhtml">
<head>
   <title>Using XPath to Locate Nodes in an XML Document</title>
   <style type = "text/css">
      #outputDiv { font: 10pt "Lucida Console", monospace; }
   </style>
   <script type = "text/javascript">
   <!--
   var doc; // variable to reference the XML document
   var outputHTML = ""; // stores text to output in outputDiv
   var browser = ""; // used to determine which browser is being used

   // load XML document based on whether the browser is IE7 or Firefox 2
   function loadXMLDocument( url )
   {
      if ( window.ActiveXObject ) // IE7
      {
```

Fig. 14.33 | Using XPath to locate nodes in an XML document. (Part 1 of 3.)

```
         // create IE7-specific XML document object
         doc = new ActiveXObject( "Msxml2.DOMDocument.6.0" );
         doc.async = false; // specifies synchronous loading of XML doc
         doc.load( url ); // load the XML document specified by url
         browser = "IE7"; // set browser
      } // end if
      else if ( document.implementation &&
         document.implementation.createDocument ) // other browsers
      {
         // create XML document object
         doc = document.implementation.createDocument( "", "", null );
         doc.load( url ); // load the XML document specified by url
         browser = "FF2"; // set browser
      } // end else
      else // not supported
         alert( 'This script is not supported by your browser' );
   } // end function loadXMLDocument

   // display the XML document
   function displayDoc()
   {
      document.getElementById( "outputDiv" ).innerHTML = outputHTML;
   } // end function displayDoc

   // obtain and apply XPath expression
   function processXPathExpression()
   {
      var xpathExpression = document.getElementById( "inputField" ).value;
      outputHTML = "";

      if ( browser == "IE7" )
      {
         var result = doc.selectNodes( xpathExpression );

         for ( var i = 0; i < result.length; i++ )
            outputHTML += "<div style='clear: both'>" +
               result.item( i ).text + "</div>";
      } // end if
      else // browser == "FF2"
      {
         var result = document.evaluate( xpathExpression, doc, null,
            XPathResult.ANY_TYPE, null );
         var current = result.iterateNext();

         while ( current )
         {
            outputHTML += "<div style='clear: both'>" +
               current.textContent + "</div>";
            current = result.iterateNext();
         } // end while
      } // end else

```

Fig. 14.33 | Using XPath to locate nodes in an XML document. (Part 2 of 3.)

```
         displayDoc();
      } // end function processXPathExpression
      // -->
      </script>
   </head>
   <body id = "body" onload = "loadXMLDocument( 'sports.xml' );">
      <form action = "" onsubmit = "return false;">
         <input id = "inputField" type = "text" style = "width: 200px"/>
         <input type = "submit" value = "Get Matches"
            onclick = "processXPathExpression()"/>
      </form><br/>
      <div id = "outputDiv"></div>
   </body>
</html>
```


Fig. 14.33 | Using XPath to locate nodes in an XML document. (Part 3 of 3.)

```
<?xml version = "1.0"?>

<!-- Fig. 14.34: sports.xml -->
<!-- Sports Database        -->
<sports>
   <game id = "783">
      <name>Cricket</name>
      <paragraph>
         More popular among commonwealth nations.
      </paragraph>
   </game>
   <game id = "239">
      <name>Baseball</name>
      <paragraph>
         More popular in America.
      </paragraph>
   </game>
   <game id = "418">
      <name>Soccer (Futbol)</name>
      <paragraph>
         Most popular sport in the world.
      </paragraph>
   </game>
</sports>
```

Fig. 14.34 | XML document that describes various sports.

The program of Fig. 14.33 loads the XML document `sports.xml` (Fig. 14.34) using the same techniques we presented in Fig. 14.26, so we focus on only the new features in this example. Internet Explorer 7 (MSXML) and Firefox 2 handle XPath processing differently, so this example declares the variable `browser` (line 17) to store the browser that loaded the page. In function `loadDocument` (lines 20–40), lines 28 and 36 assign a string to variable `browser` indicating the appropriate browser.

When the `body` of this XHTML document loads, its `onload` event calls `loadDocument` (line 81) to load the `sports.xml` file. The user specifies the XPath expression in the `input` element at line 83. When the user clicks the **Get Matches** button (lines 84–85), its `onclick` event handler invokes our `processXPathExpression` function to locate any matches and display the results in `outputDiv` (line 87).

Function `processXPathExpression` (lines 49–77) first obtains the XPath expression (line 51). The `document` object's `getElementById` method returns the element with the `id` `"inputField"`; then we use its value property to get the XPath expression. Lines 54–61 apply the XPath expression in Internet Explorer 7, and lines 62–74 apply the XPath expression in Firefox 2. In IE7, the XML document object's `selectNodes` method receives an XPath expression as an argument and returns a collection of elements that match the expression. Lines 58–60 iterate through the results and mark up each one in a separate `div` element. After this loop completes, line 76 displays the generated markup in `outputDiv`.

For Firefox 2, lines 64–65 invoke the XML document object's `evaluate` method, which receives five arguments—the XPath expression, the document to apply the expression to, a namespace resolver, a result type and an `XPathResult` object into which to place the results. If the last argument is `null`, the function simply returns a new `XPathResult` object containing the matches. The namespace resolver argument can be null if you are not using XML namespace prefixes in the XPath processing. Lines 66–73 iterate through the XPathResult and mark up the results. Line 66 invokes the XPathResult's iterateNext method to position to the first result. If there is a result, the condition in line 68 will be true, and lines 70–71 create a div for that result. Line 72 then positions to the next result. After this loop completes, line 76 displays the generated markup in outputDiv.

Figure 14.35 summarizes the XPath expressions that we demonstrate in Fig. 14.33's sample outputs. For more information on using XPath in Firefox, visit the site developer.mozilla.org/en/docs/XPath. For more information on using XPath in Internet Explorer, visit msdn.microsoft.com/msdnmag/issues/0900/xml/.

Expression	Description
/sports	Matches all sports nodes that are child nodes of the document root node.
/sports/game	Matches all game nodes that are child nodes of sports, which is a child of the document root.
/sports/game/name	Matches all name nodes that are child nodes of game. The game is a child of sports, which is a child of the document root.
/sports/game/paragraph	Matches all paragraph nodes that are child nodes of game. The game is a child of sports, which is a child of the document root.
/sports/game [@id='239']	Matches the game node with the id number 239. The game is a child of sports, which is a child of the document root.
/sports/game [name='Cricket']	Matches all game nodes that contain a child element whose name is Cricket. The game is a child of sports, which is a child of the document root.

Fig. 14.35 | XPath expressions and descriptions.

14.10 RSS

RSS stands for RDF (Resource Description Framework) Site Summary and is also known as Rich Site Summary and Really Simple Syndication. RSS is an XML format used to syndicate website content, such as news articles, blog entries, product reviews, podcasts, vodcasts and more for inclusion on other websites. An RSS feed contains an rss root element with a version attribute and a channel child element with item subelements. Depending on the RSS version, the channel and item elements have certain required and optional child elements. The item elements provide the feed subscriber with a link to a web page or file, a title and description of the page or file. The most commonly used RSS feed versions are 0.91, 1.0, and 2.0, with RSS 2.0 being the most popular version. We discuss only RSS version 2.0 in this section.

RSS version 2.0, introduced in 2002, builds upon the RSS 0.9x versions. Version 2.0 does not contain length limitations or `item` element limitations of earlier versions, makes some formerly required elements optional, and adds new `channel` and `item` subelements. Removing length limitations on `item` descriptions allows RSS feeds to contain entire articles, blog entries and other web content. You can also have partial feeds that provide only a summary of the syndicated content. Partial feeds require the RSS subscriber to visit a website to view the complete content. RSS 2.0 allows `item` elements to contain an `enclosure` element providing the location of a media file that is related to the `item`. Such `enclosures` enable syndication of audio and video (such as podcasts and vodcasts) via RSS feeds.

By providing up-to-date, linkable content for anyone to use, RSS enables website developers to draw more traffic. It also allows users to get news and information from many sources easily and reduces content development time. RSS simplifies importing information from portals, weblogs and news sites. Any piece of information can be syndicated via RSS, not just news. After putting information in RSS format, an RSS program, such as a feed reader or aggregator, can check the feed for changes and react to them. For more details on RSS and for links to many RSS sites, visit our RSS Resource Center at `www.deitel.com/RSS`.

RSS 2.0 `channel` and `item` Elements

In RSS 2.0, the required child elements of `channel` are `description`, `link` and `title`, and the required child element of an `item` is either `title` or `description`. Figures 14.36–14.37 overview the child elements of `channel`s and `item`s, respectively.

Element	Description
`title`	The name of the `channel` or feed.
`link`	The URL to the website of the `channel` or feed the RSS is coming from.
`description`	A description of the `channel` or feed.
`language`	The language the `channel` is in, using W3C language values.
`copyright`	The copyright material of the `channel` or feed.
`managingEditor`	The e-mail address of the editor of the `channel` or feed.
`webMaster`	The e-mail address for the webmaster of the `channel` or feed.
`pubDate`	The date of the `channel` or feed release, using the RFC 822 Date and Time Specification—e.g., Sun, 14 Jan 2007 8:00:00 EST.
`lastBuildDate`	The last date the `channel` or feed was changed, using the RFC 822 Date and Time Specification.
`category`	The category (or several categories) of the `channel` or feed. This element has an optional `attribute` tag.
`generator`	Indicates the program that was used to generate the `channel` or feed.

Fig. 14.36 | `channel` elements and descriptions. (Part 1 of 2.)

Element	Description
`docs`	The URL of the documentation for the format used in the RSS file.
`cloud`	Specifies a SOAP web service that supports the `rssCloud` interface (`cyber.law.harvard.edu/rss/soapMeetsRss.html#rsscloudInterface`).
`ttl`	(Time To Live) A number of minutes for how long the `channel` or feed can be cached before refreshing from the source.
`image`	The GIF, JPEG or PNG image that can be displayed with the `channel` or feed. This element contains the required children `title`, `link` and `url`, and the optional children `description`, `height` and `width`.
`rating`	The PICS (Platform for Internet Content Selection) rating for the `channel` or feed.
`textInput`	Specifies a text input box to display with the `channel` or feed. This element contains the required children `title`, `name`, `link` and `description`.
`skipHours`	Tells aggregators which hours they can skip checking for new content.
`skipDays`	Tells aggregators which days they can skip checking for new content.

Fig. 14.36 | `channel` elements and descriptions. (Part 2 of 2.)

Element	Description
`title`	The title of the `item`.
`link`	The URL of the `item`.
`description`	The description of the `item`.
`author`	The e-mail address of the author of the `item`.
`category`	The category (or several categories) of the `item`. This element has an optional `attribute` tag.
`comments`	The URL of a page for comments related to the `item`.
`enclosure`	The location of a media object attached to the `item`. This element has the required attributes `type`, `url` and `length`.
`guid`	(Globally Unique Identifier) A string that uniquely identifies the `item`.
`pubDate`	The date the item was published, using the RFC 822 Date and Time Specification—e.g., Sun, 14 Jan 2007 8:00:00 EST.
`source`	The RSS channel the `item` came from. This element has a required attribute `url`.

Fig. 14.37 | `item` elements and descriptions.

Browsers and RSS Feeds

Many of the latest web browsers can now view RSS feeds, determine whether a website offers feeds, allow you to subscribe to feeds and create feed lists. An **RSS aggregator** keeps tracks of many RSS feeds and brings together information from the separate feeds. There are many RSS aggregators available, including Bloglines, BottomFeeder, FeedDemon, Microsoft Internet Explorer 7, Mozilla Firefox 2.0, My Yahoo, NewsGator and Opera 9.

To allow browsers and search engines to determine whether a web page contains an RSS feed, a `link` element can be added to the `head` of a page as follows:

```
<link rel = "alternate" type = "application/rss+xml" title = "RSS"
href = "file">
```

Many sites provide RSS feed validators. Some examples of RSS feed validators are `validator.w3.org/feed`, `feedvalidator.org`, and `www.validome.org/rss-atom/`.

Creating a Feed Aggregator

The DOM and XSL can be used to create RSS aggregators. A simple RSS aggregator uses an XSL stylesheet to format RSS feeds as XHTML. Figure 14.38 loads two XML documents—an RSS feed (a small portion of which is shown in Fig. 14.39) and an XSL style sheet—then uses JavaScript to apply an XSL transformation to the RSS content and render it on the page. You'll notice as we discuss this program that there is little commonality between Internet Explorer 7 and Firefox with regard to programmatically applying XSL transformations. This is one of the reasons that JavaScript libraries have become popular in web development—they tend to hide such browser-specific issues from you. We discuss the Dojo toolkit—one of many popular JavaScript libraries—in Section 15.8. For more information on JavaScript libraries, see our JavaScript and Ajax Resource Centers (`www.deitel.com/JavaScript/` and `www.deitel.com/Ajax/`, respectively).

Determining the Browser Type and Loading the Documents

When this page first loads, lines 19–23 (Fig. 14.38) determine whether the browser is Internet Explorer 7 or Firefox 2 and store the result in variable `browser` for use throughout the script. After the body of this XHTML document loads, its `onload` event calls function `start` (lines 26–48) to load RSS and XSL files as XML documents, and to transform the RSS. Since Internet Explorer 7 can download the files synchronously, lines 30–33 perform the loading, transformation and display steps sequentially. As mentioned previously, Firefox 2 loads the files asynchronously. For this reason, line 37 starts loading the `rss.xsl` document (included with this example's code), and lines 38–46 register an `onload` event handler for that document. When the document finishes loading, line 40 begins loading the `deitel-20.xml` RSS document. Lines 41–45 register an `onload` event handler for this second document. When it finishes loading, lines 43–44 perform the transformation and display the results.

Transforming the RSS to XHTML

Function `applyTransform` (Fig. 14.38, lines 75–96) performs the browser-specific XSL transformations using the RSS document and XSL document it receives as arguments. Line 81 uses the MSXML object's built-in XSLT capabilities to apply the transformations. Method **`transformNode`** is invoked on the `rssDocument` object and receives the `xslDocument` object as an argument.

```
<?xml version = "1.0" encoding = "utf-8"?>
<!DOCTYPE html PUBLIC "-//W3C//DTD XHTML 1.0 Strict//EN"
   "http://www.w3.org/TR/xhtml1/DTD/xhtml1-strict.dtd">

<!-- Fig. 14.38: RssViewer.html -->
<!-- Simple RSS viewer. -->
<html xmlns = "http://www.w3.org/1999/xhtml">
<head>
   <title>Simple RSS Viewer</title>
   <style type = "text/css">
      #outputDiv { font: 12px Verdana, Geneva, Arial,
                   Helvetica, sans-serif; }
   </style>
   <script type = "text/javascript">
   <!--
   var browser = ""; // used to determine which browser is being used

   // is the browser Internet Explorer 7 or Firefox 2?
   if ( window.ActiveXObject ) // IE7
      browser = "IE7";
   else if ( document.implementation &&
      document.implementation.createDocument ) // FF2 and other browsers
      browser = "FF2";

   // load both the RSS feed and the XSL file to process it
   function start()
   {
      if ( browser == "IE7" )
      {
         var xsl = loadXMLDocument( 'rss.xsl' ); // load XSL file
         var rss = loadXMLDocument( 'deitel-20.xml' ); // load RSS feed
         var result = applyTransform( rss, xsl ); // apply transform
         displayTransformedRss( result ); // display feed info
      } // end if
      else if ( browser == "FF2" )
      {
         var xsl = loadXMLDocument( 'rss.xsl' ); // load XSL file
         xsl.onload = function() // function to execute when xsl loads
         {
            var rss = loadXMLDocument( 'deitel-20.xml' ); // load RSS feed
            rss.onload = function() // function to execute when rss loads
            {
               var result = applyTransform( rss, xsl ); // apply transform
               displayTransformedRss( result ); // display feed info
            } // end onload event handler for rss
         } // end onload event handler for xsl
      } // end else
   } // end function start

   // load XML document based on whether the browser is IE7 or Firefox 2
   function loadXMLDocument( url )
   {
      var doc = ""; // variable to manage loading file
```

Fig. 14.38 | Rendering an RSS feed in a web page using XSLT and JavaScript. (Part 1 of 3.)

```

      if ( browser == "IE7" ) // IE7
      {
         // create IE7-specific XML document object
         doc = new ActiveXObject( "Msxml2.DOMDocument.6.0" );
         doc.async = false; // specifies synchronous loading of XML doc
         doc.load( url ); // load the XML document specified by url
      } // end if
      else if ( browser == "FF2" ) // other browsers
      {
         // create XML document object
         doc = document.implementation.createDocument( "", "", null );
         doc.load( url ); // load the XML document specified by url
      } // end else
      else // not supported
         alert( 'This script is not supported by your browser' );

      return doc; // return the loaded document
   } // end function loadXMLDocument

   // apply XSL transformation and show results
   function applyTransform( rssDocument, xslDocument )
   {
      var result; // stores transformed RSS

      // transform the RSS feed to XHTML
      if ( browser == "IE7" )
         result = rssDocument.transformNode( xslDocument );
      else // browser == "FF2"
      {
         // create Firefox object to perform transformation
         var xsltProcessor = new XSLTProcessor();

         // specify XSL stylesheet to use in transformation
         xsltProcessor.importStylesheet( xslDocument );

         // apply the transformation
         result =
            xsltProcessor.transformToFragment( rssDocument, document );
      } // end else

      return result; // return the transformed RSS
   } // end function applyTransform

   // display the XML document and highlight the first child
   function displayTransformedRss( resultXHTML )
   {
      if ( browser == "IE7" )
         document.getElementById( "outputDiv" ).innerHTML = resultXHTML;
      else // browser == "FF2"
         document.getElementById( "outputDiv" ).appendChild(
            resultXHTML );
   } // end function displayTransformedRss
```

Fig. 14.38 | Rendering an RSS feed in a web page using XSLT and JavaScript. (Part 2 of 3.)

```
    // -->
    </script>
</head>
<body id = "body" onload = "start();">
    <div id = "outputDiv"></div>
</body>
</html>
```

Fig. 14.38 | Rendering an RSS feed in a web page using XSLT and JavaScript. (Part 3 of 3.)

```
<?xml version="1.0" encoding="utf-8"?>

<!-- Fig. 14.39: deitel-20.xml -->
<!-- RSS 2.0 feed of Deitel Resource Centers -->
<rss version="2.0">
   <channel>
      <title>
         Internet &#38; World Wide Web How to Program:
         Deitel Resource Centers
      </title>
```

Fig. 14.39 | RSS 2.0 sample feed. (Part 1 of 2.)

```
      <link>http://www.deitel.com/ResourceCenters.html</link>
      <description>
         Check out our growing network of Resource Centers that focus on
         many of today's hottest programming, Web 2.0 and technology
         topics. Start your search here for downloads, tutorials,
         documentation, books, e-books, blogs, RSS feeds, journals,
         articles, training, webcasts, podcasts, videos and more.
      </description>
      <languague>en-us</languague>
      <image>
         <url>
            http://www.deitel.com/Portals/0/deitel_transparent_smaller.png
         </url>
         <title>Deitel.com</title>
         <link>http://www.deitel.com/</link>
      </image>

      <item>
         <title>Adobe® Flex</title>
         <link>http://www.deitel.com/Flex/</link>
         <description>
            <p>
           Welcome to the Adobe® Flex™ Resource Center. Adobe Flex 2 is a
            rich Internet application (RIA) framework that allows you to
            create scalable, cross-platform, multimedia-rich applications
            for delivery within the enterprise or across the Internet.
            Start your search here for resources, downloads, tutorials,
            documentation, books, e-books, articles, blogs and more that
            will help you develop Flex applications.
            </p>
         </description>
         <category>Programming</category>
      </item>
   </channel>
</rss>
```

Fig. 14.39 | RSS 2.0 sample feed. (Part 2 of 2.)

Firefox provides built-in XSLT processing in the form of the `XSLTProcessor` object (created at line 85). After creating this object, you use its `importStylesheet` method to specify the XSL stylesheet you'd like to apply (line 88). Finally, lines 91–92 apply the transformation by invoking the `XSLTProcessor` object's `transformToFragment` method, which returns a document fragment—i.e., a piece of a document. In our case, the `rss.xsl` document transforms the RSS into an XHTML `table` element that we'll append to the `outputDiv` element in our XHTML page. The arguments to `transformToFragment` are the document to transform and the document object to which the transformed fragment will belong. To learn more about `XSLTProcessor`, visit `developer.mozilla.org/en/docs/The_XSLT/JavaScript_Interface_in_Gecko`.

In each browser's case, after the transformation, the resulting XHTML markup is assigned to variable `result` and returned from function `applyTransform`. Then function `displayTransformedRss` is called.

Displaying the XHTML Markup

Function `displayTransformedRss` (lines 99–106) displays the transformed RSS in the `outputDiv` element (line 111 in the `body`). In both Internet Explorer 7 and Firefox 2, we use the DOM method `getElementById` to obtain the `outputDiv` element. In Internet Explorer 7, the node's `innerHTML` property is used to add the table as a child of the `outputDiv` element (line 102). In Firefox, the node's `appendChild` method must be used to append the table (a document fragment) to the `outputDiv` element.

14.11 Wrap-Up

In this chapter, we studied Extensible Markup Language and several of its related technologies. We began by discussing some basic XML terminology, introducing the concepts of markup, XML vocabularies and XML parsers (validating and nonvalidating). We then demonstrated how to describe and structure data in XML, illustrating these points with examples marking up an article and a business letter.

The chapter discussed the concept of an XML namespace. You learned that each namespace has a unique name that provides a means for document authors to unambiguously refer to elements with the same name (i.e., prevent naming collisions). We presented examples of defining two namespaces in the same document, as well as setting the default namespace for a document.

We also discussed how to create DTDs and schemas for specifying and validating the structure of an XML document. We showed how to use various tools to confirm whether XML documents are valid (i.e., conform to a DTD or schema).

The chapter demonstrated how to create and use XSL documents to specify rules for converting XML documents between formats. Specifically, you learned how to format and sort XML data as XHTML for display in a web browser.

The final sections of the chapter presented more advanced uses of XML. We demonstrated how to retrieve and display data from an XML document using JavaScript. We illustrated how a Document Object Model (DOM) tree represents each element of an XML document as a node in the tree. You also learned how to traverse the DOM tree, interact with individual nodes in the DOM tree from JavaScript code, search for nodes using XPath and apply XSL transformations.

Chapter 15 begins our discussion of Rich Internet Applications (RIAs)—web applications that approximate the look, feel and usability of desktop applications. RIAs have two key attributes—performance and rich GUI. You'll learn about Ajax (Asynchronous JavaScript and XML), which uses all the concepts you've learned so far to build rich web applications. You'll see that Ajax techniques are key to the responsiveness of RIAs.

14.12 Web Resources

`www.deitel.com/XML/`

The Deitel XML Resource Center focuses on the vast amount of free XML content available online, plus some for-sale items. Start your search here for tools, downloads, tutorials, podcasts, wikis, documentation, conferences, FAQs, books, e-books, sample chapters, articles, newsgroups, forums, downloads from CNET's download.com, jobs and contract opportunities, and more that will help you develop XML applications.

Summary

Section 14.1 Introduction

- XML is a portable, widely supported, open (i.e., nonproprietary) technology for data storage and exchange.

Section 14.2 XML Basics

- XML documents are readable by both humans and machines.
- XML permits document authors to create custom markup for any type of information. This enables document authors to create entirely new markup languages that describe specific types of data, including mathematical formulas, chemical molecular structures, music and recipes.
- An XML parser is responsible for identifying components of XML documents (typically files with the `.xml` extension) and then storing those components in a data structure for manipulation.
- An XML document can optionally reference a Document Type Definition (DTD) or schema that defines the XML document's structure.
- An XML document that conforms to a DTD/schema (i.e., has the appropriate structure) is valid.
- If an XML parser (validating or nonvalidating) can process an XML document successfully, that XML document is well-formed.

Section 14.3 Structuring Data

- An XML document begins with an optional XML declaration, which identifies the document as an XML document. The `version` attribute specifies the version of XML syntax used in the document.
- XML comments begin with `<!--` and end with `-->`.
- An XML document contains text that represents its content (i.e., data) and elements that specify its structure. XML documents delimit an element with start and end tags.
- The root element of an XML document encompasses all its other elements.
- XML element names can be of any length and can contain letters, digits, underscores, hyphens and periods. However, they must begin with either a letter or an underscore, and they should not begin with "`xml`" in any combination of uppercase and lowercase letters, as this is reserved for use in the XML standards.
- When a user loads an XML document in a browser, a parser parses the document, and the browser uses a style sheet to format the data for display.
- IE and Firefox each display minus (–) or plus (+) signs next to all container elements. A minus sign indicates that all child elements are being displayed. When clicked, a minus sign becomes a plus sign (which collapses the container element and hides all the children), and vice versa.
- Data can be placed between tags or in attributes (name/value pairs that appear within the angle brackets of start tags). Elements can have any number of attributes.

Section 14.4 XML Namespaces

- XML allows document authors to create their own markup, and as a result, naming collisions (i.e., two different elements that have the same name) can occur. XML namespaces provide a means for document authors to prevent collisions.
- Each namespace prefix is bound to a uniform resource identifier (URI) that uniquely identifies the namespace. A URI is a series of characters that differentiate names. Document authors create their own namespace prefixes. Any name can be used as a namespace prefix, but the namespace prefix `xml` is reserved for use in XML standards.

- To eliminate the need to place a namespace prefix in each element, authors can specify a default namespace for an element and its children. We declare a default namespace using keyword `xmlns` with a URI (Uniform Resource Identifier) as its value.
- Document authors commonly use URLs (Uniform Resource Locators) for URIs, because domain names (e.g., `deitel.com`) in URLs must be unique.

Section 14.5 Document Type Definitions (DTDs)

- DTDs and schemas specify documents' element types and attributes, and their relationships to one another.
- DTDs and schemas enable an XML parser to verify whether an XML document is valid (i.e., its elements contain the proper attributes and appear in the proper sequence).
- A DTD expresses the set of rules for document structure using an EBNF (Extended Backus-Naur Form) grammar.
- In a DTD, an `ELEMENT` element type declaration defines the rules for an element. An `ATTLIST` attribute-list declaration defines attributes for a particular element.

Section 14.6 W3C XML Schema Documents

- Unlike DTDs, schemas do not use EBNF grammar. Instead, they use XML syntax and are themselves XML documents that programs can manipulate.
- Unlike DTDs, XML Schema documents can specify what type of data (e.g., numeric, text) an element can contain.
- An XML document that conforms to a schema document is schema valid.
- Two categories of types exist in XML Schema: simple types and complex types. Simple types cannot contain attributes or child elements; complex types can.
- Every simple type defines a restriction on an XML Schema-defined schema type or on a user-defined type.
- Complex types can have either simple content or complex content. Both simple and complex content can contain attributes, but only complex content can contain child elements.
- Whereas complex types with simple content must extend or restrict some other existing type, complex types with complex content do not have this limitation.

Section 14.7 XML Vocabularies

- XML allows authors to create their own tags to describe data precisely.
- Some of these XML vocabularies includ MathML (Mathematical Markup Language), Scalable Vector Graphics (SVG), Wireless Markup Language (WML), Extensible Business Reporting Language (XBRL), Extensible User Interface Language (XUL), Product Data Markup Language (PDML), W3C XML Schema and Extensible Stylesheet Language (XSL).
- MathML markup describes mathematical expressions for display. MathML is divided into two types of markup—content markup and presentation markup.
- Content markup provides tags that embody mathematical concepts. Content MathML allows programmers to write mathematical notation specific to different areas of mathematics.
- Presentation MathML is directed toward formatting and displaying mathematical notation. We focus on Presentation MathML in the MathML examples.
- By convention, MathML files end with the `.mml` filename extension.
- A MathML document's root node is the `math` element and its default namespace is `http://www.w3.org/1998/Math/MathML`.

- The `mn` element marks up a number. The `mo` element marks up an operator.
- Entity reference `⁢` indicates a multiplication operation without explicit symbolic representation.
- The `msup` element represents a superscript. It has two children—the expression to be superscripted (i.e., the base) and the superscript (i.e., the exponent). Correspondingly, the `msub` element represents a subscript.
- To display variables, use identifier element `mi`.
- The `mfrac` element displays a fraction. If either the numerator or the denominator contains more than one element, it must appear in an `mrow` element.
- An `mrow` element is used to group elements that are positioned horizontally in an expression.
- The entity reference `∫` represents the integral symbol.
- The `msubsup` element specifies the subscript and superscript of a symbol. It requires three child elements—an operator, the subscript expression and the superscript expression.
- Element `msqrt` represents a square-root expression.
- Entity reference `δ` represents a lowercase delta symbol.

Section 14.8 Extensible Stylesheet Language and XSL Transformations

- XSL can convert XML into any text-based document. XSL documents have the extension `.xsl`.
- XPath is a string-based language of expressions used by XML and many of its related technologies for effectively and efficiently locating structures and data (such as specific elements and attributes) in XML documents.
- XPath is used to locate parts of the source-tree document that match templates defined in an XSL style sheet. When a match occurs (i.e., a node matches a template), the matching template executes and adds its result to the result tree. When there are no more matches, XSLT has transformed the source tree into the result tree.
- The XSLT does not analyze every node of the source tree; it selectively navigates the source tree using XPath's `select` and `match` attributes.
- For XSLT to function, the source tree must be properly structured. Schemas, DTDs and validating parsers can validate document structure before using XPath and XSLTs.
- XSL style sheets can be connected directly to an XML document by adding an `xml:stylesheet` processing instruction to the XML document.
- Two tree structures are involved in transforming an XML document using XSLT—the source tree (the document being transformed) and the result tree (the result of the transformation).
- The XPath character `/` (a forward slash) always selects the document root. In XPath, a leading forward slash specifies that we are using absolute addressing.
- An XPath expression with no beginning forward slash uses relative addressing.
- XSL element `value-of` retrieves an attribute's value. The `@` symbol specifies an attribute node.
- XSL node-set function `name` retrieves the current node's element name.
- XSL node-set function `text` retrieves the text between an element's start and end tags.
- The XPath expression `//*` selects all the nodes in an XML document.

Section 14.9 Document Object Model (DOM)

- Although an XML document is a text file, retrieving data from the document using traditional sequential file processing techniques is neither practical nor efficient, especially for adding and removing elements dynamically.

- Upon successfully parsing a document, some XML parsers store document data as tree structures in memory. This hierarchical tree structure is called a Document Object Model (DOM) tree, and an XML parser that creates this type of structure is known as a DOM parser.
- Each element name is represented by a node. A node that contains other nodes is called a parent node. A parent node can have many children, but a child node can have only one parent node.
- Nodes that are peers are called sibling nodes.
- A node's descendant nodes include its children, its children's children and so on. A node's ancestor nodes include its parent, its parent's parent and so on.
- Many of the XML DOM capabilities are similar or identical to those of the XHTML DOM.
- The DOM tree has a single root node, which contains all the other nodes in the document.
- If `window.ActiveXObject` exists, the browser is Internet Explorer. An `ActiveXObject` that loads Microsoft's MSXML parser is used to manipulate XML documents in Internet Explorer.
- MSXML's `load` method loads an XML document.
- A document's `childNodes` property contains a list of the XML document's top-level nodes.
- If the browser is Firefox 2, then the `document` object's `implementation` property and the `implementation` property's `createDocument` method will exist.
- Firefox loads each XML document asynchronously, so you must use the XML document's `onload` property to specify a function to call when the document finishes loading to ensure that you can access the document's contents.
- A node's `nodeType` property contains the type of the node.
- Nonbreaking spaces (` `) are spaces that the browser is not allowed to collapse or that can be used to keep words together.
- The name of an element can be obtained by the node's `nodeName` property.
- If the currrent node has children, the length of the node's `childNodes` list is nonzero.
- The `nodeValue` property returns the value of an element.
- Node property `firstChild` refers to the first child of a given node. Similarly, `lastChild` refers to the last child of a given node.
- Node property `nextSibling` refers to the next sibling in a list of children of a particular node. Similarly, `previousSibling` refers to the current node's previous sibling.
- Property `parentNode` refers to the current node's parent node.
- A simpler way to locate nodes is to search for lists of node-matching search criteria that are written as XPath expressions.
- In IE7, the XML document object's `selectNodes` method receives an XPath expression as an argument and returns a collection of elements that match the expression.
- Firefox 2 searches for XPath matches using the XML document object's `evaluate` method, which receives five arguments—the XPath expression, the document to apply the expression to, a namespace resolver, a result type and an `XPathResult` object into which to place the results. If the last argument is `null`, the function simply returns a new `XPathResult` object containing the matches. The namespace resolver argument can be `null` if you are not using XML namespace prefixes in the XPath processing.

Section 14.10 RSS

- RSS stands for RDF (Resource Description Framework) Site Summary and is also known as Rich Site Summary and Really Simple Syndication.

- RSS is an XML format used to syndicate simple website content, such as news articles, blog entries, product reviews, podcasts, vodcasts and more.
- An RSS feed contains an `rss` root element with a `version` attribute and a `channel` child element with `item` subelements. Depending on the RSS version, the `channel` and `item` elements have certain required and optional child elements.
- The `item` elements provide the feed subscriber with a link to a web page or file, a title and description of the page or file.
- By providing up-to-date, free and linkable content for anyone to use, RSS enables website developers to draw more traffic.
- In RSS 2.0, the required child elements of `channel` are `description`, `link` and `title`, and the required child element of an `item` is either `title` or `description`.
- An RSS aggregator keeps tracks of many RSS feeds and brings together information from the separate feeds.
- Many sites provide RSS feed validators. Some examples of RSS feed validators are `validator.w3.org/feed`, `feedvalidator.org`, and `www.validome.org/rss-atom/`.
- The DOM and XSL can be used to create RSS aggregators. A simple RSS aggregator uses an XSL style sheet to format RSS feeds as XHTML.
- MSXML's built-in XSLT capabilities include method `transformNode` to apply an XSLT transformation. It is invoked on an RSS document object and receives the XSL document object as an argument.
- Firefox provides built-in XSLT processing in the form of the `XSLTProcessor` object. After creating this object, you use its `importStylesheet` method to specify the XSL style sheet you'd like to apply. Finally, you apply the transformation by invoking the `XSLTProcessor` object's `transformToFragment` method, which returns a document fragment.

Terminology

`δ` entity reference (MathML)
`⁢` entity reference (MathML)
`∫` entity reference (MathML)
` `
`.mml` filename extension for MathML documents
`/`, forward slash in end tags
`/`, XPath root selector
`<!--…-->`, XML comment tags
`<?` and `?>` XML processing instruction delimiters
`@`, XPath attribute symbol
absolute addressing (XPath)
`ActiveXObject` from Internet Explorer
`all` XML Schema element
Amaya (W3C browser)
ancestor node
`appendChild` method of a `Node`
asterisk (*) occurrence indicator
`ATTLIST` attribute-list declaration (DTD)
`Attr` object
`attribute` element
attribute in XML
attribute-list declaration
attribute value in XML
`base` attribute of element `extension`
base type (XML Schema)
`CDATA` keyword (DTD)
`channel` child element of an `rss` element
character data in XML
child element
child node (DOM tree)
`childNodes` property of a `Node`
complex content in XML Schema
`complexType` XML Schema element
container element
content
context node (XPath)
`createDocument` method of the `document` object's `implementation` property
`data-type` attribute (XPath)
default namespace

Self-Review Exercises

14.1 Which of the following are valid XML element names? (Select all that apply.)

a) `yearBorn`
b) `year.Born`
c) `year Born`
d) `year-Born1`
e) `2_year_born`
f) `_year_born_`

14.2 State which of the following statements are *true* and which are *false*. If *false*, explain why.

a) XML is a technology for creating markup languages.
b) XML markup is delimited by forward and backward slashes (/ and \).
c) All XML start tags must have corresponding end tags.
d) Parsers check an XML document's syntax.
e) XML does not support namespaces.
f) When creating XML elements, document authors must use the set of XML tags provided by the W3C.
g) The pound character (#), dollar sign (`$`), ampersand (&) and angle brackets (< and >) are examples of XML reserved characters.
h) XML is not case sensitive.
i) XML Schemas are better than DTDs, because DTDs lack a way of indicating what specific type of data (e.g., numeric, text) an element can contain and DTDs are not themselves XML documents.
j) DTDs are written using an XML vocabulary.
k) Schema is a technology for locating information in an XML document.

14.3 Fill in the blanks for each of the following:

a) ________ help prevent naming collisions.
b) ________ embed application-specific information into an XML document.
c) ________ is Microsoft's XML parser.
d) XSL element ________ writes a `DOCTYPE` to the result tree.
e) XML Schema documents have root element ________.
f) XSL element ________ is the root element in an XSL document.
g) XSL element ________ selects specific XML elements using repetition.
h) Nodes that contain other nodes are called ________ nodes.
i) Nodes that are peers are called ________ nodes.

14.4 In Fig. 14.2, we subdivided the `author` element into more detailed pieces. How might you subdivide the `date` element? Use the date May 5, 2005, as an example.

14.5 Write a processing instruction that includes style sheet `wap.xsl`.

14.6 Write an XPath expression that locates `contact` nodes in `letter.xml` (Fig. 14.4).

Answers to Self-Review Exercises

14.1 a, b, d, f. [Choice c is incorrect because it contains a space. Choice e is incorrect because the first character is a number.]

14.2 a) True. b) False. In an XML document, markup text is delimited by tags enclosed in angle brackets (< and >) with a forward slash just after the < in the end tag. c) True. d) True. e) False. XML does support namespaces. f) False. When creating tags, document authors can use any valid name but should avoid ones that begin with the reserved word `xml` (also `XML`, `Xml`, etc.). g) False. XML reserved characters include the ampersand (&), the left angle bracket (<) and the right angle bracket (>), but not `#` and `$`. h)False. XML is case sensitive. i) True. j) False. DTDs use EBNF grammar, which is not XML syntax. k) False. XPath is a technology for locating information in an XML document. XML Schema provides a means for type checking XML documents and verifying their validity.

14.3 a) Namespaces. b) Processing instructions. c) MSXML. d) `xsl:output`. e) `schema`. f) `xsl:stylesheet`. g) `xsl:for-each`. h) parent. i) sibling.

14.4

```
<date>
    <month>May</month>
    <day>5</day>
    <year>2005</year>
</date>.
```

14.5 `<?xsl:stylesheet type = "text/xsl" href = "wap.xsl"?>`

14.6 `/letter/contact.`

Exercises

14.7 (*Nutrition Information XML Document*) Create an XML document that marks up the nutrition facts for a package of Grandma White's cookies. A package of cookies has a serving size of 1 package and the following nutritional value per serving: 260 calories, 100 fat calories, 11 grams of fat, 2 grams of saturated fat, 5 milligrams of cholesterol, 210 milligrams of sodium, 36 grams of total carbohydrates, 2 grams of fiber, 15 grams of sugars and 5 grams of protein. Name this document `nutrition.xml`. Load the XML document into Internet Explorer. [*Hint:* Your markup should contain elements describing the product name, serving size/amount, calories, sodium, cholesterol, proteins, etc. Mark up each nutrition fact/ingredient listed above.]

14.8 (*Nutrition Information XML Schema*) Write an XML Schema document (`nutrition.xsd`) specifying the structure of the XML document created in Exercise 14.7.

14.9 (*Nutrition Information XSL Style Sheet*) Write an XSL style sheet for your solution to Exercise 14.7 that displays the nutritional facts in an XHTML table. Modify Fig. 14.38 to output the results.

14.10 (*Sorting XSLT Modification*) Modify Fig. 14.23 (`sorting.xsl`) to sort by the number of pages rather than by chapter number. Save the modified document as `sorting_byPage.xsl`.

14.11 Modify Fig. 14.38 to use `sorting.xml` (Fig. 14.22), `sorting.xsl` (Fig. 14.23) and `sorting_byPage.xsl` (from Exercise 14.10). Display the result of transforming `sorting.xml` using each style sheet. [*Hint:* Remove the `xml:stylesheet` processing instruction from line 2 of `sorting.xml` before attempting to transform the file programmatically.]

15

Ajax-Enabled Rich Internet Applications

OBJECTIVES

In this chapter you will learn:

- What Ajax is and why it is important for building Rich Internet Applications.
- What asynchronous requests are and how they help give web applications the feel of desktop applications.
- What the `XMLHttpRequest` object is and how it's used to create and manage asynchronous requests to servers and to receive asynchronous responses from servers.
- Methods and properties of the `XMLHttpRequest` object.
- How to use XHTML, JavaScript, CSS, XML, JSON and the DOM in Ajax applications.
- How to use Ajax frameworks and toolkits, specifically Dojo, to conveniently create robust Ajax-enabled Rich Internet Applications.
- About resources for studying Ajax-related issues such as security, performance, debugging, the "back-button problem" and more.

... the challenges are for the designers of these applications: to forget what we think we know about the limitations of the Web, and begin to imagine a wider, richer range of possibilities. It's going to be fun.
—Jesse James Garrett

Dojo is the standard library JavaScript never had.
—Alex Russell

To know how to suggest is the great art of teaching. To attain it we must be able to guess what will interest ...
—Henri-Fredreic Amiel

It is characteristic of the epistemological tradition to present us with partial scenarios and then to demand whole or categorical answers as it were.
—Avrum Stroll

O! call back yesterday, bid time return.
—William Shakespeare

Outline

15.1 Introduction

Despite the tremendous technological growth of the Internet over the past decade, the usability of web applications has lagged behind compared to that of desktop applications. Every significant interaction in a web application results in a waiting period while the application communicates over the Internet with a server. Rich Internet Applications (RIAs) are web applications that approximate the look, feel and usability of desktop applications. RIAs have two key attributes—performance and a rich GUI.

RIA performance comes from Ajax (Asynchronous JavaScript and XML), which uses client-side scripting to make web applications more responsive. Ajax applications separate client-side user interaction and server communication, and run them in parallel, reducing the delays of server-side processing normally experienced by the user.

There are many ways to implement Ajax functionality. "Raw" Ajax uses JavaScript to send asynchronous requests to the server, then updates the page using the DOM (see Section 15.5). "Raw" Ajax is best suited for creating small Ajax components that asynchronously update a section of the page. However, when writing "raw" Ajax you need to deal directly with cross-browser portability issues, making it impractical for developing large-scale applications. These portability issues are hidden by Ajax toolkits, such as Dojo (Section 15.8), Prototype, Script.aculo.us and ASP.NET Ajax, which provide powerful ready-to-use controls and functions that enrich web applications, and simplify JavaScript coding by making it cross-browser compatible.

Traditional web applications use XHTML forms (Chapter 4) to build simple and thin GUIs compared to the rich GUIs of Windows, Macintosh and desktop systems in general. We achieve rich GUI in RIAs with Ajax toolkits and with RIA environments such as Adobe's Flex (Chapter 18), Microsoft's Silverlight (Chapter 19) and JavaServer Faces (Chapters 26–27). Such toolkits and environments provide powerful ready-to-use controls and functions that enrich web applications.

Previous chapters discussed XHTML, CSS, JavaScript, dynamic HTML, the DOM and XML. This chapter uses these technologies to build Ajax-enabled web applications. The client-side of Ajax applications is written in XHTML and CSS, and uses JavaScript to add functionality to the user interface. XML is used to structure the data passed between the server and the client. We'll also use JSON (JavaScript Object Notation) for this purpose. The Ajax component that manages interaction with the server is usually implemented with JavaScript's XMLHttpRequest object—commonly abbreviated as XHR. The server processing can be implemented using any server-side technology, such as PHP, ASP. NET, JavaServer Faces and Ruby on Rails—each of which we cover in later chapters.

This chapter begins with several examples that build basic Ajax applications using JavaScript and the XMLHttpRequest object. We then build an Ajax application with a rich calendar GUI using the Dojo Ajax toolkit. In subsequent chapters, we use tools such as Adobe Flex, Microsoft Silverlight and JavaServer Faces to build RIAs using Ajax. In Chapter 24, we'll demonstrate features of the Prototype and Script.aculo.us Ajax libraries, which come with the Ruby on Rails framework (and can be downloaded separately). Prototype provides capabilities similar to Dojo. Script.aculo.us provides many "eye candy" effects that enable you to beautify your Ajax applications and create rich interfaces. In Chapter 27, we present Ajax-enabled JavaServer Faces (JSF) components. JSF uses Dojo to implement many of its client-side Ajax capabilities.

15.2 Traditional Web Applications vs. Ajax Applications

In this section, we consider the key differences between traditional web applications and Ajax-based web applications.

Traditional Web Applications

Figure 15.1 presents the typical interactions between the client and the server in a traditional web application, such as one that uses a user registration form. First, the user fills in the form's fields, then submits the form (Fig. 15.1, *Step 1*). The browser generates a request to the server, which receives the request and processes it (*Step 2*). The server generates and sends a response containing the exact page that the browser will render (*Step 3*), which causes the browser to load the new page (*Step 4*) and temporarily makes the browser window blank. Note that the client *waits* for the server to respond and *reloads the entire page* with the data from the response (*Step 4*). While such a synchronous request is being pro-

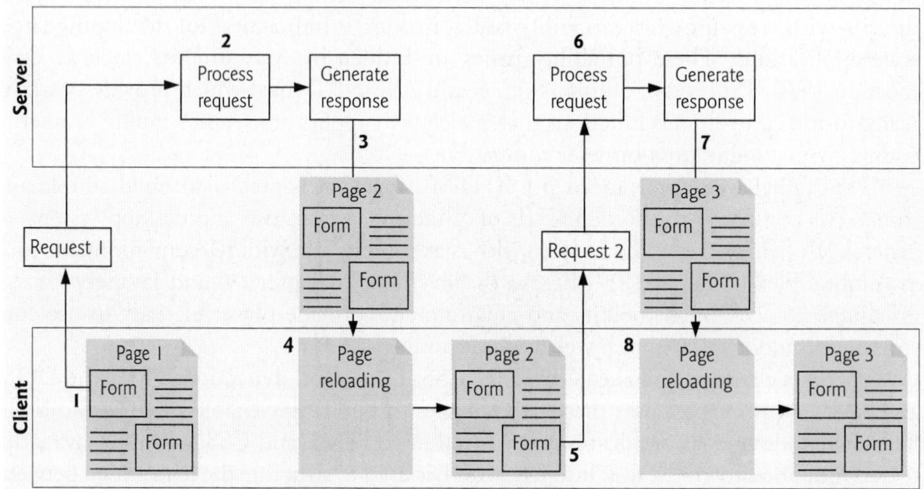

Fig. 15.1 | Classic web application reloading the page for every user interaction.

cessed on the server, the user cannot interact with the client web page. Frequent long periods of waiting, due perhaps to Internet congestion, have led some users to refer to the World Wide Web as the "World Wide Wait." If the user interacts with and submits another form, the process begins again (*Steps 5–8*).

This model was originally designed for a web of hypertext documents—what some people call the "brochure web." As the web evolved into a full-scale applications platform, the model shown in Fig. 15.1 yielded "choppy" application performance. Every full-page refresh required users to re-establish their understanding of the full-page contents. Users began to demand a model that would yield the responsive feel of desktop applications.

Ajax Web Applications

Ajax applications add a layer between the client and the server to manage communication between the two (Fig. 15.2). When the user interacts with the page, the client creates an `XMLHttpRequest` object to manage a request (*Step 1*). The `XMLHttpRequest` object sends the request to the server (*Step 2*) and awaits the response. The requests are asynchronous, so the user can continue interacting with the application on the client-side while the server processes the earlier request concurrently. Other user interactions could result in additional requests to the server (*Steps 3* and *4*). Once the server responds to the original request (*Step 5*), the `XMLHttpRequest` object that issued the request calls a client-side function to process the data returned by the server. This function—known as a callback function—uses partial page updates (*Step 6*) to display the data in the existing web page *without reloading the entire page*. At the same time, the server may be responding to the second request (*Step 7*) and the client-side may be starting to do another partial page update (*Step 8*). The callback function updates only a designated part of the page. Such partial page updates help make web applications more responsive, making them feel more like desktop applications. The web application does not load a new page while the user interacts with it.

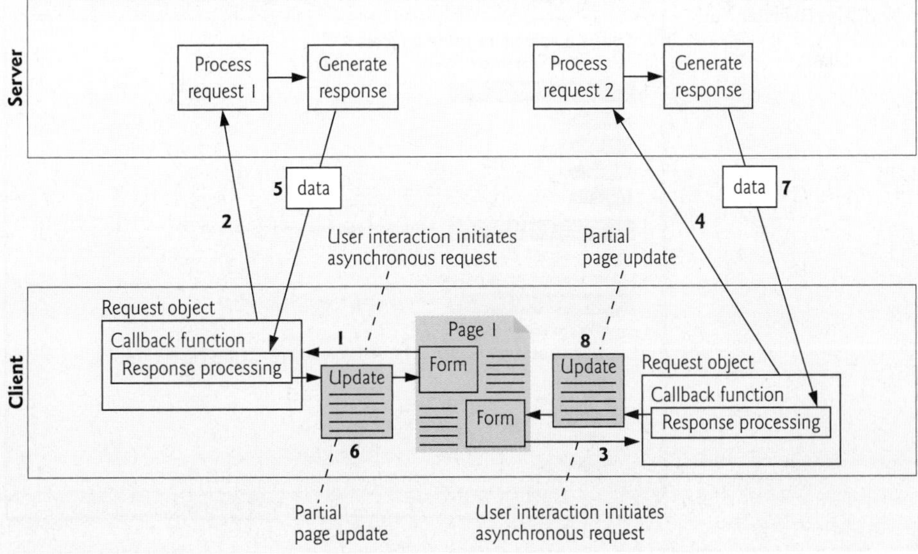

Fig. 15.2 | Ajax-enabled web application interacting with the server asynchronously.

15.3 Rich Internet Applications (RIAs) with Ajax

Ajax improves the user experience by making interactive web applications more responsive. Consider a registration form with a number of fields (e.g., first name, last name e-mail address, telephone number, etc.) and a **Register** (or **Submit**) button that sends the entered data to the server. Usually each field has rules that the user's entries have to follow (e.g., valid e-mail address, valid telephone number, etc.).

When the user clicks **Register**, a classic XHTML form sends the server all of the data to be validated (Fig. 15.3). While the server is validating the data, the user cannot interact with the page. The server finds invalid data, generates a new page identifying the errors in the form and sends it back to the client—which renders the page in the browser. Once the user fixes the errors and clicks the **Register** button, the cycle repeats until no errors are found, then the data is stored on the server. The entire page reloads every time the user submits invalid data.

Ajax-enabled forms are more interactive. Rather than sending the entire form to be validated, entries are validated dynamically as the user enters data into the fields. For example, consider a website registration form that requires a unique e-mail address. When the user enters an e-mail address into the appropriate field, then moves to the next form field to continue entering data, an asynchronous request is sent to the server to validate the e-mail address. If the e-mail address is not unique, the server sends an error message that is displayed on the page informing the user of the problem (Fig. 15.4). By sending each entry asynchronously, the user can address each invalid entry quickly, versus making edits and resubmitting the entire form repeatedly until all entries are valid. Asynchronous

a) A sample registration form in which the user has not filled in the required fields, but attempts to submit the form anyway by clicking **Register**.

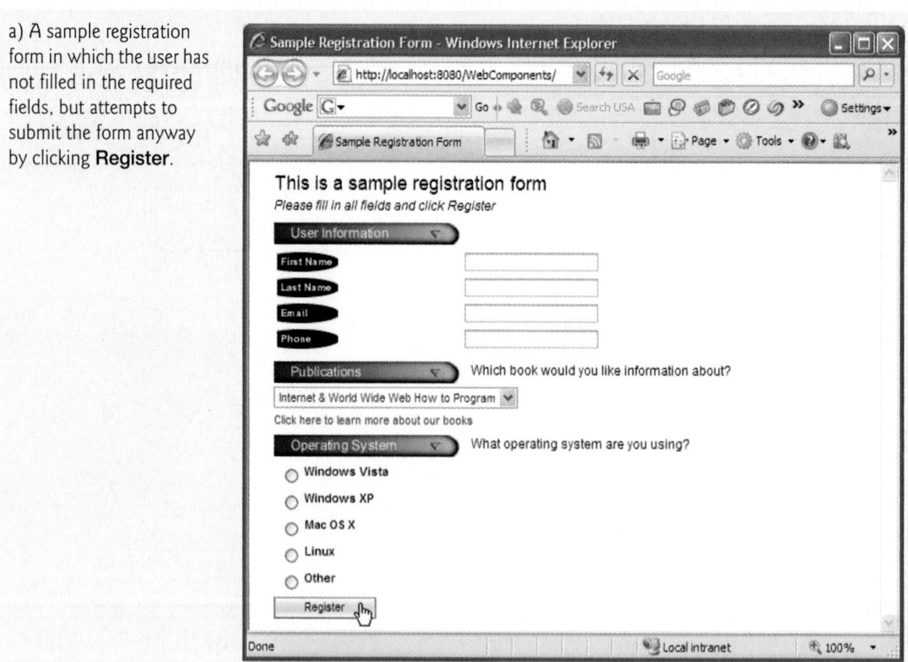

Fig. 15.3 | Classic XHTML form: User submits entire form to server, which validates the data entered (if any). Server responds indicating fields with invalid or missing data. (Part 1 of 2.)

b) The server responds by indicating all the form fields with missing or invalid data. The user must correct the problems and resubmit the entire form repeatedly until all errors are corrected.

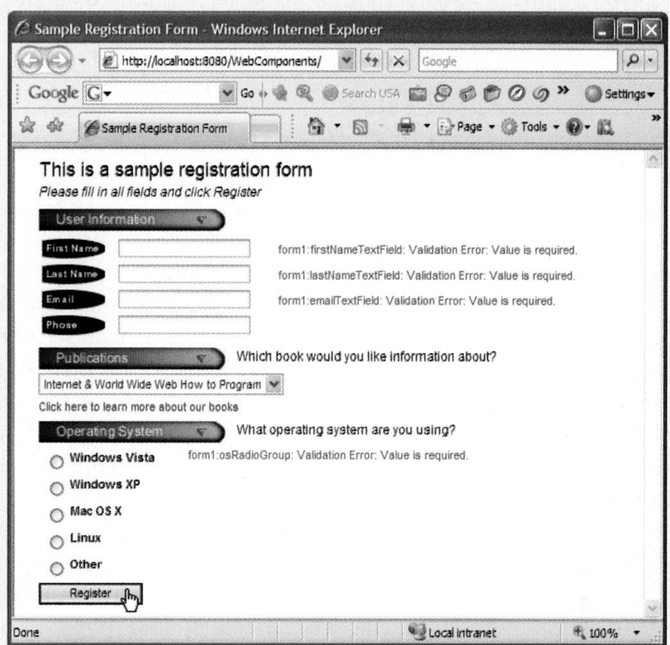

Fig. 15.3 | Classic XHTML form: User submits entire form to server, which validates the data entered (if any). Server responds indicating fields with invalid or missing data. (Part 2 of 2.)

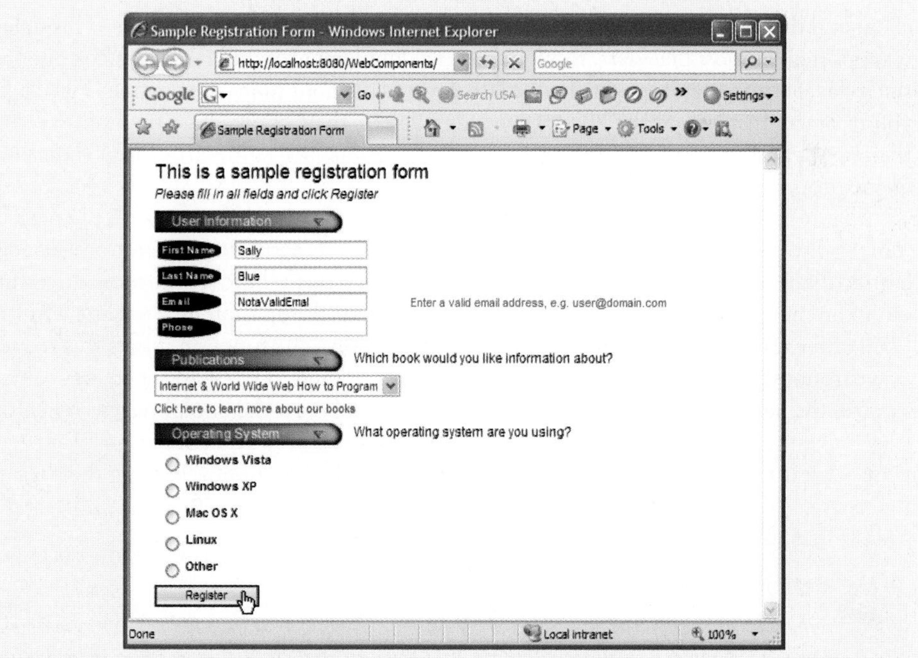

Fig. 15.4 | Ajax-enabled form shows errors asynchronously when user moves to another field.

requests could also be used to fill some fields based on previous fields (e.g., automatically filling in the "city" and "state" fields based on the zip code entered by the user).

15.4 History of Ajax

The term Ajax was coined by Jesse James Garrett of Adaptive Path in February 2005, when he was presenting the previously unnamed technology to a client. The technologies of Ajax (XHTML, JavaScript, CSS, the DOM and XML) have all existed for many years.

Asynchronous page updates can be traced back to earlier browsers. In the 1990s, Netscape's LiveScript made it possible to include scripts in web pages (e.g., web forms) that could run on the client. LiveScript evolved into JavaScript. In 1998, Microsoft introduced the `XMLHttpRequest` object to create and manage asynchronous requests and responses. Popular applications like Flickr and Google's Gmail use the `XMLHttpRequest` object to update pages dynamically. For example, Flickr uses the technology for its text editing, tagging and organizational features; Gmail continuously checks the server for new e-mail; and Google Maps allows you to drag a map in any direction, downloading the new areas on the map without reloading the entire page.

The name Ajax immediately caught on and brought attention to its component technologies. Ajax has become one of the hottest web-development technologies, enabling webtop applications to challenge the dominance of established desktop applications.

15.5 "Raw" Ajax Example Using the `XMLHttpRequest` Object

In this section, we use the `XMLHttpRequest` object to create and manage asynchronous requests. The `XMLHttpRequest` object (which resides on the client) is the layer between the client and the server that manages asynchronous requests in Ajax applications. This object is supported on most browsers, though they may implement it differently—a common issue in JavaScript programming. To initiate an asynchronous request (shown in Fig. 15.5), you create an instance of the `XMLHttpRequest` object, then use its `open` method to set up the request and its `send` method to initiate the request. We summarize the `XMLHttpRequest` properties and methods in Figs. 15.6–15.7.

Figure 15.5 presents an Ajax application in which the user interacts with the page by moving the mouse over book-cover images. We use the `onmouseover` and `onmouseout` events (discussed in Chapter 13) to trigger events when the user moves the mouse over and out of an image, respectively. The `onmouseover` event calls function `getContent` with the URL of the document containing the book's description. The function makes this request asynchronously using an `XMLHttpRequest` object. When the `XMLHttpRequest` object receives the response, the book description is displayed below the book images. When the user moves the mouse out of the image, the `onmouseout` event calls function `clearContent` to clear the display box. These tasks are accomplished without reloading the page on the client. You can test-drive this example at `test.deitel.com/examples/iw3htp4/ajax/fig15_05/SwitchContent.html`.

Performance Tip 15.1

When an Ajax application requests a file from a server, such as an XHTML document or an image, the browser typically caches that file. Subsequent requests for the same file can load it from the browser's cache rather than making the round trip to the server again.

Software Engineering Observation 15.1

For security purposes, the `XMLHttpRequest` *object doesn't allow a web application to request resources from domain names other than the one that served the application. For this reason, the web application and its resources must reside on the same web server (this could be a web server on your local computer). This is commonly known as the same origin policy (SOP). SOP aims to close a vulnerability called cross-site scripting, also known as XSS, which allows an attacker to compromise a website's security by injecting a malicious script onto the page from another domain. To learn more about XSS visit* `en.wikipedia.org/wiki/XSS`. *To get content from another domain securely, you can implement a server-side proxy—an application on the web application's web server—that can make requests to other servers on the web application's behalf.*

Asynchronous Requests

The function `getContent` (lines 19–35) sends the asynchronous request. Line 24 creates the `XMLHttpRequest` object, which manages the asynchronous request. We store the object in the global variable `asyncRequest` (declared at line 16) so that it can be accessed anywhere in the script.

```
1  <?xml version = "1.0" encoding = "utf-8"?>
2  <!DOCTYPE html PUBLIC "-//W3C//DTD XHTML 1.0 Strict//EN"
3     "http://www.w3.org/TR/xhtml1/DTD/xhtml1-strict.dtd">
4
5  <!-- Fig. 15.5: SwitchContent.html -->
6  <!-- Asynchronously display content without reloading the page. -->
7  <html xmlns = "http://www.w3.org/1999/xhtml">
8  <head>
9     <style type="text/css">
10        .box { border: 1px solid black;
11               padding: 10px }
12    </style>
13    <title>Switch Content Asynchronously</title>
14    <script type = "text/javascript" language = "JavaScript">
15       <!--
16       var asyncRequest; // variable to hold XMLHttpRequest object
17
18       // set up and send the asynchronous request
19       function getContent( url )
20       {
21          // attempt to create the XMLHttpRequest and make the request
22          try
23          {
24             asyncRequest = new XMLHttpRequest(); // create request object
25
26             // register event handler
27             asyncRequest.onreadystatechange = stateChange;
28             asyncRequest.open( 'GET', url, true ); // prepare the request
29             asyncRequest.send( null ); // send the request
30          } // end try
```

Fig. 15.5 | Asynchronously display content without reloading the page. (Part 1 of 3.)

```
         catch ( exception )
         {
            alert( 'Request failed.' );
         } // end catch
      } // end function getContent

      // displays the response data on the page
      function stateChange()
      {
         if ( asyncRequest.readyState == 4 && asyncRequest.status == 200 )
         {
            document.getElementById( 'contentArea' ).innerHTML =
               asyncRequest.responseText; // places text in contentArea
         } // end if
      } // end function stateChange

      // clear the content of the box
      function clearContent()
      {
         document.getElementById( 'contentArea' ).innerHTML = '';
      } // end function clearContent
      // -->
   </script>
</head>
<body>
   <h1>Mouse over a book for more information.</h1>
   <img src =
      "http://test.deitel.com/examples/iw3htp4/ajax/thumbs/cpphtp6.jpg"
      onmouseover = 'getContent( "cpphtp6.html" )'
      onmouseout = 'clearContent()'/>
   <img src =
      "http://test.deitel.com/examples/iw3htp4/ajax/thumbs/iw3htp4.jpg"
      onmouseover = 'getContent( "iw3htp4.html" )'
      onmouseout = 'clearContent()'/>
   <img src =
      "http://test.deitel.com/examples/iw3htp4/ajax/thumbs/jhtp7.jpg"
      onmouseover = 'getContent( "jhtp7.html" )'
      onmouseout = 'clearContent()'/>
   <img src =
      "http://test.deitel.com/examples/iw3htp4/ajax/thumbs/vbhtp3.jpg"
      onmouseover = 'getContent( "vbhtp3.html" )'
      onmouseout = 'clearContent()'/>
   <img src =
      "http://test.deitel.com/examples/iw3htp4/ajax/thumbs/vcsharphtp2.jpg"
      onmouseover = 'getContent( "vcsharphtp2.html" )'
      onmouseout = 'clearContent()'/>
   <img src =
      "http://test.deitel.com/examples/iw3htp4/ajax/thumbs/chtp5.jpg"
      onmouseover = 'getContent( "chtp5.html" )'
      onmouseout = 'clearContent()'/>
   <div class = "box" id = "contentArea"> </div>
</body>
</html>
```

Fig. 15.5 | Asynchronously display content without reloading the page. (Part 2 of 3.)

a) User hovers over *C++ How to Program* book cover image, causing an asynchronous request to the server to obtain the book's description. When the response is received, the application performs a partial page update to display the description.

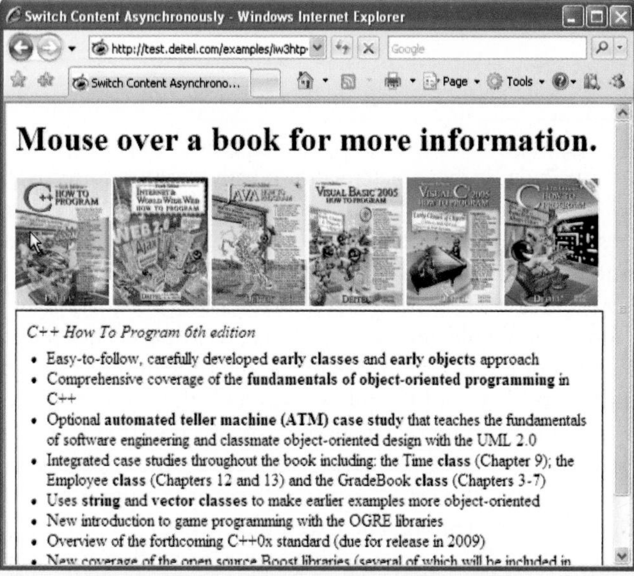

b) User hovers over *Java How to Program* book cover image, causing the process to repeat.

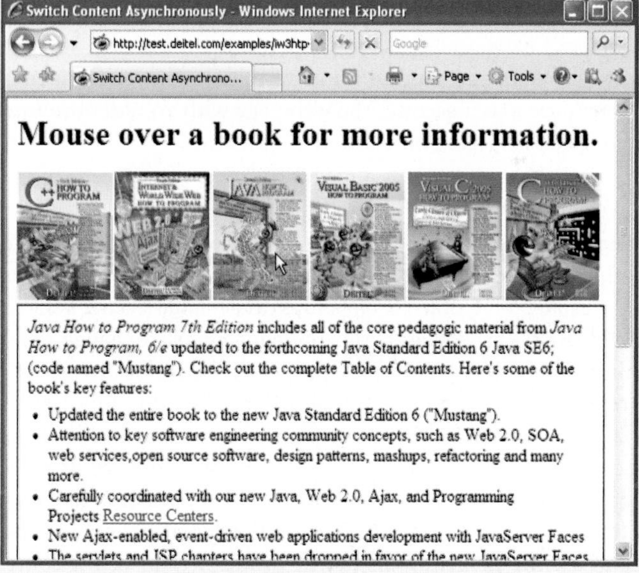

Fig. 15.5 | Asynchronously display content without reloading the page. (Part 3 of 3.)

Line 28 calls the `XMLHttpRequest` `open` method to prepare an asynchronous `GET` request. In this example, the `url` parameter specifies the address of an HTML document containing the description of a particular book. When the third argument is `true`, the request is asynchronous. The URL is passed to function `getContent` in response to the `onmouseover` event for each image. Line 29 sends the asynchronous request to the server by calling `XMLHttpRequest` `send` method. The argument `null` indicates that this request is not submitting data in the body of the request.

Exception Handling

Lines 22–34 introduce exception handling. An exception is an indication of a problem that occurs during a program's execution. The name "exception" implies that the problem occurs infrequently—if the "rule" is that a statement normally executes correctly, then the "exception to the rule" is that a problem occurs. Exception handling enables you to create applications that can resolve (or handle) exceptions—in some cases allowing a program to continue executing as if no problem had been encountered.

Lines 22–30 contain a `try` block, which encloses the code that might cause an exception and the code that should not execute if an exception occurs (i.e., if an exception occurs in a statement of the `try` block, the remaining code in the `try` block is skipped). A `try` block consists of the keyword `try` followed by a block of code enclosed in curly braces (`{}`). If there is a problem sending the request—e.g., if a user tries to access the page using an older browser that does not support `XMLHttpRequest`—the `try` block terminates immediately and a `catch` block (also called a `catch` clause or exception handler) catches (i.e., receives) and handles an exception. The `catch` block (lines 31–34) begins with the keyword `catch` and is followed by a parameter in parentheses (called the exception parameter) and a block of code enclosed in curly braces. The exception parameter's name (`exception` in this example) enables the `catch` block to interact with a caught exception object (for example, to obtain the name of the exception or an exception-specific error message via the exception object's `name` and `message` properties). In this case, we simply display our own error message `'Request Failed'` and terminate the `getContent` function. The request can fail because a user accesses the web page with an older browser or the content that is being requested is located on a different domain.

Callback Functions

The `stateChange` function (lines 38–45) is the callback function that is called when the client receives the response data. Line 27 registers function `stateChange` as the event handler for the `XMLHttpRequest` object's `onreadystatechange` event. Whenever the request makes progress, the `XMLHttpRequest` calls the `onreadystatechange` event handler. This progress is monitored by the `readyState` property, which has a value from 0 to 4. The value 0 indicates that the request is not initialized and the value 4 indicates that the request is complete—all the values for this property are summarized in Fig. 15.6. If the request completes successfully (line 40), lines 42–43 use the `XMLHttpRequest` object's `responseText` property to obtain the response data and place it in the `div` element named `contentArea` (defined at line 81). We use the DOM's `getElementById` method to get this `div` element, and use the element's `innerHTML` property to place the content in the `div`.

XMLHttpRequest Object Properties and Methods

Figures 15.6 and 15.7 summarize some of the `XMLHttpRequest` object's properties and methods, respectively. The properties are crucial to interacting with asynchronous requests. The methods initialize, configure and send asynchronous requests.

Property	Description
`onreadystatechange`	Stores the callback function—the event handler that gets called when the server responds.
`readyState`	Keeps track of the request's progress. It is usually used in the callback function to determine when the code that processes the response should be launched. The `readyState` value `0` signifies that the request is uninitialized; `1` signifies that the request is loading; `2` signifies that the request has been loaded; `3` signifies that data is actively being sent from the server; and `4` signifies that the request has been completed.
`responseText`	Text that is returned to the client by the server.
`responseXML`	If the server's response is in XML format, this property contains the XML document; otherwise, it is empty. It can be used like a `document` object in JavaScript, which makes it useful for receiving complex data (e.g. populating a table).
`status`	HTTP status code of the request. A `status` of `200` means that request was successful. A `status` of `404` means that the requested resource was not found. A status of `500` denotes that there was an error while the server was proccessing the request.
`statusText`	Additional information on the request's status. It is often used to display the error to the user when the request fails.

Fig. 15.6 | `XMLHttpRequest` object properties.

Method	Description
`open`	Initializes the request and has two mandatory parameters—method and URL. The method parameter specifies the purpose of the request—typically `GET` if the request is to take data from the server or `POST` if the request will contain a body in addition to the headers. The URL parameter specifies the address of the file on the server that will generate the response. A third optional boolean parameter specifies whether the request is asynchronous—it's set to `true` by default.
`send`	Sends the request to the sever. It has one optional parameter, `data`, which specifies the data to be POSTed to the server—it's set to `null` by default.
`setRequestHeader`	Alters the header of the request. The two parameters specify the header and its new value. It is often used to set the `content-type` field.

Fig. 15.7 | `XMLHttpRequest` object methods. (Part 1 of 2.)

Method	Description
`getResponseHeader`	Returns the header data that precedes the response body. It takes one parameter, the name of the header to retrieve. This call is often used to determine the response's type, to parse the response correctly.
`getAllResponseHeaders`	Returns an array that contains all the headers that precede the response body.
`abort`	Cancels the current request.

Fig. 15.7 | `XMLHttpRequest` object methods. (Part 2 of 2.)

15.6 Using XML and the DOM

When passing structured data between the server and the client, Ajax applications often use XML because it is easy to generate and parse. When the `XMLHttpRequest` object receives XML data, it parses and stores the data as an XML DOM object in the `responseXML` property. The example in Fig. 15.8 asynchronously requests from a server XML documents containing URLs of book-cover images, then displays the images in an HTML table. The code that configures the asynchronous request is the same as in Fig. 15.5. You can test-drive this application at `test.deitel.com/examples/iw3htp4/ajax/fig15_08/PullImagesOntoPage.html` (the book-cover images will be easier to see on the screen).

```
<?xml version = "1.0" encoding = "utf-8"?>
<!DOCTYPE html PUBLIC "-//W3C//DTD XHTML 1.0 Strict//EN"
   "http://www.w3.org/TR/xhtml1/DTD/xhtml1-strict.dtd">

<!-- Fig. 15.8: PullImagesOntoPage.html -->
<!-- Image catalog that uses Ajax to request XML data asynchronously. -->
<html xmlns = "http://www.w3.org/1999/xhtml">
<head>
<title> Pulling Images onto the Page </title>
<style type = "text/css">
   td { padding: 4px }
   img { border: 1px solid black }
</style>
<script type = "text/javascript" language = "Javascript">
   var asyncRequest; // variable to hold XMLHttpRequest object

   // set up and send the asynchronous request to the XML file
   function getImages( url )
   {
      // attempt to create the XMLHttpRequest and make the request
      try
      {
         asyncRequest = new XMLHttpRequest(); // create request object

```

Fig. 15.8 | Image catalog that uses Ajax to request XML data asynchronously. (Part 1 of 4.)

```
         // register event handler
         asyncRequest.onreadystatechange = processResponse;
         asyncRequest.open( 'GET', url, true ); // prepare the request
         asyncRequest.send( null ); // send the request
      } // end try
      catch ( exception )
      {
         alert( 'Request Failed' );
      } // end catch
   } // end function getImages

   // parses the XML response; dynamically creates a table using DOM and
   // populates it with the response data; displays the table on the page
   function processResponse()
   {
      // if request completed successfully and responseXML is non-null
      if ( asyncRequest.readyState == 4 && asyncRequest.status == 200 &&
         asyncRequest.responseXML )
      {
         clearTable(); // prepare to display a new set of images

         // get the covers from the responseXML
         var covers = asyncRequest.responseXML.getElementsByTagName(
            "cover" )

         // get base URL for the images
         var baseUrl = asyncRequest.responseXML.getElementsByTagName(
            "baseurl" ).item( 0 ).firstChild.nodeValue;

         // get the placeholder div element named covers
         var output = document.getElementById( "covers" );

         // create a table to display the images
         var imageTable = document.createElement( 'table' );

         // create the table's body
         var tableBody = document.createElement( 'tbody' );

         var rowCount = 0; // tracks number of images in current row
         var imageRow = document.createElement( "tr" ); // create row

         // place images in row
         for ( var i = 0; i < covers.length; i++ )
         {
            var cover = covers.item( i ); // get a cover from covers array

            // get the image filename
            var image = cover.getElementsByTagName( "image" ).
               item( 0 ).firstChild.nodeValue;

            // create table cell and img element to display the image
            var imageCell = document.createElement( "td" );
```

Fig. 15.8 | Image catalog that uses Ajax to request XML data asynchronously. (Part 2 of 4.)

```
            var imageTag = document.createElement( "img" );

            // set img element's src attribute
            imageTag.setAttribute( "src", baseUrl + escape( image ) );
            imageCell.appendChild( imageTag ); // place img in cell
            imageRow.appendChild( imageCell ); // place cell in row
            rowCount++; // increment number of images in row

            // if there are 6 images in the row, append the row to
            // table and start a new row
            if ( rowCount == 6 && i + 1 < covers.length )
            {
               tableBody.appendChild( imageRow );
               imageRow = document.createElement( "tr" );
               rowCount = 0;
            } // end if statement
         } // end for statement

         tableBody.appendChild( imageRow ); // append row to table body
         imageTable.appendChild( tableBody ); // append body to table
         output.appendChild( imageTable ); // append table to covers div
      } // end if
   } // end function processResponse

   // deletes the data in the table.
   function clearTable()
   {
      document.getElementById( "covers" ).innerHTML = '';
   }// end function clearTable
   </script>
</head>
<body>
   <input type = "radio" checked = "unchecked" name ="Books" value = "all"
      onclick = 'getImages( "all.xml" )'/> All Books
   <input type = "radio" checked = "unchecked"
      name = "Books" value = "simply"
      onclick = 'getImages( "simply.xml" )'/>  Simply Books
   <input type = "radio" checked = "unchecked"
      name = "Books" value = "howto"
      onclick = 'getImages( "howto.xml" )'/> How to Program Books
   <input type = "radio" checked = "unchecked"
      name = "Books" value = "dotnet"
      onclick = 'getImages( "dotnet.xml" )'/> .NET Books
   <input type = "radio" checked = "unchecked"
      name = "Books" value = "javaccpp"
      onclick = 'getImages( "javaccpp.xml" )'/> Java, C, C++ Books
   <input type = "radio" checked = "checked" name = "Books" value = "none"
      onclick = 'clearTable()'/> None
   <br/>
   <div id = "covers"></div>
</body>
</html>
```

Fig. 15.8 | Image catalog that uses Ajax to request XML data asynchronously. (Part 3 of 4.)

a) User clicks the **All Books** radio button to display all the book covers. The application sends an asynchronous request to the server to obtain an XML document containing the list of book-cover filenames. When the response is received, the application performs a partial page update to display the set of book covers.

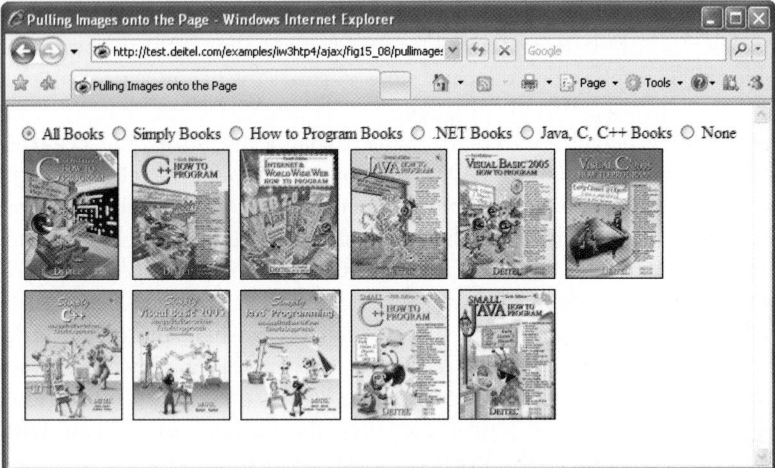

b) User clicks the **How to Program Books** radio button to select a subset of book covers to display. Application sends an asynchronous request to the server to obtain an XML document containing the appropriate subset of book-cover filenames. When the response is received, the application performs a partial page update to display the subset of book covers.

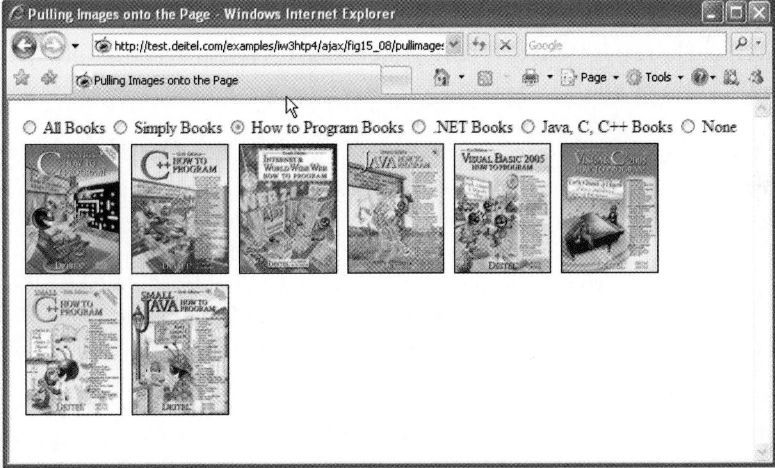

Fig. 15.8 | Image catalog that uses Ajax to request XML data asynchronously. (Part 4 of 4.)

When the `XMLHttpRequest` object receives the response, it invokes the callback function `processResponse` (lines 38–99). We use `XMLHttpRequest` object's `responseXML` property to access the XML returned by the server. Lines 41–42 check that the request was successful, and that the `responseXML` property is not empty. The XML file that we requested includes a `baseURL` node that contains the address of the image directory and a collection of `cover` nodes that contain image filenames. `responseXML` is a document object, so we can extract data from it using the XML DOM functions. Lines 47–52 use the DOM's method getElementsByTagName to extract all the image filenames from cover nodes and the URL of the directory from the baseURL node. Since the baseURL has no child nodes, we use item(0).firstChild.nodeValue to obtain the directory's address and store it in variable baseURL. The image filenames are stored in the covers array.

As in Fig. 15.5 we have a placeholder div element (line 126) to specify where the image table will be displayed on the page. Line 55 stores the div in variable output, so we can fill it with content later in the program.

Lines 58–93 generate an XHTML table dynamically, using the createElement, setAttribute and appendChild DOM methods. Method createElement creates an XHTML element of the specified type. Method setAttribute adds or changes an attribute of an XHTML element. Method appendChild inserts one XHTML element into another. Lines 58 and 61 create the table and tbody elements, respectively. We restrict each row to no more than six images, which we track with variable rowCount variable. Each iteration of the for statement (lines 67–93) obtains the filename of the image to be inserted (lines 69–73), creates a table cell element where the image will be inserted (line 76) and creates an <img> element (line 77). Line 80 sets the image's src attribute to the image's URL, which we build by concatenating the filename to the base URL of the XHTML document. Lines 81–82 insert the <img> element into the cell and the cell into the table row. When the row has six cells, it is inserted into the table and a new row is created (lines 87–92). Once all the rows have been inserted into the table, the table is inserted into the placeholder element covers that is referenced by variable output (line 97). This element is located on the bottom of the web page.

Function clearTable (lines 102–105) is called to clear images when the user switches radio buttons. The text is cleared by setting the innerHTML property of the placeholder element to the empty string.

15.7 Creating a Full-Scale Ajax-Enabled Application

Our next example demonstrates additional Ajax capabilities. The web application interacts with a web service to obtain data and to modify data in a server-side database. The web application and server communicate with a data format called JSON (JavaScript Object Notation). In addition, the application demonstrates server-side validation that occurs in parallel with the user interacting with the web application. You can test the application at test.deitel.com/examples/iw3htp4/ajax/fig15_09_10/AddressBook.html.

Using JSON

JSON (JavaScript Object Notation)—a simple way to represent JavaScript objects as strings—is an alternative way (to XML) for passing data between the client and the server. Each object in JSON is represented as a list of property names and values contained in curly braces, in the following format:

```
{ "propertyName1" : value1, "propertyName2": value2 }
```

Arrays are represented in JSON with square brackets in the following format:

```
[ value1, value2, value3 ]
```

Each value can be a string, a number, a JSON representation of an object, true, false or null. You can convert JSON strings into JavaScript objects with JavaScript's eval function. To evaluate a JSON string properly, a left parenthesis should be placed at the beginning of the string and a right parenthesis at the end of the string before the string is passed to the `eval` function.

The `eval` function creates a potential security risk—it executes any embedded JavaScript code in its string argument, possibly allowing a harmful script to be injected into JSON. A more secure way to process JSON is to use a JSON parser. In our examples, we use the open source parser from `www.json.org/js.html`. When you download its JavaScript file, place it in the same folder as your application. Then, link the `json.js` file into your XHTML file with the following statement in the `head` section:

```
<script type = "text/javascript" src = "json.js">
```

You can now call function `parseJSON` on a JSON string to convert it to a JavaScript object.

JSON strings are easier to create and parse than XML, and require fewer bytes. For these reasons, JSON is commonly used to communicate in client/server interaction. For more information on JSON, visit our JSON Resource Center at `www.deitel.com/json`.

Rich Functionality

The previous examples in this chapter requested data from static files on the server. The example in Fig. 15.9 is an address-book application that communicates with a server-side application. The application uses server-side processing to give the page the functionality and usability of a desktop application. We use JSON to encode server-side responses and to create objects on the fly.

Initially the address book loads a list of entries, each containing a first and last name (Fig. 15.9(a)). Each time the user clicks a name, the address book uses Ajax functionality to load the person's address from the server and expand the entry *without reloading the page* (Fig. 15.9(b))—and it does this *in parallel* with allowing the user to click other names. The application allows the user to search the address book by typing a last name. As the user enters each keystroke, the application asynchronously displays the list of names in which the last name starts with the characters the user has entered so far (Fig. 15.9(c), Fig. 15.9 (d) and Fig. 15.9(e))—a popular feature called **type ahead**.

```
<?xml version = "1.0" encoding = "utf-8"?>
<!DOCTYPE html PUBLIC "-//W3C//DTD XHTML 1.0 Strict//EN"
   "http://www.w3.org/TR/xhtml1/DTD/xhtml1-strict.dtd">

<!-- Fig. 15.9 addressbook.html -->
<!-- Ajax enabled address book application. -->
<html xmlns = "http://www.w3.org/1999/xhtml">
<head>
   <title>Address Book</title>
   <link rel = "stylesheet" type = "text/css" href = "address.css" />
   <script type = "text/javascript" src = "json.js"></script>
   <script type = "text/javascript">
      <!--
      // URL of the web service
      var webServiceUrl = '/AddressBookWebService/AddressService.asmx';
```

Fig. 15.9 | Ajax-enabled address-book application. (Part 1 of 10.)

```
      var phoneValid = false; // indicates if the telephone is valid
      var zipValid = false; //indicates if the zip code is valid

      // get a list of names from the server and display them
      function showAddressBook()
      {
         // hide the "addEntry" form and show the address book
         document.getElementById( 'addEntry' ).style.display = 'none';
         document.getElementById( 'addressBook' ).style.display = 'block';

         var params = "[]"; // create an empty object
         callWebService( 'getAllNames', params, parseData );
      } // end function showAddressBook

      // send the asynchronous request to the web service
      function callWebService( method, paramString, callBack )
      {
         // build request URL string
         var requestUrl = webServiceUrl + "/" + method;
         var params = paramString.parseJSON();

         // build the parameter string to add to the url
         for ( var i = 0; i < params.length; i++ )
         {
            // checks whether it is the first parameter and builds
            // the parameter string accordingly
            if ( i == 0 )
               requestUrl = requestUrl + "?" + params[ i ].param +
                  "=" + params[ i ].value; // add first parameter to url
            else
               requestUrl = requestUrl + "&" + params[ i ].param +
                  "=" + params[ i ].value; // add other parameters to url
         } // end for

         // attempt to send the asynchronous request
         try
         {
            var asyncRequest = new XMLHttpRequest(); // create request

            // set up callback function and store it
            asyncRequest.onreadystatechange = function()
            {
               callBack( asyncRequest );
            }; // end anonymous function

            // send the asynchronous request
            asyncRequest.open( 'GET', requestUrl, true );
            asyncRequest.setRequestHeader("Accept",
               "application/json; charset=utf-8" );
            asyncRequest.send(); // send request
         } // end try
```

Fig. 15.9 | Ajax-enabled address-book application. (Part 2 of 10.)

```
         catch ( exception )
         {
            alert ( 'Request Failed' );
         } // end catch
      } // end function callWebService

      // parse JSON data and display it on the page
      function parseData( asyncRequest )
      {
         // if request has completed successfully process the response
         if ( asyncRequest.readyState == 4 && asyncRequest.status == 200 )
         {
            // convert the JSON string to an Object
            var data = asyncRequest.responseText.parseJSON();
            displayNames( data ); // display data on the page
         } // end if
      } // end function parseData

      // use the DOM to display the retrieved address book entries
      function displayNames( data )
      {
         // get the placeholder element from the page
         var listBox = document.getElementById( 'Names' );
         listBox.innerHTML = ''; // clear the names on the page

         // iterate over retrieved entries and display them on the page
         for ( var i = 0; i < data.length; i++ )
         {
            // dynamically create a div element for each entry
            // and a fieldset element to place it in
            var entry = document.createElement( 'div' );
            var field = document.createElement( 'fieldset' );
            entry.onclick = handleOnClick; // set onclick event handler
            entry.id = i; // set the id
            entry.innerHTML = data[ i ].First + ' ' + data[ i ].Last;
            field.appendChild( entry ); // insert entry into the field
            listBox.appendChild( field ); // display the field
          } // end for
      } // end function displayAll

      // event handler for entry's onclick event
      function handleOnClick()
      {
         // call getAddress with the element's content as a parameter
         getAddress( eval( 'this' ), eval( 'this.innerHTML' ) );
      } // end function handleOnClick

      // search the address book for input
      // and display the results on the page
      function search( input )
      {
         // get the placeholder element and delete its content
         var listBox = document.getElementById( 'Names' );
```

Fig. 15.9 | Ajax-enabled address-book application. (Part 3 of 10.)

```
         listBox.innerHTML = ''; // clear the display box

         // if no search string is specified all the names are displayed
         if ( input == "" ) // if no search value specified
         {
            showAddressBook(); // Load the entire address book
         } // end if
         else
         {
            var params = '[{"param": "input", "value": "' + input + '"}]';
            callWebService( "search",  params , parseData );
         } // end else
      } // end function search

      // Get address data for a specific entry
      function getAddress( entry, name )
      {
         // find the address in the JSON data using the element's id
         // and display it on the page
         var firstLast = name.split(" "); // convert string to array
         var requestUrl = webServiceUrl + "/getAddress?first="
            + firstLast[ 0 ] + "&last=" + firstLast[ 1 ];

         // attempt to send an asynchronous request
         try
         {
            // create request object
            var asyncRequest = new XMLHttpRequest();

            // create a callback function with 2 parameters
            asyncRequest.onreadystatechange = function()
            {
               displayAddress( entry, asyncRequest );
            }; // end anonymous function

            asyncRequest.open( 'GET', requestUrl, true );
            asyncRequest.setRequestHeader("Accept",
            "application/json; charset=utf-8"); // set response datatype
            asyncRequest.send(); // send request
         } // end try
         catch ( exception )
         {
            alert ( 'Request Failed.' );
         } // end catch
      } // end function getAddress

      // clear the entry's data.
      function displayAddress( entry, asyncRequest )
      {
         // if request has completed successfully, process the response
         if ( asyncRequest.readyState == 4 && asyncRequest.status == 200 )
         {
```

Fig. 15.9 | Ajax-enabled address-book application. (Part 4 of 10.)

```
            // convert the JSON string to an object
            var data = asyncRequest.responseText.parseJSON();
            var name = entry.innerHTML // save the name string
            entry.innerHTML = name + '<br/>' + data.Street +
               '<br/>' + data.City + ', ' + data.State
               + ', ' + data.Zip + '<br/>' + data.Telephone;

            // clicking on the entry removes the address
            entry.onclick = function()
            {
               clearField( entry, name );
            }; // end anonymous function

         } // end if
      } // end function displayAddress

      // clear the entry's data
      function clearField( entry, name )
      {
         entry.innerHTML = name; // set the entry to display only the name
         entry.onclick = function() // set onclick event
         {
            getAddress( entry, name ); // retrieve address and display it
         }; // end function
      } // end function clearField

      // display the form that allows the user to enter more data
      function addEntry()
      {
         document.getElementById( 'addressBook' ).style.display = 'none';
         document.getElementById( 'addEntry' ).style.display = 'block';
      } // end function addEntry

      // send the zip code to be validated and to generate city and state
      function validateZip( zip )
      {
         // build parameter array
         var params = '[{"param": "zip", "value": "' + zip + '"}]';
         callWebService ( "validateZip", params, showCityState );
      } // end function validateZip

      // get city and state that were generated using the zip code
      // and display them on the page
      function showCityState( asyncRequest )
      {
         // display message while request is being processed
         document.getElementById( 'validateZip' ).
            innerHTML = "Checking zip...";

         // if request has completed successfully, process the response
         if ( asyncRequest.readyState == 4 )
         {
```

Fig. 15.9 | Ajax-enabled address-book application. (Part 5 of 10.)

```
            if ( asyncRequest.status == 200 )
            {
               // convert the JSON string to an object
               var data = asyncRequest.responseText.parseJSON();

               // update zip code validity tracker and show city and state
               if ( data.Validity == 'Valid' )
               {
                  zipValid = true; // update validity tracker

                  // display city and state
                  document.getElementById( 'validateZip' ).innerHTML = '';
                  document.getElementById( 'city' ).innerHTML = data.City;
                  document.getElementById( 'state' ).
                     innerHTML = data.State;
               } // end if
               else
               {
                  zipValid = false; // update validity tracker
                  document.getElementById( 'validateZip' ).
                     innerHTML = data.ErrorText; // display the error

                  // clear city and state values if they exist
                  document.getElementById( 'city' ).innerHTML = '';
                  document.getElementById( 'state' ).innerHTML = '';
               } // end else
            } // end if
            else if ( asyncRequest.status == 500 )
            {
               document.getElementById( 'validateZip' ).
                  innerHTML = 'Zip validation service not avaliable';
            } // end else if
         } // end if
      } // end function showCityState

      // send the telephone number to the server to validate format
      function validatePhone( phone )
      {
         var params = '[{ "param": "tel", "value": "' + phone + '"}]';
         callWebService( "validateTel", params, showPhoneError );
      } // end function validatePhone

      // show whether the telephone number has correct format
      function showPhoneError( asyncRequest )
      {
         // if request has completed successfully, process the response
         if ( asyncRequest.readyState == 4 && asyncRequest.status == 200 )
         {
            // convert the JSON string to an object
            var data = asyncRequest.responseText.parseJSON();

            if ( data.ErrorText != "Valid Telephone Format" )
            {
```

Fig. 15.9 | Ajax-enabled address-book application. (Part 6 of 10.)

```
                  phoneValid = false; // update validity tracker
               } // end if
               else
               {
                  phoneValid = true; // update validity tracker
               } // end else

               document.getElementById( 'validatePhone' ).
                  innerHTML = data.ErrorText; // display the error
            } // end if
         } // end function showPhoneError

         // enter the user's data into the database
         function saveForm()
         {
            // retrieve the data from the form
            var first = document.getElementById( 'first' ).value;
            var last = document.getElementById( 'last' ).value;
            var street = document.getElementById( 'street' ).value;
            var city = document.getElementById( 'city' ).innerHTML;
            var state = document.getElementById( 'state' ).innerHTML;
            var zip = document.getElementById( 'zip' ).value;
            var phone = document.getElementById( 'phone' ).value;

            // check if data is valid
            if ( !zipValid || !phoneValid  )
            {
               // display error message
               document.getElementById( 'success' ).innerHTML =
                  'Invalid data entered. Check form for more information';
            } // end if
            else if ( ( first == "" ) || ( last == "" ) )
            {
               // display error message
               document.getElementById( 'success').innerHTML =
                  'First Name and Last Name must have a value.';
            } // end if
            else
            {
               // hide the form and show the addressbook
               document.getElementById( 'addEntry' )
                  .style.display = 'none';
               document.getElementById( 'addressBook' ).
                  style.display = 'block';

               // build the parameter to include in the web service URL
               params = '[{"param": "first", "value": "' + first +
                  '"}, { "param": "last", "value": "' + last +
                  '"}, { "param": "street", "value": "'+ street +
                  '"}, { "param": "city", "value": "' +  city +
                  '"}, { "param":  "state", "value:": "' + state +
                  '"}, { "param": "zip", "value": "' + zip +
                  '"}, { "param": "tel", "value": "' + phone + '"}]';
```

Fig. 15.9 | Ajax-enabled address-book application. (Part 7 of 10.)

```
            // call the web service to insert data into the database
            callWebService( "addEntry", params, parseData );
         } // end else
      } // end function saveForm
      //-->
   </script>
</head>
<body onload = "showAddressBook()">
   <div>
      <input type = "button" value = "Address Book"
         onclick = "showAddressBook()"/>
      <input type = "button" value = "Add an Entry"
         onclick = "addEntry()"/>
   </div>
   <div id = "addressBook" style = "display : block;">
       Search By Last Name:
      <input onkeyup = "search( this.value )"/>
      <br/>
      <div id = "Names">
      </div>
   </div>
   <div id = "addEntry" style = "display : none">
      First Name: <input id = 'first'/>
      <br/>
      Last Name: <input id = 'last'/>
      <br/>
      <strong> Address: </strong>
      <br/>
      Street: <input id = 'street'/>
      <br/>
      City: <span id = "city" class = "validator"></span>
      <br/>
      State: <span id = "state" class = "validator"></span>
      <br/>
      Zip: <input id = 'zip' onblur = 'validateZip( this.value )'/>
      <span id = "validateZip" class = "validator">
      </span>
      <br/>
      Telephone:<input id = 'phone'
         onblur = 'validatePhone( this.value )'/>
      <span id = "validatePhone" class = "validator">
      </span>
      <br/>
      <input type = "button" value = "Submit"
         onclick = "saveForm()" />
      <br/>
      <div id = "success" class = "validator">
      </div>
   </div>
</body>
</html>
```

Fig. 15.9 | Ajax-enabled address-book application. (Part 8 of 10.)

a) Page is loaded. All the entries are displayed.

b) User clicks on an entry. The entry expands, showing the address and the telephone.

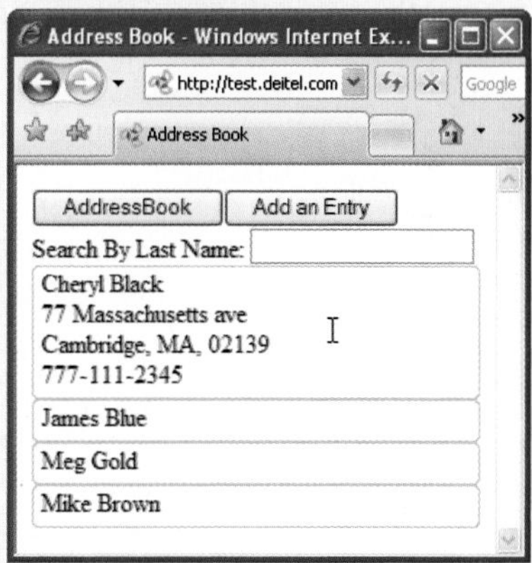

c) User types "B" in the search field. Application loads the entries whose last names start with "B".

d) User types "Bl" in the search field. Application loads the entries whose last names start with "Bl".

e) User types "Bla" in the search field. Application loads the entries whose last names start with "Bla".

f) User clicks **Add an Entry** button. The form allowing user to add an entry is displayed.

Fig. 15.9 | Ajax-enabled address-book application. (Part 9 of 10.)

g) User types in a nonexistent zip code. An error is displayed.

h) User enters a valid zip code. While the server processes it, **Checking Zip...** is displayed on the page.

i) The server finds the city and state associated with the zip code entered and displays them on the page.

j) The user enters a telephone number and tries to submit the data. The application does not allow this, because the First Name and Last Name are empty.

k) The user enters the last name and the first name and clicks the Submit button.

l) The address book is redisplayed with the new name added in.

Fig. 15.9 | Ajax-enabled address-book application. (Part 10 of 10.)

The application also enables the user to add another entry to the address book by clicking the **addEntry** button (Fig. 15.9(f)). The application displays a form that enables live field validation. As the user fills out the form, the zip-code value is validated and used to generate the city and state (Fig. 15.9(g), Fig. 15.9(h) and Fig. 15.9(i)). The telephone number is validated for correct format (Fig. 15.9(j)). When the `Submit` button is clicked, the application checks for invalid data and stores the values in a database on the server (Fig. 15.9(k) and Fig. 15.9(l)). You can test-drive this application at `test.deitel.com/examples/iw3htp4/ajax/fig15_09_10/AddressBook.html`.

Interacting with a Web Service on the Server

When the page loads, the `onload` event (line 339) calls the `showAddressBook` function to load the address book onto the page. Function `showAddressBook` (lines 21–29) shows the `addressBook` element and hides the `addEntry` element using the HTML DOM (lines 24–25). Then it calls function `callWebService` to make an asynchronous request to the server (line 28). Function `callWebService` requires an array of parameter objects to be sent to the server. In this case, the function we are invoking on the server requires no arguments, so line 27 creates an empty array to be passed to `callWebService`. Our program uses an ASP.NET web service that we created for this example to do the server-side processing. The web service contains a collection of methods that can be called from a web application.

Function `callWebService` (lines 32–72) contains the code to call our web service, given a method name, an array of parameter bindings (i.e., the method's parameter names and argument values) and the name of a callback function. The web-service application and the method that is being called are specified in the request URL (line 35). When sending the request using the `GET` method, the parameters are concatenated URL starting with a `?` symbol and followed by a list of *parameter=value* bindings, each separated by an `&`. Lines 39–49 iterate over the array of parameter bindings that was passed as an argument, and add them to the request URL. In this first call, we do not pass any parameters because the web method that returns all the entries requires none. However, future web method calls will send multiple parameter bindings to the web service. Lines 52–71 prepare and send the request, using similar functionality to the previous two examples. There are many types of user interaction in this application, each requiring a separate asynchronous request. For this reason, we pass the appropriate `asyncRequest` object as an argument to the function specified by the `callBack` parameter. However, event handlers cannot receive arguments, so lines 57–60 assign an anonymous function to `asyncRequest`'s `onreadystatechange` property. When this anonymous function gets called, it calls function `callBack` and passes the `asyncRequest` object as an argument. Lines 64–65 set an `Accept` request header to receive JSON formatted data.

Parsing JSON Data

Each of our web service's methods in this example returns a JSON representation of an object or array of objects. For example, when the web application requests the list of names in the address book, the list is returned as a JSON array, as shown in Fig. 15.10. Each object in Fig. 15.10 has the attributes `first` and `last`.

Line 11 links the `json.js` script to the XHTML file so we can parse JSON data. When the `XMLHttpRequest` object receives the response, it calls function `parseData` (lines 75–84). Line 81 calls the string's `parseJSON` function, which converts the JSON string into a JavaScript object. Then line 82 calls function `displayNames` (lines 87–106), which

```
[ { "first": "Cheryl", "last": "Black" },
  { "first": "James", "last": "Blue" },
  { "first": "Mike", "last": "Brown" },
  { "first": "Meg", "last": "Gold" } ]
```

Fig. 15.10 | Address-book data formatted in JSON.

displays the first and last name of each address-book entry passed to it. Lines 90–91 use the DOM to store the placeholder `div` element `Names` in the variable `listbox`, and clear its content. Once parsed, the JSON string of address-book entries becomes an array, which this function traverses (lines 94–105).

Creating XHTML Elements and Setting Event Handlers on the Fly

Line 99 uses an XHTML `fieldset` element to create a box in which the entry will be placed. Line 100 registers function `handleOnClick` as the `onclick` event handler for the `div` created in line 98. This enables the user to expand each address-book entry by clicking it. Function `handleOnClick` (lines 109–113) calls the `getAddress` function whenever the user clicks an entry. The parameters are generated dynamically and not evaluated until the `getAddress` function is called. This enables each function to receive arguments that are specific to the entry the user clicked. Line 102 displays the names on the page by accessing the `first` (first name) and `last` (last name) fields of each element of the `data` array.

Function `getAddress` (lines 136–166) is called when the user clicks an entry. This request must keep track of the entry where the address is to be displayed on the page. Lines 151–154 set the `displayAddress` function (lines 168–187) as the callback function, and pass it the entry element as a parameter. Once the request completes successfully, lines 174–178 parse the response and display the addresses. Lines 181–184 update the `div`'s `onclick` event handler to hide the address data when that `div` is clicked again by the user. When the user clicks an expanded entry, function `clearField` (lines 190–197) is called. Lines 192–196 reset the entry's content and its `onclick` event handler to the values they had before the entry was expanded.

Implementing Type-Ahead

The `input` element declared in line 348 enables the user to search the address book by last name. As soon as the user starts typing in the input box, the `onkeyup` event handler calls the `search` function (lines 117–133), passing the `input` element's value as an argument. The `search` function performs an asynchronous request to locate entries with last names that start with its argument value. When the response is received, the application displays the matching list of names. Each time the user changes the text in the input box, function `search` is called again to make another asynchronous request.

The `search` function (lines 117–133) first clears the address-book entries from the page (lines 120–121). If the `input` argument is the empty string, line 126 displays the entire address book by calling function `showAddressBook`. Otherwise lines 130–131 send a request to the server to search the data. Line 130 creates a JSON string to represent the parameter object to be sent as an argument to the `callWebServices` function. Line 131 converts the string to an object and calls the `callWebServices` function. When the server responds, callback function `parseData` is invoked, which calls function `displayNames` to display the results on the page.

Implementing a Form with Asynchronous Validation

When the **Add an Entry** button (lines 343–344) is clicked, the `addEntry` function (lines 200–204) is called, which hides the `addressBook` element and shows the `addEntry` element that allows the user to add a person to the address book. The `addEntry` element (lines 353–380) contains a set of entry fields, some of which have event handlers that enable validation that occurs asynchronously as the user continues to interact with the page. When a user enters a zip code, the `validateZip` function (lines 207–212) is called. This function calls an external web service to validate the zip code. If it is valid, that external web service returns the corresponding city and state. Line 210 builds a parameter object containing `validateZip`'s parameter name and argument value in JSON format. Line 211 calls the `callWebService` function with the appropriate method, the parameter object created in line 210 and `showCityState` (lines 216–258) as the callback function.

Zip-code validation can take a long time due to network delays. The `showCityState` function is called every time the request object's `readyState` property changes. Until the request completes, lines 219–220 display `"Checking zip code..."` on the page. After the request completes, line 228 converts the JSON response text to an object. The response object has four properties—`Validity`, `ErrorText`, `City` and `State`. If the request is valid, line 233 updates the `zipValid` variable that keeps track of zip-code validity (declared at line 18), and lines 237–239 show the city and state that the server generated using the zip code. Otherwise lines 243–245 update the `zipValid` variable and show the error code. Lines 248–249 clear the city and state elements. If our web service fails to connect to the zip-code validator web service, lines 252–256 display an appropriate error message.

Similarly, when the user enters the telephone number, the function `validatePhone` (lines 261–265) sends the phone number to the server. Once the server responds, the `showPhoneError` function (lines 268–288) updates the `validatePhone` variable (declared at line 17) and shows the message that the web service returned.

When the **Submit** button is clicked, the `saveForm` function is called (lines 291–335). Lines 294–300 retrieve the data from the form. Lines 303–308 check if the zip code and telephone number are valid, and display the appropriate error message in the `Success` element on the bottom of the page. Before the data can be entered into a database on the server, both the first-name and last-name fields must have a value. Lines 309–314 check that these fields are not empty and, if they are empty, display the appropriate error message. Once all the data entered is valid, lines 318–321 hide the entry form and show the address book. Lines 324–333 build the parameter object using JSON and send the data to the server using the `callWebService` function. Once the server saves the data, it queries the database for an updated list of entries and returns them; then function `parseData` displays the entries on the page.

15.8 Dojo Toolkit

Developing web applications in general, and Ajax applications in particular, involves a certain amount of painstaking and tedious work. Cross-browser compatibility, DOM manipulation and event handling can get cumbersome, particularly as an application's size increases. Dojo is a free, open source JavaScript library that takes care of these issues. Dojo reduces asynchronous request handling to a single function call. Dojo also provides cross-browser DOM functions that simplify partial page updates. It covers many more areas of web development, from simple event handling to fully functional rich GUI controls.

To install Dojo, download the Dojo version 0.4.3 from `www.Dojotoolkit.org/downloads` to your hard drive. Extract the files from the archive file you downloaded to your web development directory or web server. Including the `dojo.js` script file in your web application will give you access to all the Dojo functions. To do this, place the following script in the head element of your XHTML document:

```
<script type = "text/javascript" src = "path/Dojo.js">
```

where *path* is the relative or complete path to the Dojo toolkit's files. Quick installation instructions for Dojo are provided at `Dojotoolkit.org/book/Dojo-book-0-9/part-1-life-Dojo/quick-installation`.

Figure 15.11 is a calendar application that uses Dojo to create the user interface, communicate with the server asynchronously, handle events and manipulate the DOM. The application contains a calendar control that shows the user six weeks of dates (see the screen captures in Fig. 15.11). Various arrow buttons allow the user to traverse the calendar. When the user selects a date, an asynchronous request obtains from the server a list of the scheduled events for that date. There is an **Edit** button next to each scheduled event. When the **Edit** button is clicked, the item is replaced by a text box with the item's content, a **Save** button and a **Cancel** button. When the user presses **Save**, an asynchronous request saves the new value to the server and displays it on the page. This feature, often referred to as edit-in-place, is common in Ajax applications. You can test-drive this application at `test.deitel.com/examples/iw3htp4/ajax/fig15_11/calendar.html`.

```
<?xml version = "1.0" encoding = "utf-8"?>
<!DOCTYPE html PUBLIC "-//W3C//DTD XHTML 1.0 Strict//EN"
   "http://www.w3.org/TR/xhtml1/DTD/xhtml1-strict.dtd">

<!-- Fig. 15.11 Calendar.html -->
<!-- Calendar application built with dojo. -->
<html xmlns = "http://www.w3.org/1999/xhtml">
<head>
   <script type = "text/javascript" src = "/dojo043/dojo.js"></script>
   <script type = "text/javascript" src = "json.js"></script>
   <script type = "text/javascript">
      <!--
      // specify all the required dojo scripts
      dojo.require( "dojo.event.*" ); // use scripts from event package
      dojo.require( "dojo.widget.*" ); // use scripts from widget package
      dojo.require( "dojo.dom.*" ); // use scripts from dom package
      dojo.require( "dojo.io.*" ); // use scripts from the io package

      // configure calendar event handler
      function connectEventHandler()
      {
         var calendar = dojo.widget.byId( "calendar" ); // get calendar
         calendar.setDate( "2007-07-04" );
         dojo.event.connect(
            calendar, "onValueChanged", "retrieveItems" );
      } // end function connectEventHandler

```

Fig. 15.11 | Calendar application built with Dojo. (Part 1 of 7.)

```
      // location of CalendarService web service
      var webServiceUrl = "/CalendarService/CalendarService.asmx";

      // obtain scheduled events for the specified date
      function retrieveItems( eventDate )
      {
         // convert date object to string in yyyy-mm-dd format
         var date = dojo.date.toRfc3339( eventDate ).substring( 0, 10 );

          // build parameters and call web service
         var params = '[{ "param":"eventDate", "value":"' +
            date +  "'}]";
         callWebService( 'getItemsByDate', params, displayItems );
      } // end function retrieveItems

     // call a specific web service asynchronously to get server data
      function callWebService( method, params, callback )
      {
         // url for the asynchronous request
         var requestUrl = webServiceUrl + "/" + method;
         var params = paramString.parseJSON();

         // build the parameter string to append to the url
         for ( var i = 0; i < params.length; i++ )
         {
            // check if it is the first parameter and build
            // the parameter string accordingly
            if ( i == 0 )
               requestUrl = requestUrl + "?" + params[ i ].param +
                  "=" + params[ i ].value; // add first parameter to url
            else
               requestUrl = requestUrl + "&" + params[ i ].param +
                "=" + params[ i ].value; // add other parameters to url
         } // end for

         // call asynchronous request using dojo.io.bind
         dojo.io.bind( { url: requestUrl, handler: callback,
            accept: "application/json; charset=utf-8" } );
      } // end function callWebService

      // display the list of scheduled events on the page
      function displayItems( type, data, event )
      {
         if ( type == 'error' ) // if the request has failed
         {
            alert( 'Could not retrieve the event' ); // display error
         } // end if
         else
         {
            var placeholder = dojo.byId( "itemList" ); // get placeholder
            placeholder.innerHTML = ''; // clear placeholder
            var items = data.parseJSON(); // parse server data

```

Fig. 15.11 | Calendar application built with Dojo. (Part 2 of 7.)

```
            // check whether there are events;
            // if none then display message
            if ( items == "" )
            {
               placeholder.innerHTML = 'No events for this date.';
            }

            for ( var  i = 0; i < items.length; i++ )
            {
               // initialize item's container
               var item = document.createElement( "div" );
               item.id = items[ i ].id; // set DOM id to database id

               // obtain and paste the item's description
               var text = document.createElement( "div" );
               text.innerHTML =  items[i].description;
               text.id = 'description' + item.id;
               dojo.dom.insertAtIndex( text, item, 0 );

               // create and insert the placeholder for the edit button
               var buttonPlaceHolder = document.createElement( "div" );
               dojo.dom.insertAtIndex( buttonPlaceHolder, item, 1 );

               // create the edit button and paste it into the container
               var editButton = dojo.widget.
                  createWidget( "Button", {}, buttonPlaceHolder );
               editButton.setCaption( "Edit" );
               dojo.event.connect(
                  editButton, 'buttonClick', handleEdit );

               // insert item container in the list of items container
               dojo.dom.insertAtIndex( item, placeholder, i );
            } // end for
         } // end else
      } // end function displayItems

      // send the asynchronous request to get content for editing and
      // run the edit-in-place UI
      function handleEdit( event )
      {
         var id = event.currentTarget.parentNode.id; // retrieve id
         var params = '[{ "param":"id", "value":"' + id +  '"}]';
         callWebService( 'getItemById', params, displayForEdit );
      } // end function handleEdit

      // set up the interface for editing an item
      function displayForEdit(type, data, event)
      {
         if ( type == 'error' ) // if the request has failed
         {
            alert( 'Could not retrieve the event' ); // display error
         }
```

Fig. 15.11 | Calendar application built with Dojo. (Part 3 of 7.)

```
         else
         {
            var item = data.parseJSON(); // parse the item
            var id = item.id; // set the id

            // create div elements to insert content
            var editElement = document.createElement( 'div' );
            var buttonElement = document.createElement( 'div' );

            // hide the unedited content
            var oldItem = dojo.byId( id ); // get the original element
            oldItem.id = 'old' + oldItem.id; // change element's id
            oldItem.style.display = 'none'; // hide old element
            editElement.id = id; // change the "edit" container's id

            // create a textbox and insert it on the page
            var editArea = document.createElement( 'textarea' );
            editArea.id = 'edit' + id; // set textbox id
            editArea.innerHTML = item.description; // insert description
            dojo.dom.insertAtIndex( editArea, editElement, 0 );

            // create button placeholders and insert on the page
            // these will be transformed into dojo widgets
            var saveElement = document.createElement( 'div' );
            var cancelElement = document.createElement( 'div' );
            dojo.dom.insertAtIndex( saveElement, buttonElement, 0 );
            dojo.dom.insertAtIndex( cancelElement, buttonElement, 1 );
            dojo.dom.insertAtIndex( buttonElement, editElement, 1 );

            // create "save" and "cancel" buttons
            var saveButton =
               dojo.widget.createWidget( "Button", {}, saveElement );
            var cancelButton =
               dojo.widget.createWidget( "Button", {}, cancelElement );
            saveButton.setCaption( "Save" ); // set saveButton label
            cancelButton.setCaption( "Cancel" ); // set cancelButton text

            // set up the event handlers for cancel and save buttons
            dojo.event.connect( saveButton, 'buttonClick', handleSave );
            dojo.event.connect(
               cancelButton, 'buttonClick', handleCancel );

            // paste the edit UI on the page
            dojo.dom.insertAfter( editElement, oldItem );
         } // end else
      } // end function displayForEdit

      // sends the changed content to the server to be saved
      function handleSave( event )
      {
         // grab user entered data
         var id = event.currentTarget.parentNode.parentNode.id;
         var descr = dojo.byId( 'edit' + id ).value;
```

Fig. 15.11 | Calendar application built with Dojo. (Part 4 of 7.)

```

         // build parameter string and call the web service
         var params = '[{ "param":"id", "value":"' + id +
            '"}, {"param": "descr", "value":"' + descr + '"}]';
         callWebService( 'Save', params, displayEdited );
      } // end function handleSave

      // restores the original content of the item
      function handleCancel( event )
      {
         var voidEdit = event.currentTarget.parentNode.parentNode;
         var id = voidEdit.id; // retrieve the id of the item
         dojo.dom.removeNode( voidEdit, true ); // remove the edit UI
         var old = dojo.byId( 'old' + id ); // retrieve pre-edit version
         old.style.display = 'block'; // show pre-edit version
         old.id = id; // reset the id
      } // end function handleCancel

      // displays the updated event information after an edit is saved
      function displayEdited( type, data, event )
      {
         if ( type == 'error' )
         {
            alert( 'Could not retrieve the event' );
         }
         else
         {
            editedItem = data.parseJSON(); // obtain updated description
            var id = editedItem.id; // obtain the id
            var editElement = dojo.byId( id ); // get the edit UI
            dojo.dom.removeNode( editElement, true ); // delete edit UI
            var old = dojo.byId( 'old' + id ); // get item container

            // get pre-edit element and update its description
            var oldText = dojo.byId( 'description' + id );
            oldText.innerHTML = editedItem.description;

            old.id = id; // reset id
            old.style.display = 'block'; // show the updated item
         } // end else
      } // end function displayEdited

      // when the page is loaded, set up the calendar event handler
      dojo.addOnLoad( connectEventHandler );
      // -->
   </script>
   <title> Calendar built with dojo </title>
</head>
<body>
   Calendar
   <div dojoType = "datePicker" style = "float: left"
      widgetID = "calendar"></div>
   <div id = "itemList" style = "float: left"></div>
```

Fig. 15.11 | Calendar application built with Dojo. (Part 5 of 7.)

```
</body>
</html>
```

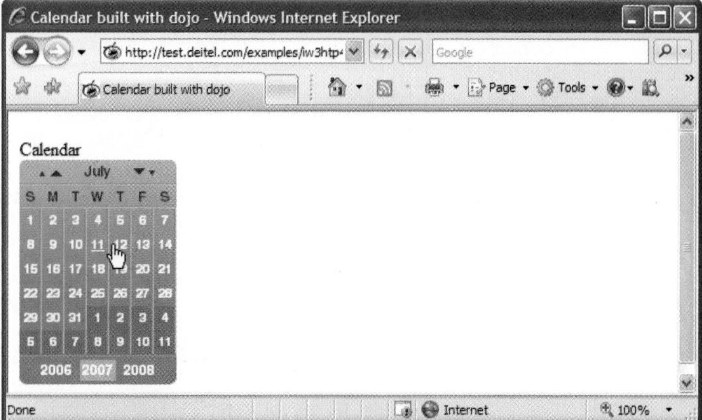

a) `DatePicker` Dojo widget after the web page loads.

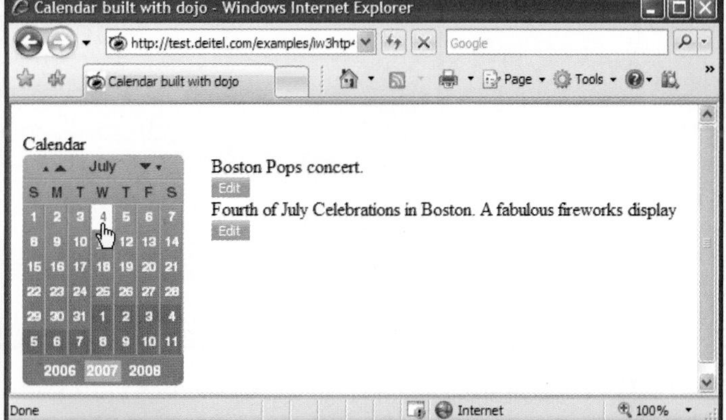

b) User selects a date and the application asynchronously requests a list of events for that date and displays the results with a partial page update.

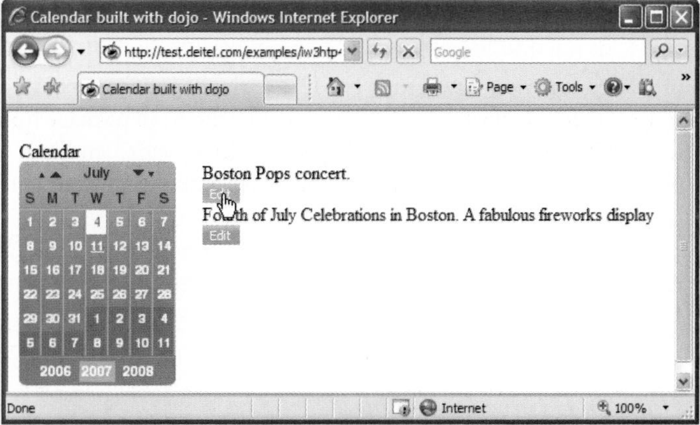

c) User clicks the **Edit** button to modify an event's description.

Fig. 15.11 | Calendar application built with Dojo. (Part 6 of 7.)

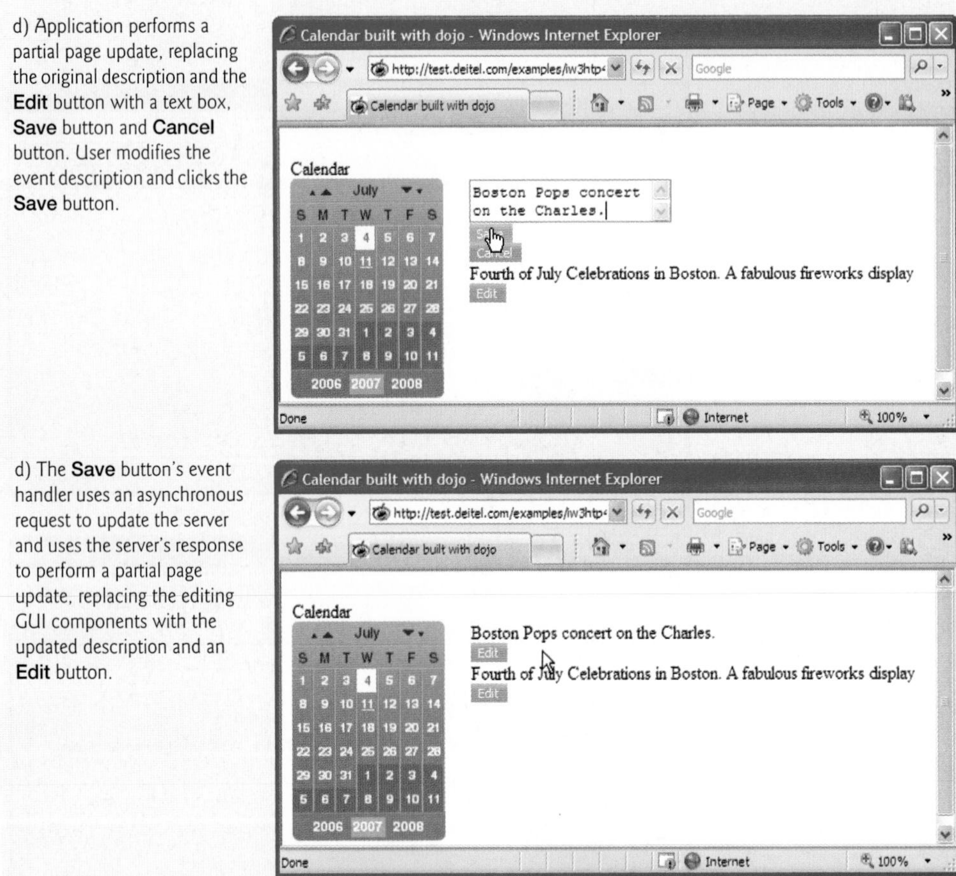

Fig. 15.11 | Calendar application built with Dojo. (Part 7 of 7.)

Loading Dojo Packages

Lines 9–17 load the Dojo framework. Line 9 links the `dojo.js` script file to the page, giving the script access to all the functions in the Dojo toolkit. Dojo is organized in packages of related functionality. Lines 14–17 use the `dojo.require` call, provided by the `dojo.js` script to include the packages we need. The `dojo.io` package functions communicate with the server, the `dojo.event` package simplifies event handling, the `dojo.widget` package provides rich GUI controls, and the `dojo.dom` package contains additional DOM functions that are portable across many different browsers.

The application cannot use any of this functionality until all the packages have been loaded. Line 229 uses the `dojo.addOnLoad` method to set up the event handling after the page loads. Once all the packages have been loaded, the `connectEventHandler` function (lines 20–26) is called.

Using an Existing Dojo Widget

A **Dojo widget** is any predefined user interface element that is part of the Dojo toolkit. The calendar control on the page is the `DatePicker` widget. To incorporate an existing

Dojo widget onto a page, you must set the `DojoType` attribute of any HTML element to the type of widget that you want it to be (line 236). Dojo widgets also have their own `widgetID` property (line 237). Line 22 uses the `dojo.widget.byId` method, rather than the DOM's `document.getElementById` method, to obtain the calendar widget element. The `dojo.events.connect` method links functions together. Lines 24–25 use it to connect the calendar's `onValueChanged` event handler to the `retrieveItems` function. When the user picks a date, a special `onValueChanged` event that is part of the `DatePicker` widget calls `retrieveItems`, passing the selected date as an argument. The `retrieveItems` function (lines 32–41) builds the parameters for the request to the server, and calls the `callWebService` function. Line 35 uses the `dojo.date.toRfc3339` method to convert the date passed by the calendar control to *yyyy-mm-dd* format.

Asynchronous Requests in Dojo

The `callWebService` function (lines 44–66) sends the asynchronous request to the specified web-service method. Lines 47–61 build the request URL using the same code as Fig. 15.9. Dojo reduces the asynchronous request to a single call to the `dojo.io.bind` method (lines 64–65), which works on all the popular browsers such as Firefox, Internet Explorer, Opera, Mozilla and Safari. The method takes an array of parameters, formatted as a JavaScript object. The `url` parameter specifies the destination of the request, the `handler` parameter specifies the callback function, and the `mimetype` parameter specifies the format of the response. The `handler` parameter can be replaced by the `load` and `error` parameters. The function passed as `load` handles successful requests and the function passed as `error` handles unsuccessful requests.

Response handling is done differently in Dojo. Rather than calling the callback function every time the request's `readyState` property changes, Dojo calls the function passed as the "handler" parameter when the request completes. In addition, in Dojo the script does not have access to the request object. All the response data is sent directly to the callback function The function sent as the `handler` argument must have three parameters—type, data and event.

In the first request, the function `displayItems` (lines 69–115) is set as the callback function. Lines 71–74 check if the request is successful, and display an error message if it isn't. Lines 77–78 obtain the place-holder element (`itemList`), where the items will be displayed, and clear its content. Line 79 converts the JSON response text to a JavaScript object, using the same code as the example in Fig. 15.9.

Partial Page Updates Using Dojo's Cross-Browser DOM Manipulation Capabilities

The Dojo toolkit (like most other Ajax libraries) provides functionality that enables you to manipulate the DOM in a cross-browser portable manner. Lines 83–86 check if the server-side returned any items, and display an appropriate message if it didn't. For each item object returned from the server, lines 91–92 create a `div` element and set its `id` to the item's `id` in the database. Lines 95–97 create a container element for the item's description. Line 98 uses Dojo's `dojo.dom.insertAtIndex` method to insert the description element as the first element in the item's element.

For each entry, the application creates an **Edit** button that enables the user to edit the event's content on the page. Lines 101–109 create a Dojo `Button` widget programmatically. Lines 101–102 create a `buttonPlaceHolder` `div` element for the button and paste it on the page. Lines 105–106 convert the `buttonPlaceHolder` element to a Dojo `Button` widget by calling the `dojo.widget.createWidget` function. This function takes three parameters—the type of widget to be created, a list of additional widget parameters and the element which is to be converted to a Dojo widget. Line 107 uses the button's `setCaption` method to set the text that appears on the button. Line 112 uses the `insertAtIndex` method to insert the items into the `itemList` placeholder, in the order in which they were returned from the server.

Adding Edit-In-Place Functionality

Dojo `Button` widgets use their own `buttonClick` event instead of the DOM `onclick` event to store the event handler. Lines 108–109 use the `dojo.event.connect` method to connect the `buttonClick` event of the Dojo `Button` widget and the `handleEdit` event handler (lines 119–124). When the user clicks the **Edit** button, the `Event` object gets passed to the event handler as an argument. The `Event` object's `currentTarget` property contains the element that initiated the event. Line 121 uses the `currentTarget` property to obtain the `id` of the item. This `id` is the same as the item's `id` in the server database. Line 123 calls the web service's `getItemById` method, using the `callWebService` function to obtain the item that needs to be edited.

Once the server responds, the function `displayForEdit` (lines 127–178) replaces the item on the screen with the user interface used for editing the item's content. The code for this is similar to the code in the `displayItems` function. Lines 129–132 make sure the request was successful and parse the data from the server. Lines 139–140 create the container elements into which we insert the new user-interface elements. Lines 143–146 hide the element that displays the item and change its `id`. Now the `id` of the user-interface element is the same as the `id` of the item that it's editing stored in the database. Lines 149–152 create the text-box element that will be used to edit the item's description, paste it into the text box, and paste the resulting text box on the page. Lines 156–173 use the same syntax that was used to create the **Edit** button widget to create **Save** and **Cancel** button widgets. Line 176 pastes the resulting element, containing the text box and two buttons, on the page.

When the user edits the content and clicks the **Cancel** button, the `handleCancel` function (lines 194–202) restores the item element to what it looked like before the button was clicked. Line 198 deletes the edit UI that was created earlier, using Dojo's `removeNode` function. Lines 200–201 show the item with the original element that was used to display the item, and change its `id` back to the item's `id` on the server database.

When the user clicks the **Save** button, the `handleSave` function (lines 181–191) sends the text entered by the user to the server. Line 185 obtains the text that the user entered in the text box. Lines 188–190 send to the server the `id` of the item that needs to be updated and the new description.

Once the server responds, `displayEdited` (lines 205–226) displays the new item on the page. Lines 214–217 contain the same code that was used in `handleCancel` to remove the user interface used to edit the item and redisplay the element that contains the item. Line 221 changes the item's description to its new value.

15.9 Wrap-Up

In this chapter, we introduced Ajax and showed how to use it to create Rich Internet Applications (RIAs) that approximate the look, feel and usability of desktop applications.

You learned that RIAs have two key attributes—performance and a rich GUI. We discussed that RIA performance comes from Ajax (Asynchronous JavaScript and XML), which uses client-side scripting to make web applications more responsive by separating client-side user interaction and server communication, and running them in parallel.

You learned various ways to develop Ajax applications. We showed how to use "raw" Ajax with its component technologies (XHTML, CSS, JavaScript, dynamic HTML, the DOM, XML and the `XMLHttpRequest` object) to manage asynchronous requests to the server, then process the server responses (via JavaScript event handling) to perform partial page updates with the DOM on the client. You learned how to implement client/server communication using XML, and how to parse server responses using the DOM.

We discussed the impracticality of "raw" Ajax for developing large-scale applications and the hiding of such portability issues by Ajax toolkits, such as Dojo, Prototype, Script.aculo.us and ASP.NET Ajax, and by RIA environments such as Adobe's Flex (Chapter 18), Microsoft's Silverlight (Chapter 19) and JavaServer Faces (Chapters 26–27). You also learned that these Ajax libraries and RIA environments provide powerful ready-to-use GUI controls and functions that enrich web applications. You used two data formats—XML and JSON (JavaScript Object Notation—for communicating between the server and client. We then built an Ajax application with a rich calendar GUI using the Dojo Ajax toolkit. In the applications we presented, you learned techniques including callback functions for handling asynchronous responses, partial page updates to display response data, JavaScript exception handling, type-ahead capabilities for making suggestions to users as they type in a text field and edit-in-place capabilities so users can edit entries directly in a web page.

In subsequent chapters, we use tools such as Adobe Flex, Microsoft Silverlight, Ruby on Rails and JavaServer Faces to build RIAs using Ajax. In Chapter 24, we'll demonstrate features of the Prototype and Script.aculo.us Ajax libraries, which come with the Ruby on Rails framework. Prototype provides capabilities similar to Dojo. Script.aculo.us provides many "eye candy" effects that enable you to beautify your Ajax applications and create rich interfaces. In Chapter 27, we present Ajax-enabled JavaServer Faces (JSF) components. JSF uses Dojo to implement many of its client-side Ajax capabilities.

15.10 Web Resources

`www.deitel.com/ajax`

Our *Ajax Resource Center* contains links to some of the best Ajax resources on the web from which you can learn more about Ajax and its component technologies. Find categorized links to Ajax tools, code, forums, books, libraries, frameworks, conferences, podcasts and more. Check out the tutorials for all skill levels, from introductory to advanced. See our comprehensive list of developer toolkits and libraries. Visit the most popular Ajax community websites and blogs. Explore many popular commercial and free open-source Ajax applications. Download code snippets and complete scripts that you can use on your own website. Also, be sure to visit our Resource Centers with information on Ajax's component technologies, including XHTML (`www.deitel.com/xhtml/`), CSS 2.1 (`www.deitel.com/css21/`), XML (`www.deitel.com/XML/`), and JavaScript (`www.deitel.com/javascript/`). For a complete list of Resource Centers, visit `www.deitel.com/ResourceCenters.html`.

Summary

Section 15.1 Introduction

- Despite the tremendous technological growth of the Internet over the past decade, the usability of web applications has lagged behind compared to desktop applications.
- Rich Internet Applications (RIAs) are web applications that approximate the look, feel and usability of desktop applications. RIAs have two key attributes—performance and rich GUI.
- RIA performance comes from Ajax (Asynchronous JavaScript and XML), which uses client-side scripting to make web applications more responsive.
- Ajax applications separate client-side user interaction and server communication, and run them in parallel, making the delays of server-side processing more transparent to the user.
- "Raw" Ajax uses JavaScript to send asynchronous requests to the server, then updates the page using the DOM.
- When writing "raw" Ajax you need to deal directly with cross-browser portability issues, making it impractical for developing large-scale applications.
- Portability issues are hidden by Ajax toolkits, such as Dojo, Prototype and Script.aculo.us, which provide powerful ready-to-use controls and functions that enrich web applications and simplify JavaScript coding by making it cross-browser compatible.
- We achieve rich GUI in RIAs with Ajax toolkits and with RIA environments such as Adobe's Flex, Microsoft's Silverlight and JavaServer Faces. Such toolkits and environments provide powerful ready-to-use controls and functions that enrich web applications.
- The client-side of Ajax applications is written in XHTML and CSS, and uses JavaScript to add functionality to the user interface.
- XML and JSON are used to structure the data passed between the server and the client.
- The Ajax component that manages interaction with the server is usually implemented with JavaScript's `XMLHttpRequest` object—commonly abbreviated as XHR.

Section 15.2 Traditional Web Applications vs. Ajax Applications

- In traditional web applications, the user fills in the form's fields, then submits the form. The browser generates a request to the server, which receives the request and processes it. The server generates and sends a response containing the exact page that the browser will render, which causes the browser to load the new page and temporarily makes the browser window blank. The client *waits* for the server to respond and *reloads the entire page* with the data from the response.
- While a synchronous request is being processed on the server, the user cannot interact with the client web browser.
- The synchronous model was originally designed for a web of hypertext documents—what some people call the "brochure web." This model yielded "choppy" application performance.
- In an Ajax application, when the user interacts with a page, the client creates an `XMLHttpRequest` object to manage a request. The `XMLHttpRequest` object sends the request to and awaits the response from the server. The requests are asynchronous, allowing the user to continue interacting with the application while the server processes the request concurrently. When the server responds, the `XMLHttpRequest` object that issued the request invokes a callback function, which typically uses partial page updates to display the returned data in the existing web page *without reloading the entire page.*
- The callback function updates only a designated part of the page. Such partial page updates help make web applications more responsive, making them feel more like desktop applications.

Section 15.3 Rich Internet Applications (RIAs) with Ajax

- A classic XHTML registration form sends all of the data to be validated to the server when the user clicks the **Register** button. While the server is validating the data, the user cannot interact with the page. The server finds invalid data, generates a new page identifying the errors in the form and sends it back to the client—which renders the page in the browser. Once the user fixes the errors and clicks the **Register** button, the cycle repeats until no errors are found, then the data is stored on the server. The entire page reloads every time the user submits invalid data.
- Ajax-enabled forms are more interactive. Entries are validated dynamically as the user enters data into the fields. If a problem is found, the server sends an error message that is asynchronously displayed to inform the user of the problem. Sending each entry asynchronously allows the user to address invalid entries quickly, rather than making edits and resubmitting the entire form repeatedly until all entries are valid. Asynchronous requests could also be used to fill some fields based on previous fields' values.

Section 15.4 History of Ajax

- The term Ajax was coined by Jesse James Garrett of Adaptive Path in February 2005, when he was presenting the previously unnamed technology to a client.
- All of the technologies involved in Ajax (XHTML, JavaScript, CSS, dynamic HTML, the DOM and XML) have existed for many years.
- In 1998, Microsoft introduced the `XMLHttpRequest` object to create and manage asynchronous requests and responses.
- Popular applications like Flickr, Google's Gmail and Google Maps use the `XMLHttpRequest` object to update pages dynamically.
- The name Ajax immediately caught on and brought attention to its component technologies. Ajax has quickly become one of the hottest technologies in web development, as it enables webtop applications to challenge the dominance of established desktop applications.

Section 15.5 "Raw" Ajax Example using the `XMLHttpRequest` Object

- The `XMLHttpRequest` object (which resides on the client) is the layer between the client and the server that manages asynchronous requests in Ajax applications. This object is supported on most browsers, though they may implement it differently.
- To initiate an asynchronous request, you create an instance of the `XMLHttpRequest` object, then use its `open` method to set up the request, and its `send` method to initiate the request.
- When an Ajax application requests a file from a server, the browser typically caches that file. Subsequent requests for the same file can load it from the browser's cache.
- For security purposes, the `XMLHttpRequest` object does not allow a web application to request resources from servers other than the one that served the web application.
- Making a request to a different server is known as cross-site scripting (also known as XSS). You can implement a server-side proxy—an application on the web application's web server—that can make requests to other servers on the web application's behalf.
- When the third argument to `XMLHttpRequest` method `open` is `true`, the request is asynchronous.
- An exception is an indication of a problem that occurs during a program's execution.
- Exception handling enables you to create applications that can resolve (or handle) exceptions—in some cases allowing a program to continue executing as if no problem had been encountered.
- A `try` block encloses code that might cause an exception and code that should not execute if an exception occurs. A `try` block consists of the keyword `try` followed by a block of code enclosed in curly braces (`{}`).

- When an exception occurs, a `try` block terminates immediately and a `catch` block (also called a `catch` clause or exception handler) catches (i.e., receives) and handles an exception.
- The `catch` block begins with the keyword `catch` and is followed by an exception parameter in parentheses and a block of code enclosed in curly braces.
- The exception parameter's name enables the `catch` block to interact with a caught exception object, which contains `name` and `message` properties.
- A callback function is registered as the event handler for the `XMLHttpRequest` object's `onreadystatechange` event. Whenever the request makes progress, the `XMLHttpRequest` calls the `onreadystatechange` event handler.
- Progress is monitored by the `readyState` property, which has a value from 0 to 4. The value 0 indicates that the request is not initialized and the value 4 indicates that the request is complete.

Section 15.6 Using XML and the DOM

- When passing structured data between the server and the client, Ajax applications often use XML because it consumes little bandwidth and is easy to parse.
- When the `XMLHttpRequest` object receives XML data, the `XMLHttpRequest` object parses and stores the data as a DOM object in the `responseXML` property.
- The `XMLHttpRequest` object's `responseXML` property contains the XML returned by the server.
- DOM method `createElement` creates an XHTML element of the specified type.
- DOM method `setAttribute` adds or changes an attribute of an XHTML element.
- DOM method `appendChild` inserts one XHTML element into another.
- The `innerHTML` property of a DOM element can be used to obtain or change the XHTML that is displayed in a particular element.

Section 15.7 Creating a Full-Scale Ajax-Enabled Application

- JSON (JavaScript Object Notation)—a simple way to represent JavaScript objects as strings—is an alternative way (to XML) for passing data between the client and the server.
- Each JSON object is represented as a list of property names and values contained in curly braces.
- An array is represented in JSON with square brackets containing a comma-separated list of values.
- Each value in a JSON array can be a string, a number, a JSON representation of an object, `true`, `false` or `null`.
- JavaScript's `eval` function can convert JSON strings into JavaScript objects. To evaluate a JSON string properly, a left parenthesis should be placed at the beginning of the string and a right parenthesis at the end of the string before the string is passed to the `eval` function.
- The `eval` function creates a potential security risk—it executes any embedded JavaScript code in its string argument, possibly allowing a harmful script to be injected into JSON. A more secure way to process JSON is to use a JSON parser
- JSON strings are easier to create and parse than XML and require fewer bytes. For these reasons, JSON is commonly used to communicate in client/server interaction.
- When a request is sent using the `GET` method, the parameters are concatenated to the URL. URL parameter strings start with a `?` symbol and have a list of *parameter-value* bindings, each separated by an `&`.
- To implement type-ahead, you can use an element's `onkeyup` event handler to make asynchronous requests.

Section 15.8 Dojo Toolkit

- Developing web applications in general, and Ajax applications in particular, involves a certain amount of painstaking and tedious work. Cross-browser compatibility, DOM manipulation and event handling can get cumbersome, particularly as an application's size increases. Dojo is a free, open source JavaScript library that takes care of these issues.
- Dojo reduces asynchronous request handling to a single function call.
- Dojo provides cross-browser DOM functions that simplify partial page updates. It also provides event handling and rich GUI controls.
- To install Dojo, download the latest release from `www.Dojotoolkit.org/downloads` to your hard drive. Extract the files from the archive file you downloaded to your web development directory or web server. To include the `Dojo.js` script file in your web application, place the following script in the head element of your XHTML document:

  ```
  <script type = "text/javascript" src = "path/Dojo.js">
  ```

  where *path* is the relative or complete path to the Dojo toolkit's files.
- Edit-in-place enables a user to modify data directly in the web page, a common feature in Ajax applications.
- Dojo is organized in packages of related functionality.
- The `dojo.require` method is used to include specific Dojo packages.
- The `dojo.io` package functions communicate with the server, the `dojo.event` package simplifies event handling, the `dojo.widget` package provides rich GUI controls, and the `dojo.dom` package contains additional DOM functions that are portable across many different browsers.
- A Dojo widget is any predefined user interface element that is part of the Dojo toolkit.
- To incorporate an existing Dojo widget onto a page, you must set the `dojoType` attribute of any HTML element to the type of widget that you want it to be.
- The `dojo.widget.byId` method can be used to obtain a Dojo widget.
- The `dojo.events.connect` method links functions together.
- The `dojo.date.toRfc3339` method converts a date to *yyyy-mm-dd* format.
- The `dojo.io.bind` method configures and sends asynchronous requests. The method takes an array of parameters, formatted as a JavaScript object. The `url` parameter specifies the destination of the request, the `handler` parameter specifies the callback function, and the `mimetype` parameter specifies the format of the response. The `handler` parameter can be replaced by the `load` and `error` parameters. The function passed as the `load` handler processes successful requests and the function passed as the `error` handler processes unsuccessful requests.
- Dojo calls the function passed as the `handler` parameter only when the request completes.
- In Dojo, the script does not have access to the request object. All the response data is sent directly to the callback function.
- The function sent as the `handler` argument must have three parameters—`type`, `data` and `event`.
- The Dojo toolkit (like most other Ajax libraries) provides functionality that enables you to manipulate the DOM in a cross-browser manner.
- Dojo's `dojo.dom.insertAtIndex` method inserts an element at the specified index in the DOM.
- Dojo's `removeNode` function removes an element from the DOM.
- Dojo `Button` widgets use their own `buttonClick` event instead of the DOM `onclick` event to store the event handler.
- The `Event` object's `currentTarget` property contains the element that initiated the event.

Terminology

Ajax
Ajax toolkit
asynchronous request
callback function
`catch` block
`catch` clause
`catch` keyword
cross-browser compatibility
cross-site scripting (XSS)
Dojo Ajax library
edit-in-place
exception
exception handler
exception handling
GET method of `XMLHttpRequest` object
`getResponseHeader` method of `XMLHttpRequest` object
JavaScript Object Notation (JSON)
`onReadyStateChange` property of the `XMLHttpRequest` object
`open` method of `XMLHttpRequest`
partial page update
Prototype Ajax library
"raw" Ajax
`readyState` property of `XMLHttpRequest` object
`responseText` property of `XMLHttpRequest` object
`responseXML` property of `XMLHttpRequest` object
same origin policy (SOP)
Script.aculo.us Ajax library
`send` method of `XMLHttpRequest`
`setRequestHeader` method of `XMLHttpRequest` object
`status` property of `XMLHttpRequest` object
`statusText` property of `XMLHttpRequest` object
synchronous request
`try` block
`try` keyword
type ahead
XHR (abbreviation for `XMLHttpRequest`)
`XMLHttpRequest` object

Self-Review Exercises

15.1 Fill in the blanks in each of the following statements:

a) Ajax applications use ________ requests to create Rich Internet Applications.
b) In Ajax applications, the ________ object manages asynchronous interaction with the server.
c) The event handler called when the server responds is known as a(n) ________ function.
d) The ________ attribute can be accessed through the DOM to update an XHTML element's content without reloading the page.
e) JavaScript's `XMLHttpRequest` object is commonly abbreviated as ________.
f) ________ is a simple way to represent JavaScript objects as strings.
g) Making a request to a different server is known as ________.
h) JavaScript's ________ function can convert JSON strings into JavaScript objects.
i) A(n) ________ encloses code that might cause an exception and code that should not execute if an exception occurs.
j) The `XMLHttpRequest` object's ________ contains the XML returned by the server.

15.2 State whether each of the following is *true* or *false*. If *false*, explain why.

a) Ajax applications must use XML for server responses.
b) The technologies that are used to develop Ajax applications have existed since the 1990s.
c) The event handler that processes the response is stored in the `readyState` property of `XMLHttpRequest`.
d) An Ajax application can be implemented so that it never needs to reload the page on which it runs.
e) The `responseXML` property of the `XMLHttpRequest` object stores the server's response as a raw XML string.

f) The Dojo toolkit (like most other Ajax libraries) provides functionality that enables you to manipulate the DOM in a cross-browser manner.
g) An exception indicates successful completion of a program's execution.
h) When the third argument to `XMLHttpRequest` method `open` is `false`, the request is asynchronous.
i) For security purposes, the `XMLHttpRequest` object does not allow a web application to request resources from servers other than the one that served the web application.
j) The `innerHTML` property of a DOM element can be used to obtain or change the XHTML that is displayed in a particular element.

Answers to Self-Review Exercises

15.1 a) asynchronous. b) `XMLHttpRequest`. c) callback. d) `innerHTML`. e) XHR. f) JSON. g) cross-site scripting (or XSS). h) `eval`. i) `try` block. j) `responseXML` property.

15.2
a) False. Ajax applications can use any type of textual data as a response. For example, we used JSON in this chapter.
b) True.
c) False. `readyState` is the property that keeps track of the request's progress. The event handler is stored in the `onReadyStateChange` property.
d) True.
e) False. If the response data has XML format, the `XMLHttpRequest` object parses it and stores it in a document object.
f) True.
g) False. An exception is an indication of a problem that occurs during a program's execution.
h) False. The third argument to `XMLHttpRequest` method `open` must be `true` to make an asynchronous request.
i) True.
j) True.

Exercises

15.3 Describe the differences between client/server interactions in traditional web applications and client/server interactions in Ajax web applications.

15.4 Consider the `AddressBook` application in Fig. 15.9. Describe how you could reimplement the type-ahead capability so that it could perform the search using data previously downloaded rather than making an asynchronous request to the server after every keystroke.

15.5 Describe each of the following terms in the context of Ajax:
a) type-ahead
b) edit-in-place
c) partial page update
d) asynchronous request
e) `XMLHttpRequest`
f) "raw" Ajax
g) callback function
h) same origin policy
i) Ajax libraries
j) RIA

[*Note to Instructors and Students:* Due to security restrictions on using `XMLHttpRequest`, Ajax applications must be placed on a web server (even one on your local computer) to enable the applications to work correctly, and when they need to access other resources, those must reside on the same web server. ***Students:*** You'll need to work closely with your instructors to understand your lab setup so you can run your solutions to the exercises (the examples are already posted on our web server) and to run many of the other server-side applications that you'll learn later in the book.]

15.6 The XML files used in the book-cover catalog example (Fig. 15.8) also store the titles of the books in a `title` attribute of each `cover` node. Modify the example so that every time the mouse hovers over an image, the book's title is displayed below the image.

15.7 Create an Ajax-enabled version of the feedback form from Fig. 4.13. As the user moves between form fields, ensure that each field is non-empty. For the e-mail field, ensure that the e-mail address has valid format. In addition, create an XML file that contains a list of email addresses that are not allowed to post feedback. Each time the user enters an e-mail address check whether it is on that list; if so, display an appropriate message.

15.8 Create an Ajax-based product catalog that obtains its data from JSON files located on the server. The data should be separated into four JSON files. The first file should be a summary file, containing a list of products. Each product should have a title, an image filename for a thumbnail image and a price. The second file should contain a list of descriptions for each product. The third file should contain a list of filenames for the full-size product images. The last file should contain a list of the thumbnail image file names. Each item in a catalogue should have a unique ID that should be included with the entries for that product in every file. Next, create an Ajax-enabled web page that displays the product information in a table. The catalog should initially display a list of product names with their associated thumbnail images and prices. When the mouse hovers over a thumbnail image, the larger product image should be displayed. When the user moves the mouse away from that image, the original thumbnail should be redisplayed. You should provide a button that the user can click to display the product description.

15.9 Create a version of Exercise 15.8 that uses Dojo's capabilities and widgets to display the product catalog. Modify the asynchronous request's to use `dojo.io.bind` functions rather than raw Ajax. Use Dojo's DOM functionality to place elements on the page. Improve the look of the page by using Dojo's button widgets rather than XHTML button elements..

3 PART

Rich Internet Application Client Technologies

The user should feel in control of the computer; not the other way around. This is achieved in applications that embody three qualities: responsiveness, permissiveness, and consistency.

—Inside Macintosh, Volume 1,
Apple Computer, Inc., 1985

16

Adobe® Flash® CS3

Science and technology and the various forms of art, all unite humanity in a single and interconnected system.
—Zhores Aleksandrovich Medvede

All the world's a stage, and all the men and women merely players; they have their exits and their entrances; and one man in his time plays many parts. . .
—William Shakespeare

Music has charms to soothe a savage breast,
To soften rocks, or bend a knotted oak.
—William Congreve

A flash and where previously the brain held a dead fact, the soul grasps a living truth! At moments we are all artists.
—Arnold Bennett

OBJECTIVES

In this chapter you will learn:

- Flash CS3 multimedia development.
- To develop Flash movies.
- Flash animation techniques.
- ActionScript 3.0, Flash's object-oriented programming language.
- To create a preloading animation for a Flash movie.
- To add sound to Flash movies.
- To publish a Flash movie.
- To create special effects with Flash.
- To create a Splash Screen.

Outline

16.1 Introduction

Adobe Flash CS3 (Creative Suite 3) is a commercial application that you can use to produce interactive, animated movies. Flash can be used to create web-based banner advertisements, interactive websites, games and web-based applications with stunning graphics and multimedia effects. It provides tools for drawing graphics, generating animations, and adding sound and video. Flash movies can be embedded in web pages, distributed on CDs and DVDs as independent applications, or converted into stand-alone, executable programs. Flash includes tools for coding in its scripting language—ActionScript 3.0—which is similar to JavaScript and enables interactive applications. A fully functional, 30-day trial version of Flash CS3 is available for download from:

```
www.adobe.com/products/flash/
```

To follow along with the examples in this chapter, please install this software before continuing. Follow the on-screen instructions to install the trial version of the Flash software.

To play Flash movies, the Flash Player plug-in must be installed in your web browser. The most recent version of the plug-in (at the time of this writing) is version 9. You can download the latest version from:

```
www.adobe.com/go/getflashplayer
```

According to Adobe's statistics, approximately 98.7 percent of web users have Flash Player version 6 or greater installed, and 83.4 percent of web users have Flash Player version 9 installed.[1] There are ways to detect whether a user has the appropriate plug-in to view Flash content. Adobe provides a tool called the Flash Player Detection Kit which contains files that work together to detect whether a suitable version of Adobe Flash Player is installed in a user's web browser. This kit can be downloaded from:

`www.adobe.com/products/flashplayer/download/detection_kit/`

This chapter introduces building Flash movies. You'll create interactive buttons, add sound to movies, create special graphic effects and integrate ActionScript in movies.

16.2 Flash Movie Development

Once Flash CS3 is installed, open the program. Flash's **Welcome Screen** appears by default. The **Welcome Screen** contains options such as **Open a Recent Item**, **Create New** and **Create from Template**. The bottom of the page contains links to useful help topics and tutorials. [*Note:* For additional help, refer to Flash's **Help** menu.]

To create a blank Flash document, click **Flash File (ActionScript 3.0)** under the **Create New** heading. Flash opens a new file called **Untitled-1** in the Flash development environment (Fig. 16.1).

At the center of the development environment is the movie stage—the white area in which you place graphic elements during movie development. Above the stage is the timeline, which represents the time period over which a movie runs. The timeline is divided into increments called frames, represented by gray and white rectangles. Each frame depicts a moment in time during the movie, into which you can insert movie elements. The playhead indicates the current frame.

Common Programming Error 16.1

Elements placed off stage can still appear if the user changes the aspect ratio of the movie. If an element should not be visible, use an alpha of 0% to hide the element.

The development environment contains several windows that provide options and tools for creating Flash movies. Many of these tools are located in the **Tools** bar, the vertical window located at the left side of the development environment. The **Tools** bar (Fig. 16.2) is divided into multiple sections, each containing tools and functions that help you create Flash movies. The tools near the top of the **Tools** bar select, add and remove graphics from Flash movies. The **Hand** and **Zoom** tools allow you to pan and zoom in the stage. Another section of tools provides colors for shapes, lines and filled areas. The last section contains settings for the active tool (i.e., the tool that is highlighted and in use). You can make a tool behave differently by selecting a new mode from the options section of the **Tools** bar.

Application windows called panels organize frequently used movie options. Panel options modify the size, shape, color, alignment and effects associated with a movie's graphic elements. By default, panels line the right and bottom edges of the window. Panels

1. Flash Player statistics from Adobe's Flash Player Penetration Survey website at `www.adobe.com/products/player_census/flashplayer/version_penetration.html`.

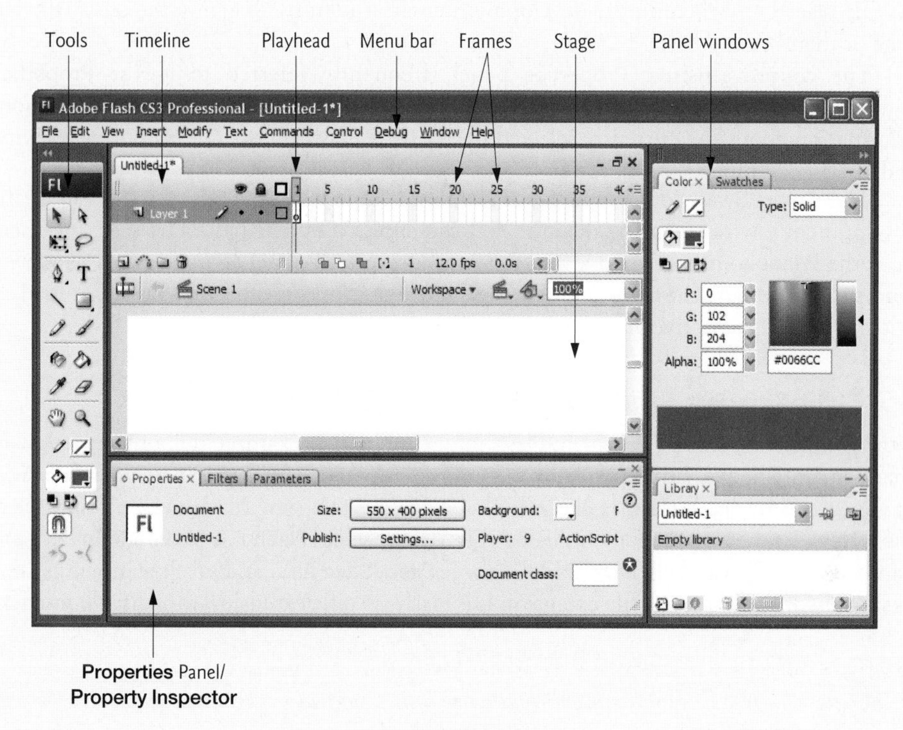

Fig. 16.1 | Flash CS3 development environment.

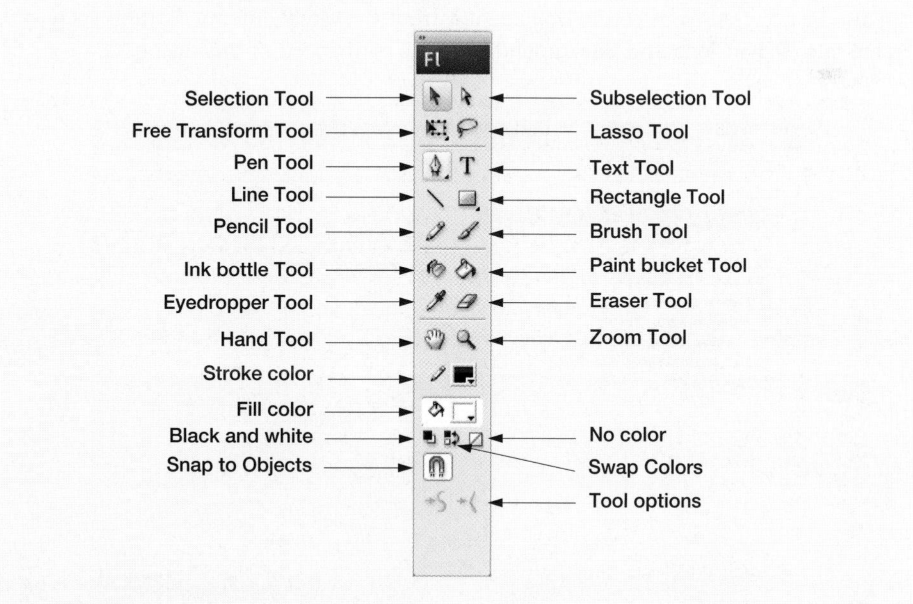

Fig. 16.2 | CS3 **Tools** bar.

may be placed anywhere in the development environment by dragging the tab at the left edge of their bars.

The context-sensitive **Properties** panel (frequently referred to as the **Properties** window) is located at the bottom of the screen by default. This panel displays various information about the currently selected object. It is Flash's most useful tool for viewing and altering an object's properties.

The **Color**, **Swatches**, **Properties**, **Filters** and **Parameters** panels also appear in the development environment by default. You can access different panels by selecting them from the **Window** menu. To save and manage customized panel layouts, select **Window > Workspace**, then use the **Save Current...** and **Manage...** options to save a layout or load an existing layout, respectively.

16.3 Learning Flash with Hands-On Examples

Now you'll create several complete Flash movies. The first example demonstrates how to create an interactive, animated button. ActionScript code will produce a random text string each time the button is clicked. To begin, create a new Flash movie. First, select **File > New**. In the **New Document** dialog (Fig. 16.3), select **Flash File (ActionScript 3.0)** under the **General** tab and click **OK**. Next, choose **File > Save As...** and save the movie as `CeoAssistant.fla`. The `.fla` file extension is a Flash-specific extension for editable movies.

Good Programming Practice 16.1

Save each project with a meaningful name in its own folder. Creating a new folder for each movie helps keep projects organized.

Right click the stage to open a menu containing different movie options. Select **Document Properties...** to display the **Document Properties** dialog (Fig. 16.4). This dialog can also be accessed by selecting **Document...** from the **Modify** menu. Settings such as the **Frame rate**, **Dimensions** and **Background color** are configured in this dialog.

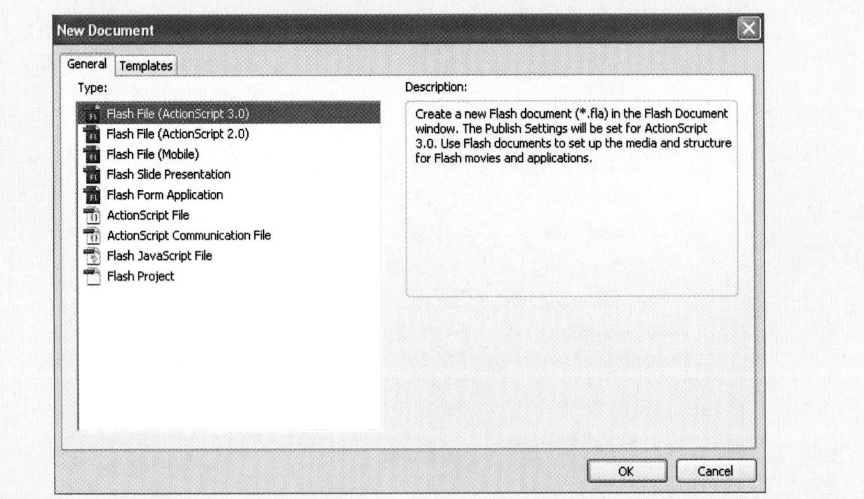

Fig. 16.3 | **New Document** dialog.

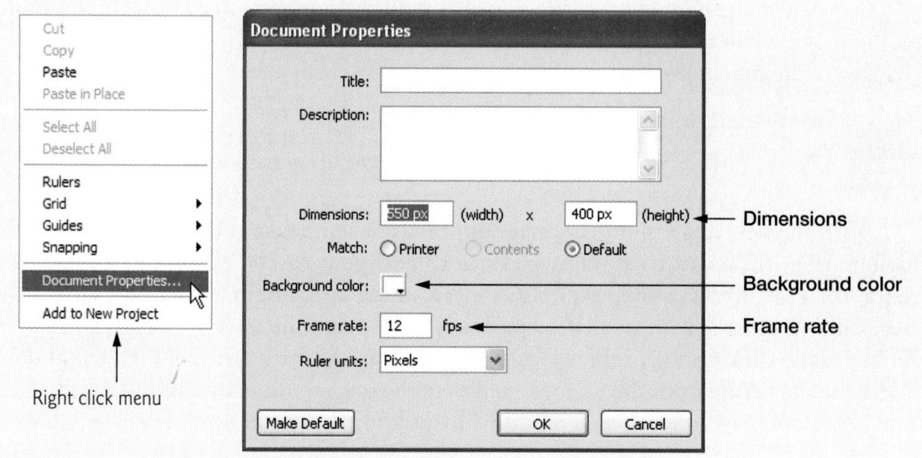

Fig. 16.4 | **Document Properties** dialog.

The **Frame rate** sets the speed at which movie frames display. A higher frame rate causes more frames to be displayed in a given unit of time (the standard measurement is seconds), thus creating a faster movie. The frame rate for Flash movies on the web is generally between 12 and 60 frames per second (**fps**). Flash's default frame rate is 12 fps. For this example, set the **Frame Rate** to 10 frames per second.

Performance Tip 16.1

Higher frame rates increase the amount of information to process, and thus increase the movie's processor usage and file size. Be especially aware of file sizes when catering to low bandwidth web users.

The background color determines the color of the stage. Click the background-color box (called a swatch) to select the background color. A new panel opens, presenting a web-safe palette. Web-safe palettes and color selection are discussed in detail in Chapter 3. Note that the mouse pointer changes into an eyedropper, which indicates that you may select a color. Choose a light blue color (Fig. 16.5).

The box in the upper-left corner of the dialog displays the new background color. The hexadecimal notation for the selected color appears to the right of this box. The hexadecimal notation is the color code that a web browser uses to render color. Hexadecimal notation is discussed in detail in Appendix E, Number Systems.

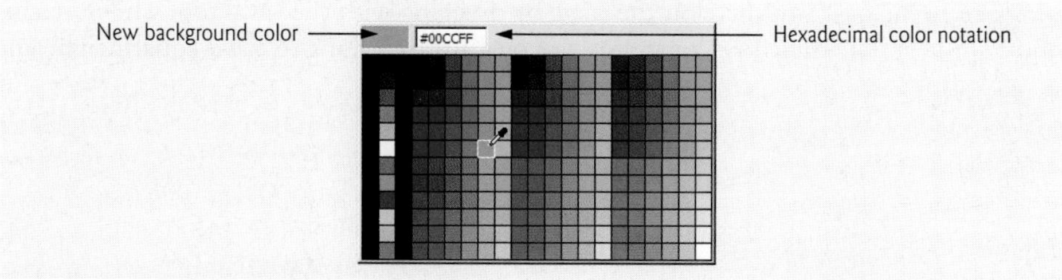

Fig. 16.5 | Selecting a background color.

Dimensions define the size of the movie as it displays on the screen. For this example, set the movie **width** to **200** pixels and the movie **height** to **180** pixels. Click **OK** to apply the changes in the movie settings.

Software Engineering Observation 16.1

A movie's contents are not resized when you change the size of the movie stage.

With the new dimensions, the stage appears smaller. Select the **Zoom Tool** from the toolbox (Fig. 16.2) and click the stage once to enlarge it to 200 percent of its size (i.e., zoom in). The current zoom percentage appears in the upper-right above the stage editing area. Editing a movie with small dimensions is easier when the stage is enlarged. Press the *Alt* key while clicking the zoom tool to reduce the size of the work area (i.e., zoom out). Select the **Hand Tool** from the toolbox, and drag the stage to the center of the editing area. The hand tool may be accessed at any time by holding down the *spacebar* key.

16.3.1 Creating a Shape with the Oval Tool

Flash provides several editing tools and options for creating graphics. Flash creates shapes using vectors—mathematical equations that Flash uses to define size, shape and color. Some other graphics applications create raster graphics or bitmapped graphics. When vector graphics are saved, they are stored using equations. Raster graphics are defined by areas of colored pixels—the unit of measurement for most computer monitors. Raster graphics typically have larger file sizes because the computer saves the information for every pixel. Vector and raster graphics also differ in their ability to be resized. Vector graphics can be resized without losing clarity, whereas raster graphics lose clarity as they are enlarged or reduced.

We will now create an interactive button out of a circular shape. You can create shapes by dragging with the shape tools. Select the Oval tool from the toolbox. If the Oval tool is not already displayed, click and hold the Rectangle/Oval tool to display the list of rectangle and oval tools. We use this tool to specify the button area. Every shape has a Stroke color and a Fill color. The stroke color is the color of a shape's outline, and the fill color is the color that fills the shape. Click the swatches in the **Colors** section of the toolbox (Fig. 16.6) to set the fill color to red and the stroke color to black. Select the colors from the web-safe palette or enter their hexadecimal values.

Clicking the **Black and white** button resets the stroke color to black and the fill color to white. Selecting the Swap colors option switches the stroke and fill colors. A shape can be created without a fill or stroke color by selecting the No color option (⊠) when you select either the stroke or fill swatch.

Create the oval anywhere on the stage by dragging with the Oval tool while pressing the *Shift* key. The *Shift* key constrains the oval's proportions to have equal height and

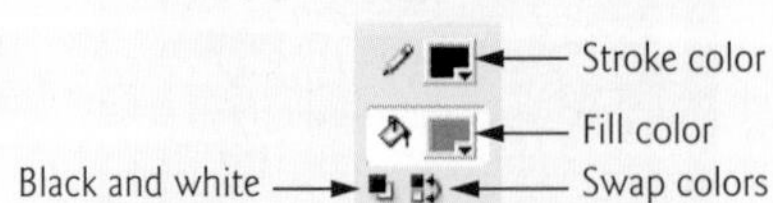

Fig. 16.6 | Setting the fill and stroke colors.

width (i.e., a circle). The same technique creates a square with the Rectangle tool or draws a straight line with the Pencil tool. Drag the mouse until the circle is approximately the size of a dime, then release the mouse button.

After you draw the oval, a dot appears in frame 1, the first frame of the timeline for **Layer 1**. This dot signifies a keyframe (Fig. 16.7), which indicates a point of change in a timeline. Whenever you draw a shape in an empty frame, Flash creates a keyframe.

The shape's fill and stroke may be edited individually. Click the red area with the Selection tool (black arrow) to select the circle fill. A grid of white dots appears over an object when it is selected (Fig. 16.8). Click the black stroke around the circle while pressing the *Shift* key to add to this selection. You can also make multiple selections by dragging with the selection tool to draw a selection box around specific items.

A shape's size can be modified with the **Properties** panel when the shape is selected (Fig. 16.9). If the panel is not open, open it by selecting **Properties** from the **Window** menu or pressing *<Ctrl>-F3*.

Set the width and height of the circle by typing **30** into the **W:** text field and **30** into the **H:** text field. Entering an equal width and height maintains a constrained aspect ratio while changing the circle's size. A constrained aspect ratio maintains an object's proportions as it is resized. Press *Enter* to apply these values.

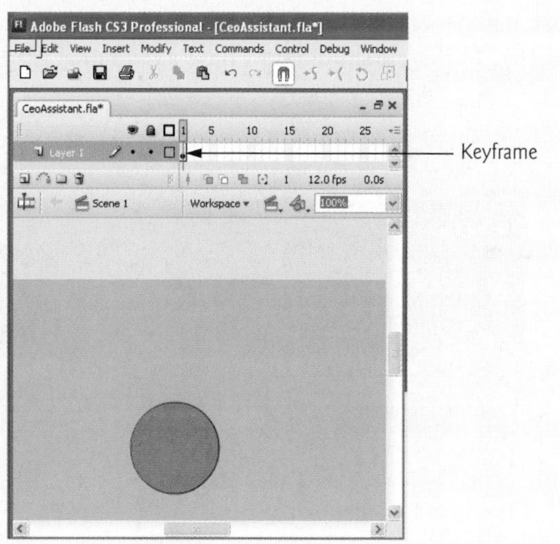

Fig. 16.7 | Keyframe added to the timeline.

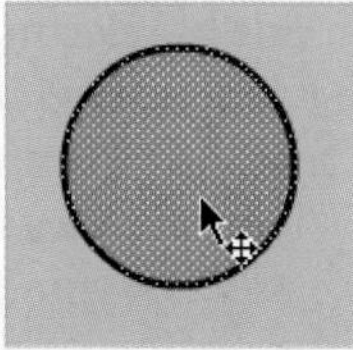

Fig. 16.8 | Making multiple selections with the Selection tool.

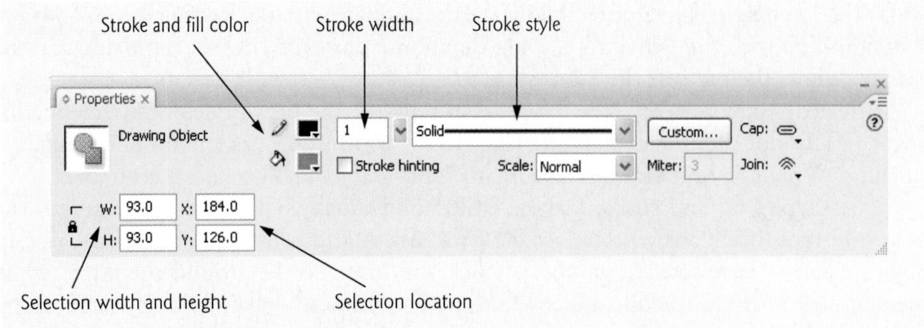

Fig. 16.9 | Modifying the size of a shape with the **Properties window.**

The next step is to modify the shape's color. We will apply a gradient fill—a gradual progression of color that fills the shape. Open the **Swatches** panel (Fig. 16.10), either by selecting **Swatches** from the **Window** menu or by pressing *<Ctrl>-F9*. The **Swatches** panel provides four radial gradients and three linear gradients, although you also can create and edit gradients with the **Color** panel.

Click outside the circle with the Selection tool to deselect the circle. Now, select only the red fill with the Selection tool. Change the fill color by clicking the red radial gradient fill in the **Swatches** panel. The gradient fills are located at the bottom of the **Swatches** panel (Fig. 16.10). The circle should now have a red radial gradient fill with a black stroke surrounding it.

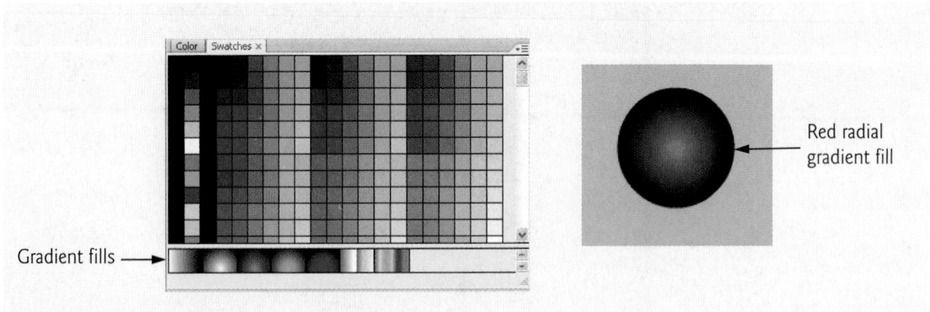

Fig. 16.10 | Choosing a gradient fill.

16.3.2 Adding Text to a Button

Button titles communicate a button's function to the user. The easiest way to create a title is with the Text tool. Create a button title by selecting the Text tool and clicking the center of the button. Next, type GO in capital letters. Highlight the text with the Text tool. Once text is selected, you can change the font, text size and font color with the **Properties** window (Fig. 16.11). Select a sans-serif font, such as **Arial** or **Verdana**, from the font drop-down list. Set the font size to **14** pt either by typing the size into the font size field or by pressing the arrow button next to it, revealing the size selection slider—a vertical slider that, when moved, changes the font size. Set the font weight to bold by clicking the bold

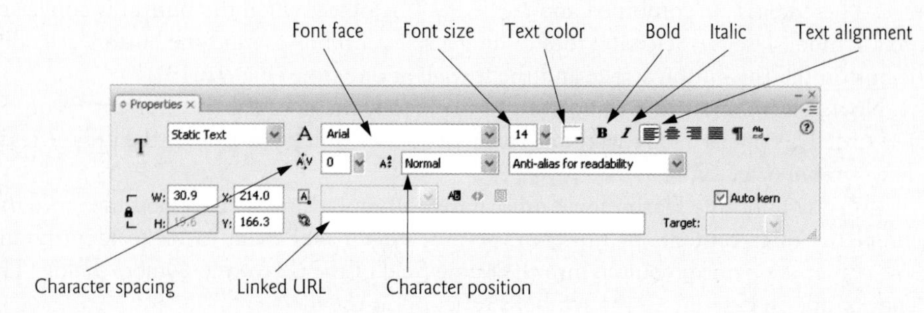

Fig. 16.11 | Setting the font face, size, weight and color with the **Properties window**.

button (**B**). Finally, change the font color by clicking the text color swatch and selecting white from the palette.

Look-and-Feel Observation 16.1

Sans-serif fonts, such as Arial, Helvetica and Verdana, are easier to read on a computer monitor, and therefore ensure better usability.

If the text does not appear in the correct location, drag it to the center of the button with the Selection tool. The button is almost complete and should look similar to Fig. 16.12.

Fig. 16.12 | Adding text to the button.

16.3.3 Converting a Shape into a Symbol

A Flash movie consists of scenes and symbols. Each scene contains all graphics and symbols. The parent movie may contain several symbols that are reusable movie elements, such as graphics, buttons and movie clips. A scene timeline can contain numerous symbols, each with its own timeline and properties. A scene may have several instances of any given symbol (i.e., the same symbol can appear multiple times in one scene). You can edit symbols independently of the scene by using the symbol's editing stage. The editing stage is separate from the scene stage and contains only one symbol.

Good Programming Practice 16.2

Reusing symbols can drastically reduce file size, thereby allowing faster downloads.

To make our button interactive, we must first convert the button into a button symbol. The button consists of distinct text, color fill and stroke elements on the parent stage. These items are combined and treated as one object when the button is converted into a symbol. Use the Selection tool to drag a selection box around the button, selecting the button fill, the button stroke and the text all at one time (Fig. 16.13).

Now, select **Convert to Symbol...** from the **Modify** menu or use the shortcut *F8* on the keyboard. This opens the **Convert to Symbol** dialog, in which you can set the properties of a new symbol (Fig. 16.14).

Every symbol in a Flash movie must have a unique name. It is a good idea to name symbols by their contents or function, because this makes them easier to identify and reuse. Enter the name **go button** into the **Name** field of the **Convert to Symbol** dialog. The **Behavior** option determines the symbol's function in the movie.

You can create three different types of symbols—movie clips, buttons and graphics. A movie clip symbol's behavior is similar to that of a scene and thus it is ideal for recurring animations. Graphic symbols are ideal for static images and basic animations. Button symbols are objects that perform button actions, such as rollovers and hyperlinking. A rollover is an action that changes the appearance of a button when the mouse passes over it. For this example, select **Button** as the type of symbol and click **OK**. The button should now be surrounded by a blue box with crosshairs in the upper-left corner, indicating that the button is a symbol. Also, in the **Properties** window panel, name this instance of the **go button** symbol **goButton** in the field containing **<Instance Name>**. Use the selection tool to drag the button to the lower-right corner of the stage.

The **Library** panel (Fig. 16.15) stores every symbol present in a movie and is accessed through the **Window** menu or by the shortcuts *<Ctrl>-L* or *F11*. Multiple instances of a symbol can be placed in a movie by dragging and dropping the symbol from the **Library** panel onto the stage.

The **Movie Explorer** displays the movie structure and is accessed by selecting **Movie Explorer** from the **Window** menu or by pressing *<Alt>-F3* (Fig. 16.16). The **Movie Explorer** panel illustrates the relationship between the current scene (**Scene 1**) and its symbols.

Fig. 16.13 | Selecting an object with the selection tool.

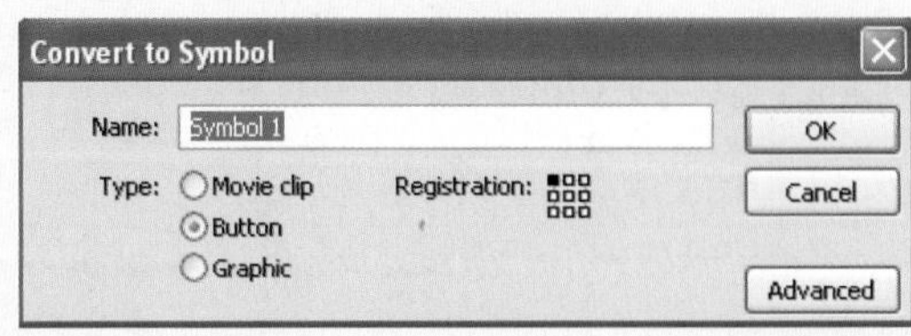

Fig. 16.14 | Creating a new symbol with the **Convert to Symbol** dialog.

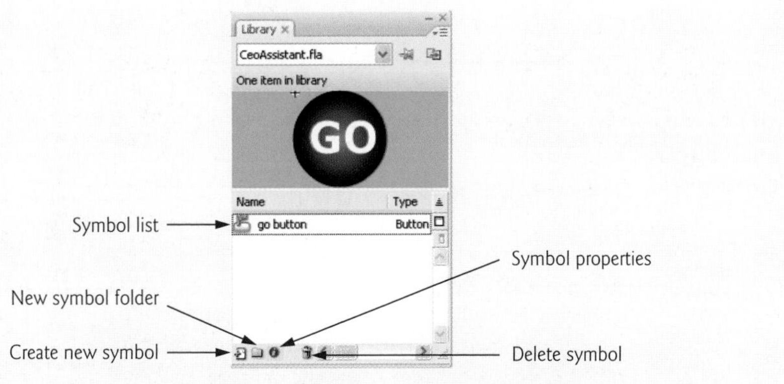

Fig. 16.15 | **Library** panel.

Fig. 16.16 | **Movie Explorer** for `CeoAssistant.fla`.

16.3.4 Editing Button Symbols

The next step in this example is to make the button symbol interactive. The different components of a button symbol, such as its text, color fill and stroke, may be edited in the symbol's editing stage, which you can access by double clicking the icon next to the symbol in the **Library**. A button symbol's timeline contains four frames, one for each of the button states (up, over and down) and one for the hit area.

The up state (indicated by the **Up** frame on screen) is the default state before the user presses the button or rolls over it with the mouse. Control shifts to the over state (i.e., the **Over** frame) when the user rolls over the button with the mouse cursor. The button's down state (i.e., the **Down** frame) plays when a user presses a button. You can create interactive, user-responsive buttons by customizing the appearance of a button in each of these states. Graphic elements in the hit state (i.e., the **Hit** frame) are not visible to a viewer of the movie; they exist simply to define the active area of the button (i.e., the area that can be clicked). The hit state will be discussed further in Section 16.6.

By default, buttons have only the up state activated when they are created. You may activate other states by adding keyframes to the other three frames. Keyframes for a button, discussed in the next section, determine how a button reacts when it is rolled over or clicked with the mouse.

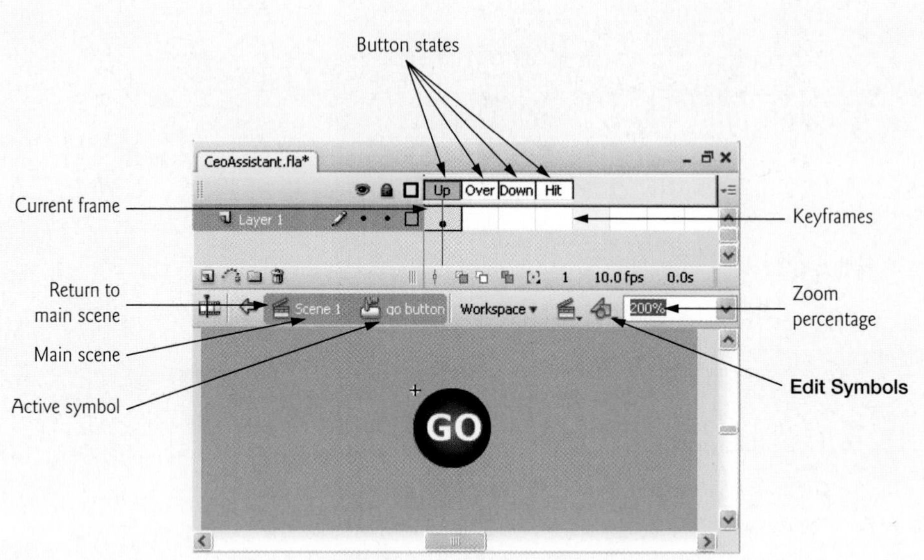

Fig. 16.17 | Modifying button states with a button's editing stage.

16.3.5 Adding Keyframes

Keyframes are points of change in a Flash movie and appear in the timeline with a dot. By adding keyframes to a button symbol's timeline, you can control how the button reacts to user interactions. The following step shows how to create a button rollover effect, which is accomplished by inserting a keyframe in the button's **Over** frame, then changing the button's appearance in that frame. Right click the **Over** frame and select **Insert Keyframe** from the resulting menu or press *F6* (Fig. 16.18).

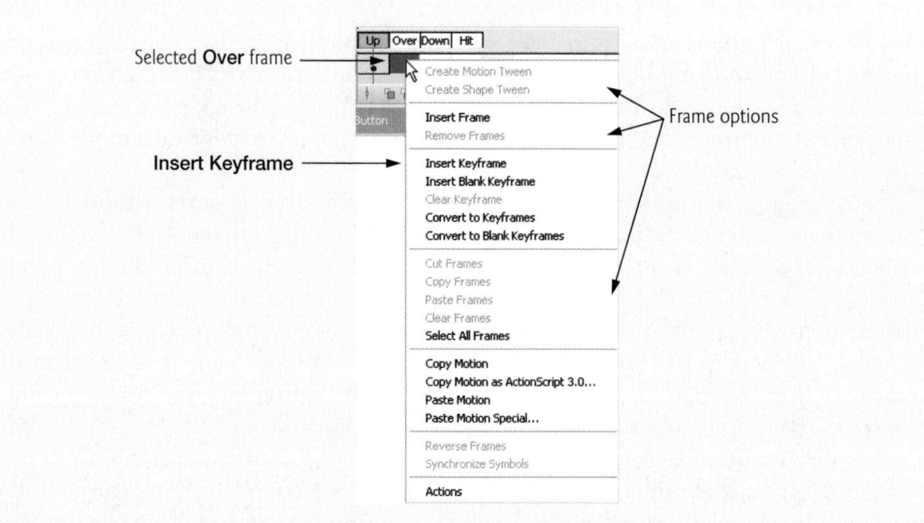

Fig. 16.18 | Inserting a keyframe.

Select the **Over** frame and click outside the button area with the selection tool to deselect the button's components. Change the color of the button in the **Over** state from red gradient fill to green gradient fill by selecting only the fill portion of the button with the Selection tool. Select the green gradient fill in the **Swatches** panel to change the color of the button in the **Over** state. Changing the color of the button in the over state does not affect the color of the button in the up state. Now, when the user moves the cursor over the button (in the up state) the button animation is replaced by the animation in the **Over** state. Here, we change only the button's color, but we could have created an entirely new animation in the **Over** state. The button will now change from red to green when the user rolls over the button with the mouse. The button will return to red when the mouse is no longer positioned over the button.

16.3.6 Adding Sound to a Button

The next step is to add a sound effect that plays when a user clicks the button. Flash imports sounds in the `WAV` (Windows), `AIFF` (Macintosh) or `MP3` formats. Several button sounds are available free for download from sites such as Flashkit (`www.flashkit.com`) and Muinar (`www.sounds.muinar.com`). For this example, download the cash register sound in `WAV` format from

```
www.flashkit.com/soundfx/Industrial_Commercial/Cash
```

Click the **Download** link to download the sound from this site. This link opens a new web page from which the user chooses the sound format. Choose `MP3` as the file format by clicking the **mp3** link. Save the file to the same folder as `CeoAssistant.fla`. Extract the sound file and save it in the same folder as `CeoAssistant.fla`.

Once the sound file is extracted, it can be imported into Flash. Import the sound into the **Library** by choosing **Import to Library...** from the **Import** submenu of the **File** menu. Select **All Formats** in the **Files of type** field of the **Import** dialog so that all available files are displayed. Select the sound file and press **Open**. This imports the sound file and places it in the movie's **Library**, making it available to use in the movie.

You can add sound to a movie by placing the sound clip in a keyframe or over a series of frames. For this example, we add the sound to the button's down state so that the sound plays when the user presses the button. Select the button's **Down** frame and press *F6* to add a keyframe.

Add the sound to the **Down** keyframe by dragging it from the **Library** to the stage. Open the **Properties** window (Fig. 16.19) and select the **Down** frame in the timeline to define the sound's properties in the movie. To ensure the desired sound has been added to the keyframe, choose the sound filename from the **Sound** drop-down list. This list contains all the sounds that have been added to the movie. Make sure the **Sync** field is set to **Event** so that the sound plays when the user clicks the button. If the **Down** frame has a blue wave or line through it, the sound effect has been added to the button.

Next, optimize the sound for the web. Double click the sound icon in the **Library** panel to open the **Sound Properties** dialog (Fig. 16.20). The settings in this dialog change the way that the sound is saved in the final movie. Different settings are optimal for different sounds and different audiences. For this example, set the **Compression** type to **MP3**, which reduces file size. Ensure that **Use imported MP3 quality** is selected. If the sound clip

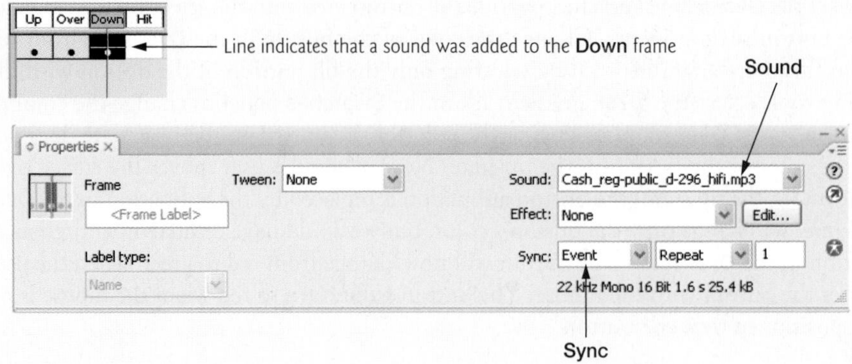

Fig. 16.19 | Adding sound to a button.

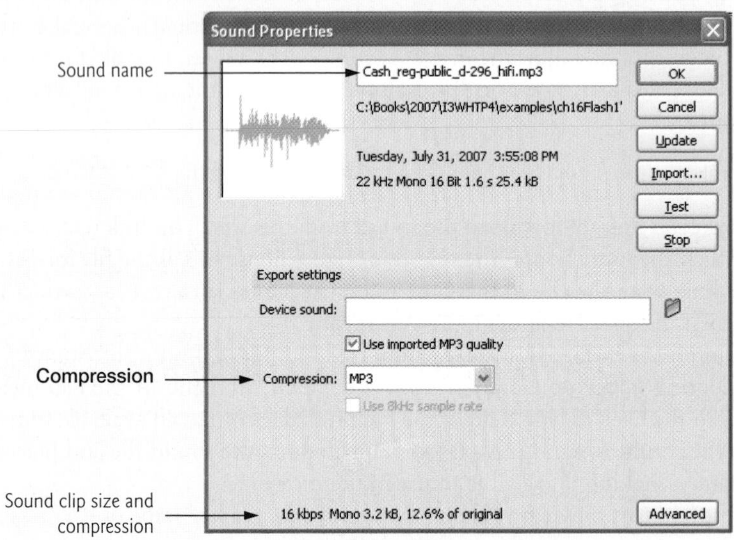

Fig. 16.20 | Optimizing sound with the **Sound Properties** dialog.

is long, or if the source MP3 was encoded with a high bitrate, you may want to deselect this and specify your own bitrate to save space.

The sound clip is now optimized for use on the web. Return to the scene by pressing the **Edit Scene** button () and selecting **Scene 1** or by clicking **Scene 1** at the top of the movie window.

16.3.7 Verifying Changes with Test Movie

It is a good idea to ensure that movie components function correctly before proceeding further with development. Movies can be viewed in their **published state** with the Flash Player. The published state of a movie is how it would appear if viewed over the web or with the Flash Player. Published Flash movies have the Shockwave Flash extension `.swf` (pronounced "swiff"). SWF files can be viewed but not edited.

Select **Test Movie** from the **Control** menu (or press *<Ctrl>-Enter*) to export the movie into the Flash Player. A window opens with the movie in its published state. Move the cursor over the **GO** button to view the color change (Fig. 16.21), then click the button to play the sound. Close the test window to return to the stage. If the button's color does not change, return to the button's editing stage and check that you followed the steps correctly.

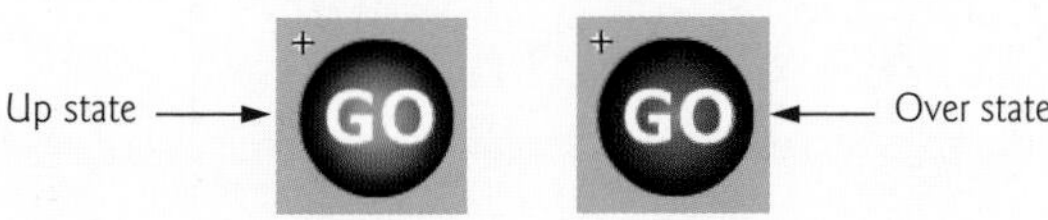

Fig. 16.21 | **GO** button in its up and over states.

16.3.8 Adding Layers to a Movie

The next step in this example is to create the movie's title animation. It's a good idea for you to create a new layer for new movie items. A movie can be composed of many layers, each having its own attributes and effects. Layers organize movie elements so that they can be animated and edited separately, making the composition of complex movies easier. Graphics in higher layers appear over the graphics in lower layers.

Before creating a new title layer, double click the text **Layer 1** in the timeline. Rename the layer by entering the text `Button` into the name field (Fig. 16.22).

Create a new layer for the title animation by clicking the Insert a new layer button or by selecting **Layer** from the **Timeline** submenu of the **Insert** menu. The Insert a new layer button places a layer named **Layer 2** above the selected layer. Change the name of **Layer 2** to **Title**. Activate the new layer by clicking its name.

Good Programming Practice 16.3

Always give movie layers descriptive names. Descriptive names are especially helpful when working with many layers.

Select the Text tool to create the title text. Click with the Text tool in the center of the stage toward the top. Use the **Property** window to set the font to **Arial**, the text color to navy blue (hexadecimal value #000099) and the font size to **20** pt (Fig. 16.23). Set the text alignment to center by clicking the center justify button.

Type the title **CEO Assistant 1.0** (Fig. 16.24), then click the selection tool. A blue box appears around the text, indicating that it is a grouped object. This text is a grouped object because each letter is a part of a text string and cannot be edited independently. Text can be broken apart for color editing, shape modification or animation (shown in a later example). Once text has been broken apart, it may not be edited with the Text tool.

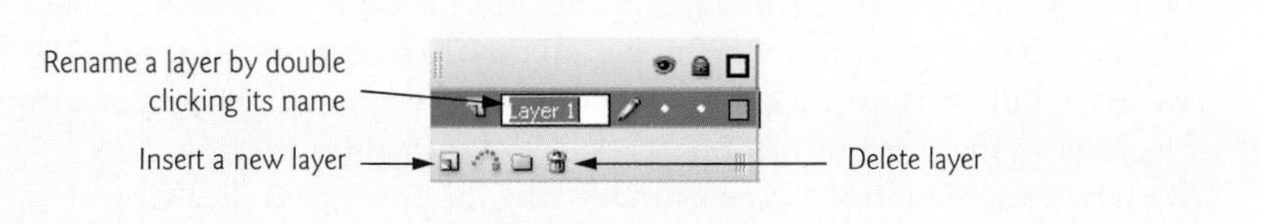

Fig. 16.22 | Renaming a layer.

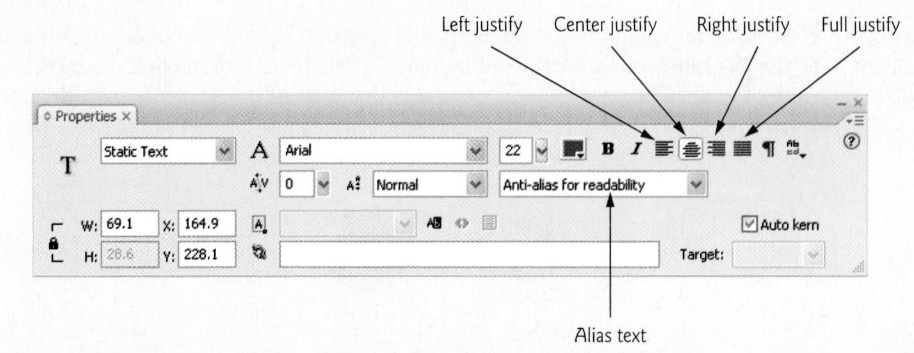

Fig. 16.23 | Setting text alignment with the **Properties window**.

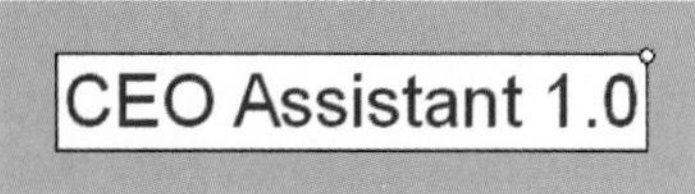

Fig. 16.24 | Creating a title with the Text tool.

16.3.9 Animating Text with Tweening

Animations in Flash are created by inserting keyframes into the timeline. Each keyframe represents a significant change in the position or appearance of the animated object.

You may use several methods to animate objects in Flash. One is to create a series of successive keyframes in the timeline. Modifying the animated object in each keyframe creates an animation as the movie plays. Another method is to insert a keyframe later in the timeline representing the final appearance and position of the object, then create a tween between the two keyframes. Tweening is an automated process in which Flash creates the intermediate steps of the animation between two keyframes.

Flash provides two tweening methods. Shape tweening morphs an object from one shape to another. For instance, the word "star" could morph into the shape of a star. Shape tweening can be applied only to ungrouped objects, not symbols or grouped objects. Be sure to break apart text before attempting to create a shape tween. Motion tweening moves objects around the stage. Motion tweening can be applied to symbols or grouped objects.

You can only have one symbol per layer if you intend to tween the symbol. At this point in the development of the example movie, only frame 1 is occupied in each layer. Keyframes must be designated in the timeline before adding the motion tween. Click frame 15 in the **Title** layer and press *F6* to add a new keyframe. All the intermediate frames in the timeline should turn gray, indicating that they are active (Fig. 16.25). Until the motion tween is added, each active frame contains the same image as the first frame.

The button disappears from the movie after the first frame because only the first frame is active in the button layer. Before the movie is completed, we'll move the button to frame 15 of its layer so that the button appears once the animation stops.

We now create a motion tween by modifying the position of the title text. Select frame 1 of the **Title** layer and select the title text with the Selection tool. Drag the title text directly above the stage. When the motion tween is added, the title will move onto the stage. Add

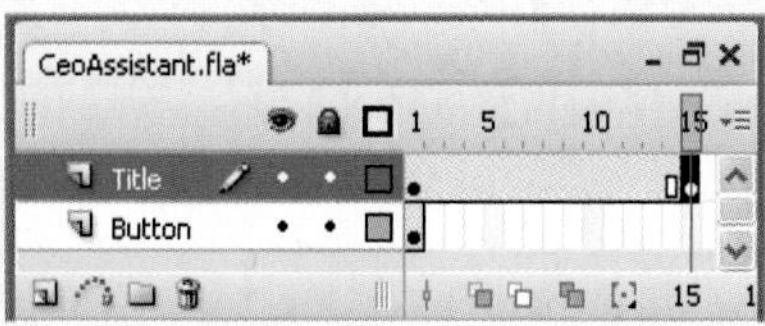

Fig. 16.25 | Adding a keyframe to create an animation.

the motion tween by right clicking frame 1 in the **Title** layer. Then select **Create Motion Tween** from the **Insert > Timeline** menu. Tweens also can be added using the **Tween type** drop down menu in the **Properties** window. Frames 2–14 should turn light blue, with an arrow pointing from the keyframe in frame 1 to the keyframe in frame 15 (Fig. 16.26).

Test the movie again with the Flash Player by pressing *<Ctrl>-Enter* to view the new animation. Note that the animation continues to loop—all Flash movies loop by default. Adding the ActionScript function `stop` to the last frame in the movie stops the movie from looping. For this example, click frame 15 of the **Title** layer, and open the **Actions** panel by selecting **Window > Actions** or by pressing *F9* (Fig. 16.27). The **Actions** panel is used to add

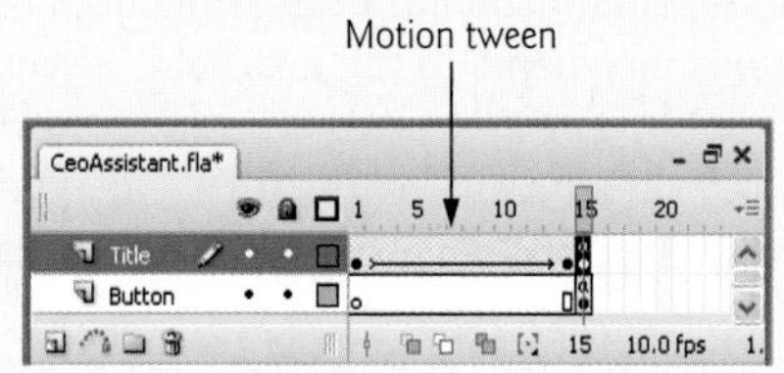

Fig. 16.26 | Creating a motion tween.

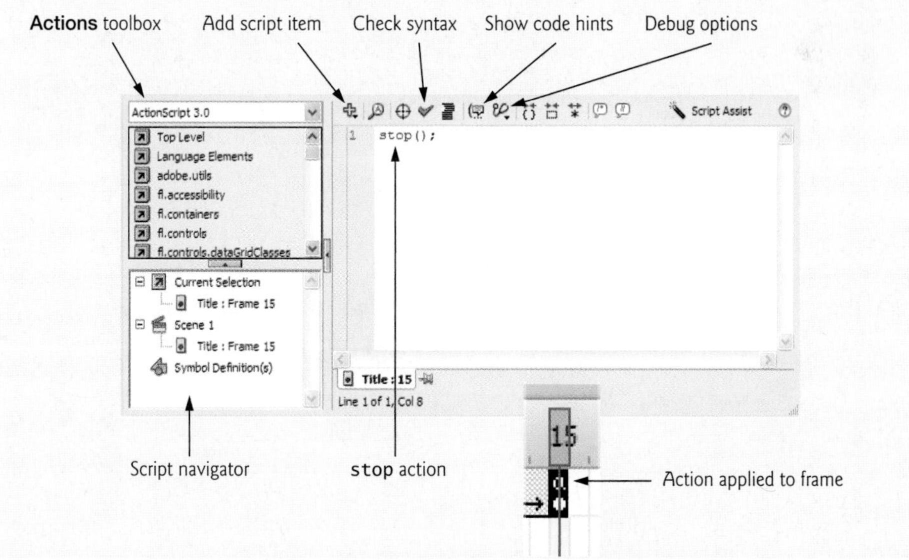

Fig. 16.27 | Adding ActionScript to a frame with the **Actions** panel.

actions (i.e., scripted behaviors) to symbols and frames. Here, add `stop();` so that the movie does not loop back to the first frame.

Minimize the **Actions** panel by clicking the down arrow in its title bar. The small letter **a** in frame 15 of the **Title** layer indicates the new action. Test the movie again in Flash Player. Now, the animation should play only once.

The next step is to move the button to frame 15 so that it appears only at the end of the movie. Add a keyframe to frame 15 of the **Button** layer. A copy of the button should appear in the new keyframe. Select the button in the first frame and delete it by pressing the *Delete* key. The button will now appear only in the keyframe at the end of the movie.

16.3.10 Adding a Text Field

The final component of our movie is a text field, which contains a string of text that changes every time the user presses the button. An instance name is given to the text field so that ActionScript added to the button can control its contents.

Create a layer named **Advice** for the new text field, and add a keyframe to frame 15 of the **Advice** layer. Select the Text tool and create the text field by dragging with the mouse in the stage (Fig. 16.28). Place the text field directly below the title. Set the text font to **Courier New, 12 pt** and the style to bold in the **Properties** window. You can alter the size of the text field by dragging the anchor that appears in its upper-right corner.

You'll now assign an instance name to the text field. Select the text field and open the **Properties** window (Fig. 16.29). The **Properties** window contains several options for modifying text fields. The top-left field contains the different types of text fields. **Static Text**, the default setting for this panel, creates text that does not change. The second option,

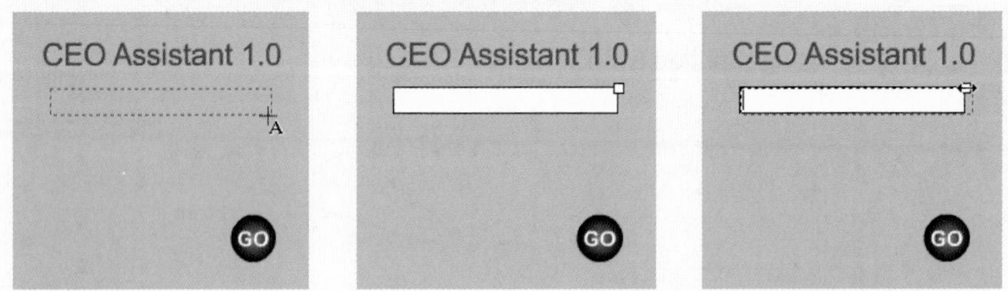

Fig. 16.28 | Creating a text field.

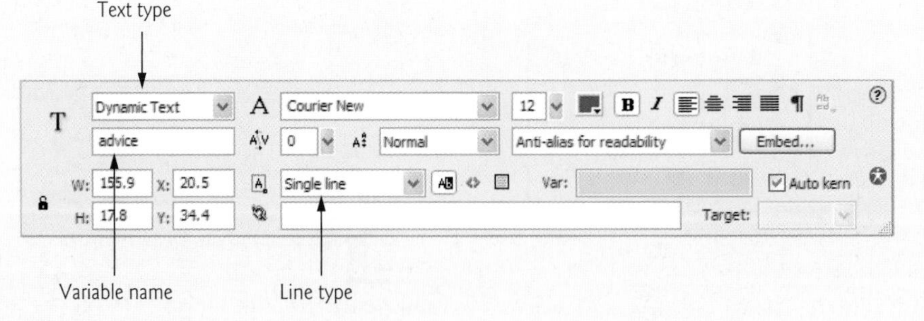

Fig. 16.29 | Creating a dynamic text field with the **Properties** window.

Dynamic Text, creates text that can be changed or determined by outside variables through ActionScript. When you select this text type, new options appear below this field. The **Line type** drop-down list specifies the text field size as either a single line or multiple lines of text. The **Instance Name** field allows you to give the text field an instance name by which it can be referenced in script. For example, if the text field instance name is `newText`, you could write a script setting `newText.text` equal to a string or a function output. The third text type, **Input Text**, creates a text field into which the viewers of the movie can input their own text. For this example, select **Dynamic Text** as the text type. Set the line type to **Single Line** and enter `advice` as the instance name. This instance name will be used in ActionScript later in this example.

16.3.11 Adding ActionScript

All the movie objects are now in place, so `CEO Assistant 1.0` is almost complete. The final step is to add ActionScript to the button, enabling the script to change the contents of the text field every time a user clicks the button. Our script calls a built-in Flash function to generate a random number. This random number corresponds to a message in a list of possible messages to display. [*Note:* The ActionScript in this chapter has been formatted to conform with the code-layout conventions of this book. The Flash application may produce code that is formatted differently.]

Select frame 15 of the **Button** layer and open the **Actions** panel. We want the action to occur when the user clicks the button. To achieve this, insert the statement:

```
goButton.addEventListener( MouseEvent.MOUSE_DOWN, goFunction );
```

This statement uses the button object's instance name (**goButton**) to call the **`addEventListener`** function, which registers an event handler (`goFunction` in this example) that will be called when the event takes place (i.e., when you click the button). The first argument, `MouseEvent.MOUSE_DOWN`, specifies that an action is performed when the user presses the button with the mouse.

The next step is to add the function that handles this event. Create a new function named `goFunction` by using the code

```
function goFunction( event : MouseEvent ) : void
{
} // end function goFunction
```

The function's one parameter is a `MouseEvent`, implying that the function has to be provided with a mouse action to be accessed. The function does not return anything, hence the `void return` value. Inside this function, add the following statement:

```
var randomNumber : int = Math.floor( ( Math.random() * 5 ) );
```

which creates an integer variable called `randomNumber` and assigns it a random value. For this example, we use the `Math.random` function to choose a random number from 0 to 1. `Math.random` returns a random floating-point number from 0.0 up to, but not including, 1.0. Then, it is scaled accordingly, depending on what the range should be. Since we want all the numbers between 0 and 4, inclusive, the value returned by the `Math.random` should be multiplied by 5 to produce a number in the range 0.0 up to, but not including, 5.0.

Finally, this new number should be rounded down to the largest integer smaller than itself, using the `Math.floor` function.

Error-Prevention Tip 16.1

ActionScript is case sensitive. Be aware of the case when entering arguments or variable names.

The value of `randomNumber` determines the text string that appears in the text field. A `switch` statement sets the text field's value based on the value of `randomNumber`. [*Note:* For more on `switch` statements, refer to Chapter 8.] On a new line in the `goFunction` function, insert the following `switch` statement:

```
switch ( randomNumber )
{
   case 0:
      advice.text = "Hire Someone!";
      break;
   case 1:
      advice.text = "Buy a Yacht!";
      break;
   case 2:
      advice.text = "Buy stock!";
      break;
   case 3:
      advice.text = "Go Golfing!";
      break;
   case 4:
      advice.text = "Hold a meeting!";
      break;
} // end switch
```

This statement displays different text in the `advice` text field based on the value of the variable `randomNumber`. The text field's `text` property specifies the text to display. If you feel ambitious, increase the number of `advice` statements by producing a larger range of random values and adding more `cases` to the `switch` statement. Minimize the **Actions** panel to continue.

Congratulations! You have now completed building `CEO Assistant 1.0`. Test the movie by pressing *<Ctrl>-Enter* and clicking the **GO** button. After testing the movie with the Flash Player, return to the main window and save the file.

16.4 Publishing Your Flash Movie

Flash movies must be published for users to view them outside the Flash CS3 environment and Flash Player. This section discusses the more common methods of publishing Flash movies. For this example, we want to publish in two formats, Flash and Windows Projector, which creates a standard Windows-executable file that works even if the user hasn't installed Flash. Select **Publish Settings...** from the **File** menu to open the **Publish Settings** dialog.

Select the **Flash**, **HTML** and **Windows Projector** checkboxes and uncheck all the others. Then click the **Flash** tab at the top of the dialog. This section of the dialog allows you to choose the Flash settings. Flash movies may be published in an older Flash version if you wish to support older Flash Players. Note that ActionScript 3.0 is not supported by older players, so choose a version with care. Publish the movie by clicking **Publish** in the **Publish Settings** dialog or by selecting **Publish** from the **File** menu. After you've published the movie, the directory in which you saved the movie will have several new files (Fig. 16.30). If you wish to place your movie on a website, be sure to copy the HTML, JavaScript and SWF files to your server.

Good Programming Practice 16.4

It is not necessary to transfer the `.fla` *version of your Flash movie to a web server unless you want other users to be able to download the editable version of the movie.*

As we can see in the `Ceo Assistant 1.0` example, Flash is a feature-rich program. We have only begun to use Flash to its full potential. ActionScript can create sophisticated programs and interactive movies. It also enables Flash to interact with ASP.NET (Chapter 25), PHP (Chapter 23), and JavaScript (Chapters 6–11), making it a program that integrates smoothly into a web environment.

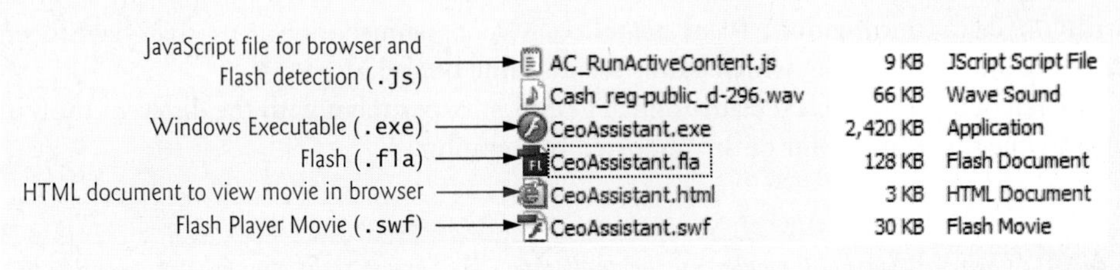

Fig. 16.30 | Published Flash files.

16.5 Creating Special Effects with Flash

The following sections introduce several Flash special effects. The preceding example familiarized you with basic movie development. The next sections cover many additional topics, from importing bitmaps to creating splash screens that display before a web page loads.

16.5.1 Importing and Manipulating Bitmaps

Some of the examples in this chapter require importing bitmapped images and other media into a Flash movie. The importing process is similar for all types of media, including images, sound and video. The following example shows how to import an image into a Flash movie.

Begin by creating a new Flash document. The image we are going to import is located in the Chapter 16 examples folder. Select **File > Import > Import to Stage...** (or press *<Ctrl>-R*) to display the **Import** dialog. Browse to the folder on your system containing this chapter's examples and open the folder labeled `images`. Select `bug.bmp` and click **OK** to continue. A bug image should appear on the stage. The **Library** panel stores imported images. You can convert imported images into editable shapes by selecting the image and pressing *<Ctrl>-B* or by choosing **Break Apart** from the **Modify** menu. Once an imported image is broken apart, it may be shape tweened or edited with editing tools, such as the

Lasso, Paint bucket, Eraser and Paintbrush. The editing tools are found in the toolbox and apply changes to a shape.

Dragging with the **Lasso tool** selects areas of shapes. The color of a selected area may be changed or the selected area may be moved. Click and drag with the Lasso tool to draw the boundaries of the selection. As with the button in the last example, when you select a shape area, a mesh of white dots covers the selection. Once an area is selected, you may change its color by selecting a new fill color with the fill swatch or by clicking the selection with the Paint bucket tool. The Lasso tool has different options (located in the **Options** section of the toolbox) including **Magic wand** and **Polygon mode**. The Magic wand option changes the Lasso tool into the Magic wand tool, which selects areas of similar colors. The polygonal lasso selects straight-edged areas.

The **Eraser tool** removes shape areas when you click and drag the tool across an area. You can change the eraser size using the tool options. Other options include settings that make the tool erase only fills or strokes.

The **Brush tool** applies color in the same way that the eraser removes color. The paintbrush color is selected with the fill swatch. The paintbrush tool options include a **Brush mode** option. These modes are **Paint behind**, which sets the tool to paint only in areas with no color information; **Paint selection**, which paints only areas that have been selected; and **Paint inside**, which paints inside a line boundary.

Each of these tools can create original graphics. Experiment with the different tools to change the shape and color of the imported bug graphic.

Portability Tip 16.1

When building Flash movies, use the smallest possible file size and web-safe colors to ensure that most people can view the movie regardless of bandwidth, processor speed or monitor resolution.

16.5.2 Creating an Advertisement Banner with Masking

Masking hides portions of layers. A masking layer hides objects in the layers beneath it, revealing only the areas that can be seen through the shape of the mask. Items drawn on a masking layer define the mask's shape and cannot be seen in the final movie. The next example, which builds a website banner, shows how to use masking frames to add animation and color effects to text.

Create a new Flash document and set the size of the stage to **470** pixels wide by **60** pixels high. Create three layers named **top**, **middle** and **bottom** according to their positions in the layer hierarchy. These names help track the masked layer and the visible layers. The **top** layer contains the mask, the **middle** layer becomes the masked animation and the **bottom** layer contains an imported bitmapped logo. Import the graphic `bug_apple.bmp` (from the `images` folder in this chapter's examples folder) into the first frame of the **top** layer, using the method described in the preceding section. This image will appear too large to fit in the stage area. Select the image with the selection tool and align it with the upper-left corner of the stage. Then select the Free transform tool in the toolbox (Fig. 16.31).

The Free transform tool allows us to resize an image. When an object is selected with this tool, anchors appear around its corners and sides. Click and drag an anchor to resize the image in any direction. Holding the *Shift* key while dragging a corner anchor ensures

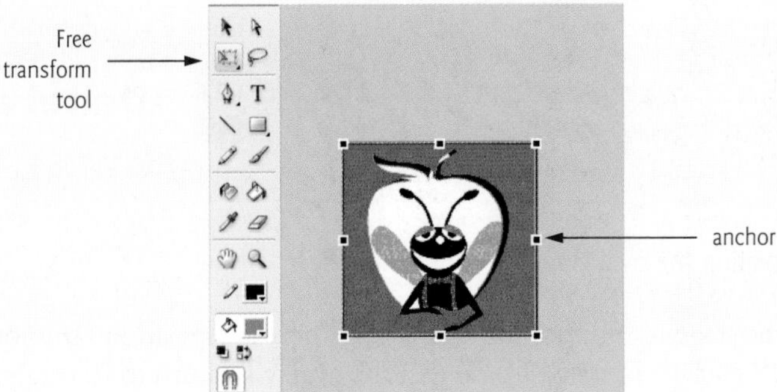

Fig. 16.31 | Resizing an image with the Free transform tool.

that the image maintains the original height and width ratio. Hold down the *Shift* key while dragging the lower-right anchor upward until the image fits on the stage.

Use the text tool to add text to frame 1 of the **top** layer. Use **Verdana, 28** pt bold, as the font. Select a blue text color, and make sure that **Static Text** is selected in the **Properties** window. Type the banner text "`Deitel and Associates`", making sure that the text fits inside the stage area, and use the Selection tool to position the text next to the image. This text becomes the object that masks an animation.

We must convert the text into a shape before using it as a mask. Click the text field with the Selection tool to ensure that it is active and select **Break Apart** twice from the **Modify** menu. Breaking the text apart once converts each letter into its own text field. Breaking it apart again converts the letters into shapes that cannot be edited with the text tool, but can be manipulated as regular graphics.

Copy the contents of the **top** layer to the **bottom** layer before creating the mask, so that the text remains visible when the mask is added. Right click frame 1 of the **top** layer, and select **Copy Frames** from the resulting menu. Paste the contents of the **top** layer into frame 1 of the **bottom** layer by right clicking frame 1 of the **bottom** layer and selecting **Paste Frames** from the menu. This shortcut pastes the frame's contents in the same positions as the original frame. Delete the extra copy of the bug image by selecting the bug image in the **top** layer with the selection tool and pressing the *Delete* key.

Next, you'll create the animated graphic that the banner text in the **top** layer masks. Click in the first frame of the **middle** layer and use the Oval tool to draw a circle to the left of the image that is taller than the text. The oval does not need to fit inside the banner area. Set the oval stroke to no color by clicking the stroke swatch and selecting the **No color** option. Set the fill color to the rainbow gradient (Fig. 16.32), found at the bottom of the **Swatches** panel.

Select the oval by clicking it with the Selection tool, and convert the oval to a symbol by pressing *F8*. Name the symbol **oval** and set the behavior to **Graphic.** When the banner is complete, the oval will move across the stage; however, it will be visible only through the text mask in the **top** layer. Move the oval just outside the left edge of the stage, indicating the point at which the oval begins its animation. Create a keyframe in frame 20 of the **middle** layer and another in frame 40. These keyframes indicate the different locations of the **oval** symbol during the animation. Click frame 20 and move the oval just outside

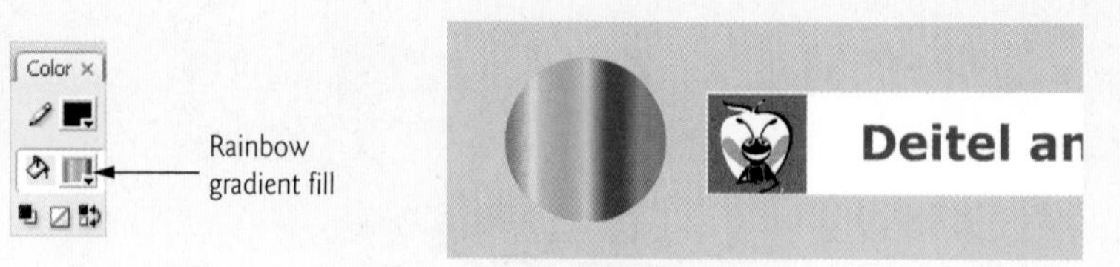

Fig. 16.32 | Creating the oval graphic.

the right side of the stage to indicate the animation's next key position. Do not move the position of the **oval** graphic in frame 40, so that the oval will return to its original position at the end of the animation. Create the first part of the animation by right clicking frame 1 of the **middle** layer and choosing **Create Motion Tween** from the menu. Repeat this step for frame 20 of the **middle** layer, making the **oval** symbol move from left to right and back. Add keyframes to frame 40 of both the **top** and **bottom** layers so that the other movie elements appear throughout the movie.

Now that all the supporting movie elements are in place, the next step is to apply the masking effect. To do so, right click the **top** layer and select **Mask** (Fig. 16.33). Adding a mask to the **top** layer masks only the items in the layer directly below it (the **middle** layer), so the bug logo in the **bottom** layer remains visible at all times. Adding a mask also locks the **top** and **middle** layers to prevent further editing.

Now that the movie is complete, save it as `banner.fla` and test it with the Flash Player. The rainbow oval is visible through the text as it animates from left to right. The text in the bottom layer is visible in the portions not containing the rainbow (Fig. 16.34).

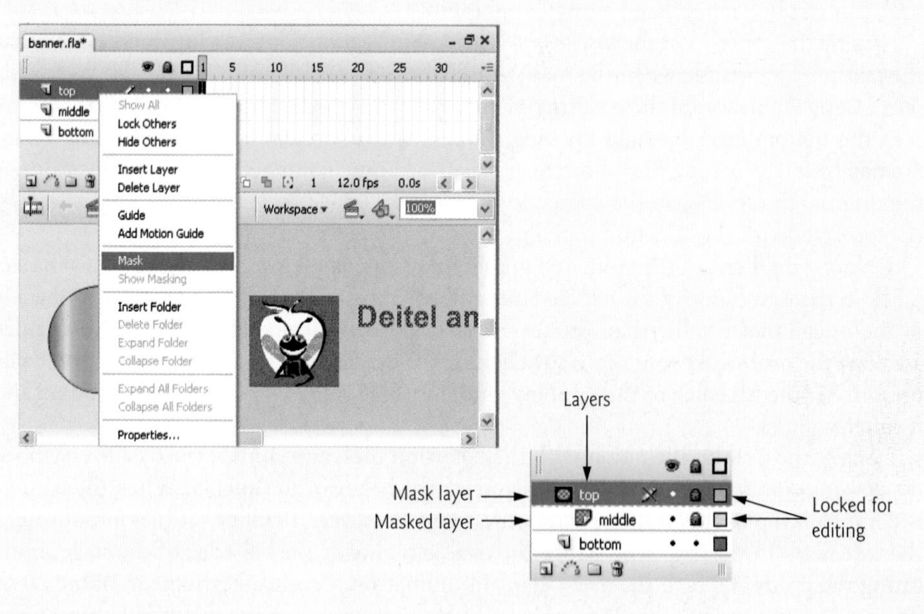

Fig. 16.33 | Creating a mask layer.

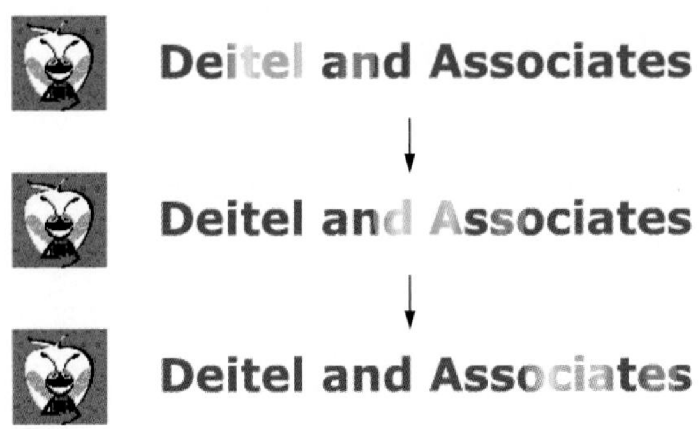

Fig. 16.34 | Completed banner.

16.5.3 Adding Online Help to Forms

In this section, we build on Flash techniques introduced earlier in this chapter, including tweening, masking, importing sound and bitmapped images, and writing ActionScript. In the following example, we apply these various techniques to create an online form that offers interactive help. The interactive help consists of animations that appear when a user presses buttons located next to the form fields. Each button contains a script that triggers an animation, and each animation provides the user with information regarding the form field that corresponds to the pressed button.

Each animation is a movie-clip symbol that is placed in a separate frame and layer of the scene. Adding a `stop` action to frame 1 pauses the movie until the user presses a button.

Begin by creating a new movie, using default movie size settings. Set the frame rate to 24 fps. The first layer will contain the site name, form title and form captions. Change the name of **Layer 1** to **text**. Add a `stop` action to frame 1 of the text layer. Create the site name `Bug2Bug.com` as static text in the **text** layer using a large, bold font, and place the title at the top of the page. Next, place the form name `Registration Form` as static text beneath the site name, using the same font, but in a smaller size and different color. The final text element added to this layer is the text box containing the form labels. Create a text box using the **Text Tool**, and enter the text: `Name:`, `Member #:` and `Password:`, pressing *Enter* after entering each label to put it on a different line. Next, adjust the value of the **Line Spacing** field (the amount of space between lines of text) found by clicking the **Edit Format Options** button (¶) in the **Properties** window. Change the form field caption line spacing to **22** in the **Format Options** dialog (Fig. 16.35) and set the text alignment (found in the **Properties** window) to right justify.

Now we'll create the form fields for our help form. The first step in the production of these form fields is to create a new layer named **form**. In the **form** layer, draw a rectangle that is roughly the same height as the caption text. This rectangle will serve as a background for the form text fields (Fig. 16.36). We set a **Rectangle corner radius** of 6 px in the **Properties** panel. Feel free to experiment with other shapes and colors.

The next step is to convert the rectangle into a symbol so that it may be reused in the movie. Select the rectangle fill and stroke with the selection tool and press *F8* to convert the selection to a symbol. Set the symbol behavior to **Graphic** and name the symbol **form**

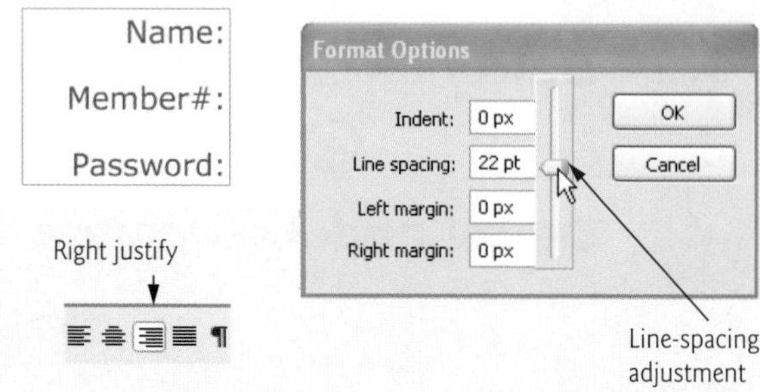

Fig. 16.35 | Adjusting the line spacing with the **Format Options** dialog.

Bug2Bug.com
Registration Form
Name:
Member#:
Password:

Fig. 16.36 | Creating a rectangle with rounded corners.

field. This symbol should be positioned next to the **Name:** caption. When the symbol is in place, open the **Library** panel by pressing *<Ctrl>-L*, select the **form** layer and drag two copies of the **form field** symbol from the **Library** onto the stage. This will create two new instances of this symbol. Use the Selection tool to align the fields with their corresponding captions. For more precise alignment, select the desired object with the Selection tool and press the arrow key on the keyboard in the direction you want to move the object. After alignment of the **form field** symbols, the movie should resemble Fig. 16.37.

We now add input text fields to our movie. An input text field is a text field into which the user can enter text. Select the Text tool and, using the **Properties** window, set the font to **Verdana**, **16** pt, with dark blue as the color. In the **Text type** pull-down menu in the **Properties** window, select **Input Text** (Fig. 16.38). Then, click and drag in the stage to create a text field slightly smaller than the **form field** symbol we just created. With the Selection tool, position the text field over the instance of the **form field** symbol associated with the name. Create a similar text field for member number and password. Select the Password text field, and select **Password** in the Line type pull-down menu in the **Properties** window. Selecting **Password** causes any text entered into the field by the user to appear as an asterisk (*). We have now created all the input text fields for our help form. In this

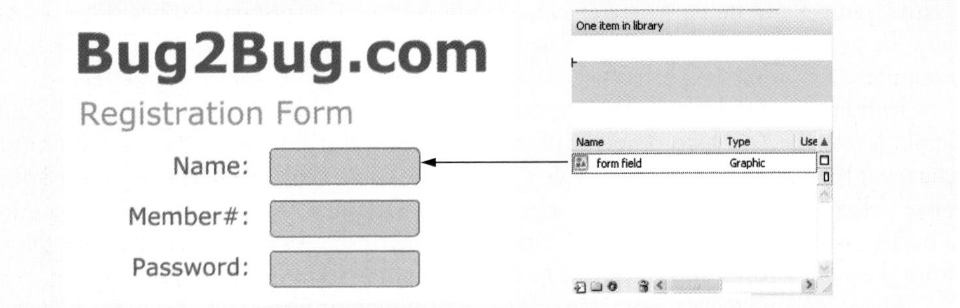

Fig. 16.37 | Creating multiple instances of a symbol with the **Library** panel.

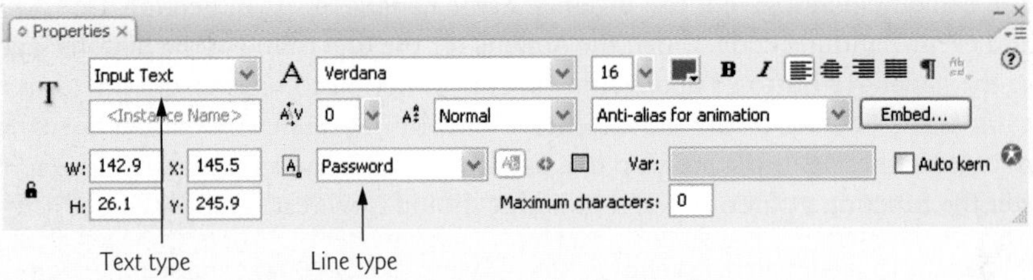

Fig. 16.38 | Input and password text-field creation.

example, we won't actually process the text entered into these fields. Using ActionScript, we could give each input text field a variable name, and send the values of these variables to a server-side script for processing.

Now that the form fields are in place, we can create the help associated with each field. Add two new layers. Name one layer **button** and the other **labels**. The **labels** layer will hold the frame label for each keyframe. A frame label is a text string that corresponds to a specific frame or series of frames. In the **labels** layer, create keyframes in frames 2, 3 and 4. Select frame 2 and enter `name` into the **Frame** field in the **Properties** window (Fig. 16.39).

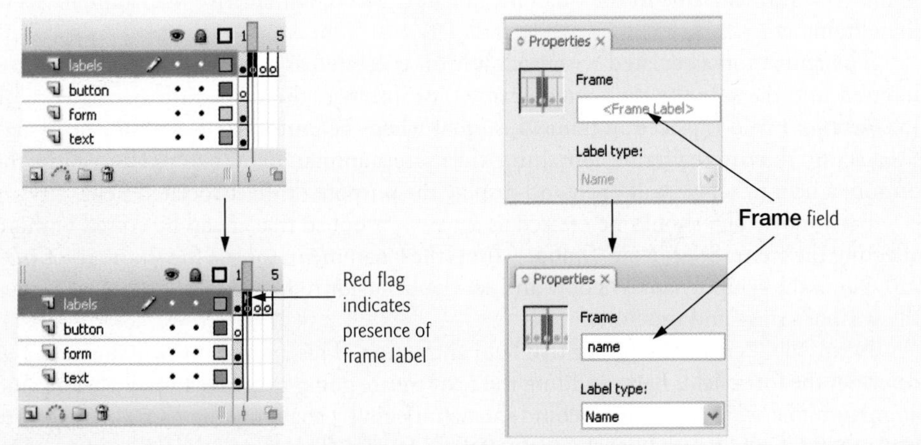

Fig. 16.39 | Adding **Frame Labels** using the **Properties window**.

Name frame 3 and frame 4 memberNumber and password, respectively. These frames can now be accessed either by number or by name. We use the labels again later in this example.

In frame 1 of the **button** layer, create a small circular button containing a question mark. [*Note:* the **Text type** property of the **Text Tool** will still be **Input Text**, so you must change it back to **Static Text**]. Position it next to the **name** field. When the button is complete, select all of its pieces with the selection tool, and press *F8* to convert the shape into a button symbol named **helpButton**. Drag two more instances of the **helpButton** symbol from the **Library** panel onto the stage next to each of the form fields.

These buttons will trigger animations that provide information about their corresponding form fields. A script will be added to each button so that the movie jumps to a particular frame when a user presses the button. Click the **helpButton** symbol associated with the **name** field and give it the instance name nameHelp. As in Section 16.3.11, we'll now add event-handling code. Open the **Actions** for the first frame of the **buttons** layer and invoke the nameHelp button's addEventListener function to register the function nameFunction as the handler of the mouse-click event. In nameFunction, add a gotoAndStop action, causing the movie play to skip to a particular frame and stop playing. Enter "name" between the function's parentheses. The script should now read as follows:

```
nameHelp.addEventListener( MouseEvent.MOUSE_DOWN, nameFunction );

function nameFunction( event : MouseEvent ) : void
{
   gotoAndStop( "name" );
}
```

When the user presses the nameHelp button, this script advances to the frame labeled name and stops. [*Note:* We could also have entered gotoAndStop(2), referenced by frame number, in place of gotoAndStop("name").] Add similar code for the memberHelp and passwordHelp buttons, changing the frame labels to memberNumber and password, the button instance names to memberHelp and passwordHelp and the function names to memberFunction and passwordFunction, respectively. Each button now has an action that points to a distinct frame in the timeline. We next add the interactive help animations to these frames.

The animation associated with each button is created as a movie-clip symbol that is inserted into the scene at the correct frame. For instance, the animation associated with the **Password** field is placed in frame 4, so that when the button is pressed, the gotoAndStop action skips to the frame containing the correct animation. When the user clicks the button, a help rectangle will open and display the purpose of the associated field.

Each movie clip should be created as a new symbol so that it can be edited without affecting the scene. Select **New Symbol...** from the **Insert** menu (or use the shortcut *<Ctrl>-F8*), name the symbol **nameWindow** and set the behavior to **Movie Clip**. Press **OK** to open the symbol's stage and timeline.

Next, you'll create the interactive help animation. This animation contains text that describes the form field. Before adding the text, we are going to create a small background animation that we will position behind the text. Begin by changing the name of **Layer 1** to **background**. Draw a dark blue rectangle with no border. This rectangle can be of any size, because we will customize its proportions with the **Properties** window. Select the rectangle with the Selection tool, then open the **Properties** window. Set the **W:** field to **200** and the **H:** field to **120**, to define the rectangle's size. Next, center the rectangle by entering **–100** and **–60** into the **X:** and **Y:** fields, respectively (Fig. 16.40).

Now that the rectangle is correctly positioned, we can begin to create its animation. Add keyframes to frames 5 and 10 of the **background** layer. Use the **Properties** window to change the size of the rectangle in frame 5, setting its height to **5.0**. Next, right click frame 5 and select **Copy Frames**. Then right click frame 1 and select **Paste Frames**. While in frame 1, change the width of the rectangle to **5.0**.

The animation is created by applying shape tweening to frames 1 and 5. Recall that shape tweening morphs one shape into another. The shape tween causes the dot in frame 1 to grow into a line by frame 5, then into a rectangle in frame 10. Select frame 1 and apply the shape tween by right clicking frame 1 and selecting **Create Shape Tween**. Do the same for frame 5. Shape tweens appear green in the timeline (Fig. 16.41). Follow the same procedure for frame 5.

Now that this portion of the animation is complete, it may be tested on the stage by pressing *Enter*. The animation should appear as the dot from frame 1 growing into a line by frame 5 and into a rectangle by frame 10.

The next step is to add a mock form field to this animation which demonstrates what the user would type in the actual field. Add two new layers above the **background** layer, named **field** and **text**. The **field** layer contains a mock form field, and the **text** layer contains the help information.

First, create an animation similar to the growing rectangle we just created for the mock form field. Add a keyframe to frame 10 in both the **field** and **text** layers. Fortunately, we have a form field already created as a symbol. Select frame 10 of the **field** layer, and drag

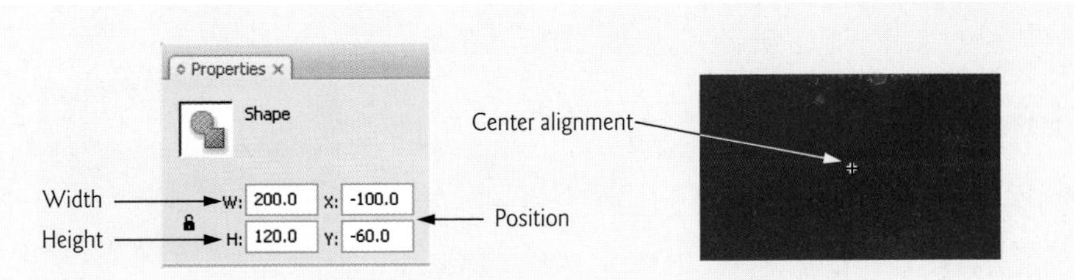

Fig. 16.40 | Centering an image on the stage with the **Properties** window.

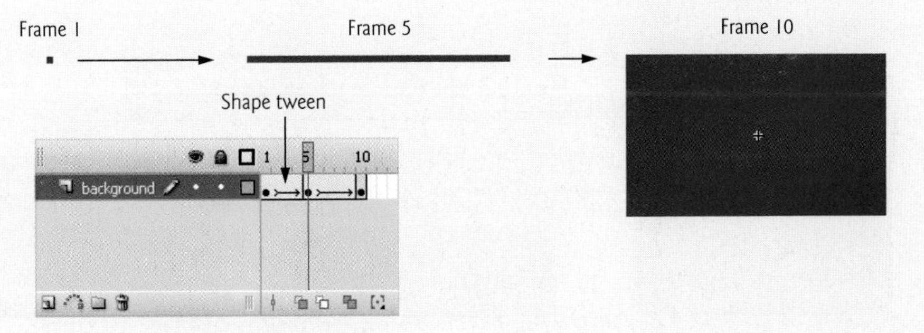

Fig. 16.41 | Creating a shape tween.

the **form field** symbol from the **Library** panel onto the stage, placing it within the current movie clip. Symbols may be embedded in one another; however, they cannot be placed within themselves (i.e., an instance of the **form field** symbol cannot be dragged onto the **form field** symbol editing stage). Align the **form field** symbol with the upper-left corner of the background rectangle, as shown in Fig. 16.42.

Next, set the end of this movie clip by adding keyframes to the **background** and **field** layers in frame 40. Also add keyframes to frames 20 and 25 of the **field** layer. These keyframes define intermediate points in the animation. Refer to Fig. 16.43 for correct keyframe positioning.

The next step in creating the animation is to make the **form field** symbol grow in size. Select frame 20 of the **field** layer, which contains only the **form field** symbol. Next open the **Transform** panel from the **Window** menu. The **Transform** panel can be used to change an object's size. Check the **Constrain** checkbox to constrain the object's proportions as it is resized. Selecting this option causes the scale factor to be equal in the width and height fields. The scale factor measures the change in proportion. Set the scale factor for the width and height to **150%**, and press *Enter* to apply the changes. Repeat the previous step for frame 10 of the **field** layer, but scale the **form field** symbol down to **0%**.

The symbol's animation is created by adding a motion tween. Adding the motion tween to **field** layer frames 10 and 20 will cause the **form field** symbol to grow from 0% of the original size to 150%, then to 100%. Figure 16.43 illustrates this portion of the animation.

Next, you'll add text to the movie clip to help the user understand the purpose of the corresponding text field. You'll set text to appear over the **form field** symbol as an example to the user. The text that appears below the **form field** symbol tells the user what should be typed in the text field.

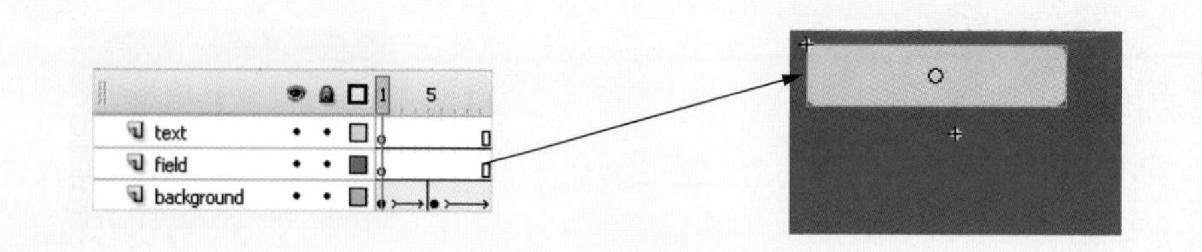

Fig. 16.42 | Adding the **field** symbol to the **nameWindow** movie clip.

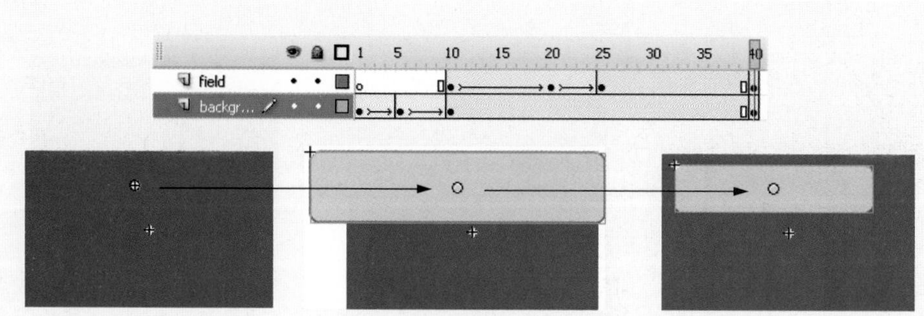

Fig. 16.43 | Creating an animation with the **form field** symbol.

To add the descriptive text, first insert a keyframe in frame 25 of the **text** layer. Use the Text tool (white, **Arial**, **16** pt text and **3** pt line spacing) to type the help information for the **Name** field. Make sure the text type is **Static Text**. This text will appear in the help window. For instance, our example gives the following directions for the **Name** field: **Enter your name in this field. First name, Last name.** Align this text with the left side of the rectangle. Next, add a keyframe to frame 40 of this layer, causing the text to appear throughout the animation.

Next, duplicate this movie clip so that it may be customized and reused for the other two help button animations. Open the **Library** panel and right click the **nameWindow** movie clip. Select **Duplicate** from the resulting menu, and name the new clip **passwordWindow**. Repeat this step once more, and name the third clip **memberWindow** (Fig. 16.44).

You must customize the duplicated movie clips so their text reflects the corresponding form fields. To begin, open the **memberWindow** editing stage by pressing the **Edit Symbols** button, which is found in the upper-right corner of the editing environment, and selecting **memberWindow** from the list of available symbols (Fig. 16.44). Select frame 25 of the **text** layer and change the form field description with the Text tool so that the box contains the directions **Enter your member number here in the form: 556677.** Copy the text in frame 25 by selecting it with the Text tool and using the shortcut *<Ctrl>-C*. Click frame 40 of the **text** layer, which contains the old text. Highlight the old text with the Text tool, and use the shortcut *<Ctrl>-V* to paste the copied text into this frame. Repeat these steps for the **passwordWindow** movie clip using the directions **Enter your secret password in this field.** [*Note:* Changing a symbol's function or appearance in its editing stage updates the symbol in the scene.]

The following steps further customize the help boxes for each form field. Open the **nameWindow** symbol's editing stage by clicking the **Edit Symbols** button (Fig. 16.44) and selecting **nameWindow.** Add a new layer to this symbol called **typedText** above the **text** layer. This layer contains an animation that simulates the typing of text into the form field.

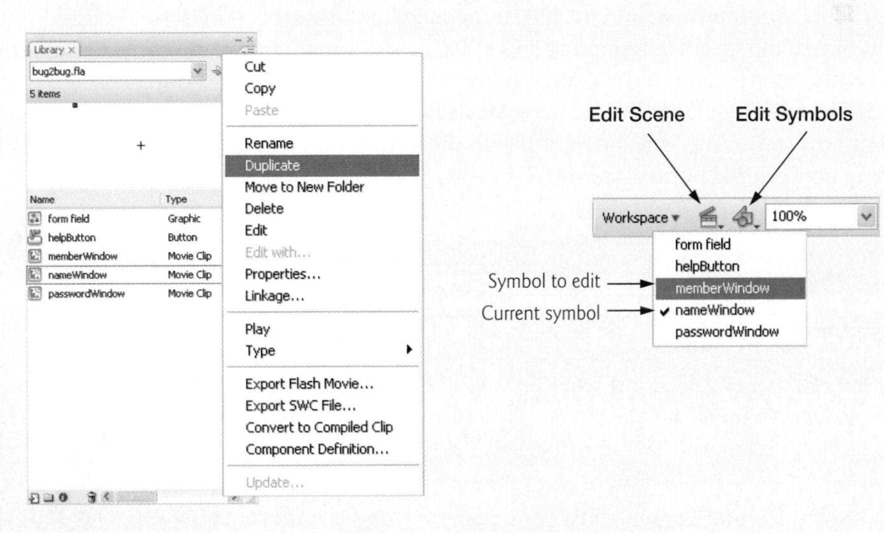

Fig. 16.44 | Duplicating movie-clip symbols with the **Library** panel.

Insert a keyframe in frame 25. Select this frame and use the Text tool to create a text box on top of the **form field** symbol. Type the name **John Doe** in the text box, then change the text color to black.

The following frame-by-frame animation creates the appearance of the name being typed into the field. Add a keyframe to frame 40 to indicate the end of the animation. Then add new keyframes to frames 26–31. Each keyframe contains a new letter being typed in the sequence, so when the playhead advances, new letters appear. Select the **John Doe** text in frame 25 and delete everything except the first **J** with the Text tool. Next, select frame 26 and delete all of the characters except the **J** and the **o**. This step must be repeated for all subsequent keyframes up to frame 31, each keyframe containing one more letter than the last (Fig. 16.45). Frame 31 should show the entire name. When this process is complete, press *Enter* to preview the frame-by-frame typing animation.

Create the same type of animation for both the **passwordWindow** and the **memberWindow** movie clips, using suitable words. For example, we use six asterisks for the **passwordWindow** movie clip and six numbers for the **memberWindow** movie clip. Add a `stop` action to frame 40 of all three movie clips so that the animations play only once.

The movie clips are now ready to be added to the scene. Click the **Edit Scene** button next to the **Edit Symbols** button, and select **Scene 1** to return to the scene. Before inserting the movie clips, add the following layers to the timeline: **nameMovie**, **memberMovie** and **passwordMovie**, one layer for each of the movie clips. Add a keyframe in frame 2 of the **nameMovie** layer. Also, add keyframes to frame 4 of the **form**, **text** and **button** layers, ensuring that the form and text appear throughout the movie.

Now you'll place the movie clips in the correct position in the scene. Recall that the ActionScript for each help button contains the script

```
function functionName( event : MouseEvent ) : void
{
   gotoAndStop( frameLabel );
}
```

in which *functionName* and *frameLabel* depend on the button. This script causes the movie to skip to the specified frame and stop. Placing the movie clips in the correct frames causes the playhead to skip to the desired frame, play the animation and stop. This effect is created by selecting frame 2 of the **nameMovie** layer and dragging the **nameWindow** movie clip onto the stage. Align the movie clip with the button next to the **Name** field, placing it halfway between the button and the right edge of the stage.

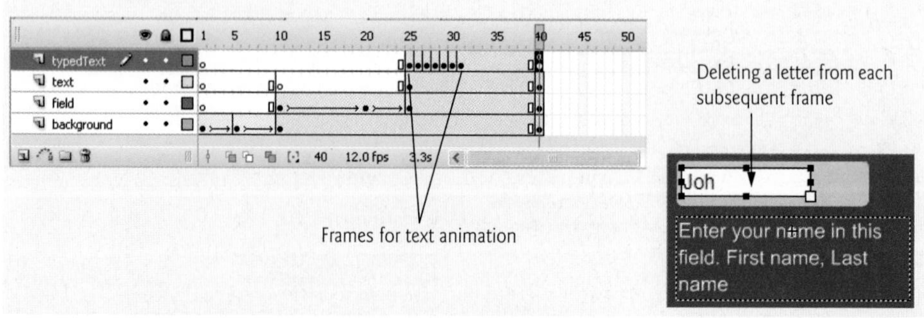

Fig. 16.45 | Creating a frame-by-frame animation.

The preceding step is repeated twice for the other two movie clips so that they appear in the correct frames. Add a keyframe to frame 3 of the **memberMovie** layer and drag the **memberWindow** movie clip onto the stage. Position this clip in the same manner as the previous clip. Repeat this step for the **passwordWindow** movie clip, dragging it into frame 4 of the **passwordMovie** layer.

The movie is now complete. Press *<Ctrl>-Enter* to preview it with the Flash Player. If the triggered animations do not appear in the correct locations, return to the scene and adjust their position. The final movie is displayed in Fig. 16.46.

In our example, we have added a picture beneath the text layer. Movies can be enhanced in many ways, such as by changing colors and fonts or by adding pictures. Our movie (`bug2bug.fla`) can be found in the this chapter's examples directory. If you want to use our symbols to recreate the movie, select **Open External Library...** from the **Import** submenu of the **File** menu and open `bug2bug.fla`. The **Open External Library...** option allows you to reuse symbols from another movie.

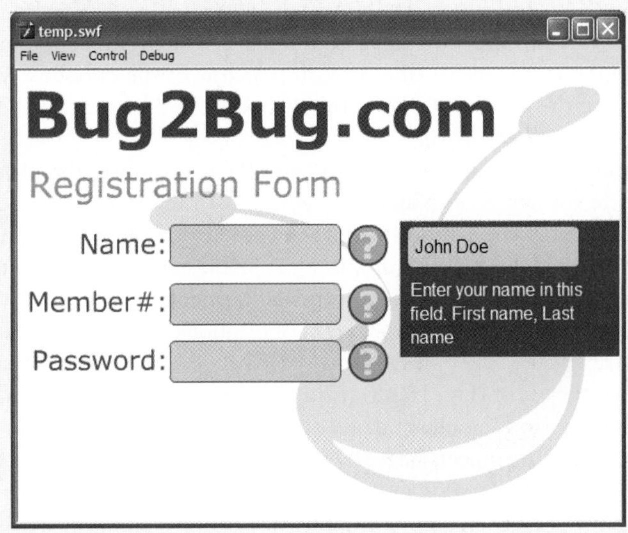

Fig. 16.46 | **Bug2Bug.com** help form.

16.6 Creating a Website Splash Screen

Flash is becoming an important tool for e-businesses. Many organizations use Flash to create website splash screens (i.e., introductions), product demos and web applications. Others use Flash to build games and interactive entertainment in an effort to attract new visitors. However, these types of applications can take a long time to load, causing visitors—especially those with slow connections—to leave the site. One way to alleviate this problem is to provide visitors with an animated Flash introduction that draws and keeps their attention. Flash animations are ideal for amusing visitors while conveying information as the rest of a page downloads "behind the scenes."

A preloader or splash screen is a simple animation that plays while the rest of the web page is loading. Several techniques are used to create animation preloaders. The following example creates an animation preloader that uses ActionScript to pause the movie at a particular frame until all the movie elements have loaded.

To start building the animation preloader, create a new Flash document. Use the default size, and set the background color to a light blue. First, you'll create the movie pieces that will be loaded later in the process. Create five new layers, and rename **Layer 2** to **C++**, **Layer 3** to **Java** and **Layer 4** to **IW3**. **Layer 5** will contain the movie's ActionScript, so rename it **actions**. Because **Layer 1** contains the introductory animation, rename this layer **animation**.

The preloaded objects we use in this example are animated movie clip symbols. Create the first symbol by clicking frame 2 of the **C++** layer, inserting a keyframe, and creating a new movie-clip symbol named **cppbook**. When the symbol's editing stage opens, import the image `cpphtp.gif` (found in the `images` folder with this chapter's examples). Place a keyframe in frame 20 of **Layer 1** and add a `stop` action to this frame. The animation in this example is produced with the motion tween Rotate option, which causes an object to spin on its axis. Create a motion tween in frame 1 with the **Properties** window, setting the **Rotate** option to **CCW** (counterclockwise) and the **times** field to **2** (Fig. 16.47). This causes the image `cpphtp.gif` to spin two times counterclockwise over a period of 20 frames.

After returning to the scene, drag and drop a copy of the **cppbook** symbol onto the stage in frame 2 of the **C++** layer. Move this symbol to the left side of the stage. Insert a frame in frame 25 of the **C++** layer.

Build a similar movie clip for the **Java** and **IW3** layers, using the files `java.gif` and `iw3.gif` to create the symbols. Name the symbol for the **Java** layer **jbook** and the **IW3** symbol **ibook** to identify the symbols with their contents. In the main scene, create a keyframe in frame 8 of the **Java** layer, and place the **jbook** symbol in the center of the stage. Insert a frame in frame 25 of the **Java** layer. Insert the **ibook** symbol in a keyframe in frame 14 of the **IW3** layer, and position it to the right of the **jbook** symbol. Insert a frame in frame 25 of the **IW3** layer. Make sure to leave some space between these symbols so that they will not overlap when they spin (Fig. 16.48). Add a keyframe to the 25th frame of the actions layer, then add a `stop` to the **Actions** panel of that frame.

Now that the loading objects have been placed, it is time to create the preloading animation. By placing the preloading animation in the frame preceding the frame that contains the objects, we can use ActionScript to pause the movie until the objects have loaded. Begin by adding a stop action to frame 1 of the **actions** layer. Select frame 1 of the **animation** layer and create another new movie-clip symbol named **loader**. Use the text tool with a medium-sized sans-serif font, and place the word **Loading** in the center of the symbol's

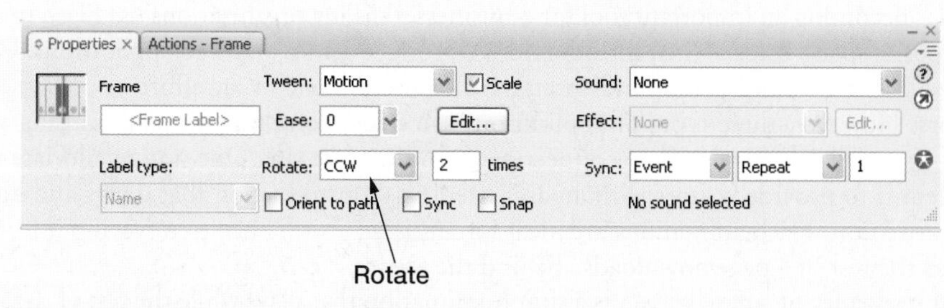

Fig. 16.47 | Creating a rotating object with the motion tween **Rotate** option.

Fig. 16.48 | Inserted movie clips.

editing stage. This title indicates to the user that objects are loading. Insert a keyframe into frame 14 and rename this layer **load**.

Create a new layer called **orb** to contain the animation. Draw a circle with no stroke about the size of a quarter above the word **Loading**. Give the circle a green-to-white radial gradient fill color. The colors of this gradient can be edited in the **Color** panel (Fig. 16.49).

The block farthest to the left on the **gradient range** indicates the innermost color of the radial gradient, whereas the block farthest to the right indicates the outermost color of the radial gradient. Click the left block to reveal the **gradient color** swatch. Click the swatch and select a medium green as the inner color of the gradient. Select the right, outer color box and change its color to white. Deselect the circle by clicking on a blank portion of the stage. Note that a white ring appears around the circle due to the colored background. To make the circle fade into the background, we adjust its **alpha** value. Alpha is a value between 0 and 100% that corresponds to a color's transparency or opacity. An alpha value of 0% appears transparent, whereas a value of 100% appears completely opaque. Select the circle again and click the right gradient box (white). Adjust the value of the **Alpha** field in the **Color Mixer** panel to 0%. Deselect the circle. It should now appear to fade into the background.

The rate of progression in a gradient can also be changed by sliding the color boxes. Select the circle again. Slide the left color box to the middle so that the gradient contains more green than transparent white, then return the slider to the far left. Intermediate colors may be added to the gradient range by clicking beneath the bar, next to one of the existing

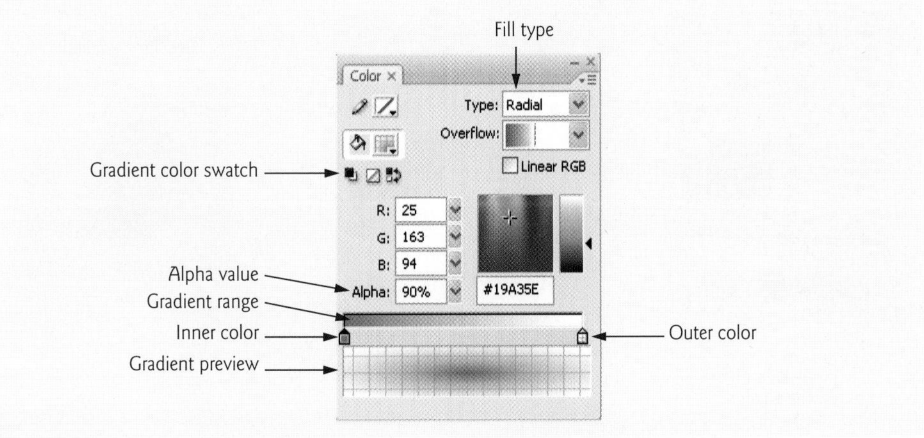

Fig. 16.49 | Changing gradient colors with the **Color** panel.

color boxes. Click to the right of the inner color box to add a new color box (Fig. 16.50). Slide the new color box to the right and change its color to a darker green. Any color box may be removed from a gradient by dragging it downward off the gradient range.

Insert keyframes into frame 7 and 14 of the **orb** layer. Select the circle in frame 7 with the selection tool. In the **Color** panel change the alpha of every color box to 0%. Select frame 1 in the **Timeline** and add shape tween. Change the value of the **Ease** field in the **Properties** window to **–100. Ease** controls the rate of change during tween animation. Negative values cause the animated change to be gradual at the beginning and become increasingly drastic. Positive values cause the animation to change quickly in the first frames, becoming less drastic as the animation progresses. Add shape tween to frame 7 and set the **Ease** value to 100. In frame 14, add the action `gotoAndPlay(1);` to repeat the animation. You can preview the animation by pressing *Enter*. The circle should now appear to pulse.

Before inserting the movie clip into the scene, we are going to create a hypertext linked button that will enable the user to skip over the animations to the final destination. Add a new layer called **link** to the **loader** symbol with keyframes in frames 1 and 14. Using the text tool, place the words **skip directly to Deitel website** below **Loading** in a smaller font size. Select the words with the selection tool and convert them into a button symbol named **skip**. Converting the text into a button simulates a text hyperlink created with XHTML. Double click the words to open the **skip** button's editing stage. For this example, we are going to edit only the hit state. When a button is created from a shape, the button's hit area is, by default, the area of the shape. It is important to change the hit state of a button created from text so that it includes the spaces between the letters; otherwise, the link will work only when the user hovers over a letter's area. Insert a keyframe in the hit state. Use the rectangle tool to draw the hit area of the button, covering the entire length and height of the text. This rectangle is not visible in the final movie, because it defines only the hit area (Fig. 16.51).

The button is activated by giving it an action that links it to another web page. After returning to the **loader** movie-clip editing stage, give the **skip** button the instance name **skipButton** and open the **Actions** panel for the first frame of the **link** layer. Invoke the `addEventListener` function using the **skipButton** instance to call function `onClick` whenever

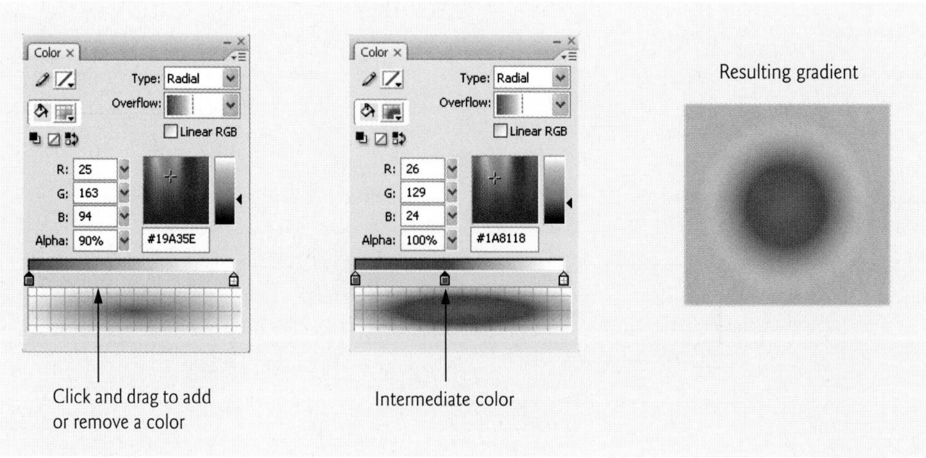

Fig. 16.50 | Adding an intermediate color to a gradient.

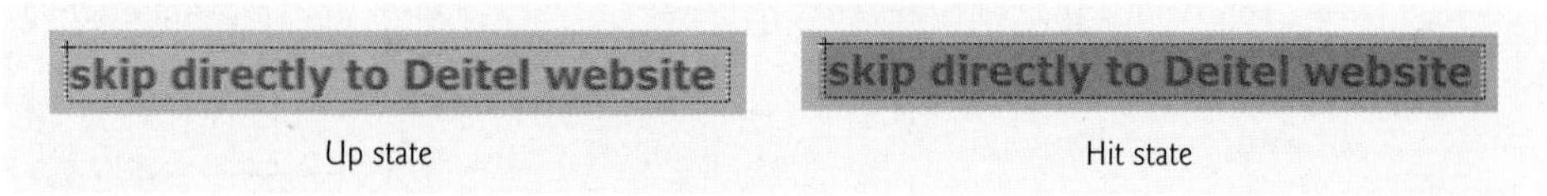

skip directly to Deitel website

Up state

skip directly to Deitel website

Hit state

Fig. 16.51 | Defining the hit area of a button.

the button is clicked. Then, create an object of type `URLRequest` and give the constructor a parameter value of `"http://www.deitel.com"`. The function `onClick` employs Flash's `navigateToURL` function to access the website given to it. Thus, the code now reads

```
skipButton.addEventListener( MouseEvent.CLICK, onClick );
var url : URLRequest = new URLRequest( "http://www.deitel.com" );

function onClick( e : MouseEvent ) : void
{
   navigateToURL( url, "_blank" );
} // end function onClick
```

The `"_blank"` parameter signifies that a new browser window displaying the Deitel website should open when the user presses the button.

Return to the scene by clicking **Scene 1** directly below the timeline, next to the name of the current symbol. Drag and drop a copy of the **loader** movie clip from the **Library** panel into frame 1 of the **animation** layer, center it on the stage, and set its **Instance name** to **loadingClip**.

The process is nearly complete. Open the **Actions** panel for the **actions** layer. The following actions direct the movie clip to play until all the scene's objects are loaded. First, add a `stop` to the frame so that it doesn't go to the second frame until we tell it to. Using the **loadingClip** movie instance, use the `addEventListener` function to invoke the function `onBegin` whenever the event `Event.ENTER_FRAME` is triggered. The `ENTER_FRAME` event occurs every time the playhead enters a new frame. Since this movie's frame rate is 12 fps (frames per second), the `ENTER_FRAME` event will occur 12 times each second.

```
loadingClip.addEventListener( Event.ENTER_FRAME, onBegin );
```

The next action added to this sequence is the function `onBegin`. The condition of the `if` statement will be used to determine how many frames of the movie are loaded. Flash movies load frame by frame. Frames that contain complex images take longer to load. Flash will continue playing the current frame until the next frame has loaded. For our movie, if the number of frames loaded (`frameLoaded`) is equal to the total number of frames (`totalFrames`), then the movie is finished loading, so it will play frame `2`. It also invokes the `removeEventListener` function to ensure that `onBegin` is not called for the remainder of the movie. If the number of frames loaded is less than the total number of frames, then the current movie clip continues to play. The code now reads:

```
stop();

loadingClip.addEventListener( Event.ENTER_FRAME, onBegin );

// check if all frames have been loaded
function onBegin( event : Event ) : void
{
   if ( framesLoaded == totalFrames )
   {
```

```
            loadingClip.removeEventListener( Event.ENTER_FRAME, onBegin );
            gotoAndPlay( 2 );
        } // end if
    } // end function onBegin
```

Create one more layer in the scene, and name the layer **title**. Add a keyframe to frame 2 of this layer, and use the Text tool to create a title that reads **Recent Deitel Publications**. Below the title, create another text hyperlink button to the Deitel website. The simplest way to do this is to duplicate the existing **skip** button and modify the text. Right click the **skip** symbol in the **Library** panel, and select **Duplicate**. Name the new button **visit**, and place it in frame 2 of the **title** layer. Label the instance **visitButton**, then create a keyframe in the second frame of the **actions** layer. Duplicate the code from the **Actions** panel of the first frame of the **link** layer in the **loader** symbol, and replace `skipButton` with `visitButton`. Double click the **visit** button and edit the text to say **visit the Deitel website**. Add keyframes to each frame of the **title** layer and manipulate the text to create a typing effect similar to the one we created in the `bug2bug` example.

The movie is now complete. Test the movie with the Flash Player (Fig. 16.52). When viewed in the testing window, the loading sequence will play for only one frame because your processor loads all the frames almost instantly. Flash can simulate how a movie would appear to an online user, though. While still in the testing window, select **56K** from the **Download Settings** submenu of the **View** menu. Also, select **Bandwidth Profiler** from the **View** menu. Then select **Simulate Download** from the **View** menu or press *<Ctrl>-Enter*. The graph at the top of the window displays the amount of bandwidth required to load each frame.

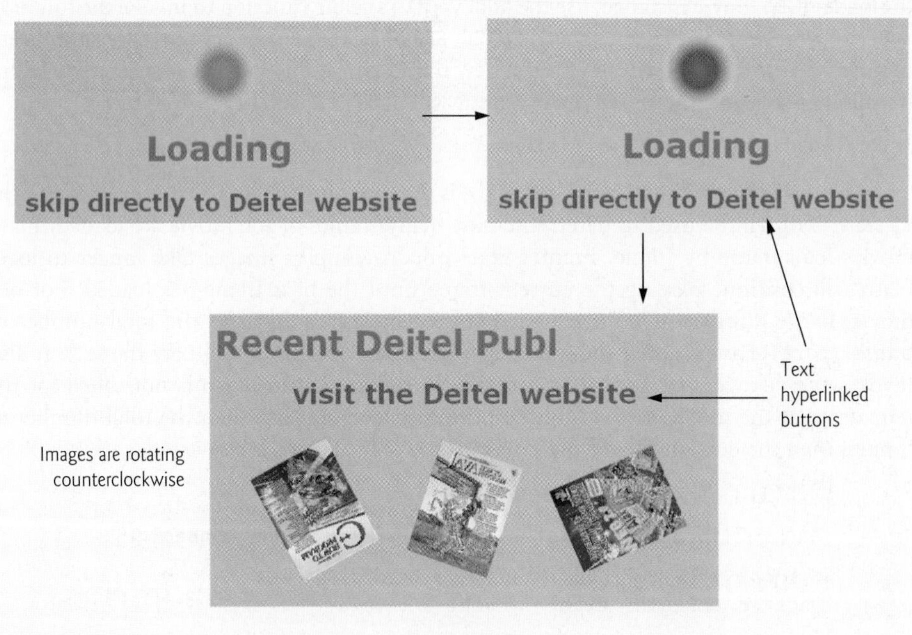

Fig. 16.52 | Creating an animation to preload images.

16.7 ActionScript

Figure 16.53 lists common Flash ActionScript 3.0 functions. By attaching these functions to frames and symbols, you can build some fairly complex Flash movies.

Function	Description
`gotoAndPlay`	Jump to a frame or scene in another part of the movie and start playing the movie.
`gotoAndStop`	Jump to a frame or scene in another part of the movie and stop the movie.
`play`	Start playing a movie from the beginning, or from wherever it has been stopped.
`stop`	Stop a movie.
`SoundMixer.stopAll`	Stop the sound track without affecting the movie.
`navigateToUrl`	Load a URL into a new or existing browser window.
`fscommand`	Insert JavaScript or other scripting languages into a Flash movie.
`Loader class`	Load a SWF or JPEG file into the Flash Player from the current movie. Can also load another SWF into a particular movie.
`framesLoaded`	Check whether certain frames have been loaded.
`addEventListener`	Assign functions to a movie clip based on specific events. The events include `load`, `unload`, `enterFrame`, `mouseUp`, `mouseDown`, `mouseMove`, `keyUp`, `keyDown` and `data`.
`if`	Set up condition statements that run only when the condition is true.
`while/do while`	Run a collection of statements while a condition statement is true.
`trace`	Display programming notes or variable values while testing a movie.
`Math.random`	Returns a random number less than or equal to 0 and less than 1.

Fig. 16.53 | Common ActionScript functions.

16.8 Wrap-Up

In this chapter, we introduced Adobe Flash CS3 (Creative Suite 3) and demonstrated how to produce interactive, animated movies. You learned that Flash CS3 can be used to create web-based banner advertisements, interactive websites, games and web-based applications, and that it provides tools for drawing graphics, generating animations, and adding sound and video. We discussed how to embed Flash movies in web pages and how to execute Flash movies as stand-alone programs. You also learned some ActionScript 3.0 programming and created interactive buttons, added sound to movies, created special graphic effects. In the next chapter, you'll build an interactive game using Flash.

16.9 Web Resources

`www.deitel.com/flash9/`

The Deitel Flash 9 Resource Center contains links to some of the best Flash 9 and Flash CS3 resources on the web. There you'll find categorized links to forums, conferences, blogs, books, open source projects, videos, podcasts, webcasts and more. Also check out the tutorials for all skill levels, from introductory to advanced. Be sure to visit the related Resource Centers on Microsoft Silverlight (`www.deitel.com/silverlight/`) and Adobe Flex (`www.deitel.com/flex/`).

Summary

Section 16.1 Introduction

- Adobe *Flash CS3* (Creative Suite 3) is a commercial application that you can use to produce interactive, animated movies.
- Flash can be used to create web-based banner advertisements, interactive websites, games and web-based applications with stunning graphics and multimedia effects.
- Flash movies can be embedded in web pages, placed on CDs or DVDs as independent applications or converted into stand alone, executable programs.
- Flash includes tools for coding in its scripting language, ActionScript 3.0. ActionScript, which is similar to JavaScript, enables interactive applications.
- To play Flash movies, the Flash Player plug-in must be installed in your web browser. This plug-in has several versions, the most recent of which is version 9.

Section 16.2 Flash Movie Development

- The stage is the white area in which you place graphic elements during movie development. Only objects in this area will appear in the final movie.
- The timeline represents the time period over which a movie runs.
- Each frame depicts a moment in the movie's timeline, into which you can insert movie elements.
- The playhead indicates the current frame.
- The **Tools** bar is divided into multiple sections, each containing tools and functions that help you create Flash movies.
- Windows called panels organize frequently used movie options. Panel options modify the size, shape, color, alignment and effects associated with a movie's graphic elements.
- The context-sensitive **Properties** panel displays information about the currently selected object. It is a useful tool for viewing and altering an object's properties.
- You can access different panels by selecting them from the **Window** menu.

Section 16.3 Learning Flash with Hands-On Examples

- The `.fla` file extension is a Flash-specific extension for editable movies.
- **Frame rate** sets the speed at which movie frames display.
- The background color determines the color of the stage.
- **Dimensions** define the size of a movie as it displays on the screen.

Section 16.3.1 Creating a Shape with the Oval Tool

- Flash creates shapes using vectors—mathematical equations that define the shape's size, shape and color. When vector graphics are saved, they are stored using equations.

- Vector graphics can be resized without losing clarity.
- You can create shapes by dragging with the shape tools.
- Every shape has a stroke color and a fill color. The stroke color is the color of a shape's outline, and the fill color is the color that fills the shape.
- Clicking the Black and white button resets the stroke color to black and the fill color to white.
- Selecting the Swap colors option switches the stroke and fill colors.
- The *Shift* key constrains a shape's proportions to have equal width and height.
- A dot in a frame signifies a keyframe, which indicates a point of change in a timeline.
- A shape's size can be modified with the **Properties** panel when the shape is selected.
- Gradient fills are gradual progressions of color.
- The **Swatches** panel provides four radial gradients and three linear gradients.

Section 16.3.2 Adding Text to a Button

- Button titles communicate a button's function to the user. You can create a title with the Text tool.
- With selected text, you can change the font, text size and font color with the **Properties** window.
- To change the font color, click the text color swatch and select a color from the palette.

Section 16.3.3 Converting a Shape into a Symbol

- The scene contains graphics and symbols. The parent movie may contain several symbols that are reusable movie elements, such as graphics, buttons and movie clips.
- A scene timeline can contain numerous symbols with their own timelines and properties.
- A scene may have several instances of any given symbol.
- Symbols can be edited independently of the scene by using the symbol's editing stage. The editing stage is separate from the scene stage and contains only one symbol.
- Selecting **Convert to Symbol...** from the **Modify** menu or using the shortcut *F8* on the keyboard opens the **Convert to Symbol** dialog, in which you can set the properties of a new symbol.
- Every symbol in a Flash movie must have a unique name.
- You can create three different types of symbols—movie clips, buttons and graphics.
- A movie-clip symbol is ideal for recurring animations.
- Graphic symbols are ideal for static images and basic animations.
- Button symbols are objects that perform button actions, such as rollovers and hyperlinking. A rollover is an action that changes the appearance of a button when the mouse passes over it.
- The **Library** panel stores every symbol in a movie and is accessed through the **Window** menu or by the shortcuts *<Ctrl>-L* or *F11*. Multiple instances of a symbol can be placed in a movie by dragging and dropping the symbol from the **Library** panel onto the stage.

Section 16.3.4 Editing Button Symbols

- The different components of a button symbol, such as its fill and type, may be edited in the symbol's editing stage. You may access a symbol's editing stage by double clicking the symbol in the **Library** or by pressing the **Edit Symbols** button and selecting the symbol name.
- The pieces that make up a button can all be changed in the editing stage.
- A button symbol's timeline contains four frames, one for each of the button states (up, over and down) and one for the hit area.

- The up state (indicated by the **Up** frame on screen) is the default state before the user presses the button or rolls over it with the mouse.
- Control shifts to the over state (i.e., the **Over** frame) when the mouse moves over the button.
- The button's down state (i.e., the **Down** frame) plays when a user presses a button. You can create interactive, user-responsive buttons by customizing the appearance of a button in each state.
- Graphic elements in the hit state (i.e., the **Hit** frame) are not visible when viewing the movie; they exist simply to define the active area of the button (i.e., the area that can be clicked).
- By default, buttons only have the up state activated when they are created. You may activate other states by adding keyframes to the other three frames.

Section 16.3.5 Adding Keyframes

- Keyframes are points of change in a Flash movie and appear in the timeline as gray with a black dot. By adding keyframes to a button symbol's timeline, you can control how the button reacts to user input.
- A rollover is added by inserting a keyframe in the button's **Over** frame, then changing the button's appearance in that frame.
- Changing the button color in the over state does not affect the button color in the up state.

Section 16.3.6 Adding Sound to a Button

- Flash imports sounds in the `WAV` (Windows), `AIFF` (Macintosh) or `MP3` formats.
- Sounds can be imported into the **Library** by choosing **Import to Library** from the **Import** submenu of the **File** menu.
- You can add sound to a movie by placing the sound clip in a keyframe or over a series of frames.
- If a frame has a blue wave or line through it, a sound effect has been added to it.

Section 16.3.7 Verifying Changes with **Test Movie**

- Movies can be viewed in their published state with the Flash Player. The published state of a movie is how it would appear if viewed over the web or with the Flash Player.
- Published Flash movies have the Shockwave Flash extension (`.swf`). SWF files can be viewed but not edited.

Section 16.3.8 Adding Layers to a Movie

- A movie can be composed of many layers, each having its own attributes and effects.
- Layers organize different movie elements so that they can be animated and edited separately, making the composition of complex movies easier. Graphics in higher layers appear over the graphics in lower layers.
- Text can be broken apart or regrouped for color editing, shape modification or animation. However, once text has been broken apart, it may not be edited with the Text tool.

Section 16.3.9 Animating Text with Tweening

- Animations in Flash are created by inserting keyframes into the timeline.
- Tweening, also known as morphing, is an automated process in which Flash creates the intermediate steps of the animation between two keyframes.
- Shape tweening morphs an ungrouped object from one shape to another.
- Motion tweening moves symbols or grouped objects around the stage.
- Keyframes must be designated in the timeline before adding the motion tween.

- Adding the `stop` function to the last frame in a movie stops the movie from looping.
- The small letter **a** in a frame indicates that it contains an action.

Section 16.3.10 Adding a Text Field

- **Static Text** creates text that does not change.
- **Dynamic Text** creates can be changed or determined by outside variables through ActionScript.
- **Input Text** creates a text field into which the viewers of the movie can input their own text.

Section 16.3.11 Adding ActionScript

- The `addEventListener` function helps make an object respond to an event by calling a function when the event takes place.
- `MouseEvent.MOUSE_DOWN` specifies that an action is performed when the user clicks the button.
- `Math.random` returns a random floating-point number from 0.0 up to, but not including, 1.0.

Section 16.4 Publishing Your Flash Movie

- Flash movies must be published for users to view them outside Flash CS3 and the Flash Player.
- Flash movies may be published in a different Flash version to support older Flash Players.
- Flash can automatically generate an XHMTL document that embeds your Flash movie.

Section 16.5.1 Importing and Manipulating Bitmaps

- Once an imported image is broken apart, it may be shape tweened or edited with editing tools such as the Lasso, Paint bucket, Eraser and Paintbrush. The editing tools are found in the toolbox and apply changes to a shape.
- Dragging with the Lasso tool selects areas of shapes. The color of a selected area may be changed, or the selected area may be moved.
- Once an area is selected, its color may be changed by selecting a new fill color with the fill swatch or by clicking the selection with the Paint bucket tool.
- The Eraser tool removes shape areas when you click and drag the tool across an area. You can change the eraser size using the tool options.

Section 16.5.2 Creating an Advertisement Banner with Masking

- Masking hides portions of layers. A masking layer hides objects in the layers beneath it, revealing only the areas that can be seen through the shape of the mask.
- Items drawn on a masking layer define the mask's shape and cannot be seen in the final movie.
- The Free transform tool allows us to resize an image. When an object is selected with this tool, anchors appear around its corners and sides.
- Breaking text apart once converts each letter into its own text field. Breaking it apart again converts the letters into shapes that cannot be edited with the Text tool, but can be manipulated as regular graphics.
- Adding a mask to a layer masks only the items in the layer directly below it.

Section 16.5.3 Adding Online Help to Forms

- Use the Selection tool to align objects with their corresponding captions. For more precise alignment, select the desired object with the Selection tool and press the arrow key on the keyboard in the direction you want to move the object.
- An input text field is a text field into which the user can type text.

- Each movie clip should be created as a new symbol so that it can be edited without affecting the scene.
- Symbols may be embedded in one another; however, they cannot be placed within themselves.
- The **Transform** panel can be used to change an object's size.
- The **Constrain** checkbox causes the scale factor to be equal in the height and width fields. The scale factor measures the change in proportion.
- Changing a symbol's function or appearance in its editing stage updates the symbol in the scene.

Section 16.6 Creating a Website Splash Screen

- Many organizations use Flash to create website splash screens (i.e., introductions), product demos and web applications.
- Flash animations are ideal for amusing visitors while conveying information as the rest of a page downloads "behind the scenes."
- A preloader is a simple animation that plays while the rest of the web page is loading.
- Alpha is a value between 0 and 100% that corresponds to a color's transparency or opacity. An alpha value of 0% appears transparent, whereas a value of 100% appears completely opaque.
- The rate of progression in a gradient can also be changed by sliding the color boxes.
- Any color box may be removed from a gradient by dragging it downward off the gradient range.
- **Ease** controls the rate of change during tween animation. Negative values cause the animated change to be gradual at the beginning and become increasingly drastic. Positive values cause the animation to change quickly in the first frames and less drastically as the animation progresses.
- When a button is created from a shape, the button's hit area is, by default, the area of the shape.
- It is important to change the hit state of a button created from text so that it includes the spaces between the letters; otherwise, the link will work only when the user hovers over a letter's area.
- The `"_blank"` signifies that a new browser window should open when the user presses the button.
- Flash movies load frame by frame, and frames containing complex images take longer to load. Flash will continue playing the current frame until the next frame has loaded.

Terminology

ActionScript 3.0
active tool
`addEventListener` function
Adobe Flash CS3
alpha value
anchor
Bandwidth Profiler
bitmapped graphics
break apart
Brush Mode
Brush Tool
constrained aspect ratio
`do while` control structure
down state
duplicate symbol
Eraser tool
`.fla` file format
frame
frame label
Frame Rate
frames per second
`framesLoaded` property
free transform tool
`fscommand` function
`gotoAndPlay` function
`gotoAndStop` function
gradients
Hand tool
hexadecimal notation
hit state
hypertext link
`if` control structure
input text field
instance

instance name
interactive animated movies
JavaScript
keyframe
Lasso tool
layer
Library panel
`Loader` class
Magic wand
masking layer
`math.random` function
motion tween
movie clip
movie clip symbol
MP3 audio compression format
`navigateToUrl` function
Oval tool
over state
`play` function
playhead
preloader
radial gradient
raster graphic
raw compression
Rectangle tool
Sample Rate
scenes
Selection tool
shape tween
`SoundMixer.stopAll` function
splash screen
stage
`stop` function
`.swf` file format
symbol
Text tool
timeline
`trace` function
tween
up state
vector graphic
web-safe palette
`while` control structure
Zoom tool

Self-Review Exercises

16.1 Fill in the blanks in each of the following statements:

a) Adobe Flash's ________ feature draws the in-between frames of an animation.
b) Graphics, buttons and movie clips are all types of ________.
c) The two types of tweening in Adobe Flash are ________ tweening and ________ tweening.
d) Morphing one shape into another over a period of time can be accomplished with ________ tweening.
e) Adobe Flash's scripting language is called ________.
f) The area in which the movie is created is called the ________.
g) Holding down the *Shift* key while drawing with the Oval tool draws a perfect ________.
h) By default, shapes in Flash are created with a fill and a(n) ________.
i) ________ tell Flash how a shape or symbol should look at the beginning and end of an animation.
j) A graphic's transparency can be altered by adjusting its ________.

16.2 State whether each of the following is *true* or *false*. If *false*, explain why.

a) A button's hit state is entered when the button is clicked.
b) To draw a straight line in Flash, hold down the *Shift* key while drawing with the Pencil tool.
c) Motion tweening moves objects within the stage.
d) The more frames you give to an animation, the slower it is.
e) Flash's `math.random` function returns a number between 1 and 100.
f) The maximum number of layers allowed in a movie is ten.
g) Flash can shape tween only one shape per layer.
h) When a new layer is created, it is placed above the selected layer.

i) The **Lasso Tool** selects objects by drawing freehand or straight-edge selection areas.
j) The **Ease** value controls an object's transparency during motion tween.

Answers to Self-Review Exercises

16.1 a) tweening. b) symbols. c) shape, motion. d) shape. e) ActionScript. f) stage. g) circle. h) stroke. i) keyframes. j) alpha value.

16.2 a) False. The down state is entered when the button is clicked. b) True. c) True. d) True. e) False. Flash's `math.random` function returns a number greater than or equal to 0 and less than 1. f) False. Flash allows an unlimited number of layers for each movie. g) False. Flash can tween as many shapes as there are on a layer. The effect is usually better when the shapes are placed on their own layers. h) True. i) True. j) False. The **Ease** value controls the acceleration of a tween animation.

Exercises

16.3 Using the combination of one movie-clip symbol and one button symbol to create a navigation bar that contains four buttons, make the buttons trigger an animation (contained in the movie clip) when the user rolls over the buttons with the mouse. Link the four buttons to `www.nasa.gov`, `www.w3c.org`, `www.flashkit.com` and `www.cnn.com`.

16.4 Download and import five `WAV` files from `www.coolarchive.com`. Create five buttons, each activating a different sound when it is pressed.

16.5 Create an animated mask that acts as a spotlight on an image. First, import the file `arches.jpg` from the `images` folder in the Chapter 16 examples directory. Then, change the background color of the movie to black. Animate the mask in the layer above to create a spotlight effect.

16.6 Create a text "morph" animation using a shape tween. Make the text that appears in the first frame of the animation change into a shape in the last frame. Make the text and the shape different colors.

16.7 Give a brief description of the following terms:
a) symbol
b) tweening
c) ActionScript
d) **Frame rate**
e) **Library** panel
f) masking
g) context-sensitive **Properties** window
h) **Bandwidth Profiler**
i) **Frame Label**

16.8 Describe what the following file extensions are used for in Flash movie development.
a) `.fla`
b) `.swf`
c) `.exe`
d) `.html`

17

Adobe® Flash® CS3: Building an Interactive Game

Knowledge must come through action.
—Sophocles

It is circumstance and proper timing that give an action its character and make it either good or bad.
—Agesilaus

Life's but a walking shadow, a poor player that struts and frets his hour upon the stage and then is heard no more: it is a tale told by an idiot, full of sound and fury, signifying nothing.
—William Shakespeare

Come, Watson, come! The game is afoot.
—Sir Arthur Conan Doyle

Cannon to right of them,
Cannon to left of them,
Cannon in front of them
Volley'd and thunder'd.
—Alfred, Lord Tennyson

OBJECTIVES

In this chapter you'll learn:

- Advanced ActionScript 3 in Flash CS3.
- How to build on Flash CS3 skills learned in Chapter 16.
- The basics of object-oriented programming in Flash CS3.
- How to create a functional, interactive Flash game.
- How to make objects move in Flash.
- How to embed sound and text objects into a Flash movie.
- How to detect collisions between objects in Flash.

Outline

17.1 Introduction

While Adobe Flash CS3 is useful for creating short animations, it is also capable of building large, interactive applications. In this chapter, we build a fully functional interactive video game. First, download the Chapter 17 examples from `www.deitel.com/books/iw3htp4`. Then, open `FullCannon.swf` and run the completed game. In the cannon game, the player has a limited amount of time to hit every part of a moving target. Hitting the target increases the remaining time, and missing the target or hitting the blocker decreases it. Some elements of the `FullCannon.swf` game are not discussed in the body of the chapter, but are presented as supplementary exercises. This case study will sharpen the Flash skills you acquired in Chapter 16 and introduce you to more advanced ActionScript. For this case study, we assume that you are comfortable with the material on Flash in Chapter 16. The completed game should run similar to what is shown in Fig. 17.1. Notice how in

a)

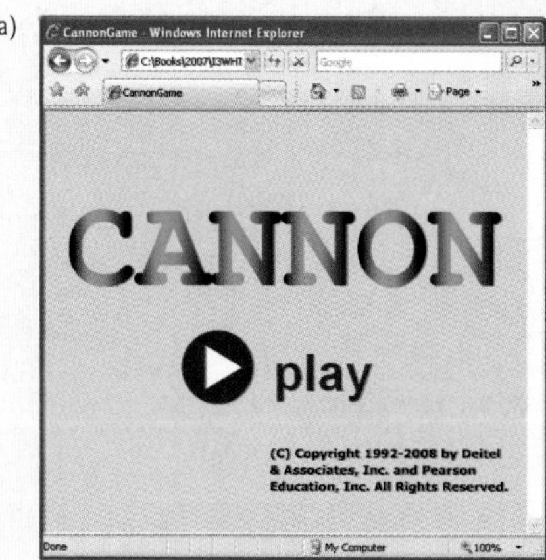

Fig. 17.1 | Ball fired from the cannon and hitting the target. (Part 1 of 3.)

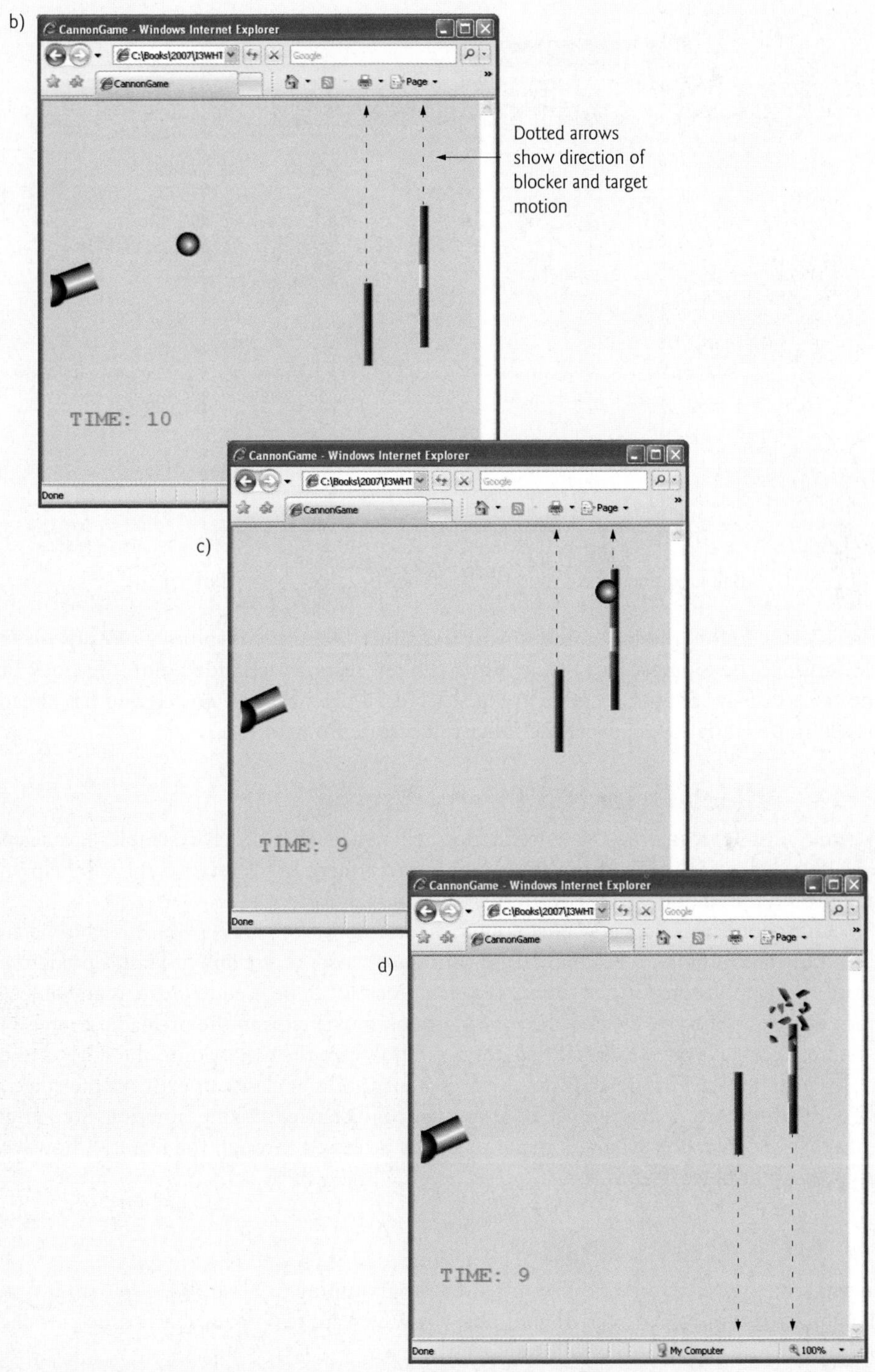

Fig. 17.1 | Ball fired from the cannon and hitting the target. (Part 2 of 3.)

e)

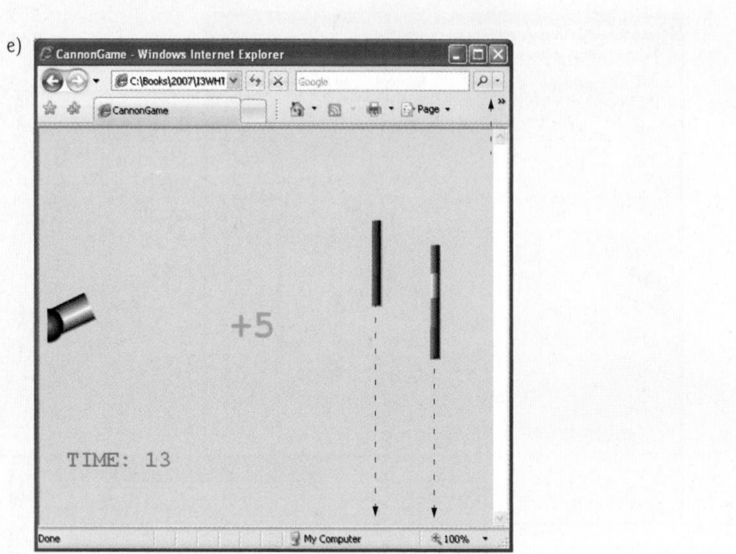

Fig. 17.1 | Ball fired from the cannon and hitting the target. (Part 3 of 3.)

Fig. 17.1(c), before the ball collides with the target, the timer displays `9` seconds on the clock. Once the topmost part of the target is hit, `5` seconds are added onto the clock but the clock displays only `13` seconds in Fig. 17.1(d). This is because one second has already passed in this duration, causing the timer to decrease from `14` to `13`.

17.2 Object-Oriented Programming

ActionScript 3.0 is an object-oriented scripting language that closely resembles JavaScript. The knowledge you gained from the JavaScript treatment in Chapters 6–11 will help you understand the ActionScript used in this case study.

An ActionScript class is a collection of characteristics known as properties and behaviors known as functions. You can create your own classes or use any of Flash's predefined classes. A symbol stored in the **Library** is a class. A class can be used to create many objects. For example, when you created the rotating-book movie clips in the preloader exercise in Chapter 16, you created a class. Dragging a symbol from the **Library** onto the stage created an instance (object) of the class. Multiple instances of one class can exist on the stage at the same time. Any changes made to an individual instance (resizing, rotating, etc.) affect only that one instance. Changes made to a class (accessed through the **Library**), however, affect every instance of the class.

17.3 Objects in Flash

In this section, we introduce object-oriented programming in Flash. We also demonstrate dynamic positioning (i.e., moving an object). We create two boxes. Each time you click on the left box, the right box will move to the left.

Start by creating a new Flash document named `Box.fla`. Set the movie's dimensions to 230 px wide and 140 px high. On the stage, draw a 100-px-wide blue box with a black

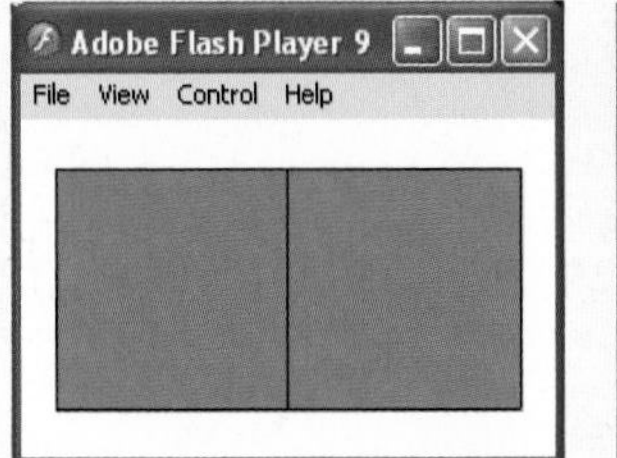

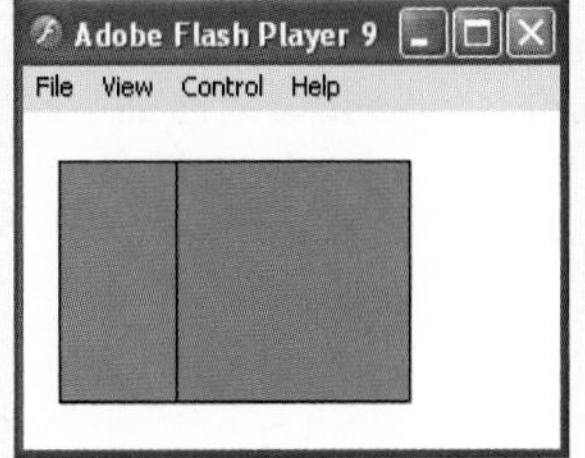

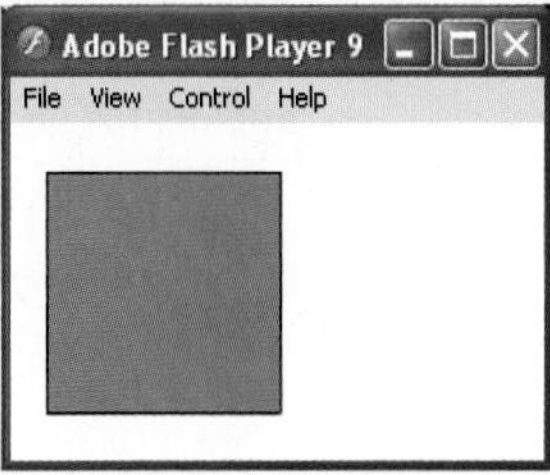

Fig. 17.2 | Dynamic positioning.

outline and convert it into a movie-clip symbol. You can name this symbol **box**, but that is not necessary. Next, select the box on the stage and delete it, leaving the stage empty. This step ensures that the box will be added using the ActionScript code and that the box is not already on the stage. Now, create a new **ActionScript File** from the **File > New** menu, save it as `BoxCode.as` in the same directory as `Box.fla`, and add the code in Fig. 17.3.

The properties `x` and `y` refer to the respective *x*- and *y*-coordinates of the boxes. The two `imports` (lines 5–6) at the top of the code allow for the code to utilize those two classes, which in this case are `MouseEvent` and `Sprite`, both of which are built-in Flash classes. Inside the class, the two `Box` instances are declared. By declaration of the two `Box` objects at the beginning of the class (lines 11–12), they become instance variables and have scope through the entire class. Once the boxes have been allocated positions (lines 18–21), they must be placed on the stage using the `addChild` function (lines 23–24). The function `handleClick` is called every time the user clicks `box1`. The `addEventListener` function, which is invoked by `box1`, specifies that `handleClick` will be called whenever `box1` is clicked (line 27).

```
1  // Fig. 17.2: BoxCode.as
2  // Object animation in ActionScript.
3  package
4  {
5     import flash.events.MouseEvent; // import MouseEvent class
6     import flash.display.Sprite; // import Sprite class
7
8     public class BoxCode extends Sprite
9     {
10       // create two new box objects
11       public var box1 = new Box();
12       public var box2 = new Box();
13
14       // initialize Box coordinates, add Boxes
15       // to the stage and register MOUSE_DOWN event handler
16       public function BoxCode() : void
17       {
18          box1.x = 15; // set box1's x-coordinate
19          box1.y = 20; // set box1's y-coordinate
20          box2.x = 115; // set box2's x-coordinate
21          box2.y = 20; // set box2's y-coordinate
```

Fig. 17.3 | Object animation in ActionScript. (Part 1 of 2.)

```

         addChild( box1 ); // add box1 to the stage
         addChild( box2 ); // add box2 to the stage

         // handleClick is called when box1 is clicked
         box1.addEventListener( MouseEvent.MOUSE_DOWN, handleClick );
      } // end BoxCode constructor

      // move box2 5 pixels to the left whenever box1 is clicked
      private function handleClick( args : MouseEvent )
      {
         box2.x -= 5;
      } // end function handleClick
   } // end class BoxCode
} // end package
```

Fig. 17.3 | Object animation in ActionScript. (Part 2 of 2.)

To test the code, return to `Box.fla`. In the **Library** panel, right click the `Box` symbol and select **Linkage**. In the pop-up box, check off the box next to **Export for ActionScript** and type `Box` in the space provided next to **Class**. Ignore Flash's warning that a definition for this class doesn't exist in the classpath. Once you return to the stage, go to the **Property Inspector** panel and in the space next to **Document Class**, type `BoxCode` and press *Enter*. Now, the `BoxCode` ActionScript file has been linked to this specific Flash document. Type *<Ctrl>-Enter* to test the movie.

17.4 Cannon Game: Preliminary Instructions and Notes

Open the template file named `CannonTemplate.fla` from Chapter 17's examples folder. We'll build our game from this template. For this case study, the graphics have already been created so that we can focus on the ActionScript. We created all the images using Flash. Chapter 16 provides a detailed coverage of Flash's graphical capabilities. Take a minute to familiarize yourself with the symbols in the **Library**. Note that the **target** movie clip has movie clips within it. Also, the **ball**, **sound**, **text** and **scoreText** movie clips have `stop` actions and labels already in place. Throughout the game, we play different sections of these movie clips by referencing their frame labels. The `stop` action at the end of each section ensures that only the desired animation will be played.

Labeling Frames

Before writing any ActionScript to build the game, we must label each frame in the main timeline to represent its purpose in the game. First, add a keyframe to frames 2 and 3 of the **Labels** layer. Select the first frame of the **Labels** layer and enter **intro** into the **Frame Label** field in the **Property Inspector**. A flag should appear in the corresponding box in the **timeline**. Label the second frame **game** and the third frame **end**. These labels will provide useful references as we create the game.

Using the `Actions` Layer

In our game, we use an **Actions** layer to hold any ActionScript attached to a specific frame. ActionScript programmers often create an **Actions** layer to better organize Flash movies.

Add keyframes in the second and third frame of the **Actions** layer, and place a `stop` function in all three frames.

17.5 Adding a Start Button

Most games start with an introductory animation. In this section, we create a simple starting frame for our game (Fig. 17.1(a)).

Select the first frame of the **Intro/End** layer. From the **Library**, drag the **introText** movie clip and the **Play** button onto the stage. Resize and position both objects any way you like. Set the **Play** button's instance name to **playButton**. Don't worry that **introText** is invisible when deselected; it will fade in when the movie is viewed.

Test the movie. The text effects were created by manipulating alpha and gradient values with shape tweening. Explore the different symbols in the **Library** to see how they were created. Now, in the first frame of the **Actions** layer, add the code shown in Fig. 17.4 in the **Actions** panel. When the **Play** button is clicked, the movie will now play the second frame, labeled **game**.

```
// Fig. 17.4: Handle playButton click event.

// call function playFunction when playButton is clicked
playButton.addEventListener( MouseEvent.MOUSE_DOWN, playFunction );

// go to game frame
function playFunction( event : MouseEvent ) : void
{
   gotoAndPlay( "game" );
} // end function playFunction
```

Fig. 17.4 | Handle `playButton` click event.

17.6 Creating Moving Objects

Adding the Target

In our game, the player's goal is to hit a moving target, which we create in this section. Create a keyframe in the second frame of the **Target** layer, then drag an instance of the **target** movie clip from the **Library** onto the stage. Using the **Property Inspector**, position the target at the *x*- and *y*-coordinates 490 and 302, respectively. The position (0, 0) is located in the upper-left corner of the screen, so the target should appear near the lower-right corner of the stage. Give the **target** symbol the instance name **target**. Right click the **target** symbol in the **Library** and select **Linkage.** In the box that pops up, select **Export for ActionScript** and enter `Target` in the **Class** field.

The **target** symbol is now linked with a class named `Target`. Create a new **ActionScript File** from the **File > New** menu. Save this file immediately and give it the name `Target.as`. This will serve as the `Target` class definition. In this file, add the code in Fig. 17.5.

The `Target` class has four instance variables—the speed of the `Target` (`speed`), the direction of the `Target` (`upDown`), the number of times the `Target` has been hit by the ball (`hitCounter`), and the `Timer` variable (`moveTargetTimer`). We specify that `moveTargetTimer` is a `Timer` using the colon syntax in line 18. The first parameter of the `Timer` constructor is the delay between timer events in milliseconds. The second parameter is the

```
// Fig. 17.5: Target.as
// Move target, set direction and speed,
// and keep track of number of blocks hit.
package
{
   // import relevant classes
   import flash.display.MovieClip;
   import flash.events.TimerEvent;
   import flash.utils.Timer;

   public class Target extends MovieClip
   {
      var speed; // speed of Target
      var upDown; // direction of Target
      var hitCounter; // number of times Target has been hit

      // timer runs indefinitely every 33 ms
      var moveTargetTimer : Timer = new Timer ( 33, 0 );

      // register function moveTarget as moveTargetTimer's
      // event handler, start timer
      public function Target() : void
      {
         moveTargetTimer.addEventListener (
            TimerEvent.TIMER, moveTarget );
         moveTargetTimer.start(); // start timer
      } // end Target constructor

      // move the Target
      private function moveTarget( t : TimerEvent )
      {
         // if Target is at the top or bottom of the stage,
         // change its direction
         if ( y > 310 )
         {
            upDown = -1; // change direction to up
         } // end if

         else if ( y < 90 )
         {
            upDown = 1; // change direction to down
         } // end else

         y += (speed * upDown); // move target
      } // end function moveTarget

      // set direction of the Target
      public function setUpDown( newUpDown : int )
      {
         upDown = newUpDown;
      } // end function setUpDown

```

Fig. 17.5 | Move target, set direction and speed, and track number of blocks hit. (Part 1 of 2.)

```
53         // get direction of the Target
54         public function getUpDown() : int
55         {
56            return upDown;
57         } // end function getUpDown
58
59        // set speed of the Target
60         public function setSpeed ( newSpeed : int )
61         {
62            speed = newSpeed;
63         } // end function setSpeed
64
65         // get speed of the Target
66         public function getSpeed() : int
67         {
68            return speed;
69         } // end function getSpeed
70
71         // set the number of times the Target has been hit
72         public function setHitCounter( newCount : int )
73         {
74            hitCounter = newCount;
75         } // end setHitCounter function
76
77         // return the number of times the Target has been hit
78         public function getHitCounter () : int
79         {
80            return hitCounter;
81         } // end function getHitCounter
82
83         // stop moveTargetTimer
84         public function stopTimers() : void
85         {
86            moveTargetTimer.stop();
87         }
88      } // end class Target
89   } // end package
```

Fig. 17.5 | Move target, set direction and speed, and track number of blocks hit. (Part 2 of 2.)

number of times the `Timer` should repeat. A value of 0 means that the `Timer` will run indefinately. The constructor function (lines 22–27) activates `moveTargetTimer`, which in turn calls the `moveTarget` function (lines 30–45) to move the `Target` every 33 milliseconds. The `moveTarget` function contains a nested `if...else` statement (lines 34–42) that sets `upDown` to `-1` (up) when the target reaches the bottom of the screen and sets `upDown` to `1` (down) when it reaches the top of the screen. It does this by testing if the target's *y*-coordinate is greater than 310 or less than 90. [*Note:* The property `y` refers specifically to the *y*-coordinate of the small white circle that appears on the main stage.] Since the stage is 400 pixels high and the target is 180 pixels high (half of which is below its *y*-coordinate), when the target's *y*-coordinate is equal to 310, the bottom end of the target is even with bottom of the stage. Similar logic applies when the target is at the top of the stage.

Line 44 moves the target by incrementing its *y*-coordinate by the result of `getSpeed() * upDown`. The remaining functions in this class are the public *get* and *set* functions for the `upDown`, `speed` and `hitCounter` variables. These allow us to retrieve and set the values outside of the class. The `stopTimers` function allows us to stop the `moveTargetTimer` from outside of the class.

Now, we can enable the target on stage, **target**, to move vertically simply by adding the calling methods `setSpeed`, `setUpDown` and `setHitCounter` in the second frame of the **Actions** layer:

```
target.setSpeed( 8 );
target.setUpDown( -1 );
target.setHitCounter( 0 );
```

Now, test the movie to see the target oscillate between the top and bottom of the stage.

Adding the Blocker

An additional moving object is used to block the ball, increasing the game's difficulty. Insert a keyframe in the second frame of the `Blocker` layer and drag an instance of the **blocker** object from the **Library** onto the stage. Give this **blocker** instance the name **blocker**. Set the blocker instance's *x*- and *y*-coordinates to 415 and 348, respectively. Create a `Blocker.as` file and class and link it to the **blocker** symbol. In this file, add the code in Fig. 17.6.

```
// Fig. 17.6: Blocker.as
// Set position and speed of Blocker.
package
{
   // import relevant classes
   import flash.display.MovieClip;
   import flash.events.TimerEvent;
   import flash.utils.Timer;

   public class Blocker extends MovieClip
   {
      var speed : int; // speed of Blocker
      var upDown : int; // direction of Blocker
      var moveBlockerTimer : Timer = new Timer ( 33, 0 );

      // call function moveBlocker as moveBlockerTimer event handler
      public function Blocker() : void
      {
         moveBlockerTimer.addEventListener (
            TimerEvent.TIMER, moveBlocker );
         moveBlockerTimer.start();
      } // end Blocker constructor

      // move the Blocker
      private function moveBlocker( t : TimerEvent )
      {
         // if Blocker is at the top or bottom of the stage,
         // change its direction
```

Fig. 17.6 | Set position and speed of `Blocker`. (Part 1 of 2.)

```
         if ( y > 347.5 )
         {
            upDown = -1;
         } // end if

         else if ( y < 52.5 )
         {
            upDown = 1;
         } // end else

         y += getSpeed() * upDown;
      } // end function moveBlocker

      // set speed for the Blocker
      public function setSpeed ( v : int )
      {
         speed = v;
      } // end function setSpeed

      // get speed of the Blocker
      public function getSpeed() : int
      {
         return speed;
      } // end function getSpeed

      // set direction for the Blocker
      public function setUpDown( newUpDown : int )
      {
         upDown = newUpDown;
      } // end function setUpDown

      // get direction of the Blocker
      public function getUpDown() : int
      {
         return upDown;
      } // end function getUpDown

      // stop moveBlockerTimer
      public function stopTimers() : void
      {
         moveBlockerTimer.stop();
      }
   } // end class Blocker
} // end package
```

Fig. 17.6 | Set position and speed of `Blocker`. (Part 2 of 2.)

This code is very similar to that of the `Target.as`. Add the following code in the second frame of the **Actions** layer to set the speed and direction of the blocker:

```
blocker.setSpeed( 5 );
blocker.setUpDown( 1 );
```

Test the movie. The blocker and target should both oscillate at different speeds (Fig. 17.7).

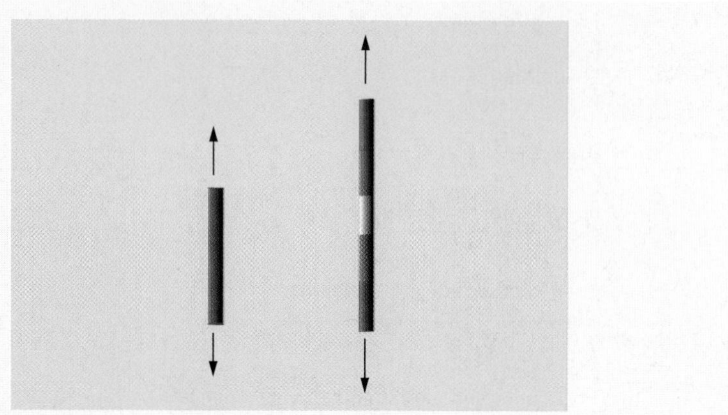

Fig. 17.7 | Oscillating blocker and target.

17.7 Adding the Rotating Cannon

Many Flash applications include animation that responds to mouse-cursor motions. In this section, we discuss how to make the cannon's barrel follow the cursor, allowing the player to aim at the moving target. The skills you learn here can be used to create many effects that respond to cursor movements.

Add a keyframe to the second frame of the **Cannon** layer and drag the **cannon** object from the **Library** onto the stage. Set its *x*- and *y*-coordinates to 0 and 200. Give this cannon instance the name **cannon**. The cannon should appear in the middle of the stage's left edge (Fig. 17.8).

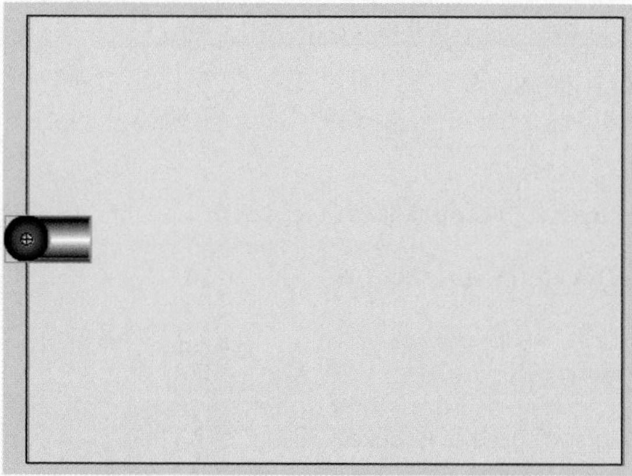

Fig. 17.8 | Cannon position.

Coding the Cannon's Rotation

Now, add the code from Fig. 17.9 to the second frame of the **Actions** layer. This code rotates the cannon barrel to point toward the cursor. The *x*- and *y*-coordinates of the cursor are directly accessed using the `stage.mouseX` and `stage.mouseY` properties. The code ex-

```
1  // Fig. 17.9: Register mouseInHandler as MOUSE_MOVE event handler.
2  stage.addEventListener( MouseEvent.MOUSE_MOVE, mouseInHandler );
3
4  // rotate cannon when mouse is moved
5  function mouseInHandler( args : MouseEvent ) : void
6  {
7     // rotates cannon if cursor is within stage
8     if ( ( stage.mouseX > 0 ) && ( stage.mouseY > 0 ) &&
9        ( stage.mouseX < 550 ) && ( stage.mouseY < 400 ) )
10    {
11       // adjust cannon rotation based on cursor position
12       var angle = Math.atan2( ( stage.mouseY - 200 ), stage.mouseX );
13       cannon.rotation = angle * ( 180 / Math.PI );
14    } // end if
15 } // end function mouseInHandler
```

Fig. 17.9 | Register `mouseInHandler` as `MOUSE_MOVE` event handler.

ecutes any time the player moves the cursor, so the cannon always points toward the mouse cursor. The `addEventListener` function of the `stage` object registers the `mouseInHandler` function as the event handler of the `MOUSE_MOVE` event (line 2). Inside the `mouseInHandler` function, an `if` statement (lines 8–9) checks whether the cursor is within the stage. If it is, the code adjusts the `cannon`'s `rotation` so that it points toward the cursor (line 13). The **`rotation` property** (line 13) controls an object's rotation, assuming its natural orientation to be 0 degrees.

ActionScript's **`Math` class** contains various mathematical functions and values that are useful when performing complex operations. For a full list of the `Math` class's functions and values, refer to the **Flash Help** in the **Help** menu. We use the `Math` class to help us compute the rotation angle required to point the cannon toward the cursor.

First, we need to find the cursor's coordinates relative to the cannon. Subtracting 200 from the cursor's *y*-coordinate gives us the cursor's vertical position, assuming (0, 0) lies at the cannon's center (Fig. 17.10). We then determine the desired angle of rotation. Note the

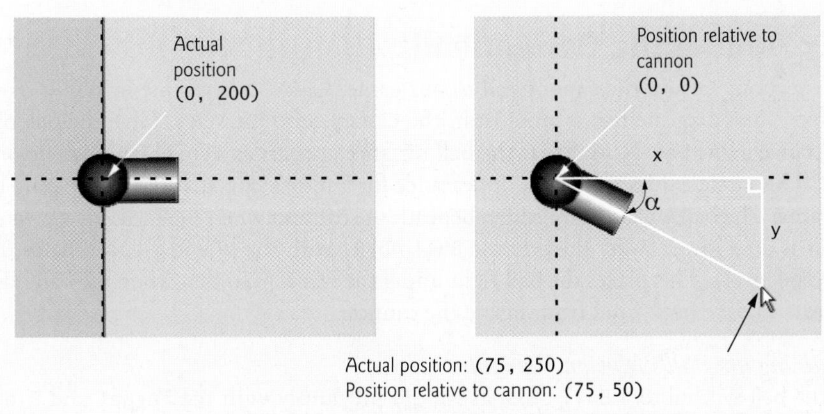

Fig. 17.10 | Trigonometry of the **cannon** object.

right triangle created by the cannon and the cursor in Fig. 17.10. From trigonometry, we know that the tangent of angle α equals the length of side *y* divided by side *x*: $\tan(\alpha) = y/x$. We want the value of α, though, not the value of tan(α). Since the arc tangent is the inverse of the tangent, we can rewrite this equation as $\alpha = \arctan(y/x)$. The `Math` object provides us with an arc tangent function: `Math.atan2(y, x)`. This function returns a value, in radians, equal to the angle opposite side y and adjacent to side x (line 12). Radians are a type of angle measurement similar to degrees that range from 0 to 2π instead of 0 to 360. To convert from radians to degrees, we multiply by 180/π (line 13). The constant `Math.PI` provides the value of π. Since this rotation adjustment is performed every time the mouse moves within the stage, the cannon barrel appears to constantly point at the cursor. Test the movie to observe this effect.

Error-Prevention Tip 17.1

If your code is not working and no error message displays, ensure that every variable points to the correct object. One incorrect reference can prevent an entire function from operating correctly.

Hiding the **Cannon** *Layer*

We won't make any other changes to the **Cannon** layer. Hide the **Cannon** layer by selecting the show/hide selector (dot) in the portion of the **Timeline** to the right of the layer name (Fig. 17.11). A red **x** should appear in place of the dot to indicate that the layer is hidden while editing the movie. The layer will still be visible when the movie is viewed. Clicking the show/hide **x** again makes the **Cannon** layer visible.

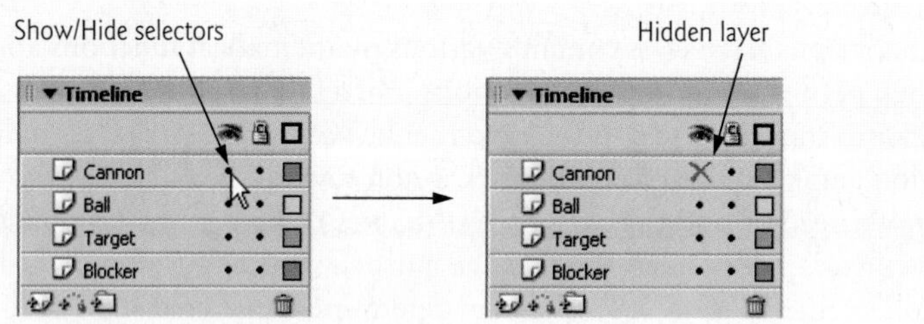

Fig. 17.11 | Using selectors to show/hide layers.

17.8 Adding the Cannonball

In this section, we add the cannonball to our game. Create a keyframe in frame 2 of the **Ball** layer, then drag the **ball** symbol from the **Library** onto the stage. Give the **ball** object the instance name **ball**. Notice that the ball instance appears as a small white circle on the `stage`. This circle is Flash's default appearance for a movie clip that has no graphic in its first frame. The ball will appear hidden beneath the cannon when the movie is viewed, because it is on a lower layer. Provide the `Ball` object with the *x*- and *y*-coordinates 0 and 200, respectively. This places the ball right under the cannon, so that when the ball is fired, it appears to have been fired from inside the cannon.

Initializing the Ball's Motion Variables

Link the **ball** symbol to a `Ball` class, as we did previously with the `Target` and `Blocker` classes. Next, create a new ActionScript 3.0 file named `Ball.as` and add the code shown in Fig. 17.12 to the file.

This code defines the `Ball` class. It has three properties—the speed in the *x*-direction, `speedX` (line 12), the speed in the *y*-direction, `speedY` (line 13), and a timer that moves the ball, `moveBallTimer` (line 16). Since the speed in the *x*-direction will be only integer values, it is of type `int`. However, the speed in the *y*-direction is also dependent on `fireRatio`, which can be a decimal value, and thus, `speedY` is of type `Number`, which is ActionScript 3's floating-point variable type. The class definition also creates the *get* and *set* functions for these properties. When the `Ball` object is created, the `Ball` constructor function starts the `moveBallTimer`, which calls the `moveBall` function every 33 ms. Function `moveBall` (lines 28–32) increments the *x*- and *y*-coordinates by `speedX` and `speedY`. The `stopTimers` function allows us to stop the `moveBallTimer` from outside of the class.

```
1  // Fig. 17.12: Ball.as
2  // Move ball and set speed.
3  package
4  {
5     // import relevant classes
6     import flash.display.MovieClip;
7     import flash.events.TimerEvent;
8     import flash.utils.Timer;
9
10    public class Ball extends MovieClip
11    {
12       var speedX : int; // speed in x-direction
13       var speedY : Number; // speed in y-direction
14
15       // Create Timer object to move ball
16       var moveBallTimer : Timer = new Timer( 33, 0 );
17
18       // Ball constructor starts moveBallTimer
19       public function Ball() : void
20       {
21          // call function moveBall as moveBallTimer event handler
22          moveBallTimer.addEventListener(
23             TimerEvent.TIMER, moveBall );
24          moveBallTimer.start();
25       } // end Ball constructor
26
27       // update the x and y coordinates using the specific speeds
28       private function moveBall( t : TimerEvent )
29       {
30          x += speedX;
31          y += speedY;
32       } // end function moveBall
33
34       // set speed in x direction
35       public function setSpeedX( v : int )
36       {
37          speedX = v;
38       } // end function setSpeedX
39
```

Fig. 17.12 | Move ball and set speed. (Part 1 of 2.)

```
      // get speed in x direction
      public function getSpeedX() : int
      {
         return speedX;
      } // end function getSpeedX

      // set speed in y direction
      public function setSpeedY( v : int, fireRatio : Number )
      {
         speedY = v * fireRatio;
      } // end function setSpeedY

      // get speed in y direction
      public function getSpeedY() : Number
      {
         return speedY;
      } // end function getSpeedY

      public function stopTimers() : void
      {
         moveBallTimer.stop();
      } // end function stopTimer
   } // end class Ball
} // end package
```

Fig. 17.12 | Move ball and set speed. (Part 2 of 2.)

Scripting the Ball's Motion

In the second frame of the **Actions** layer, add the code in Fig. 17.13. The new code moves the ball along a straight line in the direction the cannon was pointing when the mouse was clicked.

```
// Fig. 17.13: Fire ball on click event.
var firing : Boolean = false; // is ball firing?
var exploding : Boolean = false; // is ball exploding?
var fireRatio : Number = 0; // firing direction of ball
var speed : int = 30; // speed of ball
ball.setSpeedX( 0 );
ball.setSpeedY( 0, 0 );

// register function mouseDownHandler as MOUSE_DOWN event handler
stage.addEventListener( MouseEvent.MOUSE_DOWN, mouseDownHandler );

function mouseDownHandler( args : MouseEvent ) : void
{
   // if the mouse is within the stage and the ball has not been fired or
   // exploded yet, fire ball toward mouse cursor
   if ( ( !firing ) && ( !exploding ) && ( stage.mouseX > 0 ) &&
      ( stage.mouseY > 0 ) && ( stage.mouseX < 550 ) &&
      ( stage.mouseY < 400 ) )
   {
```

Fig. 17.13 | Fire ball on click event. (Part 1 of 2.)

```
20          firing = true;
21          fireRatio = ( stage.mouseY - 200 ) / stage.mouseX;
22          ball.setSpeedX( speed );
23          ball.setSpeedY( speed, fireRatio );
24       } // end if
25    } // end function mouseDownHandler
```

Fig. 17.13 | Fire ball on click event. (Part 2 of 2.)

This code initializes four variables—`firing`, `exploding`, `fireRatio` and `speed` (lines 2–5). Variables `firing` and `exploding` are set to `false` to signify that the ball is not moving or exploding. Later, we will set `exploding` to `true` and play a brief explosion animation upon collision with the target or the blocker. Variables `fireRatio` and `speed` specify the ball's firing direction and speed, respectively. The function `addEventListener` (line 10) registers the function `mouseDownHandler` (lines 12–25) as the event handler for the stage's `MOUSE_DOWN` event. The `if` statement in the `mouseDownHandler` function (lines 16–24) checks that the ball is not currently in flight (`!firing`) or exploding (`!exploding`), and the mouse is within the stage (lines 16–18). If the condition evaluates to true, `firing` is set to `true` (line 20), and `fireRatio` is set to the mouse's *y*-coordinate (relative to the cannon) divided by its *x*-coordinate (line 21). This `fireRatio` will move the ball toward the cursor's position when it is fired. Lines 22–23 set the ball's speed in the *x*-direction to `speed`, and the ball's speed in the *y*-direction to `speed * fireRatio`. The expression `speed * fireRatio` returns the appropriate change in `y` based on the given change in `x` (`speed`).

17.9 Adding Sound and Text Objects to the Movie

Next, we add sound and text to our movie. Add a keyframe to frame 2 of the **Text** layer and drag the **text** symbol from the **Library** onto the stage. Note that the **text** object, like the ball, is represented by a small white dot. This dot will not appear when the movie is viewed. Position the **text** symbol in the center of the `stage` at coordinate (275, 200), and name the instance **text**. Then, add a keyframe to the second frame of the **Sounds** and **ScoreText** layers, and add an instance of the **sound** and **scoreText** objects, respectively. Center both objects on the stage and give them instance names matching their symbol names—**sound** and **scoreText.** Lock these three layers by clicking the lock/unlock selector (dot) to the right of the layer name in the timeline (Fig. 17.14). When a layer is locked,

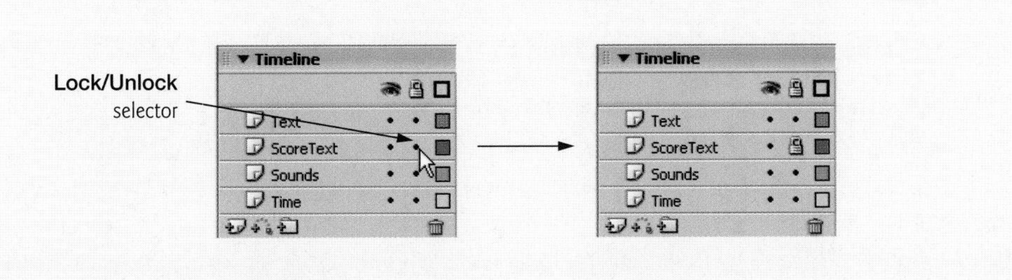

Fig. 17.14 | **Lock/Unlock** layers.

its elements are visible, but they cannot be edited. This allows you to use one layer's elements as visual references for designing another layer, while ensuring that no elements are moved unintentionally. To unlock a layer, click the lock symbol to the right of the layer name in the **Timeline**.

All the necessary sound and text capabilities have now been added to the game. In the next section, we add the time counter to the game.

17.10 Adding the Time Counter

What makes the cannon game challenging is the limited amount of time the player has to completely destroy the `target`. Time, whether increasing or decreasing, is an important aspect of many games and applications. In this section, we discuss adding a time counter that decreases as the game progresses.

Adding the Time Box

In the cannon game, the player has a limited amount of time to destroy every section of the target. The amount of time remaining appears in a dynamic text box in the bottom-left corner of the screen. To create this dynamic text box, first add a keyframe to frame 2 of the **Time** layer and add an instance of the **time** symbol to the stage. Position it at coordinate (100, 365), which should be in the lower-left corner of the stage. Name the instance **time.** Open the **time** symbol from the **Library** and select the text field. In the **Property Inspector**, change the text type to **Dynamic Text** and name the instance **timeText.** Return to the main scene, and add the code in Fig. 17.15 to the **Actions** panel in the second frame.

The variable `timer` is initialized to `10` (line 2). This variable will hold the amount of time remaining. The `countTimer` (lines 3–7) calls the `countDown` function (lines 9–18) each second. The `countDown` function decrements the `timer` by 1, and also sets the `text` of the `time` symbol's `timeText` element to `"TIME: "`, followed by the current value of `timer`.

```
1  // Fig. 17.15: Timer countdown.
2  var timer = 10; // set initial timer value to 10 seconds
3  var countTimer : Timer = new Timer( 1000, 0 );
4
5  // call function countDown as countTimer event handler
6  countTimer.addEventListener( TimerEvent.TIMER, countDown );
7  countTimer.start(); // start Timer
8
9  function countDown( t : TimerEvent )
10 {
11    --timer;    // decrement timer by 1 every second
12    time.timeText.text = "TIME: " + timer;
13    // player loses game if he/she runs out of time
14    if( ( !firing ) && timer <= 0 )
15    {
16       gotoAndPlay( "end" ); // call end frame sequence
17    } // end if
18 } // end function countDown
```

Fig. 17.15 | Timer countdown.

Lines 14–17 test whether time has run out and the ball is not firing. If the condition is `true`, the movie will skip to the (empty) `end` frame.

Test the movie. The time should decrease from 10 to 0. When the time reaches 0, the **end** frame should play. Because none of the functions or objects in the second frame currently exist in the third frame, the timers that are still active will try to call those functions and fail, returning an error message. To fix this, we must first include all of the objects on the stage in the second frame in the third frame. You can do this by inserting a new frame (not keyframe) in the third frame of the **Text**, **ScoreText**, **Sounds**, **Time**, **Cannon**, **Ball**, **Target**, and **Blocker** layers. Next, we must stop all timers and hide most of the elements at the beginning of the third frame. Add the code in Fig. 17.16 to the third frame of the `Actions` layer.

Lines 2–3 remove the event listeners for the stage's `MOUSE_MOVE` and `MOUSE_DOWN` events, which are no longer needed. Lines 4–7 stop all of the timers that we have used, either by accessing the timer's `stop` method directly (line 4), or by accessing the class's `stopTimers` method (lines 5–7). Lines 8–13 hide every element on the stage by playing the `hidden` frame of each element, which is an empty frame.

```
1  // Fig. 17.16: Stops all timers and sends objects into hidden frame.
2  stage.removeEventListener( MouseEvent.MOUSE_MOVE, mouseInHandler );
3  stage.removeEventListener( MouseEvent.MOUSE_DOWN, mouseDownHandler );
4  countTimer.stop();
5  blocker.stopTimers();
6  ball.stopTimers();
7  target.stopTimers();
8  blocker.gotoAndPlay( "hidden" );
9  cannon.gotoAndPlay( "hidden" );
10 ball.gotoAndPlay( "hidden" );
11 target.gotoAndPlay( "hidden" );
12 time.gotoAndPlay( "hidden" );
13 scoreText.gotoAndPlay( "hidden" );
```

Fig. 17.16 | Stops all timers and sends objects into `hidden` frame.

Creating a Final Animation Sequence

Games generally have a final animation sequence that informs the player of the outcome of the game. In this section, we create a final animation sequence for the game.

First, we must create a winner boolean to keep track of whether the player has won or lost the game. To do this, add the following code to the second frame of the `Actions` layer.

```
var winner : Boolean = false; // Keep track of who won
```

Next, add the code in Fig. 17.17 to the third frame of the `Actions` layer. This `if...else` statement checks the `winner` variable. If `winner` is `true`, the **text** movie clip goes to the **win** frame. Otherwise **text** goes to the **lose** frame. Test the movie again. When the time runs out, the **lose** frame, containing the text **Game Over**, should appear on an otherwise blank stage.

```
// Fig. 17.17: Check winner and show "Winner" or "Game Over".
if (winner == true)
{
   text.gotoAndPlay( "win" );
}

else
{
   text.gotoAndPlay( "lose" );
}
```

Fig. 17.17 | Check winner and show **Winner** or **Game Over**.

17.11 Detecting a Miss

We now add code to the **ball** instance that detects when the ball has moved outside of the stage. First, add the `checkBall` function in Fig. 17.18 to the second frame of the **Actions** panel.

Lines 5–6 test whether the ball is outside the bounds of the stage. If it is, the `checkBallTimer` is stopped (line 8), because the ball is no longer in motion and does not need to be checked until it has been fired again. Boolean `firing` is set to `false` (line 9). Then, lines 10–12 play the text movie clip's `miss` frame, the `scoreText` movie clip's `minusTwo` frame and the `sound` movie clip's `miss` frame. This will display **MISS** and **-2** on the stage, and play the miss sound. Also, the `timer` variable is decreased by 2 (line 13). Finally, the `Ball` object is reset to its starting position and speed (lines 14–17).

In order to check the ball at regular intervals, we create a timer that calls `checkBall` every 33 ms. First, add the following code to the second frame of the **Actions** layer:

```
// Check ball at 33-ms intervals
var checkBallTimer : Timer = new Timer( 33, 0 );
```

```
1  // Fig. 17.18: Detecting a miss.
2  function checkBall ( e : TimerEvent )
3  {
4     // if ball is not inside stage, go through miss sequence
5     if ( ( ball.x < 0 ) || ( ball.y  < 0 ) || ( ball.x > 550 ) ||
6        ( ball.y > 400 ) )
7     {
8           checkBallTimer.stop(); // stop checkBallTimer
9           firing = false; // ball is no longer being fired
10          text.gotoAndPlay( "miss" ); // display miss on the stage
11          scoreText.gotoAndPlay ( "minusTwo" ); // display "-2"
12          sound.gotoAndPlay ( "miss" ); // miss sound is played
13          timer -= 2; // deduct 2 seconds from timer
14          ball.x = 0; // set ball back to initial x-coordinate
15          ball.y = 200; // set ball back to initial y-coordinate
16          ball.setSpeedX( 0 ); // set ball speed in x-direction to 0
17          ball.setSpeedY( 0, 0 ); // set ball speed in y-direction to 0
18    } // end if
19 } // end function checkBall
```

Fig. 17.18 | Detecting a miss.

Next, we must start the timer. Since this timer needs to run only after the ball has been fired, we will start the timer in the `mouseDownHandler`. Insert the following code between lines 13 and 14 of Fig. 17.13.

```
// call function checkBall as checkBallTimer event handler
checkBallTimer.addEventListener( TimerEvent.TIMER, checkBall );
checkBallTimer.start(); // start Timer
```

We must also stop this timer at the end of the game by adding the following code to the third frame of the `Actions` layer.

```
checkBallTimer.stop();
```

Test the movie with your computer's sound turned on. At this point, every fired ball should travel off the stage and count as a miss. In the next few sections, we discuss how to add features that allow the player to gain time and win the game.

17.12 Adding Collision Detection

Before we add collision detection to the target and blocker, we add a function that handles the actions common to all of our collisions. Add the `onBallContact` function (Fig. 17.19) to the second frame of the `Actions` layer.

```
// Fig. 17.19: Common actions after collision.
function onBallContact( timeChange : int )
{
   // adjust variables to play exploding sequence
   exploding = true;
   firing = false;
   timer += timeChange; // add the amount of time passed as parameter
   ball.gotoAndPlay( "explode" ); // explode the Ball object
   ball.setSpeedX( 0 ); // set ball speed in x-direction to 0
   ball.setSpeedY( 0, 0 ); // set ball speed in y-direction to 0

   // give explode animation time to finish, then call resetBall
   explodeTimer.addEventListener( TimerEvent.TIMER, resetBall );
   explodeTimer.start();

   // play appropriate sound and text based on timeChange
   if ( timeChange < 0 )
   {
      sound.gotoAndPlay( "blocked" );
      text.gotoAndPlay( "blocked" );
      if ( timeChange == -5 )
      {
         scoreText.gotoAndPlay( "minusFive" );
      } // end if
   } // end if

   else if ( timeChange >= 0 )
   {
```

Fig. 17.19 | Common actions after collision. (Part 1 of 2.)

```
29          sound.gotoAndPlay( "hit" );
30          text.gotoAndPlay( "hit" );
31
32          // increment the hitCounter by 1
33          target.setHitCounter( target.getHitCounter() + 1 );
34
35          if ( target.getHitCounter() >= 5 )
36          {
37             // if target has been hit 5 times, then declare player winner
38             winner = true;
39             gotoAndPlay( "end" ); // go to third frame
40          } // end if
41
42          if ( timeChange == 5 )
43          {
44             scoreText.gotoAndPlay( "plusFive" );
45          } // end if
46
47          else if ( timeChange == 10 )
48          {
49             scoreText.gotoAndPlay( "plusTen" );
50          } // end else
51
52          else if ( timeChange == 20 )
53          {
54             scoreText.gotoAndPlay( "plus20" );
55          } // end else
56       } // end else
57    } // end function onBallContact
```

Fig. 17.19 | Common actions after collision. (Part 2 of 2.)

The `onBallContact` function takes a `timeChange` parameter that specifies how many seconds to add or remove from the time remaining. Line 7 adds `timeChange` to the timer. Lines 8–10 tell the ball to `explode` and stop. Lines 13–14 start a timer that calls the `resetBall` function after completion. We must create this timer by adding the following code to the second frame of the **Actions** layer:

```
// Delay for ball explosion
var explodeTimer : Timer = new Timer( 266, 1 );
```

This timer gives the `ball`'s `explode` animation time to complete before it calls `resetBall`. We must stop this timer at the end of the game, by adding the following code to the third frame of the **Actions** layer.

```
explodeTimer.stop();
```

The `resetBall` function (Fig. 17.20) sets `exploding` to `false` (line 4), then resets the ball to the starting frame and position (lines 5–7). Add the `resetBall` function to the second frame of the `Actions` layer.

The `onBallContact` function (Fig. 17.19) also plays a frame from the `sound`, `text` and `scoreText` movie clips, depending on the `timeChange`, to notify the player whether

```
// Fig. 17.20: Reset the ball to its original position.
function resetBall( t : TimerEvent )
{
   exploding = false; // set the ball explosion status to false
   ball.gotoAndPlay( "normal" );
   ball.x = 0; // set x-coordinate to original position
   ball.y = 200; // set y-coordinate to original position
} // end function resetBall
```

Fig. 17.20 | Reset the ball to its original position.

they hit a target or a blocker, and to show the player how many points they gained or lost (lines 17–56). Lines 35–40 test whether the target has been hit 5 times. If it has, `winner` is set to `true` and the **end** frame is played.

Adding Collision Detection to the Target and Blocker

Flash has a built-in collision detection function that determines whether two objects are touching. The function *object1*.`hitTestObject(`*object2*`)` returns `true` if any part of *object1* touches *object2*. Many games must detect collisions between moving objects to control game play or add realistic effects. In this game, we rely on collision detection to determine if the ball hits either the blocker or the target.

In this section, we add code to **target** and **blocker** that increases or decreases your remaining time, depending on what you hit. Note that the **target** object comprises five instances of three different symbols: one **targetCenter** (white), two **targetMiddle**s (gray) and two **targetOut**s (red). The closer to the center the **target** is hit, the more seconds get added to the total time.

Add the collision detection function shown in Fig. 17.21 to the second frame of the **Actions** layer.

```
// Fig. 17.21: Detect collision using hitTestObject.
function collisionDetection()
{
   if ( target.out1.hitTestObject( ball ) && ( !exploding ) )
   {
      onBallContact ( 5 ); // hit upper outer part of target
      target.out1.gotoAndPlay( "hit" );
   } // end if

   else if ( target.mid1.hitTestObject( ball ) && ( !exploding ) )
   {
      onBallContact ( 10 ); // hit upper middle part of target
      target.mid1.gotoAndPlay( "hit" );
   } // end else

   else if ( target.center.hitTestObject( ball ) && ( !exploding ) )
   {
      onBallContact ( 20 ); // hit center of target
      target.center.gotoAndPlay( "hit" );
   } // end else
```

Fig. 17.21 | Detect collision using `hitTestObject`. (Part 1 of 2.)

```
21
22       else if ( target.mid2.hitTestObject( ball ) && ( !exploding ) )
23       {
24          onBallContact ( 10 ); // hit lower middle part of target
25          target.mid2.gotoAndPlay( "hit" );
26       } // end else
27
28       else if ( target.out2.hitTestObject( ball ) && ( !exploding ) )
29       {
30          onBallContact ( 5 ); // hit lower outer part of target
31          target.out2.gotoAndPlay( "hit" );
32       } // end else
33
34       else if ( blocker.hitTestObject( ball ) && ( !exploding ) )
35       {
36          onBallContact ( -5 );
37
38          // if timer runs out, player loses
39          if ( timer < 0 )
40          {
41             winner = false;
42             gotoAndPlay( "end" );
43          } // end if
44       } // end else
45    } // end function collisionDetection
```

Fig. 17.21 | Detect collision using `hitTestObject`. (Part 2 of 2.)

Function `collisionDetection` consists of an `if...else` statement that tests whether the ball has hit the blocker or one of the parts of the target. It ensures that the ball is not currently exploding, to prevent the ball from hitting more than one part of the target at a time. If these conditions return true, the `onBallContact` function is called with the appropriate number of seconds to add to or subtract from the timer as the parameter. For each of the parts of the target, that part's `hit` animation is played upon being hit. For the blocker, an `if` statement (lines 39–43) checks whether time has run out (line 39). If it has, the `winner` is set to `false` and the movie moves to the `end` frame.

To run the `collisionDetection` function at a regular interval, we will call it from the `checkBall` function. Add the following at the beginning of the `checkBall` function.

```
collisionDetection();
```

Now test the movie. The target pieces should disappear when hit by the ball, as shown in Fig. 17.1. The player can now gain time by hitting the target and lose time by hitting the blocker. The ball should explode in the position where it hit the blocker, then reset to under the cannon, allowing the player to fire again.

17.13 Finishing the Game

Open the **text** symbol's editing stage from the **Library**. An action that plays the frame labeled **intro** in the main scene has already been attached to the last frame of the sections labeled **win** and **lose**. These actions, which were included in the original `CannonTemplate.fla` file, cause the game to restart after the final text animation is played.

To change the game's difficulty, adjust `speed` in the **blocker** and/or the **target**. Adjusting the time change in the `timeText` instance also changes the difficulty (a smaller decrement gives more time).

Congratulations! You have created an interactive Flash game. Now you can play the completed version. In the chapter exercises, you can improve the game and add additional levels of difficulty.

17.14 ActionScript 3.0 Elements Introduced in This Chapter

Figure 17.22 lists the Flash ActionScript 3.0 elements introduced in this chapter, which are useful in building complex Flash movies.

Element	Description
object.x	Property that refers to *object's* *x*-coordinate.
object.y	Property that refers to *object's* *y*-coordinate.
addChild(*object*)	Function that adds the object to the stage.
addEventListener(*event*, *function*)	Function that invokes another function in response to an event.
mouseX	Mouse's *x*-coordinate property.
mouseY	Mouse's *y*-coordinate property.
object.rotation	Property that rotates the *object*.
stage	Manipulates objects on the stage.
object1.hitTestObject(*object2*)	Built-in function that determines when two objects collide
Math	Built-in object that contains useful functions and properties (refer to Flash's ActionScript Dictionary for a full list).

Fig. 17.22 | ActionScript 3.0 elements.

Summary

Section 17.1 Introduction

- Adobe Flash CS3 is capable of building large, interactive applications.

Section 17.2 Object-Oriented Programming

- ActionScript 3.0 is an object-oriented scripting language that closely resembles JavaScript. The knowledge you gained from the JavaScript treatment in Chapters 6–11 will help you understand the ActionScript used in this case study.
- An ActionScript class is a collection of characteristics known as properties and of behaviors known as functions.

- You can create your own classes or use any of Flash's predefined classes.
- A symbol stored in the **Library** is a class.
- A class can be used to create many instances, or objects, of the class.
- Dragging a symbol from the **Library** onto the stage creates an instance (object) of the class. Multiple instances of one class can exist on the stage at the same time.
- Any changes made to an individual instance (resizing, rotating, etc.) affect only that one instance.
- Changes made to a class (accessed through the **Library**), affect every instance of the class.

Section 17.3 Objects in Flash

- The properties `x` and `y` refer to the respective *x*- and *y*-coordinates of an object.
- `import` allows you to utilize built-in classes of ActionScript 3.0, such as `MouseEvent` and `Sprite`.
- Instance variables have scope through the entire class.
- Movie clips in the **Library** can be placed on the stage using the `addChild` function.
- Function `addEventListener` registers an event handler to be called when an event is triggered.

Section 17.4 Cannon Game: Preliminary Instructions and Notes

- The `stop` action at the end of a section ensures that only the desired animation will be played.
- ActionScript programmers often create an **Actions** layer to better organize Flash movies.

Section 17.5 Adding a Start Button

- Most games start with an introductory animation.

Section 17.6 Creating Moving Objects

- The first parameter of a `Timer` constructor is the delay between timer events in milliseconds. The second parameter is the number of times the `Timer` should repeat. A value of 0 means that the `Timer` will run indefinitely.

Section 17.7 Adding the Rotating Cannon

- Many Flash applications include animation that responds to mouse cursor motions.
- ActionScript's `Math` class contains various mathematical functions and values that are useful when performing complex operations. For a full list of the `Math` class's functions and values, refer to the **Flash Help** dictionary from the **Help** menu.
- The `Math` object provides us with an arc tangent function: `Math.atan2(y, x)`. This function returns a value, in radians, equal to the angle opposite side `y` and adjacent to side `x`.
- The constant `Math.PI` provides the value of π.
- If your code is not working and no error message displays, ensure that every variable points to the correct object. One incorrect `stage` can prevent an entire function from operating correctly.
- Hide a layer by selecting the show/hide selector (dot) in the portion of the **Timeline** to the right of the layer name. A red **x** should appear in place of the dot to indicate that the layer is hidden while editing the movie. The layer will still be visible when the movie is viewed. Clicking the show/hide **x** again makes the layer visible.

Section 17.8 Adding the Cannonball

- A small white circle is Flash's default appearance for a movie clip that has no graphic in its first frame.
- The `Number` type is ActionScript 3's floating-point variable type.

Section 17.9 Adding Sound and Text Objects to the Movie

- Lock a layer by clicking the lock/unlock selector (dot) to the right of the layer name in the timeline. When a layer is locked, its elements are visible, but they cannot be edited. This allows you to use one layer's elements as visual references for designing another layer, while ensuring that no elements are moved unintentionally. To unlock a layer, click the lock symbol to the right of the layer name in the **Timeline**.

Section 17.10 Adding the Time Counter

- Time, whether increasing or decreasing, is an important aspect of many games and applications.
- Games generally have a final animation sequence that informs the player of the outcome of the game.

Section 17.12 Adding Collision Detection

- Flash has a built-in collision detection function that determines whether two objects are touching. The function *object1*`.hitTestObject(`*object2*`)` returns `true` if any part of *object1* touches *object2*. Many games must detect collisions between moving objects to control game play or add realistic effects. In this game, we rely on collision detection to determine if the ball hits either the blocker or the target.

Terminology

ActionScript 3.0
`addChild`
`addEventListener`
Adobe Flash CS 3
function
`hitTestObject` ActionScript collision detection method
`import`
instance
instance name
instance variable
Library
lock/unlock layer
`Math` class
`MouseEvent`
`Number`
property
Property Inspector
`rotation` property
show/hide layers
`Sprite`
`stage`
`stage.mouseX`
`stage.mouseY`
`stop`

Self-Review Exercises

17.1 State whether each of the following is *true* or *false*. If *false*, explain why.

a) ActionScript 3.0 is an object-oriented scripting language that contains functions and classes.
b) There can be multiple instances of one symbol.
c) Locking a layer is the same as hiding it, except that a hidden layer can still be edited.
d) New functions can never be created in Flash. We must rely on Flash's predefined functions.

17.2 Fill in the blanks for each of the following statements.

a) Property _______ accesses the main timeline object.
b) A movie clip with no animation in its first frame appears as a(n) _______.
c) Flash has a built-in _______ function that returns `true` when two objects touch.

Answers to Self-Review Exercises

17.1 a) True. b) True. d) False. Neither locked nor hidden layers can be edited. Locked layers are visible, though, whereas hidden layers are not. e) False. New functions can be created inside a `package`, or inside a frame's **Actions** using the keyword `function`.

17.2 a) `stage`. b) small white circle. c) collision detection.

Exercises

17.3 Add an **instructions** button to the **intro** frame of the main scene. Make it play a brief movie clip explaining the rules of the game. The instructions should not interfere with the actual game play.

17.4 Use Flash's `random(` *n* `)` function (discussed in Chapter 16) to assign a random speed between 1 and 4 to the blocker, and a speed between 5 and 7 to the target. Remember that `random(` *n* `)` returns a random integer between 0 and *n*.

17.5 Add a text field to the **end** frame that displays the player's final score (i.e., the time remaining) if the player wins. Output different phrases depending on the player's final score (e.g., 1–10: `Nice job`, 11–15: `Great!`, 16–20: `Amazing!`). [*Hint:* Create a new global variable `finalTime` if the player wins. Create an `if...else` statement to determine which text phrase to use based on `finalTime`.]

17.6 Add a second level to the game with two blockers instead of one. Try to do this without adding a fourth frame to the timeline. Instead, create a duplicate **blocker** symbol and modify it to appear invisible at first. Think about reversing the process we used to make the sections of the **target** invisible. The final score should be a combination of first- and second-round scores. [*Hint:* Create an instance variable `level` that stores the current level (i.e., `1` or `2`). Make the second blocker visible only if `level == 2`.]

17.7 Give a brief description of each of the following terms:

a) Lock/unlock
b) Instance
c) Collision detection
d) `x` and `y`
e) Event handler
f) Function

18

Adobe® Flex™ 2 and Rich Internet Applications

Becoming more flexible, open-minded, having a capacity to deal with change is a good thing.
—Eda Le Shan

We wove a web in childhood, A web of sunny air.
—Charlotte Brontë

Genius is the ability to put into effect what is on your mind.
—F. Scott Fitzgerald

A fair request should be followed by the deed in silence.
—Dante

The transition from cause to effect, from event to event, is often carried on by secret steps, which our foresight cannot divine, and our sagacity is unable to trace.
—Joseph Addison

OBJECTIVES

In this chapter you will learn:

- What Flex is and what it's used for.
- How to design user interfaces in Flex's user interface markup language, MXML.
- How to embed multimedia in a Flex application.
- How to use data binding to create responsive user interfaces.
- How to access XML data from a Flex application.
- Client-side scripting in ActionScript 3.0, Flex's object-oriented scripting language.
- How to interact with a web service.
- How to create an advanced user interface.
- How the Adobe Integrated Runtime allows Flex applications to run on the desktop without an Internet connection.

Outline

18.1 Introduction

In Chapter 15, we introduced Ajax, which uses a combination of XHTML, JavaScript and XML to produce a web application with a desktop-like feel through client-side processing. In this chapter, we introduce Adobe Flex, another means of achieving that same goal. Flex uses Adobe's ubiquitous Flash platform to deliver a rich graphical user interface backed by ActionScript 3, Adobe's implementation of ECMAScript 4 (better known as JavaScript 2). The relationship between Flex and ActionScript is similar to that between Ajax libraries and JavaScript. The powerful graphical capabilities and cross-platform nature of Flash allow web developers to deliver Rich Internet Applications (RIAs) to a large user base. The term RIA was coined in 2001 by Macromedia, the creator of Flash and Flex; Adobe acquired Macromedia in 2005.

Flex provides user interface library elements that can easily be accessed and customized. You can see these user interface elements in action using Adobe's Flex 2 Component Explorer at `examples.adobe.com/flex2/inproduct/sdk/explorer/explorer.html`. The user interface library helps you present a consistent user experience in all applications, a quality that various Ajax and Flash applications lack. Additionally, Flash has the advantage of a large installed base—98.6% penetration for Flash 6 and up, and 84.0% penetration for Flash 9 in the United States as of March 2007.[1] This allows applications developed in Flex to be used on most Windows, Mac and Linux computers. Since the Flash engine is virtually equivalent across browsers and platforms, Flex developers can avoid the cross-platform conflicts of Ajax and even Java. This significantly reduces development time.

The Flex framework enables a wide variety of web applications, from simple image viewers to RSS feed readers to complex data analysis tools. This flexibility is partly derived from Flex's separation of the user interface from the data. Visually appealing and consistent user interfaces are easily described using the MXML markup language, which is converted to Flash's executable SWF (Shockwave Flash) format when the application is compiled.

---

1. Adobe Flash Player Version Penetration, March 2007, `www.adobe.com/products/player_census/flashplayer/version_penetration.html`.

Flex is appropriate for online stores, where Flex's versatile user interface library allows for drag-and-drop, dynamic content, multimedia, visual feedback and more. Applications that require real-time streaming data benefit from Flex's ability to accept data "pushed" from the server and instantly update content, without constantly polling the server as some Ajax applications do. Applications that require data visualization benefit from Flex's Charting library which can create interactive and customized charts and graphs. ActionScript adds to the power of the Flex user interface library by allowing you to code powerful logic into your Flex applications.

In this chapter, you'll learn how to implement these elements in real-world applications. You'll run the examples from your local computer as well as from `deitel.com`. A comprehensive list of Flex resources is available in our Flex Resource Center at `www.deitel.com/flex`. Another helpful resource is Adobe's Flex 2 Language Reference at `www.adobe.com/go/flex2_apiref`.

18.2 Flex Platform Overview

The Flex platform requires the Flash Player 9 runtime environment. Flash Player 9 provides the ActionScript Virtual Machine and graphical capabilities that execute Flex applications. Flash Player 9, as described in Chapters 16–17, is a multimedia-rich application environment that runs on most platforms. Flash Player installation is detailed in those chapters, but for end users, only the Flash Player 9 browser plug-in is required. The plug-in, including a debug version, is included as part of the Flex SDK (Software Development Kit) installation. Flex applications are essentially Flash programs that use the Flex framework of user interface elements, web services, animations and more. The Flex development environment is programming-centric in contrast to the animation-centric Flash authoring tool.

In addition to describing user interfaces, MXML can describe web services, data objects, visual effects and more. Flex's user interface elements are much richer and more consistent than those of HTML and AJAX because they're rendered the same way on all platforms by the Flash player. The root element of every MXML application is the `Application` element (`<mx:Application>`), inside which all Flex elements reside.

The Flex SDK is a free download, which you can get from `www.adobe.com/products/flex/downloads`. It includes an MXML compiler and debugger, the Flex framework, the user interface components, and some templates and examples. You can extract the `zip` file anywhere on your computer. The compiler and debugger included with the Flex SDK are command-line utilities. They're written in Java, so you must have Java Runtime Edition 1.4.2_06 (or later) installed. To check your current version, run `java -version` in your command line.

ActionScript 3 is Adobe's object-oriented scripting language. Flash Player 9 uses version 2 of the ActionScript Virtual Machine (AVM2), which adds support for ActionScript 3 and provides many performance improvements over the previous version. This virtual machine is being submitted as open source to the Mozilla Firefox project to provide support for ActionScript 3 and JavaScript 2. This engine, called Tamarin, is slated to be included in Firefox 4.

ActionScript 3 supports such object-oriented capabilities as inheritance, encapsulation and polymorphism. Also, it uses an asynchronous programming model. This means that the program will continue to execute while another operation is being completed, such as a call to a web service. This ensures that the user interface is responsive even while the application is busy processing data, an important feature of RIAs. In many cases, you'll need to take advantage of event handling and data binding to handle asynchronous operations.

Flex Builder is Adobe's graphical IDE for Flex applications. A 30-day free trial is available at `www.adobe.com/go/tryflex`. It is based on Eclipse, a popular open source IDE. Because Flex Builder costs money, and because you can develop Flex applications without it, we won't use Flex Builder in this book.

Adobe LiveCycle Data Services ES extends Flex's built-in data connectivity, allowing for such features as data push and synchronization. It also enables Flex applications to handle disconnection from the server, synchronizing data upon reconnection. The Express edition of Adobe LiveCycle Data Services ES is available for free at `www.adobe.com/go/trylivecycle_dataservices/`. This version is limited to use on a single server with a single CPU (the license agreement is included with the download).

Flex Charting provides an extensible library of plotting and graphing elements, including pie charts, line graphs, bar graphs, bubble charts and plots. Flex Charting also provides appealing animations for dynamic data representations. Flex Charting is available for purchase from Adobe, and a 30-day free trial is available at `www.adobe.com/go/tryflex`. An excellent demonstration of Flex Charting is the **Flex Charting Sampler** available at `demo.quietlyscheming.com/ChartSampler/app.html`.

18.3 Creating a Simple User Interface

Our first example application is a simple image viewer (Fig. 18.1) that displays thumbnail (i.e., small) images of several Deitel book covers. In this example, we specify the images with a static array within the MXML, but you could load this type of data dynamically from a web service. You can select a thumbnail to view a larger cover image, or use the horizontal slider to select an image. These two elements are bound to each other, meaning that when the user changes one, the other is updated. The image viewer also allows you to zoom the image. You can try this application at `test.deitel.com/examples/iw3htp4/flex/coverViewer/` (Fig. 18.2).

```
<?xml version = "1.0" encoding = "utf-8"?>
<!-- Fig. 18.1: coverViewer.mxml -->
<!-- Creating a simple book cover viewer in Flex 2 -->
<mx:Application xmlns:mx = "http://www.adobe.com/2006/mxml">
   <!-- an array of images -->
   <mx:ArrayCollection id = "bookCovers">
      <!-- each image has a name and source attribute -->
      <mx:Object name = "C How to Program" source = "chtp5.jpg" />
      <mx:Object name = "C++ How to Program" source = "cpphtp6.jpg" />
      <mx:Object name = "Internet How to Program"
         source = "iw3htp4.jpg" />
      <mx:Object name = "Java How to Program" source = "jhtp7.jpg" />
      <mx:Object name = "VB How to Program" source = "vbhtp3.jpg" />
      <mx:Object name = "Visual C# How to Program"
         source = "vcsharphtp2.jpg" />
      <mx:Object name = "Simply C++" source = "simplycpp.jpg" />
      <mx:Object name = "Simply VB 2005" source = "simplyvb2005.jpg" />
```

Fig. 18.1 | Creating a simple book cover viewer in Flex 2. (Part 1 of 3.)

```
      <mx:Object name = "Simply Java" source = "simplyjava.jpg" />
      <mx:Object name = "Small C++ How to Program"
         source = "smallcpphtp5.jpg" />
      <mx:Object name = "Small Java" source = "smalljavahtp6.jpg" />
   </mx:ArrayCollection>

   <!-- bind largeImage's source to the slider and selected thumbnail -->
   <mx:Binding
      source = "'fullsize/' +
       bookCovers.getItemAt( selectCoverSlider.value ).source"
      destination = "largeImage.source" />
   <mx:Binding source = "'fullsize/' + thumbnailList.selectedItem.source"
      destination = "largeImage.source" />

   <!-- user interface begins here -->
   <mx:Panel id = "viewPanel" title = "Deitel Book Cover Viewer"
      width = "100%" height = "100%" horizontalAlign = "center">

      <mx:HBox height = "100%" width = "100%">
         <mx:VSlider id = "zoomSlider" value = "100" minimum = "0"
            maximum = "100" liveDragging = "true"
            change = "largeImage.percentWidth = zoomSlider.value;
               largeImage.percentHeight = zoomSlider.value;"
            height = "100%" width = "0%"
            labels = "[ '0%', 'Zoom', '100%' ]" />
         <mx:VBox width = "100%" height = "100%"
            horizontalAlign = "center">

            <!-- We bind the source of this image to the source of -->
            <!-- the selected thumbnail, and center it in the VBox. -->
            <!-- completeEffect tells Flex to fade the image in -->
            <mx:Image id = "largeImage"
               source = ""
               horizontalAlign = "center"
               verticalAlign = "middle"
               width = "100%" height = "100%"
               completeEffect = "Fade" />

            <!-- bind this Label to the name of the selected thumbnail -->
            <mx:Label text = "{ thumbnailList.selectedItem.name }" />
         </mx:VBox>
      </mx:HBox>

      <!-- slider can switch between images -->
      <mx:HSlider id = "selectCoverSlider" height = "0%"
            minimum = "0" maximum = "{ bookCovers.length - 1 }"
            showDataTip = "false" snapInterval = "1" tickInterval = "1"
            liveDragging = "true"
            change = "thumbnailList.selectedIndex =
               selectCoverSlider.value;
               thumbnailList.scrollToIndex( selectCoverSlider.value )" />

```

Fig. 18.1 | Creating a simple book cover viewer in Flex 2. (Part 2 of 3.)

```
70       <!-- display thumbnails of the images in bookCovers horizontally -->
71       <mx:HorizontalList id = "thumbnailList"
72          dataProvider = "{ bookCovers }" width = "100%" height = "160"
73          selectedIndex = "0"
74          change = "selectCoverSlider.value = thumbnailList.selectedIndex">
75
76          <!-- define how each item is displayed -->
77          <mx:itemRenderer>
78             <mx:Component>
79                <mx:VBox width = "140" height = "160"
80                   horizontalAlign = "center" verticalAlign = "middle"
81                   verticalScrollPolicy = "off"
82                   horizontalScrollPolicy = "off" paddingBottom = "20">
83
84                   <!-- display a thumbnail of each image -->
85                   <mx:Image source = "{ 'thumbs/' + data.source }"
86                      verticalAlign = "middle" />
87
88                   <!-- display the name of each image -->
89                   <mx:Label text = "{ data.name }" />
90                </mx:VBox>
91             </mx:Component>
92          </mx:itemRenderer>
93       </mx:HorizontalList>
94    </mx:Panel>
95 </mx:Application>
```

Fig. 18.1 | Creating a simple book cover viewer in Flex 2. (Part 3 of 3.)

Line 1 of Fig. 18.1 declares the document to be an XML document, because MXML is a type of XML. The `mx` **prefix**, defined in line 4, is commonly associated with the `"http://www.adobe.com/2006/mxml"` **namespace**, which is used for the Flex elements in an MXML document. The `Panel` **element** (lines 33–94 is a container, and is generally the outermost container of a Flex application. This element has many attributes, including `title`, `width`, `height`, `horizontalAlign` and `verticalAlign`. The `id = "viewPanel"` attribute allows us to reference this item in ActionScript using the identifier `viewPanel`. Flex elements can contain an `id` **attribute**, so that their properties can be accessed programatically. The value of the `title` attribute is displayed at the top of the `Panel`, in the border. Inside the `Panel` element, there is an `HBox` **element** (lines 36–59), which is a container that organizes its enclosed elements horizontally. There is also a `VBox` **element** available for organizing elements vertically, which we will use later.

In the `HBox`, we have a `VSlider` (lines 37–42) and a `VBox` (lines 43–58) containing an `Image` **element** (lines 49–54) and a `Label` **element** (line 57). The `VSlider` **element** provides a vertically oriented slider user interface element. The `VSlider` controls the zoom level of the image. The `value` attribute sets the slider's initial value (`100` in this example). The `minimum` and `maximum` attributes set the range of values you can select with the slider. The `change` attribute (lines 39–40) allows ActionScript to execute whenever the user changes the slider's `value`. Lines 39–40 scale the image by setting its `percentWidth` and `percentHeight` properties to the slider's `value`. The `liveDragging` attribute with the value `"true"` indicates that the ActionScript in the `change` attribute executes immediately

Fig. 18.2 | Deitel cover Viewer displaying *C How to Program* cover.

when the user changes the slider value, even if the user is still clicking it. The `labels` attribute places text next to the slider. You can give it any number of labels, and it will equidistantly space them.

The `Image` element has the attribute `source = ""` (line 50). This is because in lines 25–28, we use a **`Binding` element** to bind the value of `largeImage`'s `source` attribute (line 50) to the value of the `source` attribute of an element in the `bookCovers` `ArrayCollection` (defined in lines 6–22). In line 27, we use the horizontal slider's value to select an element from `bookCovers` and set the `largeImage`'s `source`. Lines 29–30 set up a second `Binding` element that binds the image's `source` to the `source` of the selected item in `thumbnailList` (defined in lines 71–74). For each binding, we prepend `'fullsize/'`, the directory containing the full-sized images. When the user selects an image with the selectCoverSlider or thumbnailList, largeImage shows the full-size version of the corresponding image.

The Image element's other attributes specify that the element is centered (lines 51–52) and takes up as much space in the containing element as possible (line 53). The completeEffect attribute of the Image element is set to "Fade" (line 54), which means that when the image is loaded, it will be presented using Flex's built-in Fade effect. You can view the list of built-in effects at livedocs.adobe.com/flex/201/langref/mx/effects/package-detail.html.

The **Label element** (line 57) has a text attribute, in which we indicate that the string displayed by the Label is bound to the name of thumbnailList's selectedItem. The curly braces surrounding this ActionScript are another way to indicate data binding.

Following the HBox is an HSlider (lines 62–68) that gives the user another way to navigate through the images. The **HSlider element** is the horizontal equivalent of the VSlider. The change attribute (lines 66–68) changes the selected thumbnail from the thumbnailList based on the value of the HSlider and ensures that the thumbnailList is showing the selected thumbnail by scrolling to the HSlider's value. We set the HSlider's maximum value to { bookCovers.length - 1 }, the index of the last element of the bookCovers array. We set showDataTip to "false" (line 64) to turn off the tool tip showing the HSlider's current value while the user is dragging the slider. Finally, we set snapInterval and tickInterval to "1" (line 64), so that the slider's values increment by 1, and the tick marks are displayed at intervals of 1.

The **HorizontalList element** with id thumbnailList (lines 71–93) takes an array of items from a **dataProvider** and displays them in a horizontal configuration. This HorizontalList's dataProvider is the ArrayCollection of Objects called bookCovers (lines 6–22). **Object** is the root class of the ActionScript hierarchy, and is used here to simply hold attributes. An **ArrayCollection** is a type of Array that provides methods for manipulating an Array. Each of the items in the HorizontalList is selectable, and the selectedIndex attribute dictates that the first array element is selected initially.

The thumbnailList contains an inline itemRenderer (lines 77–92), which gives you complete control over the contents of the list. At runtime, the HorizontalList will create an instance of the itemRenderer for each of the elements in the dataProvider array. If you don't provide an itemRenderer, Flex will render each item with the default item renderer, which depends on the item's type. An itemRenderer can also be defined externally by giving the HorizontalList an itemRenderer attribute equal to the filename (without the extension) of an external MXML file containing the elements you want.

This itemRenderer contains a **Component element** (lines 78–91), which encloses the item to render. Inside the Component element, there is a VBox containing an Image (lines 85–86) and a Label (line 89). The verticalScrollPolicy and horizontalScrollPolicy attributes (lines 81–82) are set to off so that even if the Image or Label elements don't fit in the VBox, they won't show scroll bars. The paddingBottom attribute (line 82) ensures that there is 20 pixels of space for the HorizontalList's horizontal scroll bar. The Image element's source attribute has the specifies the location of the image file. The thumbs/ directory contains the thumbnails we want to display, and data refers to the corresponding item from the list's dataProvider, in this case the bookCovers ArrayCollection. We must use the keyword data because everything inside the Component element is located in a new, separate scope, meaning that it cannot access the variables of the enclosing program. The `Label` element displays the `name` element of the corresponding item in the `ArrayCollection`. The `Spacer` element ensures that there will be enough room for a horizontal scroll bar at the bottom of the `thumbnailList` in case the window is not wide enough to display all of the thumbnails.

Compiling an Application

Flex applications are converted from MXML into ActionScript, which is then compiled and output as SWF files. We'll compile our applications using the `mxmlc` command-line compiler, included in the Flex SDK. If you do not want to specify the compiler's path every time you run it, you can add the directory to your `Path` system variable. To do this in Windows XP, first right click **My Computer**, click **Properties**, select the **Advanced** tab, click **Environment Variables**, select **Path** in the list of **System variables**, and append your path to the `flex_sdk_2\bin` directory (e.g. `C:\flex_sdk_2\bin` if you extracted it into the `C:\` directory). For Mac OS X and Linux, visit `www.linuxheadquarters.com/howto/basic/path.shtml` for instructions. The simplest syntax of the `mxmlc` command is `mxmlc` *filename*. You can see a full list of the compiler's parameters by executing `mxmlc -help`. For instance, if we're in the directory containing `coverViewer.mxml`, and we have added the `bin` directory to the **Path** system variable, the command for compiling `coverViewer.mxml` would be `mxmlc coverViewer.mxml` (Fig. 18.3).

This command creates `coverViewer.swf` in the current directory. If you'd like, you can test `coverViewer.swf` in the standalone Flash 9 Player by double clicking the file `coverViewer.swf`. If this does not work, you can locate the Flash 9 Player at `flex_sdk_2\player\debug\SAFlashPlayer.exe` for Windows or `flex_sdk_2/player/debug/SAFlashPlayer.dmg` for Mac OS X.

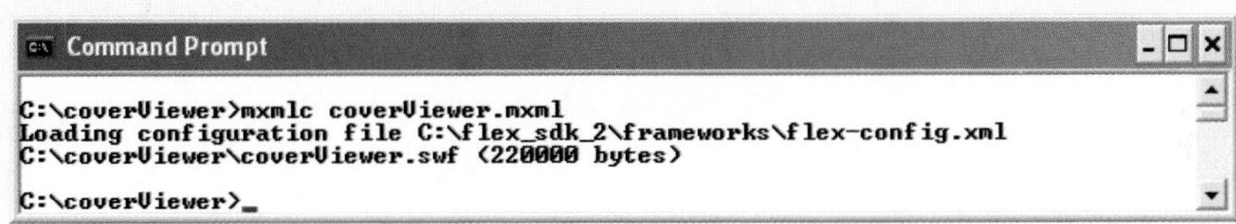

Fig. 18.3 | `mxmlc` running in Windows XP **Command Prompt**.

Running a Flex Application in the Browser

Because Flex applications run using the Flash Player, they can be embedded into a web page, then run with the Flash Player browser plug-in. The Flex SDK install includes a folder of HTML templates for embedding your application. You can copy a template and edit it to point to your SWF file. These templates are located in the folder `flex_sdk_2/resources/html-templates/`. The six templates give you different combinations of Flash installation and version detection (checks the user's Flash Player version) as well as browser history support. For our examples, we use the `no-player-detection` template. If you would like to implement the install and history features, more information is available at `livedocs.adobe.com/flex/201/html/wrapper_131_05.html`.

To create an HTML wrapper for the application, first copy the files `AC_OETags.js` and `index.template.html` from `flex_sdk_2/resources/html-templates/no-player-detection` to your Flex application's base directory. Rename `index.template.html` to `index.html` if you want it to be the default HTML file of the directory on a web server. Now, open the HTML file in your text editor, and replace the variables `${title}`, `${swf}`, and `${application}` with your application's filename without `.swf` (in this case, `coverViewer`). For `${height}` and `${width}`, use `100%`. For `${bgcolor}`, use `#869ca7` (this is Flex's default color). The modified HTML wrapper for `coverViewer` is shown in Fig. 18.4.

```
<!-- Fig. 18.4: index.html -->
<!-- HTML wrapper for coverViewer.swf -->
<!-- saved from url=(0014)about:internet -->
<html lang="en">
<head>
<meta http-equiv="Content-Type" content="text/html; charset=utf-8" />
<title>coverViewer</title>
<script src="AC_OETags.js" language="javascript"></script>
<style>
   body { margin: 0px; overflow: hidden; }
</style>
</head>

<body scroll='no'>
<script language="JavaScript" type="text/javascript">
<!--
   AC_FL_RunContent(
      "src", "coverViewer",
      "width", "100%",
      "height", "100%",
      "align", "middle",
      "id", "coverViewer",
      "quality", "high",
      "bgcolor", "#869ca7",
      "name", "coverViewer",
      "allowScriptAccess","sameDomain",
      "type", "application/x-shockwave-flash",
      "pluginspage", "http://www.adobe.com/go/getflashplayer"
   );
// -->
</script>
<noscript>
   <object classid="clsid:D27CDB6E-AE6D-11cf-96B8-444553540000"
      id="coverViewer" width="100%" height="100%"
      codebase="http://fpdownload.macromedia.com/get/
         flashplayer/current/swflash.cab">
      <param name="movie" value="coverViewer.swf" />
      <param name="quality" value="high" />
      <param name="bgcolor" value="#869ca7" />
      <param name="allowScriptAccess" value="sameDomain" />
      <embed src="coverViewer.swf" quality="high" bgcolor="#869ca7"
         width="100%" height="100%" name="coverViewer" align="middle"
         play="true"
         loop="false"
         quality="high"
         allowScriptAccess="sameDomain"
```

Fig. 18.4 | HTML wrapper for `coverViewer.swf`. (Part 1 of 2.)

```
            type="application/x-shockwave-flash"
            pluginspage="http://www.adobe.com/go/getflashplayer">
         </embed>
      </object>
   </noscript>
   </body>
   </html>
```

Fig. 18.4 | HTML wrapper for `coverViewer.swf`. (Part 2 of 2.)

Embedding Images

Instead of referencing external images, we could embed the images into the SWF file to make it more portable. We specify that an image is embedded by enclosing the source attribute inside an `@Embed` directive, as in `source = "@Embed( 'image.jpg' )"`. This tells the compiler to include the image in the SWF file, which results in a program that not only loads faster, but also is less dependent on external resources, since the SWF includes all resources it needs. In this case, embedding images would significantly increase the size of the SWF. Also, we may later want to update or change the images.

Using View States

Next, we'll add the ability to hide the thumbnail `HorizontalList` and to increase the size of the current image. We'll accomplish this using view states (Fig. 18.5), which enable us to change an application's layout on the fly, allowing for more usable interfaces. You can test this application at `test.deitel.com/examples/iw3htp4/flex/coverViewerStates/` (Fig. 18.6).

```
<?xml version = "1.0" encoding = "utf-8"?>
<!-- Fig. 18.5: coverViewerStates.mxml -->
<!-- Using States to dynamically modify a user interface -->
<mx:Application xmlns:mx = "http://www.adobe.com/2006/mxml">

   <!-- ActionScript goes in this section -->
   <mx:Script>
      // import the Cubic easing function for state transitions
      import mx.effects.easing.Cubic;
   </mx:Script>

   <!-- an array of images -->
   <mx:ArrayCollection id = "bookCovers">
      <!-- each image has a name and source attribute -->
      <mx:Object name = "C How to Program" source = "chtp5.jpg" />
      <mx:Object name = "C++ How to Program" source = "cpphtp6.jpg" />
      <mx:Object name = "Internet How to Program"
         source = "iw3htp4.jpg" />
      <mx:Object name = "Java How to Program" source = "jhtp7.jpg" />
      <mx:Object name = "VB How to Program" source = "vbhtp3.jpg" />
      <mx:Object name = "Visual C# How to Program"
         source = "vcsharphtp2.jpg" />
      <mx:Object name = "Simply C++" source = "simplycpp.jpg" />
```

Fig. 18.5 | Using `States` to dynamically modify a user interface. (Part 1 of 3.)

```
      <mx:Object name = "Simply VB 2005" source = "simplyvb2005.jpg" />
      <mx:Object name = "Simply Java" source = "simplyjava.jpg" />
      <mx:Object name = "Small C++ How to Program"
         source = "smallcpphtp5.jpg" />
      <mx:Object name = "Small Java" source = "smalljavahtp6.jpg" />
   </mx:ArrayCollection>

   <!-- define the application's states -->
   <mx:states>
      <mx:State name = "HideThumbnails">
         <mx:RemoveChild target = "{ thumbnailList }" />

         <!-- switch the showHideButton to hide -->
         <mx:SetEventHandler target = "{ showHideButton }" name = "click"
            handler = "currentState = ''" />
      </mx:State>
   </mx:states>

   <!-- define the transition effect for application state changes -->
   <mx:transitions>
      <mx:Transition>
            <mx:Resize
               target = "{ largeImage }"
               duration = "750" easingFunction = "Cubic.easeOut" />
      </mx:Transition>
   </mx:transitions>

   <!-- bind the source of largeImage to the selected thumbnail -->
   <mx:Binding
      source = "'fullsize/' +
         bookCovers.getItemAt( selectCoverSlider.value ).source"
      destination = "largeImage.source" />
   <mx:Binding source = "'fullsize/' + thumbnailList.selectedItem.source"
      destination = "largeImage.source" />

   <!-- user interface begins here -->
   <mx:Panel id = "viewPanel" title = "Deitel Book Cover Viewer"
      width = "100%" height = "100%" horizontalAlign = "center">

      <mx:HBox height = "100%" width = "100%">
         <mx:VSlider id = "zoomSlider" value = "100" minimum = "0"
            maximum = "100" liveDragging = "true"
            change = "largeImage.percentWidth = zoomSlider.value;
               largeImage.percentHeight = zoomSlider.value;"
            height = "100%" width = "0%"
            labels = "[ '0%', 'Zoom', '100%' ]" />
         <mx:VBox width = "100%" height = "100%"
            horizontalAlign = "center">

            <!-- We bind the source of this image to the source of -->
            <!-- the selected thumbnail, and center it in the VBox. -->
            <!-- completeEffect tells Flex to fade the image in -->
            <mx:Image id = "largeImage"
```

Fig. 18.5 | Using `States` to dynamically modify a user interface. (Part 2 of 3.)

```
               source = ""
               horizontalAlign = "center"
               verticalAlign = "middle"
               width = "100%" height = "100%"
               completeEffect = "Fade" />

            <!-- bind this Label to the name of the selected thumbnail -->
            <mx:Label text = "{ thumbnailList.selectedItem.name }" />
         </mx:VBox>
      </mx:HBox>

      <!-- slider can switch between images -->
      <mx:HSlider id = "selectCoverSlider" height = "0%"
            minimum = "0" maximum = "{ bookCovers.length - 1 }"
            showDataTip = "false" snapInterval = "1" tickInterval = "1"
            liveDragging = "true"
            change = "thumbnailList.selectedIndex =
               selectCoverSlider.value;
               thumbnailList.scrollToIndex( selectCoverSlider.value )" />

      <!-- display thumbnails of the images in bookCovers horizontally -->
      <mx:HorizontalList id = "thumbnailList"
         dataProvider = "{ bookCovers }" width = "100%" height = "160"
         selectedIndex = "0"
         change = "selectCoverSlider.value = thumbnailList.selectedIndex">

         <!-- define how each item is displayed -->
         <mx:itemRenderer>
            <mx:Component>
               <mx:VBox width = "140" height = "160"
                  horizontalAlign = "center" verticalAlign = "middle"
                  verticalScrollPolicy = "off"
                  horizontalScrollPolicy = "off" paddingBottom = "20">

                  <!-- display a thumbnail of each image -->
                  <mx:Image source = "{ 'thumbs/' + data.source }"
                     verticalAlign = "middle" />

                  <!-- display the name of each image -->
                  <mx:Label text = "{ data.name }" />
               </mx:VBox>
            </mx:Component>
         </mx:itemRenderer>
      </mx:HorizontalList>

      <!-- this will exist in the bottom border of the Panel -->
      <mx:ControlBar>
         <mx:LinkButton label = "Show/Hide Thumbnails"
            click = "currentState = 'HideThumbnails';"
            id = "showHideButton" />
      </mx:ControlBar>
   </mx:Panel>
</mx:Application>
```

Fig. 18.5 | Using `States` to dynamically modify a user interface. (Part 3 of 3.)

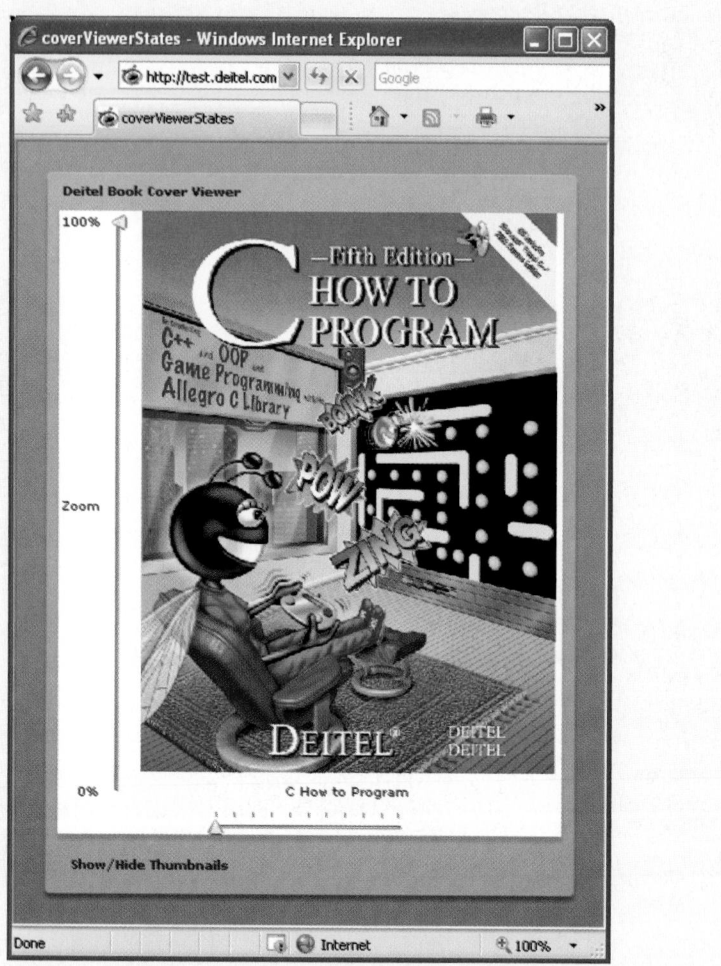

Fig. 18.6 | Deitel Cover Viewer using States to hide thumbnails.

We define an application's states in a states element (lines 32–40). An application has a default state that contains its initial elements, layout and properties. Each additional state is enclosed in a State element, with a name attribute, which is the identifier for the State. View states allow you to add elements via the AddChild element, remove elements via the RemoveChild element, modify elements' properties via the SetProperty element, set style via the SetStyle element, and set event handlers via the SetEventHandler element. The RemoveChild element in line 34 removes the thumbnailList. After the RemoveChild element, there is a SetEventHandler element (lines 39–38). Whenever the State is activated, this event handler will be registered. In this case, we change the click event handler of the showHideButton LinkButton (lines 124–126) to set the currentState to an empty string, signifying the application's default state (with the thumbnail viewer displayed). This LinkButton is enclosed in a ControlBar element (lines 123–127)—this embeds the elements it encloses into the bottom border of the Panel. The `showHideButton` element initially has a `click` attribute set to `"currentState = 'HideThumbnails';"`.

After we define the application's `states`, we define a transition effect for the `State` change. Any `State` transition effects are enclosed in the **`transitions` element** (lines 43–49). For each **`Transition`**, you can specify a `fromState` and `toState`, using the `State`'s name. In this case, we leave out these attributes so that the transition effect applies to all `State` changes. Inside the `Transition`, we have a `Resize` effect (lines 45–47). This effect has a `targets` attribute that specifies which elements it applies to. It also has a `duration` attribute, which defines how long the effect lasts in milliseconds. Finally, we define the optional `easingFunction` attribute. Normally, the `Resize` effect would go at a linear speed. Instead, we have specified that it should use the `Cubic.easeOut` function[2] (line 47), which controls the acceleration of the `Resize` animation. We import this function from the Flex library using ActionScript. A **`Script` element** (lines 7–10) encapsulates the application's ActionScript code. Line 9 allows the `Cubic` function to be used anywhere in the program.

18.4 Accessing XML Data from Your Application

Flex has the ability to access XML natively, using the **E4X (ECMAScript for XML)** standard. In this example, we use this capability to create an address book application. Figure 18.7 loads an XML file containing names and addresses into the application and displays its contents in a `DataGrid` (Fig. 18.8). The application also displays the selected contact's location in an embedded Yahoo! Map (Fig. 18.9). Finally, the application allows you to edit any of the selected contact's data (Fig. 18.10). You can test a live version of this application at `test.deitel.com/examples/iw3htp4/flex/addressBook/`. Note that because this application makes requests over HTTP, it must be run from a web server. To learn how to set up your own web server, see Chapter 21.

```
<?xml version = "1.0" encoding = "utf-8"?>
<!-- Fig. 18.7: addressBook.mxml -->
<!-- HTTPService, Validators, and new UI elements -->
<mx:Application xmlns:mx = "http://www.adobe.com/2006/mxml"
   layout = "vertical"
   xmlns:yahoo = "com.yahoo.webapis.maps.*"
   creationComplete = "getContacts.send(); initMap();">

   <!-- import XML file -->
   <mx:HTTPService
      id = "getContacts"
      url = "contacts.xml"
      showBusyCursor = "true"
      resultFormat = "object"
      result = "addressCollection = ArrayCollection(
         getContacts.lastResult.contacts.contact )"
      fault = "Alert.show( event.fault.message )" />
```

Fig. 18.7 | `HTTPService`, validators and new UI elements. (Part 1 of 5.)

2. A list of the available easing functions is available at `livedocs.adobe.com/flex/201/langref/mx/effects/easing/package-detail.html`.

```

   <!-- validators for "Edit Contact" fields -->
   <mx:StringValidator id = "firstnameValidator" source = "{ firstName }"
      property = "text" required = "true" trigger = "{ save }"
      triggerEvent = "click" valid = "saveContact()" />
   <mx:StringValidator id = "lastnameValidator" source = "{ lastName }"
      property = "text" required = "false" />
   <mx:ZipCodeValidator id = "zipValidator" source = "{ zipCode }"
      property = "text" required = "false" />
   <mx:EmailValidator id = "emailValidator" source = "{ eMail }"
      property = "text" required = "false" />
   <mx:PhoneNumberValidator id = "phoneValidator" source = "{ phone }"
      property = "text" required = "false" />

   <mx:Script>
      import mx.collections.ArrayCollection;

      // tell compiler to register an event for the addressCollection
      // variable, allowing it to be bound to another object
      [Bindable]
      private var addressCollection : ArrayCollection;
   </mx:Script>

   <!-- include ActionScript to implement search filter -->
   <mx:Script source = "search.as" />

   <!-- include ActionScript to implement Yahoo! Maps component -->
   <mx:Script source = "map.as" />

   <!-- include ActionScript to implement button actions -->
   <mx:Script source = "buttonActions.as" />

   <mx:Panel
      layout = "vertical" width = "100%" height = "100%"
      title = "Address Book">
      <mx:Accordion id = "accordion" width = "100%" height = "100%"
         creationPolicy = "all">
         <mx:VBox label = "View Contacts">
            <!-- search box, calls filter function on any change -->
            <mx:ApplicationControlBar>
               <mx:Label text = "Search:" />
               <mx:TextInput id = "textFilter"
                  width = "100%"
                  change = "filter();"/>
            </mx:ApplicationControlBar> <!-- End Search Box -->

            <!-- contacts data grid, populated with addressCollection -->
            <!-- call setMarkerByAddress on change of selection -->
            <mx:DataGrid id = "contactsView"
               dataProvider = "{ addressCollection }"
               width = "100%" height = "100%"
               change = "setMarkerByAddress();">
               <mx:columns>
```

Fig. 18.7 | `HTTPService`, validators and new UI elements. (Part 2 of 5.)

```
               <mx:DataGridColumn dataField = "firstname"
                  headerText = "First Name" />
               <mx:DataGridColumn dataField = "lastname"
                  headerText = "Last Name" />
               <mx:DataGridColumn dataField = "street"
                  headerText = "Street" />
               <mx:DataGridColumn dataField = "city"
                  headerText = "City" />
               <mx:DataGridColumn dataField = "state"
                  headerText = "State" />
               <mx:DataGridColumn dataField = "zip"
                  headerText = "Zip" />
               <mx:DataGridColumn dataField = "email"
                  headerText = "E-Mail" />
               <mx:DataGridColumn dataField = "phone"
                  headerText = "Phone Number" />
            </mx:columns>
         </mx:DataGrid>

         <mx:ControlBar>
            <!-- start contact action buttons -->
            <mx:Button label = "New"
               click = "newContact()" />
            <mx:Button label = "Delete"
               click = "Alert.show( 'Are you sure?',
               'Delete Contact',
               mx.controls.Alert.YES | mx.controls.Alert.CANCEL,
               this, deleteContact );" />
            <mx:Button label = "Get Directions"
               click = "getDirections();" />
            <mx:Button label = "Edit"
               click = "accordion.selectedIndex = 2;" />
            <mx:Button label = "View on Map"
               click = "accordion.selectedIndex = 1;" />
            <mx:Button label = "E-Mail"
               click = "emailContact();" />
            <!-- end contact action buttons -->
         </mx:ControlBar>
      </mx:VBox> <!-- end "View Contacts" Section -->

      <mx:VBox label = "Map View">
         <!-- create Yahoo! Map -->
         <yahoo:YahooMapService id = "yahooMap" UUID = "{ UUID }"
            swfDomId = "{ swfDomID }"
            apiId = "{ YahooAPIKey }"
            mapURL = "{ mapURL }" width = "600" height = "400" />
         <mx:Button label = "Back to Contacts"
            click = "accordion.selectedIndex = 0;" />
      </mx:VBox> <!-- end "Map View" Section -->

      <mx:VBox label = "Edit Contact">
         <!-- begin edit contact form, set default button to "save" -->
```

Fig. 18.7 | HTTPService, validators and new UI elements. (Part 3 of 5.)

```
         <mx:Form width = "100%" backgroundColor = "#ffffff"
            defaultButton = "{ save }">
            <!-- edit contact text fields, bound to data -->
            <mx:FormItem label = "First Name:" required = "true">
               <mx:TextInput id = "firstName"
                  text = "{ contactsView.selectedItem.firstname }" />
            </mx:FormItem>
            <mx:FormItem label = "Last Name:">
               <mx:TextInput id = "lastName"
                  text = "{ contactsView.selectedItem.lastname }" />
            </mx:FormItem>
            <mx:FormItem label = "Street Address:">
               <mx:TextInput id = "streetAddress"
                  text = "{ contactsView.selectedItem.street }" />
            </mx:FormItem>
            <mx:FormItem label = "City:">
               <mx:TextInput id = "city"
                  text = "{ contactsView.selectedItem.city }" />
            </mx:FormItem>
            <mx:FormItem label = "State:">
               <mx:TextInput id = "state"
                  text = "{ contactsView.selectedItem.state }" />
            </mx:FormItem>
            <mx:FormItem label = "Zip Code:">
               <mx:TextInput id = "zipCode"
                  text = "{ contactsView.selectedItem.zip }" />
            </mx:FormItem>
            <mx:FormItem label = "E-Mail Address:">
               <mx:TextInput id = "eMail"
                  text = "{ contactsView.selectedItem.email }" />
            </mx:FormItem>
            <mx:FormItem label = "Phone Number:">
               <mx:TextInput id = "phone"
                  text = "{ contactsView.selectedItem.phone }" />
            </mx:FormItem>
            <!-- end contact text fields -->

            <!-- edit contact action buttons -->
            <mx:FormItem>
               <mx:Button id = "save" label = "Save" />
            </mx:FormItem>
            <mx:FormItem>
               <!-- cancel button reverts fields to previous values -->
               <!-- return user to "View Contacts" section -->
               <mx:Button id = "cancel" label = "Cancel"
                  click = "cancelContact()" />
            </mx:FormItem>
            <mx:FormItem>
               <!-- pull up "Delete Contact" dialog box -->
               <mx:Button label = "Delete"
                  click = "Alert.show( 'Are you sure?',
                     'Delete Contact',
```

Fig. 18.7 | HTTPService, validators and new UI elements. (Part 4 of 5.)

```
175                         mx.controls.Alert.YES | mx.controls.Alert.CANCEL,
176                         this, deleteContact );" />
177                 </mx:FormItem>
178             </mx:Form> <!-- end edit contact form -->
179          </mx:VBox> <!-- end "Edit Contact" Section -->
180       </mx:Accordion> <!-- end Accordion navigation element -->
181    </mx:Panel> <!-- end UI layout -->
182 </mx:Application>
```

Fig. 18.7 | `HTTPService`, validators and new UI elements. (Part 5 of 5.)

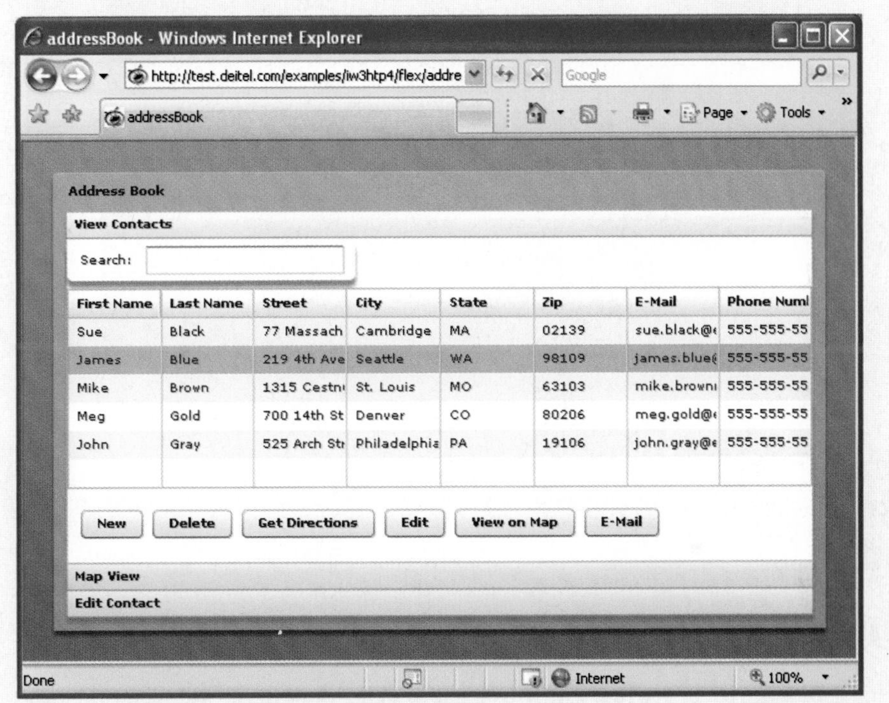

Fig. 18.8 | Address book's **View Contacts** mode.

We begin by looking at the user interface code in the `Panel` element (lines 50–181, Fig. 18.7). An **`Accordion` element** (lines 53–180) allows the user to easily navigate between multiple `VBox`es. As you click the title of one `VBox`, it slides on top of the previously active `VBox`. This `Accordion` contains three `VBox`es, **View Contacts**, **Map View**, and **Edit Contact** (lines 55–109, 111–119, and 121–179, respectively). The `Accordion` attribute `creationPolicy` with the value `"all"` (line 54) forces the Flash player to load all components, even those that are not initially visible to the user. This is necessary to allow the Yahoo! Map to load before we create the map navigation elements.

Inside the **View Contacts** `VBox` (as seen in Fig. 18.8), we first define an **`ApplicationControlBar`** container for the search field (line 57–62). An `ApplicationControlBar` is a type of `ControlBar` that can be placed anywhere or docked at the top of an application.

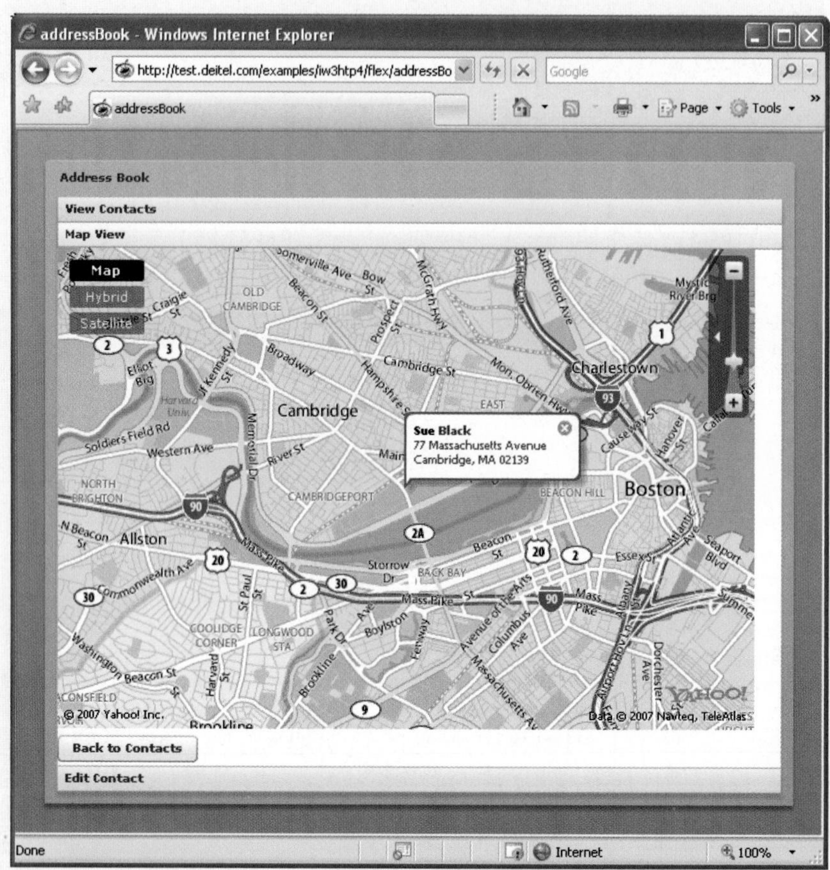

Fig. 18.9 | Address book's **Map View** mode.

This `ApplicationControlBar` contains a `Label` explaining to the user what the text field is for, followed by the `TextInput` element itself (lines 59–61). This element's `change` attribute indicates that the `filter` function (located in the `search.as` file) should be called whenever a change is made to the field, such as adding or removing characters. We'll discuss the `filter` function in detail when we review the ActionScript code.

Lines 66–88 create a **`DataGrid` element** with a `dataProvider` attribute that specifies what data will fill the rows and columns. The `dataProvider` `addressCollection` is placed in curly braces (line 67) to indicate that the `dataProvider` is being bound to the `DataGrid`—any changes to the `addressCollection` will be displayed in the `DataGrid`. This `DataGrid` also has a `change` attribute. This is set to call the `setMarkerByAddress` function located in the `map.as` file whenever the user selects a different contact, so that the map will update to display that contact's location. In the `DataGrid`, we define each column using **`DataGridColumn` elements** inside a parent `columns` element. Each `DataGridColumn` (e.g., lines 71–72) has a `dataField` attribute that tells the element which data it should display, and a `headerText` attribute that defines the text in the column header.

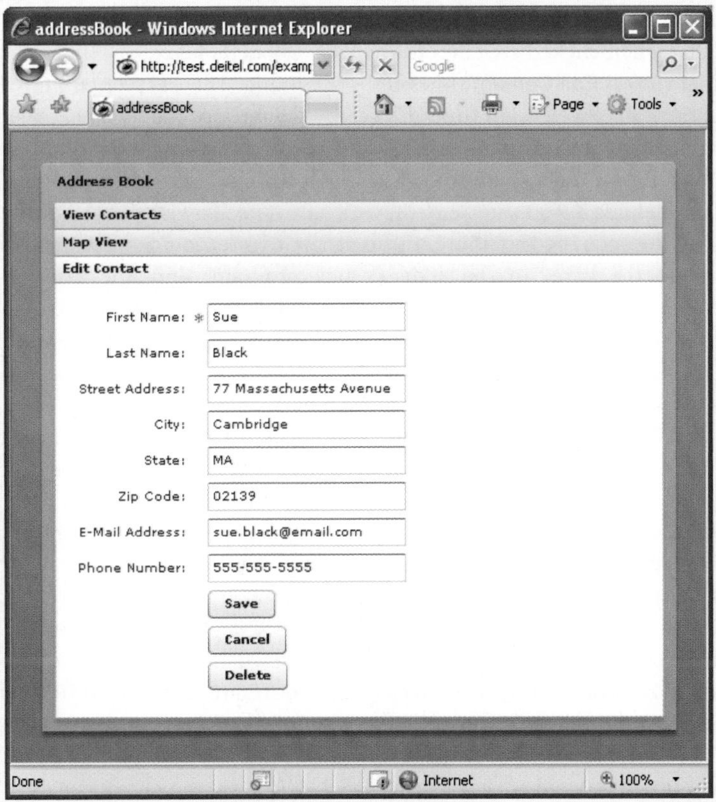

Fig. 18.10 | Address book's **Edit Contact** mode.

Following the `DataGrid` are a series of `Buttons` that perform actions. These `Buttons` reside in a `ControlBar` container (lines 90–108), and each has a `click` attribute that defines the ActionScript code that will be executed when the user clicks the `Button`. For the **New** (lines 92–93), **Get Directions** (lines 99–100), and **E-Mail** (lines 105–106) `Buttons`, the code executed by `click` calls a function specific to that `Button`, located in `buttonActions.as`. For the **Delete** `Button` (94–98), the code executed by `click` calls the `Alert.show` function to display a dialog box confirming the user's action. This specific call to the `Alert.show` function sends five parameters—`text`, `title`, `flags` (specifies which buttons should appear), `parent`, and `closeHandler`. For the **Edit** (lines 101–102) and **View on Map** (lines 103–104) `Buttons`, the `click` attribute sets the `selectedIndex` of the `Accordion` to the index of the appropriate `VBox`.

The next `VBox` is **Map View** (lines 111–119 in Fig. 18.7, as seen in Fig. 18.9), which contains two items. The first is the `YahooMapService` element (lines 113–116). Note that the namespace of this element is `yahoo`—line 6 defines the `yahoo` namespace, which directs the compiler to the `com/yahoo/webapis/maps` directory located in the base directory of your application. This directory contains the `YahooMapService.as` file, which defines the `YahooMapService` element. This element has seven attributes. After the `id`, the next four are constants that we set in the ActionScript file for the Yahoo! Map, `map.as`.

The last two define the width and height of the map element. We discuss using the Yahoo! Maps API when we describe the map.as file. Following the map is a Button (lines 117–118) that when clicked switches to the **View Contacts** VBox.

The final VBox is **Edit Contact** (lines 121–179 in Fig. 18.7, as seen in Fig. 18.10). This element contains a Form element (lines 123–178) that groups the TextInput elements and the Button elements into a single entity. This aligns the elements and also allows us to specify such things as defaultButton (line 124), which is set to the **Save** Button. Each TextInput resides in a FormItem element, which can specify whether or not the item must be filled in via the required attribute. If this attribute is set to true, Flex will display a red asterisk next to the item. In the addressBook program, only the firstName field is required. When a user leaves this field blank and clicks the **Save** Button, the action is ignored and the firstName field is highlighted. This is an improvement over HTML forms, with which the user is notified of invalid data only after the form is sent to the server (though client-side validation can be performed with JavaScript).

Lines 20–30 create validator elements that check the contents of the TextInput elements to ensure that the user entered data correctly. Flex provides preconfigured validators for Strings, zip codes, e-mail addresses, phone numbers and more. There are several attributes for a validator element. The source attribute specifies which object to validate. The required attribute specifies whether the user is required to fill in data. The trigger attribute determines which button to listen to. The triggerEvent attribute specifies which event from the trigger initiates validation. The valid attribute specifies what ActionScript to execute if the triggerEvent is triggered and the data is valid.

Lines 10–17 create an HTTPService named getContacts. An HTTPService downloads a URL using the HTTP protocol. The send method of an HTTPService executes a request to the service, and can include parameters if the service requires them. We specify the url attribute to be contacts.xml (Fig. 18.11). We set the showBusyCursor attribute to true (line 13) so that the application displays a busy cursor while a request is being processed. We set the resultFormat to object (line 14), so that the XML is parsed as a tree of ActionScript objects. Some other valid resultFormats are array (which parses the tree as an array object), text (which returns the raw XML) and e4x (which allows you to use E4X expressions, explained in Section 18.4). The expression in the result attribute is executed when the HTTP request is complete. It stores each contact node from the HTTPService's lastResult property into an ArrayCollection called addressCollection. We create this ArrayCollection in lines 37–38. The [Bindable] metadata tag allows the variable that follows to be bound. It does this by registering an event to keep track of changes to the variable. The fault attribute (line 17) of an HTTPService specifies what to do in the event of a failed request. In this example, a failed request triggers an Alert displaying the error message. Finally, we call the send method at line 7, using the Application's creationComplete attribute. This attribute registers an event handler that is triggered after the Flash Player creates all of the interface elements.

```
<?xml version = "1.0" encoding = "utf-8" ?>
<!-- Fig. 18.11: contacts.xml -->
<!-- XML file containing contacts -->
```

Fig. 18.11 | XML file containing contacts. (Part 1 of 2.)

```
<contacts>
    <contact id = "1">
       <firstname>Sue</firstname>
        <lastname>Black</lastname>
        <street>77 Massachusetts Avenue</street>
        <city>Cambridge</city>
        <state>MA</state>
        <zip>02139</zip>
        <email>sue.black@email.com</email>
        <phone>555-555-5555</phone>
    </contact>
    <contact id = "2">
        <firstname>James</firstname>
        <lastname>Blue</lastname>
        <street>219 4th Avenue</street>
        <city>Seattle</city>
        <state>WA</state>
        <zip>98109</zip>
        <email>james.blue@email.com</email>
        <phone>555-555-5555</phone>
    </contact>
    <contact id = "3">
        <firstname>Mike</firstname>
        <lastname>Brown</lastname>
        <street>1315 Cestnut Street</street>
        <city>St. Louis</city>
        <state>MO</state>
        <zip>63103</zip>
        <email>mike.brown@email.com</email>
        <phone>555-555-5555</phone>
    </contact>
    <contact id = "4">
        <firstname>Meg</firstname>
        <lastname>Gold</lastname>
        <street>700 14th Street</street>
        <city>Denver</city>
        <state>CO</state>
        <zip>80206</zip>
        <email>meg.gold@email.com</email>
        <phone>555-555-5555</phone>
    </contact>
    <contact id = "5">
        <firstname>John</firstname>
        <lastname>Gray</lastname>
        <street>525 Arch Street</street>
        <city>Philadelphia</city>
        <state>PA</state>
        <zip>19106</zip>
        <email>john.gray@email.com</email>
        <phone>555-555-5555</phone>
    </contact>
</contacts>
```

Fig. 18.11 | XML file containing contacts. (Part 2 of 2.)

You can embed ActionScript in MXML through use of the `Script` tag (lines 32–39). To better organize the code, we also place ActionScript in separate `.as` files. The `addressBook.mxml` file includes these files using a `Script` element with a `source` attribute (lines 42–48). There are three script files—`search.as`, `map.as` and `buttonActions.as`. We now explain each of these ActionScript files.

Search Function ActionScript

The `search.as` ActionScript file (Fig. 18.12) contains the function `filter` (lines 3–8), which is called any time a change is made in the `textFilter` `TextInput`—as specified by the `change` attribute in line 61 of Fig. 18.7. This function defines `addressCollection`'s `filterFunction` (line 6) to be `testMatch` (lines 10–31). An `ArrayCollection`'s `filterFunction` is passed each item of the collection and returns `true` if the item matches the search criteria, and `false` otherwise. Function `testMatch` tests whether the `searchTerm` matches the text in any of the data fields of each `item`.

```
1  // Fig. 18.12: search.as
2  // Using a filterFunction for a live search feature
3  private function filter() : void
4  {
5     // define filter function
6     addressCollection.filterFunction = testMatch;
7     addressCollection.refresh(); // refresh data to only display matches
8  } // end function filter
9
10 private function testMatch( item : Object ) : Boolean
11 {
12    // save search term to variable
13    var searchTerm:String = textFilter.text.toLowerCase();
14
15    // return whether search parameter matches any field for each item
16    return( item.firstname.toLowerCase().search( searchTerm ) != -1 ||
17       item.lastname.toLowerCase().search( searchTerm ) != -1 ||
18       item.street.toLowerCase().search( searchTerm ) != -1 ||
19       item.city.toLowerCase().search( searchTerm ) != -1 ||
20       item.state.toLowerCase().search( searchTerm ) != -1 ||
21       String( item.zip ).search( searchTerm ) != -1 ||
22       item.email.toLowerCase().search( searchTerm ) != -1 ||
23       item.phone.toLowerCase().search( searchTerm ) != -1 )
24 } // end function testMatch
```

Fig. 18.12 | Using a `filterFunction` for a live search feature.

Yahoo! Map ActionScript

The `map.as` ActionScript file (Fig. 18.13) handles the `addressBook` application's map functionality. We use the Yahoo! Maps API, because Yahoo! provides the ability to embed maps in Flex 2 applications[3] (the map itself is a Flash application). The first step in using the Yahoo! Maps API is to get a Yahoo! account and Application ID. These are available at `developer.yahoo.com`. You then need to download the Yahoo! AS3 API Libraries at `developer.yahoo.com/flash/as3_api_libraries.html`. Move the `source/as3/com/`

3. For more information see `developer.yahoo.com/flash/howto-maps-as3.html`.

folder and the `source/as2/as2map.swf` file into the base directory of your application. This allows you to use the `as2map.swf` file, which contains the ActionScript 2-based map, as well as use the ActionScript 3 functions Yahoo! provides to control the map.

```
// Fig. 18.13: map.as
// Handle the map functions for the Address Book application
import mx.managers.CursorManager;
import com.yahoo.webapis.maps.methodgroups.*;
import mx.controls.Alert;

// define constants
private const swfDomID : String = "addressBook";
private const UUID : int = Math.random() * 10000;

// YahooAPIKey string must be your own from developer.yahoo.com
private const YahooAPIKey : String = "Your Yahoo API Key Here";
private const mapURL : String = "as2map.swf";
private var mapController : MapController;

private function initMap() : void
{
   CursorManager.setBusyCursor(); // turn on busy cursor

   // wait for map to load, then call onMapLoaded method
   yahooMap.addEventListener( 'onMapLoad', onMapLoaded );
   yahooMap.addEventListener( 'onMapError', onMapError );
} // end function initMap

// handle map after it has loaded
public function onMapLoaded( event : Object ) : void
{
   // instantiate map controller
   mapController = new MapController( yahooMap );

   // instantiate panTool method
   var panTools : PanTool = new PanTool( yahooMap );

   // allow user to pan across the map
   panTools.setPanTool( true );

   // instantiate the maps widget class
   var widgets : Widgets = new Widgets( yahooMap );

   // activate Navigator widget
   widgets.showNavigatorWidget();

   // activate map-type selection widget
   widgets.showSatelliteControlWidget();

   // turn off busy cursor
   CursorManager.removeBusyCursor();
} // end function onMapLoaded
```

Fig. 18.13 | Handle the map functions for the Address Book application. (Part 1 of 2.)

```
49
50   public function onMapError( errorCode:String, httpStatus:String ) : void
51   {
52      Alert.show( errorCode + '\n' + httpStatus, 'Map Load Error' );
53   } // end function onMapError
54
55   // place a labeled marker at the currently selected address
56   public function setMarkerByAddress() : void
57   {
58      mapController.removeAllMarkers(); // clear previous markers
59
60      // add marker at specified address,
61      // labeled with contact's name and address
62      mapController.addCustomPOIMarker(
63         ( contactsView.selectedItem.street + " " +
64         contactsView.selectedItem.city + " " +
65         contactsView.selectedItem.state ),
66         contactsView.selectedItem.firstname,
67         contactsView.selectedItem.lastname,
68         (contactsView.selectedItem.street + "\n" +
69         contactsView.selectedItem.city + ", " +
70         contactsView.selectedItem.state + " " +
71         contactsView.selectedItem.zip ),
72         0x990099, 0xFFFFFF );
73
74      // instantly center on address and zoom in
75      mapController.setCenterByAddressAndZoom(
76         contactsView.selectedItem.street + " " +
77         contactsView.selectedItem.city + " " +
78         contactsView.selectedItem.state, 5, 0 );
79   } // end function setMarkerByAddress
```

Fig. 18.13 | Handle the map functions for the Address Book application. (Part 2 of 2.)

We first import the classes that we use in this ActionScript file (lines 3–5). The `CursorManager` class allows us to set and remove the busy cursor. We also import all of the classes located in the `com/yahoo/webapis/maps/methodgroups` directory, which provide us with the ability to control the map and to create the map's user interface widgets. We set the constants necessary for using a Yahoo! Map in lines 8–13. `swfDomID` (line 8) is a `string` that must be equal to the `object id` used in the `.html` file containing the application. `UUID` (line 9) is the unique ID of the map element and is set to `Math.random()*10000` so that it is a random integer from 0 up to 9999. `YahooAPIKey` (lines 12) should be set to the Yahoo Application ID you obtained from `developer.yahoo.com`. Constant `mapURL` (line 13) is the path to the `as2map.swf` file. Because we placed that file in the base directory of the application, we can simply specify the file's name. Line 14 creates the `mapController` variable that we will instantiate at line 29.

The function `initMap` (lines 16–23) is called when the application has finished creating the user interface elements, as specified by `addressBook`'s `creationComplete` attribute (line 7 in Fig. 18.7). This function sets the busy cursor, then registers event handlers for the `onMapLoad` and `onMapError` events for the map. The `onMapError` event handler (lines 50–53) triggers an Alert displaying the error. The onMapLoaded event handler (lines 26–48) adds MapController, PanTool and Widgets objects to the map.

MapController enables programmatic control of the map's location and zoom and the placing of markers on the map at a specified address.[4] PanTool (line 32) enables the user to click and drag the map, as well as double click a location to center on it. Widgets (line 38) add the ability to show a navigator widget (line 41), which provides zoom controls and an overview map, and a satellite control widget (line 44), which provides the user with a selection of the regular map view, the satellite view, or the hybrid view. After loading all of the map's functions, initMap removes the busy cursor (line 47).

Function setMarkerByAddress (lines 56–79) provides the ability to place a marker at the location of the selected contact's location. It uses the mapController's addCustomPOIMarker function (lines 62–72) to place a marker at the contact's address that contains the contact's first and last name as well as the address. It also uses the mapController's setCenterByAddressAndZoom function (lines 75–78) to center the map on that contact's location and zoom down to the street level (zoom level 5). The final parameter of the setCenterByAddressAndZoom function is the amount of time in milliseconds the map should take to pan to the new location. We set this to 0, because the map will not be visible when this function is called.

Button Event-Handling ActionScript

The buttonActions.as ActionScript file (Fig. 18.14) handles the functionality of most of the addressBook application's Buttons. Each Button has a corresponding function. The first Button it handles is the **Cancel** Button (lines 167–168 of Fig. 18.7). The cancelContact function (lines 6–19 of Fig. 18.14) reverts **Edit Contact**'s fields back to the previous value of the selected contact, then switches the Accordion to **View Contacts**. The deleteContact function (lines 22–35) handles when the user clicks a **Delete** Button (lines 94–98 or 172–176 of Fig. 18.7), then clicks **Yes** in the confirmation dialog box. It switches the Accordion to **View Contacts** if the user was not already there, and removes the currently selected contact. The emailContact function (lines 38–46 of Fig. 18.14) creates a new URLRequest object that contains a mailto URL for the current contact's e-mail address. The call to navigateToURL opens that URL in _self, which refers to the current browser window. Since the URL is a mailto URL, however, the browser tells the user's default e-mail client to open and to compose a new message addressed to the specified e-mail address. The getDirections function (lines 49–60) uses the same method to open a URL; however, instead of forming a mailto URL, it forms a URL pointing to the Yahoo! Maps page, specifying that we want directions ending at the currently selected contact's address. It opens this URL in _blank, which creates a new browser window with the specified URL. The saveContact function (lines 63–82) sets the data in the addressCollection item corresponding to the currently selected contact to be equal to that of the text in **Edit Contact**'s TextInputs. It then refreshes addressCollection in case the contactsView DataGrid is being filtered (the refresh ensures that the filter results are current). The newContact function (lines 85–93) creates a new item in addressCollection whose firstname is set to "New" and whose lastname is set to "Contact". It then sets the selectedIndex of the contactsView DataGrid to be the new item, and switches to the **Edit Contacts** view.

---

4. The full list of functions this enables is available at developer.yahoo.com/flash/as3webapis/docs/com/yahoo/webapis/maps/methodgroups/MapController.html.

```
// Fig. 18.14: buttonActions.as
// Implement the actions of each button
import mx.events.CloseEvent;

// "Cancel" button
private function cancelContact() : void
{
   // revert edit fields to original value
   firstName.text = contactsView.selectedItem.firstname;
   lastName.text = contactsView.selectedItem.lastname;
   streetAddress.text = contactsView.selectedItem.street;
   city.text = contactsView.selectedItem.city;
   state.text = contactsView.selectedItem.state;
   zipCode.text = contactsView.selectedItem.zip;
   eMail.text = contactsView.selectedItem.email;
   phone.text = contactsView.selectedItem.phone;
   // return user to "View Contacts" section
   accordion.selectedIndex = 0;
} // end function cancelContact

// "Delete" button
private function deleteContact( event : CloseEvent ) : void
{
   // handle if user clicked "Yes" in "Delete Contact" dialog box
   if ( event.detail == Alert.YES )
   {
      // return user to "View Contacts" section if
      // the user was in "Edit Contacts" section
      if ( accordion.selectedIndex == 2 )
         accordion.selectedIndex = 0;

      // remove selected contact
      addressCollection.removeItemAt( contactsView.selectedIndex );
   } // end if
} // end function deleteContact

// "E-Mail" button
public function emailContact() : void
{
   // form "mailto" URL given the selected e-mail address
   var mailURL : URLRequest = new URLRequest( 'mailto:' +
      contactsView.selectedItem.email );

   // open the URL without opening new window
   navigateToURL( mailURL, "_self" );
} // end function emailContact

// "Directions" button
public function getDirections() : void
{
   // form directions URL given the selected address
   var directionsURL : URLRequest = new URLRequest(
      'http://maps.yahoo.com/broadband#mvt=m&q2=' +
```

Fig. 18.14 | Implement the actions of each button. (Part 1 of 2.)

```
            contactsView.selectedItem.street + ' ' +
            contactsView.selectedItem.city + ' ' +
            contactsView.selectedItem.state + ' ' +
            contactsView.selectedItem.zip );
         // open URL in a new window
         navigateToURL( directionsURL, "_blank" );
      } // end function getDirections

      // "Save" button
      private function saveContact() : void
      {
         // write changes to data array
         addressCollection.setItemAt( {
            firstname : firstName.text,
            lastname : lastName.text,
            street : streetAddress.text,
            city : city.text,
            state : state.text,
            zip : zipCode.text,
            email : eMail.text,
            phone : phone.text },
            contactsView.selectedIndex );

         // refresh data collection so that search will still work
         addressCollection.refresh();

         // return user to "View Contacts" section
         accordion.selectedIndex = 0;
      } // end function saveContact

      // "New" button
      private function newContact() : void
      {
         addressCollection.addItem( {
            firstname : 'New', lastname : 'Contact',
            street : null, city : null, state : null,
            zip : null, email : null, phone : null } );
         contactsView.selectedIndex = addressCollection.length;
         accordion.selectedIndex = 2;
      } // end function newContact
```

Fig. 18.14 | Implement the actions of each button. (Part 2 of 2.)

18.5 Interacting with Server-Side Applications

Flex makes it easy to consume web services. In this example (Fig. 18.15), we use a web service from `WebServiceX.net` to obtain weather data based on a zip code. The user inputs the zip code, clicks a button and a five-day forecast is displayed on the screen (Fig. 18.16). Additionally, a marker is placed on a Yahoo! Map at the zip code's location, and the forecast information is displayed in the marker's tool tip (Fig. 18.17). You can test a live version of this application at `test.deitel.com/examples/iw3htp4/flex/weather/`. More information on web services is available in Chapter 28, Web Services, and at our Web Services Resource Center at `www.deitel.com/webservices`.

```
<?xml version = "1.0" encoding = "utf-8" ?>
<!-- Fig. 18.15: weather.mxml -->
<!-- Weather Forecast application in Flex 2 -->
<mx:Application xmlns:mx = "http://www.adobe.com/2006/mxml"
   layout = "absolute" xmlns:yahoo = "com.yahoo.webapis.maps.*"
   creationComplete = "initMap();" >

   <mx:Script source = "map.as" />

   <mx:Script>
   <![CDATA[
      import mx.controls.dataGridClasses.DataGridColumn;
      import mx.rpc.events.ResultEvent;
      import mx.managers.CursorManager;
      import mx.controls.Alert;
      import mx.collections.ArrayCollection;
      import flash.events.MouseEvent;

      // define default namespace
      default xml namespace = "http://www.webservicex.net";

      [Bindable]
      private var xmlData : XML;
      [Bindable]
      private var highLowTemp : String;
      [Bindable]
      private var fiveDayForecast : String = "";
      [Bindable]
      private var placeName : String;

      // handle getWeatherButton click action
      private function getWeather() : void
      {
         // disable button while request is pending
         getWeatherButton.enabled = false;

         // hide the old forecast data before displaying new data
         forecastBox.visible = false;

         // reset place name while loading new data
         placeNameText.text = "";

         // show the loading progress bar
         loadingBar.visible = true;

         // request the new data
         weatherService.GetWeatherByZipCode.send();
      } // end function getWeather

      private function weatherResultHandler(event : ResultEvent) : void
      {
         // save the result of the web service as XML
         xmlData = XML( event.result );
```

Fig. 18.15 | Weather Forecast application in Flex 2. (Part 1 of 5.)

```

         // check that result is valid by checking length of StateCode
         if ( xmlData.GetWeatherByZipCodeResult[ 0 ].
            StateCode.text().length() != 0 )
         {
            // set placeNameText to the city and state of the zip code
            placeName = xmlData.GetWeatherByZipCodeResult[ 0 ].
               PlaceName.text() + ", " +
               xmlData.GetWeatherByZipCodeResult[ 0 ].StateCode.text();
            placeNameText.text = "5 Day Forecast for " + placeName;

            // set image, temperature and date for each day
            setData( weatherImage0, weatherTemp0, weatherDay0, 0 );
            setData( weatherImage1, weatherTemp1, weatherDay1, 1 );
            setData( weatherImage2, weatherTemp2, weatherDay2, 2 );
            setData( weatherImage3, weatherTemp3, weatherDay3, 3 );
            setData( weatherImage4, weatherTemp4, weatherDay4, 4 );

            forecastBox.visible = true;

            // save today's high/low as a string
            highLowTemp =  xmlData.GetWeatherByZipCodeResult.
               Details.WeatherData.MaxTemperatureF[ 0 ].text() +
               "/" + xmlData.GetWeatherByZipCodeResult.Details.
               WeatherData.MinTemperatureF[ 0 ].text();

            // save the five-day forecast as a string
            fiveDayForecast = highLowTemp;

            for ( var i : int = 1; i < 5; i++ )
            {
               fiveDayForecast += ", " + xmlData.
                  GetWeatherByZipCodeResult.Details.WeatherData.
                     MaxTemperatureF[ i ].text() + "/" + xmlData.
                     GetWeatherByZipCodeResult.Details.
                     WeatherData.MinTemperatureF[ i ].text();
            } // end for

            // place a marker on the map with the forecast
            mapController.addCustomPOIMarker(
               zipcode.text, placeName, highLowTemp, fiveDayForecast,
               0x990099, 0xFFFFFF);

            mapController.setCenterByAddressAndZoom(
               zipcode.text, 7, 0 );
         }
         else
         {
            Alert.show( "Invalid zip code" );
         }
         // hide the loading progress bar
         loadingBar.visible = false;

```

Fig. 18.15 | Weather Forecast application in Flex 2. (Part 2 of 5.)

```
         // enable getWeatherButton
         getWeatherButton.enabled = true;
      } // end function weatherResultHandler

      private function setData( forecastImage : Image,
         tempText : Text, dateText : Text, i : int ) : void
      {
         // set the image for each day
         forecastImage.source = xmlData.GetWeatherByZipCodeResult.
            Details.WeatherData.WeatherImage[ i ].text();

         // set the temperature for each day
         tempText.text = xmlData.GetWeatherByZipCodeResult.
            Details.WeatherData.MaxTemperatureF[ i ].text() +
            "\n" + xmlData.GetWeatherByZipCodeResult.Details.
            WeatherData.MinTemperatureF[ i ].text();

         // set the date for each day
         dateText.text = xmlData.GetWeatherByZipCodeResult.
            Details.WeatherData.Day[ i ].text();
      }
   ]]>
   </mx:Script>

   <!-- show/hide animations for forecast boxes -->
   <mx:Parallel id = "forecastAnimationIn">
      <mx:Fade duration = "1000" alphaFrom = "0.0" alphaTo = "1.0" />
      <mx:Zoom zoomWidthTo = "1" zoomHeightTo = "1" zoomWidthFrom = "0"
         zoomHeightFrom = "0" />
   </mx:Parallel>

   <mx:Parallel id = "forecastAnimationOut">
      <mx:Fade duration = "500" alphaFrom = "1.0" alphaTo = "0.0" />
      <mx:Zoom zoomWidthTo = "0" zoomHeightTo = "0" zoomWidthFrom = "1"
         zoomHeightFrom = "1" />
   </mx:Parallel>

   <!-- WebService description -->
   <mx:WebService id = "weatherService"
      wsdl = "http://www.webservicex.net/WeatherForecast.asmx?WSDL"
      fault = "Alert.show( event.fault.faultString )"
      result = "weatherResultHandler( event )"
      showBusyCursor = "true">
      <mx:operation name = "GetWeatherByZipCode" resultFormat = "e4x">
         <mx:request>
            <ZipCode>{ zipcode.text }</ZipCode>
         </mx:request>
      </mx:operation>
   </mx:WebService>

   <!-- user interface begins here -->
   <mx:Panel title = "Weather" width = "100%" height = "100%">
      <mx:Accordion id = "accordion" width = "100%" height = "100%"
```

Fig. 18.15 | Weather Forecast application in Flex 2. (Part 3 of 5.)

```
            creationPolicy = "all">
            <mx:VBox label = "Forecast View" width = "100%" height = "100%">
               <mx:ApplicationControlBar
                  defaultButton = "{ getWeatherButton }">
                  <mx:Label width = "100%"
                     text = "Enter a zip code:" />
                  <mx:TextInput id = "zipcode" left = "10" />
                  <mx:Button id = "getWeatherButton" label = "Get Weather"
                     click = "getWeather()" left = "10" />
               </mx:ApplicationControlBar>

               <mx:Text fontWeight = "bold" id = "placeNameText" />
               <mx:ProgressBar id = "loadingBar" indeterminate = "true"
                  labelPlacement = "bottom" visible = "false" minimum = "0"
                  maximum = "100" label = "Loading Weather Data"
                  direction = "right" width = "75%" />

               <!-- forecastBox holds the five-day forecast -->
               <!-- start off as hidden, define show and hide effects -->
               <mx:HBox id = "forecastBox" width = "100%" height = "100%"
                  visible = "false" showEffect = "{ forecastAnimationIn }"
                  hideEffect = "{ forecastAnimationOut }">
                  <mx:VBox id = "forecastBox0" horizontalAlign = "center"
                     borderStyle = "solid" width = "20%" height = "0%">
                     <mx:Text id = "weatherDay0" />
                     <mx:Image id = "weatherImage0" />
                     <mx:Text id = "weatherTemp0" />
                  </mx:VBox>

                  <mx:VBox horizontalAlign = "center"
                     borderStyle = "solid" width = "20%">
                     <mx:Text id = "weatherDay1" />
                     <mx:Image id = "weatherImage1" />
                     <mx:Text id = "weatherTemp1" />
                  </mx:VBox>

                  <mx:VBox horizontalAlign = "center"
                     borderStyle = "solid" width = "20%">
                     <mx:Text id = "weatherDay2" />
                     <mx:Image id = "weatherImage2" />
                     <mx:Text id = "weatherTemp2" />
                  </mx:VBox>

                  <mx:VBox horizontalAlign = "center"
                     borderStyle = "solid" width = "20%">
                     <mx:Text id = "weatherDay3" />
                     <mx:Image id = "weatherImage3" />
                     <mx:Text id = "weatherTemp3" />
                  </mx:VBox>

                  <mx:VBox horizontalAlign = "center"
                     borderStyle = "solid" width = "20%">
                     <mx:Text id = "weatherDay4" />
```

Fig. 18.15 | Weather Forecast application in Flex 2. (Part 4 of 5.)

```
213                         <mx:Image id = "weatherImage4" />
214                         <mx:Text id = "weatherTemp4" />
215                      </mx:VBox>
216                   </mx:HBox>
217                </mx:VBox>
218                <mx:VBox label = "Map View" width = "100%" height = "100%">
219                   <!-- create Yahoo! Map -->
220                   <yahoo:YahooMapService id = "yahooMap" UUID = "{ UUID }"
221                      swfDomId = "{ swfDomID }"
222                      apiId = "{ YahooAPIKey }"
223                      mapURL = "{ mapURL }" width = "600" height = "400" />
224                   <mx:HBox>
225                      <mx:Button label = "Back"
226                         click = "accordion.selectedIndex=0;" />
227                      <mx:Button label = "Clear"
228                         click = "mapController.removeAllMarkers();" />
229                   </mx:HBox>
230                </mx:VBox> <!-- end "Map View" Section -->
231             </mx:Accordion>
232          </mx:Panel>
233       </mx:Application>
```

Fig. 18.15 | Weather Forecast application in Flex 2. (Part 5 of 5.)

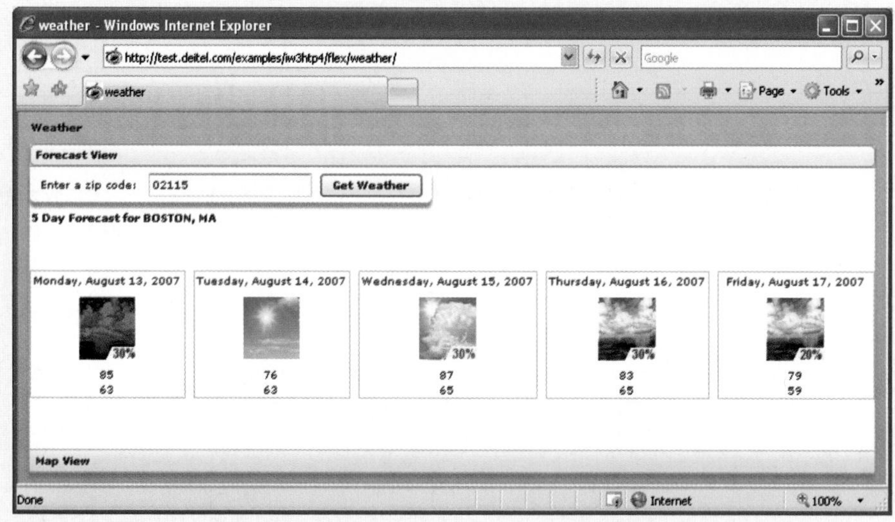

Fig. 18.16 | **Forecast View** of five-day weather forecast for Boston, MA.

We first look at the user interface part of `weather.mxml` (lines 158–232). Line 158 begins the user interface definition with a `Panel`, which holds an `Accordion`. In the `Accordion` (lines 159–231), there are two `VBox`es, one for the **Forecast View** section (lines 161–217) and one for the **Map View** section (lines 218–230). The **Forecast View** `VBox` holds a `ApplicationControlBar` (lines 162–169) that contains the `zipcode` `TextInput` box, the **Get Weather** `Button` and a `ProgressBar` that notifies the user that the web service call is

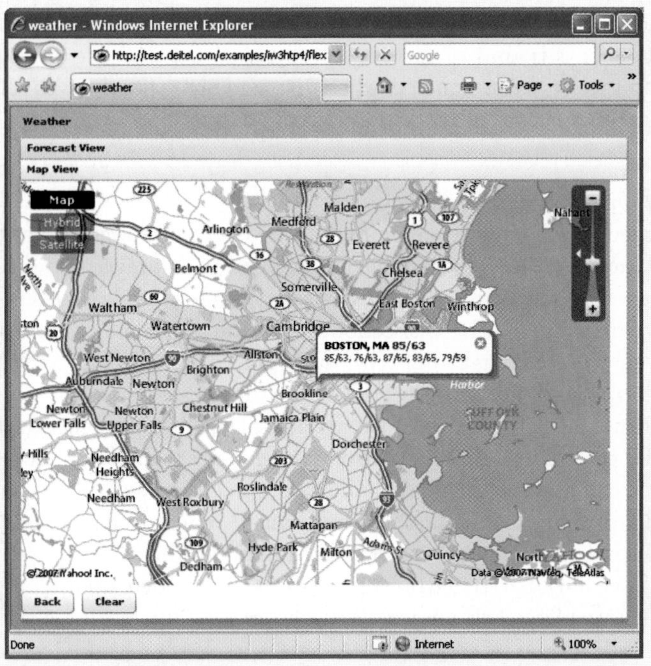

Fig. 18.17 | **Map View** of 5-Day Weather Forecast for Boston, MA.

being processed. The `ProgressBar` element allows you to give the user an idea of an operation's state. We set the `indeterminate` attribute of this `ProgressBar` to `true` because the application doesn't know when the web service call will complete.

The `VBox` also holds an `HBox` (lines 179–216) that contains the five-day forecast. Each day's forecast is held in a `VBox` that displays the date, an image representing the weather, and the high and low temperature in Fahrenheit. The `HBox` containing the forecast is not initially visible (line 180) because we do not want to see the borders of its `VBoxes` before there is any content. It also has the attributes `showEffect` and `hideEffect` (lines 180–181). These tell Flex which animation to use when the element is shown or hidden. These animations (lines 132–142) use the `Parallel` element to play effects simultaneously. Each `Parallel` element contains two effects, `Fade` and `Zoom`. The **Map View** `VBox` (lines 218–230) contains the `YahooMapService` element, as well as two `Buttons`. The first `Button` simply returns the user to the **Forecast View**, and the second `Button` tells the `YahooMapService` object to remove any markers from the map.

The `weatherService` `WebService` element (lines 145–155) specifies the URL of the Web Services Description Language (WSDL) file for the web service. A WSDL file is an XML file describing what services are available on a server, how to consume those services, what parameters they accept and what they return. Flex uses this WSDL file to make it easy to access the services without further configuration. We specify the `fault` event handler for the web service (line 147) to show an `Alert` dialog, and the `result` event handler to be `weatherResultHandler` (line 148). We then describe a specific method using the `operation` element (lines 150–154), which specifies the name of the method (`GetWeath-`

erByZipCode), and the desired format of the result (e4x). One way to send parameters to the web service is to enclose request elements in the operation element. In this case, the ZipCode parameter is bound to the text property of the zipcode TextInput. Alternatively, you can specify the parameters when you actually make the web service call using the same syntax that is used to send parameters to a function.

ActionScript for Weather Application

A Script element (lines 10–129) contains most of this application's ActionScript. Because the code is located in a CDATA section, the MXML compiler knows not to parse this section as XML in case it contains any reserved characters, such as angle brackets (< and >), that might confuse the compiler. In this section, we define the default XML namespace to be http://www.webservicex.net (line 20). This prevents us from having to specify this namespace every time we access the XML returned by the web service. Function getWeather (lines 32–48) is invoked when getWeatherButton is clicked. It first disables getWeatherButton and sets the busy cursor. It then hides the HBox containing the forecast data, because it is about to be changed, and resets placeNameText. It continues by showing the loadingBar ProgressBar (line 44) and finally requests the weather data through weatherService.GetWeatherByZipCode's send method (line 47).

Method weatherResultHandler (lines 50–109) is called upon completion of this request. It first saves the web service's result as an XML object (line 53). It then checks whether the result is valid by seeing if the StateCode returned by the service is not empty. If it is empty, an Alert (line 102) will notify the user that the zip code is invalid. If the StateCode exists, that indicates that the zip code was valid, and that we have received weather data. In this case, the program continues to set placeNameText (line 63) based on the city and state returned by the service, traversing the XML's tree down to the PlaceName and StateCode items using dot operators (lines 60–62). Next, it displays the data for each data with multiple calls to the setData function (lines 66–70).

This function (lines 111–127) sets the source URL of the forecast image for a given day to the URL in the XML's corresponding WeatherImage element (lines 115–116). The first WeatherImage in the XML has an index of 0. We apply a similar technique to populate the high and low temperature (lines 119–122) and the date for a given day (lines 125–126). Lines 75–78 save today's high and low temperature, as well as the five-day forecast, as strings for use in the map marker.

Finally, we place a marker on the map using mapController's addCustomPOIMarker function (lines 93–95). We specify the location of the marker to be the zip code we obtained data for, and title of the marker to be the name of that town or city, as well as today's high and low temperature. The body of the marker is set to display the five-day forecast. The setCenterByAddressAndZoom function (lines 97–98) zooms in and centers the map on the zip code's location. The function finally hides the ProgressBar, removes the busy cursor, and enables getWeatherButton.

The map.as ActionScript file (Fig. 18.18) handles the map functionality of the weather application. You need to copy the Yahoo! Map com folder and as2map.swf file into the application's base directory, just as we did for the addressBook application. This version of map.as contains the same initMap, onMapLoaded and onMapError functions as addressBook's version of map.as, but doesn't include the function setMarkerByAddress. The only other change is the swfDomID, which is set to weather (line 10).

```
// Fig. 18.18: map.as
// Handle the map functions for the Weather application
import mx.managers.CursorManager;
import com.yahoo.webapis.maps.methodgroups.*;
import mx.controls.Alert;

// define constants
private const swfDomID : String = "weather";
private const UUID : int = Math.random() * 10000;

// YahooAPIKey string must be your own from developer.yahoo.com
private const YahooAPIKey : String = "Your Yahoo API Key Here";
private const mapURL : String = "as2map.swf";
private var mapController : MapController;

private function initMap() : void
{
   CursorManager.setBusyCursor(); // turn on busy cursor

   // wait for map to load, then call onMapLoaded method
   yahooMap.addEventListener( 'onMapLoad', onMapLoaded );
   yahooMap.addEventListener( 'onMapError', onMapError );
} // end function initMap

// handle map after it has loaded
public function onMapLoaded( event : Object ) : void
{
   // instantiate map controller
   mapController = new MapController( yahooMap );

   // instantiate panTool method
   var panTools : PanTool = new PanTool( yahooMap );

   // allow user to pan across the map
   panTools.setPanTool( true );

   // instantiate the maps widget class
   var widgets : Widgets = new Widgets( yahooMap );

   // activate Navigator widget
   widgets.showNavigatorWidget();

   // activate map-type selection widget
   widgets.showSatelliteControlWidget();

   // turn off busy cursor
   CursorManager.removeBusyCursor();
} // end function onMapLoaded

public function onMapError( errorCode:String, httpStatus:String ) : void
{
   Alert.show(errorCode + '\n' + httpStatus, 'Map Load Error');
} // end function onMapError
```

Fig. 18.18 | Handle the map functions for the Weather application.

18.6 Customizing Your User Interface

Flex allows you to customize the style of your user interface. Just as in XHTML, you can include the styles inline, put them in a separate style section, or place them in a separate style-sheet file. The syntax is similar to that of CSS, but the names of the properties are different when used inline. Here, we add a style section and an inline style to our `coverViewer` application (Fig. 18.19). You can try this application at `test.deitel.com/examples/iw3htp4/flex/coverViewerStyles/`.

The first change we make is to add a **`Style` element** (lines 7–15). Inside the `Style` element is a format virtually identical to CSS (Chapter 5). We first give all `LinkButton` and `HorizontalList` elements custom styles, by setting the font family, size and color. We specify a custom style by using a dot before the style name, `customStyle`. We can then apply that style to any eligible element by adding a `styleName = "customStyle"` attribute, as we do in line 101. Finally, we can specify a style inline as we do for the `Panel` element (lines 74–76). Some of the names of the inline style attributes are different from those in the `Style` element and in CSS, using a camel-case naming convention instead of hyphenation (e.g. `font-family` becomes `fontFamily`).

```
1  <?xml version = "1.0" encoding = "utf-8" ?>
2  <!-- Fig. 18.19: coverViewerStyles.mxml -->
3  <!-- Using a Style element and inline styles -->
4  <mx:Application xmlns:mx = "http://www.adobe.com/2006/mxml">
5
6     <!-- define styles for application -->
7     <mx:Style>
8        LinkButton     { font-family: "Helvetica, sans-serif";
9                         font-size: 14 }
10       HorizontalList { font-size: 12;
11                        color: black }
12       .customStyle   { font-size: 16;
13                        font-weight: bold;
14                        color: black }
15    </mx:Style>
16
17    <!-- ActionScript goes in this section -->
18    <mx:Script>
19       <![CDATA[
20          // import the Cubic easing function for state transitions
21          import mx.effects.easing.Cubic;
22       ]]>
23    </mx:Script>
24
25    <!-- an array of images -->
26    <mx:ArrayCollection id = "bookCovers">
27       <!-- each image has a name and source attribute -->
28       <mx:Object name = "C How to Program" source = "chtp5.jpg" />
29       <mx:Object name = "C++ How to Program" source = "cpphtp6.jpg" />
30       <mx:Object name = "Internet How to Program"
31          source = "iw3htp4.jpg" />
32       <mx:Object name = "Java How to Program" source = "jhtp7.jpg" />
```

Fig. 18.19 | Using a `Style` element and inline styles. (Part 1 of 4.)

```
      <mx:Object name = "VB How to Program" source = "vbhtp3.jpg" />
      <mx:Object name = "Visual C# How to Program"
         source = "vcsharphtp2.jpg" />
      <mx:Object name = "Simply C++" source = "simplycpp.jpg" />
      <mx:Object name = "Simply VB 2005" source = "simplyvb2005.jpg" />
      <mx:Object name = "Simply Java" source = "simplyjava.jpg" />
      <mx:Object name = "Small C++ How to Program"
         source = "smallcpphtp5.jpg" />
      <mx:Object name = "Small Java" source = "smalljavahtp6.jpg" />
   </mx:ArrayCollection>

   <!-- define the application's states -->
   <mx:states>
      <mx:State name = "HideThumbnails">
         <mx:RemoveChild target = "{ thumbnailList }" />

         <!-- switch the showHideButton to hide -->
         <mx:SetEventHandler target = "{ showHideButton }" name = "click"
            handler = "currentState = ''" />
      </mx:State>
   </mx:states>

   <!-- define the transition effect for application state changes -->
   <mx:transitions>
      <mx:Transition>
            <mx:Resize
               targets = "{ [ thumbnailList, viewPanel, largeImage ] }"
               duration = "750" easingFunction = "Cubic.easeOut" />
      </mx:Transition>
   </mx:transitions>

   <!-- bind the source of largeImage to the selected thumbnail -->
   <mx:Binding
      source = "'fullsize/' +
         bookCovers.getItemAt( selectCoverSlider.value ).source"
      destination = "largeImage.source" />
   <mx:Binding source = "'fullsize/' + thumbnailList.selectedItem.source"
      destination = "largeImage.source" />

   <!-- user interface begins here -->
   <mx:Panel id = "viewPanel" title = "Deitel Book Cover Viewer"
      width = "100%" height = "100%" horizontalAlign = "center"
      color = "blue" fontSize = "18" fontFamily = "Helvetica"
      textAlign = "center">

      <mx:HBox height = "100%" width = "100%">
         <mx:VSlider id = "zoomSlider" value = "100" minimum = "0"
            maximum = "100" liveDragging = "true"
            change = "largeImage.percentWidth = zoomSlider.value;
               largeImage.percentHeight = zoomSlider.value;"
            height = "100%" width = "0%"
            labels = "[ '0%', 'Zoom', '100%' ]" />
```

Fig. 18.19 | Using a `Style` element and inline styles. (Part 2 of 4.)

```
      <mx:VBox width = "100%" height = "100%"
         horizontalAlign = "center">

         <!-- We bind the source of this image to the source of -->
         <!-- the selected thumbnail, and center it in the VBox. -->
         <!-- completeEffect tells Flex to fade the image in -->
         <mx:Image id = "largeImage"
            source = ""
            horizontalAlign = "center"
            verticalAlign = "middle"
            width = "100%" height = "100%"
            completeEffect = "Fade" />

         <!-- bind this Label to the name of the selected thumbnail -->
         <!-- also specify a styleName to use the customStyle style -->
         <mx:Label text = "{ thumbnailList.selectedItem.name }"
            styleName = "customStyle" />
      </mx:VBox>
   </mx:HBox>

   <!-- slider can switch between images -->
   <mx:HSlider id = "selectCoverSlider" height = "0%"
         minimum = "0" maximum = "{ bookCovers.length - 1 }"
         showDataTip = "false" snapInterval = "1" tickInterval = "1"
         liveDragging = "true"
         change = "thumbnailList.selectedIndex =
            selectCoverSlider.value;
            thumbnailList.scrollToIndex( selectCoverSlider.value )" />

   <!-- display thumbnails of the images in bookCovers horizontally -->
   <mx:HorizontalList id = "thumbnailList"
      dataProvider = "{ bookCovers }" width = "100%" height = "160"
      selectedIndex = "0"
      change = "selectCoverSlider.value = thumbnailList.selectedIndex">

      <!-- define how each item is displayed -->
      <mx:itemRenderer>
         <mx:Component>
            <mx:VBox width = "140" height = "160"
               horizontalAlign = "center" verticalAlign = "middle"
               verticalScrollPolicy = "off"
               horizontalScrollPolicy = "off" paddingBottom = "20">

               <!-- display a thumbnail of each image -->
               <mx:Image source = "{ 'thumbs/' + data.source }"
                  verticalAlign = "middle" />

               <!-- display the name of each image -->
               <mx:Label text = "{ data.name }" />
            </mx:VBox>
         </mx:Component>
      </mx:itemRenderer>
   </mx:HorizontalList>
```

Fig. 18.19 | Using a `Style` element and inline styles. (Part 3 of 4.)

```

      <!-- this will exist in the bottom border of the Panel -->
      <mx:ControlBar>
         <mx:LinkButton label = "Show/Hide Thumbnails"
            click = "currentState = 'HideThumbnails';"
            id = "showHideButton" />
      </mx:ControlBar>
   </mx:Panel>
</mx:Application>
```

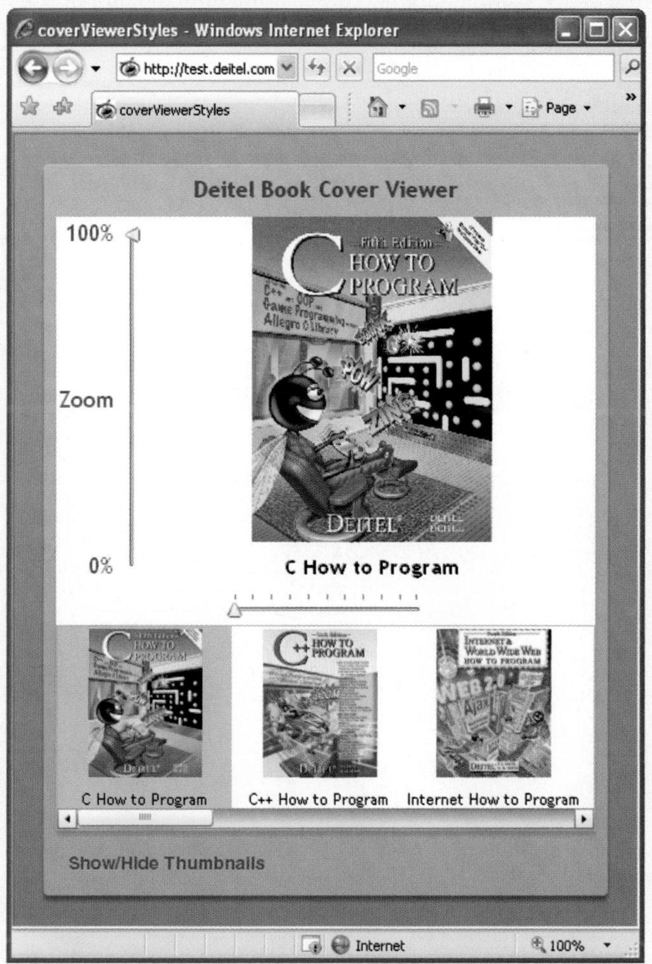

Fig. 18.19 | Using a `Style` element and inline styles. (Part 4 of 4.)

To specify an external style-sheet, which uses syntax identical to the contents of a `Style` element, you simply add a `Style` element with a source attribute pointing to the style-sheet file, as in `<mx:Style source = "styles.css" />`.

A great way to try out different styles is Adobe's Flex Style Explorer, which you can find at `weblogs.macromedia.com/mc/archives/FlexStyleExplorer.html`. This allows you to visually create styles for most Flex user interface elements and generate the CSS you need to apply that style to your application.

Another way to customize the look of your application is through themes. The default theme of Flex applications is Halo. Other themes available with the Flex 2 SDK are Halo Classic (the former default), Ice, Institutional, Smoke and Wooden. All of these are defined in CSS files, but some of them also reference outside images and SWF files. These theme files can be found in `flex_sdk_2/frameworks/themes/`. You can specify that you want your application to use any of these themes at compile time by adding a `theme` parameter to the `mxmlc` command. Fig. 18.20 shows how to compile `coverViewer.mxml` with the `ice.css` theme. You can see how it looks in Fig. 18.21.

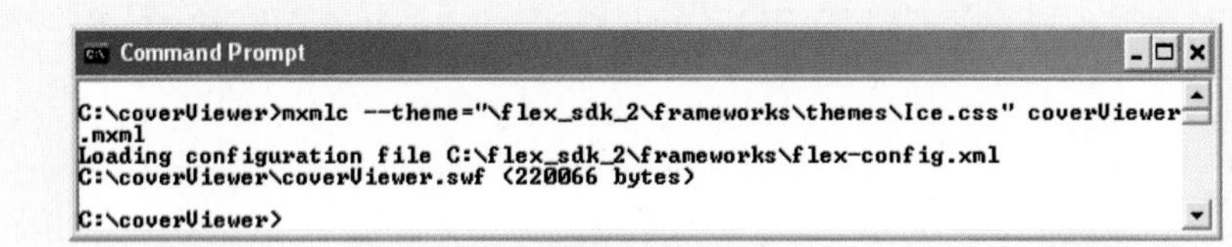

Fig. 18.20 | Running `mxmlc` with the `theme` parameter in Windows XP **Command Prompt**.

Fig. 18.21 | Deitel Cover Viewer compiled with the Ice theme.

18.7 Creating Charts and Graphs

To use Flex's charting components, you must first install Flex Charting. A trial version is available at `www.adobe.com/go/tryflex`. Installation instructions are available at `www.adobe.com/support/documentation/en/flex/2/install.html#installingcharts`.

To demonstrate Flex's charting capabilities, we've added a **Chart View** section to our `weather` application (Fig. 18.22) and populated it with two charts. The first is a `LineChart` that separately plots the high and low temperatures against the date. The user can mouse over any point of data and a data tip will tell the user whether it is a high or low temperature, the date and the temperature. The second chart is a `CandlestickChart`, displaying the range of temperatures for each day. This element also uses data tips to show greater detail. You can test a live version of this application at `test.deitel.com/examples/iw3htp4/flex/weatherChart/`.

A chart is just another type of user interface element. In addition to the chart types mentioned in Section 18.2, a full list of charting components is available from Adobe at `livedocs.adobe.com/flex/201/html/charts_intro_108_03.html`.

Figure 18.23 is a listing of the weather application with charting capabilities added. The first change we make in the code is to create an `ArrayCollection` to make our weather data available to a chart. To do this, we add the code `[Bindable] public var weatherArray : ArrayCollection;` in lines 31–32. We want it to be `Bindable` so that whenever the `ArrayCollection` is changed, the chart updates automatically. Next, we add lines 47 and 70 to create text showing the place name in the **Chart View** that acts just like the text in our **Forecast View**. We also add line 182 to animate changes in a chart's data.

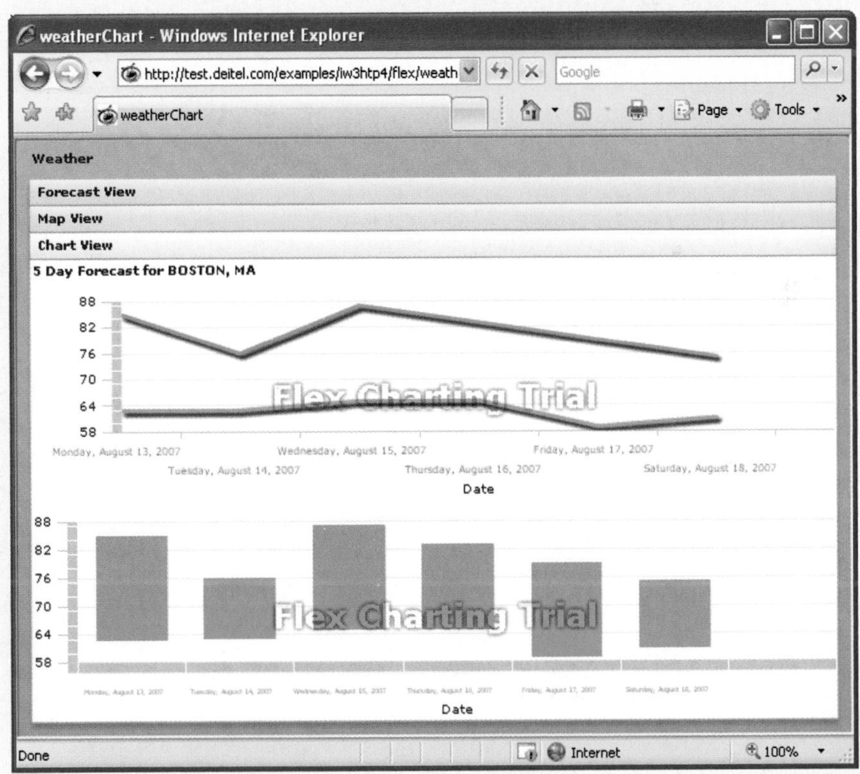

Fig. 18.22 | **Chart View** showing Boston, MA, forecast.

```
<?xml version = "1.0" encoding = "utf-8" ?>
<!-- Fig. 18.23: weatherChart.mxml -->
<!-- Charting weather data in Flex 2 -->
<mx:Application xmlns:mx = "http://www.adobe.com/2006/mxml"
   layout = "absolute"
   xmlns = "*" xmlns:yahoo = "com.yahoo.webapis.maps.*"
   creationComplete = "initMap();" >

   <mx:Script source = "map.as" />

   <mx:Script>
   <![CDATA[
      import mx.controls.dataGridClasses.DataGridColumn;
      import mx.rpc.events.ResultEvent;
      import mx.managers.CursorManager;
      import mx.controls.Alert;
      import mx.collections.ArrayCollection;
      import flash.events.MouseEvent;

      // define default namespace so we don't have to write it every time
      default xml namespace = "http://www.webservicex.net";

      [Bindable]
      private var xmlData : XML;
      [Bindable]
      private var highLowTemp : String;
      [Bindable]
      private var fiveDayForecast : String = "";
      [Bindable]
      public var weatherArray : ArrayCollection;
      [Bindable]
      private var placeName : String;

      // handle getWeatherButton click action
      private function getWeather() : void
      {
         // disable button while request is pending
         getWeatherButton.enabled = false;

         // hide the old forecast data before displaying new data
         forecastBox.visible = false;

         // reset place name while loading new data
         placeNameText.text = "";

         // reset place name while loading new data
         placeNameChartText.text = "";

         // show the loading progress bar
         loadingBar.visible = true;

```

Fig. 18.23 | Charting weather data in Flex 2. (Part 1 of 6.)

```
         // request the new data
         weatherService.GetWeatherByZipCode.send();
      } // end function getWeather

      private function weatherResultHandler(event : ResultEvent) : void
      {
         // save the result of the web service as XML
         xmlData = XML( event.result );

         // check that result is valid by checking length of StateCode
         if ( xmlData.GetWeatherByZipCodeResult[ 0 ].
            StateCode.text().length() != 0 )
         {
            // set placeNameText to the city and state of the zip code
            placeName = xmlData.GetWeatherByZipCodeResult[ 0 ].
               PlaceName.text() + ", " +
               xmlData.GetWeatherByZipCodeResult[ 0 ].StateCode.text();
            placeNameText.text = "5 Day Forecast for " + placeName;
            placeNameChartText.text = "5 Day Forecast for " + placeName;

            // set image, temperature and date for each day
            setData( weatherImage0, weatherTemp0, weatherDay0, 0 );
            setData( weatherImage1, weatherTemp1, weatherDay1, 1 );
            setData( weatherImage2, weatherTemp2, weatherDay2, 2 );
            setData( weatherImage3, weatherTemp3, weatherDay3, 3 );
            setData( weatherImage4, weatherTemp4, weatherDay4, 4 );

            forecastBox.visible = true;

            // save today's high/low as a string
            highLowTemp =  xmlData.GetWeatherByZipCodeResult.
               Details.WeatherData.MaxTemperatureF[ 0 ].text() +
               "/" + xmlData.GetWeatherByZipCodeResult.Details.
               WeatherData.MinTemperatureF[ 0 ].text();

            // save the five-day forecast as a string
            fiveDayForecast = highLowTemp;

            for ( var i : int = 1; i < 5; i++ )
            {
               fiveDayForecast += ", " + xmlData.
                  GetWeatherByZipCodeResult.Details.WeatherData.
                     MaxTemperatureF[ i ].text() + "/" + xmlData.
                     GetWeatherByZipCodeResult.Details.
                     WeatherData.MinTemperatureF[ i ].text();
            } // end for

            // place a marker on the map with the forecast
            mapController.addCustomPOIMarker(
               zipcode.text, placeName, highLowTemp, fiveDayForecast,
               0x990099, 0xFFFFFF);

```

Fig. 18.23 | Charting weather data in Flex 2. (Part 2 of 6.)

```
            mapController.setCenterByAddressAndZoom(
               zipcode.text, 7, 0 );

            // begin charting functionality

            // saves date, high and low temp into an ArrayCollection
            // so it can act as a chart's dataProvider
            weatherArray = new ArrayCollection( );

            for ( var j : int = 0; j < weatherService.GetWeatherByZipCode.
               lastResult.GetWeatherByZipCodeResult.Details.
               WeatherData.length(); j++ )
            {
               // create the object to be added to the array
               var weatherDataObject : Object = new Object();

               // extract the data from the e4x-formatted result
               weatherDataObject.Date =  weatherService.
                  GetWeatherByZipCode.lastResult.
                  GetWeatherByZipCodeResult.Details.WeatherData[ j ].Day;
               weatherDataObject.HighTemp = weatherService.
                  GetWeatherByZipCode.lastResult.
                  GetWeatherByZipCodeResult.Details.
                  WeatherData[ j ].MaxTemperatureF;
               weatherDataObject.LowTemp = weatherService.
                  GetWeatherByZipCode.lastResult.
                  GetWeatherByZipCodeResult.Details.
                  WeatherData[ j ].MinTemperatureF;

               // add the object to the array
               weatherArray.addItem( weatherDataObject );
            } //end for
         // end charting functionality
         }
         else
         {
            Alert.show( "Invalid zip code" );
         }
         // hide the loading progress bar
         loadingBar.visible = false;

         // enable getWeatherButton
         getWeatherButton.enabled = true;
      } // end function weatherResultHandler

      private function setData( forecastImage : Image,
         tempText : Text, dateText : Text, i : int ) : void
      {
         // set the image for each day
         forecastImage.source = xmlData.GetWeatherByZipCodeResult.
            Details.WeatherData.WeatherImage[ i ].text();

```

Fig. 18.23 | Charting weather data in Flex 2. (Part 3 of 6.)

```
         // set the temperature for each day
         tempText.text = xmlData.GetWeatherByZipCodeResult.
            Details.WeatherData.MaxTemperatureF[ i ].text() +
            "\n" + xmlData.GetWeatherByZipCodeResult.Details.
            WeatherData.MinTemperatureF[ i ].text();

         // set the date for each day
         dateText.text = xmlData.GetWeatherByZipCodeResult.
            Details.WeatherData.Day[ i ].text();
      }
   ]]>
   </mx:Script>

   <!-- show/hide animations for forecast boxes -->
   <mx:Parallel id = "forecastAnimationIn">
      <mx:Fade duration = "1000" alphaFrom = "0.0" alphaTo = "1.0" />
      <mx:Zoom zoomWidthTo = "1" zoomHeightTo = "1" zoomWidthFrom = "0"
         zoomHeightFrom = "0" />
   </mx:Parallel>

   <mx:Parallel id = "forecastAnimationOut">
      <mx:Fade duration = "500" alphaFrom = "1.0" alphaTo = "0.0" />
      <mx:Zoom zoomWidthTo = "0" zoomHeightTo = "0" zoomWidthFrom = "1"
         zoomHeightFrom = "1" />
   </mx:Parallel>

   <mx:SeriesInterpolate id = "interpolateEffect" duration = "1000" />

   <!-- WebService description -->
   <mx:WebService id = "weatherService"
      wsdl = "http://www.webservicex.net/WeatherForecast.asmx?WSDL"
      fault = "Alert.show( event.fault.faultString )"
      result = "weatherResultHandler( event )"
      showBusyCursor = "true">
      <mx:operation name = "GetWeatherByZipCode" resultFormat = "e4x">
         <mx:request>
            <ZipCode>{ zipcode.text }</ZipCode>
         </mx:request>
      </mx:operation>
   </mx:WebService>

   <!-- user interface begins here -->
   <mx:Panel title = "Weather" width = "100%" height = "100%">
      <mx:Accordion id = "accordion" width = "100%" height = "100%"
         creationPolicy = "all">
         <mx:VBox label = "Forecast View" width = "100%" height = "100%">
            <mx:ApplicationControlBar
               defaultButton = "{ getWeatherButton }">
               <mx:Label width = "100%"
                  text = "Enter a zip code:" />
               <mx:TextInput id = "zipcode" left = "10" />
               <mx:Button id = "getWeatherButton" label = "Get Weather"
                  click = "getWeather()" left = "10" />
```

Fig. 18.23 | Charting weather data in Flex 2. (Part 4 of 6.)

```
         </mx:ApplicationControlBar>

         <mx:Text fontWeight = "bold" id = "placeNameText" />
         <mx:ProgressBar id = "loadingBar" indeterminate = "true"
            labelPlacement = "bottom" visible = "false" minimum = "0"
            maximum = "100" label = "Loading Weather Data"
            direction = "right" width = "75%" />

         <!-- forecastBox holds the five-day forecast -->
         <!-- start off as hidden, define show and hide effects -->
         <mx:HBox id = "forecastBox" width = "100%" height = "100%"
            visible = "false" showEffect = "{ forecastAnimationIn }"
            hideEffect = "{ forecastAnimationOut }">
            <mx:VBox id = "forecastBox0" horizontalAlign = "center"
               borderStyle = "solid" width = "20%" height = "0%">
               <mx:Text id = "weatherDay0" />
               <mx:Image id = "weatherImage0" />
               <mx:Text id = "weatherTemp0" />
            </mx:VBox>

            <mx:VBox horizontalAlign = "center"
               borderStyle = "solid" width = "20%">
               <mx:Text id = "weatherDay1" />
               <mx:Image id = "weatherImage1" />
               <mx:Text id = "weatherTemp1" />
            </mx:VBox>

            <mx:VBox horizontalAlign = "center"
               borderStyle = "solid" width = "20%">
               <mx:Text id = "weatherDay2" />
               <mx:Image id = "weatherImage2" />
               <mx:Text id = "weatherTemp2" />
            </mx:VBox>

            <mx:VBox horizontalAlign = "center"
               borderStyle = "solid" width = "20%">
               <mx:Text id = "weatherDay3" />
               <mx:Image id = "weatherImage3" />
               <mx:Text id = "weatherTemp3" />
            </mx:VBox>

            <mx:VBox horizontalAlign = "center"
               borderStyle = "solid" width = "20%">
               <mx:Text id = "weatherDay4" />
               <mx:Image id = "weatherImage4" />
               <mx:Text id = "weatherTemp4" />
            </mx:VBox>
         </mx:HBox>
      </mx:VBox>
      <mx:VBox label = "Map View" width = "100%" height = "100%">
         <!-- create Yahoo! Map -->
         <yahoo:YahooMapService id = "yahooMap" UUID = "{ UUID }"
            swfDomId = "{ swfDomID }"
```

Fig. 18.23 | Charting weather data in Flex 2. (Part 5 of 6.)

```
               apiId = "{ YahooAPIKey }"
               mapURL = "{ mapURL }" width = "600" height = "400" />
            <mx:HBox>
               <mx:Button label = "Back"
                  click = "accordion.selectedIndex=0;" />
               <mx:Button label = "Clear"
                  click = "mapController.removeAllMarkers();" />
            </mx:HBox>
         </mx:VBox> <!-- end "Map View" Section -->

         <!-- begin "Chart View" pane -->
         <mx:VBox label = "Chart View" width = "100%" height = "100%">
            <mx:Text fontWeight = "bold" id = "placeNameChartText" />
            <mx:LineChart id = "lineChart" width = "100%" height = "100%"
               dataProvider = "{ weatherArray }" showDataTips = "true">
               <mx:verticalAxis>
                   <mx:LinearAxis baseAtZero = "false" />
               </mx:verticalAxis>
               <mx:horizontalAxis>
                  <mx:CategoryAxis categoryField = "Date"
                     title = "Date" />
               </mx:horizontalAxis>
               <mx:series>
                  <mx:LineSeries yField = "HighTemp"
                     displayName = "High Temp"
                     showDataEffect = "{ interpolateEffect }" />
                  <mx:LineSeries yField = "LowTemp"
                     displayName = "Low Temp"
                     showDataEffect = "{ interpolateEffect }" />
               </mx:series>
            </mx:LineChart>
            <mx:CandlestickChart id = "candlestickChart" width = "100%"
               height = "100%" showDataTips = "true"
               dataProvider = "{ weatherArray }">
               <mx:verticalAxis>
                   <mx:LinearAxis baseAtZero = "false" />
               </mx:verticalAxis>
               <mx:horizontalAxis>
                  <mx:CategoryAxis categoryField = "Date"
                     title = "Date"/>
               </mx:horizontalAxis>
               <mx:series>
                  <mx:CandlestickSeries openField = "HighTemp"
                     highField = "HighTemp" lowField = "LowTemp"
                     closeField = "LowTemp"
                     showDataEffect = "{ interpolateEffect }" />
               </mx:series>
            </mx:CandlestickChart>
         </mx:VBox> <!-- end "Chart View" section -->
      </mx:Accordion>
   </mx:Panel>
</mx:Application>
```

Fig. 18.23 | Charting weather data in Flex 2. (Part 6 of 6.)

Lines 113–135 declare a for statement that iterates over the WeatherData objects returned by the weatherService WebService. Inside the for statement, we create a weatherDataObject and give it the attributes Date, HighTemp, and LowTemp (lines 121–131). We give these attributes values from the XML returned by the web service. Finally, we add each weatherDataObject to weatherArray (line 134).

We also add a new pane in the Accordion for our chart, a VBox called **Chart View** (lines 273–310). This contains a Text element called placeNameChartText (line 274). This element serves an identical purpose to placeNameText (line 211). Next, we add a LineChart element (lines 275–292). This LineChart has the dataProvider attribute set to { weatherArray } to indicate that the data presented in the chart is bound to weatherArray. We also specify that showDataTips is true (line 276), meaning that when the user mouses over a data point on the graph, a data tip will pop up, giving the user more detailed information about that point. Line 278 specifies that the baseAtZero attribute of the verticalAxis' LinearAxis is false. This way, the graph displays the range of temperatures only from lowest to highest, rather than starting at zero. Inside the horizontalAxis element (lines 280–283), we specify one CategoryAxis named Date. The CategoryAxis' categoryField attribute is set to "Date", meaning that the axis receives data from the Date field of weatherArray. Next, we specify LineSeries elements, located in the series element (lines 284–291). The first LineSeries' yField attribute is set to "HighTemp", which means that the LineSeries gets its data from the HighTemp field of weatherArray. We also set showDataEffect to "{ interpolateEffect }". This calls the interpolateEffect SeriesEffect that we created every time the data is updated. We also create a second LineSeries displaying LowTemp from weatherArray, using the same effect.

The second chart is a CandlestickChart (lines 293–309). This chart also sets showDataTips to "true" and uses the same dataProvider (weatherArray). It also sets the verticalAxis' baseAtZero attribute to "false" and has a horizontalAxis that displays the Date. In the CandlestickChart's series element (lines 303–307) is a CandlestickSeries with several attributes. The four attributes that define the data it displays are openField, highField, lowField and closeField. A CandlestickChart is designed to display financial data, such as stock prices. Therefore, it requires a start value and end value in addition to a high and low value. Since we have only high and low data for the weather, we place HighTemp in both openField and highField. Similarly, we place LowTemp in both closeField and lowField. We use interpolateEffect as the showDataEffect. Finally, the swfDomID constant in map.as must point to the filename of our application without .swf (in this case, weatherChart).

18.8 Connection-Independent RIAs on the Desktop: Adobe Integrated Runtime (AIR)

The Adobe Integrated Runtime (AIR) allows developers to deploy Ajax, Flash and Flex web applications to the desktop. It requires the user to download and install the runtime (planned to be between 5 and 9 MB). Once installed, the user can download and run AIR applications as if they were native desktop applications, including running them while disconnected from the server. This ability to function while disconnected is similar to that of Google's Gears.[5]

5. Information on Google Gears can be found at code.google.com/apis/gears/.

AIR (as of the Beta version) supports Mac OS X 10.4.8 and up, Windows XP with Service Pack 2 (SP2) and Windows Vista. Adobe plans to add Linux support "shortly after the 1.0. release".[6] AIR uses Flash Player 9 as well as the the open source WebKit HTML rendering and JavaScript engine (also found in Apple's Safari and KDE's Konqueror browsers).

AIR provides an API for file input and output, a SQLite embedded database, windowing support, and file-type association (so that you can make it the operating system's default application for a type of document). It is also planned to support native menus (the Beta version supports this for Mac OS X), and contextual (right click) menus.

Adobe's AIR web page is currently located at `labs.adobe.com/technologies/air/`. From there, you will find links to learn more about AIR, download the runtime environment, download the SDK, and try sample applications.

18.9 Flex 3 Beta

At the time of publication, Flex 3 was in beta. The Flex 3 beta homepage is `labs.adobe.com/technologies/flex/`. The final version of Flex 3 is planned to be released in Q4 2007[7]. You can download the Flex SDK beta from `labs.adobe.com/technologies/flex/sdk/flex3sdk.html`. Install instructions are available at `labs.adobe.com/wiki/index.php/Flex_3:Release_Notes#Installation_Instructions`.

An introduction to the features planned for Flex 3 is available at `labs.adobe.com/wiki/index.php/Flex_3:Feature_Introductions`. Flex Builder 3, for instance, will add a wizard to easily consume web services, improve the user interface designer, and also add support for AIR development. Some of the new features are discussed at `www.adobe.com/devnet/flex/articles/flex3_whatsnew.html`.

18.10 Wrap-Up

In this chapter, you learned how to describe Flex applications using MXML, how to compile them, and how to embed them in web pages. You also learned how to use ActionScript 3 to manipulate data and programatically control the user interface. Finally, you learned how to consume web services in Flex and present data from those web services in a visual and interactive manner. In the next chapter, you'll learn about Microsoft's new RIA technology—Silverlight.

18.11 Web Resources

`www.deitel.com/flex`
The Deitel Flex Resource Center contains many resources, downloads, tutorials, documentation, books, e-books, articles, blogs and more that will help you develop Flex applications. The Deitel Flex Resource Center will provide you resources to allow you to pursue more advanced Flex programming.

---

6. From `labs.adobe.com/wiki/index.php/AIR:Developer_FAQ`.
7. From `flexwiki.adobe.com/confluence/display/ADOBE/Flex+3+Planning`.

Summary

Section 18.1 Introduction

- Flex uses Adobe's ubiquitous Flash platform to deliver a rich graphical user interface backed by ActionScript 3, Adobe's implementation of ECMAScript 4 (better known as JavaScript 2).
- The term Rich Internet Application (RIA) was coined in 2001 by Macromedia, the creator of Flash and Flex.
- Flash has the advantage of a large installed base. This allows applications developed in Flex to be used on most Windows, Mac and Linux computers.
- Because the Flash engine is virtually equivalent no matter what the browser or platform, Flex developers avoid having to deal with the cross-platform conflicts of Ajax and even Java.
- Flex user interfaces are easily described using the MXML markup language.
- MXML is compiled into Flash's executable SWF format.

Section 18.2 Flex Platform Overview

- Flash 9 provides the ActionScript Virtual Machine and graphical capabilities that allow Flex applications to run.
- Flex's user interface elements are much richer and more consistent than those of HTML and AJAX, because they're rendered by the Flash player the same way on all platforms.
- The Flex development environment is programming-centric in contrast to the animation-centric Flash development environment.
- In addition to describing user interfaces, MXML allows for the description of web services, data objects, visual effects and more.
- The root element of every MXML application is `<mx:Application>`, inside which all Flex elements reside.
- The Flex SDK available at `www.adobe.com/products/flex/downloads/` includes an MXML compiler and debugger, the Flex framework, and user interface components and some templates and examples.
- ActionScript 3 is Adobe's object-oriented scripting language, forming the basis of Flash 9 and the associated Flex 2 technology.
- ActionScript 3 uses an asynchronous programming model. This means that the program will continue to execute while another operation is being completed, such as a call to a web service. This ensures that the user interface is responsive even while the application is busy processing data, an important feature of Ajax.
- In many cases, you'll need to take advantage of event handling and data binding to handle asynchronous operations.
- Flex Builder is Adobe's graphical IDE for Flex applications.
- Adobe LiveCycle Data Services ES, formerly Flex Data Services, extends Flex's built-in messaging to enable data push and synchronization. It also gives Flex applications the ability to handle disconnection from the server and synchronizing of data upon reconnection.
- Flex Charting provides an extensible library of plotting and graphing elements, including pie charts, line graphs, bar graphs, bubble charts and plots, as well as visually stunning animations that can present the user with a dynamic representation of data.

Section 18.3 Creating a Simple User Interface

- The first line of an MXML file declares the document to be an XML document, because MXML is a type of XML.

- The mx namespace is commonly used for the Flex elements in an MXML document.
- The VSlider element provides a vertically oriented slider user interface element.
- The HSlider is the horizontal equivalent of the VSlider.
- The value attribute of a slider sets its initial value.
- The minimum and maximum attributes set the range of values you can select with a slider.
- The change attribute specifies ActionScript to execute whenever the user changes a slider's value.
- A slider's liveDragging = "true" attribute causes the ActionScript in the change attribute to execute when the user changes the slider value, even if the user is still clicking the slider.
- The labels attribute of a slider places text next to itself.
- The showDataTip attribute allows you to turn off the tool tip showing the current value of the slider while the user is dragging it.
- The snapInterval attribute specifies the possible increment in values.
- The tickInterval attribute specifies at what intervals tick marks are displayed.
- The Image element has attributes specifying the source URL, as well as size and positioning.
- The Image element's completeEffect attribute specifies an effect to apply when an image is loaded.
- The Label element has a text attribute to indicate the string displayed by the Label.
- The Binding element indicate that its destination is bound to its source.
- Curly braces are another way to indicate data binding.
- A HorizontalList takes an array of items from a dataProvider and displays them in a horizontal configuration. A HorizontalList has attribute selectedIndex and scrollToIndex. Each of the items in the horizontalList is selectable.
- An ArrayCollection provides methods for manipulating an Array.
- A HorizontalList can contain an inline itemRenderer.
- An itemRenderer gives you complete control over the contents of each item in a list.
- Keyword data refers to the corresponding item from the dataProvider of the HorizonalList. We must use the keyword data because everything inside the Component element is located in a new, separate scope, meaning that it cannot access the variables of the enclosing program.
- Flex applications are converted from MXML into ActionScript, which is then compiled and output as SWF files using the mxmlc command-line compiler, included in the Flex SDK.
- You can see a list of the compiler's runtime parameters by executing mxmlc -help.
- The most basic syntax of the mxmlc command is mxmlc *filename*.
- You can embed images into an SWF file to make it more portable. To do so, enclose the source attribute inside an @Embed, as in source = "@Embed('image.jpg')". This tells the compiler to include the image in the SWF file, which results in a program that not only loads faster, but also is less dependent on external resources, since the SWF includes all resources it needs.
- Because Flex applications run using the Flash Player, they can be embedded into a web page, then run with the Flash Player browser plug-in.
- The Flex SDK install includes a folder of HTML templates for embedding your application in the resources directory.
- Application states give you the ability to change the layout of an application on the fly.
- An application's states are defined inside a states element. Each state is enclosed in a State element, with a name attribute that is used as the identifier for the State. The current state is set by changing the currentState property, as in currentState = "HideThumbnails".

- The State element allows you to add elements via the AddChild element, remove elements via the RemoveChild element, modify elements' properties via the SetProperty element, set style via the SetStyle element, and set event handlers via the SetEventHandler element.
- Whenever a State is activated, the ActionScript in the SetEventHandler element executes.
- A ControlBar element embeds its nested elements into the bottom border of a Panel.
- State transition effects are enclosed in a transitions element.
- For each Transition, you can specify a fromState and toState, using the State's name.
- Each effect, such as Resize, has a targets attribute that specifies which elements it applies to.
- An effect has a duration attribute, which defines how long the effect will last in milliseconds.
- An effect has an optional easingFunction attribute. One possible value is the Cubic.easeOut function, which controls the acceleration of the animation.

Section 18.4 Accessing XML Data from Your Application

- Flex can access XML natively, using the E4X (ECMAScript for XML) standard.
- An Accordion element instantiates a new navigation user interface, in which multiple containers can be placed, providing easy navigation between them.
- An Accordion with the attribute creationPolicy = "all" forces the Flash player to load all components, even those that are not initially visible to the user.
- The TextInput element uses the change attribute to specify ActionScript to execute whenever a change is made to the field, such as adding or removing characters.
- The DataGrid element has a dataProvider attribute, which defines what data will fill the rows and columns. The object defined as the dataProvider is located within curly brackets so that any changes to the data object will be written back to the grid.
- The DataGrid has a change attribute that calls ActionScript whenever the user clicks a different item in the grid.
- In a DataGrid, each column is defined using a DataGridColumn element. All DataGridColumns reside in a parent columns element. Each DataGridColumn has a dataField attribute that tells the element which data it should display, and a headerText attribute that defines the text in the column header.
- The Button element has a click attribute that defines the ActionScript code that will be executed when the user clicks the Button.
- Function Alert displays a dialog box and has attributes text, title, flags (specifies which buttons should appear), parent, and closeHandler.
- The Form element groups elements, such as TextInputs and Buttons, into a single entity that aligns the elements and allows you to specify a defaultButton.
- Each element in a Form resides in a FormItem element, which has a required attribute that specifies whether the item is required. If true, Flex displays a red asterisk next to the item.
- Validators check the contents of a TextInput element to make sure that the user entered data correctly.
- Flex provides preconfigured validators for Strings, zip codes, e-mail addresses, phone numbers, and more.
- The validator element's source attribute specifies which object is to be validated. The required attribute specifies whether the user is required to fill in data. The trigger attribute determines which object to listen to. The triggerEvent attribute specifies which event to listen for. The valid attribute specifies what happens if the triggerEvent is triggered and the data is valid.

- You can reference external ActionScript by using a `Script` element with a `source` attribute set to the path of the `.as` file.
- The `HTTPService` downloads a `url` using the HTTP protocol. The `send` operation of an `HTTPService` executes a request to the service, and can include parameters if the service requires them.
- The `creationComplete` attribute of the `Application` element executes ActionScript when the Flash Player has finished creating the interface components.
- An `HTTPService`'s `invoke` attribute specifies a function to call when the `HTTPService` is first invoked.
- An `HTTPService`'s `result` attribute specifies a function to call when the `HTTPService` has completed retrieving the `url`.
- An `HTTPService`'s `fault` attribute specifies a function to call if an error occured while the `HTTPService` was retrieving the `url`.
- An `arrayCollection`'s `filterFunction` is handed each item of the `arrayCollection` and returns `true` if the item matches the search criteria, and `false` otherwise.
- The `URLRequest` object contains a URL that can be opened using the function `navigateToURL`, which also specifies where to open the URL.

Section 18.5 Interacting with Server-Side Applications

- A container can have attributes `showEffect` and `hideEffect` that specify which animations to use when the element is shown or hidden.
- The `Parallel` element groups effects, such as `Fade` and `Zoom`.
- The `WebService` element specifies the URL of the Web Services Description Language (WSDL) file for a web service. A WSDL file is an XML file describing what services are available on a server, how to consume those services, what parameters they accept and what they return. Flex uses a WSDL file to make it easy to access the services, without needing further configuration.
- Like an `HTTPService`, a `WebService` element allows us to specify an `invoke`, `fault`, and `result` function.
- We describe a specific web-service method using the `operation` element, which specifies the method name and the desired result format. The `operation` element can enclose specific `request` elements.
- The `CDATA` element tells the MXML compiler not to parse a section as XML in case it contains any reserved characters.
- You can traverse an `XML` object's tree using dot operators.
- The `ProgressBar` element allows you to give the user an idea of an operation's state.

Section 18.6 Customizing Your User Interface

- Flex allows you to customize the style of your user interface. Just as in XHTML, you can include the styles inline, put them in a separate style section or place them in a separate style-sheet file.
- We give user interface elements custom styles either by setting attributes such as `fontFamily`, `fontSize`, and `color`, or by applying a custom style to any eligible element by adding a `styleName = "customStyle"` attribute.
- To specify an external style-sheet, which will be identical to the contents of a `Style` element, add a `Style` element with a source attribute pointing to the style-sheet file, as in `<mx:Style source="styles.css"/>`.
- Another way to customize the look of your application is by using themes, found in `flex_sdk_2/frameworks/themes/`.

- You can specify that you want your application to use a different theme at compile time by adding a theme argument to the mxmlc command.

Section 18.7 Creating Charts and Graphs

- A chart is just another type of user interface element.
- The SeriesInterpolate element allows us to animate changes in a chart's data. The duration attribute specifies how long the animation takes in milliseconds.
- We can use a for statement that iterates over the objects in an XML object to fill an ArrayCollection with data from the XML.
- The LineChart element creates a line chart, using data from the object specified by the dataProvider attribute. The showDataTips attribute, if true, displays a tool tip giving the user more detailed information about a point when the user mouses over a data point on the graph.
- The verticalAxis' LinearAxis has a baseAtZero attribute that specifies whether the chart starts at zero.
- The CategoryAxis element of a horizontalAxis or verticalAxis element defines the values located on the axes. The categoryField attribute defines what data object the values come from.
- The LineSeries element, located within the series element, defines a series of data values to chart as a line. The yField and xField attributes define the data source. We can also specify a showDataEffect that calls the effect when the data is changed.
- The CandlestickChart element is designed to display financial data, such as stock prices. Inside the series element of the CandlestickChart, we have a CandlestickSeries with the attributes openField, highField, lowField, closeField and interpolateEffect.

Section 18.8 Connection-Independent RIAs on the Desktop: Adobe Integrated Runtime (AIR)

- AIR (Adobe Integrated Runtime) allows developers to deploy web applications written in Ajax and Flex to the desktop. It requires that the user download and install the runtime.
- The user can download and run AIR applications as if they were native desktop applications, including running them while disconnected from the server.
- Adobe's AIR homepage is currently located at labs.adobe.com/technologies/air/.

Section 18.9 Flex 3 Beta

- An introduction to the features planned for Flex 3 is available at labs.adobe.com/wiki/index.php/Flex_3:Feature_Introductions.

Terminology

Accordion element
ActionScript
ActionScript Virtual Machine
AddChild element
AIR (Adobe Integrated Runtime)
angle brackets
Application
ApplicationControlBar
asynchronous programming model
Bindable
CandlestickChart
CategoryAxis
CDATA
Component
ControlBar
creationComplete attribute
CSS
Cubic.easeOut
data push
DataGrid
dataProvider attribute
E4X (ECMAScript for XML)
ECMAScript 4
Embed

encapsulation
external style-sheet
`Fade`
`filterFunction`
five-day forecast
Flash 9
Flash Player
Flex 3
Flex Builder
Flex Charting
Flex SDK
`Form`
Google Gears
Halo Classic theme
`HBox`
`hideEffect`
`horizontalAxis`
`HorizontalList`
`HSlider`
`HTTPService`
Ice theme
`Image`
Institutional theme
JavaScript 2
Konqueror web browser
`Label`
`LinearAxis`
`LineChart`
`LineSeries`
LiveCycle Data Services ES
Macromedia
`mailto`
`MapController`
`mx` namespace
MXML markup language
`mxmlc`
`navigateToURL`
open source
`operation`
`Panel`
`PanTool`
`Parallel`
`Path` system variable
polling
polymorphism
`ProgressBar`
`Resize`
RIAs (Rich Internet Applications)
Safari web browser
`Script`
`series`
`SeriesEffect`
`showEffect`
Smoke theme
`Spacer`
SQLite database
`State`
`states`
`Style`
SWF (Shockwave Flash) File
synchronization
temperature
`TextInput`
`theme`
`Transition`
`transitions`
`URLRequest`
`VBox`
`verticalAxis`
`VSlider`
web services
WebKit rendering engine
`WebServiceX.net`
Wooden theme
WSDL (Web Services Description Language)
Yahoo! Map
Yahoo! Maps API
`YahooMapService`
`Zoom`

Self-Review Exercises

18.1 Fill in the blanks in each of the following statements:

a) _______ braces indicate data binding.
b) _______ is the prefix commonly used to specify the XML namespace of Flex elements.
c) The _______ tag is the root tag of an MXML application.
d) A(n) _______ element defines the contents of a `HorizontalList`.
e) You can change an `Application`'s current `State` using the _______ property.
f) The `Application` tag's _______ attribute specifies ActionScript to execute when the user interface has finished loading.

g) The content of a `DataGrid` comes from its _______.
h) An `arrayCollection`'s _______ allows you to implement a search feature.
i) _______ are used to make sure that the user's input is in the correct format.
j) The _______ tag allows you to define a group of effects that occur simultaneously.
k) You can modify an application's look and feel in a CSS-like syntax in the _______ tag.
l) A(n) _______ allows you to chart data points with opening, closing, high and low values.

18.2 State whether each of the following is *true* or *false*. If *false*, explain why.
a) Flex applications can run only on Windows.
b) The Flex SDK is available for free.
c) ActionScript 3 executes synchronously.
d) Flex 2 applications need the Flash Player 9 to run.
e) `Buttons` can execute ActionScript when clicked using the `onClick` attribute.

Answers to Self-Review Exercises

18.1 a) Curly ({ }). b) `mx`. c) `Application`. d) `itemRenderer`. e) `currentState` f) `creationComplete`. g) `dataProvider`. h) `filterFunction`. i) Validators. j) `Parallel`. k) `Style`. l) `CandlestickChart`.

18.2 a) False. Flex applications can run on Mac OS X, Windows and Linux.
b) True.
c) False. ActionScript 3 is executed in an asynchronous manner.
d) True.
e) False. ActionScript in the `click` attribute is executed when the user clicks a button.

Exercises

18.3 For the `coverViewer` application, add effects to the `itemRenderer` of the thumbnail images so that the image zooms in when you roll over it (`rollOverEffect`) using the `Zoom` effect, zooms back out when you roll back out (`rollOutEffect`) using the `Zoom` effect, and glows red when you click it (`mouseDownEffect`) using the `Glow` effect. Learn how to configure these effects by referring to Adobe's Flex 2 Language Reference at `livedocs.adobe.com/flex/201/langref/mx/effects/Zoom.html` and `livedocs.adobe.com/flex/201/langref/mx/effects/Glow.html`. [The effects must be defined locally in the `itemRenderer`, inside the `VBox`.] An example of how your solution may look is available at `test.deitel.com/examples/iw3htp4/flex/coverViewerExercise/`.

18.4 Combine the XML handling techniques of the `addressBook` example with the `coverViewer` example to display the 20 most recent photos from Flickr's Public RSS feed. See `www.flickr.com/services/feeds/docs/photos_public/` for information on how to use the RSS feed, and Chapter 14 for more information on XML in general. The application should show thumbnails of the images at the bottom, as well as a large version of the selected image. You must set the width and height of the thumbnails to fit in the thumbnails bar. The thumbnails should be labeled with the image's title, and the large image should be accompanied by the image's title and author. Include a button that refreshes the RSS feed and loads the most recent images. You may find it beneficial to use an `ArrayCollection` similar to that in the `weatherChart` example (Fig. 18.23) to store each image's source and title. One feature you may want to include is the ability for the user to search for specific tags. By adding `?tags=`*stringOfTags* to the end of the RSS URL, where *stringOfTags* is replaced by your own string, the RSS feed will return only images containing those tags. Other features you may want to include are the abilities for the user to chose how many photos to display and to click the author's name to open the Flickr homepage. An example of how your solution may look is available at `test.deitel.com/examples/iw3htp4/flex/flickrPhotoViewerExercise/`.

18.5 Add a cellphone number field to the addressBook application. [*Hint:* You must add the field in contacts.xml, then modify buttonActions.as, search.as and the DataGrid and **Edit Contact** form in addressBook.mxml.] An example of how your solution may look is available at our web site test.deitel.com/examples/iw3htp4/flex/addressBookExercise/.

18.6 Create a currency-converter application using the web service at www.webservicex.net/CurrencyConvertor.asmx. The application should let you select a currency. You can base your application on the weather example. Use the web service's ConversionRate operation, sending it FromCurrency and ToCurrency from the list in the web service's description. One important change you must make from the weather example is that the XML namespace must be the URI http://www.webserviceX.NET/ instead of http://www.webserviceX.net/. See how your solution may look at test.deitel.com/examples/iw3htp4/flex/currencyConverterExercise/.

19

Microsoft® Silverlight™ and Rich Internet Applications

Had I the heavens' embroidered cloths, Enwrought with gold and silver light.
—William Butler

This world is but a canvas to our imaginations.
—Henry David Thoreau

Something deeply hidden had to be behind things.
—Albert Einstein

Individuality of expression is the beginning and end of all art.
—Johann Wolfgang von Goethe

The path of duty lies in what is near, and man seeks for it in what is remote.
—Mencius

OBJECTIVES

In this chapter you will learn:

- What Silverlight is and what its capabilities are.
- The differences between Silverlight 1.0 and 1.1.
- To create user interfaces in XAML.
- To embed multimedia in a Silverlight application.
- To program for Silverlight with JavaScript.
- To embed Silverlight in web pages.
- To host Silverlight applications online with Microsoft's Silverlight Streaming Service.
- To program for Silverlight with .NET languages, specifically Visual Basic.
- To parse RSS feeds in Silverlight 1.1.

Outline

19.1 Introduction

Silverlight™, formerly code named "Windows Presentation Foundation Everywhere (WPF/E)," is Microsoft's platform for Rich Internet Applications (RIAs). It is designed to complement Ajax and other RIA technologies, such as Adobe Flash and Flex, Sun's JavaFX and Microsoft's own ASP.NET Ajax. Silverlight currently runs as a browser plug-in for Internet Explorer, Firefox and Safari on recent versions of Microsoft Windows and Mac OS X. In addition, developers from the Mono project (`www.mono-project.com`) are developing an open-source implementation of Silverlight for Linux distributions called Moonlight.

Microsoft announced Silverlight 1.0 Beta and 1.1 Alpha at the 2007 MIX conference (`www.visitmix.com`), Microsoft's annual conference for web developers and designers. The demos were compelling, and many technology bloggers who attended the conference blogged about Silverlight's excitement and potential. Since then, Microsoft has continued developing and enhancing Silverlight. At the time of this writing, Silverlight is currently available in version 1.0 Release Candidate and version 1.1 Alpha Refresh.

Despite the generally unstable nature of alpha-level software, we felt compelled to include examples using the Silverlight 1.1 Alpha Refresh because of Silverlight 1.1's potential to become an important RIA development platform. Silverlight 1.1 is still early in its development cycle, so you may encounter bugs while running this software. Also, it is possible that Silverlight 1.1 will change substantially in future releases, breaking our 1.1-based example applications. For updated examples, please visit our website for this book at `www.deitel.com/books/iw3htp4/`. For information on the latest version(s) of Silverlight and to find additional Silverlight web resources, please visit our Silverlight Resource Center at `www.deitel.com/silverlight`.

19.2 Platform Overview

Silverlight applications consist of a user interface described in Extensible Application Markup Language (XAML) and a code-behind file (or files) containing the program logic. XAML (pronounced "zammel") is Microsoft's XML vocabulary for describing user interfaces and is also used in Microsoft's Windows Presentation Foundation (WPF)—the preferred user-interface technology of the .NET Platform as of version 3.0.

Silverlight currently runs in Internet Explorer 6+ and Firefox 1.5.0.8+ on Windows XP SP2 and Vista, as well as Safari 2.0.4+ and Firefox 1.5.0.8+ on Mac OS X. Support for Windows 2000 and for the Opera browser is planned in a future release.

Silverlight 1.0 focuses primarily on media and supports programming only in JavaScript. Its primary purpose is to take advantage of the increasing popularity of web-based video to drive user adoption—it is well known that users are willing to install software to watch video. Microsoft also provides a service called Silverlight Streaming that allows you to distribute video-based Silverlight applications for free.

When Silverlight 1.1 is released, computers with Silverlight 1.0 will automatically be upgraded. This could immediately make Silverlight 1.1 a widespread platform for RIA development. Silverlight 1.1's key benefit is that it adds an implementation of the .NET runtime, allowing developers to create Silverlight applications in .NET languages such as Visual Basic, Visual C#, IronRuby and IronPython. This makes it easy for developers familiar with .NET programming for Windows to create applications that run in a web browser. Two of our 1.1 Alpha Refresh examples borrow their user interfaces and code from examples in our *Visual Basic 2005 How to Program, 3/e* textbook. This straightforward conversion was made possible by Silverlight 1.1's .NET runtime and a set of third-party Silverlight user-interface controls (available at `www.netikatech.com`) designed to replicate the standard Windows Forms controls. Microsoft plans to implement their own built-in set of controls in a future release of Silverlight 1.1. Version 1.1 also provides a substantial performance improvement over 1.0 because .NET code is compiled by the developer then executed on the client, unlike JavaScript, which is interpreted and executed on the client at runtime. For a detailed feature comparison of 1.0 Release Candidate and 1.1 Alpha Refresh, visit `silverlight.net/GetStarted/overview.aspx`.

19.3 Silverlight 1.0 Installation and Overview

You can download the Silverlight 1.0 Release Candidate plug-in from `www.microsoft.com/silverlight/install.aspx`. After installing the plug-in, go to `silverlight.net/themes/silverlight/community/gallerydetail.aspx?cat=1` and try some of the sample applications. We list many other demo websites in Section 19.11.

We developed our Silverlight 1.0 application using Microsoft's Expression Blend 2, a WYSIWYG editor for XAML user interfaces. You can download a free trial of Expression Blend 2 from

```
www.microsoft.com/Expression/products/download.aspx?key=blend2preview
```

Follow the instructions on the web page to install the software. Note that Expression Blend runs only on Windows XP SP2 and Vista. Also, note that you do not need to install Visual Studio 2005 Express.

19.4 Creating a Movie Viewer for Silverlight 1.0

Our first example application is a movie viewer (Fig. 19.1) that plays Windows Media Video (WMV) videos. This example runs on Silverlight 1.0 Release Candidate, and the user interface was created using Expression Blend 2 August Preview. The XAML was generated primarily by Expression Blend. We discuss the XAML as we show you how to build the user interface.

The movie viewer's GUI includes play/pause, stop and full-screen buttons, a timeline with a marker at the current time, a volume control and thumbnails of other videos that you can view. The timeline also shows the percentage of the video that has been downloaded. In this example, you'll learn to create user interfaces in XAML and to use JavaScript to handle events. We'll also demonstrate how to use JavaScript to manipulate the Silverlight DOM (Document Object Model). You can test a live version of this application at `test.deitel.com/examples/iw3htp4/silverlight/MovieViewer/index.html`.

To create the project in Expression Blend, open Expression Blend and select **New Project** in the **Project** tab. To create a Silverlight 1.0 application, select **Silverlight Application (JavaScript)**. Name the project `MovieViewer` and select the location where you would like to save it.

Fig. 19.1 | Silverlight Movie Viewer.

19.4.1 Creating a User Interface In XAML Using Expression Blend

To show how XAML works, we first create elements in Expression Blend, then discuss the corresponding generated XAML in `Scene.xaml` (which you'll see in Fig. 19.12).

Canvas Elements

The root element of the XAML file is a Canvas element. A **Canvas element** acts as a container for other user interface elements and controls their position. The parent Canvas element is created when you create a new Silverlight project in Expression Blend. The parent Canvas has a default Name of Page, Width of 640 px and Height of 480 px. The **Name attribute** provides an ID to access the element programmatically. The Canvas's properties can be edited in the **Properties** panel (Fig. 19.2). Additional Canvas elements can be created in Expression Blend using the Canvas tool in the toolbar, shown in Fig. 19.3. The XAML can be manually edited by selecting **XAML** in Expression Blend's **View** menu.

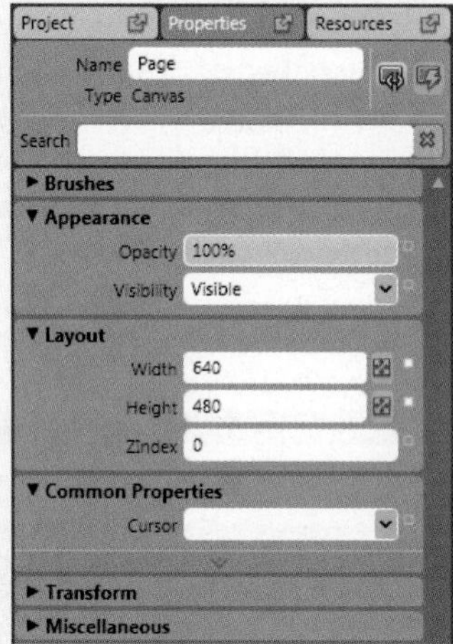

Fig. 19.2 | Expression Blend's **Properties** inspector.

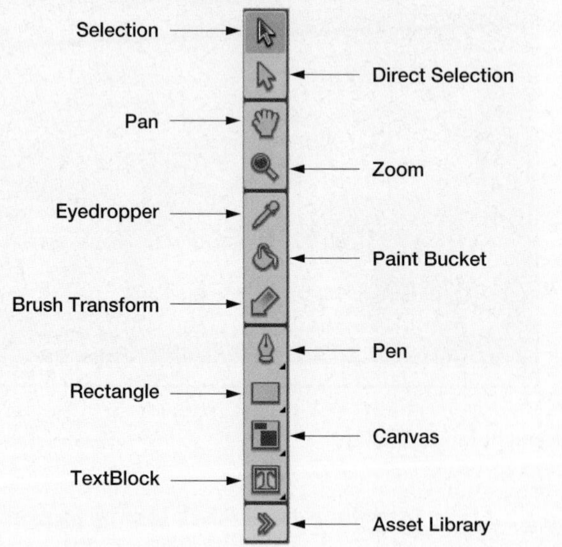

Fig. 19.3 | Expression Blend's toolbar.

19.4.2 Using Storyboards

The **Storyboard element** allows you to define animations. In Expression Blend, you can create a `Storyboard` by opening the **Open, create or manage Storyboards** panel and clicking the **Create new Storyboard** button (Fig. 19.4). Select the **Create as a Resource** checkbox (Fig. 19.5). This enables you to start the `Storyboard` from anywhere in the application's JavaScript at any time (as opposed to starting the `Storyboard` automatically when the application loads). Name the `Storyboard` `timelineTimer` and click **OK**. This `Storyboard` will be used as a timer, because a dedicated timer object does not exist in Silverlight 1.0. A `Storyboard` must have a target object, so we will create an invisible object. Create a `Rectangle` of any size in any location using the **Rectangle** tool, name it `invisibleRectangle`, then set its **Visiblity** to **Collapsed** using the **Properties** panel. Move the timeline playhead to 0.1 seconds, then click the **Record Keyframe** button (Fig. 19.6). In this

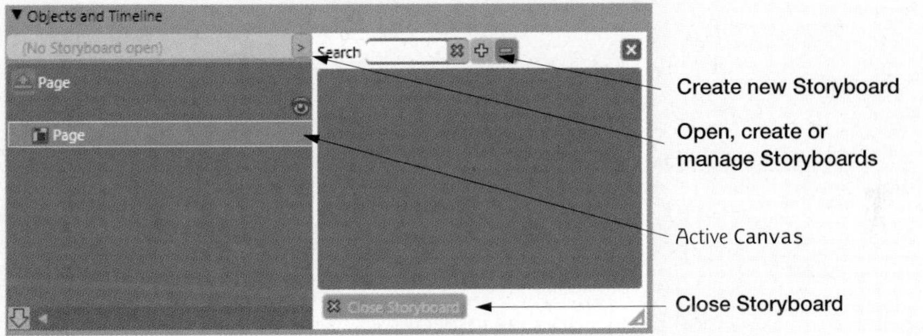

Fig. 19.4 | Expression Blend's **Objects and Timeline** inspector.

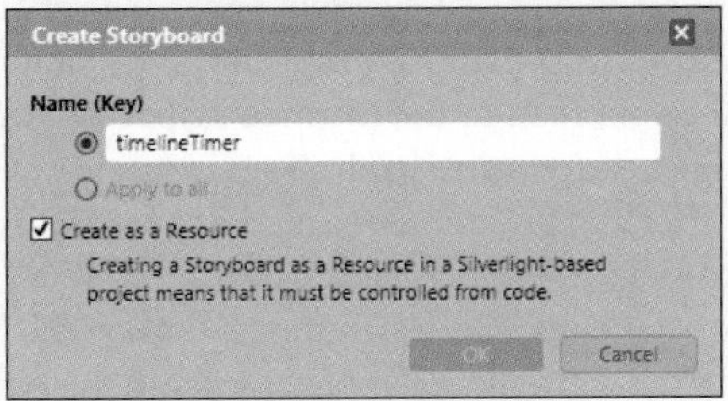

Fig. 19.5 | Expression Blend's **Create Storyboard** dialog box.

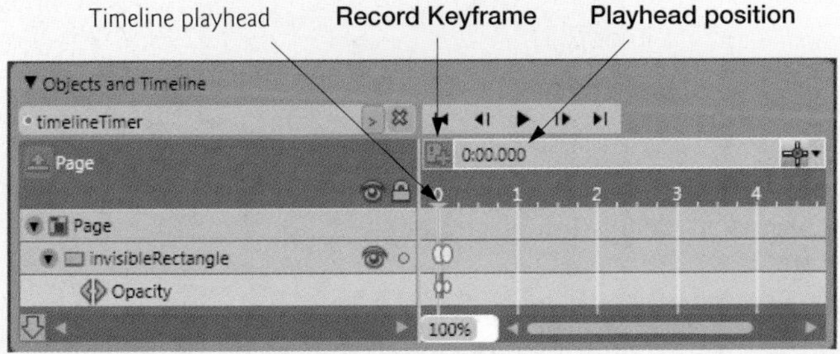

Fig. 19.6 | **Objects and Timeline** inspector showing the `TimelineTimer Storyboard`.

new keyframe, change any property of the rectangle. If you create the keyframe without changing a property, the `Storyboard` will not do anything. Close the `Storyboard` by opening the **Open, create or manage Storyboards** menu and clicking **Close Storyboard.**

Expression Blend provides the `Gradient` brush tool (Fig. 19.7) to visually create and modify gradients. First, use the **Selection** tool to select the `Page Canvas` in the design area. Then, select the **Gradient brush** for the **Background** and select the gradient slider on the right (Fig. 19.7). Change the red, green and blue values to 71.

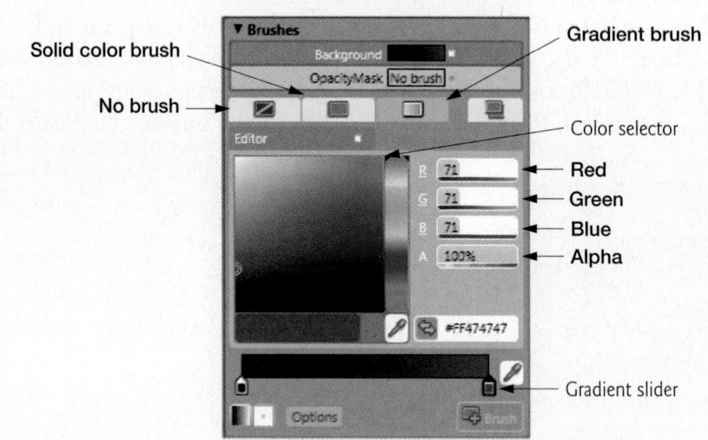

Fig. 19.7 | Expression Blend's **Brushes** inspector.

19.4.3 Creating Controls

We use a `TextBlock` element to display **Silverlight Movie Viewer** at the top of the page. Create this element using Expression Blend's **TextBlock** tool, name the element `titleText`, then change to the **Solid color brush** in the **Brushes** inspector and use the color selector to make the text white. Adjust the text size in the **Text** inspector to **24** (Fig. 19.8).

Next, we create another `Canvas` element called `controls`, using the **Canvas** tool. The `controls Canvas` will contain the application's buttons, which are themselves `Canvases`. This `Canvas` is a child of the `Page Canvas` element. Create this `Canvas` at the bottom of the application, spanning the width of the application. Set the **Height** to **160** and make sure that the `Canvas` is at the bottom of the application by moving it until it snaps into place.

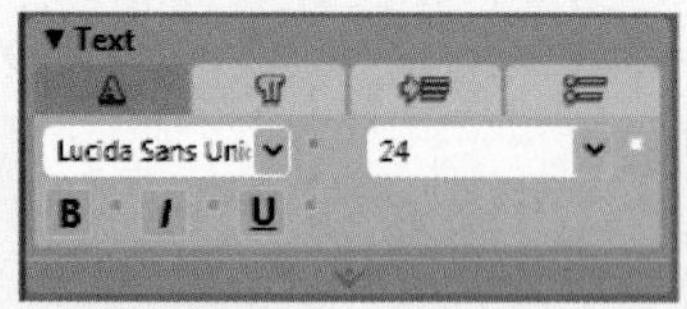

Fig. 19.8 | Expression Blend's **Text** inspector.

Creating the Video Thumbnail Buttons

For each video, we create a button consisting of the video's thumbnail and title. Double-click the `controls Canvas` with the **Selection** tool to activate it, then create four new `Can-`

vases in the controls Canvas. Set each Canvas's **Width** to **120** and **Height** to **114**. In each Canvas, create an Image element, with the **Source** attribute pointing to the video's thumbnail JPEG image, for example baileyThumb.jpg (Fig. 19.9). You can select the **Image** tool by clicking the **Asset Library** button (Fig. 19.3), checking **Show All** and selecting **Image** (Fig. 19.10). Set the Image's **Width** and **Height** to **120** and **90**, and place it at the top of the Canvas. Add a TextBlock containing the text Crazy Dog. Do the same for the other three Canvases, setting the Image's Sources to featherAndHammerThumb.jpg, apollo15Launch-Thumb.jpg and F35Thumb.jpg. The TextBlocks for the three Canvases should contain Gravity, Apollo 15 and F35 Landing, respectively. Name the Canvases crazyDogButton, gravityButton, apollo15Button, and f35Button, and space them evenly across the controls Canvas. Finally, to make each of these Canvases appear to act like a button, we will set their **Cursor** properties to **Hand** in the **Common Properties** inspector. This way, the user's cursor will change to a hand when the cursor is moved over each button Canvas.

Fig. 19.9 | Expression Blend's **Common Properties** inspector for an **Image** element.

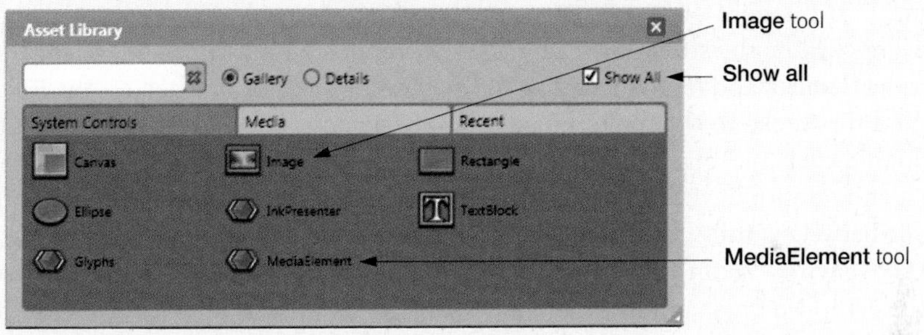

Fig. 19.10 | Expression Blend's **Asset Library**.

Creating the Video Playback Control Buttons

Next, we create a play button, a stop button, a pause button, and a full-screen button. These buttons are all contained in the controls Canvas. To create the play button, first create a Canvas named playButton, then set its **Width** and **Height** to **30**. Set the **RadiusX** and **RadiusY** to **2** to give the button rounded corners. These properties are located in the **advanced properties** section of the **Appearance** inspector (Fig. 19.11). Inside this Canvas, use the **Rectangle** tool to draw a Rectangle with the same width and height as the Canvas, and set its background to a gradient going from dark blue to light blue. Then, using the **Pen** tool, draw two Paths to make an arrow pointing right (a play button). Use the **Pen** tool to click once at each endpoint of the line. After drawing each line, use the **Select** tool to move the line into place. The Path element allows you to draw shapes that include curves and arcs, but here we are just using it to draw simple lines. Set each Path's **Stroke**

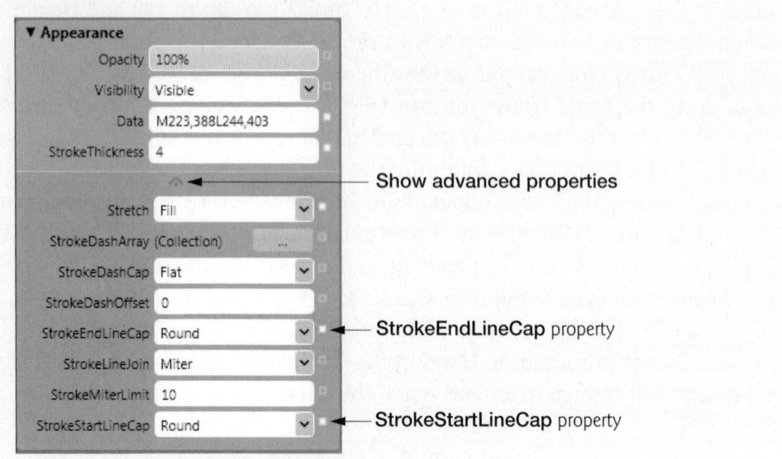

Fig. 19.11 | Expression Blend's **Appearance** inspector.

color to white. Set the **StrokeThickness** property in the **Appearance** inspector to **4**. Set each `Path`'s **StrokeEndLineCap** and **StrokeStartLineCap** to **Round** in the **Appearance** inspector. Finally, set the **Cursor** property of the `playButton Canvas` to **Hand**.

Copy the `playButton Canvas` and paste it three times. Move one copy just to the right of the `playButton`, then move another to the right side of the application. Double-click the button to the right of the `playButton` to make it the active `Canvas`, and remove the `Paths`. This will be the stop button. Draw a `Rectangle` with a **Width** of **14** and **Height** of **18**. Set the **RadiusX** and **RadiusY** to **2** in the **Appearance** inspector, then set the **Fill** to solid white and the **Stroke** to **No Brush**. Finally, set the **Name** of the `Canvas` to `stopButton`.

Double-click the button at the far right of the application to make it the active `Canvas`, and remove the `Paths`. This will be the full-screen button that will enable the user to toggle between a full-screen view and a browser window view of the application. Draw a `Rectangle` with a **Width** and **Height** of **22**. Set the **RadiusX**, **RadiusY** and **StrokeThickness** to **2**, the **Fill** to **No Brush**, and the **Stroke** to solid white. Then, draw a second `Rectangle` with a **Width** and **Height** of **10**, starting at the bottom-left of the previous `Rectangle`. Give this `Rectangle` the same **StrokeThickness** and **Fill** and **Stroke** colors as the larger `Rectangle`. Finally, name this `Canvas fullscreenButton`.

Double-click the button that is still on top of the `playButton` to make it the active `Canvas`, and remove the `Paths`. This will be the pause button. Draw two vertical `paths` with the same properties as the `paths` in the play button, and space them apart by a few pixels. Name this `Canvas pauseButton` and set its **Visibility** attribute to **Collapsed** (i.e., hidden). We'll programmatically display this button when it is needed.

The application displays the current time of the video in *hh*:*mm*:*ss* format in the `timeText TextBlock`, located inside the `timeCanvas Canvas`. To create this element, first create a `Canvas` named `timeCanvas` to the left of the full-screen button, and give it a **Width** of **75** and **Height** of **23**. Inside this `Canvas`, create a `Rectangle` that takes up the entire `Canvas`. Set this `Rectangle`'s **RadiusX** and **RadiusY** to **2**, and its **StrokeThickness** to **1**. Set the **Stroke** color to solid black, and the **Fill** to a gradient going from grey to white. Create a `TextBlock` named `timeText` using the **TextBlock** tool, and set its initial text value to `"00:00:00"`. Use the default font (**Lucida Sans Unicode**) and font size (**14.667**). This TextBlock's text value will be updated programmatically in our JavaScript code-behind file.

Creating the Volume and Timeline Controls

The application allows the user to select the volume level through a volume control. To create this control, first create a Canvas named volumeCanvas with a **Width** of **15** and a **Height** of **30** to the right of the full-screen button. Use the **Rectangle** tool to create a vertical Rectangle (the slider). Give the Rectangle a **Width** of **4** and **Height** of **30**. Set the **Fill** of the Rectangle to light grey. Set the **Stroke** of the Rectangle to black, with a **StrokeThickness** of **1**.

Use the **Rectangle** tool to create a horizontal Rectangle (to mark the current volume). Give the Rectangle a **Width** of **14** and **Height** of **2**. Set its **Fill** to white, its **Stroke** to **No Brush** and its **Opacity** to **50%** (in the **Appearance** inspector). Center the horizontal Rectangle on the center of the vertical Rectangle. Finally, name the horizontal Rectangle volumeHead and the Canvas volumeCanvas.

Next, we create a video timeline that serves two purposes. The timeline acts as a progress bar while the video is being downloaded. This is accomplished by having a dark grey Rectangle with a Width of 400 located underneath a light grey Rectangle with an initial Width of 0. The light Rectangle's Width is set programmatically in the JavaScript code-behind file to indicate the download progress. Also, a vertical Rectangle acts as the playhead, indicating the current playback progress of the video. To create the video timeline, first create a Canvas named timelineCanvas to the right of the stop button. Give this Canvas a **Width** of **400** and a **Height** of **20**, and a **Cursor** of **Hand**. Inside this Canvas, create a Rectangle named timelineRectangle with a **Width** of **400** and a **Height** of **4**. Set its **StrokeThickness** to **1**, its **Fill** to dark grey and its **Stroke** to black. Center the Rectangle vertically, then copy and paste the Rectangle. Name the copy downloadProgressRectangle, set its **Fill** to a lighter grey and set its **Width** to **0**. Note that because downloadProgressRectangle appears after the timelineRectangle in the **Objects and Timeline** inspector, it appears on top of the timelineRectangle. You can also specify the *z*-order of elements (discussed in Section 5.6) using an object's ZIndex attribute. Higher ZIndex integer values position the element closer to the foreground and in front of other elements with smaller ZIndex values.

Create a Rectangle named playHead with a **Width** of **2** and a **Height** of **20**. Place this Rectangle at the far left of the Canvas and center it vertically. Set this Rectangle's **Fill** to **No brush**, its **StrokeThickness** to **1**, its **Stroke** to white, and its **Opacity** to **50%**.

Using a MediaElement to Display Audio/Video

The MediaElement allows you to include video and/or audio in your Silverlight application. It supports WMV/VC-1 (including high-definition video), WMA and MP3 formats.

First, create a Canvas named movieViewCanvas and set its **Height** to **260** and **Width** to **640**. Inside the Canvas, add a MediaElement named movieMediaElement. To access the **MediaElement** tool, click the **Asset Library** button (Fig. 19.3), check **Show All** and select **MediaElement** (Fig. 19.10). Set the MediaElement's **Width** and **Height** to those of the Canvas. Set the **Source** attribute to point to bailey.wmv in the **Media** inspector.

This Canvas also contains a **Play** button overlaid on the video. First, create a Canvas named playOverlayCanvas with an **Opacity** of **60%**, a **Width** of **200** and a **Height** of **180**. Inside this Canvas, create a Rectangle with the same **Width** and **Height** as the Canvas, a **Fill** of black, a **Stroke** of **No brush**, and a **RadiusX** and **RadiusY** of **40**. Create an Ellipse using the **Ellipse** tool with a **Width** of **100** and a **Height** of **100**. Set its **Fill** to **No brush**, its **Stroke** to white, and its **StrokeThickness** to **6**. In the middle of this `Ellipse`, draw two `Paths` in the shape of a right arrow, both with a **Width** and **Height** of **30**, a **StrokeThickness** of **6**, and a **StrokeStartLineCap** and **StrokeEndLineCap** of **Round**. Underneath the `Ellipse`, create a `TextBlock` containing the text **Play**. Set the font size to **36** in the **Text** inspector.

Finally, set the `playOverlayCanvas` **Visibility** attribute to **Collapsed**, since we will show this `Canvas` programmatically.

Creating Event Handlers in XAML

Expression Blend 2 August Preview does not currently have a user interface to set event handlers, so we will manually set them in `Scene.xaml` (Fig. 19.12). The `timelineTimer` `Storyboard`'s **`Completed` attribute** (line 8) registers an event that calls the `updateTime` function located in our JavaScript code-behind file (Fig. 19.13) when the animation has completed. This JavaScript function updates user-interface elements such as the timeline marker.

```
1  <!-- Fig. 19.12: Page.xaml -->
2  <!-- Movie Viewer user interface described in XAML. -->
3
4  <Canvas xmlns="http://schemas.microsoft.com/client/2007"
5     xmlns:x="http://schemas.microsoft.com/winfx/2006/xaml"
6     Width="640" Height="480" x:Name="Page" Loaded="canvasLoaded">
7     <Canvas.Resources>
8        <Storyboard x:Name="timelineTimer" Completed="updateTime" >
9           <DoubleAnimationUsingKeyFrames BeginTime="00:00:00"
10             Storyboard.TargetName="invisibleRectangle"
11             Storyboard.TargetProperty="(UIElement.Opacity)">
12             <SplineDoubleKeyFrame KeyTime="00:00:00" Value="1"/>
13             <SplineDoubleKeyFrame KeyTime="00:00:00.1000000" Value="0"/>
14          </DoubleAnimationUsingKeyFrames>
15          <ColorAnimationUsingKeyFrames BeginTime="00:00:00"
16             Duration="00:00:00.0010000" Storyboard.TargetName="Page"
17             Storyboard.TargetProperty="(Panel.Background).
18                (GradientBrush.GradientStops)[1].(GradientStop.Color)">
19             <SplineColorKeyFrame KeyTime="00:00:00" Value="#FF474747"/>
20          </ColorAnimationUsingKeyFrames>
21       </Storyboard>
22    </Canvas.Resources>
23    <Canvas.Background>
24       <LinearGradientBrush EndPoint="1,0.5" StartPoint="0,0.5">
25          <GradientStop Color="#FF000000" Offset="0"/>
26          <GradientStop Color="#FF505050" Offset="1"/>
27       </LinearGradientBrush>
28    </Canvas.Background>
29    <Rectangle Visibility="Collapsed" x:Name="invisibleRectangle"
30       Width="21" Height="16" Fill="#FFFFFFFF" Stroke="#FF000000"
31       Canvas.Left="7" Canvas.Top="103"/>
32    <TextBlock Width="278" Height="60" Canvas.Left="192" Canvas.Top="8"
33       FontSize="24" TextWrapping="Wrap" x:Name="titleText"><Run
34       Foreground="#FFFFFFFF" Text="Silverlight Movie Viewer"/></TextBlock>
```

Fig. 19.12 | Movie Viewer user interface described in XAML. (Part 1 of 5.)

```
      <Canvas x:Name="controls" Width="640" Height="160" Canvas.Top="320">
         <Canvas MouseLeftButtonDown="movieThumbHandler" Cursor="Hand"
            Width="120" Height="114" Canvas.Left="33" Canvas.Top="38"
            x:Name="crazyDogButton">
            <Image Width="120" Height="90" Source="baileyThumb.jpg"/>
            <TextBlock Width="78" Height="24" Canvas.Left="23"
               Canvas.Top="90" TextWrapping="Wrap"><Run
               Foreground="#FFFFFFFF" Text="Crazy Dog"/></TextBlock>
         </Canvas>
         <Canvas MouseLeftButtonDown="movieThumbHandler" Width="120"
            Height="114" Canvas.Left="184" Canvas.Top="38" Cursor="Hand"
            x:Name="gravityButton">
            <Image Width="120" Height="90"
               Source="featherAndHammerThumb.jpg"/>
            <TextBlock Width="52" Height="24" Canvas.Top="90"
               TextWrapping="Wrap" Canvas.Left="34"><Run
               Foreground="#FFFFFFFF" Text="Gravity"/></TextBlock>
         </Canvas>
         <Canvas MouseLeftButtonDown="movieThumbHandler" Width="120"
            Height="114" Canvas.Left="335" Canvas.Top="38" Cursor="Hand"
            x:Name="apollo15Button">
            <Image Width="120" Height="90" Source="apollo15LaunchThumb.jpg"/>
            <TextBlock Width="72" Height="24" Canvas.Left="26"
               Canvas.Top="90" TextWrapping="Wrap">
                  <Run Foreground="#FFFFFFFF" Text="Apollo 15"/></TextBlock>
         </Canvas>
         <Canvas MouseLeftButtonDown="movieThumbHandler" Width="120"
            Height="114" Canvas.Left="487" Canvas.Top="38" Cursor="Hand"
            x:Name="f35Button">
            <Image Width="120" Height="90" Source="F35Thumb.jpg"/>
            <TextBlock Width="88" Height="24" Canvas.Left="16"
               Canvas.Top="90" TextWrapping="Wrap"><Run
               Foreground="#FFFFFFFF" Text="F35 Landing"/></TextBlock>
         </Canvas>

         <!-- define the buttons -->
         <Canvas MouseLeftButtonDown="playAndPauseButtonEventHandler"
            Width="30" Height="30" x:Name="playButton" Cursor="Hand"
            Canvas.Left="10">
            <Rectangle Stroke="#FF000000" Width="30" Height="30"
               RadiusX="4" RadiusY="4">
               <Rectangle.Fill>
                  <LinearGradientBrush EndPoint="1,0.5" StartPoint="0,0.5"
                     MappingMode="RelativeToBoundingBox" SpreadMethod="Pad">
                     <GradientStop Color="#FF0000FF" Offset="0"/>
                     <GradientStop Color="#FF0084FF" Offset="1"/>
                  </LinearGradientBrush>
               </Rectangle.Fill>
            </Rectangle>
            <Path Stretch="Fill" Stroke="#FFFFFFFF"
               StrokeThickness="4" Width="12" Height="12" Data="M223,388
               L244,403" StrokeEndLineCap="Round" StrokeStartLineCap="Round"
               Canvas.Left="10" Canvas.Top="4"/>
```

Fig. 19.12 | Movie Viewer user interface described in XAML. (Part 2 of 5.)

```
         <Path Stretch="Fill" Stroke="#FFFFFFFF"
            StrokeThickness="4" Width="12" Height="12" Data="M223,388
            L244,403" RenderTransformOrigin="0.5,0.5"
            StrokeEndLineCap="Square" StrokeStartLineCap="Round"
            Canvas.Left="10" Canvas.Top="13">
            <Path.RenderTransform>
               <TransformGroup>
                  <ScaleTransform ScaleX="1" ScaleY="-1"/>
                  <SkewTransform AngleX="0" AngleY="0"/>
                  <RotateTransform Angle="0"/>
                  <TranslateTransform X="0" Y="0"/>
               </TransformGroup>
            </Path.RenderTransform>
         </Path>
      </Canvas>
      <Canvas x:Name="timeCanvas" Width="75" Height="23" Canvas.Left="497"
         Canvas.Top="3">
         <Rectangle Stroke="#FF000000" Width="75" Height="25" RadiusX="2"
            RadiusY="2" StrokeThickness="1">
            <Rectangle.Fill>
               <LinearGradientBrush EndPoint="1,0.5" StartPoint="0,0.5">
                  <GradientStop Color="#FF9A9A9A" Offset="0"/>
                  <GradientStop Color="#FFFFFFFF" Offset="1"/>
               </LinearGradientBrush>
            </Rectangle.Fill>
         </Rectangle>
         <TextBlock x:Name="timeText" Width="68" Height="17"
            Foreground="#FF000000" TextWrapping="Wrap" Canvas.Left="4"
            Canvas.Top="3"><Run Text="00:00:00"/></TextBlock>
      </Canvas>
      <Canvas MouseLeftButtonDown="volumeHandler" Cursor="Hand"
         x:Name="volumeCanvas" Width="15" Height="30"
         Canvas.Left="616">
         <Rectangle Fill="#FF868686"
            Stroke="#FF000000" Width="4" Height="30" Canvas.Left="6"/>
         <Rectangle Opacity="0.5" x:Name="volumeHead" Width="14"
            Height="2" Fill="#FFFFFFFF" Stroke="#FFFFFFFF"
            StrokeThickness="0" RadiusX="0" RadiusY="0" Canvas.Left="1"
            Canvas.Top="14"/>
      </Canvas>
      <Canvas x:Name="timelineCanvas" Width="401" Height="26"
         Canvas.Left="87" Canvas.Top="2" Cursor="Hand" >
         <Rectangle x:Name="timelineRectangle" Width="400" Height="4"
            Fill="#FFA6A6A6" Stroke="#FF000000" Canvas.Top="11"/>
         <Rectangle MouseLeftButtonDown="timelineHandler"
            x:Name="downloadProgressRectangle" Width="0"
            Height="4" Fill="#FFD5D5D5" Stroke="#FF000000"
            Canvas.Top="11"/>
         <Rectangle Opacity="0.5" x:Name="playHead" Width="2" Height="20"
            Stroke="#FFFFFFFF" Canvas.Left="1" Canvas.Top="3"/>
      </Canvas>
      <Canvas MouseLeftButtonDown="playAndPauseButtonEventHandler"
         Width="30" Height="30" x:Name="pauseButton" Cursor="Hand"
```

Fig. 19.12 | Movie Viewer user interface described in XAML. (Part 3 of 5.)

```
            Canvas.Left="10" Visibility="Collapsed" >
            <Rectangle Stroke="#FF000000" Width="30" Height="30"
               RadiusX="4" RadiusY="4">
               <Rectangle.Fill>
                  <LinearGradientBrush EndPoint="1,0.5" StartPoint="0,0.5"
                     MappingMode="RelativeToBoundingBox" SpreadMethod="Pad">
                     <GradientStop Color="#FF0000FF" Offset="0"/>
                     <GradientStop Color="#FF0084FF" Offset="1"/>
                  </LinearGradientBrush>
               </Rectangle.Fill>
            </Rectangle>
            <Path Stretch="Fill" Stroke="#FFFFFFFF"
               StrokeThickness="4" Width="4" Height="18"
               RenderTransformOrigin="0.5,0.5" StrokeEndLineCap="Round"
               StrokeStartLineCap="Round" Canvas.Left="9"
               StrokeDashCap="Flat" Canvas.Top="6" Data="M223,388L223,308"/>
            <Path Stretch="Fill" Stroke="#FFFFFFFF"
               StrokeThickness="4" Width="4" Height="18"
               Data="M223,388L223,403" RenderTransformOrigin="0.5,0.5"
               StrokeEndLineCap="Round" StrokeStartLineCap="Round"
               Canvas.Left="17" StrokeDashCap="Flat" Canvas.Top="6"/>
         </Canvas>
         <Canvas MouseLeftButtonDown="toggleFullScreen" Width="30"
            Height="30" x:Name="fullscreenButton" Cursor="Hand"
            Canvas.Left="582" Canvas.Top="1">
            <Rectangle Stroke="#FF000000" Width="30" Height="30"
               RadiusX="4" RadiusY="4">
               <Rectangle.Fill>
                  <LinearGradientBrush EndPoint="1,0.5" StartPoint="0,0.5"
                     MappingMode="RelativeToBoundingBox" SpreadMethod="Pad">
                     <GradientStop Color="#FF0000FF" Offset="0"/>
                     <GradientStop Color="#FF0084FF" Offset="1"/>
                  </LinearGradientBrush>
               </Rectangle.Fill>
            </Rectangle>
            <Rectangle Width="22" Height="22" Stroke="#FFFFFFFF"
               StrokeEndLineCap="Square" StrokeStartLineCap="Round"
               StrokeThickness="2" RadiusX="2" RadiusY="2" Canvas.Left="4"
               Canvas.Top="4"/>
            <Rectangle Width="10" Height="10" Stroke="#FFFFFFFF"
               StrokeEndLineCap="Square" StrokeStartLineCap="Round"
               StrokeThickness="2" RadiusX="2" RadiusY="2" Canvas.Left="4"
               Canvas.Top="16"/>
         </Canvas>
         <Canvas MouseLeftButtonDown="stopButtonEventHandler" Width="30"
            Height="30" x:Name="stopButton" Cursor="Hand" Canvas.Left="46">
            <Rectangle Stroke="#FF000000" Width="30" Height="30"
               RadiusX="4" RadiusY="4">
               <Rectangle.Fill>
                  <LinearGradientBrush EndPoint="1,0.5" StartPoint="0,0.5"
                     MappingMode="RelativeToBoundingBox" SpreadMethod="Pad">
                     <GradientStop Color="#FF0000FF" Offset="0"/>
                     <GradientStop Color="#FF0084FF" Offset="1"/>
```

Fig. 19.12 | Movie Viewer user interface described in XAML. (Part 4 of 5.)

```
               </LinearGradientBrush>
            </Rectangle.Fill>
         </Rectangle>
         <Rectangle RadiusX="2" RadiusY="2" Width="14"
            Height="18" Canvas.Left="8" Fill="#FFFFFFFF"
            StrokeThickness="0" Canvas.Top="6"/>
      </Canvas>
   </Canvas>
   <Canvas x:Name="movieViewCanvas" Width="640" Height="260"
      Canvas.Top="46">
      <MediaElement AutoPlay="false" MediaEnded="movieEndedHandler"
         MediaOpened="movieOpenedHandler" x:Name="movieMediaElement"
         Width="640" Height="260" Source="bailey.wmv" />
      <Canvas MouseLeftButtonDown="playAndPauseButtonEventHandler"
         Width="200" Height="180" Canvas.Left="220" Canvas.Top="35"
         Opacity="0.6" Visibility="Collapsed" x:Name="playOverlayCanvas">
         <Canvas.RenderTransform>
            <TransformGroup>
               <ScaleTransform ScaleX="1" ScaleY="1"/>
               <SkewTransform AngleX="0" AngleY="0"/>
               <RotateTransform Angle="0"/>
               <TranslateTransform X="0" Y="0"/>
            </TransformGroup>
         </Canvas.RenderTransform>
         <Rectangle Fill="#FF000000"
            Width="200" Height="180" RadiusX="40"
            RadiusY="40" Canvas.Left="0" Canvas.Top="0"/>
         <Ellipse Stroke="#FFFFFFFF" StrokeThickness="6"
            Width="100" Height="100" Canvas.Left="49" Canvas.Top="14"/>
         <Path Fill="#FF010000" Stretch="Fill" Stroke="#FFDFDFDF"
            StrokeThickness="6" Width="30" Height="30" Canvas.Left="86"
            Canvas.Top="36" Data="M295,189 L319,213"
            StrokeEndLineCap="Round" StrokeStartLineCap="Round"/>
         <Path Fill="#FF010000" Stretch="Fill" Stroke="#FFDFDFDF"
            StrokeThickness="6" Width="30" Height="30" Canvas.Left="86"
            Canvas.Top="61" Data="M295,189 L319,213"
            RenderTransformOrigin="0.5,0.5" StrokeEndLineCap="Round"
            StrokeStartLineCap="Round">
            <Path.RenderTransform>
               <TransformGroup>
                  <ScaleTransform ScaleX="1" ScaleY="1"/>
                  <SkewTransform AngleX="0" AngleY="0"/>
                  <RotateTransform Angle="-90"/>
                  <TranslateTransform X="0" Y="0"/>
               </TransformGroup>
            </Path.RenderTransform>
         </Path>
         <TextBlock Width="74" Height="49" Canvas.Left="64"
            Canvas.Top="120" FontSize="36" Foreground="#FFFFFFFF"
            Text="Play" TextWrapping="Wrap"/>
      </Canvas>
   </Canvas>
</Canvas>
```

Fig. 19.12 | Movie Viewer user interface described in XAML. (Part 5 of 5.)

Configuring the Event Handlers

For each of the thumbnail button Canvases (crazyDogButton, gravityButton, apollo15Button and f35Button), we specify a MouseLeftButtonDown attribute (lines 36, 44, 53 and 61, respectively). This registers the movieThumbHandler function (Fig. 19.13, lines 157–178) as the event handler to call when the user clicks one of these Canvases with the left mouse button. Each of the playback control buttons also has a MouseLeftButton-Down attribute (lines 71, 139, 163, 185 and 207 for the play, pause, full-screen, stop, play overlay buttons, respectively). Each of these buttons has a separate event handler function.

The volumeCanvas has a MouseLeftButtonDown attribute (line 118) that allows the user to change the volume by calling volumeHandler (Fig. 19.13, lines 239–245) when the user clicks somewhere on the volumeCanvas.

The downloadProgressRectangle has a MouseLeftButtonDown attribute (line 132) that allows the user to jump anywhere in the video by calling the timelineHandler function (lines 225–236, Fig. 19.13) when the user clicks somewhere on the downloadProgressRectangle.

The movieMediaElement's MediaOpened attribute (line 205) is set to movieOpened-Handler. When a new video is opened, function movieOpenedHandler (Fig. 19.13, lines 137–143) is called to ensure that the **Play** overlay button is visible, and to start the timer that keeps the timeline and time up to date. When you open a movie the MediaElement begins playing the movie by default. We don't want this to happen until the user clicks the play button, so we set its AutoPlay attribute to false (line 204). The movieMediaElement's MediaEnded attribute (line 204) is set to movieEndedHandler. When the video finishes playing, the movieEndedHandler function (Fig. 19.13, lines 146–155) is called to reset the video to the beginning and to ensure that the **Play** overlay button is visible.

Registering Event Handlers in JavaScript

An alternative to registering event handlers in the XAML is to register event handlers in the JavaScript code. While this technique requires a few more lines of code, it has two key advantages. First, it keeps the application's logic (in this case, event handling) separate from the application's user interface. Second, it allows you to add and remove event listeners dynamically. The JavaScript for adding an event handler is:

```
variableName = objectName.addEventHandler( "EventName", eventHandler );
```

The JavaScript for removing an event handler is:

```
objectName.removeEventHandler( "EventName", variableName );
```

When an event is registered in JavaScript using the addEventListener method, we must assign the return value of the method to a variable. This way, if we wish to remove an event listener using the removeEventListener, we can remove only that specific event listener.

19.4.4 Using JavaScript for Event Handling and DOM Manipulation

The JavaScript code-behind file, Page.xaml.js (Fig. 19.13), defines the event handlers for the various elements in the XAML. In the event handlers, we use JavaScript to manipulate the Silverlight DOM, similar to how we manipulated the XHTML DOM in Chapter 12 and the XML DOM in Chapter 14. To edit the JavaScript code files, use your preferred text editor.

```
// Fig. 19.13: Page.xaml.js
// JavaScript code-behind for Movie Viewer.

// variables for accessing the Silverlight elements
var host; // allow access to host plug-in
var Page;
var movieMediaElement;
var downloadProgressRectangle;
var timeText;
var timelineRectangle;
var playHead;
var timelineTimer;
var playButton;
var pauseButton;
var playOverlayCanvas;
var timelineTimer;
var volumeCanvas;
var volumeHead;
var crazyDogButton;
var gravityButton;
var apollo15Button;
var f35Button;
var controls;
var fullscreenButton;
var timeCanvas;
var titleText;
var playOverlayCanvasListener; // token for event listener

function canvasLoaded( sender, eventArgs )
{
   // set variables to more easily access the Silverlight elements
   host = sender.getHost(); // allow access to host plug-in
   Page = sender.findName( "Page" );
   movieMediaElement = sender.findName( "movieMediaElement" );
   downloadProgressRectangle = sender.findName(
      "downloadProgressRectangle" );
   timeText = sender.findName( "timeText" );
   timelineRectangle = sender.findName( "timelineRectangle" );
   playHead = sender.findName( "playHead" );
   timelineTimer = sender.findName( "timelineTimer" );
   playButton = sender.findName( "playButton" );
   pauseButton = sender.findName( "pauseButton" );
   playOverlayCanvas = sender.findName( "playOverlayCanvas" );
   volumeCanvas = sender.findName( "volumeCanvas" );
   volumeHead = sender.findName( "volumeHead" );
   crazyDogButton = sender.findName( "crazyDogButton" );
   gravityButton = sender.findName( "gravityButton" );
   apollo15Button = sender.findName( "apollo15Button" );
   f35Button = sender.findName( "f35Button" );
   controls = sender.findName( "controls" );
   fullscreenButton = sender.findName( "fullscreenButton" );
   timeCanvas = sender.findName( "timeCanvas" );
   titleText = sender.findName( "titleText" );
```

Fig. 19.13 | JavaScript code-behind file for Movie Viewer. (Part 1 of 6.)

```
   // add an event handler for the onFullScreenChange event
   host.content.onFullScreenChange = onFullScreenChangedHandler;

   // start the timer
   timelineTimer.begin();
} // end function canvasLoaded

// timelineTimer event handler
function updateTime()
{
   // get the video's current position in seconds
   var elapsedTime = movieMediaElement.position.Seconds;
   var hours = convertToHHMMSS( elapsedTime )[ 0 ]; // saves hours
   var minutes = convertToHHMMSS( elapsedTime )[ 1 ]; // saves minutes
   var seconds = convertToHHMMSS( elapsedTime )[ 2 ]; // saves seconds

   // set text of timeText to current time in hh:mm:ss format
   timeText.text = hours + ":" + minutes + ":" + seconds;

   // set width of downloadProgressRectangle
   downloadProgressRectangle.width = movieMediaElement.downloadProgress *
      timelineRectangle.width;

   // if the movie is playing, place the playHead at a
   // position representing the playback progress
   if ( movieMediaElement.position.Seconds &&
      movieMediaElement.naturalDuration )
   {
      playHead[ "Canvas.Left" ] = ( ( movieMediaElement.position.Seconds /
         movieMediaElement.naturalDuration.Seconds ) *
         timelineRectangle.Width ) + timelineRectangle[ "Canvas.Left" ];
   } // end if

   // if movie is not playing, place the playHead at the beginning
   else
   {
      playHead[ "Canvas.Left" ] = timelineRectangle[ "Canvas.Left" ];
   } // end else

   // if download is incomplete or movie is playing
   if ( movieMediaElement.downloadProgress != 1 ||
      movieMediaElement.CurrentState == "Playing" )
   {
      timelineTimer.begin(); // run timelineTimer again
   } // end if
} // end function updateTime

// handle play and pause buttons
function playAndPauseButtonEventHandler( sender, eventArgs )
{
   // check the CurrentState of the movie;
   // pause if playing, play if paused or stopped
```

Fig. 19.13 | JavaScript code-behind file for Movie Viewer. (Part 2 of 6.)

```
      if ( movieMediaElement.CurrentState == "Playing" )
      {
         movieMediaElement.pause();

         playButton.Visibility = "Visible"; // show play button
         pauseButton.Visibility = "Collapsed"; // hide pause button
      } // end if
      else
      {
         movieMediaElement.play();
         timelineTimer.begin(); // start timelineTimer again
         pauseButton.Visibility = "Visible"; // show pause button
         playButton.Visibility = "Collapsed"; // hide play button
         playOverlayCanvas.Visibility = "Collapsed"; // hide "Play" overlay
      } // end if
   } // end function playAndPauseButtonEventHandler

   // handle stop button
   function stopButtonEventHandler( sender, eventArgs )
   {
      movieMediaElement.stop(); // stop the movie
      playButton.Visibility = "Visible"; // show play button
      pauseButton.Visibility = "Collapsed"; // hide pause button

      // show "Play" overlay
      playOverlayCanvas.Visibility = "Visible";
      updateTime();
   } // end function stopButtonEventHandler

   // handle MediaOpened event
   function movieOpenedHandler( sender, eventArgs )
   {
      timelineTimer.begin();

      // show "Play" overlay
      playOverlayCanvas.Visibility = "Visible";
   } // end function movieOpenedHandler

   // handle when movie has reached end
   function movieEndedHandler( sender, eventArgs )
   {
      movieMediaElement.stop(); // stop the movie
      playButton.Visibility = "Visible"; // show play button
      pauseButton.Visibility = "Collapsed"; // hide pause button

      // show "Play" overlay
      playOverlayCanvas.Visibility = "Visible";
      updateTime();
   } // end function movieEndedHandler

   function movieThumbHandler ( sender, eventArgs ) // a thumb was clicked
   {
      movieMediaElement.stop(); // stop movie
```

Fig. 19.13 | JavaScript code-behind file for Movie Viewer. (Part 3 of 6.)

```
   playButton.Visibility = "Visible"; // show play button
   pauseButton.Visibility = "Collapsed"; // hide pause button

   switch ( sender.name )
   {
      case "crazyDogButton": // open Crazy Dog video
         movieMediaElement.source = "bailey.wmv";
         break;
      case "gravityButton": // open Gravity video
         movieMediaElement.source = "featherAndHammer.wmv";
         break;
      case "apollo15Button": // open Apollo 15 video
         movieMediaElement.source = "apollo15Launch.wmv";
         break;
      case "f35Button": // open F35 Landing video
         movieMediaElement.source = "F35.wmv";
         break;
   } // end switch
} // end function movieThumbHandler

// handle toggle full-screen button by toggling fullScreen state
function toggleFullScreen( sender, eventArgs )
{
   host.content.fullScreen = !host.content.fullScreen;
} // end function toggleFullScreen

// handle onFullScreenChange event
function onFullScreenChangedHandler( sender, eventArgs )
{
   // update layout based on current dimensions
   updateLayout( host.content.actualWidth,
      host.content.actualHeight );

   // update time and timeline
   updateTime();
} // end function onFullScreenChangedHandler

// reposition and resize elements based on new dimensions
function updateLayout( width, height )
{
   // resize and reposition the elements based on the screen dimensions
   Page.width = width;
   Page.height = height;
   movieMediaElement.width = width;
   movieMediaElement.height = height - 220;
   movieMediaElement[ "Canvas.Left" ] =
      ( width / 2 ) - ( ( movieMediaElement.width ) / 2 );
   movieMediaElement[ "Canvas.Top" ] =
      ( ( height - 220 ) / 2 ) - ( movieMediaElement.height / 2 );
   controls.width = width;
   playOverlayCanvas[ "Canvas.Left" ] =
      ( width / 2 ) - ( ( playOverlayCanvas.width ) / 2 );
```

Fig. 19.13 | JavaScript code-behind file for Movie Viewer. (Part 4 of 6.)

```
   playOverlayCanvas[ "Canvas.Top" ] =
      ( ( height - 220 ) / 2 ) - ( playOverlayCanvas.height / 2 );
   controls[ "Canvas.Left" ] = ( width / 2 ) - ( ( controls.width ) / 2 );
   controls[ "Canvas.Top" ] = height - controls.height;
   timelineRectangle.width = controls.width - 235;
   fullscreenButton[ "Canvas.Left" ] = controls.width - 55;
   timeCanvas[ "Canvas.Left" ] = controls.width - 140;
   volumeCanvas[ "Canvas.Left" ] = controls.width - 22;
   titleText[ "Canvas.Left" ] =
      ( width / 2 ) - ( ( titleText.width ) / 2 );
} // end function updateLayout

// handle timelineCanvas's MouseLeftButtonDown event
function timelineHandler( sender, eventArgs )
{
   // determine new time from mouse position
   var elapsedTime = ( ( eventArgs.getPosition( timelineRectangle ).x ) /
      timelineRectangle.Width ) *
      movieMediaElement.NaturalDuration.seconds;
   var hours = convertToHHMMSS( elapsedTime )[ 0 ]; // Saves hours
   var minutes = convertToHHMMSS( elapsedTime )[ 1 ]; // Saves minutes
   var seconds = convertToHHMMSS( elapsedTime )[ 2 ]; // Saves seconds
   movieMediaElement.Position = hours + ":" + minutes + ":" + seconds;
   updateTime();
} // end function timelineHandler

// handle volume's MouseLeftButtonDown event
function volumeHandler( sender, eventArgs )
{
   movieMediaElement.volume = 1 - ( ( eventArgs.getPosition(
      volumeCanvas ).y ) / 30 );
   volumeHead[ "Canvas.Top" ] =
      eventArgs.getPosition( volumeCanvas ).y;
} // end function volumeHandler

// get the hours, minutes and seconds of the video's current position
// Date object converts seconds to hh:mm:ss format
function convertToHHMMSS( seconds )
{
   var datetime = new Date( 0, 0, 0, 0, 0, seconds );
   var hours = datetime.getHours(); // saves hours to var
   var minutes = datetime.getMinutes(); // saves minutes to var
   var seconds = datetime.getSeconds(); // saves seconds to var

   // ensure hh:mm:ss format
   if ( seconds < 10 )
   {
      seconds = "0" + seconds;
   } // end if

   if ( minutes < 10 )
   {
```

Fig. 19.13 | JavaScript code-behind file for Movie Viewer. (Part 5 of 6.)

```
264          minutes = "0" + minutes;
265       } // end if
266
267       if ( hours < 10 )
268       {
269          hours = "0" + hours;
270       } // end if
271
272       return [ hours, minutes, seconds ]
273    } // end function convertToHHMMSS
```

Fig. 19.13 | JavaScript code-behind file for Movie Viewer. (Part 6 of 6.)

Handling Events and Accessing XAML Elements in JavaScript

Lines 5–27 declare variables that our event handler functions use to access the XAML elements in our video player. In the `canvasLoaded` function (lines 29–60), which handles the `Page Canvas`'s **`Loaded` event** (Fig. 19.12, line 6), these variables are set to reference their corresponding XAML elements using the `sender`'s **`findName`** method (lines 33–53). Every event handler receives **`sender`** and **`eventArgs`** parameters. The `sender` parameter is a reference to the element with which the user interacted, and the `eventArgs` parameter passes information about the event that occurred. Line 32 sets the `host` variable to the Silverlight plug-in object using the **`getHost`** method. This allows us to access properties of the Silverlight plug-in, such as its screen dimensions, throughout the program. Line 56 registers an event handler for the plug-in's **`onFullScreenChange`** event. Line 59 calls the `timelineTimer Storyboard`'s `begin` function, to start the `Storyboard` that we are using as a timer. When this `Storyboard`'s `Completed` event (Fig. 19.12, line 8) occurs—i.e., its 0.1-second-long animation completes (Fig. 19.12, lines 9–14)—the event handler `updateTime` (lines 63–100) is invoked.

Creating a Timer

The `updateTime` function (lines 63–100) updates the `timeText`, the `downloadProgressRectangle`, the `playHead`, and starts the `timelineTimer` again if necessary. It uses the `convertToHHMMSS` function (lines 249–273) to convert the `movieMediaElement`'s **`position.Seconds`**—its elapsed time in seconds—to hours, minutes and seconds (lines 66–69), then displays that time in *hh:mm:ss* format in the `timeText textBlock` (line 72). The `updateTime` function also updates the download progress indicator (lines 75–76) by setting the width of the `downloadProgressRectangle` to the width of the `timelineRectangle` multiplied by the `movieMediaElement`'s **`downloadProgress`**, which is a value from 0 to 1 representing the fraction of the video that has downloaded so far. Lines 80–81 check whether `movieMediaElement`'s **`naturalDuration`** and `position.Seconds` properties exist. If they do, lines 83–85 set the `playHead`'s position to the current playback position in the video. This is accomplished by setting the `playHead`'s `Canvas.Left` attribute to the sum of the `timelineRectangle`'s `Canvas.Left` attribute and the `width` of the `timelineRectangle` multiplied by the ratio of current time (`movieMediaElement.position.Seconds`) and total time (`movieMediaElement.naturalDuration.Seconds`). `Left` is a **dependency property** of `Canvas`, meaning that the `Left` value is relative to that of the `Canvas`. Since the `Canvas.Left` dependency property already has a dot in its notation, we must enclose the attribute name in quotes and square brackets, as in *element*`["`*attributeName*`"]`. If movieMediaElement's naturalDuration and position.Seconds attributes do not exist, line 91 sets the playHead's Canvas.Left attribute to be equal to the timelineRectangle's to indicate that the movie has not started playing. Finally, lines 95–99 check whether the download is not finished or the movie is playing, in which case it calls timelineTimer's begin function to run the timer again. This way, the downloadProgressRectangle and playHead will be updated.

Handling Button Events

The playAndPauseButtonEventHandler function (lines 103–122) handles the play and pause buttons' MouseLeftButtonDown events (Fig. 19.12, lines 71 and 139). Line 107 checks whether the movieMediaElement is currently playing. If it is, the video should be paused and the play button should be shown. If not, lines 116–120 play the video, start the timelineTimer, show the pause button and hide the playOverlayCanvas.

The stopButtonEventHandler function (lines 125–134) handles the stop button. It stops the video (line 127), then shows the play button and the **Play** overlay button (lines 128–132). Finally, it calls the updateTime function to ensure that the timeText TextBlock displays **00:00:00**.

Function movieThumbHandler (lines 157–178) handles the movie thumbnail buttons. Lines 159–161 stop the video and show the play button. Lines 163–177 contain a switch statement that checks the sender element's name attribute (the name of the button that was clicked) and sets the Source of movieMediaElement to the corresponding video file.

Adding a Full-Screen Feature

Function toggleFullScreen (lines 181–184) handles the full-screen button. Line 183 sets the Silverlight plug-in's fullScreen attribute to the opposite of its previous value. This means that if the plug-in was previously in full-screen mode, it will switch to windowed mode, and if it was previously in windowed mode, it will switch to full-screen mode.

The onFullScreenChangeHandler function (lines 208–216) handles the onFullScreenChange event. Lines 190–191 uses the updateLayout function to update the layout of the application based on its current width and height. Then, line 194 calls the updateTime function.

Dynamically Changing XAML Layout

Function updateLayout (lines 198–222) repositions the user interface elements relative to the width and height parameters. Lines 201–202 set the width and height of the Page Canvas to the width and height parameters. Lines 203–204 set the width and height of movieMediaElement to the width parameter and the height parameter minus 220 (leaving room for the controls). Lines 205–208 move the movieMediaElement in the application. Line 209 sets the width of the controls Canvas. Lines 210–213 center the playOverlayCanvas over the movieMediaElement. Lines 214–215 center the controls at the bottom of the application. Line 216 sets the width of the timelineRectangle to be the width of the controls Canvas minus 235, to allow room for the other controls. Lines 217–219 move the full-screen button, timeCanvas and volumeCanvas to the right side of the controls Canvas. Finally, lines 220–221 center titleText at the top of the application.

The movieOpenedHandler function (lines 137–143) handles movieMediaElement's MediaOpened event (Fig. 19.12, line 205). Line 139 starts the timelineTimer to update the loading progress rectangle, and line 142 shows the playOverlayCanvas.

The `movieEndedHandler` function (lines 146–155) handles the `movieMediaElement`'s `MediaEnded` event (Fig. 19.12, line 204). It stops the video (line 148), which resets the playback position to the beginning, then shows the play button and hides the pause button (lines 149–150). Lines 153 shows the `playOverlayCanvas`. Finally, line 154 calls the `updateTime` function to ensure that the `timeText` `textBox` displays **00:00:00**.

Creating a Timeline for a MediaElement

The `timelineHandler` function (lines 225–236) handles the `downloadProgressRectangle`'s `MouseLeftButtonDown` event (Fig. 19.12, line 132). Lines 228–234 set `elapsedTime` to the position that was clicked on the timeline, convert the number of seconds to *hh:mm:ss* format using the `convertToHHMMSS` function and set the `Position` of the `movieMediaElement` to that time string. Finally, line 235 calls the `updateTime` function to show the new position.

Controlling Volume of a MediaElement

Function `volumeHandler` (lines 239–245) handles the `volumeCanvas`'s `MouseLeftButtonDown` event (Fig. 19.12, line 118). Lines 241–242 set `movieMediaElement`'s **`volume` property** based on the position the user clicked on the `volumeCanvas`. We convert the *y*-coordinate of the mouse relative to the volume rectangle to a value between 0 and 1 (0 being muted and 1 being full volume). Lines 243–244 move the `volumeHead` to the new position.

19.5 Embedding Silverlight in HTML

Expression Blend generates an HTML wrapper named `Default.html` for your Silverlight application when you first create the Silverlight project. Figure 19.14 shows a version of this file that we formatted for readability. You can open `Default.html` in a supported web browser to test your application. You can embed a Silverlight application into an existing HTML file by including the `scripts` (lines 8–10), the `silverlightHost` style class (lines 12–13) and the `SilverlightControlHost` `div` (lines 17–21). You can adjust the width and height of your application by changing the `width` and `height` attributes of the `silverlightHost` style class (lines 12–13).

```
1  <!-- Fig. 19.14: Default.html -->
2  <!-- HTML wrapper for Movie Viewer. -->
3  <!DOCTYPE HTML PUBLIC "-//W3C//DTD HTML 4.01 Transitional//EN"
4     "http://www.w3c.org/TR/1999/REC-html401-19991224/loose.dtd">
5  <html xmlns = "http://www.w3.org/1999/xhtml">
6     <head>
7        <title>MovieViewer</title>
8        <script type = "text/javascript" src = "Silverlight.js"></script>
9        <script type = "text/javascript" src = "Default_html.js"></script>
10       <script type = "text/javascript" src = "Page.xaml.js"></script>
11       <style type = "text/css">
12          .silverlightHost { height: 480px;
13                             width: 640px }
14       </style>
15    </head>
```

Fig. 19.14 | HTML wrapper for Movie Viewer. (Part 1 of 2.)

```
16    <body>
17       <div id = "SilverlightControlHost" class = "silverlightHost">
18          <script type = "text/javascript">
19             createSilverlight();
20          </script>
21       </div>
22    </body>
23 </html>
```

Fig. 19.14 | HTML wrapper for Movie Viewer. (Part 2 of 2.)

The `createSilverlight` function (line 19) is located in `Default_html.js` (Fig. 19.15). This function inserts the Silverlight plug-in object in the `SilverlightControlHost` div. The `Default_html.js` file that Expression Blend creates will not work with our project because it tries to access function `Page` in the JavaScript, which no longer exists. You must remove the lines instantiating the `scene` variable and set the `onLoad` event to `null` (line 15).

```
1  // Fig. 19.15: Default_html.js
2  // Create Silverlight object in SilverlightControlHost div.
3  function createSilverlight()
4  {
5     Silverlight.createObjectEx( {
6        source: "Page.xaml",
7        parentElement: document.getElementById( "SilverlightControlHost" ),
8        id: "SilverlightControl",
9        properties: {
10          width: "100%",
11          height: "100%",
12          version: "1.0"
13       },
14       events: {
15          onLoad: null
16       }
17    } );
18 }
19
20 if ( !window.Silverlight )
21    window.Silverlight = {};
22
23 Silverlight.createDelegate = function( instance, method ) {
24    return function() {
25       return method.apply( instance, arguments );
26    }
27 }
```

Fig. 19.15 | Creates Silverlight object in `SilverlightControlHost` div.

19.6 Silverlight Streaming

Microsoft provides a service called Silverlight Streaming at `silverlight.live.com`. This service currently hosts your Silverlight applications for free, which allows individuals and businesses to share video content online without having to provide and pay for the significant bandwidth that video requires. While in prerelease status, Silverlight Streaming provides you with "up to 4GB storage and unlimited outbound streaming, and no limit on the number of users that can view those streams."[1] Eventually, Microsoft intends to allow "up to 1 million minutes of free video streaming at 700 Kbps per site per month. Unlimited streaming will also be available for free with advertising, or with payment of a nominal fee for the service for use without advertising."[2] You can easily embed Silverlight applications that are hosted by this service into your web pages.

Encoding Your Video with Expression Media Encoder

According to `dev.live.com/silverlight/`, the bit rate of video files included with Silverlight applications must not exceed 700 Kbps. To ensure that your video adheres to these requirements, it is recommended that you encode your video using Microsoft Expression Blend Media Encoder. A free trial of Media Encoder is available at `www.microsoft.com/expression/products/download.aspx?key=encoder`. Once Media Encoder is installed, open it and select **Import...** from the **File** menu. Select the video file you would like to encode (Media Encoder supports many video types) and click **Open**. If the video is encoded in VC-1 and doesn't open properly, you may need to install Windows Media Player 11. In the **Profile** panel of the **Settings** inspector (Fig. 19.16), you can select the **Video** and **Audio** type. For the Movie Viewer example, we encoded the video using **VC-1 Streaming Broadband** and the audio using the **Default Profile**. In the **Output** inspector (Fig. 19.16), you can have Media Encoder save a thumbnail of a frame of your choosing, and have the output include one of 14 prebuilt Silverlight media player templates for your video. To start the encoding process, either select **Encode** from the **File** menu, or click the **Encode** button at the bottom of the **Media Content** inspector.

Uploading an Application to the Silverlight Streaming Service

To use the Silverlight Streaming service, you must go to `silverlight.live.com` and register for an account. Once you have an account, log in and select **Manage Applications** from the navigation links on the left side of the page. This page will show you what applications are currently being hosted on your account, and it also enables you to upload applications.

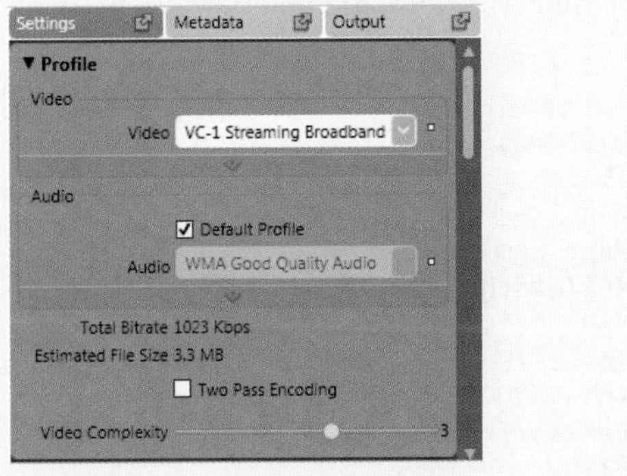

Fig. 19.16 | Microsoft's Expression Media Encoder. (Part 1 of 2.)

---

1. `dev.live.com/terms/`
2. `dev.live.com/silverlight/`

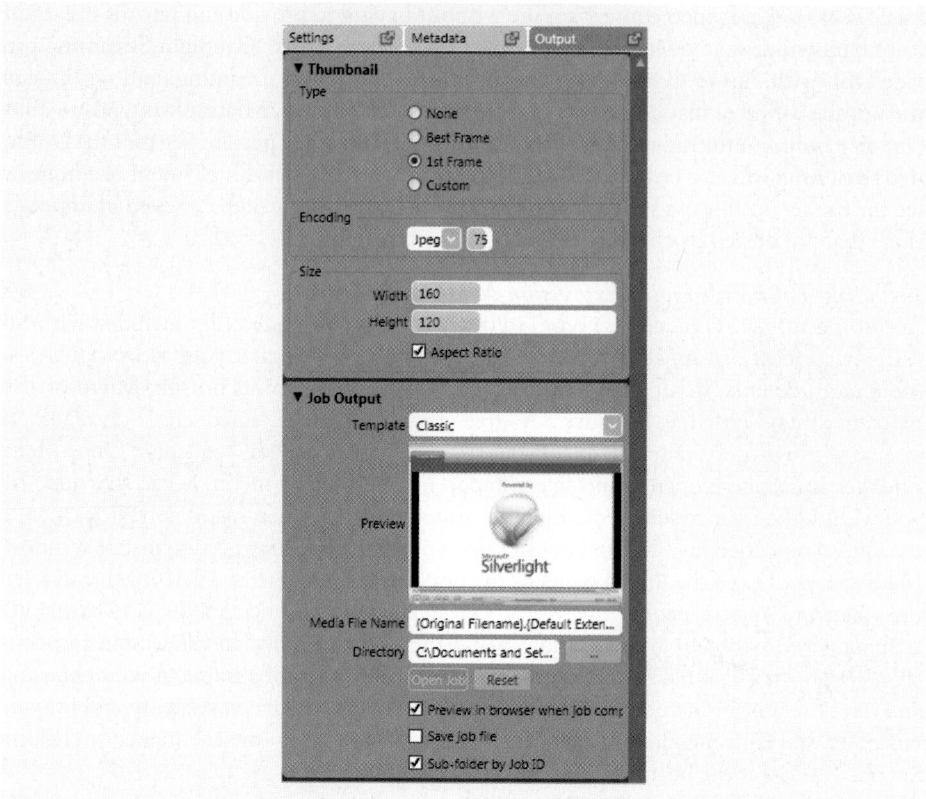

Fig. 19.16 | Microsoft's Expression Media Encoder. (Part 2 of 2.)

To upload an application, you must package it into a Zip archive. This archive must contain your XAML, your code-behind file, any media elements you use in the application, and a `manifest.xml` file (Fig. 19.17). The `manifest.xml` file specifies the filename of your XAML file (line 4), width and height (lines 5–6), and more.

```
1  <!-- Fig. 19.17: manifest.xml -->
2  <!-- Manifest for Movie Viewer on Silverlight Streaming. -->
3  <SilverlightApp>
4     <source>Page.xaml</source>
5     <width>640</width>
6     <height>480</height>
7     <inplaceInstallPrompt>true</inplaceInstallPrompt>
8     <background>#000000</background>
9     <framerate>24</framerate>
10    <version>1.0</version>
11    <isWindowless>false</isWindowless>
12 </SilverlightApp>
```

Fig. 19.17 | Manifest for Movie Viewer on Silverlight Streaming.

On the **Manage Applications** page, click the **Upload a Silverlight Application** link. You must enter an **Application Name** and select the Zip archive you wish to upload. If the application uploads successfully after you click **Upload**, you will see the **Manage Application** page for the application. On this page, Microsoft provides instructions for adding the application to an existing web page. First, you must create a new JavaScript file to handle the `CreateSilverlight` function that adds the Silverlight application inside a `div` in your HTML. For the `div` element that you add to your HTML, make sure to set the `width` and `height` parameters to the `width` and `height` of your application. Figures 19.18 and 19.19 show the HTML and JavaScript needed to embed the Movie Viewer application that is hosted on Silverlight Streaming.

```
<?xml version = "1.0" encoding = "utf-8"?>
<!DOCTYPE html PUBLIC "-//W3C//DTD XHTML 1.0 Strict//EN"
   "http://www.w3.org/TR/xhtml1/DTD/xhtml1-strict.dtd">

<!-- Fig. 19.18: silverlightStreaming.html -->
<!-- HTML wrapper for Movie Viewer hosted on Silverlight Streaming -->
<html xmlns = "http://www.w3.org/1999/xhtml">
   <head>
      <title>MovieViewer Hosted on Silverlight Streaming</title>
      <script type = "text/javascript"
         src = "http://agappdom.net/h/silverlight.js"></script>
      <script type = "text/javascript"
         src = "CreateSilverlight.js"></script>
      <style type = "text/css">
         .silverlightHost { height: 480px;
                            width: 640px; }
      </style>
   </head>
   <body>
      <div id = "Wrapper_MovieViewer"
         style = "width: 640px; height: 480px; overflow: hidden;"></div>
      <script type = "text/javascript">
         var Wrapper_MovieViewer =
            document.getElementById( "Wrapper_MovieViewer" );
            CreateSilverlight();
      </script>
   </body>
</html>
```

Fig. 19.18 | HTML wrapper for Movie Viewer hosted on Silverlight Streaming.

```
// Fig. 19.19: CreateSilverlight.js
// JavaScript to add the Silverlight object to the Wrapper_MovieViewer div
function CreateSilverlight()
{
   Silverlight.createHostedObjectEx( {
      source: "streaming:/16645/MovieViewer",
      parentElement: Wrapper_MovieViewer } );
}
```

Fig. 19.19 | JavaScript to add the Silverlight object to `Wrapper_MovieViewer` `div`.

19.7 Silverlight 1.1 Installation and Overview

Silverlight 1.1 uses a lightweight version of the .NET CLR (Common Language Runtime) in the browser plug-in. This allows you to program Silverlight applications in C#, Visual Basic, Python, Ruby and JavaScript. Silverlight 1.1 applications use the .NET CLR's just-in-time (JIT) compiler to compile the code to machine language, allowing for a significant improvement in performance over the interpreted JavaScript used in Silverlight 1.0 and Ajax.

To install the Silverlight 1.1 Alpha Refresh browser plug-in, go to `silverlight.net/GetStarted/` and download the Silverlight 1.1 Alpha Refresh runtime for your platform. Once you have installed it, you can see some 1.1 applications in action at the website `silverlight.net/themes/silverlight/community/gallerydetail.aspx?cat=2`.

A chess game that serves as an excellent demonstration of the performance improvement is located at `silverlight.net/samples/1.1/chess/run/default.html`. This game allows you to compare the performance of a computer player coded in .NET to the performance of a computer player coded in JavaScript. As you will see, the .NET player usually wins because it can analyze many more moves than the JavaScript player in the same amount of time.

We will develop our Silverlight 1.1 applications using Microsoft Expression Blend 2 and Microsoft Visual Studio 2008. After you have installed these tools, download and install the **Silverlight Tools Alpha for Visual Studio** from `go.microsoft.com/fwlink/?LinkID=89149&clcid=0x409`. Now, you can create a Silverlight 1.1 Alpha Refresh project.

19.8 Creating a Cover Viewer for Silverlight 1.1 Alpha

Our next example is a Deitel book cover viewer (Fig. 19.20) written in XAML (Fig. 19.21) with a Visual Basic code-behind file (Fig. 19.22) for Silverlight 1.1 Alpha

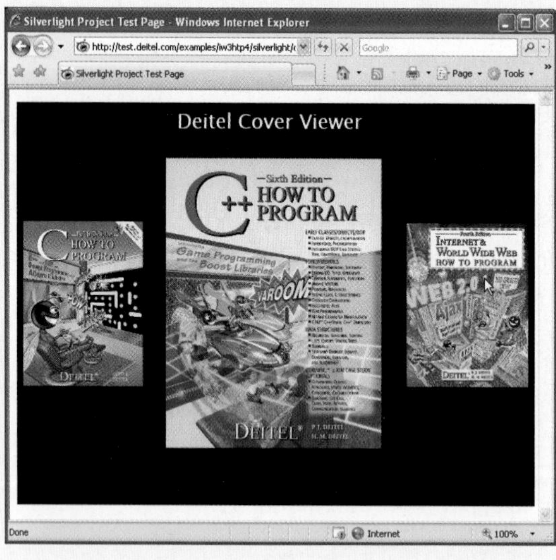

a) The user clicking the *Internet & World Wide Web How To Program* cover

Fig. 19.20 | Deitel book-cover viewer running on Silverlight 1.1 Alpha Refresh. (Part 1 of 2.)

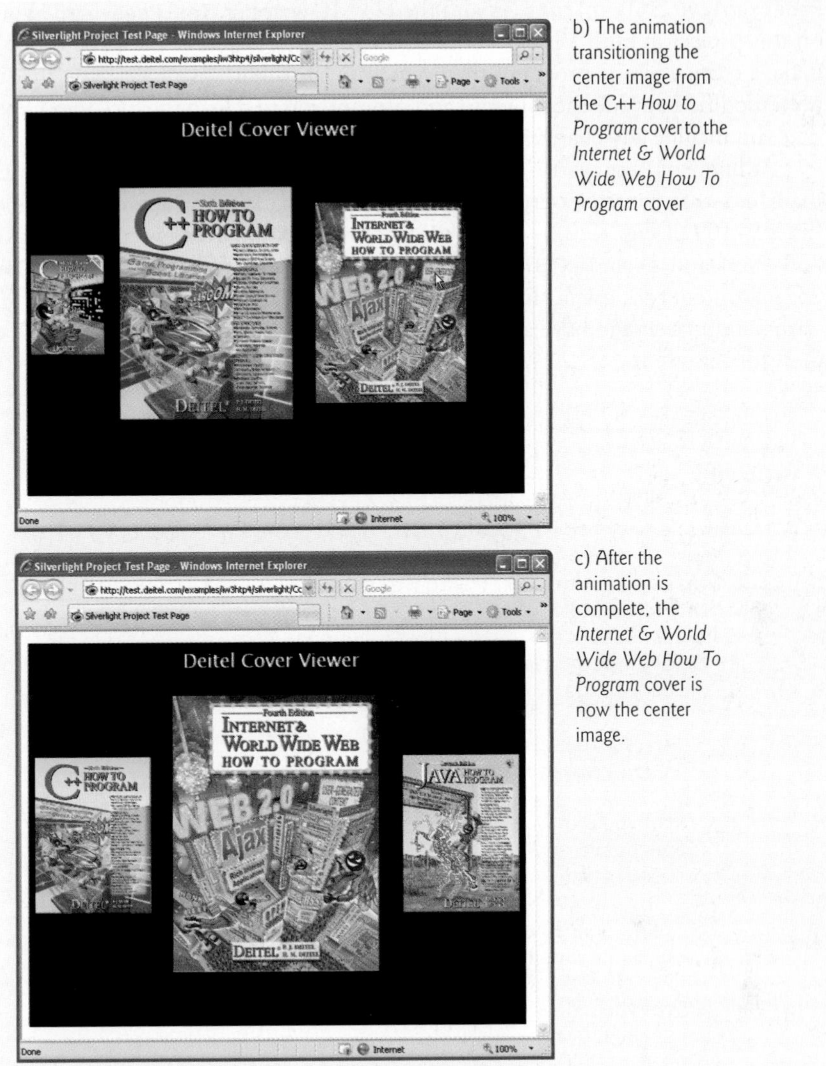

b) The animation transitioning the center image from the C++ *How to Program* cover to the *Internet & World Wide Web How To Program* cover

c) After the animation is complete, the *Internet & World Wide Web How To Program* cover is now the center image.

Fig. 19.20 | Deitel book-cover viewer running on Silverlight 1.1 Alpha Refresh. (Part 2 of 2.)

Refresh. This cover viewer retrieves an RSS feed containing the image URIs, and displays three covers at a time. Clicking the cover on the left or right triggers an animation that moves the cover the user clicked to the center. You can test a live version of this application at `test.deitel.com/examples/iw3htp4/silverlight/CoverViewer/index.html`.

Creating a Silverlight 1.1 Application in Visual Studio 2008

To create a Silverlight 1.1 Alpha Refresh project, open Visual Studio 2008 and select **New Project** in the **File** menu. Next, select **Visual Basic** (for your later projects, you can also select **Visual C#**), then **Silverlight**, then specify the name and location of your project, and click **OK**. The project will initially contain a XAML file, `Page.xaml`, a code-behind file,

`Page.xaml.vb`, `Silverlight.js` and the HTML wrapper, `TestPage.html`. You can work on this project in both Visual Studio and Expression Blend at the same time. When you make a change in one program, then switch to the other, it will alert you that the file has been modified outside the program and prompt you to reload the file. Select **Yes** to ensure that you include any changes you made in the other program.

At line 7 of `Page.xaml` (Fig. 19.21), we define the **`x:Class`** attribute, which specifies the `Class` that contains our event handlers, in this case the `Page` class in `Page.xaml.vb` (lines 9–159 of Fig. 19.22). The GUI contains two `TextBlocks`—`titleTextBlock` (lines 230–233) and `errorTextBlock` (lines 234–236)–and three `Images`—`prevImage` (lines 237–248), `currentImage` (lines 249–250) and `nextImage` (lines 251–262). Both `nextImage` and `prevImage` have a `MouseLeftButtonDown` attribute, registering the event handlers for this event.

```
1   <!-- Fig. 19.21: Page.xaml -->
2   <!-- Deitel Cover Viewer in Silverlight 1.1 Alpha Refresh -->
3   <Canvas
4      xmlns = "http://schemas.microsoft.com/client/2007"
5      xmlns:x = "http://schemas.microsoft.com/winfx/2006/xaml"
6      x:Name = "parentCanvas" Loaded = "Page_Loaded"
7      x:Class = "CoverViewer.Page;assembly=ClientBin/CoverViewer.dll"
8      Width = "640" Height = "480" Background = "Black">
9      <Canvas.Resources>
10        <Storyboard x:Name = "nextImageAnimation"
11           Completed = "nextImageSwitch">
12
13           <!-- Lines 12-99 of the autogenerated code were -->
14           <!-- removed to save space. -->
15
100       </Storyboard>
101       <Storyboard x:Name = "prevImageAnimation"
102          Completed = "prevImageSwitch">
103
104          <!-- Lines 103-226 of the autogenerated code were -->
105          <!-- removed to save space. -->
106
227       </Storyboard>
228    </Canvas.Resources>
229
230    <TextBlock x:Name = "titleTextBlock" Canvas.Left = "199.994"
231       Canvas.Top = "5" FontSize = "24" Width = "238.308"
232       TextWrapping = "Wrap" Foreground = "#FFFFFFFF"
233       Text = "Deitel Cover Viewer" />
234    <TextBlock x:Name = "errorTextBlock" Canvas.Left = "0"
235       Canvas.Top = "400" FontSize = "12" Width = "640"
236       TextWrapping = "Wrap" Foreground = "#FFFFFFFF" />
237    <Image x:Name = "prevImage" MouseLeftButtonDown = "prevImageHandler"
238       Width = "149.64" Height = "196.652" Canvas.Left = "8"
239       Canvas.Top = "142" RenderTransformOrigin = "0.5, 0.5" >
240       <Image.RenderTransform>
241          <TransformGroup>
242             <ScaleTransform ScaleX = "1" ScaleY = "1" />
```

Fig. 19.21 | Deitel Cover Viewer in Silverlight 1.1 Alpha Refresh. (Part 1 of 2.)

```
243                 <SkewTransform AngleX = "0" AngleY = "0" />
244                 <RotateTransform Angle = "0" />
245                 <TranslateTransform X = "0" Y = "0" />
246              </TransformGroup>
247           </Image.RenderTransform>
248        </Image>
249        <Image x:Name = "currentImage" Width = "265.302" Height = "348.652"
250           Canvas.Left = "186" Canvas.Top = "64.79" />
251        <Image x:Name = "nextImage" MouseLeftButtonDown = "nextImageHandler"
252           Width = "149.64" Height = "196.652" Canvas.Left = "482.36"
253           Canvas.Top = "142" RenderTransformOrigin = "0.5, 0.5" >
254           <Image.RenderTransform>
255              <TransformGroup>
256                 <ScaleTransform ScaleX = "1" ScaleY = "1" />
257                 <SkewTransform AngleX = "0" AngleY = "0" />
258                 <RotateTransform Angle = "0" />
259                 <TranslateTransform X = "0" Y = "0" />
260              </TransformGroup>
261           </Image.RenderTransform>
262        </Image>
263     </Canvas>
```

Fig. 19.21 | Deitel Cover Viewer in Silverlight 1.1 Alpha Refresh. (Part 2 of 2.)

In lines 10–100 (of which lines 12–99 are not shown to save space), the `nextImageAnimation` `Storyboard` moves and resizes the three images so that the `nextImage` replaces the `currentImage`, the `currentImage` replaces the `prevImage`, and the `prevImage` disappears. This animation code was generated using Expression Blend. To create this animation, first click the **Create new Storyboard** button (Fig. 19.4). Name the `Storyboard` `nextImageAnimation`, and select the **Create as a Resource** checkbox. Then, select `nextImage` and click **Record Keyframe.** Move the time slider to 0.5 seconds, then move and resize the element so that it replaces `currentImage`. You can click the **Play** button to see a preview of the animation.

`Storyboard` `nextImageAnimation` has a `Completed` attribute (line 11) that specifies the event handler to be called when the animation is complete. In lines 101–227 (of which lines 103–226 are not shown to save space), the `prevImageAnimation` `Storyboard` moves and resizes the three images so that the `prevImage` replaces the `currentImage`, the `currentImage` replaces the `nextImage`, and the `nextImage` disappears. This animation also has a `Completed` attribute (line 102) that specifies the event handler to be called when the animation is complete.

Visual Basic Code-Behind File

The Visual Basic code-behind file, `Page.xaml.vb` (Fig. 19.22), begins by importing the class libraries the application will use (lines 3–7). Lines 9–10 specify that the `Page` class `Inherits` methods and properties from the `Canvas` class. Lines 13–15 declare the instance variables the application will use. These include `imageURIArrayList` (a **`List`** of the image `Uri`s), `currentImageIndex` (which holds the index number of the `Uri` in `imageURIArrayList` to be displayed as the `currentImage`), and `appRootURI` (which uses the `appRootURIGen` method (lines 151–158) to find the root URI of the application at runtime).

```
' Fig. 19.22: Page.xaml.vb
' VB code-behind file for Cover Viewer.
Imports System.IO
Imports System.Text
Imports System.Windows.Browser
Imports System.Windows.Browser.Net
Imports System.Collections.Generic

Partial Public Class Page
   Inherits Canvas

   ' Instance variables
   Dim currentImageIndex = 0 ' Initialize index of currentImage as 0
   Dim imageURIArrayList As New List(Of Uri)() ' Create ArrayList of URIs
   Dim appRootURI = appRootURIGen() ' Store application root URI

   Public Sub Page_Loaded(ByVal o As Object, ByVal e As EventArgs)
      ' Required to initialize variables
      InitializeComponent()
      Try
         Dim httpRequest As New _
            BrowserHttpWebRequest( _
               New Uri(appRootURI + "bookCoversRSS.xml"))

         ' Save response in variable
         Dim httpResponse = httpRequest.GetResponse()

         ' Save response stream in variable
         Dim httpResponseStream = httpResponse.GetResponseStream()

         Dim currentImageURI ' Store Image URI

         ' Create an XmlReader to parse the response stream
         Using xmlReader As XmlReader = xmlReader.Create( _
            New StreamReader(httpResponseStream))

            ' Start reading response stream, exit loop when done
            While (xmlReader.Read())

               ' Find item element in response stream
               If ((xmlReader.IsStartElement()) And _
                  ("item" = xmlReader.LocalName)) Then

                  ' Create an XmlReader for item element
                  Using itemXMLReader As XmlReader = _
                     xmlReader.ReadSubtree()

                     ' Start reading item element, exit loop when done
                     While (itemXMLReader.Read())

                        ' Find image child element of item
                        If (itemXMLReader.IsStartElement()) Then
                           If ("image" = itemXMLReader.LocalName) Then
```

Fig. 19.22 | VB code-behind file for Cover Viewer. (Part 1 of 3.)

```

                              ' Save Uri of image into ArrayList
                              currentImageURI = appRootURI + _
                              itemXMLReader.ReadElementContentAsString
                              imageURIArrayList.Add( _
                                 New Uri(currentImageURI))
                           End If
                        End If
                     End While
                  End Using
               End If
            End While
         End Using

         ' Close BrowserHttpWebRequest
         httpResponse.Close()

         ' Initialize currentImage and nextImage Sources
         currentImage.Source = imageURIArrayList(currentImageIndex)
         nextImage.Source = imageURIArrayList(currentImageIndex + 1)

         Catch ex As Exception
            errorTextBlock.Text = "Error: " & ex.Message
      End Try
   End Sub ' Page_Loaded

   ' Handle nextImageAnimation's Completed event
   Private Sub nextImageSwitch(ByVal sender As Object, _
      ByVal e As EventArgs)
      nextImageAnimation.Stop()

      ' Test if at end of images
      If (currentImageIndex = (imageURIArrayList.Count - 2)) Then
         currentImageIndex += 1 ' Increment currentImageIndex

         ' Set Source of prevImage and currentImage
         prevImage.Source = imageURIArrayList(currentImageIndex - 1)
         currentImage.Source = imageURIArrayList(currentImageIndex)
         nextImage.Opacity = 0 ' Hide nextImage
      Else
         currentImageIndex += 1 ' Increment currentImageIndex

         ' Set Source of prevImage, currentImage and nextImage
         prevImage.Source = imageURIArrayList(currentImageIndex - 1)
         currentImage.Source = imageURIArrayList(currentImageIndex)
         nextImage.Source = imageURIArrayList(currentImageIndex + 1)
         prevImage.Opacity = 1 ' Show prevImage
      End If
   End Sub ' nextImageSwitch

   ' Handle prevImageAnimation's Completed event
   Private Sub prevImageSwitch(ByVal sender As Object, _
      ByVal e As EventArgs)
```

Fig. 19.22 | VB code-behind file for Cover Viewer. (Part 2 of 3.)

```
      prevImageAnimation.Stop()

      ' Test if at beginning of images
      If (currentImageIndex = 1) Then
         currentImageIndex -= 1 ' Decrement currentImageIndex
         prevImage.Opacity = 0 ' Hide prevImage

         ' Set Source of currentImage and nextImage
         currentImage.Source = imageURIArrayList(currentImageIndex)
         nextImage.Source = imageURIArrayList(currentImageIndex + 1)
      Else
         currentImageIndex -= 1 ' Decrement currentImageIndex

         ' Set Source of prevImage, currentImage and nextImage
         prevImage.Source = imageURIArrayList(currentImageIndex - 1)
         currentImage.Source = imageURIArrayList(currentImageIndex)
         nextImage.Source = imageURIArrayList(currentImageIndex + 1)
         nextImage.Opacity = 1 ' Show nextImage
      End If
   End Sub ' prevImageSwitch

   ' Handle nextImage's MouseLeftButtonDown event
   Private Sub nextImageHandler(ByVal sender As Object, _
      ByVal e As EventArgs)

      ' Make sure there are more images to the right
      If (currentImageIndex < (imageURIArrayList.Count - 1)) Then
         nextImageAnimation.Begin()
      End If
   End Sub ' nextImageHandler

   ' Handle prevImage's MouseLeftButtonDown event
   Private Sub prevImageHandler(ByVal sender As Object, _
      ByVal e As EventArgs)

      ' Make sure there are more images to the left
      If (currentImageIndex > 1) Then
         prevImageAnimation.Begin()
      ElseIf (currentImageIndex > 0) Then
         prevImageAnimation.Begin()
      End If
   End Sub ' prevImageHandler

   ' Generate root URI of application
   Public Function appRootURIGen() As String

      ' Find root directory of application
      Dim path = HtmlPage.DocumentUri.AbsolutePath
      Dim lastSlash = path.LastIndexOf("/")
      path = path.Substring(0, lastSlash + 1)
      Return "http://" & HtmlPage.DocumentUri.Host & path
   End Function ' appRootURIGen
End Class ' Page
```

Fig. 19.22 | VB code-behind file for Cover Viewer. (Part 3 of 3.)

In method Page_Loaded (lines 17–78), line 19 initializes the application using the InitializeComponent method located in the autogenerated Page.g.vb file (located in the obj\Debug directory). This file takes any XAML elements that have an x:Name attribute, and uses the **FindName** method to map each element to a variable of the same name. This means that we do not have to do this manually, as we did for the Silverlight 1.0 **Movie Viewer** example. It also allows us to use Visual Studio's IntelliSense feature to autocomplete XAML element names in our code-behind file.

Lines 20–77 try to download an RSS file, bookCoversRSS.xml (Fig. 19.23), and create an array of image Uris. First, lines 21–23 create a **BrowserHttpWebRequest** object that downloads the RSS file located at the URI created by concatenating the appRootURI variable with bookCoversRSS.xml. Note that the BrowserHttpWebRequest object does not currently support cross-domain requests, so the application and the RSS file must be located on the same server. Lines 26 and 29 get the object used to manipulate the request's response, then get the stream associated with that object. Lines 34–35 create an **XmlReader** object to parse the RSS content. The XmlReader class provides read-only access to the elements in an XML document. Lines 38–65 contain a While loop in which the condition remains True until the XmlReader has reached the end of the RSS. Lines 41–42 search for an item element in the RSS, and lines 45–53 read the contents of that element and search for an image element inside the item element. Upon finding an image element, lines 56–59 add the contents of the image element (the image's filename) to the imageURIArrayList as a complete Uri including the application's root Uri (appRootURI). Line 69 closes the BrowserHttpWebRequest. Lines 72–73 set the Source attribute of the currentImage and nextImage to the first and second elements of the imageURIArrayList. Lines 75–76 catch any exceptions and display the error message in the errorTextBlock.

```
<?xml version = "1.0" encoding = "ISO-8859-1" ?>
<!-- Fig. 19.23: bookCoversRSS.xml -->
<!-- RSS for Deitel book-cover viewer -->
<rss version = "2.0">
   <link rel = "alternate" type = "application/rss+xml"
      title = "Deitel Cover Viewer" href = "http://www.deitel.com/" />
   <channel>
      <title>Deitel Cover Viewer</title>
      <link>http://www.deitel.com/</link>
      <description>View the Deitel book covers.</description>
      <copyright>2008 Deitel And Associates</copyright>
      <language>en-us</language>

      <item>
         <title>C How to Program</title>
         <link>images/chtp5.jpg</link>
         <image>images/chtp5.jpg</image>
      </item>
      <item>
         <title>C++ How to Program</title>
         <link>images/cpphtp6.jpg</link>
         <image>images/cpphtp6.jpg</image>
      </item>
```

Fig. 19.23 | RSS for Deitel book-cover viewer. (Part 1 of 2.)

```
        <item>
            <title>Internet How to Program</title>
            <link>images/iw3htp4.jpg</link>
            <image>images/iw3htp4.jpg</image>
        </item>
        <item>
            <title>Java How to Program</title>
            <link>images/jhtp7.jpg</link>
            <image>images/jhtp7.jpg</image>
        </item>
        <item>
            <title>VB How to Program</title>
            <link>images/vbhtp3.jpg</link>
            <image>images/vbhtp3.jpg</image>
        </item>
        <item>
            <title>Visual C# How to Program</title>
            <link>images/vcsharphtp2.jpg</link>
            <image>images/vcsharphtp2.jpg</image>
        </item>
        <item>
            <title>Simply C++</title>
            <link>images/simplycpp.jpg</link>
            <image>images/simplycpp.jpg</image>
        </item>
        <item>
            <title>Simply VB 2005</title>
            <link>images/simplyvb2005.jpg</link>
            <image>images/simplyvb2005.jpg</image>
        </item>
        <item>
            <title>Simply Java</title>
            <link>images/simplyjava.jpg</link>
            <image>images/simplyjava.jpg</image>
        </item>
        <item>
            <title>Small C++ How to Program</title>
            <link>images/smallcpphtp5.jpg</link>
            <image>images/smallcpphtp5.jpg</image>
        </item>
        <item>
            <title>Small Java</title>
            <link>images/smalljavahtp6.jpg</link>
            <image>images/smalljavahtp6.jpg</image>
        </item>
    </channel>
</rss>
```

Fig. 19.23 | RSS for Deitel book-cover viewer. (Part 2 of 2.)

Method appRootURIGen (Fig. 19.22, lines 151–158) first uses the **HtmlPage** element to find the **AbsolutePath** of the page. Lines 155–156 find the last forward slash (/) of the Uri and save the Uri up to that last slash as a string, using the Substring method. Line

157 returns a string concatenating "http://", the Silverlight application's Host (the domain name or IP address of the server) and the path string.

Method nextImageHandler (lines 129–136) handles nextImage's MouseLeftButtonDown event. Line 133 checks whether there are, in fact, additional book covers to the right. If so, line 134 begins the nextImageAnimation Storyboard. Upon completion, this Storyboard will call the nextImageSwitch method (lines 81–102). Line 86 checks whether there is only one more book cover to the right, in which case it will increment the currentImageIndex by one (line 87), update the Source of prevImage and currentImage (90–91), and hide nextImage (line 92). If there is more than one book cover to the right, lines 94–100 will increment the currentImageIndex by one (line 94), update the Source of all three Images (lines 97–99), and ensure that prevImage is visible (line 100), in case the user is going from the first book cover (where prevImage would be hidden) to the second book cover. Methods prevImageHandler (lines 139–148) and prevImageSwitch (lines 105–126) provide the corresponding functionality for prevImage.

19.9 Building an Application with Third-Party Controls

Though Silverlight 1.1 Alpha Refresh does not yet include pre-built controls, a number of third-party control libraries have been created. One such third-party library is Netika's GOA WinForms library for Silverlight. This library is an implementation of .NET's System.Windows.Form library for both Silverlight and Flash. This allows us to create Silverlight applications by using .NET desktop applications as templates. The free version of GOA WinForms includes 40+ controls, including buttons, text boxes, calendars and more. Netika's website at www.netikatech.com includes demos and documentation for all the controls. To download the library, go to www.netikatech.com/downloads and select the standard Silverlight version of GOA WinForms. After installation, open Visual Studio 2008 and create a new project. Select **Visual Basic**, then **GOA WinForms VB Application** in **My Templates**. Name this project **InterestRateCalculator**, as we will be creating a Silverlight application that calculates interest. For a GOA WinForms project, the Visual Basic code-behind file is located in MyForm.vb. In this file, you will find an InitializeComponent function (lines 27–42) that creates a Button. Select **Build InterestRateCalculator** from the **Build** menu, then open TestPage.html in your browser to see a sample button.

Open up the InterestRateCalculatorForWindows project from the examples directory. We are going to be creating a Silverlight application from this desktop application (Fig. 19.24). First, build and run the project to see how the application looks on the desktop. Next, replace the InitializeComponent function in the InterestRateCalculator project's MyForm.vb with the InitializeComponent in the InterestRateCalculatorForWindows project's InterestRateCalculatorForWindows.Designer.vb. Then replace the Friend WithEvents line (line 26) in the InterestRateCalculator project's MyForm.vb with the Friend WithEvents lines (lines 139–147) in the InterestRateCalculatorForWindows project's InterestRateCalculatorForWindows.Designer.vb file. Finally, copy the btnCalculate_Click function from the InterestRateCalculatorForWindows project's InterestRateCalculatorForWindows.vb into the MyForm class in the InterestRateCalculator project's MyForm.vb.

Try to build the InterestRateCalculator project. You will see several errors. This is because not every property of the Windows Form controls has been implemented in GOA WinForms. Looking at Fig. 19.25, you will see that we commented out lines 47, 60, 82,

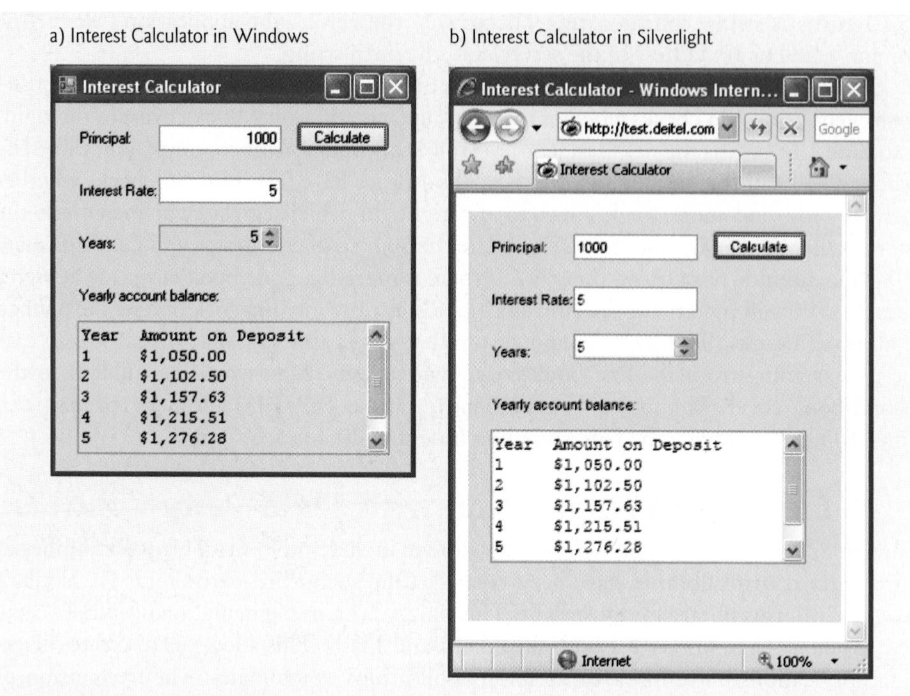

Fig. 19.24 | Interest Calculator in Windows and Silverlight

100, 118 and 128–129. These lines all accessed properties not supported in GOA WinForms. We kept these lines as comments to show you the relatively easy process of converting a Visual Basic desktop application to a Silverlight 1.1 application when using GOA WinForms controls.

```
1  ' Fig. 19.25: MyForm.vb
2  ' Using third-party controls in Silverlight 1.1 Alpha Refresh.
3  Public Class MyForm
4     Inherits System.Windows.Forms.Form
5
6     Public Sub New()
7        MyBase.New()
8        InitializeComponent()
9      End Sub ' New
10
11    Protected Overloads Overrides Sub Dispose( _
12       ByVal disposing As Boolean)
13       If disposing Then
14          If Not (components Is Nothing) Then
15             components.Dispose()
16          End If
17       End If
```

Fig. 19.25 | Using third-party controls in Silverlight 1.1 Alpha Refresh. (Part 1 of 5.)

```
        MyBase.Dispose(disposing)
    End Sub ' Dispose

    Private components As System.ComponentModel.IContainer

    Private Sub InitializeComponent()
        Me.btnCalculate = New System.Windows.Forms.Button
        Me.txtDisplay = New System.Windows.Forms.TextBox
        Me.lblBalance = New System.Windows.Forms.Label
        Me.updYear = New System.Windows.Forms.NumericUpDown
        Me.lblYears = New System.Windows.Forms.Label
        Me.txtInterest = New System.Windows.Forms.TextBox
        Me.lblInterest = New System.Windows.Forms.Label
        Me.txtPrincipal = New System.Windows.Forms.TextBox
        Me.lblPrincipal = New System.Windows.Forms.Label
        CType(Me.updYear, _
           System.ComponentModel.ISupportInitialize).BeginInit()
        Me.SuspendLayout()

        ' btnCalculate
        Me.btnCalculate.Location = New System.Drawing.Point(197, 14)
        Me.btnCalculate.Name = "btnCalculate"
        Me.btnCalculate.Size = New System.Drawing.Size(75, 23)
        Me.btnCalculate.TabIndex = 17
        Me.btnCalculate.Text = "Calculate"

        ' txtDisplay
        ' the following line was commented out because it accessed
        ' a property that is not supported in GOA WinForms
        ' Me.txtDisplay.BackColor = System.Drawing.SystemColors.Control
        Me.txtDisplay.Location = New System.Drawing.Point(18, 170)
        Me.txtDisplay.Multiline = True
        Me.txtDisplay.Name = "txtDisplay"
        Me.txtDisplay.ReadOnly = True
        Me.txtDisplay.ScrollBars = System.Windows.Forms.ScrollBars.Vertical
        Me.txtDisplay.Size = New System.Drawing.Size(254, 104)
        Me.txtDisplay.TabIndex = 16
        Me.txtDisplay.Font = New Font("Courier New", 10)

        ' lblBalance
        ' the following line was commented out because it accessed
        ' a property that is not supported in GOA WinForms
        ' Me.lblBalance.AutoSize = True
        Me.lblBalance.Location = New System.Drawing.Point(17, 143)
        Me.lblBalance.Name = "lblBalance"
        Me.lblBalance.Size = New System.Drawing.Size(122, 13)
        Me.lblBalance.TabIndex = 15
        Me.lblBalance.Text = "Yearly account balance:"

        ' updYear
        Me.updYear.Location = New System.Drawing.Point(85, 95)
        Me.updYear.Maximum = New Decimal(New Integer() {10, 0, 0, 0})
        Me.updYear.Minimum = New Decimal(New Integer() {1, 0, 0, 0})
```

Fig. 19.25 | Using third-party controls in Silverlight 1.1 Alpha Refresh. (Part 2 of 5.)

```
        Me.updYear.Name = "updYear"
        Me.updYear.ReadOnly = True
        Me.updYear.Size = New System.Drawing.Size(100, 20)
        Me.updYear.TabIndex = 14
        Me.updYear.TextAlign = _
           System.Windows.Forms.HorizontalAlignment.Right
        Me.updYear.Value = New Decimal(New Integer() {1, 0, 0, 0})

        ' lblYears
        ' the following line was commented out because it accessed
        ' a property that is not supported in GOA WinForms
        ' Me.lblYears.AutoSize = True
        Me.lblYears.Location = New System.Drawing.Point(17, 102)
        Me.lblYears.Name = "lblYears"
        Me.lblYears.Size = New System.Drawing.Size(37, 13)
        Me.lblYears.TabIndex = 13
        Me.lblYears.Text = "Years:"

        ' txtInterest
        Me.txtInterest.Location = New System.Drawing.Point(85, 58)
        Me.txtInterest.Name = "txtInterest"
        Me.txtInterest.Size = New System.Drawing.Size(100, 20)
        Me.txtInterest.TabIndex = 12
        Me.txtInterest.TextAlign = _
           System.Windows.Forms.HorizontalAlignment.Right

        ' lblInterest
        ' the following line was commented out because it accessed
        ' a property that is not supported in GOA WinForms
        ' Me.lblInterest.AutoSize = True
        Me.lblInterest.Location = New System.Drawing.Point(17, 61)
        Me.lblInterest.Name = "lblInterest"
        Me.lblInterest.Size = New System.Drawing.Size(71, 13)
        Me.lblInterest.TabIndex = 11
        Me.lblInterest.Text = "Interest Rate:"

        ' txtPrincipal
        Me.txtPrincipal.Location = New System.Drawing.Point(85, 17)
        Me.txtPrincipal.Name = "txtPrincipal"
        Me.txtPrincipal.Size = New System.Drawing.Size(100, 20)
        Me.txtPrincipal.TabIndex = 10
        Me.txtPrincipal.TextAlign = _
           System.Windows.Forms.HorizontalAlignment.Right

        ' lblPrincipal
        ' the following line was commented out because it accessed
        ' a property that is not supported in GOA WinForms
        ' Me.lblPrincipal.AutoSize = True
        Me.lblPrincipal.Location = New System.Drawing.Point(17, 20)
        Me.lblPrincipal.Name = "lblPrincipal"
        Me.lblPrincipal.Size = New System.Drawing.Size(50, 13)
        Me.lblPrincipal.TabIndex = 9
        Me.lblPrincipal.Text = "Principal:"
```

Fig. 19.25 | Using third-party controls in Silverlight 1.1 Alpha Refresh. (Part 3 of 5.)

```

      ' FrmInterestCalculator
      ' the following two lines were commented out because they
      ' accessed properties that are not supported in GOA WinForms
      ' Me.AutoScaleDimensions = New System.Drawing.SizeF(6.0!, 13.0!)
      ' Me.AutoScaleMode = System.Windows.Forms.AutoScaleMode.Font
      Me.ClientSize = New System.Drawing.Size(289, 288)
      Me.Controls.Add(Me.btnCalculate)
      Me.Controls.Add(Me.txtDisplay)
      Me.Controls.Add(Me.lblBalance)
      Me.Controls.Add(Me.updYear)
      Me.Controls.Add(Me.lblYears)
      Me.Controls.Add(Me.txtInterest)
      Me.Controls.Add(Me.lblInterest)
      Me.Controls.Add(Me.txtPrincipal)
      Me.Controls.Add(Me.lblPrincipal)
      Me.Name = "FrmInterestCalculator"
      Me.Text = "Interest Calculator"
      CType(Me.updYear, _
         System.ComponentModel.ISupportInitialize).EndInit()
      Me.ResumeLayout(False)
      Me.PerformLayout()
   End Sub ' InitializeComponent

   Friend WithEvents btnCalculate As System.Windows.Forms.Button
   Friend WithEvents txtDisplay As System.Windows.Forms.TextBox
   Friend WithEvents lblBalance As System.Windows.Forms.Label
   Friend WithEvents updYear As System.Windows.Forms.NumericUpDown
   Friend WithEvents lblYears As System.Windows.Forms.Label
   Friend WithEvents txtInterest As System.Windows.Forms.TextBox
   Friend WithEvents lblInterest As System.Windows.Forms.Label
   Friend WithEvents txtPrincipal As System.Windows.Forms.TextBox
   Friend WithEvents lblPrincipal As System.Windows.Forms.Label

   Public Shared Sub Main()
      Application.Run(New MyForm)
   End Sub ' Main

   Private Sub btnCalculate_Click(ByVal sender As System.Object, _
      ByVal e As System.EventArgs) Handles btnCalculate.Click

      Dim principal As Decimal
      Dim rate As Double
      Dim year As Integer
      Dim amount As Decimal

      principal = Convert.ToDecimal(Me.txtPrincipal.Text)
      rate = Convert.ToDouble(Me.txtInterest.Text)
      year = Convert.ToInt32(Me.updYear.Value)

      txtDisplay.Text = String.Format("{0,-6}{1}" & vbCrLf, "Year", _
         "Amount on Deposit")

```

Fig. 19.25 | Using third-party controls in Silverlight 1.1 Alpha Refresh. (Part 4 of 5.)

```
177         For yearCounter As Integer = 1 To year
178            amount = principal * Convert.ToDecimal( _
179               Math.Pow(1 + rate / 100, yearCounter))
180            txtDisplay.Text &= String.Format("{0,-6:D}{1:C}" & vbCrLf, _
181               yearCounter, amount)
182         Next
183      End Sub ' btnCalculate_Click
184   End Class ' MyForm
```

Fig. 19.25 | Using third-party controls in Silverlight 1.1 Alpha Refresh. (Part 5 of 5.)

Build the `InterestRateCalculator` project, then open up `TestPage.html` in a web browser. You will see an **"AG_E_UNKNOWN_ERROR"** error message because the application is not running from a web server. You can safely ignore this error message for now. Test the application, and compare it with the desktop version (Fig. 19.24). Some of the controls function slightly differently, as GOA WinForms is not an exact replica of the standard Windows Forms controls.

The `InitializeComponent` function (lines 23–146) was generated in the `InterestRateCalculatorForWindows` project using Visual Studio's design mode. `TextBoxes` are used to input the principal and interest-rate amounts, and a `NumericUpDown` control is used to input the number of years for which we want to calculate interest.

The `btnCalculate_Click` function (lines 162–183) handles `btnCalculate`'s `Click` event (line 163). Lines 165 and 168 declare two `Decimal` variables, `principal` and `amount`. Line 166 declares `rate` as type `Double`, and line 167 declares `year` as type `Integer`. Lines 170–171 take the `Text` from the `txtPrincipal` and `txtInterest` text boxes, convert them to the correct type, then store the value in the corresponding variable. Line 172 takes the `Value` from the `updYear` `NumericUpDown`, converts it to an integer, and stores the value to `year`. Lines 174–175 set the `txtDisplay`'s `Text` to display `"Year"` and `"Amount on Deposit"` column headers followed by a carriage return. These are formatted using the `String.Format` method.

Lines 177–182 count from 1 to `year` in increments of `1`. Lines 178–179 perform a calculation based on the following formula:

$$a = p(1 + r)^{n}$$

where a is the `amount`, p is the `principal`, r is the `rate` and n is the `year`. Lines 180–181 set `txtDisplay`'s `Text` to display two columns containing the current `yearCounter` and `amount` values.

19.10 Consuming a Web Service

In the next example, we consume a web service from a Silverlight application. The web service is designed to perform calculations with integers that contain a maximum of 100 digits. Most programming languages cannot easily perform calculations using integers this large. The web service provides client applications with methods that take two "huge integers" and determine their sum, their difference, which one is larger or smaller and whether the two numbers are equal. We've placed the web service is on our website at `test.deitel.com/hugeinteger/hugeinteger.asmx`.

We provide a Visual Basic program that consumes this web service. We will create a Silverlight application using that application's code, then we'll add a proxy class to the project that allows the Silverlight application to access the web service. The proxy class (or proxy) is generated from the web service's WSDL file and enables the client to call web methods over the Internet. The proxy class handles all the details of communicating with the web service. The proxy class is hidden from you by default—you can view it in the **Solution Explorer** by clicking the **Show All Files** button. The proxy class's purpose is to make clients think that they are calling the web methods directly.

When you add a web reference to the Silverlight project, Visual Studio will generate the appropriate proxy class. You will then create an instance of the proxy class and use it to call the web service's methods. First, create a new **GOA WinForms VB Application** named `HugeInteger` in Visual Studio 2008, then perform the following steps:

Step 1: Opening the **Add Web Reference** *Dialog*
Right click the project name in the **Solution Explorer** and select **Add Web Reference...** (Fig. 19.26).

Step 2: Locating Web Services on Your Computer
In the **Add Web Reference** dialog that appears (Fig. 19.26), enter `http://test.deitel.com/hugeinteger/hugeinteger.asmx` in the **URL** field and press **Go**. You will see a list of the operations that the `HugeInteger` web service provides. Note that for the application to work, it must reside on the same server as the web service, because Silverlight 1.1 does not yet allow for cross-domain requests. These steps demonstrate the process we went through to create the application on our server at `test.deitel.com/examples/iw3htp4/silverlight/HugeInteger/`.

Step 3: Adding the Web Reference
Add the web reference by clicking the **Add Reference** button (Fig. 19.27).

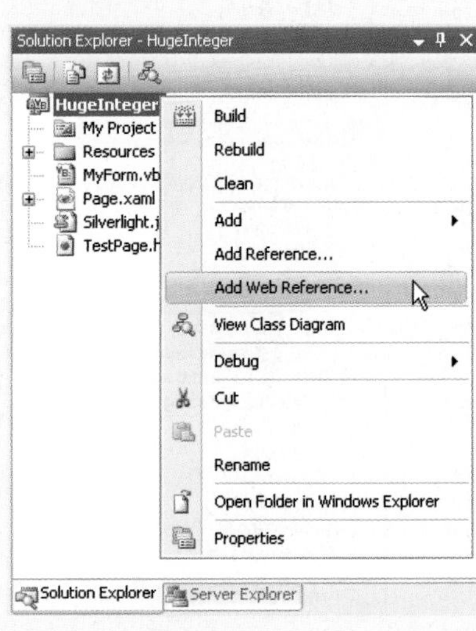

Fig. 19.26 | Adding a web service reference to a project.

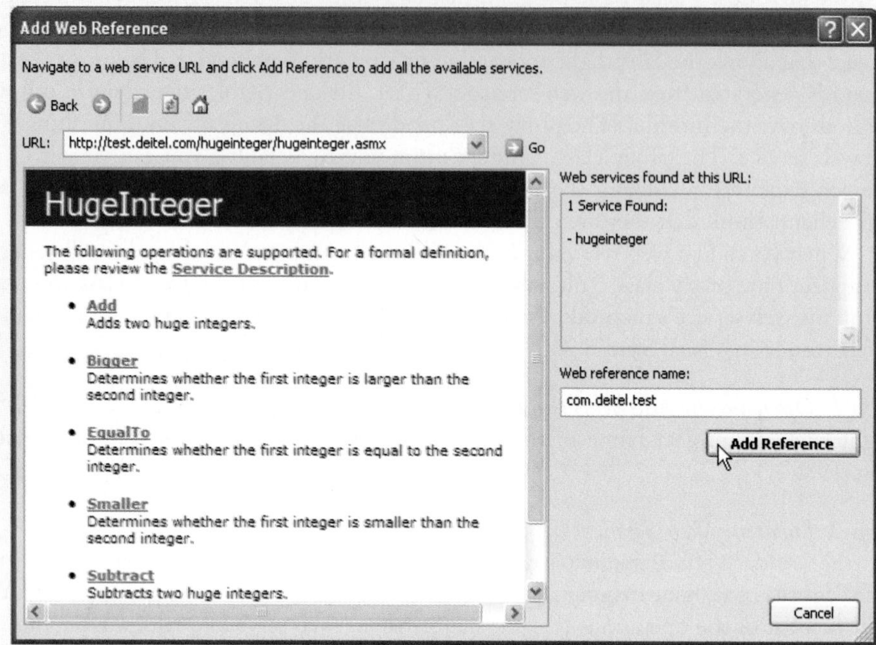

Fig. 19.27 | Web reference selection and description.

Step 4: Viewing the Web Reference in the Solution Explorer

The **Solution Explorer** (Fig. 19.28) should now contain a **Web References** folder with a node named after the domain name where the web service is located. In this case, the name is `com.deitel.test` because we are using a web service from `test.deitel.com`. When we reference class `HugeInteger` in the client application, we will do so through the `com.deitel.test` namespace.

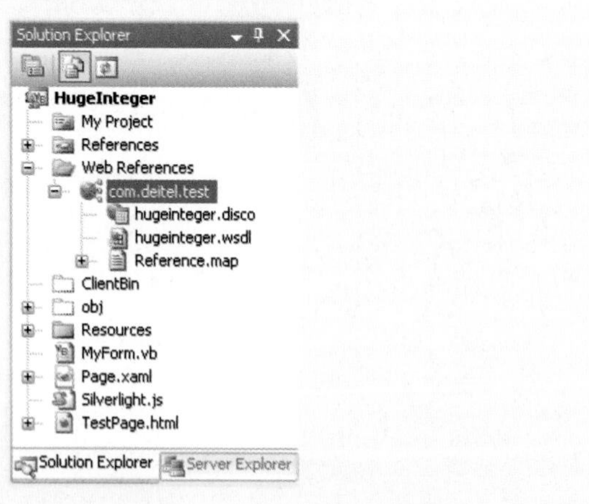

Fig. 19.28 | **Solution Explorer** after adding a web reference to a project.

19.10.1 Consuming the HugeInteger Web Service

Now, copy the `InitializeComponent` function (lines 14–109) and `Private WithEvents` section (lines 111–119) from `HugeIntegerForWindows.Designer.vb` in the `HugeIntegerForWindows` project to `MyForm.vb` in the `HugeInteger` project. Delete the old `InitializeComponent` function and `Friend WithEvents` line in `MyForm.vb`. Then, copy lines 6–117 from `HugeIntegerForWindows.vb` in the `HugeIntegerForWindows` project into the `MyForm Class` located in `MyForm.vb` in the `HugeInteger` project. If you try to build the project now, you will notice that the code is trying to access properties not supported by GOA WinForms. In Fig. 19.29, we commented out lines 38–41, 85–86, 95–95, 105–107 and 118–119 to remove statements that access unsupported properties in GOA WinForms. If you were running this application from the same server as the web service, you could now build this application and run it by opening `TestPage.html`. Try the completed application at `test.deitel.com/examples/iw3htp4/silverlight/HugeInteger/`.

```
1  ' Fig. 19.29: MyForm.vb
2  ' Consuming the HugeInteger web service in Silverlight 1.1 Alpha Refresh
3  Public Class MyForm
4     Inherits System.Windows.Forms.Form
5
6     Public Sub New()
7        MyBase.New()
8        InitializeComponent()
9     End Sub
10
11     'Form overrides dispose to clean up the component list.
12     Protected Overloads Overrides Sub Dispose(ByVal disposing As Boolean)
13         If disposing Then
14             If Not (components Is Nothing) Then
15                 components.Dispose()
16             End If
17         End If
18         MyBase.Dispose(disposing)
19     End Sub
20
21    Private components As System.ComponentModel.IContainer
22
23    Private Sub InitializeComponent()
24       Me.lblResult = New System.Windows.Forms.Label
25       Me.btnEqual = New System.Windows.Forms.Button
26       Me.btnSmaller = New System.Windows.Forms.Button
27       Me.btnLarger = New System.Windows.Forms.Button
28       Me.btnSubtract = New System.Windows.Forms.Button
29       Me.btnAdd = New System.Windows.Forms.Button
30       Me.txtSecond = New System.Windows.Forms.TextBox
31       Me.txtFirst = New System.Windows.Forms.TextBox
32       Me.lblPrompt = New System.Windows.Forms.Label
33       Me.SuspendLayout()
34
35       ' lblResult
36       ' the following four lines were commented out because they
```

Fig. 19.29 | Consuming the `HugeInteger` web service in Silverlight 1.1 Alpha. (Part 1 of 6.)

```
        ' accessed properties that are not supported in GOA WinForms
        ' Me.lblResult.BorderStyle = System.Windows.Forms.BorderStyle.
           ' FixedSingle()
        ' Me.lblResult.Font = New System.Drawing.Font(
           ' "Microsoft Sans Serif", 9.75!)
        Me.lblResult.Location = New System.Drawing.Point(13, 122)
        Me.lblResult.Name = "lblResult"
        Me.lblResult.Size = New System.Drawing.Size(714, 37)
        Me.lblResult.TabIndex = 17

        ' btnEqual
        Me.btnEqual.Location = New System.Drawing.Point(562, 91)
        Me.btnEqual.Name = "btnEqual"
        Me.btnEqual.Size = New System.Drawing.Size(85, 23)
        Me.btnEqual.TabIndex = 16
        Me.btnEqual.Text = "Equal"

        ' btnSmaller
        Me.btnSmaller.Location = New System.Drawing.Point(445, 91)
        Me.btnSmaller.Name = "btnSmaller"
        Me.btnSmaller.Size = New System.Drawing.Size(85, 23)
        Me.btnSmaller.TabIndex = 15
        Me.btnSmaller.Text = "Smaller Than"

        ' btnLarger
        Me.btnLarger.Location = New System.Drawing.Point(328, 91)
        Me.btnLarger.Name = "btnLarger"
        Me.btnLarger.Size = New System.Drawing.Size(85, 23)
        Me.btnLarger.TabIndex = 14
        Me.btnLarger.Text = "Larger Than"

        ' btnSubtract
        Me.btnSubtract.Location = New System.Drawing.Point(211, 91)
        Me.btnSubtract.Name = "btnSubtract"
        Me.btnSubtract.Size = New System.Drawing.Size(85, 23)
        Me.btnSubtract.TabIndex = 13
        Me.btnSubtract.Text = "Subtract"

        ' btnAdd
        Me.btnAdd.Location = New System.Drawing.Point(94, 91)
        Me.btnAdd.Name = "btnAdd"
        Me.btnAdd.Size = New System.Drawing.Size(85, 23)
        Me.btnAdd.TabIndex = 12
        Me.btnAdd.Text = "Add"

        ' txtSecond
        ' the following two lines were commented out because they
        ' accessed a property that is not supported in GOA WinForms
        ' Me.txtSecond.Font = New System.Drawing.Font(
           ' "Microsoft Sans Serif", 9.75!)
        Me.txtSecond.Location = New System.Drawing.Point(13, 63)
        Me.txtSecond.Name = "txtSecond"
        Me.txtSecond.Size = New System.Drawing.Size(714, 22)
```

Fig. 19.29 | Consuming the `HugeInteger` web service in Silverlight 1.1 Alpha. (Part 2 of 6.)

```
        Me.txtSecond.TabIndex = 11

        ' txtFirst
        ' the following two lines were commented out because they
        ' accessed a property that is not supported in GOA WinForms
        ' Me.txtFirst.Font = New System.Drawing.Font(
           ' "Microsoft Sans Serif", 9.75!)
        Me.txtFirst.Location = New System.Drawing.Point(13, 35)
        Me.txtFirst.Name = "txtFirst"
        Me.txtFirst.Size = New System.Drawing.Size(714, 22)
        Me.txtFirst.TabIndex = 10

        ' lblPrompt
        ' the following three lines were commented out because they
        ' accessed properties that are not supported in GOA WinForms
        ' Me.lblPrompt.AutoSize = True
        ' Me.lblPrompt.Font = New System.Drawing.Font(
           ' "Microsoft Sans Serif", 9.75!)
        Me.lblPrompt.Location = New System.Drawing.Point(13, 16)
        Me.lblPrompt.Name = "lblPrompt"
        Me.lblPrompt.Size = New System.Drawing.Size(339, 16)
        Me.lblPrompt.TabIndex = 9
        Me.lblPrompt.Text = "Please enter two positive numbers" & _
           "up to 100 digits each."

        ' UsingHugeIntegerWebService
        ' the following two lines were commented out because they
        ' accessed properties that are not supported in GOA WinForms
        ' Me.AutoScaleDimensions = New System.Drawing.SizeF(6.0!, 13.0!)
        ' Me.AutoScaleMode = System.Windows.Forms.AutoScaleMode.Font
        Me.ClientSize = New System.Drawing.Size(740, 175)
        Me.Controls.Add(Me.lblResult)
        Me.Controls.Add(Me.btnEqual)
        Me.Controls.Add(Me.btnSmaller)
        Me.Controls.Add(Me.btnLarger)
        Me.Controls.Add(Me.btnSubtract)
        Me.Controls.Add(Me.btnAdd)
        Me.Controls.Add(Me.txtSecond)
        Me.Controls.Add(Me.txtFirst)
        Me.Controls.Add(Me.lblPrompt)
        Me.Name = "UsingHugeIntegerWebService"
        Me.Text = "Using Huge Integer Web Service"
        Me.ResumeLayout(False)
        Me.PerformLayout()
    End Sub

    Private WithEvents lblResult As System.Windows.Forms.Label
    Private WithEvents btnEqual As System.Windows.Forms.Button
    Private WithEvents btnSmaller As System.Windows.Forms.Button
    Private WithEvents btnLarger As System.Windows.Forms.Button
    Private WithEvents btnSubtract As System.Windows.Forms.Button
    Private WithEvents btnAdd As System.Windows.Forms.Button
    Private WithEvents txtSecond As System.Windows.Forms.TextBox
```

Fig. 19.29 | Consuming the `HugeInteger` web service in Silverlight 1.1 Alpha. (Part 3 of 6.)

```
   Private WithEvents txtFirst As System.Windows.Forms.TextBox
   Private WithEvents lblPrompt As System.Windows.Forms.Label

   Public Shared Sub Main()
      Application.Run(New MyForm)
   End Sub

   ' declare a reference to Web service
   Private remoteInteger As New com.deitel.test.HugeInteger

   ' character to trim from strings
   Private zeros As Char() = New Char() {"0"c}

   ' adds two numbers input by user
   Private Sub btnAdd_Click(ByVal sender As System.Object, _
      ByVal e As System.EventArgs) Handles btnAdd.Click
      ' make sure numbers do not exceed 100 digits and that both
      ' are not 100 digits long, which would result in overflow
      If txtFirst.Text.Length > 100 Or txtSecond.Text.Length > 100 _
         Or (txtFirst.Text.Length = 100 And _
            txtSecond.Text.Length = 100) Then
         MessageBox.Show( _
            "HugeIntegers must not be more than 100 digits" & _
            vbCrLf & "Both integers cannot be of length 100: " & _
            " this causes an overflow", "Error", _
            MessageBoxButtons.OK, MessageBoxIcon.Information)
      Else
         ' perform addition
         lblResult.Text = remoteInteger.Add( _
            txtFirst.Text, txtSecond.Text).TrimStart(zeros)
      End If
   End Sub ' btnAdd_Click

   ' subtracts two numbers input by user
   Private Sub btnSubtract_Click(ByVal sender As System.Object, _
      ByVal e As System.EventArgs) Handles btnSubtract.Click
      ' ensure that HugeIntegers do not exceed 100 digits
      If Not NumbersTooBig(txtFirst.Text, txtSecond.Text) Then
         ' perform subtraction
         Try
            Dim result As String = remoteInteger.Subtract( _
               txtFirst.Text, txtSecond.Text).TrimStart(zeros)

            If result = "" Then
               lblResult.Text = "0"
            Else
               lblResult.Text = result
            End If
         Catch exception As Exception
            ' if WebMethod throws an exception,
            ' then first argument was smaller than second
            MessageBox.Show( _
               "First argument was smaller than the second")
```

Fig. 19.29 | Consuming the HugeInteger web service in Silverlight 1.1 Alpha. (Part 4 of 6.)

```
            End Try
         End If
      End Sub ' btnSubtract_Click

      ' determines whether first number input is larger than the second
      Private Sub btnLarger_Click(ByVal sender As System.Object, _
         ByVal e As System.EventArgs) Handles btnLarger.Click
         ' ensure that HugeIntegers do not exceed 100 digits
         If Not NumbersTooBig(txtFirst.Text, txtSecond.Text) Then
            ' call Web-service method to determine whether
            ' first integer is larger than the second
            If remoteInteger.Bigger(txtFirst.Text, txtSecond.Text) Then
               lblResult.Text = txtFirst.Text.TrimStart(zeros) & _
                  " is larger than " & txtSecond.Text.TrimStart(zeros)
            Else
               lblResult.Text = txtFirst.Text.TrimStart(zeros) & _
                  " is not larger than " + txtSecond.Text.TrimStart(zeros)
            End If
         End If
      End Sub ' btnLarger_Click

      ' determines whether first number input is smaller than the second
      Private Sub btnSmaller_Click(ByVal sender As System.Object, _
         ByVal e As System.EventArgs) Handles btnSmaller.Click
         ' make sure HugeIntegers do not exceed 100 digits
         If Not NumbersTooBig(txtFirst.Text, txtSecond.Text) Then
            ' call Web-service method to determine if
            ' first integer is smaller than second
            If remoteInteger.Smaller(txtFirst.Text, txtSecond.Text) Then
               lblResult.Text = txtFirst.Text.TrimStart(zeros) & _
                  " is smaller than " + txtSecond.Text.TrimStart(zeros)
            Else
               lblResult.Text = txtFirst.Text.TrimStart(zeros) & _
                  " is not smaller than " & txtSecond.Text.TrimStart(zeros)
            End If
         End If
      End Sub ' btnSmaller_Click

      ' determines whether the two numbers input are equal
      Private Sub btnEqual_Click(ByVal sender As System.Object, _
         ByVal e As System.EventArgs) Handles btnEqual.Click
         ' ensure that HugeIntegers do not exceed 100 digits
         If Not NumbersTooBig(txtFirst.Text, txtSecond.Text) Then
            ' call Web-service method to determine if integers are equal
            If remoteInteger.EqualTo(txtFirst.Text, txtSecond.Text) Then
               lblResult.Text = txtFirst.Text.TrimStart(zeros) & _
                  " is equal to " & txtSecond.Text.TrimStart(zeros)
            Else
               lblResult.Text = txtFirst.Text.TrimStart(zeros) & _
                  " is not equal to " & txtSecond.Text.TrimStart(zeros)
            End If
         End If
      End Sub ' btnEqual_Click
```

Fig. 19.29 | Consuming the HugeInteger web service in Silverlight 1.1 Alpha. (Part 5 of 6.)

```
249
250     ' determines whether numbers input by user are too big
251     Private Function NumbersTooBig(ByVal first As String, _
252        ByVal second As String) As Boolean
253        ' display an error message if either number has too many digits
254        If (first.Length > 100) Or (second.Length > 100) Then
255           MessageBox.Show("HugeIntegers must be less than 100 digits", _
256              "Error", MessageBoxButtons.OK, MessageBoxIcon.Information)
257           Return True
258        End If
259
260        Return False
261     End Function ' NumbersTooBig
262
263  End Class
```

Fig. 19.29 | Consuming the `HugeInteger` web service in Silverlight 1.1 Alpha. (Part 6 of 6.)

The code in Fig. 19.29 uses the `HugeInteger` web service to perform computations with positive integers up to `100` digits long. You are already familiar with converting a Visual Basic Windows Forms application to Silverlight, so we focus our discussion on the web services concepts in this example.

Line 151 creates variable `remoteInteger` and initializes it with a proxy object of type `com.deitel.test.HugeInteger`. This variable is used in each of the application's event handlers to call methods of the `HugeInteger` web service. Lines 171–172, 183–184, 207, 224 and 240 in the various button event handlers invoke methods of the web service. Note that each call is made on the local proxy object, which then communicates with the web service on the client's behalf.

The user inputs two integers, each up to 100 digits long. Clicking a button causes the application to invoke a web method to perform the appropriate task and return the result. Note that client application `HugeInteger` cannot perform operations using 100-digit numbers directly. Instead the application creates `String` representations of these numbers and passes them as arguments to web methods that handle such tasks for the client. It then uses the return value of each operation to display an appropriate message.

Note that the application eliminates leading zeros in the numbers before displaying them by calling `String` method `TrimStart`, which removes all occurrences of characters specified by a `Char` array (line 154) from the beginning of a `String`.

19.11 Silverlight Demos, Games and Web Resources

In this section we provide links to, and descriptions of, several websites where you'll find Silverlight demos, games, controls, sample code and tutorials. For additional Silverlight resources (including tutorials, articles, blogs, books, sample chapters, community sites, FAQs, RSS feeds, podcasts, videos and more), visit the Deitel Silverlight Resource Center at `www.deitel.com/silverlight`.

`silverlight.net/community/communitygallery.aspx`

The Silverlight Gallery provides a large collection of Silverlight 1.0 and 1.1 sample applications. Check out the top-rated and recently added samples, or view the complete list. Each sample includes a star rating, a description and options for viewing and downloading the samples. Become a member to upload and share your Silverlight applications with the community.

`www.hanselman.com/blog/SilverlightSamples.aspx`
A collection of Silverlight sample applications (many overlap with Microsoft's Silverlight Gallery) compiled by Scott Hanselman, a Microsoft MVP.

`community.netikatech.com/demos/`
GOA WinForms demos from Netika Tech, available for Silverlight and Flash. GOA WinForms is an implementation of the .NET System.Windows.Form library in Silverlight and Flash for developing RIAs. The simple demos include quick tours of GOA WinForms controls, a `DataGrid`, an Outlook-like calendar and a Visual Studio-like form designer.

`www.andybeaulieu.com/Home/tabid/67/EntryID/73/Default.aspx`
Silverlight Rocks! is a simple shooter game built with Silverlight 1.1. Using four buttons on your keyboard, you can turn the spaceship left or right, shoot and thrust forward. The goal is to destroy the asteroids. The author provides a walkthrough of how he wrote the game. The source code is available for download.

`www.andybeaulieu.com/Home/tabid/67/EntryID/75/Default.aspx`
Destroy All Invaders is a shooter game built with Silverlight 1.1. Select a location from the drop-down list (options include rural upstate New York, Microsoft's Redmond campus and Las Vegas, to name a few) or enter a specific address. The game brings up a satellite image of the location and an animated helicopter. The point of the game is to shoot and destroy the UFOs. The author provides a walkthrough of how he wrote the game. The source code is available for download.

`www.bluerosegames.com/brg/drpopper/default.html`
Dr. Popper Silverlight Edition by Bill Reiss of Blue Rose Games is written for Silverlight 1.1. The game consists of multiple colored bubbles arranged on a 10-bubble by 8-bubble board. You can remove the bubbles in groups of two or more, gaining more points for bigger groups. The source code is available for download.

`www.aisto.com/Roeder/Silverlight/Monotone/Default.aspx`
Monotone is an animated graphics demo built for Silverlight (using C#) and MP3 audio. Download the source code at `www.aisto.com/Roeder/Silverlight/`.

`www.aisto.com/Roeder/Silverlight/Inplay/Default.aspx`
InPlay is an in-browser audio and video player. The demo includes stunning audio and video, and you can use the controls to adjust the volume and position. Source code for InPlay is available at `www.aisto.com/Roeder/Silverlight/`.

`zerogravity.terralever.com/`
Zero Gravity is an adventure game, created by Terralever using Silverlight and C#. The game features animation and audio. Using your keyboard controls, the goal is to get Lieutenant Bennett back to his spaceship safely, jumping between blocks, teleports, switches and more.

`silverlight.net/samples/1.0/Sprawl/default.html`
Sprawl, written for Silverlight, is a tile-capture game in which you play against the computer. The goal is to capture more tiles than the computer without paving over tiles you have already captured.

`cosmik.members.winisp.net/BubbleFactory/`
The Bubble Factory game, built with Silverlight, is a simple animated game in which you use keyboard controls to move the bubble dropper left or right and to drop the bubbles. The key is to align three bubbles of the same color (horizontally, vertically or diagonally) to make them explode.

`silverlight.net/samples/1.1/chess/run/default.html`
A simple game of chess built with Silverlight 1.1.

`microsoft.blognewschannel.com/archives/2007/06/29/barrel-o-silverlight-games/`
The Inside Microsoft blog entry entitled "Barrel O' Silverlight Games" includes links to several Silverlight games including Chess, Zero Gravity, Sprawl, Destroy All Invaders, Digger and more.

`silverlightrocks.com/community/blogs/silverlight_games_101/default.aspx`
A tutorial entitled "Silverlight Games 101: Beginning game programming in Microsoft Silverlight 1.1 using C#" by Bill Reiss and Silverlight Rocks! Topics include the Zero Gravity game, loading XAML dynamically, adding thrusts, a better game loop, keyboard input, creating a game loop and drawing a sprite. All of the source code for the tutorial is available for download.

`blogs.msdn.com/tims/default.aspx`
Microsoft's Tim Sneath blogs about Silverlight and other Microsoft technologies. He includes links to 50+ Silverlight samples, information about the latest Silverlight releases and other Silverlight news.

`www.junkship.org:8000/silverlightdemo/`
The Amazon Search Visualization demo, built with Silverlight. Click the "New Search" button, then enter the title of the book or author for which you would like to search. Images of each book and related books appear on the screen. Click the green button on the image to get the book details (including title, author(s), reviewer rating, lowest new price and lowest used price). You will also see a visual presentation of book covers for related books. Click the red button on the book cover to close that item. Click the "Clear All" button to search for a new book.

`dnnsilverlight.adefwebserver.com/Samples/SilverlightVideo/tabid/55/Default.aspx`
A Silverlight Video module for DotNetNuke allows you to embed a video player in your DotNetNuke site. Check out the demo to view a video in a web page or to view the video full-screen. The site includes installation and configuration instructions.

`www.chriscavanagh.com/Chris/Silverlight/Physics2D-1/TestPage.html`
A 2-D Physics Engine has numerous platforms. Click the "Drop Wheels" button to drop tires from the top of the page onto the varying platforms to see which direction they will roll. Click the "Move Platforms" button and "Drop Wheels" to try again.

`dev.aol.com/mail`
The AOL Social Mail Gadget, built with Silverlight, gives AOL mail users easy access to email, IM, photos and video and more with just one click. It also allows you to set up an "A-List" of your most important contacts so you are aware when they are online, when a message from someone on the list is received and more.

`mlb.mlb.com/media/video.jsp`
Check out a sample of a Silverlight video player embedded in a Major League Baseball web page. You can pause and rewind the video and adjust the volume. A link is provided so you can link to the video from your website.

`silverlight.net/samples/1.0/Grand-Piano/default.html`
A Grand Piano application built with Silverlight includes audio and animation. Click on the key with your mouse to play a note.

`www.telerik.com/products/silverlight/overview.aspx`
RadControls for Microsoft Silverlight help you build RIAs without using JavaScript or XAML coding. Features include layouts, animation effects, integration with ASP.NET Ajax and more. Check out the demos to see the features, functionality, appearance and more.

`blogs.msdn.com/cbowen/archive/2007/07/30/controls-and-control-libraries-for-silverlight.aspx`
The blog entry entitled "Controls and Control Libraries for Silverlight" by Microsoft's Chris Bowen, provides links to some of the reusable Silverlight controls and libraries that allow you to develop Silverlight applications faster and more efficiently. You'll also find links to samples and tutorials.

`silverlight.net/QuickStarts/BuildUi/CustomControl.aspx`
The tutorial "How to Create Custom Silverlight Controls" discusses the control UI and object model, starting from the Silverlight Class Library Project, defining the UI, getting object references, add-

ing properties and events for control customization, testing your control and shadowing inherited properties.

`silverlight.net/learn/learnvideo.aspx?video=207`
The video tutorial "How to Build a Silverlight Control" by Jesse Liberty, shows you how to create an HTML application that interacts with a Silverlight control.

`www.codeplex.com/Project/ProjectDirectory.aspx?ProjectSearchText=silverlight`
CodePlex, Microsoft's open source project hosting website, includes a collection of 14 open source Silverlight projects including iTunes 2.0, Dynamic Silverlight Samples, Silverlight 1.0 JavaScript Intellisense, Silverlight Playground, Balder, Silverlight Audio Player and more. Each project includes a description of the project, a demo and the source code.

`www.aisto.com/Roeder/Silverlight/`
Lutz Roeder's Silverlight page provides several sample applications including Monotone (`www.aisto.com/Roeder/Silverlight/Monotone/Default.aspx`), a graphics application written in XAML and C#; Digger (`www.aisto.com/Roeder/Silverlight/Digger/Default.aspx`), a clone of the Boulderdash game, written in C#; and Inplay (`www.aisto.com/Roeder/Silverlight/Inplay/Default.aspx?Audio=play:false&Video=source:http://download.microsoft.com/download/2/C/4/2C433161-F56C-4BAB-BBC5-B8C6F240AFCC/SL_0410_448x256_300kb_2passCBR.wmv`), an audio and video player that can be embedded in a web page, built with C#. Download demos of each application and get the source code.

19.12 Wrap-Up

In this chapter, you learned how to build Silverlight XAML user interfaces in Microsoft Expression Blend. You also learned how to program Silverlight event handlers with JavaScript in Silverlight 1.0 and Visual Basic in Silverlight 1.1 Alpha Refresh. We showed how to embed Silverlight applications in HTML pages, and how to distribute media over the web using Microsoft's Silverlight Streaming service. We used Netika's GOA WinForms library to port two Visual Basic desktop applications to Silverlight 1.1. Finally, you learned how to consume an ASP.NET web service in Silverlight. In the next chapter, you'll learn how to use Adobe Dreamweaver CS3 to design web pages.

Summary

Section 19.1 Introduction

- Silverlight is Microsoft's RIA platform. It is designed to complement Ajax and other RIA technologies, such as Adobe Flash and Flex, Sun's JavaFX and Microsoft's own ASP.NET Ajax.
- Silverlight currently runs as a browser plug-in for Internet Explorer, Firefox and Safari on recent versions of Microsoft Windows and Mac OS X.
- Developers from the Mono project are developing an open-source implementation of Silverlight for Linux distributions called Moonlight.
- At the time of this writing, Silverlight is currently available in version 1.0 Release Candidate and version 1.1 Alpha Refresh.

Section 19.2 Platform Overview

- Silverlight applications consist of a user interface described in Extensible Application Markup Language (XAML) and a code-behind file (or files) containing the program logic.
- XAML is Microsoft's XML vocabulary for describing user interfaces.

- Silverlight 1.0 focuses primarily on media and supports programming only in JavaScript.
- Microsoft provides a service called Silverlight Streaming that allows you to distribute video-based Silverlight applications for free.
- When Silverlight 1.1 is released, computers with Silverlight 1.0 will automatically be upgraded. This could immediately make Silverlight 1.1 a widespread platform for RIA development.
- Silverlight 1.1's key benefit is that it adds an implementation of the .NET runtime, allowing developers to create Silverlight applications in .NET languages.
- Microsoft plans to implement a built-in set of controls in a future release of Silverlight 1.1.
- Version 1.1 provides a substantial performance improvement over 1.0 because .NET code is compiled by the developer then executed on the client, unlike JavaScript, which is interpreted and executed on the client at runtime.

Section 19.3 Silverlight 1.0 Installation and Overview

- We developed our Silverlight 1.0 application using Microsoft's Expression Blend 2, a WYSIWYG editor for building XAML user interfaces.

Section 19.4 Creating a Movie Viewer for Silverlight 1.0

- To create the project in Expression Blend, open Expression Blend and select **New Project** in the **Project** tab. To create a Silverlight 1.0 application, select **Silverlight Application (JavaScript).**

Section 19.4.1 Creating a User Interface In XAML Using Expression Blend

- The root element of the XAML file is a `Canvas` element. A `Canvas` element acts as a container for other user interface elements and controls their position.
- The parent `Canvas` element is created when you create a new Silverlight project in Expression Blend. The parent `Canvas` has a default `Name` of `Page`, `Width` of 640 px and `Height` of 480 px.
- An element's `Name` attribute provides an ID to access the element programmatically.
- An element's properties can be edited in the **Properties** panel.
- Additional `Canvas` elements can be created in Expression Blend using the toolbar's `Canvas` tool.
- The XAML can be manually edited by selecting **XAML** in Expression Blend's **View** menu.

Section 19.4.2 Using `Storyboards`

- The `Storyboard` element allows you to define animations.
- In Expression Blend, you can create a `Storyboard` by opening the **Open, create or manage Storyboards** panel and clicking the **Create new Storyboard** button. Selecting the **Create as a Resource** checkbox enables you to start the `Storyboard` from anywhere in the application's JavaScript.
- A `Storyboard` must have a target object.
- Expression Blend provides the Gradient brush tool to visually create and modify gradients.

Section 19.4.3 Creating Controls

- You can create a `TextBlock` element using Expression Blend's **TextBlock** tool.
- Use the **Solid color brush** in the **Brushes** inspector to set a solid color.
- You can adjust the text size in the **Text** inspector.
- A `Canvas` element can be a child of another `Canvas` element.
- Double-click a `Canvas` element with the **Selection** tool to activate it.
- The `Image` element's **Source** attribute points to an image file. You can select the **Image** tool by clicking the **Asset Library** button, checking **Show All**, and selecting **Image**.

- The user's cursor will change to a hand when the cursor is moved over a `Canvas` if its **Cursor** property is set to **Hand** in the **Common Properties** inspector.
- Set the **RadiusX** and **RadiusY** to give a `Rectangle` rounded corners. These properties are located in the **advanced properties** section of the **Appearance** inspector.
- Use the **Pen** tool to draw a `Path`. The `Path` element allows you to draw shapes that include curves and arcs, but here we are just using it to draw simple lines.
- You can set the **StrokeThickness**, **StrokeEndLineCap** and **StrokeStartLineCap** properties of a `Path` in the **Appearance** inspector.
- One element appears on top of another if it appears after the other element in the **Objects and Timeline** inspector. You can also specify the *z*-order of elements using an object's `ZIndex` attribute. Higher `ZIndex` integer values position the element closer to the foreground.
- The `MediaElement` allows you to include video and/or audio. To access the **MediaElement** tool, click the **Asset Library** button, check **Show All** and select **MediaElement.**
- The `MediaElement`'s **Source** attribute points to the source video file.
- Expression Blend 2 August Preview does not currently have a user interface to set event handlers, so you must manually set them in the XAML.
- `Storyboard` attribute `Completed` registers an event that is triggered when an animation completes.
- The `MouseLeftButtonDown` attribute registers an event that is triggered when the user left-clicks on the element.
- `MediaElement` attribute `MediaOpened` registers an event that is triggered when a video opens.
- When a `MediaElement` is loaded, it will begin playing the movie. To change this, set its `AutoPlay` attribute to `false`.
- `MediaElement` attribute `MediaEnded` registers an event that is triggered when a video has reaches the end.
- An alternative to registering event handlers in the XAML is to register event handlers in the JavaScript code. This has two key advantages—it keeps the application's logic separate from the application's user interface, and it allows you to add and remove event listeners dynamically.
- When registering an event in JavaScript using the `addEventListener` method, store the method's return value, so you can remove the event listener using the `removeEventListener` later.

Section 19.4.4 Using JavaScript for Event Handling and DOM Manipulation

- The JavaScript code-behind file, `Page.xaml.js`, defines the event handlers for the various elements in the XAML.
- A `Canvas`'s `Loaded` event is triggered when the `Canvas` finishes loading
- You can create a reference to a XAML element using the `sender`'s `findName` method.
- Every event handler receives `sender` and `eventArgs` parameters. The `sender` parameter is a reference to the element with which the user interacted, and the `eventArgs` parameter passes information about the event that occurred.
- Method `getHost` returns a reference to the Silverlight plug-in so you can access its properties.
- The plug-in's `onFullScreenChange` event occurts when the application switches to or from full-screen mode.
- A `Storyboard`'s `begin` function starts the `Storyboard`.
- A `Storyboard`'s `Completed` event occurs when the animation completes.
- The `MediaElement`'s `position.Seconds` attribute contains the media's elapsed time in seconds.

- In the `Canvas.Left` attribute, `Left` is a dependency property of `Canvas`, meaning that the `Left` value is relative to the `Canvas`. To access a dependency property, enclose the attribute name in quotes and square brackets, as in *element*`["`*attributeName*`"]`.
- The plug-in's `fullScreen` attribute specifies whether the application is in full-screen mode.
- `MediaElement` property `volume` is a value between 0 (muted) and 1 (full volume).

Section 19.5 Embedding Silverlight in HTML

- Expression Blend generates an HTML wrapper named `Default.html` for your Silverlight application when you first create the Silverlight project.
- You can embed a Silverlight application into an existing HTML file by including the `scripts`, the `silverlightHost` style class and the `SilverlightControlHost` `div` from `Default.html`.
- You can adjust the width and height of your application by changing the `width` and `height` attributes of the `silverlightHost` style class.

Section 19.6 Silverlight Streaming

- Microsoft's Silverlight Streaming (`silverlight.live.com`) enables individuals and businesses to share video content online. You can easily embed Silverlight applications that are hosted by this service into your web pages.

Section 19.7 Silverlight 1.1 Installation and Overview

- Silverlight 1.1 uses a lightweight version of the .NET CLR (Common Language Runtime) in the browser plug-in. This allows you to program Silverlight applications in many .NET languages.
- Silverlight 1.1 applications use the .NET CLR's just-in-time (JIT) compiler to compile the code to machine language, providing significant performance improvements over the interpreted JavaScript used in Silverlight 1.0 and Ajax.
- We developed our Silverlight 1.1 applications using Microsoft Expression Blend 2 and Microsoft Visual Studio 2008. The **Silverlight Tools Alpha for Visual Studio** enable you to create a Silverlight 1.1 Alpha Refresh project.

Section 19.8 Creating a Cover Viewer for Silverlight 1.1 Alpha

- To create a Silverlight 1.1 Alpha Refresh project, open Visual Studio 2008 and select **New Project** in the **File** menu.
- A Silverlight 1.1 Alpha Refresh project will initially contain a XAML file, `Page.xaml`, a code-behind file, `Page.xaml.vb`, `Silverlight.js` and the HTML wrapper, `TestPage.html`.
- The `x:Class` attribute specifies the class that contains the event handlers.
- The `InitializeComponent` method in the autogenerated `Page.g.vb` file, takes any XAML elements that have an `x:Name` attribute and uses the `FindName` method to map each element to a variable of the same name.
- Note that the `BrowserHttpWebRequest` object does not currently support cross-domain requests, so your application and its resources must be located on the same server.
- Use the `HtmlPage` element to find the `AbsolutePath` of the page.

Section 19.9 Building an Application with Third-Party Controls

- Though Silverlight 1.1 Alpha Refresh does not yet include pre-built controls, a number of third-party control libraries have been created.
- Netika's GOA WinForms library implements .NET's `System.Windows.Form` library for both Silverlight and Flash.

- To create a GOA WinForms Silverlight application, open Visual Studio 2008 and create a new project. Select **Visual Basic**, then **GOA WinForms VB Application** in **My Templates.**
- For a GOA WinForms project, the Visual Basic code-behind file is located in `MyForm.vb`.
- To convert a Visual Basic desktop application to a Silverlight application using GOA WinForms, copy code from the user interface and code-behind files into `MyForm.vb`.
- You may see errors because not every property of the Windows Form controls has been implemented in GOA WinForms.
- Some of the controls function slightly differently, as GOA WinForms is not an exact replica of the standard Windows Forms controls.

Section 19.10 Consuming a Web Service

- A proxy class (or proxy) is generated from a web service's WSDL file and enables the client to call web methods over the Internet. The proxy class handles all the details of communicating with the web service.
- When you add a web reference to the Silverlight project, Visual Studio will generate the appropriate proxy class. You will then create an instance of the proxy class and use it to call the web service's methods.
- At this time, a Silverlight application that invokes a web service must reside on the same domain as that web service, because Silverlight 1.1 does not yet allow for cross-domain requests.
- Add the web reference by clicking the **Add Reference** button (Fig. 19.27).

Terminology

`addEventListener` method
`AutoPlay` attribute of `MediaElement` element
`BrowserHttpWebRequest` object
C#
`Canvas` element
`Canvas.Left` attribute
code-behind file
`Collapsed` value of `Visibility`
`Completed` attribute of `Storyboard` element
dependency property
`Ellipse` element
`eventArgs` parameter
Expression Blend 2
`Fill` attribute
`findName` method of the Silverlight 1.0 plug-in
`FindName` method of the Silverlight 1.1 plug-in
`fullScreen` attribute of Silverlight plug-in
`getHost` method
`Gradient` brush tool
`Hand` value of `Cursor` attribute
`Height` attribute
HTML wrapper
`HtmlPage` element
`Image` element
IntelliSense
JavaScript
just-in-time (JIT) compiler
`Loaded` event of `Canvas` element
Manifest for Silverlight Streaming
`MediaElement` element
`MediaEnded` attribute of `MediaElement`
`MediaOpened` attribute of `MediaElement`
`MouseLeftButtonDown` attribute
`naturalDuration` attribute of a `MediaElement`
.NET Common Language Runtime (CLR)
`onFullScreenChange` event (Silverlight plug-in)
`Opacity` attribute
`Path` element
`position.Seconds` attribute of `MediaElement`
proxy class for a web service
`Rectangle` element
`removeEventListener` method
`sender` parameter
Silverlight
Silverlight Document Object Model (DOM)
Silverlight plug-in
Silverlight Streaming
Silverlight Tools Alpha for Visual Studio
`Source` attribute of `Image`
`Source` attribute of `MediaElement`

`Storyboard` element
`Stroke` attribute
`TextBlock` element
`Uri`
`Visibility` attribute of `Canvas` element
Visual Basic
`volume` attribute of `MediaElement` element
Web reference selection and description
`Width` attribute
Windows Media Video (WMV)
Windows Presentation Foundation (WPF)
Windows Presentation Foundation Everywhere (WPF/E)
WMV (Windows Media Video)
`x:Class` attribute of `Canvas` element
`x:Name` attribute
XAML (Extensible Application Markup Language)
`XmlReader` object
`ZIndex` attribute of `Canvas`
z-order

Self-Review Exercises

19.1 Fill in the blanks in each of the following statements:

a) A(n) _______ is the parent element of a XAML file.
b) A(n) _______ is used to embed video and audio in a Silverlight application.
c) Visual Basic's _______ class can be used to parse RSS in Silverlight.
d) The _______ event is triggered by clicking an element with the left mouse button.
e) Animations are described using the _______ XAML element.
f) _______ allows you to distribute Silverlight applications containing audio and video for free.
g) _______ allows you to visually edit XAML.
h) You can use an object's _______ attribute to specify the *z*-order of elements.
i) A `MediaElement`'s _______ attribute determines whether the media will start playing immediately after it has loaded.
j) The Silverlight plug-in's _______ method retrieves an element of a specific name.
k) In Silverlight 1.1, the _______ attribute specifies the `Class` that contains the XAML elements' event handlers.

19.2 State whether each of the following is *true* or *false*. If *false*, explain why.

a) The Silverlight browser plug-in runs on IE and Firefox on Windows XP and Vista, and Safari and Firefox on Mac OS X.
b) Silverlight applications can be embedded in an existing HTML file.
c) Silverlight requires server-side software.
d) You can program Silverlight event handlers in XAML.
e) Silverlight 1.1 supports programming in C#, Visual Basic, and other .NET languages.
f) Silverlight applications can run in full-screen mode.
g) The `BrowserHttpWebRequest` object allows for cross-domain requests.
h) A Silverlight application must have at least one `Canvas` element.
i) There is no way to implement a timer in Silverlight 1.0.
j) You can hide an element only by setting its `Opacity` to `0`.

Answers to Self-Review Exercises

19.1 a) `Canvas`. b) `MediaElement`. c) `XmlReader`. d) `MouseLeftButtonDown`. e) `Storyboard`. f) Silverlight Streaming. g) Expression Blend. h) `ZIndex`. i) `AutoPlay`. j) `findName`. k) `x:Class`.

19.2

a) True.
b) True.
c) False. Silverlight applications can be served by any server, or run locally.
d) False. XAML is used to describe the user interface.

e) True.
f) True.
g) False. The `BrowserHttpWebRequest` object allows for requests only to the Silverlight application's host domain.
h) True.
i) False. You can use a `Storyboard` as a timer.
j) False. You can set the element's `Visibility` to `Collapsed`.

Exercises

19.3 Add mouse-over and mouse-down graphics for the controls in the Movie Viewer, to improve the feel of the user interface. To do this, add the `MouseEnter`, `MouseLeave` and `MouseLeftButtonUp` events in the XAML and corresponding event handlers in the JavaScript code-behind. An example of how your solution may look is available at `test.deitel.com/examples/iw3htp4/silverlight/MovieViewer2/index.html`.

19.4 Enhance the book-cover viewer application so that when the user switches covers, the new image zooms in instead of instantly appearing. Do this by adding `nextNextImage` and `prevPrevImage` elements that are initially hidden. An example of how your solution may look is available at `test.deitel.com/examples/iw3htp4/silverlight/CoverViewer2/index.html`.

19.5 Create a Silverlight 1.1 Alpha Visual Basic application based on the book-cover viewer that plays an MP3 audio file using a `MediaElement` when the user clicks a corresponding `Image`, such as an album cover. An example of how your solution may look is available at `test.deitel.com/examples/iw3htp4/silverlight/AudioPlayer/index.html`.

20

Adobe® Dreamweaver® CS3

OBJECTIVES

In this chapter you will learn:

- To use Dreamweaver CS3 effectively.
- To develop web pages in a visual environment.
- To insert images and links into web pages.
- To create XHTML elements such as tables and forms.
- To insert scripts into Dreamweaver pages.
- To use the Spry framework to create richer, more dynamic web applications.
- To use Dreamweaver's site-management capabilities.

We must select the illusion which appeals to our temperament, and embrace it with passion, if we want to be happy.
—Cyril Connolly

The symbolic view of things is a consequence of long absorption in images. Is sign language the real language of Paradise?
—Hugo Ball

What you see is what you get (WYSIWYG).
—Anonymous

All human knowledge takes the form of interpretation.
—Walter Benjamin

Outline

20.1 Introduction

This chapter presents Adobe's *Dreamweaver CS3*, perhaps the most popular visual HTML editor. A fully functional, 30–day trial version of Dreamweaver is available for download at `www.adobe.com/cfusion/tdrc/index.cfm?product=dreamweaver`. Please download and install the software before studying this chapter.

Using Dreamweaver, you can easily perform many of the tasks you learned in previous chapters. You can insert and edit text, as well as create more complex XHTML elements, such as tables, forms, frames and much more. In addition, this latest version of Dreamweaver now enables you to develop Ajax applications with Adobe's Spry framework.

20.2 Adobe Dreamweaver CS3

Upon starting, Dreamweaver displays the default **Start Page**, which offers various options, such as **Open a Recent Item**, **Create New** and **Create from Samples** (Fig. 20.1). For example, you can click the **HTML** option under the **Create New** heading to open a blank page in the default viewing mode (Fig. 20.2). Dreamweaver is a WYSIWYG (What You See Is What You Get) editor. Unlike editors that simply display XHTML code, Dreamweaver renders XHTML elements much as a browser would, using the WYSIWYG screen. This functionality enables you to design your web pages as they will appear on the web.

We will now recreate the book's first XHTML example (Fig. 4.1) using Dreamweaver. To see a more detailed list of options for creating new files, create a new document by selecting **New...** from the **File** menu. In the **New Document** dialog, select the **Blank page** tab from the leftmost column, and **HTML** from the **Page Type:** list (Fig. 20.3). By default, Dreamweaver's **DocType** (in the lower-right corner) is set to **XHMTL 1.0 Transitional**. Select the drop-down **DocType** menu and select **XHTML 1.0 Strict**—this will cause Dreamweaver to generate XHTML-compliant code. In the **Layout:** list, make sure **<none>** is selected. Click the **Create** button to open the new document.

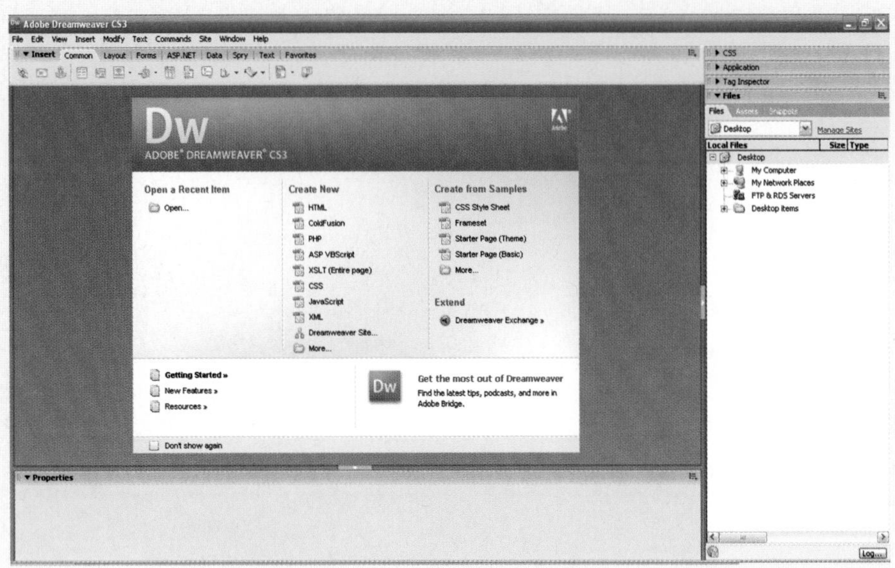

Fig. 20.1 | Dreamweaver **Start Page**.

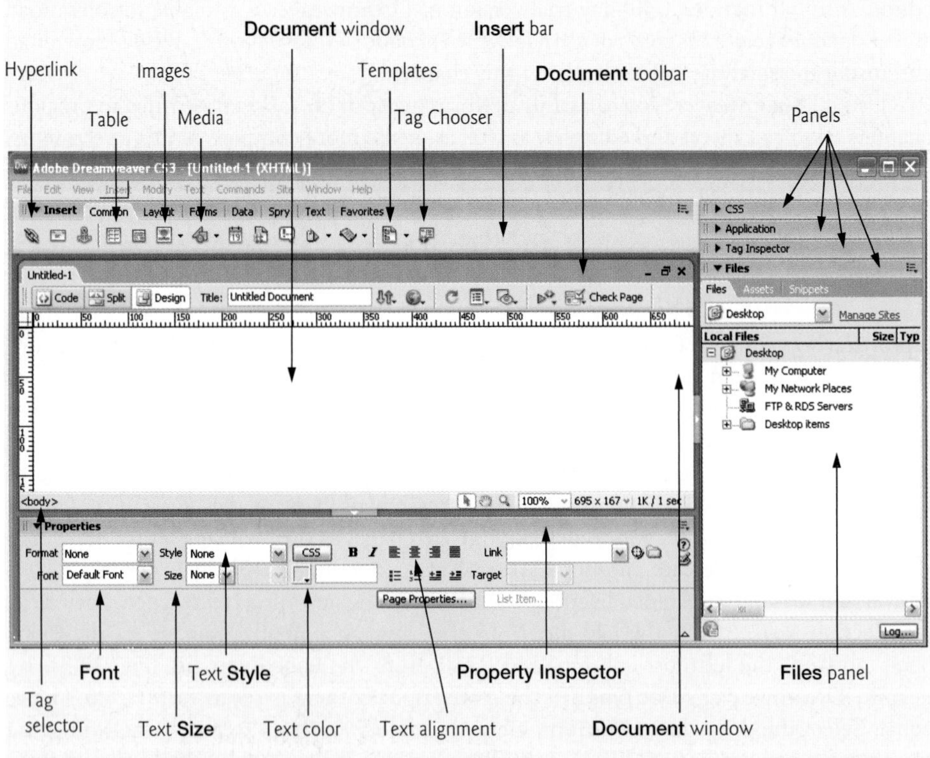

Fig. 20.2 | Dreamweaver editing environment.

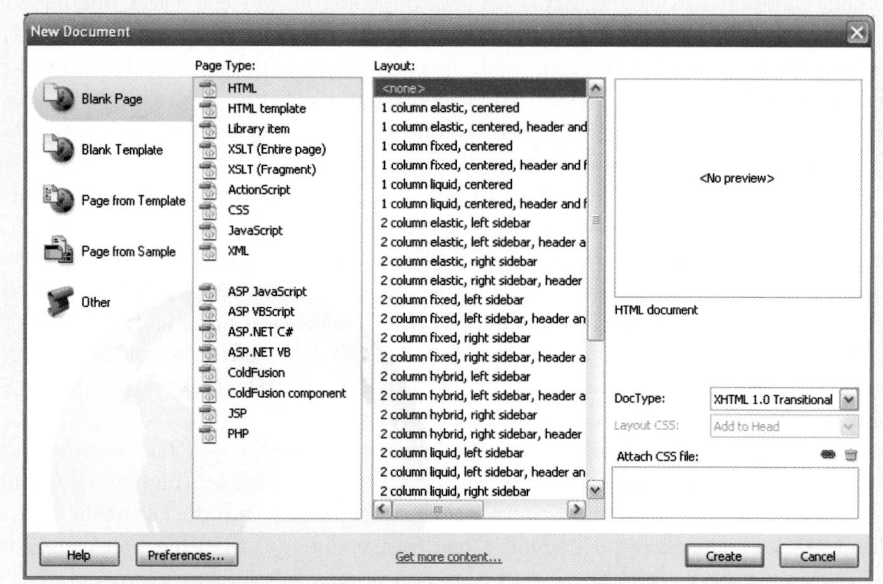

Fig. 20.3 | **New Document** dialog.

Type

```
Welcome to XHTML!
```

in the **Document** window. Dreamweaver automatically places this text in the body element. Note that XHTML tags are not currently visible. We will switch to an alternate view in a moment to see the code that Dreamweaver generates. Now, to insert a title as we did in Fig. 4.1, right click in the **Document** window and select **Page Properties...** from the pop-up menu to view the **Page Properties** dialog (Fig. 20.4).

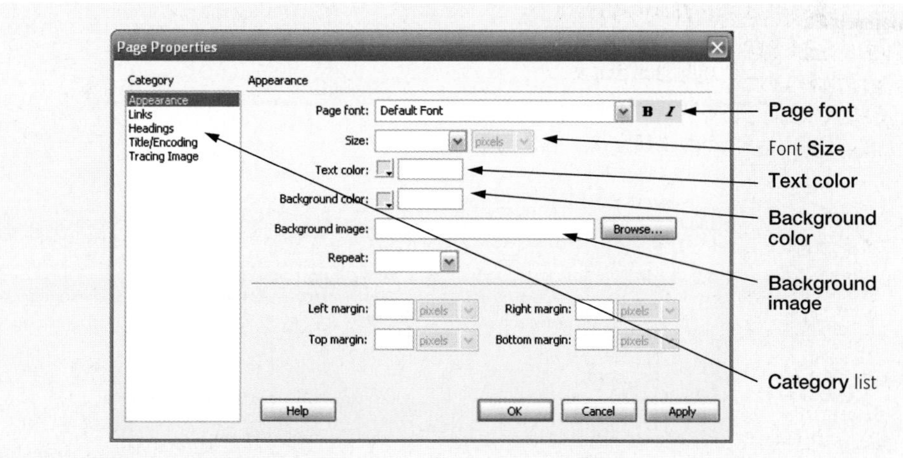

Fig. 20.4 | **Page Properties** dialog.

The **Category list** lets the user select a set of properties to view. Select **Title/Encoding** from the **Category** list and enter **Internet and WWW How to Program** into the **Title** field. Clicking **OK** inserts a `title` element with the corresponding title text inside the `head` element of your XHTML code. [*Note:* You can also create a `title` by entering text directly into the Document title box (Fig. 20.6).] You now have a representation of the code in Fig. 4.1 in the WYSIWYG display (Fig. 20.5).

Though you have been editing using the WYSIWYG display, remember that you are still programming in XHTML. To view or edit the XHTML that Dreamweaver generated, you must switch from **Design view**, the mode you are currently working in, to **Code view**. To do so, click the **Code button** in the **Document toolbar** (Fig. 20.6). Note that Dreamweaver automatically color-codes XHTML to make viewing easier (Fig. 20.7). The tag names, attribute values and page text are all displayed in different colors. The code-coloring scheme can be accessed (and modified) by selecting **Preferences...** from the **Edit** menu and clicking **Code Coloring** in the **Category** list.

To save your file, click **Save** in the **File** menu or press *<Ctrl>-S*. The **Save As dialog** will appear, allowing you to specify a filename, type and location (Fig. 20.8). Create a folder in your `C:` drive named **Dreamweaver sites**. Type `main` into the **File name** field and select **HTML Documents** as the file type. Dreamweaver adds an `.html` filename extension if no extension is specified.

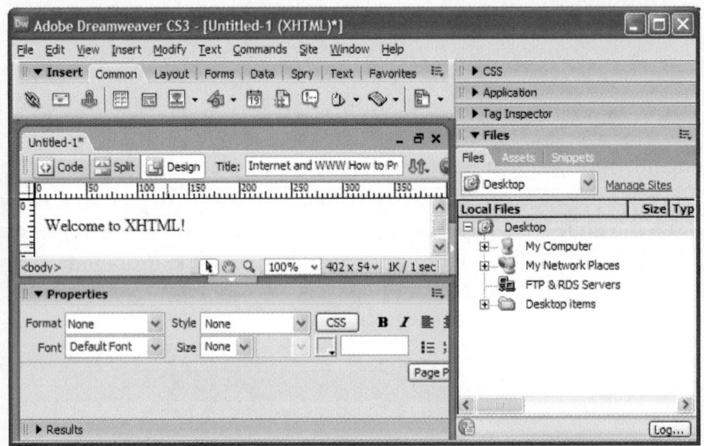

Fig. 20.5 | Example of Fig. 4.1 in Dreamweaver.

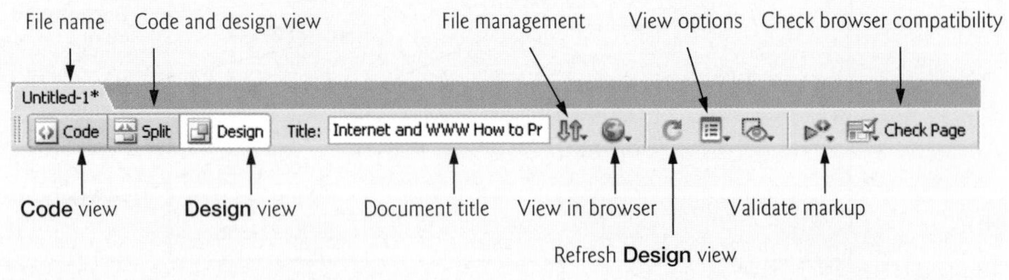

Fig. 20.6 | **Document** toolbar.

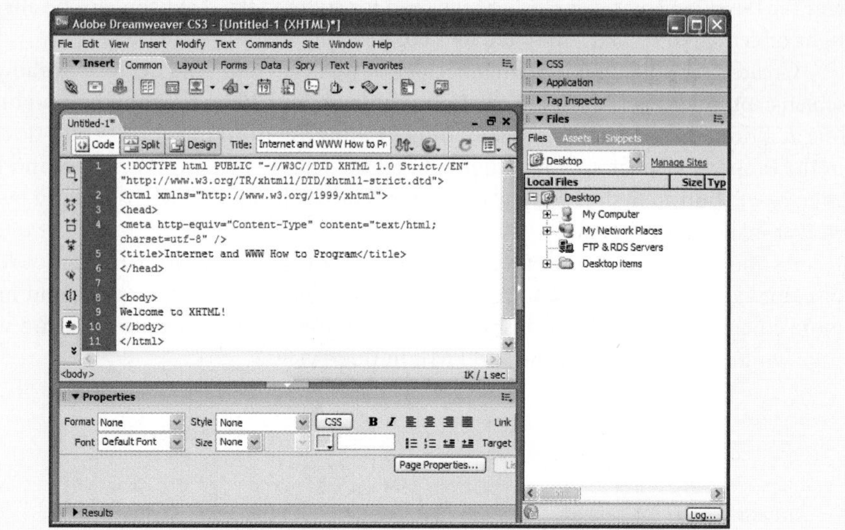

Fig. 20.7 | **Code** view.

Fig. 20.8 | **Save As** dialog.

To view your page in a browser, press *F12* or select **Preview in Browser** from the **File** menu. Note that the **File** menu option provides several browsers in which to view your code—more browsers can be added with the **Edit Browser List...** option. Your page should appear identical to the one in Fig. 4.1.

20.3 Text Styles

In Dreamweaver, we can alter text properties with the **Text menu** or the **Property Inspector** (Fig. 20.2). Using these tools, we can quickly apply heading tags (`<h1>`, `<h2>`, etc.), list tags (<ol>, <ul>) and several other tags used for styling text. Text can also be aligned left, right or centered, resized, indented and colored.

Create a new document, switch back to **Design** view and type the text, as shown in the screen capture of Fig. 20.9, into the **Document** window. Drag the mouse to highlight one line at a time and select the corresponding heading tag from the **Format** pull-down menu in the **Property Inspector**. Then, highlight all the text by pressing *<Ctrl>-A*, and click the align center button in the **Property Inspector**. The resulting XHTML produced by Dreamweaver is shown in Fig. 20.9.

As you can see, Dreamweaver is prone to produce somewhat inefficient code. In this case, for example, using Cascading Style Sheets (CSS) to center the text would have been more efficient. At the end of this section, we discuss how to integrate CSS into your web page without having to edit the XHTML in **Code** view.

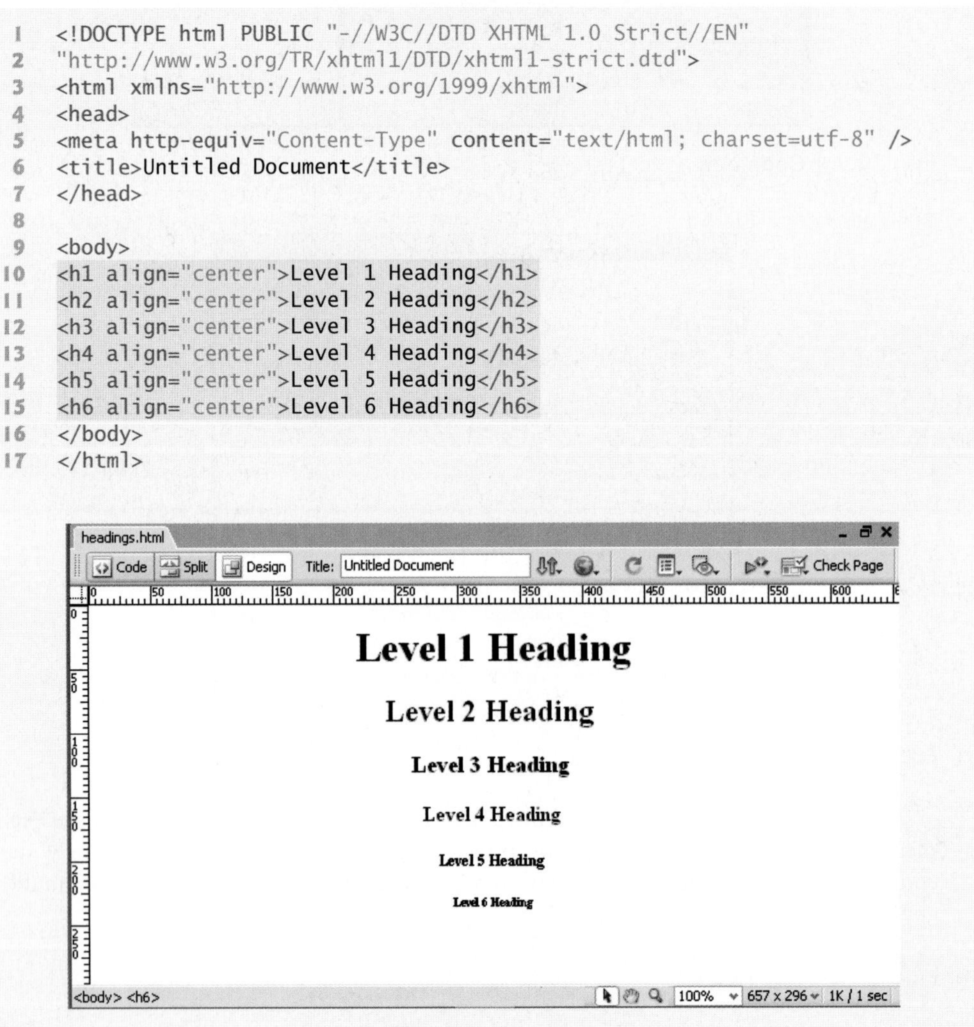

```
<!DOCTYPE html PUBLIC "-//W3C//DTD XHTML 1.0 Strict//EN"
"http://www.w3.org/TR/xhtml1/DTD/xhtml1-strict.dtd">
<html xmlns="http://www.w3.org/1999/xhtml">
<head>
<meta http-equiv="Content-Type" content="text/html; charset=utf-8" />
<title>Untitled Document</title>
</head>

<body>
<h1 align="center">Level 1 Heading</h1>
<h2 align="center">Level 2 Heading</h2>
<h3 align="center">Level 3 Heading</h3>
<h4 align="center">Level 4 Heading</h4>
<h5 align="center">Level 5 Heading</h5>
<h6 align="center">Level 6 Heading</h6>
</body>
</html>
```


Fig. 20.9 | Applying heading tags and centering using Dreamweaver.

Software Engineering Observation 20.1

Dreamweaver uses text-manipulation techniques that sometimes produce inefficient code. Make sure to check the code often to know exactly the kind of XHTML Dreamweaver is producing. Thorough knowledge of a page and what XHTML elements are present is necessary for advanced scripting.

Dreamweaver is capable of much more extensive text formatting, such as creating mathematical formulas. For example, type

```
e = mc2
```

into a new WYSIWYG window, then highlight the text. You can now change the formatting of the equation by selecting **Style** from the **Text** menu, and selecting **Code**. The **Code** option applies a `code` element to the highlighted text, which designates formulas or computer code. Many other useful text-formatting options are located in the **Text** menu, as well. Click the **Code** button in the **Document** toolbar to view the code, and find the `2` in the equation. Surround the `2` with a `<sup>...</sup>` tag. The `<sup>...</sup>` tag formats the enclosed text as a superscript. Notice that after typing `<sup>`, Dreamweaver automatically completes a matching end tag (`</sup>`) after you have entered the `</` characters. Click the **Design** button in the **Document** toolbar to view the fully formatted text (Fig. 20.10).

The formula can be further emphasized by selecting a **Color...** attribute from the **Text** menu. You can also access most of the elements in the **Text** menu (though not the color attribute) by right clicking highlighted text.

Look-and-Feel Observation 20.1

When you press Enter *after typing text in* **Design** *view, Dreamweaver encloses that text in a new paragraph (*`p`*) element. If you want to insert only a* `<br />` *tag into a page, hold* Shift *while pressing* Enter.

Look-and-Feel Observation 20.2

You can manipulate the properties of almost any element displayed in the Dreamweaver window by right clicking an element and selecting its properties from the menu that pops up.

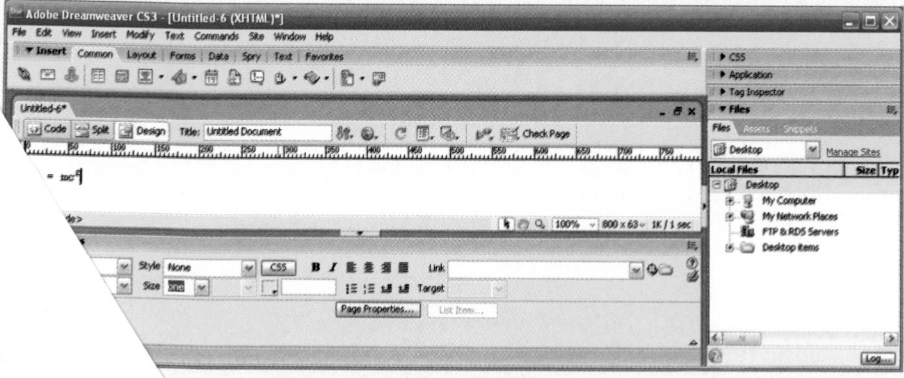

ling text using **code** and **sup** elements.

The **Property Inspector** is also useful for creating lists. Try entering the contents of a shopping list, as shown in Fig. 20.11, and applying the **Unordered List style** to the list elements. Apply an `h2` element to the title of the list.

Select **List** from the **Text** menu for more list-related tags, such as the definition list (`<dl>`). There are two list elements in a definition list—the defined term (`<dt>`) and the definition data (`<dd>`). Figure 20.12 shows the formatting produced by a definition list and the code Dreamweaver uses to produce it.

To apply the definition list as shown, select **Definition List** from the **List** submenu of the **Text** menu. In the **Document** window, type the first term you want to define. When you press *Enter*, Dreamweaver changes the style to match that of a definition. Pressing *Enter* again lets you enter another defined term. The bold style of the defined terms is applied by clicking the **Bold** button in the **Property Inspector**, which applies the `strong` element.

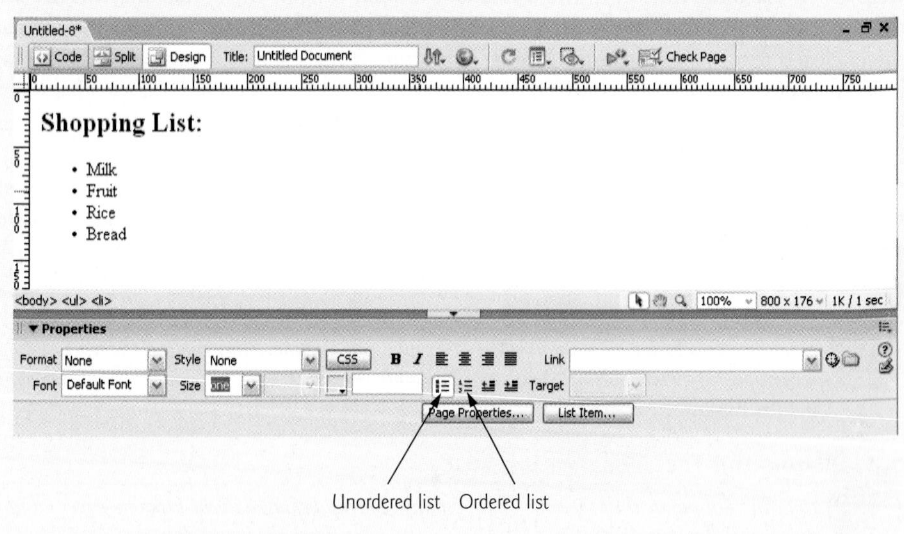

Fig. 20.11 | List creation in Dreamweaver.

```
<!DOCTYPE html PUBLIC "-//W3C//DTD XHTML 1.0 Strict//EN"
"http://www.w3.org/TR/xhtml1/DTD/xhtml1-strict.dtd">
<html xmlns="http://www.w3.org/1999/xhtml">
<head>
<meta http-equiv="Content-Type" content="text/html; charset=utf-8" />
<title>Untitled Document</title>
</head>

<body>
<dl>
    <dt><strong>FTP</strong></dt>
    <dd>File Transfer Protocol</dd>
```

Fig. 20.12 | Definition list inserted using the **Text** menu. (Part 1 of 2.)

```
    <dt><strong>GIF</strong></dt>
    <dd>Graphics Interchange Format</dd>
    <dt><strong>XHTML</strong></dt>
    <dd>Extensible HyperText Markup Language</dd>
    <dt><strong>PNG</strong></dt>
    <dd>Portable Network Graphics</dd>
 </dl>
 </body>
 </html>
```

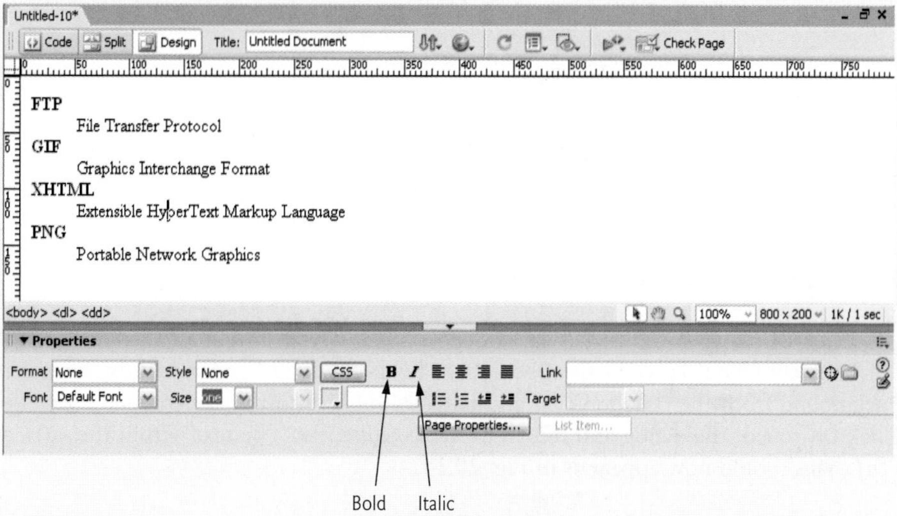

Fig. 20.12 | Definition list inserted using the **Text** menu. (Part 2 of 2.)

Creating Style Sheets

Dreamweaver provides powerful tools to integrate CSS easily into existing code. Type

```
Deitel Textbooks
Internet & World Wide Web How to Program, 4/e
Java How to Program, 7/e
Visual Basic 2005 How to Program, 3/e
C# For Programmers, 2/e
```

into the WYSIWYG display. Make the last four lines into unordered list elements using the method described above.

Select **CSS Styles** from the `Window` menu, or press *<Shift>-F11*. The **CSS Styles** panel will appear on the right-hand side of the page (Fig. 20.13). Now, click the **New CSS Rule** icon (Fig. 20.13) to open the **New CSS Rule dialog**. Next to the **Selector Type:** prompt, select the **Tag** option. This designates your style selections to the particular tag selected in the **Tag:** prompt. Enter `ul` into this menu's text box, or select it from the drop-down list. Next to the **Define in:** field, select the **This document only** radio button to create an embedded style sheet. The **(New Style Sheet File)** option generates an external style sheet.

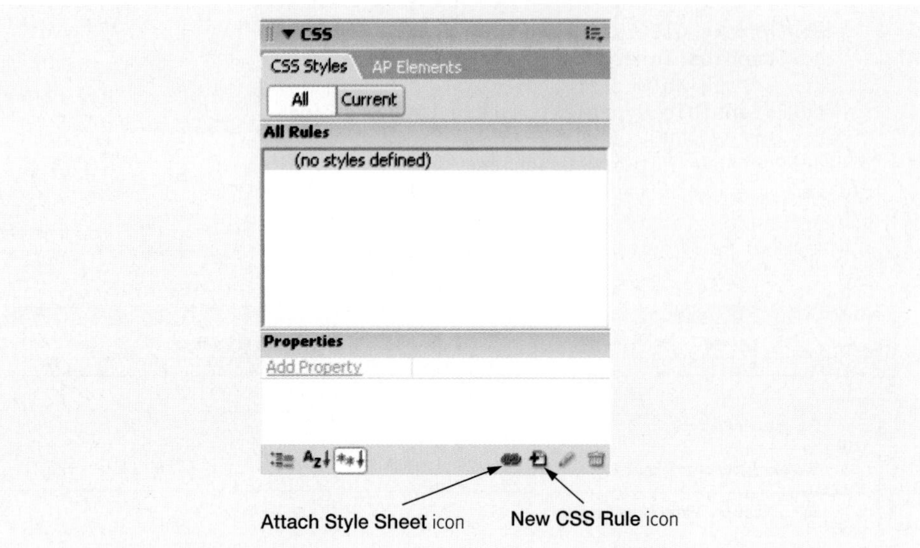

Fig. 20.13 | CSS Styles panel.

Click OK to open the CSS Rule definition dialog. Type should already be selected in the Category menu. Next to the Decoration: field, check the underline box. Now select Background from the Category list, and enter #66ffff into the Background color: field. Click OK to exit the dialog and return to the Design view. The text within the <ul> and </ul> tags should now appear as in Fig. 20.14.

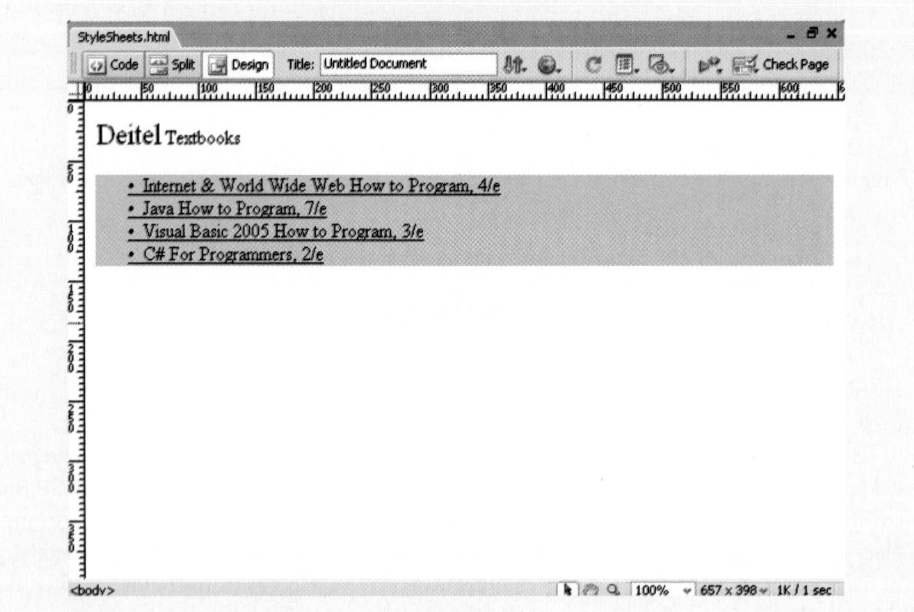

Fig. 20.14 | List with styles applied using CSS.

Now click the **New CSS Rule** icon to bring up the dialog again. This time, select **Class** under **Selector Type:**, and next to **Name:** enter `special`. In the **CSS Rule definition** dialog, select **x-large** from the **Size:** menu. Click **OK** to return to **Style** view, and highlight the word `Deitel`. Then right click the text and select **CSS styles** from the menu that appears. In the new menu, click **special** to apply the new class to the selected text. Your page should now appear as in Fig. 20.14.

Select the **All** option under the **CSS Styles** tab of the **CSS Styles** panel. There should now be a `<style>` tag in the **All Rules** window. Click the plus sign to its left to expand the category. Note that the two style rules that you created are present in this menu, and that additional properties can be added by selecting the rule, then clicking the **Add Property** link in the panel. Also, clicking a property's value in the **CSS Styles** panel creates a drop-down menu, allowing you to specify a new value for the property.

Switch to **Code** view to see the style sheet that Dreamweaver has generated for you. Note that a `<span>` element was automatically created to contain the `special` class.

Please refer to

```
www.adobe.com/devnet/dreamweaver/css.html
```

for additional information on using CSS in Dreamweaver.

20.4 Images and Links

Inserting images using Dreamweaver is simply a matter of clicking a button and selecting an image to insert. Open the **Select Image Source dialog** (Fig. 20.15) either by selecting **Image** from the **Insert** menu, clicking the **Images** menu (Fig. 20.2) in the **Insert** bar and selecting **Image**, or pressing *<Ctrl><Alt>-I*. Browse your local hard-drive directory for a `JPEG`, `GIF` or `PNG` image. You can view the image's URL in the **URL** field—this will become the image's `src` attribute, which can also be viewed in the **Src** field of the **Property Inspector**.

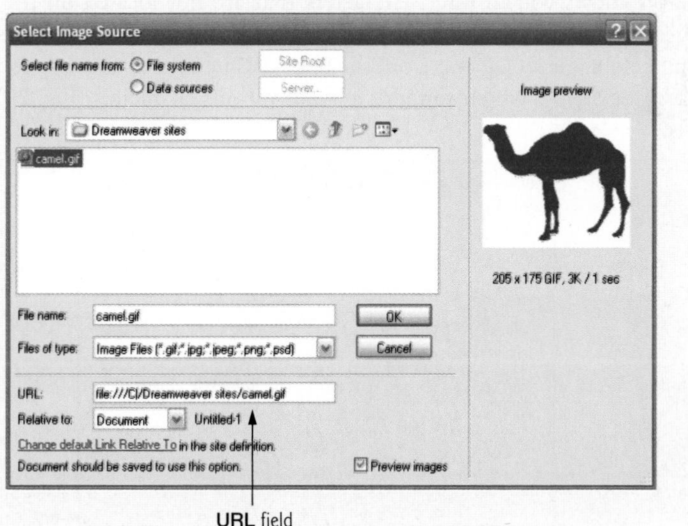

Fig. 20.15 | Image source selection in Dreamweaver.

Software Engineering Observation 20.2

When you insert a local image into an unsaved document, Dreamweaver sets an absolute path, such as `file:///C|/Dreamweaver sites/camel.gif`*. If the image is stored in the same folder as the .html file, saving the document sets the image source to a relative path, starting at the folder in which the document is saved (e.g.,* `camel.gif`*).*

After inserting your image, select it in the **Document** window and create a hyperlink using the **Link** field in the **Property Inspector** (Fig. 20.16). Type in the URL to which the hyperlink will point, `http://www.deitel.com`. Using the **Border** field of the **Property Inspector**, add a `border = 0` attribute to the `<img>` tag to remove the blue rectangle that normally appears around the image.

You can also change other image attributes in the **Property Inspector**. Try resizing the image using the height and width fields and changing its alignment in the **Align pull-down menu**. Clicking and dragging an image's borders also resizes the image.

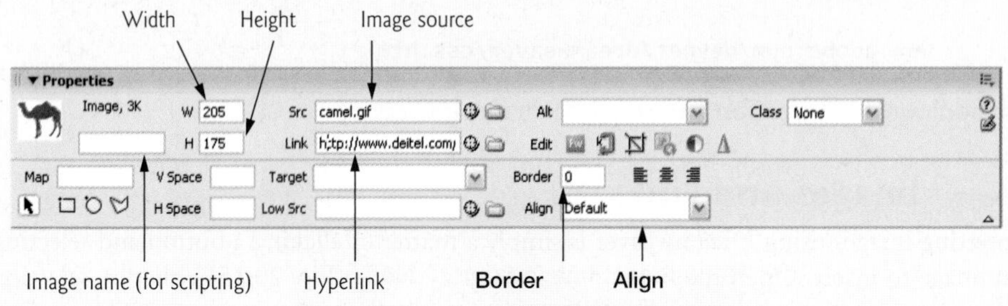

Fig. 20.16 | Image properties in the **Property Inspector**.

20.5 Symbols and Lines

Dreamweaver allows you to insert characters that are not located on the standard keyboard. These characters are accessed by selecting **HTML** in the **Insert** menu, then selecting **Special Characters**. Select **Other...** from the **Special Characters** submenu to view the **Insert Other Character dialog**, which contains a list of various characters (Fig. 20.17).

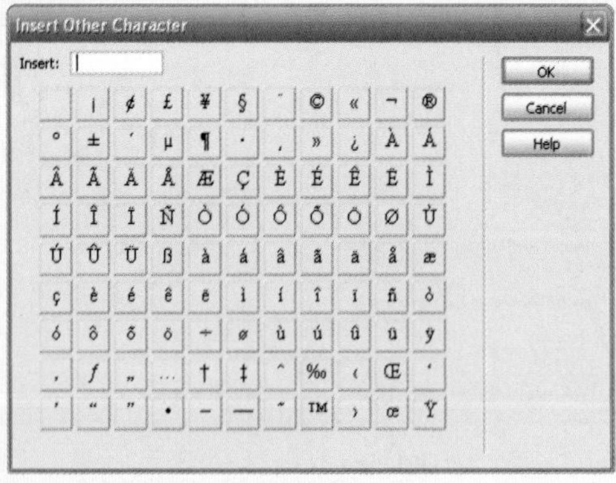

Fig. 20.17 | **Insert Other Character** dialog.

In the next example, we demonstrate how these symbols can be used in a web page, along with Dreamweaver's horizontal rule feature. Begin by typing

```
10 ÷ 5 =
```

Use the **Insert Other Character** dialog to insert the division symbol. Then, select **HTML** from the **Insert** menu and click the **Horizontal Rule button**. This action inserts a line (`hr` element) onto the page directly below the cursor's position. The line should be selected by default; if it is not, select the line by clicking it once. Using the **Property Inspector**, set the width to **60** pixels by entering **60** in the **W** field and selecting **pixels** from the pull-down menu directly to its right (Fig. 20.18). The other value in the menu, **%**, sets the line's length to the specified percentage of the screen. Make the line **5** pixels high by entering **5** in the **H** field (values in this field always have pixels as their units). Select **Left** from the **Align** pull-down menu.

On a new line, type the number `2`. Insert another horizontal rule below the `2`. Set its height to 10 pixels and width to 100%. The page should now resemble Fig. 20.19.

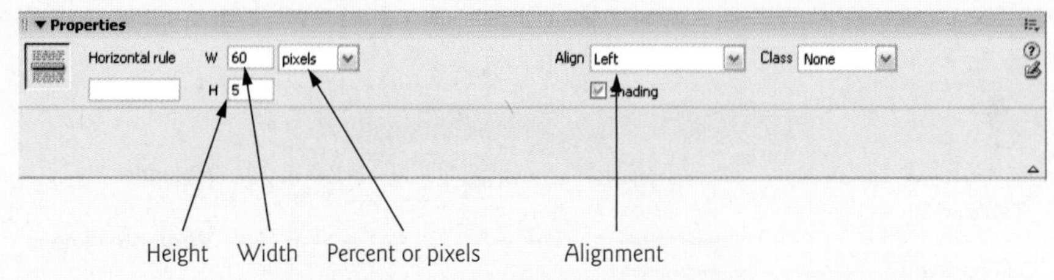

Fig. 20.18 | **Horizontal Rule** properties.

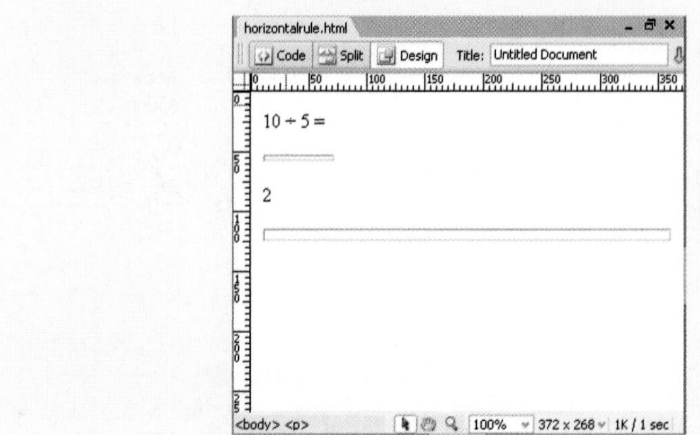

Fig. 20.19 | Special characters and `hr` elements in Dreamweaver.

20.6 Tables

As useful as tables are, they often are time consuming and confusing to code by hand in XHTML. Dreamweaver offers easy-to-use table-editing commands. Open the **Table** dialog by selecting **Table** from the **Insert** menu, clicking the **Table** button in the **Insert** bar or pressing *<Ctrl><Alt>-T*. The **Table dialog** (Fig. 20.20) allows us to select the number of rows and columns, the width of the table and several other related settings.

Figure 20.21 is a simple table with two rows, two columns and no border. Once the table is placed, you can manipulate its size. Click in a cell and press **<tr>** in the tag selector (Fig. 20.2) at the bottom of the **Document** window to select that row. Pressing the *Delete* key removes the row from the table. You can highlight an individual cell by clicking **<td>** in the tag selector. Holding down the *Ctrl* key, then clicking multiple cells allows them all to be selected simultaneously. Clicking the **Merge Cells** button in the **Property Inspector** while two adjacent cells are selected combines the cells into one (Fig. 20.22). Dreamweaver uses the `colspan` and `rowspan` attributes of the `<td>` tag to merge cells. Select a cell and click the **Split Cell** button in the **Property Inspector** to open the **Split Cell** dialog, which allows you to divide the selected cell into any number of rows or columns (Fig. 20.23).

The **Property Inspector** allows us to manipulate the selected table, or a portion of the table. While a cell is selected, its text attributes can be adjusted just as we demonstrated earlier in the chapter. In addition, background and border colors can be assigned to cells, groups of cells or an entire table. We can adjust a cell's height and width in the **Property Inspector**. To manually adjust a cell's size, you can also click and drag its border lines.

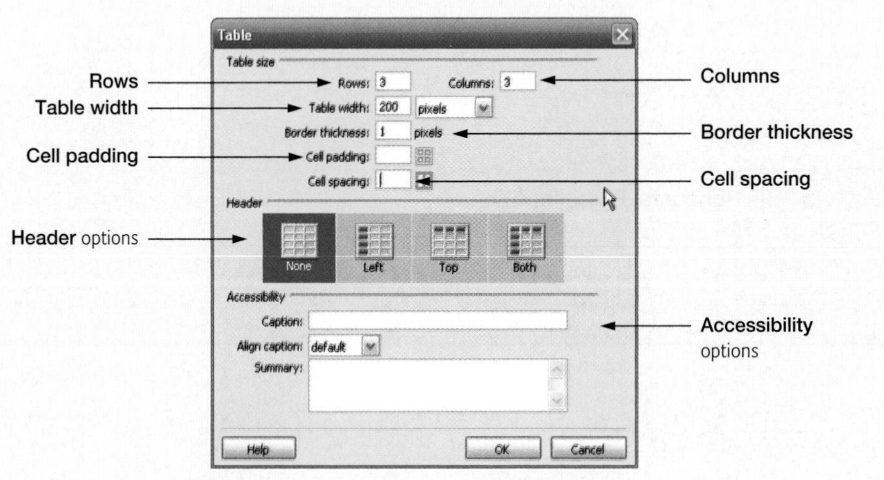

Fig. 20.20 | **Table** dialog.

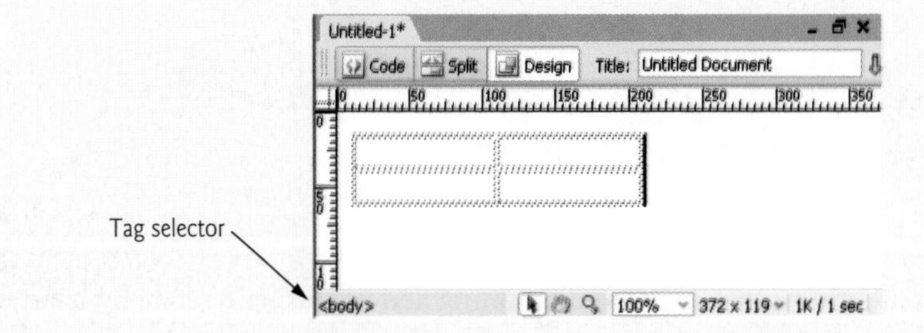

Fig. 20.21 | Table with two rows and two columns.

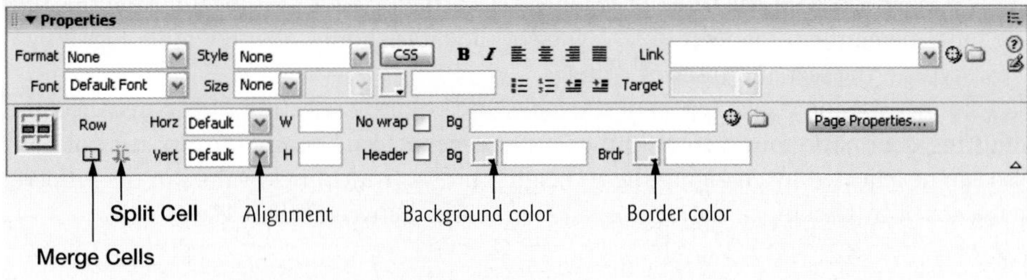

Fig. 20.22 | Table **Property Inspector**.

Fig. 20.23 | **Split Cell** dialog.

We now recreate the table of Fig. 4.11. Make a four-row and five-column table that spans 90% of the page with a one-pixel border. Click the top-left cell, hold the *Shift* key and click the cell below it—another way to select multiple cells. Two of the leftmost cells should now be selected. Merge them by right clicking in either cell and selecting **Table > Merge Cells** (Fig. 20.24) or select **Merge Cells** in the **Property Inspector** as we did before.

Fig. 20.24 | Merging cells in a table.

To make space for the title of the table, select the top four cells (again using the *Shift* key) and merge them together. The layout of the table should now resemble Fig. 20.25. Now, type in the text and insert the image.

To increase the visual appeal of the table, add color by selecting the desired cells and adjusting their background color in the **Property Inspector**. The size of rows and columns also can be adjusted by changing the **H** (height) and **W** (width) field values in the **Property Inspector** or by clicking and dragging the boundaries between cells.

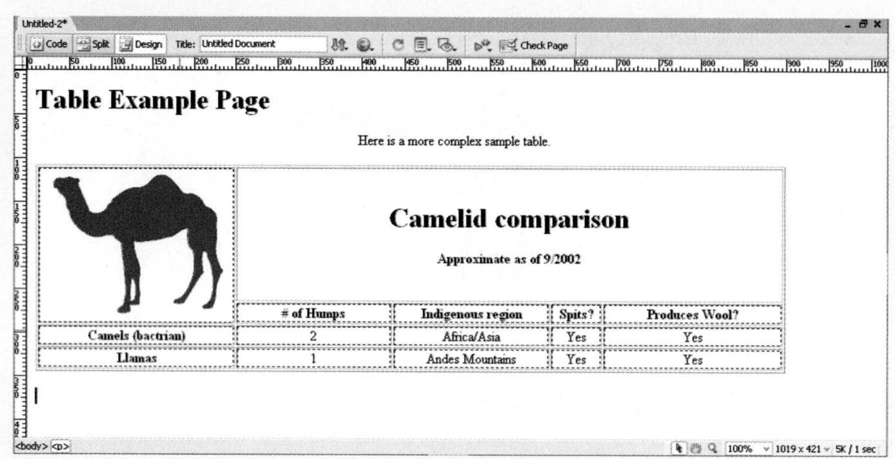

Fig. 20.25 | Almost completed table.

20.7 Forms

All the necessary XHTML coding needed for creating a feedback form or any other forms can be done in Dreamweaver. To insert a form, first select **Forms** from the insert menu in the **Insert** bar (Fig. 20.26). The **Insert** bar will now contain various options for creating forms. Click the leftmost button to insert an empty form into the document. Forms can also be inserted by selecting **Form** from the **Insert** menu's **Form** submenu.

After a form is inserted into a document, Dreamweaver displays a dotted line to delineate the bounds of the form. Any form objects (i.e., text fields, buttons, etc.) placed inside

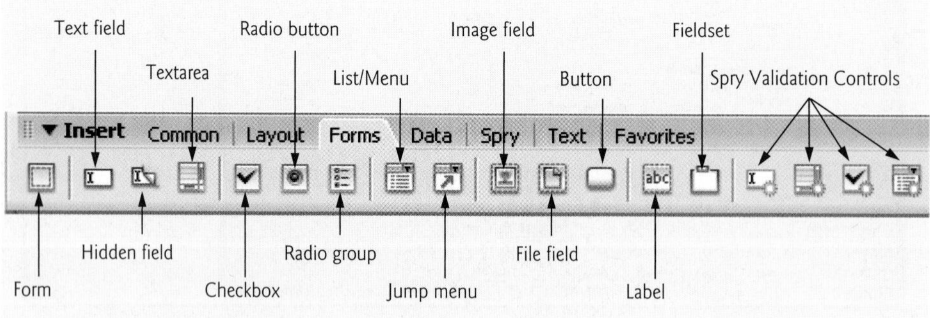

Fig. 20.26 | **Forms Insert** bar.

this dotted line will be part of the same `form` element in the XHTML code that Dreamweaver generates.

We can modify the properties of a form by clicking anywhere inside the dotted line that delineates the form, then clicking **<form#*name*>** (where *name* is the `name` of the `form` element) in the tag selector at the bottom of the **Document** window. Dreamweaver assigns default names to forms in sequential order (i.e., the first form inserted is named **form1**, the second form is named **form2** and so on). The name of the form can be altered in the **Form name** field in the **Property Inspector**. The **Property Inspector** can also be used to set the **Action** and **Method** attributes of the form, which are required for server-side processing. Server-side technology is discussed later in this book.

You can insert text field by clicking the **Text Field** button in the **Insert** bar or by selecting **Text Field** from the **Insert** menu's **Form** submenu. The **Input Tag Accessibility Attributes dialog** that appears allows you to set an `id` and `label` for the text field, and to specify some of its other properties. Once placed, a text field's attributes can be adjusted using the **Property Inspector.** Its `name`, `id` and `value` attributes can be set or modified along with the `size` and `maxlength` (Fig. 20.27). The text field type also can be set to **Multi line**, allowing multiple lines of text, or **Password**, making all entered text appear as asterisks (*).

Scrollable **Textareas** also can be selected from the **Form Insert** bar. Their properties are almost identical to those of a text field, except that they have the additional attributes for the number of lines (specified in the **Num lines** field in the **Property Inspector**) and **Wrap** (i.e., how the text area handles lines of text that exceed its width).

A drop-down select menu can be added by clicking the **List/Menu button** in the **Insert** bar. To add entries and values to the list or menu, click the **List Values... button** in the **Property Inspector** (Fig. 20.28). In the **List Values** dialog, you can add entries by pressing the **+** button, and remove entries by pressing the **-** button. Each entry has an **Item Label** and a **Value.** An entry can be made the default selection by selecting it in the **Initially selected** list in the **Property Inspector.**

Now that we've discussed the basics of forms in Dreamweaver, we're ready to create a "rate my website" form. To start, insert a form into a new page, followed by text fields, menus and text. The elements should appear as in Fig. 20.29.

Make the text fields the proper width by adjusting the **Char width** value in the **Property Inspector**. Now select the drop-down menu to the right of the text **How would you rate our site?** and click the **List Values...** button in the **Property Inspector** to add appropriate entries to the list (e.g., **Excellent**, **Good**, **Fair**, **Poor** and **Terrible**).

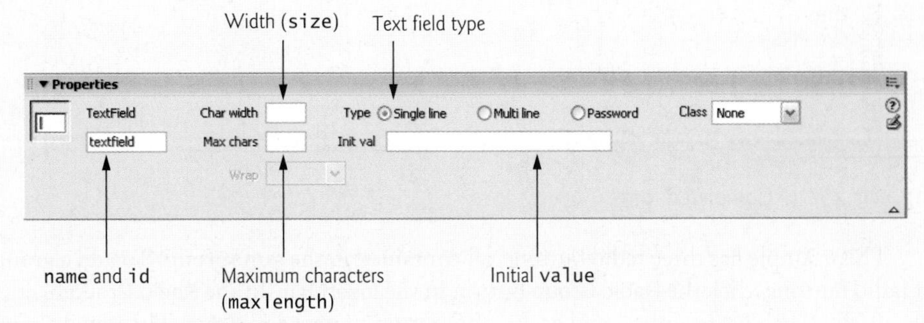

Fig. 20.27 | Text field **Property Inspector.**

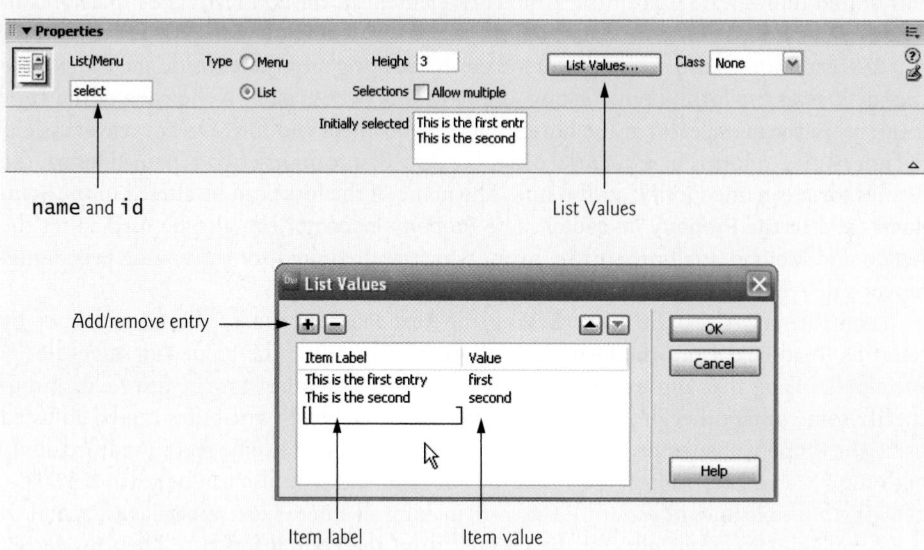

Fig. 20.28 | **List Values** dialog box.

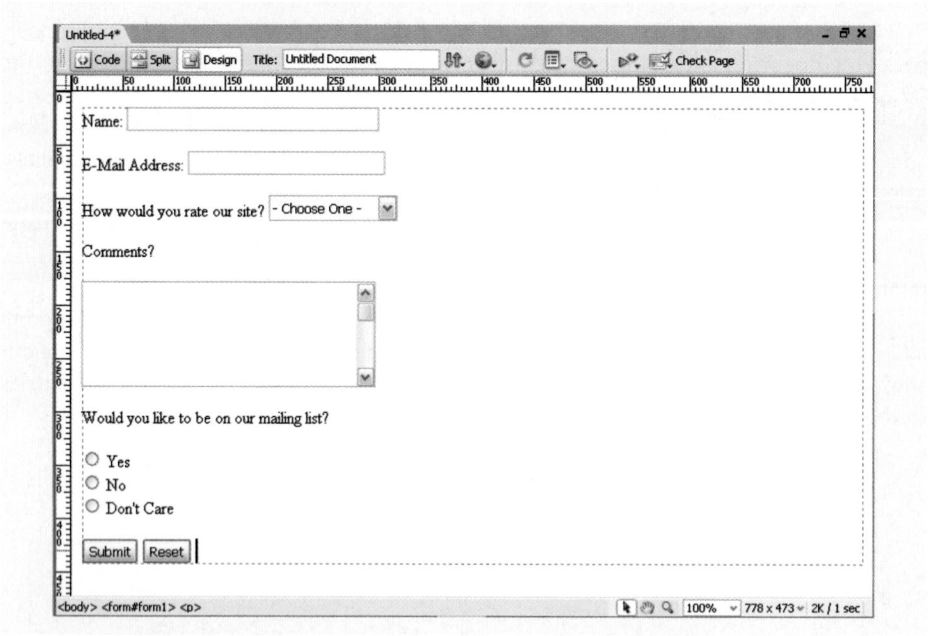

Untitled-4*
Code Split Design Title: Untitled Document Check Page
Name:
E-Mail Address:
How would you rate our site? - Choose One -
Comments?
Would you like to be on our mailing list?
Yes
No
Don't Care
Submit Reset
<body> <form#form1> <p> 100% 778 x 473 2K / 1 sec

Fig. 20.29 | Completed form.

This example has three radio buttons, all contained in the same group. To add a group of radio buttons, click the **Radio Group** button in the **Insert** bar. In the **Radio Group** dialog, specify the **Name** of the group, and each radio button's **Label** and **Value**. The **Radio Group** dialog works similarly to the **List Values** dialog.

To create the **Reset** and **Submit** buttons, click the **Button** selection in the **Insert** bar. The **Value** of each new button defaults to **Submit**, but can be changed to **Reset** or any other value using the **Property Inspector**. The button's **Property Inspector** can also be used to assign a **Button name**, which is assigned to the button's `name` and `id` attributes, or to specify its **Action**, or `type` attribute.

For a complete list and description of Dreamweaver's XHTML tags, open the **Reference** panel by selecting **Reference** from the **Window** menu. Select the desired XHTML element from the **Tag** pull-down list in the **Reference** panel.

20.8 Scripting in Dreamweaver

Dreamweaver also allows us to add JavaScript to our pages manually in the **Code** view or automatically using the **Behaviors panel**. To open the **Behaviors** panel, either select **Behaviors** from the **Window** menu, or press *<Shift>-F4*. The **Behaviors** panel appears as a tab option in the **Tag panel** (Fig. 20.30).

The **Behaviors** panel allows us to add commands to elements of a web page that trigger various JavaScript actions in response to browser events. To add an action, select an element on the page. Click the **+** button in the **Behaviors** panel to display a pop-up menu of applicable actions. The pop-up menu offers several predefined JavaScript actions, such as **Go To URL** or **Popup Message**. A developer also can manually write an action by selecting **Call JavaScript** from the pop-up menu and entering the desired code into the **Call JavaScript** dialog. Selecting **Get More Behaviors...** opens a web page that provides options to download or purchase additional behaviors, extensions, functions and code. After completing the dialog associated with the selected action, the action and a default event appear in the **Behaviors** panel. A developer can change the event that triggers this action by clicking the event field and choosing an event from the drop-down list that appears.

Dreamweaver supports several server-side scripting languages, discussed later in the book, such as ASP.NET, JSF, PHP and ColdFusion. Server-side scripting elements, such

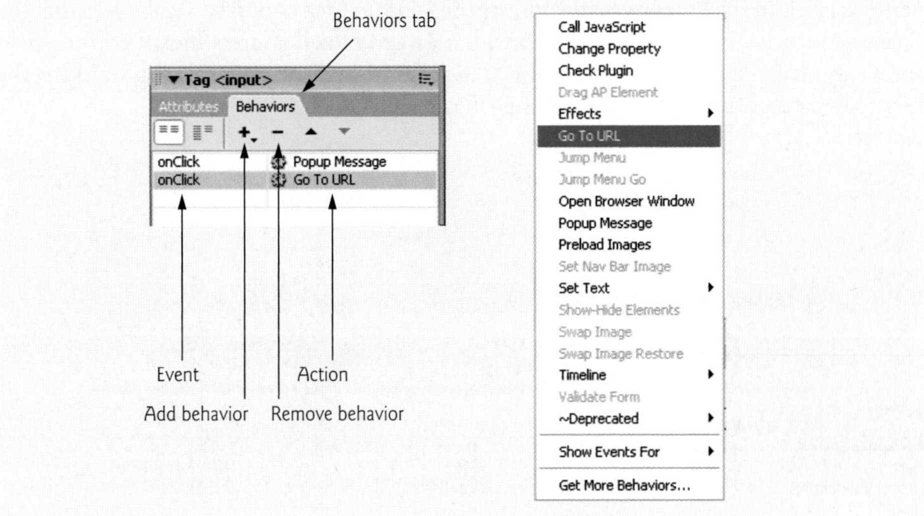

Fig. 20.30 | **Behaviors** panel and menu to add behaviors.

as **Databases** and **Bindings**, can be accessed in the **Window** menu. Tags of the various languages can also be selected from the **Tag Chooser**, which is accessed by selecting **Tag...** from the **Insert** menu, or from the icon in the **Insert** bar (Fig. 20.2). Dreamweaver allows the user to add scripting elements only where applicable.

20.9 Spry Framework for Creating Ajax Applications

Many toolkits are available that provide prebuilt controls to enhance web applications and make it easier to include JavaScript functions in your applications with minimal coding (such as the Dojo toolkit mentioned in Chapter 15, and the Prototype and Script.aculo.us toolkits in Chapter 24). Adobe also created its own toolkit for Dreamweaver to develop dynamic and more robust web pages known as the Spry Framework.

The Spry Framework enables web developers with basic knowledge of HTML, CSS and JavaScript to create richer websites and dynamic pages. The framework includes a ready-to-use JavaScript library, which contains prebuilt, but customizable, widgets (such as a **Validation Textarea**, **Validation Text Field** and a **Menu Bar**), effects (such as grow, shrink, fade and highlight) and Ajax capabilities. To view all of the available spry tools, click the **Spry** tab in the **Insert** bar (Fig. 20.31).

Recall that Ajax applications separate client-side user interaction and server communication and run them in parallel, making the delays of server-side processing more transparent to the user. Consider the form example that you built in Fig. 20.29. None of the data entered into the form is transmitted to the server until the user clicks the **Submit** button. At that time, any errors in the form are sent back to the user for correction. With Ajax and the Spry framework, text field input is validated on the client side. When the page loads, the files that provide the validation are loaded directly into the page, so you can check for errors in any given field as soon as the user moves to the next field in the form.

Now, let's rebuild the form in Fig. 20.29 using Spry controls. First, insert **Spry Validation Text Fields** next to the **Name** and **E-mail Address** labels.

Select the blue **Spry** box connected to the text field you created next to the **E-mail Address** label. In the **Property Inspector**, set the **Type:** to **Email Address**. Make sure that the **Change** checkbox is selected. This means that a valid e-mail address must be in the field and if any changes are made to the address, the client will display a message prompting the user to make a change before continuing (Fig. 20.33).

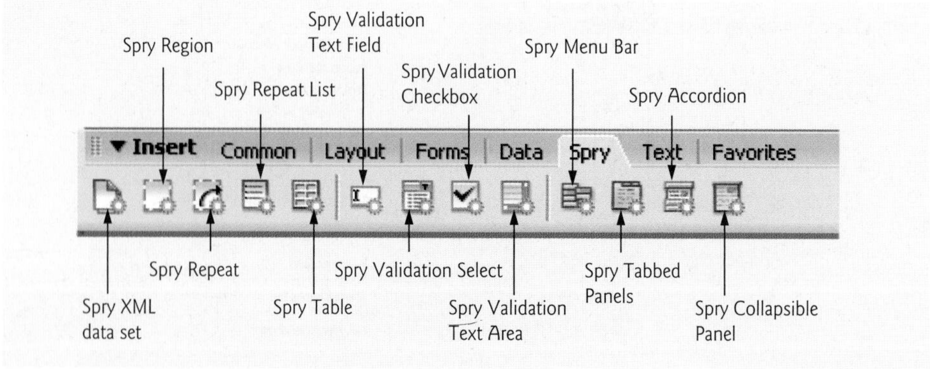

Fig. 20.31 | Spry Tools.

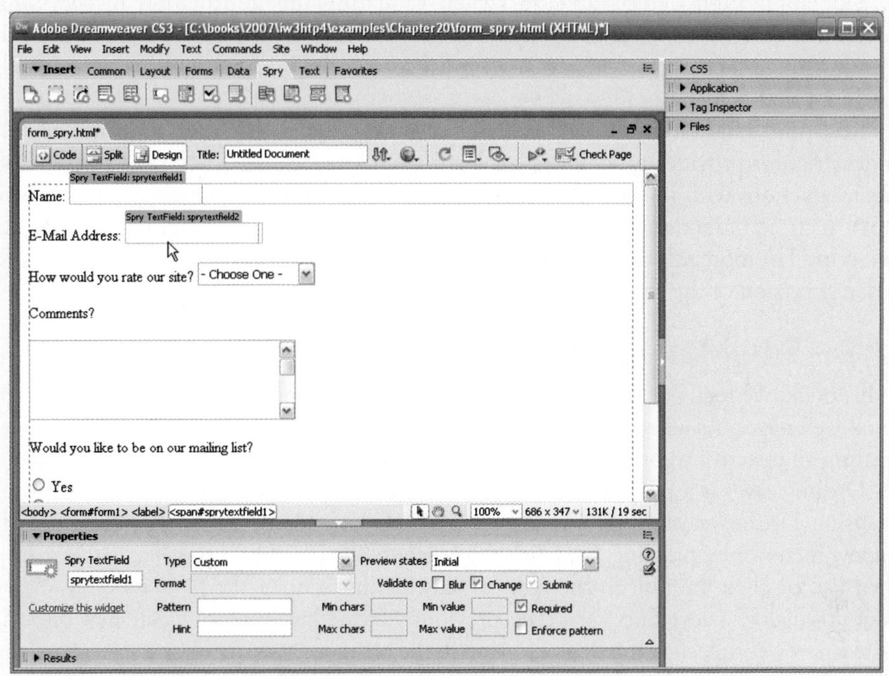

Fig. 20.32 | Inserting Spry Validation Text Fields.

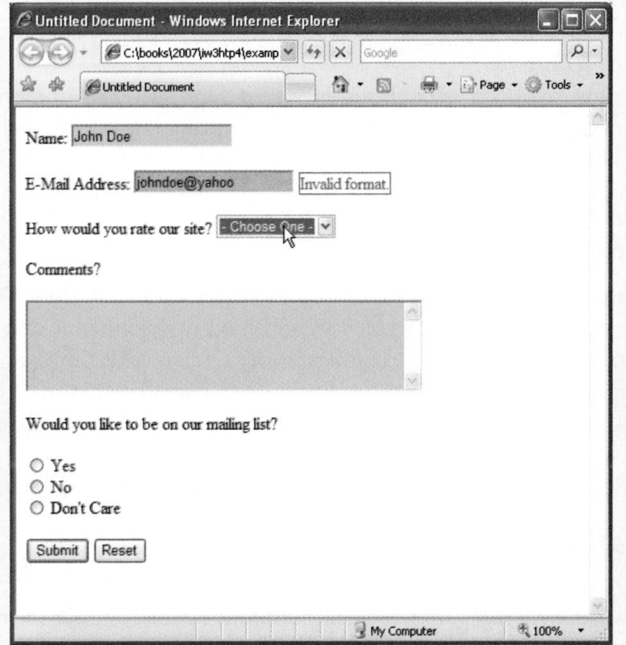

Fig. 20.33 | Using a Spry Text Field to validate data before continuing to fill out a form.

Our application detects an error when validating the information in the e-mail address text field. As soon as we try to move to the next field, the application displays the error **Invalid format** to let us know that we must correct the information that we originally typed into that field.

Real-time validation is a key element in Ajax and rich Internet applications. The framework also provides capabilities for loading and processing XML data obtained via Ajax interactions with the server. Using the Spry Framework, developers can take advantage of such rich functionality, even if they don't have a deep understanding of XML and JavaScript. For more information on the Spry framework, for Ajax-based examples and for the latest version of the framework, visit `labs.adobe.com/technologies/spry/`.

20.10 Site Management

In this book, we focus primarily on the skills and technologies involved in creating individual web pages. As a result, we do not spend much time discussing complete websites. Creating an effective website is a difficult process, requiring planning, effort and time.

Dreamweaver is a powerful tool for creating and maintaining a website. To create a site using Dreamweaver, first open the **Files panel** either by selecting **Files** from the **Window** menu or by pressing *F8*. Click the **Manage Sites...** link in the **Files** panel's drop-down list, or click the link to the right of this menu, to open the **Manage Sites dialog**. From this dialog, a developer can access previously created websites or create new ones. To create a new website, click the **New...** button in the **Manage Sites** dialog and select **Site** from the pop-up list. Then, follow the instructions provided by Dreamweaver's **Site Definition Wizard**. Once completed, site files can be viewed, accessed and added in the **File** panel.

In general, pages in a website should have consistent colors and styles to maintain site uniformity. Dreamweaver's **Assets panel** holds elements common to a website, such as pictures, colors and links. Open the **Assets** panel by selecting **Assets** from the **Window** menu or pressing *F11*.

While Dreamweaver is a valuable aid in website creation, it is not a replacement for thorough knowledge of XHTML and the related scripting languages taught in this book. Be sure to familiarize yourself with these other technologies before using Dreamweaver to accelerate the development process.

20.11 Wrap-Up

This chapter provided an introduction to Dreamweaver CS3, a WYSIWYG visual XHTML editor. We described how to create, save and modify documents, and explained how to implement many of Chapter 4's examples in the Dreamweaver environment. We also discussed incorporating more advanced scripting into pages created in Dreamweaver. Finally, we introduced Dreamweaver's Spry framework, which allows us to create richer websites and dynamic pages by incorporating XML into documents. The next chapter will discuss web servers, and how they can be used to exchange information over the Internet.

20.12 Web Resources

`www.adobe.com/devnet/dreamweaver`

Adobe's *Dreamweaver Developer Center* contains numerous tutorials and sample files intended for beginner, intermediate and expert users. This site explores some of the more advanced features of Dreamweaver in addition to the topics covered in this chapter.

www.adobe.com/software/dreamweaver
This site contains detailed product information, software downloads and links to featured sites created with Dreamweaver CS3.

Summary

Section 20.1 Introduction

- Dreamweaver CS3 is a popular HTML editor that can create complex XHTML elements, such as tables, forms and frames.

Section 20.2 Adobe Dreamweaver CS3

- Unlike editors that simply display XHTML code, Dreamweaver renders XHTML elements much as a browser would, using the WYSIWYG screen. This functionality enables you to design your web pages as they will appear on the web.
- Create a new document by selecting **New...** from the **File** menu. In the **New Document** dialog, select the **Blank page** tab from the leftmost column, and **HTML** from the **Page Type:** list.
- Dreamweaver automatically encloses text in a paragraph (p) element for proper formatting.
- The **Category** list in the **Page Properties** dialogue lets the user select a set of properties to view.
- To view or edit the XHTML that Dreamweaver has generated, you must switch from **Design** view to **Code** view.
- The tag names, attribute values and page text are all displayed in different colors.
- To save your file, click **Save** in the **File** menu or press *<Ctrl>-S*.
- To view your page in a browser, press *F12* or select **Preview in Browser** from the **File** menu. Note that the **File** menu option provides several browsers in which to view your code—more browsers can be added with the **Edit Browser List...** option.

Section 20.3 Text Styles

- In Dreamweaver, we can alter text properties with the **Text** menu or the **Property Inspector.**
- Dreamweaver is prone to produce somewhat inefficient code.
- Dreamweaver is capable of extensive text formatting, such as creating mathematical formulas.
- Many useful text-formatting options are located in the **Text** menu and can be applied to highlighted code.
- You can also access most of the elements in the **Text** menu by right clicking highlighted text.
- Dreamweaver automatically inserts a matching end tag in Code view.
- The **Property Inspector** can be used to create lists.
- Dreamweaver can integrate CSS easily into existing code using the **CSS Styles** panel. You can create both embedded and external style sheets with this tool.

Section 20.4 Images and Links

- Images can be inserted into Dreamweaver by selecting **Image** from the **Insert** menu or clicking the **Images** button in the **Insert** bar.

Section 20.5 Symbols and Lines

- Dreamweaver allows you to insert characters that are not located on the standard keyboard by selecting **HTML** in the **Insert** menu, then selecting **Special Characters.**
- Select **HTML** from the **Insert** menu and click the **Horizontal Rule** button to insert a horizontal rule.

Section 20.6 Tables

- Open the **Table** dialog by selecting **Table** from the **Insert** menu, clicking the **Table** button in the **Insert** bar or pressing *<Ctrl><Alt>-T*.
- The **Table** dialog allows us to select the number of rows and columns, the overall width of the table and several other related settings.
- The **Property Inspector** allows us to manipulate the selected table, or a portion of the table.

Section 20.7 Forms

- To insert a form, first select **Forms** from the insert menu in the **Insert** bar, which will now contain various options for creating forms.
- Dreamweaver displays a dotted line to delineate the bounds of the form. Any form objects (i.e., text fields, buttons, etc.) placed inside this dotted line will be part of the same `form` element in the XHTML code that Dreamweaver generates.
- We can modify the properties of a form by clicking anywhere inside the dotted line that delineates the form, then clicking **<form#*name*>** (where *name* is the `name` of the `form` element) in the tag selector at the bottom of the **Document** window.
- For a complete list and description of Dreamweaver's XHTML tags, open the **Reference** panel by selecting **Reference** from the **Window** menu. Select the desired XHTML element from the **Tag** pull-down list in the **Reference** panel.

Section 20.8 Scripting in Dreamweaver

- Dreamweaver also allows us to add JavaScript to our pages manually in the Code view, or automatically using the **Behaviors** panel.
- The **Behaviors** panel allows us to add commands to elements of a web page that trigger various JavaScript actions in response to browser events.
- Dreamweaver supports several server-side scripting languages such as ASP.NET, JSF, PHP and ColdFusion. Server-side scripting elements, such as **Databases** and **Bindings**, can be accessed in the **Window** menu.

Section 20.9 Spry Framework for Creating Ajax Applications

- The Spry Framework promotes the creation of richer websites and dynamic pages by incorporating XML into documents for those web developers with basic knowledge of HTML, CSS and JavaScript.
- To view all of the available spry tools, click the **Spry** tab in the **Insert** bar.
- Ajax applications, including the Spry Framework, separate client-side user interaction and server communication, and run them in parallel, making the delays of server-side processing more transparent to the user.
- With Ajax and the Spry framework, text field input is validated on the client side. When the page loads, the files that provide the validation are loaded directly into the page, so you can check for errors in any given field as soon as the user moves to the next field in the form.
- You can manipulate the properties of Spry elements by selecting the blue **Spry** box connected to the element you created, then using the **Property Inspector**.

Section 20.10 Site Management

- Dreamweaver can help you create and maintain a website with the Files panel and the Site Definition Wizard.
- Dreamweaver's **Assets** panel holds elements common to a website, such as pictures, colors and links.

Terminology

Assets panel
Background Color
Behaviors panel
Button button
Category list
Code view
CSS Rule definition dialog
dd element (definition; <dd>...</dd>)
Design view
dl element (definition list; <dl>...</dl>)
Document toolbar
Document window
dt element (defined term; <dt>...</dt>)
Files panel
Font field in Property Inspector
Form button in Insert bar
Form tab in Insert bar
Horizontal Rule in HTML option in Insert menu
Images button in Insert bar
Insert bar
Insert menu
Link field in the Property Inspector
List Values button
List/Menu button
Manage Sites dialog
Merge Cells button in Property Inspector
New CSS Rule dialog
Page Property... dialog
Property Inspector
Preview in Browser
Save in File menu
Special Characters dialog
Split Cell button in Property Inspector
Style in Text menu
Table button in Insert bar
Table dialog
Tag selector
Text Field button
Text menu
WYSIWYG (What You See Is What You Get)

Self-Review Exercises

20.1 State whether each of the following is *true* or *false*. If *false*, explain why.
a) Dreamweaver renders XHTML elements correctly in its WYSIWYG display.
b) Dreamweaver allows web-page authors to insert images simply by clicking a button and selecting an image to insert.
c) Dreamweaver requires the user to manually write special characters into the code.
d) Dreamweaver delineates a form element in the WYSIWYG editor with a dotted line.
e) Dreamweaver can be used to create only XHTML documents.

20.2 Fill in the blanks for each of the following statements.
a) A(n) ________ editor renders web-page elements exactly as a browser would.
b) The ________ allows you to adjust the selected element's attributes.
c) Dreamweaver's ________ option combines selected table cells into one cell.
d) The ________ panel allows a developer to add JavaScript to an XHTML document.

Answers to Self-Review Exercises

20.1 a) True.
b) True.
c) False. Selecting Special Characters from the HTML submenu of the Insert menu provides a list of special characters.
d) True.
e) False. Dreamweaver supports several server-side scripting languages, such as ASP.NET, JSF and PHP.

20.2 a) WYSIWYG (What You See Is What You Get). b) Property Inspector. c) Merge Cells. d) Behaviors.

Exercises

20.3 Create the following table using Dreamweaver:

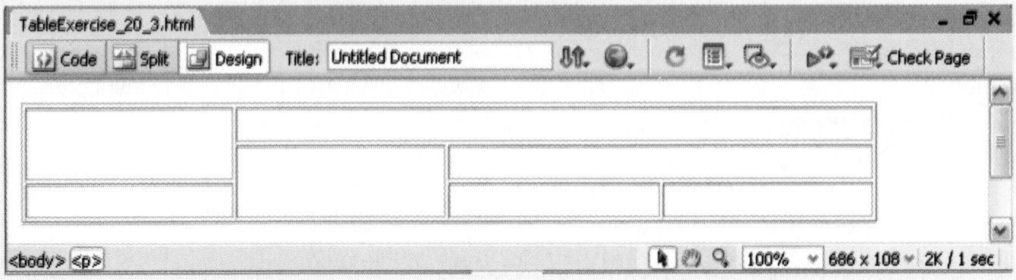

20.4 Create the following form using Dreamweaver:

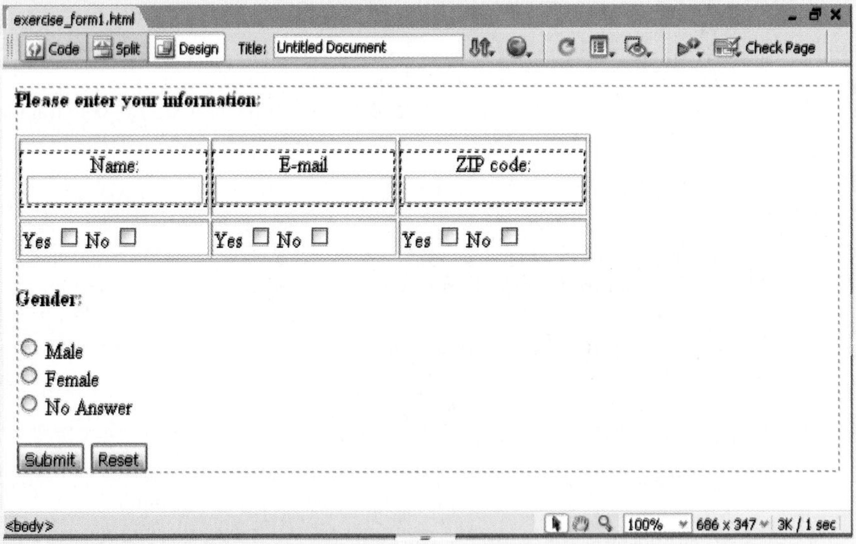

20.5 Add a feature to your solution to Exercise 20.4 that displays an `alert` dialog reading "`form submitted`" when the user clicks the **Submit** button, and that displays an `alert` dialog "`form reset`" appear when the user clicks the **Reset** button.

20.6 Create a personal web page using Dreamweaver that features an image and a list of interests. Experiment with different text-formatting options. Link the image to your favorite website.

20.7 Recreate the page in Fig. 5.2 using an external style sheet.

Rich Internet Application Server Technologies

One of the powerful things about networking technology like the Internet or the Web or the Semantic Web...is that the things we've just done with them far surpass the imagination of the people who invented them.

—Tim Berners-Lee, interviewed by Peter Moon, IDG Now

21

Web Servers (IIS and Apache)

Stop abusing my verses, or publish some of your own.
—Martial

There are three difficulties in authorship: to write anything worth the publishing, to find honest men to publish it, and to get sensible men to read it.
—Charles Caleb Colton

When your Daemon is in charge, do not try to think consciously. Drift, wait and obey.
—Rudyard Kipling

OBJECTIVES

In this chapter you will learn:

- To understand a web server's functionality.
- To introduce Microsoft Internet Information Services (IIS) and Apache HTTP Server.
- To set up virtual directories from which content can be served.
- To test whether you set up the virtual directory properly.

Outline

21.1 Introduction

In this chapter, we discuss the specialized software—called a web server—that responds to client requests (typically from a web browser) by providing resources such as XHTML documents. For example, when users enter a Uniform Resource Locator (URL) address, such as `www.deitel.com`, into a web browser, they are requesting a specific document from a web server. The web server maps the URL to a resource on the server (or to a file on the server's network) and returns the requested resource to the client. During this interaction, the web server and the client communicate using the platform-independent Hypertext Transfer Protocol (HTTP), a protocol for transferring requests and files over the Internet or a local intranet.

Our web server discussion introduces Microsoft Internet Information Services (IIS) and the open source Apache HTTP Server. Sections 21.6 and 21.7 discuss IIS and Apache, respectively.

21.2 HTTP Transactions

In this section, we discuss what occurs behind the scenes when a user requests a web page in a browser. The HTTP protocol allows clients and servers to interact and exchange information in a uniform and reliable manner.

In its simplest form, a web page is nothing more than an XHTML document that describes to a web browser how to display and format the document's information. XHTML documents normally contain hyperlinks that link to different pages or to other parts of the same page. When the user clicks a hyperlink, the requested web page loads into the user's web browser. Similarly, the user can type the address of a page into the browser's address field.

URIs

HTTP uses URIs (Uniform Resource Identifiers) to identify data on the Internet. URIs that specify document locations are called URLs (Uniform Resource Locators). Common URLs refer to files, directories or objects that perform complex tasks, such as database lookups and Internet searches. If you know the URL of a publicly available resource or file anywhere on the web, you can access it through HTTP.

Parts of a URL

A URL contains information that directs a browser to the resource that the user wishes to access. Computers that run web server software make such resources available. Let's examine the components of the URL

```
http://www.deitel.com/books/downloads.html
```

The `http://` indicates that the resource is to be obtained using the HTTP protocol. The middle portion, `www.deitel.com`, is the server's fully qualified hostname—the name of the server on which the resource resides. This computer usually is referred to as the host, because it houses and maintains resources. The hostname `www.deitel.com` is translated into an IP address—a unique numerical value that identifies the server much as a telephone number uniquely defines a particular phone line. More information on IP addresses is available at `en.wikipedia.org/wiki/IP_address`. This translation is performed by a domain name system (DNS) server—a computer that maintains a database of hostnames and their corresponding IP addresses—and the process is called a DNS lookup.

The remainder of the URL (i.e., `/books/downloads.html`) specifies both the name of the requested resource (the XHTML document `downloads.html`) and its path, or location (`/books`), on the web server. The path could specify the location of an actual directory on the web server's file system. For security reasons, however, the path normally specifies the location of a virtual directory. The server translates the virtual directory into a real location on the server (or on another computer on the server's network), thus hiding the true location of the resource. Some resources are created dynamically using other information stored on the server computer, such as a database. The hostname in the URL for such a resource specifies the correct server; the path and resource information identify the resource with which to interact to respond to the client's request.

Making a Request and Receiving a Response

When given a URL, a web browser performs a simple HTTP transaction to retrieve and display the web page found at that address. Figure 21.1 illustrates the transaction, showing the interaction between the web browser (the client side) and the web server application (the server side).

In Fig. 21.1, the web browser sends an HTTP request to the server. The request (in its simplest form) is

```
GET /books/downloads.html HTTP/1.1
```

The word `GET` is an HTTP method indicating that the client wishes to obtain a resource from the server. The remainder of the request provides the path name of the resource (e.g., an XHTML document) and the protocol's name and version number (`HTTP/1.1`). The client's request also contains some required and optional headers.

Any server that understands HTTP (version 1.1) can translate this request and respond appropriately. Figure 21.2 depicts the server responding to a request. The server first responds by sending a line of text that indicates the HTTP version, followed by a numeric code and a phrase describing the status of the transaction. For example,

```
HTTP/1.1 200 OK
```

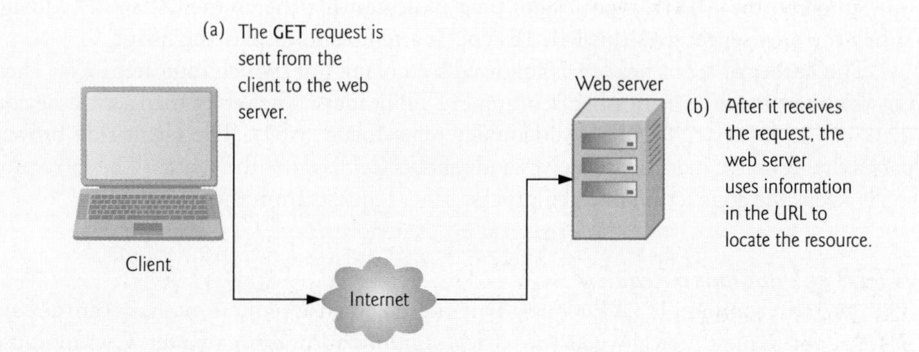

Fig. 21.1 | Client interacting with web server. *Step 1:* The GET request.

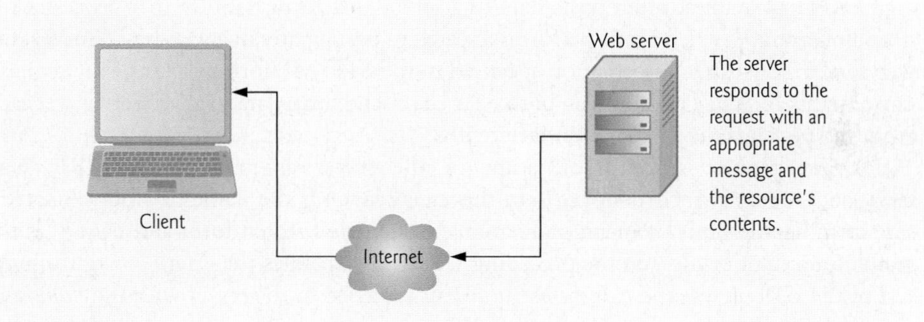

Fig. 21.2 | Client interacting with web server. *Step 2:* The HTTP response.

indicates success, whereas

```
HTTP/1.1 404 Not found
```

informs the client that the web server could not locate the requested resource. A complete list of numeric codes indicating the status of an HTTP transaction can be found at `www.w3.org/Protocols/rfc2616/rfc2616-sec10.html`.

HTTP Headers

The server then sends one or more HTTP headers, which provide additional information about the data that will be sent. In this case, the server is sending an XHTML text document, so one HTTP header for this example would read:

```
Content-type: text/html
```

The information provided in this header specifies the Multipurpose Internet Mail Extensions (MIME) type of the content that the server is transmitting to the browser. MIME is an Internet standard that specifies data formats so that programs can interpret data correctly. For example, the MIME type `text/plain` indicates that the sent information is text that can be displayed directly, without any interpretation of the content as XHTML markup. Similarly, the MIME type `image/jpeg` indicates that the content is a JPEG image. When the browser receives this MIME type, it attempts to display the image.

The header or set of headers is followed by a blank line, which indicates to the client browser that the server is finished sending HTTP headers. The server then sends the contents of the requested XHTML document (`downloads.html`). The client-side browser parses the XHTML markup it receives and renders (or displays) the results. The server normally keeps the connection open to process other requests from the client.

HTTP `get` *and* `post` *Requests*

The two most common HTTP request types (also known as request methods) are `get` and `post`. A `get` request typically gets (or retrieves) information from a server. Common uses of `get` requests are to retrieve an XHTML document or an image, or to fetch search results based on a user-submitted search term. A `post` request typically posts (or sends) data to a server. Common uses of `post` requests are to send form data or documents to a server.

An HTTP request often posts data to a server-side form handler that processes the data. For example, when a user performs a search or participates in a web-based survey, the web server receives the information specified in the XHTML form as part of the request. `Get` requests and `post` requests can both be used to send form data to a web server, yet each request type sends the information differently.

A `get` request sends information to the server as part of the URL, e.g., `www.google.com/search?q=deitel`. In this case `search` is the name of Google's server-side form handler, `q` is the `name` of a variable in Google's search form and `deitel` is the search term. Notice the `?` in the preceding URL. A `?` separates the query string from the rest of the URL in a request. A *name*/*value* pair is passed to the server with the *name* and the *value* separated by an equals sign (`=`). If more than one *name*/*value* pair is submitted, each pair is separated by an ampersand (`&`). The server uses data passed in a query string to retrieve an appropriate resource from the server. The server then sends a response to the client. A `get` request may be initiated by submitting an XHTML form whose `method` attribute is set to `"get"`, or by typing the URL (possibly containing a query string) directly into the browser's address bar (See Chapter 2 for more information on how various search engines operate and Chapter 4 for an in-depth discussion of XHTML forms.)

A `post` request is specified in an XHTML form by the `method "post"`. The `post` method sends form data as part of the HTTP message, not as part of the URL. A `get` request typically limits the query string (i.e., everything to the right of the `?`) to a specific number of characters (2083 in IE; more in other browsers), so it is often necessary to send large pieces of information using the `post` method. The `post` method is also sometimes preferred because it hides the submitted data from the user by embedding it in an HTTP message. If a form submits several hidden input values along with user-submitted data, the `post` method might generate a URL like `www.searchengine.com/search`. The form data still reaches the server and is processed in a similar fashion to a `get` request, but the user does not see the exact information sent.

Software Engineering Observation 21.1

The data sent in a `post` *request is not part of the URL and the user can't see the data by default. However there are tools available that expose this data, so you should not assume that the data is secure just because a* `post` *request is used.*

Client-Side Caching

Browsers often cache (save on disk) web pages for quick reloading. If there are no changes between the version stored in the cache and the current version on the web, this speeds up your browsing experience. An HTTP response can indicate the length of time for which the content remains "fresh." If this amount of time has not been reached, the browser can avoid another request to the server. If not, the browser loads the document from the cache. Thus, the browser minimizes the amount of data that must be downloaded for you to view a web page. Browsers typically do not cache the server's response to a `post` request, because the next `post` might not return the same result. For example, in a survey, many users could visit the same web page and answer to a question. The survey results could then be displayed for the user. Each new answer changes the overall results of the survey.

When you use a web-based search engine, the browser normally supplies the information you specify in an HTML form to the search engine with a `get` request. The search engine performs the search, then returns the results to you as a web page. Such pages are sometimes cached by the browser in case you perform the same search again.

21.3 Multitier Application Architecture

Web-based applications are multitier applications (sometimes referred to as *n*-tier applications) that divide functionality into separate tiers (i.e., logical groupings of functionality). Although tiers can be located on the same computer, the tiers of web-based applications often reside on separate computers. Figure 21.3 presents the basic structure of a three-tier web-based application.

The bottom tier (also called the data tier or the information tier) maintains the application's data. This tier typically stores data in a relational database management system (RDBMS). We discuss RDBMSs in Chapter 22. For example, a retail store might have an inventory information database containing product descriptions, prices and quantities in stock. Another database might contain customer information, such as user names, billing addresses and credit card numbers. These may reside on one or more computers, which together comprise the application's data.

The middle tier implements business logic, controller logic and presentation logic to control interactions between the application's clients and its data. The middle tier acts as an intermediary between data in the information tier and the application's clients. The middle-tier controller logic processes client requests (such as requests to view a product

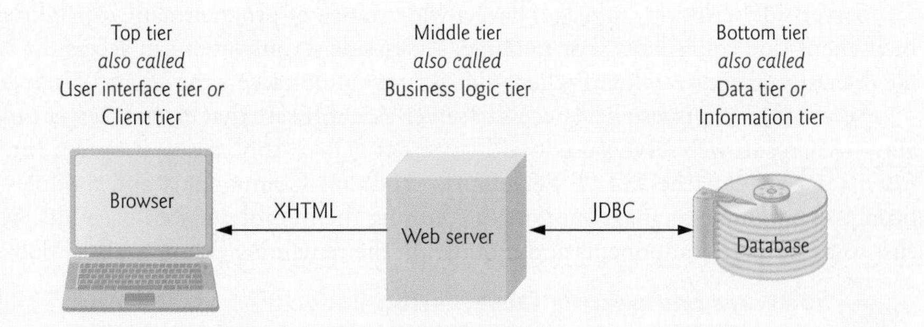

Fig. 21.3 | Three-tier architecture.

catalog) and retrieves data from the database. The middle-tier **presentation logic** then processes data from the information tier and presents the content to the client. Web applications typically present data to clients as XHTML documents.

Business logic in the middle tier enforces **business rules** and ensures that data is reliable before the application updates a database or presents data to users. Business rules dictate how clients access data, and how applications process data. For example, a business rule in the middle tier of a retail store's web-based application might ensure that all product quantities remain positive. A client request to set a negative quantity in the bottom tier's product information database would be rejected by the middle tier's business logic.

The **top tier**, or client tier, is the application's user interface, which gathers input and displays output. Users interact directly with the application through the user interface, which is typically a web browser, keyboard and mouse, or a mobile device. In response to user actions (e.g., clicking a hyperlink), the client tier interacts with the middle tier to make requests and to retrieve data from the information tier. The client tier then displays the data retrieved for the user. The client tier never directly interacts with the information tier.

21.4 Client-Side Scripting versus Server-Side Scripting

In earlier chapters, we focused on client-side scripting with JavaScript. Client-side scripting can be used to validate user input, to interact with the browser, to enhance web pages by manipulating the DOM of a page, and to add Ajax functionality.

Client-side scripting does have limitations, such as browser dependency; the browser or **scripting host** must support the scripting language and capabilities. Scripts are restricted from accessing the local hardware and filesystem for security reasons. Another issue is that client-side scripts can be viewed by the client by using the browser's source-viewing capability. Sensitive information, such as passwords or other personally identifiable data, should not be on the client. All client-side data validation should be mirrored on the server. Also, placing certain operations in JavaScript on the client can open web applications to attack and other security issues.

Programmers have more flexibility with **server-side scripts**, which often generate custom responses for clients. For example, a client might connect to an airline's web server and request a list of flights from Boston to San Antonio between April 19th and May 5th. The server queries the database, dynamically generates XHTML content containing the flight list and sends the XHTML to the client. This technology allows clients to obtain the most current flight information from the database by connecting to an airline's web server.

Server-side scripting languages have a wider range of programmatic capabilities than their client-side equivalents. For example, server-side scripts often can access the server's file directory structure, whereas client-side scripts cannot access the client's directories.

Server-side scripts also have access to server-side software that extends server functionality—Microsoft web servers use **ISAPI (Internet Server Application Program Interface) extensions** and Apache HTTP Servers use **modules**. Components and modules range from programming language support to counting the number of web-page hits. We discuss some of these components and modules in the remaining chapters of the book.

Software Engineering Observation 21.2

Properly configured server-side script source code is not visible to the client; only XHTML and any client-side scripts are visible to the client.

21.5 Accessing Web Servers

To request documents from web servers, users must know the hostnames on which the web server software resides. Users can request documents from local web servers (i.e., ones residing on users' machines) or remote web servers (i.e., ones residing on different machines).

Local web servers can be accessed through your computer's name or through the name `localhost`—a hostname that references the local machine and normally translates to the IP address `127.0.0.1` (known as the loopback address). We sometimes use `localhost` in this book for demonstration purposes. To display the machine name in Windows XP, Windows Server 2003, Windows Vista, Mac OS X or Linux, run the `hostname` command in a command prompt or terminal window.

A remote web server referenced by a fully qualified hostname or an IP address can also serve documents. In the URL `http://www.deitel.com/books/downloads.html`, the middle portion, `www.deitel.com`, is the server's fully qualified hostname.

Windows Firewall Settings

If you'd like to test your web server over a network, you may need to change your Windows Firewall settings. For security reasons, Windows Firewall does not allow remote access to a web server on your local computer by default. To change this, open the Windows Firewall utility in the Windows Control Panel. Click the **Advanced** tab and select your network connection from the **Network Connection Settings** list, then click **Settings....** On the **Services** tab of the **Advanced Settings** dialog, ensure that **Web Server (HTTP)** is checked.

21.6 Microsoft Internet Information Services (IIS)

Microsoft Internet Information Services (IIS) is a web server that is included with several versions of Windows. Installing IIS enables a computer to serve documents. To install IIS 5.1 on Windows XP Professional, open the **Add or Remove Programs** control panel, click **Add/Remove Windows Components**, check the checkbox next to **Internet Information Services (IIS)**, and click **Next >**. You may need the original operating system disk to complete the installation. For IIS 6.0 on Windows Server 2003 and IIS 7.0 on Windows Vista, the software should already be installed (but is also on your installation disk). The remainder of this section assumes that either IIS 5.1, IIS 6.0 or IIS 7.0 is installed on your system. In Windows Server 2003, you'll need to use the **Manager Your Server** window to add the **Application Server** role. In Windows Vista, go to the **Control Panel**, select **Programs**, then select **Turn Windows Features On or Off**.

The following subsections explain how to configure IIS 5.1, IIS 6.0 and IIS 7.0 to serve documents via HTTP. If you are using Windows XP or Windows Server 2003, see Section 21.6.1. If you are using Windows Vista, skip to Section 21.6.2.

21.6.1 Microsoft Internet Information Services (IIS) 5.1 and 6.0

Start the Internet services manager by clicking the **Start** button and opening the **Control Panel**. If the **Control Panel** is currently in **Category View**, click **Switch to Classic View**. Then, double click the **Administrative Tools** icon and double click the **Internet Services Manager** icon (**Internet Information Services (IIS) Manager** in Windows Server 2003). For Windows XP, this opens the **Internet Information Services** window (Fig. 21.4)—the administration

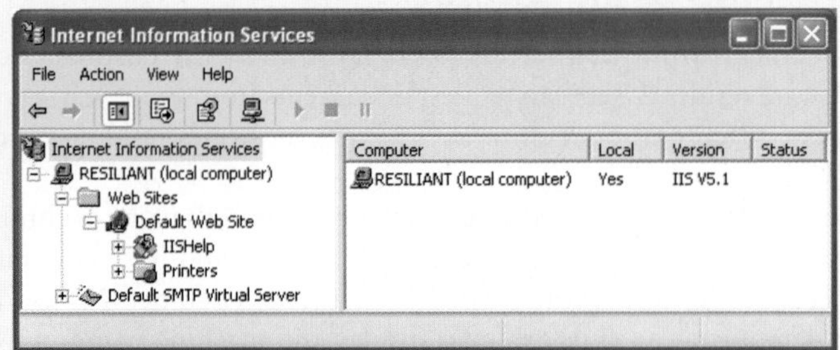

Fig. 21.4 | **Internet Information Services** window of IIS 5.1.

program for IIS 5.1. For Windows Server 2003, this opens the (**Internet Information Services (IIS) Manager**, which provides the same capabilities. Alternatively, you can type `inetmgr` at the **Start** menu's **Run...** command prompt to open this window. You place documents that will be requested from IIS either in the website's **default directory** (i.e., `C:\Inetpub\wwwroot`) or in a **virtual directory**. A virtual directory is an alias for an existing directory that resides on the local machine (e.g., `C:\`) or on the network. When a server is accessed from a web browser, content in the default directory and virtual directories is visible to the client.

In the window, the left pane contains the web server's directory structure. The name of the machine running IIS (e.g., **RESILIANT**) is listed under **Internet Information Services**. Clicking the + symbol to the left of the machine name displays **Default Web Site** (and possibly several other nodes).

Expand the **Default Web Site** directory by clicking the + to the left of it. In this directory, we will create a virtual directory for the website. Most web documents are placed in the web server's `wwwroot` directory or one of its subdirectories. For this example, we create a directory in the `wwwroot` directory and have our virtual directory point to it. To create a virtual directory in this directory, right click **Default Web Site** and select **New > Virtual Directory...**. This starts the **Virtual Directory Creation Wizard** (Fig. 21.5), which guides you through creating a virtual directory.

Fig. 21.5 | **Virtual Directory Creation Wizard** welcome page.

To begin, click **Next >** in the **Virtual Directory Creation Wizard** welcome page. In the **Virtual Directory Alias** page (Fig. 21.6), enter a name for the virtual directory and click **Next >**. We use the name `Chapter21Test`, although the virtual directory may have any name, provided that it does not conflict with an existing virtual directory name.

In the **Web Site Content Directory** page (Fig. 21.7), enter the path for the directory containing the documents that clients will view. We created a directory named `C:\Chapter21Examples` that serves our documents. You can select the **Browse** button to navigate to the desired directory or to create a new one. Click **Next >**.

The **Access Permissions** page (Fig. 21.8) presents the virtual directory security level choices. Choose the access level appropriate for a web document. The **Read** option allows users to read and download files located in the directory. The **Run scripts (such as ASP)**

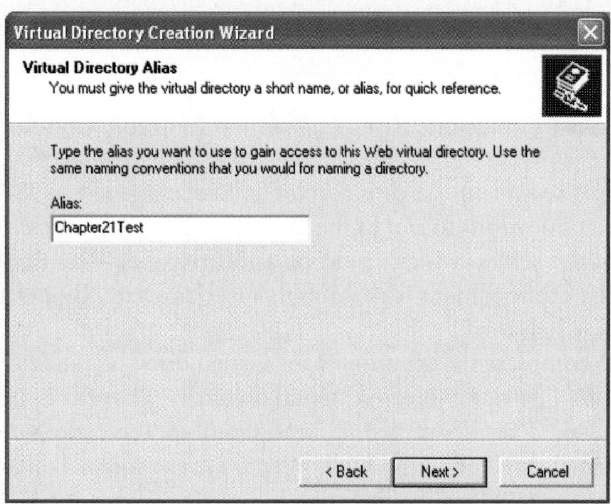

Fig. 21.6 | **Virtual Directory Alias** page of the **Virtual Directory Creation Wizard.**

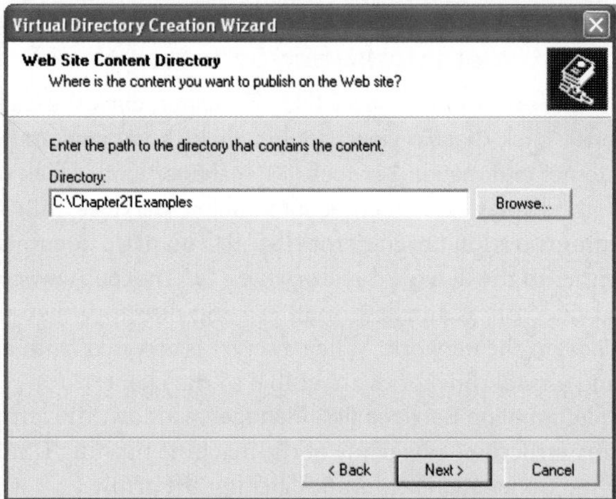

Fig. 21.7 | **Web Site Content Directory** page of the **Virtual Directory Creation Wizard.**

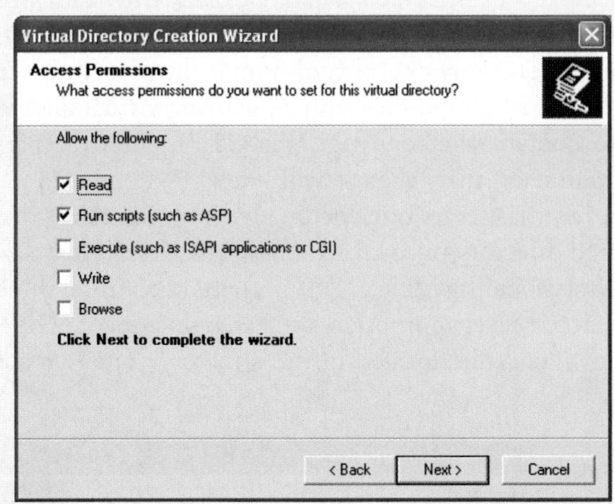

Fig. 21.8 | **Access Permissions** page of the **Virtual Directory Creation Wizard.**

option allows scripts to run in the directory. The **Execute (such as ISAPI applications or CGI)** option allows applications to run in the directory. The **Write** option allows a web page to write to files on the server, which could be a security risk. The **Browse** option allows users to see a full list of the folder's files through a web browser. By default, **Read** and **Run scripts** are enabled. Click **Next >**.

Click **Finish** to complete the creation of the virtual directory and exit the **Virtual Directory Creation Wizard**. The newly created virtual directory, `Chapter21Test`, is now part of the **Default Web Site**. The IIS server is configured to serve documents through the `Chapter21Test` virtual directory. The URL `http://localhost/Chapter21Test` now references the `C:\Chapter21Examples` directory.

To start IIS so it can serve content, right click **Default Web Site** and select **Start**. If you need to stop IIS, right click **Default Web Site** and select **Stop**. The web server is not available to serve content if it is stopped.

21.6.2 Microsoft Internet Information Services (IIS) 7.0

To start the Internet Information Services (IIS) Manager, click the start ( ) button, select the **Control Panel**, click **Classic View**, double click the **Administrative Tools** icon and double click the **Internet Information Services (IIS) Manager** icon. Click **Continue** in the dialog that appears to display the **Internet Information Services (IIS) Manager** window (Fig. 21.9)—the administration program for IIS 7.0. You place documents that will be requested from IIS either in the default directory (i.e., `C:\Inetpub\wwwroot`) or in a virtual directory. A virtual directory is an alias for an existing directory that resides on the local machine (e.g., `C:\`) or on the network. When a server is accessed from a browser, only the default directory and virtual directories are visible to the client.

In the **Internet Information Services (IIS) Manager** window, the left pane contains the web server's directory structure. The name of the machine running IIS (e.g., **QUALIFLY**) is listed at the top of the **Connections** column. Clicking the arrow (▷) symbol to the left of the machine name displays **Application Pools** and **Web Sites**. The **Application Pools** folder contains tools for configuring advanced features of IIS 7.0.

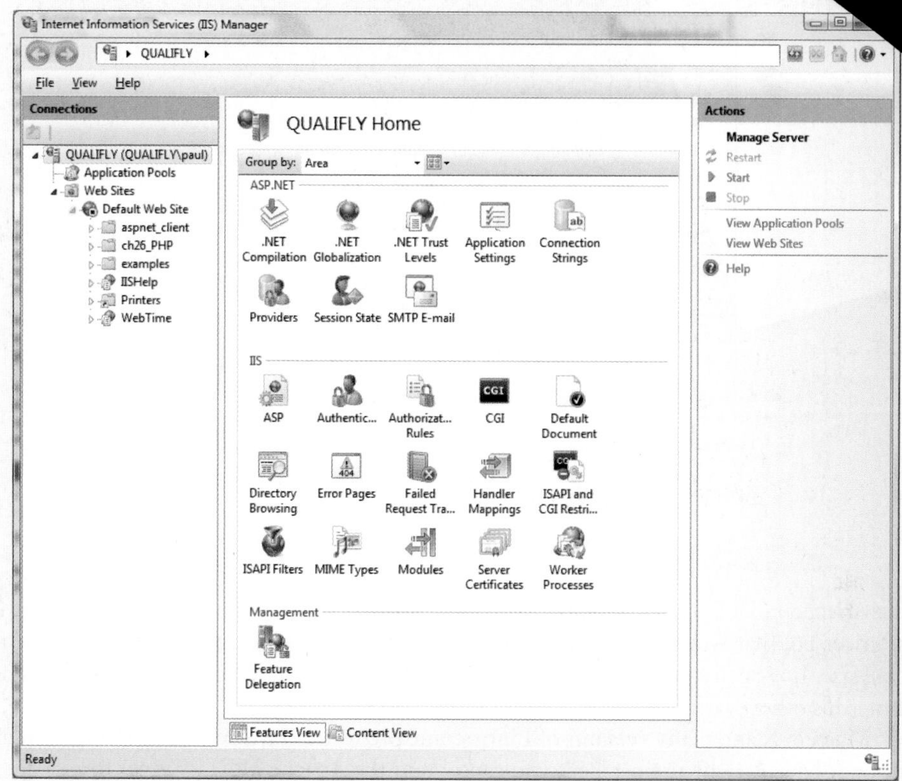

Fig. 21.9 | **Internet Information (IIS) Services Manager** window (IIS 7.0).

Expand **Web Sites** by clicking the arrow (▷) to the left of it. This should display **Default Web Site.** Expand **Default Web Site** by clicking the arrow (▷) to the left of it. These are the folders and virtual directories in the default website. For this example, we create a virtual directory from which we request our documents. To create a virtual directory, right click **Default Web Site** and select **Add Virtual Directory....** This displays the **Add Virtual Directory** dialog (Fig. 21.10). In the **Alias:** field, enter a name for the virtual directory. We use the name `Chapter21Test`, although the virtual directory may have any name, provided that it does not conflict with an existing virtual directory. In the **Physical path:** field, enter the path for the directory containing the documents that clients will view. We created a directory named `C:\Chapter21Examples` for our documents. If necessary, select the ... button to navigate to the desired directory or to create a new one. Click **OK** to create the new virtual directory.

In Windows Vista, before you can use IIS, you must enable the World Wide Web Publishing Service (W3SVC). To do so, go to the start ( ) button, select **Control Panel**, select **Classic View**, double click **Administrative Tools** and double click **Services**. This displays the **Services** window. Locate **World Wide Web Publishing Service** in the list of services, then right click it and select **Properties**. In the window that appears, change the **Startup type:** option to **Automatic**, then click **OK**. Next, right click **World Wide Web Publishing Service** again and select **Start** to run IIS so that it can accept requests.

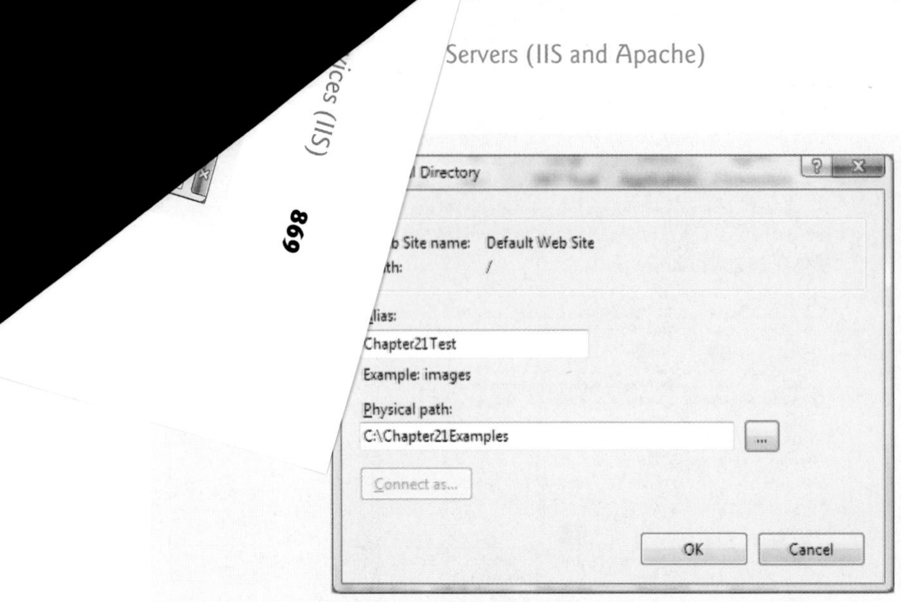

Fig. 21.10 | **Add Virtual Directory** dialog.

21.7 Apache HTTP Server

The Apache HTTP Server, maintained by the Apache Software Foundation, is currently the most popular web server because of its stability, efficiency, portability, security and small size. It is open source software that runs on UNIX, Linux, Mac OS X, Windows and numerous other platforms.

Mac OS X and many versions of Linux come preinstalled with Apache. If your system does not have Apache preinstalled, you can obtain the Apache HTTP Server for a variety of platforms from `httpd.apache.org/download.cgi`. For instructions on installing version 2.2 of the Apache HTTP Server on Windows, please visit

```
http://httpd.apache.org/docs-2.2/platform/windows.html
```

After installing the Apache HTTP Server, start the application. For Windows, open the **Start** menu, select **Programs > Apache HTTP Server** [*version number*] **> Control Apache Server > Monitor Apache Servers**. Double click on the **Apache Service Monitor** that appears in your **Taskbar**, select **Apache2**, and click **Start** (Fig. 21.11). For Mac OS X, you can start Apache from the **System Preferences** by opening the **Sharing** preference pane and checking the checkbox next to **Web Sharing**. To stop Apache in Windows, open the **Apache Service Monitor**, select your server, and click **Stop**. For Mac OS X, open the **Sharing** preference pane and uncheck the checkbox next to **Web Sharing**.

All documents that will be requested from an Apache HTTP Server must either be in the default directory (i.e., `C:\Program Files\Apache Software Foundation\Apache2.2\htdocs` for Windows, `/Library/WebServer/Documents` for Mac OS X, and `/var/www/html` or `/var/www` for most Linux distros) or in a directory for which an Apache HTTP Server alias is configured. An alias is Apache's equivalent to Microsoft IIS's virtual directory. It is a pointer to an existing directory that resides on the local machine or on the network. We will create an alias for the examples in this chapter.

Instead of using an administrative utility or set of wizards, we configure the Apache HTTP Server by editing the `httpd.conf` file. This file contains all the information that

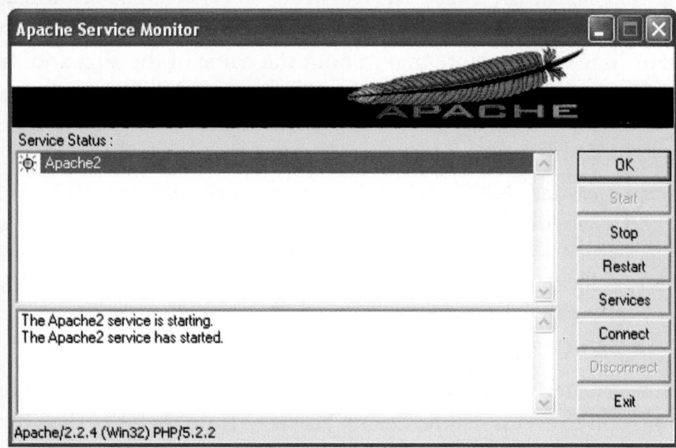

Fig. 21.11 | **Apache Service Monitor**. (Courtesy of The Apache Software Foundation, `<http://www.apache.org/>`.)

the Apache HTTP Server needs to run correctly and serve web documents. For Windows, the `httpd.conf` file is located in the `conf` subdirectory of Apache's installation directory. For Mac OS X and most Linux distros, it is located in the `/etc/apache2/` directory. To edit this file, either open the `httpd.conf` in a text editor, or in Windows go to the **Start** menu and select **Programs > Apache HTTP Server** [*version number*] **> Configure Apache Server > Edit the Apache httpd.conf Configuration File.** `httpd.conf` is a large text file containing all of Apache HTTP Server's configuration information. In this file, any line that starts with a # is a comment that explains the various configuration options.

Good Programming Practice 21.1

Place a small comment near any changes you make to the Apache `httpd.conf` *file.*

An introductory comment at the top of the `httpd.conf` file explains how the file is organized. After this comment, the configuration information starts with the most important, global settings. These should have been configured correctly by the Apache installer. Scroll down in the file until you have reached the section titled `DocumentRoot` (using your text editor's search function will save time). The `DocumentRoot` setting specifies Apache's default directory. In Windows, the default setting is:

```
DocumentRoot "C:/Program Files/Apache Software Foundation/Apache2.2/
htdocs"
```

Now, find the section starting with `<IfModule alias_module>` and ending with `</IfModule>`. To create an alias, we add the following lines below the comment.

```
# This alias is for the examples used in Chapter 21
Alias /Chapter21Test "C:/Chapter21Examples"
```

This creates an alias called `Chapter21Test` that points to the physical directory `C:\Chapter21Examples`. We use the name `Chapter21Test`, but any name that does not conflict with an existing alias is allowed. We created a directory named C:\Chapter21Examples that contains our documents (you should specify an appropriate path on Linux or Mac OS X). Note that in both the name of the alias and the path of the directory to which the alias points we must use forward slashes (/), not backslashes (\).

Error-Prevention Tip 21.1

If you place a forward slash (/) at the end of the alias name, Apache will require this slash when a document is requested from the server. For example, if your alias is /myExamples/*, then a user request for* http://localhost/myExamples *will not work as expected. The user will need to request* http://localhost/myExamples/ *to access the alias. If the forward slash (/) is not placed at the end of the alias name, Apache will not require this slash, and will work as expected whether or not it is present in the request.*

Once we have created the alias, we must set the access settings of that directory so that users have permission to access it. The default access settings for every directory are to deny access to everybody. In order to override those settings for our new directory, C:\Chapter21Examples, we must create a new Directory entry. We append this new Directory entry to the end of the file:

```
# Begin Chapter21Examples directory access settings
<Directory "C:/Chapter21Examples">

    Options Indexes
    Order allow,deny
    Allow from all

</Directory>
# End Chapter21Examples directory access settings
```

We begin by specifying the location of the directory, then proceed to configure that directory. Indexes on the Options line specifies that if an index file, such as index.html, does not exist, Apache will generate one for you that contains the filenames of every document in the directory. Order allow,deny specifies that users are permitted access by default, and are denied only if they are specifically blocked. Allow from all specifies that all users are permitted access.

Now, the Apache HTTP Server is configured to serve our web document from the C:\Chapter21Examples directory. We need to restart the server so that our changes to httpd.conf file will take effect. Then we will be ready to request documents from the Apache HTTP Server. To restart the server, we must first stop it and start it again. Please refer to the beginning of this section for instructions on how to stop and start the Apache HTTP Server.

21.8 Requesting Documents

This section demonstrates how an HTTP server responds to requests for XHTML documents. Requesting other types of documents is similar. We discuss serving these documents using the IIS and Apache HTTP Servers. The server sends XHTML documents to the client as static web pages. The server response for a given XHTML document is always the same. For other types of documents, such as PHP, Ruby on Rails, ASP.NET and JavaServer Faces, the appropriate language interpreter or scripting engine first generates XHTML content, then transmits it to the client over HTTP. These are often referred to as dynamic web pages, because the results of these requests might vary based on numerous factors, such as user input, the time of day and current database content.

Copy `test.html` from the Chapter 21 examples directory into the directory `C:\Chapter21Examples` (or to the directory you created in Section 21.6 or 21.7). This is the directory that is referenced by our virtual directory (`Chapter21Test`). [*Note*: A file cannot be copied directly to a virtual directory, because a virtual directory is only a name referring to a physical local directory.] To request the document from IIS or Apache, start the server, launch a web browser and enter the XHTML document's URL (i.e., `http://localhost/Chapter21Test/test.html`) in the **Address** field. Figure 21.12 displays the result of requesting `test.html` in Internet Explorer 7.

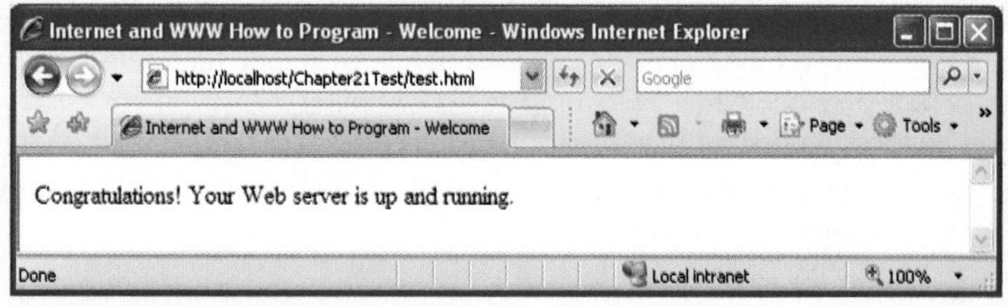

Fig. 21.12 | Requesting `test.html`.

21.9 Web Resources

`www.deitel.com/WebServers/`

The Web Servers Resource Center guides you through learning the basics behind web servers, deciding which server is best suited to you, and configuring and maintaining your own web server. Start your search here for resources, downloads, tutorials, documentation, books, e-books, articles, blogs and more that will help you run your own web server.

`www.fiddlertool.com/fiddler/`

Fiddler is a freeware web debugging proxy that logs all HTTP traffic between your computer and the Internet. Fiddler allows you to inspect traffic, set breakpoints, and "fiddle" with incoming or outgoing data. The tool includes a JavaScript-based scripting system, and can be extended using any .NET language.

`addons.mozilla.org/en-US/firefox/addon/3829`

An add-on for Firefox that enables you to view HTTP traffic as you browse the web. This can help you learn more about HTTP.

Summary

Section 21.1 Introduction

- A web server responds to client requests (typically from a web browser) by providing resources such as XHTML documents. When users enter a Uniform Resource Locator (URL) address, such as `www.deitel.com`, into a web browser, they are requesting a specific document from a web server. The web server maps the URL to a resource on the server (or to a file on the server's network) and returns the requested resource to the client.
- A web server and a client communicate using the platform-independent Hypertext Transfer Protocol (HTTP), a protocol for transferring requests and files over the Internet or an intranet.

Section 21.2 HTTP Transactions

- The HTTP protocol allows clients and servers to interact and exchange information in a uniform and reliable manner.
- HTTP uses URIs (Uniform Resource Identifiers) to identify data on the Internet.
- URIs that specify document locations are called URLs (Uniform Resource Locators). Common URLs refer to files, directories or objects that perform complex tasks, such as database lookups and Internet searches.
- A URL contains information that directs a browser to the resource that the user wishes to access.
- `http://` indicates that the resource is to be obtained using the HTTP protocol.
- The server's fully qualified hostname is the name of the server on which the resource resides, called the host.
- A hostname is translated into an IP address—a unique numerical value which identifies the server much as a telephone number uniquely defines a particular phone line. This translation is performed by a domain name system (DNS) server—a computer that maintains a database of hostnames and their corresponding IP addresses—and the process is called a DNS lookup.
- The remainder of the URL after the hostname specifies both the name of the requested resource and its path, or location, on the web server.
- For security reasons the path normally specifies the location of a virtual directory. The server translates the virtual directory into a real location on the server (or on another computer on the server's network), thus hiding the true location of the resource.
- Some resources are created dynamically and do not reside anywhere on the server.
- When given a URL, a web browser performs a simple HTTP transaction to retrieve and display the web page found at that address.
- HTTP method `get` indicates that the client wishes to obtain a resource from the server. The remainder of the request provides the path name of the resource (e.g., an XHTML document) and the protocol's name and version number (`HTTP/1.1`).
- Any server that understands HTTP can receive a `get` request and respond appropriately.
- HTTP status code `200` indicates success. Status code `404` informs the client that the web server could not locate the requested resource. A complete list of numeric codes indicating the status of an HTTP transaction can be found at `www.w3.org/Protocols/rfc2616/rfc2616-sec10.html`.
- In a response, the server sends one or more HTTP headers, which provide additional information about the data that will be sent.
- Multipurpose Internet Mail Extensions (MIME) is an Internet standard that specifies data formats so that programs can interpret data correctly. The MIME type `text/plain` indicates that the sent information is text that can be displayed directly, without any interpretation of the content as XHTML markup. The MIME type `image/jpeg` indicates that the content is a JPEG image. When the browser receives this MIME type, it attempts to display the image.
- The header or set of headers is followed by a blank line, which indicates to the client browser that the server is finished sending HTTP headers.
- The two most common HTTP request types (also known as request methods) are `get` and `post`.
- A `get` request typically gets (or retrieves) information from a server. Common uses of `get` requests are to retrieve an XHTML document or an image, or to fetch search results based on a user-submitted search term.
- A `post` request typically posts (or sends) data to a server. Common uses of `post` requests are to send information to a server, such as authentication information or data from a form that gathers user input.

- An HTTP request often posts data to a server-side form handler that processes the data.
- A `get` request sends information to the server as part of the URL in a query string. A `?` separates the query string from the rest of the URL in a `get` request. A *name/value* pair is passed to the server with the *name* and the *value* separated by an equals sign (`=`). If more than one *name/value* pair is submitted, each pair is separated by an ampersand (`&`).
- A `get` request may be initiated by submitting an XHTML form whose `method` attribute is set to `"get"`, or by typing the URL (possibly containing a query string) directly into the browser's address bar.
- A `post` request is specified in an XHTML form by the `method "post"`. The `post` method sends form data as an HTTP message, not as part of the URL.
- A `get` request limits the query string to a specific number of characters (2083 in IE; more in other browsers).
- Large pieces of information must be sent using the `post` method.
- Browsers often cache web pages so they can quickly reload the pages. If there are no changes between the version stored in the cache and the current version on the web, this helps speed up your browsing experience.

Section 21.3 Multitier Application Architecture

- Web-based applications are multitier applications that divide functionality into separate tiers. Although tiers can be located on the same computer, the tiers of web-based applications typically reside on separate computers.
- The bottom tier (also called the data tier or the information tier) maintains the application's data.
- The middle tier implements business logic, controller logic and presentation logic to control interactions between the application's clients and its data.
- Business logic in the middle tier enforces business rules and ensures that data is reliable before the server application updates the database or presents the data to users. Business rules dictate how clients can and cannot access application data, and how applications process data.
- The top tier, or client tier, is the application's user interface. In response to user actions, the client tier interacts with the middle tier to make requests and to retrieve data from the information tier. The client tier then displays the data retrieved for the user. The client tier never directly interacts with the information tier.

Section 21.4 Client-Side Scripting versus Server-Side Scripting

- Client-side scripting can be used to validate user input, to interact with the browser, to enhance web pages by manipulating the DOM of a page, and to add Ajax functionality.
- Client-side scripting does have limitations, such as browser dependency; the browser or scripting host must support the scripting language and capabilities.
- Client-side scripts can be viewed by the client by using the browser's source-viewing capability.
- Sensitive information, such as passwords or other personally identifiable data, should not be stored or validated on the client.
- Placing large amounts of JavaScript on the client can open web applications to attack and other security issues.
- Code executed on the server often generate custom responses for clients.
- Server-side scripting languages have a wider range of programmatic capabilities than their client-side equivalents. For example, server-side scripts often can access the server's file directory structure, whereas client-side scripts cannot access the client's directories.

- Properly configured server-side scripts are not visible to the client; only XHTML and any client-side scripts are visible to the client.
- To request documents from web servers, users must know the hostnames on which the web server software resides.
- Users can request documents from local web servers or remote web servers.
- Local web servers can be accessed through your computer's name or through the name `localhost`—a hostname that references the local machine and normally translates to the IP address `127.0.0.1` (also known as the loopback address).

Section 21.6 Microsoft Internet Information Services (IIS)

- Microsoft Internet Information Services (IIS) is a web server that is included with several versions of Windows. Installing IIS on a machine allows that computer to serve documents.
- To install IIS 5.1 on Windows XP, you may need your original operating-system disk. For IIS 6.0 (Windows Server 2003) and IIS 7.0 (Windows Vista), the software should already be installed, but is also available on your installation disk.
- You place documents that will be requested from IIS either in the default directory or in a virtual directory. A virtual directory is an alias for an existing directory that resides on the local machine or on the network.
- In Windows Vista, before you can use IIS, you must enable the World Wide Web Publishing Service (W3SVC).

Section 21.7 Apache HTTP Server

- The Apache HTTP Server, maintained by the Apache Software Foundation, is currently the most popular web server. It is open source software that runs on UNIX, Linux, Mac OS X, Windows and numerous other platforms.
- Mac OS X and many versions of Linux come preinstalled with Apache.
- You can obtain the Apache HTTP Server for a variety of platforms from `httpd.apache.org/download.cgi`.
- All documents that will be requested from an Apache HTTP Server must be either in the default directory or in a directory for which an Apache HTTP Server alias is configured. An alias is Apache's equivalent to Microsoft IIS's virtual directory. It is a pointer to an existing directory that resides on the local machine or on the network.
- The `httpd.conf` file contains all the information that the Apache HTTP Server needs to run correctly and serve web documents. An introductory comment at the top of the `httpd.conf` file explains how the file is organized. After this comment, the configuration information starts with the most important, global settings.

Terminology

Apache HTTP Server
bottom tier
business logic
cache
client-side scripting
client tier
controller logic
data tier
DNS lookup
DNS server
domain name
domain name system (DNS)
dynamic web page
fully qualified hostname
`get` (HTTP request)
hostname
`htdocs` directory
HTTP request type

Hypertext Transfer Protocol (HTTP)
information tier
IIS 5.1
IIS 6.0
IIS 7.0
Internet Information Services (IIS)
Internet Protocol (IP) address
Linux
local web server
`localhost`
Mac OS X
middle tier
module
multitier application
n-tier application
open source
`post` (HTTP request)
presentation logic
relational database management system (RDBMS)
remote web server
request method
request type
scripting host
security level
server-side form handler
server-side script
static web page
top tier
Uniform Resource Locator (URL)
validation
virtual directory
web server
Windows XP
Windows Server 2003
Windows Vista

Self-Review Exercises

21.1 State whether each of the following is *true* or *false*. If *false*, explain why.

a) Web servers and clients communicate with each other through the platform-independent HTTP.
b) Web servers often cache web pages for quick reloading.
c) The information tier implements business logic to control the type of information that is presented to a particular client.
d) Client-side scripts can access the browser, use features specific to that browser and manipulate browser documents.
e) A virtual directory is an alias for an existing directory on a remote machine.
f) The Apache HTTP Server is said to be platform independent because it runs on various operating systems, such as UNIX, Linux, Windows and Max OS X.
g) The path in a URL normally specifies the location of an actual directory on the server.

21.2 Fill in the blanks in each of the following statements:

a) The two most common HTTP request types are _______ and _______.
b) In a three-tier application, a web server is typically part of the _______ tier.
c) The most popular client-side scripting language is _______.
d) A(n) _______ translates a fully qualified hostname to an IP address.
e) _______ is a hostname that references the local computer.
f) A(n) _______ is Apache's equivalent to Microsoft IIS's virtual directory.
g) The bottom tier (also called the _______ or the _______) maintains the application's data.
h) _______ is an Internet standard that specifies data formats so that programs can interpret data correctly.

Answers to Self-Review Exercises

21.1 a.) True. b) False. Web browsers cache web pages for quick reloading. c) False. The middle tier implements business logic and presentation logic to control interactions between application clients and application data. d) True. e) False. A virtual directory is an alias for an existing directory on the local machine or network. f) True. g) False. For security reasons the path normally specifies the location of a virtual directory.

21.2 a) `get`, `post`. b) middle. c) JavaScript. d) domain name system (DNS) server. e) `localhost`. f) alias. g) data tier, information tier. h) Multipurpose Internet Mail Extensions (MIME).

Exercises

21.3 Define the following terms:

a) HTTP.
b) Multitier application.
c) Request method.
d) Virtual directory.
e) Web server.

21.4 In a three-tier application, explain how the middle tier (e.g., web server) interacts with the client tier (e.g., web browser).

21.5 Explain the difference between the `get` request type and the `post` request type. When is it ideal to use the `post` request type?

21.6 Configure Apache to serve a home page from your computer.

21.7 Discuss the benefits and disadvantages of client-side vs. server-side scripting.

22

Database: SQL, MySQL, ADO.NET 2.0 and Java DB

It is a capital mistake to theorize before one has data.
—Arthur Conan Doyle

Now go, write it before them in a table, and note it in a book, that it may be for the time to come for ever and ever.
—The Holy Bible, Isaiah 30:8

Get your facts first, and then you can distort them as much as you please.
—Mark Twain

I like two kinds of men: domestic and foreign.
—Mae West

OBJECTIVES

In this chapter you will learn:

- Relational database concepts.
- To use Structured Query Language (SQL) to retrieve data from and manipulate data in a database.
- To install and configure MySQL.
- To create a MySQL database.
- The ADO.NET 2.0 object model.

Outline

22.1 Introduction

A database is an organized collection of data. There are many different strategies for organizing data to facilitate easy access and manipulation. A database management system (DBMS) provides mechanisms for storing, organizing, retrieving and modifying data. Database management systems allow for the access and storage of data without concern for the internal representation of the data in the database.

Today's most popular database systems are relational databases, where the data is stored without consideration of its physical structure (Section 22.2). A language called SQL—pronounced "sequel," or as its individual letters—is the international standard language used almost universally with relational databases to perform queries (i.e., to request information that satisfies given criteria) and to manipulate data. [*Note:* As you learn about SQL, you will see some authors writing "a SQL statement" (which assumes the pronunciation "sequel") and others writing "an SQL statement" (which assumes that the individual letters are pronounced). In this book we pronounce SQL as "sequel."] Some popular relational database management systems (RDBMSs) are Microsoft SQL Server, Oracle, Sybase, IBM DB2, Informix, PostgreSQL and MySQL.

Programs connect to, and interact with, a relational database via an interface—software that facilitates communication between a database management system and a program. For example, Java developers can use the JDBC interface to interact with databases. Similarly, ASP.NET programmers communicate with databases and manipulate their data through the interface provided by ADO.NET.

22.2 Relational Databases

A relational database is a logical representation of data that allows the data to be accessed without consideration of its physical structure. A relational database stores data in tables. Figure 22.1 illustrates a sample table that might be used in a personnel system. The table name is `Employee`, and its primary purpose is to store the attributes of an employee. Tables are composed of rows, and rows are composed of columns in which values are stored. This table consists of six rows. The `Number` column of each row in this table is the table's primary key—a column (or group of columns) in a table with a unique value that cannot be duplicated in other rows. This guarantees that each row can be identified by its primary key. Good examples of primary key columns are a social security number, an employee ID number and a part number in an inventory system, as values in each of these columns are guaranteed to be unique. The rows in Fig. 22.1 are displayed in order by primary key. In this case, the rows are listed in increasing order, but we could also use decreasing order.

Rows in tables are not guaranteed to be stored in any particular order. As we will demonstrate in an upcoming example, programs can specify ordering criteria when requesting data from a database.

Each column represents a data attribute. Rows are normally unique (by primary key) within a table, but particular column values may be duplicated between rows—e.g., three different rows in the `Employee` table's `Department` column contain number 413.

Different users of a database are often interested in different data and different relationships among the data. Most users require only subsets of the rows and columns. To obtain these subsets, we use queries to specify which data to select from a table. We use SQL to define complex queries that select data from a table. For example, we might select data from the `Employee` table to create a result that shows where each department is located, and present the data sorted in increasing order by department number. This result is shown in Fig. 22.2. SQL queries are discussed in Section 22.4.

Number	Name	Department	Salary	Location
23603	Jones	413	1100	New Jersey
24568	Kerwin	413	2000	New Jersey
34589	Larson	642	1800	Los Angeles
35761	Myers	611	1400	Orlando
47132	Neumann	413	9000	New Jersey
78321	Stephens	611	8500	Orlando

Row (34589 Larson row); Primary key (Number column); Column (Department column)

Fig. 22.1 | `Employee` table sample data.

Department	Location
413	New Jersey
611	Orlando
642	Los Angeles

Fig. 22.2 | Result of selecting distinct `Department` and `Location` data from table `Employee`.

22.3 Relational Database Overview: A books Database

We now overview relational databases in the context of a sample books database we created for this chapter. Before we discuss SQL, we overview the tables of the books database. We use this database to introduce various database concepts, including how to use SQL to obtain information from the database and to manipulate the data. We provide a script to create the database. You can find the script in the examples directory for this chapter. Section 22.8 explains how to use this script.

The database consists of three tables—authors, authorISBN and titles. The authors table (described in Fig. 22.3) consists of three columns that maintain each author's unique ID number, first name and last name. Figure 22.4 contains sample data from the authors table of the books database.

The authorISBN table (described in Fig. 22.5) has two columns that maintain each ISBN and the corresponding author's ID number. This table associates authors with their books. The columns represent the relationship between the authors and titles tables—

Column	Description
authorID	Author's ID number in the database. In the books database, this integer column is defined as autoincremented—for each row inserted in this table, the authorID value is increased by 1 automatically to ensure that each row has a unique authorID. This column represents the table's primary key.
firstName	Author's first name (a string).
lastName	Author's last name (a string).

Fig. 22.3 | authors table from the books database.

authorID	firstName	lastName
1	Harvey	Deitel
2	Paul	Deitel
3	Andrew	Goldberg
4	David	Choffnes

Fig. 22.4 | Sample data from the authors table.

Column	Description
authorID	The author's ID number, a foreign key to the authors table.
isbn	The ISBN for a book, a foreign key to the titles table.

Fig. 22.5 | authorISBN table from the books database.

one row in authors may be associated with many rows in titles, and vice versa. Figure 22.6 contains sample data from the authorISBN table. [*Note:* To save space, we split the table's contents into two columns, each containing the authorID and isbn columns.] The authorID column (and similarly, the isbn column) is a **foreign key**—a column in this table that matches the primary-key column in another table (i.e., authorID in the authors table). Foreign keys are specified when creating a table. The foreign key helps maintain the **Rule of Referential Integrity**—every foreign-key value must appear as another table's primary-key value. This enables the DBMS to determine whether the authorID value for a particular book is valid. Foreign keys also allow related data in multiple tables to be selected from those tables for analytic purposes—this is known as **joining** the data. If you were to remove an author from the authors table, you'd also want to remove the corresponding rows in the authorISBN table.

The titles table described in Fig. 22.7 consists of four columns that stand for each book's ISBN, the title, the edition number and the copyright year. The table is in Fig. 22.8.

authorID	isbn	authorID	isbn
1	0131869000	2	0131450913
2	0131869000	1	0131828274
1	0131483986	2	0131828274
2	0131483986	3	0131450913
1	0131450913	4	0131828274

Fig. 22.6 | Sample data from the authorISBN table of books.

Column	Description
isbn	ISBN of the book (a string). The table's primary key. ISBN is an abbreviation for "International Standard Book Number"—a numbering scheme that publishers use to give every book a unique identification number.
title	Title of the book (a string).
editionNumber	Edition number of the book (an integer).
copyright	Copyright year of the book (a string).

Fig. 22.7 | titles table from the books database.

isbn	title	editionNumber	copyright
0131869000	Visual Basic How to Program	3	2006
0131525239	Visual C# How to Program	2	2006

Fig. 22.8 | Sample data from the titles table of the books database. (Part 1 of 2.)

isbn	title	editionNumber	copyright
0132222205	Java How to Program	7	2007
0131857576	C++ How to Program	5	2005
0132404168	C How to Program	5	2007
0131450913	Internet and World Wide Web How to Program	3	2004

Fig. 22.8 | Sample data from the `titles` table of the `books` database. (Part 2 of 2.)

There is a one-to-many relationship between a primary key and a corresponding foreign key (e.g., one author can write many books). A foreign key creates a relationship between two tables in which the record with a given primary key can be referenced many times in the foreign key's table. Figure 22.9 is an entity-relationship (ER) diagram for the `books` database. This diagram shows the database tables and the relationships among them. The first compartment in each box contains the table's name. The names in italic are primary keys. A table's primary key uniquely identifies each row in the table. Every row must have a primary-key value, and that value must be unique in the table. This is known as the Rule of Entity Integrity.

Common Programming Error 22.1

Not providing a value for every column in a primary key breaks the Rule of Entity Integrity and causes the DBMS to report an error.

Common Programming Error 22.2

Providing the same value for the primary key in multiple rows causes the DBMS to report an error.

The lines connecting the tables in Fig. 22.9 represent the relationships between the tables. Consider the line between the `authorISBN` and `authors` tables. On the `authors` end of the line, there is a `1`, and on the `authorISBN` end, there is an infinity symbol (∞), indicating a one-to-many relationship in which every author in the `authors` table can have an arbitrary number of ISBNs in the `authorISBN` table. Note that the relationship line links the `authorID` column in the table `authors` (i.e., its primary key) to the `authorID` column in table `authorISBN` (i.e., its foreign key). The `authorID` column in the `authorISBN` table is a foreign key.

Fig. 22.9 | Table relationships in the `books` database.

Common Programming Error 22.3

Providing a foreign-key value that does not appear as a primary-key value in another table breaks the Rule of Referential Integrity and causes the DBMS to report an error.

The line between the `titles` and `authorISBN` tables illustrates another one-to-many relationship; a title can be written by any number of authors. In fact, the sole purpose of the `authorISBN` table is to provide a many-to-many relationship between the `authors` and `titles` tables—an author can write any number of books and a book can have any number of authors. The primary key for `authorISBN` is the combination of `authorID` and `ISBN`.

22.4 SQL

We now provide an overview of SQL in the context of our `books` database. You will be able to use the SQL discussed here in the examples later in the chapter and in examples in Chapters 23–28.

The next several subsections discuss most of the SQL keywords listed in Fig. 22.10 in the context of SQL queries and statements. Other SQL keywords are beyond this text's scope. To learn other keywords, refer to the SQL reference guide supplied by the vendor of the RDBMS you are using. [*Note:* For more information on SQL, refer to the web resources in Section 22.12.]

SQL keyword	Description
`SELECT`	Retrieves data from one or more tables.
`FROM`	Tables involved in the query. Required in every `SELECT`.
`WHERE`	Criteria for selection that determine the rows to be retrieved, deleted or updated. Optional in a SQL query or a SQL statement.
`GROUP BY`	Criteria for grouping rows. Optional in a `SELECT` query.
`ORDER BY`	Criteria for ordering rows. Optional in a `SELECT` query.
`INNER JOIN`	Combine rows from multiple tables.
`INSERT`	Insert rows into a specified table.
`UPDATE`	Update rows in a specified table.
`DELETE`	Delete rows from a specified table.

Fig. 22.10 | SQL query keywords.

22.4.1 Basic SELECT Query

Let us consider several SQL queries that extract information from database `books`. A SQL query "selects" rows and columns from one or more tables in a database. Such selections are performed by queries with the `SELECT` keyword. The basic form of a `SELECT` query is

```
SELECT * FROM tableName
```

in which the asterisk (*) indicates that all rows and columns from the *tableName* table should be retrieved. For example, to retrieve all the data in the authors table, use

```
SELECT * FROM authors
```

Most programs do not require all the data in a table. To retrieve only specific columns from a table, replace the asterisk (*) with a comma-separated list of the column names. For example, to retrieve only the columns authorID and lastName for all rows in the authors table, use the query

```
SELECT authorID, lastName FROM authors
```

This query returns the data listed in Fig. 22.11.

Software Engineering Observation 22.1

For most queries, the asterisk (*) should not be used to specify column names. In general, you process results by knowing in advance the order of the columns in the result—for example, selecting authorID *and* lastName *from table* authors *ensures that the columns will appear in the result with* authorID *as the first column and* lastName *as the second column. Programs typically process result columns by specifying the column number in the result (starting from number 1 for the first column). Selecting columns by name also avoids returning unneeded columns and protects against changes in the actual order of the columns in the table(s).*

Common Programming Error 22.4

If you assume that the columns are always returned in the same order from a query that uses the asterisk (*), the program may process the results incorrectly. If the column order in the table(s) changes or if additional columns are added at a later time, the order of the columns in the result changes accordingly.

authorID	lastName
1	Deitel
2	Deitel
3	Goldberg
4	Choffnes

Fig. 22.11 | Sample authorID and lastName data from the authors table.

22.4.2 WHERE Clause

In most cases, it is necessary to retrieve rows in a database that satisfy certain selection criteria. Only rows that satisfy the selection criteria (formally called predicates) are selected. SQL uses the optional WHERE clause in a query to specify the selection criteria for the query. The basic form of a query with selection criteria is

```
SELECT columnName1, columnName2, ... FROM tableName WHERE criteria
```

For example, to select the title, editionNumber and copyright columns from table titles for which the copyright year is greater than 2005, use the query

```
SELECT title, editionNumber, copyright
   FROM titles
   WHERE copyright > '2005'
```

Figure 22.12 shows the result of the preceding query. The `WHERE` clause criteria can contain the operators <, >, <=, >=, =, <> and `LIKE`. Operator `LIKE` is used for pattern matching with wildcard characters percent (%) and underscore (_). Pattern matching allows SQL to search for strings that match a given pattern.

A pattern that contains a percent character (%) searches for strings that have zero or more characters at the percent character's position in the pattern. For example, the next query locates the rows of all the authors whose last name starts with the letter `D`:

```
SELECT authorID, firstName, lastName
   FROM authors
   WHERE lastName LIKE 'D%'
```

This query selects the two rows shown in Fig. 22.13—two of the four authors have a last name starting with the letter `D` (followed by zero or more characters). The `%` in the `WHERE` clause's `LIKE` pattern indicates that any number of characters can appear after the letter `D` in the `lastName`. Note that the pattern string is surrounded by single-quote characters.

Portability Tip 22.1

See the documentation for your database system to determine whether SQL is case sensitive on your system and to determine the syntax for SQL keywords (i.e., should they be all uppercase letters, all lowercase letters or some combination of the two?).

An underscore (_) in the pattern string indicates a single wildcard character at that position in the pattern. For example, the following query locates the rows of all the authors

title	editionNumber	copyright
Visual C# How to Program	2	2006
Visual Basic 2005 How to Program	3	2006
Java How to Program	7	2007
C How to Program	5	2007

Fig. 22.12 | Sampling of titles with copyrights after 2005 from table `titles`.

authorID	firstName	lastName
1	Harvey	Deitel
2	Paul	Deitel

Fig. 22.13 | Authors whose last name starts with `D` from the `authors` table.

whose last names start with any character (specified by _), followed by the letter o, followed by any number of additional characters (specified by %):

```
SELECT authorID, firstName, lastName
   FROM authors
   WHERE lastName LIKE '_o%'
```

The preceding query produces the row shown in Fig. 22.14, because only one author in our database has a last name that contains the letter o as its second letter.

authorID	firstName	lastName
3	Andrew	Goldberg

Fig. 22.14 | The only author from the `authors` table whose last name contains `o` as the second letter.

22.4.3 ORDER BY Clause

The rows in the result of a query can be sorted into ascending or descending order by using the optional **ORDER BY clause**. The basic form of a query with an `ORDER BY` clause is

```
SELECT columnName1, columnName2, ... FROM tableName ORDER BY column ASC
SELECT columnName1, columnName2, ... FROM tableName ORDER BY column DESC
```

where `ASC` specifies ascending order (lowest to highest), `DESC` specifies descending order (highest to lowest) and *column* specifies the column on which the sort is based. For example, to obtain the list of authors in ascending order by last name (Fig. 22.15), use the query

```
SELECT authorID, firstName, lastName
   FROM authors
   ORDER BY lastName ASC
```

Note that the default sorting order is ascending, so `ASC` is optional. To obtain the same list of authors in descending order by last name (Fig. 22.16), use the query

authorID	firstName	lastName
4	David	Choffnes
1	Harvey	Deitel
2	Paul	Deitel
3	Andrew	Goldberg

Fig. 22.15 | `authors` sample data in ascending order by `lastName`.

authorID	firstName	lastName
3	Andrew	Goldberg
1	Harvey	Deitel
2	Paul	Deitel
4	David	Choffnes

Fig. 22.16 | `authors` sample data in descending order by `lastName`.

```
SELECT authorID, firstName, lastName
   FROM authors
   ORDER BY lastName DESC
```

Multiple columns can be used for sorting with an `ORDER BY` clause of the form

`ORDER BY` *column1 sortingOrder*, *column2 sortingOrder*, ...

where *sortingOrder* is either `ASC` or `DESC`. Note that the *sortingOrder* does not have to be identical for each column. The query

```
SELECT authorID, firstName, lastName
   FROM authors
   ORDER BY lastName, firstName
```

sorts all the rows in ascending order by last name, then by first name. If any rows have the same value in the `lastName` column, they are returned sorted by `firstName` (Fig. 22.17).

The `WHERE` and `ORDER BY` clauses can be combined in one query, as in

```
SELECT isbn, title, editionNumber, copyright
   FROM titles
   WHERE title LIKE '%How to Program'
   ORDER BY title ASC
```

which returns the `isbn`, `title`, `editionNumber` and `copyright` of each book in the `titles` table that has a `title` ending with `"How to Program"` and sorts them in ascending order by `title`. The query results are shown in Fig. 22.18.

authorID	firstName	lastName
4	David	Choffnes
1	Harvey	Deitel
2	Paul	Deitel
3	Andrew	Goldberg

Fig. 22.17 | `authors` sample data in ascending order by `lastName` and `firstName`.

isbn	title	editionNumber	copyright
0132404168	C How to Program	5	2007
0131857576	C++ How to Program	5	2005
0131450913	Internet and World Wide Web How to Program	3	2004
0132222205	Java How to Program	7	2007
0131869000	Visual Basic 2005 How to Program	3	2006
0131525239	Visual C# How to Program	2	2006

Fig. 22.18 | Sampling of books from table `titles` whose titles end with `How to Program` in ascending order by `title`.

22.4.4 Combining Data from Multiple Tables: INNER JOIN

Database designers often split related data into separate tables to ensure that a database does not store data redundantly. For example, the `books` database has tables `authors` and `titles`. We use an `authorISBN` table to store the relationship data between authors and their corresponding titles. If we did not separate this information into individual tables, we would need to include author information with each entry in the `titles` table. Then the database would store duplicate author information for authors who wrote multiple books. Often, it is necessary to combine data from multiple tables into a single result. Referred to as joining the tables, this is specified by an `INNER JOIN` operator in the query. An `INNER JOIN` combines rows from two tables by matching values in columns that are common to the tables. The basic form of an `INNER JOIN` is:

```
SELECT columnName1, columnName2, ...
FROM table1
INNER JOIN table2
   ON table1.columnName = table2.columnName
```

The **ON clause** of the `INNER JOIN` specifies a condition (often comparing columns from each table) that determines which rows are combined. For example, the following query produces a list of authors accompanied by the ISBNs for books written by each author:

```
SELECT firstName, lastName, isbn
FROM authors
INNER JOIN authorISBN
   ON authors.authorID = authorISBN.authorID
ORDER BY lastName, firstName
```

The query combines the `firstName` and `lastName` columns from table `authors` with the `isbn` column from table `authorISBN`, sorting the result in ascending order by `lastName` and `firstName`. Only rows in which the `authorID`s match are combined. Note the use of the syntax *tableName*`.`*columnName* in the `ON` clause. This syntax, called a **qualified name**, specifies the columns from each table that should be compared to join the tables. The "*tableName*`.`" syntax is required if the columns have the same name in both tables. The same syntax can be used in any query to distinguish columns in different tables that have the same name. In some systems, table names qualified with the database name can be used to perform cross-database queries. As always, the query can contain an `ORDER BY` clause. Figure 22.19 depicts a portion of the results of the preceding query, ordered by `lastName` and `firstName`. [*Note:* To save space, we split the result of the query into two columns, each containing the `firstName`, `lastName` and `isbn` columns.]

Software Engineering Observation 22.2

If a SQL statement includes columns with the same name from multiple tables, the statement must precede those column names with their table names and a dot (e.g., `authors.authorID`*).*

Common Programming Error 22.5

Failure to qualify names for columns that have the same name in two or more tables is an error.

firstName	lastName	isbn	firstName	lastName	isbn
David	Choffnes	0131828274	Paul	Deitel	0131869000
Harvey	Deitel	0131869000	Paul	Deitel	0131525239
Harvey	Deitel	0131525239	Paul	Deitel	0132222205
Harvey	Deitel	0132222205	Paul	Deitel	0131857576
Harvey	Deitel	0131857576	Paul	Deitel	0132404168
Harvey	Deitel	0132404168	Paul	Deitel	0131450913
Harvey	Deitel	0131450913	Paul	Deitel	0131869000
Harvey	Deitel	0131869000	Paul	Deitel	0131828274
Harvey	Deitel	0131828274	Andrew	Goldberg	0131450913

Fig. 22.19 | Sampling of authors and ISBNs for the books they have written in ascending order by `lastName` and `firstName`.

22.4.5 INSERT Statement

The `INSERT` statement inserts a row into a table. The basic form of this statement is

```
INSERT INTO tableName ( columnName1, columnName2, …, columnNameN )
   VALUES ( value1, value2, …, valueN )
```

where *tableName* is the table in which to insert the row. The *tableName* is followed by a comma-separated list of column names in parentheses (this list is not required if the `INSERT` operation specifies a value for every column of the table in the correct order). The list of column names is followed by the SQL keyword `VALUES` and a comma-separated list of values in parentheses. The values specified here must match the columns specified after the table name in both order and type (e.g., if *columnName1* is supposed to be the `firstName` column, then *value1* should be a string in single quotes representing the first name).

Good Programming Practice 22.1

Always explicitly list the columns when inserting rows. If the table's column order changes or a new column is added, omitting the columns list may cause an error.

The INSERT statement

```
INSERT INTO authors ( firstName, lastName )
   VALUES ( 'Sue', 'Smith' )
```

inserts a row into the authors table. The statement indicates that values are provided for the firstName and lastName columns. The corresponding values are 'Sue' and 'Smith'. We do not specify an authorID in this example because authorID is an autoincremented column in the authors table. For every row added to this table, the database assigns a unique authorID value that is the next value in the autoincremented sequence (i.e., 1, 2, 3 and so on). In this case, Sue Smith would be assigned authorID number 5. Figure 22.20 shows the authors table after the INSERT operation. [*Note:* Not every database management system supports autoincremented columns. Check the documentation for your DBMS for alternatives to autoincremented columns.]

Common Programming Error 22.6

It is normally an error to specify a value for an autoincrement column.

Common Programming Error 22.7

SQL uses the single-quote (') character as a delimiter for strings. To specify a string containing a single quote (e.g., O'Malley) in a SQL statement, the string must have two single quotes in the position where the single-quote character appears in the string (e.g., 'O''Malley'*). The first of the two single-quote characters acts as an escape character for the second. Not escaping single-quote characters in a string that is part of a SQL statement is a SQL syntax error.*

authorID	firstName	lastName
1	Harvey	Deitel
2	Paul	Deitel
3	Andrew	Goldberg
4	David	Choffnes
5	Sue	Smith

Fig. 22.20 | Sample data from table Authors after an INSERT operation.

22.4.6 UPDATE Statement

An UPDATE statement modifies data in a table. The basic form of the UPDATE statement is

```
UPDATE tableName
   SET columnName1 = value1, columnName2 = value2, …, columnNameN = valueN
   WHERE criteria
```

where *tableName* is the table to update. The *tableName* is followed by keyword SET and a comma-separated list of column name/value pairs in the format *columnName* = *value*. The *value* can be an expression that yields a value. The optional WHERE clause provides criteria that determine which rows to update. Though not required, the WHERE clause is typically used, unless a change is to be made to every row. The UPDATE statement

```
UPDATE authors
   SET lastName = 'Jones'
   WHERE lastName = 'Smith' AND firstName = 'Sue'
```

updates a row in the authors table. The statement indicates that lastName will be assigned the value Jones for the row in which lastName is equal to Smith and firstName is equal to Sue. [*Note:* If there are multiple rows with the first name "Sue" and the last name "Smith," this statement will modify all such rows to have the last name "Jones."] If we know the authorID in advance of the UPDATE operation (possibly because we searched for it previously), the WHERE clause can be simplified as follows:

```
WHERE authorID = 5
```

Figure 22.21 shows the authors table after the UPDATE operation has taken place.

authorID	firstName	lastName
1	Harvey	Deitel
2	Paul	Deitel
3	Andrew	Goldberg
4	David	Choffnes
5	Sue	Jones

Fig. 22.21 | Sample data from table authors after an UPDATE operation.

22.4.7 DELETE Statement

A SQL DELETE statement removes rows from a table. The basic form of a DELETE is

```
DELETE FROM tableName WHERE criteria
```

where *tableName* is the table from which to delete. The optional WHERE clause specifies the criteria used to determine which rows to delete. If this clause is omitted, all the table's rows are deleted. The DELETE statement

```
DELETE FROM authors
   WHERE lastName = 'Jones' AND firstName = 'Sue'
```

deletes the row (or rows) for Sue Jones in the authors table. If we know the authorID in advance of the DELETE operation, the WHERE clause can be simplified as follows:

```
WHERE authorID = 5
```

Figure 22.22 shows the authors table after the DELETE operation has taken place.

authorID	firstName	lastName
1	Harvey	Deitel
2	Paul	Deitel
3	Andrew	Goldberg
4	David	Choffnes

Fig. 22.22 | Sample data from table `authors` after a `DELETE` operation.

22.5 MySQL

In 1994, TcX, a Swedish consulting firm, needed a fast and flexible way to access its tables. Unable to find a database server that could accomplish the required task adequately, Michael Widenius, the principal developer at TcX, decided to create his own database server. The resulting product was called *MySQL* (pronounced "my sequel"), a robust and scalable relational database management system (RDBMS).

MySQL is a multiuser, multithreaded (i.e., allows multiple simultaneous connections) RDBMS server that uses SQL to interact with and manipulate data. The MySQL Manual (`www.mysql.com/why-mysql/topreasons.html`) lists numerous benefits of MySQL. A few important benefits include:

1. Scalability. You can embed in an application or use it in massive data warehousing environments.
2. Performance. You can optimize performance based on the purpose of the database in your application.
3. Support for many programming languages. Later chapters demonstrate how to access a MySQL database from PHP (Chapter 23) and Ruby on Rails (Chapter 24).
4. Implementations of MySQL for Windows, Mac OS X, Linux and UNIX.
5. Handling large databases (e.g., tens of thousands of tables with millions of rows).

For these reasons and more, MySQL is the database of choice for many businesses, universities and individuals. MySQL is an open source software product. [*Note:* Under certain situations, a commercial license is required for MySQL. See `www.mysql.com/company/legal/licensing/` for details]

22.6 Instructions for Installing MySQL

MySQL 5.0 Community Edition is an open source database management system that executes on many platforms, including Windows, Solaris, Linux, and Macintosh. Complete information about MySQL is available from `www.mysql.com`.

Installing MySQL

To install MySQL Community Edition:

1. To learn about the installation requirements for your platform, visit the site `dev.mysql.com/doc/refman/5.0/en/general-installation-issues.html`.

2. Visit `dev.mysql.com/downloads/mysql/5.0.html` and download the installer for your platform. For our MySQL examples, you need only the Windows Essentials package on Microsoft Windows, or the Standard package on most other platforms. [*Note:* For these instructions, we assume you are running Microsoft Windows. Complete installation instructions for other platforms are available at `dev.mysql.com/doc/refman/5.0/en/installing.html`.]
3. Double click `mysql-essential-5.0.45-win32.msi` to start the installer. [*Note:* This filename may differ, based on the current version of MySQL 5.0.]
4. Choose **Typical** for the **Setup Type** and click **Next >**. Then click **Install**.

When the installation completes, you will be asked to set up an account on MySQL.com. If you do not wish to do this, select **Skip Sign-up** and click **Next >**. After completing the sign-up process or skipping it, you can configure the MySQL Server. Click **Finish** to start the **MySQL Server Instance Configuration Wizard**. To configure the server:

1. Click **Next >**, then select **Standard Configuration** and click **Next >** again.
2. You have the option of installing MySQL as a Windows service, which enables the MySQL server to begin executing automatically each time your system starts. For our examples, this is unnecessary, so uncheck **Install as a Windows Service**, then check **Include Bin Directory in Windows PATH**. This will enable you to use the MySQL commands in the Windows Command Prompt.
3. Click **Next >**, then click **Execute** to perform the server configuration.
4. Click **Finish** to close the wizard.

22.7 Instructions for Setting Up a MySQL User Account

For the MySQL examples to execute correctly, you need to set up a user account that allows users to create, delete and modify a database. After MySQL is installed, follow the steps below to set up a user account (these steps assume MySQL is installed in its default installation directory):

1. Open a Command Prompt and start the database server by executing the command `mysqld-nt.exe`. (On Linux, execute `mysqld start` from a shell or terminal window.) Note that this command has no output—it simply starts the MySQL server. Do not close this window—doing so terminates the server.
2. Next, you'll start the MySQL command-line client tool so you can set up a user account, open another Command Prompt and execute the command

   ```
   mysql -h localhost -u root
   ```

   The `-h` option indicates the host (i.e., computer) on which the MySQL server is running—in this case your local computer (`localhost`). The `-u` option indicates the user account that will be used to log in to the server—`root` is the default user account that is created during installation to allow you to configure the server. Once you've logged in, you'll see a `mysql>` prompt at which you can type commands to interact with the MySQL server.

3. Next, you'll add the iw3htp4 user account to the mysql built-in database. To create the iw3htp4 user account with the password iw3htp4, execute the following commands from the mysql> prompt:

```
create user 'iw3htp4'@'localhost' identified by 'iw3htp4';

grant select, insert, update, delete, create, drop, references,
   execute on *.* to 'iw3htp4'@'localhost';
```

   This creates the iw3htp4 user with the privileges needed to create the databases used in this chapter and manipulate those databases.

4. Type the command

```
exit;
```

   to terminate the MySQL monitor.

22.8 Creating a Database in MySQL

For each MySQL database we discuss in this book, we provide a SQL script in a file with the .sql extension that sets up the database and its tables. You can execute these scripts in the MySQL command-line client tool. In the examples directory for this chapter, you'll find the SQL script books.sql to create the books database. For the following steps, we assume that the MySQL server (mysqld-nt.exe) is still running. To execute the books.sql script:

1. Open a command prompt and use the cd command to change directories to the location that contains the books.sql script.

2. Start the MySQL monitor by typing

```
mysql -h localhost -u iw3htp4 -p
```

   The -p option prompts you for the password for the iw3htp4 user account. When prompted, enter the password iw3htp4.

3. Execute the script by typing

```
source books.sql;
```

   This creates a books database in the server's data directory—located on Windows at C:\Program Files\MySQL\MySQL Server 5.0\data by default.

4. Type the command

```
exit;
```

   to terminate the MySQL command-line client tool. You are now ready to use your MySQL database.

22.9 ADO.NET Object Model

Several examples in Chapter 25, ASP.NET 2.0 and ASP.NET Ajax, use ADO.NET 2.0 to access and manipulate SQL Server 2005 Express databases. The ADO.NET object model provides an API for accessing database management systems programmatically. ADO.NET was created for the .NET framework to replace Microsoft's ActiveX Data Objects™ (ADO) technology. Microsoft's Visual Studio IDE features visual programming tools that simplify the process of using a database in your projects. While you may not need to work directly with many ADO.NET objects to develop simple applications, basic knowledge of how the ADO.NET object model works is important for understanding data access in Visual Basic (the programming language we use in Chapter 25).

Namespaces `System.Data`*,* `System.Data.OleDb` *and* `System.Data.SqlClient`

Namespace `System.Data` is the root namespace for the ADO.NET API. The other important ADO.NET namespaces, `System.Data.OleDb` and `System.Data.SqlClient`, contain classes that enable programs to connect with and manipulate data sources—locations that contain data, such as a database or an XML file. Namespace `System.Data.OleDb` contains classes that are designed to work with any data source that supports the OLE DB API, whereas `System.Data.SqlClient` contains classes that are optimized to work with Microsoft SQL Server databases. The Chapter 25 examples manipulate SQL Server 2005 Express databases, so we use the classes of namespace `System.Data.SqlClient`. SQL Server 2005 Express is available at `msdn.microsoft.com/vstudio/express/sql/default.aspx`.

An object of class `SqlConnection` (namespace `System.Data.SqlClient`) represents a connection to a data source—specifically a Microsoft SQL Server database. A `SqlConnection` object keeps track of the location of the data source and any settings that specify how the data source is to be accessed. A connection is either active (i.e., open and permitting data to be sent to and retrieved from the data source) or closed.

An object of class `SqlCommand` (namespace `System.Data.SqlClient`) represents a SQL command that a DBMS can execute on a database. A program can use `SqlCommand` objects to manipulate a data source through a `SqlConnection`. The program must open the connection to the data source before executing one or more `SqlCommands` and close the connection once no further access to the data source is required. A connection that remains active for some length of time to permit multiple data operations is known as a persistent connection.

Class `DataTable` (namespace `System.Data`) represents a table of data. A `DataTable` contains a collection of `DataRows` that represent the table's data. A `DataTable` also has a collection of `DataColumns` that describe the columns in a table. `DataRow` and `DataColumn` are both located in namespace `System.Data`. An object of class `System.Data.DataSet`, which consists of a set of `DataTables` and the relationships among them, represents a cache of data—data that a program stores temporarily in local memory. The structure of a `DataSet` mimics the structure of a relational database.

ADO.NET's Disconnected Model

An advantage of using class `DataSet` is that it is disconnected—the program does not need a persistent connection to the data source to work with data in a `DataSet`. Instead, the program connects to the data source to populate the `DataSet` (i.e., fill the `DataSet`'s `DataTables` with data), but disconnects from the data source immediately after retrieving the desired data. The program then accesses and potentially manipulates the data stored in the `DataSet`. The program operates on this local cache of data, rather than the original data in the data source. If the program makes changes to the data in the `DataSet` that need to be permanently saved in the data source, the program reconnects to the data source to perform an update, then disconnects promptly. Thus the program does not require any active, persistent connection to the data source.

An object of class **SqlDataAdapter** (namespace System.Data.SqlClient) connects to a SQL Server data source and executes SQL statements to both populate a DataSet and update the data source based on the current contents of a DataSet. A SqlDataAdapter maintains a SqlConnection object that it opens and closes as needed to perform these operations, using SqlCommands.

22.10 Java DB/Apache Derby

As of the Java SE 6 Development Kit (JDK), Sun Microsystems now bundles the open source, pure Java database Java DB (the Sun branded version of Apache Derby) with the JDK. Chapters 27–28 use Java DB in data-driven web applications. Similar to MySQL, Java DB has both an embedded version and a network (client/server) version. The tools we use in Chapters 27–28 come with Java DB. For those examples, we use Java DB's network version, and we provide all the information you need to configure each example's database. You can learn more about Apache Derby at db.apache.org/derby. You can learn more about Java DB at developers.sun.com/javadb/.

22.11 Wrap-Up

In this chapter, you learned basic database concepts and how to interact with data in a database using SQL. You learned about the SQL statements SELECT, INSERT, UPDATE and DELETE, as well as clauses such as WHERE, ORDER BY and INNER JOIN. You learned how to install MySQL, to create and configure a MySQL user account, and to execute scripts that create databases in MySQL. We also discussed ADO.NET 2.0 and introduced Java DB. In the next chapter, you'll learn one of the most popular server-side scripting languages—PHP.

22.12 Web Resources

Many database-related resources are available on the web. This section lists several database resources.

www.sql.org

The sql.org site is an online resource that provides a tutorial on the SQL programming language. It offers links to news groups, discussion forums, free software and various database vendors.

www.deitel.com/mysql/

The Deitel MySQL Resource Center focuses on the vast amount of free MySQL content available online, plus some for-sale items. Start your search here for tools, downloads, tutorials, podcasts, wikis, documentation, conferences, FAQs, books, sample chapters, articles, newsgroups, forums, jobs, contract opportunities, and more that will help you develop MySQL database applications.

www.mysql.com

This site is the MySQL database home page. You can download the latest version of MySQL and access its online documentation.

www.mysql.com/products/enterprise/server.html

Introduction to the MySQL database server and links to its documentation and download sites.

dev.mysql.com/doc/mysql/en/index.html

MySQL reference manual.

developers.sun.com/prodtech/javadb/reference/docs/10.2.1.6/devguide/index.html

The *Java DB Developer's Guide*.

`www.microsoft.com/sql`
The *Microsoft SQL Server* website contains product information, technical support, SQL news and tips on using the SQL Server to solve business problems.

`msdn.microsoft.com/vstudio/express/sql/`
The *Microsoft SQL Server Express* website.

`www.w3schools.com/sql`
The *SQL School* website provides a tutorial on basic to advanced SQL commands. The site contains a short quiz that reinforces SQL concepts.

`www.sqlmag.com`
SQL Server Magazine is an excellent SQL Server resource. Subscribers receive monthly issues filled with articles on SQL design and information on current developments involving SQL. Certain articles are available for free at the website.

`db.apache.org/derby/`
The Apache Derby website provides downloads and resources for Apache Derby.

Summary

Section 22.1 Introduction

- A database is an integrated collection of data. A database management system (DBMS) provides mechanisms for storing, organizing, retrieving and modifying data.
- Today's most popular database management systems are relational database systems.
- SQL is the international standard language used almost universally with relational database systems to perform queries and manipulate data.
- Programs connect to, and interact with, relational databases systems via an interface—software that facilitates communications between a database management system and a program.

Section 22.2 Relational Databases

- A relational database stores data in tables. Tables are composed of rows, and rows are composed of columns in which values are stored.
- A primary key provides a unique value that cannot be duplicated in other rows of the same table.
- Each column of a table represents a different attribute in a row of data.
- The primary key can be composed of more than one column.
- SQL provides a rich set of language constructs that enable you to define complex queries to retrieve data from a database.
- Every column in a primary key must have a value, and the value of the primary key must be unique. This is known as the Rule of Entity Integrity.
- A one-to-many relationship between tables indicates that a row in one table can have many related rows in a separate table.
- A foreign key is a column in a table that matches the primary-key column in another table.
- The foreign key helps maintain the Rule of Referential Integrity: Every foreign-key value must appear as another table's primary-key value. Foreign keys can be used to combine information from multiple tables. There is a one-to-many relationship between a primary key and its corresponding foreign key.

Section 22.4.1 Basic **SELECT** *Query*

- The basic form of a query is

```
SELECT * FROM tableName
```

  where the asterisk (*) indicates that all columns from *tableName* should be selected, and *tableName* specifies the table in the database from which rows will be retrieved.
- To retrieve specific columns from a table, replace the asterisk (*) with a comma-separated list of column names.

Section 22.4.2 **WHERE** *Clause*

- The optional `WHERE` clause in a query specifies the selection criteria for the query. The basic form of a query with selection criteria is

```
SELECT columnName1, columnName2, ... FROM tableName WHERE criteria
```

- The `WHERE` clause can contain operators <, >, <=, >=, =, <> and `LIKE`. Operator `LIKE` is used for string pattern matching with wildcard characters percent (`%`) and underscore (`_`).
- A percent character (`%`) in a pattern indicates that a string matching the pattern can have zero or more characters at the percent character's location in the pattern.
- An underscore (`_`) in the pattern string indicates a single character at that position in the pattern.

Section 22.4.3 **ORDER BY** *Clause*

- The result of a query can be sorted in ascending or descending order using the optional `ORDER BY` clause. The simplest form of an `ORDER BY` clause is

```
SELECT columnName1, columnName2, ... FROM tableName ORDER BY column ASC
SELECT columnName1, columnName2, ... FROM tableName ORDER BY column DESC
```

  where `ASC` specifies ascending order, `DESC` specifies descending order and *column* specifies the column on which the sort is based. The default sorting order is ascending, so `ASC` is optional.
- Multiple columns can be used for ordering purposes with an `ORDER BY` clause of the form

```
ORDER BY column1 sortingOrder, column2 sortingOrder, ...
```

- The `WHERE` and `ORDER BY` clauses can be combined in one query. If used, `ORDER BY` must be the last clause in the query.

Section 22.4.4 Merging Data from Multiple Tables: **INNER JOIN**

- An `INNER JOIN` combines rows from two tables by matching values in columns that are common to the tables. The basic form for the `INNER JOIN` operator is:

```
SELECT columnName1, columnName2, ...
FROM table1
INNER JOIN table2
   ON table1.columnName = table2.columnName
```

  The `ON` clause specifies a condition that determines which rows are joined. This condition often compares columns from each table If a SQL statement uses columns with the same name from multiple tables, the column names must be fully qualified by prefixing them with their table names and a dot (`.`).

Section 22.4.5 **INSERT** *Statement*

- An `INSERT` statement inserts a new row into a table. The basic form of this statement is

```
INSERT INTO tableName ( columnName1, columnName2, ..., columnNameN )
   VALUES ( value1, value2, ..., valueN )
```

where *tableName* is the table in which to insert the row. The *tableName* is followed by a comma-separated list of column names in parentheses. The list of column names is followed by the SQL keyword `VALUES` and a comma-separated list of values in parentheses.

- SQL uses single quotes (`'`) as the delimiter for strings. To specify a string containing a single quote in SQL, the single quote must be escaped with another single quote.

Section 22.4.6 **UPDATE** *Statement*

- An `UPDATE` statement modifies data in a table. The basic form of an `UPDATE` statement is

```
UPDATE tableName
    SET columnName1 = value1, columnName2 = value2, …, columnNameN = valueN
    WHERE criteria
```

where *tableName* is the table in which to update data. The *tableName* is followed by keyword `SET` and a comma-separated list of column name/value pairs in the format *columnName* = *value*. The optional `WHERE` clause *criteria* determines which rows to update.

Section 22.4.7 **DELETE** *Statement*

- A `DELETE` statement removes rows from a table. The simplest form for a `DELETE` statement is

```
DELETE FROM tableName WHERE criteria
```

where *tableName* is the table from which to delete a row (or rows). The optional `WHERE` *criteria* determines which rows to delete. If this clause is omitted, all the table's rows are deleted.

Section 22.5 MySQL

- MySQL (pronounced "my sequel") is a robust and scalable relational database management system (RDBMS) that was created by the Swedish consulting firm TcX in 1994.
- MySQL is a multiuser, multithreaded RDBMS server that uses SQL to interact with and manipulate data.
- Multithreading capabilities enable MySQL database to perform multiple tasks concurrently, allowing the server to process client requests efficiently.
- Implementations of MySQL are available for Windows, Mac OS X, Linux and UNIX.

Section 22.9 ADO.NET Object Model

- The ADO.NET object model provides an API for accessing database systems programmatically.
- ADO.NET was created for the .NET framework to replace Microsoft's ActiveX Data Objects (ADO) technology.
- Namespace `System.Data` is the root namespace for the ADO.NET API.
- Namespace `System.Data.OleDb` contains classes that are designed to work with any data source that supports the OLE DB API, whereas `System.Data.SqlClient` contains classes that are optimized to work with Microsoft SQL Server databases.
- An object of class `SqlConnection` represents a connection to a SQL Server data source.
- A `SqlConnection` object keeps track of the location of the data source and any settings that specify how the data source is to be accessed.
- A `SqlCommand` object represents a SQL command that a DBMS can execute on a database.
- A connection that remains active for some length of time to permit multiple data operations is known as a persistent connection.
- A `DataTable` contains a collection of `DataRows` that represent the table's data. A `DataTable` also has a collection of `DataColumns` that describe the columns in a table.

- A DataSet, which consists of a set of DataTables and the relationships among them, represents a cache of data—data that a program stores temporarily in local memory.
- The structure of a DataSet mimics the structure of a relational database.
- An advantage of using class DataSet is that it is disconnected—the program does not need a persistent connection to the data source to work with data in a DataSet.
- A SqlDataAdapter object connects to a SQL Server data source and executes SQL statements to both populate a DataSet and update the data source based on the current contents of a DataSet.

Section 22.10 Java DB/Apache Derby

- As of the Java SE 6 Development Kit (JDK), Sun Microsystems now bundles the open source, pure Java database Java DB (the Sun branded version of Apache Derby) with the JDK.

Terminology

% SQL wildcard character
* SQL wildcard character
_ SQL wildcard character
active database connection
ADO.NET object model
AND SQL keyword
Apache Derby
ASC SQL keyword
ascending order
asterisk (*) SQL wildcard character
autoincremented column value
column
column number in a result set
combine records from tables
data source
database
database management system (DBMS)
DataColumn class
DataRow class
DataSet class
DataTable class
DELETE SQL statement
DESC SQL keyword
disconnected object model
entity-relationship diagram
escape character
foreign key
FROM SQL clause
GROUP BY SQL clause
INNER JOIN SQL clause
INSERT SQL statement
Java DB
joining database tables
LIKE SQL clause
many-to-many relationship
Microsoft SQL Server
MySQL
mysqld-nt.exe
ON SQL clause
one-to-many relationship
ORDER BY SQL clause
pattern matching
percent (%) SQL wildcard character
persistent database connection
populating a DataSet
predicate
primary key
qualified name
query
relational database
relational database management system (RDBMS)
relational database table
row
Rule of Entity Integrity
Rule of Referential Integrity
SELECT SQL keyword
selecting data from a table
selection criteria
SET SQL clause
single-quote character
.sql filename extension
SQL script
SqlCommand class
SqlConnection class
SqlDataAdapter class
Structured Query Language (SQL)
System.Data namespace
System.Data.OleDb namespace
System.Data.SqlClient namespace
table
underscore (_) SQL wildcard character

`UPDATE` SQL statement
`VALUES` SQL clause
`WHERE` SQL clause

Self-Review Exercise

22.1 Fill in the blanks in each of the following statements:

a) The international standard database language is ________.
b) A table in a database consists of ________ and ________.
c) The ________ uniquely identifies each row in a table.
d) SQL keyword ________ is followed by the selection criteria that specify the rows to select in a query.
e) SQL keywords ________ specify the order in which rows are sorted in a query.
f) Merging rows from multiple database tables is called ________ the tables.
g) A(n) ________ is an organized collection of data.
h) A(n) ________ is a set of columns whose values match the primary key values of another table.

Answers to Self-Review Exercise

22.1 a) SQL. b) rows, columns. c) primary key. d) `WHERE`. e) `ORDER BY`. f) joining. g) database. h) foreign key.

Exercises

22.2 Define the following terms:

a) Qualified name.
b) Rule of Referential Integrity.
c) Rule of Entity Integrity.
d) `System.Data`.
e) selection criteria.

22.3 State the purpose of the following SQL keywords:

a) `ASC`
b) `FROM`
c) `DESC`
d) `INSERT`
e) `LIKE`
f) `UPDATE`
g) `SET`
h) `VALUES`
i) `ON`

22.4 Write SQL queries for the `books` database (discussed in Section 22.3) that perform each of the following tasks:

a) Select all authors from the `Authors` table with the columns in the order `lastName`, `firstName` and `authorID`.
b) Select a specific author and list all books for that author. Include the title, year and ISBN number. Order the information alphabetically by title.
c) Add a new author to the `Authors` table.
d) Add a new title for an author (remember that the book must have an entry in the `AuthorISBN` table).

22.5 Fill in the blanks in each of the following statements:

a) The ________ states that every column in a primary key must have a value, and the value of the primary key must be unique
b) The ________ states that every foreign-key value must appear as another table's primary-key value.
c) A(n) ________ in a pattern indicates that a string matching the pattern can have zero or more characters at the percent character's location in the pattern.
d) Java DB is the Sun branded version of ________.
e) A(n) ________ in a `LIKE` pattern string indicates a single character at that position in the pattern.
f) There is a(n) ________ relationship between a primary key and its corresponding foreign key.
g) SQL uses ________ as the delimiter for strings.
h) Microsoft's ________ object model provides an API for accessing database systems programmatically.

22.6 Correct each of the following SQL statements that refer to the `books` database.

a) `SELECT firstName FROM author WHERE authorID = 3`
b) `SELECT isbn, title FROM Titles ORDER WITH title DESC`
c) `INSERT INTO Authors ( authorID, firstName, lastName )`
`VALUES ( "2", "Jane", "Doe" )`

23

PHP

Conversion for me was not a Damascus Road experience. I slowly moved into an intellectual acceptance of what my intuition had always known.
—Madeleine L'Engle

Be careful when reading health books; you may die of a misprint.
—Mark Twain

Reckoners without their host must reckon twice.
—John Heywood

There was a door to which I found no key;
There was the veil through which I might not see.
—Omar Khayyam

OBJECTIVES

In this chapter you will learn:

- To manipulate data of various types.
- To use operators, arrays and control statements.
- To use regular expressions to search for patterns.
- To construct programs that process form data.
- To store data on the client using cookies.
- To create programs that interact with MySQL databases.

Outline

23.1 Introduction

PHP, or **PHP: Hypertext Preprocessor**, has become one of the most popular server-side scripting languages for creating dynamic web pages. PHP was created by Rasmus Lerdorf to track users at his website. In 1995, Lerdorf released it as a package called the "Personal Home Page Tools." Two years later, PHP 2 featured built-in database support and form handling. In 1997, PHP 3 was released with a rewritten parser, which substantially increased performance and led to an explosion of PHP use. The release of PHP 4 featured the new *Zend Engine* from Zend, a PHP software company. This version was considerably faster and more powerful than its predecessor, further increasing PHP's popularity. It is estimated that over 15 million domains now use PHP, accounting for more than 20 percent of web pages.[1] Currently, PHP 5 features the *Zend Engine 2*, which provides further speed increases, exception handling and a new object-oriented programming model.[2] More information about the Zend Engine can be found at `www.zend.com`.

PHP is an open-source technology that is supported by a large community of users and developers. PHP is platform independent—implementations exist for all major UNIX, Linux, Mac and Windows operating systems. PHP also supports many databases, including MySQL.

After introducing the basics of the PHP scripting language, we discuss form processing and business logic, which are vital to e-commerce applications. Next, we build a three-tier web application that queries a MySQL database. We also show how PHP can use cookies to store information on the client that can be retrieved during future visits to the website. Finally, we revisit the form-processing example to demonstrate some of PHP's more dynamic capabilities.

---

1. "History of PHP," 30 June 2007, *PHP* <`us.php.net/history`>.
2. Suraski, Z., "The OO Evolution of PHP," 16 March 2004, *Zend* <`devzone.zend.com/node/view/id/1717`>.

23.2 PHP Basics

The power of the web resides not only in serving content to users, but also in responding to requests from users and generating web pages with dynamic content. Interactivity between the user and the server has become a crucial part of web functionality, making PHP—a language written specifically for interacting with the web—a valuable tool.

Installing PHP

PHP code is embedded directly into XHTML documents, though these script segments are interpreted by the server before being delivered to the client. This allows the document author to write XHTML in a clear, concise manner. PHP script file names end with `.php`.

To run a PHP script, PHP must first be installed on your system. All examples and exercises in this chapter have been verified using PHP 5.2.3, the most current release at the time of publication. The most recent version of PHP can be downloaded from `www.php.net/downloads.php`, and installation instructions are available at `www.php.net/manual/en/installation.php`. Be sure to check for specific instructions that pertain to the server you want to use. During setup, when the **Choose Items to Install** window is displayed, expand the **Extensions** menu by clicking the small plus sign to its left. Then click the down arrow to the left of the MySQL option, and select the **Will be installed on local hard drive** option. This will ensure that your PHP script will be able to access your MySQL database server for examples later in this chapter.

Although PHP can be used from the command line, a web server is necessary to take full advantage of the scripting language. Before continuing, files from the Chapter 23 examples directory to the web server's root directory (e.g., `C:\Inetpub\wwwroot` for IIS or `C:\Program Files\Apache Software Foundation\Apache2\htdocs` for Apache on Windows or `/var/www/html` or similar on Linux).

Simple PHP Program

Figure 23.1 presents a simple PHP program that displays a welcome message. In PHP, code is inserted between the scripting delimiters `<?php` and `?>`. PHP code can be placed anywhere in XHTML markup, as long as the code is enclosed in these delimiters. Line 1 uses function `print` to output the XML declaration. This avoids the <? in the XML dec-

```
1  <?php print( '<?xml version = "1.0" encoding = "utf-8"?>' ) ?>
2  <!DOCTYPE html PUBLIC "-//W3C//DTD XHTML 1.0 Strict//EN"
3     "http://www.w3.org/TR/xhtml1/DTD/xhtml1-strict.dtd">
4
5  <!-- Fig. 23.1: first.php -->
6  <!-- Simple PHP program. -->
7  <html xmlns = "http://www.w3.org/1999/xhtml">
8  <?php
9     $name = "Harvey"; // declaration and initialization
10 ?><!-- end PHP script -->
11    <head>
12       <title>Using PHP document</title>
13    </head>
14    <body style = "font-size: 2em">
```

Fig. 23.1 | Simple PHP program. (Part 1 of 2.)

```
15          <p>
16             <strong>
17                <!-- print variable name's value -->
18                Welcome to PHP, <?php print( "$name" ); ?>!
19             </strong>
20          </p>
21       </body>
22    </html>
```

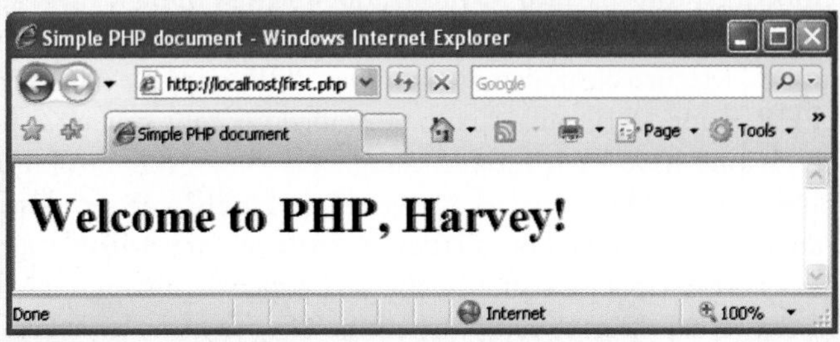

Fig. 23.1 | Simple PHP program. (Part 2 of 2.)

laration getting interpreted as an incorrect PHP scripting delimiter. Line 9 declares variable `$name` and assigns it the string `"Harvey"`. All variables are preceded by a `$` and are created the first time they are encountered by the PHP interpreter. PHP statements terminate with a semicolon (`;`).

Common Programming Error 23.1

Failing to precede a variable name with a $ is a syntax error.

Common Programming Error 23.2

Variable names in PHP are case sensitive. Failure to use the proper mixture of cases to refer to a variable will result in a logic error, since the script will create a new variable for any name it doesn't recognize as a previously used variable.

Common Programming Error 23.3

Forgetting to terminate a statement with a semicolon (;) is a syntax error.

Line 9 also contains a single-line comment, which begins with two forward slashes (`//`). Text to the right of the slashes is ignored by the interpreter. Single-line comments can also begin with the pound sign (`#`). Multiline comments begin with delimiter `/*` and end with delimiter `*/`.

Line 18 outputs the value of variable `$name` by calling function `print`. The actual value of `$name` is printed, not the string `"$name"`. When a variable is encountered inside a double-quoted (`""`) string, PHP interpolates the variable. In other words, PHP inserts the variable's value where the variable name appears in the string. Thus, variable `$name` is replaced by `Harvey` for printing purposes. All operations of this type execute on the server before the XHTML document is sent to the client. You can see by viewing the source of a PHP document that the code sent to the client does not contain any PHP code.

PHP variables are loosely typed—they can contain different types of data (e.g., integers, doubles or strings) at different times. Figure 23.2 introduces these data types.

Type	Description
`int, integer`	Whole numbers (i.e., numbers without a decimal point).
`float, double, real`	Real numbers (i.e., numbers containing a decimal point).
`string`	Text enclosed in either single (`''`) or double (`""`) quotes. [*Note:* Using double quotes allows PHP to recognize more escape sequences.]
`bool, boolean`	True or false.
`array`	Group of elements.
`object`	Group of associated data and methods.
`resource`	An external source—usually information from a database.
`NULL`	No value.

Fig. 23.2 | PHP types.

Converting Between Data Types

Converting between different data types may be necessary when performing arithmetic operations with variables. Type conversions can be performed using function `settype`. Figure 23.3 demonstrates type conversion of some types introduced in Fig. 23.2.

```
<?php print( '<?xml version = "1.0" encoding = "utf-8"?>' ) ?>
<!DOCTYPE html PUBLIC "-//W3C//DTD XHTML 1.0 Strict//EN"
   "http://www.w3.org/TR/xhtml1/DTD/xhtml1-strict.dtd">

<!-- Fig. 23.3: data.php -->
<!-- Data type conversion. -->
<html xmlns = "http://www.w3.org/1999/xhtml">
   <head>
      <title>Data type conversion</title>
   </head>
   <body>
      <?php
         // declare a string, double and integer
         $testString = "3.5 seconds";
         $testDouble = 79.2;
         $testInteger = 12;
      ?><!-- end PHP script -->

      <!-- print each variable's value and type -->
      <?php
         print( "$testString is a(n) " . gettype( $testString )
            . "<br />" );
```

Fig. 23.3 | Data type conversion. (Part 1 of 2.)

```
         print( "$testDouble is a(n) " . gettype( $testDouble )
            . "<br />" );
         print( "$testInteger is a(n) " . gettype( $testInteger)
            . "<br />" );
      ?><!-- end PHP script -->
      <br />
      converting to other data types:<br />
      <?php
         // call function settype to convert variable
         // testString to different data types
         print( "$testString" );
         settype( $testString, "double" );
         print( " as a double is $testString <br />" );
         print( "$testString" );
         settype( $testString, "integer" );
         print( " as an integer is $testString <br />" );
         settype( $testString, "string" );
         print( "converting back to a string results in
            $testString <br /><br />" );

         // use type casting to cast variables to a different type
         $data = "98.6 degrees";
         print( "before casting, $data is a " .
            gettype( $data ) . "<br /><br />" );
         print( "using type casting instead: <br />
            as a double: " . (double) $data .
            "<br />as an integer: " . (integer) $data );
         print( "<br /><br />after casting, $data is a " .
           gettype( $data ) );
      ?><!-- end PHP script -->
   </body>
</html>
```

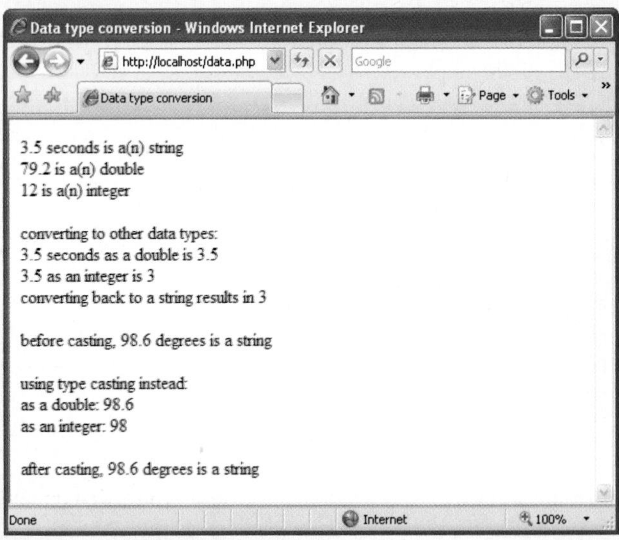

Fig. 23.3 | Data type conversion. (Part 2 of 2.)

Lines 14–16 of Fig. 23.3 assign a string to variable `$testString`, a floating-point number to variable `$testDouble` and an integer to variable `$testInteger`. Variables are automatically converted to the type of the value they are assigned. For example, variable `$testString` becomes a string when assigned the value `"3.5 seconds"`. Lines 22–27 `print` the value of each variable and their types using function **`gettype`**, which returns the current type of its argument. Note that when a variable is in a `print` statement but not part of a string, enclosing the variable name in double quotes is unnecessary. Lines 35, 38 and 40 call **`settype`** to modify the type of each variable. Function `settype` takes two arguments—the variable whose type is to be changed and the variable's new type.

Calling function `settype` can result in loss of data. For example, doubles are truncated when they are converted to integers. When converting from a string to a number, PHP uses the value of the number that appears at the beginning of the string. If no number appears at the beginning, the string evaluates to `0`. In line 35, the string `"3.5 seconds"` is converted to a double, storing `3.5` in variable `$testString`. In line 38, double `3.5` is converted to integer `3`. When we convert this variable to a string (line 40), the variable's value becomes `"3"`—much of the original content from the variable's declaration in line 14 is lost.

Another option for conversion between types is **casting** (or **type casting**). Unlike `settype`, casting does not change a variable's content—it creates a temporary copy of a variable's value in memory. Lines 48–49 cast variable `$data`'s value (declared in line 17) from a `string` to a `double` and an `integer`. Casting is useful when a different type is required in a specific operation but you would like to retain the variable's original value and type. Lines 45–51 show that the type and value of `$data` remain unchanged even after it has been cast several times.

The **concatenation operator** (`.`) combines multiple strings in the same `print` statement, as demonstrated in lines 45–51. A `print` statement may be split over multiple lines—all data that is enclosed in the parentheses and terminated by a semicolon is printed to the XHTML document.

Error-Prevention Tip 23.1

Function `print` can be used to display the value of a variable at a particular point during a program's execution. This is often helpful in debugging a script.

Arithmetic Operators

PHP provides several arithmetic operators, which we demonstrate in Fig. 23.4. Line 13 declares variable `$a` and assigns to it the value `5`. Line 17 calls function `define` to create a **named constant**. Function `define` takes two arguments—the name and value of the constant. An optional third argument accepts a `bool` value that specifies whether the constant is case insensitive—constants are case sensitive by default.

Common Programming Error 23.4

Assigning a value to a constant after it is declared is a syntax error.

Line 20 adds constant `VALUE` to variable `$a`. Line 25 uses the **multiplication assignment operator** `*=` to yield an expression equivalent to `$a = $a * 2` (thus assigning `$a` the value `20`). Arithmetic assignment operators—like the ones described in Chapter 7—are syntactical shortcuts. Line 33 adds `40` to the value of variable `$a`.

```
<?php print( '<?xml version = "1.0" encoding = "utf-8"?>' ) ?>
<!DOCTYPE html PUBLIC "-//W3C//DTD XHTML 1.0 Strict//EN"
   "http://www.w3.org/TR/xhtml1/DTD/xhtml1-strict.dtd">

<!-- Fig. 23.4: operators.php -->
<!-- Using arithmetic operators. -->
<html xmlns = "http://www.w3.org/1999/xhtml">
   <head>
      <title>Using arithmetic operators</title>
   </head>
   <body>
      <?php
         $a = 5;
         print( "The value of variable a is $a <br />" );

         // define constant VALUE
         define( "VALUE", 5 );

         // add constant VALUE to variable $a
         $a = $a + VALUE;
         print( "Variable a after adding constant VALUE
            is $a <br />" );

         // multiply variable $a by 2
         $a *= 2;
         print( "Multiplying variable a by 2 yields $a <br />" );

         // test if variable $a is less than 50
         if ( $a < 50 )
            print( "Variable a is less than 50 <br />" );

         // add 40 to variable $a
         $a += 40;
         print( "Variable a after adding 40 is $a <br />" );

         // test if variable $a is 50 or less
         if ( $a < 51 )
            print( "Variable a is still 50 or less<br />" );

         // test if variable $a is between 50 and 100, inclusive
         elseif ( $a < 101 )
            print( "Variable a is now between 50 and 100,
               inclusive<br />" );
         else
            print( "Variable a is now greater than 100 <br />" );

         // print an uninitialized variable
         print( "Using a variable before initializing:
            $nothing <br />" ); // nothing evaluates to ""

         // add constant VALUE to an uninitialized variable
         $test = $num + VALUE; // num evaluates to 0
```

Fig. 23.4 | Using arithmetic operators. (Part 1 of 2.)

```
53            print( "An uninitialized variable plus constant
54               VALUE yields $test <br />" );
55
56            // add a string to an integer
57            $str = "3 dollars";
58            $a += $str;
59            print( "Adding a string to variable a yields $a <br />" );
60         ?><!-- end PHP script -->
61      </body>
62   </html>
```

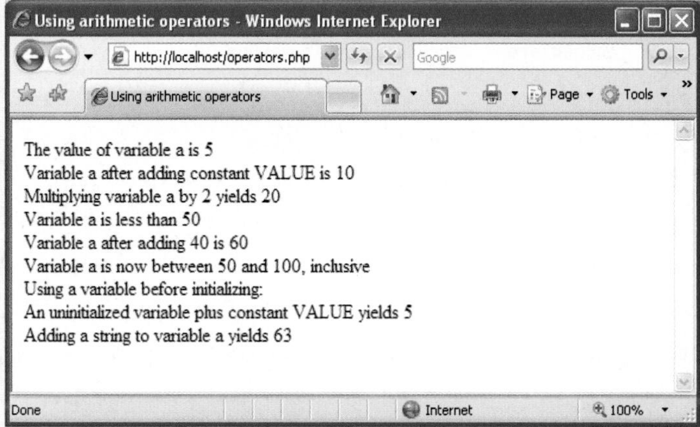

Using arithmetic operators - Windows Internet Explorer
http://localhost/operators.php
Google
Using arithmetic operators
Page
Tools
The value of variable a is 5
Variable a after adding constant VALUE is 10
Multiplying variable a by 2 yields 20
Variable a is less than 50
Variable a after adding 40 is 60
Variable a is now between 50 and 100, inclusive
Using a variable before initializing:
An uninitialized variable plus constant VALUE yields 5
Adding a string to variable a yields 63
Done
Internet
100%

Fig. 23.4 | Using arithmetic operators. (Part 2 of 2.)

Uninitialized variables have the value **`undef`**, which evaluates to different values, depending on its context. For example, when `undef` is used in a numeric context (e.g., `$num` in line 52), it evaluates to `0`. In contrast, when `undef` is interpreted in a string context (e.g., `$nothing` in line 49), it evaluates to an empty string (`""`).

Error-Prevention Tip 23.2

Initialize variables before they are used to avoid subtle errors. For example, multiplying a number by an uninitialized variable results in `0`*.*

Strings are automatically converted to integers or doubles when they are used in arithmetic operations. In line 58, a copy of the value of variable `str`, `"3 dollars"`, is converted to the integer `3` for use in the calculation. The type and value of variable `$str` are left unchanged.

Keywords (examples from Fig. 23.4 include `if`, `elseif` and `else`) may not be used as identifiers. Figure 23.5 lists all keywords.

Initializing and Manipulating Arrays

PHP provides the capability to store data in arrays. Arrays are divided into elements that behave as individual variables. Array names, like other variables, begin with the `$` symbol. Figure 23.6 demonstrates initializing and manipulating arrays. Individual array elements are accessed by following the array's variable name with an index enclosed in square brackets (`[]`). If a value is assigned to an array that does not exist, then the array is created (line

PHP keywords				
abstract	die	exit	interface	require
and	do	extends	isset	require_once
array	echo	__FILE__	__LINE__	return
as	else	file	line	static
break	elseif	final	list	switch
case	empty	for	__METHOD__	throw
catch	enddeclare	foreach	method	try
__CLASS__	endfor	__FUNCTION__	new	unset
class	endforeach	function	or	use
clone	endif	global	php_user_filter	var
const	endswitch	if	print	while
continue	endwhile	implements	private	xor
declare	eval	include	protected	
default	exception	include_once	public	

Fig. 23.5 | PHP keywords.

15). Likewise, assigning a value to an element where the index is omitted appends a new element to the end of the array (line 18). The `for` statement (lines 21–22) `print`s each element's value. Function **`count`** returns the total number of elements in the array. In this example, the `for` statement terminates when the counter (`$i`) is equal to the number of array elements.

Line 28 demonstrates a second method of initializing arrays. Function **`array`** creates an array that contains the arguments passed to it. The first item in the argument list is stored as the first array element (recall that the first element's index is 0), the second item is stored as the second array element and so on. Lines 30–31 display the array's contents.

```
1   <?php print( '<?xml version = "1.0" encoding = "utf-8"?>' ) ?>
2   <!DOCTYPE html PUBLIC "-//W3C//DTD XHTML 1.0 Strict//EN"
3      "http://www.w3.org/TR/xhtml1/DTD/xhtml1-strict.dtd">
4
5   <!-- Fig. 23.6: arrays.php -->
6   <!-- Array manipulation. -->
7   <html xmlns = "http://www.w3.org/1999/xhtml">
8      <head>
9         <title>Array manipulation</title>
10     </head>
11     <body>
12        <?php
```

Fig. 23.6 | Array manipulation. (Part 1 of 3.)

```
         // create array first
         print( "<strong>Creating the first array</strong><br />" );
         $first[ 0 ] = "zero";
         $first[ 1 ] = "one";
         $first[ 2 ] = "two";
         $first[] = "three";

         // print each element's index and value
         for ( $i = 0; $i < count( $first ); $i++ )
            print( "Element $i is $first[$i] <br />" );

         print( "<br /><strong>Creating the second array
            </strong><br />" );

         // call function array to create array second
         $second = array( "zero", "one", "two", "three" );

         for ( $i = 0; $i < count( $second ); $i++ )
            print( "Element $i is $second[$i] <br />" );

         print( "<br /><strong>Creating the third array
            </strong><br />" );

         // assign values to entries using nonnumeric indices
         $third[ "Amy" ] = 21;
         $third[ "Bob" ] = 18;
         $third[ "Carol" ] = 23;

         // iterate through the array elements and print each
         // element's name and value
         for ( reset( $third ); $element = key( $third ); next( $third ) )
            print( "$element is $third[$element] <br />" );

         print( "<br /><strong>Creating the fourth array
            </strong><br />" );

         // call function array to create array fourth using
         // string indices
         $fourth = array(
            "January"   => "first",    "February" => "second",
            "March"     => "third",    "April"    => "fourth",
            "May"       => "fifth",    "June"     => "sixth",
            "July"      => "seventh",  "August"   => "eighth",
            "September" => "ninth",    "October"  => "tenth",
            "November"  => "eleventh","December" => "twelfth"
            );

         // print each element's name and value
         foreach ( $fourth as $element => $value )
            print( "$element is the $value month <br />" );
      ?><!-- end PHP script -->
   </body>
</html>
```

Fig. 23.6 | Array manipulation. (Part 2 of 3.)

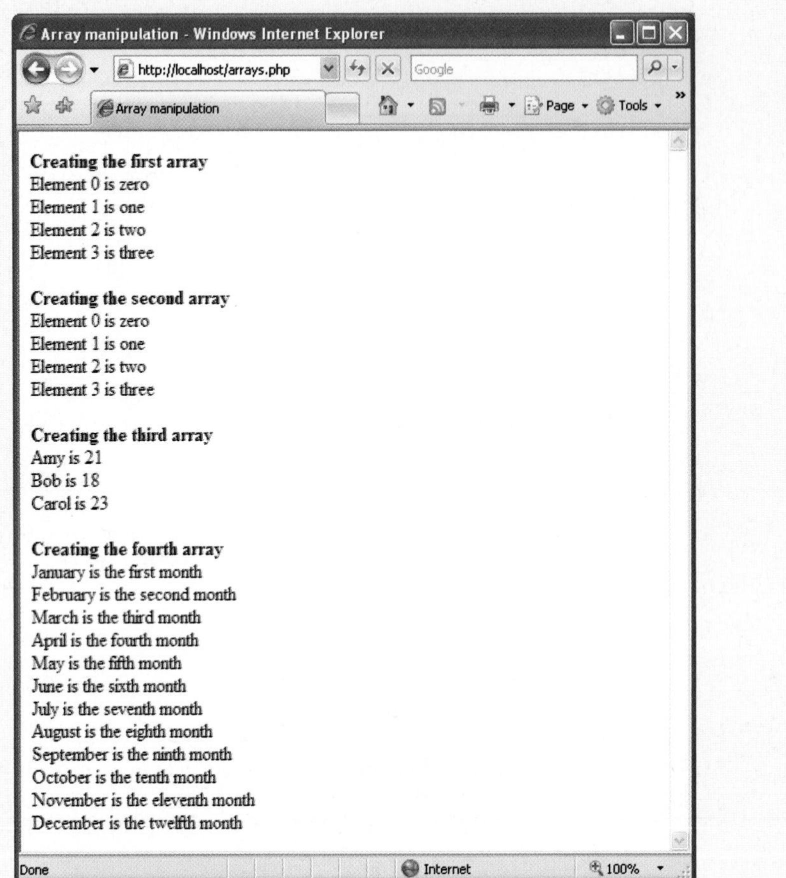

Fig. 23.6 | Array manipulation. (Part 3 of 3.)

In addition to integer indices, arrays can have float or nonnumeric indices (lines 37–39). An array with noninteger indices is called an associative array. For example, indices `Amy`, `Bob` and `Carol` are assigned the values `21`, `18` and `23`, respectively.

PHP provides functions for iterating through the elements of an array (line 43). Each array has a built-in internal pointer, which points to the array element currently being referenced. Function `reset` sets the internal pointer to the first array element. Function `key` returns the index of the element currently referenced by the internal pointer, and function `next` moves the internal pointer to the next element and returns the element. In our script, the `for` statement continues to execute as long as function `key` returns an index. Function `next` returns `false` when there are no more elements in the array. When this occurs, function `key` cannot return an index, `$element` is set to `false` and the `for` statement terminates. Line 44 `print`s the index and value of each element.

The array `$fourth` is also associative. To override the automatic numeric indexing performed by function `array`, you can use operator `=>`, as demonstrated in lines 51–58. The value to the left of the operator is the array index and the value to the right is the element's value.

The foreach control statement (lines 61–62) is specifically designed for iterating through arrays, especially associative arrays, because it does not assume that the array has consecutive integer indices that start at 0. The foreach statement starts with the array to iterate through, followed by the keyword as, followed by two variables—the first is assigned the index of the element, and the second is assigned the value of that index. (If there is only one variable listed after as, it is assigned the value of the array element.) We use the foreach statement to print the index and value of each element in array $fourth.

23.3 String Processing and Regular Expressions

PHP can process text easily and efficiently, enabling straightforward searching, substitution, extraction and concatenation of strings. Text manipulation is usually done with regular expressions—a series of characters that serve as pattern-matching templates (or search criteria) in strings, text files and databases.

23.3.1 Comparing Strings

Many string-processing tasks can be accomplished by using the equality and comparison operators, demonstrated in Fig. 23.7. Line 14 declares and initializes array $fruits. Lines 17–36 iterate through each element in the $fruits array.

```
1  <?php print( '<?xml version = "1.0" encoding = "utf-8"?>' ) ?>
2  <!DOCTYPE html PUBLIC "-//W3C//DTD XHTML 1.0 Strict//EN"
3     "http://www.w3.org/TR/xhtml1/DTD/xhtml1-strict.dtd">
4
5  <!-- Fig. 23.7: compare.php -->
6  <!-- Using the string-comparison operators. -->
7  <html xmlns = "http://www.w3.org/1999/xhtml">
8     <head>
9        <title>String Comparison</title>
10    </head>
11    <body>
12       <?php
13          // create array fruits
14          $fruits = array( "apple", "orange", "banana" );
15
16          // iterate through each array element
17          for ( $i = 0; $i < count( $fruits ); $i++ )
18          {
19             // call function strcmp to compare the array element
20             // to string "banana"
21             if ( strcmp( $fruits[ $i ], "banana" ) < 0 )
22                print( $fruits[ $i ] . " is less than banana " );
23             elseif ( strcmp( $fruits[ $i ], "banana" ) > 0 )
24                print( $fruits[ $i ] . " is greater than banana " );
25             else
26                print( $fruits[ $i ] . " is equal to banana " );
27
28             // use relational operators to compare each element
29             // to string "apple"
```

Fig. 23.7 | Using the string-comparison operators. (Part 1 of 2.)

```
30                  if ( $fruits[ $i ] < "apple" )
31                     print( "and less than apple! <br />" );
32                  elseif ( $fruits[ $i ] > "apple" )
33                     print( "and greater than apple! <br />" );
34                  elseif ( $fruits[ $i ] == "apple" )
35                     print( "and equal to apple! <br />" );
36               } // end for
37            ?><!-- end PHP script -->
38         </body>
39      </html>
```

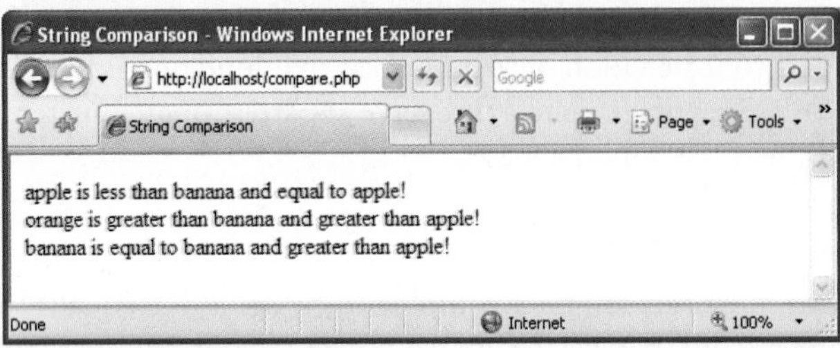

Fig. 23.7 | Using the string-comparison operators. (Part 2 of 2.)

Lines 21 and 23 call function **strcmp** to compare two strings. The function returns -1 if the first string alphabetically precedes the second string, 0 if the strings are equal, and 1 if the first string alphabetically follows the second. Lines 21–26 compare each element in the $fruits array to the string "banana", printing whether each is greater than, less than or equal to the string.

Relational operators (==, !=, <, <=, > and >=) can also be used to compare strings. Lines 30–35 use relational operators to compare each element of the array to the string "apple".

23.3.2 Regular Expressions

Functions **ereg** and **preg_match** use regular expressions to search a string for a specified pattern. Function ereg recognizes Portable Operating System Interface (POSIX) extended regular expressions, while function preg_match provides Perl-compatible regular expressions (PCRE). To use preg_match, you must install the PCRE library on your web server and add support for the library to PHP. More information on PCRE can be found at www.pcre.org. PHP 5 supports POSIX regular expressions, so we use function ereg in this section. Figure 23.8 demonstrates regular expressions.

```
<?php print( '<?xml version = "1.0" encoding = "utf-8"?>' ) ?>
<!DOCTYPE html PUBLIC "-//W3C//DTD XHTML 1.0 Strict//EN"
   "http://www.w3.org/TR/xhtml1/DTD/xhtml1-strict.dtd">

<!-- Fig. 23.8: expression.php -->
<!-- Regular expressions. -->
<html xmlns = "http://www.w3.org/1999/xhtml">
   <head>
```

Fig. 23.8 | Regular expressions. (Part 1 of 2.)

```
      <title>Regular expressions</title>
   </head>
   <body>
      <?php
         $search = "Now is the time";
         print( "Test string is: '$search'<br /><br />" );

         // call ereg to search for pattern 'Now' in variable search
         if ( ereg( "Now", $search ) )
            print( "String 'Now' was found.<br />" );

         // search for pattern 'Now' in the beginning of the string
         if ( ereg( "^Now", $search ) )
            print( "String 'Now' found at beginning
               of the line.<br />" );

         // search for pattern 'Now' at the end of the string
         if ( ereg( "Now$", $search ) )
            print( "String 'Now' was found at the end
               of the line.<br />" );

         // search for any word ending in 'ow'
         if ( ereg( "[[:<:]]([a-zA-Z]*ow)[[:>:]]", $search, $match ) )
            print( "Word found ending in 'ow': " .
               $match[ 1 ] . "<br />" );

         // search for any words beginning with 't'
         print( "Words beginning with 't' found: ");

         while ( eregi( "[[:<:]](t[[:alpha:]]+)[[:>:]]",
            $search, $match ) )
         {
            print( $match[ 1 ] . " " );

           // remove the first occurrence of a word beginning
           // with 't' to find other instances in the string
           $search = ereg_replace( $match[ 1 ], "", $search );
         } // end while
      ?><!-- end PHP script -->
   </body>
</html>
```

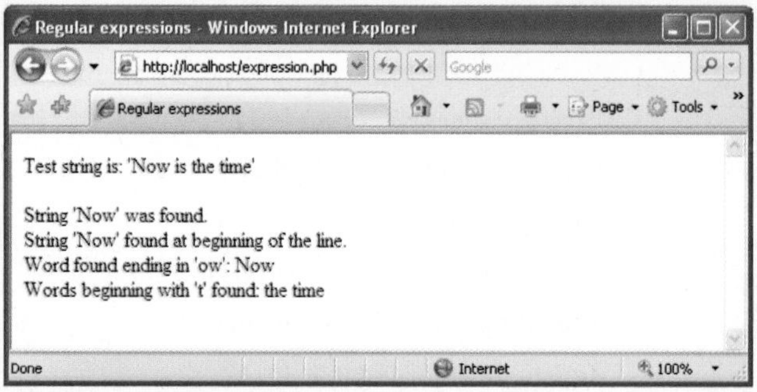

Fig. 23.8 | Regular expressions. (Part 2 of 2.)

Searching for Expressions

Line 13 assigns the string "Now is the time" to variable $search. The condition in line 17 calls function ereg to search for the literal characters "Now" inside variable $search. If the pattern is found, ereg returns the length of the matched string—which evaluates to true in a boolean context—and line 18 prints a message indicating that the pattern was found. We use single quotes ('') inside the string in the print statement to emphasize the search pattern. Anything enclosed in single quotes is not interpolated (unless the single quotes are nested in a double-quoted string literal, as in line 14). For example, '$name' in a print statement would output $name, not variable $name's value.

Function ereg takes two arguments—a regular expression pattern to search for and the string to search. Although case mixture is often significant in patterns, PHP provides function eregi for specifying case-insensitive pattern matches.

Representing Patterns

In addition to literal characters, regular expressions can include metacharacters that specify patterns. Examples of metacharacters include the ^, $ and . characters. The caret (^) metacharacter matches the beginning of a string (line 21), while the dollar sign ($) matches the end of a string (line 26). The period (.) metacharacter matches any single character. Line 21 searches for the pattern "Now" at the beginning of $search. Line 26 searches for "Now" at the end of the string. Since the pattern is not found in this case, the body of the if statement (lines 27–28) does not execute. Note that Now$ is not a variable—it is a pattern that uses $ to search for the characters "Now" at the end of a string.

Line 31 searches (from left to right) for the first word ending with the letters ow. Bracket expressions are lists of characters enclosed in square brackets ([]) that match any single character from the list. Ranges can be specified by supplying the beginning and the end of the range separated by a dash (-). For instance, the bracket expression [a-z] matches any lowercase letter and [A-Z] matches any uppercase letter. In this example, we combine the two to create an expression that matches any letter. The special bracket expressions [[:<:]] and [[:>:]] match the beginning and end of a word, respectively.

The expression [a-zA-Z]*ow inside the parentheses represents any word ending in ow. The quantifier * matches the preceding pattern zero or more times. Thus, [a-zA-Z]*ow matches any number of letters followed by the literal characters ow. Quantifiers are used in regular expressions to denote how often a particular character or set of characters can appear in a match. Some PHP quantifiers are listed in Fig. 23.9.

Quantifier	Matches
{*n*}	Exactly *n* times.
{*m*,*n*}	Between *m* and *n* times, inclusive.
{*n*,}	*n* or more times.
+	One or more times (same as {1,}).
*	Zero or more times (same as {0,}).
?	Zero or one time (same as {0,1}).

Fig. 23.9 | Some PHP quantifiers.

Finding Matches

The optional third argument to function `ereg` is an array that stores matches to the regular expression. When the expression is broken down into parenthetical sub-expressions, function `ereg` stores the first encountered instance of each expression in this array, starting from the leftmost parenthesis. The first element (i.e., index 0) stores the string matched for the entire pattern. The match to the first parenthetical pattern is stored in the second array element, the second in the third array element and so on. If the parenthetical pattern is not encountered, the value of the array element remains uninitialized. Because the statement in line 31 is the first parenthetical pattern, `Now` is stored in variable `$match[ 1 ]` (and, because it is the *only* parenthetical statement in this case, it is also stored in `$match[ 0 ]`).

Searching for multiple instances of a single pattern in a string is slightly more complicated, because the `ereg` function returns only the first instance it encounters. To find multiple instances of a given pattern, we must make multiple calls to `ereg`, and remove any matched instances before calling the function again. Lines 38–46 use a **`while`** statement and the **`ereg_replace`** function to find all the words in the string that begin with `t`. We'll say more about this function momentarily.

Character Classes

The pattern in line 38, `[[:<:]](t[[:alpha:]]+)[[:>:]]`, matches any word beginning with the character `t` followed by one or more letters. The pattern uses the **character class** `[[:alpha:]]` to recognize any letter—this is equivalent to the `[a-zA-Z]`. Figure 23.10 lists some character classes that can be matched with regular expressions.

Character classes are enclosed by the delimiters `[:` and `:]`. When this expression is placed in another set of brackets, such as `[[:alpha:]]` in line 38, it is a regular expression matching a single character that is a member of the class. A bracketed expression containing two or more adjacent character classes in the class delimiters represents those character sets combined. For example, the expression `[[:upper:][:lower:]]*` represents all strings of uppercase and lowercase letters in any order, while `[[:upper:]][[:lower:]]*` matches strings with a single uppercase letter followed by any number of lowercase characters. Also, note that `([[:upper:]][[:lower:]])*` is an expression for all strings that alternate between uppercase and lowercase characters (starting with uppercase and ending with lowercase).

Character class	Description
`alnum`	Alphanumeric characters (i.e., letters `[a-zA-Z]` or digits `[0-9]`).
`alpha`	Word characters (i.e., letters `[a-zA-Z]`).
`digit`	Digits.
`space`	White space.
`lower`	Lowercase letters.
`upper`	Uppercase letters.

Fig. 23.10 | Some PHP character classes.

Finding Multiple Instances of a Pattern

The quantifier + matches one or more consecutive instances of the preceding expression. The result of the match is stored in `$match[ 1 ]`. Once a match is found, we `print` it in line 41. We then remove it from the string in line 45, using function `ereg_replace`. This function takes three arguments—the pattern to match, a string to replace the matched string and the string to search. The modified string is returned. Here, we search for the word that we matched with the regular expression, replace the word with an empty string, then assign the result back to `$search`. This allows us to match any other words beginning with the character `t` in the string and print them to the screen.

23.4 Form Processing and Business Logic

Superglobal Arrays

Knowledge of a client's execution environment is useful to system administrators who want to access client-specific information such as the client's web browser, the server name or the data sent to the server by the client. One way to obtain this data is by using a **superglobal array**. Superglobal arrays are associative arrays predefined by PHP that hold variables acquired from user input, the environment or the web server, and are accessible in any variable scope. Some of PHP's superglobal arrays are listed in Figure 23.11.

Superglobal arrays are useful for verifying user input. The arrays `$_GET` and `$_POST` retrieve information sent to the server by HTTP `get` and `post` requests, respectively, making it possible for a script to have access to this data when it loads another page. For example, if data entered by a user into a form is posted to a script, the `$_POST` array will contain all of this information in the new script. Thus, any information entered into the form can be accessed easily from a confirmation page, or a page that verifies whether fields have been entered correctly.

Variable name	Description
`$_SERVER`	Data about the currently running server.
`$_ENV`	Data about the client's environment.
`$_GET`	Data sent to the server by a `get` request.
`$_POST`	Data sent to the server by a `post` request.
`$_COOKIE`	Data contained in cookies on the client's computer.
`$GLOBALS`	Array containing all global variables.

Fig. 23.11 | Some useful superglobal arrays.

Using PHP to Process XHTML Forms

XHTML forms enable web pages to collect data from users and send it to a web server for processing. Such capabilities allow users to purchase products, request information, send and receive web-based e-mail, create profiles in online networking services and take advantage of various other online services. The XHTML form in Fig. 23.12 gathers information to add a user to a mailing list.

```
<?xml version = "1.0" encoding = "utf-8"?>
<!DOCTYPE html PUBLIC "-//W3C//DTD XHTML 1.0 Strict//EN"
   "http://www.w3.org/TR/xhtml1/DTD/xhtml1-strict.dtd">

<!-- Fig. 23.12: form.html -->
<!-- XHTML form for gathering user input. -->
<html xmlns = "http://www.w3.org/1999/xhtml">
   <head>
      <title>Sample form to take user input in XHTML</title>
      <style type = "text/css">
         .prompt { color: blue;
                   font-family: sans-serif;
                   font-size: smaller }
      </style>
   </head>
   <body>
      <h1>Sample Registration Form</h1>
      <p>Please fill in all fields and click Register.</p>

      <!-- post form data to form.php -->
      <form method = "post" action = "form.php">
         <div>
            <img src = "images/user.gif" alt = "User" /><br />
            <span class = "prompt">
               Please fill out the fields below.<br />
            </span>

            <!-- create four text boxes for user input -->
            <img src = "images/fname.gif" alt = "First Name" />
            <input type = "text" name = "fname" /><br />

            <img src = "images/lname.gif" alt = "Last Name" />
            <input type = "text" name = "lname" /><br />

            <img src = "images/email.gif" alt = "Email" />
            <input type = "text" name = "email" /><br />

            <img src = "images/phone.gif" alt = "Phone" />
            <input type = "text" name = "phone" /><br />

            <span style = "font-size: 10pt">
               Must be in the form (555)555-5555</span>
            <br /><br />

            <img src = "images/downloads.gif"
            alt = "Publications" /><br />

            <span class = "prompt">
               Which book would you like information about?
            </span><br />

            <!-- create drop-down list containing book names -->
            <select name = "book">
```

Fig. 23.12 | XHTML form for gathering user input. (Part 1 of 2.)

```
                  <option>Internet and WWW How to Program 4e</option>
                  <option>C++ How to Program 6e</option>
                  <option>Java How to Program 7e</option>
                  <option>Visual Basic 2005 How to Program 3e</option>
               </select>
               <br /><br />

               <img src = "images/os.gif" alt = "Operating System" />
               <br /><span class = "prompt">
                  Which operating system are you currently using?
               <br /></span>

               <!-- create five radio buttons -->
               <input type = "radio" name = "os" value = "Windows XP"
                  checked = "checked" /> Windows XP
               <input type = "radio" name = "os" value =
                  "Windows Vista" /> Windows Vista<br />
               <input type = "radio" name = "os" value =
                  "Mac OS X" /> Mac OS X
               <input type = "radio" name = "os" value = "Linux" /> Linux
               <input type = "radio" name = "os" value = "Other" />
                  Other<br />

               <!-- create a submit button -->
               <input type = "submit" value = "Register" />
            </div>
         </form>
      </body>
   </html>
```

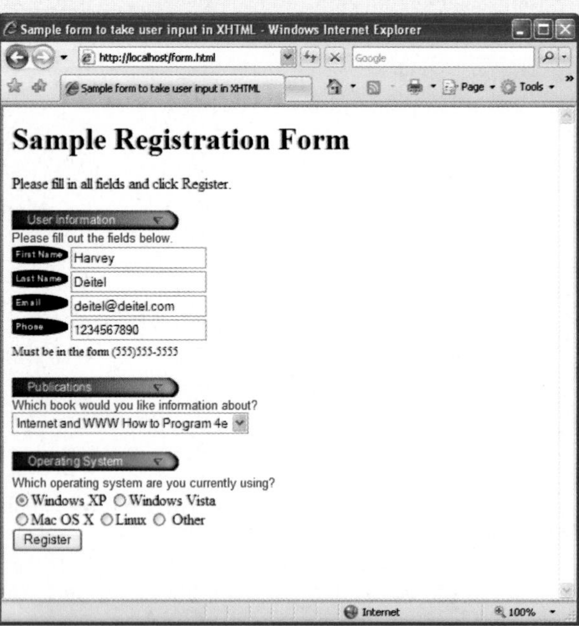

Fig. 23.12 | XHTML form for gathering user input. (Part 2 of 2.)

The `form`'s `action` attribute (line 21) indicates that when the user clicks the **Register** button, the `form` data will be `post`ed to `form.php` (Fig. 23.13) for processing. Using `method = "post"` appends form data to the browser request that contains the protocol (i.e., HTTP) and the URL of the requested resource (specified by the `action` attribute). Scripts located on the web server's machine can access the form data sent as part of the request.

We assign a unique `name` (e.g., `email`) to each of the `form`'s controls. When **Register** is clicked, each field's `name` and `value` are sent to the web server. Script `form.php` accesses the value for each field through the superglobal array `$_POST`, which contains key/value pairs corresponding to name/value pairs for variables submitted through the form. [*Note:* The superglobal array `$_GET` would contain these key/value pairs if the form had been submitted using the HTTP *get* method. In general, `get` is not as secure as `post`, because it appends the information directly to the URL, which is visible to the user.] Figure 23.13 processes the data `post`ed by `form.html` and sends XHTML back to the client.

Good Programming Practice 23.1

Use meaningful XHTML object names for `input` fields. This makes PHP scripts that retrieve `form` data easier to understand.

Function `extract` (line 29 in Fig. 23.13) creates a variable/value pair corresponding to each key/value pair in the associative array passed as an argument (i.e., `$_POST`). This creates variables whose respective names and values correspond to the names and values of each posted `form` field. For example, line 36 in Fig. 23.12 creates an XHTML text box with the name `email`. In line 70 of our PHP script (Fig. 23.13), after having called function `extract`, we access the field's value by using variable `$email`. Elements in `$_POST` can also be accessed using standard array notation. For example, we could have accessed the form field `email`'s value by referring to `$_POST[ 'email' ]`.

```
1  <?php print( '<?xml version = "1.0" encoding = "utf-8"?>' ) ?>
2  <!DOCTYPE html PUBLIC "-//W3C//DTD XHTML 1.0 Strict//EN"
3     "http://www.w3.org/TR/xhtml1/DTD/xhtml1-strict.dtd">
4
5  <!-- Fig. 23.13: form.php -->
6  <!-- Process information sent from form.html. -->
7  <html xmlns = "http://www.w3.org/1999/xhtml">
8     <head>
9        <title>Form Validation</title>
10       <style type = "text/css">
11          body      { font-family: arial, sans-serif }
12          div       { font-size: 10pt;
13                      text-align: center }
14          table     { border: 0 }
15          td        { padding-top: 2px;
16                      padding-bottom: 2px;
17                      padding-left: 10px;
18                      padding-right: 10px }
19          .error    { color: red }
20          .distinct { color: blue }
21          .name     { background-color: #ffffaa }
```

Fig. 23.13 | Process information sent from `form.html`. (Part 1 of 4.)

```
         .email    { background-color: #ffffbb }
         .phone    { background-color: #ffffcc }
         .os       { background-color: #ffffdd }
      </style>
   </head>
   <body>
      <?php
         extract( $_POST );

         // determine whether phone number is valid and print
         // an error message if not
         if ( !ereg( "^\([0-9]{3}\)[0-9]{3}-[0-9]{4}$", $phone ) )
         {
            print( "<p><span class = 'error'>
               Invalid phone number</span><br />
               A valid phone number must be in the form
               <strong>(555)555-5555</strong><br />
               <span class = 'distinct'>
               Click the Back button, enter a valid phone
               number and resubmit.<br /><br />
               Thank You.</span></p>" );
            die( "</body></html>" ); // terminate script execution
         }
      ?><!-- end PHP script -->
      <p>Hi
         <span class = "distinct">
            <strong><?php print( "$fname" ); ?></strong>
         </span>.
         Thank you for completing the survey.<br />
         You have been added to the
         <span class = "distinct">
            <strong><?php print( "$book " ); ?></strong>
         </span>
         mailing list.
      </p>
      <p><strong>The following information has been saved
          in our database:</strong></p>
      <table>
         <tr>
            <td class = "name">Name </td>
            <td class = "email">Email</td>
            <td class = "phone">Phone</td>
            <td class = "os">OS</td>
         </tr>
         <tr>
            <?php
               // print each form field's value
               print( "<td>$fname $lname</td>
                  <td>$email</td>
                  <td>$phone</td>
                  <td>$os</td>" );
            ?><!-- end PHP script -->
         </tr>
```

Fig. 23.13 | Process information sent from `form.html`. (Part 2 of 4.)

```
      </table>
      <br /><br /><br />
      <div>This is only a sample form.
         You have not been added to a mailing list.</div>
   </body>
</html>
```

a) The form in `form.html` is filled out with an incorrect phone number.

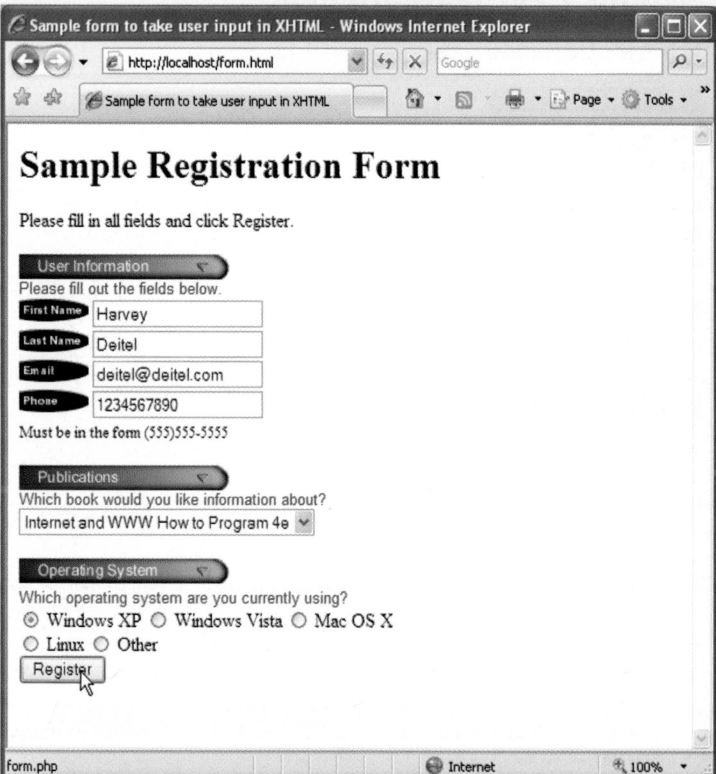

b) The user is redirected to `form.php`, which gives appropriate instructions.

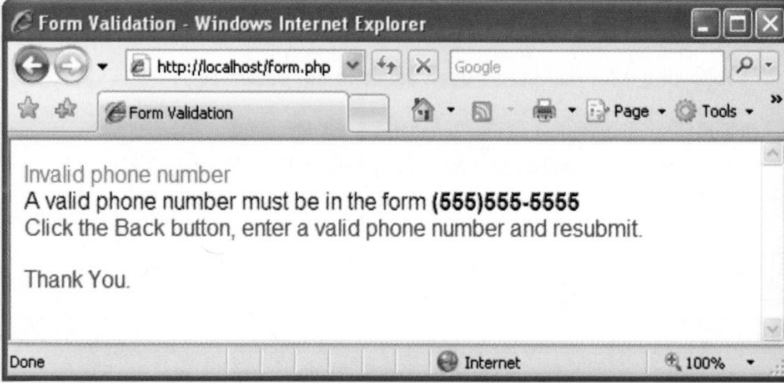

Fig. 23.13 | Process information sent from `form.html`. (Part 3 of 4.)

c) The form is now filled out correctly.

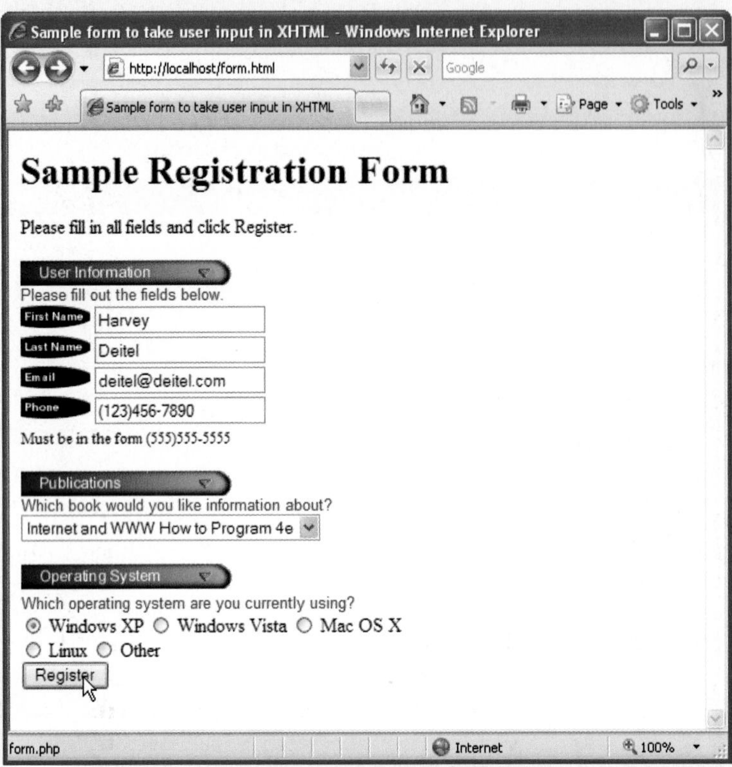

d) The user is directed to an acceptance page, which displays the entered information.

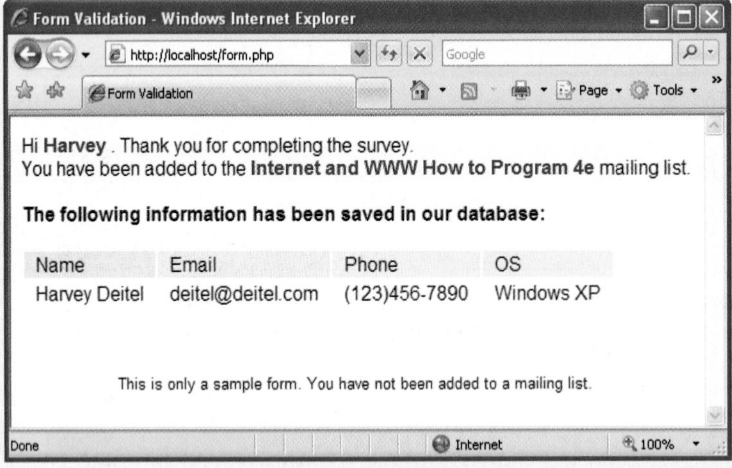

Fig. 23.13 | Process information sent from `form.html`. (Part 4 of 4.)

Line 33 determines whether the phone number entered by the user is valid. In this case, the phone number must begin with an opening parenthesis, followed by an area code, a closing parenthesis, an exchange, a hyphen and a line number. It is crucial to validate information that will be entered into databases or used in mailing lists. For example, validation can be used to ensure that credit card numbers contain the proper number of digits before the numbers are encrypted and sent to a merchant. This script implements the business logic, or business rules, of our application.

Software Engineering Observation 23.1

Use business logic to ensure that invalid information is not stored in databases. When possible, validate important or sensitive form data on the server, since JavaScript may be disabled by the client. Some data, such as passwords, must always be validated on the server side.

The expression `\(` matches the opening parenthesis of the phone number. We want to match the literal character `(`, so we escape its normal meaning by preceding it with the backslash character (\). This parenthesis in the expression must be followed by three digits (`[0-9]{3}`), a closing parenthesis, three more digits, a literal hyphen and four additional digits. Note that we use the `^` and `$` symbols to ensure that no extra characters appear at either end of the string.

If the regular expression is matched, the phone number has a valid format, and an XHTML document is sent to the client that thanks the user for completing the form. Otherwise, the body of the `if` statement executes and displays an error message.

Function `die` (line 43) terminates script execution. This function is called if the user did not enter a correct telephone number, since we do not want to continue executing the rest of the script. The function's optional argument is a string, which is printed as the script exits.

Error-Prevention Tip 23.3

Be sure to close any open XHTML tags when calling function `die`. Not doing so can produce invalid XHTML output that will not display properly in the client browser. Function `die` has an optional parameter that specifies a message to output when exiting, so one technique for closing tags is to close all open tags using `die`, as in `die("</body></html>")`.

23.5 Connecting to a Database

Databases enable companies to enter the world of e-commerce by maintaining crucial data. Database connectivity allows system administrators to maintain and update such information as user accounts, passwords, credit card numbers, mailing lists and product inventories. PHP offers built-in support for many databases. In this example, we use MySQL. Install MySQL using the instructions in Sections 22.6–22.7. Then execute the `Products` script (refer to Section 22.8) from the Script Examples folder of the Chapter 23 examples directory at `www.deitel.com/books/iw3HTP4`.

In this example, the client selects the name of a column in the database. The PHP script then executes—it builds a `SELECT` query, queries the database to obtain the column's data and sends a record set in the form of XHTML to the client. Chapter 22 discusses how to build SQL queries.

Figure 23.14 is a web page that `posts` form data consisting of a selected database column to the server. The script in Fig. 23.15 processes the form data.

```
<?xml version = "1.0" encoding = "utf-8"?>
<!DOCTYPE html PUBLIC "-//W3C//DTD XHTML 1.0 Strict//EN"
   "http://www.w3.org/TR/xhtml1/DTD/xhtml1-strict.dtd">

<!-- Fig. 23.14: data.html -->
<!-- Form to query a MySQL database. -->
<html xmlns = "http://www.w3.org/1999/xhtml">
   <head>
      <title>Sample Database Query</title>
      <style type = "text/css">
         body  { background-color: #F0E68C }
         h2    { font-family: arial, sans-serif;
                 color: blue }
         input { background-color: blue;
                 color: yellow;
                 font-weight: bold }
      </style>
   </head>
   <body>
      <h2> Querying a MySQL database.</h2>
      <form method = "post" action = "database.php">
         <div>
            <p>Select a field to display:
               <!-- add a select box containing options -->
               <!-- for SELECT query -->
               <select name = "select">
                  <option selected = "selected">*</option>
                  <option>ID</option>
                  <option>Title</option>
                  <option>Category</option>
                  <option>ISBN</option>
               </select></p>
            <input type = "submit" value = "Send Query" />
         </div>
      </form>
   </body>
</html>
```

Fig. 23.14 | Form to query a MySQL database.

```
<?php print( '<?xml version = "1.0" encoding = "utf-8"?>' ) ?>
<!DOCTYPE html PUBLIC "-//W3C//DTD XHTML 1.0 Strict//EN"
   "http://www.w3.org/TR/xhtml1/DTD/xhtml1-strict.dtd">

<!-- Fig. 23.15: database.php -->
<!-- Querying a database and displaying the results. -->
<html xmlns = "http://www.w3.org/1999/xhtml">
   <head>
      <title>Search Results</title>
   <style type = "text/css">
         body  { font-family: arial, sans-serif;
                 background-color: #F0E68C }
         table { background-color: #ADD8E6 }
         td    { padding-top: 2px;
                 padding-bottom: 2px;
                 padding-left: 4px;
                 padding-right: 4px;
                 border-width: 1px;
                 border-style: inset }
      </style>
   </head>
   <body>
      <?php
         extract( $_POST );

         // build SELECT query
         $query = "SELECT " . $select . " FROM books";

         // Connect to MySQL
         if ( !( $database = mysql_connect( "localhost",
            "iw3htp4", "iw3htp4" ) ) )
            die( "Could not connect to database </body></html>" );

         // open Products database
         if ( !mysql_select_db( "products", $database ) )
            die( "Could not open products database </body></html>" );

         // query Products database
         if ( !( $result = mysql_query( $query, $database ) ) )
         {
            print( "Could not execute query! <br />" );
            die( mysql_error() . "</body></html>" );
         } // end if

         mysql_close( $database );
      ?><!-- end PHP script -->
      <h3>Search Results</h3>
      <table>
         <?php
            // fetch each record in result set
            for ( $counter = 0; $row = mysql_fetch_row( $result );
               $counter++ )
            {
```

Fig. 23.15 | Querying a database and displaying the results. (Part 1 of 2.)

```
54                // build table to display results
55                print( "<tr>" );
56
57                foreach ( $row as $key => $value )
58                   print( "<td>$value</td>" );
59
60                print( "</tr>" );
61             } // end for
62          ?><!-- end PHP script -->
63       </table>
64       <br />Your search yielded <strong>
65       <?php print( "$counter" ) ?> results.<br /><br /></strong>
66       <h5>Please email comments to
67          <a href = "mailto:deitel@deitel.com">
68             Deitel and Associates, Inc.</a>
69       </h5>
70    </body>
71 </html>
```

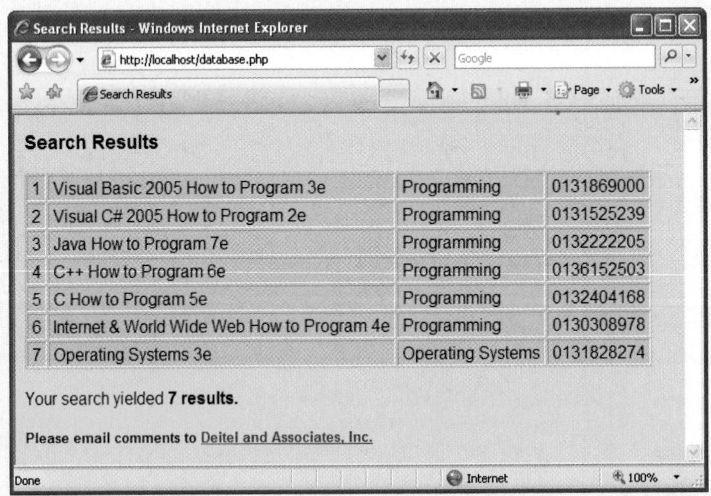

Fig. 23.15 | Querying a database and displaying the results. (Part 2 of 2.)

Line 21 of Fig. 23.14 creates an XHTML `form`, specifying that the data submitted from the `form` will be sent to script `database.php` (Fig. 23.15) in a `post` request. Lines 26–32 add a select box to the `form`, set the name of the select box to `select` and set its default selection to *. This value specifies that all rows and columns are to be retrieved from the database. Each database column is set as an option in the select box.

Script `database.php` (Fig. 23.15) builds a SQL query with the specified field name and sends it to the database management system. Line 27 concatenates the `posted` field name to a SELECT query. Line 30 calls function **`mysql_connect`** to connect to the MySQL database. We pass three arguments to function `mysql_connect`—the server's hostname, a username and a password (in this case, both our username and password are `iw3htp4`, based on the account we set up in Chapter 22). This function returns a **database handle**—

a representation of PHP's connection to the database—which we assign to variable `$database`. If the connection to MySQL fails, the function returns `false` and function `die` is called to output an error message and terminate the script. Line 35 calls function `mysql_select_db` to specify the database to be queried (in this case, `products`), which returns `true` on success or `false` on failure. Function `die` is called if the database cannot be opened.

To query the database, line 39 calls function `mysql_query`, specifying the query string and the database to query. If the query fails, the function returns `false`. Function `die` is then called with a call to function `mysql_error` as an argument. Function `mysql_error` returns any error strings from the database. If the query succeeds, `mysql_query` returns a `resource` containing the query result, which we assign to variable `$result`. Once we have stored the data in `$result`, we call `mysql_close` in line 45 to close the connection to the database. Function `mysql_query` can also execute SQL statements such as `INSERT` or `DELETE` that do not return results.

Lines 51–61 iterate through each record in the result set and construct an XHTML table from the results. The `for` statement's condition calls function `mysql_fetch_row` to return an array containing the values for each column of the current row in the query result (`$result`). The array is stored in variable `$row`. Lines 57–58 construct individual cells for each column in the row. The `foreach` statement takes the name of the array (`$row`), iterates through each index value of the array (`$key`) and stores the value in variable `$value`. Each element of the array is then printed as an individual cell. When the result has no more rows, `false` is returned by function `mysql_fetch_row`, which terminates the `for` statement.

After all the rows in the result have been displayed, the table's closing tag is written (line 63). The number of rows contained in `$counter` is printed in line 65. Alternatively, calling function `mysql_num_rows( $result )` would return the number of rows in the result.

23.6 Using Cookies

A cookie is a piece of information stored in a text file on a client's computer to maintain information about the client during and between browsing sessions. A website can store a cookie on a client's computer to record user preferences and other information that the website can retrieve during the client's subsequent visits. For example, a website can use cookies to store clients' zip codes, so that it can provide weather reports and news updates tailored to the user's region. Websites also can use cookies to track information about client activity. Analysis of information collected via cookies can reveal the popularity of websites or products. In addition, marketers can use cookies to determine the effects of advertising campaigns.

Websites store cookies on users' hard drives, which raises issues regarding security and privacy. Websites should not store critical information, such as credit card numbers or passwords, in cookies, because cookies are typically stored in text files that any program can read. Several cookie features address security and privacy concerns. A server can access only the cookies that it has placed on the client. For example, a web application running on `www.deitel.com` cannot access cookies that the website `www.prenhall.com` has placed on the client's computer. A cookie also has an expiration date, after which the web browser deletes it. Users who are concerned about the privacy and security implications of cookies can disable cookies in their web browsers. However, disabling cookies can make it impossible for the user to interact with websites that rely on cookies to function properly.

The information stored in a cookie is sent back to the web server from which it originated whenever the user requests a web page from that particular server. The web server can send the client XHTML output that reflects the preferences or information that is stored in the cookie.

Writing Cookies

Figure 23.16 uses a script to write a cookie to the client's machine. The `cookies.html` file displays an XHTML `form` that allows a user to enter a name, height and favorite color. When the user clicks the **Write Cookie** button, the `cookies.php` script (Fig. 23.17) executes.

```
<?xml version = "1.0" encoding = "utf-8"?>
<!DOCTYPE html PUBLIC "-//W3C//DTD XHTML 1.0 Strict//EN"
   "http://www.w3.org/TR/xhtml1/DTD/xhtml1-strict.dtd">

<!-- Fig. 23.16: cookies.html -->
<!-- Gathering data to be written as a cookie. -->
<html xmlns = "http://www.w3.org/1999/xhtml">
   <head>
      <title>Writing a cookie to the client computer</title>
      <style type = "text/css">
         body    { font-family: arial, sans-serif;
                   background-color: #99CCFF }
         form    { font-size: 10pt }
         .submit { background-color: #F0E86C;
                   color: navy;
                   font-weight: bold }
      </style>
   </head>
   <body>
      <h2>Click Write Cookie to save your cookie data.</h2>
      <form method = "post" action = "cookies.php">
         <div>
            <strong>Name:</strong><br />
            <input type = "text" name = "Name" /><br />

            <strong>Height:</strong><br />
            <input type = "text" name = "Height" /><br />

            <strong>Favorite Color:</strong><br />
            <input type = "text" name = "Color" /><br />

            <input type = "submit" value = "Write Cookie"
               class = "submit" />
         </div>
      </form>
   </body>
</html>
```

Fig. 23.16 | Gathering data to be written as a cookie. (Part 1 of 2.)

Fig. 23.16 | Gathering data to be written as a cookie. (Part 2 of 2.)

```
<?php
   // Fig. 23.17: cookies.php
   // Writing a cookie to the client.
   extract( $_POST );

   // write each form field's value to a cookie and set the
   // cookie's expiration date
   setcookie( "Name", $Name, time() + 60 * 60 * 24 * 5 );
   setcookie( "Height", $Height, time() + 60 * 60 * 24 * 5 );
   setcookie( "Color", $Color, time() + 60 * 60 * 24 * 5 );
?><!-- end PHP script -->

<?php print( '<?xml version = "1.0" encoding = "utf-8"?>' ) ?>
<!DOCTYPE html PUBLIC "-//W3C//DTD XHTML 1.0 Strict//EN"
   "http://www.w3.org/TR/xhtml1/DTD/xhtml1-strict.dtd">

<html xmlns = "http://www.w3.org/1999/xhtml">
   <head>
      <title>Cookie Saved</title>
      <style type = "text/css">
         body { font-family: arial, sans-serif }
         span { color: blue }
      </style>
   </head>
   <body>
      <p>The cookie has been set with the following data:</p>

      <!-- print each form field's value -->
      <br /><span>Name:</span><?php print( $Name ) ?><br />
```

Fig. 23.17 | Writing a cookie to the client. (Part 1 of 2.)

```
30          <span>Height:</span><?php print( $Height ) ?><br />
31          <span>Favorite Color:</span>
32          <span style = "color: <?php print( "$Color\">$Color" ) ?>
33          </span><br />
34          <p>Click <a href = "readCookies.php">here</a>
35             to read the saved cookie.</p>
36       </body>
37    </html>
```

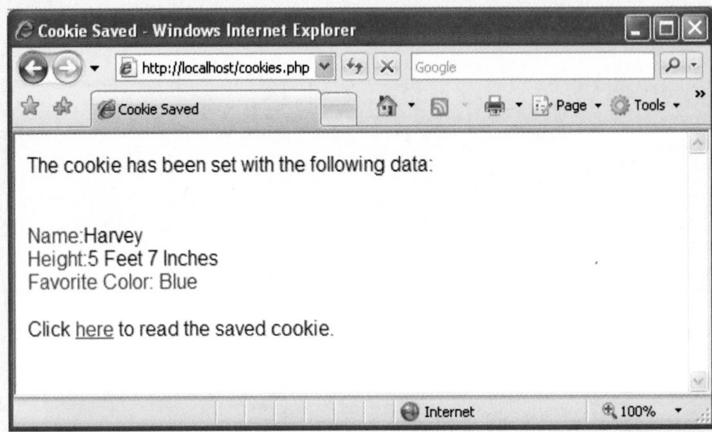

Fig. 23.17 | Writing a cookie to the client. (Part 2 of 2.)

Software Engineering Observation 23.2

Some clients do not accept cookies. When a client declines a cookie, the browser application normally informs the user that the site may not function correctly without cookies enabled.

Software Engineering Observation 23.3

Cookies should not be used to store e-mail addresses or private data on a client's computer.

Script `cookies.php` (Fig. 23.17) calls function `setcookie` (lines 8–10) to set the cookies to the values passed from `cookies.html`. The cookies defined in function `setcookie` are sent to the client at the same time as the information in the HTTP header; therefore, `setcookie` needs to be called before any XHTML (including comments) is printed.

Function `setcookie` takes the name of the cookie to be set as the first argument, followed by the value to be stored in the cookie. For example, line 8 sets the name of the cookie to `"Name"` and the value to variable `$Name`, which is passed to the script from `cookies.html`. The optional third argument indicates the expiration date of the cookie. In this example, we set the cookies to expire in five days by taking the current time, which is returned by function `time`, and adding the number of seconds after which the cookie is to expire (60 seconds/minute `* 60` minutes/hour `* 24` hours/day `* 5 = 5` days). If no expiration date is specified, the cookie lasts only until the end of the current session, which is the total time until the user closes the browser. This type of cookie is known as a session cookie, while one with an expiration date is a persistent cookie. If only the `name` argument is passed to function `setcookie`, the cookie is deleted from the client's computer. Lines 13–37 send a web page to the client indicating that the cookie has been written and listing the values that are stored in the cookie.

When using Internet Explorer, cookies are stored in a **Cookies** directory on the client's machine, while Firefox stores them in a single file called `cookies.txt`. Figure 23.18 shows the contents of this directory (for a Windows XP and IE7 user `harvey`) prior to the execution of `cookies.php`. After the cookie is written, a text file is added to the directory. In Fig. 23.19, the file `harvey@localhost[1].txt` appears in the **Cookies** directory. [*Note:* The name of the file created will vary from user to user.]

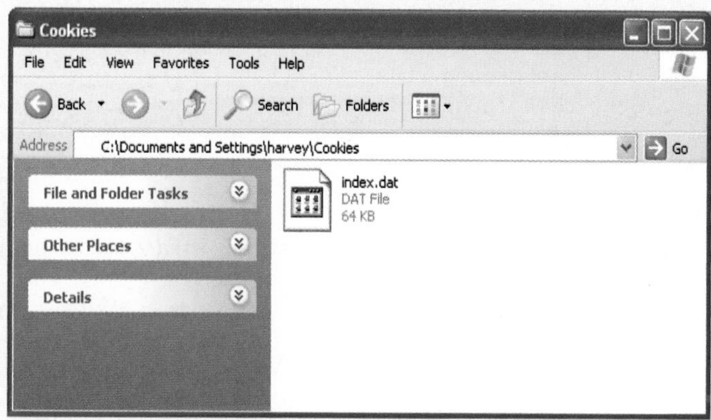

Fig. 23.18 | IE7's `Cookies` directory before a cookie is written.

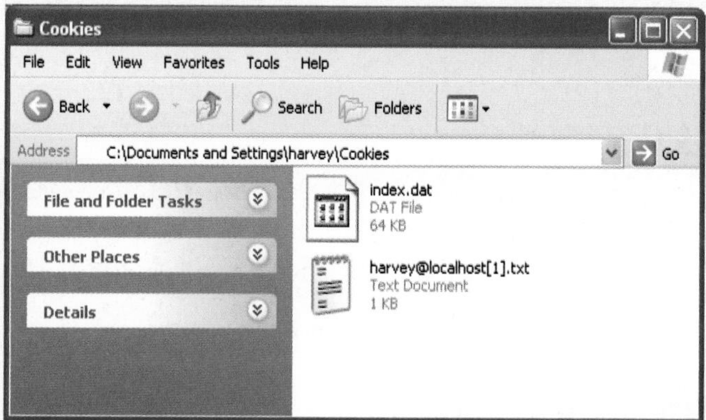

Fig. 23.19 | IE7's `Cookies` directory after a cookie is written.

Reading an Existing Cookie

Figure 23.20 reads the cookie that was written in Fig. 23.17 and displays the cookie's information in a table. PHP creates the superglobal array `$_COOKIE`, which contains all the cookie values indexed by their names, similar to the values stored in array `$_POST` when an XHTML form is posted (see Section 23.4).

```
<?php print( '<?xml version = "1.0" encoding = "utf-8"?>' ) ?>
<!DOCTYPE html PUBLIC "-//W3C//DTD XHTML 1.0 Strict//EN"
   "http://www.w3.org/TR/xhtml1/DTD/xhtml1-strict.dtd">

<!-- Fig. 23.20: readCookies.php -->
<!-- Displaying the cookie's contents. -->
<html xmlns = "http://www.w3.org/1999/xhtml">
   <head>
      <title>Read Cookies</title>
      <style type = "text/css">
         body   { font-family: arial, sans-serif }
         table  { border-width: 5px;
                  border-style: outset }
         td     { padding: 10px }
         .key   { background-color: #F0E68C }
         .value { background-color: #FFA500 }
      </style>
   </head>
   <body>
      <p>
         <strong>The following data is saved in a cookie on your
            computer.</strong>
      </p>
      <table>
         <?php
            // iterate through array $_COOKIE and print
            // name and value of each cookie
            foreach ( $_COOKIE as $key => $value )
               print( "<tr><td class = 'key' >$key</td>
                  <td class = 'value' >$value</td></tr>" );
         ?><!-- end PHP script -->
      </table>
   </body>
</html>
```

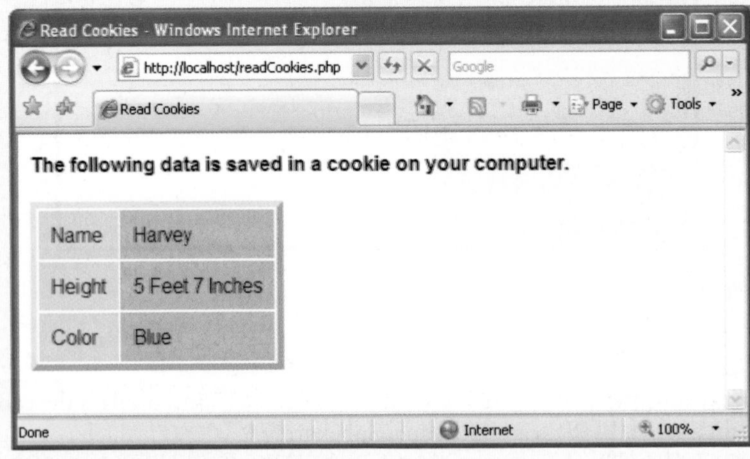

Fig. 23.20 | Displaying the cookie's contents.

Lines 28–30 iterate through the `$_COOKIE` array using a `foreach` statement, printing out the name and value of each cookie in an XHTML table. The `foreach` statement takes the name of the array (`$_COOKIE`) and iterates through each index value of the array (`$key`). In this case, the index values are the names of the cookies. Each element is then stored in variable `$value`, and these values become the individual cells of the table.

We could have also used the function `extract` to create individual variables out of the key-value pairs in `$_COOKIE`, just as we did with `$_POST`. For example, after the function `extract( $_COOKIE )` is called, the value of a cookie set with the name `"Color"` is assigned to variable `$Color`. Try closing your browser and revisiting readCookies.php to confirm that the cookie has persisted.

23.7 Dynamic Content

PHP can dynamically change the XHTML it outputs based on a user's input. We now build on Section 23.4's example by combining the XHTML form of Fig. 23.12 and the PHP script of Fig. 23.13 into one dynamic document. The form in Fig. 23.21 is created using a series of loops, arrays and conditionals. We add error checking to each of the text input fields and inform the user of invalid entries on the form itself, rather than on an error page. If an error exists, the script maintains the previously submitted values in each form element. Finally, after the form has been successfully completed, we store the input from the user in a MySQL database. Before running the following example, make sure MySQL is installed, then execute the `MailingList` script (refer to Section 22.8) from the Script Examples folder of the Chapter 23 examples directory at `www.deitel.com/books/iw3HTP4`.

Lines 36–47 create three arrays, $booklist, `$systemlist` and `$inputlist`, that are used to dynamically create the form's input fields. We specify that the `form` created in this document is self-submitting (i.e., it `posts` to itself) by setting the `action` to `'dynamicForm.php'` in line 148. [*Note:* We enclose XHTML attribute values in the string argument of a `print` statement in single quotes so that they do not interfere with the double quotes that delimit the string. We could alternatively have used the escape sequence \" to print double quotes instead of single quotes.] Line 50 uses function `isset` to determine whether the **Register** button has been pressed. If it has, each of the text input fields' values is validated. If an error is detected (e.g., a text field is blank or the phone number is improperly formatted), an entry is added to array `$formerrors` containing a key corresponding to the field name with the error and a value of true. Also, variable `$iserror` is set to `true`. If the **Register** button has not been pressed, we skip ahead to line 138.

```
1  <?php print( '<?xml version = "1.0" encoding = "utf-8"?>' ) ?>
2  <!DOCTYPE html PUBLIC "-//W3C//DTD XHTML 1.0 Strict//EN"
3     "http://www.w3.org/TR/xhtml1/DTD/xhtml1-strict.dtd">
4
5  <!-- Fig. 23.21: dynamicForm.php -->
6  <!-- Dynamic form. -->
7  <html xmlns = "http://www.w3.org/1999/xhtml">
8     <head>
9        <title>Sample form to take user input in XHTML</title>
10       <style type = "text/css">
```

Fig. 23.21 | Dynamic form. (Part 1 of 7.)

```
        td          { padding-top: 2px;
                      padding-bottom: 2px;
                      padding-left: 10px;
                      padding-right: 10px }
        div         { text-align: center }
        div div     { font-size: larger }
        .name       { background-color: #ffffaa }
        .email      { background-color: #ffffbb }
        .phone      { background-color: #ffffcc }
        .os         { background-color: #ffffdd }
        .smalltext  { font-size: smaller }
        .prompt     { color: blue;
                      font-family: sans-serif;
                      font-size: smaller }
        .largeerror { color: red }
        .error      { color: red;
                      font-size: smaller }
      </style>
   </head>
   <body>
      <?php
        extract( $_POST );
        $iserror = false;

        // array of book titles
        $booklist = array( "Internet and WWW How to Program 4e",
           "C++ How to Program 6e", "Java How to Program 7e",
           "Visual Basic 2005 How to Program 3e" );

        // array of possible operating systems
        $systemlist = array( "Windows XP", "Windows Vista",
           "Mac OS X", "Linux", "Other");

        // array of name values for the text input fields
        $inputlist = array( "fname" => "First Name",
           "lname" => "Last Name", "email" => "Email",
           "phone" => "Phone" );

        // ensure that all fields have been filled in correctly
        if ( isset ( $submit ) )
        {
           if ( $fname == "" )
           {
              $formerrors[ "fnameerror" ] = true;
              $iserror = true;
           } // end if

           if ( $lname == "" )
           {
              $formerrors[ "lnameerror" ] = true;
              $iserror = true;
           } // end if

```

Fig. 23.21 | Dynamic form. (Part 2 of 7.)

```
         if ( $email == "" )
         {
            $formerrors[ "emailerror" ] = true;
            $iserror = true;
         } // end if

         if ( !ereg( "^\([0-9]{3}\)[0-9]{3}-[0-9]{4}$", $phone ) )
         {
            $formerrors[ "phoneerror" ] = true;
            $iserror = true;
         } // end if

         if ( !$iserror )
         {
            // build INSERT query
            $query = "INSERT INTO contacts " .
               "( LastName, FirstName, Email, Phone, Book, OS ) " .
               "VALUES ( '$lname', '$fname', '$email', " .
               "'" . quotemeta( $phone ) . "', '$book', '$os' )";

            // Connect to MySQL
            if ( !( $database = mysql_connect( "localhost",
               "iw3htp4", "iw3htp4" ) ) )
               die( "Could not connect to database" );

            // open MailingList database
            if ( !mysql_select_db( "MailingList", $database ) )
               die( "Could not open MailingList database" );

            // execute query in MailingList database
            if ( !( $result = mysql_query( $query, $database ) ) )
            {
               print( "Could not execute query! <br />" );
               die( mysql_error() );
            } // end if

            mysql_close( $database );

            print( "<p>Hi<span class = 'prompt'>
               <strong>$fname</strong></span>.
               Thank you for completing the survey.<br />

               You have been added to the
               <span class = 'prompt'>
               <strong>$book</strong></span>
               mailing list.</p>
               <strong>The following information has been saved
               in our database:</strong><br />

               <table><tr>
               <td class = 'name'>Name </td>
               <td class = 'email'>Email</td>
               <td class = 'phone'>Phone</td>
```

Fig. 23.21 | Dynamic form. (Part 3 of 7.)

```
                  <td class = 'os'>OS</td>
                  </tr><tr>

                  <!-- print each form field's value -->
                  <td>$fname $lname</td>
                  <td>$email</td>
                  <td>$phone</td>
                  <td>$os</td>
                  </tr></table>

                  <br /><br /><br />
                  <div><div>
                  <a href = 'formDatabase.php'>
                  Click here to view entire database.</a>
                  </div>This is only a sample form.
                  You have not been added to a mailing list.
                  </div></body></html>" );
               die();
            } // end if
         } // end if

         print( "<h1>Sample Registration Form.</h1>
            Please fill in all fields and click Register." );

         if ( $iserror )
         {
            print( "<br /><span class = 'largeerror'>
               Fields with * need to be filled in properly.</span>" );
         } // end if

         print( "<!-- post form data to form.php -->
            <form method = 'post' action = 'dynamicForm.php'>
            <img src = 'images/user.gif' alt = 'User' /><br />
            <span class = 'prompt'>
            Please fill out the fields below.<br /> </span>

            <!-- create four text boxes for user input -->" );
         foreach ( $inputlist as $inputname => $inputalt )
         {
            $inputtext = $inputvalues[ $inputname ];

            print( "<img src = 'images/$inputname.gif'
               alt = '$inputalt' /><input type = 'text'
               name = '$inputname' value = '" . $$inputname . "' />" );

            if ( $formerrors[ ( $inputname )."error" ] == true )
               print( "<span class = 'error'>*</span>" );

            print( "<br />" );
         } // end foreach

         if ( $formerrors[ "phoneerror" ] )
            print( "<span class = 'error'>" );
```

Fig. 23.21 | Dynamic form. (Part 4 of 7.)

```
         else
            print("<span class = 'smalltext'>");

         print( "Must be in the form (555)555-5555
            </span><br /><br />

            <img src = 'images/downloads.gif'
               alt = 'Publications' /><br />

            <span class = 'prompt'>
            Which book would you like information about?
            </span><br />

            <!-- create drop-down list containing book names -->
            <select name = 'book'>" );

         foreach ( $booklist as $currbook )
         {
            print( "<option" );

            if ( ( $currbook == $book ) )
               print( " selected = 'true'" );

            print( ">$currbook</option>" );
         } // end foreach

         print( "</select><br /><br />
            <img src = 'images/os.gif' alt = 'Operating System' />
            <br /><span class = 'prompt'>
            Which operating system are you currently using?
            <br /></span>

            <!-- create five radio buttons -->" );

         $counter = 0;

         foreach ( $systemlist as $currsystem )
         {
            print( "<input type = 'radio' name = 'os'
               value = '$currsystem'" );

            if ( $currsystem == $os )
                  print( "checked = 'checked'" );
            elseif ( !$os && $counter == 0 )
               print( "checked = 'checked'" );

            print( " />$currsystem" );

            // put a line break in list of operating systems
            if ( $counter == 1 ) print( "<br />" );
            ++$counter;
         } // end foreach

```

Fig. 23.21 | Dynamic form. (Part 5 of 7.)

```
            print( "<!-- create a submit button -->
               <br /><input type = 'submit' name = 'submit'
               value = 'Register' /></form></body></html>" );
      ?><!-- end PHP script -->
```

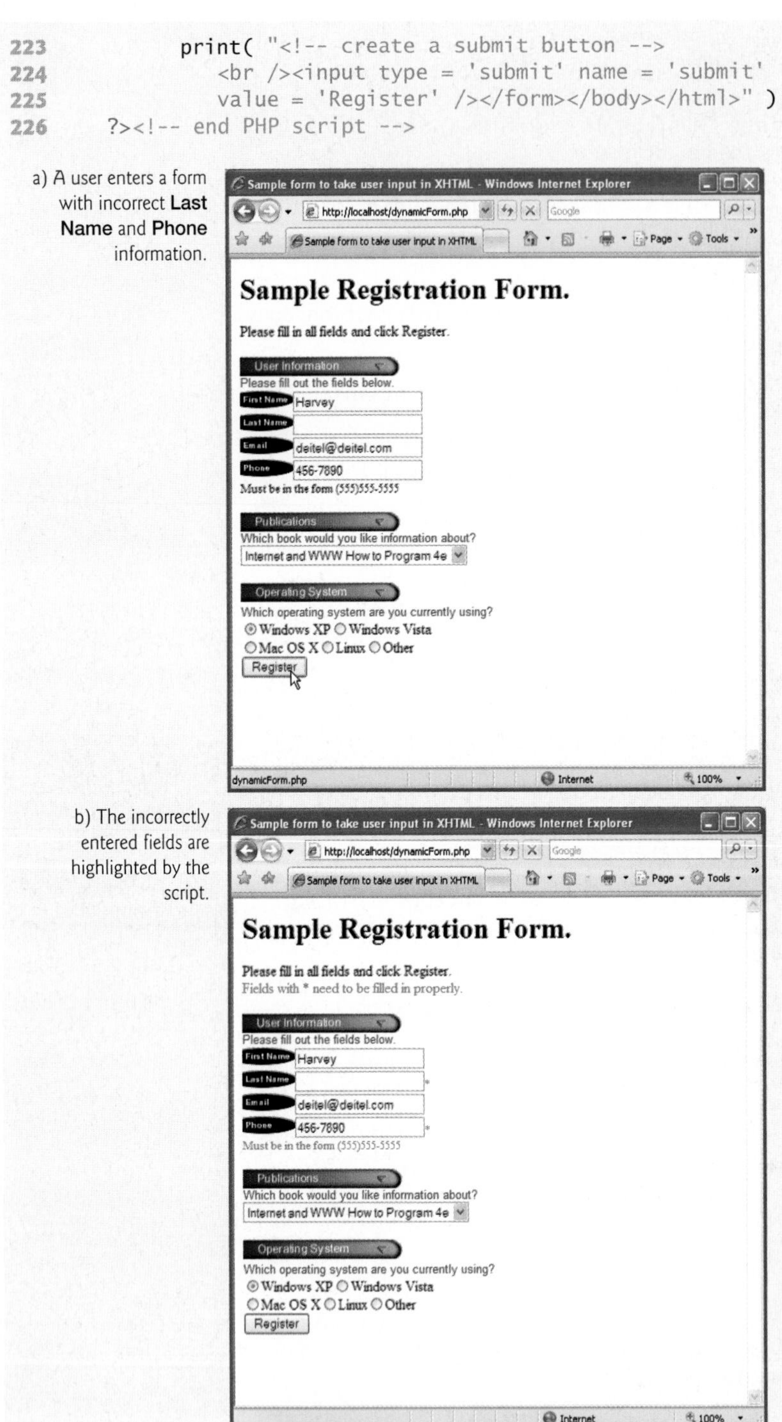

Fig. 23.21 | Dynamic form. (Part 6 of 7.)

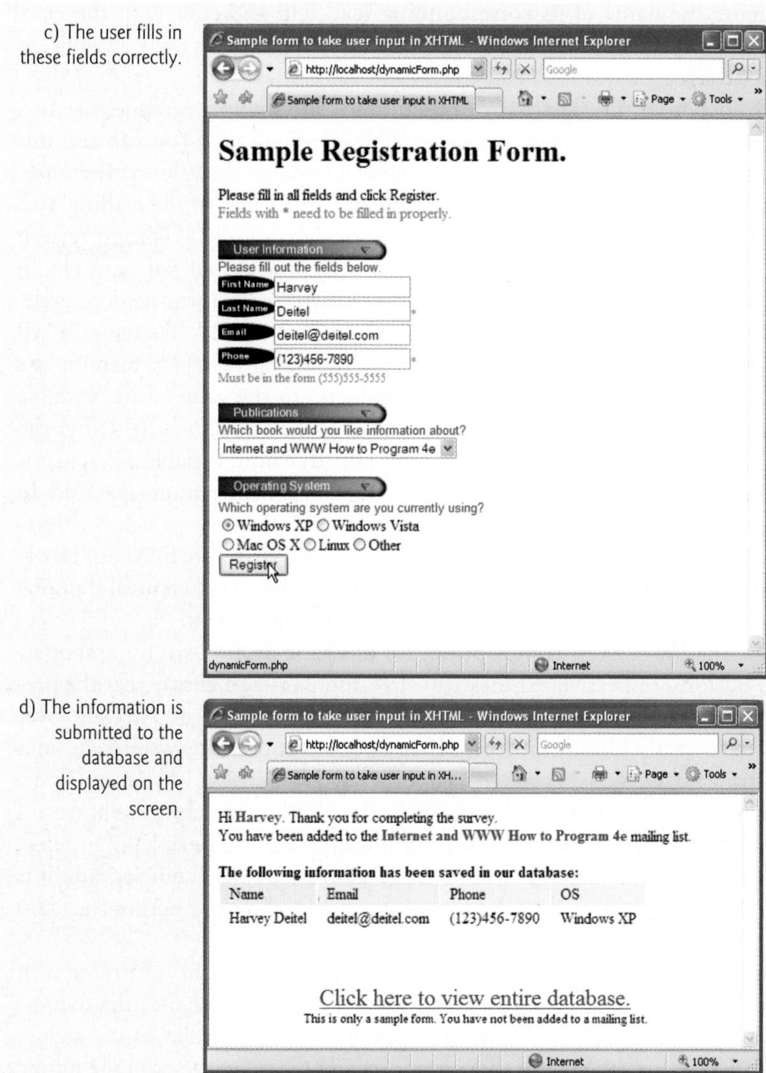

Fig. 23.21 | Dynamic form. (Part 7 of 7.)

Line 76 determines whether any errors were detected. If `$iserror` is `false` (i.e., there were no input errors), lines 79–133 display the page indicating that the form was submitted successfully. We will say more about lines 79–133 later. If `$iserror` is `true`, the script from lines 79–133 is skipped, and the code from lines 138–224 executes. These lines include a series of `print` statements and conditionals to output the form, as seen in Fig. 23.21(a). Lines 154–166 iterate through each element in the `$inputlist` array. In line 156 the value of variable `$inputtext` is assigned to the text field's `value` attribute. If the form has not yet been submitted, variable `$inputtext`'s value will be the empty string `""`. Lines 158–159 output the image that corresponds to each text field. The image `src` is set to `'images/$inputname.gif'` because the images are stored in the `images` directory, and each image shares the name of its corresponding text field and ends with the `.gif` extension. Lines 159–160 initialize the `input` text field. The text field's `name` attribute is set to variable `$inputname`.

In line 160 we encounter the **`$$variable`** notation for specifying a **variable variable**. A variable variable allows the code to reference variables dynamically. You can use this expression to obtain the value of the variable whose name is equal to the value of `$`*variable*. PHP first determines the value of `$`*variable*, then appends this value to the leading `$` to form the identifier of the variable you wish to reference dynamically. (The expression `$$`*variable* can also be written as `${$`*variable*`}` to convey this procedure.) For example, in lines 154–166, we write `$$inputname` to reference the value of each form-field variable. During the iteration of the loop, `$inputname` contains the value `"email"`. Therefore, PHP replaces `$inputname` in the expression `$$inputname` with the string `"email"`, forming the expression `${"email"}`. The entire expression then evaluates to the value of the variable `$email`. Thus, the variable `$email`, which stores the value of the e-mail text field after the form has been submitted, is dynamically referenced. This dynamic variable reference is added to the string as the value of the input field (using the concatenation operator) to maintain data over multiple submissions of the form.

Lines 162–163 add a red asterisk next to the text input fields that were filled out incorrectly. Lines 168–169 color the phone instructions red if the user entered an invalid phone number by assigning the class `error` to the span tag surrounding the text.

Lines 186–194 and 206–221 generate options for the book drop-down list and operating-system radio buttons, respectively. Lines 190–191 and 211–214 ensure that the previously selected or checked element (if one exists) remains selected or checked over multiple attempts to correctly fill out the form. If any book was previously selected, lines 190–191 add the string `selected = 'true'` to its option tag. Lines 211–214 select an operating system radio button under two conditions. First, lines 211–212 select the button if it was previously selected, before an unsuccessful submit operation. Lines 213–214 select the first radio button only if the form has not yet been submitted (`$os` is not set) and it is the first radio button. This ensures that the form cannot be submitted without a radio button selected.

If the form has been filled out correctly, lines 79–98 place the form information in the MySQL database `MailingList` using an `INSERT` statement. Line 82 uses the **`quotemeta`** function to insert a backslash (\) before any special characters in the passed string. We must use this function so that MySQL does not interpret the parentheses in the phone number as having a special meaning aside from being part of a value to insert into the database. Lines 102–133 generate the web page indicating a successful form submission, which also provides a link to `formDatabase.php` (Fig. 23.22). This script displays the contents of the `MailingList` database.

```
<?php print( '<?xml version = "1.0" encoding = "utf-8"?>' ) ?>
<!DOCTYPE html PUBLIC "-//W3C//DTD XHTML 1.0 Strict//EN"
   "http://www.w3.org/TR/xhtml1/DTD/xhtml1-strict.dtd">

<!-- Fig. 23.22: formDatabase.php -->
<!-- Displaying the MailingList database. -->
```

Fig. 23.22 | Displaying the `MailingList` database. (Part 1 of 3.)

```
<html xmlns = "http://www.w3.org/1999/xhtml">
   <head>
      <title>Search Results</title>
      <style type = "text/css">
         body  { font-family: arial, sans-serif;
                 background-color: #F0E68C }
         h3    { color: blue }
         table { background-color: #ADD8E6 }
         td    { padding-top: 2px;
                 padding-bottom: 2px;
                 padding-left: 4px;
                 padding-right: 4px;
                 border-width: 1px;
                 border-style: inset }
      </style>
   </head>
   <body>
      <?php
         extract( $_POST );

         // build SELECT query
         $query = "SELECT * FROM contacts";

         // Connect to MySQL
         if ( !( $database = mysql_connect( "localhost",
            "iw3htp4", "iw3htp4" ) ) )
            die( "Could not connect to database </body></html>" );

         // open MailingList database
         if ( !mysql_select_db( "MailingList", $database ) )
            die( "Could not open MailingList database </body></html>" );

         // query MailingList database
         if ( !( $result = mysql_query( $query, $database ) ) )
         {
            print( "Could not execute query! <br />" );
            die( mysql_error() . "</body></html>" );
         } // end if
      ?><!-- end PHP script -->

      <h3>Mailing List Contacts</h3>
      <table>
         <tr>
            <td>ID</td>
            <td>Last Name</td>
            <td>First Name</td>
            <td>E-mail Address</td>
            <td>Phone Number</td>
            <td>Book</td>
            <td>Operating System</td>
         </tr>
         <?php
```

Fig. 23.22 | Displaying the `MailingList` database. (Part 2 of 3.)

```
            // fetch each record in result set
            for ( $counter = 0; $row = mysql_fetch_row( $result );
               $counter++ )
            {
               // build table to display results
               print( "<tr>" );

               foreach ( $row as $key => $value )
                  print( "<td>$value</td>" );

               print( "</tr>" );
            } // end for

            mysql_close( $database );
         ?><!-- end PHP script -->
      </table>
   </body>
</html>
```

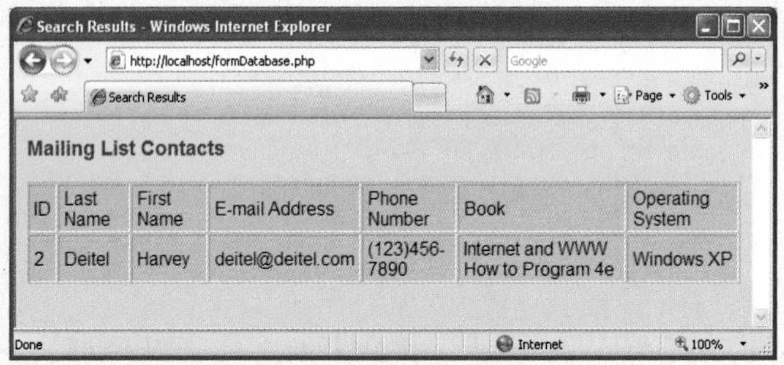

Fig. 23.22 | Displaying the `MailingList` database. (Part 3 of 3.)

23.8 Operator Precedence Chart

This section contains the operator precedence chart for PHP. In Fig. 23.23, the operators are shown from top to bottom in decreasing order of precedence.

Operator	Type	Associativity
`new`	constructor	none
`[]`	subscript	right to left
`~`	bitwise not	right to left
`!`	not	
`++`	increment	
`--`	decrement	
`-`	unary negative	
`@`	error control	

Fig. 23.23 | PHP operator precedence and associativity. (Part 1 of 2.)

Operator	Type	Associativity
*	multiplication	left to right
/	division	
%	modulus	
+	addition	left to right
-	subtraction	
.	concatenation	
<<	bitwise shift left	left to right
>>	bitwise shift right	
<	less than	none
>	greater than	
<=	less than or equal	
>=	greater than or equal	
==	equal	none
!=	not equal	
===	identical	
!==	not identical	
&	bitwise AND	left to right
^	bitwise XOR	left to right
|	bitwise OR	left to right
&&	logical AND	left to right
||	logical OR	left to right
=	assignment	left to right
+=	addition assignment	
-=	subtraction assignment	
*=	multiplication assignment	
/=	division assignment	
&=	bitwise AND assignment	
|=	bitwise OR assignment	
^=	bitwise exclusive OR assignment	
.=	concatenation assignment	
<<=	bitwise shift left assignment	
>>=	bitwise shift right assignment	
and	logical AND	left to right
xor	exclusive OR	left to right
or	logical OR	left to right
,	list	left to right

Fig. 23.23 | PHP operator precedence and associativity. (Part 2 of 2.)

23.9 Wrap-Up

In this chapter, we introduced the popular server-side scripting language PHP. We discussed the basics of how to embed PHP code into XHTML documents, and introduced string processing, regular expressions and form handling, which allow for interaction with users. We also learned how to interact with a database, which allows for full three-tier web application development. We then discussed how to use cookies to store data on the client between sessions, and finished off with a dynamic web page that combines many of the techniques we've learned. The next chapter discusses Ruby on Rails, another server-side technology that streamlines the process of creating three-tier web applications.

23.10 Web Resources

www.deitel.com/PHP/

The Deitel PHP Resource Center contains links to some of the best PHP information on the web. There you'll find categorized links to PHP tools, code generators, forums, books, libraries, frameworks and more. Also check out the tutorials for all skill levels, from introductory to advanced. Be sure to visit the related Resource Centers on XHTML (www.deitel.com/xhtml/) and CSS 2.1 (www.deitel.com/css21/).

Summary

Section 23.1 Introduction

- PHP, or PHP: Hypertext Preprocessor, has become one of the most popular server-side scripting languages for creating dynamic web pages.
- PHP is open source and platform independent—implementations exist for all major UNIX, Linux, Mac and Windows operating systems. PHP also supports a large number of databases.

Section 23.2 PHP Basics

- The power of the web resides not only in serving content to users, but also in responding to requests from users and generating web pages with dynamic content.
- PHP code is embedded directly into XHTML documents, though these script segments are interpreted by a server before being delivered to the client.
- PHP script file names end with .php.
- Although PHP can be used from the command line, a web server is necessary to take full advantage of the scripting language.
- In PHP, code is inserted between the scripting delimiters <?php and ?>. PHP code can be placed anywhere in XHTML markup, as long as the code is enclosed in these delimiters.
- Variables are preceded by a $ and are created the first time they are encountered.
- PHP statements terminate with a semicolon (;).
- Single-line comments which begin with two forward slashes (//) or a pound sign (#). Text to the right of the delimiter is ignored by the interpreter. Multiline comments begin with delimiter /* and end with delimiter */.
- When a variable is encountered inside a double-quoted ("") string, PHP interpolates the variable. In other words, PHP inserts the variable's value where the variable name appears in the string.
- All operations requiring PHP interpolation execute on the server before the XHTML document is sent to the client.

- PHP variables are loosely typed—they can contain different types of data at different times.
- Type conversions can be performed using function `settype`. This function takes two arguments—a variable whose type is to be changed and the variable's new type.
- Variables are automatically converted to the type of the value they are assigned.
- Function `gettype` returns the current type of its argument.
- Calling function `settype` can result in loss of data. For example, doubles are truncated when they are converted to integers.
- When converting from a string to a number, PHP uses the value of the number that appears at the beginning of the string. If no number appears at the beginning, the string evaluates to `0`.
- Another option for conversion between types is casting (or type casting). Casting does not change a variable's content—it creates a temporary copy of a variable's value in memory.
- The concatenation operator (`.`) combines multiple strings.
- A `print` statement split over multiple lines prints all the data that is enclosed in its parentheses.
- Function `define` creates a named constant. It takes two arguments—the name and value of the constant. An optional third argument accepts a boolean value that specifies whether the constant is case insensitive—constants are case sensitive by default.
- Uninitialized variables have the value `undef`, which has different values, depending on its context. In a numeric context, it evaluates to `0`. In a string context, it evaluates to an empty string (`""`).
- Keywords may not be used as identifiers.
- PHP provides the capability to store data in arrays. Arrays are divided into elements that behave as individual variables. Array names, like other variables, begin with the `$` symbol.
- Individual array elements are accessed by following the array's variable name with an index enclosed in square brackets (`[]`).
- If a value is assigned to an array that does not exist, then the array is created. Likewise, assigning a value to an element where the index is omitted appends a new element to the end of the array.
- Function `count` returns the total number of elements in the array.
- Function `array` creates an array that contains the arguments passed to it. The first item in the argument list is stored as the first array element (index `0`), the second item is stored as the second array element and so on.
- Arrays with nonnumeric indices are called associative arrays. You can create an associative array using the operator `=>`, where the value to the left of the operator is the array index and the value to the right is the element's value.
- PHP provides functions for iterating through the elements of an array. Each array has a built-in internal pointer, which points to the array element currently being referenced. Function `reset` sets the internal pointer to the first array element. Function `key` returns the index of the element currently referenced by the internal pointer, and function `next` moves the internal pointer to the next element.
- The `foreach` statement, designed for iterating through arrays, starts with the array to iterate through, followed by the keyword `as`, followed by two variables—the first is assigned the index of the element and the second is assigned the value of that index. (If only one variable is listed after `as`, it is assigned the value of the array element.)

Section 23.3 String Processing and Regular Expressions

- A regular expression is a series of characters used for pattern-matching templates in strings, text files and databases.

- Many string-processing tasks can be accomplished using the equality and relational operators.
- Function `strcmp` compares two strings. The function returns `-1` if the first string alphabetically precedes the second string, `0` if the strings are equal, and `1` if the first string alphabetically follows the second.
- Functions `ereg` and `preg_match` use regular expressions to search a string for a specified pattern.
- If a pattern is found using `ereg`, it returns the length of the matched string—which evaluates to `true` in a boolean context.
- Anything enclosed in single quotes in a `print` statement is not interpolated (unless the single quotes are nested in a double-quoted string literal).
- Function `ereg` receives a regular expression pattern to search for and the string to search.
- Function `eregi` performs case-insensitive pattern matches.
- Regular expressions can include metacharacters that specify patterns. For example, the caret (`^`) metacharacter matches the beginning of a string, while the dollar sign (`$`) matches the end of a string. The period (`.`) metacharacter matches any single character.
- Bracket expressions are lists of characters enclosed in square brackets (`[]`) that match any single character from the list. Ranges can be specified by supplying the beginning and the end of the range separated by a dash (-).
- The special bracket expressions `[[:<:]]` and `[[:>:]]` match the beginning and end of a word, respectively.
- Quantifiers are used in regular expressions to denote how often a particular character or set of characters can appear in a match.
- The optional third argument to function `ereg` is an array that stores matches to each parenthetical statement of the regular expression. The first element stores the string matched for the entire pattern, and the remaining elements are indexed from left to right.
- To find multiple instances of a given pattern, we must make multiple calls to `ereg`, and remove matched instances before calling the function again by using a function such as `ereg_replace`.
- Character classes, or sets of specific characters, are enclosed by the delimiters `[:` and `:]`. When this expression is placed in another set of brackets, it is a regular expression matching all of the characters in the class.
- A bracketed expression containing two or more adjacent character classes in the class delimiters represents those character sets combined.
- Function `ereg_replace` takes three arguments—the pattern to match, a string to replace the matched string and the string to search. The modified string is returned.

Section 23.4 Form Processing and Business Logic

- Superglobal arrays are associative arrays predefined by PHP that hold variables acquired from user input, the environment or the web server and are accessible in any variable scope.
- The arrays `$_GET` and `$_POST` retrieve information sent to the server by HTTP `get` and `post` requests, respectively.
- Using method = `"post"` appends form data to the browser request that contains the protocol and the requested resource's URL. Scripts located on the web server's machine can access the form data sent as part of the request.
- Function `extract` creates a variable/value pair corresponding to each key/value pair in the associative array passed as an argument.
- Business logic, or business rules, ensures that only valid information is stored in databases.

- We escape the normal meaning of a character in a string by preceding it with the backslash character (\).
- Function `die` terminates script execution. The function's optional argument is a string, which is printed as the script exits.

Section 23.5 Connecting to a Database

- Function `mysql_connect` connects to the MySQL database. It takes three arguments—the server's hostname, a username and a password, and returns a database handle—a representation of PHP's connection to the database, or `false` if the connection fails.
- Function `mysql_select_db` specifies the database to be queried, and returns a `bool` indicating whether or not it was successful.
- To query the database, we call function `mysql_query`, specifying the query string and the database to query. This returns a resource containing the result of the query, or `false` if the query fails. It can also execute SQL statements such as `INSERT` or `DELETE` that do not return results.
- Function `mysql_error` returns any error strings from the database.

Section 23.6 Using Cookies

- A cookie is a text file that a website stores on a client's computer to maintain information about the client during and between browsing sessions.
- A server can access only the cookies that it has placed on the client.
- Function `setcookie` takes the name of the cookie to be set as the first argument, followed by the value to be stored in the cookie. The optional third argument indicates the expiration date of the cookie. A cookie without a third argument is known as a session cookie, while one with an expiration date is a persistent cookie. If only the name argument is passed to function `setcookie`, the cookie is deleted from the client's computer.
- Cookies defined in function `setcookie` are sent to the client at the same time as the information in the HTTP header; therefore, it needs to be called before any XHTML is printed.
- The current time is returned by function `time`.
- When using Internet Explorer, cookies are stored in a **Cookies** directory on the client's machine. In Firefox, cookies are stored in a file named `cookies.txt`.
- PHP creates the superglobal array `$_COOKIE`, which contains all the cookie values indexed by their names.

Section 23.7 Dynamic Content

- Function `isset` allows you to find out if a variable has a value.
- A variable variable (`$$variable`) allows the code to reference variables dynamically. You can use this expression to obtain the value of the variable whose name is equal to the value of `$variable`.
- The `quotemeta` function inserts a backslash (\) before any special characters in the passed string.

Terminology

- range separator
`$_COOKIE`
`$_GET`
`$_POST`
`array` function
`as` keyword
associative array
bracket expressions
business logic
business rules
caret metacharacter (^)
casting
character classes
comparison operators

concatenation operator (.)
cookie
count function
database handle
die function
dollar-sign metacharacter
double data type
equality operators
ereg function
ereg_replace function
eregi function
escape sequence
foreach statement
gettype function
internal pointer
interpolation
isset function
iteration through an array
key function
literal characters
metacharacters
multiplication assignment operator
MySQL
mysql_close function
mysql_connect function
mysql_error function
mysql_fetch_row function
mysql_num_rows function
mysql_query function
mysql_select_db function
named constant
next function
Perl-compatible regular expressions (PCRE)
persistent cookie
PHP
POSIX extended regular expressions
post request type
preg_match function
print function
quantifier
quotemeta function
time function
type casting
variable variables
while statement

Self-Review Exercises

23.1 State whether each of the following is *true* or *false*. If *false*, explain why.
a) PHP script is never in the same file as XHTML script.
b) PHP variable names are case sensitive.
c) The settype function only temporarily changes the type of a variable.
d) Conversion between data types happens automatically when a variable is used in a context that requires a different data type.
e) The foreach statement is designed specifically for iterating over arrays.
f) Relational operators can only be used for numeric comparison.
g) The quantifier +, when used in a regular expression, matches any number of the preceding pattern.
h) Function die never takes arguments.
i) Cookies are stored on the server computer.
j) The * arithmetic operator has higher precedence than the + operator.

23.2 Fill in the blanks in each of the following statements:
a) PHP scripts typically have the file extension ________.
b) The two numeric types that PHP variables can store are ________ and ________.
c) In PHP, uninitialized variables have the value ________.
d) ________ are divided into elements, each of which acts like an individual variable.
e) Function ________ returns the total number of elements in an array.
f) To use POSIX regular expressions, use the ________ function.
g) A(n) ________ in a regular expression matches a predefined set of characters.
h) Data submitted through the HTTP post method is stored in array ________.
i) Function ________ terminates script execution.
j) ________ can be used to maintain state information on a client's computer.

Answers to Self-Review Exercises

23.1 a) False. PHP is directly embedded directly into XHTML. b) True. c) False. Function `settype` permanently changes the type of a variable. d) True. e) True. f) False. Relational operators can also be used for alphabetic comparison. g) False. The quantifier + matches one or more of the preceding pattern. h) False. Function `die` has an optional argument—a string to be printed as the script exits. i) False. Cookies are stored on the client's computer. j) True.

23.2 a) `.php`. b) `int` or `integer`, float or `double`. c) `undef`. d) Arrays. e) `count`. f) `ereg`. g) character class. h) `$_POST`. i) `die`. j) Cookies.

Exercises

23.3 Identify and correct the error in each of the following PHP code examples:

a) `<?php print( "Hello World" ); >`

b)
```
<?php
   $name = "Paul";
   print( "$Name" );
?><!-- end PHP script -->
```

23.4 Write a PHP regular expression pattern that matches a string that satisfies the following description: The string must begin with the (uppercase) letter A. Any three alphanumeric characters must follow. After these, the letter B (uppercase or lowercase) must be repeated one or more times, and the string must end with two digits.

23.5 Describe how input from an XHTML `form` is retrieved in a PHP program.

23.6 Describe how cookies can be used to store information on a computer and how the information can be retrieved by a PHP script. Assume that cookies are not disabled on the client.

23.7 Write a PHP script named `states.php` that creates a variable `$states` with the value `"Mississippi Alabama Texas Massachusetts Kansas"`. The script should perform the following tasks:

a) Search for a word in `$states` that ends in `xas`. Store this word in element 0 of an array named `$statesArray`.
b) Search for a word in `$states` that begins with `k` and ends in `s`. Perform a case-insensitive comparison. Store this word in element 1 of `$statesArray`.
c) Search for a word in `$states` that begins with `M` and ends in `s`. Store this element in element 2 of the array.
d) Search for a word in `$states` that ends in `a`. Store this word in element 3 of the array.
e) Search for a word in `$states` at the beginning of the string that starts with `M`. Store this word in element 4 of the array.
f) Output the array `$statesArray` to the screen.

23.8 Write a PHP script that tests whether an e-mail address is input correctly. Verify that the input begins with series of characters, followed by the `@` character, another series of characters, a period (`.`) and a final series of characters. Test your program, using both valid and invalid e-mail addresses.

23.9 Write a PHP script that obtains a URL and its description from a user and stores the information into a database using `MySQL`. Create and run a SQL script with a database named `URL` and a table named `Urltable`. The first field of the table should contain an actual URL, and the second, which is named `Description`, should contain a description of the URL. Use `www.deitel.com` as the first URL, and input `Cool site!` as its description. The second URL should be `www.php.net`, and the description should be `The official PHP site`. After each new URL is submitted, print the contents of the database in a table.

24

Ruby on Rails

Convention is the ruler of all.

—Pindar

Where the telescope ends, the microscope begins. Which of the two has the grander view?

—Victor Hugo

. . . We grow more partial for the observer's sake.

—Alexander Pope

Those who cannot remember the past are condemned to repeat it.

—George Santayana

Let's look at the record.

—Alfred Emanuel Smith

All that matters is that the miraculous become the norm.

—Henry Miller

In this chapter you will learn:

- Basic Ruby programming.
- How to use the Rails framework.
- The Model-View-Controller paradigm.
- How to use `ActiveRecord` to model a database.
- How to construct web applications that interact with a database.
- How to create a web-based message forum.
- How to develop Ajax-enabled applications in Ruby on Rails.
- How to use the built-in Script.aculo.us library to add visual effects to your programs.

Outline

24.1 Introduction

Ruby on Rails (also known as RoR or just Rails) is a framework for developing data-driven web applications using the Ruby scripting language. A web framework is a set of libraries and useful tools that can be used to build dynamic web applications. Ruby on Rails is different from most other programming languages because it takes advantage of many conventions to reduce development time. If you follow these conventions, the Rails framework generates substantial functionality and perform many tasks for you. Ruby on Rails has built-in libraries for performing common web development tasks, such as interacting with a database, sending mass e-mails to clients or generating web services. In addition, Rails has built-in libraries that provide Ajax functionality (discussed in Chapter 15), to improve the user experience. Rails is quickly becoming a popular web development environment.

Ruby on Rails was created by David Heinemeier Hansson of the company 37Signals. After developing Basecamp, a web application written in Ruby that allows a business to organize multiple projects. Hansson extracted the reusable components to create the Rails framework. Since then, many developers have enhanced the Rails framework. For more information, visit our Ruby on Rails Resource Center at `www.deitel.com/RubyOnRails`. Full documentation of the Rails Framework can be found at `api.rubyonrails.org`.

24.2 Ruby

The first several examples are simple command-line programs that demonstrate fundamental Ruby programming concepts. The Ruby scripting language was developed by Yukihiro "Matz" Matsumoto in 1995 to be a flexible, object-oriented scripting language. Ruby's syntax and conventions are intuitive—they attempt to mimic the way a developer thinks. Ruby is an interpreted language.

Installing Instant Rails

To run the Ruby scripts in this chapter, Ruby must first be installed on your system. In this chapter we use the **Instant Rails** package to run our applications. Instant Rails includes Ruby, Rails, MySQL, Apache, PHP and other components necessary to create and run Rails applications. PHP is used specifically for **phpMyAdmin**, a web interface to MySQL. Instant Rails is a stand-alone Rails development and testing environment.

To install Instant Rails, download Instant Rails 1.7 from `//rubyforge.org/frs/?group_id=904`. Once the zip file is downloaded, extract its contents to a folder on your hard drive.

After installing Instant Rails, make sure that you stop any existing web servers on your computer such as IIS or Apache— Instant Rails needs port 80 to be available for using **phpMyAdmin** to administer MySQL. If you are not using this tool then you don't need to stop other web servers on your computer. To run Instant Rails, navigate to the folder where you extracted the contents of the zip file and run **InstantRails.exe**. You should see a window similar to Fig. 24.1.

If you are using Mac OS X, there is an application similar to Instant Rails called Locomotive. You can download Locomotive from `locomotive.raaum.org`. Linux users might want to try LinRails (available from `linrails.thembid.com`). Another program useful for Rails development is Aptana Radrails—a free, open-source IDE. Radrails can be downloaded from `www.aptana.com/download_rails_rdt.php`.

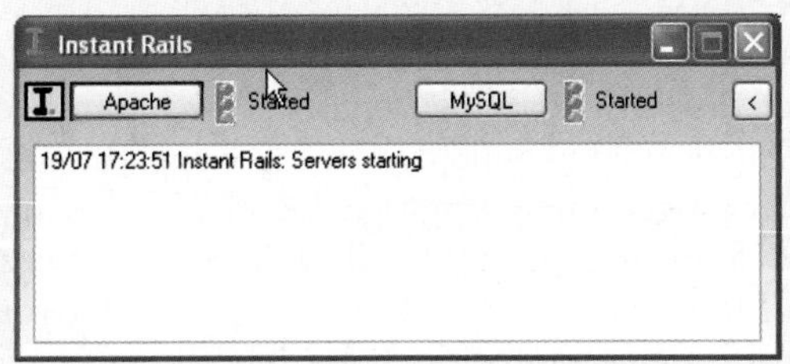

Fig. 24.1 | Instant Rails application running.

Printing a Line of Text

Figure 24.2 presents a simple Ruby program that prints the text `"Welcome to Ruby!"`. Lines 1–2 are single-line comments that instruct the interpreter to ignore everything on the current line following the # symbol. Line 3 uses the method **`puts`** that takes a single parameter (a string) and prints the text to the terminal, followed by a newline. A method can have parentheses surrounding its parameters, but this is not typical in Ruby unless they are used to avoid ambiguity. A line of Ruby code does not have to end with a semicolon, although one can be placed there. The `puts` method automatically adds a newline escape sequence (`\n`) at the end of the string if one is not explicitly added.

```
1  # Fig. 24.2: welcome.rb
2  # Simple Ruby program.
3  puts "Welcome to Ruby!"
```

Fig. 24.2 | Simple Ruby program. (Part 1 of 2.)

```
Welcome to Ruby!
```

Fig. 24.2 | Simple Ruby program. (Part 2 of 2.)

Running a Ruby Script

A Ruby script can be run several ways. One is to use the Ruby interpreter. To do so, launch Instant Rails, click the I button in the top-left corner and select **Rails Applications > Open Ruby Console Window** from the drop-down menu (see Fig. 24.3).

In the console, use the `cd` command to navigate to the directory where `welcome.rb` is located, then enter `ruby welcome.rb`. Figure 24.4 shows the Ruby interpreter executing the Ruby file from Fig. 24.2 in the **Ruby Console** window.

Ruby can also execute interactively, using IRB (Interactive Ruby). IRB interprets Ruby code statement by statement. This is useful for debugging code and for experimenting with Ruby functionality. IRB can be run through Instant Rails by typing `IRB` in the Ruby Console. Figure 24.5 shows simple Ruby statements interpreted in IRB.

The code after the prompt (`irb(main):001:0>`) shows the statement that was executed using the Ruby interpreter in Fig. 24.4. It sends the same string to the output, then returns the value of method `puts`, which is `nil`, an object that represents nothing in Ruby.

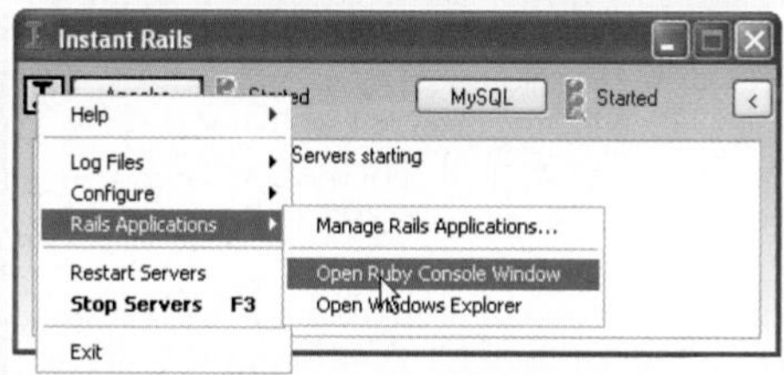

Fig. 24.3 | Launching the Ruby Interpreter in Instant Rails.

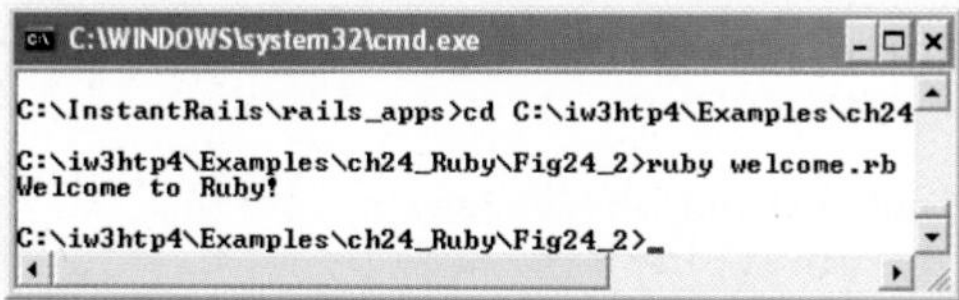

Fig. 24.4 | Using the Ruby interpreter to run a simple Ruby script.

```
C:\WINDOWS\system32\cmd.exe - IRB

C:\InstantRails\rails_apps>IRB
irb(main):001:0> puts "Welcome to Ruby!"
Welcome to Ruby!
=> nil
irb(main):002:0> 2+2
=> 4
irb(main):003:0> 4.class
=> Fixnum
irb(main):004:0> 4.5.ceil
=> 5
irb(main):005:0>
```

Fig. 24.5 | Using Interactive Ruby to execute Ruby statements.

The code after the second IRB prompt sends the arithmetic expression `2+2` to the interpreter, which evaluates the expression and returns `4`. The code after the third prompt requests the class type of the number `4`. The interpreter returns `Fixnum`—a class that represents integers in Ruby. Last, the code after the fourth prompt calls the `ceil` method of `4.5` to round the number up to the next whole-number value. The IRB returns `5`. Type `exit` to quit IRB.

Variables and Data Types in Ruby

Like most scripting languages, Ruby uses dynamic typing, which allows changes to a variable's type during runtime. There are several variable types in Ruby, including `String` and `Fixnum`. Everything is an object in Ruby, so you can call methods on any piece of data. Figure 24.6 invokes methods on numeric and string data.

Line 3 initializes the variable `myvar`. Setting `myvar` to `7.5` temporarily makes it a `Float` object. The highlighted portion of line 4 is an example of interpolation in Ruby. It inserts the object value of the variable inside the braces into the string. Lines 6 and 12 invoke the

```
1  # Fig. 24.6: types.rb
2  # Method calls on numeric and string data
3  myvar = 5.7 # binds the value 5.7 to myvar
4  puts "The value of myvar is #{myvar}"
5
6  myvar = myvar.round # return a rounded value Fixnum
7  puts "The rounded value of myvar is #{myvar}"
8
9  myvar = 5.4 # bind the value 5.4 to myvar
10 puts "The value of myvar is #{myvar}"
11
12 myvar = myvar.round # return a rounded value Fixnum
13 puts "The rounded value of myvar is #{myvar}"
14
15 myvar = "mystring" # bind the value 'mystring' to myvar
16 puts "The value of myvar is '#{myvar}'"
17
18 myvar = myvar.capitalize # capitalize the value of myvar
19 puts "The capitalized form of myvar is '#{myvar}'"
20
21 myvar = "my string" # bind the value 'my string' to myvar
22 puts "The value of myvar is '#{myvar}'"
23
24 myvar = myvar.capitalize # capitalize the value of myvar
25 puts "The capitalized form of myvar is '#{myvar}'"
```

```
The value of myvar is 5.7
The rounded value of myvar is 6
The value of myvar is 5.4
The rounded value of myvar is 5
The value of myvar is 'mystring'
The capitalized form of myvar is 'Mystring'
The value of myvar is 'my string'
The capitalized form of myvar is 'My string'
```

Fig. 24.6 | Method calls on numeric and string data.

`round` method on the `Float` object to demonstrate rounding a value up or down, respectively. The type of `myvar` changes to `String` in line 15. Lines 18 and 24 changes the first letter of the first word of this `String` by calling its `capitalize` method. A list of the available methods for the Ruby types can be found at `www.ruby-doc.org/core/`.

Using **Arrays** *and* **Hashes**

Ruby provides both **`Arrays`** and **`Hashes`** to store data. Each stores a list of objects. In an `Array`, indices of type `Fixnum` are used to select an `Object` from the `Array`. In a `Hash`, `Objects` are mapped to other `Objects` in key/value pairs. Figure 24.7 shows an example of using both an `Array` and a `Hash` to store information.

Line 3 instantiates a Ruby `Array`. `Array` elements can be accessed by their index number in square brackets (line 5). You may also traverse `Arrays` backward by using negative number indices. For example line 6 outputs the last array element. Line 8 reverses the elements in the `Array` with method **`reverse!`**. The exclamation point after the method name is a Ruby convention indicating that the object on which the method is called will be modified. Method `reverse` without an exclamation point returns a copy of the original array with its elements reversed. Many Ruby methods follow this convention.

Line 14 is an example of a `Hash`. The key/value pairs are separated by commas, and each key points to its corresponding value using the => operator. The value of a hash element can be found by passing in the key in square brackets, as shown in lines 16–17.

```
1  # Fig. 24.7: arraysAndHashes.rb
2  # Arrays and hashes in Ruby.
3  fruits = [ "mango", "orange",  "apple", "pear" ] # create an array
4  puts "The length of the fruits array is #{fruits.length}" # output length
5  puts "The first fruit is #{fruits[0]}" # output first element
6  puts "The last fruit is #{fruits[-1]}\n\n" # output last element
7
8  fruits.reverse! # reverse the order of the elements in the fruits array
9  puts "The length of the fruits array is #{fruits.length}" # output length
10 puts "The first fruit is #{fruits[0]}" # output first element
11 puts "The last fruit is #{fruits[-1]}\n\n" # output last element
12
13 # a simple hash
14 food = { "mango" => "fruit", "banana" => "fruit", "onion" => "vegetable" }
15 puts "The length of the food hash is #{food.length}" # output length
16 puts "A mango is a #{food["mango"]}" # output value of key mango
17 puts "An onion is a #{food["onion"]}" # output value of key onion
```

```
The length of the fruits array is 4
The first fruit is mango
the last fruit is pear

The length of the fruits array is 4
The first fruit is pear
the last fruit is mango

The length of the food hash is 3
A mango is a fruit
An onion is a vegetable
```

Fig. 24.7 | Arrays and hashes in Ruby.

Conditionals, Loops and Code Blocks

Like any other programming language, Ruby provides selection and repetition statements. In addition, Ruby has support for code blocks—groupings of Ruby statements that can be passed to a method as an argument. Figure 24.8 shows a program that returns a student's letter grade based on a numerical grade.

Lines 3–15 of Fig. 24.8 contain a Ruby method definition. Methods must be defined in a program before they are used. All methods start with `def` and end with `end`. Methods do not have to specify parameter types, but they must specify the name of each parameter. Lines 4–14 show a nested `if...elsif...else` statement that returns an appropriate letter grade based on the numeric value the method receives as an argument. If a method does not include an explicit return statement Ruby returns the last value or variable it encounters when executing the function.

Line 17 defines a `Hash` of students and their numeric grades. Lines 19–21 show an example of a code block. A method may have a parameter containing a block of code, such as the `each` method. The block of code appears in brackets directly after the method call. A code block is similar to a method, in that parameters can be passed into it. The parameters for a code block are given between pipe characters (`|`) and are separated by commas. The parameters are followed immediately by the code block's statements. The code block in lines 19–21 outputs a line of text based on the key/value pair of every key in the `Hash`.

```
1  # Fig. 24.8: controlStatements.rb
2  # Conditionals, loops, and codeblocks.
3  def letter_grade( x ) # define method letterGrade
4     if x >= 90 # if x is greater than or equal to 90
5        "A" # grade is A
6     elsif x >= 80 # if x is greater than or equal to 80
7        "B" # grade is B
8     elsif x >= 70 # if x is greater than or equal to 70
9        "C" # grade is C
10    elsif x >= 60 # if x is greater than or equal to 60
11       "D" # grade is D
12    else # grade is less than 60
13       "F" # grade is F
14    end # if
15 end # method letterGrade
16
17 students = { "John" => 100, "Sue" => 92, "Tom" => 56, "Jill" => 80 }
18
19 students.each() { |key, value| # display the letter grade for each student
20    puts "#{key} received a #{letter_grade(value)}"
21 } # end codeblock
```

```
Jill received a B
Sue received a A
John received a A
Tom received a F
```

Fig. 24.8 | Conditionals, loops and codeblocks.

Classes

You can create your own classes and instantiate objects. Classes enable you to encapsulate methods and data. Figure 24.9 shows a class named `Point` that stores *x-y* coordinates.

Line 3 begins the class definition with the keyword `class` followed by the class name. The `initialize` method (lines 7–11), like constructors in other object-oriented languages, is used to declare and initialize an object's data. When each instance of a class maintains its own copy of a variable, the variable is known as an instance variable. Lines 8–9 use the `@` symbol to define the instance variables `x` and `y`. Classes can also have class variables that are shared by all copies of a class. Class variables always begin with `@@` (line 4) and are visible to all instances of the class in which they are defined. Line 10 increments `@@num_points` every time a new `Point` is defined.

You can create new classes by inheriting from existing ones and providing your own additional or enhanced functionality. Lines 14–16 override the inherited `to_s` method, which is a method of all Ruby objects. When an object is concatenated with a string, the `to_s` method is implicitly called to convert the object to its string representation. Class `Point`'s `to_s` method for the `Point` class returns a string containing the *x-y* coordinates.

```
1  # Fig. 24.9: Classes.rb
2  # A Ruby class.
3  class Point
4     @@num_points = 0 # initialize numPoints
5
6     # create a new Point object
7     def initialize(x, y)
8        @x = x # initialize x-coordinate
9        @y = y # initialize y-coordinate
10       @@num_points +=1  # increment numPoints counter
11    end # method initialize
12
13    # return a string containing the x-y values
14    def to_s
15       return "x: #{@x}; y: #{@y}"
16    end # method to_s
17
18    # return how many Points have been instantiated
19    def num_points
20       return @@num_points
21    end # method numPoints
22 end # class Point
23
24 p = Point.new( 8, 9 ) # instantiate a Point
25 q = Point.new( 1, 1 ) # instantiate another Point
26 puts "the value of p is '#{p}'"
27 puts "the value of q is '#{q}'"
28 puts "the number of points created is #{p.num_points}"
```

```
the value of p is 'x: 8; y: 9'
the value of q is 'x: 1; y: 1'
the number of points created is 2
```

Fig. 24.9 | A Ruby class.

24.3 Rails Framework

While users have benefitted from the rise of database-driven web applications, web developers have had to implement rich functionality with technology that was not designed for this purpose. The Rails framework combines the simplicity of Ruby with the ability to rapidly develop database-driven web applications.

Model-View-Controller

Ruby on Rails is built on the philosophies of Convention over Configuration and Don't Repeat Yourself (DRY). If you follow certain programming idioms, your applications will require minimal configuration, and Rails will generate substantial portions of your web applications for you. One of these conventions is using the Model-View-Controller (MVC) design pattern, which splits the application into the business logic aspects handled by the model and the design aspects handled by the view. The controller handles client requests by obtaining information from the model and rendering it to the view.

The MVC architectural pattern separates application data (contained in the model) from graphical presentation components (the view) and input-processing logic (the controller). Figure 24.10 shows the relationships between components in MVC.

The controller implements logic for processing user input. The model contains application data, and the view presents the data from the model. When a user provides input, the controller modifies the model with the given input. When the model changes, the controller notifies the view so that it can update its presentation with the changed data.

MVC does not restrict an application to a single view and a single controller. In a more sophisticated program, there might be two views of a document model. One view might display an outline of the document and the other might display the complete document. An application also might implement multiple controllers—one for handling keyboard input and another for handling mouse selections. If either controller makes a change in the model, both the outline view and the print-preview window will show the change immediately when the controller notifies all views of changes.

The primary benefit to the MVC architectural pattern is that developers can modify each component individually without having to modify the others. For example, developers could modify the view that displays the document outline without having to modify either the model or other views or controllers.

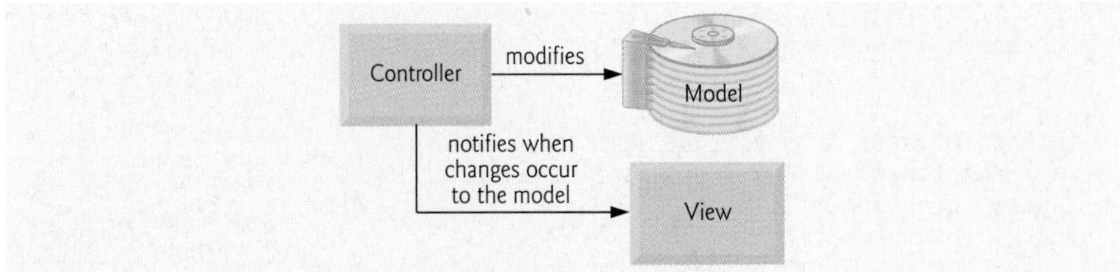

Fig. 24.10 | Model-View-Controller architecture.

Overview

In the following examples, we show how to create a Ruby on Rails application. We show how a controller can be used to send information to the client directly, and how a controller can render a view for a cleaner and more organized design. We then show how to set up a database in a Ruby on Rails application. Finally, we show how to generate a model to be the front end of a database in a dynamic web application.

Creating a Rails Application

The Instant Rails package comes with a full install of Rails that includes `ActiveRecord`, `ActionView`, and `ActionController`. `ActiveRecord` is used to map a database table to an Object. `ActionView` is a set of helper methods to modify user interfaces. `ActionController` is a set of helper methods to create controllers. To generate an empty Rails application in Instant Rails, click the [I] button and select **Rails Applications > Manage Rails Applications...** from the drop-down menu to display the **Rails Applications** window. In that window click the **Create New Rails App...** button. In the console that appears, type `rails` *Application Name* at the command line to create a directory named *Application Name* with a prebuilt directory structure inside. For the first example, use `Welcome` as the application name. Figure 24.11 shows the directory structure that is automatically generated by Rails. The directories that we'll be primarily concerned with are `app\controllers`, `app\models`, and `app\views`.

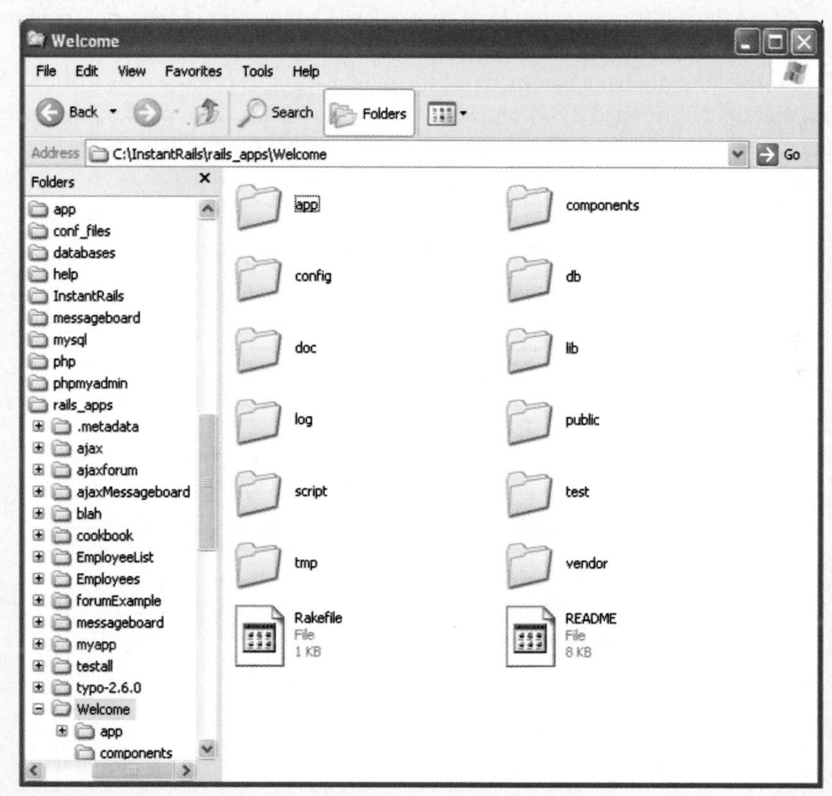

Fig. 24.11 | Rails directory structure for a new Rails application.

24.4 ActionController and ActionView

Ruby on Rails has two classes that work together to process a client request and render a view. These classes are `ActionController` and `ActionView`.

Rails Controller

To generate a controller in Rails, you can use the built-in `Controller generator`. To do that, open the **Ruby Console** window and navigate to the application directory by typing in:

cd *pathToInstantRails*\rails_apps*applicationName*

To generate a controller for the welcome application type:

```
ruby script/generate controller Welcome
```

This creates several files including `welcome_controller.rb`, which contains a class named `WelcomeController`. Figure 24.12 shows a controller for our Welcome example containing only one method.

Line 3 defines a class `WelcomeController` that inherits from `ApplicationController`. `ApplicationController` inherits from `ActionController::Base`, which provides all of the default functionality for a controller. The method in lines 5–7 renders text in XHTML format to the browser using the `render` method

Line 6 specifies the `text` parameter of the render variable using a ruby symbol. Symbols are identifiers preceded by a colon that have a particular value or variable associated with them. When specifying a parameter in a method the notation is as follows:

parameter_symbol => *parameter_value*

```
1  # Fig. 24.12: app/controllers/welcome_controller.rb
2  # Simple controller that renders a message on a web page.
3  class WelcomeController < ApplicationController
4     # render text in page
5     def index
6        render :text => "Welcome to Ruby on Rails!"
7     end # method index
8  end # class WelcomeController
```

Fig. 24.12 | Simple controller that renders a message on the web page.

Running Ruby on Rails

A Ruby on Rails application must be run from a web server. In addition to Apache, Instant Rails comes with a built-in web server named Mongrel, which is easy to use to test Rails applications on the local machine. You can start the Mongrel server through Instant Rails by going to the **Rails Application** window, selecting the **Welcome** application from the list and clicking the **Start with Mongrel** button (Fig. 24.13).

One important feature of Rails is its URL mapping ability. Rails automatically sets up your web application in a tree structure, where the controller's name in lowercase is the directory, and the method name is the subdirectory. Since the controller name is `Welcome` and the method name is `index`, the URL to display the text in Figure 24.12 is `http://localhost:3000/welcome/index`. Notice in the screen capture of Figure 24.12 that the URL is simply `http://localhost:3000/welcome`. The default action called on any controller is the one specified by the method `index`. So, you do not need to explicitly invoke the `index` in the URL to render the text in line 6.

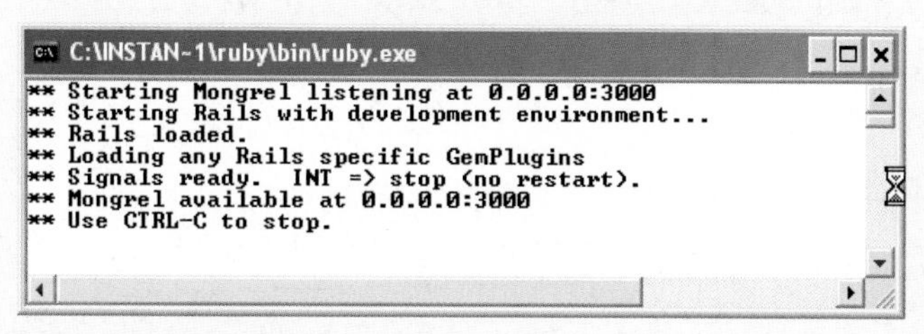

Fig. 24.13 | Starting the Mongrel web server.

Rendering a View

When generating output, a controller usually renders a template—an XHTML document with embedded Ruby that has the `.rhtml` filename extension. [*Note:* The next version of Rails will use the extension `.html.erb` rather than `.rhtml`.] The embedded Ruby comes from a library named `erb`. A method in a controller will automatically render a view with the same name by default. For example, an empty `hello` method would look for a `hello.rhtml` view to render. Fig. 24.14 is the `Welcome` controller with a `hello` method added. The `index` method has been removed for simplicity.

The `server_software` method (line 6) is called on the request object—an object that contains all of the environment variables and other information for that web page. The method `server_software` returns the name of the server that is running the web application. This name is stored in an instance variable that will be used by the view. Our `hello` method looks for a `hello.rhtml` file in the web application's `app/views/welcome` directory. Figure 24.15 shows a sample `hello.rhtml` file.

The view consists mostly of XHTML. The `erb` is shown in line 14, surrounded by <%= and %> tags. Everything between these tags is parsed as Ruby code and formatted as text. Ruby delimiters without an equals sign—<% %>—represents statements to execute as Ruby code but not formatted as text. The `@server_name` variable is passed in directly from the controller in the view. To run this application, modify the `welcome.rb` controller file to look like Figure 24.14. Then go to the `/app/views/welcome` directory, create the `hello.rhtml` file in Fig. 24.15. Run the welcome application on the Mongrel server (if it is not already running) and direct your browser to the URL `http://localhost:3000/welcome/hello`.

```
# Fig. 24.14: app/controllers/welcome_controller.rb
# Simple controller that passes a parameter to the view.
class WelcomeController < ApplicationController
   # set server_name to server information
   def hello
      @server_name = request.server_software # retrieve software of server
   end # method hello
end # class WelcomeController
```

Fig. 24.14 | Simple controller that passes a parameter to the view.

```
<?xml version = "1.0" encoding = "utf-8"?>
<!DOCTYPE html PUBLIC "-//W3C//DTD XHTML 1.0 Strict//EN"
   "http://www.w3.org/TR/xhtml1/DTD/xhtml1-strict.dtd">

<!-- Fig. 24.15: app/views/welcome/hello.rhtml -->
<!-- View that displays the server name. -->
<html xmlns = "http://www.w3.org/1999/xhtml">
<head>
   <title>hello</title>
</head>
<body style = "background-color: lightyellow">
   <strong>Hello from the view!</strong><br />
   The server you are coming from is
   <em><%= @server_name %></em>
</body>
</html>
```

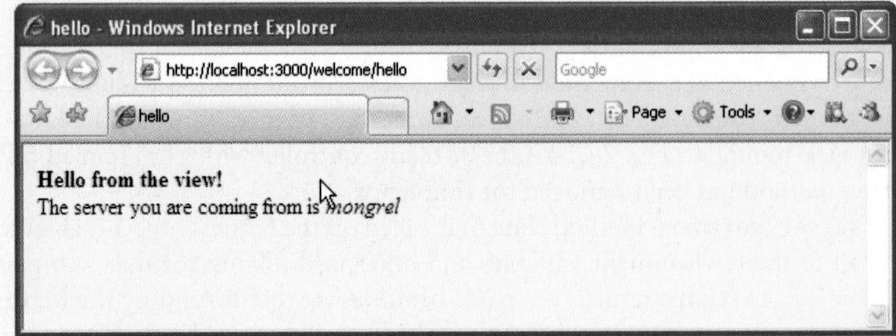

Fig. 24.15 | View that displays the name of the server.

Using a Layout

Often, information spans multiple web pages that could be viewed as a header or footer. Rails allows you to add headers and footers with a **layout**—a master view that is displayed by every method in a controller. A layout can refer to a template of the method that is being called, using `yield`. A layout has the same name as the controller, and is placed in the app/views/layouts directory. Figure 24.16 is a layout for the Welcome controller. To add a layout to the application create a welcome.rhtml file in the apps/views/layouts directory. To run this application, re-load the page from Fig. 24.15.

Line 9 invokes the **action_name** method on the controller object. This displays the name of the method that is currently being called in the controller. Instance variables defined in the controller are copied to both the layout and the view that the layout renders. Line 14 is a placeholder for the view content (hello.rhtml in this example) that is specific to the action called in the controller.

```
1  <?xml version = "1.0" encoding = "utf-8"?>
2  <!DOCTYPE html PUBLIC "-//W3C//DTD XHTML 1.0 Strict//EN"
3     "http://www.w3.org/TR/xhtml11/DTD/xhtml11-strict.dtd">
4
5  <!-- Fig. 24.16: app/views/layouts/welcome.rhtml -->
6  <!-- Layout that displays a greeting. -->
7  <html xmlns = "http://www.w3.org/1999/xhtml">
8  <head>
9      <title><%= controller.action_name %></title>
10 </head>
11 <body style = "background-color: lightyellow">
12    Hello from the Layout!<br />
13    <hr />
14    <%= yield %> <!-- render template -->
15 </body>
16 </html>
```

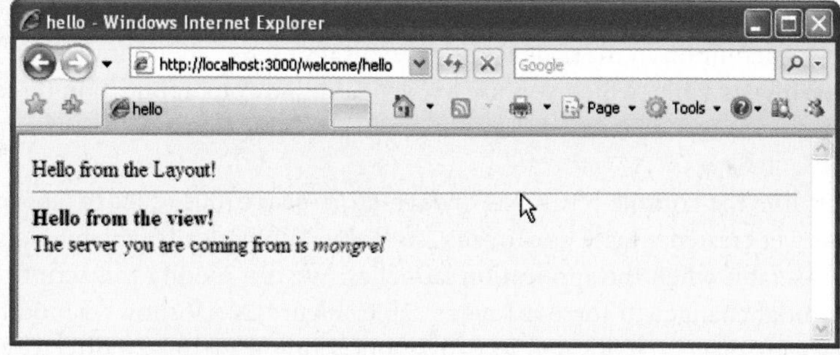

Fig. 24.16 | Layout that displays a greeting.

24.5 A Database-Driven Web Application

The third tier of a typical Rails application—the model—manages the data used in the application. In this section, we set up a database and build a fully functional web application using the ActionView and ActionController classes that we introduced in Section 24.4. We create an application that allows the user to browse and edit an employee list. To create this application's structure, type rails Employees in the **Ruby Console** window.

Object Relational Mapping

Rails makes extensive use of Object-Relational Mapping (ORM) in its web framework. ORM maps a table to application objects. The objects that Rails uses to encapsulate a database inherit from ActiveRecord. By using ActiveRecord and Rails conventions, you can avoid a lot of explicit configuration.

One ActiveRecord convention is that every model that extends ActiveRecord::Base in an application represents a table in a database. The table that the model represents is, by convention, the lowercase, pluralized form of the model. For example, if there were a messages table in your database, Message would be the name of the model representing it. ActiveRecord follows many standard English pluralization rules as well, which means that a Person model would automatically correspond to a people table. Furthermore, if a people table has a first_name column, the Person model would have a method named first_name that returns the value in that column. ActiveRecord does this for you with no additional configuration.

Creating the Database

Before creating a model using ActiveRecord, we need to create the database it will use. You can do that using MySQL's mysqladmin command. Rails will automatically look for a database with the name *applicationName*_development to use as the development database. To create a database for the Employees application, launch the **Ruby Console** and type in mysqladmin -u root create employees_development. If no error is returned, the database was created successfully in the mysql/data directory of your InstantRails installation.

By default MySQL has the user name root and no password. If your settings are different you can modify the appropriate fields database.yml, located in the config folder in your application directory.

Creating the Employee Model

Since Rails separates the model from the rest of the application, we simply need to put the Employee class definition in the models directory. Rails uses a generator to create the model for the employees table, which you use by navigating to your application directory then typing ruby script/generate model employee in the **Ruby Console.** The result is shown in Fig. 24.17.

The last line the console returns is create db/migrate/001_create_employees.rb. We have not yet created a table employees, so Ruby automatically generates a script that will create this table when the application launches. We can modify this script to perform additional initial changes to the employees table. Figure 24.19 shows a modification of 001_create_employees.rb (located in your application's db/migrate directory) that creates the table and adds three records to it.

ActiveRecord has a special feature called Migration, which allows you to preform database operations within Rails. Each object that inherits from ActiveRecord::Migra-

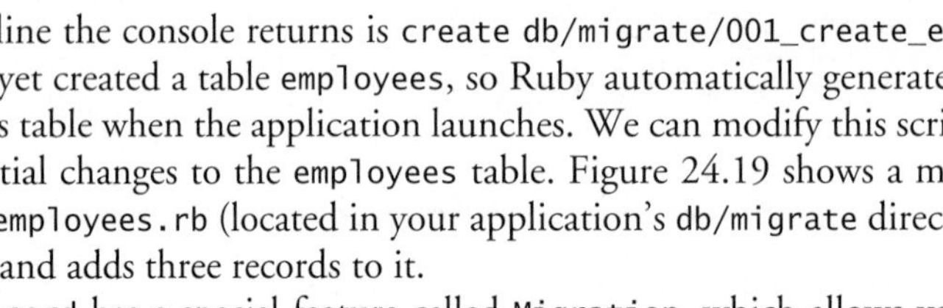

```
C:\WINDOWS\system32\cmd.exe

C:\InstantRails\rails_apps\Employees>ruby script/generate model employee
      exists  app/models/
      exists  test/unit/
      exists  test/fixtures/
   identical  app/models/employee.rb
   identical  test/unit/employee_test.rb
   identical  test/fixtures/employees.yml
      exists  db/migrate
      create  db/migrate/001_create_employees.rb

C:\InstantRails\rails_apps\Employees>_
```

Fig. 24.17 | Creating a model in the Ruby Console.

```
1  # Fig. 24.18: db/migrate/001_create_employees.rb
2  # Database migration script modified to add data to the table
3  class CreateEmployees < ActiveRecord::Migration
4     # create the table with three columns and insert some rows.
5     def self.up
6        create_table  :employees do |t|
7           t.column :first_name, :string
8           t.column :last_name, :string
9           t.column :job_title, :string
10       end # do block
11
12       Employee.create :first_name => "Sue", :last_name => "Green",
13          :job_title => "Programmer"
14       Employee.create :first_name => "Meg", :last_name => "Gold",
15          :job_title => "Programmer"
16       Employee.create :first_name => "John", :last_name => "Gray",
17          :job_title => "Programmer"
18    end # method self.up
19
20    # reverse the migration, delete the table that was created
21    def self.down
22       drop_table :employees
23    end # method self.down
24 end # class CreateEmployees
```

Fig. 24.18 | Database migration script modified to add data to the table.

tion must implement two methods—`self.up` (lines 5–18), which preforms a set of database operations, and `self.down` (lines 21–23), which reverses the database operations performed in `self.up`. In this case `self.up` creates the table with three columns and adds data to it, and `self.down` deletes the table. Line 6 calls the `create_table` function passing as a parameter a code block, inside the `do`, containing the table's column names and types. Lines 12–17 use `ActiveRecord`'s built in `create` method to add data to the `Employees` table. `ActiveRecord` has built-in functionality for many create, retrieve, update, and destroy methods—known in Rails as CRUD. These methods represent the trivial operations that you would want to do with a database.

We can execute the migration using Ruby's `rake` command. To do so open up the **Ruby Console**, navigate to your application's directory and type `rake db:migrate`. This command will call the `self.up` method of all the migrations located in your `db/migrate` directory. If you ever want to roll back the migrations you can type in `rake db:migrate VERSION=0`, which calls each migration's `self.down` method. Specifying a version number other than 0 will call the `self.down` method of all the migrations whose number is greater then the version number.

Common Programming Error 24.1

If the code that comes after the creation of the table in the `self.up` is erroneous, the migration will fail, and will not be able to execute again because the table will already exist. Also, Rails will not have marked the migration as successfully completed, so the version will still be 0 and the migration cannot be rolled back. One way to prevent this problem is to force the table to be dropped every time before creating it. Another solution is splitting up the migration into smaller discrete migrations, one to create the table and another to insert data in the table.

Because our model will never be modified by the application, we do not need to add any functionality to it. Figure 24.19, which represents the `employee.rb` file located in the `app/Models` directory, contains all the code that is needed to integrate the `employees` database table into the application.

```
# Fig. 24.19: employee.rb
# Generated code for an Employee Model.
class Employee < ActiveRecord::Base
end # class Employee
```

Fig. 24.19 | Generated code for an `Employee` model.

Employee Controller

Next, create the controller with the `ruby script/generate controller employees` command as shown in Section 24.4. Figure 24.20 shows the example controller for the Employee application. Line 4 calls the scaffold method. This is a powerful tool that automatically creates CRUD functionality. It creates methods such as `new`, `edit` and `list` so you don't have to create them yourself. It also defines default views for these methods that are rendered when each method is called. You can override the default functionality by defining your own methods. If you override all the CRUD methods you can delete the `scaffold` method. When you override a method, you must also create the corresponding view. Since we will not modify the `new` method created by the scaffold you can see the new method's view with the URL `http://localhost:3000/employee/new` (Figure 24.21). Line 7–9 override the `list` method. Line 8 queries the database and returns a list of all of the `Employee` objects, which gets stored in an `@employees` instance array. This data will be passed to the view.

The `list` View

The `list` template is rendered by the `list` method from the `EmployeeController`. Code for the `list` template is shown in Fig. 24.22. This file should be placed in your application's `app/views/employee` directory. While most of it is just standard XHTML, lines 14–17 contain Ruby code that iterates through all the employees in the `@employees` array instance variable, and outputs each employee's first and last name (line 16). A `for` statement like this in a `list` view is common in database-driven web applications.

```
1  # Fig. 24.20: app/controllers/employees_controller.rb
2  # Provides all of the functionality for the application.
3  class EmployeesController < ApplicationController
4     scaffold :employee  # create scaffold code for controller
5
6     # override scaffold list method
7     def list
8        @employees = Employee.find( :all ) # return an array of Employees
9     end # method list
10 end # class EmployeeController
```

Fig. 24.20 | `Employee` controller provides all of the functionality for the application.

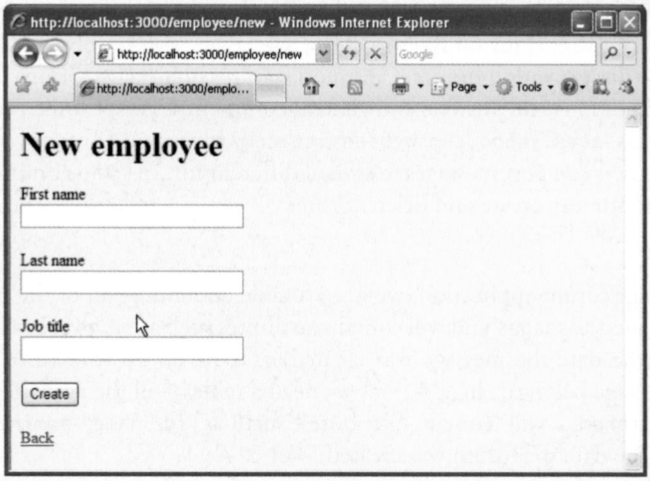

Fig. 24.21 | View of the new action when generated by the `scaffold`.

```
<?xml version = "1.0" encoding = "utf-8"?>
<!DOCTYPE html PUBLIC "-//W3C//DTD XHTML 1.0 Strict//EN"
   "http://www.w3.org/TR/xhtml1/DTD/xhtml1-strict.dtd">

<!-- Fig. 24.22 app/views/employees/list.rhtml -->
<!-- A view that displays a list of Employees. -->
<html xmlns = "http://www.w3.org/1999/xhtml">
<head>
   <title>List of Employees</title>
</head>
<body style="background-color: lightyellow">
   <h1>List of Employees</h1>
   <ol>
   <% for employee in @employees %>
   <!-- create a list item for every employee with his full name -->
      <li><%= employee.first_name %> <%= employee.last_name %></li>
   <% end %>
   </ol>
</body>
</html>
```

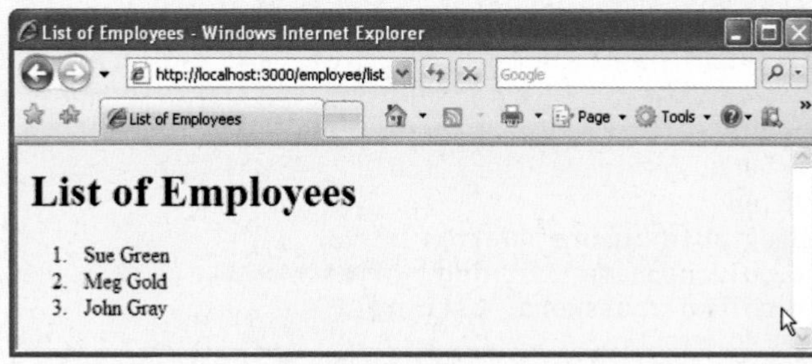

Fig. 24.22 | A view that displays a list of `employees`.

24.6 Case Study: Message Forum

Our next example uses Ruby on Rails to create a message forum website. Message forums enable users to discuss various topics. Common features of message forums include discussion groups, questions and answers and general comments. To see some popular message forums, visit messages.yahoo.com, web.eesite.com/forums and groups.google.com. In this example, users can post messages to several different forums, and administrators of the message forum site can create and delete forums.

Design

For our message forum application, we need a table containing all of the messages. This table will be called messages and will contain attributes such as id, title, author, e-mail, created_on (the date the message was created) and forum_id (the id of the forum to which the message belongs). In addition, we need a table of all the available forums. This table, called forums, will contain attributes such as id, name, administrator and created_on (the date the forum was created).

In our message forum application, we want to have the functionality to create and delete forums, but we don't want everyone who uses our application to be able to do this. Therefore, we will also have a users table, which contains the username/password combinations of all the application's administrators.

Before we implement this design we must create the empty application called messageboard and the database for this application. Type in rails Messageboard and then mysqladmin -u root create messageboard_development in the **Ruby Console**.

24.6.1 Logging In and Logging Out

Use the model generator to generate the User model by typing ruby script/generate model User into the **Ruby Console** (from the Messageboard directory). Next, create the table that will be associated with the model. To do that, modify the migration created by the model generator to set up the users table and add some data to it. Figure 24.23 is the 001_create_users.rb migration (from the db/migrate directory) which sets up the user table.

The create_table function call (lines 6–9) specifies the table's columns. By default a primary key id column is created, so it is not included here. Lines 7–8 create the name and password columns with appropriate types. Note that the name has a limit of 11 characters. Line 11 adds data to the table. To execute this migration type rake db:migrate in the **Ruby Console**.

```
1  # Fig. 24.23: db/migrate/001_create_users.rb
2  # Database migration script modified to add data to the table.
3  class CreateUsers < ActiveRecord::Migration
4     # create and configure users table
5     def self.up
6        create_table :users do |t|
7           t.column :name, :string, :limit => 11
8           t.column :password, :string
9        end # do block
```

Fig. 24.23 | Database migration script modified to add data to the table. (Part 1 of 2.)

```
      User.create :name => "user1", :password => "54321"
   end # method self.up

   # remove users table
   def self.down
      drop_table :users
   end # method self.down
end # class CreateUsers
```

Fig. 24.23 | Database migration script modified to add data to the table. (Part 2 of 2.)

Common Programming Error 24.2

Creating a column without explicitly specifying a limit on length will cause Rails to truncate the data entered into the database with database-defined limits.

Since the `users` table never changes, nothing needs to be specified in the `User` model, but one still needs to exist. This will allow the controller to access a `User` as an `ActiveRecord`. Figure 24.24 shows the empty model for the `users` table.

Next, we need to provide user creation, field validation and user logout functionality through the use of a controller (Fig. 24.25). Create this controller by typing `ruby script/generate controller user`. When a user logs in, we will keep track of that `User` object in a session variable—a variable that maintains information across multiple pages of a web application. The purpose of the `admin` method (lines 5–7) is to pass a blank `user` object into the `admin` page, which will get filled with information, then render the `admin.rhtml` template. The `validate` method (lines 10–21) checks the `user` model to determine

```
# Fig. 24.24: app/models/user.rb
# Generated code for the User model.
class User < ActiveRecord::Base
end # method User
```

Fig. 24.24 | Generated code for the `User` model.

```
1  # Fig. 24.25: app/controllers/users_controller.rb
2  # UsersController provides validation functionality for the table.
3  class UsersController < ApplicationController
4     # create a new User object
5     def admin
6        @user = User.new # create a new User object
7     end # method admin
8
9     # validate that user exists
10    def validate
11       # find a user with the correct name and password
12       @user = User.find_by_name_and_password( params[ :user ][ :name ],
13          params[ :user ][ :password ] )
14
```

Fig. 24.25 | `UsersController` provides validation functionality for the table. (Part 1 of 2.)

```
15       if ( @user == nil ) # if the user dosn't exist
16          redirect_to :action => "admin" # redirect to admin action
17       else # user does exist
18          session[ :user ] = @user # store the user in a session variable
19          redirect_to :controller => "forums", :action => "index"
20       end # if
21    end # method validate
22
23    # log user out
24    def logout
25       reset_session # delete all session variables
26       redirect_to :controller => "forums", :action => "index" # redirect
27    end # method logout
28 end # class UserController
```

Fig. 24.25 | `UsersController` provides validation functionality for the table. (Part 2 of 2.)

whether the username exists, then redirects the application to the next action based on the result of that check.

Rails allows us to generate methods dynamically to serve a specific purpose. Lines 12–13 call the `find_by_name_and_password` method, which searches the model with the `name` and `password`, passed as a parameter.

The `validate` method assigns to an instance variable named `@user` (line 12) the value of the `User` that was returned by the `find_by_name_and_password` method. If no such `User` exists, the client is redirected to the `admin` page and asked to log in again (line 16). If the `User` does exist, a session variable is created (line 18), and line 19 redirects the client to the `index` of the `forums` controller, which we create in Section 24.6.4. The `logout` method (lines 24–27) uses the `reset_session` method to delete all the user's session variables, forcing the user to sign in again to use administrative options.

Performance Tip 24.1

Storing full objects in the session is inefficient. The user object is one of the rare exceptions, because it doesn't change very often and is frequently needed in web applications that manage the state information for unique clients.

Method `admin`'s view is a simple login form. The template is shown in Fig. 24.26. It asks the user for a name and password using the **`text_field`** (line 6) and **`password_field`** (line 9) helpers, then sends the information to the `validate` method when the user clicks **Sign In**.

```
1 <!-- Fig. 24.26: app/views/users/admin.rhtml -->
2 <!-- Login form used to send data to the user controller. -->
3 <h1>Please Log In</h1>
4 <% form_tag :action => 'validate' do %> <!-- create form tag -->
5    <p><label for="user_name">Name</label><br/>
6    <%= text_field 'user', 'name'  %></p> <!-- create input tag -->
7
```

Fig. 24.26 | Login form used to send data to the `user` controller. (Part 1 of 2.)

```
8       <p><label for="user_password">Password</label><br/>
9       <%= password_field 'user', 'password'  %></p> <!-- create input tag -->
10      <%= submit_tag "Sign In" %> <!-- create submit tag -->
11   <% end %> <!-- create an end form tag -->
```

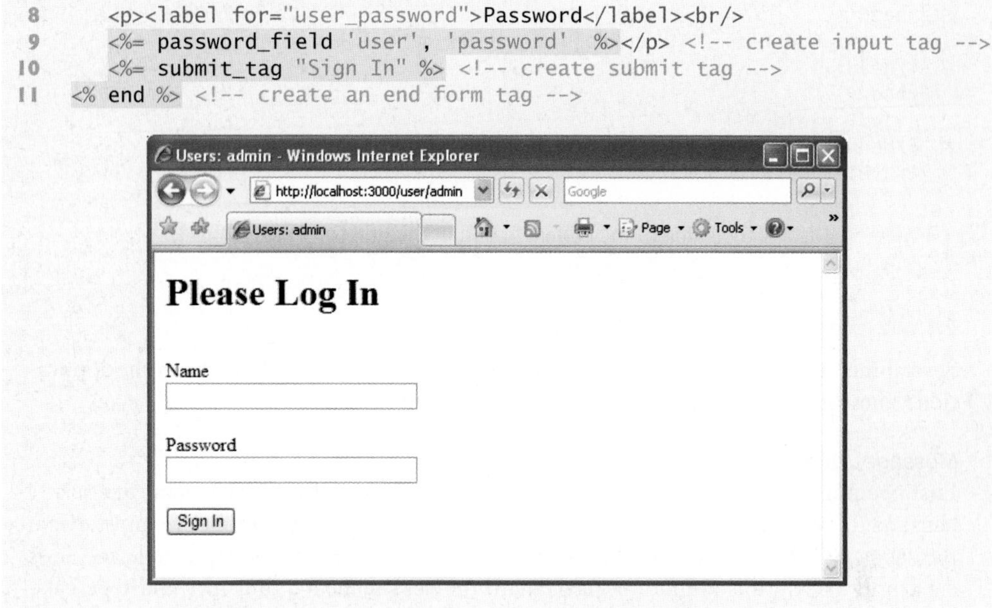

Fig. 24.26 | Login form used to send data to the `user` controller. (Part 2 of 2.)

Rails **helpers** are methods that generate XHTML content for the view. The `password_field` helper method generates a text field that masks the text inside it. Both `text_field` and `password_field` specify a model and the column. This information is used to determine the validation properties for each column when validating the text typed into these fields. When the user clicks the submit button defined in line 10, the **`form_tag`** method (line 4) automatically generates a `Hash`, where the keys are the names of the input fields and the values are what the user entered, and sends it to the `validate` action. The link to the `validate` action is specified by the `action` option. To display this action, run the Mongrel server and navigate your browser to `http://localhost:3000/user/admin`.

We define the `user` controller's template in Fig. 24.27. Because the `user` controller has only a single view to render, we could have simply include this XHTML in the view. The benefit of a template is that it allows us to easily add more views in the future that are all based on the same template and adhere to Ruby on Rails' DRY (Don't Repeat Yourself) philosophy. Line 9 displays the current action in the title bar. Line 12 is the placeholder for the content of the action's view.

```
1   <?xml version = "1.0" encoding = "utf-8"?>
2   <!DOCTYPE html PUBLIC "-//W3C//DTD XHTML 1.0 Strict//EN"
3      "http://www.w3.org/TR/xhtml1/DTD/xhtml1-strict.dtd">
4
5   <!-- Fig. 24.27: app/views/layouts/users.rhtml-->
6   <!-- Display the name of the current action in the title bar -->
7   <html xmlns = "http://www.w3.org/1999/xhtml">
```

Fig. 24.27 | Display the name of the current action in the title bar. (Part 1 of 2.)

```
<head>
   <title>Users: <%= controller.action_name %></title>
</head>
<body>
   <%= yield %>
</body>
</html>
```

Fig. 24.27 | Display the name of the current action in the title bar. (Part 2 of 2.)

24.6.2 Embellishing the Models

Several methods must be added to the model so that it can be modified from the application. These methods are all defined by `ActiveRecord`.

`Message` Model

First, we must create an empty `Message` model by typing `ruby script/generate model Message` in the **Ruby Console**. Before we make any change to the model we must create the `messages` table. Figure 24.28 is the migration that creates the messages table and adds data to it. To run this migration, navigate to the `messageboard` directory and type `rake db:migrate`.

```
# Fig. 24.28: db/migrate/002_create_messages.rb
# Database migration script modified to add data to the table.
class CreateMessages < ActiveRecord::Migration
   # create and configure messages table
   def self.up
      create_table :messages, do |t|
         t.column :title, :string, :limit => 64
         t.column :author, :string, :limit => 20
         t.column :created_on, :timestamp
         t.column :email, :string, :limit => 40
         t.column :message, :text
         t.column :forum_id, :integer
      end # do block

      Message.create :title => "Welcome to the Fourth Edition",
         :author => "Bob Green",
         :email => "noone@deitel.com",
         :message => "We hope you enjoy the book.",
         :forum_id => 2
   end # method self.up

   # remove messages table
   def self.down
      drop_table :messages
   end # method self.down
end # class CreateForums
```

Fig. 24.28 | Database migration script modified to add data to the table.

The `create_table` function call (lines 6–13) specifies the columns of the table. Lines 7–12 create the `title`, `author`, `created_on`, `email`, `message` and `forum_id` columns with appropriate variable types and length limits. Lines 15–20 add data to the table. Rails fills the `created_on` column value automatically when a new row is created. To apply the migration, type `rake db:migrate` in the console window.

Figure 24.29 shows the `Message` model that encapsulates the `messages` table in the database. Line 4 invokes the `belongs_to` method, which defines an association with the `forums` table that can be used to access elements of the `forums` table. This method will allow the `Message` to access the `forum` to which the given `Message` belongs simply by calling a method named `forum` on the `Message`. This is known as an association method.

Lines 7–9 are examples of validators that can be applied to an object that inherits from `ActiveRecord`. These validations occur when the `save` method is called on a `message` object in an attempt to store it in the database. If the validations are successful, then the object is saved to the database and the method returns `true`. If the validations fail, an `Errors` object associated with the `Message` object is updated and the method returns `false`. The method `validates_presence_of` ensures that all of the fields specified by its parameters are not empty. The method `validates_format_of` matches all of the fields specified by its parameters with a regular expression. The regular expression in line 9 represents a valid e-mail address. This regular expression can be found in the Rails framework documentation at `api.rubyonrails.org`.

```
1  # Fig. 24.29: app/models/message.rb
2  # Message Model containing validation and initialization functionality.
3  class Message < ActiveRecord::Base
4     belongs_to :forum # adds a forum method to Message
5
6     # validators (validates automatically before ActiveRecord.save)
7     validates_presence_of :title, :author, :email, :message
8     validates_format_of :email,
9        :with => /^([^@\s]+)@((?:[-a-z0-9]+\.)+[a-z]{2,})$/i
10 end # class Message
```

Fig. 24.29 | `Message` model containing validation and initialization functionality.

`Forum` Model

Next, create an empty `forum` model by typing in `ruby script/generate model forum`. Then create the `forums` table in a similar fashion to `messages` and `users`. Figure 24.30 is the `Migration` that sets up the `messages` table.

The `create_table` function call (lines 6–10) specifies the columns of the table. Lines 7–9 create the `name`, `administrator` and `created_on` columns with appropriate variable types and length limits. Lines 12–16 add data to the table. To apply the migration, type in `rake db:migrate`.

The model for the `forums` table (Fig. 24.31) looks similar to the model for the `messages` table. We can create an association method that allows a `Forum` to access every `Message` that is associated with it. Line 4 shows the `has_many` method, which will create a method called `messages` for every `Forum` object. The `messages` method will return an array of all the `messages` in the `Forum`.

```
# Fig. 24.30 db/migrate/003_create_forums.rb
# Database migration script modified to add data to the table.
class CreateForums < ActiveRecord::Migration
   # Create and configure forums table
   def self.up
      create_table :forums do |t|
         t.column :name, :string, :limit => 64
         t.column :administrator, :string, :limit => 20
         t.column :created_on, :timestamp
      end # do block

      Forum.create :name => "Ruby On Rails",
         :administrator => "user1"
      Forum.create :name => "Internet and World Wide Web: 4th Edition",
         :administrator => "user1"
   end # method self.up

   # remove forums table
   def self.down
      drop_table :forums
   end # method self.down
end # class CreateForums
```

Fig. 24.30 | Database migration script modified to add data to the table.

```
1 # Fig. 24.31: app/models/forum.rb
2 # Forum model that includes validation and initialization functionality.
3 class Forum < ActiveRecord::Base
4    has_many :messages, :dependent => :destroy
5    validates_presence_of :name
6 end # class Forum
```

Fig. 24.31 | `Forum` model that includes validation and initialization functionality.

When a `forum` is deleted, all of that `forum`'s `messages` should also be deleted. Line 4 sets the `dependent` parameter of the `has_many` method to `:destroy` to ensure that when a forum is destroyed all the messages that are associated with it are destroyed as well.

24.6.3 Generating Scaffold Code

Now that the user can log in and out of our application, we need to create the `messages` and `forums` views and controllers. Since much of this code is standard CRUD, we can use the Rails `scaffold` generator by typing `ruby script/generate scaffold message` and `ruby script/generate scaffold forum` in the **Ruby Console**. The `scaffold generator` creates the scaffold code that would be generated using the `scaffold` method in the controller. When using the `scaffold` method, notice that the controller name and the view directory are both pluralized forms of the name, rather than the singular form that the model generator and controller generator would create.

24.6.4 Forum Controller and Forum Views

The ForumsController (Fig. 24.32), which was initially generated as part of the scaffolding, handles all incoming requests from the client. The index, list, new, and delete methods are all responsible for rendering a view, while the create and destroy methods are responsible for processing incoming data and then redirecting to another action. We will not use the edit or show methods so you may delete the .rhtml view files associated with them.

The verify method call in lines 4–5 is edited scaffold code, which ensures a post request is used to send data to the server for each request that modifies the database. Whenever a method modifies a database, the arguments should be from a post so that they don't show up in the URL. The :only argument specifies which actions this verification should be applied (create and destroy in this case). If a call to create or destroy is not made via a post request, line 5 redirects the request to the list action.

```
1  # Fig. 24.32: app/controllers/forums_controller.rb
2  # ForumsController implements CRUD functionality.
3  class ForumsController < ApplicationController
4     verify :method => :post, :only => [ :destroy, :create ],
5        :redirect_to => { :action => :list }
6
7     # shortcut to the list method
8     def index
9        list
10       render :action => 'list'
11    end # method index
12
13    # set up the list web page that lists all forums
14    def list
15       @forums = Forum.find( :all )
16    end # method list
17
18    # set up the new web page that adds a new forum
19    def new
20       if ( session[ :user ] == nil ) # if user is not logged in
21          flash[ :error ] = 'you must be logged in to complete this action'
22          redirect_to :action => "index" and return
23       end # if
24
25       @forum = Forum.new
26    end # method new
27
28    # attempt to create a new forum with the parameters passed in
29    def create
30       @forum = Forum.new( params[ :forum ] )
31       @forum.administrator = session[ :user ].name
32
33       if @forum.save # if save method was successful
34          flash[ :notice ] = 'Forum was successfully created.'
35          redirect_to :action => 'list'
```

Fig. 24.32 | ForumsController implements CRUD functionality. (Part 1 of 2.)

```
36         else # save was unsuccessful
37            render :action => 'new' # go to new
38         end # if...else
39      end # method create
40
41      # set up the delete web page
42      def delete
43         if ( session[ :user ] == nil ) # if user is not logged in
44            flash[ :error ] = 'you must be logged in to complete this action'
45            redirect_to :action => "index" and return
46         else
47            @forums = Forum.find( :all,
48               :conditions => "administrator = '#{ session[:user].name }'" )
49         end # if else
50      end # method delete
51
52      # delete a forum with a specified parameter
53      def destroy
54         # find the forum and delete it
55         Forum.destroy( params[ :forum ][ :id ] ) # delete the forum
56         redirect_to :action => 'list' # redirect to list
57      end # method destroy
58   end # class ForumsController
```

Fig. 24.32 | `ForumsController` implements CRUD functionality. (Part 2 of 2.)

Method `index` (line 8–11) redirects the client to the `list` method (lines 14–16), which obtains a list of forums from the database to be displayed on the page. The `new` method (lines 19–26) checks whether the user has privileges to create a new forum. If not, lines 21–22 display an error and redirect the user to the `index` action. The hash called `flash` in line 21 is used to display `messages` in the view. `Flash` is a special type of session storage that is always automatically cleared after every request to the controller. If the user has privileges, line 25 creates a new instance of the forum object which is initialized with data from the user input.

The `create` method (lines 29–39) is similar to the scaffold code, but differs in that the `administrator` attribute of the `forum` being saved must be the `name` of the user who is logged in. Line 33 attempts to save the forum, and either renders a template if the method returns `false` (line 37), or redirects to the `list` method and updates the `flash` object if the method returns `true` (lines 34–35). The `delete` method (lines 42–50) sets up the deletion operation by finding all the forums created by the user currently logged in. Once the user picks a forum to delete in the view, the `destroy` method (lines 53–58) destroys the forum specified by the user (line 55) and re-displays the list (line 56).

List View

Figure 24.33 is the template that is rendered by the `list` method from the `Forum` controller. [*Note:* We replaced the auto-generated `list.rhtml` from the scaffolding]. This is also the template rendered by the `index` method. Line 10 uses the `link_to` method to create a link with the name of the forum and the `list` action of its messages, which we build in Section 24.6.5.. Lines 12–13 contain a conditional statement which make the forum italicized for five minutes after it has been created by using the `minutes.ago` method of the

```
1  <!-- Fig. 24.33: app/views/forums/list.rhtml -->
2  <!-- Template for the list action that displays a list of forums. -->
3  <h1>Deitel Message Forums</h1>
4  <h2>Available Forums</h2>
5  <ul>
6     <% for forum in @forums %>
7     <!-- create a list item for every forum -->
8        <li>
9           <!-- link to list action in messages -->
10          <%= link_to ( forum.name, {:controller => 'messages',
11             :action => 'list', :forum_id => forum.id},
12             { :class => (forum.created_on < 5.minutes.ago ?
13             'recent': nil ) } ) %>
14       </li>
15    <% end %> <!-- end for -->
16 </ul>
17 <% if ( session[ :user ] ) then %>
18    <!-- a user is logged in -->
19    <h2>Forum Management</h2>
20    <ul>
21       <li><%= link_to 'Add a Forum', :action => 'new' %></li>
22       <li><%= link_to 'Delete a Forum', :action => 'delete' %></li>
23    </ul>
24 <% end %> <!-- end if -->
```

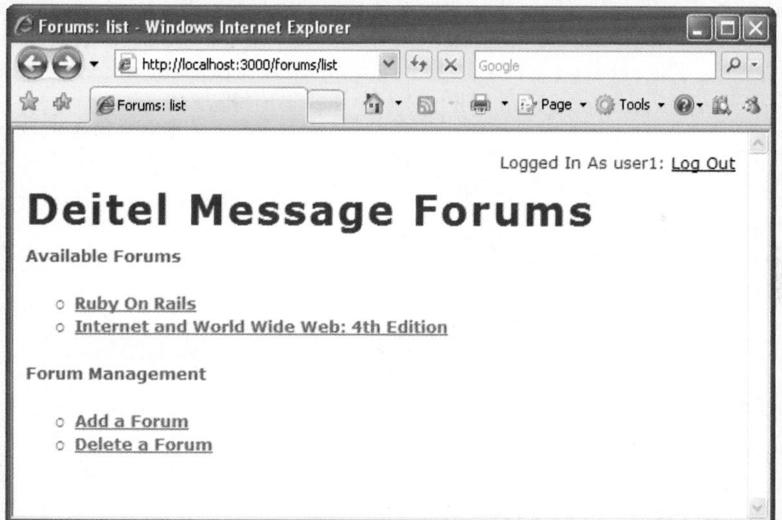

Fig. 24.33 | Template for the list action that displays a list of forums.

`Fixnum` class. The `if` statement in lines 17–24 displays the XHTML in lines 19–23 only if there is a user logged in.

New View

Figure 24.34 shows the template for the `Forum` controller's `new` method. This is code generated by the `scaffold`. Lines 4–7 create a form that is rendered to the page, and indicate

```
1 <!-- Fig. 24.34 app/views/forums/new.rhtml -->
2 <!-- Template for a new action that adds a forum to the forums table. -->
3 <h1>New forum</h1>
4 <% form_tag :action => 'create' do %>
5    <%= render :partial => 'form' %>
6    <%= submit_tag "Create" %>
7 <% end %>
8
9 <%= link_to 'Back', :action => 'list' %>
```

Fig. 24.34 | Template for a `new` action that adds a `forum` to the `forums` table.

that the action `create` will be called when the **Create** button is pressed. This template renders a partial—a block of HTML and embedded Ruby code stored in another file and inserted directly into the document. A partial allows the same block of code to be used across multiple documents. In this example, line 5 renders the partial named `form`, which inserts the file `_form.rhtml` at that line of code. A partial filename always begins with an underscore.

Line 6 uses the `submit_tag` method to create a submit button that when clicked will create a `Hash` with the form's fields as keys and the user's input as values. Line 9 uses the `link_to` function to allow the user to go back to the forums list by redirecting the client to the `list` action of the `forum` controller.

The partial in Fig. 24.35 renders the input text field for the form. The `administrator` and `created_on` fields will be generated on the server, so they've been deleted from the scaffold's code. The `created_on` field will be automatically set to the time when the forum is created. The administrator field will be set by the controller.

```
<!-- Fig. 24.35: app/views/forums/_form.rhtml -->
<!-- Partial that contains a form used to add a new forum. -->
<%= error_messages_for 'forum' %>
<p><label for="forum_name">Name</label><br/>
<%= text_field 'forum', 'name'  %></p>
```

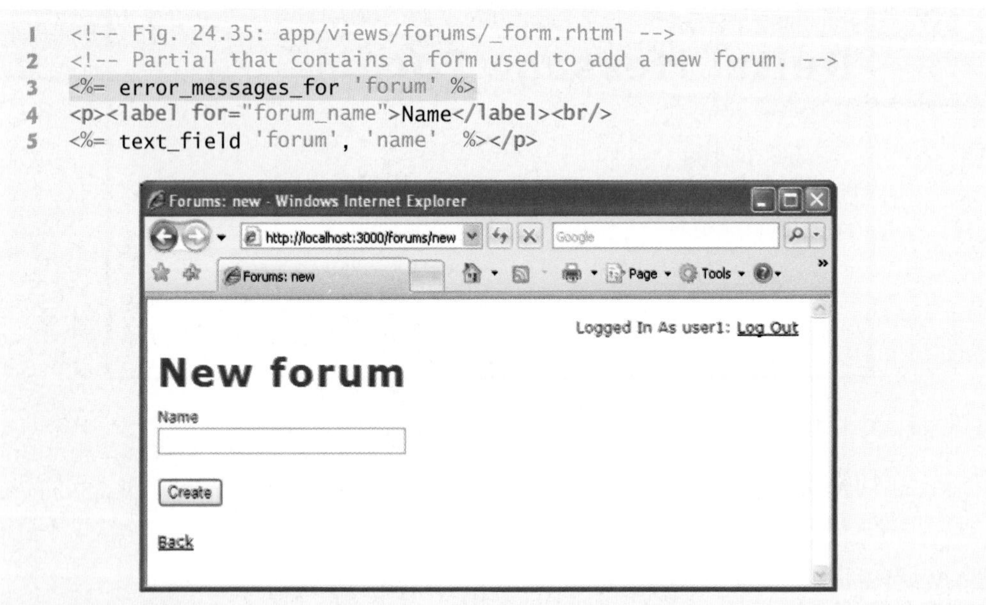

Fig. 24.35 | Partial that contains a form used to add a new `forum`.

`delete` *View*

The `delete` view (Fig. 24.36) is not generated by the scaffold, so we create it ourselves. It is similar to `create` in that it renders a form, but uses the `collection_select` method to display for that administrator the list of available forums to delete. The `collection_select` takes five parameters—the type of object to be selected, the field which the options are to be grouped by, the collection from that to obtain the list of objects, the field that will be sent once an option is selected and the field that is to be displayed on the screen for each option.

```
<!-- Fig. 24.36: app/views/forums/delete.rhtml -->
<!-- Template for delete action used to delete a Forum. -->
<h1>Delete a Forum</h1><br />

<% form_tag  :action => :destroy do %> <!-- create from tag -->
   <p><label for="forum_id">Forum Name</label><br />
   <%= collection_select "forum", "id", @forums, "id", "name" %></p>
   <%= submit_tag "Delete" %> <!-- create submit tag -->
<% end %> <!-- create end form tag -->

<%= link_to 'Back', :action => 'list' %> <!-- link back to list method -->
```

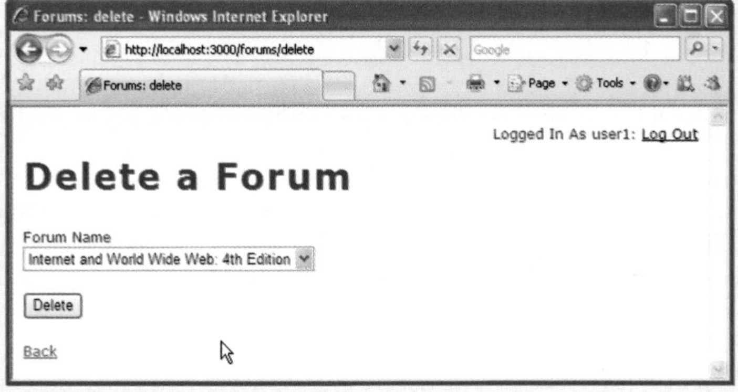

Fig. 24.36 | Template for `Delete` action used to delete a `forum`.

`Forum` Layout

Figure 24.37 is the layout that renders every template for the `ForumsController`. It has all the necessary XHTML, and contains the login/logout text (lines 13–25). Line 29 automatically renders the template of any action that uses the template.

```
1  <?xml version = "1.0" encoding = "utf-8"?>
2  <!DOCTYPE html PUBLIC "-//W3C//DTD XHTML 1.0 Strict//EN"
3     "http://www.w3.org/TR/xhtml1/DTD/xhtml1-strict.dtd">
4
5  <!-- Fig. 24.37: app/views/layouts/forums.rhtml -->
6  <!-- Layout that displays the logged-in user for every Forums action. -->
```

Fig. 24.37 | Layout that displays the logged-in user for every `Forums` action. (Part 1 of 2.)

```
7  <html xmlns = "http://www.w3.org/1999/xhtml">
8  <head>
9     <title>Forums: <%= controller.action_name %></title>
10    <%= stylesheet_link_tag 'scaffold' %> <!-- link to a stylesheet -->
11 </head>
12 <body>
13    <div style = "text-align: right">
14       <% if ( session[ :user ] ) then %> <!-- if user is logged on -->
15          <!-- code to display if user is logged on -->
16          <%= "Logged In As #{ session[ :user ].name }: " %>
17          <%= link_to 'Log Out',
18             :controller => 'users', :action => 'logout' %>
19       <% else %> <!-- user is not logged on -->
20          <!-- code to display if user is not logged on -->
21          <%= "Not Currently Logged In:" %>
22          <%= link_to 'Log In',
23             :controller => 'users', :action => 'admin' %>
24       <% end %> <!-- end if -->
25    </div>
26    <p style="color: green"><%= flash[ :notice ] %></p>
27    <p style="color: red"><%= flash[ :error ] %></p>
28 
29    <%= yield %> <!-- displays template -->
30 </body>
31 </html>
```

Fig. 24.37 | Layout that displays the logged-in user for every `Forums` action. (Part 2 of 2.)

If the user is logged in (line 14), lines 16–18 display the username on the page and use the `link_to` method to enable the user to log out by redirecting to the `logout` action. Otherwise, lines 21–23 allow the user to log in, using the `link_to` helper method to redirect the user to the `admin` action. Lines 26–27 display any error messages or success messages that result from user interactions.

24.6.5 Message Controller and Message Views

The `MessagesController` (Fig. 24.38) is similar to the `ForumsController`, except that its `list` method (lines 8–22) doesn't list all of the `messages`—it lists only the ones with the specified `forum_id` that is passed in as a URL parameter from the `Forum list` view. Line 10 updates the `session` variable to match the URL parameter. If no parameter value is specified, the `forum_id` session variable is used. If neither of these exists, line 14 displays an error and line 15 redirects the client to the `list` action of the forum `controller`. The `find` method which is called on `Message` (line 18–19) specifies that the messages should be ordered by their `created_on` dates in descending order. Line 20 also calls the `find` method to obtain the `forum` object, which we will need to add messages to the `forum`.

The `create` method (lines 30–40) replaces the method generated by the scaffold. Line 31 obtains the `id` of the forum to which the message should be added and line 32 obtains the new message entered by the user. If the message is added to the database successfully, lines 35–36 set the appropriate message to be displayed in the view using the `flash` object and redirect the client to the `list` action. Otherwise, line 38 redirects the client to the `new` action, prompting the user to enter the message again.

```
# Fig. 24.38: app/controllers/messages_controller.rb
# MessagesController that implements CRUD functionality.
class MessagesController < ApplicationController
   verify :method => :post, :only => [ :destroy, :create ],
      :redirect_to => { :action => :list }

   # sets up the list web page that lists all messages
   def list
      if ( params[ :forum_id ] ) # if parameter forum_id is provided
         session[ :forum_id ] = params[ :forum_id ]
      end # if

      if ( session[ :forum_id ] == nil ) # if no forum_id is provided
         flash[ :notice ]  = 'there has been an error.'
         redirect_to :controller => "forums", :action => "list" and return
      end # if

      @messages = Message.find( :all, :order => "created_on desc",
         :conditions => "forum_id = #{ session[:forum_id ] }" )
      @forum = Forum.find( :first,
         :conditions => "id = #{ session[ :forum_id ] }" )
   end # method list

   # sets up the new web page that creates a message
   def new
      @message = Message.new
   end # method new

   # attempts to create a new message with the parameters passed in
   def create
      @message = Message.new( params[ :message ] )
      @message.forum_id = session[ :forum_id ]

      if @message.save  # if save method was successful
         flash[ :notice ] = 'Message was successfully created.'
         redirect_to :action => 'list'
      else # save was unsuccessful
         render :action => 'new'
      end # if
   end # method create
end # class MessagesController
```

Fig. 24.38 | `MessagesController` that implements CRUD functionality.

List View

The `list` view (Fig. 24.39) for the `Message` controller is similar to the `list` view for the `Forum` controller, except that more information is displayed in the messages `list` view. It uses CSS to format the output. In this view, every `message` object acts like a `Hash`—passing a column name as a key returns the corresponding value in the `message` object. To obtain an a column's value, include the attribute method's name in square brackets after the name of the object. For each `message` in the forum, line 12 displays the title, line 13 displays the author and line 19 displays the message's text. At line 14, the Ruby `Time` object that is returned by the `message['created on']` is formatted using the Ruby `Time` class formatting

```
1  <!-- Fig. 24.39: app/views/messages/list.rhtml -->
2  <!-- Template for the list action that displays a list of Forums. -->
3  <div style = "text-align: center">
4     <table style = "width: 600px; margin: 0 auto 0 auto">
5        <tr class="msgHeader">
6           <td><%= @forum.name %></td>
7        </tr>
8        <% for message in @messages %>
9           <!-- create two table rows for every message -->
10          <tr class="msgTitle">
11             <td>
12             <strong><%= message[ 'title' ] %></strong><br />
13             by <em><%= message[ 'author' ] %></em> at
14             <%= message[ 'created_on' ].strftime("%m/%d/%Y at %I:%M%p") %>
15             </td>
16          </tr>
17          <tr class="msgPost">
18             <!-- message content -->
19             <td><%= message[ 'message' ] %></td>
20          </tr>
21       <% end %>
22    </table>
23
24    <%= link_to 'New message', :action => 'new' %> |
25    <%= link_to 'list forums',
26       :controller => 'forums', :action => 'index' %>
27 </div>
```

Fig. 24.39 | Template for the `list` action that displays a list of messages.

options. Lines 24–26 use the `link_to` method to allow the user to create a message in the current forum or to go back to the list of the forums.

New View

The new template for the `Message` controller is omitted here because it is scaffold code that is nearly identical to the `new` template for the `Forum` controller. The partial shown in Fig. 24.40 for the `messages` form is also similar. Lines 8, 12 and 16 use the `text_field` helper method to create fields for specifying the `title`, `author` and `email`. Line 20 uses the `text_area` helper method to create an input area of a certain size, to be used to input the message. These fields are validated when the `Message` model's `save` method is called. If the model does not deem the data valid, line 3 displays the error messages.

```
<!-- Fig. 24.40: app/views/messages/_form.rhtml -->
<!-- A form that allows the user to enter a new message. -->
<%= error_messages_for 'message' %>

<table>
   <tr class = "alignRight">
      <td>Title</td>
      <td><%= text_field 'message', 'title'  %></td>
   </tr>
   <tr class = "alignRight">
      <td>Author</td>
      <td><%= text_field 'message', 'author' %></td>
   </tr>
   <tr class = "alignRight">
      <td>Email</td>
      <td><%= text_field 'message', 'email'  %></td>
   </tr>
   <tr><td colspan = "2">Message</td></tr>
   <tr><td colspan = "2">
      <%= text_area 'message', 'message', :cols => "30", :rows => "4"%>
   </td></tr>
</table>
```

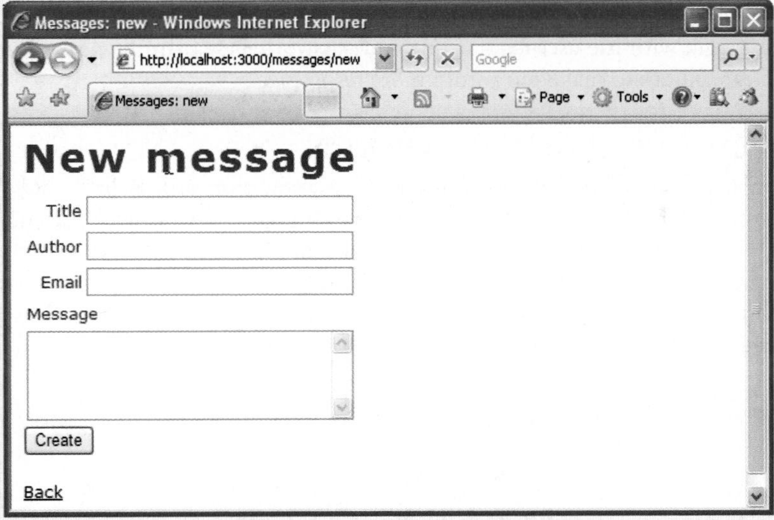

Fig. 24.40 | Form that allows the user to enter a new message.

`Message` Layout

Figure 24.41 shows the layout used to render all `Message` templates. Line 10 invokes the `scaffold.css` style sheet, which we changed slightly to improve our page's presentation. To make the style sheet available for import it must be placed in the `public/stylesheets` directory of the application. When a forum has been modified, line 14 displays the appropriate message.

```
<?xml version = "1.0" encoding = "utf-8"?>
<!DOCTYPE html PUBLIC "-//W3C//DTD XHTML 1.0 Strict//EN"
   "http://www.w3.org/TR/xhtml1/DTD/xhtml1-strict.dtd">

<!-- Fig. 24.41: app/views/layouts/messages.rhtml -->
<!-- Message layout that links a style sheet and displays a message. -->
<html xmlns = "http://www.w3.org/1999/xhtml">
<head>
   <title>Messages: <%= controller.action_name %></title>
   <%= stylesheet_link_tag 'scaffold' %>
</head>
<body>
   <% if ( flash[ :notice ] ) then %>
      <p style="color: green"><%= flash[ :notice ] %></p>
   <% end %>
   <%= yield %>
</body>
</html>
```

Fig. 24.41 | Message layout that links a style sheet and displays a message.

We have now implemented the basic functionality of the forum application. To test this application execute it on Mongrel and browse to `http://localhost:3000/forums`. To test the administrative privileges of the forum go to `http://localhost:3000/user/admin` and login with the username `user1` and password `54321`. In the next section we'll add Ajax capabilities to make our forum more responsive.

24.6.6 Ajax-Enabled Rails Applications

Adding Ajax functionality to Rails applications is straightforward. Rails includes a JavaScript library called Prototype that contains easy-to-use cross-browser Ajax functions. Figure 24.42 is the modified layout for the forum file, which now links the prototype library to the application. For the application to have the correct look, make sure you insert the modified style sheet, which can be found in our examples folder, into the `public/stylesheets` directory of the application.

```
<?xml version = "1.0" encoding = "utf-8"?>
<!DOCTYPE html PUBLIC "-//W3C//DTD XHTML 1.0 Strict//EN"
   "http://www.w3.org/TR/xhtml1/DTD/xhtml1-strict.dtd">

<!-- Fig. 24.42: app/views/layouts/forums.rhtml -->
<!-- Forums layout that uses the default JavaScript libraries. -->
<html xmlns = "http://www.w3.org/1999/xhtml">
<head>
   <title>Forums: <%= controller.action_name %></title>
   <%= stylesheet_link_tag 'scaffold' %> <!-- link to a stylesheet -->
   <%= javascript_include_tag :defaults %>
</head>
<body>
```

Fig. 24.42 | Forums layout that uses the default JavaScript libraries. (Part 1 of 2.)

```
14      <div style = "text-align: right">
15         <% if ( session[ :user ] ) then %> <!-- if user is logged on -->
16            <!-- code to display if user is logged on -->
17            <%= "Logged In As #{ session[ :user ].name }: " %>
18            <%= link_to 'Log Out',
19               :controller => 'users', :action => 'logout' %>
20         <% else %> <!-- user is not logged on -->
21            <!-- code to display if user is not logged on -->
22            <%= "Not Currently Logged In:" %>
23            <%= link_to 'Log In',
24               :controller => 'users', :action => 'admin' %>
25         <% end %> <!-- end if -->
26      </div>
27      <p style="color: green"><%= flash[ :notice ] %></p>
28      <p style="color: red"><%= flash[ :error ] %></p>
29
30      <%= yield %> <!-- displays template -->
31   </body>
32   </html>
```

Fig. 24.42 | Forums layout that uses the default JavaScript libraries. (Part 2 of 2.)

Line 11 links in the JavaScript library using the **`javascript_include_tag`** helper method. The defaults parameter tells `javascript_include_tag` to link all the `defaults` JavaScript Rails libraries including Prototype and Script.aculo.us. The rest of the layout file is the same as in the non-Ajax version.

Figure 24.43 changes the `Forum` object's `list` view to perform Ajax requests rather than load a new page. Now, whenever the user clicks a forum's name, the page loads the forum's messages to the right of the forums list with a partial page update.

```
<!-- Fig. 24.43: app/views/forums/list.rhtml -->
<!-- Displaying a list of messages without reloading the page. -->
<h1>Deitel Message Forums</h1>
<div class = "forumList">
   <h2>Available Forums</h2>
   <ul>
      <% for forum in @forums %>
         <li>
            <%= link_to_remote ( forum.name,
               { :url => { :controller => 'messages',
               :action => 'list', :forum_id => forum.id },
               :update => 'currentForum' },
               { :class => ( forum.created_on < 5.minutes.ago ?
               'recent': nil ) } ) %>
         </li>
      <% end %>
   </ul>
   <% if ( session[ :user ] ) then %>
      <h2>Forum Management</h2>
      <ul>
```

Fig. 24.43 | Displaying a list of messages without reloading the page. (Part 1 of 2.)

```
21             <li><%= link_to 'Add a Forum', :action => 'new' %></li>
22             <li><%= link_to 'Delete a Forum', :action => 'delete' %></li>
23          </ul>
24       <% end %>
25    </div>
26    <div id = 'currentForum' class = "ajaxComponent">
27    </div>
```

Fig. 24.43 | Displaying a list of messages without reloading the page. (Part 2 of 2.)

The key change is lines 9–12, which have been changed to call the `link_to_remote` helper method instead of the `link_to` helper method. The `link_to_remote` method allows us to link to JavaScript that we included in the layout file. By specifying the `url` and `update` parameters inside the `link_to_remote` method we are telling Rails to convert these tags into prototype `Ajax.Updater` objects that will update the page asynchronously. The `url` argument (line 10) specifies the `controller` in which to look for the action. The `action` parameter (line 11) specifies the action to invoke. The `forum_id` parameter (line 11) specifies the id to pass to the action. Line 12 specifies `currentForum` as the `id` of the placeholder `div` in the page that needs to be updated. Lines 26–27 define the placeholder `div` element where the list of messages will be inserted. The rest of the code is the same as in the non-Ajax version of this application.

In similar fashion, we modify the `list` and `new` views of the `message` object, to be able to add a message to a forum without reloading the page. First we include all the default JavaScript libraries in the `message.rhtml` layout file (not shown here), ensuring all the views in the message object have access to Prototype. After that we modify all the calls to other actions to be asynchronous. Figure 24.44 is the updated `list.rhtml`.

```
<!-- Fig. 24.44: app/views/messages/list.rhtml -->
<!-- Forum that allows the user to add a message on the same page. -->
<div class = "messageList">
<table style = "width: 400">
   <tr class="msgHeader">
```

Fig. 24.44 | Forum that allows the user to add a message on the same page. (Part 1 of 2.)

```
        <td><%= @forum.name %></td>
    </tr>
    <% for message in @messages %>
        <tr class="msgTitle">
            <td>
                <strong><%= message.title %></strong><br/>
                by <em><%= message.author %></em> at
                <%= message.created_on.strftime( "%m/%d/%Y at %I:%M%p" ) %>
            </td>
        </tr>
        <tr class="msgPost">
            <td><%= message.message %></td>
        </tr>
    <% end %>
</table>

<%= link_to_remote 'New message',
    :url => { :action => 'new' },
    :update => 'currentForum'%>
</div>
```

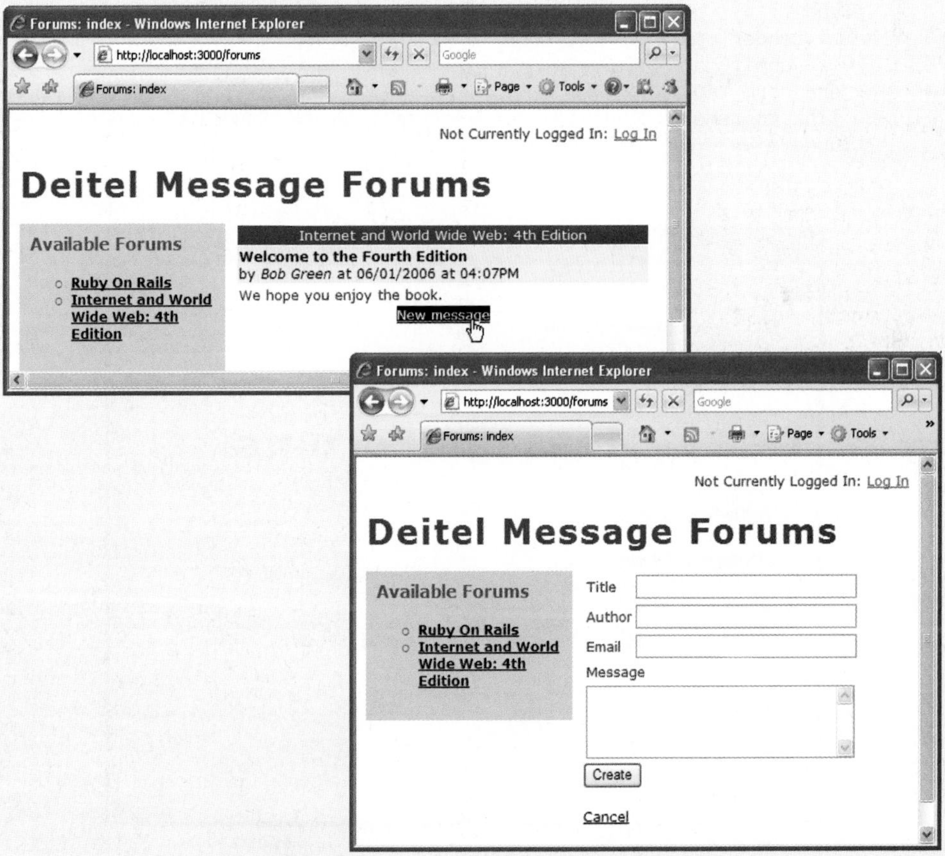

Fig. 24.44 | Forum that allows the user to add a message on the same page. (Part 2 of 2.)

Lines 22–24 use the `link_to_remote` helper method to allow the user to add new messages without reloading the page. The `url` is the `new` action, which returns the form and the placeholder to update is `currentForum`, defined in the `list.rhtml` view of the `forum` object (Fig. 24.43). The `new` view is also modified, so that once the user submits the new message, the updated `div` named `currentForum` is shown without reloading the page. Figure 24.45 shows the modified `new.rhtml`.

Lines 3–7 have been changed to use the **`form_remote_tag`** helper method, which redirects the client to the next action without reloading the page. Once the user clicks the **Submit** button, generated by `submit_tag` (line 6), the form will generate a Prototype `Ajax.Updater` object that will send the data to the action specified and display the result in the specified placeholder. This placeholder is set to `currentForum`, the same element inside which this forum will be displayed. When the user finishes adding the new message, a new forum will replace this form, without reloading the page. Lines 8–9 provide the user a way to cancel the new-message operation, in which case the original forum displays.

```
1 <!-- Fig. 24.45: app/views/messages/new.rhtml -->
2 <!-- Allows the user to add a new message without reloading the page. -->
3 <%= form_remote_tag :url=> { :action => 'create' },
4    :update => 'currentForum' %>
5    <%= render :partial => 'form' %>
6    <%= submit_tag "Create" %>
7 <%= end_form_tag %>
8 <%= link_to_remote 'Cancel', :url=> { :action => 'list' },
9    :update => 'currentForum' %>
```

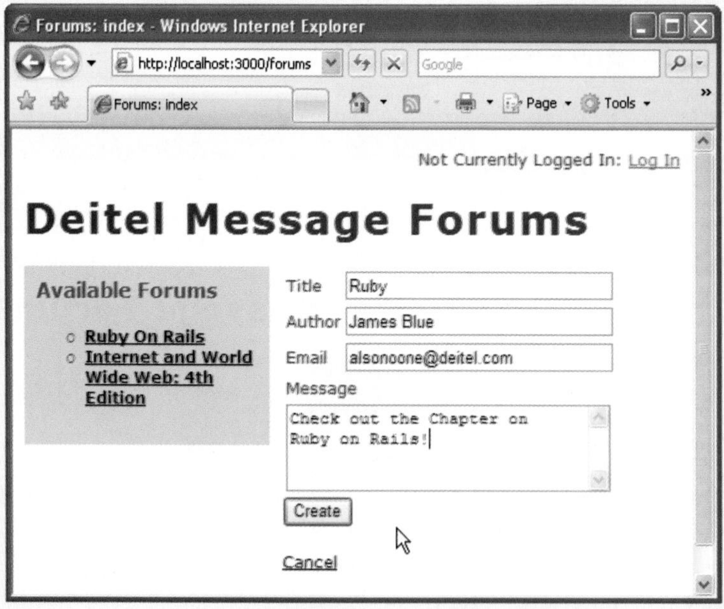

Fig. 24.45 | Adding a new message without reloading the page. (Part 1 of 2.)

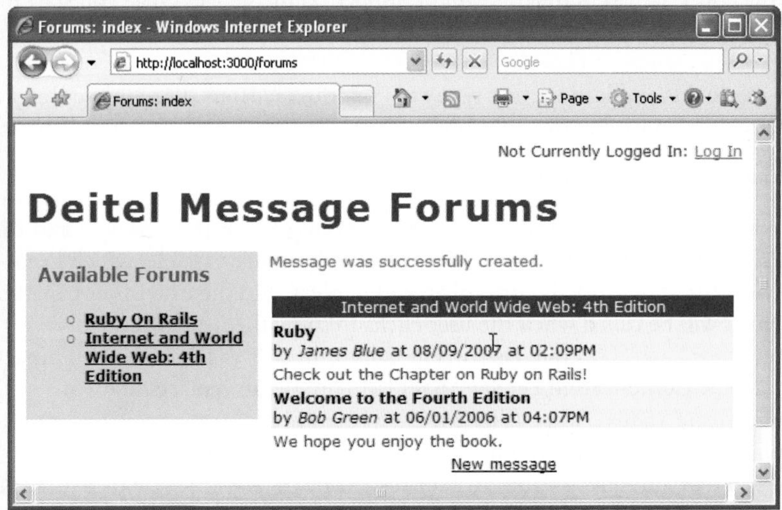

Fig. 24.45 | Adding a new message without reloading the page. (Part 2 of 2.)

24.7 Script.aculo.us

Visual Effects

Rails includes the Script.aculo.us JavaScript library, which allows you to easily create visual effects similar to those in Adobe Flash and Microsoft Silverlight. The library provides many pre-defined effects, as well as the ability to create your own effects from the predefined ones. The following example demonstrates many of the effects provided by this library. Figure 24.46 demonstrates the Fade effect. When the user clicks the link above the

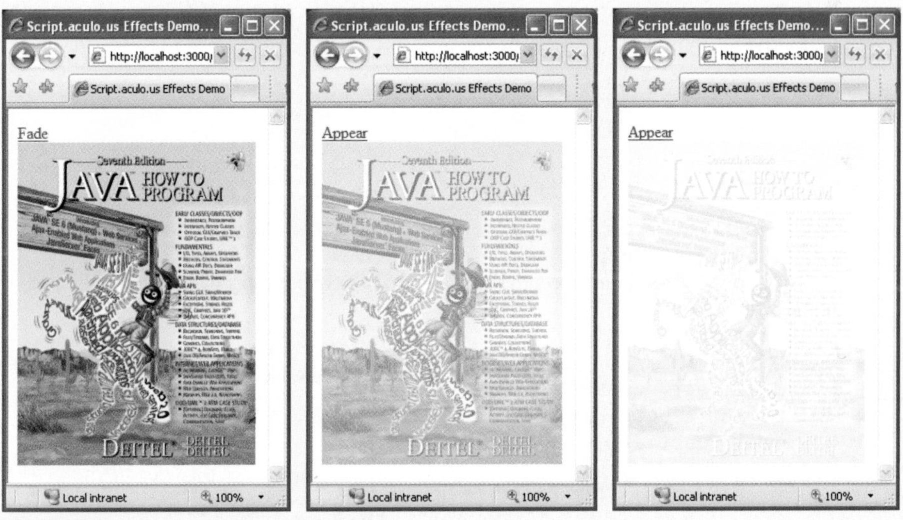

Fig. 24.46 | Script.aculo.us's Fade effect.

image, the effect named in the link will be applied to the image. Once you start the application with Mongrel, open `http://localhost:3000/scriptaculous_demo/` in your web browser.

To create this application, first type `rails scriptaculous_demo` in the Ruby console. Next, create the controller by executing

```
ruby script/generate controller ScriptaculousDemo
```

In `app/controllers/scriptaculous_demo_controller.rb` (Fig. 24.47), add the `index` method. This method sets to `0` the `currentEffect` instance variable, which keeps track of which effect the application is currently playing. Next, add the `PlayEffect` method (lines 4–6), which will be called when the user clicks to show the next effect.

Now, create `application.rhtml` (Fig. 24.48) in `app/view/layouts`. This acts as the default layout. Content from `render :partial` commands replaces line 13.

Next, create `index.rhtml` (Fig. 24.49) in `app/views/scriptaculous_demo`. This is the application's default view. The `"link"` `div` (lines 3–8) contains a `link_to_remote` (lines 4–7) that initially is labeled `'Shrink'`, calls `playEffect` with a `effect_index` parameter of `0`, updates itself and plays an effect on the `before` event. The effect is created using the `visual_effect` method (lines 6–7). The parameters of this method call are the effect name, the name of the element the effect should apply to, the `duration` and the loca-

```
1  <!-- Fig. 24.47: app/views/scriptaculous_demo/index.rhtml -->
2  <!-- Default view for Script.aculo.us demo. -->
3  <div id = "link">
4     <%= link_to_remote 'Shrink', :url => {:action => 'playEffect',
5        :effect_index => 0}, :update => "link",
6        :before => visual_effect(
7           :Shrink, 'image', :duration => 1.0, :queue => 'end') %>
8  </div>
9  
10 <div id = "image" style = "width: 244px; height: 320px;">
11    <%= image_tag "jhtp7medium.jpg" %>
12 </div>
```

Fig. 24.47 | Default view for Script.aculo.us demo.

```
1  # Fig. 24.48: app/controllers/scriptaculous_demo_controller.rb
2  # Script.aculo.us Demo controller
3  class ScriptaculousDemoController < ApplicationController
4    def index
5       @currentEffect = 0
6    end
7    def playEffect
8       @currentEffect = params[ :effect_index ]
9       render :partial => "link"
10   end # method playEffect
11 end # class ScriptaculousDemoController
```

Fig. 24.48 | Script.aculo.us Demo controller.

```
<?xml version = "1.0" encoding = "utf-8"?>
<!DOCTYPE html PUBLIC "-//W3C//DTD XHTML 1.0 Strict//EN"
   "http://www.w3.org/TR/xhtml1/DTD/xhtml1-strict.dtd">

<!-- Fig. 24.49: app/views/layouts/application.rhtml -->
<!-- Default layout of Script.aculo.us demo. -->
<html xmlns = "http://www.w3.org/1999/xhtml">
   <head>
      <title>Script.aculo.us Effects Demo</title>
      <%= javascript_include_tag :defaults %>
   </head>
   <body>
      <%= yield %>
   </body>
</html>
```

Fig. 24.49 | Default layout of Script.aculo.us demo.

tion in the queue. The queue is set to end so that any new effects will be played after all the others are complete. The image in line 11 must be in the public/images directory.

The playEffect method (lines 7–10, Fig. 24.47) sets the currentEffect instance variable to the effect_index parameter, then renders the link view in the link div. In app/views/scriptaculous_demo/_link.rhtml (Fig. 24.50), the application demonstrates several Script.aculo.us effects by using nested if statements to check the currentEffect, apply it, then increment currentEffect after each effect with the effect_index parameter. The link text corresponds to the name of the effect the link activates.

```
<!-- Fig. 24.50: app/views/scriptaculous_demo/_link.rhtml -->
<!-- link partial view for Script.aculo.us demo -->
<!-- Grow effect -->
<% if @currentEffect == '0' %>
   <%= link_to_remote 'Grow', :url => { :action => 'playEffect',
   :effect_index => 1 }, :update => "link",
      :before => ( visual_effect(
         :Grow, 'image', :duration => 1.0, :queue => 'end' ) ) %>

<!-- Fade effect -->
<% elsif @currentEffect == '1' %>
   <%= link_to_remote 'Fade', :url => { :action => 'playEffect',
      :effect_index => 2 }, :update => "link",
      :before => ( visual_effect(
         :Fade, 'image', :duration => 1.0, :queue => 'end' ) ) %>

<!-- Appear effect -->
<% elsif @currentEffect == '2' %>
   <%= link_to_remote 'Appear', :url => {:action => 'playEffect',
      :effect_index => 3 }, :update => "link",
      :before => ( visual_effect(
         :Appear, 'image', :duration => 1.0, :queue => 'end' ) ) %>
```

Fig. 24.50 | link partial view for Script.aculo.us demo. (Part 1 of 3.)

```

<!-- BlindUp effect -->
<% elsif @currentEffect == '3' %>
   <%= link_to_remote 'BlindUp', :url => { :action => 'playEffect',
      :effect_index => 4 }, :update => "link",
      :before => ( visual_effect(
         :BlindUp, 'image', :duration => 1.0, :queue => 'end' ) ) %>

<!-- BlindDown effect -->
<% elsif @currentEffect == '4' %>
   <%= link_to_remote 'BlindDown', :url => { :action => 'playEffect',
      :effect_index => 5 }, :update => "link",
      :before => ( visual_effect(
         :BlindDown, 'image', :duration => 1.0, :queue => 'end' ) ) %>

<!-- Puff effect -->
<% elsif @currentEffect == '5' %>
   <%= link_to_remote 'Puff', :url => { :action => 'playEffect',
      :effect_index => 6 }, :update => "link",
      :before => ( visual_effect(
         :Puff, 'image', :duration => 1.0, :queue => 'end' ) ) %>

<!-- SwitchOff effect -->
<% elsif @currentEffect == '6' %>
   <%= link_to_remote 'SwitchOff', :url => { :action => 'playEffect',
      :effect_index => 7 }, :update => "link",
      :before => ( visual_effect(
         :SwitchOff, 'image', :duration => 1.0, :queue => 'end' ) ) %>

<!-- SlideUp effect -->
<% elsif @currentEffect == '7' %>
   <%= link_to_remote 'SlideUp', :url => { :action => 'playEffect',
      :effect_index => 8 }, :update => "link",
      :before => ( visual_effect(
         :SlideUp, 'image', :duration => 1.0, :queue => 'end' ) ) %>

<!-- SlideDown effect -->
<% elsif @currentEffect == '8' %>
   <%= link_to_remote 'SlideDown', :url => { :action => 'playEffect',
      :effect_index => 9 }, :update => "link",
      :before => ( visual_effect(
         :SlideDown, 'image', :duration => 1.0, :queue => 'end' ) ) %>

<!-- Shake effect -->
<% elsif @currentEffect == '9' %>
   <%= link_to_remote 'Shake', :url => { :action => 'playEffect',
      :effect_index => 10 }, :update => "link",
      :before => ( visual_effect(
         :Shake, 'image', :duration => 1.0, :queue => 'end' ) ) %>

<!-- Pulsate effect -->
<% elsif @currentEffect == '10' %>
   <%= link_to_remote 'Pulsate', :url => { :action => 'playEffect',
```

Fig. 24.50 | `link` partial view for Script.aculo.us demo. (Part 2 of 3.)

```
         :effect_index => 11 }, :update => "link",
         :before => ( visual_effect(
            :Pulsate, 'image', :duration => 1.0, :queue => 'end' ) ) %>

   <!-- Squish effect -->
   <% elsif @currentEffect == '11' %>
      <%= link_to_remote 'Squish', :url => { :action => 'playEffect',
         :effect_index => 12 }, :update => "link",
         :before => ( visual_effect(
            :Squish, 'image', :duration => 1.0, :queue => 'end' ) ) %>

   <!-- Grow effect -->
   <% elsif @currentEffect == '12' %>
      <%= link_to_remote 'Grow', :url => { :action => 'playEffect',
         :effect_index => 13 }, :update => "link",
         :before => ( visual_effect(
            :Grow, 'image', :duration => 1.0, :queue => 'end' ) ) %>

   <!-- Fold effect -->
   <% elsif @currentEffect == '13' %>
      <%= link_to_remote 'Fold', :url => { :action => 'playEffect',
         :effect_index => 14 }, :update => "link",
         :before => ( visual_effect(
            :Fold, 'image', :duration => 1.0, :queue => 'end' ) ) %>

   <!-- Grow effect -->
   <% elsif @currentEffect == '14' %>
      <%= link_to_remote 'Grow', :url => { :action => 'playEffect',
         :effect_index => 15 }, :update => "link",
         :before => ( visual_effect(
            :Grow, 'image', :duration => 1.0, :queue => 'end' ) ) %>

   <!-- DropOut effect -->
   <% elsif @currentEffect == '15' %>
      <%= link_to_remote 'DropOut', :url => { :action => 'playEffect',
         :effect_index => 16 }, :update => "link",
         :before => ( visual_effect(
            :DropOut, 'image', :duration => 1.0, :queue => 'end' ) ) %>

   <!-- Grow effect -->
   <% elsif @currentEffect == '16' %>
      <%= link_to_remote 'Grow', :url => { :action => 'playEffect',
         :effect_index => 17 }, :update => "link",
         :before => ( visual_effect(
            :Grow, 'image', :duration => 1.0, :queue => 'end' ) ) %>

   <!-- Shrink effect -->
   <% elsif @currentEffect == '17' %>
      <%= link_to_remote 'Shrink', :url => { :action => 'playEffect',
         :effect_index => 0 }, :update => "link",
         :before => ( visual_effect(
            :Shrink, 'image', :duration => 1.0, :queue => 'end' ) ) %>
   <% end %>
```

Fig. 24.50 | `link` partial view for Script.aculo.us demo. (Part 3 of 3.)

Other Script.aculo.us Features

The Script.aculo.us library also brings other features to Rails. It provides drag-and-drop capability through the `draggable_element` and `drop_receiving_element` methods. A live example of this can be found at `demo.script.aculo.us/shop`.

Script.aculo.us also provides the `sortable_element` method which allows you to describe a list that allows the user to drag and drop list items to reorder them. A live example of this can be found at `demo.script.aculo.us/ajax/sortable_elements`.

Another intereresting capability is the `text_field_with_auto_complete` method, which enables server-side auto completion of a text field. A live example of this can be found at `demo.script.aculo.us/ajax/autocompleter`.

Flickr Photo Viewer with Effects

The Script.aculo.us library's effects are useful for adding a desktop-like feel to a web page. In the following example (Fig. 24.51), the user can search for photos with specific tags and can specify the number of images for each search to return. The application uses the Script.aculo.us sliding effect to show when the thumbnails for the specified tags have finished loading from Flickr. The application also uses the grow effect when the user clicks an image to display the full-size version of the image.

After creating the `FlickrPhotoViewer` application, you must install the Flickr library for Ruby. This library can be installed by executing `gem install flickr` in the Ruby console. More information about this library is available at `redgreenblu.com/flickr/`. Once

Fig. 24.51 | Flickr Photo Viewer showing search results for **bugs**.

installed, you must configure the library to use your own Flickr API key. You can sign up for a free API key at `www.flickr.com/services/api/misc.api_keys.html`. Once you receive your API key, you *must* replace the key in `flickr.rb` with your own. If you are using Instant Rails, `flickr.rb` will be located in the Instant Rails directory, in the folder If you are running Mac OS X, or otherwise have installed Ruby system-wide, this file will be harder to find. If you cannot locate it with a normal search in Mac OS X, open **Terminal** and use `find / -name flickr.rb` to locate it. The API key to replace should be located at line 57, in the `initialize` method. Finally, you must tell the application to include the Flickr library by adding `require 'flickr'` to the end of `config/environment.rb`.

Create the controller with `ruby script/generate controller flickr`. In `app/views/flickr/index.rhtml` (Fig. 24.52), we create the application's main view. Be sure to copy the `flickrPhotoViewer.css` file from this chapter's folder into the `public/stylesheets/` directory. Lines 15–31 contain a `form_remote_tag` element that implements the application's photo tag search functionality. Line 17 creates a `BlindDown` `visual_effect` for the `thumbs div` (line 32) when the `search action` is complete. Lines 18–19 create the corresponding `BlindUp` `visual_effect` for the `loading div` (lines 28–29). Lines 20–21 hide the `loading div` on `failure` and `success` events, respectively. The `fullsizeImage div` (line 33) will be populated later with an `img` element.

```
1  <?xml version = "1.0" encoding = "utf-8"?>
2  <!DOCTYPE html PUBLIC "-//W3C//DTD XHTML 1.0 Strict//EN"
3     "http://www.w3.org/TR/xhtml1/DTD/xhtml1-strict.dtd">
4
5  <!-- Fig. 24.52: app/view/flickr/index.rhtml -->
6  <!-- Main view for Flickr Photo Viewer. -->
7  <html xmlns = "http://www.w3.org/1999/xhtml">
8     <head>
9        <title>Flickr Photo Viewer</title>
10       <%= javascript_include_tag :defaults %>
11       <%= stylesheet_link_tag 'flickrPhotoViewer' %>
12    </head>
13    <body>
14       <!-- Form to search for tags -->
15       <%= form_remote_tag :url => { :action => 'search' },
16          :update => 'thumbs',
17          :complete => visual_effect( :BlindDown, 'thumbs' ),
18          :before => { visual_effect( :BlindUp, 'thumbs' ),
19             %( Element.show( 'loading' ) ) },
20          :failure => %( Element.hide( 'loading' ) ),
21          :success => %( Element.hide( 'loading' ) ) %>
22          <div id = "search">
23             Tags:
24             <%= text_field_tag "tags" %>
25             #:
26             <%= text_field_tag "numImages", "8", :size => "3" %>
27             <%= submit_tag "Search" %>
28             <div id = "loading"
29                style = "display: none">Loading...</div>
30          </div>
```

Fig. 24.52 | Main view for Flickr Photo Viewer. (Part 1 of 2.)

```
31          <%= end_form_tag %>
32          <div id = "thumbs"></div>
33          <div id = "fullsizeImage"></div>
34       </body>
35    </html>
```

Fig. 24.52 | Main view for Flickr Photo Viewer. (Part 2 of 2.)

The controller located at `app/controllers/flickr_controller.rb` (Fig. 24.53) handles the `search action` called by the form in line 15 of Fig. 24.52 and the `fullsizeImage` action called by the `link_to_remote` in lines 3–9 of Fig. 24.54. In the `search` method, line 6 creates the `flickr` object using the `Flickr` class we installed previously. Lines 7–9 use the `flickr` object to populate `thumbs` with `photos`, supplying as arguments the `tags` and `numImages` values from the corresponding `text_field_tags` in lines 24 and 26 of Fig. 24.52. The `fullsizeImage` method (lines 13–15) takes the `imageURL` parameter's value and uses it to set the `currentURL` variable.

The `thumbs` view (Fig. 24.54) defines each thumbnail as a `link_to_remote` with an `image_tag` as the link's contents. The source of the image is retrieved from the `thumbs` collection that was passed by line 8 of Fig. 24.53. The first index, 0, specifies the image size to be the smallest provided by Flickr. In lines 5–6 of Fig. 24.54, we specify that the `url` should

```
1  # Fig. 24.53: app/controllers/flickr_controller.rb
2  # Controller for Flickr Photo Viewer.
3  class FlickrController < ApplicationController
4     # handle the search request
5     def search
6        flickr = Flickr.new
7        render :partial => "thumbs",
8           :collection => flickr.photos( :tags => params[ :tags ],
9           :per_page => params[ :numImages ] )
10    end # method search
11
12    # handle the thumbnail click, sets the currentURL variable
13    def fullsizeImage
14       @currentURL = params[ :imageURL ]
15    end # method fullsizeImage
16 end # class FlickrController
```

Fig. 24.53 | Controller for Flickr Photo Viewer.

```
1  <!-- Fig. 24.54: app/views/flickr/_thumbs.rhtml -->
2  <!-- thumbs view of Flickr Photo Viewer. -->
3  <%= link_to_remote image_tag( thumbs.sizes[ 0 ][ 'source' ],
4        :class => "image" ),
5     :url => { :action => 'fullsizeImage',
6        :imageURL => thumbs.sizes[ 3 ][ 'source' ] },
7     :update => "fullsizeImage",
8     :success => visual_effect( :grow, 'fullsizeImage',
9        :queue => 'last' ) %>
```

Fig. 24.54 | `thumbs` view of Flickr photo viewer.

activate the `fullsizeImage` action and pass an `imageURL` parameter. This parameter is set to the source of the image's large version. Lines 8–9 apply the `grow` `visual_effect` to `fullsizeImage`.

The `fullsizeImage` view (Fig. 24.55) fills the `fullsizeImage` `div` in line 33 of Fig. 24.52 with an `image_tag`. The source of this image is set to the `currentURL` variable. Try the program out with different tag searches and numbers of images.

```
<!-- Fig. 24.55: app/views/flickr/fullsizeImage.rhtml -->
<!-- fullsizeImage view of Flickr Photo Viewer. -->
<%= image_tag( @currentURL, :class => "image" ) %>
```

Fig. 24.55 | `fullsizeImage` view of Flickr Photo Viewer.

24.8 Wrap-Up

In this chapter, you first learned basic Ruby programming concepts, including classes, control structures, and data types such as `Fixnum`, `String`, `Array` and `Hash`. Next, you learned how to develop web applications using the Rails framework. You installed Instant Rails, an all-in-one environment for building and testing Rails applications. We then discussed the MVC (Model-View-Controller) design pattern that is used by Rails applications, and the many conventions that allow Rails to generate a significant amount of functionality for you. This included using the `controller` generator to create an application's controller, using the `scaffold` generator to quickly generate a user interface to view and modify a database, and combining Ruby script and HTML into RHTML files that define an application's view. You learned how to include rich AJAX functionality (such as partial page updates, advanced controls, and visual effects) in Rails applications through the use of the built-in Prototype and Script.aculo.us libraries. These libraries allow for Ajax functionality such as In the next chapter, we discuss how to build web applications using Microsoft's ASP.NET 2.0.

24.9 Web Resources

`www.deitel.com/Ruby/`
`www.deitel.com/RubyOnRails/`

The Deitel Ruby and Ruby on Rails Resource Centers contain links to some of the best Ruby and Rails resources on the web. There you'll find categorized links to forums, conferences, blogs, books, open source projects, videos, podcasts, webcasts and more. Also check out the tutorials for all skill levels, from introductory to advanced.

Summary

Section 24.1 Introduction

- Ruby on Rails (also known as RoR or just Rails) is a framework for developing data-driven web applications.
- A web framework is a set of libraries and useful tool that can be used to build dynamic web applications.

- Ruby on Rails is different from most other programming languages because it takes advantage of many conventions to reduce development time. If you follow these conventions, the Rails framework generates substantial functionality and perform many tasks for you.
- Ruby on Rails has built-in libraries for performing common web development tasks, such as interacting with a database, sending mass e-mails to clients or generating web services.
- Rails has built-in libraries that provide Ajax functionality, improving the user experience. Rails is quickly becoming a popular environment for web development.
- Ruby on Rails was created by David Heinemeier Hansson of the company 37Signals.

Section 24.2 Ruby

- The Ruby scripting language was developed by Yukihiro "Matz" Matsumoto in 1995 to be a flexible, object-oriented scripting language.
- Ruby's syntax and conventions are intuitive—they attempt to mimic the way a developer thinks. Ruby is an interpreted language.
- Instant Rails is a stand-alone Rails development and testing environment that includes Ruby, Rails, MySQL, Apache, PHP and other components necessary to create and run Rails applications.
- If you are using Mac OS X, there is an application similar to Instant Rails called Locomotive.
- The method `puts` prints the text to the terminal, followed by a newline.
- A method can have parentheses surrounding its parameters, but this is not typical in Ruby unless they are used to avoid ambiguity.
- A line of Ruby code does not have to end with a semicolon, although one can be placed there.
- One way to run a Ruby script is to use the Ruby interpreter.
- IRB (Interactive Ruby) can be used to interpret Ruby code statement by statement.
- Ruby uses dynamic typing, which allows changes to a variable's type at execution time.
- Everything is an object in Ruby, so you can call methods on any piece of data.
- `Hash` `Objects` are mapped to other `Objects` in key/value pairs.
- The exclamation point after a method name is a Ruby convention indicating that the object on which the method is called will be modified.
- Ruby has support for code blocks—groupings of Ruby statements that can be passed to a method as an argument.
- The `initialize` method acts like a constructor in other object-oriented languages—it is used to declare and initialize an object's data.
- When each instance of a class maintains its own copy of a variable, the variable is known as an instance variable and is declared in Ruby using the `@` symbol.
- Classes can also have class variables, declared using the `@@` symbol, that are shared by all copies of a class.
- When an object is concatenated with a string, the object's `to_s` method is called to convert the object to its string representation.

Section 24.3 Rails Framework

- While users have benefitted from the rise of database-driven web applications, web developers have had to implement rich functionality with technology that was not designed for this purpose.
- The Rails framework combines the simplicity of development that has become associated with Ruby with the ability to rapidly develop database-driven web applications.

- Ruby on Rails is built on the philosophy of convention over configuration—if you follow certain programming idioms, your applications will require little or no configuration and Rails will generate substantial portions of the applications for you.
- The Model-View-Controller (MVC) architectural pattern separates application data (contained in the model) from graphical presentation components (the view) and input-processing logic (the controller).
- `ActiveRecord` is used to map a database table to an object.
- `ActionView` is a set of helper methods to modify user interfaces.
- `ActionController` is a set of helper methods to create controllers.

Section 24.4 `ActionController` *and* `ActionView`

- Ruby on Rails has two classes, `ActionController` and `ActionView`, that work together to process a client request and render a view.
- To generate a controller in Rails, you can use the built-in `Controller generator` by typing `ruby script/generate controller` *name*.
- A Ruby on Rails application must be run from a web server
- Instant Rails comes with a built-in web server named Mongrel, which is easy to use to test Rails applications on the local machine.
- When generating output, a controller usually renders a template—an XHTML document with embedded Ruby that has the `.rhtml` filename extension.
- The `request` object contains the environment variables and other information for a web page.
- Erb (embedded Ruby) that is located between the `<%= %>` tags in rhtml files is parsed as Ruby code and formatted as text.
- A set of Ruby tags without an equals sign—`<% %>`—represents statements to execute as Ruby code but not formatted as text.
- Rails allows you to add headers and footers with a layout—a master view that is displayed by every method in a controller.
- A layout can generate a template for a specific method using `yield`.

Section 24.5 A Database-Driven Web Application

- Rails makes extensive use of Object-Relational Mapping (ORM) that maps a database to application objects.
- The objects that Rails uses to encapsulate a database inherit from `ActiveRecord`.
- One `ActiveRecord` convention is that every model that extends `ActiveRecord::Base` in an application represents a table in a database.
- By convention, the table that the model represents has a name which is the lowercase, pluralized form of the model's name.
- Rails uses a generator to create the `Employee` model. You use a generator by typing `ruby script/server model employee` in the **Ruby Console**, after navigating to your application directory.
- The `ActiveRecord` object has a special feature called `Migration`, which allows you to perform database operations within Rails.
- `ActiveRecord` has built-in functionality for many create, retrieve, update and destroy methods known in Rails as CRUD.
- We can execute the migration using Ruby's `rake` command by typing in `rake db:migrate`, which will call the `self.up` method of all the migrations located in your `db/migrate` directory.

- If you ever want to roll back the migrations, you can type in `rake db:migrate VERSION=0`, which calls each migration's `self.down` method.
- The scaffold method is a powerful tool that automatically creates CRUD functionality. It creates methods such as `new`, `edit` and `list` so you don't have to create them yourself.

Section 24.6 Case Study: Message Forum

- Validators that will be called when the database is modified, can be applied to an object that inherits from `ActiveRecord`.
- The method `validates_presence_of` ensures that all the fields specified by its parameters are not empty.
- The method `validates_format_of` matches all the fields specified by its parameters with a regular expression.
- The `link_to` method is used to link to an action in the controller and pass arguments to it.
- A partial is a block of HTML and embedded Ruby code stored in another file and inserted directly into the document.
- Rails includes a JavaScript library called Prototype that contains easy-to-use cross-browser Ajax functions.
- The `javascript_include_tag` helper method is used to link in JavaScript libraries.
- The `link_to_remote` method allows us to link to JavaScript that we included in the layout file.
- Specifying the `url` and `update` parameters inside the `link_to_remote` method tells Rails to convert these tags into prototype `Ajax.Updater` objects that will update the page asynchronously.

Section 24.7 Script.aculo.us.

- Script.aculo.us also provides the `text_field_with_auto_complete` method, which enables server-side autocompletion of a text field.

Terminology

`ActionController`
`ActionView`
`ActiveRecord`
Ajax
Apache
`ApplicationController`
arrays
association
`before_create`
`before_destroy`
`belongs_to`
class variable
code block
comments
controller generator
Convention over Configuration
CRUD
`def`
Don't Repeat Yourself (DRY)
`draggable_element` method
`drop_recieving_element` method
dynamic typing
embedded Ruby (erb)
end
`Errors` Object
escape sequence
`find_all`
`Fixnum`
Gem
`Hash`
initialize
instance variable
Instant Rails
IRB
layout
`link_to` method
`link_to_remote` method
message forum
Model-View-Controller
Mongrel

MySQL
Object Relational Mapping
partial
password_field method
PHP
Prototype JavaScript Library
puts
relational integrity
reset_session
request object
Rails
RoR
Ruby
Ruby interpreter
Ruby on Rails
scaffold
scaffold generator
Script.aculo.us JavaScript library
session variable
sortable_element method
String
template
text_field method
text_field_with_autocomplete method
to_s method
validate
validates_format_of
validates_presence_of
validations
verify
web framework
web server
web services

Self-Review Exercises

24.1 Fill in the blanks in each of the following statements:

a) _______ is a stand-alone Rails development and testing environment for Windows.
b) Ruby on Rails is built on the philosophy of _______.
c) The _______ architectural pattern separates application data from graphical presentation components and input processing.
d) The objects that Rails uses to encapsulate a database inherit from class _______.
e) A(n) _______ is a master view that is displayed by every method in a controller.
f) The _______ method automatically creates CRUD functionality in Ruby on Rails.
g) The _______ helper method creates a link in HTML that calls a partial page update.
h) The _______ helper method calls effects from the Script.aculo.us library.

24.2 State whether each of the following is *true* or *false*. If *false*, explain why.

a) Every line in Ruby must end with a semicolon.
b) Rails is a programming language.
c) Rails makes creating database-driven Internet applications easy.
d) The name of the model must be the same as the name of the table that is associated with it.
e) By following Ruby on Rails naming conventions you can build a Rails application with no configuration.
f) Each controller in Ruby has one layout file which is rendered for every action of that controller.
g) Embedded Ruby located between the <% %> delimiters is evaluated and rendered on the page.
h) Rails implements Ajax functionality using the JavaScript Prototype library.

Answers to Self-Review Exercises

24.1 a) Instant Rails. b) convention over configuration. c) Model-View-Controller. d) ActiveRecord. e) layout. f) scaffold method. g) link_to_remote. h) playEffect.

24.2 a) False. A line of Ruby code does not have to end with a semicolon, although one can be placed there.

b) False. Rails is a framework for internet applications built in the Ruby programming language.
c) True.
d) False. The name of the table must be the plural version of the Model associated with it.
e) True.
f) True.
g) False. The Ruby between the `<% %>` tags is evaluated but is *not* rendered on the page. Only the Ruby between the `<%= %>` tags is evaluated then rendered on the page.
h) True.

Exercises

24.3 Write a series of `ActiveRecord::Migration` scripts to set up the structure for a book catalog database. The book catalog should have two tables—`Books` and `Authors`. The `Authors` table should have fields containing the author ID (the primary key for the table) the first name and the last name. The `Books` table should have fields containing the book's id (primary key for the table) the title, the author's ID that corresponds to an id in the authors table, the most current edition number and the year the most current edition was released. The migration scripts should also add a few rows of data to both tables.

24.4 Assume you have a book catalog database with tables `Books` and `Authors`. Write down the Ruby commands you would put in the **Command Prompt** to set up a structure for a Book Catalog application. Do not create your own directories or files—let the scripts do that for you. Both `Books` and `Authors` should have a model, a view and a controller component associated with them. There should be a structure set up for CRUD functionality associated with them.

24.5 Add code to the employee catalog example from Fig. 24.21 and 24.22 to make it a fully functional application. Make sure the user can add new employees, edit existing employees and delete existing employees.

24.6 Modify the Forum case study to be completely Ajax enabled. Make the Create Forum and Delete Forum links open up on the same page instead of linking to a different page. You will have to modify the `list.rhtml`, `new.rhtml` and `delete.rhtml` files in the `Forum` section of the `View` directory.

24.7 Add Script.aculo.us effects to the Ajax version of the Forum example. Pick an effect and have it play when the Forum is selected or gets updated.

24.8 Create an Address Book application like the one in Fig. 15.9. Enable the user to expand and contract, add and remove address-book entries.

25

ASP.NET 2.0 and ASP.NET Ajax

If any man will draw up his case, and put his name at the foot of the first page, I will give him an immediate reply. Where he compels me to turn over the sheet, he must wait my leisure.
—Lord Sandwich

Rule One: Our client is always right.
Rule Two: If you think our client is wrong, see Rule One.
—Anonymous

A fair question should be followed by a deed in silence.
—Dante Alighieri

You will come here and get books that will open your eyes, and your ears, and your curiosity, and turn you inside out or outside in.
—Ralph Waldo Emerson

OBJECTIVES

In this chapter you will learn:

- Web application development using Active Server Pages .NET (ASP.NET).
- To create Web Forms.
- To create ASP.NET applications consisting of multiple Web Forms.
- To maintain state information about a user with session tracking and cookies.
- To use the **Web Site Administration Tool** to modify web application configuration settings.
- To control user access to web applications using forms authentication and ASP.NET login controls.
- To use databases in ASP.NET applications.
- To design a master page and content pages to create a uniform look-and-feel for a website.

Outline

25.1 Introduction

This chapter introduces web application development with Microsoft's Active Server Pages .NET (ASP.NET) 2.0 technology. Web-based applications create web content for web-browser clients. This web content includes Extensible HyperText Markup Language (XHTML), client-side scripting, images and binary data. If you are not familiar with XHTML, you should read Chapter 4 before studying this chapter. [*Note:* This chapter assumes that you know Visual Basic and are familiar with the .NET platform version 2.0. To learn more about Visual Basic, check out *Visual Basic 2005 How to Program, Third Edition*, or visit our Visual Basic Resource Center at `www.deitel.com/visualbasic`.]

We present several examples that demonstrate web application development using Web Forms, web controls (also called ASP.NET server controls) and Visual Basic programming. We also introduce ASP.NET Ajax and use it to enhance one of the earlier examples. Web Form files have the filename extension `.aspx` and contain the web page's GUI. You customize Web Forms by adding web controls including labels, text boxes, images, buttons and other GUI components. The Web Form file generates the web page that is sent to the client browser. From this point onward, we refer to Web Form files as ASPX files.

An ASPX file created in Visual Studio is implemented as a class written in a .NET language, such as Visual Basic. This class contains event handlers, initialization code, utility methods and other supporting code. The file that contains this class is called the code-behind file and provides the ASPX file's programmatic implementation.

To develop the code and GUIs in this chapter, we used Microsoft Visual Web Developer 2005 Express—an IDE designed for developing ASP.NET web applications. Visual Web Developer and Visual Basic 2005 Express share many common features and visual programming tools that simplify building complex applications, such as those that access a database (Sections 25.5–25.6). The full version of Visual Studio 2005 includes the functionality of Visual Web Developer, so the instructions we present for Visual Web Developer also apply to Visual Studio 2005. Note that you must install either Visual Web Developer 2005 Express (available from `msdn.microsoft.com/vstudio/express/vwd/default.aspx`) or a complete version of Visual Studio 2005 to implement the programs in this chapter.

25.2 Creating and Running a Simple Web Form Example

Our first example displays the web server's time of day in a browser window. When run, this program displays the text `A Simple Web Form Example`, followed by the web server's time. As mentioned previously, the program consists of two related files—an ASPX file (Fig. 25.1) and a Visual Basic code-behind file (Fig. 25.2), which we'll discuss in Section 25.2.5. We first display the markup, code and output, then we carefully guide you through the step-by-step process of creating this program. [*Note:* The markup in Fig. 25.1 and other ASPX file listings in this chapter is the same as the markup that appears in Visual Web Developer, but we've reformatted it for presentation purposes to make the code more readable.]

Visual Web Developer generates all the markup shown in Fig. 25.1 when you set the web page's title, type text in the Web Form, drag a `Label` onto the Web Form and set the properties of the page's text and the `Label`. We discuss these steps in Section 25.2.6.

```
<%-- Fig. 25.1: WebTime.aspx --%>
<%-- A page that displays the current time in a Label. --%>
<%@ Page Language="VB" AutoEventWireup="false" CodeFile="WebTime.aspx.vb"
   Inherits="WebTime" EnableSessionState="False" %>

<!DOCTYPE html PUBLIC "-//W3C//DTD XHTML 1.0 Transitional//EN"
   "http://www.w3.org/TR/xhtml1/DTD/xhtml1-transitional.dtd">

<html xmlns="http://www.w3.org/1999/xhtml" >
<head runat="server">
   <title>A Simple Web Form Example</title>
</head>
<body>
   <form id="form1" runat="server">
   <div>
      <h2>
      Current time on the Web server:</h2>
```

Fig. 25.1 | ASPX file that displays the web server's time. (Part 1 of 2.)

```
18              <p>
19                  <asp:Label ID="timeLabel" runat="server" BackColor="Black"
20                      EnableViewState="False" Font-Size="XX-Large"
21                      ForeColor="Yellow"></asp:Label>
22              </p>
23          </div>
24          </form>
25      </body>
26      </html>
```

Fig. 25.1 | ASPX file that displays the web server's time. (Part 2 of 2.)

25.2.1 Examining an ASPX File

The ASPX file contains other information in addition to XHTML. Lines 1–2 are ASP.NET **comments** that indicate the figure number, the filename and the purpose of the file. ASP.NET comments begin with `<%--` and terminate with `--%>`. We added these comments to the file. ASP.NET comments are not output as part of the XHTML sent to the client. Lines 3–4 use a **Page** directive (in an ASPX file a **directive** is delimited by `<%@` and `%>`) to specify information needed by ASP.NET to process this file. The **Language** attribute of the Page directive specifies the language of the code-behind file as Visual Basic ("VB"); the code-behind file (i.e., the **CodeFile**) is WebTime.aspx.vb. A code-behind filename usually consists of the full ASPX filename (e.g., WebTime.aspx) followed by a filename extension indicating the programming language (.vb in this chapter's examples).

The **AutoEventWireup** attribute (line 3) determines how Web Form events are handled. When AutoEventWireup is set to true, ASP.NET determines which methods in the class are called in response to events generated in the Page. For example, ASP.NET will call methods Page_Init and Page_Load in the code-behind file to handle the Page's Init and Load events, respectively. AutoEventWireup requires the event-handling methods to follow specific naming copnventions. (We discuss these events later in the chapter.)

The **Inherits** attribute (line 4) specifies the page's class name—in this case, WebTime. We say more about Inherits momentarily. [*Note:* We explicitly set the **EnableSessionState** attribute (line 4) to False. We explain the significance of this attribute later in the chapter. The IDE sometimes generates attribute values (e.g., true and false) and control names (as you will see later in the chapter) that do not adhere to our standard code capitalization conventions (i.e., True and False). Like Visual Basic, ASP.NET markup is not case sensitive, so using a different case is not problematic. To remain consistent with the code generated by the IDE, we do not modify these values in our code listings or in our accompanying discussions.]

For this first ASPX file, we provide a brief discussion of the XHTML markup. For more information on XHTML, see Chapter 4. Lines 6–7 contain the document type declaration, which specifies the document element name (HTML) and the PUBLIC Uniform Resource Identifier (URI) for the DTD that defines the XHTML vocabulary.

Lines 9–10 contain the <html> and <head> start tags, respectively. XHTML documents have the root element html and mark up information about the document in the head element. Also note that the html element specifies the XML namespace of the document using the xmlns attribute (see Section 14.4).

Notice the runat attribute in line 10, which is set to "server". This attribute indicates that when a client requests this ASPX file, ASP.NET processes the head element and its nested elements on the server and generates the corresponding XHTML, which is then sent to the client. In this case, the XHTML sent to the client will be identical to the markup in the ASPX file. However, as you will see, ASP.NET can generate complex XHTML markup from simple elements in an ASPX file.

Line 11 sets the title of this web page. We demonstrate how to set the title through a property in the IDE shortly. Line 13 contains the <body> start tag, which begins the body of the XHTML document; the body contains the main content that the browser displays. The form that contains our XHTML text and controls is defined in lines 14–24. Again, the runat attribute in the form element indicates that this element executes on the server, which generates equivalent XHTML and sends it to the client. Lines 15–23 contain a div element that groups the elements of the form in a block of markup.

Software Engineering Observation 25.1

Most ASP.NET controls must be placed in a form element in which the <form> tag has the runat="server" attribute.

Lines 16–17 are an XHTML h2 heading element. As we demonstrate shortly, the IDE generates this element in response to typing text directly in the Web Form and selecting the text as a second-level heading.

Lines 18–22 contain a p element to mark up a paragraph of content in the browser. Lines 19–21 mark up a Label web control. The properties that we set in the **Properties** window, such as Font-Size and BackColor (i.e., background color), are attributes here. The ID attribute (line 19) assigns a name to the control so that it can be manipulated programmatically in the code-behind file. We set the control's EnableViewState attribute (line 20) to False. We explain the significance of this attribute later in the chapter.

The asp: tag prefix in the declaration of the Label tag (line 19) indicates that the label is an ASP.NET web control, not an XHTML element. Each web control maps to a corresponding XHTML element (or group of elements)—when processing a web control on the server, ASP.NET generates XHTML markup that will be sent to the client to represent that control in a web browser.

Portability Tip 25.1

The same web control can map to different XHTML elements, depending on the client browser and the web control's property settings.

In this example, the asp:Label control maps to the XHTML span element (i.e., ASP.NET creates a span element to represent this control in the client's web browser). A span element particular element is used because span elements allow formatting styles to be applied to text. Several of the property values that were applied to our label are represented as part of the style attribute of the span element. You will soon see what the generated span element's markup looks like.

The web control in this example contains the runat="server" attribute–value pair (line 19), because this control must be processed on the server so that the server can translate the control into XHTML that can be rendered in the client browser. If this attribute pair is not present, the asp:Label element is written as text to the client (i.e., the control is not converted into a span element and does not render properly).

25.2.2 Examining a Code-Behind File

Figure 25.2 presents the code-behind file. Recall that the ASPX file in Fig. 25.1 references `WebTime.aspx.vb` in line 3.

Line 3 (Fig. 25.2) begins the declaration of class `WebTime`. A class declaration can span multiple source-code files, and the separate portions of the class declaration in each file are known as partial classes. The `Partial` modifier in line 3 indicates that the code-behind file is a partial class. We discuss the remainder of this class shortly.

Line 4 indicates that `WebTime` inherits from class `Page` in namespace `System.Web.UI`. This namespace contains classes and controls that assist in building web-based applications. Class `Page` provides events and objects necessary for creating web-based applications. In addition to class `Page`, `System.Web.UI` also includes class `Control`—the base class that provides common functionality for all web controls.

Lines 7–11 define method `Page_Init`, which handles the page's `Init` event. This event indicates that all the controls on the page have been created and initialized and additional application-specific initialization can now be performed. The only initialization required for this page is setting `timeLabel`'s `Text` property to the time on the server (i.e., the computer on which this code executes). The statement in line 10 retrieves the current time and formats it as *hh*:*mm*:*ss*. For example, 9 AM is formatted as 09:00:00, and 2:30 PM is formatted as 14:30:00. Notice that the code-behind file can access `timeLabel` (the `ID` of the `Label` in the ASPX file) programmatically, even though the file does not contain a declaration for a variable named `timeLabel`. You will learn why momentarily.

```
1  ' Fig. 25.5: WebTime.aspx.vb
2  ' Code-behind file for a page that displays the current time.
3  Partial Class WebTime
4     Inherits System.Web.UI.Page
5
6     ' initializes the contents of the page
7     Protected Sub Page_Init(ByVal sender As Object, _
8        ByVal e As System.EventArgs) Handles Me.Init
9        ' display the server's current time in timeLabel
10       timeLabel.Text = DateTime.Now.ToString("hh:mm:ss")
11    End Sub ' Page_Init
12 End Class ' WebTime
```

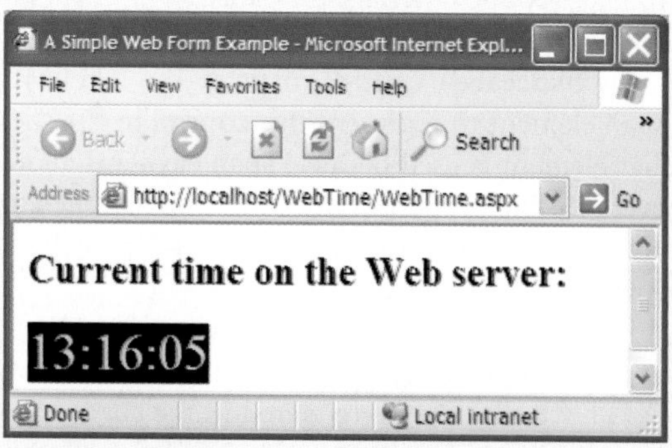

Fig. 25.2 | Code-behind file for a page that displays the web server's time.

25.2.3 Relationship Between an ASPX File and a Code-Behind File

How are the ASPX and code-behind files used to create the web page that is sent to the client? First, recall that class `WebTime` is the base class specified in line 4 of the ASPX file (Fig. 25.1). This class (partially declared in the code-behind file) inherits from `Page`, which defines general web page functionality. Partial class `WebTime` inherits this functionality and defines some of its own (i.e., displaying the current time). The code in the code-behind file displays the time, whereas the code in the ASPX file defines the GUI.

When a client requests an ASPX file, ASP.NET creates two partial classes behind the scenes. The code-behind file contains one partial class named `WebTime` and ASP.NET generate another partial class containing the remainder of class `WebTime`, based on the markup in the ASPX file. For example, `WebTime.aspx` contains a `Label` web control with `ID` `timeLabel`, so the generated partial class would contain a declaration for a variable named `timeLabel` of type `System.Web.UI.WebControls.Label`. Class `Label` represents a web control for displaying text. It is defined in namespace `System.Web.UI.WebControls`, which contains web controls for designing a page's user interface. Web controls in this namespace derive from class `WebControl`. When compiled, the partial class that declares `timeLabel` combines with the code-behind file's partial class declaration to form the complete `WebTime` class. This explains why line 10 in Fig. 25.2 can access `timeLabel`, which is created in lines 19–21 of `WebTime.aspx` (Fig. 25.1)—method `Page_Init` and control `timeLabel` are actually members of the same class, but defined in separate partial classes.

The partial class generated by ASP.NET is based on the ASPX file that defines the page's visual representation. This partial class is combined with the one in Fig. 25.2, which defines the page's logic. The first time the web page is requested, this class is compiled and an instance is created. This instance represents the page and creates the XHTML that is sent to the client. The assembly created from the compiled partial classes is placed in a subdirectory of

```
C:\WINDOWS\Microsoft.NET\Framework\VersionNumber\
   Temporary ASP.NET Files\WebTime
```

where *VersionNumber* is the version number of the .NET Framework (e.g., `v2.0.50727`) installed on your computer.

Once the web page has been compiled, no recompilation is required on subsequent requeses. New instances of the web page class will be created to serve each request. The project will be recompiled only when you modify the application; changes are detected by the runtime environment, and the application is recompiled to reflect the altered content.

25.2.4 How the Code in an ASP.NET Web Page Executes

Let's look briefly at how the code for our web page executes. When an instance of the page is created, the `PreInit` event occurs first, invoking method `Page_PreInit`, which can be used to set a page's theme and look-and-feel (and perform other tasks that are beyond this chapter's scope). The `Init` event occurs next, invoking method `Page_Init`. Method `Page_Init` is used to initialize objects and other aspects of the page. After `Page_Init` executes, the `Load` event occurs, and the `Page_Load` event handler executes. Although not present in this example, the `PreInit` and `Load` events are inherited from class `Page`. You will see examples of the `Page_Load` event handler later in the chapter. After the `Load` event handler finishes executing, the page processes events that are generated by the page's controls, such as user interactions with the GUI. When the user's request is considered fully processed, an Unload event occurs, which calls the Page_Unload event handler. This event, too, is inherited from class Page. Page_Unload typically contains code that releases resources used by the page. Other events occur as well, but are typically used only by ASP.NET controls to generate XHTML to render client-side controls. You can learn more about a Page's event life cycle at msdn2.microsoft.com/en-US/library/ms178472.aspx.

25.2.5 Examining the XHTML Generated by an ASP.NET Application

Figure 25.3 shows the XHTML generated by ASP.NET when a client browser requests WebTime.aspx (Fig. 25.1). To view this code, select **View > Source** in Internet Explorer. We added the comments in lines 1–2 and reformatted the XHTML for readability.

The markup in this page is similar to the ASPX file. Lines 7–9 define a document header comparable to that in Fig. 25.1. Lines 10–25 define the document's body. Line 11 begins the form, a mechanism for collecting user information and sending it to the web server. In this particular program, the user does not submit data to the web server for processing; however, processing user data is a crucial part of many applications that is facilitated by forms. We demonstrate how to submit form data to the server in later examples.

XHTML forms can contain visual and nonvisual components. Visual components include buttons and other GUI components with which users interact. Nonvisual components, called hidden inputs, store data, such as e-mail addresses, that the document author specifies. A hidden input is defined in lines 13–14. We discuss the precise meaning of this

```
1  <!-- Fig. 25.3: WebTime.html -->
2  <!-- The XHTML generated when WebTime.aspx is loaded. -->
3  <!DOCTYPE html PUBLIC "-//W3C//DTD XHTML 1.1//EN"
4     "http://www.w3.org/TR/xhtml11/DTD/xhtml11.dtd">
5
6  <html xmlns="http://www.w3.org/1999/xhtml" >
7  <head>
8     <title>A Simple Web Form Example</title>
9  </head>
10 <body>
11    <form name="form1" method="post" action="WebTime.aspx" id="form1">
12       <div>
13          <input type="hidden" name="__VIEWSTATE" id="__VIEWSTATE" value=
14             "/wEPDwUJODExMDE5NzY5ZGSzVbs789nqEeoNueQCnCJQEUgykw==" />
15       </div>
16
17       <div>
18          <h2>Current time on the Web server:</h2>
19          <p>
20             <span id="timeLabel" style="color:Yellow;
21                background-color:Black;font-size:XX-Large;">13:51:12</span>
22          </p>
23       </div>
24    </form>
25 </body>
26 </html>
```

Fig. 25.3 | XHTML response when the browser requests WebTime.aspx.

hidden input later in the chapter. Attribute **method** of the `form` element (line 11) specifies the method by which the web browser submits the form to the server. The **action** attribute identifies the name and location of the resource that will be requested when this form is submitted—in this case, `WebTime.aspx`. Recall that the ASPX file's `form` element contained the `runat="server"` attribute–value pair (line 14 of Fig. 25.1). When the `form` is processed on the server, the `runat` attribute is removed. The `method` and `action` attributes are added, and the resulting XHTML `form` is sent to the client browser.

In the ASPX file, the form's `Label` (i.e., `timeLabel`) is a web control. Here, we are viewing the XHTML created by our application, so the `form` contains a `span` element (lines 20–21 of Fig. 25.3) to represent the text in the label. In this particular case, ASP.NET maps the `Label` web control to an XHTML `span` element. The formatting options that were specified as properties of `timeLabel`, such as the font size and color of the text in the `Label`, are now specified in the `style` attribute of the `span` element.

Notice that only those elements in the ASPX file marked with the `runat="server"` attribute–value pair or specified as web controls are modified or replaced when the file is processed by the server. The pure XHTML elements, such as the `h2` in line 18, are sent to the browser as they appear in the ASPX file.

25.2.6 Building an ASP.NET Web Application

Now that we have presented the ASPX file, the code-behind file and the resulting web page sent to the web browser, we show the steps we used to create this application in Visual Web Developer.

Step 1: Creating the Website

In Visual Web Developer, select **File > New Web Site...** to display the **New Web Site** dialog (Fig. 25.4). In this dialog, select **ASP.NET Web Site** in the **Templates** pane. Below this pane, there are two fields in which you can specify the type and location of the web appli-

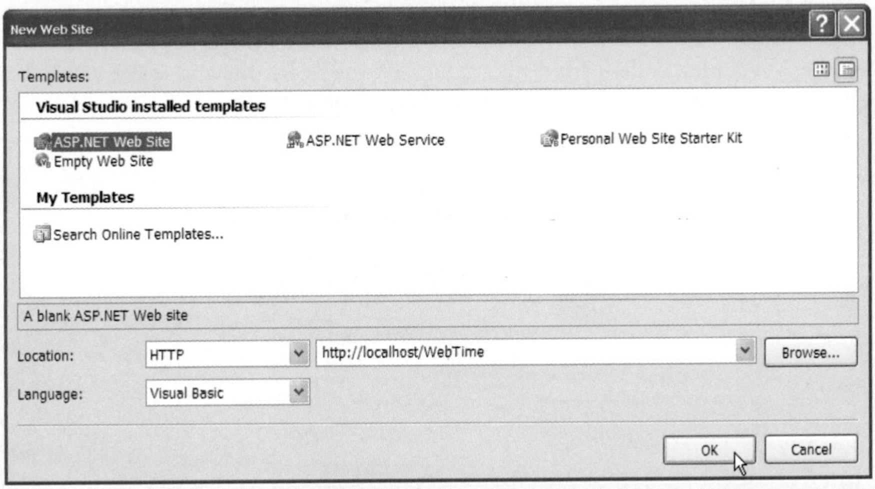

Fig. 25.4 | Creating an **ASP.NET Web Site** in Visual Web Developer.

cation you are creating. If it is not already selected, select **HTTP** from the drop-down list closest to **Location**. This indicates that the web application should be configured to run as an IIS application using HTTP (either on your computer or on a remote computer). We want our project to be located in `http://localhost`, which is the URL for IIS's root directory (this URL normally corresponds to the `C:\InetPub\wwwroot` directory on your machine). The name `localhost` indicates that the server resides on local computer. If the web server were located on a different computer, `localhost` would be replaced with the appropriate IP address or hostname. By default, Visual Web Developer sets the location where the website will be created to `http://localhost/WebSite`, which we change to `http://localhost/WebTime`.

If you do not have IIS on your computer or do not have permission to access it, you can select **File System** from the drop-down list next to **Location** to create the web application in a folder on your computer. You will be able to test the application using Visual Web Developer's internal ASP.NET Development Server, but you will not be able to access the application remotely over the Internet.

The **Language** drop-down list in the **New Web Site** dialog allows you to specify the language (i.e., Visual Basic, Visual C# or Visual J#) in which you will write the code-behind file(s) for the web application. Change the setting to Visual Basic. Click **OK** to create the website. This creates the directory `C:\Inetpub\wwwroot\WebTime` (in IIS) and makes it accessible through the URL `http://localhost/WebTime`. This action also creates a `WebTime` directory in the directory `My Documents\Visual Studio 2005\Projects` in which the project's solution files (e.g., `WebTime.sln`) are stored.

Step 2: Examining the Solution Explorer *of the Newly Created Project*

The next several figures describe the new project's content, beginning with the **Solution Explorer** shown in Fig. 25.5. Like Visual Basic 2005 Express, Visual Web Developer creates several files when you create a new project. It creates an ASPX file (i.e., Web Form) named `Default.aspx` for each new **ASP.NET Web Site** project. This file is open by default in the Web Forms Designer in **Source** mode when the project first loads (we discuss this momentarily). As mentioned previously, a code-behind file is included as part of the project. Visual Web Developer creates a code-behind file named `Default.aspx.vb`. To open the ASPX file's code-behind file, right click the ASPX file and select **View Code** or click the **View Code** button (▤) at the top of the **Solution Explorer**. Alternatively, you can

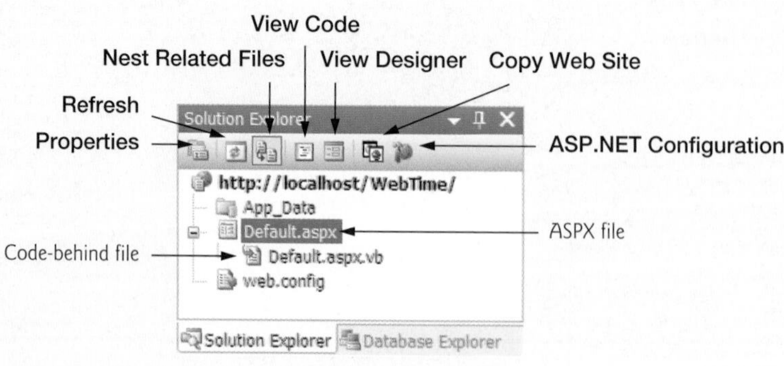

Fig. 25.5 | **Solution Explorer** window for project `WebTime`.

expand the node for the ASPX file to reveal the node for the code-behind file (see Fig. 25.5). You can also choose to list all the files in the project individually (instead of nested) by clicking the **Nest Related Files** button—this option is turned on by default, so clicking the button toggles the option off.

The **Properties** and **Refresh** buttons in Visual Web Developer's **Solution Explorer** behave like those in Visual Basic 2005 Express. Visual Web Developer's **Solution Explorer** also contains the buttons **View Designer**, **Copy Web Site** and **ASP.NET Configuration**. The **View Designer** button allows you to open the Web Form in **Design** mode, which we discuss shortly. The **Copy Web Site** button opens a dialog that allows you to move the files in this project to another location, such as a remote web server. This is useful if you are developing the application on your local computer, but want to make it available to the public from a different location. Finally, the **ASP.NET Configuration** button takes you to a web page called the **Web Site Administration Tool**, where you can manipulate various settings and security options for your application. We discuss this tool in greater detail in Section 25.6.

Step 3: Examining the Toolbox *in Visual Web Developer*

Figure 25.6 shows the **Toolbox** displayed in the IDE when the project loads. Figure 25.6(a) displays the beginning of the **Standard** list of web controls, and Fig. 25.6(b) displays the remaining web controls, and the list of **Data** controls used in ASP.NET. We discuss specific controls in Fig. 25.6 as they are used throughout the chapter. Notice that some controls in the **Toolbox** are similar to Windows controls.

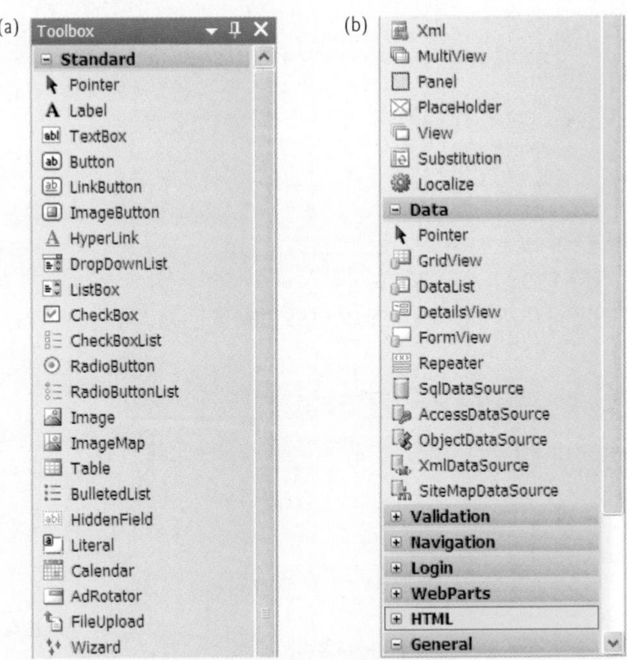

Fig. 25.6 | **Toolbox** in Visual Web Developer.

Step 4: Examining the Web Forms Designer

Figure 25.7 shows the Web Forms Designer in **Source** mode, which appears in the center of the IDE. When the project loads for the first time, the Web Forms Designer displays the autogenerated ASPX file (i.e., `Default.aspx`) in **Source** mode, which allows you to view and edit the markup that comprises the web page. The markup listed in Fig. 25.7 was created by the IDE and serves as a template that we will modify shortly. Clicking the **Design** button in the lower-left corner of the Web Forms Designer switches to **Design** mode (Fig. 25.8), which allows you to drag and drop controls from the **Toolbox** onto the Web Form and see the controls. You can also type at the current cursor location to add text to the web page. We demonstrate this shortly. In response to such actions, the IDE generates the appropriate markup in the ASPX file. Notice that **Design** mode indicates the XHTML element where the cursor is currently located. Clicking the **Source** button returns the Web Forms Designer to **Source** mode, where you can see the generated markup.

Default.aspx

Client Objects & Events | (No Events)

```
<%@ Page Language="VB" AutoEventWireup="false"
    CodeFile="Default.aspx.vb" Inherits="_Default" %>

<!DOCTYPE html PUBLIC "-//W3C//DTD XHTML 1.0 Transitional//EN"
    "http://www.w3.org/TR/xhtml1/DTD/xhtml1-transitional.dtd">

<html xmlns="http://www.w3.org/1999/xhtml" >
<head runat="server">
    <title>Untitled Page</title>
</head>
<body>
    <form id="form1" runat="server">
    <div>

    </div>
    </form>
</body>
</html>
```

Source mode button

Design mode button

Design | Source | <!DOCTYPE>

Fig. 25.7 | **Source** mode of the Web Forms Designer.

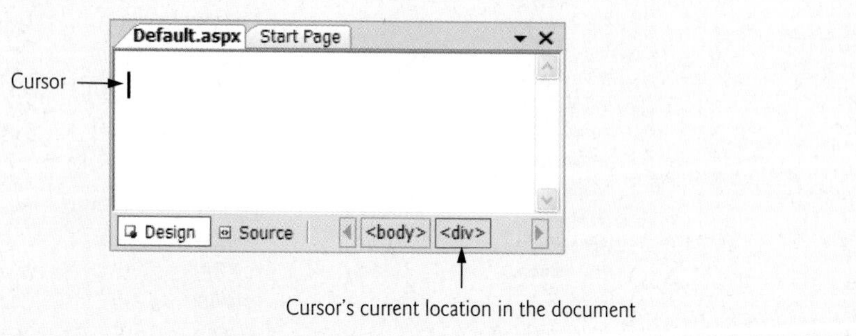

Fig. 25.8 | **Design** mode of the Web Forms Designer.

Step 5: Examining the Code-Behind File in the IDE

The next figure (Fig. 25.9) displays `Default.aspx.vb`—the code-behind file generated by Visual Web Developer for `Default.aspx`. Right click the ASPX file in the **Solution Explorer** and select **View Code** to open the code-behind file. When it is first created, this file contains nothing more than a partial class declaration. We will add the `Page_Init` event handler to this code momentarily.

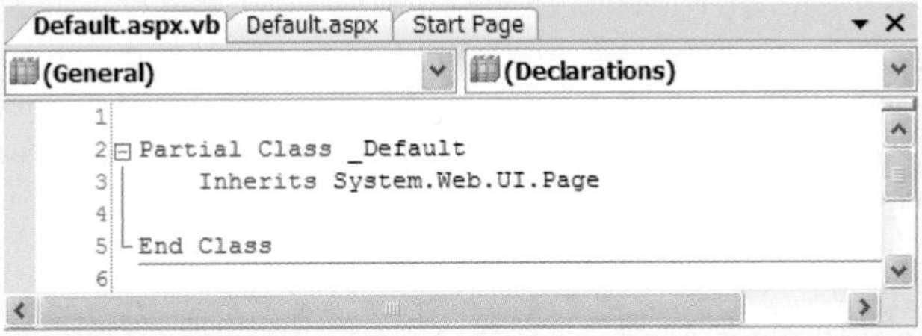

```
Default.aspx.vb | Default.aspx | Start Page
(General)        (Declarations)
1
2  Partial Class _Default
3       Inherits System.Web.UI.Page
4
5  End Class
6
```

Fig. 25.9 | Code-behind file for `Default.aspx` generated by Visual Web Developer.

Step 6: Renaming the ASPX File

Now that you've seen the contents of the default ASPX and code-behind files, let's rename these files. Right click the ASPX file in the **Solution Explorer** and select **Rename**. Enter the new filename `WebTime.aspx` and press *Enter*. This updates the name of both the ASPX file and the code-behind file. The IDE also updates the `Page` directive's `CodeFile` attribute in `WebTime.aspx`.

Step 7: Renaming the Class in the Code-Behind File and Updating the ASPX File

Although renaming the ASPX file causes the name of the code-behind file to change, this action does not affect the name of the partial class declared in the code-behind file. Open the code-behind file and change the class name from `_Default` (line 2 in Fig. 25.9) to `WebTime`, so the partial class declaration appears as in line 3 of Fig. 25.2. Recall that this class is also referenced by the `Page` directive in the ASPX file. Using the Web Forms Designer's **Source** mode, modify the `Inherits` attribute of the `Page` directive in `WebTime.aspx`, so it appears as in line 4 of Fig. 25.1. The value of the `Inherits` attribute and the class name in the code-behind file must be identical; otherwise, you'll get errors when you build the web application.

Step 8: Changing the Title of the Page

Before designing the content of the Web Form, we change its title from the default `Untitled Page` (line 9 of Fig. 25.7) to `A Simple Web Form Example`. To do so, open the ASPX file in **Source** mode and modify the text in the `title` element—i.e., the text between the tags `<title>` and `</title>`. Alternatively, you can open the ASPX file in **Design** mode and modify the Web Form's `Title` property in the **Properties** window. To view the Web Form's properties, select `DOCUMENT` from the drop-down list in the **Properties** window; `DOCUMENT` represents the Web Form in the **Properties** window.

Step 9: Designing the Page

Designing a Web Form is as simple as designing a Windows Form. To add controls to the page, drag-and-drop them from the **Toolbox** onto the Web Form in **Design** mode. Like the

Web Form itself, each control is an object that has properties, methods and events. You can set these properties and events visually using the **Properties** window or programmatically in the code-behind file. However, unlike working with a Windows Form, you can type text directly on a Web Form at the cursor location or insert XHTML elements from the **Toolbox**.

Controls and other elements are placed sequentially on a Web Form, much as text and images are placed in a document using word-processing software like Microsoft Word. Controls are placed one after another in the order in which you drag-and-drop them onto the Web Form. The cursor indicates the point at which text and XHTML elements will be inserted. If you want to position a control between existing text or controls, you can drop the control at a specific position within the existing elements. You can also rearrange existing controls using drag-and-drop actions. By default, controls flow based on the width of the page. An alternate type of layout is known as **absolute positioning**, in which controls are located exactly where they are dropped on the Web Form. You can enable absolute positioning in **Design** mode by selecting **Layout > Position > Auto-position Options...**., clicking the first checkbox in the **Positioning options** pane of the **Options** dialog that appears, then selecting the appropriate positioning option from the drop-down menu.

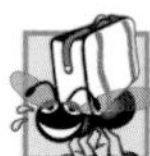

Portability Tip 25.2

Absolute positioning is discouraged, because pages designed in this manner may not render correctly on computers with different screen resolutions and font sizes. This could cause absolutely positioned elements to overlap each other or display off-screen, requiring the client to scroll to see the full page content.

In this example, we use one piece of text and one `Label`. To add the text to the Web Form, click the blank Web Form in **Design** mode and type `Current time on the Web server:`. Visual Web Developer is a **WYSIWYG (What You See Is What You Get)** editor—whenever you make a change to a Web Form in **Design** mode, the IDE creates the markup (visible in **Source** mode) necessary to achieve the desired visual effects seen in **Design** mode. After adding the text to the Web Form, switch to **Source** mode. You should see that the IDE added this text to the `div` element that appears in the ASPX file by default. Back in **Design** mode, highlight the text you added. From the **Block Format** drop-down list (see Fig. 25.10), choose **Heading 2** to format this text as a heading that will appear bold in a font slightly larger than the default. This action encloses the text in an `h2` element. Finally, click to the right of the text and press the *Enter* key to start a new paragraph. This action generates a `p` (paragraph) element in the ASPX file's markup. The IDE should now look like Fig. 25.10.

You can place a `Label` on a Web Form either by dragging-and-dropping or by double clicking the **Toolbox**'s **Label** control. Ensure that the cursor is in the new paragraph, then add a `Label` that will be used to display the time. Using the **Properties** window, set the `(ID)` property of the `Label` to `timeLabel`. In the `Text` property, delete `timeLabel`'s text—this text will be set programmatically in the code-behind file. When a `Label` does not contain text, its name is displayed in square brackets in the Web Forms Designer (Fig. 25.11) as a placeholder for design and layout purposes. This text is not displayed at execution time. We set `timeLabel`'s `BackColor`, `ForeColor` and `Font-Size` properties to `Black`, `Yellow` and `XX-Large`, respectively. To change the `Label`'s font properties, select the `Label`, expand the `Font` node in the **Properties** window and change each relevant property.

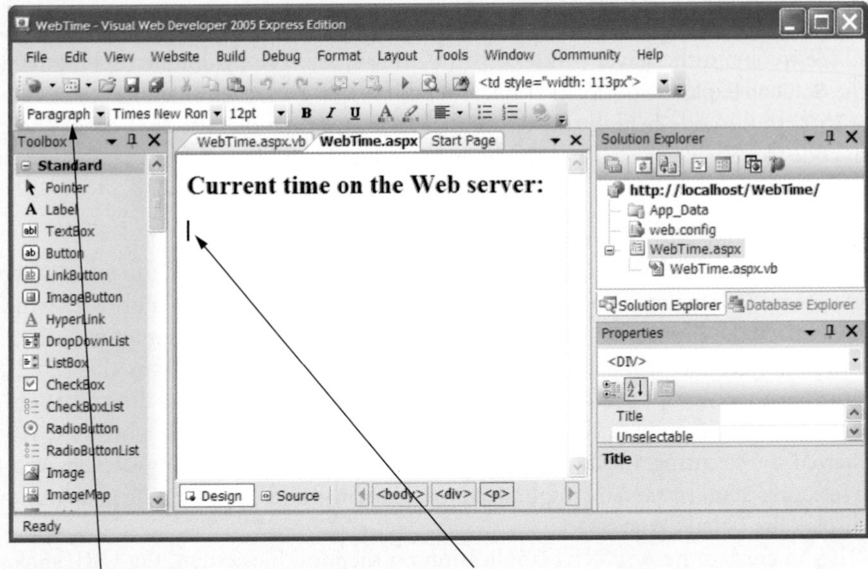

Fig. 25.10 | `WebTime.aspx` after inserting text and a new paragraph.

As the `Label`'s properties are set, Visual Web Developer updates the ASPX file's contents. Figure 25.11 shows the IDE after setting these properties.

Next, set the `Label`'s `EnableViewState` property to `False`. Finally, select `DOCUMENT` from the drop-down list in the **Properties** window and set the Web Form's `EnableSessionState` property to `False`. We discuss both of these properties later in the chapter.

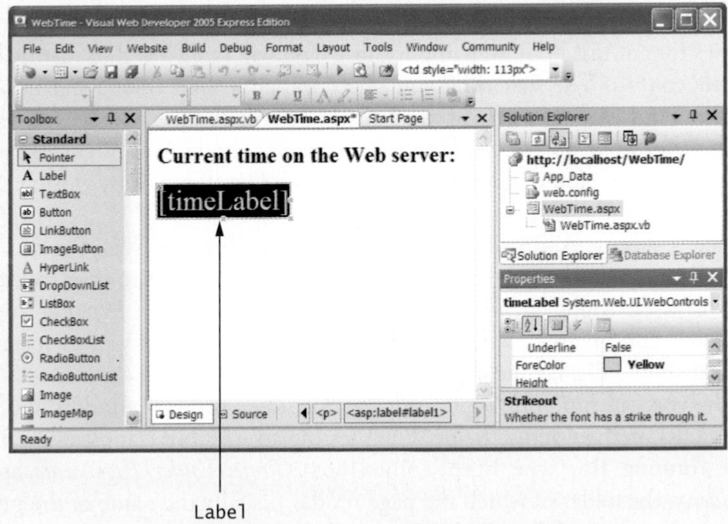

Fig. 25.11 | `WebTime.aspx` after adding a `Label` and setting its properties.

Step 10: Adding Page Logic

Now that you've designed the user interface, you'll add Visual Basic code to the code-behind file to obtain the server's time. Open `WebTime.aspx.vb` by double clicking its node in the **Solution Explorer**. In this example, we add a `Page_Init` event handler (lines 7–11 of Fig. 25.2) to the code-behind file. Recall that `Page_Init` handles the `Init` event and contains code to initialize the page. The statement in line 10 of Fig. 25.2 sets `timeLabel`'s text to the server's current time.

Step 11: Running the Program

After creating the Web Form, you can view it several ways. First, you can select **Debug > Start Without Debugging**, which runs the application by opening it in a browser window. If you created the application on your local IIS server (as we did in this example), the URL shown in the browser will be `http://localhost/WebTime/WebTime.aspx` (Fig. 25.2), indicating that the web page (the ASPX file) is located within the virtual directory `WebTime` on the local IIS web server. IIS must be running to test the website in a browser. IIS can be started by executing `inetmgr.exe` from **Start > Run...**, right clicking **Default Web Site** and selecting **Start**. [*Note:* You might need to expand the node representing your computer to display the **Default Web Site**.]

If you created the ASP.NET application on the local file system, the URL shown in the browser will be `http://localhost:`*PortNumber*`/WebTime/WebTime.aspx`, where *PortNumber* is the number of the randomly assigned port on which Visual Web Developer's built-in test server runs. The IDE assigns the port number on a per-solution basis. This URL indicates that the `WebTime` project folder is being accessed through the root directory of the test server running at `localhost:`*PortNumber*. When you select **Debug > Start Without Debugging**, a tray icon appears near the bottom-right of your screen next to the computer's date and time to show that the **ASP.NET Development Server** is running. The test server stops when you exit Visual Web Developer.

To debug your application, you can select **Debug > Start Debugging** to view the web page in a web browser with debugging enabled. You cannot debug a web application unless debugging is explicitly enabled by the **`Web.config`** file—a file that stores configuration settings for an ASP.NET web application. You will rarely need to manually create or modify `Web.config`. The first time you select **Debug > Start Debugging** in a project, a dialog appears and asks whether you want the IDE to modify the `Web.config` file to enable debugging. After you click **OK**, the IDE enters **Running** mode. You can exit **Running** mode by selecting **Debug > Stop Debugging** in Visual Web Developer or by closing the browser window in which the ASPX file is displayed.

To view a specific ASPX file, you can right click either the Web Forms Designer or the ASPX filename (in the **Solution Explorer**) and select **View In Browser** to load the page in a web browser. Right clicking the ASPX file in the **Solution Explorer** and selecting **Browse With...** also opens the page in a browser, but first allows you to specify the web browser that should display the page and its screen resolution.

Finally, you can run your application by opening a browser window and typing the web page's URL in the **Address** field. When testing an ASP.NET application on the same computer running IIS, type `http://localhost/`*ProjectFolder*`/`*PageName*`.aspx`, where *ProjectFolder* is the folder in which the page resides (usually the name of the project), and *PageName* is the name of the ASP.NET page. If your application resides on the local file system, you must first start the **ASP.NET Development Server** by running the application using one of the methods described above. Then you can type the URL (including the *PortNumber* found in the test server's tray icon) in the browser to execute the application.

Note that all of these methods of running the application compile the project for you. In fact, ASP.NET compiles your web page whenever it changes between HTTP requests. For example, suppose you browse the page, then modify the ASPX file or add code to the code-behind file. When you reload the page, ASP.NET recompiles the page on the server before returning the HTTP response to the browser. This important new behavior of ASP.NET 2.0 ensures that clients always see the latest version of the page. You can manually compile a web page or an entire website by selecting **Build Page** or **Build Site**, respectively, from the **Build** menu in Visual Web Developer.

Windows Firewall Settings

If you would like to test your web application over a network, you may need to change your Windows Firewall settings. For security reasons, Windows Firewall does not allow remote access to a web server on your local computer by default. To change this, open the Windows Firewall utility in the Windows Control Panel. In Windows XP, Click the **Advanced** tab and select your network connection from the **Network Connection Settings** list, then click **Settings...**. On the **Services** tab of the **Advanced Settings** dialog, ensure that **Web Server (HTTP)** is checked. In Windows Vista click the **Change settings** link, then click **Continue** in dialog that appears. Select the **Exceptions** tab and place a check next to **World Wide Web Services (HTTP)**.

25.3 Web Controls

This section introduces some of the web controls located in the **Standard** section of the **Toolbox** (Fig. 25.6). Figure 25.12 summarizes some of the web controls used in the chapter examples.

Web control	Description
`Label`	Displays text that the user cannot edit.
`TextBox`	Gathers user input and displays text.
`Button`	Triggers an event when clicked.
`HyperLink`	Displays a hyperlink.
`DropDownList`	Displays a drop-down list of choices from which you can select an item.
`RadioButtonList`	Groups radio buttons.
`Image`	Displays images (e.g., GIF and JPG).

Fig. 25.12 | Commonly used web controls.

25.3.1 Text and Graphics Controls

Figure 25.13 depicts a simple form for gathering user input. This example uses all the controls listed in Fig. 25.12, except `Label`, which you used in Section 25.2. The code in

Fig. 25.13 was generated by Visual Web Developer in response to dragging controls onto the page in **Design** mode. To begin, create an ASP.NET website named `WebControls`. [*Note:* This example does not contain any functionality—i.e., no action occurs when the user clicks **Register**. We ask you to provide the functionality as an exercise. In subsequent examples, we demonstrate how to add functionality to many of these web controls.]

```
<%-- Fig. 25.13: WebControls.aspx --%>
<%-- Registration form that demonstrates Web controls. --%>
<%@ Page Language="VB" AutoEventWireup="false"
   CodeFile="WebControls.aspx.vb" Inherits="WebControls" %>

<!DOCTYPE html PUBLIC "-//W3C//DTD XHTML 1.0 Transitional//EN"
   "http://www.w3.org/TR/xhtml1/DTD/xhtml1-transitional.dtd">

<html xmlns="http://www.w3.org/1999/xhtml">
<head runat="server">
    <title>Web Controls Demonstration</title>
</head>
<body>
   <form id="form1" runat="server">
   <div>
      <h3>This is a sample registration form.</h3>
      <p>
         <em>Please fill in all fields and click Register.</em></p>
      <p>
         <asp:Image ID="userInformationImage" runat="server"
            EnableViewState="False" ImageUrl="~/Images/user.png" />  
         <span style="color: teal">
            Please fill out the fields below.</span>
      </p>
      <table id="TABLE1">
         <tr>
            <td style="width: 230px; height: 21px" valign="top">
               <asp:Image ID="firstNameImage" runat="server"
                  EnableViewState="False" ImageUrl="~/Images/fname.png" />
               <asp:TextBox ID="firstNameTextBox" runat="server"
                  EnableViewState="False"></asp:TextBox>
            </td>
            <td style="width: 231px; height: 21px" valign="top">
               <asp:Image ID="lastNameImage" runat="server"
                  EnableViewState="False" ImageUrl="~/Images/lname.png" />
               <asp:TextBox ID="lastNameTextBox" runat="server"
                  EnableViewState="False"></asp:TextBox>
            </td>
         </tr>
         <tr>
            <td style="width: 230px" valign="top">
               <asp:Image ID="emailImage" runat="server"
                  EnableViewState="False" ImageUrl="~/Images/email.png" />
               <asp:TextBox ID="emailTextBox" runat="server"
                  EnableViewState="False"></asp:TextBox>
            </td>
```

Fig. 25.13 | Web Form that demonstrates web controls. (Part 1 of 3.)

```
            <td style="width: 231px" valign="top">
               <asp:Image ID="phoneImage" runat="server"
                  EnableViewState="False" ImageUrl="~/Images/phone.png" />
               <asp:TextBox ID="phoneTextBox" runat="server"
                  EnableViewState="False"></asp:TextBox>
               Must be in the form (555) 555-5555.
            </td>
         </tr>
      </table>
      <p>
         <asp:Image ID="publicationsImage" runat="server"
            EnableViewState="False"
            ImageUrl="~/Images/publications.png" />  
         <span style="color: teal">
            Which book would you like information about?</span>
      </p>
      <p>
         <asp:DropDownList ID="booksDropDownList" runat="server"
            EnableViewState="False">
            <asp:ListItem>Visual Basic 2005 How to Program 3e
                </asp:ListItem>
            <asp:ListItem>Visual C# 2005 How to Program 2e
                </asp:ListItem>
            <asp:ListItem>Java How to Program 6e</asp:ListItem>
            <asp:ListItem>C++ How to Program 5e</asp:ListItem>
            <asp:ListItem>XML How to Program 1e</asp:ListItem>
         </asp:DropDownList>
      </p>
      <p>
         <asp:HyperLink ID="booksHyperLink" runat="server"
            EnableViewState="False" NavigateUrl="http://www.deitel.com"
            Target="_blank">
            Click here to view more information about our books
         </asp:HyperLink>
      </p>
      <p>
         <asp:Image ID="osImage" runat="server" EnableViewState="False"
            ImageUrl="~/Images/os.png" />  
         <span style="color: teal">
            Which operating system are you using?</span>
      </p>
      <p>
         <asp:RadioButtonList ID="operatingSystemRadioButtonList"
            runat="server" EnableViewState="False">
            <asp:ListItem>Windows XP</asp:ListItem>
            <asp:ListItem>Windows 2000</asp:ListItem>
            <asp:ListItem>Windows NT</asp:ListItem>
            <asp:ListItem>Linux</asp:ListItem>
            <asp:ListItem>Other</asp:ListItem>
         </asp:RadioButtonList>
      </p>
      <p>
```

Fig. 25.13 | Web Form that demonstrates web controls. (Part 2 of 3.)

```
99              <asp:Button ID="registerButton" runat="server"
100                EnableViewState="False" Text="Register" />
101           </p>
102       </div>
103       </form>
104  </body>
105  </html>
```

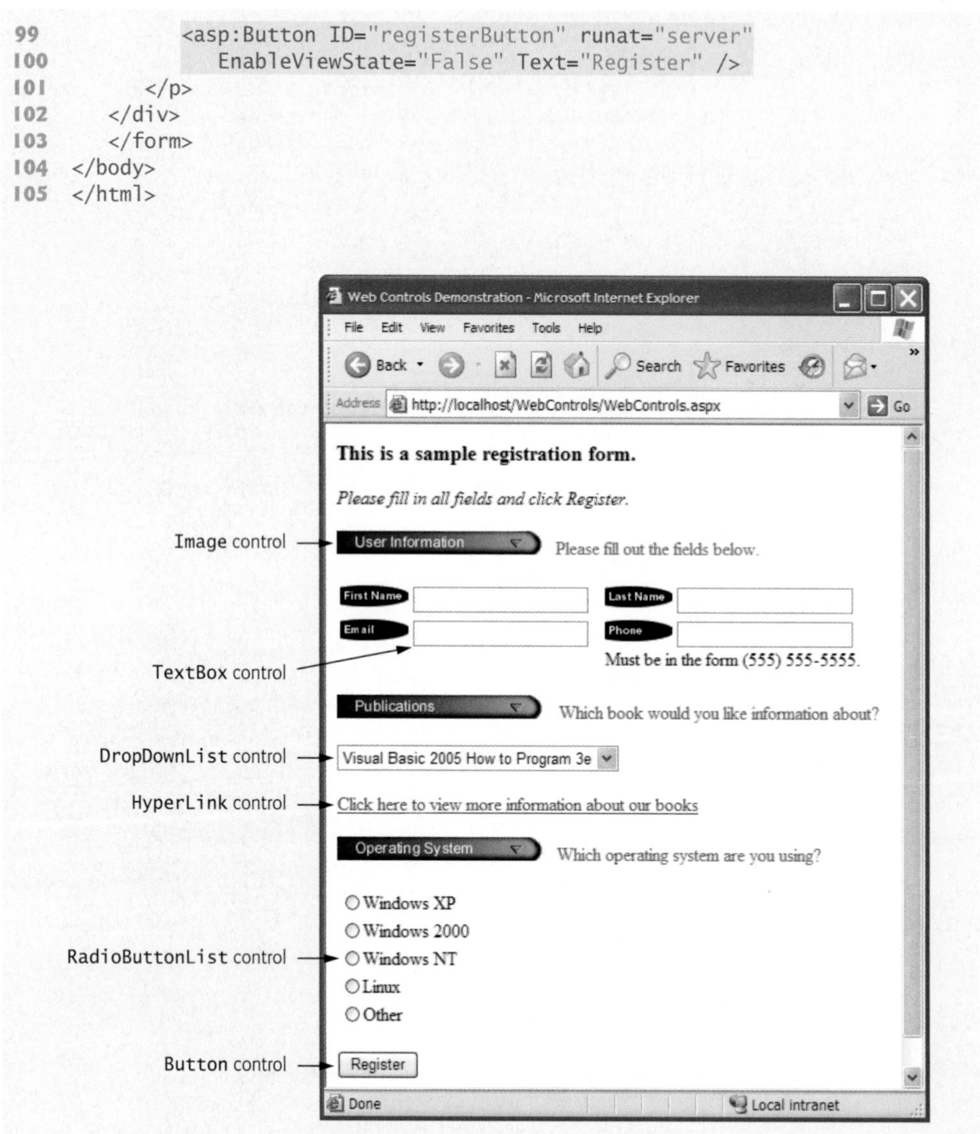

Fig. 25.13 | Web Form that demonstrates web controls. (Part 3 of 3.)

Before discussing the web controls used in this ASPX file, we explain the XHTML that creates the layout seen in Fig. 25.13. The page contains an `h3` heading element (line 16), followed by a series of additional XHTML blocks. We place most of the web controls inside `p` elements (i.e., paragraphs), but we use an XHTML `table` element (lines 25–55) to organize the `Image` and `TextBox` controls in the user information section of the page. In the preceding section, we described how to add heading elements and paragraphs visually without manipulating any XHTML in the ASPX file directly. Visual Web Developer allows you to add a table in a similar manner.

Adding an XHTML Table to a Web Form

To create a table with two rows and two columns in **Design** mode, select the **Insert Table** command from the **Layout** menu. In the **Insert Table** dialog that appears, select the **Custom** radio button. In the **Layout** group box, change the values of **Rows** and **Columns** to `2`. By default, the contents of a table cell are aligned vertically in the middle of the cell. We changed the vertical alignment of all cells in the table by clicking the **Cell Properties...** button, then selecting **top** from the **Vertical align** combo box in the resulting dialog. This causes the content of each table cell to align with the top of the cell. Click **OK** to close the **Cell Properties** dialog, then click **OK** to close the **Insert Table** dialog and create the table. Once a table is created, controls and text can be added to particular cells to create a neatly organized layout.

Setting the Color of Text on a Web Form

Notice that some of the instructions to the user on the form appear in a teal color. To set the color of a specific piece of text, highlight the text and select **Format > Foreground color...**. In the **Color Picker** dialog, click the **Named Colors** tab and choose a color. Click **OK** to apply the color. Note that the IDE places the colored text in an XHTML `span` element (e.g., lines 22–23) and applies the color using the `span`'s `style` attribute.

Examining Web Controls on a Sample Registration Form

Lines 20–21 of Fig. 25.13 define an **`Image`** control, which inserts an image into a web page. The images used in this example are located in the chapter's examples directory. You can download the examples from `www.deitel.com/books/iw3htp4`. Before an image can be displayed on a web page using an `Image` web control, the image must first be added to the project. We added an `Images` folder to this project (and to each example project in the chapter that uses images) by right clicking the location of the project in the **Solution Explorer**, selecting **New Folder** and entering the folder name `Images`. We then added each of the images used in the example to this folder by right clicking the folder, selecting **Add Existing Item...** and browsing for the files to add. You can also drag a folder full of images onto the project's location in the **Solution Explorer** to add the folder and all the images to the project.

The **`ImageUrl`** property (line 21) specifies the location of the image to display in the `Image` control. To select an image, click the ellipsis next to the `ImageUrl` property in the **Properties** window and use the **Select Image** dialog to browse for the desired image in the project's `Images` folder. When the IDE fills in the `ImageUrl` property based on your selection, it includes a tilde and forward slash (`~/`) at the beginning of the `ImageUrl`—this indicates that the `Images` folder is in the root directory of the project.

Lines 25–55 contain the `table` element created by the steps discussed previously. Each `td` element contains an `Image` control and a **`TextBox`** control, which allows you to obtain text from the user and display text to the user. For example, lines 30–31 define a `TextBox` control used to collect the user's first name.

Lines 64–73 define a **`DropDownList`**. This control is similar to the XHTML `select` control. When a user clicks the drop-down list, it expands and displays a list from which the user can make a selection. Each item in the drop-down list is defined by a **`ListItem`** element (lines 66–72). After dragging a `DropDownList` control onto a Web Form, you can add items to it using the **ListItem Collection Editor**. This process is similar to customizing a `ListBox` in a Windows application. In Visual Web Developer, you can access the **ListItem Collection Editor** by clicking the ellipsis next to the `Items` property of the `DropDownList`, or by using the **DropDownList Tasks** menu. You can open this menu by clicking the small arrowhead that appears in the upper-right corner of the control in **Design** mode (Fig. 25.14). This menu is called a smart tag menu. Visual Web Developer displays smart tag menus for many ASP.NET controls to facilitate common tasks. Clicking **Edit Items...** in the **DropDownList Tasks** menu opens the **ListItem Collection Editor**, which allows you to add `ListItem` elements to the `DropDownList`.

The `HyperLink` control (lines 76–80 of Fig. 25.13) adds a hyperlink to a web page. The `NavigateUrl` property (line 77) of this control specifies the resource (i.e., `http://www.deitel.com`) that is requested when a user clicks the hyperlink. Setting the `Target` property to `_blank` specifies that the requested web page should open in a new browser window. By default, `HyperLink` controls cause pages to open in the same browser window.

Lines 89–96 define a `RadioButtonList` control, which provides a series of radio buttons from which the user can select only one. Like options in a `DropDownList`, individual radio buttons are defined by `ListItem` elements. Note that, like the **DropDownList Tasks** smart tag menu, the **RadioButtonList Tasks** smart tag menu also provides an **Edit Items...** link to open the **ListItem Collection Editor**.

The final web control in Fig. 25.13 is a `Button` (lines 99–100). A `Button` web control represents a button that triggers an action when clicked. This control typically maps to an XHTML `input` element with attribute `type` set to `"submit"`. As stated earlier, clicking the **Register** button in this example does not do anything.

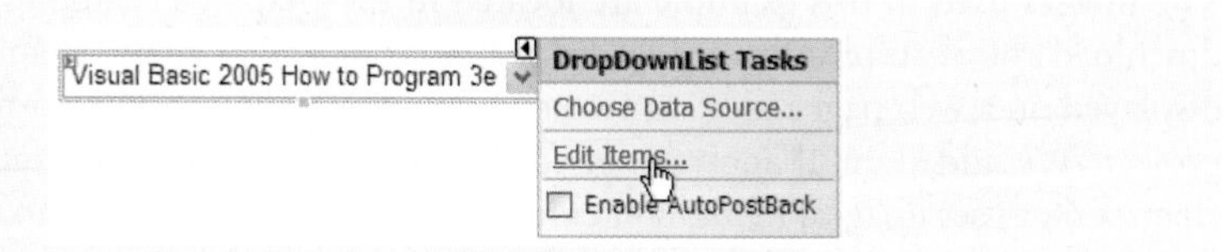

Fig. 25.14 | **DropDownList Tasks** smart tag menu.

25.3.2 AdRotator Control

Web pages often contain product or service advertisements, which usually consist of images. Although website authors want to include as many sponsors as possible, web pages can display only a limited number of advertisements. To address this problem, ASP.NET provides the `AdRotator` web control for displaying advertisements. Using advertisement data located in an XML file, an `AdRotator` randomly selects an image to display and generates a hyperlink to the web page associated with that image. Browsers that do not support images display alternate text that is specified in the XML document. If a user clicks the image or substituted text, the browser loads the web page associated with that image.

Demonstrating the `AdRotator` *Web Control*

Figure 25.15 demonstrates the `AdRotator` web control. In this example, the "advertisements" that we rotate are the flags of 10 countries. When a user clicks the displayed flag image, the browser is redirected to a web page containing information about the country that the flag represents. If a user refreshes the browser or requests the page again, one of the 10 flags is again chosen at random and displayed.

The ASPX file in Fig. 25.15 is similar to that in Fig. 25.1. However, instead of XHTML text and a `Label`, this page contains XHTML text (the `h3` element in line 16) and an `AdRotator` control named `countryRotator` (lines 18–19). This page also contains an `XmlDataSource` control (lines 20–22), which supplies the data to the `AdRotator` control. The `background` attribute of the page's `body` element (line 13) is set to the image `background.png`, located in the project's `Images` folder. To specify this file, click the ellipsis provided next to the `Background` property of `DOCUMENT` in the **Properties** window and use the resulting dialog to select `background.png` from the `Images` folder. The images and XML file used in this example are both located in the chapter's examples directory.

You do not need to add any code to the code-behind file, because the `AdRotator` control "does all the work." The output depicts two different requests. Figure 25.15(a) shows

```
1  <%-- Fig. 25.15: FlagRotator.aspx --%>
2  <%-- A Web Form that displays flags using an AdRotator control. --%>
3  <%@ Page Language="VB" AutoEventWireup="false"
4     CodeFile="FlagRotator.aspx.vb" Inherits="FlagRotator" %>
5
6  <!DOCTYPE html PUBLIC "-//W3C//DTD XHTML 1.0 Transitional//EN"
7     "http://www.w3.org/TR/xhtml1/DTD/xhtml1-transitional.dtd">
8
9  <html xmlns="http://www.w3.org/1999/xhtml" >
10 <head runat="server">
11     <title>Flag Rotator</title>
12 </head>
13 <body background="Images/background.png">
14     <form id="form1" runat="server">
15     <div>
16        <h3>AdRotator Example</h3>
17        <p>
18           <asp:AdRotator ID="countryRotator" runat="server"
19              DataSourceID="adXmlDataSource" />
20           <asp:XmlDataSource ID="adXmlDataSource" runat="server"
21              DataFile="~/App_Data/AdRotatorInformation.xml">
22           </asp:XmlDataSource>
23        </p>
24     </div>
25     </form>
26 </body>
27 </html>
```

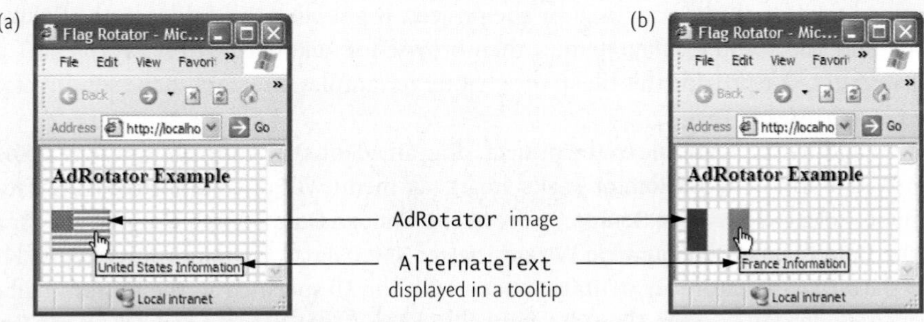

Fig. 25.15 | Web Form that demonstrates the `AdRotator` web control. (Part 1 of 2.)

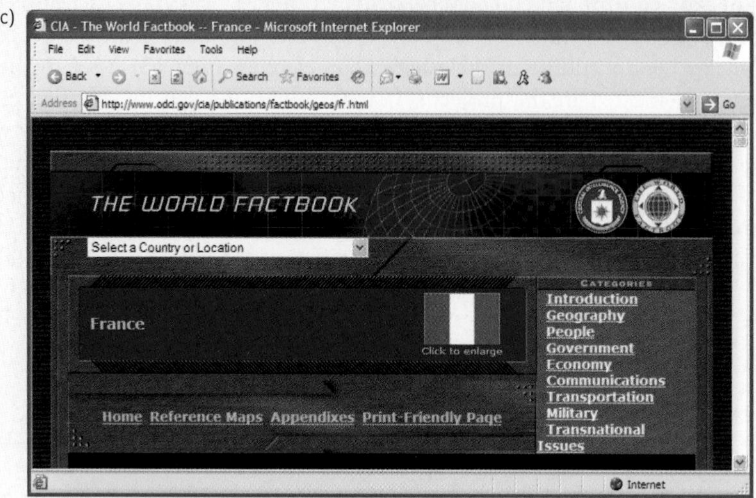

Fig. 25.15 | Web Form that demonstrates the `AdRotator` web control. (Part 2 of 2.)

the first time the page is requested, when the American flag is shown. In the second request, as shown in Fig. 25.15(b), the French flag is displayed. Figure 25.15(c) depicts the web page that loads when the French flag is clicked.

Connecting Data to an `AdRotator` *Control*

An `AdRotator` control accesses an XML file (presented shortly) to determine what advertisement (i.e., flag) image, hyperlink URL and alternate text to display and include in the page. To connect the `AdRotator` control to the XML file, we create an **`XmlDataSource`** control—one of several ASP.NET data controls (found in the **Data** section of the **Toolbox**) that encapsulate data sources and make such data available for web controls. An `XmlDataSource` references an XML file containing data that will be used in an ASP.NET application. Later in the chapter, you will learn more about data-bound web controls, as well as the `SqlDataSource` control, which retrieves data from a SQL Server database, and the `ObjectDataSource` control, which encapsulates an object that makes data available.

To build this example, we first add the XML file `AdRotatorInformation.xml` to the project. Each project created in Visual Web Developer contains an `App_Data` folder, which is intended to store all the data used by the project. Right click this folder in the **Solution Explorer** and select **Add Existing Item...**, then browse for `AdRotatorInformation.xml` on your computer. We provide this file in the chapter's examples directory in the subdirectory named `exampleXMLFiles`.

After adding the XML file to the project, drag an `AdRotator` control from the **Toolbox** to the Web Form. The **AdRotator Tasks** smart tag menu will open automatically. From this menu, select **<New Data Source...>** from the **Choose Data Source** drop-down list to start the **Data Source Configuration Wizard**. Select **XML File** as the data-source type. This causes the wizard to create an `XmlDataSource` with the `ID` specified in the bottom half of the wizard dialog. We set the `ID` of the control to `adXmlDataSource`. Click **OK** in the **Data Source Configuration Wizard** dialog. The **Configure Data Source - adXmlDataSource** dialog appears next. In this dialog's **Data File** section, click **Browse...** and, in the **Select XML File** dialog, locate and select the XML file you added to the `App_Data` folder. Click **OK** to exit this dialog, then click **OK** to exit the **Configure Data Source - adXmlDataSource** dialog. After completing these steps, the `AdRotator` is configured to use the XML file to determine which advertisements to display.

Examining an XML File Containing Advertisement Information

XML document `AdRotatorInformation.xml` (Fig. 25.16)—or any XML document used with an `AdRotator` control—must contain one **`Advertisements`** root element (lines 4–94). Within that element can be several **`Ad`** elements (e.g., lines 5–12), each of which provides information about a different advertisement. Element **`ImageUrl`** (line 6) specifies the path (location) of the advertisement's image, and element **`NavigateUrl`** (lines 7–9) specifies the URL for the web page that loads when a user clicks the advertisement. Note that we reformatted this file for presentation purposes. The actual XML file cannot contain any whitespace before or after the URL in the `NavigateUrl` element, or the whitespace will be considered part of the URL, and the page will not load properly.

The **`AlternateText`** element (line 10) nested in each `Ad` element contains text that displays in place of the image when the browser cannot locate or render the image for some reason (i.e., the file is missing, or the browser is not capable of displaying it), or to assist the visually impaired. The `AlternateText` element's text is also a tooltip that Internet Explorer displays when a user places the mouse pointer over the image (Fig. 25.15). The **`Impressions`** element (line 11) specifies how often a particular image appears, relative to the other images. An advertisement that has a higher `Impressions` value displays more frequently than an advertisement with a lower value. In our example, the advertisements display with equal probability, because the value of each `Impressions` element is set to `1`.

```
1  <?xml version="1.0" encoding="utf-8"?>
2  <!-- Fig. 25.16: AdRotatorInformation.xml -->
3  <!-- XML file containing advertisement information. -->
4  <Advertisements>
5     <Ad>
6        <ImageUrl>Images/france.png</ImageUrl>
7        <NavigateUrl>http://www.cia.gov/library/publications/
8           the-world-factbook/geos/fr.html
9        </NavigateUrl>
10       <AlternateText>France Information</AlternateText>
11       <Impressions>1</Impressions>
12    </Ad>
13
14    <Ad>
15       <ImageUrl>Images/germany.png</ImageUrl>
16       <NavigateUrl>http://www.cia.gov/library/publications/
17          the-world-factbook/geos/gm.html
18       </NavigateUrl>
19       <AlternateText>Germany Information</AlternateText>
20       <Impressions>1</Impressions>
21    </Ad>
22
```

Fig. 25.16 | XML file containing advertisement information used in `AdRotator` example. (Part 1 of 3.)

```
   <Ad>
      <ImageUrl>Images/italy.png</ImageUrl>
      <NavigateUrl>http://www.cia.gov/library/publications/
         the-world-factbook/geos/it.html
      </NavigateUrl>
      <AlternateText>Italy Information</AlternateText>
      <Impressions>1</Impressions>
   </Ad>

   <Ad>
      <ImageUrl>Images/spain.png</ImageUrl>
      <NavigateUrl>http://www.cia.gov/library/publications/
         the-world-factbook/geos/sp.html
      </NavigateUrl>
      <AlternateText>Spain Information</AlternateText>
      <Impressions>1</Impressions>
   </Ad>

   <Ad>
      <ImageUrl>Images/latvia.png</ImageUrl>
      <NavigateUrl>http://www.cia.gov/library/publications/
         the-world-factbook/geos/lg.html
      </NavigateUrl>
      <AlternateText>Latvia Information</AlternateText>
      <Impressions>1</Impressions>
   </Ad>

   <Ad>
      <ImageUrl>Images/peru.png</ImageUrl>
      <NavigateUrl>http://www.cia.gov/library/publications/
         the-world-factbook/geos/pe.html
      </NavigateUrl>
      <AlternateText>Peru Information</AlternateText>
      <Impressions>1</Impressions>
   </Ad>

   <Ad>
      <ImageUrl>Images/senegal.png</ImageUrl>
      <NavigateUrl>http://www.cia.gov/library/publications/
         the-world-factbook/geos/sg.html
      </NavigateUrl>
      <AlternateText>Senegal Information</AlternateText>
      <Impressions>1</Impressions>
   </Ad>

   <Ad>
      <ImageUrl>Images/sweden.png</ImageUrl>
      <NavigateUrl>http://www.cia.gov/library/publications/
         the-world-factbook/geos/sw.html
      </NavigateUrl>
      <AlternateText>Sweden Information</AlternateText>
```

Fig. 25.16 | XML file containing advertisement information used in `AdRotator` example. (Part 2 of 3.)

```
        <Impressions>1</Impressions>
    </Ad>

    <Ad>
        <ImageUrl>Images/thailand.png</ImageUrl>
        <NavigateUrl>http://www.cia.gov/library/publications/
            the-world-factbook/geos/th.html
        </NavigateUrl>
        <AlternateText>Thailand Information</AlternateText>
        <Impressions>1</Impressions>
    </Ad>

    <Ad>
        <ImageUrl>Images/unitedstates.png</ImageUrl>
        <NavigateUrl>http://www.cia.gov/library/publications/
            the-world-factbook/geos/us.html
        </NavigateUrl>
        <AlternateText>United States Information</AlternateText>
        <Impressions>1</Impressions>
    </Ad>
</Advertisements>
```

Fig. 25.16 | XML file containing advertisement information used in `AdRotator` example. (Part 3 of 3.)

25.3.3 Validation Controls

This section introduces a different type of web control, called a **validation control** (or **validator**), which determines whether the data in another web control is in the proper format. For example, validators could determine whether a user has provided information in a required field or whether a zip-code field contains exactly five digits. Validators provide a mechanism for validating user input on the client. When the XHTML for our page is created, the validator is converted into JavaScript that performs the validation. However, some clients do not support scripting or disable scripting. So, for security reasons, validation is always performed on the server too—whether or not scripting is enabled on the client. For this example, we assume the client has JavaScript enabled.

Validating Input in a Web Form

The example in this section prompts the user to enter a name, e-mail address and phone number. A website could use a form like this to collect contact information from site visitors. After the user enters any data, but before the data is sent to the web server, validators ensure that the user entered a value in each field and that the e-mail address and phone number values are in an acceptable format. In this example, (555) 123-4567, 555-123-4567 and 123-4567 are all considered valid phone numbers. Once the data is submitted, the web server responds by displaying an appropriate message and an XHTML table repeating the submitted information. Note that a real business application would typically store the submitted data in a database or in a file on the server. We simply send the data back to the form to demonstrate that the server received the data.

Figure 25.17 presents the ASPX file. Like the Web Form in Fig. 25.13, this Web Form uses a `table` to organize the page's contents. Lines 24–25, 36–37 and 58–59 define

`TextBoxes` for retrieving the user's name, e-mail address and phone number, respectively, and line 78 defines a **Submit** button. Lines 80–82 create a `Label` named `outputLabel` that displays the response from the server when the user successfully submits the form. Notice that `outputLabel`'s `Visible` property is initially set to `False` (line 81), so the `Label` does not appear in the client's browser when the page loads for the first time.

Using `RequiredFieldValidator` *Controls*

In this example, we use three `RequiredFieldValidator` controls (found in the **Validation** section of the **Toolbox**) to ensure that the name, e-mail address and phone number `TextBoxes` are not empty when the form is submitted. A `RequiredFieldValidator` makes an input control a required field. If such a field is empty, validation fails. For example, lines 26–30 define `RequiredFieldValidator nameInputValidator`, which confirms that `nameTextBox` is not empty. Line 28 associates `nameTextBox` with `nameInputValidator` by setting the validator's `ControlToValidate` property to `nameTextBox`. This indicates that `nameInputValidator` verifies the `nameTextBox`'s contents. We set the value of this property (and the validator's other properties) by selecting the validator in **Design** mode and using the **Properties** window to specify property values. Property `ErrorMessage`'s text (line 29) is displayed on the Web Form if the validation fails. If the user does not input any data in `nameTextBox` and attempts to submit the form, the `ErrorMessage` text is displayed in red. Because we set the validator's `Display` property to `Dynamic` (line 28), the validator is displayed on the Web Form only when validation fails. Space is allocated dynamically when validation fails, causing the controls below the validator to shift downward to accommodate the `ErrorMessage`, as seen in Fig. 25.17(a)–(c).

Using `RegularExpressionValidator` *Controls*

This example also uses `RegularExpressionValidator` controls to match the e-mail address and phone number entered by the user against regular expressions. These controls determine whether the e-mail address and phone number were each entered in a valid format. For example, lines 44–51 create a `RegularExpressionValidator` named `emailFormatValidator`. Line 46 sets property `ControlToValidate` to `emailTextBox` to indicate that `emailFormatValidator` verifies the `emailTextBox`'s contents.

```
1  <%-- Fig. 25.17: Validation.aspx --%>
2  <%-- Form that demonstrates using validators to validate user input. --%>
3  <%@ Page Language="VB" AutoEventWireup="false"
4     CodeFile="Validation.aspx.vb" Inherits="Validation" %>
5
6  <!DOCTYPE html PUBLIC "-//W3C//DTD XHTML 1.0 Transitional//EN"
7     "http://www.w3.org/TR/xhtml1/DTD/xhtml1-transitional.dtd">
8
9  <html xmlns="http://www.w3.org/1999/xhtml" >
10 <head runat="server">
11     <title>Demonstrating Validation Controls</title>
12 </head>
13 <body>
14    <form id="form1" runat="server">
15    <div>
```

Fig. 25.17 | Form that demonstrates using validators to validate user input. (Part 1 of 4.)

```
        Please fill out the following form.<br /><em>All fields are
        required and must contain valid information.</em><br />
        <br />
        <table>
           <tr>
              <td style="width: 100px" valign="top">
                 Name:</td>
              <td style="width: 450px" valign="top">
                 <asp:TextBox ID="nameTextBox" runat="server">
                 </asp:TextBox><br />
                 <asp:RequiredFieldValidator
                    ID="nameInputValidator" runat="server"
                    ControlToValidate="nameTextBox" Display="Dynamic"
                    ErrorMessage="Please enter your name.">
                 </asp:RequiredFieldValidator>
              </td>
           </tr>
           <tr>
              <td style="width: 100px" valign="top">E-mail address:</td>
              <td style="width: 450px" valign="top">
                 <asp:TextBox ID="emailTextBox" runat="server">
                 </asp:TextBox>
                  e.g., user@domain.com<br />
                 <asp:RequiredFieldValidator
                    ID="emailInputValidator" runat="server"
                    ControlToValidate="emailTextBox" Display="Dynamic"
                    ErrorMessage="Please enter your e-mail address.">
                 </asp:RequiredFieldValidator>
                 <asp:RegularExpressionValidator
                    ID="emailFormatValidator" runat="server"
                    ControlToValidate="emailTextBox" Display="Dynamic"
                    ErrorMessage=
                       "Please enter an e-mail address in a valid format."
                    ValidationExpression=
                       "\w+([-+.']\w+)*@\w+([-.]\w+)*\.\w+([-.]\w+)*">
                 </asp:RegularExpressionValidator>
              </td>
           </tr>
           <tr>
              <td style="width: 100px; height: 21px" valign="top">
                 Phone number:</td>
              <td style="width: 450px; height: 21px" valign="top">
                 <asp:TextBox ID="phoneTextBox" runat="server">
                 </asp:TextBox>
                  e.g., (555) 555-1234<br />
                 <asp:RequiredFieldValidator
                    ID="phoneInputValidator" runat="server"
                    ControlToValidate="phoneTextBox" Display="Dynamic"
                    ErrorMessage="Please enter your phone number.">
                 </asp:RequiredFieldValidator>
                 <asp:RegularExpressionValidator
                    ID="phoneFormatValidator" runat="server"
                    ControlToValidate="phoneTextBox" Display="Dynamic"
```

Fig. 25.17 | Form that demonstrates using validators to validate user input. (Part 2 of 4.)

```
                    ErrorMessage=
                       "Please enter a phone number in a valid format."
                    ValidationExpression=
                       "((\(\d{3}\) ?)|(\d{3}-))?\d{3}-\d{4}">
                 </asp:RegularExpressionValidator>
              </td>
           </tr>
        </table>
        <br />
        <asp:Button ID="submitButton" runat="server" Text="Submit" /><br />
        <br />
        <asp:Label ID="outputLabel" runat="server"
           Text="Thank you for your submission." Visible="False">
        </asp:Label>
     </div>
     </form>
</body>
</html>
```

(a)

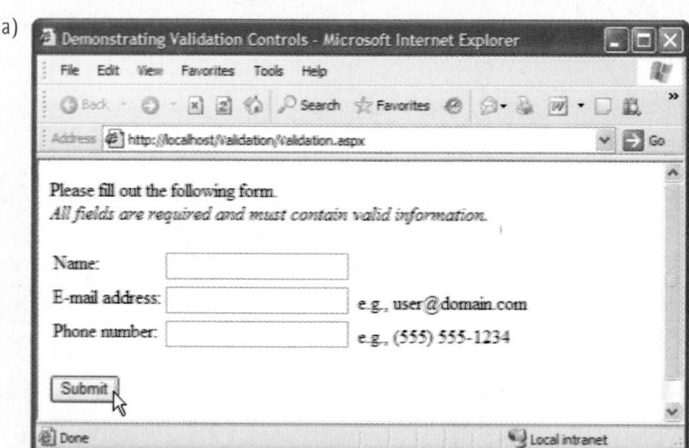

(b)

Fig. 25.17 | Form that demonstrates using validators to validate user input. (Part 3 of 4.)

(c)

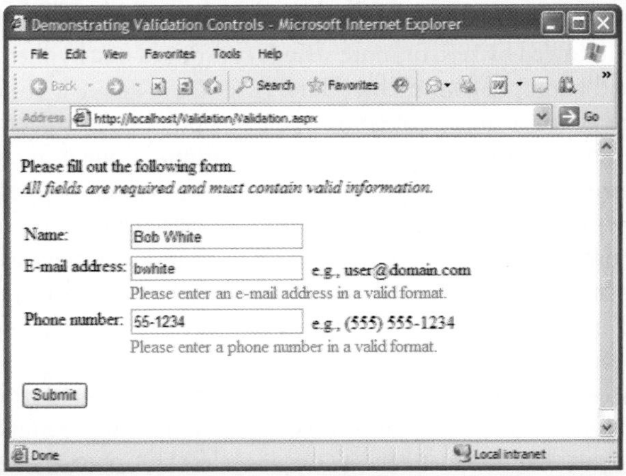

(d)

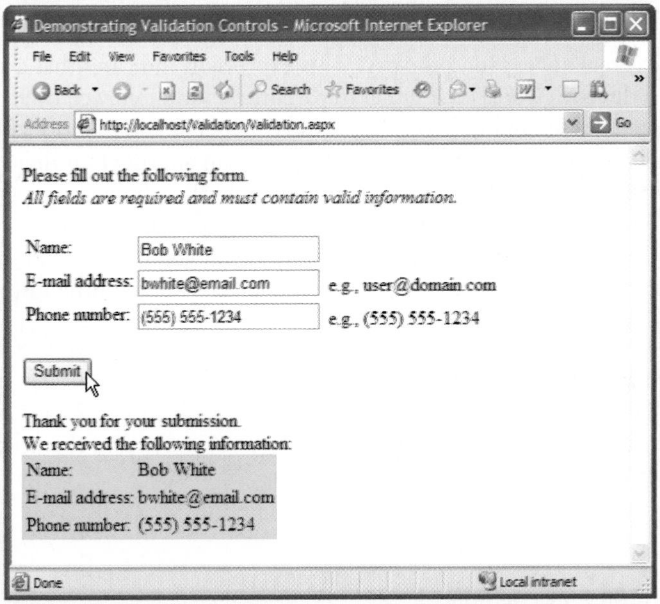

Fig. 25.17 | Form that demonstrates using validators to validate user input. (Part 4 of 4.)

A `RegularExpressionValidator`'s **`ValidationExpression`** property specifies the regular expression that validates the `ControlToValidate`'s contents. Clicking the ellipsis next to property `ValidationExpression` in the **Properties** window displays the **Regular Expression Editor** dialog, which contains a list of **Standard expressions** for phone numbers, zip codes and other formatted information. You can also write your own custom expression. For the `emailFormatValidator`, we selected the standard expression **Internet e-mail address**, which uses the validation expression

```
\w+([-+.']\w+)*@\w+([-.]\w+)*\.\w+([-.]\w+)*
```

This regular expression indicates that an e-mail address is valid if the part of the address before the `@` symbol contains one or more word characters (i.e., alphanumeric characters or underscores), followed by zero or more strings comprised of a hyphen, plus sign, period or apostrophe and additional word characters. After the `@` symbol, a valid e-mail address must contain one or more groups of word characters potentially separated by hyphens or periods, followed by a required period and another group of one or more word characters potentially separated by hyphens or periods. For example, `bob.white@email.com`, `bob-white@my-email.com` and `bob's-personal.email@white.email.com` are all valid e-mail addresses. If the user enters text in the `emailTextBox` that does not have the correct format and either clicks in a different text box or attempts to submit the form, the `ErrorMessage` text is displayed in red. You can learn more about regular expressions at `www.regular-expressions.info`.

We also use `RegularExpressionValidator phoneFormatValidator` (lines 66–73) to ensure that the `phoneTextBox` contains a valid phone number before the form is submitted. In the **Regular Expression Editor** dialog, we select **U.S. phone number**, which assigns

```
((\(\d{3}\) ?)|(\d{3}-))?\d{3}-\d{4}
```

to the `ValidationExpression` property. This expression indicates that a phone number can contain a three-digit area code either in parentheses and followed by an optional space or without parentheses and followed by required hyphen. After an optional area code, a phone number must contain three digits, a hyphen and another four digits. For example, `(555) 123-4567`, `555-123-4567` and `123-4567` are all valid phone numbers.

If all five validators are successful (i.e., each `TextBox` is filled in, and the e-mail address and phone number provided are valid), clicking the **Submit** button sends the form's data to the server. As shown in Fig. 25.17(d), the server then responds by displaying the submitted data in the `outputLabel` (lines 80–82).

Examining the Code-Behind File for a Web Form That Receives User Input

Figure 25.18 depicts the code-behind file for the ASPX file in Fig. 25.17. Notice that this code-behind file does not contain any implementation related to the validators. We say more about this soon.

```
' Fig. 25.18: Validation.aspx.vb
' Code-behind file for the form demonstrating validation controls.
Partial Class Validation
   Inherits System.Web.UI.Page

   ' Page_Load event handler executes when the page is loaded
   Protected Sub Page_Load(ByVal sender As Object, _
      ByVal e As System.EventArgs) Handles Me.Load
      ' if this is not the first time the page is loading
      ' (i.e., the user has already submitted form data)
      If IsPostBack Then
         ' retrieve the values submitted by the user
         Dim name As String = nameTextBox.Text
         Dim email As String = emailTextBox.Text
```

Fig. 25.18 | Code-behind file for the form demonstrating validation controls. (Part 1 of 2.)

```
15          Dim phone As String = phoneTextBox.Text
16
17          ' create a table indicating the submitted values
18          outputLabel.Text &= _
19             "<br />We received the following information:" & _
20             "<table style=""background-color: yellow"">" & _
21             "<tr><td>Name: </td><td>" & name & "</td></tr>" & _
22             "<tr><td>E-mail address: </td><td>" & email & "</td></tr>" & _
23             "<tr><td>Phone number: </td><td>" & phone & "</td></tr>" & _
24             "<table>"
25          outputLabel.Visible = True ' display the output message
26       End If
27    End Sub ' Page_Load
28 End Class ' Validation
```

Fig. 25.18 | Code-behind file for the form demonstrating validation controls. (Part 2 of 2.)

Web programmers using ASP.NET often design their web pages so that the current page reloads when the user submits the form; this enables the program to receive input, process it as necessary and display the results in the same page when it is loaded the second time. These pages usually contain a form that, when submitted, sends the values of all the controls to the server and causes the current page to be requested again. This event is known as a **postback**. Line 11 uses the **`IsPostBack`** property of class `Page` to determine whether the page is being loaded due to a postback. The first time that the web page is requested, `IsPostBack` is `False`, and the page displays only the form for user input. When the postback occurs (from the user clicking **Submit**), `IsPostBack` is `True`.

Lines 13–15 retrieve the values of `nameTextBox`, `emailTextBox` and `phoneTextBox`. When data is posted to the web server, the XHTML form's data is accessible to the web application through the properties of the ASP.NET controls. Lines 18–24 append to `outputLabel`'s `Text` a line break, an additional message and an XHTML table containing the submitted data, so the user knows that the server received the data correctly. In a real business application, the data would be stored in a database or file at this point in the application. Line 25 sets the `outputLabel`'s `Visible` property to `True`, so the user can see the thank you message and submitted data.

Examining the Client-Side XHTML for a Web Form with Validation

Figure 25.19 shows the XHTML and ECMAScript sent to the client browser when `Validation.aspx` loads after the postback. (We added the comments in lines 1–2.) To view this code, select **View > Source** in Internet Explorer. Lines 27–55, lines 126–190 and lines 196–212 contain the ECMAScript that provides the implementation for the validation controls and for performing the postback. ASP.NET generates this ECMAScript. You do not need to be able to create or even understand ECMAScript—the functionality defined for the controls in our application is converted to working ECMAScript for us.

The `EnableViewState` attribute determines whether a web control's value is retained when a postback occurs. Previously, we explicitly set this attribute to `False`. The default value, `True`, indicates that the control's value is retained. In Fig. 25.17(d), notice that the user input is retained after the postback occurs. A `hidden` input in the XHTML document (lines 17–25 of Fig. 25.19) contains the data of the controls on this page. This element is always named **`__VIEWSTATE`** and stores the controls' data as an encoded string.

```
<!-- Fig. 25.19 -->
<!-- The XHTML and ECMAScript generated for Validation.aspx -->
<!DOCTYPE html PUBLIC "-//W3C//DTD XHTML 1.0 Transitional//EN"
   "http://www.w3.org/TR/xhtml1/DTD/xhtml1-transitional.dtd">
<html xmlns="http://www.w3.org/1999/xhtml" >
<head>
<title>Demonstrating Validation Controls</title>
</head>
<body>
<form name="form1" method="post" action="Validation.aspx"
   onsubmit="javascript:return WebForm_OnSubmit();" id="form1">
   <div>
      <input type="hidden" name="__EVENTTARGET" id="__EVENTTARGET"
         value="" />
      <input type="hidden" name="__EVENTARGUMENT" id="__EVENTARGUMENT"
         value="" />
      <input type="hidden" name="__VIEWSTATE" id="__VIEWSTATE"
         value="/wEPDwUJMzg4NDI1NzgzD2QWAgIDD2QWAgITDw8WBB4EVGV4dAWVAlRoY
         W5rIHlvdSBmb3IgeW91ciBzdWJtaXNzaW9uLjxiciAvPldlIHJlY2VpdmVkIHRoZ
         SBmb2xsb3dpbmcgaW5mb3JtYXRpb246PHRhYmxlIHN0eWxlPSJiYWNrZ3JvdW5kL
         WNvbG9yOiB5ZWxsb3ciPjx0cj48dGQ+TmFtZTogPC90ZD48dGQ+Qm9iIFdoaXRlP
          C90ZD48L3RyPjx0cj48dGQ+RS1tYWlsIGFkZHJlc3M6IDwvdGQ+PHRkPmJ3aGl0
         ZUBlbWFpbC5jb208L3RkPjwvdHI+PHRyPjx0ZD5QaG9uZSBudW1iZXI6IDwvdGQ+
         PHRkPig1NTUpIDU1NS0xMjM0PC90ZD48L3RyPjx0YWJsZT4eB1Zpc2libGVnZGRk
         qbjgKg1/lLZfogqihtkd1C7nmSk=" />
   </div>
   <script type="text/javascript">
   <!--
   var theForm = document.forms['form1'];
   if (!theForm) {
      theForm = document.form1;
   }
   function __doPostBack(eventTarget, eventArgument) {
      if (!theForm.onsubmit || (theForm.onsubmit() != false)) {
         theForm.__EVENTTARGET.value = eventTarget;
         theForm.__EVENTARGUMENT.value = eventArgument;
         theForm.submit();
      }
   }
   // -->
   </script>
   <script src="/Validation/WebResource.axd?d=g4BXOwpt2-OjwFwNi7BCNQ2
      &amp;t=632670465355304640" type="text/javascript"></script>
   <script src="/Validation/WebResource.axd?d=ZlFGPYdcOpaOPqraRf9s2PN8QeuH
      PzQxnkR5mPVtAVc1&amp;t=632670465355304640"
      type="text/javascript"></script>
   <script type="text/javascript">
   <!--
   function WebForm_OnSubmit() {
      if (typeof(ValidatorOnSubmit) == "function" &&
         ValidatorOnSubmit() == false) return false;
```

Fig. 25.19 | XHTML and ECMAScript generated by ASP.NET and sent to the browser when `Validation.aspx` is requested. (Part 1 of 5.)

```
            return true;
         }
         // -->
         </script>
         <div>
            Please fill out the following form.<br />
            <em>All fields are required and must contain valid information.
            </em><br />
            <br />
            <table>
               <tr>
                  <td style="width: 100px" valign="top"> Name:</td>
                  <td style="width: 450px" valign="top">
                     <input name="nameTextBox" type="text" value="Bob White"
                        id="nameTextBox" />
                     <br />
                     <span id="nameInputValidator"
                        style="color:Red;display:none;">
                        Please enter your name.</span> </td>
               </tr>
               <tr>
                  <td style="width: 100px" valign="top">E-mail address:</td>
                  <td style="width: 450px" valign="top">
                     <input name="emailTextBox" type="text"
                        value="bwhite@email.com" id="emailTextBox" />
                      e.g., user@domain.com<br />
                     <span id="emailInputValidator"
                        style="color:Red;display:none;">
                        Please enter your e-mail address.</span>
                     <span id="emailFormatValidator"
                        style="color:Red;display:none;">Please enter an e-mail
                        address in a valid format.</span> </td>
               </tr>
               <tr>
                  <td style="width: 100px; height: 21px" valign="top">
                     Phone number:</td>
                  <td style="width: 450px; height: 21px" valign="top">
                     <input name="phoneTextBox" type="text"
                        value="(555) 555-1234" id="phoneTextBox" />
                      e.g., (555) 555-1234<br />
                     <span id="phoneInputValidator"
                        style="color:Red;display:none;">
                        Please enter your phone number.</span>
                     <span id="phoneFormatValidator"
                        style="color:Red;display:none;">Please enter a phone
                        number in a valid format.</span> </td>
               </tr>
            </table>
            <br />
            <input type="submit" name="submitButton" value="Submit"
               onclick="javascript:WebForm_DoPostBackWithOptions(
```

Fig. 25.19 | XHTML and ECMAScript generated by ASP.NET and sent to the browser when `Validation.aspx` is requested. (Part 2 of 5.)

```
         new WebForm_PostBackOptions(&quot;submitButton&quot;,
            &quot;&quot;, true, &quot;&quot;, &quot;&quot;, false,
            false))" id="submitButton" />
   <br />
   <br />
   <span id="outputLabel">Thank you for your submission.<br />
      We received the following information:
      <table style="background-color: yellow">
         <tr>
            <td>Name: </td>
            <td>Bob White</td>
         </tr>
         <tr>
            <td>E-mail address: </td>
            <td>bwhite@email.com</td>
         </tr>
         <tr>
            <td>Phone number: </td>
            <td>(555) 555-1234</td>
         </tr>
      <table>
   </span>
</div>
<script type="text/javascript">
<!--
   var Page_Validators = new Array(
      document.getElementById("nameInputValidator"),
      document.getElementById("emailInputValidator"),
      document.getElementById("emailFormatValidator"),
      document.getElementById("phoneInputValidator"),
      document.getElementById("phoneFormatValidator"));
// -->
</script>
<script type="text/javascript">
<!--
   var nameInputValidator = document.all ?
      document.all["nameInputValidator"] :
      document.getElementById("nameInputValidator");
   nameInputValidator.controltovalidate = "nameTextBox";
   nameInputValidator.errormessage = "Please enter your name.";
   nameInputValidator.display = "Dynamic";
   nameInputValidator.evaluationfunction =
      "RequiredFieldValidatorEvaluateIsValid";
   nameInputValidator.initialvalue = "";
   var emailInputValidator = document.all ?
      document.all["emailInputValidator"] :
      document.getElementById("emailInputValidator");
   emailInputValidator.controltovalidate = "emailTextBox";
   emailInputValidator.errormessage =
      "Please enter your e-mail address.";
   emailInputValidator.display = "Dynamic";
```

Fig. 25.19 | XHTML and ECMAScript generated by ASP.NET and sent to the browser when `Validation.aspx` is requested. (Part 3 of 5.)

```
      emailInputValidator.evaluationfunction =
         "RequiredFieldValidatorEvaluateIsValid";
      emailInputValidator.initialvalue = "";
      var emailFormatValidator = document.all ?
         document.all["emailFormatValidator"] :
         document.getElementById("emailFormatValidator");
      emailFormatValidator.controltovalidate = "emailTextBox";
      emailFormatValidator.errormessage =
         "Please enter an e-mail address in a valid format.";
      emailFormatValidator.display = "Dynamic";
      emailFormatValidator.evaluationfunction =
         "RegularExpressionValidatorEvaluateIsValid";
      emailFormatValidator.validationexpression =
         "\\w+([-+.\']\\w+)*@\\w+([-.]\\w+)*\\.\\w+([-.]\\w+)*";
      var phoneInputValidator = document.all ?
         document.all["phoneInputValidator"] :
         document.getElementById("phoneInputValidator");
      phoneInputValidator.controltovalidate = "phoneTextBox";
      phoneInputValidator.errormessage =
         "Please enter your phone number.";
      phoneInputValidator.display = "Dynamic";
      phoneInputValidator.evaluationfunction =
         "RequiredFieldValidatorEvaluateIsValid";
      phoneInputValidator.initialvalue = "";
      var phoneFormatValidator = document.all ?
         document.all["phoneFormatValidator"] :
         document.getElementById("phoneFormatValidator");
      phoneFormatValidator.controltovalidate = "phoneTextBox";
      phoneFormatValidator.errormessage =
         "Please enter a phone number in a valid format.";
      phoneFormatValidator.display = "Dynamic";
      phoneFormatValidator.evaluationfunction =
         "RegularExpressionValidatorEvaluateIsValid";
      phoneFormatValidator.validationexpression =
         "((\\(\\d{3}\\) ?)|(\\d{3}-))?\\d{3}-\\d{4}";
   // -->
   </script>
   <div>
     <input type="hidden" name="__EVENTVALIDATION" id="__EVENTVALIDATION"
        value="/wEWBQL6jZCbCAKLsYSOBwKCkfPgDAKE8IO1CQKSuuDUC0eNO37OTaQqZQ
           OWPApDOKktGC5N" />
   </div>
   <script type="text/javascript">
   <!--
      var Page_ValidationActive = false;
      if (typeof(ValidatorOnLoad) == "function") {
         ValidatorOnLoad();
      }

      function ValidatorOnSubmit() {
         if (Page_ValidationActive) {
```

Fig. 25.19 | XHTML and ECMAScript generated by ASP.NET and sent to the browser when `Validation.aspx` is requested. (Part 4 of 5.)

```
                return ValidatorCommonOnSubmit();
            }
            else {
              return true;
            }
        }
      // -->
      </script>
   </form>
   </body>
   </html>
```

Fig. 25.19 | XHTML and ECMAScript generated by ASP.NET and sent to the browser when `Validation.aspx` is requested. (Part 5 of 5.)

Performance Tip 25.1

Setting `EnableViewState` to `False` reduces the amount of data passed to the web server with each request.

Software Engineering Observation 25.2

Client-side validation cannot be trusted by the server because there are too many ways top circumvent client-side validation. For this reason, all important validation should be peformed on the server.

25.4 Session Tracking

Originally, critics accused the Internet and e-businesses of failing to provide the kind of customized service typically experienced in "brick-and-mortar" stores. To address this problem, e-businesses began to establish mechanisms by which they could personalize users' browsing experiences, tailoring content to individual users while enabling them to bypass irrelevant information. Businesses achieve this level of service by tracking each customer's movement through the Internet and combining the collected data with information provided by the consumer, including billing information, personal preferences, interests and hobbies.

Personalization

Personalization makes it possible for e-businesses to communicate effectively with their customers and also improves users' ability to locate desired products and services. Companies that provide content of particular interest to users can establish relationships with customers and build on those relationships over time. Furthermore, by targeting consumers with personal offers, recommendations, advertisements, promotions and services, e-businesses create customer loyalty. Websites can use sophisticated technology to allow visitors to customize home pages to suit their individual needs and preferences. Similarly, online shopping sites often store personal information for customers, tailoring notifications and special offers to their interests. Such services encourage customers to visit sites more frequently and make purchases more regularly.

Privacy

A trade-off exists, however, between personalized e-business service and protection of privacy. Some consumers embrace the idea of tailored content, but others fear the possible adverse consequences if the info they provide to e-businesses is released or collected by tracking technologies. Consumers and privacy advocates ask: What if the e-business to which we give personal data sells or gives that information to another organization without our knowledge? What if we do not want our actions on the Internet—a supposedly anonymous medium—to be tracked and recorded by unknown parties? What if unauthorized parties gain access to sensitive private data, such as credit card numbers or medical history? All of these are questions that must be debated and addressed by programmers, consumers, e-businesses and lawmakers alike.

Recognizing Clients

To provide personalized services to consumers, e-businesses must be able to recognize clients when they request information from a site. As we have discussed, the request/response system on which the web operates is facilitated by HTTP. Unfortunately, HTTP is a stateless protocol. This means that web servers cannot determine whether a request comes from a particular client or whether the same or different clients generate a series of requests.

To circumvent this problem, sites can use the concept of a "session" to identify individual clients. A session represents a unique client on a website. If the client leaves a site and then returns later, the client will still be recognized as the same user. To help the server distinguish among clients, each client must identify itself to the server. Tracking individual clients, known as session tracking, can be achieved in a number of ways. One popular technique uses cookies (Section 25.4.1); another uses ASP.NET's `HttpSessionState` object (Section 25.4.2). Additional session-tracking techniques include the use of `input` `form` elements of type `"hidden"` and URL rewriting. Using `"hidden"` form elements, a Web Form can write session-tracking data into a `form` in the web page that it returns to the client in response to a prior request. When the user submits the form in the new web page, all the form data, including the `"hidden"` fields, is sent to the form handler on the web server. When a website performs URL rewriting, the Web Form embeds session-tracking information directly in the URLs of hyperlinks that the user clicks to send subsequent requests to the web server.

Note that our previous examples set the Web Form's `EnableSessionState` property to `False`. However, because we wish to use session tracking in the following examples, we keep this property's default setting—`True`.

25.4.1 Cookies

Cookies provide web developers with a tool for identifying and tracking web users. A cookie is a piece of data stored in a small text file on the user's computer. A cookie maintains information about the client during and between browser sessions. The first time a user visits the website, the user's computer might receive a cookie; this cookie is then retrieved each time the user revisits that site. The collected information is intended to be an anonymous record containing data that is used to personalize the user's future visits to the site. For example, cookies in a shopping application might store unique identifiers for users. When a user adds items to an online shopping cart or performs another task resulting in a request to the web server, the server receives a cookie containing the user's unique identifier. The server then uses the unique identifier to locate the shopping cart and perform any necessary processing.

In addition to identifying users, cookies also can indicate users' shopping preferences. When a web server receives a request from a client, the server can examine the cookie(s) it sent to the client during previous communications, identify the users's preferences and immediately return products of interest to the client.

Every HTTP-based interaction between a client and a server includes a header containing information either about the request (when the communication is from the client to the server) or about the response (when the communication is from the server to the client). When a web server receives a request, the header includes information such as the request type (e.g., `Get`) and any cookies that have been sent previously from the server to be stored on the client machine. When the server formulates its response, the header information contains any cookies the server wants to store on the client computer and other information, such as the MIME type of the response.

The expiration date of a cookie determines how long the cookie remains on the client's computer. If you do not set an expiration date for a cookie, the web browser maintains the cookie for the duration of the browsing session. Otherwise, the Web browser maintains the cookie until the expiration date occurs. When the browser requests a resource from a web server, cookies previously sent to the client by that Web server are returned to the web server as part of the request formulated by the browser. Cookies are deleted when they expire.

Portability Tip 25.3

Users may disable cookies in their browsers to ensure that their privacy is protected. Such users will experience difficulty using sites that depend on cookies to maintain state information.

Using Cookies to Provide Book Recommendations

The next web application demonstrates the use of cookies. The example contains two pages. In the first page (Figs. 25.20–25.21), users select a favorite programming language from a group of radio buttons and submit the XHTML form to the web server for processing. The web server responds by creating a cookie that stores a record of the chosen language, as well as the ISBN number for a book on that topic. The server then returns an XHTML document to the browser, allowing the user either to select another favorite programming language or to view the second page in our application (Figs. 25.22–25.23), which lists recommended books pertaining to the programming language that the user selected previously. When the user clicks the hyperlink, the cookies previously stored on the client are read and used to form the list of book recommendations.

The ASPX file in Fig. 25.20 contains five radio buttons (lines 20–26) with the values **Visual Basic 2005**, **Visual C# 2005**, **C**, **C++**, and **Java**. Recall that you can set the values of radio buttons via the **ListItem Collection Editor**, which you open either by clicking the `RadioButtonList`'s `Items` property in the **Properties** window or by clicking the **Edit Items...** link in the **RadioButtonList Tasks** smart tag menu. The user selects a programming language by clicking one of the radio buttons. When the user clicks **Submit**, we'll create a cookie containing the selected language. Then, we'll add this cookie to the HTTP response header, so the cookie will be stored on the user's computer. Each time the user chooses a language and clicks **Submit**, a cookie is written to the client. Each time the client requests information from our web application, the cookies are sent back to the server.

When the postback occurs, certain controls are hidden and others are displayed. The `Label`, `RadioButtonList` and `Button` used to select a language are hidden. Toward the bottom of the page, a `Label` and two `HyperLink`s are displayed. One link requests this page (lines 32–35), and the other requests `Recommendations.aspx` (lines 37–40). Clicking the first hyperlink (the one that requests the current page) does not cause a postback to occur. The file `Options.aspx` is specified in the `NavigateUrl` property of the hyperlink. When the hyperlink is clicked, a new request for this page occurs. Recall that earlier in the chapter, we set `NavigateUrl` to a remote website (`http://www.deitel.com`). To set this property to a page within the same ASP.NET application, click the ellipsis button next to the `NavigateUrl` property in the **Properties** window to open the **Select URL** dialog. Use this dialog to select a page within your project as the destination for the `HyperLink`.

```
1  <%-- Fig. 25.20: Options.aspx --%>
2  <%-- Allows client to select programming languages and access --%>
3  <%-- book recommendations. --%>
4  <%@ Page Language="VB" AutoEventWireup="false"
5     CodeFile="Options.aspx.vb" Inherits="Options" %>
6
7  <!DOCTYPE html PUBLIC "-//W3C//DTD XHTML 1.0 Transitional//EN"
8     "http://www.w3.org/TR/xhtml1/DTD/xhtml1-transitional.dtd">
9
10 <html xmlns="http://www.w3.org/1999/xhtml" >
11 <head runat="server">
12     <title>Cookies</title>
13 </head>
14 <body>
15    <form id="form1" runat="server">
16    <div>
17       <asp:Label ID="promptLabel" runat="server" Font-Bold="True"
18          Font-Size="Large" Text="Select a programming language:">
19       </asp:Label>
20       <asp:RadioButtonList ID="languageList" runat="server">
21          <asp:ListItem>Visual Basic 2005</asp:ListItem>
22          <asp:ListItem>Visual C# 2005</asp:ListItem>
23          <asp:ListItem>C</asp:ListItem>
24          <asp:ListItem>C++</asp:ListItem>
25          <asp:ListItem>Java</asp:ListItem>
26       </asp:RadioButtonList>
27       <asp:Button ID="submitButton" runat="server" Text="Submit" />
28       <asp:Label ID="responseLabel" runat="server" Font-Bold="True"
29          Font-Size="Large" Text="Welcome to cookies!" Visible="False">
30       </asp:Label><br />
31       <br />
32       <asp:HyperLink ID="languageLink" runat="server"
33          NavigateUrl="~/Options.aspx" Visible="False">
34          Click here to choose another language
35       </asp:HyperLink><br />
36       <br />
37       <asp:HyperLink ID="recommendationsLink" runat="server"
38          NavigateUrl="~/Recommendations.aspx" Visible="False">
```

Fig. 25.20 | ASPX file that presents a list of programming languages. (Part 1 of 2.)

```
            Click here to get book recommendations
         </asp:HyperLink>
      </div>
      </form>
   </body>
   </html>
```

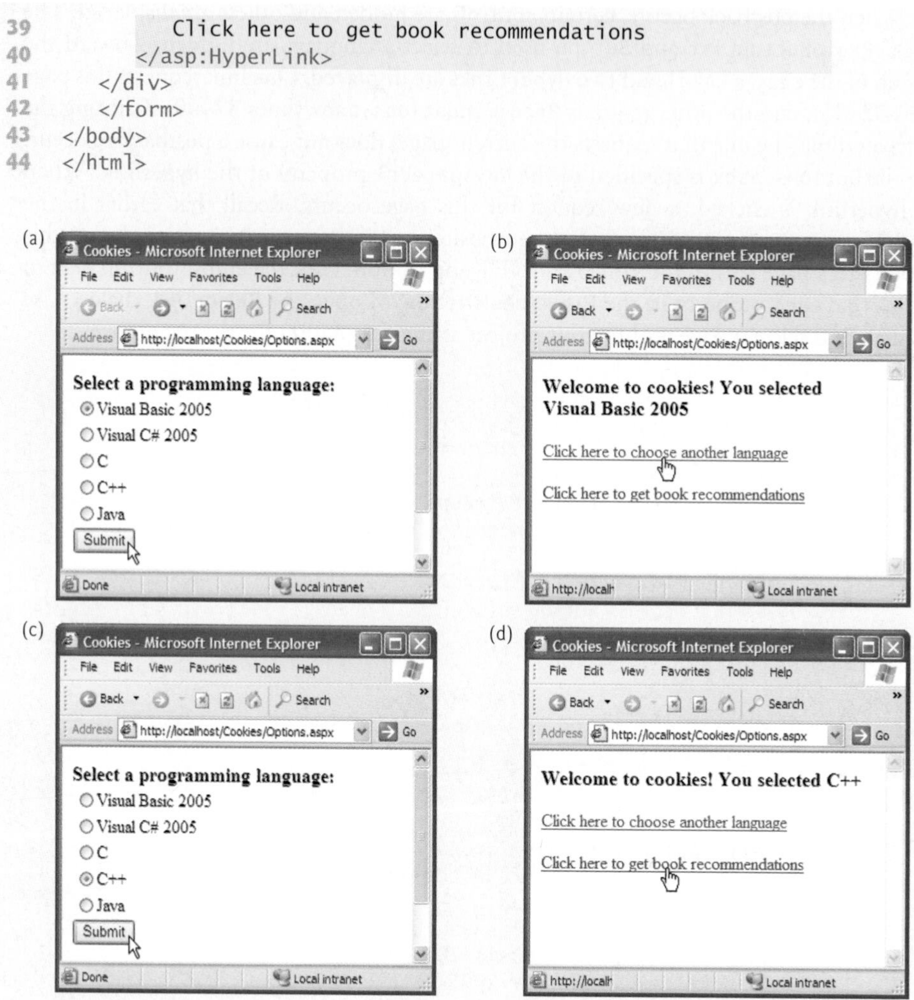

Fig. 25.20 | ASPX file that presents a list of programming languages. (Part 2 of 2.)

Adding and Linking to a New Web Form

Setting the `NavigateUrl` property to a page in the current application requires that the destination page exist already. Thus, to set the `NavigateUrl` property of the second link (the one that requests the page with book recommendations) to `Recommendations.aspx`, you must first create this file by right clicking the project location in the **Solution Explorer** and selecting **Add New Item...** from the menu that appears. In the **Add New Item** dialog, select **Web Form** from the **Templates** pane and change the name of the file to `Recommendations.aspx`. Finally, check the box labeled **Place code in separate file** to indicate that the IDE should create a code-behind file for this ASPX file. Click **Add** to create the file. (We discuss the contents of this ASPX file and code-behind file shortly.) Once the `Recommendations.aspx` file exists, you can select it as the `NavigateUrl` value for a `HyperLink` in the **Select URL** dialog.

Writing Cookies in a Code-Behind File

Figure 25.21 presents the code-behind file for `Options.aspx` (Fig. 25.20). This file contains the code that writes a cookie to the client machine when the user selects a programming language. The code-behind file also modifies the appearance of the page in response to a postback.

```
' Fig. 25.21: Options.aspx.vb
' Processes user's selection of a programming language
' by displaying links and writing a cookie to the user's machine.
Partial Class Options
   Inherits System.Web.UI.Page
   ' stores values to represent books as cookies
   Private books As New System.Collections.Hashtable()

   ' initializes the Hashtable of values to be stored as cookies
   Protected Sub Page_Init(ByVal sender As Object, _
      ByVal e As System.EventArgs) Handles Me.Init
      books.Add("Visual Basic 2005", "0-13-186900-0")
      books.Add("Visual C# 2005", "0-13-152523-9")
      books.Add("C", "0-13-142644-3")
      books.Add("C++", "0-13-185757-6")
      books.Add("Java", "0-13-148398-6")
   End Sub ' Page_Init

   ' if postback, hide form and display links to make additional
   ' selections or view recommendations
   Protected Sub Page_Load(ByVal sender As Object, _
      ByVal e As System.EventArgs) Handles Me.Load

      If IsPostBack Then
         ' user has submitted information, so display message
         ' and appropriate hyperlinks
         responseLabel.Visible = True
         languageLink.Visible = True
         recommendationsLink.Visible = True

         ' hide other controls used to make language selection
         promptLabel.Visible = False
         languageList.Visible = False
         submitButton.Visible = False

         ' if the user made a selection, display it in responseLabel
         If languageList.SelectedItem IsNot Nothing Then
            responseLabel.Text &= " You selected " & _
               languageList.SelectedItem.Text.ToString()
         Else
            responseLabel.Text &= " You did not select a language."
         End If
      End If
   End Sub ' Page_Load

```

Fig. 25.21 | Code-behind file that writes a cookie to the client. (Part 1 of 2.)

```
46      ' write a cookie to record the user's selection
47      Protected Sub submitButton_Click(ByVal sender As Object, _
48         ByVal e As System.EventArgs) Handles submitButton.Click
49         ' if the user made a selection
50         If languageList.SelectedItem IsNot Nothing Then
51            Dim language As String = languageList.SelectedItem.ToString()
52
53            ' get ISBN number of book for the given language
54            Dim ISBN As String = books(language).ToString()
55
56            ' create cookie using language-ISBN name-value pair
57            Dim cookie As New HttpCookie(language, ISBN)
58
59            ' add cookie to response to place it on the user's machine
60            Response.Cookies.Add(cookie)
61         End If
62      End Sub ' submitButton_Click
63   End Class ' Options
```

Fig. 25.21 | Code-behind file that writes a cookie to the client. (Part 2 of 2.)

Line 7 creates variable books as a **Hashtable** (namespace System.Collections)—a data structure that stores key–value pairs. A program uses the key to store and retrieve the associated value in the Hashtable. In this example, the keys are strings containing the programming languages' names, and the values are strings containing the ISBN numbers for the recommended books. Class Hashtable provides method **Add**, which takes as arguments a key and a value. A value that is added via method Add is placed in the Hashtable at a location determined by the key. The value for a specific Hashtable entry can be determined by indexing the Hashtable with that value's key. The expression

HashtableName(*keyName*)

returns the value in the key–value pair in which *keyName* is the key. For example, the expression books(language) in line 54 returns the value that corresponds to the key contained in language.

Clicking the **Submit** button creates a cookie if a language is selected and causes a postback to occur. In the submitButton_Click event handler (lines 47–62), a new cookie object (of type **HttpCookie**) is created to store the language and its corresponding ISBN number (line 57). This cookie is then Added to the **Cookies** collection sent as part of the HTTP response header (line 60). The postback causes the condition in the If statement of Page_Load (line 24) to evaluate to True, and lines 27–42 execute. Lines 27–29 reveal the initially hidden controls responseLabel, languageLink and recommendationsLink. Lines 32–34 hide the controls used to obtain the user's language selection. Line 37 determines whether the user selected a language. If so, that language is displayed in responseLabel (lines 38–39). Otherwise, text indicating that a language was not selected is displayed in responseLabel (line 41).

Displaying Book Recommendations Based on Cookie Values

After the postback of Options.aspx, the user may request a book recommendation. The book recommendation hyperlink forwards the user to Recommendations.aspx (Fig. 25.22) to display the recommendations based on the user's language selections.

```
1  <%-- Fig. 25.22: Recommendations.aspx --%>
2  <%-- Displays book recommendations using cookies. --%>
3  <%@ Page Language="VB" AutoEventWireup="false"
4     CodeFile="Recommendations.aspx.vb" Inherits="Recommendations" %>
5
6  <!DOCTYPE html PUBLIC "-//W3C//DTD XHTML 1.0 Transitional//EN"
7     "http://www.w3.org/TR/xhtml1/DTD/xhtml1-transitional.dtd">
8
9  <html xmlns="http://www.w3.org/1999/xhtml" >
10 <head runat="server">
11     <title>Book Recommendations</title>
12 </head>
13 <body>
14     <form id="form1" runat="server">
15     <div>
16        <asp:Label ID="recommendationsLabel" runat="server"
17           Font-Bold="True" Font-Size="X-Large" Text="Recommendations">
18        </asp:Label><br />
19        <br />
20        <asp:ListBox ID="booksListBox" runat="server" Height="125px"
21           Width="450px"></asp:ListBox><br />
22        <br />
23        <asp:HyperLink ID="languageLink" runat="server"
24           NavigateUrl="~/Options.aspx">
25           Click here to choose another language
26        </asp:HyperLink> </div>
27     </form>
28 </body>
29 </html>
```

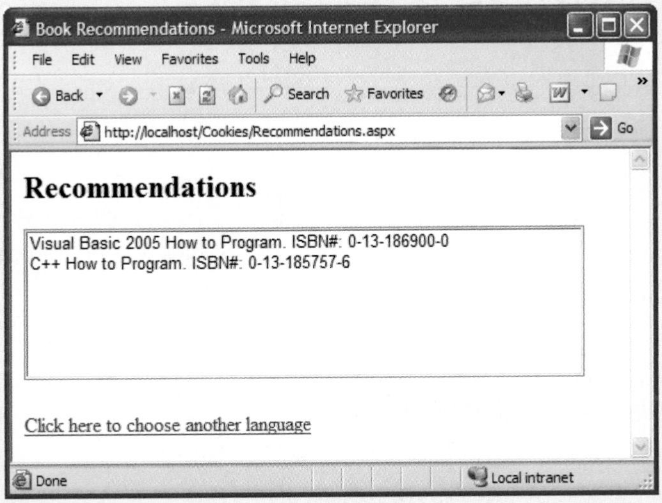

Fig. 25.22 | ASPX file that displays book recommendations based on cookies.

`Recommendations.aspx` contains a `Label` (lines 16–18), a `ListBox` (lines 20–21) and a `HyperLink` (lines 23–26). The `Label` displays the text **Recommendations** if the user selects one or more languages; otherwise, it displays **No Recommendations.** The `ListBox` displays the recommendations specified by the code-behind file (Fig. 25.23). The `HyperLink` allows the user to return to `Options.aspx` to select additional languages.

Code-Behind File That Creates Book Recommendations from Cookies

In the code-behind file (Fig. 25.23), method `Page_Init` (lines 7–28) retrieves the cookies from the client, using the `Request` object's **`Cookies`** property (line 10). This returns a collection of type **`HttpCookieCollection`**, containing cookies that have previously been written to the client. Cookies can be read by an application only if they were created in the domain in which the application is running—a web server can never access cookies created outside the domain associated with that server. For example, a cookie created by a web server in the `deitel.com` domain cannot be read by a web server in any other domain. [*Note:* Depending on the settings in `web.config` and whether other pages store cookies, other cookie values may be displayed by this web application.]

Line 13 determines whether at least one cookie exists. Lines 14–17 add the information in the cookie(s) to the `booksListBox`. The `loop` retrieves the name and value of each cookie using `i`, the loop's control variable, to determine the current value in the cookie collection. The **`Name`** and **`Value`** properties of class `HttpCookie`, which contain the language and corresponding ISBN, respectively, are concatenated with `" How to Program.`

```
1   ' Fig. 25.23: Recommendations.aspx.vb
2   ' Creates book recommendations based on cookies.
3   Partial Class Recommendations
4      Inherits System.Web.UI.Page
5
6      ' read cookies and populate ListBox with any book recommendations
7      Protected Sub Page_Init(ByVal sender As Object, _
8         ByVal e As System.EventArgs) Handles Me.Init
9         ' retrieve client's cookies
10        Dim cookies As HttpCookieCollection = Request.Cookies
11
12        ' if there are cookies, list the appropriate books and ISBN numbers
13        If cookies.Count <> 0 Then
14           For i As Integer = 0 To cookies.Count - 1
15              booksListBox.Items.Add(cookies(i).Name & _
16                 " How to Program. ISBN#: " & cookies(i).Value)
17           Next
18        Else
19           ' if there are no cookies, then no language was chosen, so
20           ' display appropriate message and clear and hide booksListBox
21           recommendationsLabel.Text = "No Recommendations"
22           booksListBox.Items.Clear()
23           booksListBox.Visible = False
24
25           ' modify languageLink because no language was selected
26           languageLink.Text = "Click here to choose a language"
27        End If
28     End Sub ' Page_Init
29  End Class ' Recommendations
```

Fig. 25.23 | Reading cookies from a client to determine book recommendations.

ISBN# " and added to the ListBox. Lines 21–26 execute if no language was selected. We summarize some commonly used HttpCookie properties in Fig. 25.24.

Properties	Description
Domain	Returns a String containing the cookie's domain (i.e., the domain of the web server running the application that wrote the cookie). This determines which web servers can receive the cookie. By default, cookies are sent to the web server that originally sent the cookie to the client. Changing the Domain property causes the cookie to be returned to a web server other than the one that originally wrote it.
Expires	Returns a DateTime object indicating when the browser can delete the cookie.
Name	Returns a String containing the cookie's name.
Path	Returns a String containing the path to a directory on the server (i.e., the Domain) to which the cookie applies. Cookies can be "targeted" to specific directories on the web server. By default, a cookie is returned only to applications operating in the same directory as the application that sent the cookie or a subdirectory of that directory. Changing the Path property causes the cookie to be returned to a directory other than the one from which it was originally written.
Secure	Returns a Boolean value indicating whether the cookie should be transmitted through a secure protocol. The value True causes a secure protocol to be used.
Value	Returns a String containing the cookie's value.

Fig. 25.24 | HttpCookie properties.

25.4.2 Session Tracking with HttpSessionState

Session-tracking capabilities are provided by the FCL class **HttpSessionState**. To demonstrate basic session-tracking techniques, we modified the example of Figs. 25.20–25.23 to use HttpSessionState objects. Figures 25.25–25.26 present the ASPX file and code-behind file for Options.aspx. Figures 25.28–25.29 present the ASPX file and code-behind file for Recommendations.aspx. Options.aspx is similar to the version presented in Fig. 25.20, but Fig. 25.25 contains two additional Labels (lines 32–33 and lines 35–36), which we discuss shortly.

Every Web Form includes an HttpSessionState object, which is accessible through property **Session** of class Page. Throughout this section, we use property Session to manipulate our page's HttpSessionState object. When the web page is requested, an HttpSessionState object is created and assigned to the Page's Session property. As a result, we often refer to property Session as the Session object.

Adding Session Items

When the user presses **Submit** on the Web Form, submitButton_Click is invoked in the code-behind file (Fig. 25.26, lines 55–66). Method submitButton_Click responds by adding a key–value pair to our Session object, specifying the language chosen and the ISBN number for a book on that language. These key–value pairs are often referred to as session items. Next, a postback occurs. Each time the user clicks **Submit**, `submitButton_Click` adds a new session item to the `HttpSessionState` object. Because much of this example is identical to the last example, we concentrate on the new features.

```
<%-- Fig. 25.25: Options.aspx --%>
<%-- Allows client to select programming languages and access --%>
<%-- book recommendations. --%>
<%@ Page Language="VB" AutoEventWireup="false"
   CodeFile="Options.aspx.vb" Inherits="Options" %>

<!DOCTYPE html PUBLIC "-//W3C//DTD XHTML 1.0 Transitional//EN"
   "http://www.w3.org/TR/xhtml1/DTD/xhtml1-transitional.dtd">

<html xmlns="http://www.w3.org/1999/xhtml" >
<head id="Head1" runat="server">
    <title>Sessions</title>
</head>
<body>
   <form id="form1" runat="server">
   <div>
      <asp:Label ID="promptLabel" runat="server" Font-Bold="True"
         Font-Size="Large" Text="Select a programming language:">
      </asp:Label>
      <asp:RadioButtonList ID="languageList" runat="server">
         <asp:ListItem>Visual Basic 2005</asp:ListItem>
         <asp:ListItem>Visual C# 2005</asp:ListItem>
         <asp:ListItem>C</asp:ListItem>
         <asp:ListItem>C++</asp:ListItem>
         <asp:ListItem>Java</asp:ListItem>
      </asp:RadioButtonList>
      <asp:Button ID="submitButton" runat="server" Text="Submit" />
      <asp:Label ID="responseLabel" runat="server" Font-Bold="True"
         Font-Size="Large" Text="Welcome to sessions!" Visible="False">
      </asp:Label><br />
      <br />
      <asp:Label ID="idLabel" runat="server" Visible="False">
      </asp:Label><br />
      <br />
      <asp:Label ID="timeoutLabel" runat="server" Visible="False">
      </asp:Label><br />
      <br />
      <asp:HyperLink ID="languageLink" runat="server"
         NavigateUrl="~/Options.aspx" Visible="False">
         Click here to choose another language
      </asp:HyperLink><br />
      <br />
      <asp:HyperLink ID="recommendationsLink" runat="server"
         NavigateUrl="~/Recommendations.aspx" Visible="False">
         Click here to get book recommendations
      </asp:HyperLink>
   </div>
   </form>
```

Fig. 25.25 | ASPX file that presents a list of programming languages. (Part 1 of 2.)

```
</body>
</html>
```

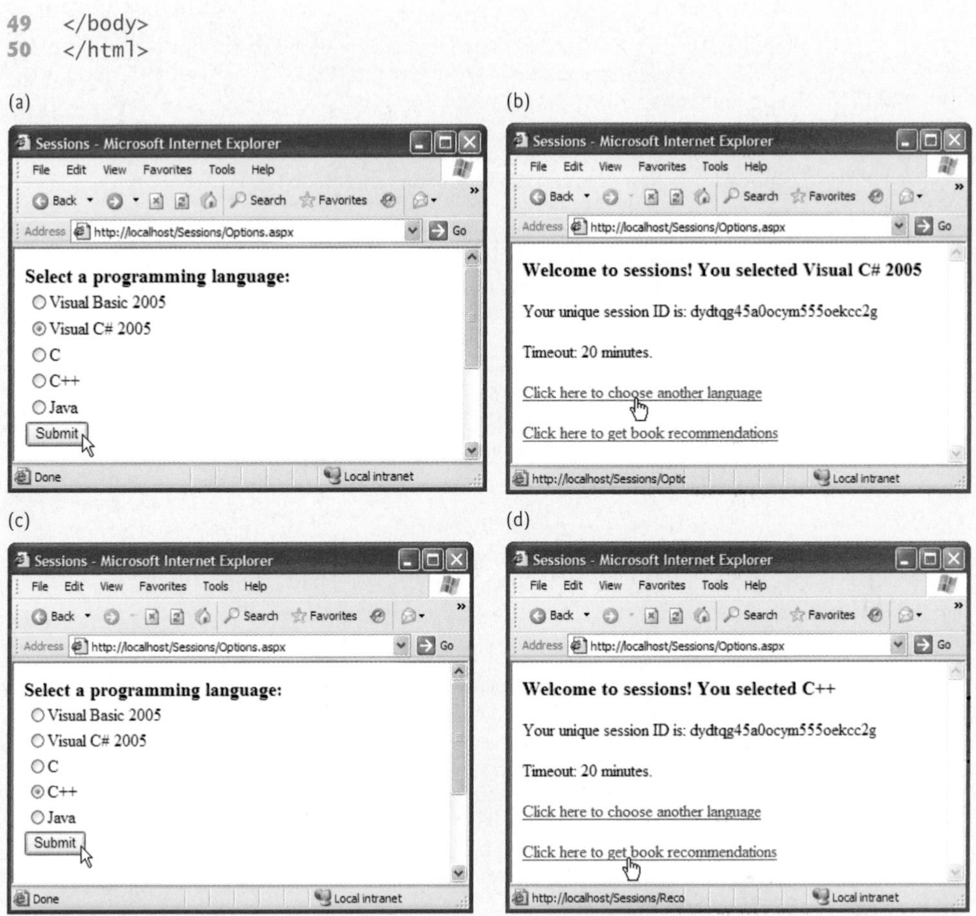

Fig. 25.25 | ASPX file that presents a list of programming languages. (Part 2 of 2.)

Software Engineering Observation 25.3

A Web Form should not use instance variables to maintain client state information, because each new request or postback is handled by a new instance of the page. Instead, maintain client state information in `HttpSessionState` objects, because such objects are specific to each client.

Like a cookie, an `HttpSessionState` object can store name–value pairs. These session items are placed in an `HttpSessionState` object by calling method **Add**. Line 64 calls `Add` to place the language and its corresponding recommended book's ISBN number in the `HttpSessionState` object. If the application calls method `Add` to add an attribute that has the same name as an attribute previously stored in a session, the object associated with that attribute is replaced.

Software Engineering Observation 25.4

A benefit of using `HttpSessionState` objects (rather than cookies) is that `HttpSessionState` objects can store any type of object (not just `String`s) as attribute values. This provides you with increased flexibility in determining the type of state information to maintain for clients.

```
' Fig. 25.26: Options.aspx.vb
' Processes user's selection of a programming language
' by displaying links and writing information in a Session object.
Partial Class Options
   Inherits System.Web.UI.Page
   ' stores values to represent books
   Private books As New System.Collections.Hashtable()

   ' initializes the Hashtable of values to be stored in a Session
   Protected Sub Page_Init(ByVal sender As Object, _
      ByVal e As System.EventArgs) Handles Me.Init
      books.Add("Visual Basic 2005", "0-13-186900-0")
      books.Add("Visual C# 2005", "0-13-152523-9")
      books.Add("C", "0-13-142644-3")
      books.Add("C++", "0-13-185757-6")
      books.Add("Java", "0-13-148398-6")
   End Sub ' Page_Init

   ' if postback, hide form and display links to make additional
   ' selections or view recommendations
   Protected Sub Page_Load(ByVal sender As Object, _
      ByVal e As System.EventArgs) Handles Me.Load

      If IsPostBack Then
         ' user has submitted information, so display message
         ' and appropriate hyperlinks
         responseLabel.Visible = True
         idLabel.Visible = True
         timeoutLabel.Visible = True
         languageLink.Visible = True
         recommendationsLink.Visible = True

         ' hide other controls used to make language selection
         promptLabel.Visible = False
         languageList.Visible = False
         submitButton.Visible = False

         ' if the user made a selection, display it in responseLabel
         If languageList.SelectedItem IsNot Nothing Then
            responseLabel.Text &= " You selected " & _
               languageList.SelectedItem.Text.ToString()
         Else
            responseLabel.Text &= " You did not select a language."
         End If

         ' display session ID
         idLabel.Text = "Your unique session ID is: " & Session.SessionID

         ' display the timeout
         timeoutLabel.Text = "Timeout: " & Session.Timeout & " minutes."
      End If
   End Sub ' Page_Load
```

Fig. 25.26 | Processes user's selection of a programming language by displaying links and writing information in a `Session` object. (Part 1 of 2.)

```
53
54    ' record the user's selection in the Session
55    Protected Sub submitButton_Click(ByVal sender As Object, _
56       ByVal e As System.EventArgs) Handles submitButton.Click
57       ' if the user made a selection
58       If languageList.SelectedItem IsNot Nothing Then
59          Dim language As String = languageList.SelectedItem.ToString()
60
61          ' get ISBN number of book for the given language
62          Dim ISBN As String = books(language).ToString()
63
64          Session.Add(language, ISBN) ' add name/value pair to Session
65       End If
66    End Sub ' submitButton_Click
67 End Class ' Options
```

Fig. 25.26 | Processes user's selection of a programming language by displaying links and writing information in a `Session` object. (Part 2 of 2.)

The application handles the postback event (lines 24–51) in method `Page_Load`. Here, we retrieve information about the current client's session from the `Session` object's properties and display this information in the web page. The ASP.NET application contains information about the `HttpSessionState` object for the current client. Property **`SessionID`** (line 47) contains the **unique session ID**—a sequence of random letters and numbers. The first time a client connects to the web server, a unique session ID is created for that client and a temporary cookie is written to the client so the server can identify the client on subsequent requests. When the client makes additional requests, the client's session ID from that temporary cookie is compared with the session IDs stored in the web server's memory to retrieve the client's `HttpSessionState` object. Recall that clients may disable cookies in their web browsers to ensure that their privacy is protected. Such clients will experience difficulty using web applications that depend on `HttpSessionState` objects and cookies to maintain state information. The `HttpSessionStrate` property `IsCookieless` indicates whether URL rewriting or cookies are used for session tracking. Property **`Timeout`** (line 50) specifies the maximum amount of time that an `HttpSessionState` object can be inactive before it is discarded. Figure 25.27 lists some common `HttpSessionState` properties.

Properties	Description
`Count`	Specifies the number of key–value pairs in the `Session` object.
`IsNewSession`	Indicates whether this is a new session (i.e., whether the session was created during loading of this page).
`IsReadOnly`	Indicates whether the `Session` object is read-only.

Fig. 25.27 | `HttpSessionState` properties. (Part 1 of 2.)

Properties	Description
`Keys`	Returns a collection containing the `Session` object's keys.
`SessionID`	Returns the session's unique ID.
`Timeout`	Specifies the maximum number of minutes during which a session can be inactive (i.e., no requests are made) before the session expires. By default, this property is set to 20 minutes.

Fig. 25.27 | `HttpSessionState` properties. (Part 2 of 2.)

Displaying Recommendations Based on Session Values

As in the cookies example, this application provides a link to `Recommendations.aspx` (Fig. 25.28), which displays a list of book recommendations based on the user's language selections. Lines 20–21 define a `ListBox` web control that is used to present the recommendations to the user.

```
1  <%-- Fig. 25.28: Recommendations.aspx --%>
2  <%-- Displays book recommendations using a Session object. --%>
3  <%@ Page Language="VB" AutoEventWireup="false"
4     CodeFile="Recommendations.aspx.vb" Inherits="Recommendations" %>
5
6  <!DOCTYPE html PUBLIC "-//W3C//DTD XHTML 1.0 Transitional//EN"
7     "http://www.w3.org/TR/xhtml1/DTD/xhtml1-transitional.dtd">
8
9  <html xmlns="http://www.w3.org/1999/xhtml" >
10 <head id="Head1" runat="server">
11     <title>Book Recommendations</title>
12 </head>
13 <body>
14     <form id="form1" runat="server">
15     <div>
16        <asp:Label ID="recommendationsLabel" runat="server"
17           Font-Bold="True" Font-Size="X-Large" Text="Recommendations">
18        </asp:Label><br />
19        <br />
20        <asp:ListBox ID="booksListBox" runat="server" Height="125px"
21           Width="450px"></asp:ListBox><br />
22        <br />
23        <asp:HyperLink ID="languageLink" runat="server"
24           NavigateUrl="~/Options.aspx">
25           Click here to choose another language
26        </asp:HyperLink> </div>
27     </form>
28 </body>
29 </html>
```

Fig. 25.28 | Session-based book recommendations displayed in a `ListBox`. (Part 1 of 2.)

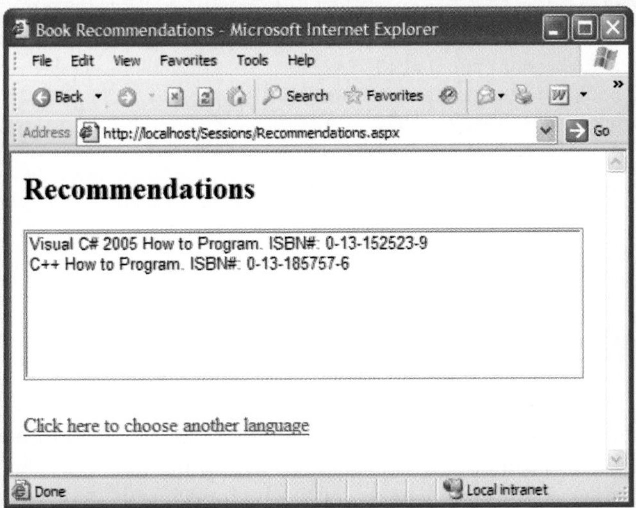

Fig. 25.28 | Session-based book recommendations displayed in a `ListBox`. (Part 2 of 2.)

Code-Behind File That Creates Book Recommendations from a Session

Figure 25.29 presents the code-behind file for `Recommendations.aspx`. Event handler `Page_Init` (lines 7–30) retrieves the session information. If a user has not selected a language on `Options.aspx`, our `Session` object's **`Count`** property will be `0`. This property provides the number of session items contained in a `Session` object. If `Session` object's `Count` property is `0` (i.e., no language was selected), then we display the text **No Recommendations** and update the `Text` of the `HyperLink` back to `Options.aspx`.

```
1  ' Fig. 25.29: Recommendations.aspx.vb
2  ' Creates book recommendations based on a Session object.
3  Partial Class Recommendations
4     Inherits System.Web.UI.Page
5
6     ' read Session items and populate ListBox with any book recommendations
7     Protected Sub Page_Init(ByVal sender As Object, _
8        ByVal e As System.EventArgs) Handles Me.Init
9        ' determine whether Session contains any information
10       If Session.Count <> 0 Then
11          For i As Integer = 0 To Session.Count - 1
12             ' get current key name from Session object
13             Dim keyName As String = Session.Keys(i)
14
15             ' use keyName to display one of Session's name-value pairs
16             booksListBox.Items.Add(keyName & _
17                " How to Program. ISBN#: " & _
18                Session(keyName).ToString())
19          Next
20       Else
```

Fig. 25.29 | Session data used to provide book recommendations to the user. (Part 1 of 2.)

```
21            ' if there are no session items, no language was chosen, so
22            ' display appropriate message and clear and hide booksListBox
23            recommendationsLabel.Text = "No Recommendations"
24            booksListBox.Items.Clear()
25            booksListBox.Visible = False
26
27            ' modify languageLink because no language was selected
28            languageLink.Text = "Click here to choose a language"
29         End If
30      End Sub ' Page_Init
31   End Class ' Recommendations
```

Fig. 25.29 | Session data used to provide book recommendations to the user. (Part 2 of 2.)

If the user has chosen a language, the loop in lines 11–19 iterates through our `Session` object's session items, temporarily storing each key name (line 13). The value in a key–value pair is retrieved from the `Session` object by indexing the `Session` object with the key name, using the same process by which we retrieved a value from our `Hashtable` in the preceding section.

Line 13 accesses the **`Keys`** property of class `HttpSessionState`, which returns a collection containing all the keys in the session. Line 13 indexes this collection to retrieve the current key. Lines 16–18 concatenate `keyName`'s value to the `String` `" How to Program. ISBN#: "` and the value from the `Session` object for which `keyName` is the key. This `String` is the recommendation that appears in the `ListBox`.

25.5 Case Study: Connecting to a Database in ASP.NET

Many websites allow users to provide feedback about the website in a **guestbook**. Typically, users click a link on the website's home page to request the guestbook page. This page usually consists of an XHTML form that contains fields for the user's name, e-mail address, message/feedback and so on. Data submitted on the guestbook form is then stored in a database located on the web server's machine.

In this section, we create a guestbook Web Form application. This example's GUI is slightly more complex than that of earlier examples. It contains a **`GridView`** ASP.NET data control, as shown in Fig. 25.30, which displays all the entries in the guestbook in tabular format. We explain how to create and configure this data control shortly. Note that the `GridView` displays **abc** in **Design** mode to indicate string data that will be retrieved from a data source at runtime.

The XHTML form presented to the user consists of a name field, an e-mail address field and a message field. The form also contains a **Submit** button to send the data to the server and a **Clear** button to reset each of the fields on the form. The application stores the guestbook information in a SQL Server database called `Guestbook.mdf` located on the web server. (We provide this database in the examples directory for this chapter. You can download the examples from `www.deitel.com/books/iw3htp4`.) Below the XHTML form, the `GridView` displays the data (i.e., guestbook entries) in the database's `Messages` table.

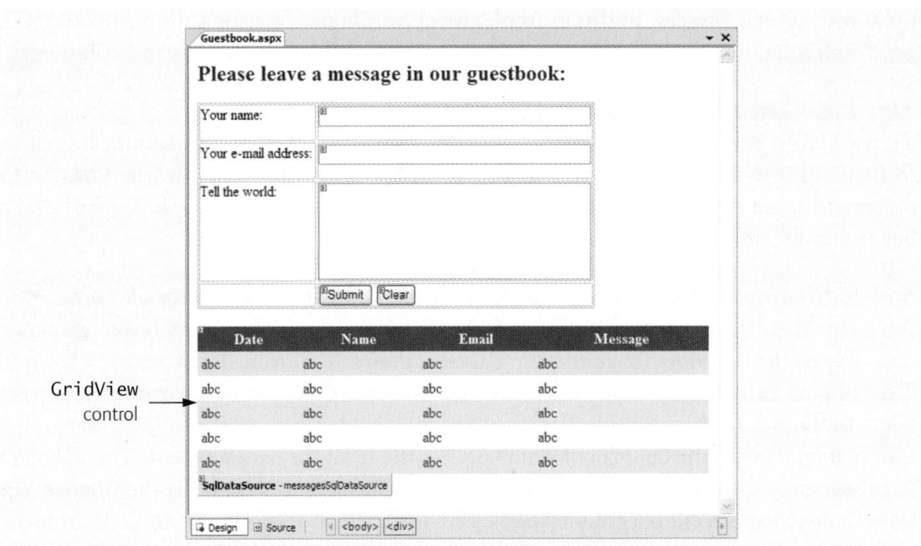

Fig. 25.30 | Guestbook application GUI in **Design** mode.

25.5.1 Building a Web Form That Displays Data from a Database

We now explain how to build this GUI and set up the data binding between the `GridView` control and the database. We present the ASPX file generated from the GUI later in the section, and we discuss the related code-behind file in the next section. To build the guestbook application, perform the following steps:

Step 1: Creating the Project

Create an **ASP.NET Web Site** named `Guestbook` and name the ASPX file `Guestbook.aspx`. Rename the class in the code-behind file `Guestbook`, and update the `Page` directive in the ASPX file accordingly.

Step 2: Creating the Form for User Input

In **Design** mode for the ASPX file, add the text `Please leave a message in our guestbook:` formatted as an `h2` header. As discussed in Section 25.3.1, insert an XHTML table with two columns and four rows, configured so that the text in each cell aligns with the top of the cell. Place the appropriate text (see Fig. 25.30) in the top three cells in the table's left column. Then place `TextBoxes` named `nameTextBox`, `emailTextBox` and `messageTextBox` in the top three table cells in the right column. Set `messageTextBox` to be a multiline `TextBox`. Finally, add `Buttons` named `submitButton` and `clearButton` to the bottom-right table cell. Set the buttons' `Text` properties to `Submit` and `Clear`, respectively. We discuss the buttons' event handlers when we present the code-behind file.

*Step 3: Adding a **`GridView`** Control to the Web Form*

Add a `GridView` named `messagesGridView` that will display the guestbook entries. This control appears in the **Data** section of the **Toolbox**. The colors for the `GridView` are specified through the **Auto Format...** link in the **GridView Tasks** smart tag menu that opens when you place the `GridView` on the page. Clicking this link causes an **Auto Format** dialog to open with several choices. In this example, we chose **Simple**. We soon show how to set the `GridView`'s data source (i.e., where it gets the data to display in its rows and columns).

Step 4: Adding a Database to an ASP.NET Web Application

To use a SQL Server 2005 Express database in an ASP.NET web application, it is easiest to first add it to the project's `App_Data` folder. Right click this folder in the **Solution Explorer** and select **Add Existing Item...**. Locate the `Guestbook.mdf` file in the `exampleDatabases` subdirectory of the chapter's examples directory, then click **Add**.

Step 5: Binding the `GridView` to the `Messages` Table of the `Guestbook` Database

Now that the database is part of the project, we can configure the `GridView` to display its data. Open the **GridView Tasks** smart tag menu, then select **<New data source...>** from the **Choose Data Source** drop-down list. In the **Data Source Configuration Wizard** that appears, select **Database**. In this example, we use a **`SqlDataSource`** control that allows the application to interact with the `Guestbook` database. Set the `ID` of the data source to `messagesSqlDataSource` and click **OK** to begin the **Configure Data Source** wizard. In the **Choose Your Data Connection** screen, select `Guestbook.mdf` from the drop-down list (Fig. 25.31), then click **Next >** twice to continue to the **Configure the Select Statement** screen.

The **Configure the Select Statement** screen (Fig. 25.32) allows you to specify which data the `SqlDataSource` should retrieve from the database. Your choices on this page design a `SELECT` statement, shown in the bottom pane of the dialog. The **Name** drop-down list identifies a table in the database. The `Guestbook` database contains only one table named `Messages`, which is selected by default. In the **Columns** pane, click the checkbox marked with an asterisk (*) to indicate that you want to retrieve the data from all the columns in the **Message** table. Click the **Advanced** button, then check the box next to **Gen-**

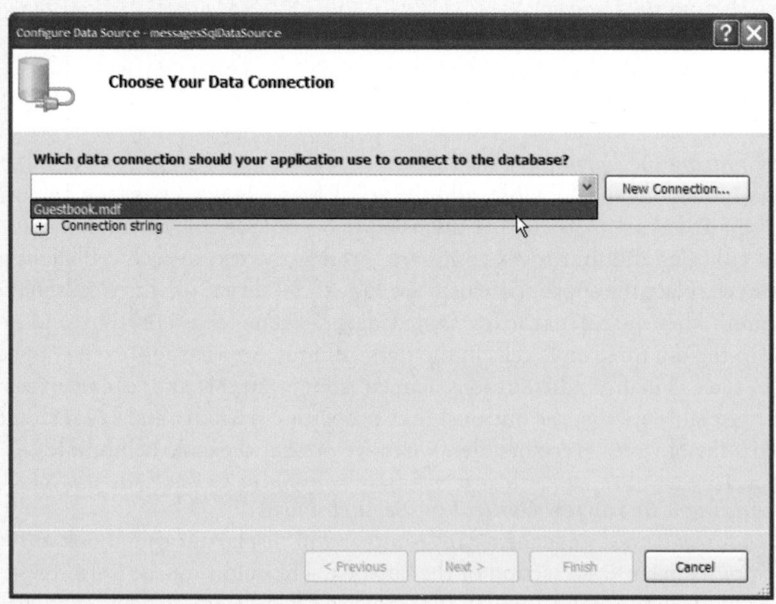

Fig. 25.31 | **Configure Data Source** dialog in Visual Web Developer.

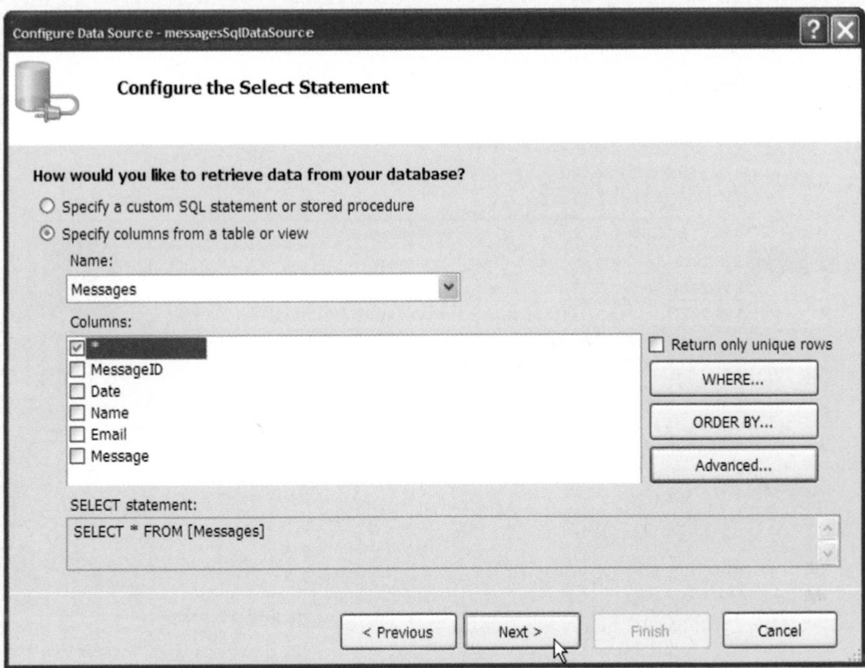

Fig. 25.32 | Configuring the `SELECT` statement used by the `SqlDataSource` to retrieve data.

erate **UPDATE, INSERT and DELETE statements**. This configures the `SqlDataSource` control to allow us to change data in, insert new data into and delete data from the database. We discuss inserting new guestbook entries based on users' form submissions shortly. Click **OK**, then click **Next >** to continue the **Configure Data Source** wizard.

The next screen of the wizard allows you to test the query that you just designed. Click **Test Query** to preview the data that will be retrieved by the `SqlDataSource` (shown in Fig. 25.33).

Finally, click **Finish** to complete the wizard. Notice that a control named `messagesSqlDataSource` now appears on the Web Form directly below the `GridView` (Fig. 25.34). This control is represented in **Design** mode as a gray box containing its type and name. This control will *not* appear on the web page—the gray box simply provides a way to manipulate the control visually through **Design** mode. Also notice that the `GridView` now has column headers that correspond to the columns in the `Messages` table and that the rows each contain either a number (which signifies an autoincremented column) or **abc** (which indicates string data). The actual data from the `Guestbook` database file will appear in these rows when the ASPX file is executed and viewed in a web browser.

Step 6: Modifying the Columns of the Data Source Displayed in the `GridView`

It is not necessary for site visitors to see the `MessageID` column when viewing past guestbook entries—this column is merely a unique primary key required by the `Messages` table within the database. Thus, we modify the `GridView` so that this column does not display

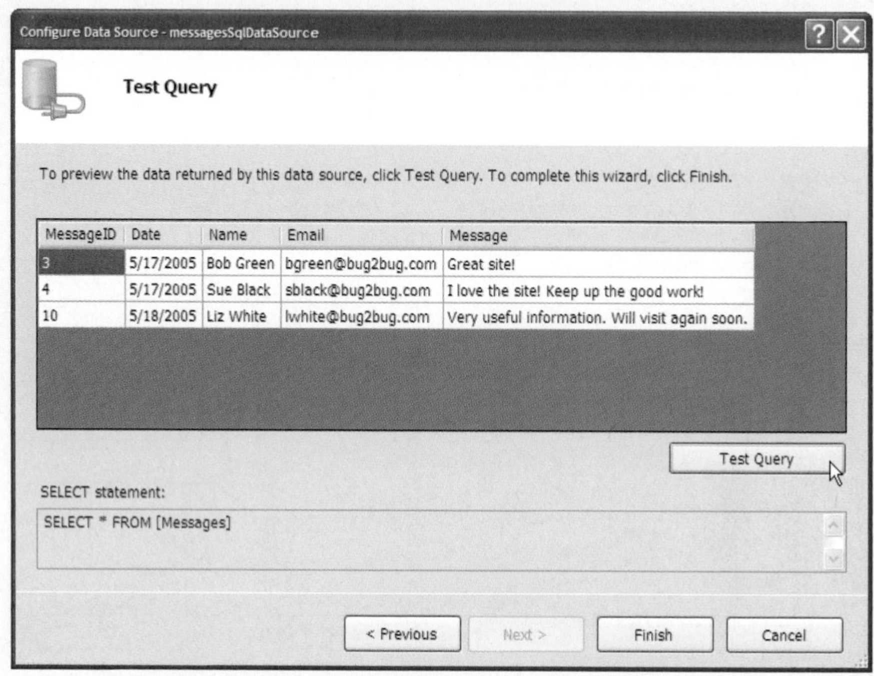

Fig. 25.33 | Previewing the data retrieved by the `SqlDataSource`.

Default.aspx

Please leave a message in our guestbook:

Your name:

Your e-mail address:

Tell the world:

Submit Clear

MessageID	Date	Name	Email	Message
0	abc	abc	abc	abc
1	abc	abc	abc	abc
2	abc	abc	abc	abc
3	abc	abc	abc	abc
4	abc	abc	abc	abc

SqlDataSource - messagesSqlDataSource

`SqlDataSource` control

Design Source <body> <asp:gridview#gridview1>

Fig. 25.34 | **Design** mode displaying `SqlDataSource` control for a `GridView`.

on the Web Form. In the **GridView Tasks** smart tag menu, click **Edit Columns**. In the resulting **Fields** dialog (Fig. 25.35), select **MessageID** in the **Selected fields** pane, then click the **X**. This removes the `MessageID` column from the `GridView`. Click **OK** to return to the main IDE window. The `GridView` should now appear as in Fig. 25.30.

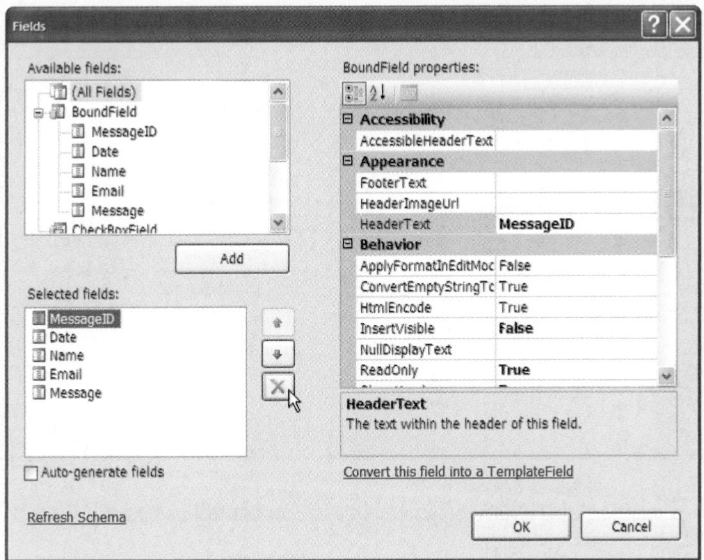

Fig. 25.35 | Removing the `MessageID` column from the `GridView`.

Step 7: Modifying the Way the `SqlDataSource` *Control Inserts Data*

When you create a `SqlDataSource` in the manner described here, it is configured to permit `INSERT` SQL operations against the database table from which it gathers data. You must specify the values to insert either programmatically or through other controls on the Web Form. In this example, we wish to insert the data entered by the user in the `nameTextBox`, `emailTextBox` and `messageTextBox` controls. We also want to insert the current date—we will specify the date to insert programmatically in the code-behind file, which we present shortly.

To configure the `SqlDataSource` to allow such an insertion, select the `messagesSqlDataSource` control then click the ellipsis button next to the control's `InsertQuery` property of the `messagesSqlDataSource` control in the **Properties** window. The **Command and Parameter Editor** (Fig. 25.36) that appears displays the `INSERT` command used by the `SqlDataSource` control. This command contains parameters `@Date`, `@Name`, `@Email` and `@Message`. You must provide values for these parameters before they are inserted into the database. Each parameter is listed in the **Parameters** section of the **Command and Parameter Editor**. Because we will set the **Date** parameter programmatically, we do not modify it here. For each of the remaining three parameters, select the parameter, then select **Control** from the **Parameter source** drop-down list. This indicates that the value of the parameter should be taken from a control. The **ControlID** drop-down list contains all the controls on the Web Form. Select the appropriate control for each parameter, then click **OK**. Now the `SqlDataSource` is configured to insert the user's name, e-mail address and message in the

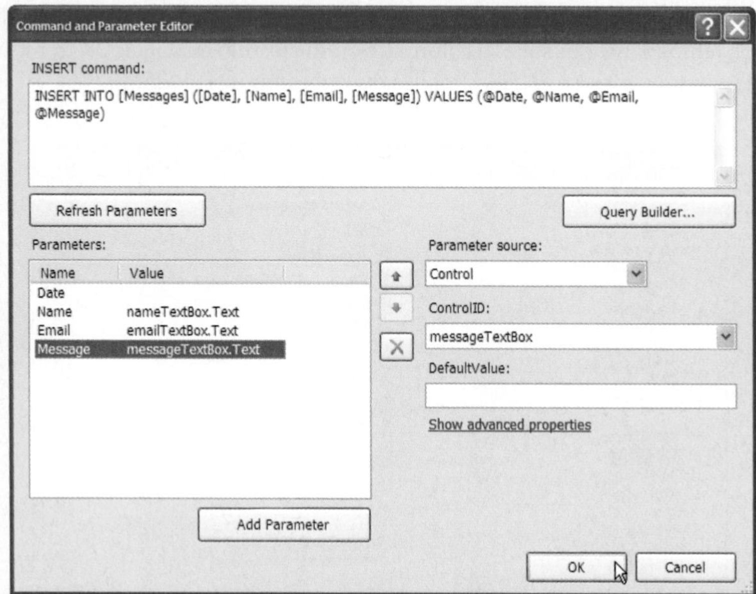

Fig. 25.36 | Setting up `INSERT` parameters based on control values.

`Messages` table of the `Guestbook` database. We show how to set the date parameter and initiate the insert operation when the user clicks **Submit** shortly.

ASPX File for a Web Form That Interacts with a Database

The ASPX file generated by the guestbook GUI (and `messagesSqlDataSource` control) is shown in Fig. 25.37. This file contains a large amount of generated markup. We discuss only those parts that are new or noteworthy for the current example. Lines 19–58 contain the XHTML and ASP.NET elements that comprise the form that gathers user input. The `GridView` control appears in lines 60–85. The `<asp:GridView>` start tag (lines 60–63) contains properties that set various aspects of the `GridView`'s appearance and behavior, such as whether grid lines should be displayed between rows and columns. The **`DataSourceID`** property identifies the data source that is used to fill the `GridView` with data at runtime.

Lines 66–75 define the `Columns` that appear in the `GridView`. Each column is represented as a **`BoundField`**, because the values in the columns are bound to values retrieved from the data source (i.e., the `Messages` table of the `Guestbook` database). The `DataField` property of each `BoundField` identifies the column in the data source to which the column in the `GridView` is bound. The `HeaderText` property indicates the text that appears as the column header. By default, this is the name of the column in the data source, but you can change this property as desired. Lines 76–84 contain nested elements that define the styles used to format the `GridView`'s rows. The IDE configured these styles based on your selection of the **Simple** style in the **Auto Format** dialog for the `GridView`.

The `messagesSqlDataSource` is defined by the markup in lines 86–115 in Fig. 25.37. Line 87 contains a **`ConnectionString`** property, which indicates the connection through which the `SqlDataSource` control interacts with the database. The value of this property uses an ASP.NET expression, delimited by `<%$` and `%>`, to access the `GuestbookConnectionString` stored in the `ConnectionStrings` section of the application's `Web.config` configuration file. Recall that we created this connection string earlier in this section using the **Configure Data Source** wizard.Lines 88–95 define the **`DeleteCommand`**, **`InsertCommand`**, **`SelectCommand`** and **`UpdateCommand`** properties, which contain the `DELETE`, `INSERT`, `SELECT` and `UPDATE` SQL statements, respectively. These were generated by the **Configure Data Source** wizard. In this example, we use only the `InsertCommand`. We discuss invoking this command shortly.

```
1  <%-- Fig. 25.37: Guestbook.aspx --%>
2  <%-- Guestbook Web application with a form for users to submit --%>
3  <%-- guestbook entries and a GridView to view existing entries. --%>
4  <%@ Page Language="VB" AutoEventWireup="false"
5     CodeFile="Guestbook.aspx.vb" Inherits="Guestbook" %>
6
7  <!DOCTYPE html PUBLIC "-//W3C//DTD XHTML 1.0 Transitional//EN"
8     "http://www.w3.org/TR/xhtml11/DTD/xhtml11-transitional.dtd">
9
10 <html xmlns="http://www.w3.org/1999/xhtml" >
11 <head runat="server">
12     <title>Guestbook</title>
13 </head>
14 <body>
15     <form id="form1" runat="server">
16     <div>
17        <h2>
18           Please leave a message in our guestbook:</h2>
19        <table>
20           <tr>
21              <td style="width: 130px; height: 21px" valign="top">
22                 Your name:<br />
23              </td>
24              <td style="width: 300px; height: 21px" valign="top">
25                 <asp:TextBox ID="nameTextBox" runat="server"
26                    Width="300px"></asp:TextBox>
27              </td>
28           </tr>
29           <tr>
30              <td style="width: 130px" valign="top">
31                 Your e-mail address:<br />
32              </td>
33              <td style="width: 300px" valign="top">
34                 <asp:TextBox ID="emailTextBox" runat="server"
35                    Width="300px"></asp:TextBox>
36              </td>
37           </tr>
38           <tr>
39              <td style="width: 130px" valign="top">
40                 Tell the world:<br />
41              </td>
```

Fig. 25.37 | ASPX file for the guestbook application. (Part 1 of 4.)

```
            <td style="width: 300px" valign="top">
               <asp:TextBox ID="messageTextBox" runat="server"
                  Height="100px" Rows="8" Width="300px">
                  </asp:TextBox>
            </td>
         </tr>
         <tr>
            <td style="width: 130px" valign="top">
            </td>
            <td style="width: 300px" valign="top">
               <asp:Button ID="submitButton" runat="server"
                  Text="Submit" />
               <asp:Button ID="clearButton" runat="server"
                  Text="Clear" />
            </td>
         </tr>
      </table>
      <br />
      <asp:GridView ID="messagesGridView" runat="server"
         AutoGenerateColumns="False" CellPadding="4"
         DataKeyNames="MessageID" DataSourceID="messagesSqlDataSource"
         ForeColor="#333333" GridLines="None" Width="600px">
         <FooterStyle BackColor="#1C5E55" Font-Bold="True"
            ForeColor="White" />
         <Columns>
            <asp:BoundField DataField="Date" HeaderText="Date"
               SortExpression="Date" />
            <asp:BoundField DataField="Name" HeaderText="Name"
               SortExpression="Name" />
            <asp:BoundField DataField="Email" HeaderText="Email"
               SortExpression="Email" />
            <asp:BoundField DataField="Message" HeaderText="Message"
               SortExpression="Message" />
         </Columns>
         <RowStyle BackColor="#E3EAEB" />
         <EditRowStyle BackColor="#7C6F57" />
         <SelectedRowStyle BackColor="#C5BBAF" Font-Bold="True"
            ForeColor="#333333" />
         <PagerStyle BackColor="#666666" ForeColor="White"
            HorizontalAlign="Center" />
         <HeaderStyle BackColor="#1C5E55" Font-Bold="True"
            ForeColor="White" />
         <AlternatingRowStyle BackColor="White" />
      </asp:GridView>
      <asp:SqlDataSource ID="messagesSqlDataSource" runat="server"
         ConnectionString="<%$ ConnectionStrings:ConnectionString %>"
         DeleteCommand="DELETE FROM [Messages] WHERE [MessageID] =
            @MessageID" InsertCommand="INSERT INTO [Messages]
            ([Date], [Name], [Email], [Message])
            VALUES (@Date, @Name, @Email, @Message)"
         SelectCommand="SELECT * FROM [Messages]" UpdateCommand=
            "UPDATE [Messages] SET [Date] = @Date, [Name] = @Name,
            [Email] = @Email, [Message] = @Message
```

Fig. 25.37 | ASPX file for the guestbook application. (Part 2 of 4.)

```
            WHERE [MessageID] = @MessageID">
         <DeleteParameters>
            <asp:Parameter Name="MessageID" Type="Int32" />
         </DeleteParameters>
         <UpdateParameters>
            <asp:Parameter Name="Date" Type="String" />
            <asp:Parameter Name="Name" Type="String" />
            <asp:Parameter Name="Email" Type="String" />
            <asp:Parameter Name="Message" Type="String" />
            <asp:Parameter Name="MessageID" Type="Int32" />
         </UpdateParameters>
         <InsertParameters>
            <asp:Parameter Name="Date" Type="String" />
            <asp:ControlParameter ControlID="nameTextBox" Name="Name"
               PropertyName="Text" Type="String" />
            <asp:ControlParameter ControlID="emailTextBox" Name="Email"
               PropertyName="Text" Type="String" />
            <asp:ControlParameter ControlID="messageTextBox"
               Name="Message" PropertyName="Text" Type="String" />
         </InsertParameters>
      </asp:SqlDataSource>
   </div>
   </form>
</body>
</html>
```

(a)

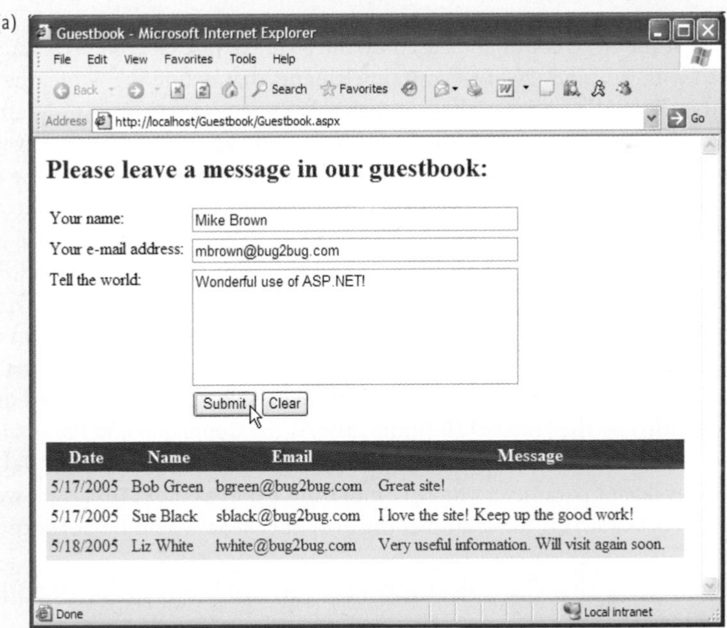

Fig. 25.37 | ASPX file for the guestbook application. (Part 3 of 4.)

(b)

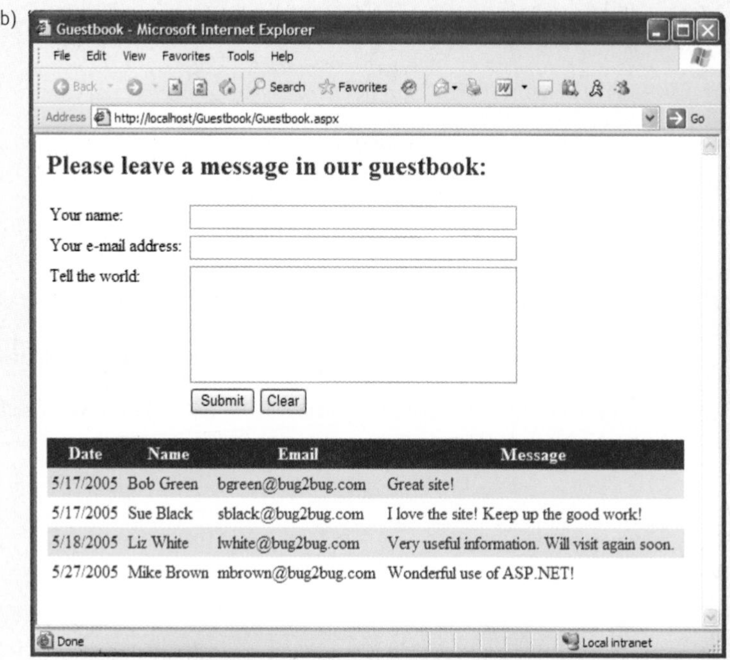

Fig. 25.37 | ASPX file for the guestbook application. (Part 4 of 4.)

Notice that the SQL commands used by the `SqlDataSource` contain several parameters (prefixed with `@`). Lines 96–114 contain elements that define the name, the type and, for some parameters, the source of the parameter. Parameters that are set programmatically are defined by **`Parameter`** elements containing `Name` and `Type` properties. For example, line 107 defines the `Date` parameter of `Type String`. This corresponds to the `@Date` parameter in the `InsertCommand` (line 91). Parameters that obtain their values from controls are defined by **`ControlParameter`** elements. Lines 108–113 contain markup that sets up the relationships between the `INSERT` parameters and the Web Form's `TextBoxes`. We established these relationships in the **Command and Parameter Editor** (Fig. 25.36). Each `ControlParameter` contains a `ControlID` property indicating the control from which the parameter gets its value. The `PropertyName` specifies the property that contains the actual value to be used as the parameter value. The IDE sets the `PropertyName` based on the type of control specified by the `ControlID` (indirectly via the **Command and Parameter Editor**). In this case, we use only `TextBoxes`, so the `PropertyName` of each `ControlParameter` is `Text` (e.g., the value of parameter `@Name` comes from `nameTextBox.Text`). However, if we were using a `DropDownList`, for example, the `PropertyName` would be `SelectedValue`.

25.5.2 Modifying the Code-Behind File for the Guestbook Application

After building the Web Form and configuring the data controls used in this example, double click the **Submit** and **Clear** buttons in **Design** view to create their corresponding `Click` event handlers in the `Guestbook.aspx.vb` code-behind file (Fig. 25.38). The IDE generates empty event handlers, so we must add the appropriate code to make these but-

```
1  ' Fig. 25.38: Guestbook.aspx.vb
2  ' Code-behind file that defines event handlers for the guestbook.
3  Partial Class Guestbook
4     Inherits System.Web.UI.Page
5  
6     ' Submit Button adds a new guestbook entry to the database,
7     ' clears the form and displays the updated list of guestbook entries
8     Protected Sub submitButton_Click(ByVal sender As Object, _
9        ByVal e As System.EventArgs) Handles submitButton.Click
10       ' create a date parameter to store the current date
11       Dim currentDate As New System.Web.UI.WebControls.Parameter( _
12          "Date", TypeCode.String, DateTime.Now.ToShortDateString())
13 
14       ' set the @Date parameter to the date parameter
15       messagesSqlDataSource.InsertParameters.RemoveAt(0)
16       messagesSqlDataSource.InsertParameters.Add(currentDate)
17 
18       ' execute an INSERT SQL statement to add a new row to the
19       ' Messages table in the Guestbook database that contains the
20       ' current date and the user's name, e-mail address and message
21       messagesSqlDataSource.Insert()
22 
23       ' clear the TextBoxes
24       nameTextBox.Text = ""
25       emailTextBox.Text = ""
26       messageTextBox.Text = ""
27 
28       ' update the GridView with the new database table contents
29       messagesGridView.DataBind()
30    End Sub ' submitButton_Click
31 
32    ' Clear Button clears the Web Form's TextBoxes
33    Protected Sub clearButton_Click(ByVal sender As Object, _
34       ByVal e As System.EventArgs) Handles clearButton.Click
35       nameTextBox.Text = ""
36       emailTextBox.Text = ""
37       messageTextBox.Text = ""
38    End Sub ' clearButton_Click
39 End Class ' Guestbook
```

Fig. 25.38 | Code-behind file for the guestbook application.

tons work properly. The event handler for `clearButton` (lines 33–38) clears each `TextBox` by setting its `Text` property to an empty string. This resets the form for a new guestbook submission.

Lines 8–30 contain the event-handling code for `submitButton`, which adds the user's information to the `Messages` table of the `Guestbook` database. Recall that we configured `messagesSqlDataSource`'s `INSERT` command to use the values of the `TextBoxes` on the Web Form as the parameter values inserted into the database. We have not yet specified the date value to be inserted, though. Lines 11–12 assign a `String` representation of the current date (e.g., `"3/27/06"`) to a `new` object of type `Parameter`. This `Parameter` object is identified as `"Date"` and is given the current date as a default value. The `SqlData-`

Source's InsertParameters collection contains an item named Date (at position 0), which we Remove in line 15 and replace in line 16 by Adding our currentDate parameter. Invoking SqlDataSource method Insert in line 21 executes the INSERT command against the database, thus adding a row to the Messages table. After the data is inserted into the database, lines 24–26 clear the TextBoxes, and line 29 invokes messagesGridView's DataBind method to refresh the data that the GridView displays. This causes messagesSqlDataSource (the data source of the GridView) to execute its SELECT command to obtain the Messages table's newly updated data.

25.6 Case Study: Secure Books Database Application

This case study presents a web application in which a user logs into a secure website to view a list of publications by an author of the user's choosing. The application consists of several ASPX files. Section 25.6.1 presents the application and explains the purpose of each of its web pages. Section 25.6.2 provides step-by-step instructions to guide you through building the application and presents the markup in the ASPX files.

25.6.1 Examining the Completed Secure Books Database Application

This example uses a technique known as forms authentication to protect a page so that only users known to the website can access it. Such users are known as the site's members. Authentication is a crucial tool for sites that allow only members to enter the site or a portion of the site. In this application, website visitors must log in before they are allowed to view the publications in the Books database. The first page that a user would typically request is Login.aspx (Fig. 25.39). You will soon learn to create this page using a Login control, one of several ASP.NET login controls that help create secure applications using authentication. These controls are found in the **Login** section of the **Toolbox**.

The Login.aspx page allows a site visitor to enter an existing user name and password to log into the website. A first-time visitor must click the link below the **Log In** button to create a new user before logging in. Doing so redirects the visitor to CreateNewUser.aspx

Fig. 25.39 | Login.aspx page of the secure books database application.

(Fig. 25.40), which contains a `CreateUserWizard` control that presents the visitor with a user registration form. We discuss the `CreateUserWizard` control in detail in Section 25.6.2. In Fig. 25.40, we use the password `pa$$word` for testing purposes—as you will learn, the `CreateUserWizard` requires that the password contain special characters for security purposes. Clicking **Create User** establishes a new user account. After creating the account, the user is automatically logged in and shown a success message (Fig. 25.41).

Fig. 25.40 | `CreateNewUser.aspx` page of the secure books database application.

Fig. 25.41 | Message displayed to indicate that a user account was created successfully.

Clicking the **Continue** button on the confirmation page sends the user to `Books.aspx` (Fig. 25.42), which provides a drop-down list of authors and a table containing the ISBNs, titles, edition numbers and copyright years of books in the database. By default, all the books by Harvey Deitel are displayed. Links appear at the bottom of the table that allow you to access additional pages of data. When the user chooses an author, a postback occurs, and the page is updated to display information about books written by the selected author (Fig. 25.43).

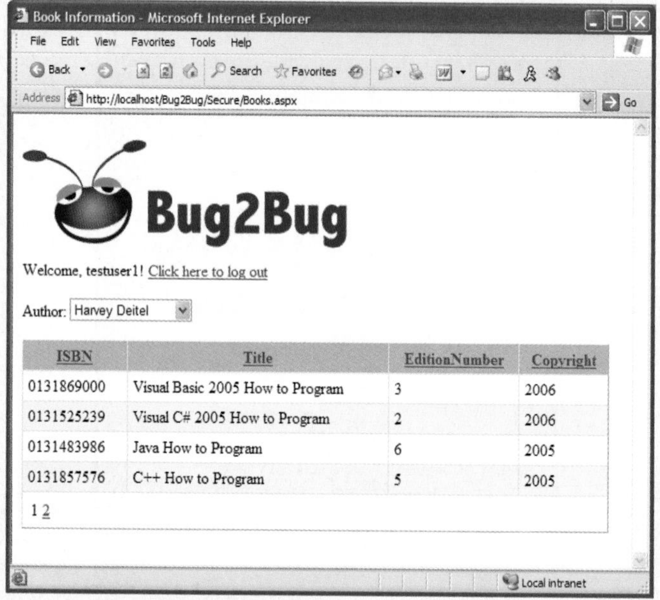

Fig. 25.42 | `Books.aspx` displaying books by Harvey Deitel (by default).

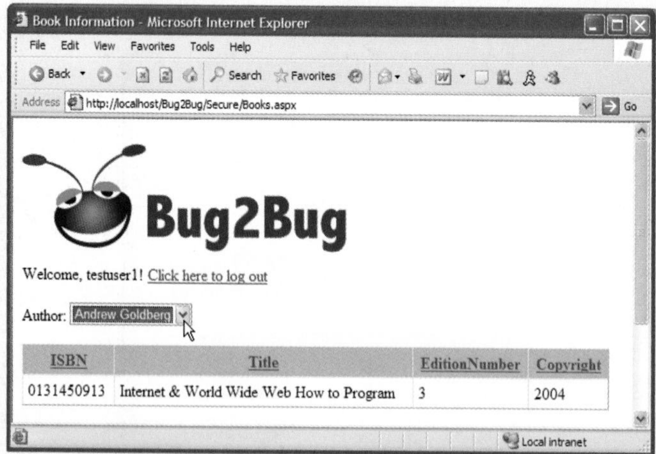

Fig. 25.43 | `Books.aspx` displaying books by Andrew Goldberg.

Note that once the user creates an account and is logged in, `Books.aspx` displays a welcome message customized for the particular logged-in user. As you will soon see, a `LoginName` control provides this functionality. After you add this control to the page, ASP.NET handles the details of determining the user name.

Clicking the **Click here to log out** link logs the user out, then sends the user back to `Login.aspx` (Fig. 25.44). This link is created by a `LoginStatus` control, which handles the log out details. After logging out, the user would need to log in through `Login.aspx` to view the book listing again. The `Login` control on this page receives the user name and password entered by a visitor. ASP.NET compares these values with user names and passwords stored in a database on the server. If there is a match, the visitor is **authenticated** (i.e., the user's identity is confirmed). We explain the authentication process in detail in Section 25.6.2. When an existing user is successfully authenticated, `Login.aspx` redirects the user to `Books.aspx` (Fig. 25.42). If the user's login attempt fails, an appropriate error message is displayed (Fig. 25.45).

Fig. 25.44 | Logging in using the `Login` control.

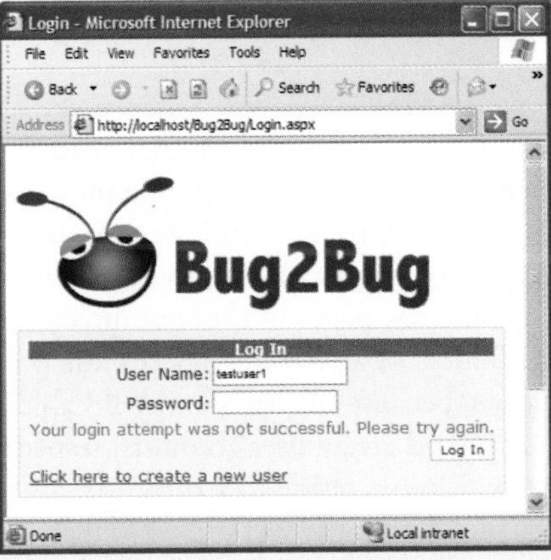

Fig. 25.45 | Error message displayed for an unsuccessful login attempt.

Notice that `Login.aspx`, `CreateNewUser.aspx` and `Books.aspx` share the same page header containing the logo image from the fictional company Bug2Bug. Instead of placing this image at the top of each page, we use a master page to achieve this. As we demonstrate shortly, a master page defines common GUI elements that are inherited by each page in a set of content pages. Just as Visual Basic classes can inherit instance variables and methods from existing classes, content pages inherit elements from master pages—this is known as visual inheritance.

25.6.2 Creating the Secure Books Database Application

Now that you are familiar with how this application behaves, you'll learn how to create it from scratch. Thanks to the rich set of login and data controls provided by ASP.NET, you will not have to write *any* code to create this application. In fact, the application does not contain any code-behind files. All of the functionality is specified through properties of controls, many of which are set through wizards and other visual programming tools. ASP.NET hides the details of authenticating users against a database of user names and passwords, displaying appropriate success or error messages and redirecting the user to the correct page based on the authentication results. We now discuss the steps you must perform to create the secure books database application.

Step 1: Creating the Website

Create a new **ASP.NET Web Site** at `http://localhost/Bug2Bug` as described previously. We will explicitly create each of the ASPX files that we need in this application, so delete the IDE-generated `Default.aspx` file (and its corresponding code-behind file) by selecting `Default.aspx` in the **Solution Explorer** and pressing the *Delete* key. Click **OK** in the confirmation dialog to delete these files.

Step 2: Setting Up the Website's Folders

Before building the pages in the website, we create folders to organize its contents. First, create an `Images` folder by right clicking the location of the website in the **Solution Explorer** and selecting **New Folder**, then add the `bug2bug.png` file to it. This image can be found in the examples directory for this chapter. Next, add the `Books.mdf` database file (located in the `exampleDatabases` subdirectory of the chapter's examples directory) to the project's `App_Data` folder. We show how to retrieve data from this database later in the section.

Step 3: Configuring the Application's Security Settings

In this application, we want to ensure that only authenticated users are allowed to access `Books.aspx` (created in *Step 9* and *Step 10*) to view the information in the database. Previously, we created all of our ASPX pages in the web application's root directory (e.g., `http://localhost/`*ProjectName*). By default, any website visitor (regardless of whether the visitor is authenticated) can view pages in the root directory. ASP.NET allows you to restrict access to particular folders of a website. We do not want to restrict access to the root of the website, however, because all users must be able to view `Login.aspx` and `CreateNewUser.aspx` to log in and create user accounts, respectively. Thus, if we want to restrict access to `Books.aspx`, it must reside in a directory other than the root directory. Create a folder named `Secure`. Later in the section, we will create `Books.aspx` in this folder. First, let's enable forms authentication in our application and configure the `Secure` folder to restrict access to authenticated users only.

Select **Website > ASP.NET Configuration** to open the **Web Site Administration Tool** in a web browser (Fig. 25.46). This tool allows you to configure various options that determine how your application behaves. Click either the **Security** link or the **Security** tab to open a web page in which you can set security options (Fig. 25.47), such as the type of authentication the application should use. In the **Users** column, click **Select authentication type.** On the resulting page (Fig. 25.48), select the radio button next to **From the internet** to indicate that users will log in via a form on the website in which the user can enter a username and password (i.e., the application will use forms authentication). The default setting—**From a local network**—relies on users' Windows user names and passwords for authentication purposes. Click the **Done** button to save this change.

Now that forms authentication is enabled, the **Users** column on the main page of the **Web Site Administration Tool** (Fig. 25.49) provides links to create and manage users. As you saw in Section 25.6.1, our application provides the `CreateNewUser.aspx` page in which users can create their own accounts. Thus, while it is possible to create users through the **Web Site Administration Tool**, we do not do so here.

Even though no users exist at the moment, we configure the `Secure` folder to grant access only to authenticated users (i.e., deny access to all unauthenticated users). Click the **Create access rules** link in the **Access Rules** column of the **Web Site Administration Tool** (Fig. 25.49) to view the **Add New Access Rule** page (Fig. 25.50). This page is used to create an access rule—a rule that grants or denies access to a particular web application directory for a specific user or group of users. Click the `Secure` directory in the left column of the page to identify the directory to which our access rule applies. In the middle column, select the radio button marked **Anonymous users** to specify that the rule applies to users who

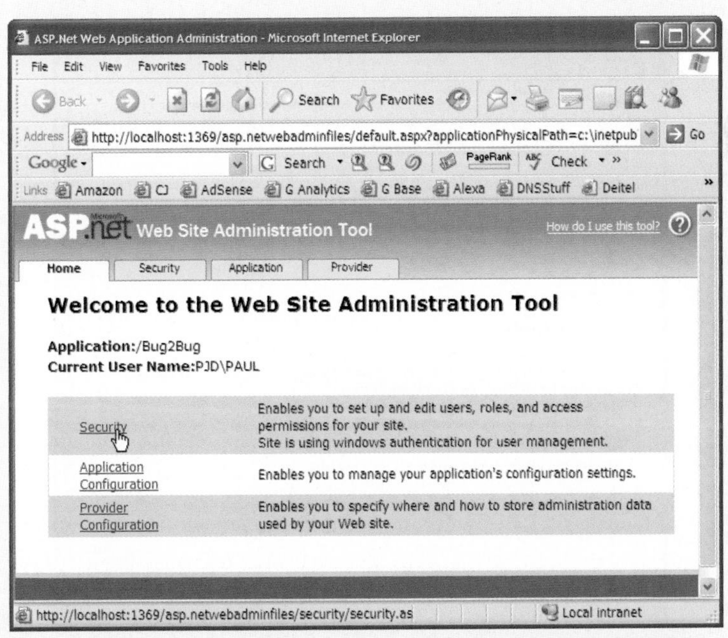

Fig. 25.46 | **Web Site Administration Tool** for configuring a web application.

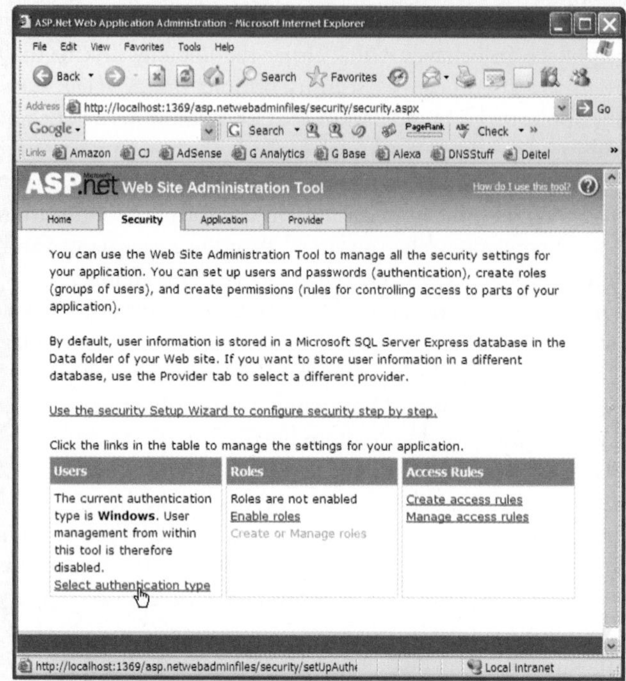

Fig. 25.47 | **Security** page of the **Web Site Administration Tool**.

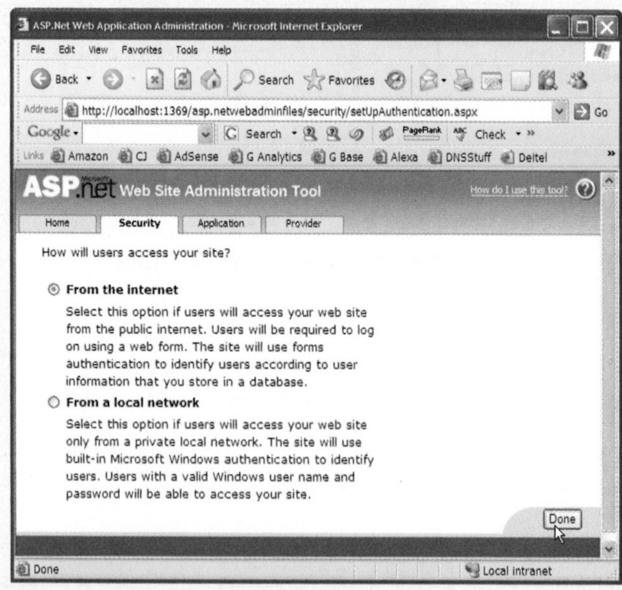

Fig. 25.48 | Choosing the type of authentication used by an ASP.NET web application.

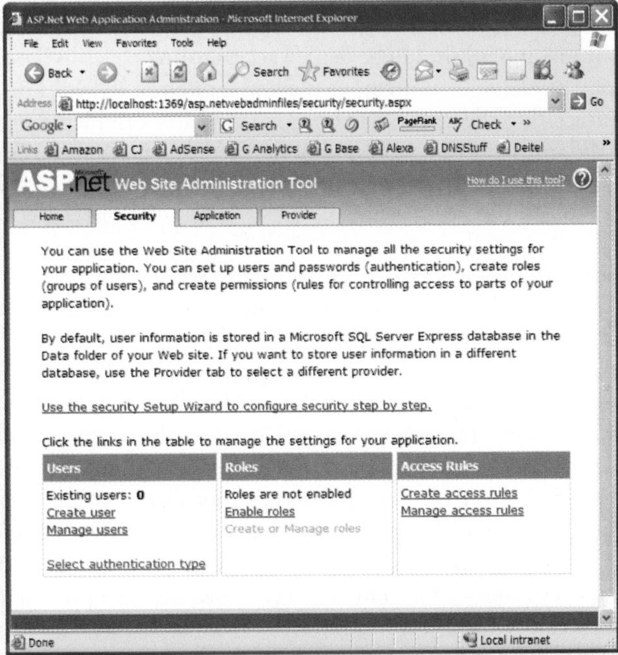

Fig. 25.49 | Main page of the **Web Site Administration Tool** after enabling forms authentication.

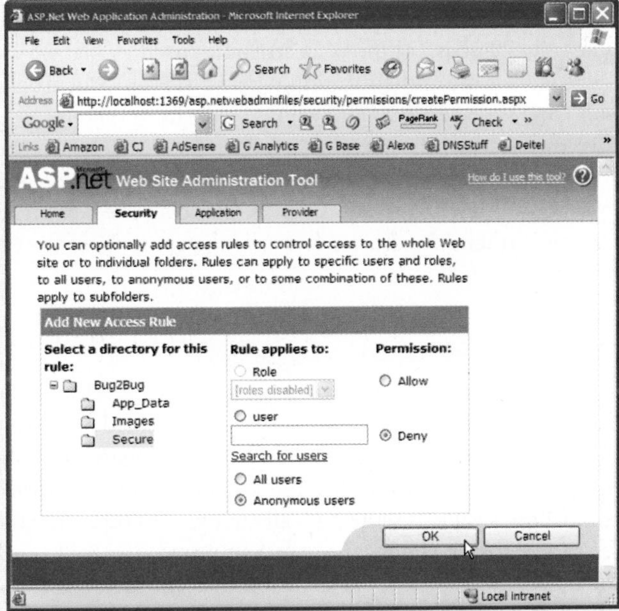

Fig. 25.50 | **Add New Access Rule** page used to configure directory access.

have not been authenticated. Finally, select **Deny** in the right column, labeled **Permission**, then click **OK**. This rule indicates that anonymous users (i.e., users who have not identified themselves by logging in) should be denied access to any pages in the `Secure` directory (e.g., `Books.aspx`). By default, anonymous users who attempt to load a page in the `Secure` directory are redirected to the `Login.aspx` page so that they can identify themselves. Note that because we did not set up any access rules for the `Bug2Bug` root directory, anonymous users may still access pages there (e.g., `Login.aspx`, `CreateNewUser.aspx`). We create these pages momentarily.

Step 4: Examining the Autogenerated `Web.config` Files

We have now configured the application to use forms authentication and created an access rule to ensure that only authenticated users can access the `Secure` folder. Before creating the website's content, we examine how the changes made through the **Web Site Administration Tool** appear in the IDE. Recall that `Web.config` is an XML file used for application configuration, such as enabling debugging or storing database connection strings. Visual Web Developer generates two `Web.config` files in response to our actions using the **Web Site Administration Tool**—one in the application's root directory and one in the `Secure` folder. [*Note:* You may need to click the **Refresh** button in the **Solution Explorer** to see these files.] In an ASP.NET application, a page's configuration settings are determined by the current directory's `Web.config` file. The settings in this file take precedence over the settings in the root directory's `Web.config` file.

After setting the authentication type for the web application, the IDE generates a `Web.config` file at `http://localhost/Bug2Bug/Web.config`, which contains an `authentication` element

```
<authentication mode="Forms" />
```

This element appears in the root directory's `Web.config` file, so the setting applies to the entire website. The value `"Forms"` of the `mode` attribute specifies that we want to use forms authentication. Had we left the authentication type set to **From a local network** in the **Web Site Administration Tool**, the `mode` attribute would be set to `"Windows"`.

After creating the access rule for the `Secure` folder, the IDE generates a second `Web.config` file in that folder. This file contains an `authorization` element that indicates who is, and who is not, authorized to access this folder over the web. In this application, we want to allow only authenticated users to access the contents of the `Secure` folder, so the authorization element appears as

```
<authorization>
   <deny users="?" />
</authorization>
```

Rather than grant permission to each individual authenticated user, we deny access to those who are not authenticated (i.e., those who have not logged in). The `deny` element inside the `authorization` element specifies the users to whom we wish to deny access. When the `users` attribute's value is set to `"?"`, all anonymous (i.e., unauthenticated) users are denied access to the folder. Thus, an unauthenticated user will not be able to load `http://localhost/Bug2Bug/Secure/Books.aspx`. Instead, such a user will be redirected to the `Login.aspx` page—when a user is denied access to a part of a site, ASP.NET by default sends the user to a page named `Login.aspx` in the application's root directory.

Step 5: Creating a Master Page

Now that you have established the application's security settings, you can create the application's web pages. We begin with the master page, which defines the elements we want to appear on each page. A master page is like a base class in a visual inheritance hierarchy, and content pages are like derived classes. The master page contains placeholders for custom content created in each content page. The content pages visually inherit the master page's content, then add content in place of the master page's placeholders.

For example, you might want to include a **navigation bar** (i.e., a series of buttons for navigating a website) on every page of a site. If the site encompasses a large number of pages, adding markup to create the navigation bar for each page can be time consuming. Moreover, if you subsequently modify the navigation bar, every page on the site that uses it must be updated. By creating a master page, you can specify the navigation bar markup in one file and have it appear on all the content pages, with only a few lines of markup. If the navigation bar changes, only the master page changes—any content pages that use it are updated the next time the page is requested.

In this example, we want the Bug2Bug logo to appear as a header at the top of every page, so we will place an `Image` control in the master page. Each subsequent page we create will be a content page based on this master page and thus will include the header. To create a master page, right click the location of the website in the **Solution Explorer** and select **Add New Item....** In the **Add New Item** dialog, select **Master Page** from the template list and specify `Bug2Bug.master` as the filename. Master pages have the filename extension `.master` and, like Web Forms, can optionally use a code-behind file to define additional functionality. In this example, we do not need to specify any code for the master page, so leave the box labeled **Place code in a separate file** unchecked. Click **Add** to create the page.

The IDE opens the master page in **Source** mode (Fig. 25.51) when the file is first created. [*Note:* We added a line break in the `DOCTYPE` element for presentation purposes.] The

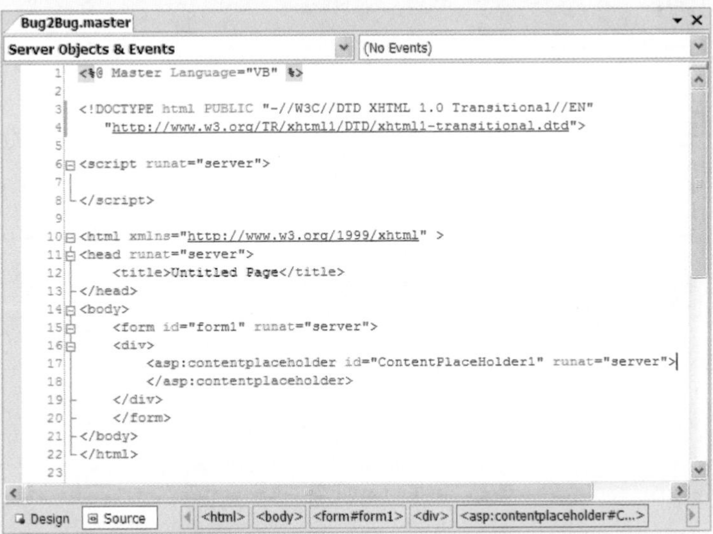

Fig. 25.51 | Master page in **Source** mode.

markup for a master page is almost identical to that of a Web Form. One difference is that a master page contains a `Master` directive (line 1 in Fig. 25.51), which specifies that this file defines a master page using the indicated `Language` for any code. Because we chose not to use a code-behind file, the master page also contains a `script` element (lines 6–8). Code that would usually be placed in a code-behind file can be placed in a `script` element. However, we remove the `script` element from this page, because we do not need to write any additional code. After deleting this block of markup, set the `title` of the page to `Bug2Bug`. Finally, notice that the master page contains a `ContentPlaceHolder` control (lines 17–18 of Fig. 25.51). This control serves as a placeholder for content that will be defined by a content page. You will see how to define content to replace the `ContentPlaceHolder` shortly.

At this point, you can edit the master page in **Design** mode (Fig. 25.52) as if it were an ASPX file. Notice that the `ContentPlaceHolder` control appears as a large rectangle with a gray bar indicating the control's type and `ID`. Using the **Properties** window, change the `ID` of this control to `bodyContent`.

To create a header in the master page that will appear at the top of each content page, we insert a table into the master page. Place the cursor to the left of the `ContentPlaceHolder` and select **Layout > Insert Table**. In the **Insert Table** dialog, click the **Template** radio button, then select **Header** from the drop-down list of available table templates. Click **OK** to create a table that fills the page and contains two rows. Drag and drop the `ContentPlaceHolder` into the bottom table cell. Change the `valign` property of this cell to `top`, so the `ContentPlaceHolder` vertically aligns with the top of the cell. Next, set the `Height` of the top table cell to `130`. Add to this cell an `Image` control named `headerImage` with its `ImageUrl` property set to the `bug2bug.png` file in the project's `Images` folder. Figure 25.53 shows the markup and **Design** view of the completed master page. As you will see in *Step*

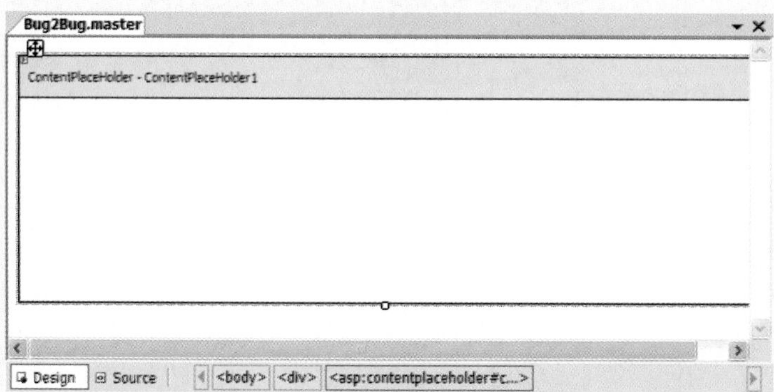

Fig. 25.52 | Master page in **Design** mode.

```
<%-- Fig. 25.53: Bug2bug.master --%>
<%-- Master page that defines common features of all pages in the --%>
<%-- secure book database application. --%>
```

Fig. 25.53 | `Bug2Bug.master` page that defines a logo image header for all pages in the secure book database application. (Part 1 of 2.)

```
<%@ Master Language="VB" %>

<!DOCTYPE html PUBLIC "-//W3C//DTD XHTML 1.0 Transitional//EN"
   "http://www.w3.org/TR/xhtml1/DTD/xhtml1-transitional.dtd">

<html xmlns="http://www.w3.org/1999/xhtml" >
<head runat="server">
    <title>Bug2Bug</title>
</head>
<body>
    <form id="form1" runat="server">
    <div>
       <table border="0" cellpadding="0" cellspacing="0"
          style="width: 100%; height: 100%">
          <tr>
             <td height="130" style="width: 887px">
                <asp:Image ID="headerImage" runat="server"
                   ImageUrl="~/Images/bug2bug.png" />
             </td>
          </tr>
          <tr>
             <td style="width: 887px" valign="top">
                <asp:contentplaceholder id="bodyContent" runat="server">
                </asp:contentplaceholder>
             </td>
          </tr>
       </table>
        
    </div>
    </form>
</body>
</html>
```

Fig. 25.53 | `Bug2Bug.master` page that defines a logo image header for all pages in the secure book database application. (Part 2 of 2.)

6, a content page based on this master page displays the logo image defined here, as well as the content designed for that specific page (in place of the `ContentPlaceHolder`).

Step 6: Creating a Content Page

We now create a content page based on `Bug2Bug.master`. We begin by building `CreateNewUser.aspx`. To create this file, right click the master page in the **Solution Explorer** and select **Add Content Page**. This action causes a `Default.aspx` file, configured to use the master page, to be added to the project. Rename this file `CreateNewUser.aspx`, then open it in **Source** mode (Fig. 25.54). Note that this file contains a `Page` directive with a `Language` property, a `MasterPageFile` property and a `Title` property. The `Page` directive indicates the **`MasterPageFile`** that is used as a starting point for this new page's design. In this case, the `MasterPageFile` property is set to `"~/Bug2Bug.master"` to indicate that the current file is based on the master page we just created. The **`Title`** property specifies the title that will be displayed in the web browser's title bar when the content page is loaded. This value, which we set to `Create a New User`, replaces the value (i.e., `Bug2Bug`) set in the `title` element of the master page.

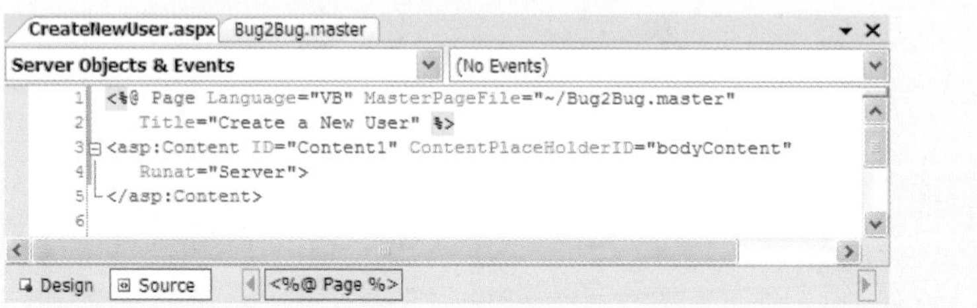

Fig. 25.54 | Content page `CreateNewUser.aspx` in **Source** mode.

Because `CreateNewUser.aspx`'s `Page` directive specifies `Bug2Bug.master` as the page's `MasterPageFile`, the content page implicitly contains the contents of the master page, such as the `DOCTYPE`, `html` and `body` elements. The content page file does not duplicate the XHTML elements found in the master page. Instead, the content page contains a **`Content`** control (lines 3–5 in Fig. 25.54), in which we will place page-specific content that will replace the master page's `ContentPlaceHolder` when the content page is requested. The `ContentPlaceHolderID` property of the `Content` control identifies the `ContentPlaceHolder` in the master page that the control should replace—in this case, `bodyContent`.

The relationship between a content page and its master page is more evident in **Design** mode (Fig. 25.55). The gray shaded region contains the contents of the master page `Bug2Bug.master` as they will appear in `CreateNewUser.aspx` when rendered in a web browser. The only editable part of this page is the `Content` control, which appears in place of the master page's `ContentPlaceHolder`.

Step 7: Adding a **`CreateUserWizard`** *Control to a Content Page*

Recall from Section 25.6.1 that `CreateNewUser.aspx` is the page in our website that allows first-time visitors to create user accounts. To provide this functionality, we use a **`CreateUserWizard`** control. Place the cursor inside the `Content` control in **Design** mode and double click `CreateUserWizard` in the **Login** section of the **Toolbox** to add it to the

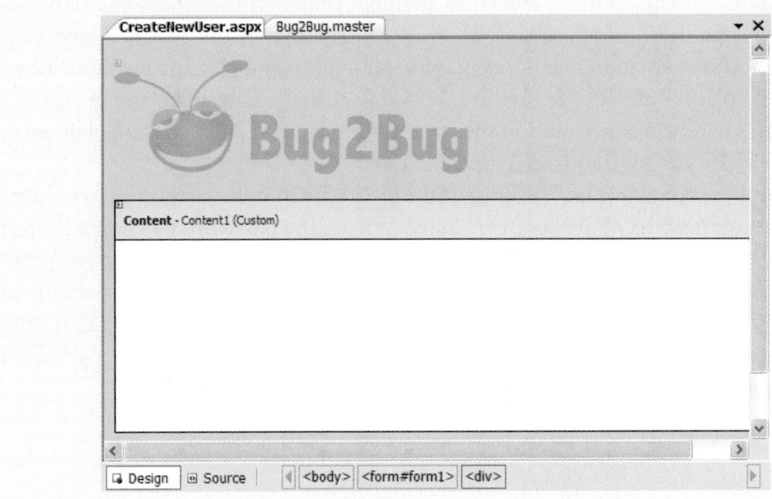

Fig. 25.55 | Content page `CreateNewUser.aspx` in **Design** mode.

page at the current cursor position. You can also drag-and-drop the control onto the page. To change the `CreateUserWizard`'s appearance, open the **CreateUserWizard Tasks** smart tag menu, and click **Auto Format**. Select the **Professional** color scheme.

As discussed previously, a `CreateUserWizard` provides a registration form that site visitors can use to create a user account. ASP.NET creates a SQL Server database (named `ASPNETDB.MDF` and located in the `App_Data` folder) to store the user names, passwords and other account information of the application's users. ASP.NET also enforces a default set of requirements for filling out the form. Each field on the form is required, the password must contain at least seven characters (including at least one nonalphanumeric character) and the two passwords entered must match. The form also asks for a security question and answer that can be used to identify a user in case the user needs to reset or recover the account's password.

After the user fills in the form's fields and clicks the **Create User** button to submit the account information, ASP.NET verifies that all the form's requirements were fulfilled and attempts to create the user account. If an error occurs (e.g., the user name already exists), the `CreateUserWizard` displays a message below the form. If the account is created successfully, the form is replaced by a confirmation message and a button that allows the user to continue. You can view this confirmation message in **Design** mode by selecting **Complete** from the **Step** drop-down list in the **CreateUserWizard Tasks** smart tag menu.

When a user account is created, ASP.NET automatically logs the user into the site (we say more about the login process shortly). At this point, the user is authenticated and allowed to access the `Secure` folder. After we create `Books.aspx` later in this section, we set the `CreateUserWizard`'s `ContinueDestinationPageUrl` property to `~/Secure/Books.aspx` to indicate that the user should be redirected to `Books.aspx` after clicking the **Continue** button on the confirmation page.

Figure 25.56 presents the completed `CreateNewUser.aspx` file (reformatted for readability). Inside the `Content` control, the `CreateUserWizard` control is defined by the markup in lines 7–36. The start tag (lines 7–10) contains several properties that specify formatting styles for the control, as well as the `ContinueDestinationPageUrl` property, which you will set later in the chapter. Lines 11–16 specify the wizard's two steps—`CreateUserWizardStep` and `CompleteWizardStep`—in a `WizardSteps` element. `CreateUserWizardStep` and `CompleteWizardStep` are classes that encapsulate the details of creating a user and issuing a confirmation message. Finally, lines 17–35 contain elements that define additional styles used to format specific parts of the control.

The sample outputs in Fig. 25.56(a) and Fig. 25.56(b) demonstrate successfully creating a user account with `CreateNewUser.aspx`. We use the password `pa$$word` for testing purposes. This password satisfies the minimum length and special character requirement imposed by ASP.NET, but in a real application, you should use a password that is more difficult for someone to guess. Figure 25.56(c) illustrates the error message that appears when you attempt to create a second user account with the same user name—ASP.NET requires that each user name be unique.

```
1  <%-- Fig. 25.56: CreateNewUser.aspx --%>
2  <%-- Content page using a CreateUserWizard control to register users. --%>
3  <%@ Page Language="VB" MasterPageFile="~/Bug2Bug.master"
4     Title="Create a New User" %>
5  <asp:Content ID="Content1" ContentPlaceHolderID="bodyContent"
6     Runat="Server">
7     <asp:CreateUserWizard ID="CreateUserWizard1" runat="server"
8        BackColor="#F7F6F3" BorderColor="#E6E2D8" BorderStyle="Solid"
9        BorderWidth="1px" Font-Names="Verdana" Font-Size="0.8em"
10       ContinueDestinationPageUrl="~/Secure/Books.aspx">
11       <WizardSteps>
12          <asp:CreateUserWizardStep runat="server">
13          </asp:CreateUserWizardStep>
14          <asp:CompleteWizardStep runat="server">
15          </asp:CompleteWizardStep>
16       </WizardSteps>
17       <SideBarStyle BackColor="#5D7B9D" BorderWidth="0px"
18          Font-Size="0.9em" VerticalAlign="Top" />
19       <TitleTextStyle BackColor="#5D7B9D" Font-Bold="True"
20          ForeColor="White" />
21       <SideBarButtonStyle BorderWidth="0px" Font-Names="Verdana"
22          ForeColor="White" />
23       <NavigationButtonStyle BackColor="#FFFBFF" BorderColor="#CCCCCC"
24          BorderStyle="Solid" BorderWidth="1px" Font-Names="Verdana"
25          ForeColor="#284775" />
26       <HeaderStyle BackColor="#5D7B9D" BorderStyle="Solid"
27          Font-Bold="True" Font-Size="0.9em"
28          ForeColor="White" HorizontalAlign="Center" />
29       <CreateUserButtonStyle BackColor="#FFFBFF" BorderColor="#CCCCCC"
30         BorderStyle="Solid" BorderWidth="1px" Font-Names="Verdana"
31         ForeColor="#284775" />
32       <ContinueButtonStyle BackColor="#FFFBFF" BorderColor="#CCCCCC"
33          BorderStyle="Solid" BorderWidth="1px" Font-Names="Verdana"
34          ForeColor="#284775" />
```

Fig. 25.56 | `CreateNewUser.aspx` content page that provides a user registration form. (Part 1 of 2.)

```
            <StepStyle BorderWidth="0px" />
        </asp:CreateUserWizard>
</asp:Content>
```

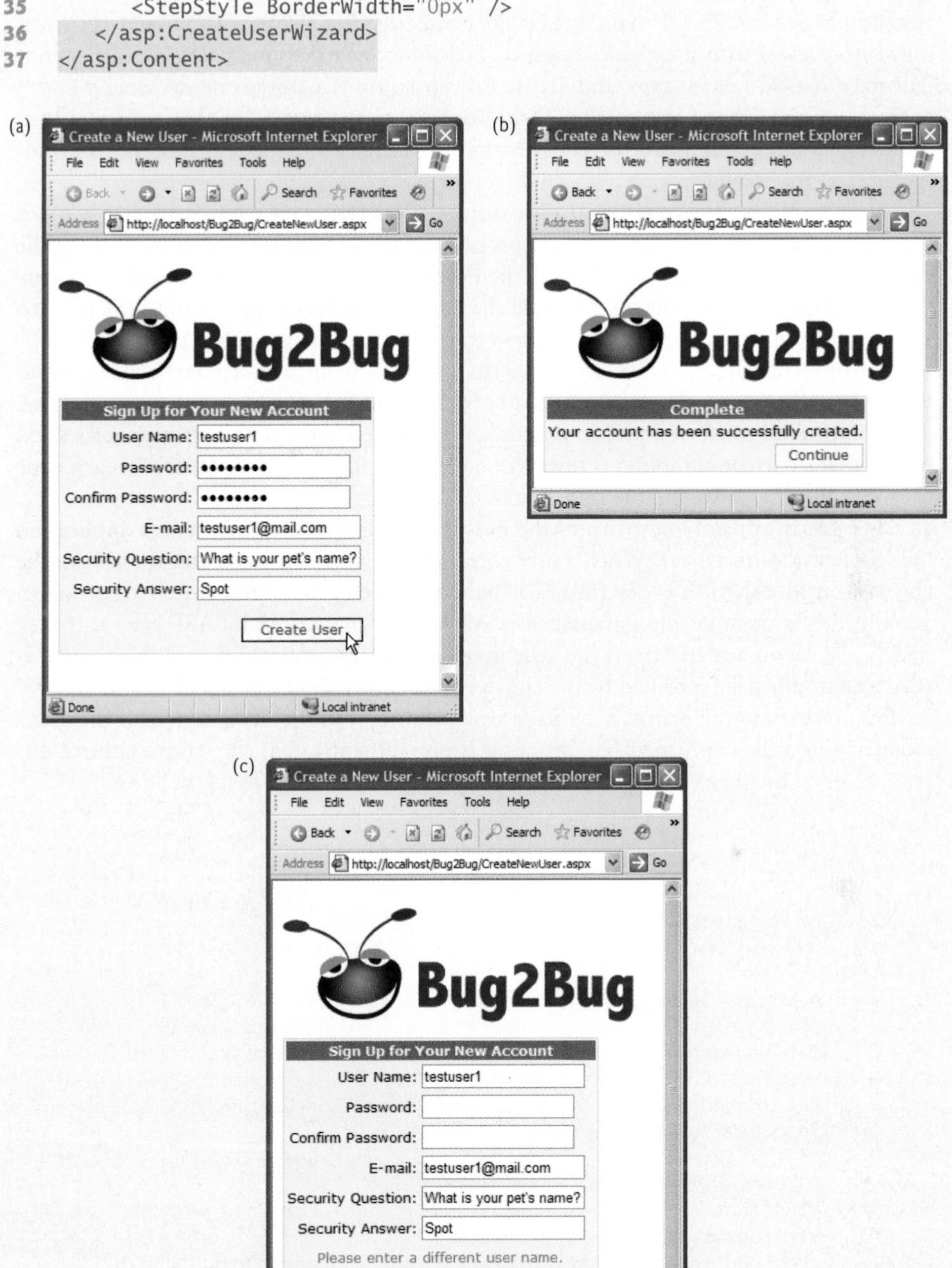

Fig. 25.56 | `CreateNewUser.aspx` content page that provides a user registration form. (Part 2 of 2.)

Step 8: Creating a Login Page

Recall from Section 25.6.1 that `Login.aspx` is the page in our website that allows returning visitors to log into their user accounts. To create this functionality, add another content page named `Login.aspx` and set its title to `Login`. In **Design** mode, drag a `Login` control (located in the **Login** section of the **Toolbox**) to the page's `Content` control. Open the **Auto Format** dialog from the **Login Tasks** smart tag menu and set the control's color scheme to **Professional**.

Next, configure the `Login` control to display a link to the page for creating new users. Set the `Login` control's `CreateUserUrl` property to `CreateNewUser.aspx` by clicking the ellipsis button to the property's right in the **Properties** window and selecting the `CreateNewUser.aspx` file in the dialog. Then set the `CreateUserText` property to `Click here to create a new user`. These property values cause a link to appear in the `Login` control.

Finally, change the value of the `Login` control's `DisplayRememberMe` property to `False`. By default, the control displays a checkbox and the text `Remember me next time`. This can be used to allow a user to remain authenticated beyond a single browser session on the user's current computer. However, we want to require that users log in each time they visit the site, so we disable this option.

The `Login` control encapsulates the details of logging a user into a web application (i.e., authenticating a user). When a user enters a user name and password, then clicks the **Log In** button, ASP.NET determines whether the items provided match those of an account in the membership database (i.e., `ASPNETDB.MDF` created by ASP.NET). If they match, the user is authenticated (i.e., the user's identity is confirmed), and the browser is redirected to the page specified by the `Login` control's `DestinationPageUrl` property. We set this property to the `Books.aspx` page after creating it in the next section. If the user's identity cannot be confirmed (i.e., the user is not authenticated), the `Login` control displays an error message (see Fig. 25.57), and the user can attempt to log in again.

```
<%-- Fig. 25.57: Login.aspx --%>
<%-- Content page using a Login control that authenticates users. --%>
<%@ Page Language="VB" MasterPageFile="~/Bug2Bug.master" Title="Login" %>
<asp:Content ID="Content1" ContentPlaceHolderID="bodyContent"
   Runat="Server">
   <asp:Login ID="Login1" runat="server" BackColor="#F7F6F3"
      BorderColor="#E6E2D8" BorderPadding="4" BorderStyle="Solid"
      BorderWidth="1px" CreateUserText="Click here to create a new user"
      CreateUserUrl="~/CreateNewUser.aspx" DisplayRememberMe="False"
      Font-Names="Verdana" Font-Size="0.8em" ForeColor="#333333"
      DestinationPageUrl="~/Secure/Books.aspx">
      <TitleTextStyle BackColor="#5D7B9D" Font-Bold="True"
         Font-Size="0.9em" ForeColor="White" />
      <InstructionTextStyle Font-Italic="True" ForeColor="Black" />
      <TextBoxStyle Font-Size="0.8em" />
      <LoginButtonStyle BackColor="#FFFBFF" BorderColor="#CCCCCC"
         BorderStyle="Solid" BorderWidth="1px" Font-Names="Verdana"
         Font-Size="0.8em" ForeColor="#284775" />
   </asp:Login>
</asp:Content>
```

Fig. 25.57 | `Login.aspx` content page using a `Login` control. (Part 1 of 2.)

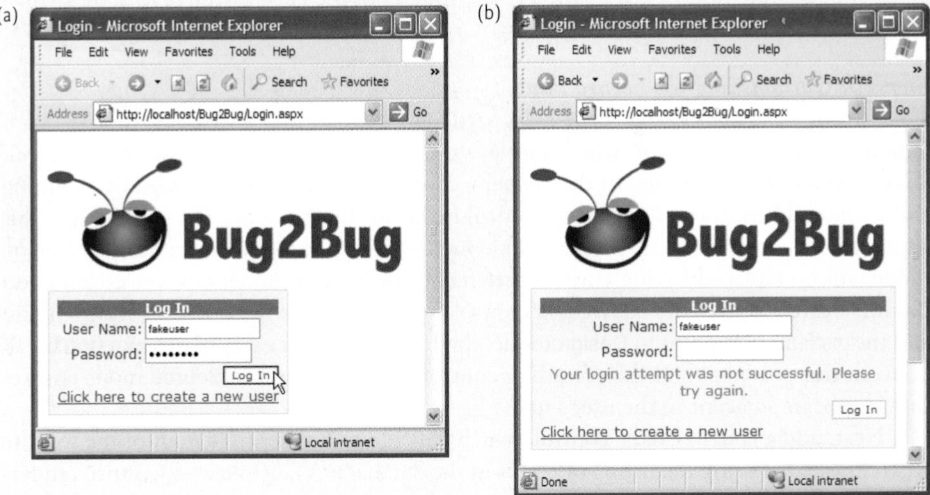

Fig. 25.57 | `Login.aspx` content page using a `Login` control. (Part 2 of 2.)

Figure 25.57 presents the completed `Login.aspx` file. Note that, as in `CreateNewUser.aspx`, the `Page` directive indicates that this content page inherits content from `Bug2Bug.master`. In the `Content` control that replaces the master page's `ContentPlaceHolder` with `ID bodyContent`, lines 6–19 create a `Login` control. Note the `CreateUserText` and `CreateUserUrl` properties (lines 8–9) that we set using the **Properties** window. Line 11 in the start tag for the `Login` control contains the `DestinationPageUrl` (you will set this property in the next step). The elements in lines 12–18 define various formatting styles applied to parts of the control. Note that all of the functionality related to actually logging the user in or displaying error messages is completely hidden from you.

When a user enters the user name and password of an existing user account, ASP.NET authenticates the user and writes to the client an encrypted cookie containing information about the authenticated user. Encrypted data is data translated into a code that only the sender and receiver can understand—thereby keeping it private. The encrypted cookie contains a `String` user name and a `Boolean` value that specifies whether this cookie should persist (i.e., remain on the client's computer) beyond the current session. Our application authenticates the user only for the current session.

Step 9: Creating a Content Page That Only Authenticated Users Can Access

A user who has been authenticated will be redirected to `Books.aspx`. We now create the `Books.aspx` file in the `Secure` folder—the folder for which we set an access rule denying access to anonymous users. If an unauthenticated user requests this file, the user will be redirected to `Login.aspx`. From there, the user can either log in or a create a new account, both of which will authenticate the user, thus allowing the user to return to `Books.aspx`.

To create `Books.aspx`, right click the `Secure` folder in the **Solution Explorer** and select **Add New Item...**. In the resulting dialog, select **Web Form** and specify the filename `Books.aspx`. Check the box **Select Master Page** to indicate that this Web Form should be created as a content page that references a master page, then click **Add**. In the **Select a Master Page** dialog, select `Bug2Bug.master` and click **OK**. The IDE creates the file and opens it in **Source** mode. Change the `Title` property of the `Page` directive to `Book Information`.

Step 10: Customizing the Secure Page

To customize the `Books.aspx` page for a particular user, we add a welcome message containing a **`LoginName`** control, which displays the current authenticated user name. Open `Books.aspx` in **Design** mode. In the `Content` control, type `Welcome` followed by a comma and a space. Then drag a `LoginName` control from the **Toolbox** onto the page. When this page executes on the server, the text `[UserName]` that appears in this control in **Design** mode will be replaced by the current user name. In **Source** mode, type an exclamation point (`!`) directly after the `LoginName` control (with no spaces in between). [*Note:* If you add the exclamation point in **Design** mode, the IDE may insert extra spaces or a line break between this character and the preceding control. Entering the `!` in **Source** mode ensures that it appears adjacent to the user's name.]

Next, add a `LoginStatus` control, which will allow the user to log out of the website when finished viewing the listing of books in the database. A **`LoginStatus`** control renders on a web page in one of two ways—by default, if the user is not authenticated, the control displays a hyperlink with the text `Login`; if the user is authenticated, the control displays a hyperlink with the text `Logout`. Each link performs the stated action. Add a `LoginStatus` control to the page by dragging it from the **Toolbox** onto the page. In this example, any user who reaches this page must already be authenticated, so the control will always render as a `Logout` link. The **LoginStatus Tasks** smart tag menu allows you switch between the control's **Views**. Select the **Logged In** view to see the `Logout` link. To change the actual text of this link, modify the control's `LogoutText` property to `Click here to log out`. Next, set the `LogoutAction` property to `RedirectToLoginPage`.

Step 11: Connecting the `CreateUserWizard` and `Login` Controls to the Secure Page

Now that we have created `Books.aspx`, we can specify that this is the page to which the `CreateUserWizard` and `Login` controls redirect users after they are authenticated. Open `CreateNewUser.aspx` in **Design** mode and set the `CreateUserWizard` control's `ContinueDestinationPageUrl` property to `Books.aspx`. Next, open `Login.aspx` and select `Books.aspx` as the `DestinationPageUrl` of the `Login` control.

At this point, you can run the web application by selecting **Debug > Start Without Debugging**. First, create a user account on `CreateNewUser.aspx`, then notice how the `LoginName` and `LoginStatus` controls appear on `Books.aspx`. Next, log out of the site and log back in using `Login.aspx`.

Step 12: Generating a `DataSet` Based on the `Books.mdf` Database

Now, let's add the content (i.e., book information) to the secure page `Books.aspx`. This page will provide a `DropDownList` containing authors' names and a `GridView` displaying information about books written by the author selected in the `DropDownList`. A user will select an author from the `DropDownList` to cause the `GridView` to display information about only the books written by the selected author. As you will see, we create this functionality entirely in **Design** mode without writing any code.

To work with the `Books` database, we use an approach slightly different than in the preceding case study, in which we accessed the `Guestbook` database using a `SqlDataSource` control. Here we use an **`ObjectDataSource`** control, which encapsulates an object that provides access to a data source. An ObjectDataSource can encapsulate a TableAdapter and use its methods to access the data in the database. This helps separate the data-access logic from the presentation logic. As you will see shortly, the SQL statements used to retrieve data do not appear in the ASPX page when using an ObjectDataSource.

The first step in accessing data using an ObjectDataSource is to create a DataSet that contains the data from the Books database required by the application. In Visual Basic 2005 Express, this occurs automatically when you add a data source to a project. In Visual Web Developer, however, you must explicitly generate the DataSet. Right click the project's location in the **Solution Explorer** and select **Add New Item....** In the resulting dialog, select **DataSet** and specify BooksDataSet.xsd as the filename, then click **Add.** A dialog will appear that asks you whether the DataSet should be placed in an App_Code folder—a folder whose contents are compiled and made available to all parts of the project. Click **Yes** for the IDE to create this folder to store BooksDataSet.xsd.

Step 13: Creating and Configuring an ***AuthorsTableAdapter***

Once the DataSet is added, the **Dataset Designer** will appear, and the **TableAdapter Configuration Wizard** will open. This wizard allows you to configure a TableAdapter for filling a DataTable in a DataSet with data from a database. The Books.aspx page requires two sets of data—a list of authors that will be displayed in the page's DropDownList (created shortly) and a list of books written by a specific author. We focus on the first set of data here—the authors. Thus, we use the **TableAdapter Configuration Wizard** first to configure an AuthorsTableAdapter. In the next step, we will configure a TitlesTableAdapter.

In the **TableAdapter Configuration Wizard**, select Books.mdf from the drop-down list. Then click **Next >** twice to save the connection string in the application's Web.config file and move to the **Choose a Command Type** screen.

In the wizard's **Choose a Command Type** screen, select **Use SQL statements** and click **Next >**. The next screen allows you to enter a SELECT statement for retrieving data from the database, which will then be placed in an Authors DataTable within the BooksDataSet. Enter the SQL statement

```
SELECT AuthorID, FirstName + ' ' + LastName AS Name FROM Authors
```

in the text box on the **Enter a SQL Statement** screen. This query selects the AuthorID of each row. This query's result will also contain the column Name that is created by concatenating each row's FirstName and LastName, separated by a space. The AS SQL keyword allows you to generate a column in a query result—called an alias—that contains a SQL expression's result (e.g., FirstName + ' ' + LastName). You'll soon see how we use this query's result to populate the DropDownList with items containing the authors' full names.

After entering the SQL statement, click the **Advanced Options...** button and uncheck **Generate Insert, Update and Delete statements**, since this application does not need to modify the database's contents. Click **OK** to close the **Advanced Options** dialog. Click **Next >** to advance to the **Choose Methods to Generate** screen. Leave the default names and click **Finish.** Notice that the **DataSet Designer** (Fig. 25.58) now displays a DataTable named Authors with AuthorID and Name members, and Fill and GetData methods.

Step 14: Creating and Configuring a ***TitlesTableAdapter***

Books.aspx needs to access a list of books by a specific author and a list of authors. Thus we must create a TitlesTableAdapter that will retrieve the desired information from the

Fig. 25.58 | `Authors` `DataTable` in the **Dataset Designer**.

database's `Titles` table. Right click the **Dataset Designer** and from the menu that appears, select **Add > TableAdapter...** to launch the **TableAdapter Configuration Wizard**. Make sure the `BooksConnectionString` is selected as the connection in the wizard's first screen, then click **Next >**. Choose **Use SQL statements** and click **Next >**.

In the **Enter a SQL Statement** screen, open the **Advanced Options** dialog and uncheck **Generate Insert, Update and Delete statements**, then click **OK**. Our application allows users to filter the books displayed by the author's name, so we need to build a query that takes an `AuthorID` as a parameter and returns the rows in the `Titles` table for books written by that author. To build this complex query, click the **Query Builder...** button.

In the **Add Table** dialog that appears, select **AuthorISBN** and click **Add**. Then **Add** the **Titles** table, too. Our query requires access to data in both of these tables. Click **Close** to exit the **Add Table** dialog. In the **Query Builder** window's top pane (Fig. 25.59), check the box marked *** (All Columns)** in the **Titles** table. Next, in the middle pane, add a row with **Column** set to `AuthorISBN.AuthorID`. Uncheck the **Output** box, because we do not want

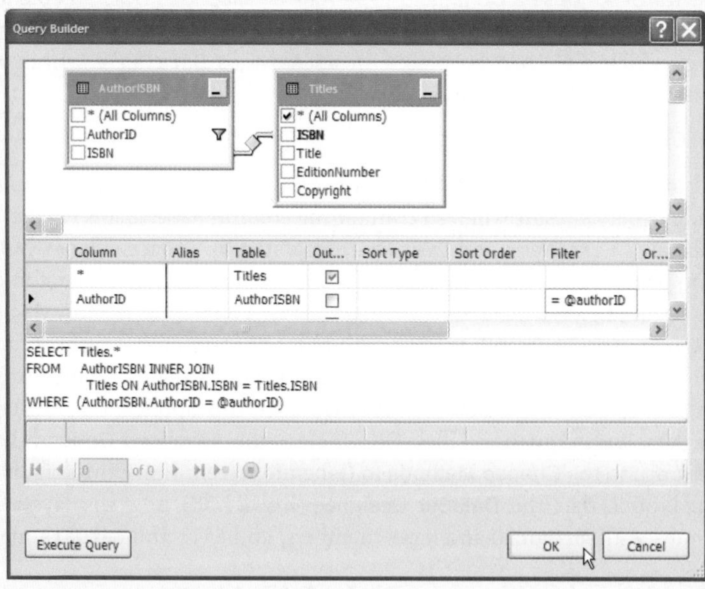

Fig. 25.59 | **Query Builder** for designing a query that selects books written by a particular author.

the **AuthorID** to appear in our query result. Add an `@authorID` parameter in this row's **Filter** column. The SQL statement generated by these actions retrieves information about all books written by the author specified by parameter `@authorID`. The statement first merges the data from the `AuthorISBN` and `Titles` tables. The `INNER JOIN` clause specifies that the `ISBN` columns of each table are compared to determine which rows are merged. The `INNER JOIN` results in a temporary table containing the columns of both tables. The `WHERE` clause of the SQL statement restricts the book information from this temporary table to a specific author (i.e., all rows in which the `AuthorID` column is equal to `@authorID`).

Click **OK** to exit the **Query Builder**, then in the **TableAdapter Configuration Wizard**, click **Next >**. On the **Choose Methods to Generate** screen, enter `FillByAuthorID` and `GetDataByAuthorID` as the names of the two methods to be generated for the `TitlesTableAdapter`. Click **Finish** to exit the wizard. You should now see a `Titles DataTable` in the **Dataset Designer** (Fig. 25.60).

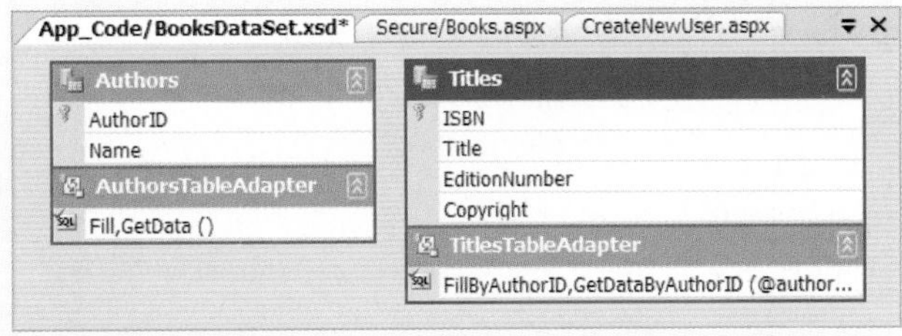

Fig. 25.60 | **Dataset Designer** after adding the `TitlesTableAdapter`.

Step 15: Adding a `DropDownList` *Containing Authors' First and Last Names*

Now that we have created a `BooksDataSet` and configured the necessary `TableAdapters`, we add controls to `Books.aspx` that will display the data on the web page. We first add the `DropDownList` from which users can select an author. Open `Books.aspx` in **Design** mode, then add the text `Author:` and a `DropDownList` control named `authorsDropDownList` in the page's `Content` control, below the existing content. The `DropDownList` initially displays the text `[Unbound]`. We now bind the list to a data source, so the list displays the author information placed in the `BooksDataSet` by the `AuthorsTableAdapter`. In the **DropDownList Tasks** smart tag menu, click **Choose Data Source...** to start the **Data Source Configuration Wizard**. Select **<New data source...>** from the **Select a data source** drop-down list in the first screen of the wizard. Doing so opens the **Choose a Data Source Type** screen. Select **Object** and set the ID to `authorsObjectDataSource`, then click **OK**.

An `ObjectDataSource` accesses data through another object, often called a business object. Recall that the middle tier of a three-tier application contains business logic that controls the way an application's top-tier user interface (in this case, `Books.aspx`) accesses the bottom tier's data (in this case, the `Books.mdf` database file). Thus, a business object represents the middle tier of an application and mediates interactions between the other two tiers. In an ASP.NET web application, a `TableAdapter` typically serves as the business object that retrieves the data from the bottom-tier database and makes it available to the top-tier user interface through a `DataSet`. In the **Choose a Business Object** screen of the **Configure Data Source** wizard (Fig. 25.61), select `BooksDataSetTableAdapters.AuthorsTableAdapter`. [*Note:* You may need to save the project to see the `AuthorsTableAdapter`.]

`BooksDataSetTableAdapters` is a namespace declared by the IDE when you create `Books-DataSet`. Click **Next >** to continue.

The **Define Data Methods** screen (Fig. 25.62) allows you to specify which of the business object's methods (in this case, `AuthorsTableAdapter`) should be used to obtain the data accessed through the `ObjectDataSource`. You can choose only methods that return data, so the only choice is method `GetData`, which returns an `AuthorsDataTable`. Click **Finish** to close the **Configure Data Source** wizard and return to the **Data Source Configuration Wizard** for the `DropDownList` (Fig. 25.63). The new data source (i.e., `authorsObject-`

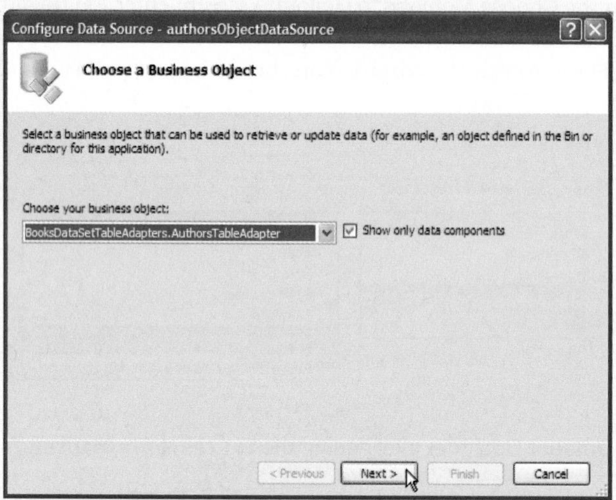

Fig. 25.61 | Choosing a business object for an `ObjectDataSource`.

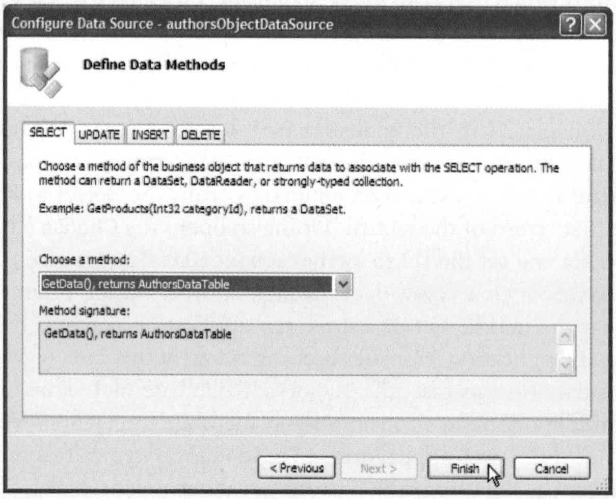

Fig. 25.62 | Choosing a data method of a business object for use with an `ObjectDataSource`.

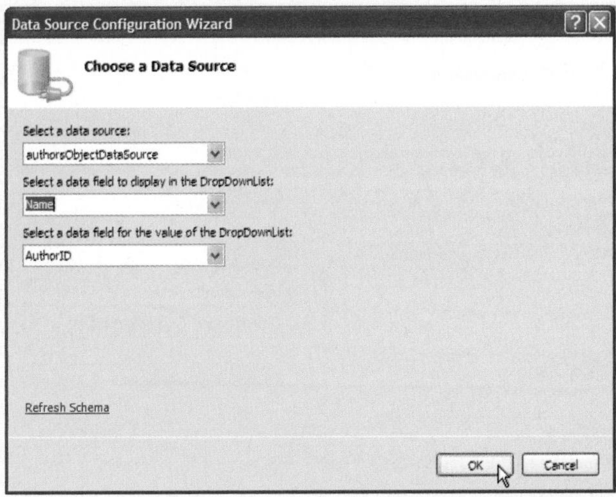

Fig. 25.63 | Choosing a data source for a `DropDownList`.

`DataSource`) should be selected in the top drop-down list. The other two drop-down lists on this screen allow you to configure how the `DropDownList` control uses the data from the data source. Set `Name` as the data field to display and `AuthorID` as the data field to use as the value. Thus, when `authorsDropDownList` is rendered in a web browser, the list items display the author names, but the underlying values associated with each item are the author `AuthorID`s. Finally, click **OK** to bind the `DropDownList` to the specified data.

The last step in configuring the `DropDownList` on `Books.aspx` is to set the control's `AutoPostBack` property to `True`. This property indicates that a postback occurs each time the user selects an item in the `DropDownList`. As you will see shortly, this causes the page's `GridView` (created in the next step) to display new data.

Step 16: Creating a `GridView` to Display the Selected Author's Books

We now add a `GridView` to `Books.aspx` for displaying the book information by the author selected in the `authorsDropDownList`. Add a `GridView` named `titlesGridView` below the other controls in the page's `Content` control.

To bind the `GridView` to data from the `Books` database, select **<New data source...>** from the **Choose Data Source** drop-down list in the **GridView Tasks** smart tag menu. When the **Data Source Configuration Wizard** opens, select **Object** and set the `ID` of the data source to `titlesObjectDataSource`, then click **OK**. In the **Choose a Business Object** screen, select the `BooksDataSetTableAdapters.TitlesTableAdapter` from the drop-down list to indicate the object that will be used to access the data. Click **Next >**. In the **Define Data Methods** screen, leave the default selection of `GetDataByAuthorID` as the method that will be invoked to obtain the data for display in the `GridView`. Click **Next >**.

Recall that `TitlesTableAdapter` method `GetDataByAuthorID` requires a parameter to indicate the `AuthorID` for which data should be retrieved. The **Define Parameters** screen (Fig. 25.64) allows you to specify where to obtain the value of the `@authorID` parameter in the SQL statement executed by `GetDataByAuthorID`. Select **Control** from the **Parameter source** drop-down list. Select `authorsDropDownList` as the **ControlID** (i.e., the `ID` of the

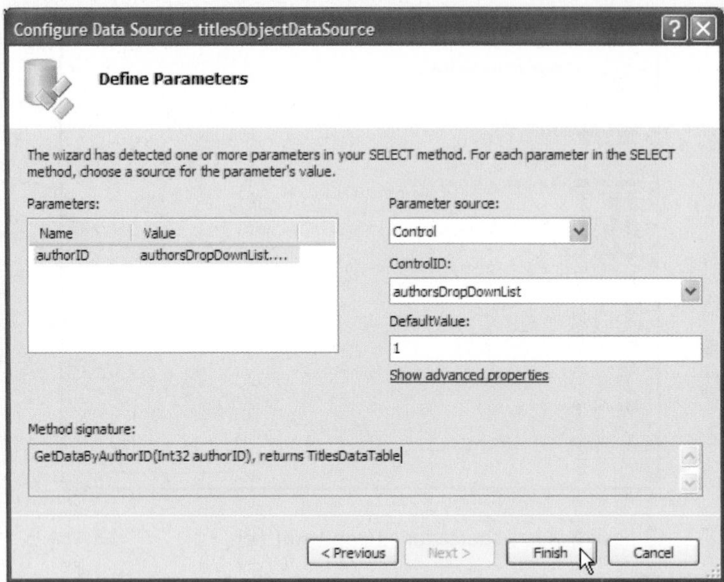

Fig. 25.64 | Choosing the data source for a parameter in a business object's data method.

parameter source control). Next, enter `1` as the **DefaultValue**, so books by Harvey Deitel (who has `AuthorID 1` in the database) display when the page first loads (i.e., before the user has made any selections using the `authorsDropDownList`). Finally, click **Finish** to exit the wizard. The `GridView` is now configured to display the data retrieved by `TitlesTableAdapter.GetDataByAuthorID`, using the value of the current selection in `authorsDropDownList` as the parameter. Thus, when the user selects a new author and a postback occurs, the `GridView` displays a new set of data.

Now that the `GridView` is tied to a data source, we modify several of the control's properties to adjust its appearance and behavior. Set the `GridView`'s `CellPadding` property to `5`, set the `BackColor` of the `AlternatingRowStyle` to `LightYellow`, and set the `BackColor` of the `HeaderStyle` to `LightGreen`. Change the `Width` of the control to `600px` to accommodate long data values.

Next, in the **GridView Tasks** smart tag menu, check **Enable Sorting**. This causes the column headings in the `GridView` to turn into hyperlinks that allow users to sort the data in the `GridView`. For example, clicking the `Titles` heading in the web browser will cause the displayed data to appear sorted in alphabetical order. Clicking this heading a second time will cause the data to be sorted in reverse alphabetical order. ASP.NET hides the details required to achieve this functionality.

Finally, in the **GridView Tasks** smart tag menu, check **Enable Paging**. This causes the `GridView` to split across multiple pages. The user can click the numbered links at the bottom of the `GridView` control to display a different page of data. `GridView`'s **`PageSize`** property determines the number of entries per page. Set the `PageSize` property to `4` using the **Properties** window so that the `GridView` displays only four books per page. This technique for displaying data makes the site more readable and enables pages to load more quickly (because less data is displayed at one time). Note that, as with sorting data in a `GridView`, you do not need to add any code to achieve paging functionality. Figure 25.65 displays the completed `Books.aspx` file in **Design** mode.

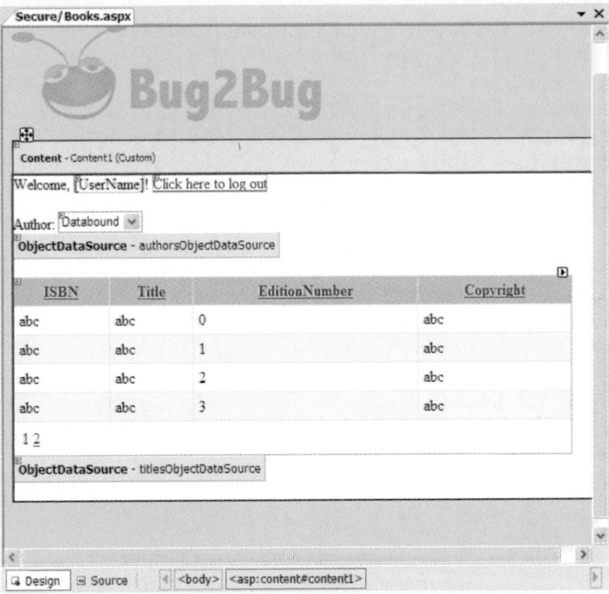

Fig. 25.65 | Completed `Books.aspx` in **Design** mode.

Step 17: Examining the Markup in **`Books.aspx`**

Figure 25.66 presents the markup in `Books.aspx` (reformatted for readability). Aside from the exclamation point in line 8, which we added manually in **Source** mode, all the remaining markup was generated by the IDE in response to the actions we performed in **Design** mode. The `Content` control (lines 5–53) defines page-specific content that will replace the `ContentPlaceHolder` named `bodyContent`. Recall that this control is located in the master page specified in line 3. Line 8 creates the `LoginName` control, which displays the authenticated user's name when the page is requested and viewed in a browser. Lines 9–11 create the `LoginStatus` control. Recall that this control is configured to redirect the user to the login page after logging out (i.e., clicking the hyperlink with the `LogoutText`).

Lines 15–18 define the `DropDownList` that displays the names of the authors in the `Books` database. Line 16 contains the control's `AutoPostBack` property, which indicates that changing the selected item in the list causes a postback to occur. The `DataSourceID` property in line 16 specifies that the `DropDownList`'s items are created based on the data obtained through the `authorsObjectDataSource` (defined in lines 19–23). Line 21 specifies that this `ObjectDataSource` accesses the `Books` database by calling method `GetData` of the `BooksDataSet`'s `AuthorsTableAdapter` (line 22).

Lines 26–42 create the `GridView` that displays information about the books written by the selected author. The start tag (lines 26–29) indicates that paging (with a page size of `4`) and sorting are enabled in the `GridView`. The `AutoGenerateColumns` property indicates whether the columns in the `GridView` are generated at runtime based on the fields in the data source. This property is set to `False`, because the IDE-generated `Columns` element

```
<%-- Fig. 25.66: Books.aspx --%>
<%-- Displays information from the Books database. --%>
<%@ Page Language="VB" MasterPageFile="~/Bug2Bug.master"
   Title="Book Information" %>
<asp:Content ID="Content1" ContentPlaceHolderID="bodyContent"
   Runat="Server">
   Welcome,
   <asp:LoginName ID="LoginName1" runat="server" />!
   <asp:LoginStatus ID="LoginStatus1" runat="server"
      LogoutAction="RedirectToLoginPage"
      LogoutText="Click here to log out" />
   <br />
   <br />
   Author:
   <asp:DropDownList ID="authorsDropDownList" runat="server"
      AutoPostBack="True" DataSourceID="authorsObjectDataSource"
      DataTextField="Name" DataValueField="AuthorID">
   </asp:DropDownList>
   <asp:ObjectDataSource ID="authorsObjectDataSource"
      runat="server" OldValuesParameterFormatString="original_{0}"
      SelectMethod="GetData"
      TypeName="BooksDataSetTableAdapters.AuthorsTableAdapter">
   </asp:ObjectDataSource>
   <br />
   <br />
   <asp:GridView ID="titlesGridView" runat="server" AllowPaging="True"
      AllowSorting="True" AutoGenerateColumns="False" CellPadding="5"
      DataKeyNames="ISBN" DataSourceID="titlesObjectDataSource"
      PageSize="4" Width="600px">
      <Columns>
         <asp:BoundField DataField="ISBN" HeaderText="ISBN"
            ReadOnly="True" SortExpression="ISBN" />
         <asp:BoundField DataField="Title" HeaderText="Title"
            SortExpression="Title" />
         <asp:BoundField DataField="EditionNumber"
            HeaderText="EditionNumber" SortExpression="EditionNumber" />
         <asp:BoundField DataField="Copyright" HeaderText="Copyright"
            SortExpression="Copyright" />
      </Columns>
      <HeaderStyle BackColor="LightGreen" />
      <AlternatingRowStyle BackColor="LightYellow" />
   </asp:GridView>
   <asp:ObjectDataSource ID="titlesObjectDataSource" runat="server"
      OldValuesParameterFormatString="original_{0}"
      SelectMethod="GetDataByAuthorID"
      TypeName="BooksDataSetTableAdapters.TitlesTableAdapter">
      <SelectParameters>
         <asp:ControlParameter ControlID="authorsDropDownList"
            DefaultValue="1" Name="authorID"
            PropertyName="SelectedValue" Type="Int32" />
      </SelectParameters>
   </asp:ObjectDataSource>
</asp:Content>
```

Fig. 25.66 | Markup for the completed Books.aspx file. (Part 1 of 2.)

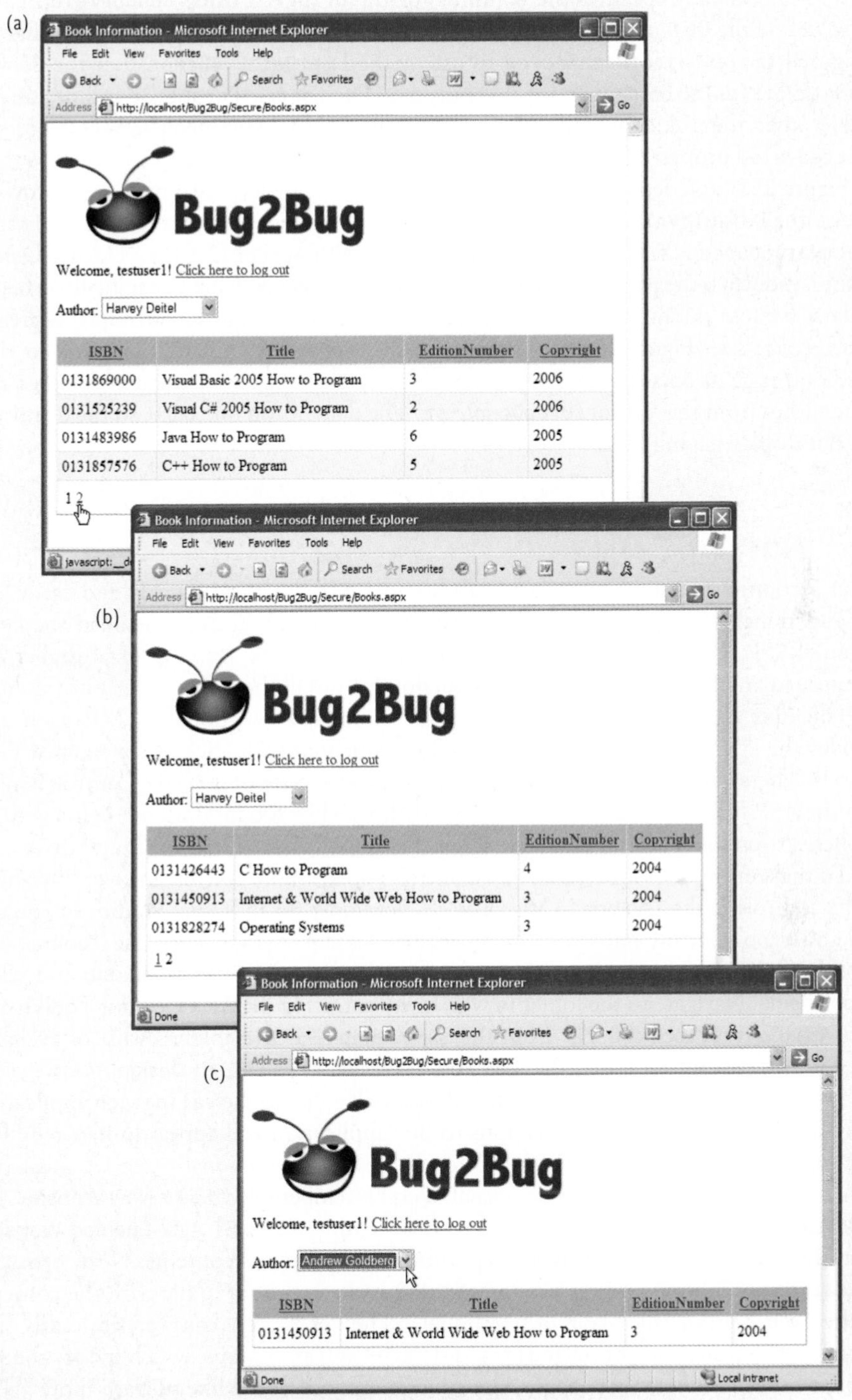

Fig. 25.66 | Markup for the completed `Books.aspx` file. (Part 2 of 2.)

(lines 30–39) already specifies the columns for the GridView using BoundFields. Lines 43–52 define the ObjectDataSource used to fill the GridView with data. Recall that we configured titlesObjectDataSource to use method GetDataByAuthorID of the Books-DataSet's TitlesTableAdapter for this purpose. The ControlParameter in lines 48–50 specifies that the value of method GetDataByAuthorID's parameter comes from the SelectedValue property of the authorsDropDownList.

Figure 25.66(a) depicts the default appearance of Books.aspx in a web browser. Because the DefaultValue property (line 49) of the ControlParameter for the titles-ObjectDataSource is set to 1, books by the author with AuthorID 1 (i.e., Harvey Deitel) are displayed when the page first loads. Note that the GridView displays paging links below the data, because the number of rows of data returned by GetDataByAuthorID is greater than the page size. Figure 25.66(b) shows the GridView after clicking the 2 link to view the second page of data. Figure 25.66(c) presents Books.aspx after the user selects a different author from the authorsDropDownList. The data fits on one page, so the GridView does not display paging links.

25.7 ASP.NET Ajax

In this section, we introduce how you can use ASP.NET Ajax to quickly and easily add Ajax functionality to existing ASP.NET web applications. You can download the latest version of ASP.NET Ajax from www.asp.net/ajax/downloads. Run the .msi installer you downloaded and follow the on-screen instructions to install the Ajax Extensions package.

The Ajax Extensions package implements basic Ajax functionality. Microsoft also provides the ASP.NET Ajax Control Toolkit, which contains rich, Ajax-enabled GUI controls. There is also a link to the download the latest version of the Ajax Control Toolkit from the ASP.NET Ajax download page listed above. The toolkit does not come with an installer, so you must extract the contents of the toolkit's ZIP file to your hard drive.

To make using the ASP.NET Ajax Control Toolkit more convenient, you'll want to add its controls to the **Toolbox** in Visual Web Developer (or in Visual Studio) so you can drag and drop controls onto your Web Forms. To do so, right click the **Toolbox** and choose **Add Tab**. Type Ajax Toolkit in the new tab. Then right click the tab and select **Choose Items**. Navigate to the folder in which you extracted the Ajax Control Toolkit and select AjaxControlToolkit.dll from the SampleWebSite\Bin folder. A list of available Ajax controls will appear under the **Ajax Toolkit** tab when you are in **Design** mode.

To demonstrate ASP.NET Ajax capabilities we'll enhance the Validation application from Fig. 25.17. The only modifications to this application will appear in its .aspx file. This application was not initially set up to support Ajax functionality, so we must first modify the web.config file. First, in Visual Web Developer select **File > New Website...** to display the **New Website** dialog. Then, create an empty **ASP.NET Ajax-Enabled Website**. Open the web.config file in this new application and copy its contents. Next, open the Validation application and replace the contents of its web.config file with the contents of the web.config file you just copied. The new web.config file adds the system.web.extensions, httpHandlers and httpModules sections, which specify the settings for running scripts that enable Ajax functionality. If you'd like to learn more about the details of these web.config modifications, please visit the site www.asp.net/ajax/documentation/live/configuringASPNETAJAX.aspx.

We'll now use Ajax-enabled controls to add Ajax features to this application. Figure 25.67 is a modified `validation.aspx` file that enhances the application by using the `ToolkitScriptManager`, `UpdatePanel` and `ValidatorCalloutExtender` controls.

```
<%-- Fig. 25.67: Validation.aspx --%>
<%-- Validation application enhanced by ASP.NET Ajax. --%>
<%@ Page Language="VB" AutoEventWireup="false"
   CodeFile="Validation.aspx.vb" Inherits="Validation" %>
<%@ Register Assembly="AjaxControlToolkit" Namespace="AjaxControlToolkit"
   TagPrefix="ajax" %>

<!DOCTYPE html PUBLIC "-//W3C//DTD XHTML 1.0 Transitional//EN"
   "http://www.w3.org/TR/xhtml1/DTD/xhtml1-transitional.dtd">

<html xmlns="http://www.w3.org/1999/xhtml" >
<head runat="server">
    <title>Demonstrating Validation Controls</title>
</head>
<body>
   <form id="form1" runat="server">
   <div>
      <ajax:ToolkitScriptManager ID="ToolkitScriptManager1"
         runat="server">
      </ajax:ToolkitScriptManager>
       Please fill out the following form.<br /><em>All fields are
      required and must contain valid information.</em><br /><br />
      <table>
         <tr>
            <td style="width: 100px" valign="top">
               Name:</td>
            <td style="width: 450px" valign="top">
               <asp:TextBox ID="nameTextBox" runat="server">
               </asp:TextBox>
               <br />
               <asp:RequiredFieldValidator
                  ID="nameInputValidator" runat="server"
                  ControlToValidate="nameTextBox" Display="None"
                  ErrorMessage="Please enter your name.">
               </asp:RequiredFieldValidator>
               <ajax:ValidatorCalloutExtender ID="nameInputCallout"
                  runat="server" TargetControlID="nameInputValidator"/>
            </td>
         </tr>
         <tr>
            <td style="width: 100px" valign="top">E-mail address:</td>
            <td style="width: 450px" valign="top">
               <asp:TextBox ID="emailTextBox" runat="server">
               </asp:TextBox>
                e.g., user@domain.com<br />
               <asp:RequiredFieldValidator
                  ID="emailInputValidator" runat="server"
```

Fig. 25.67 | `Validation` application enhanced by ASP.NET Ajax. (Part 1 of 3.)

```
            ControlToValidate="emailTextBox" Display="None"
            ErrorMessage="Please enter your e-mail address.">
         </asp:RequiredFieldValidator>
         <ajax:ValidatorCalloutExtender ID="emailInputCallout"
            runat="server" TargetControlID="emailInputValidator"/>
         <asp:RegularExpressionValidator
            ID="emailFormatValidator" runat="server"
            ControlToValidate="emailTextBox" Display="None"
            ErrorMessage=
               "Please enter an e-mail address in a valid format."
            ValidationExpression=
               "\w+([-+.']\w+)*@\w+([-.]\w+)*\.\w+([-.]\w+)*">
         </asp:RegularExpressionValidator>
         <ajax:ValidatorCalloutExtender ID="emailFormatCallout"
            runat="server"
            TargetControlID="emailFormatValidator"/>
      </td>
   </tr>
   <tr>
      <td style="width: 100px; height: 21px" valign="top">
         Phone number:</td>
      <td style="width: 450px; height: 21px" valign="top">
         <asp:TextBox ID="phoneTextBox" runat="server">
         </asp:TextBox>
           e.g., (555) 555-1234<br />
         <asp:RequiredFieldValidator
            ID="phoneInputValidator" runat="server"
            ControlToValidate="phoneTextBox" Display="None"
            ErrorMessage="Please enter your phone number.">
         </asp:RequiredFieldValidator>
         <ajax:ValidatorCalloutExtender ID="phoneInputCallout"
            runat="server" TargetControlID="phoneInputValidator"/>
         <asp:RegularExpressionValidator
            ID="phoneFormatValidator" runat="server"
            ControlToValidate="phoneTextBox" Display="None"
            ErrorMessage=
               "Please enter a phone number in a valid format."
            ValidationExpression=
               "((\(\d{3}\) ?)|(\d{3}-))?\d{3}-\d{4}">
         </asp:RegularExpressionValidator>
         <ajax:ValidatorCalloutExtender ID="PhoneFormatCallout"
            runat="server"
            TargetControlID="phoneFormatValidator"/>
      </td>
   </tr>
</table>
<asp:UpdatePanel ID="UpdatePanel1" runat="server">
   <ContentTemplate>
      <asp:Button ID="submitButton" runat="server" Text="Submit" />
      <br /><br /><br /> 
      <asp:Label ID="outputLabel" runat="server"
         Text="Thank you for your submission." Visible="False">
      </asp:Label>
```

Fig. 25.67 | `Validation` application enhanced by ASP.NET Ajax. (Part 2 of 3.)

```
            </ContentTemplate>
        </asp:UpdatePanel>
    </div>
    </form>
</body>
</html>
```

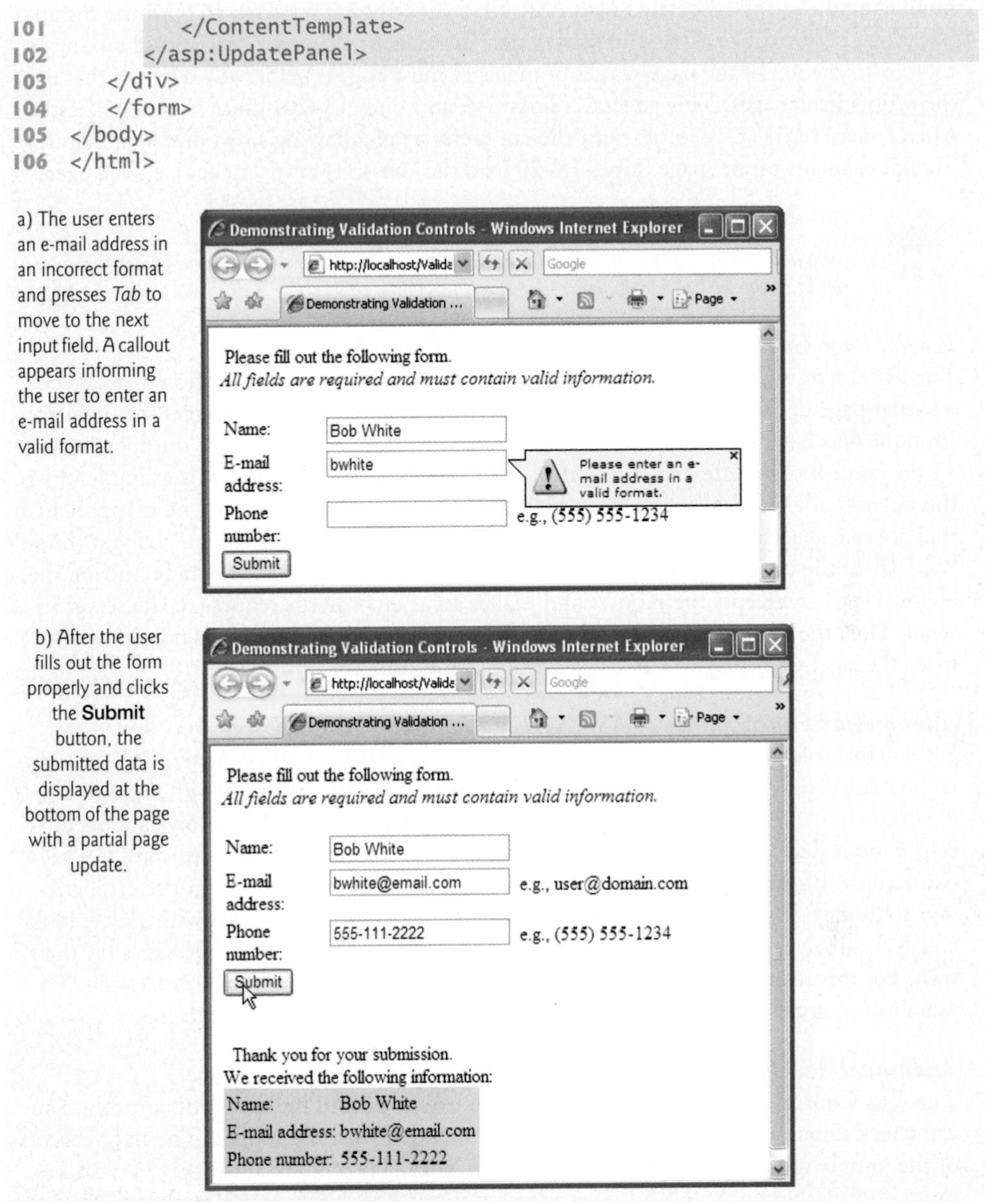

a) The user enters an e-mail address in an incorrect format and presses *Tab* to move to the next input field. A callout appears informing the user to enter an e-mail address in a valid format.

b) After the user fills out the form properly and clicks the **Submit** button, the submitted data is displayed at the bottom of the page with a partial page update.

Fig. 25.67 | `Validation` application enhanced by ASP.NET Ajax. (Part 3 of 3.)

`ScriptManager` Control

The key control in every ASP.NET Ajax-enabled application is the `ScriptManager`, which manages the client-side scripts that enable asynchronous Ajax functionality. There can be only one `ScriptManager` per page. To incorporate controls from the Ajax Control Toolkit you should use the `ToolkitScriptManager` that comes with the toolkit contorls, rather than the `ScriptManager` from the ASP.NET Ajax Extensions. The `ToolkitScriptManager` bundles all the scripts associated with ASP. NET Ajax Toolkit controls to optimize the application's performance. Drag the `ToolkitScriptManager` from the **Ajax Toolkit** tab in the toolbox to the top of the page—a script manager must appear before any controls that use the scripts it manages. This generates lines 5–6 and lines 18–20. Lines 5–6 associate the `AjaxControlToolkit` assembly with the tag prefix `ajax`, allowing us to put Ajax Control Toolkit elements on the page. Lines 18–20 load the `ToolkitScriptManager` on the page.

Common Programming Error 25.1

Putting more than one instance of the `ScriptManager` control on a Web Form causes the application to throw an `InvalidOperationException` when the page is initialized.

Partial Page Updates Using the `UpdatePanel` *Control*

The `UpdatePanel` control eliminates full-page refreshes by isolating a section of a page for a partial-page update. To implement a partial-page update, drag the `UpdatePanel` control from the **Ajax Extensions** tab in the **Toolbox** to your form. Then, drag into the `UpdatePanel` the control to update and the control that triggers the update. For this example, drag the `outputLabel` and `submitButton` elements into the `UpdatePanel`. The components that are managed by the `UpdatePanel` are placed in the `ContentTemplate` element (lines 95–101) of the `UpdatePanel` (lines 94–102). When the user clicks the **Submit** button, the `UpdatePanel` intercepts the request and makes an asynchronous request to the server instead. Then the response is inserted in the `outputLabel` element, and the `UpdatePanel` reloads the label to display the new text without refreshing the entire page.

Adding Ajax Functionality to ASP.NET Validation Controls Using Ajax Extenders

Several controls in the Ajax Control Toolkit are extenders—components that enhance regular ASP.NET controls. Lines 36–37, 51–52, 61–63, 78–79 and 88–90 define `ValidatorCalloutExtender` controls that display error messages in small yellow callouts next to the input fields. Line 37 sets the `targetControlID` property, which indicates the validator control from which the `ValidatorCalloutExtender` should obtain the error message to display. The `ValidatorCalloutExtenders` display error messages with a nicer look and feel, so we no longer need the validator controls to display these messages on their own. For this reason, line 33 sets the `Display` property of the first validator to `None`. The remaining control extenders and validator controls are configured similarly.

Additional ASP.NET Information

The Ajax Control Toolkit contains many other extenders and independent controls. You can check them out using the sample website included with the toolkit. The live version of the sample website can be found at `www.asp.net/ajax/control-toolkit/live/`. For more information on ASP.NET Ajax, check out our ASP.NET Ajax Resource Center at `www.deitel.com/aspdotnetajax`.

25.8 Wrap-Up

In this chapter, we introduced web application development using ASP.NET and Visual Web Developer 2005 Express. We began by discussing the simple HTTP transactions that take place when you request and receive a web page through a web browser. You then learned about the three tiers (i.e., the client or top tier, the business logic or middle tier and the information or bottom tier) that comprise most web applications.

Next, we explained the role of ASPX files (i.e., Web Form files) and code-behind files, and the relationship between them. We discussed how ASP.NET compiles and executes web applications so that they can be displayed as XHTML in a web browser. You also learned how to build an ASP.NET web application using Visual Web Developer.

The chapter demonstrated several common ASP.NET web controls used for displaying text and images on a Web Form. You learned how to use an `AdRotator` control to display randomly selected images. We also discussed validation controls, which allow you to ensure that user input on a web page satisfies certain requirements.

We discussed the benefits of maintaining a user's state information across multiple pages of a website. We then demonstrated how you can include such functionality in a web application using either cookies or session tracking with `HttpSessionState` objects.

We presented two case studies on building ASP.NET applications that interact with databases. First, we showed how to build a guestbook application that allows users to submit comments about a website. You learned how to save the user input in a SQL Server database and how to display past submissions on the web page.

Finally, we introduced ASP.NET Ajax and the Ajax Control Toolkit. You learned how to add Ajax functionality to an existing application by using the `ToolkitScript-Manager` and the `UpdatePanel`. You also learned how to use validation extenders.

The second case study presented a secure web application that requires users to log in before accessing information from the `Books` database. You used the **Web Site Administration Tool** to configure the application to use forms authentication and prevent anonymous users from accessing the book information. This case study explained how to use the new ASP.NET 2.0 `Login`, `CreateUserWizard`, `LoginName` and `LoginStatus` controls to simplify user authentication. You also learned to create a uniform look-and-feel for a website using a master page and several content pages. In the next chapter, you will learn about similar web application development techniques with JavaServer Faces, which is implemented with the Java programming language.

25.9 Web Resources

`www.deitel.com/aspdotnet/`

The Deitel ASP.NET Resource Center focuses on the vast amount of free ASP.NET content available online, plus some for-sale items. Start your search here for tools, downloads, text and video tutorials, webcasts, podcasts, wikis, documentation, reference manuals, conferences, FAQs, books, e-books, sample chapters, articles, newsgroups, forums, downloads from CNET's download.com, jobs and contract opportunities, and more that will help you develop ASP.NET-based applications. Keep track of ASP.NET blogs for the latest news and developments, or sign up for RSS feeds to be notified promptly of each new development. Also, download free open-source ASP.NET projects.

Summary

Section 25.1 Introduction

- Microsoft's ASP.NET technology is used for web application development.
- Web-based applications create web content for web-browser clients. This web content includes XHTML, client-side scripting, images and binary data.
- A Web Form file generates a web page that is sent to the client browser. Web Form files have the filename extension `.aspx` and contain a web page's GUI. You customize Web Forms by adding web controls.

- Every ASPX file created in Visual Studio has a corresponding class written in a .NET language. The file that contains this class is called the code-behind file and provides the ASPX file's programmatic implementation.

Section 25.2 Creating and Running a Simple Web Form Example
- An ASP.NET Web Form typically consists of an ASPX file and a code-behind file.
- Visual Web Developer generates markup when you change a Web Form's properties and when you add text or controls to a Web Form.

Section 25.2.1 Examining an ASPX File
- ASP.NET comments begin with `<%--` and terminate with `--%>`.
- A `Page` directive (delimited by `<%@` and `%>`) specifies information needed by ASP.NET to process an ASPX file. The `CodeFile` attribute of the `Page` directive indicates the name of the corresponding code-behind file. The `Language` attribute specifies the .NET language used in this file.
- When a control's `runat` attribute is set to `"server"`, the control is processed by ASP.NET on the server, generating an XHTML equivalent.
- The `asp:` tag prefix in a control declaration indicates that a control is an ASP.NET web control.
- Each web control maps to a corresponding XHTML element (or group of elements)—when processing a web control on the server, ASP.NET generates XHTML markup that will be sent to the client to represent that control in a web browser.

Section 25.2.2 Examining a Code-Behind File
- The code-behind file is a partial class.
- Namespace `System.Web.UI` contains classes for the creation of web applications and controls.
- Class `Page` defines a standard web page, providing events and objects necessary for creating Web-based applications. All web pages directly or indirectly inherit from class `Page`.
- Class `Control` is the base class that provides common functionality for all web controls.
- Method `Page_Init` handles the `Init` event, which indicates that a page is initialized and ready to execute application-specific initialization code..

Section 25.2.3 Relationship Between an ASPX File and a Code-Behind File
- When a client requests an ASPX file, ASP.NET combines two partial classes—the one defined in the code-behind file and the one that ASP.NET generates based on the markup in the ASPX file that defines the page's GUI.
- ASP.NET compiles the combined partial classes and creates a class that represents the page. An instance of this class creates the XHTML that is sent to the client.
- Namespace `System.Web.UI.WebControls` contains web controls (derived from class `WebControl`) for designing a page's user interface.

Section 25.2.4 How the Code in an ASP.NET Web Page Executes
- When an instance of a page is created, the `PreInit` event occurs first, invoking method `Page_PreInit`. The `Init` event occurs next, invoking method `Page_Init`. Then the `Load` event occurs, invoking method `Page_Load`.
- After `Page_Load` finishes executing, the page processes any events raised by the page's controls.
- When a Web Form object completes the response to the user, an `Unload` event occurs. Event handler `Page_Unload` is inherited from class `Page` and contains any code that releases resources.

Section 25.2.5 Examining the XHTML Generated by an ASP.NET Application

- A form is a mechanism for collecting user information and sending it to the web server.
- XHTML forms can contain visual and nonvisual components.
- Nonvisual components in an XHTML form, called hidden inputs, store any data that the document author specifies.

Section 25.2.6 Building an ASP.NET Web Application

- The name `localhost` indicates that the server resides on the local computer. If the web server were located on a different computer, `localhost` would be replaced with the appropriate IP address or hostname.
- `DOCUMENT` is the name used to represent a Web Form in the **Properties** window.
- The Web Forms Designer's **Source** mode allows you to view the markup that represents the user interface of a page. The **Design** mode allows you to view the page as it will look and modify it by dragging and dropping controls from the **Toolbox** onto the Web Form.
- Controls and other elements are placed sequentially on a Web Form, much as text and images are placed in a document using word-processing software like Microsoft Word. The positions of controls and other elements flow based on the width of the page by default.
- An alternate type of layout is known as absolute positioning, in which controls are located exactly where they are dropped on the Web Form.
- Visual Web Developer is a WYSIWYG (What You See Is What You Get) editor—whenever you make a change to a Web Form in **Design** mode, the IDE creates the markup (visible in **Source** mode) necessary to achieve the desired visual effects seen in **Design** mode.
- `Web.config` is a file that stores configuration settings for an ASP.NET web application.

Section 25.3 Web Controls

- The **Standard** section of the **Toolbox** in Visual Web Developer contains several web controls.

Section 25.3.1 Text and Graphics Controls

- The **Insert Table** command from the **Layout** menu in **Design** mode allows you to add an XHTML table to a Web Form.
- An `Image` control inserts an image into a web page. The `ImageUrl` property specifies the file location of the image to display.
- A `TextBox` control allows the you to obtain text from the user and display text to the user.
- A `DropDownList` control provides a list of options to the user. Each item in the drop-down list is defined by a `ListItem` element.
- Visual Web Developer displays smart tag menus for many ASP.NET controls to facilitate performing common tasks. A smart tag menu is opened by clicking the small arrowhead that appears in the upper-right corner of the control in **Design** mode.
- A `HyperLink` control adds a hyperlink to a web page. The `NavigateUrl` property of this control specifies the resource that is requested when a user clicks the hyperlink.
- A `RadioButtonList` control provides a series of radio buttons for the user.

Section 25.3.2 `AdRotator` Control

- ASP.NET provides the `AdRotator` web control for displaying advertisements (or any other images). Using data from an XML file, the `AdRotator` control randomly selects an image to display and generates a hyperlink to the web page associated with that image.

- An `XmlDataSource` references an XML file containing data that will be used in an ASP.NET application. The **AdRotator Tasks** smart tag menu allows you to create a new `XmlDataSource` that retrieves advertisement data from an XML file.
- The advertisement file used for an `AdRotator` control contains `Ad` elements, each of which provides information about a different advertisement.
- Element `ImageUrl` in an advertisement file specifies the path (location) of the advertisement's image, and element `NavigateUrl` specifies the URL that loads when a user clicks the advertisement.
- The `AlternateText` element contains text that displays in place of the image when the browser cannot locate or render the image for some reason, or to assist the visually impaired.
- Element `Impressions` specifies how often an image appears, relative to the other images.

Section 25.3.3 Validation Controls

- A validation control (or validator) determines whether the data in another web control is in the proper format. Validators provide a mechanism for validating user input on the client.
- When the XHTML for a page is created, a validator is converted into ECMAScript, scripting language that enhances the functionality and appearance of Web pages.
- The `Visible` property of a control indicates whether the control appears in the client's browser.
- A `RequiredFieldValidator` ensures that a control receives user input before a form is submitted.
- A validator's `ControlToValidate` property indicates which control will be validated.
- A validator's `ErrorMessage` property contains text to be displayed if the validation fails.
- A `RegularExpressionValidator` matches a web control's content against a regular expression. The regular expression that validates the input is assigned to property `ValidationExpression`.
- Web programmers using ASP.NET often design their web pages so that the current page reloads when the user submits the form. This event is known as a postback.
- A `Page`'s `IsPostBack` property determines whether the page is being loaded due to a postback.
- When data is posted to the web server, the XHTML form's data is accessible to the web application through properties of the ASP.NET controls.
- The `EnableViewState` attribute determines whether a web control's state persists (i.e., is retained) when a postback occurs.

Section 25.4 Session Tracking

- Personalization makes it possible for e-businesses to communicate effectively with their customers and also improves users' ability to locate desired products and services.
- To provide personalized services to consumers, e-businesses must be able to recognize clients when they request information from a site.
- The request/response system on which the web operates is facilitated by HTTP.
- HTTP is a stateless protocol.
- A session represents a unique client on a website. If the client leaves a site and then returns later, the client will still be recognized as the same user. To help the server distinguish among clients, each client must identify itself to the server.
- Tracking individual clients is known as session tracking.

Section 25.4.1 Cookies

- A cookie is a piece of data stored in a small text file on the user's computer. A cookie maintains information about the client during and between browser sessions.

- A cookie object is of type `HttpCookie`. Properties `Name` and `Value` of class `HttpCookie` can be used to retrieve the key and value in a key–value pair (both strings) in a cookie.
- Cookies are sent and received as a collection of type `HttpCookieCollection`. An application on a server can write cookies to a client using the `Response` object's `Cookies` property. Cookies can be accessed programmatically using the `Request` object's `Cookies` property. Cookies can be read by an application only if they were created in the domain in which the application is running.
- When a Web Form receives a request, the header includes information such as the request type and any cookies that have been sent previously from the server to be stored on the client machine.
- When the server formulates its response, the header information includes any cookies the server wants to store on the client computer.
- The expiration date of a cookie determines how long the cookie remains on the client's computer. If you do not set an expiration date for a cookie, the web browser maintains the cookie for the duration of the browsing session.
- Clients can disable cookies. If they do, they may not be able to use certain web applications.

Section 25.4.2 Session Tracking with `HttpSessionState`

- Session-tracking capabilities are provided by FCL class `HttpSessionState`. Every Web Form includes an `HttpSessionState` object, which is accessible through property `Session` of class `Page`.
- When the web page is requested, an `HttpSessionState` object is created and assigned to the `Page`'s `Session` property. A unique session ID is created for that client, and a temporary cookie is written to the client so the server can identify the client on subsequent requests. Recall that clients may disable cookies in their web browsers to ensure that their privacy is protected. Such clients will experience difficulty using web applications that depend on `HttpSessionState` objects to maintain state information, unless `HttpSessionState` is configured to use URL rewriting.
- The `Page`'s `Session` property is often referred to as the `Session` object.
- The `Session` object's key–value pairs are often referred to as session items.
- Session items are placed into an `HttpSessionState` object by calling method `Add`.
- `HttpSessionState` objects can store any type of object (not just `string`s) as attribute values. This provides increased flexibility in maintaining client state information.
- Property `SessionID` contains the unique session ID. The first time a client connects to the web server, a unique session ID is created for that client. When the client makes additional requests, the client's session ID is compared with the session IDs stored in the web server's memory to retrieve the `HttpSessionState` object for that client.
- Property `Timeout` specifies the maximum amount of time that an `HttpSessionState` object can be inactive before it is discarded.
- Property `Count` provides the number of session items contained in a `Session` object.
- Indexing the `Session` object with a key name retrieves the corresponding value.
- Property `Keys` of class `HttpSessionState` returns a collection containing all the session's keys.

Section 25.5 Case Study: Connecting to a Database in ASP.NET

- A `GridView` ASP.NET data control displays data on a Web Form in a tabular format.

Section 25.5.1 Building a Web Form That Displays Data from a Database

- A `GridView`'s colors can be set using the **Auto Format...** link in the **GridView Tasks** smart tag menu.
- A SQL Server 2005 Express database used by an ASP.NET website should be located in the project's `App_Data` folder.

- A SqlDataSource control allows a web application to interact with a database.
- When a SqlDataSource is configured to perform INSERT SQL operations against the database table from which it gathers data, you must specify the values to insert either programmatically or through other controls on the Web Form.
- The **Command and Parameter Editor**, accessed by clicking the ellipsis next to a SqlDataSource's InsertQuery property, allows you to specify that parameter values come from controls.
- Each column in a GridView is represented as a BoundField.
- SqlDataSource property ConnectionString indicates the connection through which the SqlDataSource control interacts with the database.
- An ASP.NET expression, delimited by <%$ and %>, can be used to access a connection string stored in an application's Web.config configuration file.

Section 25.5.2 Modifying the Code-Behind File for the Guestbook Application

- A SqlDataSource's InsertParameters collection contains an item corresponding to each parameter in the SqlDataSource's INSERT command.
- SqlDataSource method Insert executes the control's INSERT command against the database.
- GridView method DataBind refreshes the information displayed in the GridView.

Section 25.6.1 Examining the Completed Secure Books Database Application

- Forms authentication is a technique that protects a page so that only users known to the website can access it. Such users are known as the site's members.
- ASP.NET login controls help create secure applications using authentication. These controls are found in the **Login** section of the **Toolbox**.
- When a user's identity is confirmed, the user is said to have been authenticated.
- A master page defines common GUI elements that are inherited by each page in a set of content pages. Just as Visual Basic classes can inherit instance variables and methods from existing classes, content pages inherit elements from master pages—this is known as visual inheritance.

Section 25.6.2 Creating the Secure Books Database Application

- ASP.NET hides the details of authenticating users, displaying appropriate success or error messages and redirecting the user to the correct page based on the authentication results.
- The **Web Site Administration Tool** allows you to configure an application's security settings, add site users and create access rules that determine who is allowed to access the site.
- By default, anonymous users who attempt to load a page in a directory to which they are denied access are redirected to a page named Login.aspx so that they can identify themselves.
- In an ASP.NET application, a page's configuration settings are determined by the current directory's Web.config file. The settings in this file take precedence over the settings in the root directory's Web.config file.
- A master page contains placeholders for custom content created in a content page, which visually inherits the master page's content, then adds content in place of the placeholders.
- Master pages have the filename extension .master and, like Web Forms, can optionally use a code-behind file to define additional functionality.
- A Master directive in an ASPX file specifies that the file defines a master page.
- A ContentPlaceHolder control serves as a placeholder for page-specific content defined by a content page using a Content control. The Content control will appear in place of the master page's ContentPlaceHolder when the content page is requested.

- A `CreateUserWizard` control provides a registration form that site visitors can use to create a user account. ASP.NET handles the details of creating a SQL Server database to store the user names, passwords and other account information of the application's users.
- A `Login` control encapsulates the details of logging a user into a web application (i.e., authenticating a user by comparing the provided user name and password with those of an account in the ASP.NET-created membership database). If the user is authenticated, the browser is redirected to the page specified by the `Login` control's `DestinationPageUrl` property. If the user is not authenticated, the `Login` control displays an error message.
- ASP.NET writes to the client an encrypted cookie containing data about an authenticated user.
- Encrypted data is data translated into a code that only the sender and receiver can understand.
- A `LoginName` control displays the current authenticated user name on a Web Form.
- A `LoginStatus` control renders on a web page in one of two ways—by default, if the user is not authenticated (the **Logged Out** view), the control displays a hyperlink with the text `Login`; if the user is authenticated (the **Logged In** view), the control displays a hyperlink with the text `Logout`. The `LogoutText` determines the text of the link in the **Logged In** view.
- An `ObjectDataSource` control encapsulates a business object that provides access to a data source. A business object (e.g., a `TableAdapter`) represents the middle tier of an application and mediates interactions between the bottom tier and the top tier.
- The `AS` SQL keyword allows you to generate a column in a query result—called an alias—that contains the result of a SQL expression.
- A `DropDownList`'s `AutoPostBack` property indicates whether a postback occurs each time the user selects an item.
- When you **Enable Sorting** for a `GridView`, the column headings in the `GridView` turn into hyperlinks that allow users to sort the data it displays.
- When you **Enable Paging** for a `GridView`, the `GridView` divides its data among multiple pages. The user can click the numbered links at the bottom of the `GridView` control to display a different page of data. `GridView`'s `PageSize` property determines the number of entries per page.

Section 25.7 ASP.NET Ajax

- ASP.NET Ajax is an extension of ASP.NET that provides a fast and simple way to create Ajax-enabled applications.
- The ASP.NET Ajax Control Toolkit contains rich controls that implement Ajax functionality.
- The key part of every ASP.NET Ajax-enabled application is the `ScriptManager` control, which manages the client-side scripts that enable asynchronous functionality.
- The `ToolkitScriptManager` bundles all the scripts associated with ASP. NET Ajax Toolkit controls to optimize the application's performance.
- The `UpdatePanel` control eliminates full-page refreshes by isolating a section of a page for a partial-page update.
- The components that an `UpdatePanel` reloads are placed in the `ContentTemplate` element.
- Several controls in the Ajax Control Toolkit are extenders—components that enhance regular ASP.NET controllers.

Terminology

`<%-- --%>` ASP.NET comment delimiters
`<%$ %>` ASP.NET expression delimiters
`<%@ %>` ASP.NET directive delimiters
absolute positioning

access rule in ASP.NET
action attribute of XHTML element form
Ad XML element in an AdRotator advertisement file
Add method of class Hashtable
Add method of class HttpSessionState
AdRotator ASP.NET web control
Advertisements XML element in an AdRotator advertisement file
Ajax Control Toolkit
Ajax Control Toolkit TooklitScriptManager control
Ajax Control Toolkit ValidatorCalloutExtender control
alias in SQL
AlternateText element in an AdRotator advertisement file
AS SQL keyword
asp: tag prefix
ASP.NET 20
ASP.NET Ajax
ASP.NET Ajax extender
ASP.NET Ajax ScriptManager control
ASP.NET Ajax UpdatePanel control
ASP.NET comment
ASP.NET expression
ASP.NET login control
ASP.NET server control
ASP.NET Web Site in Visual Web Developer
ASPX file
.aspx filename extension
authenticating a user
authentication element in Web.config
authorization element in Web.config
AutoEventWireup attribute of ASP.NET page
AutoPostBack property of a DropDownList
bottom tier
BoundField ASP.NET element
Build Page command in Visual Web Developer
Build Site command in Visual Web Developer
business logic
business object
business rule
Button ASP.NET Web control
client tier
code-behind file
CodeFile attribute in a Page directive
ConnectionString property of a SqlDataSource
Content ASP.NET control
content page in ASP.NET
ContentPlaceHolder ASP.NET control
Control class
controller logic
ControlParameter ASP.NET element
ControlToValidate property of a validation control
cookie
Cookies collection of the Response object
Cookies property of class Request
Count property of class HttpSessionState
CreateUserWizard ASP.NET login control
data tier
DataSourceID property of a GridView
DeleteCommand property of a SqlDataSource
deny element in Web.config
Design mode in Visual Web Developer
directive in ASP.NET
Display property of a validation control
DNS (domain name system) server
DNS lookup
DOCUMENT property of a Web Form
domain name system (DNS) server
DropDownList ASP.NET web control
ECMAScript
Enable Paging setting for a GridView
Enable Sorting setting for a GridView
EnableSessionState property of a Web Form
EnableViewState property of a web control
encrypted data
ErrorMessage property of a validation control
expiration date of a cookie
forms authentication
GET HTTP request
GridView ASP.NET data control
guestbook on a website
hidden input in an XHTML form
host
hostname
HTTP (Hypertext Transfer Protocol)
HTTP header
HTTP method
HttpCookie class
HttpCookieCollection class
HttpSessionState class
hyperlink
HyperLink ASP.NET web control
hypertext
ID attribute of an ASP.NET web control
IIS (Internet Information Services)
Image ASP.NET web control

ImageUrl element in an AdRotator advertisement file
ImageUrl property of an Image web control
Impressions element in an AdRotator advertisement file
information tier
Inherits attribute of an ASP.NET page
Init event of an ASP.NET Web page
InsertCommand property of a SqlDataSource
InsertQuery property of a SqlDataSource
IP address
IsPostBack property of class Page
JavaScript
key–value pair
Keys property of HttpSessionState class
Label ASP.NET Web control
Language attribute in a Page directive
ListItem ASP.NET control
Load event of an ASP.NET web page
localhost
Login ASP.NET control
LoginName ASP.NET login control
LoginStatus ASP.NET login control
Master directive
.master filename extension
master page in ASP.NET
MasterPageFile property of a Page directive
method attribute of XHTML element form
middle tier
MIME (Multipurpose Internet Mail Extensions)
mode attribute of element authentication in Web.config
multitier application
n-tier application
Name property of class HttpCookie
NavigateUrl element in an AdRotator advertisement file
NavigateUrl property of a HyperLink control
navigation bar on a website
ObjectDataSource ASP.NET data control
Page class
Page directive in ASP.NET
Page_Init event handler
Page_Load event handler
Page_PreInit event handler
Page_Unload event handler
PageSize property of a GridView
Parameter ASP.NET element
personalization
postback event of an ASP.NET page
PreInit event of an ASP.NET web page
presentation logic
RadioButtonList ASP.NET web control
RegularExpressionValidator ASP.NET validation control
relative positioning
rendering XHTML in a web browser
Request object in ASP.NET
RequiredFieldValidator ASP.NET validation control
runat ASP.NET attribute
script element in ASP.NET
SelectCommand property of a SqlDataSource
server
server control
session item
Session property of class Page
session tracking
SessionID property of class HttpSessionState
smart tag menu in Visual Web Developer
Source mode in Visual Web Developer
span XHTML element
SqlDataSource ASP.NET data control
System.Web.UI namespace
System.Web.UI.WebControls namespace
Target property of a HyperLink control
TextBox ASP.NET web control
tier in a multitier application
Timeout property of class HttpSessionState
Title property of a Page directive
Title property of a Web Form
title XHTML element
top tier
unique session ID of an ASP.NET client
Unload event of an ASP.NET page
UpdateCommand property of a SqlDataSource
validation control
ValidationExpression property of a RegularExpressionValidator control
validator
Value property of class HttpCookie
View In Browser command in Visual Web Developer
__VIEWSTATE hidden input
virtual directory
Visible property of an ASP.NET Web control
visual inheritance
web application development
web control

Web Form
Web Site Administration Tool
`Web.config` ASP.NET configuration file
`WebControl` class
WYSIWYG (What You See Is What You Get) editor
XHTML markup
XHTML tag
`XmlDataSource` ASP.NET data control

Self-Review Exercises

25.1 State whether each of the following is *true* or *false*. If *false*, explain why.
a) Web Form filenames end in `.aspx`.
b) `App.config` is a file that stores configuration settings for an ASP.NET web application.
c) A maximum of one validation control can be placed on a Web Form.
d) If no expiration date is set for a cookie, that cookie will be destroyed at the end of the browser session.
e) A `LoginStatus` control displays the current authenticated user name on a Web Form.
f) ASP.NET directives are delimited by `<%@` and `%>`.
g) An `AdRotator` control always displays all ads with equal frequency.
h) Each web control maps to exactly one corresponding XHTML element.
i) A `SqlDataSource` control allows a web application to interact with a database.

25.2 Fill in the blanks in each of the following statements:
a) Web applications contain three basic tiers: ________, ________, and ________.
b) A control which ensures that the data in another control is in the correct format is called a(n) ________.
c) A(n) ________ occurs when a page requests itself.
d) Every ASP.NET page inherits from class ________.
e) When a page loads, the ________ event occurs first, followed by the ________ event.
f) The ________ file contains the functionality for an ASP.NET page.
g) A(n) ________ control provides a registration form that site visitors can use to create a user account.
h) A(n) ________ defines common GUI elements that are inherited by each page in a set of ________.
i) In a multitier application, the ________ tier controls interactions between the application's clients and the application's data.

Answers to Self-Review Exercises

25.1 a) True. b) False. `Web.config` is the file that stores configuration settings for an ASP.NET web application. c) False. An unlimited number of validation controls can be placed on a Web Form. d) True. e) False. A `LoginName` control displays the current authenticated user name on a Web Form. A `LoginStatus` control displays a link to either log in or log out, depending on whether the user is currently authenticated. f) True. g) False. The frequency with which the `AdRotator` displays ads is specified in the `AdvertisementFile`. h) False. A web control can map to a group of XHTML elements—ASP.NET can generate complex XHTML markup from simple elements in an ASPX file. i) True.

25.2 a) bottom (information), middle (business logic), top (client). b) validator. c) postback. d) `Page`. e) `PreInit`, `Init`. f) code-behind. g) `CreateUserWizard`. h) master page, content pages. i) middle.

Exercises

25.3 *(`WebTime` Modification)* Modify the `WebTime` example to contain drop-down lists that allow the user to modify such `Label` properties as `BackColor`, `ForeColor` and `Font-Size`. Configure these drop-down lists so that a postback occurs whenever the user makes a selection. When the page reloads, it should reflect the specified changes to the properties of the `Label` displaying the time.

25.4 *(Page Hit Counter)* Create an ASP.NET page that uses a persistent cookie (i.e., a cookie with a distant expiration date) to keep track of how many times the client computer has visited the page. Set the `HttpCookie` object's `Expires` property to `DateTime.Now.AddMonths(1)` to cause the cookie to remain on the client's computer for one month. Display the number of page hits (i.e., the cookie's value) every time the page loads.

25.5 *(`WebControls` Modification)* Provide the following functionality for the example in Section 25.3.1: When users click **Register**, store their information in the `Users` table of the `Registration.mdf` database (provided in the chapter's examples directory). On postback, thank the user for providing the information.

25.6 *(Guestbook Application Modification)* Add validation to the guestbook application in Section 25.5. Use validation controls to ensure that the user provides a name, a valid e-mail address and a message.

25.7 Modify the `WebTime` example to asynchronously update the label every second. To do so, use the `UpdatePanel` and `Timer` ASP.NET Ajax controls. The `Timer` control refreshes the `UpdatePanel` each time its `Tick` even occurs. The `interval` property of the `Timer` control determines how often the `UpdatePanel` should be refreshed.

26

JavaServer™ Faces Web Applications

If any man will draw up his case, and put his name at the foot of the first page, I will give him an immediate reply. Where he compels me to turn over the sheet, he must wait my leisure.
—Lord Sandwich

Rule One: Our client is always right.
Rule Two: If you think our client is wrong, see Rule One.
—Anonymous

A fair question should be followed by a deed in silence.
—Dante Alighieri

You will come here and get books that will open your eyes, and your ears, and your curiosity, and turn you inside out or outside in.
—Ralph Waldo Emerson

OBJECTIVES

In this chapter you will learn:

- Web application development using Java Technologies and Netbeans.
- To create JavaServer Pages with JavaServer Faces components.
- To create web applications consisting of multiple pages.
- To validate user input on a web page.
- To maintain state information about a user with session tracking and cookies.

Outline

26.1 Introduction

In this chapter, we introduce web application development with Java-based technology. Web-based applications create web content for web browser clients. This web content includes Extensible HyperText Markup Language (XHTML), client-side scripting, images and binary data. If you are not familiar with XHTML, you should read Chapter 4 before studying this chapter. [*Note:* This chapter assumes that you know Java. To learn more about Java, check out *Java How to Program, Seventh Edition*, or visit our Java Resource Centers at `www.deitel.com/ResourceCenters.html`.]

This chapter begins with an overview of multitier application architecture and Java's web technologies for implementing multitier applications. We then present several examples that demonstrate web application development. The first example introduces you to Java web development. In the second example, we build a web application that simply shows the look-and-feel of several web application GUI components. Next, we demonstrate how to use validation components and custom validation methods to ensure that user input is valid before it is submitted for processing on the server. The chapter finishes with two examples of customizing a user's experience with session tracking.

In Chapter 27, we continue our discussion of Java web application development with more advanced concepts, including the AJAX-enabled components from Sun's Java BluePrints. AJAX helps web-based applications provide the interactivity and responsiveness that users typically expect of desktop applications.

Throughout this chapter and Chapter 27, we use the Netbeans 5.5.1 IDE, its Visual Web Pack and the Sun Java System Application Server (SJSAS). The Visual Web Pack helps you build web applications using Java technologies such as JavaServer Pages and JavaServer Faces. To implement the examples presented in this chapter, you must install all three software products. A bundle of Netbeans 5.5.1 and SJSAS is available at

```
www.netbeans.info/downloads/index.php?rs=22&p=3
```

The Visual Web Pack is available at

```
www.netbeans.org/products/visualweb/
```

26.2 Java Web Technologies

Java web technologies continually evolve to provide developers with higher levels of abstraction and greater separation of the application's tiers. This separation makes web applications more maintainable and extensible. It also allows for an effective division of labor. A graphic designer can build the application's user interface without concern for the underlying page logic, which will be handled by a programmer. Meanwhile, the programmer is free to focus on the application's business logic, leaving the details of building an attractive and easy-to-use application to the designer. Netbeans is the latest step in this evolution, allowing you to develop a web application's GUI in a drag-and-drop design tool, while handling the business logic in separate Java classes.

Java multitier applications are typically implemented using the features of Java Enterprise Edition (Java EE). The technologies we use to develop web applications in Chapters 26–27 are part of Java EE 5 (`java.sun.com/javaee`).

26.2.1 Servlets

Servlets are the lowest-level view of web development technologies in Java that we will discuss in this chapter. They use the HTTP request/response model of communication between client and server.

Servlets extend a server's functionality by allowing it to generate dynamic content. For instance, servlets can dynamically generate custom XHTML documents, help provide secure access to a website, interact with databases on behalf of a client and maintain unique session information for each client. A web server component called the servlet container executes and interacts with servlets. Packages `javax.servlet` and `javax.servlet.http` provide the classes and interfaces to define servlets. The servlet container receives HTTP requests from a client and directs each request to the appropriate servlet. The servlet processes the request and returns an appropriate response to the client—usually in the form of an XHTML or XML (Extensible Markup Language) document to display in the browser. XML is a language used to exchange structured data on the web.

Architecturally, all servlets must implement the `Servlet` interface of package `javax.servlet`, which ensures that each servlet can execute in the framework provided by the servlet container. Interface `Servlet` declares methods used by the servlet container to manage the servlet's life cycle. A servlet's life cycle begins when the servlet container loads it into memory—usually in response to the first request for the servlet. Before the servlet can handle that request, the container invokes the servlet's `init` method, which is called only once during a servlet's life cycle to initialize the servlet. After `init` completes execution, the servlet is ready to respond to its first request. All requests are handled by a servlet's service method, which is the key method in defining a servlet's functionality. The service method receives the request, processes it and sends a response to the client. During a servlet's life cycle, service is called once per request. Each new request is typically handled in a separate thread of execution (managed by the servlet container), so each servlet must be thread safe. When the servlet container terminates the servlet (e.g. when the servlet container needs more memory or when it is shut down), the servlet's destroy method is called to release any resources held by the servlet.

26.2.2 JavaServer Pages

JavaServer Pages (JSP) technology is an extension of servlet technology. Each JSP is translated by the JSP container into a servlet. Unlike servlets, JSPs help you separate presentation from content. JavaServer Pages enable web application programmers to create dynamic content by reusing predefined components and by interacting with components using server-side scripting. JSP programmers can use special software components called JavaBeans and custom tag libraries that encapsulate complex, dynamic functionality. A JavaBean is a reusable component that follows certain conventions for class design. For example, JavaBeans classes that allow reading and writing of instance variables must provide appropriate *get* and *set* methods. The complete set of class design conventions is discussed in the JavaBeans specification (java.sun.com/products/javabeans/glasgow/index.html).

Custom Tag Libraries

Custom tag libraries are a powerful feature of JSP that allows Java developers to hide code for database access and other complex operations in custom tags. To use such capabilities, you simply add the custom tags to the page. This simplicity enables web-page designers who are not familiar with Java to enhance web pages with powerful dynamic content and dynamic processing capabilities. The JSP classes and interfaces are located in the packages javax.servlet.jsp and javax.servlet.jsp.tagext.

JSP Components

There are four key components to JSPs—directives, actions, scripting elements and tag libraries. Directives are messages to the JSP container—the web server component that executes JSPs. Directives enable you to specify page settings, to include content from other resources and to specify custom tag libraries for use in JSPs. Actions encapsulate functionality in predefined tags that programmers can embed in JSPs. Actions often are performed based on the information sent to the server as part of a particular client request. They also can create Java objects for use in JSPs. Scripting elements enable you to insert Java code that interacts with components in a JSP (and possibly other web application components) to perform request processing. Tag libraries are part of the tag extension mechanism that enables programmers to create custom tags. Such tags enable web-page designers to manipulate JSP content without prior Java knowledge. The JavaServer Pages Standard Tag Library (JSTL) provides the functionality for many common web application tasks, such as iterating over a collection of objects and executing SQL statements.

Static Content

JSPs can contain other static content. For example, JSPs normally include XHTML or XML markup. Such markup is known as fixed-template data or fixed-template text. Any literal text or XHTML markup in a JSP is translated to a `String` literal in the servlet representation of the JSP.

Processing a JSP Request

When a JSP-enabled server receives the first request for a JSP, the JSP container translates the JSP into a servlet that handles the current request and future requests to the JSP. JSPs thus rely on the same request/response mechanism as servlets to process requests from and send responses to clients.

Performance Tip 26.1

Some JSP containers translate JSPs into servlets at the JSP's deployment time (i.e., when the application is placed on a web server). This eliminates the translation overhead for the first client that requests each JSP, as the JSP will be translated before it is ever requested by a client.

26.2.3 JavaServer Faces

JavaServer Faces (JSF) is a web application framework (similar to ASP.NET) that simplifies the design of an application's user interface and further separates a web application's presentation from its business logic. A framework simplifies application development by providing libraries and sometimes software tools to help you organize and build your applications. Though the JSF framework can use many technologies to define the pages in web applications, this chapter focuses on JSF applications that use JavaServer Pages. JSF provides a set of user interface components, or JSF components, that simplify web-page design. These components are similar to the Swing components used to build GUI applications. JSF provides two JSP custom tag libraries for adding these components to a JSP page. JSF also includes APIs for handling component events (such as processing component state changes and validating user input), navigating between web application pages and more. You design the look-and-feel of a page with JSF by adding tags to a JSP file and manipulating their attributes. You define the page's behavior separately in a related Java source-code file.

Though the standard JSF components are sufficient for most basic web applications, you can also write custom component libraries. Additional component libraries are available through the Java BluePrints project—which shows best practices for developing Java applications. Many other vendors provide JSF component libraries. For example, Oracle provides almost 100 components in its ADF Faces library. In the next chapter, we discuss one such component library, the BluePrints AJAX components library, which can be found at `blueprints.dev.java.net/ajaxcomponents.html`.

26.2.4 Web Technologies in Netbeans

Netbeans web applications consist of one or more JSP web pages built in the JavaServer Faces framework. These JSP files have the filename extension `.jsp` and contain the web pages' GUI elements. The JSPs can also contain JavaScript to add functionality to the page. JSPs can be customized in Netbeans by adding JSF components, including labels, text fields, images, buttons and other GUI components. The IDE allows you to design pages visually by dragging and dropping these components onto a page; you can also customize a web page by editing the `.jsp` file manually.

Every JSP file created in Netbeans represents a web page and has a corresponding JavaBean class called the page bean. A JavaBean class must have a default (or no-argument) constructor, and *get* and *set* methods for all of the bean's properties (i.e., instance variables). The page bean defines properties for each of the page's elements. The page bean also contains event handlers and page life-cycle methods for managing tasks such as page initialization and rendering, and other supporting code for the web application.

Every Netbeans web application has three other JavaBeans. The `RequestBean` object is maintained in request scope—this object exists only for an HTTP request's duration. A `SessionBean` object has session scope—the object exists throughout a user's browsing session or until the session times out. There is a unique `SessionBean` object for each user. Finally, the `ApplicationBean` object has application scope—this object is shared by all instances of an application and exists as long as the application remains deployed on a web server. This object is used for application-wide data storage or processing; only one instance exists for the application, regardless of the number of open sessions.

26.3 Creating and Running a Simple Application in Netbeans

Our first example displays the web server's time of day in a browser window. When run, this program displays the text `"Current Time on the Web Server"`, followed by the web server's time. The application contains a single web page and, as mentioned previously, consists of two related files—a JSP file (Fig. 26.1) and a supporting page bean file (Fig. 26.3). The application also has the three scoped data beans for request, session, and application scopes. Since this application does not store data, these beans are not used in this example. We first discuss the markup in the JSP file, the code in the page bean file and the application output, then we provide step-by-step instructions for creating the program. [*Note:* The markup in Fig. 26.1 and other JSP file listings in this chapter is the same as the markup that appears in Netbeans, but we have reformatted these listings for presentation purposes to make the code more readable.]

```
<?xml version = "1.0" encoding = "UTF-8"?>

<!-- Fig. 26.1: Time.jsp -->
<!-- JSP file generated by Netbeans that displays -->
<!-- the current time on the web server -->
<jsp:root version = "1.2"
   xmlns:f = "http://java.sun.com/jsf/core"
   xmlns:h = "http://java.sun.com/jsf/html"
   xmlns:jsp = "http://java.sun.com/JSP/Page"
   xmlns:webuijsf = "http://www.sun.com/webui/webuijsf">
   <jsp:directive.page contentType = "text/html;charset=UTF-8"
      pageEncoding = "UTF-8" />
   <f:view>
      <webuijsf:page binding = "#{Time.page1}" id = "page1">
         <webuijsf:html binding = "#{Time.html1}" id = "html1">
```

Fig. 26.1 | JSP file generated by Netbeans that displays the current time on the web server. (Part 1 of 2.)

```
16            <webuijsf:head binding = "#{Time.head1}" id = "head1"
17               title = "Web Time: A Simple Example">
18               <webuijsf:link binding = "#{Time.link1}" id = "link1"
19                  url = "/resources/stylesheet.css"/>
20               <webuijsf:meta content = "60" httpEquiv = "refresh" />
21            </webuijsf:head>
22            <webuijsf:body binding = "#{Time.body1}" id = "body1"
23               style = "-rave-layout: grid">
24               <webuijsf:form binding = "#{Time.form1}" id = "form1">
25                  <webuijsf:staticText binding = "#{Time.timeHeader}"
26                     id = "timeHeader" style = "font-size: 18px;
27                        left: 24px; top: 24px; position: absolute"
28                     text = "Current time on the web server:" />
29                  <webuijsf:staticText binding = "#{Time.clockText}"
30                     id = "clockText" style = "background-color: black;
31                        color: yellow; font-size: 18px; left: 24px;
32                        top: 48px; position: absolute" />
33               </webuijsf:form>
34            </webuijsf:body>
35         </webuijsf:html>
36      </webuijsf:page>
37   </f:view>
38 </jsp:root>
```

Fig. 26.1 | JSP file generated by Netbeans that displays the current time on the web server. (Part 2 of 2.)

Netbeans generates all the markup shown in Fig. 26.1 when you set the web page's title, drag two **Static Text** components onto the page and set the properties of the **Static Text** components. **Static Text** components display text that cannot be edited by the user. We show these steps shortly.

26.3.1 Examining a JSP File

The JSP files used in this and the following examples are generated almost entirely by Netbeans, which provides a Visual Editor that allows you to build a page's GUI by dragging and dropping components onto a design area. The IDE generates a JSP file in response to your interactions. Line 1 of Fig. 26.1 is the XML declaration, indicating the fact that the JSP is expressed in XML syntax and the version of XML that is used. Lines 3–5 are comments that we added to the JSP to indicate its figure number, filename and purpose.

Line 6 begins the JSP's root element. All JSPs must have this **`jsp:root`** element, which has a `version` attribute to indicate the JSP version being used (line 6) and one or more `xmlns` attributes (lines 7–10). Each **`xmlns` attribute** specifies a prefix and a URL for a tag library, allowing the page to use tags from that library. For example, line 9 allows the page to use the standard JSP elements. To use these elements, each element's tag must be preceded by the `jsp` prefix. All JSPs generated by Netbeans include the tag libraries specified in lines 7–10 (the JSF core components library, the JSF HTML components library, the JSP standard components library and the JSF user interface components library).

Lines 11–12 are the **`jsp:directive.page`** element. Its `contentType` attribute specifies the MIME type (`text/html`) and the character set (`UTF-8`) the page uses. The `page-`

Encoding attribute specifies the character encoding used by the page source. These attributes help the client (typically a web browser) determine how to render the content.

All pages containing JSF components are represented in a component tree (Fig. 26.2) with the root JSF element `f:view`, which is of type `UIViewRoot`. This component tree structure is represented in a JSP by enclosing all JSF component tags inside the `f:view` element (lines 13–37).

Lines 14–21 begin the JSP's definition with the `webuijsf:page`, `webuijsf:html` and `webuijsf::head` tags, all from the `webuijsf` (JSF user interface components) tag library. These and many other `webuijsf` page elements have a `binding` attribute. For example, the `webuijsf:head` element (line 16) has the attribute `binding = "#{Time.head1}."` This attribute uses JSF Expression Language notation (i.e., `#{Time.head1}`) to reference the `head1` property in the `Time` class that represents the page bean (you'll see this class in Fig. 26.3). You can bind an attribute of a JSP element to a property in any of the web application's JavaBeans. For instance, the `text` attribute of a `webuijsf:label` component can be bound to a `String` property in the application's `SessionBean` (shown in Section 26.5.2).

The `webuijsf:head` element (lines 16–21) has a `title` attribute that specifies the page's title. This element also contains a `webuijsf:link` element (lines 18–19) that specifies the CSS stylesheet used by the page, and a `webuijsf:meta` element (line 20) that specifies the page's refresh rate. The `webuijsf:body` element (lines 22–34) contains a `webuijsf:form` element (lines 24–33), which contains two `webuijsf:staticText` components (lines 25–28 and 29–32) that display the page's text. The `timeHeader` component (lines 25–28) has a `text` attribute (line 28) that specifies the text to display (i.e., `"Current time on the web server"`). The `clockText` component (lines 29–32) does not specify a `text` attribute because this component's text will be set programmatically.

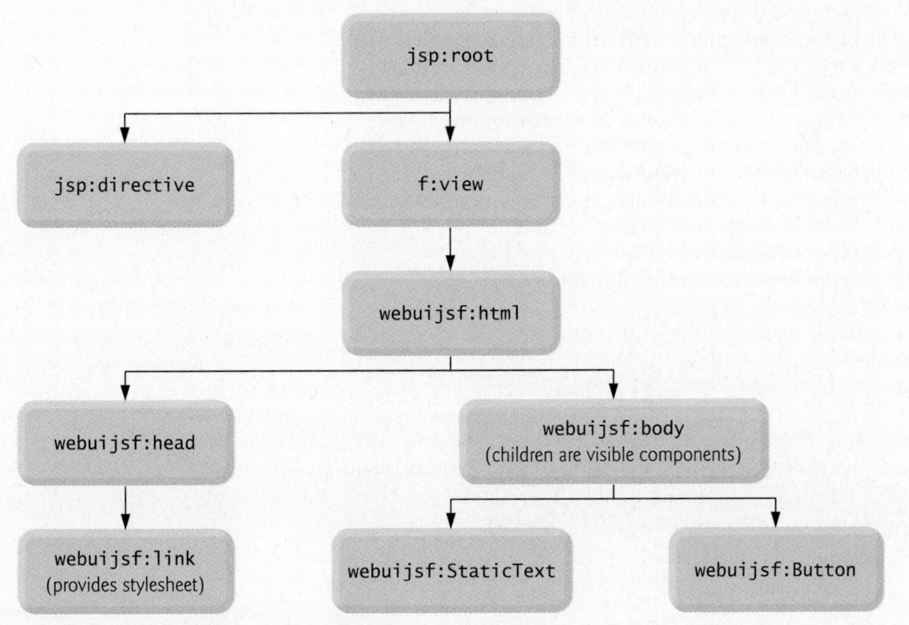

Fig. 26.2 | Sample JSF component tree.

For the markup in this file to be displayed in a browser, all the JSP's elements are automatically mapped to XHTML elements that the browser recognizes. The same web component can map to different XHTML elements, depending on the client browser and the component's property settings. In this example, the `webuijsf:staticText` components (lines 25–28, 29–32) map to XHTML **span** elements. A `span` element contains text that is displayed on a web page and is typically used to control the formatting of the text. The `style` attributes of a JSP's `webuijsf:staticText` element will be represented as part of the corresponding `span` element's `style` attribute when the browser renders the page. We show momentarily the XHTML document that results when `Time.jsp` is requested by a browser.

26.3.2 Examining a Page Bean File

Figure 26.3 presents the page bean file. Line 3 indicates that this class belongs to package `webtime`. This line is autogenerated and specifies the project's name as the package name. Line 18 begins class `Time`'s declaration and indicates that it inherits from class **`AbstractPageBean`** (from package **`com.sun.rave.web.ui.appbase`**). All page bean classes that support JSP files with JSF components must inherit from the abstract class `AbstractPageBean`, which provides page life-cycle methods. Note that the IDE makes the class name match the page name. Package **`com.sun.webui.jsf.component`** includes classes for many of the basic JSF components (see the `import` statements at lines 6–13).

```
1  // Fig. 26.3: Time.java
2  // Page bean file that sets clockText to the time on the Web server.
3  package webtime;
4
5  import com.sun.rave.web.ui.appbase.AbstractPageBean;
6  import com.sun.webui.jsf.component.Body;
7  import com.sun.webui.jsf.component.Form;
8  import com.sun.webui.jsf.component.Head;
9  import com.sun.webui.jsf.component.Html;
10 import com.sun.webui.jsf.component.Link;
11 import com.sun.webui.jsf.component.Meta;
12 import com.sun.webui.jsf.component.Page;
13 import com.sun.webui.jsf.component.StaticText;
14 import java.text.DateFormat;
15 import java.util.Date;
16 import javax.faces.FacesException;
17
18 public class Time extends AbstractPageBean
19 {
20    private int __placeholder;
21
22    // auto-generated component initialization method.
23    private void _init() throws Exception
24    {
25    } // end method _init
26
27    private Page page1 = new Page();
28
```

Fig. 26.3 | Page bean file that sets `clockText` to the time on the web server. (Part 1 of 5.)

```
   public Page getPage1()
   {
      return page1;
   } // end method getPage1

   public void setPage1( Page p )
   {
      this.page1 = p;
   } // end method setPage1

   private Html html1 = new Html();

   public Html getHtml1()
   {
      return html1;
   } // end method getHtml1

   public void setHtml1( Html h )
   {
      this.html1 = h;
   } // end method setHtml1

   private Head head1 = new Head();

   public Head getHead1()
   {
      return head1;
   } // end method getHead1

   public void setHead1( Head h )
   {
      this.head1 = h;
   } // end method setHead1

   private Link link1 = new Link();

   public Link getLink1()
   {
      return link1;
   } // end method getLink1

   public void setLink1( Link l )
   {
      this.link1 = l;
   } // end method setLink1

   private Body body1 = new Body();

   public Body getBody1()
   {
      return body1;
   } // end method getBody1

```

Fig. 26.3 | Page bean file that sets `clockText` to the time on the web server. (Part 2 of 5.)

```
   public void setBody1( Body b )
   {
      this.body1 = b;
   } // end method setBody1

   private Form form1 = new Form();

   public Form getForm1()
   {
      return form1;
   } // end method getForm1

   public void setForm1( Form f )
   {
      this.form1 = f;
   } // end method setForm1

   private StaticText timeHeader = new StaticText();

   public StaticText getTimeHeader()
   {
      return timeHeader;
   } // end method getTimeHeader

   public void setTimeHeader( StaticText st )
   {
      this.timeHeader = st;
   } // end method setTimeHeader

   private StaticText clockText = new StaticText();

   public StaticText getClockText()
   {
      return clockText;
   } // end method getClockText

   public void setClockText( StaticText st )
   {
      this.clockText = st;
   } // end method setClockText

   private Meta meta1 = new Meta();

   public Meta getMeta1()
   {
      return meta1;
   } // end method getMeta1

   public void setMeta1( Meta m )
   {
      this.meta1 = m;
   } // end method setMeta1

```

Fig. 26.3 | Page bean file that sets `clockText` to the time on the web server. (Part 3 of 5.)

```
   public Time()
   {
   } // end Time constructor

   // initializes page content
   public void init()
   {
      super.init();

      try
      {
         _init();
      } // end try
      catch ( Exception e )
      {
         log( "Time Initialization Failure", e );
         throw e instanceof FacesException ? ( FacesException ) e :
            new FacesException( e );
      } // end catch
   } // end method init

   // method called when postback occurs
   public void preprocess()
   {
   } // end method preprocess

   // method called before the page is rendered
   public void prerender()
   {
      clockText.setValue( DateFormat.getTimeInstance(
         DateFormat.LONG ).format( new Date() ) );
   } // end method prerender

   // method called after rendering completes, if init was called
   public void destroy()
   {
   } // end method destroy

   // return a reference to the scoped data bean
   protected SessionBean1 getSessionBean1()
   {
      return ( SessionBean1 ) getBean( "SessionBean1" );
   } // end method getSessionBean1

   // return a reference to the scoped data bean
   protected ApplicationBean1 getApplicationBean1()
   {
      return ( ApplicationBean1 ) getBean( "ApplicationBean1" );
   } // end method getApplicationBean1

   // return a reference to the scoped data bean
   protected RequestBean1 getRequestBean1()
   {
```

Fig. 26.3 | Page bean file that sets `clockText` to the time on the web server. (Part 4 of 5.)

```
188         return ( RequestBean1 ) getBean( "RequestBean1" );
189     } // end method getRequestBean1
190 } // end class Time
```

Fig. 26.3 | Page bean file that sets `clockText` to the time on the web server. (Part 5 of 5.)

This page bean file provides *get* and *set* methods for every element of the JSP file of Fig. 26.1. These methods are generated automatically by the IDE. We included the complete page bean file in this first example, but in future examples these properties and their *get* and *set* methods will be omitted to save space. Lines 99–109 and 111–121 of the page bean file define the two **Static Text** components that we dropped onto the page and their *get* and *set* methods. These components are objects of class `StaticText` in package `com.sun.webui.jsf.component`.

The only logic required in this page is to set the `clockText` component's text to read the current time on the server. We do this in the `prerender` method (lines 162–166). The meaning of this and other page bean methods will be discussed shortly. Lines 164–165 fetch and format the time on the server and set the value of `clockText` to that time.

26.3.3 Event-Processing Life Cycle

Netbeans's application model places several methods in the page bean that tie into the JSF event-processing life cycle. These methods represent four major stages—initialization, preprocessing, prerendering and destruction. Each corresponds to a method in the page bean class—`init`, `preprocess`, `prerender` and `destroy`, respectively. Netbeans automatically creates these methods, but you can customize them to handle life-cycle processing tasks, such as rendering an element on a page only if a user clicks a button.

The `init` method (Fig. 26.3, lines 140–154) is called by the JSP container the first time the page is requested and on postbacks. A postback occurs when form data is submitted, and the page and its contents are sent to the server to be processed. Method `init` invokes its superclass version (line 142) then tries to call the method `_init` (declared in lines 23–25). The `_init` method is also automatically generated and handles component initialization tasks (if there are any), such as setting the options for a group of radio buttons.

The `preprocess` method (lines 157–159) is called after `init`, but only if the page is processing a postback. The `prerender` method (lines 162–166) is called just before a page is rendered (i.e., displayed) by the browser. This method should be used to set component properties; properties that are set sooner (such as in method `init`) may be overwritten before the page is actually rendered by the browser. For this reason, we set the value of `clockText` in the `prerender` method.

Finally, the **destroy method** (lines 169–171) is called after the page has been rendered, but only if the `init` method was called. This method handles tasks such as freeing resources used to render the page.

26.3.4 Relationship Between the JSP and Page Bean Files

The page bean has a property for every element that appears in the JSP file of Fig. 26.1, from the `html` element to the two `Static Text` components. Recall that the elements in the JSP file were explicitly bound to these properties by each element's `binding` attribute using a JSF Expression Language statement. Because this is a JavaBean class, *get* and *set* methods for each of these properties are also included (lines 27–133). This code is automatically generated by the IDE for every web application project.

26.3.5 Examining the XHTML Generated by a Java Web Application

Figure 26.4 shows the XHTML generated when `Time.jsp` (Fig. 26.1) is requested by a client web browser. To view this XHTML, select **View > Source** in Internet Explorer or **View > Page Source** in Firefox. [*Note:* We reformatted the XHTML to conform to our coding conventions.]

```
<!DOCTYPE html PUBLIC "-//W3C//DTD XHTML 1.0 Transitional//EN"
   "http://www.w3.org/TR/xhtml1/DTD/xhtml1-transitional.dtd">
<html xmlns = "http://www.w3.org/1999/xhtml"
   xmlns:wairole = "http://www.w3.org/2005/01/wai-rdf/GUIRoleTaxonomy#"
   xmlns:waistate = "http://www.w3.org/2005/07/aaa">
   <head>
      <meta content = "no-cache" http-equiv = "Pragma" />
      <meta content = "no-cache" http-equiv = "Cache-Control" />
      <meta content = "no-store" http-equiv = "Cache-Control" />
      <meta content = "max-age=0" http-equiv = "Cache-Control" />
      <meta content = "1" http-equiv = "Expires" />
      <title>Web Time: A Simple Example</title>
      <link rel = "stylesheet" type = "text/css" href = "/WebTime/theme/
         com/sun/webui/jsf/suntheme/css/css_master.css" />
      <link rel = "stylesheet" type = "text/css" href = "/WebTime/theme/
         com/sun/webui/jsf/suntheme/css/ie7.css" />
      <script type = "text/javascript">
         djConfig = {
            "isDebug": false,
            "parseWidgets": false,
            "debugAtAllCosts": false
         };
      </script>
      <script type = "text/javascript"
         src = "/WebTime/theme/META-INF/dojo/dojo.js"></script>
      <script type = "text/javascript"
         src = "/WebTime/theme/META-INF/json/json.js"></script>
      <script type = "text/javascript"
         src = "/WebTime/theme/META-INF/prototype/prototype.js"></script>
      <script type = "text/javascript"
         src = "/WebTime/theme/META-INF/com_sun_faces_ajax.js"></script>
```

Fig. 26.4 | XHTML response generated when the browser requests `Time.jsp`. (Part 1 of 2.)

```
32          <script type = "text/javascript">
33             dojo.hostenv.setModulePrefix( "webui.suntheme",
34                "/WebTime/theme/com/sun/webui/jsf/suntheme/javascript" );
35             dojo.require( 'webui.suntheme.*' );
36          </script>
37          <link id = "link1" rel = "stylesheet" type = "text/css"
38             href = "/WebTime/resources/stylesheet.css" />
39          <meta id = "j_id_id7" http-equiv = "refresh" content = "60" />
40       </head>
41       <body id = "body1" style = "-rave-layout:grid" onload="" onunload="">
42          <form id = "form1" class = "form" method = "post"
43             action = "/WebTime/faces/Time.jsp"
44             enctype = "application/x-www-form-urlencoded">
45          <span id = "form1:timeHeader" style = "font-size: 18px; left: 24px;
46             top: 24px; position: absolute">Current time on the web server:
47          </span>
48          <span id = "form1:clockText" style = "background-color: black;
49             color: yellow; font-size: 18px; left: 24px; top: 48px;
50             position: absolute">12:30:49 PM EDT</span>
51          <input id = "form1_hidden" name = "form1_hidden"
52             value = "form1_hidden" type = "hidden" />
53          <input type = "hidden" name = "javax.faces.ViewState"
54             id = "javax.faces.ViewState" value = "j_id173:j_id174" />
55          </form>
56          <script type = "text/javascript">
57             webui.suntheme.common.body = new webui.suntheme.body(
58                '/Time.jsp', '/WebTime/faces/Time.jsp', null, null,
59                'com_sun_webui_util_FocusManager_focusElementId');</script>
60       </body>
61    </html>
```

Fig. 26.4 | XHTML response generated when the browser requests `Time.jsp`. (Part 2 of 2.)

The XHTML document in Fig. 26.4 is similar in structure to the JSP file of Fig. 26.1. Lines 1–2 are the document type declaration, which declares this document to be an `XHTML 1.0 Transitional` document. The XHTML `meta` tags in lines 7–11 are equivalent to HTTP headers and are used to control browser behavior.

Lines 41–60 define the `body` of the document. Lines 42–55 define an XHTML `form`. In this particular program, the user does not submit data to the web server for processing. We demonstrate how to submit data to the server in later examples. Attribute `method` of the `form` element (line 42) specifies the method by which the web browser submits the form to the server. By default, JSPs use the `post` method. The `form`'s `action` attribute (line 43) identifies the resource that will be requested when this form is submitted—in this case, `/WebTime/faces/Time.jsp`.

Note that the two **Static Text** components (i.e., `timeHeader` and `clockText`) are represented by two `span` elements in the XHTML document (lines 45–47, 48–50) as previously discussed. The formatting options that were specified as properties of `timeHeader` and `clockText`, such as the font size and text color in the components, are now specified in each `span` element's `style` attribute.

26.3.6 Building a Web Application in Netbeans

Now that we have presented the JSP file, the page bean file and the resulting XHTML web page sent to the web browser, we discuss the steps to create this application. To build the `WebTime` application, perform the following steps in Netbeans:

Step 1: Creating the Web Application Project
Select **File > New Project...** to display the **New Project** dialog. In this dialog, select **Web** in the **Categories** pane, **Visual Web Application** in the **Projects** pane and click **Next**. Change the project name to `WebTime`. In the **Project Location** field, specify where you'd like to store the project. These settings will create a `WebTime` directory to store the project's files in the parent directory you specified. Keep the other default settings and click **Finish** to create the web application project.

Step 2: Examining the Visual Editor Window of the New Project
The next several figures describe important features of the IDE, beginning with the Visual Editor window (Fig. 26.5). Netbeans creates a single web page named `Page1` when a new project is created. This page is open by default in the Visual Editor in **Design mode** when the project first loads. As you drag and drop new components onto the page, **Design** mode allows you to see how your page will be rendered in the browser. The JSP file for this page, named `Page1.jsp`, can be viewed by clicking the **JSP** button at the top of the visual editor or by right clicking anywhere in the Visual Editor and selecting **Edit JSP Source**. As mentioned previously, each web page is supported by a page bean file. Netbeans creates a file named `Page1.java` when a new project is created. To open this file, click the **Java** button at the top of the Visual Editor or right click anywhere in the Visual Editor and select **Edit Java Source**.

The **Preview in Browser** button at the top of the Visual Editor window allows you to view your pages in a browser without having to build and run the application. The **Refresh** button redraws the page in the Visual Editor. The **Show Virtual Forms** button allows you to see which form elements are participating in virtual forms (we discuss this concept in Chapter 27). The **Target Browser Size** drop-down list lets you specify the optimal browser

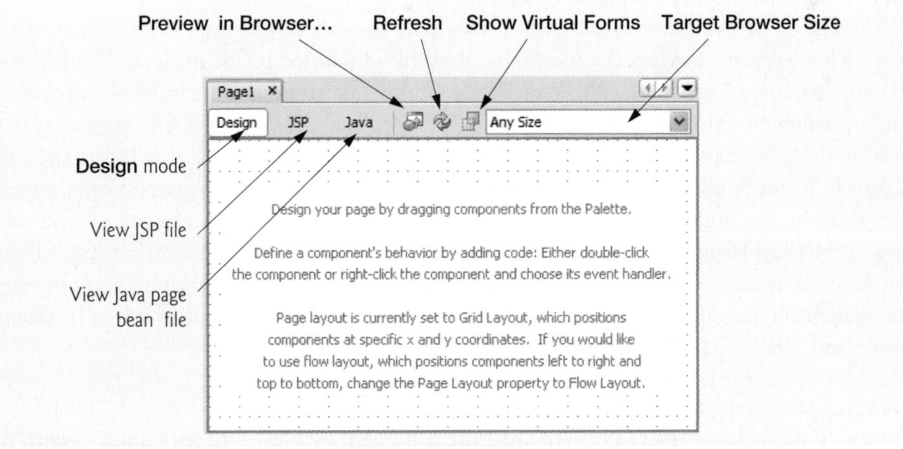

Fig. 26.5 | Visual Editor window in **Design** mode.

resolution for viewing the page and lets you see what the page will look like in different screen resolutions.

Step 3: Examining the **Palette** *in Netbeans*

Figure 26.6 shows the **Palette** displayed in the IDE when the project loads. Part (a) displays the beginning of the **Basic** list of web components, and part (b) displays the remaining **Basic** components, as well as the list of **Layout** components. We discuss specific components in Fig. 26.6 as they are used throughout the chapter.

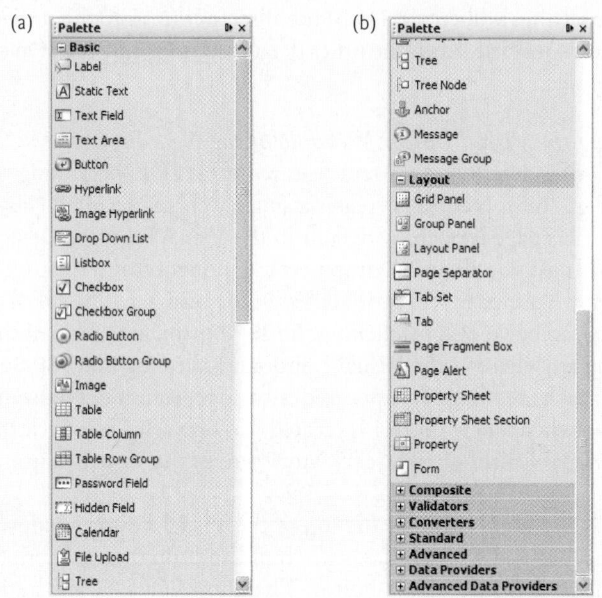

Fig. 26.6 | **Palette** in Netbeans.

Step 4: Examining the **Projects** *Window*

Figure 26.7 displays the **Projects** window, which appears in the upper-left corner of the IDE. This window displays the hierarchy of all files included in the project. The JSP files for each page are listed under the **Web Pages** node. This node also includes the **resources** folder, which contains the CSS stylesheet for the project and any other files the pages may need to display properly, such as image files. All of the Java source code, including the page bean file for each web page and the application, session and request scope beans, can be found under the **Source Packages** node. Another useful file displayed in the project window is the **Page Navigation** file, which defines rules for navigating the project's pages based on the outcome of some user-initiated event, such as clicking a button or a link. The **Page Navigation** file can also be accessed by right clicking in the Visual Editor while in **Design** mode and selecting **Page Navigation**.

Step 5: Examining the JSP and Java Files in the IDE

Figure 26.8 displays `Page1.jsp`—the JSP file generated by Netbeans for `Page1`. [*Note:* We reformatted the code to match our coding conventions.] Click the **JSP** button at the top

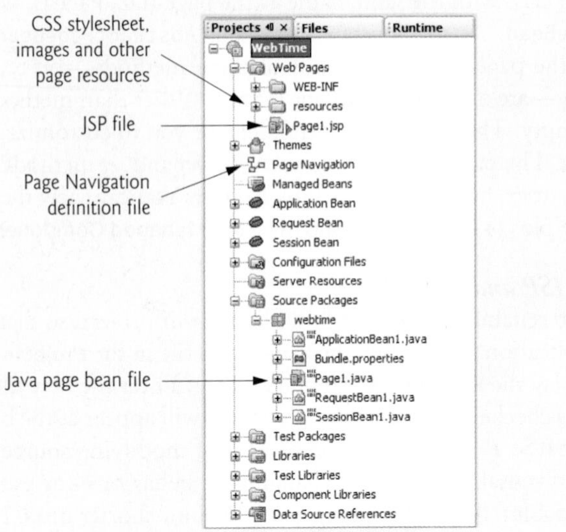

Fig. 26.7 | **Projects** window for the `WebTime` project.

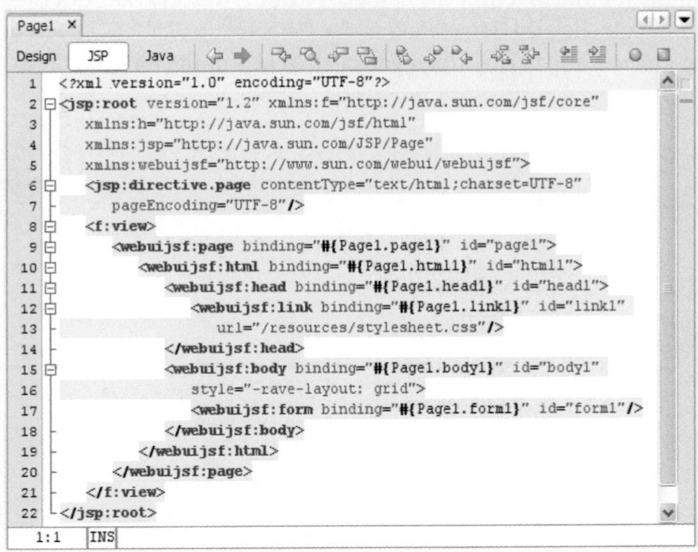

Fig. 26.8 | JSP file generated for Page1 by Netbeans.

of the Visual Editor to open the JSP file. When it is first created, this file contains some tags for setting up the page, including linking to the page's style sheet and defining the necessary JSF libraries. Otherwise, the JSP file's tags are empty, as no components have been added to the page yet.

Figure 26.9 displays part of `Page1.java`—the page bean file generated by Netbeans for `Page1`. Click the **Java** button at the top of the Visual Editor to open the page bean file.

This file contains a Java class with the same name as the page (i.e., `Page1`), which extends the class `AbstractPageBean`. As previously mentioned, `AbstractPageBean` has several methods that manage the page's life cycle. Four of these methods—`init`, `preprocess`, `prerender` and `destroy`—are overridden by `Page1.java`. Other than method `init`, these methods are initially empty. They serve as placeholders for you to customize the behavior of your web application. The page bean file also includes *get* and *set* methods for all of the page's elements—`page`, `html`, `head`, `body` and `link` to start. You can view these *get* and *set* methods by clicking the plus (+) sign on the line that says **Managed Component Definition**.

Step 6: Renaming the JSP and JSF Files

Typically, you'll want to rename the JSP and Java files in your project, so that their names are relevant to your application. Right click the `Page1.jsp` file in the **Projects Window** and select **Rename...** to display the **Rename Class Page1** dialog. Enter the new filename `Time`. If **Preview All Changes** is checked, the **Refactoring Window** will appear at the bottom of the IDE when you click **Next >**. Refactoring is the process of modifying source code to improve its readability and reusability without changing its behavior—for example, by renaming methods or variables, or breaking long methods into shorter ones. Netbeans has built-in refactoring tools that automate some refactoring tasks. Using these tools to rename the project files updates the name of both the JSP file and the page bean file. The refactoring tool also changes the class name in the page bean file and all of the attribute bindings in the JSP file to reflect the new class name. Note that none of these changes will be made until you click **Do Refactoring** in the **Refactoring Window**. If you do not preview the changes, refactoring occurs when you click **Next >** in the **Rename Class Page1** dialog.

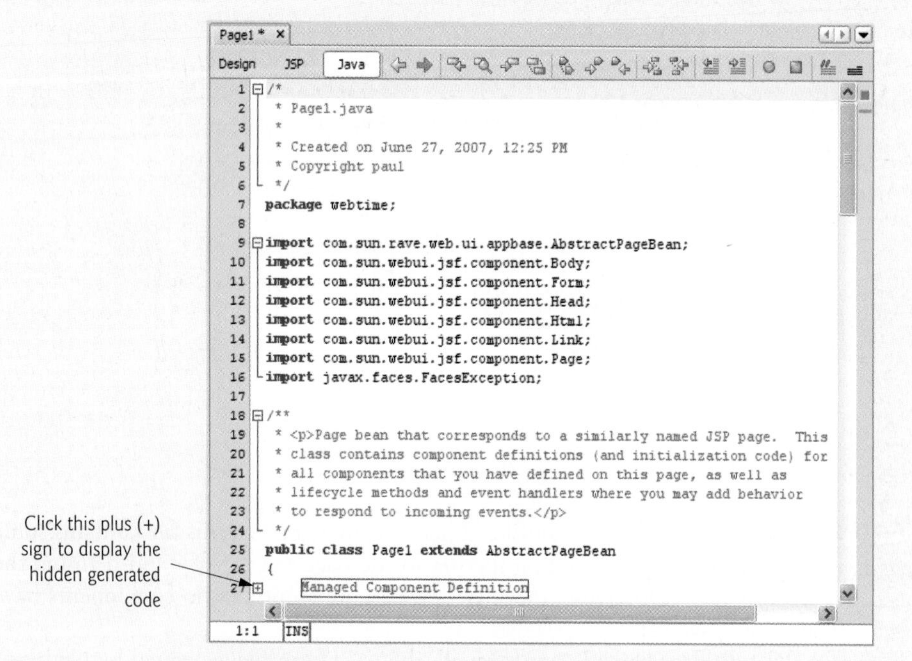

Fig. 26.9 | Page bean file for `Page1.jsp` generated by Netbeans.

Step 7: Changing the Title of the Page

Before designing the content of the web page, we give it the title `"Web Time: A Simple Example"`. By default, the page does not have a title when it is generated by the IDE. To add a title, open the JSP file in **Design** mode. In the **Properties** window, enter the new title next to the **Title** property and press *Enter*. View the JSP to see that the attribute `title = "Web Time: A Simple Example"` was automatically added to the `webuijsf:head` tag.

Step 8: Designing the Page

Designing a web page is simple in Netbeans. To add components to the page, you can drag and drop them from the **Palette** onto the page in **Design** mode. Like the web page itself, each component is an object that has properties, methods and events. You can set these properties and events visually using the **Properties** window or programmatically in the page bean file. *Get* and *set* methods are automatically added to the page bean file for each component you add to the page.

The IDE generates the JSP tags for the components you drag and drop using a grid layout, as specified in the `webuijsf:body` tag. The components are rendered using absolute positioning—they appear exactly where they are dropped on the page. As you add components, the `style` attribute in each component's JSP element will include the number of pixels from the top and left margins of the page at which the component is positioned.

This example uses two **Static Text** components. To add the first one to the page, drag and drop it from the **Palette**'s **Basic** components list to the page in **Design** mode. Edit the component's text by typing `"Current time on the web server:"` directly into the component. The text can also be edited by changing the component's `text` property in the **Properties** window. Netbeans is a WYSIWYG (What You See Is What You Get) editor—whenever you make a change to a web page in **Design** mode, the IDE creates the markup (visible in **JSP** mode) necessary to achieve the desired visual effects seen in **Design** mode. After adding the text to the web page, switch to **JSP** mode. You should see that the IDE added a `webuijsf:staticText` element to the page body, which is bound to the object `staticText1`, in the page bean file and whose `text` attribute matches the text you just entered. Back in **Design** mode, click the **Static Text** component to select it. In the **Properties** window, click the ellipsis button next to the `style` property to open a dialog box to edit the text's style. Select `18 px` for the font size and click **OK**. Again in the **Properties** window, change the `id` property to `timeHeader`. Setting the `id` property also changes the name of the component's corresponding property in the page bean and updates its `binding` attribute in the JSP accordingly. Notice that `font-size: 18 px` has been added to the `style` attribute and the `id` attribute has been changed to `timeHeader` in the component's tag in the JSP file. The IDE should now appear as in Fig. 26.10.

Drop a second **Static Text** component onto the page and set its `id` to `clockText`. Edit its `style` property so that the font size is `18 px`, the text color is `yellow`, and the background color is `black`. Do not edit the component's text, as this will be set programmatically in the page bean file. The component will display with the text ***Static Text*** in the IDE, but will not display any text at runtime unless the text is set programmatically. Figure 26.11 shows the IDE after the second component is added.

Step 9: Adding Page Logic

After designing the user interface, you can modify the page bean file to set the text of the `clockText` element. In this example, we add a statement to method `prerender` (lines 170–

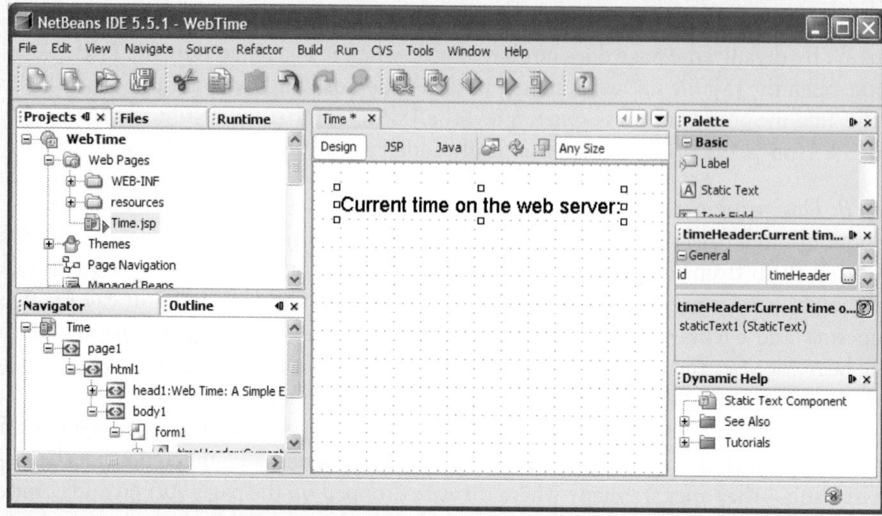

Fig. 26.10 | `Time.jsp` after inserting the first **Static Text** component.

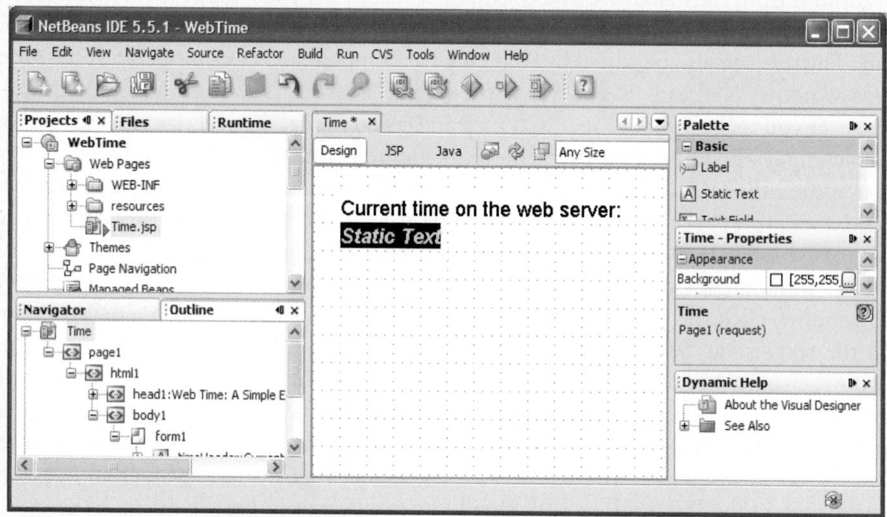

Fig. 26.11 | `Time.jsp` after adding the second `StaticText` component.

174 of Fig. 26.3). Recall that we use method `prerender` to ensure that `clockText` will be updated each time the page is refreshed. Lines 164–165 of Fig. 26.3 programmatically set the text of `clockText` to the current time on the server. For this statement to work, you'll also need the two imports shown in lines 14–15 of Fig. 26.3.

We would like this page to refresh automatically to display an up-to-date time. To accomplish this, add `<webuijsf:meta content = "60" httpEquiv = "refresh" />` to the JSP file, before the end of the `webuijsf:head` tag. This tag tells the browser to reload the page automatically every 60 seconds. You can also add this tag by dragging a **Meta** component from the **Advanced** section of the **Palette** to your page, then setting the component's `content` attribute to `60` and its `httpEquiv` attribute to `refresh`. If you do this, the **Meta** component will show up in the **Outline** window.

Step 10: Examining the Outline Window

Figure 26.12 displays the **Outline** window in Netbeans. The **Time** node representing the page bean file is expanded and shows the contents of the component tree. The request, session and application scope beans are collapsed by default, as we have not added any properties to these beans in this example. Clicking an item in the page's component tree selects the item in the Visual Editor.

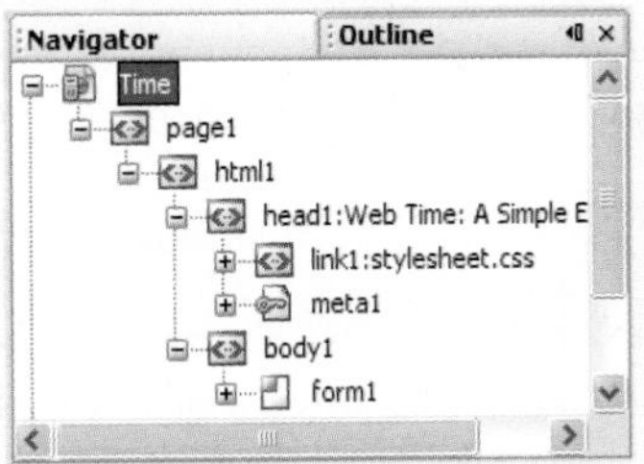

Fig. 26.12 | **Outline** window in Netbeans.

Step 11: Running the Application

After creating the web page, you can view it several ways. First, you can select **Build > Build Main Project**, and after the build completes, select **Run > Run Main Project**, to run the application in a browser window. You can run a project that has already been built by pressing the **Run Main Project** icon ( ) in the toolbar at the top of the IDE. Note that if changes are made to a project, the project must be rebuilt before they will be reflected when the application is viewed in a browser. Because this application was built on the local file system, the URL displayed in the address bar of the browser when the application is run will be `http://localhost:8080/WebTime/` (Fig. 26.3), where `8080` is the port number on which the test server—Sun Java System Application Server (SJSAS)—runs by default. [*Note:* The port number will depend on the server to which you deploy your web application.]

Alternatively, you can press *F5* to build the application, then run it in debug mode—the Netbeans built-in debugger can help you troubleshoot applications. If you type *F6*, the program executes without debugging enabled.

Error-Prevention Tip 26.1

If you have trouble building your project due to errors in the Netbeans-generated XML files used for building, try cleaning the project and building again. You can do this by selecting **Build > Clean and Build Main Project** *or by pressing* Shift + F11.

Finally, you can run your built application by opening a browser window and typing the web page's URL in the **Address** field. Since your application resides on the local file system, you must first start the Sun Java System Application Server. If you have previously run the application using one of the methods above, the server will already be started. Otherwise, you can start the server from the IDE by opening the **Runtime** tab (located in the same panel as the **Projects**), expanding the **Servers** node, right clicking **Sun Java System Application Server 9** and selecting **Start**. Then you can type the URL (including the port number for the application server, 8080) in the browser to execute the application. For this example it is not necessary to type the entire URL, `http://localhost:8080/WebTime/faces/Time.jsp`. The path to the file `Time.jsp` (i.e., `faces/Time.jsp`) can be omitted, because this file was set by default as the project's start page. For projects with multiple pages, you can change the start page by right clicking the desired page in the **Projects** window and selecting **Set As Start Page**. The start page is indicated by a green arrow next to the page's name in the **Projects** window.

26.4 JSF Components

This section introduces some of the JSF components featured in the **Palette** (Fig. 26.6). Figure 26.13 summarizes some of the JSF components used in the chapter examples.

JSF component	Description
Label	Displays text that can be associated with an input element.
Static Text	Displays text that the user cannot edit.
Text Field	Gathers user input and displays text.
Button	Triggers an event when clicked.
Hyperlink	Displays a hyperlink.
Drop Down List	Displays a drop-down list of choices.
Radio Button Group	Groups radio buttons.
Image	Displays images (e.g., GIF and JPG).

Fig. 26.13 | Commonly used JSF components.

26.4.1 Text and Graphics Components

Figure 26.14 displays a simple form for gathering user input. This example uses all the components listed in Fig. 26.13, except `Label`, which you will see in later examples. All the code in Fig. 26.14 was generated by Netbeans in response to actions performed in **Design** mode. This example does not perform any tasks when the user clicks **Register**. We ask you to add functionality to this example as an exercise. In successive examples, we demonstrate how to add functionality to many of these JSF components.

Before discussing the JSF components used in this JSP file, we explain the XHTML that creates the layout in Fig. 26.14. As discussed previously, Netbeans uses absolute positioning, so components are rendered wherever they were dropped in the Visual Editor. In this example, in addition to absolute positioning, we use a **Grid Panel** component (lines 37–61) from the **Palette**'s **Layout** component group. The `h:` prefix indicates that it can be found in the JSF HTML tag library. This component, an object of class `HtmlPanelGrid` in package `javax.faces.component.html`, controls the positioning of the components it contains. The **Grid Panel** component allows the designer to specify the number of columns the grid should contain. Components may then be dropped anywhere inside the panel, and they will automatically be repositioned into evenly spaced columns in the order in which they are dropped. When the number of components exceeds the number of columns, the panel moves the additional components to a new row. In this way, the **Grid Panel** behaves like an XHTML table, and is in fact rendered to the browser as an XHTML table. In this example, we use the **Grid Panel** to control the positions of the **Image** and **Text Field** components in the user information section of the page.

```
<?xml version = "1.0" encoding = "UTF-8" ?>

<!-- Fig. 26.14: WebComponents.jsp -->
<!-- Registration form that demonstrates JSF components -->
<jsp:root version = "1.2"
   xmlns:f = "http://java.sun.com/jsf/core"
   xmlns:h = "http://java.sun.com/jsf/html"
   xmlns:jsp = "http://java.sun.com/JSP/Page"
   xmlns:webuijsf = "http://www.sun.com/webui/webuijsf">
   <jsp:directive.page contentType = "text/html;charset=UTF-8"
      pageEncoding = "UTF-8" />
   <f:view>
   <webuijsf:page binding = "#{WebComponents.page1}" id = "page1">
      <webuijsf:html binding = "#{WebComponents.html1}" id = "html1">
         <webuijsf:head binding = "#{WebComponents.head1}" id = "head1"
            title = "Sample Registration Form">
            <webuijsf:link binding = "#{WebComponents.link1}"
               id = "link1" url = "/resources/stylesheet.css" />
         </webuijsf:head>
         <webuijsf:body binding = "#{WebComponents.body1}" id = "body1"
            style = "-rave-layout: grid">
            <webuijsf:form binding = "#{WebComponents.form1}"
               id = "form1">
                <webuijsf:staticText binding = "#{WebComponents.header}"
                   id = "header" style = "font-size: 18px; left: 24px;
                   top: 24px; position: absolute; width: 264px"
                   text = "This is a sample registration form" />
                <webuijsf:staticText
                   binding = "#{WebComponents.instructions}"
                   id = "instructions" style = "font-size: 12px;
                   font-style: italic; left: 24px; top: 48px;
                   position: absolute"
                   text = "Please fill in all fields and click Register"/>
                <webuijsf:image binding = "#{WebComponents.userImage}"
                   id = "userImage" style = "left: 24px; top: 72px;
                   position: absolute" url = "/resources/user.JPG" />
                <h:panelGrid binding = "#{WebComponents.gridPanel}"
                   columns = "4" id = "gridPanel" style = "height: 96px;
                   left: 24px; top: 96px; position: absolute"
                   width = "576">
                   <webuijsf:image binding = "#{WebComponents.image1}"
                      id = "image1" url = "/resources/fname.JPG" />
```

Fig. 26.14 | Registration form that demonstrates JSF components. (Part 1 of 3.)

```
                  <webuijsf:textField
                     binding = "#{WebComponents.firstNameTextField}"
                     id = "firstNameTextField" />
                  <webuijsf:image binding = "#{WebComponents.image2}"
                     id = "image2" url = "/resources/lname.JPG" />
                  <webuijsf:textField
                     binding = "#{WebComponents.lastNameTextField}"
                     id = "lastNameTextField" />
                  <webuijsf:image binding = "#{WebComponents.image4}"
                     id = "image4" url = "/resources/email.JPG" />
                  <webuijsf:textField
                     binding = "#{WebComponents.emailTextField}"
                     id = "emailTextField" />
                  <webuijsf:image binding = "#{WebComponents.image3}"
                     id = "image3" url = "/resources/phone.JPG" />
                  <webuijsf:textField
                     binding = "#{WebComponents.phoneTextField}"
                     id = "phoneTextField" />
               </h:panelGrid>
               <webuijsf:image binding = "#{WebComponents.image5}"
                  id = "image5" style = "left: 24px; top: 216px;
                  position: absolute"
                  url = "/resources/publications.JPG" />
               <webuijsf:staticText
                  binding = "#{WebComponents.publicationLabel}"
                  id = "publicationLabel" style = "font-size: 12px;
                  left: 216px; top: 216px; position: absolute"
                  text = "Which book would you like information about?"/>
               <webuijsf:dropDown
                  binding = "#{WebComponents.booksDropDown}"
                  id = "booksDropDown" items =
                  "#{WebComponents.booksDropDownDefaultOptions.options}"
                  selected= "#{WebComponents.booksDropDownDefaultOptions.
                  selectedValue}" style = "left: 24px; top: 240px;
                  position: absolute" />
               <webuijsf:radioButtonGroup
                  binding = "#{WebComponents.osRadioGroup}"
                  id = "osRadioGroup" items =
                  "#{WebComponents.osRadioGroupDefaultOptions.options}"
                  selected = "#{WebComponents.osRadioGroupDefaultOptions.
                  selectedValue}" style = "left: 24px; top: 336px;
                  position: absolute" />
               <webuijsf:button binding =
                  "#{WebComponents.registerButton}" id = "registerButton"
                  style = "left: 23px; top: 480px; position: absolute;
                  width: 100px" text = "Register" />
               <webuijsf:image binding = "#{WebComponents.image6}"
                  id = "image6" style = "left: 24px; top: 312px;
                  position: absolute" url = "/resources/os.JPG" />
               <webuijsf:staticText binding = "#{WebComponents.osLabel}"
                  id = "osLabel" style = "font-size: 12px; left: 216px;
                  top: 312px; position: absolute"
                  text = "What operating system are you using?" />
```

Fig. 26.14 | Registration form that demonstrates JSF components. (Part 2 of 3.)

```
                <webuijsf:hyperlink
                  binding = "#{WebComponents.deitelHyperlink}"
                  id = "deitelHyperlink" style = "left: 24px; top: 264px;
                  position: absolute" target = "_blank"
                  text = "Click here to learn more about our books"
                  url = "http://www.deitel.com" />
              </webuijsf:form>
            </webuijsf:body>
          </webuijsf:html>
        </webuijsf:page>
      </f:view>
    </jsp:root>
```

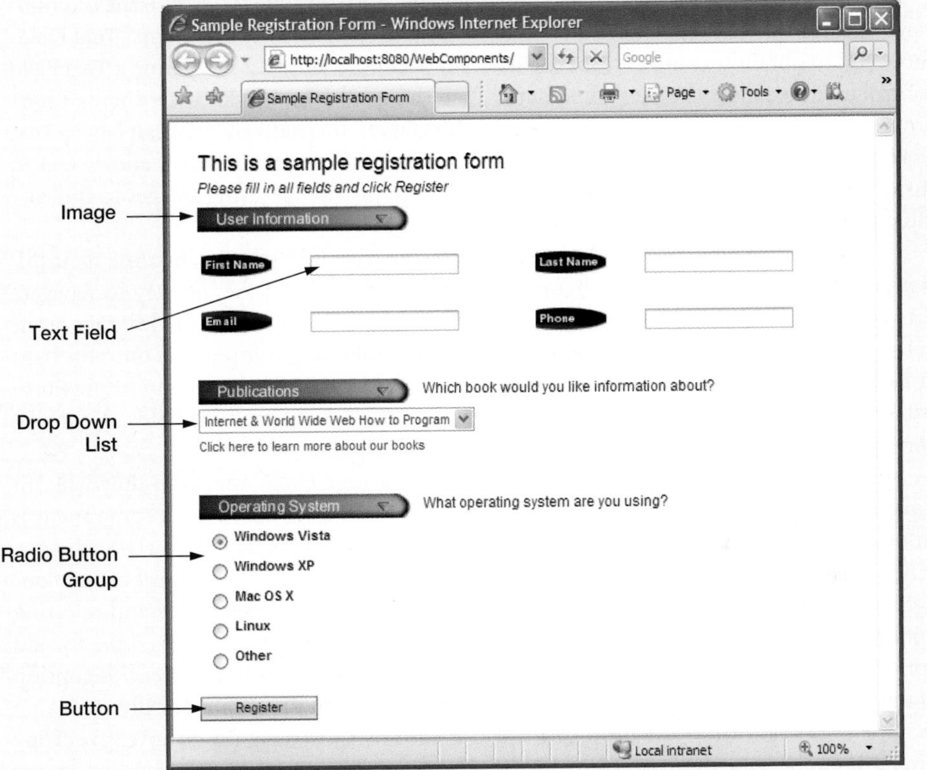

Fig. 26.14 | Registration form that demonstrates JSF components. (Part 3 of 3.)

Adding a Formatting Component to a Web Page

To create the layout for the **User Information** section of the form shown in Fig. 26.14, drag a **Grid Panel** component onto the page. In the **Properties** window, change the component's `id` to `gridPanel` and set the component's `columns` property to `4`. The component also has properties to control the cell padding, cell spacing and other elements of the component's appearance. In this case, accept the defaults for these properties. Now you can simply drag the **Images** and **Text Fields** for user information into the **Grid Panel**. The **Grid Panel** will manage their spacing and their organization into rows and columns.

Examining Web Components on a Sample Registration Form

Lines 34–36 of Fig. 26.14 define an **Image** component, an object of class `ImageComponent` which inserts an image into a web page. The images used in this example are located in this chapter's examples directory. Images to be displayed on a web page must be placed in the project's `resources` folder. To add images to the project, drop an **Image** component onto the page and click the ellipsis button next to the **url** property in the **Properties** window. This opens a dialog in which you can select the image to display. Since no images have been added to the `resources` folder yet, click the **Add File** button, locate the image on your computer's file system and click **Add File.** This copies the file you selected into the project's `resources` directory. Now you can select the image from the list of files in the `resources` folder and click **OK** to insert the image into the page.

Lines 37–61 contain an `h:panelGrid` element representing the **Grid Panel** component. Within this element, there are eight **Image** and **Text Field** components. **Text Field**s allow you to obtain text input from the user. For example, lines 43–45 define a **Text Field** control used to collect the user's first name. You can label a **Text Field** by setting its `label` property, which places text directly above the **Text Field.** Alternatively, you can label a **Text Field** by dragging and dropping a **Label** component onto the page, which allows you to customize the **Label**'s position and style. In this example, we are using images to indicate the purpose of each **Text Field.**

The order in which **Text Fields** are dragged to the page is important, because their JSP tags are added to the JSP file in that order. When a user presses the *Tab* key to navigate between input fields, they will navigate the fields in the order in which the JSP tags occur in the JSP file. To specify the navigation order, you should drag components onto the page in that order. Alternatively, you can set each input field's `tabIndex` property in the **Properties** window to control the order in which the user will tab through the fields. A component with a tab index of 1 will be the first in the tab sequence.

Lines 71–77 define a **Drop Down List**. When a user clicks the drop-down list, it expands and displays a list from which the user can make a selection. This component is an object of class `DropDown` and is bound to the object `booksDropDownDefaultOptions`, a `SingleSelectOptionsList` object that controls the list of options. This object can be configured automatically by right clicking the drop-down list in **Design** mode and selecting **Configure Default Options...**, which opens the **Options Customizer** dialog box to add options to the list. Each option consists of a display `String` that will represent the option in the browser and a value `String` that will be returned when programmatically retrieving the user's selection from the drop-down list. Netbeans constructs the `SingleSelectOptionsList` object in the page bean file based on the display-value pairs entered in the **Options Customizer** dialog box. To view the code that constructs the object, close the dialog box by clicking **OK**, open the page bean file, and expand the **Creator-managed Component Definition** node near the top of the file. The object is constructed in the `_init` method, which is called from method `init` the first time the page loads.

Lines 78–84 define a **Radio Button Group** component of class `RadioButtonGroup`, which provides a series of radio buttons from which the user can select only one. Like **Drop Down List**, a **Radio Button Group** is bound to a `SingleSelectOptionList` object. The options can be edited by right clicking the component and selecting **Configure Default Options....** Also like the drop-down list, the `SingleSelectOptionsList` is automatically generated by the IDE and placed in the `_init` method of the page bean class.

Lines 85–88 define a **Button** component of class `Button` that triggers an action when clicked. A **Button** component typically maps to an `input` XHTML element with attribute `type` set to `submit`. As stated earlier, clicking the **Register** button in this example does not do anything.

The **Hyperlink** component (lines 96–101) of class `Hyperlink` adds a link to a web page. The `url` property of this component specifies the resource (`http://www.deitel.com` in this case) that is requested when a user clicks the hyperlink. Setting the `target` property to `_blank` specifies that the requested web page should open in a new browser window. By default, **Hyperlink** components cause pages to open in the same browser window.

26.4.2 Validation Using Validator Components and Custom Validators

This section introduces form **validation**. Validating user input is an important step in collecting information from users. Validation helps prevent processing errors due to incomplete or improperly formatted user input. For example, you may perform validation to ensure that all required fields have been filled out or that a zip-code field contains exactly five digits. Netbeans provides three validator components. A **Length Validator** determines whether a field contains an acceptable number of characters. **Double Range Validators** and **Long Range Validators** determine whether numeric input falls within acceptable ranges. Package **`javax.faces.validators`** contains the classes for these validators. Netbeans also allows custom validation with validator methods in the page bean file. The following example demonstrates validation using both a validator component and custom validation.

Validating Form Data in a Web Application

The example in this section prompts the user to enter a name, e-mail address and phone number. After the user enters any data, but before the data is sent to the web server, validation ensures that the user entered a value in each field, that the entered name does not exceed 30 characters, and that the e-mail address and phone number values are in an acceptable format. If the client does not have JavaScript enabled, then the validation would be performed on the server. In this example, (555) 123-4567, 555-123-4567 and 123-4567 are all considered valid phone numbers. Once the data is submitted, the web server responds by displaying an appropriate message and a **Grid Panel** component repeating the submitted information. Note that a real business application would typically store the submitted data in a database or in a file on the server. We simply send the data back to the page to demonstrate that the server received the data.

Building the Web Page

This web application introduces two additional JSF components—**Label** and **Message** from the **Basic** section of the **Palette**. Each of the page's three text fields should have its own label and message. **Label** components describe other components and can be associated with user input fields by setting their `for` property. **Message** components display error messages when validation fails. This page requires three **Text Fields**, three **Labels** and three **Messages**, as well as a submit **Button**. To associate the **Label** components and **Message** components with their corresponding **Text Field** components, hold the *Ctrl* and *Shift* keys, then drag the label or message to the appropriate **Text Field**. In the **Properties** window, notice that each **Label** and **Message** component's `for` property is set to the appropriate **Text Field**.

You should also add a **Static Text** component to display a validation success message at the bottom of the page. Set the text to `"Thank you for your submission.<br/>We received the following information:"` and change the component's `id` to `resultText`. In the **Properties** window, unset the component's `rendered` and `escaped` properties. The **`rendered`** property controls whether the component will be displayed the first time the page loads. Setting **`escaped`** to `false` enables the browser to recognize the `<br/>` tag so it can start a new line of text rather than display the characters `"<br/>"` in the web page.

Finally, add a **Grid Panel** component below the `resultText` component. The panel should have two columns, one for displaying **Static Text** components that label the user's validated data, and one for displaying **Static Text** components that echo back that data. The panel's `rendered` property should be set to `false` so that it is not initialially displayed.

The JSP file for this page is displayed in Fig. 26.15. Lines 34–40, 48–52 and 60–64 define `webuijsf:textFields` for retrieving the user's name, e-mail address and phone number, respectively. Lines 31–33, 45–47 and 57–59 define `webuijsf:labels` for each of these text fields. Lines 41–44, 53–56 and 65–68 define the text fields' **`webuijsf:message`** elements. Lines 69–73 define a **Submit** `webuijsf:button`. Lines 74–78 create a `webuijsf:staticText` named `resultText` that displays the response from the server when the user successfully submits the form, and lines 79–99 define a `webuijsf:panelGrid` that contains components for echoing validated user input to the browser.

```
1  <?xml version = "1.0" encoding = "UTF-8"?>
2
3  <!-- Fig. 26.15: Validation.jsp -->
4  <!-- JSP that demonstrates validation of user input. -->
5  <jsp:root version = "1.2"
6     xmlns:f = "http://java.sun.com/jsf/core"
7     xmlns:h = "http://java.sun.com/jsf/html"
8     xmlns:jsp = "http://java.sun.com/JSP/Page"
9     xmlns:webuijsf = "http://www.sun.com/webui/webuijsf">
10    <jsp:directive.page contentType = "text/html;charset=UTF-8"
11       pageEncoding = "UTF-8"/>
12    <f:view>
13    <webuijsf:page binding = "#{Validation.page1}" id = "page1">
14       <webuijsf:html binding = "#{Validation.html1}" id = "html1">
15          <webuijsf:head binding = "#{Validation.head1}" id = "head1">
16             <webuijsf:link binding = "#{Validation.link1}" id = "link1"
17                url = "/resources/stylesheet.css"/>
18          </webuijsf:head>
19          <webuijsf:body binding = "#{Validation.body1}" id = "body1"
20             style = "-rave-layout: grid">
21             <webuijsf:form binding = "#{Validation.form1}" id = "form1">
22                <webuijsf:staticText binding = "#{Validation.headerText}"
23                   id = "headerText" style = "font-size: 14px; font-weight:
24                   bold; left: 24px; top: 24px; position: absolute"
25                   text = "Please fill out the following form:"/>
26                <webuijsf:staticText binding =
27                   "#{Validation.instructionText}" id = "instructionText"
28                   style = "font-size: 12px; font-style: italic; left:
```

Fig. 26.15 | JSP that demonstrates validation of user input. (Part 1 of 4.)

```
                    24px; top: 48px; position: absolute" text = "All fields
                    are required and must contain valid information."/>
                <webuijsf:label binding = "#{Validation.nameLabel}" for =
                    "nameTextField" id = "nameLabel" style = "left: 24px;
                    top: 75px; position: absolute" text = "Name:"/>
                <webuijsf:textField binding = "#{Validation.nameTextField}"
                    id = "nameTextField" required = "true" style = "left:
                    96px; top: 72px; position: absolute; width: 216px"
                    validatorExpression =
                    "#{Validation.nameLengthValidator.validate}"
                    valueChangeListenerExpression =
                    "#{Validation.nameTextField_processValueChange}"/>
                <webuijsf:message binding = "#{Validation.nameMessage}"
                    for = "nameTextField" id = "nameMessage" showDetail =
                    "false" showSummary = "true"
                    style = "left: 336px; top: 74px; position: absolute"/>
                <webuijsf:label binding = "#{Validation.emailLabel}" for =
                    "emailTextField" id = "emailLabel" style = "left: 24px;
                    top: 109px; position: absolute" text = "E-Mail:"/>
                <webuijsf:textField binding =
                    "#{Validation.emailTextField}" id = "emailTextField"
                    required = "true" style = "left: 96px; top: 106px;
                    position: absolute; width: 216px" validatorExpression =
                    "#{Validation.emailTextField_validate}"/>
                <webuijsf:message binding = "#{Validation.emailMessage}"
                    for = "emailTextField" id = "emailMessage" showDetail =
                    "false" showSummary = "true" style = "left: 336px; top:
                    108px; position: absolute"/>
                <webuijsf:label binding = "#{Validation.phoneLabel}" for =
                    "phoneTextField" id = "phoneLabel" style = "left: 24px;
                    top: 143px; position: absolute" text = "Phone:"/>
                <webuijsf:textField binding =
                    "#{Validation.phoneTextField}" id = "phoneTextField"
                    required = "true" style = "left: 96px; top: 140px;
                    position: absolute; width: 216px" validatorExpression =
                    "#{Validation.phoneTextField_validate}"/>
                <webuijsf:message binding = "#{Validation.phoneMessage}"
                    for = "phoneTextField" id = "phoneMessage" showDetail =
                    "false" showSummary = "true" style = "left: 336px; top:
                    142px; position: absolute"/>
                <webuijsf:button actionExpression =
                    "#{Validation.submitButton_action}" binding =
                   "#{Validation.submitButton}" id = "submitButton" style =
                    "left: 23px; top: 192px; position: absolute; width:
                    100px" text = "Submit"/>
                <webuijsf:staticText binding = "#{Validation.resultText}"
                    escape = "false" id = "resultText" rendered = "false"
                    style = "left: 24px; top: 216px; position: absolute"
                    text = "Thank you for your submission.&lt;br/&gt;We
                    received the following information:"/>
                <h:panelGrid binding = "#{Validation.resultGridPanel}"
                    columns = "2" id = "resultGridPanel" rendered = "false"
                    style = "border-width: 1px; border-style: solid;
```

Fig. 26.15 | JSP that demonstrates validation of user input. (Part 2 of 4.)

```
                  background-color: #ffff99; height: 96px; left: 24px;
                  top: 264px; position: absolute" width = "288">
                  <webuijsf:staticText binding =
                     "#{Validation.nameResultLabel}"
                     id = "nameResultLabel" text = "Name:"/>
                  <webuijsf:staticText binding =
                     "#{Validation.nameResult}" id = "nameResult"/>
                  <webuijsf:staticText binding =
                     "#{Validation.emailResultLabel}"
                     id = "emailResultLabel" text = "E-Mail:"/>
                  <webuijsf:staticText binding =
                     "#{Validation.emailResult}" id = "emailResult"/>
                  <webuijsf:staticText binding =
                     "#{Validation.phoneResultLabel}"
                     id = "phoneResultLabel" text = "Phone:"/>
                  <webuijsf:staticText binding =
                     "#{Validation.phoneResult}" id = "phoneResult"/>
               </h:panelGrid>
            </webuijsf:form>
         </webuijsf:body>
      </webuijsf:html>
   </webuijsf:page>
   </f:view>
</jsp:root>
```

(a)

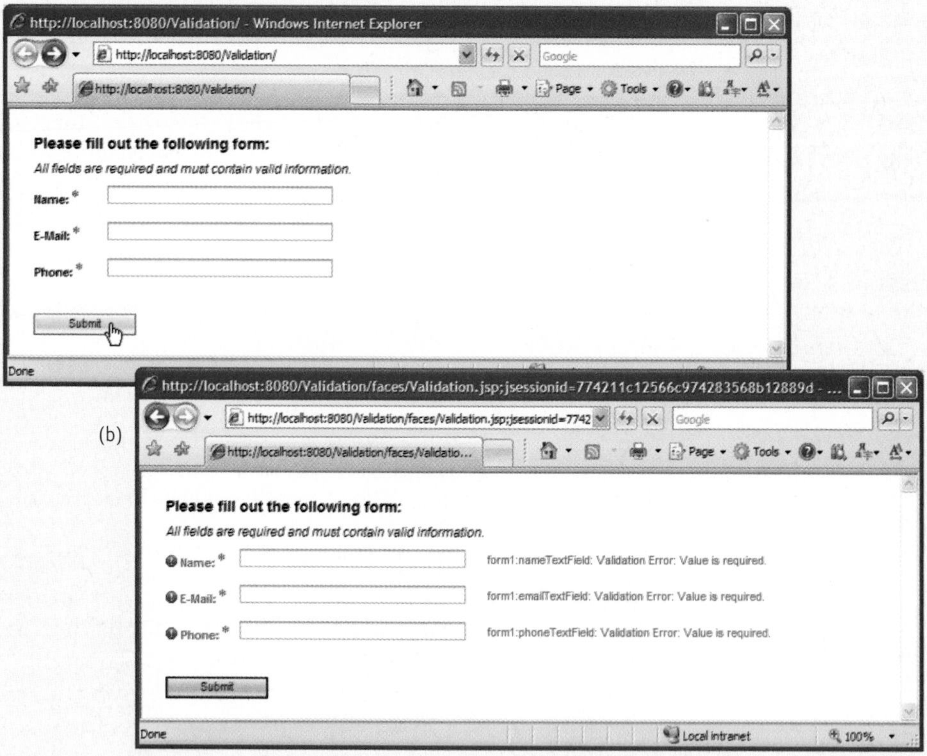

(b)

Fig. 26.15 | JSP that demonstrates validation of user input. (Part 3 of 4.)

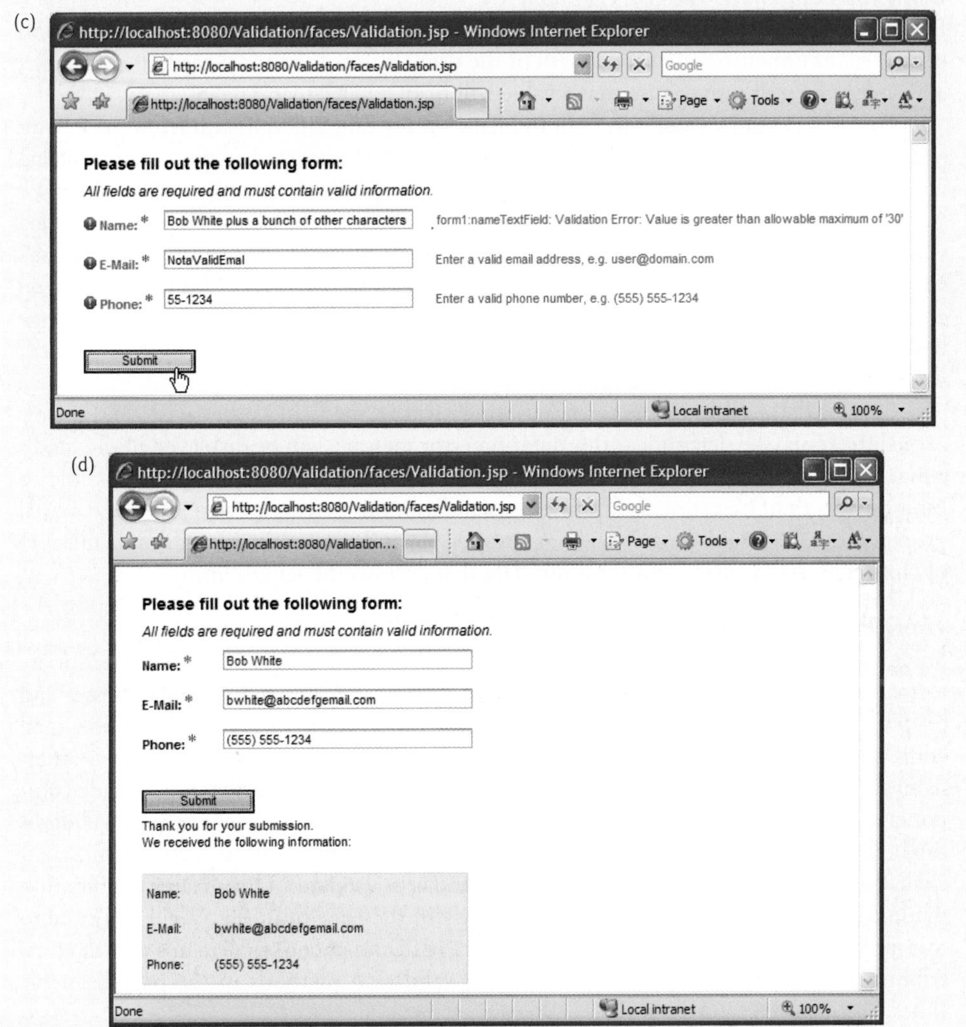

Fig. 26.15 | JSP that demonstrates validation of user input. (Part 4 of 4.)

Setting the `required` *Property of an Input Component*

Ensuring that the user has made a selection or entered some text in a required input element is a basic type of validation. This is accomplished by checking the **`required`** box in the element's **Properties** window. If you add a validator component or custom validator method to an input field, the field's `required` property must be set to `true` for validation to occur. Notice that each of the three input `webuijsf:textField`s in this example has its `required` property set to `true`. Also note in the Visual Editor that the label for a required field is automatically marked by a red asterisk. If a user submits this form with empty text fields, the default error message for a required field will be displayed in the empty field's associated `webuijsf:message` component. To customize the error message, you must provide a custom validator.

Using the **`LengthValidator`** *Component*

In this example, we use the **Length Validator** component (found in the **Validators** section of the **Palette**) to ensure that the length of the user's name does not exceed 30 characters. This might be useful to ensure that a value will fit in a particular database field.

To add a **Length Validator** to a component, simply drag the validator from the **Palette** and drop it onto the field to validate. A **lengthValidator1** node will appear in the **Outline** window. To edit the validation component's properties, click this node and set the `maximum` and `minimum` properties to the desired number of characters in the **Properties** window. Here, we set only the `maximum` property to 30. We also changed the component's `id` to `nameLengthValidator`. Notice that the `nameTextField`'s `validationExpression` property has been bound to the `nameLengthValidator`'s `validate` method in the page bean file (lines 37–38). Remember that most client-side validation can be circumvented, so important validation should always be performed on the server.

This validator allows users to type as much text in the field as they wish, and if they exceed the limit, the default length validation error message will be displayed in the field's `webuijsf:message` component after the user clicks the **Submit** button. It is possible to limit the length of user input without using validation. By setting a **Text Field**'s `maxLength` property, the **Text Field**'s cursor will not advance beyond the maximum allowable number of characters, so the user cannot submit data that exceeds the length limit.

Using Regular Expressions to Perform Custom Validation

Some of the most common validation tasks involve checking user input for appropriate formatting. For instance, it may be necessary to check user-entered e-mail addresses and telephone numbers to ensure that they conform to the standard formatting for valid e-mail addresses and phone numbers. Matching user input against a regular expression is an effective way to ensure that the input is properly formatted. Netbeans does not provide components for validation using regular expressions, so we will add our own custom validator methods to the page bean file. To add a custom validator to an input component, right click the component and select **Edit Event Handler > validate**. This creates a validation method for the component with an empty body in the page bean file. We'll add code to this method shortly. Note that both `emailTextField` and `phoneTextField`'s `validate` attributes are bound to their respective custom validation methods in the page bean file (lines 51–52 and 63–64).

Examining the Page Bean File for a Form That Receives User Input

Figure 26.16 contains the page bean file for the JSP file in Fig. 26.15. Line 31 sets the maximum length for the `nameLengthValidator`, which is a property of this page bean. Recall that the name text field was bound to this property in the JSP file. Method `emailTextField_validate` (lines 410–422) and `phoneTextField_validate` (lines 426–438) are the custom validator methods that verify the user-entered e-mail address and phone number, respectively. The `submitButton_action` method (lines 441–452) echoes the data back to the user if validation succeeds. The validator methods are called before the event handler, so if validation fails, `submitButton_action` will not be called and the user input will not be echoed.

The two custom validator methods in this page bean file validate a text field's contents against a regular expression using the `String` method `match`, which takes a regular expression as an argument and returns `true` if the `String` conforms to the specified format.

```
// Fig. 26.16: Validation.java
// Validating user input.
package validation;

import com.sun.rave.web.ui.appbase.AbstractPageBean;
import com.sun.webui.jsf.component.Body;
import com.sun.webui.jsf.component.Button;
import com.sun.webui.jsf.component.Form;
import com.sun.webui.jsf.component.Head;
import com.sun.webui.jsf.component.Html;
import com.sun.webui.jsf.component.Label;
import com.sun.webui.jsf.component.Link;
import com.sun.webui.jsf.component.Message;
import com.sun.webui.jsf.component.Page;
import com.sun.webui.jsf.component.StaticText;
import com.sun.webui.jsf.component.TextField;
import javax.faces.FacesException;
import javax.faces.application.FacesMessage;
import javax.faces.component.UIComponent;
import javax.faces.component.html.HtmlPanelGrid;
import javax.faces.context.FacesContext;
import javax.faces.validator.LengthValidator;
import javax.faces.validator.ValidatorException;

public class Validation extends AbstractPageBean
{
   private int __placeholder;

   private void _init() throws Exception
   {
      nameLengthValidator.setMaximum( 30 );
   } // end method _init

   // To save space, we omitted the code in lines 34-407. The complete
   // source code is provided with this chapter's examples.

   // validates entered email address against the regular expression
   // that represents the form of a valid email address.
   public void emailTextField_validate( FacesContext context,
      UIComponent component, Object value )
   {
      String email = String.valueOf( value );

      // if entered email address is not in a valid format
      if ( !email.matches(
         "\\w+([-+.']\\w+)*@\\w+([-.]\\w+)*\\.\\w+([-.]\\w+)*" ) )
      {
         throw new ValidatorException( new FacesMessage(
            "Enter a valid email address, e.g. user@domain.com" ) );
      } // end if
   } // end method emailTextField_validate

```

Fig. 26.16 | Page bean for validating user input and redisplaying that input if valid. (Part 1 of 2.)

```
424       // validates entered phone number against the regular expression
425       // that represents the form of a valid phone number.
426       public void phoneTextField_validate( FacesContext context,
427          UIComponent component, Object value )
428       {
429          String phone = String.valueOf( value );
430
431          // if entered phone number is not in a valid format
432          if ( !phone.matches(
433             "((\\(\\d{3}\\) ?)|(\\d{3}-))?\\d{3}-\\d{4}" ) )
434          {
435             throw new ValidatorException( new FacesMessage(
436                "Enter a valid phone number, e.g. (555) 555-1234" ) );
437          } // end if
438       } // end method phoneTextField_validate
439
440       // displays the values the user entered
441       public String submitButton_action()
442       {
443          String name = String.valueOf( nameTextField.getValue() );
444          String email = String.valueOf( emailTextField.getValue() );
445          String phone = String.valueOf( phoneTextField.getValue() );
446          nameResult.setValue( name );
447          emailResult.setValue( email );
448          phoneResult.setValue( phone );
449          resultGridPanel.setRendered( true );
450          resultText.setRendered( true );
451          return null;
452       } // end method submitButton_action
453    } // end class Validation
```

Fig. 26.16 | Page bean for validating user input and redisplaying that input if valid. (Part 2 of 2.)

For the `emailTextField_validate` method, we use the validation expression

```
\w+([-+.']\w+)*@\w+([-.]\w+)*\.\w+([-.]\w+)*
```

Note that each backslash in the regular expression `String` (line 417) must be escaped with another backslash (as in \\), because the backslash character normally represents the beginning of an escape sequence in Java. This regular expression indicates that an e-mail address is valid if the part before the `@` symbol contains one or more word characters (i.e., alphanumeric characters or underscores), followed by zero or more `Strings` comprised of a hyphen, plus sign, period or apostrophe and additional word characters. After the `@` symbol, a valid e-mail address must contain one or more groups of word characters potentially separated by hyphens or periods, followed by a required period and another group of one or more word characters potentially separated by hyphens or periods. For example, the e-mail addresses `bob's-personal.email@white.email.com`, `bob-white@my-email.com` and `bob.white@email.com` are all valid. If the user enters text in `emailTextField` that does not have the correct format and attempts to submit the form, lines 419–420 throw a `ValidatorException`. The `Message` component catches this exception and displays the message in red.

The regular expression in `phoneTextField_validate` ensures that the `phoneTextBox` contains a valid phone number before the form is submitted. The user input is matched against the regular expression

```
((\(\d{3}\) ?)|(\d{3}-))?\d{3}-\d{4}
```

(Again, each backslash is escaped in the regular expression `String` in line 433.) This expression indicates that a phone number can contain a three-digit area code either in parentheses and followed by an optional space or without parentheses and followed by a required hyphen. After an optional area code, a phone number must contain three digits, a hyphen and another four digits. For example, `(555) 123-4567`, `555-123-4567` and `123-4567` are all valid phone numbers. If a user enters an invalid phone number, lines 435–436 throw a `ValidatorException` The `Message` component catches this exception and displays the error message in red.

If all six validators are successful (i.e., each `TextField` contains data, the name is less than 30 characters and the e-mail address and phone number are valid), clicking the **Submit** button sends the form's data to the server. As shown in Fig. 26.15(d), the `submitButton_action` method displays the submitted data in a `gridPanel` (lines 446–449) and a success message in `resultsText` (line 450).

26.5 Session Tracking

In the early days of the Internet, e-businesses could not provide the kind of customized service typically experienced in "brick-and-mortar" stores. To address this problem, e-businesses began to establish mechanisms by which they could personalize users' browsing experiences, tailoring content to individual users while enabling them to bypass irrelevant information. Businesses achieve this level of service by tracking each customer's movement through their websites and combining the collected data with information provided by the consumer, including billing information, personal preferences, interests and hobbies.

Personalization

Personalization makes it possible for e-businesses to communicate effectively with their customers and also improves the user's ability to locate desired products and services. Companies that provide content of particular interest to users can establish relationships with customers and build on those relationships over time. Furthermore, by targeting consumers with personal offers, recommendations, advertisements, promotions and services, e-businesses create customer loyalty. Websites can use sophisticated technology to allow visitors to customize home pages to suit their individual needs and preferences. Similarly, online shopping sites often store personal information for customers, tailoring notifications and special offers to their interests. Such services encourage customers to visit sites and make purchases more frequently.

Privacy

A trade-off exists, however, between personalized e-business service and protection of privacy. Some consumers embrace the idea of tailored content, but others fear the possible adverse consequences if the info they provide to e-businesses is released or collected by tracking technologies. Consumers and privacy advocates ask: What if the e-business to which we give personal data sells or gives that information to another organization without our knowledge? What if we do not want our actions on the Internet—a supposedly anonymous medium—to be tracked and recorded by unknown parties? What if unauthorized parties gain access to sensitive private data, such as credit card numbers or medical history? All of these are questions that must be debated and addressed by programmers, consumers, e-businesses and lawmakers alike.

Recognizing Clients

To provide personalized services to consumers, e-businesses must be able to recognize clients when they request information from a site. As we have discussed, the request/response system on which the web operates is facilitated by HTTP. Unfortunately, HTTP is a stateless protocol—it does not support persistent connections that would enable web servers to maintain state information regarding particular clients. So, web servers cannot determine whether a request comes from a particular client or whether a series of requests comes from one or several clients. To circumvent this problem, sites can provide mechanisms to identify individual clients. A session represents a unique client on a website. If the client leaves a site and then returns later, the client will still be recognized as the same user. To help the server distinguish among clients, each client must identify itself to the server.

Tracking individual clients, known as session tracking, can be achieved in a number of ways in JSPs. One popular technique uses cookies (Section 26.5.1); another uses the `SessionBean` object (Section 26.5.2). Additional session-tracking techniques include using `input` `form` elements of type `"hidden"` and URL rewriting. With `"hidden"` form elements, a Web Form can write session-tracking data into a `form` in the web page that it returns to the client in response to a prior request. When the user submits the form in the new web page, all the form data, including the `"hidden"` fields, is sent to the form handler on the web server. With URL rewriting, the web server embeds session-tracking information directly in the URLs of hyperlinks that the user clicks to send subsequent requests to the web server.

26.5.1 Cookies

Cookies provide web developers with a tool for personalizing web pages. A cookie is a piece of data typically stored in a text file on the user's computer. A cookie maintains information about the client during and between browser sessions. The first time a user visits the website, the user's computer might receive a cookie; this cookie is then reactivated each time the user revisits that site. The aim is to create an anonymous record containing data that is used to personalize the user's future visits to the site. For example, cookies in a shopping application might store unique identifiers for users. When a user adds items to an online shopping cart or performs another task resulting in a request to the web server, the server receives a cookie from the client containing the user's unique identifier. The server then uses the unique identifier to locate the shopping cart and perform any necessary processing.

In addition to identifying users, cookies also can indicate clients' shopping preferences. When a web server receives a request from a client, the server can examine the cookie(s) it sent to the client during previous communications, identify the client's preferences and immediately display products of interest to the client.

Every HTTP-based interaction between a client and a server includes a header containing information either about the request (when the communication is from the client to the server) or about the response (when the communication is from the server to the client). When a page receives a request, the header includes information such as the request type (e.g., GET or POST) and any cookies that have been sent previously from the server to be stored on the client machine. When the server formulates its response, the header information contains any cookies the server wants to store on the client computer and other information, such as the MIME type of the response.

The **expiration date** of a cookie determines how long the cookie remains on the client's computer. If you do not set an expiration date for a cookie, the web browser maintains the cookie for the duration of the browsing session. Otherwise, the web browser maintains the cookie until the expiration date occurs. When the browser requests a resource from a web server, cookies previously sent to the client by that web server are returned to the web server as part of the request formulated by the browser. Cookies are deleted when they **expire**.

Portability Tip 26.1

Clients may disable cookies in their web browsers for more privacy. When such clients use web applications that depend on cookies to maintain state information, the applications will not execute correctly.

Using Cookies to Provide Book Recommendations

The next web application shows how to use cookies. The example contains two pages. In the first page (Figs. 26.17 and 26.19), users select a favorite programming language from a group of radio buttons and submit the form to the web server for processing. The web server responds by creating a cookie that stores the selected language and the ISBN number for a recommended book on that topic. The server then renders new components in the browser that allow the user either to select another favorite programming language or to view the second page in our application (Figs. 26.20–26.21), which lists recommended books pertaining to the programming language(s) that the user selected. When the user clicks the hyperlink, the cookies previously stored on the client are read and used to form the list of book recommendations.

The JSP file in Fig. 26.17 contains a **Radio Button Group** (lines 26–30) with the options **Java, C++, Visual Basic 2005, Visual C# 2005** and **Internet & Web** (set in the page bean). Recall that you can set the display and value Strings of radio buttons by right clicking the **Radio Button Group** and selecting **Configure Default Options....** The user selects a programming language by clicking a radio button. When the user presses **Submit**, the web application creates a cookie containing the selected language. This cookie is added to the HTTP response header and sent to the client as part of the response.

```
1  <?xml version = "1.0" encoding = "UTF-8"?>
2
3  <!-- Fig. 26.17: Options.jsp -->
4  <!-- JSP file that allows the user to select a programming language -->
5  <jsp:root version = "1.2"
6     xmlns:f = "http://java.sun.com/jsf/core"
```

Fig. 26.17 | JSP file that allows the user to select a programming language. (Part 1 of 4.)

```
    xmlns:h = "http://java.sun.com/jsf/html"
    xmlns:jsp = "http://java.sun.com/JSP/Page"
    xmlns:webuijsf = "http://www.sun.com/webui/webuijsf">
    <jsp:directive.page contentType = "text/html;charset=UTF-8"
       pageEncoding = "UTF-8"/>
    <f:view>
    <webuijsf:page binding = "#{Options.page1}" id = "page1">
       <webuijsf:html binding = "#{Options.html1}" id = "html1">
          <webuijsf:head binding = "#{Options.head1}" id = "head1">
             <webuijsf:link binding = "#{Options.link1}" id = "link1"
                url = "/resources/stylesheet.css"/>
          </webuijsf:head>
          <webuijsf:body binding = "#{Options.body1}" id = "body1"
             style = "-rave-layout: grid">
             <webuijsf:form binding = "#{Options.form1}" id = "form1">
                <webuijsf:staticText binding = "#{Options.instructionText}"
                   id = "instructionText" style = "font-size: 18px;
                   left: 24px; top: 24px; position: absolute"
                   text = "Select a programming language:"/>
                <webuijsf:radioButtonGroup binding =
                   "#{Options.languageRadioGroup}" id =
                   "languageRadioGroup" items =
                   "#{Options.languageRadioGroupDefaultOptions.options}"
                   style = "left: 24px; top: 48px; position: absolute"/>
                <webuijsf:button actionExpression =
                   "#{Options.submitButton_action}" binding =
                   "#{Options.submitButton}" id = "submitButton" style =
                   "left: 23px; top: 192px; position: absolute;
                   width: 100px" text = "Submit"/>
                <webuijsf:staticText binding = "#{Options.responseText}"
                   id = "responseText" rendered = "false" style =
                   "font-size: 18px; left: 24px; top: 24px;
                   position: absolute"/>
                <webuijsf:hyperlink actionExpression =
                   "#{Options.languagesLink_action}" binding =
                   "#{Options.languagesLink}" id = "languagesLink"
                   rendered = "false" style = "left: 24px; top: 72px;
                   position: absolute" text =
                   "Click here to choose another language."/>
                <webuijsf:hyperlink actionExpression =
                   "#{Options.recommendationsLink_action}" binding =
                   "#{Options.recommendationsLink}" id =
                   "recommendationsLink" rendered = "false" style =
                   "left: 24px; top: 96px; position: absolute"
                   text = "Click here to get book recommendations."
                   url = "/faces/Recommendations.jsp"/>
               </webuijsf:form>
          </webuijsf:body>
       </webuijsf:html>
    </webuijsf:page>
    </f:view>
</jsp:root>
```

Fig. 26.17 | JSP file that allows the user to select a programming language. (Part 2 of 4.)

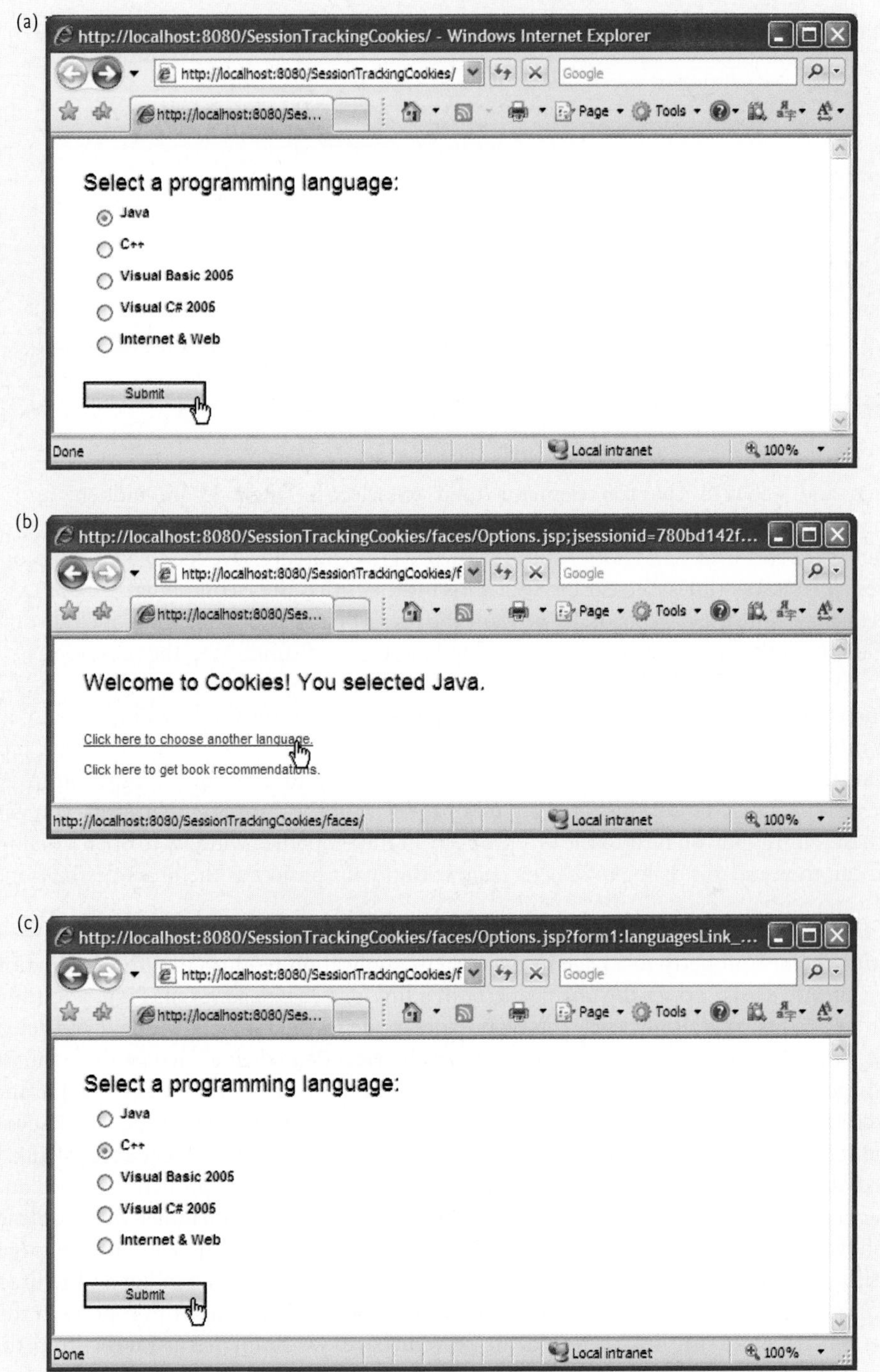

Fig. 26.17 | JSP file that allows the user to select a programming language. (Part 3 of 4.)

Fig. 26.17 | JSP file that allows the user to select a programming language. (Part 4 of 4.)

When the user clicks **Submit**, the `webuijsf:staticText`, `webuijsf:radioButtonGroup` and `webuijsf:button` elements used to select a language are hidden, and a `webuijsf:staticText` and two `webuijsf:hyperlink` elements are displayed. One `webuijsf:staticText` and both `webuijsf:hyperlinks` initially have their `rendered` properties set to `false` (lines 37, 43, and 49). This indicates that these components are not visible the first time the page loads, as we want the user's first view of the page to include only the components for selecting a programming language and submitting the selection.

The first hyperlink (lines 40–45) requests this page, and the second (lines 46–52) requests `Recommendations.jsp`. The `url` property is not set for the first link; we discuss this momentarily. The second link's `url` property is set to `/faces/Recommendations.jsp`. Recall that earlier in the chapter, we set a `url` property to a remote website (`http://www.deitel.com`). To set this property to a page within the current application, you can click the ellipsis button next to the `url` property in the **Properties** window to open a dialog. You can then use this dialog to select a page within your project as the link's destination.

Adding and Linking to a New Web Page

Setting the `url` property to a page in the current application requires that the destination page already exists. To set the `url` property of a link to `Recommendations.jsp`, you must first create this page. Right click the **Web Pages** node in the **Projects** window and select **New > Page...** from the menu that appears. In the **New Page** dialog, change the name of the page to `Recommendations` and click **Finish** to create the files `Recommendations.jsp` and `Recommendations.java`. (We discuss the contents of these files shortly.) Once the `Recommendations.jsp` file exists, you can select it as the `url` value for `recommendationsLink`.

For `Options.jsp`, rather than setting the `languagesLink`'s `url` property, we will add an action handler for this component to the page bean. The action handler will enable us to show and hide components of the page without redirecting the user to another page. Specifying a destination `url` would override the component's action handler and redirect the user to the specified page, so it is important that we do not set the `url` property in this case. Since we use this link to reload the current page, we simply return `null` from the action handler, causing `Options.jsp` to reload.

To add an action handler to a hyperlink that should also direct the user to another page, you must add a rule to the **Page Navigation** file (Fig. 26.18). To edit this file, right

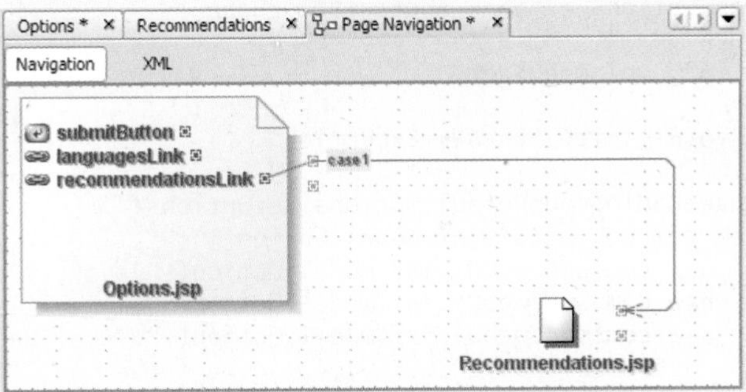

Fig. 26.18 | Editing the **Page Navigation** file.

click anywhere in the Visual Designer and select **Page Navigation**. Click `Options.jsp` in the navigation designer to display its components that might cause the page to request another page. Locate the link whose navigation rule you would like to set (`recommendationsLink` in this case) and drag it to the destination page. Now the link can direct the user to a new page (`Recommendations.jsp`) without overriding its action handler. Editing the **Page Navigation** file is also useful when you would like action elements that cannot specify a `url` property, such as buttons, to direct users to another page. You'll configure a link from `Recommendations.asp` to `Options.jsp` later in this section.

Figure 26.19 contains the code that writes a cookie to the client machine when the user selects a programming language. The file also determines which components appear on the page, displaying either the components for choosing a language or the links for navigating the application, depending on the user's actions.

```
// Fig. 26.19: Options.java
// Page bean that stores user's language selection as a client cookie.
package sessiontrackingcookies;

import com.sun.rave.web.ui.appbase.AbstractPageBean;
import com.sun.webui.jsf.component.Body;
import com.sun.webui.jsf.component.Button;
import com.sun.webui.jsf.component.Form;
import com.sun.webui.jsf.component.Head;
import com.sun.webui.jsf.component.Html;
import com.sun.webui.jsf.component.Hyperlink;
import com.sun.webui.jsf.component.Link;
import com.sun.webui.jsf.component.Page;
import com.sun.webui.jsf.component.RadioButtonGroup;
import com.sun.webui.jsf.component.StaticText;
import com.sun.webui.jsf.model.SingleSelectOptionsList;
import java.util.Properties;
import javax.faces.FacesException;
import javax.servlet.http.Cookie;
import javax.servlet.http.HttpServletResponse;

```

Fig. 26.19 | Page bean that stores the user's language selection in a client cookie. (Part 1 of 3.)

```
22  public class Options extends AbstractPageBean
23  {
24     private int __placeholder;
25
26     private void _init() throws Exception
27     {
28        languageRadioGroupDefaultOptions.setOptions(
29           new com.sun.webui.jsf.model.Option[] {
30              new com.sun.webui.jsf.model.Option( "Java", "Java" ),
31              new com.sun.webui.jsf.model.Option( "C++", "C++" ),
32              new com.sun.webui.jsf.model.Option( "Visual-Basic-2005",
33                 "Visual Basic 2005" ),
34              new com.sun.webui.jsf.model.Option( "Visual-C#-2005",
35                 "Visual C# 2005" ),
36              new com.sun.webui.jsf.model.Option( "Internet-&-Web",
37                 "Internet & Web" )
38           } // end array initializer
39        ); // end call to setOptions
40     } // end method _init
41
42     // To save space, we omitted the code in lines 42-199. The complete
43     // source code is provided with this chapter's examples.
44
200    private Properties books = new Properties();
201
202    // Construct a new page bean instance and initialize the properties
203    // that map languages to ISBN numbers of recommended books.
204    public Options()
205    {
206       // initialize the Properties object of values to be stored as
207       // cookies.
208       books.setProperty( "Java", "0132222205" );
209       books.setProperty( "C++", "0136152503" );
210       books.setProperty( "Visual Basic 2005", "0131869000" );
211       books.setProperty( "Visual C# 2005", "0131525239" );
212       books.setProperty( "Internet & Web", "0131752421" );
213    } // end Options constructor
214
215    // To save space, we omitted the code in lines 215-257. The complete
216    // source code is provided with this chapter's examples.
217
258    // Action handler for the Submit button. Checks whether a language
259    // was selected and, if so, registers a cookie for that language and
260    // sets the responseText to indicate the chosen language.
261    public String submitButton_action()
262    {
263       String msg = "Welcome to Cookies! You ";
264
265       // if the user made a selection
266       if ( languageRadioGroup.getSelected() != null )
267       {
268          String language = languageRadioGroup.getSelected().toString();
269          msg += "selected " + language.replace( '-', ' ' ) + ".";
```

Fig. 26.19 | Page bean that stores the user's language selection in a client cookie. (Part 2 of 3.)

```
270
271             // get ISBN number of book for the given language
272             String ISBN = books.getProperty( language );
273
274             // create cookie using language-ISBN name-value pair
275             Cookie cookie = new Cookie( language, ISBN );
276
277             // add cookie to response header to place it on user's machine
278             HttpServletResponse response =
279                ( HttpServletResponse ) getExternalContext().getResponse();
280             response.addCookie( cookie );
281          } // end if
282          else
283             msg += "did not select a language.";
284
285          responseText.setValue( msg );
286          languageRadioGroup.setRendered( false );
287          instructionText.setRendered( false );
288          submitButton.setRendered( false );
289          responseText.setRendered( true );
290          languagesLink.setRendered( true );
291          recommendationsLink.setRendered( true );
292          return null; // reloads the page
293       } // end method submitButton_action
294
295       // redisplay the components for selecting a language
296       public String languagesLink_action()
297       {
298          responseText.setRendered( false );
299          languagesLink.setRendered( false );
300          recommendationsLink.setRendered( false );
301          languageRadioGroup.setRendered( true );
302          instructionText.setRendered( true );
303          submitButton.setRendered( true );
304          return null;
305       } // end method languagesLink_action
306    } // end class Options
```

Fig. 26.19 | Page bean that stores the user's language selection in a client cookie. (Part 3 of 3.)

As mentioned previously, the `_init` method handles component initialization. Since this page contains a `RadioButtonGroup` object that requires initialization, method `_init` (lines 26–40) constructs an array of `Option` objects to be displayed by the buttons.

Lines 208–212 in the constructor initialize a `Properties` object—a data structure that stores `String` key/value pairs. The application uses the key to store and retrieve the associated value in the `Properties` object. In this example, the keys are `Strings` containing the programming language names, and the values are `Strings` containing the ISBN numbers for the recommended books. Class `Properties` provides method `setProperty`, which takes as arguments a key and a value. A value that is added via method `setProperty` is placed in the `Properties` at a location determined by the key. The value for a specific `Properties` entry can be determined by invoking the method `getProperty` on the `Properties` object with that value's key as an argument.

Software Engineering Observation 26.1

Netbeans can automatically import any missing packages your Java file needs. For example, after adding the `Properties` *object to* `Options.java`*, you can right click in the Java editor window and select* **Fix Imports** *to automatically import* `java.util.Properties`*.*

Clicking **Submit** invokes the event handler `submitButton_action` (lines 261–293), which displays a message indicating the selected language in the `responseText` element and adds a new cookie to the response. If a language was selected (line 266), the selected item is retrieved (line 268). Line 269 adds the selected language to the results message.

Line 272 retrieves the ISBN for the selected language from the `books` `Properties` objectc. Then line 275 creates a new `Cookie` object (in package `javax.servlet.http`), using the selected language as the cookie's name and a corresponding ISBN as the cookie's value. This cookie is added to the HTTP response header in lines 278–280. An object of class `HttpServletResponse` (from package `javax.servlet.http`) represents the response. This object can be accessed by invoking the method `getExternalContext` on the page bean, then invoking `getResponse` on the resulting object. If a language was not selected, line 283 sets the results message to indicate that no selection was made.

Lines 285–291 control the appearance of the page after the user clicks **Submit**. Line 285 sets the `responseText` to display the `String` `msg`. Since the user has just submitted a language selection, the components used to collect the selection are hidden (lines 286–288) and `responseText` and the links used to navigate the application are displayed (lines 289–291). The action handler returns `null` at line 292, which reloads `Options.jsp`.

Lines 296–305 contain the `languagesLink`'s event handler. When the user clicks this link, `responseText` and the two links are hidden (lines 298–300), and the components that allow the user to select a language are redisplayed (lines 301–303). The method returns `null` at line 304, causing `Options.jsp` to reload.

Displaying Book Recommendations Based on Cookie Values

After clicking **Submit**, the user may request a book recommendation. The book recommendations hyperlink forwards the user to `Recommendations.jsp` (Fig. 26.20) to display recommendations based on the user's language selections.

```
<?xml version = "1.0" encoding = "UTF-8"?>

<!-- Fig. 26.20: Recommendations.jsp -->
<!-- Displays book recommendations using cookies -->
<jsp:root version = "1.2"
   xmlns:f = "http://java.sun.com/jsf/core"
   xmlns:h = "http://java.sun.com/jsf/html"
   xmlns:jsp = "http://java.sun.com/JSP/Page"
   xmlns:webuijsf = "http://www.sun.com/webui/webuijsf">
   <jsp:directive.page contentType = "text/html;charset=UTF-8"
      pageEncoding = "UTF-8"/>
   <f:view>
   <webuijsf:page binding = "#{Recommendations.page1}" id = "page1">
      <webuijsf:html binding = "#{Recommendations.html1}" id = "html1">
         <webuijsf:head binding = "#{Recommendations.head1}" id = "head1">
```

Fig. 26.20 | JSP file that displays book recommendations based on cookies. (Part 1 of 2.)

```
16             <webuijsf:link binding = "#{Recommendations.link1}"
17                id = "link1" url = "/resources/stylesheet.css"/>
18             </webuijsf:head>
19             <webuijsf:body binding = "#{Recommendations.body1}"
20                id = "body1" style = "-rave-layout: grid">
21                <webuijsf:form binding = "#{Recommendations.form1}"
22                   id = "form1">
23                   <webuijsf:label binding =
24                      "#{Recommendations.recommendationsLabel}" for =
25                      "recommendationsListbox" id = "recommendationsLabel"
26                      style = "font-size: 18px; left: 24px; top: 24px;
27                      position: absolute" text = "Recommendations"/>
28                   <webuijsf:listbox binding =
29                      "#{Recommendations.recommendationsListbox}" id =
30                      "recommendationsListbox" items = "#{Recommendations.
31                      recommendationsListboxDefaultOptions.options}"
32                      style = "height: 96px; left: 24px; top: 48px;
33                      position: absolute; width: 360px"/>
34                   <webuijsf:hyperlink actionExpression =
35                      "#{Recommendations.optionsLink_action}" binding =
36                      "#{Recommendations.optionsLink}" id = "optionsLink"
37                      style = "left: 24px; top: 168px; position: absolute"
38                      text = "Click here to choose another language."/>
39                </webuijsf:form>
40             </webuijsf:body>
41          </webuijsf:html>
42       </webuijsf:page>
43       </f:view>
44    </jsp:root>
```

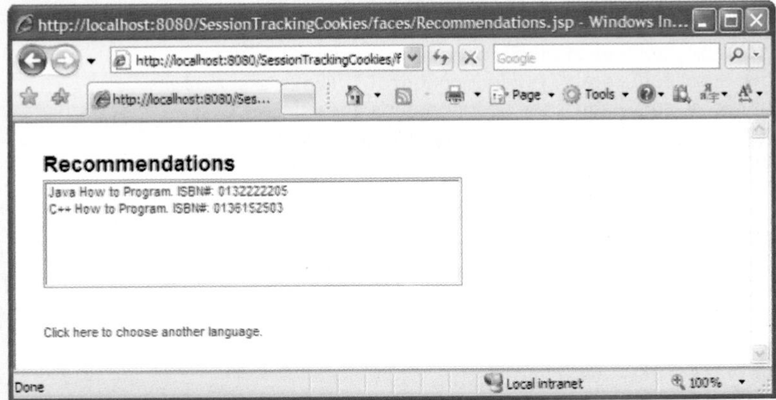

Fig. 26.20 | JSP file that displays book recommendations based on cookies. (Part 2 of 2.)

`Recommendations.jsp` contains a **Label** (lines 23–27), a **Listbox** (lines 28–33) and a **Hyperlink** (lines 34–38). The **Label** displays the text `Recommendations` at the top of the page. A **Listbox** component displays a list of options from which a user can make multiple selections. The **Listbox** in this example displays the recommendations created by the `Recommendations.java` page bean (Fig. 26.21), or the text `"No Recommendations. Please` select a language." The **Hyperlink** allows the user to return to Options.jsp to select additional languages. You can configure this hyperlink using the **Page Navigation** file as described earlier in this section.

Page Bean That Creates Book Recommendations from Cookies

In Recommendations.java (Fig. 26.21), method prerender (lines 180–210) retrieves the cookies from the client, using the request object's getCookies method (lines 183–185). An object of class HttpServletRequest (from package javax.servlet.http) represents the request. This object can be obtained by invoking method getExternalContext on the page bean, then invoking getRequest on the resulting object. The call to getCookies returns an array of the cookies previously written to the client. Cookies can be read by an application only if they were created by a server in the domain in which the application is running—a web server cannot access cookies created by servers in other domains. For example, a cookie created by a web server in the deitel.com domain cannot be read by a web server in any other domain.

```
1  // Fig. 26.21: Recommendations.java
2  // Displays book recommendations based on cookies storing user's selected
3  // programming languages.
4  package sessiontrackingcookies;
5
6  import com.sun.rave.web.ui.appbase.AbstractPageBean;
7  import com.sun.webui.jsf.component.Body;
8  import com.sun.webui.jsf.component.Form;
9  import com.sun.webui.jsf.component.Head;
10 import com.sun.webui.jsf.component.Html;
11 import com.sun.webui.jsf.component.Hyperlink;
12 import com.sun.webui.jsf.component.Label;
13 import com.sun.webui.jsf.component.Link;
14 import com.sun.webui.jsf.component.Listbox;
15 import com.sun.webui.jsf.component.Page;
16 import com.sun.webui.jsf.component.StaticText;
17 import com.sun.webui.jsf.model.DefaultOptionsList;
18 import com.sun.webui.jsf.model.Option;
19 import javax.faces.FacesException;
20 import javax.servlet.http.Cookie;
21 import javax.servlet.http.HttpServletRequest;
22
23 public class Recommendations extends AbstractPageBean
24 {
25    private int __placeholder;
26
27    private void _init() throws Exception
28    {
29       recommendationsListboxDefaultOptions.setOptions(
30          new com.sun.webui.jsf.model.Option[] {} );
31    }
32
```

Fig. 26.21 | Page bean that displays book recommendations based on cookies storing user's selected languages. (Part 1 of 2.)

```
33     // To save space, we omitted the code in lines 33-178. The complete
34     // source code is provided with this chapter's examples.
35
179    // displays the book recommendations in the Listbox
180    public void prerender()
181    {
182       // retrieve client's cookies
183       HttpServletRequest request =
184          ( HttpServletRequest ) getExternalContext().getRequest();
185       Cookie [] cookies = request.getCookies();
186
187       // if there are cookies, store the corresponding books and ISBN
188       // numbers in an array of Options
189       Option [] recommendations;
190
191       if ( cookies.length > 1 )
192       {
193          recommendations = new Option[ cookies.length - 1 ];
194
195          for ( int i = 0; i < cookies.length - 1; i++ )
196          {
197             String language = cookies[ i ].getName().replace( '-', ' ' );
198             recommendations[ i ] = new Option( language +
199                " How to Program.  ISBN#: " + cookies[ i ].getValue() );
200          } // end for
201       } // end if
202       else
203       {
204          recommendations = new Option[ 1 ];
205          recommendations[ 0 ] = new Option(
206             "No recommendations. Please select a language." ) ;
207       } // end else
208
209       recommendationsListbox.setItems( recommendations );
210    } // end method prerender
211
212    // To save space, we omitted the code in lines 212-230. The complete
213    // source code is provided with this chapter's examples.
214
231    // redirects user to Options.jsp
232    public String optionsLink_action()
233    {
234       return "case1"; // returns to Options.jsp
235    } // end method optionsLink_action
236 } // end class Recommendations
```

Fig. 26.21 | Page bean that displays book recommendations based on cookies storing user's selected languages. (Part 2 of 2.)

Line 191 determines whether at least one cookie exists. Lines 195–200 add the information in the cookie(s) to an `Option` array. Arrays of `Option` objects can be displayed as a list of items in a **Listbox** component. The loop retrieves the name and value of each cookie, using the control variable to determine the current value in the cookie array. If no language was selected, lines 204–206 add to an `Options` array a message instructing the user to select a language. Line 209 sets `recommendationsListBox` to display the resulting `Options` array. We summarize commonly used `Cookie` methods in Fig. 26.22.

Method	Description
`getDomain`	Returns a `String` containing the cookie's domain (i.e., the domain from which the cookie was written). This determines which web servers can receive the cookie. By default, cookies are sent to the web server that originally sent the cookie to the client. Changing the `Domain` property causes the cookie to be returned to a web server other than the one that originally wrote it.
`getMaxAge`	Returns an `int` indicating how many seconds the cookie will persist on the browser. This is –1 by default, meaning the cookie will persist until the browser is shut down.
`getName`	Returns a `String` containing the cookie's name.
`getPath`	Returns a `String` containing the path to a directory on the server to which the cookie applies. Cookies can be "targeted" to specific directories on the web server. By default, a cookie is returned only to applications operating in the same directory as the application that sent the cookie or a subdirectory of that directory. Changing the `Path` property causes the cookie to be returned to a directory other than the one from which it was originally written.
`getSecure`	Returns a `bool` value indicating whether the cookie should be transmitted through a secure protocol. The value `true` causes a secure protocol to be used.
`getValue`	Returns a `String` containing the cookie's value.

Fig. 26.22 | `javax.servlet.http.Cookie` methods.

26.5.2 Session Tracking with the `SessionBean` Object

You can also perform session tracking with the `SessionBean` class that is provided in each web application created with Netbeans. When a web page in the project is requested, a `SessionBean` object is created. Properties of this object can be accessed throughout a browser session by invoking the method `getSessionBean` on the page bean. To demonstrate session-tracking techniques using the `SessionBean`, we modified the page bean files in Figs. 26.19 and 26.21 so that they use the `SessionBean` to store the user's selected languages. We begin with the updated `Options.jsp` file (Fig. 26.23). Figure 26.26 presents the `SessionBean.java` file, and Fig. 26.27 presents the modified page bean file for `Options.jsp`.

The `Options.jsp` file in Fig. 26.23 is similar to that presented in Fig. 26.17 for the cookies example. Lines 40–48 define two `webuijsf:staticText` elements that were not present in the cookies example. The first element displays the text `"Number of selections so far:"`. The second element's `text` attribute is bound to property `numSelections` in the `SessionBean` (line 48). We discuss how to bind the `text` attribute to a `SessionBean` property momentarily.

```
<?xml version = "1.0" encoding = "UTF-8"?>

<!-- Fig. 26.23: Options.jsp -->
<!-- JSP file that allows the user to select a programming language -->
<jsp:root version = "1.2"
   xmlns:f = "http://java.sun.com/jsf/core"
   xmlns:h = "http://java.sun.com/jsf/html"
   xmlns:jsp = "http://java.sun.com/JSP/Page"
   xmlns:webuijsf = "http://www.sun.com/webui/webuijsf">
   <jsp:directive.page contentType = "text/html;charset=UTF-8"
      pageEncoding = "UTF-8"/>
   <f:view>
   <webuijsf:page binding = "#{Options.page1}" id = "page1">
      <webuijsf:html binding = "#{Options.html1}" id = "html1">
         <webuijsf:head binding = "#{Options.head1}" id = "head1">
            <webuijsf:link binding = "#{Options.link1}" id = "link1"
               url = "/resources/stylesheet.css"/>
         </webuijsf:head>
         <webuijsf:body binding = "#{Options.body1}" id = "body1"
            style = "-rave-layout: grid">
            <webuijsf:form binding = "#{Options.form1}" id = "form1">
               <webuijsf:staticText binding = "#{Options.instructionText}"
                  id = "instructionText" style = "font-size: 18px;
                  left: 24px; top: 24px; position: absolute"
                  text = "Select a programming language:"/>
               <webuijsf:radioButtonGroup binding =
                  "#{Options.languageRadioGroup}" id =
                  "languageRadioGroup" items =
                  "#{Options.languageRadioGroupDefaultOptions.options}"
                  style = "left: 24px; top: 48px; position: absolute"/>
               <webuijsf:button actionExpression =
                  "#{Options.submitButton_action}" binding =
                  "#{Options.submitButton}" id = "submitButton" style =
                  "left: 23px; top: 192px; position: absolute;
                  width: 100px" text = "Submit"/>
               <webuijsf:staticText binding = "#{Options.responseText}"
                  id = "responseText" rendered = "false" style =
                  "font-size: 18px; left: 24px; top: 24px;
                  position: absolute"/>
               <webuijsf:staticText binding = "#{Options.selectionsText}"
                  id = "selectionsText" rendered = "false" style =
                  "position: absolute; left: 24px; top: 72px" text =
                  "Number of selections so far:"/>
               <webuijsf:staticText binding =
                  "#{Options.selectionsValueText}" id =
                  "selectionsValueText" rendered = "false" style =
                  "left: 168px; top: 72px; position: absolute"
                  text = "#{SessionBean1.numSelections}"/>
               <webuijsf:hyperlink actionExpression =
                  "#{Options.languagesLink_action}" binding =
                  "#{Options.languagesLink}" id = "languagesLink"
                  rendered = "false" style = "left: 24px; top: 120px;
```

Fig. 26.23 | JSP file that allows the user to select a programming language. (Part 1 of 3.)

```
                    position: absolute"
                    text = "Click here to choose another language."/>
                 <webuijsf:hyperlink actionExpression =
                    "#{Options.recommendationsLink_action}" binding =
                    "#{Options.recommendationsLink}" id =
                    "recommendationsLink" rendered = "false" style =
                    "left: 24px; top: 144px; position: absolute"
                    text = "Click here to get book recommendations."
                    url = "/faces/Recommendations.jsp"/>
              </webuijsf:form>
           </webuijsf:body>
        </webuijsf:html>
     </webuijsf:page>
     </f:view>
</jsp:root>
```

(a)

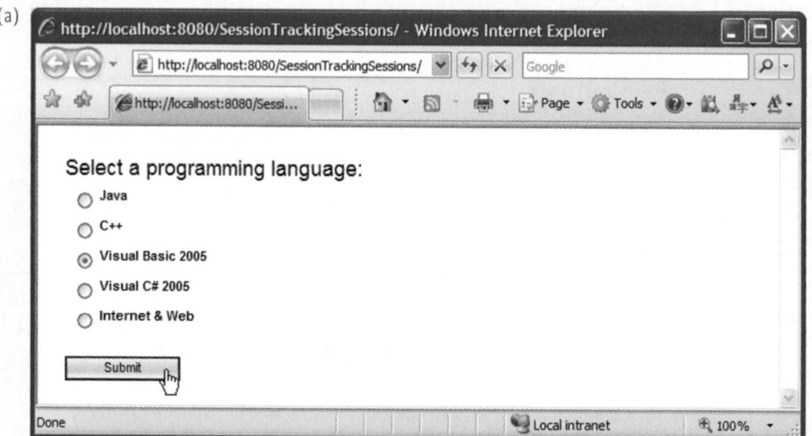

(b)

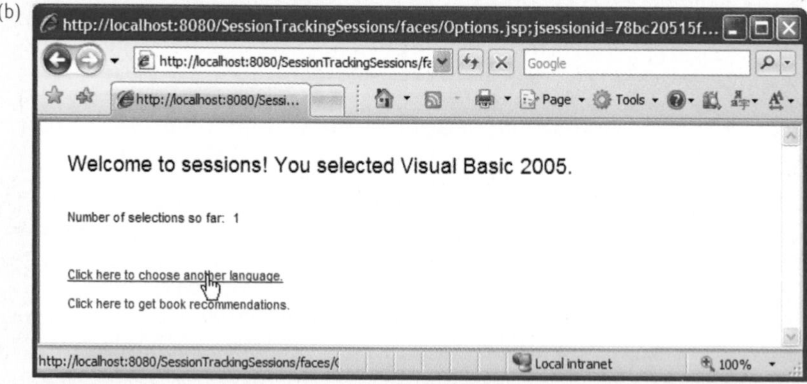

Fig. 26.23 | JSP file that allows the user to select a programming language. (Part 2 of 3.)

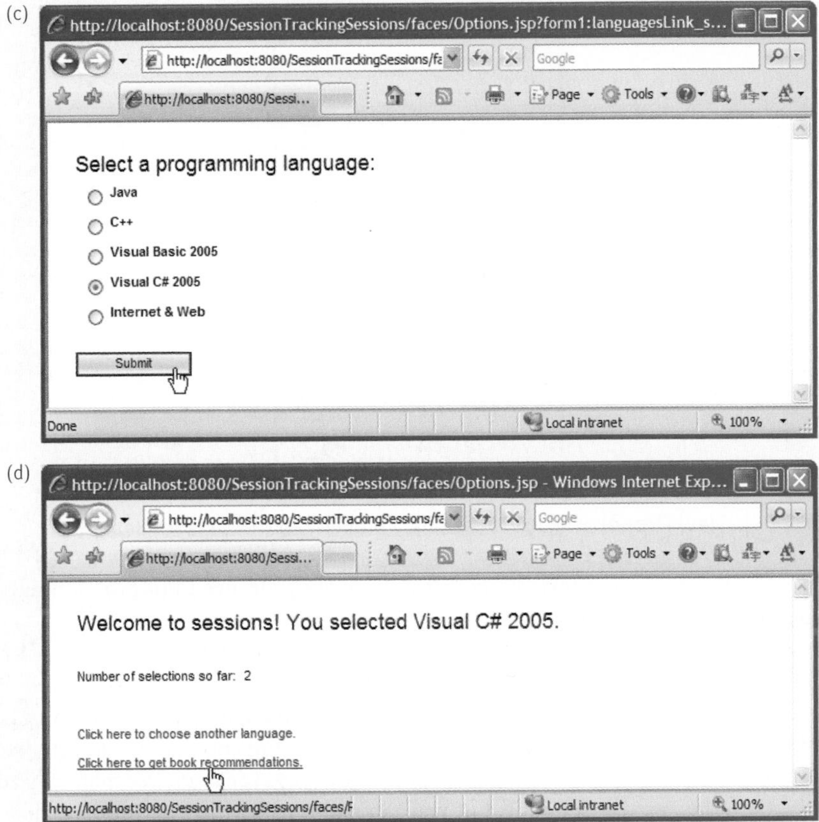

Fig. 26.23 | JSP file that allows the user to select a programming language. (Part 3 of 3.)

Adding Properties to the **SessionBean**

In this example, we use session tracking to store not only the user's selected languages, but also the number of selections made. To store this information in the `SessionBean`, we add properties to the `SessionBean` class.

To add a property that will store the number of selections so far, right click the `SessionBean1` node in the **Outline** window and select **Add > Property** to display the **New Property Pattern** dialog (Fig. 26.24). This dialog allows you to add primitive, `String` or primitive type-wrapper (e.g., `Integer`, `Double`) properties to the `SessionBean`. Add an `int` property named `numSelections` and click **OK** to accept the default settings for this property. Open the `SessionBean` file, and at the bottom of the source code you'll see a new property definition, a *get* method and *set* method for `numSelections`.

Property `numSelections` is manipulated in the page bean file to store the number of languages the user selected. To display the value of this property in the `selectionsValueText` element in the JSP file, right click the element in the **Outline** window and select **Bind to Data...**. In the **Bind to Data** dialog (Fig. 26.25), select the **Bind to an Object** tab, locate property `numSelections` under the `SessionBean1` node and click **OK**. The **Static Text** element will now always display the value of `SessionBean1`'s `numSelections` property. If the

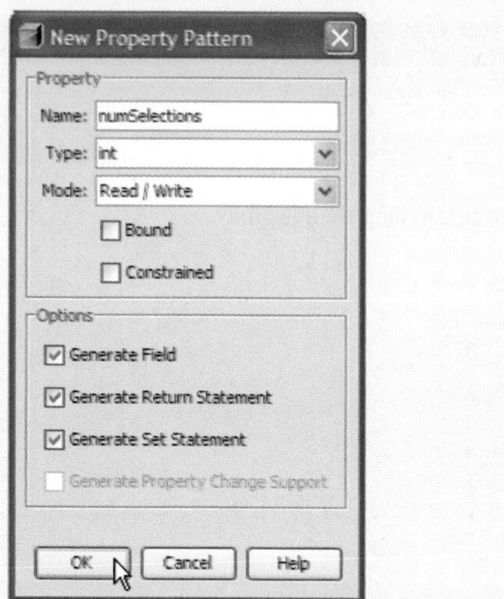

Fig. 26.24 | **New Property** dialog for adding a property to the `SessionBean`.

property's value changes, the text changes as well, so that you need not programmatically set the text in the page bean file.

Now that we've added a property to store the number of selections in the `SessionBean1`, we must add a second property to store the selections themselves. We'd like to store selections as key/value pairs of the selected language and the ISBN number of a related book, similar to the way selections were stored using cookies. To do this, we add a `Properties` object named `selectedLanguages` to the `SessionBean`. We manually added this property to the `SessionBean` file, but you can add it using the **New Property** dialog in Fig. 26.24. Simply type `java.util.Properties` in the **Type** drop-down list's field, configure the property and click **OK**. The modified `SessionBean` file (after the two properties have been added) is displayed in Fig. 26.26.

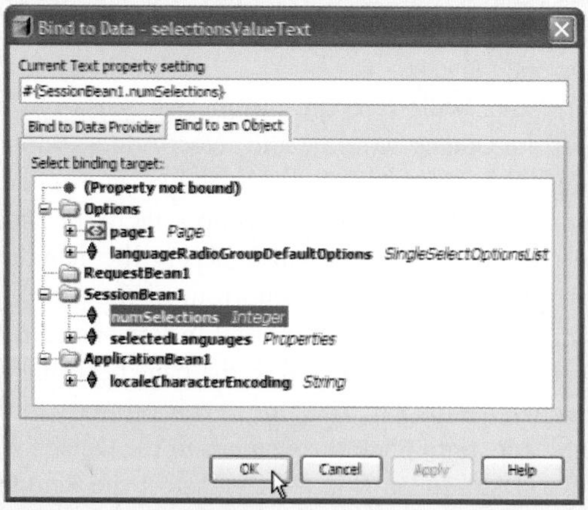

Fig. 26.25 | **Bind to Data** dialog.

```
1  // Fig. 26.26: SessionBean.java
2  // SessionBean file for storing language selections.
3  package sessiontrackingsessions;
4
5  import com.sun.rave.web.ui.appbase.AbstractSessionBean;
6  import javax.faces.FacesException;
7
8  public class SessionBean1 extends AbstractSessionBean
9  {
10    // To save space, we omitted the code in lines 10-52. The complete
11    // source code is provided with this chapter's examples.
12
53    // holds value of property numSelections
54    private int numSelections;
55
56    // returns value of numSelections
57    public int getNumSelections()
58    {
59       return this.numSelections;
60    } // end method getNumSelections
61
62    // sets new value of numSelections
63    public void setNumSelections(int numSelections)
64    {
65       this.numSelections = numSelections;
66    } // end method setNumSelections
67
68    // holds value of property selectedLanguages
69    private java.util.Properties selectedLanguages =
70       new java.util.Properties();
71
72    // returns selectedLanguages
73    public java.util.Properties getSelectedLanguages()
74    {
75       return this.selectedLanguages;
76    } // end method getSelectedLanguages
77
78    // sets new value of property selectedLanguages
79    public void setSelectedLanguages(
80       java.util.Properties selectedLanguages )
81    {
82       this.selectedLanguages = selectedLanguages;
83    } // end method setSelectedLanguages
84 } // end class SessionBean1
```

Fig. 26.26 | `SessionBean` file for storing language selections.

Line 54 declares the `numSelections` property, and lines 57–60 and 63–66 declare its *get* and *set* methods, respectively. This portion of the code was generated automatically when we used the **New Property** dialog. Lines 69–70 define the `Properties` object `selectedLanguages` that will store user selections. Lines 73–76 and 79–83 are the *get* and *set* methods for this property.

Manipulating **SessionBean** *Properties in a Page Bean File*

The page bean file for the `Options.jsp` page is displayed in Fig. 26.27. Because much of this example is identical to the preceding one, we concentrate on the new features.

```
// Fig. 26.27: Options.java
// Page bean that stores language selections in a SessionBean property.
package sessiontrackingsessions;

import com.sun.rave.web.ui.appbase.AbstractPageBean;
import com.sun.webui.jsf.component.Body;
import com.sun.webui.jsf.component.Button;
import com.sun.webui.jsf.component.Form;
import com.sun.webui.jsf.component.Head;
import com.sun.webui.jsf.component.Html;
import com.sun.webui.jsf.component.Hyperlink;
import com.sun.webui.jsf.component.Link;
import com.sun.webui.jsf.component.Page;
import com.sun.webui.jsf.component.RadioButtonGroup;
import com.sun.webui.jsf.component.StaticText;
import com.sun.webui.jsf.model.SingleSelectOptionsList;
import java.util.Properties;
import javax.faces.FacesException;
import javax.servlet.http.Cookie;
import javax.servlet.http.HttpServletResponse;

public class Options extends AbstractPageBean
{
   private int __placeholder;

   private void _init() throws Exception
   {
      languageRadioGroupDefaultOptions.setOptions(
         new com.sun.webui.jsf.model.Option[] {
            new com.sun.webui.jsf.model.Option( "Java", "Java" ),
            new com.sun.webui.jsf.model.Option( "C++", "C++" ),
            new com.sun.webui.jsf.model.Option( "Visual Basic 2005",
               "Visual Basic 2005" ),
            new com.sun.webui.jsf.model.Option( "Visual C# 2005",
               "Visual C# 2005" ),
            new com.sun.webui.jsf.model.Option( "Internet & Web",
               "Internet & Web")
         } // end array initializer
      ); // end call to setOptions
   } // end method _init

   // To save space, we omitted the code in lines 42-225. The complete
   // source code is provided with this chapter's examples.

   // Construct a new page bean instance and initialize the properties
   // that map languages to ISBN numbers of recommended books.
   public Options()
   {
```

Fig. 26.27 | Page bean that stores language selections in a `SessionBean` property. (Part 1 of 3.)

```
      // initialize the Properties object of values to be stored
      // in the session
      books.setProperty( "Java", "0132222205" );
      books.setProperty( "C++", "0136152503" );
      books.setProperty( "Visual Basic 2005", "0131869000" );
      books.setProperty( "Visual C# 2005", "0131525239" );
      books.setProperty( "Internet & Web", "0131752421" );
   } // end Options constructor

   // To save space, we omitted the code in lines 239-281. The complet
   // source code is provided with this chapter's examples.

   // Action handler for the Submit button. Checks whether a language
   // was selected and, if so, registers a cookie for that language and
   // sets the responseText to indicate the chosen language.
   public String submitButton_action()
   {
      String msg = "Welcome to sessions!  You ";

      // if the user made a selection
      if ( getLanguageRadioGroup().getSelected() != null )
      {
         String language = languageRadioGroup.getSelected().toString();
         msg += "selected " + language + ".";

         // get ISBN number of book for the given language.
         String ISBN = books.getProperty( language );

         // add the selection to the SessionBean's Properties object
         Properties selections = getSessionBean1().getSelectedLanguages();
         Object result = selections.setProperty( language, ISBN );

         // increment numSelections in the SessionBean and update
         // selectedLanguages if user has not made this selection before
         if ( result == null )
         {
            int numSelected = getSessionBean1().getNumSelections();
            getSessionBean1().setNumSelections( ++numSelected );
         } // end if
      } // end if
      else
         msg += "did not select a language.";

      responseText.setValue( msg );
      languageRadioGroup.setRendered( false );
      instructionText.setRendered( false );
      submitButton.setRendered( false );
      responseText.setRendered( true );
      selectionsText.setRendered( true );
      selectionsValueText.setRendered( true );
      languagesLink.setRendered( true );
      recommendationsLink.setRendered( true );
```

Fig. 26.27 | Page bean that stores language selections in a `SessionBean` property. (Part 2 of 3.)

```
322          return null; // reloads the page
323       } // end method submitButton_action
324
325       // redisplay the components for selecting a language
326       public String languagesLink_action()
327       {
328          responseText.setRendered( false );
329          selectionsText.setRendered( false );
330          selectionsValueText.setRendered( false );
331          languagesLink.setRendered( false );
332          recommendationsLink.setRendered( false );
333          languageRadioGroup.setRendered( true );
334          instructionText.setRendered( true );
335          submitButton.setRendered( true );
336          return null;
337       } // end method languagesLink_action
338
339       // forwards user to Recommendations.jsp
340       public String recommendationsLink_action()
341       {
342          return "case1";
343       } // end method recommendationsLink_action
344    } // end class Options
```

Fig. 26.27 | Page bean that stores language selections in a `SessionBean` property. (Part 3 of 3.)

The `submitButton`'s action handler (lines 285–323) stores the user's selections in the `SessionBean` and increments the number of selections made, if necessary. Line 299 retrieves from the `SessionBean` the `Properties` object that contains the user's selections. Line 300 adds the current selection to the `Properties` object. Method `setProperty` returns the value previously associated with the new key, or `null` if this key was not already stored in the `Properties` object. If adding the new property returns `null`, then the user has made a new selection. In this case, lines 306–307 increment the `numSelections` property in the `SessionBean`. Lines 313–321 and the `languaguesLink` action handler (lines 326–337) control the components that are displayed, just as in the cookies examples.

Software Engineering Observation 26.2

A benefit of using `SessionBean` properties (rather than cookies) is that they can store any type of object (not just `Strings`) as attribute values. This provides you with increased flexibility in maintaining client-state information.

Displaying Recommendations Based on Session Values

As in the cookies example, this application provides a link to `Recommendations.jsp`, which displays a list of book recommendations based on the user's language selections. Since this JSP is identical to the version in Fig. 26.20, we show only the sample output of this page in Fig. 26.28.

Page Bean That Creates Book Recommendations from a `SessionBean` Property

Figure 26.29 presents the page bean for `Recommendations.jsp`. Again, much of it is similar to the page bean used in the cookies example. We discuss only the new features.

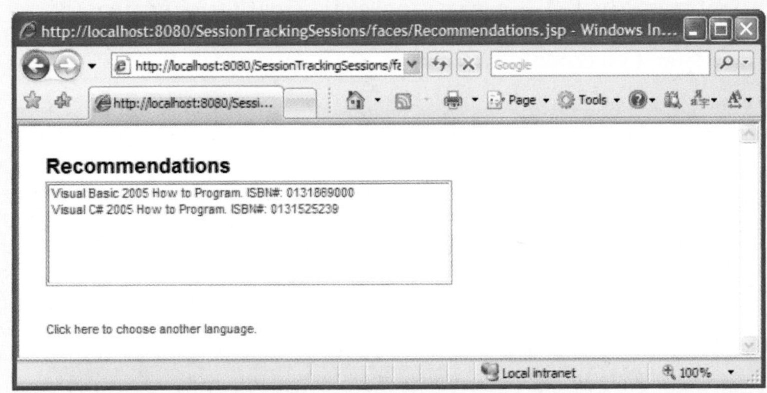

Fig. 26.28 | JSP file that displays book recommendations based on language selections stored in session scope.

```java
// Fig. 26.29: Recommendations.java
// Page bean that displays book recommendations based on a SessionBean
// property.
package sessiontrackingsessions;

import com.sun.rave.web.ui.appbase.AbstractPageBean;
import com.sun.webui.jsf.component.Body;
import com.sun.webui.jsf.component.Form;
import com.sun.webui.jsf.component.Head;
import com.sun.webui.jsf.component.Html;
import com.sun.webui.jsf.component.Hyperlink;
import com.sun.webui.jsf.component.Label;
import com.sun.webui.jsf.component.Link;
import com.sun.webui.jsf.component.Listbox;
import com.sun.webui.jsf.component.Page;
import com.sun.webui.jsf.model.DefaultOptionsList;
import com.sun.webui.jsf.model.Option;
import java.util.Enumeration;
import java.util.Properties;
import javax.faces.FacesException;

public class Recommendations extends AbstractPageBean
{
   // To save space, we omitted the code in lines 24-177. The complete
   // source code is provided with this chapter's examples.

   // displays the book recommendations in the Listbox
   public void prerender()
   {
      // retrieve user's selections and number of selections made
      Properties languages = getSessionBean1().getSelectedLanguages();
      Enumeration selectionsEnum = languages.propertyNames();
```

Fig. 26.29 | Displays book recommendations based on a `SessionBean` property. (Part 1 of 2.)

```
184         int numSelected = getSessionBean1().getNumSelections();
185
186         Option [] recommendations;
187
188         // if at least one selection was made
189         if ( numSelected > 0 )
190         {
191            recommendations = new Option[ numSelected ];
192
193            for ( int i = 0; i < numSelected; i++ )
194            {
195               String language = (String) selectionsEnum.nextElement();
196               recommendations[ i ] = new Option( language +
197                  " How to Program.  ISBN#: " +
198                  languages.getProperty( language ) );
199            } // end for
200         } // end if
201         else
202         {
203            recommendations = new Option[ 1 ];
204            recommendations[ 0 ] = new Option(
205               "No recommendations. Please select a language." );
206         } // end else
207
208         recommendationsListbox.setItems( recommendations );
209      } // end method prerender
210
211      // To save space, we omitted the code in lines 211-229. The complete
212      // source code is provided with this chapter's examples.
213
230      // redirects user to Options.jsp
231      public String optionsLink_action()
232      {
233         return "case1"; // returns to Options.jsp
234      } // end method optionsLink_action
235   } // end class Recommendations
```

Fig. 26.29 | Displays book recommendations based on a `SessionBean` property. (Part 2 of 2.)

Line 182 retrieves the `Properties` object containing the user's selections from the `SessionBean`, and line 183 gets an enumeration of all of the keys in that `Properties` object. Line 184 retrieves the number of selections made from the `SessionBean`. If any selections were made, line 191 constructs an appropriately sized `Option` array to display the selections in the `webuijsf:listBox` element of `Recommendations.jsp`. Lines 193–199 add each of the user's selections to this `Option` array. Line 195 gets the next key from the enumeration of keys, and lines 196–198 add a recommendation to the `Option` array.

26.6 Wrap-Up

In this chapter, we introduced web application development using JavaServer Pages and JavaServer Faces in Netbeans. We began by discussing the simple HTTP transactions that take place when you request and receive a web page through a web browser. We then discussed the three tiers (i.e., the client or top tier, the business logic or middle tier and the information or bottom tier) that comprise most web applications.

You learned the role of JSP files and page bean files, and the relationship between them. You learned how to use Netbeans to visually build web applications using Netbeans's drag-and-drop capabilities, then you compiled and executed them.

We demonstrated several common JSF components used for displaying text and images on web pages. We also discussed validation components and custom validator methods, which allow you to ensure that user input satisfies certain requirements.

We discussed the benefits of maintaining user information across multiple pages of a website. We then demonstrated how you can include such functionality in a web application using either cookies or properties in the `SessionBean` class. In the next chapter, we continue our discussion of web application development. You'll learn how to access a database from a JSF web application, how to use several of the AJAX-enabled JSF components from Sun's Java Blueprints and how to use virtual forms.

26.7 Web Resources

Our Java Resource Centers focus on the enormous amount of free Java content available online. We currently provide six Java-related Resource Centers:

```
www.deitel.com/java/
www.deitel.com/JavaCertification/
www.deitel.com/JavaDesignPatterns/
www.deitel.com/JavaEE5/
www.deitel.com/JavaFX/
www.deitel.com/JavaSE6Mustang/
```

You can view our complete list of Resource Centers at

```
www.deitel.com/ResourceCenters.html
```

Summary

Section 26.1 Introduction

- Web-based applications create web content for web browser clients.
- AJAX helps web-based applications provide the interactivity and responsiveness that users typically expect of desktop applications.

Section 26.2 Java Web Technologies

- Java web technologies continually evolve to provide developers with higher levels of abstraction and greater separation of the application's tiers. This separation makes web applications more maintainable and extensible.
- Netbeans allows you to develop a web application's GUI in a drag-and-drop design tool, while handling the business logic in separate Java classes.

Section 26.2.1 Servlets

- Servlets use the HTTP request/response model of communication between client and server.
- Servlets extend a server's functionality by allowing the server to generate dynamic content. A servlet container executes and interacts with servlets.

- Packages `javax.servlet` and `javax.servlet.http` contain the servlet classes and interfaces.
- The servlet container receives HTTP requests from a client and directs each request to the appropriate servlet. The servlet processes the request and returns an appropriate response to the client—usually in the form of an XHTML or XML document.
- All servlets implement the `Servlet` interface of package `javax.servlet`, which ensures that each servlet can execute in the framework provided by the servlet container. Interface `Servlet` declares methods used by the servlet container to manage the servlet's life cycle.
- A servlet's life cycle begins when the servlet container loads it into memory. The container invokes the servlet's `init` method, which is called only once during a servlet's life cycle to initialize the servlet. After `init` completes execution, the servlet is ready to respond to requests. Requests are handled by a servlet's `service` method, which receives the request, processes it and sends a response. Method `service` is called once per request. When the servlet container terminates the servlet, the servlet's `destroy` method is called to release any resources held by the servlet.

Section 26.2.2 JavaServer Pages

- JavaServer Pages (JSP) are an extension of servlet technology. Each JSP is translated by the JSP container into a servlet.
- Unlike servlets, JSPs help you separate presentation from content.
- JavaServer Pages enable web application programmers to create dynamic content by reusing predefined components and by interacting with components using server-side scripting.
- JSP programmers can use special software components called JavaBeans and custom tag libraries that encapsulate complex, dynamic functionality.
- Custom tag libraries allow Java developers to hide code for database access and other complex operations in custom tags. To use such capabilities, you simply add the custom tags to the page. This simplicity enables web-page designers who are not familiar with Java to enhance web pages with powerful dynamic content and processing capabilities.
- The JSP classes and interfaces are located in packages `javax.servlet.jsp` and `javax.servlet.jsp.tagext`.
- There are four key components to JSPs—directives, actions, scripting elements and tag libraries.
- Directives are messages to the JSP container that enable you to specify page settings, to include content from other resources and to specify custom tag libraries for use in JSPs.
- Actions encapsulate functionality in predefined tags that programmers can embed in JSPs. Actions often are performed based on the information sent to the server as part of a particular client request. They also can create Java objects for use in JSPs.
- Scripting elements enable you to insert Java code that interacts with components in a JSP.
- Tag libraries enable programmers to create custom tags and web-page designers to manipulate JSP content without prior Java knowledge.
- The JavaServer Pages Standard Tag Library (JSTL) provides the functionality for many common web application tasks.
- JSPs can contain static content such as XHTML or XML markup, which is known as fixed-template data or fixed-template text. Any literal text or XHTML markup in a JSP is translated to a `String` literal in the servlet representation of the JSP.
- When a JSP-enabled server receives the first request for a JSP, the JSP container translates the JSP into a servlet that handles the current request and future requests to the JSP.
- JSPs rely on the same request/response mechanism as servlets to process requests from and send responses to clients.

Section 26.2.3 JavaServer Faces

- JavaServer Faces (JSF) is a web application framework that simplifies the design of an application's user interface and further separates a web application's presentation from its business logic.
- A framework simplifies application development by providing libraries and sometimes software tools to help you organize and build your applications.
- JSF provides custom tag libraries containing user interface components that simplify web-page design. JSF also includes a set of APIs for handling component events.
- You design the look-and-feel of a page with JSF by adding custom tags to a JSP file and manipulating their attributes. You define the page's behavior in a separate Java source-code file.

Section 26.2.4 Web Technologies in Netbeans

- Netbeans web applications consist of one or more JSPs built in the JavaServer Faces framework. Each has the filename extension `.jsp` and contains the web page's GUI elements.
- Netbeans allows you to design pages visually by dragging and dropping JSF components onto a page; you can also customize a web page by editing its `.jsp` file manually.
- Every JSP file created in Netbeans represents a web page and has a corresponding JavaBean class called the page bean.
- A JavaBean class must have a default (or no-argument) constructor, and *get* and *set* methods for all of its properties.
- The page bean defines properties for each of the page's elements, and contains event handlers, page life-cycle methods and other supporting code for the web application.
- Every web application built with Netbeans has a page bean, a `RequestBean`, a `SessionBean` and an `ApplicationBean`.
- The `RequestBean` object is maintained in request scope—this object exists only for the duration of an HTTP request.
- A `SessionBean` object has session scope—the object exists throughout a user's browsing session or until the session times out. There is a unique `SessionBean` object for each user.
- The `ApplicationBean` object has application scope—this object is shared by all instances of an application and exists as long as the application remains deployed on a web server. This object is used for applicationwide data storage or processing; only one instance exists for the application, regardless of the number of open sessions.

Section 26.3.1 Examining a JSP File

- Netbeans generates a JSP file in response to your interactions with the Visual Editor.
- All JSPs have a `jsp:root` element with a `version` attribute to indicate the version of JSP being used and one or more `xmlns` attributes. Each `xmlns` attribute specifies a prefix and a URL for a tag library, allowing the page to use tags specified in that library.
- All JSPs generated by Netbeans include the tag libraries for the JSF core components library, the JSF HTML components library, the JSP standard components library and the JSP user interface components library.
- The `jsp:directive.page` element's `contentType` attribute specifies the MIME type and the character set the page uses. The `pageEncoding` attribute specifies the character encoding used by the page source. These attributes help the client determine how to render the content.
- All pages containing JSF components are represented in a component tree with the root JSF element `f:view` (of type `UIViewRoot`). All JSF component elements are placed in this element.

- Many `ui` page elements have a `binding` attribute to bind their values to properties in the web application's JavaBeans. JSF Expression Language is used to perform these bindings.
- The `webuijsf:head` element has a `title` attribute that specifies the page's title.
- A `webuijsf:link` element can be used to specify the CSS style sheet used by a page.
- A `webuijsf:body` element defines the body of the page.
- A `webuijsf:form` element defines a form in a page.
- A `webuijsf:staticText` component displays text that does not change.
- JSP elements are mapped to XHTML elements for rendering in a browser. The same JSP element can map to different XHTML elements, depending on the client browser and the component's property settings.
- A `webuijsf:staticText` component typically maps to an XHTML `span` element. A `span` element contains text that is displayed on a web page and is used to control the formatting of the text. The `style` attribute of a `webuijsf:staticText` element will be represented as part of the corresponding `span` element's `style` attribute when the browser renders the page.

Section 26.3.2 Examining a Page Bean File

- Page bean classes inherit from class `AbstractPageBean` (package `com.sun.rave.web.ui.appbase`), which provides page life-cycle methods.
- Package `com.sun.webui.jsf.component` includes classes for many basic JSF components.
- A `webuijsf:staticText` component is a `StaticText` object (package `com.sun.webui.jsf.component`).

Section 26.3.3 Event-Processing Life Cycle

- Netbeans's application model places several methods (`init`, `preprocess`, `prerender` and `destroy`) in the page bean that tie into the JSF event-processing life cycle. These methods represent four major stages—initialization, preprocessing, prerendering and destruction.
- The `init` method is called by the JSP container the first time the page is requested and on postbacks. A postback occurs when form data is submitted, and the page and its contents are sent to the server to be processed.
- Method `init` invokes its superclass version, then tries to call the method `_init`, which handles component initialization tasks.
- The `preprocess` method is called after `init`, but only if the page is processing a postback. The `prerender` method is called just before a page is rendered by the browser. This method should be used to set component properties; properties that are set sooner (such as in method `init`) may be overwritten before the page is actually rendered by the browser.
- The `destroy` method is called after the page has been rendered, but only if the `init` method was called. This method handles tasks such as freeing resources used to render the page.

Section 26.3.4 Relationship Between the JSP and Page Bean Files

- The page bean has a property for every element that appears in the JSP file.

Section 26.3.6 Building a Web Application in Netbeans

- To create a new web application, select **File > New Project...** to display the **New Project** dialog. In this dialog, select **Web** in the **Categories** pane, **Visual Web Application** in the **Projects** pane and click **Next**. Specify the project name and location. Click **Finish** to create the web application project.
- Netbeans creates a single web page named `Page1` when you create a new project. This page is open by default in the Visual Editor in **Design** mode when the project first loads. As you drag

and drop new components onto the page, **Design** mode allows you to see how your page will be rendered in the browser. The JSP file for this page, named `Page1.jsp`, can be viewed by clicking the **JSP** button at the top of the Visual Editor or by right clicking anywhere in the Visual Editor and selecting **Edit JSP Source.**

- To open the corresponding page bean file, click the **Java** button at the top of the Visual Editor or right click anywhere in the Visual Editor and select **Edit Java Source.**
- The **Preview in Browser** button at the top of the Visual Editor window allows you to view your pages in a browser without having to build and run the application.
- The **Refresh** button redraws the page in the Visual Editor.
- The **Target Browser Size** drop-down list allows you to specify the optimal browser resolution for viewing the page and allows you to see what the page will look like in different screen resolutions.
- The **Projects** window in the upper-left corner of the IDE displays the hierarchy of all the project's files. The **Web Pages** node contains the JSP files and includes the **resources** folder, which contains the project's CSS style sheet and any other files the pages may need to display properly (e.g., images). The Java source code, including the page bean file for each web page and the application, session and request scope beans, can be found under the **Source Packages** node.
- The **Page Navigation** file defines rules for navigating the project's pages based on the outcome of user-initiated events, such as clicking a button or a link. This file can also be accessed by right clicking in the Visual Editor while in **Design** mode and selecting **Page Navigation.**
- Methods `init`, `preprocess`, `prerender` and `destroy` are overridden in each page bean. Other than method `init`, these methods are initially empty. They serve as placeholders for you to customize the behavior of your web application.
- Typically, you'll want to rename the JSP and Java files in your project, so that their names are relevant to your application. To do so, right click the JSP file in the **Projects Window** and select **Rename** to display the **Rename** dialog. Enter the new filename. If **Preview All Changes** is checked, the **Refactoring Window** will appear at the bottom of the IDE when you click **Next >**. No changes will be made until you click **Do Refactoring** in the **Refactoring Window**. If you do not preview the changes, refactoring occurs when you click **Next >** in the **Rename** dialog.
- Refactoring is the process of modifying source code to improve its readability and reusability without changing its behavior. Netbeans has built-in refactoring tools that automate some refactoring tasks.
- To add a title, open the JSP file in **Design** mode. In the **Properties** window, enter the new title next to the **Title** property and press *Enter*.
- To add components to a page, drag and drop them from the **Palette** onto the page in **Design** mode. Each component is an object that has properties, methods and events. You can set these properties and events in the **Properties** window or programmatically in the page bean file. *Get* and *set* methods are added to the page bean file for each component you add to the page.
- Components are rendered by default using absolute positioning, so that they appear exactly where they are dropped on the page.
- Netbeans is a WYSIWYG (What You See Is What You Get) editor—whenever you make a change to a web page in **Design** mode, the IDE creates the markup (visible in **JSP** mode) necessary to achieve the desired visual effects seen in **Design** mode.
- After designing the user interface, you can modify the page bean to add your business logic.
- The **Outline** window displays the page bean and the request, session and application scope beans. Clicking an item in the page bean's component tree selects the item in the Visual Editor.
- Select **Build > Build Main Project** then **Run > Run Main Project** to run the application.

- You can run a project that has already been built by pressing the **Run Main Project** icon ( ) in the toolbar at the top of the IDE.
- If changes are made to a project, the project must be rebuilt before the changes will be reflected when the application is viewed in a browser.
- Press *F5* to build the application, then run it in debug mode. If you type *F6*, the program executes without debugging enabled.

Section 26.4.1 Text and Graphics Components

- The **Grid Panel** component allows the designer to specify the number of columns the grid should contain. Components may then be dropped anywhere inside the panel, and they will automatically be repositioned into evenly spaced columns in the order in which they are dropped. When the number of components exceeds the number of columns, the panel moves the additional components to a new row.
- An **Image** component (of class `ImageComponent`) inserts an image into a web page. Images to be displayed on a web page must be placed in the project's `resources` folder. To add images to the project, drop an **Image** component onto the page and click the ellipsis button next to the **url** property in the **Properties** window. This opens a dialog in which you can select the image to display.
- **Text Field**s allow you to obtain text input from the user.
- Note that the order in which components are dragged to the page is important, because their JSP tags will be added to the JSP file in that order. Tabbing between components navigates the components in the order in which the JSP tags occur in the JSP file. If you would like the user to navigate the components in a certain order, you should drag them onto the page in that order. Alternatively, you can set each input field's `tabIndex` property in the **Properties** window. A component with a tab index of 1 will be the first in the tab sequence.
- A **Drop Down List** displays a list from which the user can make a selection. This object can be configured by right clicking the drop-down list in **Design** mode and selecting **Configure Default Options**, which opens the **Options Customizer** dialog box to add options to the list.
- A **Hyperlink** component of class `Hyperlink` adds a link to a web page. The `url` property of this component specifies the resource that is requested when a user clicks the hyperlink.
- A **Radio Button Group** component of class `RadioButtonGroup` provides a series of radio buttons from which the user can select only one. The options can be edited by right clicking the component and selecting **Configure Default Options.**
- A **Button** is a JSF component of class `Button` that triggers an action when clicked. A **Button** component typically maps to an `input` XHTML element with attribute `type` set to `submit`.

Section 26.4.2 Validation Using Validator Components and Custom Validators

- Validation helps prevent processing errors due to incomplete or improperly formatted user input.
- A **Length Validator** determines whether a field contains an acceptable number of characters.
- **Double Range Validator**s and **Long Range Validator**s determine whether numeric input falls within acceptable ranges.
- Package `javax.faces.validators` contains the classes for these validators.
- **Label** components describe other components and can be associated with user input fields by setting their `for` property.
- **Message** components display error messages when validation fails.
- To associate a **Label** or **Message** component with another component, hold the *Ctrl* and *Shift* keys, then drag the label or message to the appropriate component.

- Set the `required` property of a component to `true` to ensure that the user enters data for it.
- If you add a validator component or custom validator method to an input field, the field's `required` property must be set to `true` for validation to occur.
- In the Visual Editor the label for a required field is automatically marked by a red asterisk.
- If a user submits a form with an empty text field for which a value is required, the default error message for that field will be displayed in its associated `webuijsf:message` component.
- To edit a **Double Range Validator**'s or a **Long Range Validator**'s properties, click its node in the **Outline** window in **Design** mode and set the `maximum` and `minimum` properties in the **Properties** window.
- It is possible to limit the length of user input without using validation by setting a **Text Field**'s `maxLength` property.
- Matching user input against a regular expression is an effective way to ensure that the input is properly formatted.
- Netbeans does not provide components for validation using regular expressions, but you can add your own custom validator methods to the page bean file.
- To add a custom validator method to an input component, right click the component and select **Edit Event Handler > validate** to create the component's validation method in the page bean file.

Section 26.5 Session Tracking

- Personalization makes it possible for e-businesses to communicate effectively with their customers and also improves the user's ability to locate desired products and services.
- A trade-off exists between personalized e-business service and protection of privacy. Some consumers embrace the idea of tailored content, but others fear the possible adverse consequences if the information they provide to e-businesses is released or collected by tracking technologies.
- To provide personalized services to consumers, e-businesses must be able to recognize clients when they request information from a site. Unfortunately, HTTP is a stateless protocol—it does not support persistent connections that would enable web servers to maintain state information regarding particular clients. So, web servers cannot determine whether a request comes from a particular client or whether a series of requests comes from one or several clients.
- To help the server distinguish among clients, each client must identify itself to the server. Tracking individual clients, known as session tracking, can be achieved in a number of ways. One popular technique uses cookies; another uses the `SessionBean` object.
- With `"hidden"` form elements, a web form can write session-tracking data into a `form` in the web page that it returns to the client in response to a prior request. When the user submits the form in the new web page, all the form data, including the `"hidden"` fields, is sent to the form handler on the web server. With URL rewriting, the web server embeds session-tracking information directly in the URLs of hyperlinks that the user clicks to send subsequent requests.

Section 26.5.1 Cookies

- A cookie is a piece of data typically stored in a text file on the user's computer. A cookie maintains information about the client during and between browser sessions.
- The first time a user visits the website, the user's computer might receive a cookie; this cookie is then reactivated each time the user revisits that site. The aim is to create an anonymous record containing data that is used to personalize the user's future visits to the site.
- Every HTTP-based interaction between a client and a server includes a header containing information either about the request (when the communication is from the client to the server) or about the response (when the communication is from the server to the client).

- When a page receives a request, the header includes information such as the request type and any cookies that have been sent previously from the server to be stored on the client machine. When the server formulates its response, the header information contains any cookies the server wants to store on the client computer and other information, such as the MIME type of the response.
- A cookie's expiration date determines how long the cookie remains on the client's computer. If you do not set a cookie's expiration date, the web browser maintains the cookie for the browsing session's duration. Otherwise, it maintains the cookie until the expiration date.
- Setting the action handler for a **Hyperlink** enables you to respond to a click without redirecting the user to another page.
- To add an action handler to a **Hyperlink** that should also direct the user to another page, you must add a rule to the **Page Navigation** file. To edit this file, right click in the Visual Designer and select **Page Navigation...**, then drag the appropriate **Hyperlink** to the destination page.
- A cookie object is an instance of class `Cookie` in package `javax.servlet.http`.
- An object of class `HttpServletResponse` (from package `javax.servlet.http`) represents the response. This object can be accessed by invoking the method `getExternalContext` on the page bean, then invoking `getResponse` on the resulting object.
- An object of class `HttpServletRequest` (from package `javax.servlet.http`) represents the request. This object can be obtained by invoking method `getExternalContext` on the page bean, then invoking `getRequest` on the resulting object.
- `HttpServletRequest` method `getCookies` returns an array of the cookies previously written to the client.
- `HttpServletResponse` method `AddCookie` adds a cookie to the response to the client.
- A web server cannot access cookies created by servers in other domains.

Section 26.5.2 Session Tracking with the `SessionBean` Object

- You can perform session tracking with the `SessionBean` class that is provided in each web application created with Netbeans. When a new client requests a web page in the project, a `SessionBean` object is created.
- The `SessionBean` can be accessed throughout a session by invoking the method `getSessionBean` on the page bean. You can then use the `SessionBean` object to access stored session properties.
- To store information in the `SessionBean`, add properties to the `SessionBean` class. To add a property, right click the `SessionBean` node in the **Outline** window and select **Add > Property** to display the **New Property Pattern** dialog. Configure the property and click **OK** to create it.

Terminology

absolute positioning
`AbstractPageBean`
`action` attribute of XHTML element `form`
action in a JSP
`ApplicationBean`
Button JSF component
`com.sun.webui.jsf.component`
component tree
controller logic
cookie
custom tag library
custom tag
Design mode
`destroy` event-processing life-cycle method
directive in a JSP
Double Range Validator JSF component
Drop Down List JSF component
end tag
`escaped` property
event-processing life cycle
expiration date of a cookie
fixed-template data
fixed-template text
framework

Grid Panel JSF component
hidden input in an XHTML form
Hyperlink JSF component
Image JSF component
init event-processing life-cycle method
IP address
JavaBeans
Java BluePrints
javax.servlet package
javax.servlet.http package
JSF (JavaServer Faces)
JSF components
JSF Expression Language
JSP (JavaServer Pages)
.jsp filename extension
JSP container
JSTL (JSP Standard Tag Library)
Label JSF component
Length Validator JSF component
Listbox JSF component
Long Range Validator JSF component
Message JSF component
method attribute of XHTML element form
Netbeans
Outline window
page bean
Palette
personalization
postback
preprocess event-processing life-cycle method
prerender event-processing life-cycle method
Radio Button Group JSF component
refactoring
rendered property
rendering XHTML in a web browser
RequestBean
required property
scripting element in a JSP
service method of Interface Servlet
servlet
Servlet interface
servlet container
SessionBean
session tracking
span element
start tag
Static Text JSF component
Sun Java System Application Server
tag extension mechanism
tag library
Text Field JSF component
title XHTML element
validation
virtual directory
Visual Editor
web application development
WYSIWYG (What You See Is What You Get) editor
xmlns attributes

Self-Review Exercises

26.1 State whether each of the following is *true* or *false*. If *false*, explain why.

a) Every JSP web page created in Netbeans has its own ApplicationBean, SessionBean, and RequestBean files.
b) Event-processing life-cycle method init is invoked every time a page loads.
c) Every component on a JSP web page is bound to a property in the Java page bean file.
d) A single JSF component may have multiple validation components placed on it.
e) If no expiration date is set for a cookie, that cookie will be destroyed at the end of the browser session.
f) Each JSF component maps to exactly one corresponding XHTML element.
g) Expressions in the JSF Expression Language syntax are delimited by <!-- and -->.
h) The SessionBean can store only primitive properties and properties of type String.

26.2 Fill in the blanks in each of the following statements:

a) The ________ JSF component is used to display error messages if validation fails.
b) A component that checks the input in another component before submitting that input to the server is called a(n) ________.
c) Every page bean class inherits from class ________.
d) When a page loads the first time, the ________ event occurs first, followed by the ________ event.

e) The ________ file contains the functionality for a JSP.
f) A(n) ________ can be used in a custom validator method to validate the format of user input.
g) The array of `Cookie` objects stored on the client can be obtained by calling `getCookies` on the ________ object.

Answers to Self-Review Exercises

26.1 a) False. If an application contains multiple JSPs, those JSPs will share the scoped data beans. b) False. `init` is invoked the first time the page is requested, but not on page refreshes. c) True. d) True. e) True. f) False. A web component can map to a group of XHTML elements—JSPs can generate complex XHTML markup from simple components. g) False. `#{` and `}` delimit JSF Expression Language statements. h) False. The scoped data beans may store any type of property.

26.2 a) **Message**. b) validator. c) `AbstractPageBean`. d) `init`, `prerender`. e) page bean. f) regular expression. g) Request (`HttpServletRequest`).

Exercises

26.3 *(`WebTime` Modification)* Modify the `WebTime` example to contain drop-down lists that allow the user to modify such **Static Text** component properties as `background-color`, `color` and `font-size`. Configure these drop-down lists so that the page refreshes whenever the user makes a selection. When the page reloads, it should reflect the specified changes to the properties of the **Static Text** displaying the time.

26.4 *(Registration Form Modification)* Modify the `WebComponents` application to add functionality to the **Register** button. When the user clicks **Submit**, validate all input fields to make sure the user has filled out the form completely and entered a valid e-mail address and phone number. Then, direct the user to another page that displays a message indicating successful registration and echoes back the user's registration information.

26.5 *(Page Hit Counter with Cookies)* Create a JSP that uses a persistent cookie (i.e., a cookie with an expiration date in the future) to keep track of how many times the client computer has visited the page. Use the `setMaxAge` method to cause the cookie to remain on the client's computer for one month. Display the number of page hits (i.e., the cookie's value) every time the page loads.

26.6 *(Page Hit Counter with **ApplicationBean**)* Create a JSP that uses the `ApplicationBean` to keep track of how many times a page has been visited. [*Note:* If you were to deploy this page on the web, it would count the number of times that any computer requested the page, unlike in the previous exercise.] Display the number of page hits (i.e., the value of an `int` property in the `ApplicationBean`) every time the page loads.

27

Ajax-Enabled JavaServer™ Faces Web Applications

Whatever is in any way beautiful hath its source of beauty in itself, and is complete in itself; praise forms no part of it.
—Marcus Aurelius Antoninus

There is something in a face, An air, and a peculiar grace, Which boldest painters cannot trace.
—William Somerville

Cato said the best way to keep good acts in memory was to refresh them with new.
—Francis Bacon

I never forget a face, but in your case I'll make an exception.
—Groucho Marx

Painting is only a bridge linking the painter's mind with that of the viewer.
—Eugéne Delacroix

OBJECTIVES

In this chapter you will learn:

- To use data providers to access databases from web applications built in Netbeans.
- To include Ajax-enabled JSF components in a Netbeans web application project.
- To configure virtual forms that enable subsets of a form's input components to be submitted to the server.

Outline

27.1 Introduction

This chapter continues our discussion of web application development with several advanced concepts. We discuss accessing, updating and searching databases in a web application, adding virtual forms to web pages to enable subsets of a form's input components to be submitted to the server, and using Ajax-enabled component libraries to improve application performance and component responsiveness. [*Note:* This chapter assumes that you know Java. To learn more about Java, check out *Java How to Program, Seventh Edition*, or visit our Java Resource Centers at `www.deitel.com/ResourceCenters.html`.]

We present a single address book application developed in three stages to illustrate these concepts. The application is backed by a Java DB database for storing the contact names and their addresses.

The address book application presents a form that allows the user to enter a new name and address to store in the address book and displays the contents of the address book in table format. It also provides a search form that allows the user to search for a contact and, if found, display the contact's address on a map. The first version of this application demonstrates how to add contacts to the database and how to display the list of contacts in a JSF **Table** component. In the second version, we add an Ajax-enabled **AutoComplete Text Field** component and enable it to suggest a list of contact names as the user types. The last version allows you to search the address book for a contact and display the corresponding address on a map using the Ajax-enabled **Map Viewer** component that is powered by Google Maps (`maps.google.com`).

As in Chapter 26, this chapter's examples were developed in Netbeans. We installed a supplementary component library—the Java BluePrints Ajax component library—which provides the Ajax-enabled components used in the address book application.

Instructions for installing this library are included in Section 27.3. These Ajax-enabled components use the Dojo Toolkit (which we introduced in Chapter 15) on the client side.

27.2 Accessing Databases in Web Applications

Many web applications access databases to store and retrieve persistent data. In this section, we build a web application that uses a Java DB database to store contacts in the address book and display contacts from the address book on a web page.

The web page enables the user to enter new contacts in a form. This form consists of **Text Field** components for the contact's first name, last name, street address, city, state and zip code. The form also has a **Submit** button to send the data to the server and a **Clear** button to reset the form's fields. The application stores the address book information in a database named `AddressBook`, which has a single table named `Addresses`. (We provide this database in the examples directory for this chapter. You can download the examples from `www.deitel.com/books/iw3htp4/`). This example also introduces the **Table** JSF component, which displays the addresses from the database in tabular format. We show how to configure the **Table** component shortly.

27.2.1 Building a Web Application That Displays Data from a Database

We now explain how to build the `AddressBook` application's GUI and set up a data binding that allows the **Table** component to display information from the database. We present the generated JSP file later in the section, and we discuss the related page bean file in Section 27.2.2. To build the `AddressBook` application, perform the following steps:

Step 1: Creating the Project

In Netbeans, create a **Visual Web Application** project named `AddressBook`. Rename the JSP and page bean files to `AddressBook` using the refactoring tools.

Step 2: Creating the Form for User Input

In **Design** mode, add a **Static Text** component to the top of the page that reads `"Add a contact to the address book:"` and use the component's `style` property to set the font size to `18px`. Add six **Text Field** components to the page and rename them `fnameTextField`, `lnameTextField`, `streetTextField`, `cityTextField`, `stateTextField` and `zipTextField`. Set each **Text Field**'s `required` property to `true` by selecting the **Text Field**, then clicking the `required` property's checkbox. Label each **Text Field** with a **Label** component and associate the **Label** with its corresponding **Text Field**. Finally, add a **Submit** and a **Clear** button. Set the **Submit** button's `primary` property to `true` to make it stand out more on the page than the **Clear** button and to allow the user to submit a new contact by pressing *Enter* rather than by clicking the **Submit** button. Set the **Clear** button's `reset` property to `true` to prevent validation when the user clicks the **Clear** button. Since we are clearing the fields, we don't need to ensure that they contain information. We discuss the action handler for the **Submit** button after we present the page bean file. The **Clear** button does not need an action-handler method, because setting the `reset` property to `true` automatically configures the button to reset all of the page's input fields. When you have finished these steps, your form should look like Fig. 27.1.

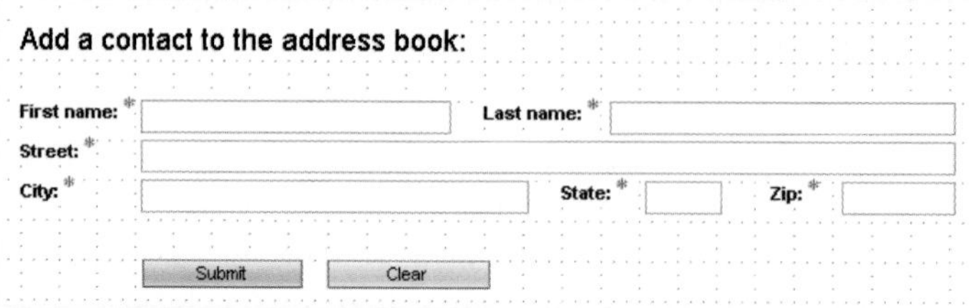

Add a contact to the address book:

First name: * Last name: *
Street: *
City: * State: * Zip: *
Submit Clear

Fig. 27.1 | `AddressBook` application form for adding a contact.

Step 3: Adding a **Table** *Component to the Page*

Drag a **Table** component from the **Basic** section of the **Palette** to the page and place it just below the two **Button** components. Name it `addressesTable`. The **Table** component formats and displays data from database tables. In the **Properties** window, change the **Table**'s `title` property to `Contacts`. We show how to configure the **Table** to interact with the `AddressBook` database shortly.

Step 4: Creating a Java DB Database

This example uses a database called `AddressBook` to store the address information. To create this database, perform the following steps:

1. Select **Tools > Java DB Database > Create Java DB Database....**
2. Enter the name of the database to create (`AddressBook`), a username (`iw3htp4`) and a password (`iw3htp4`), then click **OK** to create the database.

In the Netbeans **Runtime** tab (to the right of the **Projects** and **Files** tabs), the preceding steps create a new entry in the **Databases** node showing the URL of the database (`jdbc:derby://localhost:1527/AddressBook`). This URL indicates that the database resides on the local machine and accepts connections on port 1527.

Step 5: Adding a Table and Data to the **AddressBook** *Database*

You can use the **Runtime** tab to create tables and to execute SQL statements that populate the database with data:

1. Click the **Runtime** tab and expand the **Databases** node.
2. Netbeans must be connected to the database to execute SQL statements. If Netbeans is already connected, proceed to *Step 3*. If Netbeans is not connected to the database, the icon appears next to the database's URL (`jdbc:derby://localhost:1527/AddressBook`). In this case, right click the icon and click **Connect....** Once connected, the icon changes to .
3. Expand the node for the `AddressBook` database, right click the **Tables** node and select **Execute Command...** to open a **SQL Command** editor in Netbeans. We provided the file `AddressBook.sql` in this chapter's examples folder. Open that file in a text editor, copy the SQL statements and paste them into the **SQL Command** editor in Netbeans. Then, highlight all the SQL commands, right click inside the **SQL Command** editor and select **Run Selection**. This will create the Addresses table with the sample data shown in Fig. 27.2. You may need to refresh the **Tables** node of the **Runtime** tab to see the new table.

FirstName	LastName	Street	City	State	Zip
Bob	Green	5 Bay St.	San Francisco	CA	94133
Liz	White	100 5th Ave.	New York	NY	10011
Mike	Brown	3600 Delmar Blvd.	St. Louis	MO	63108
Mary	Green	300 Massachusetts Ave.	Boston	MA	02115
John	Gray	500 South St.	Philadelphia	PA	19147
Meg	Gold	1200 Stout St.	Denver	CO	80204
James	Blue	1000 Harbor Ave.	Seattle	WA	98116
Sue	Black	1000 Michigan Ave.	Chicago	IL	60605

Fig. 27.2 | `Addresses` table data.

Step 6: Binding the **Table** *Component to the* **`Addresses`** *Table of the* **`AddressBook`** *Database*

Now that we've configured a data source for the `Addresses` database table, we can configure the **Table** component to display the `AddressBook` data. Simply drag the database table from the **Servers** tab and drop it on the **Table** component to create the binding.

To select specific columns to display, right click the **Table** component and select **Bind to Data** to display the **Bind to Data** dialog containing the list of the columns in the `Addresses` database table (Fig. 27.3). The items under the **Selected** heading will be displayed in the **Table**. To remove a column, select it and click the **<** button. We'd like to display all the columns in this example, so you should simply click **OK** to exit the dialog.

By default, the **Table** uses the database table's column names in all uppercase letters as headings. To change these headings, select a column and edit its `headerText` property in the **Properties** window. To select a column, click the column's name in the **Design** mode. We also changed the `id` property of each column to make the variable names in the code more readable. In **Design** mode, your **Table**'s column heads should appear as in Fig. 27.4.

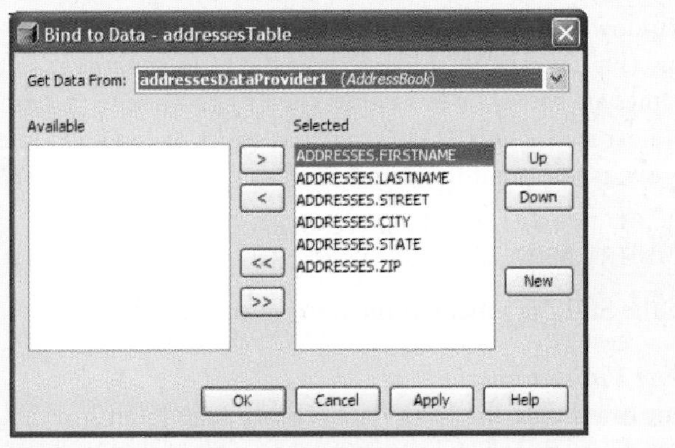

Fig. 27.3 | Dialog for binding to the `Addresses` table.

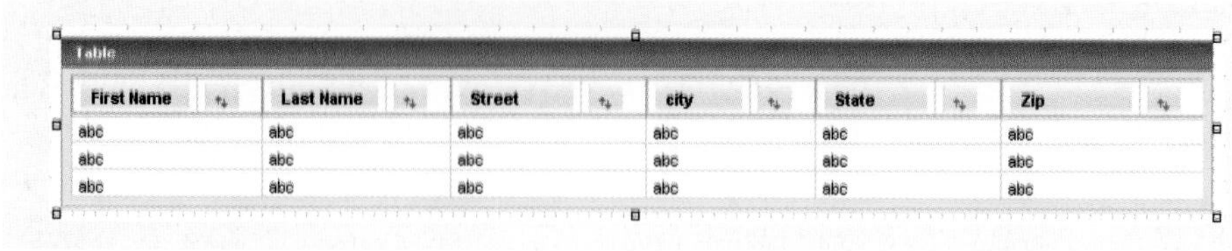

Fig. 27.4 | `Table` component after binding it to a database table and editing its column names for display purposes.

An address book might contain many contacts, so we'd like to display only a few at a time. Clicking the checkbox next to the table's `paginationControls` property in the **Properties** window configures this **Table** for automatic pagination. This adds buttons to the bottom of the **Table** for moving forward and backward between groups of contacts. You may use the **Table Layout** dialog's **Options** tab to select the number of rows to display at a time. To view this tab, right click the **Table**, select **Table Layout...**, then click the **Options** tab. For this example, we set the **Page Size** property to `5`.

Next, set the `addressesTable`'s `internalVirtualForm` property. Virtual forms allow subsets of a form's input components to be submitted to the server. Setting this property prevents the pagination control buttons on the **Table** from submitting the **Text Fields** on the form every time the user wishes to view the next group of contacts. Virtual forms are discussed in Section 27.4.1.

Binding the **Table** to a data provider added a new `addressesDataProvider` object (an instance of class `CachedRowSetDataProvider`) to the **AddressBook** node in the **Outline** window. A `CachedRowSetDataProvider` provides a scrollable `RowSet` that can be bound to a **Table** component to display the `RowSet`'s data. This data provider is a wrapper for a `CachedRowSet` object. If you click the **addressesDataProvider** element in the **Outline** window, you'll see in the **Properties** window that its `CachedRowSet` property is set to `addressesRowSet`, an object (in the session bean) that implements interface `CachedRowSet`.

Step 7: Modifying `addressesRowSet`*'s SQL Statement*

The `CachedRowSet` object wrapped by our `addressesDataProvider` is configured by default to execute a SQL query that selects all the data in the `Addresses` table of the `AddressBook` database. You can edit this SQL query by expanding the `SessionBean` node in the **Outline** window and double clicking the `addressesRowSet` element to open the query editor window (Fig. 27.5). We'd like to edit the SQL statement so that records with duplicate last names are sorted by last name, then by first name. To do this, click in the **Sort Type** column next to the **LASTNAME** row and select **Ascending**. Then, repeat this for the **FIRSTNAME** row. Notice that the expression

```
ORDER BY IW3HTP4.ADDRESSES.LASTNAME ASC,
   IW3HTP4.ADDRESSES.FIRSTNAME ASC
```

was added to the SQL statement at the bottom of the editor.

Step 8: Adding Validation

It is important to validate the form data on this page to ensure that the data can be successfully inserted into the `AddressBook` database. All of the database's columns are of type `varchar` (except the ID column) and have length restrictions. For this reason, you should

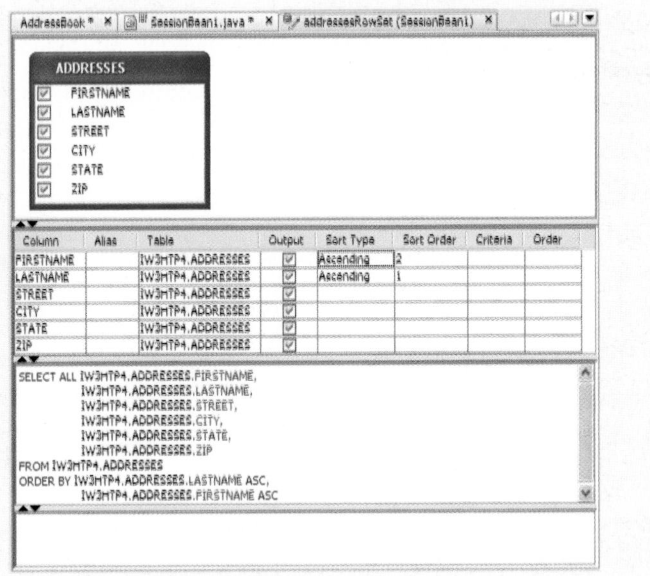

Fig. 27.5 | Editing `addressesRowSet`'s SQL statement.

either add a **Length Validator** to each **Text Field** component or set each **Text Field** component's `maxLength` property. We chose to set the `maxLength` property of each. The first name, last name, street, city, state and zip code **Text Field** components may not exceed 30, 30, 150, 30, 2 and 5 characters, respectively.

Finally, drag a **Message Group** component onto your page to the right of the **Text Fields**. A **Message Group** component displays system messages. We use this component to display an error message when an attempt to add a contact to the database fails. Set the **Message Group**'s `showGlobalOnly` property to `true` to prevent component-level validation error messages from being displayed here.

JSP File for a Web Page That Interacts with a Database

The JSP file for the application is shown in Fig. 27.6. This file contains a large amount of generated markup for components you learned in Chapter 26. We discuss the markup for only the components that are new in this example.

```
<?xml version="1.0" encoding="UTF-8"?>
<!-- Fig. 27.6: AddressBook.jsp -->
<!-- AddressBook JSP with an add form and a Table JSF component. -->
<jsp:root version="1.2"
   xmlns:f="http://java.sun.com/jsf/core"
   xmlns:h="http://java.sun.com/jsf/html"
   xmlns:jsp="http://java.sun.com/JSP/Page"
   xmlns:webuijsf="http://www.sun.com/webui/webuijsf">
   <jsp:directive.page contentType="text/html;charset=UTF-8"
      pageEncoding="UTF-8"/>
```

Fig. 27.6 | `AddressBook` JSP with an add form and a **Table** JSF component (Part 1 of 5.)

```
      <f:view>
      <webuijsf:page binding="#{AddressBook.page1}" id="page1">
         <webuijsf:html binding="#{AddressBook.html1}" id="html1">
            <webuijsf:head binding="#{AddressBook.head1}" id="head1">
              <webuijsf:link binding="#{AddressBook.link1}" id="link1"
                 url="/resources/stylesheet.css"/>
            </webuijsf:head>
            <webuijsf:body binding="#{AddressBook.body1}" id="body1"
               style="-rave-layout: grid">
               <webuijsf:form binding="#{AddressBook.form1}" id="form1">
                  <webuijsf:staticText binding="#{AddressBook.staticText1}"
                     id="staticText1" style="font-size: 18px; left: 24px;
                     top: 24px; position: absolute"
                     text="Add a contact to the address book:"/>
                  <webuijsf:label binding="#{AddressBook.fnameLabel}"
                     for="fnameTextField" id="fnameLabel" style=
                     "position: absolute; left: 24px; top: 72px"
                     text="First name:"/>
                  <webuijsf:textField binding="#{AddressBook.fnameTextField}"
                     id="fnameTextField" maxLength="30" required="true"
                     style="left: 100px; top: 72px; position: absolute;
                     width: 192px"/>
                  <webuijsf:label binding="#{AddressBook.lnameLabel}"
                     for="lnameTextField" id="lnameLabel" style="left: 312px;
                     top: 72px; position: absolute" text="Last name:"/>
                  <webuijsf:textField binding="#{AddressBook.lnameTextField}"
                     id="lnameTextField" maxLength="30" required="true"
                     style="left: 390px; top: 72px; position: absolute;
                     width: 214px"/>
                  <webuijsf:label binding="#{AddressBook.streetLabel}"
                     for="streetTextField" id="streetLabel" style="position:
                     absolute; left: 24px; top: 96px" text="Street:"/>
                  <webuijsf:textField binding=
                     "#{AddressBook.streetTextField}" id="streetTextField"
                     maxLength="150" required="true" style="left: 100px;
                     top: 96px; position: absolute; width: 504px"/>
                  <webuijsf:label binding="#{AddressBook.cityLabel}"
                     for="cityTextField" id="cityLabel" style="left: 24px;
                     top: 120px; position: absolute" text="City:"/>
                  <webuijsf:textField binding="#{AddressBook.cityTextField}"
                     id="cityTextField" maxLength="30" required="true"
                     style="left: 100px; top: 120px; position: absolute;
                     width: 240px"/>
                  <webuijsf:label binding="#{AddressBook.stateLabel}"
                     for="stateTextField" id="stateLabel" style="left: 360px;
                     top: 120px; position: absolute" text="State:"/>
                  <webuijsf:textField binding="#{AddressBook.stateTextField}"
                     id="stateTextField" maxLength="2" required="true"
                     style="left: 412px; top: 120px; position: absolute;
                     width: 48px"/>
                  <webuijsf:label binding="#{AddressBook.zipLabel}"
                     for="zipTextField" id="zipLabel" style="left: 490px;
                     top: 120px; position: absolute" text=" Zip:"/>
```

Fig. 27.6 | AddressBook JSP with an add form and a **Table** JSF component (Part 2 of 5.)

```
            <webuijsf:textField binding="#{AddressBook.zipTextField}"
               id="zipTextField" maxLength="5" required="true"
               style="left: 534px; top: 120px; position: absolute;
               width: 70px"/>
            <webuijsf:button actionExpression=
               "#{AddressBook.submitButton_action}" binding=
               "#{AddressBook.submitButton}" id="submitButton"
               primary="true" style="left: 100px; top: 168px;
               position: absolute; width: 100px" text="Submit"/>
            <webuijsf:button binding="#{AddressBook.clearButton}"
               id="clearButton" reset="true" style="left: 215px; top:
               168px; position: absolute; width: 100px" text="Clear"/>
            <webuijsf:messageGroup binding=
               "#{AddressBook.messageGroup1}" id="messageGroup1"
               showGlobalOnly="true" style="left: 624px; top: 72px;
               position: absolute"/>
            <webuijsf:table augmentTitle="false" binding=
               "#{AddressBook.addressesTable}" id="addressesTable"
               paginateButton="true" paginationControls="true"
               style="left: 24px; top: 216px; position: absolute"
               title="Contacts" width="816">
               <webuijsf:tableRowGroup binding=
                  "#{AddressBook.tableRowGroup1}" id="tableRowGroup1"
                  rows="5"
                  sourceData="#{AddressBook.addressesDataProvider}"
                  sourceVar="currentRow">
                  <webuijsf:tableColumn binding=
                     "#{AddressBook.fnameColumn}" headerText=
                     "First Name" id="fnameColumn"
                     sort="ADDRESSES.FIRSTNAME">
                     <webuijsf:staticText binding=
                        "#{AddressBook.staticText2}" id="staticText2"
                        text="#{currentRow.value[
                        'ADDRESSES.FIRSTNAME']}"/>
                  </webuijsf:tableColumn>
                  <webuijsf:tableColumn binding=
                     "#{AddressBook.lnameColumn}"
                     headerText="Last Name" id="lnameColumn"
                     sort="ADDRESSES.LASTNAME">
                     <webuijsf:staticText binding=
                        "#{AddressBook.staticText3}" id="staticText3"
                        text="#{currentRow.value[
                        'ADDRESSES.LASTNAME']}"/>
                  </webuijsf:tableColumn>
                  <webuijsf:tableColumn binding=
                     "#{AddressBook.streetColumn}" headerText="Street"
                     id="streetColumn" sort="ADDRESSES.STREET">
                     <webuijsf:staticText binding=
                        "#{AddressBook.staticText4}" id="staticText4"
                        text="#{currentRow.value[
                        'ADDRESSES.STREET']}"/>
                  </webuijsf:tableColumn>
```

Fig. 27.6 | AddressBook JSP with an add form and a **Table** JSF component (Part 3 of 5.)

```
                              <webuijsf:tableColumn binding=
                                 "#{AddressBook.cityColumn}" headerText="City"
                                 id="cityColumn" sort="ADDRESSES.CITY">
                                 <webuijsf:staticText binding=
                                    "#{AddressBook.staticText5}" id="staticText5"
                                    text="#{currentRow.value['ADDRESSES.CITY']}"/>
                              </webuijsf:tableColumn>
                              <webuijsf:tableColumn binding=
                                 "#{AddressBook.stateColumn}" headerText="State"
                                 id="stateColumn" sort="ADDRESSES.STATE">
                                 <webuijsf:staticText binding=
                                    "#{AddressBook.staticText6}" id="staticText6"
                                    text="#{currentRow.value['ADDRESSES.STATE']}"/>
                              </webuijsf:tableColumn>
                              <webuijsf:tableColumn binding=
                                 "#{AddressBook.zipColumn}" headerText="Zip"
                                 id="zipColumn" sort="ADDRESSES.ZIP" width="106">
                                 <webuijsf:staticText binding=
                                    "#{AddressBook.staticText7}" id="staticText7"
                                    text="#{currentRow.value['ADDRESSES.ZIP']}"/>
                              </webuijsf:tableColumn>
                           </webuijsf:tableRowGroup>
                        </webuijsf:table>
                     </webuijsf:form>
                  </webuijsf:body>
               </webuijsf:html>
            </webuijsf:page>
         </f:view>
      </jsp:root>
```

a)

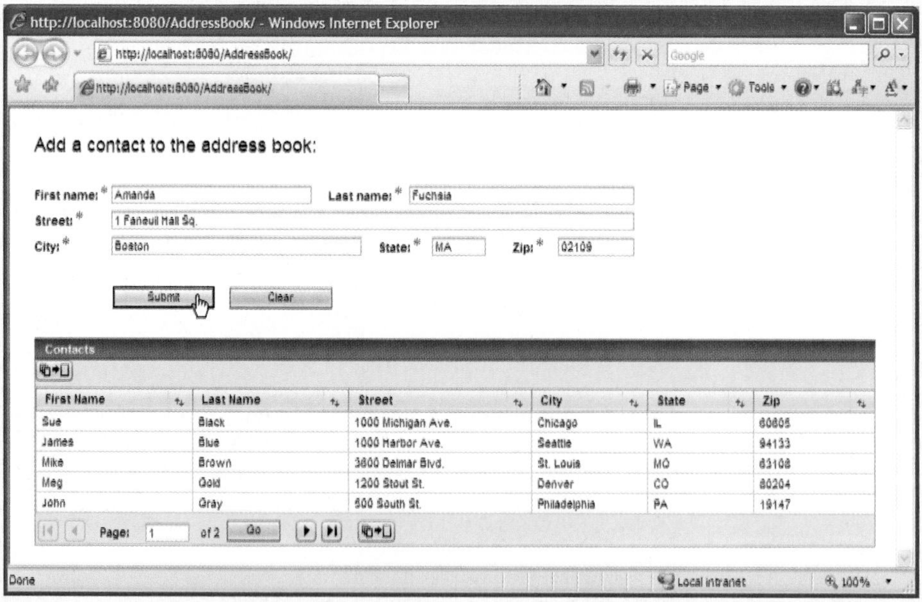

http://localhost:8080/AddressBook/ - Windows Internet Explorer

Add a contact to the address book:

First name: * Amanda Last name: * Fuchsia
Street: * 1 Faneuil Hall Sq.
City: * Boston State: * MA Zip: * 02109

Submit Clear

Contacts

First Name	Last Name	Street	City	State	Zip
Sue	Black	1000 Michigan Ave.	Chicago	IL	60605
James	Blue	1000 Harbor Ave.	Seattle	WA	94133
Mike	Brown	3600 Delmar Blvd.	St. Louis	MO	63108
Meg	Gold	1200 Stout St.	Denver	CO	80204
John	Gray	500 South St.	Philadelphia	PA	19147

Page: 1 of 2 Go

Done Local intranet 100%

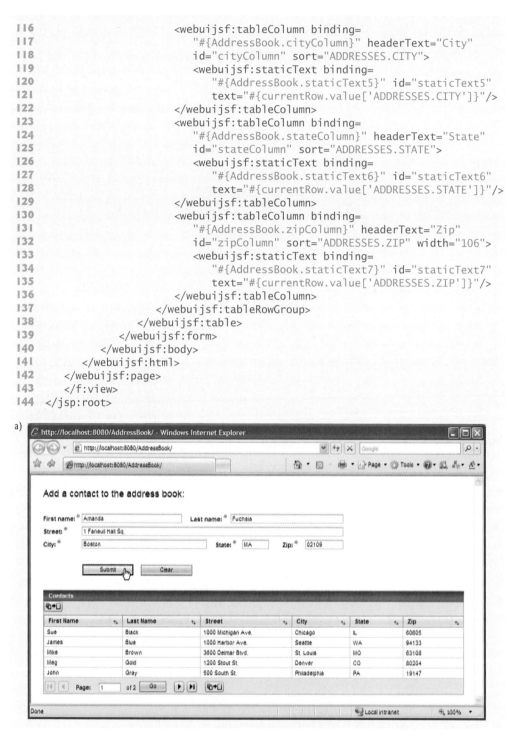

Fig. 27.6 | AddressBook JSP with an add form and a **Table** JSF component (Part 4 of 5.)

b)

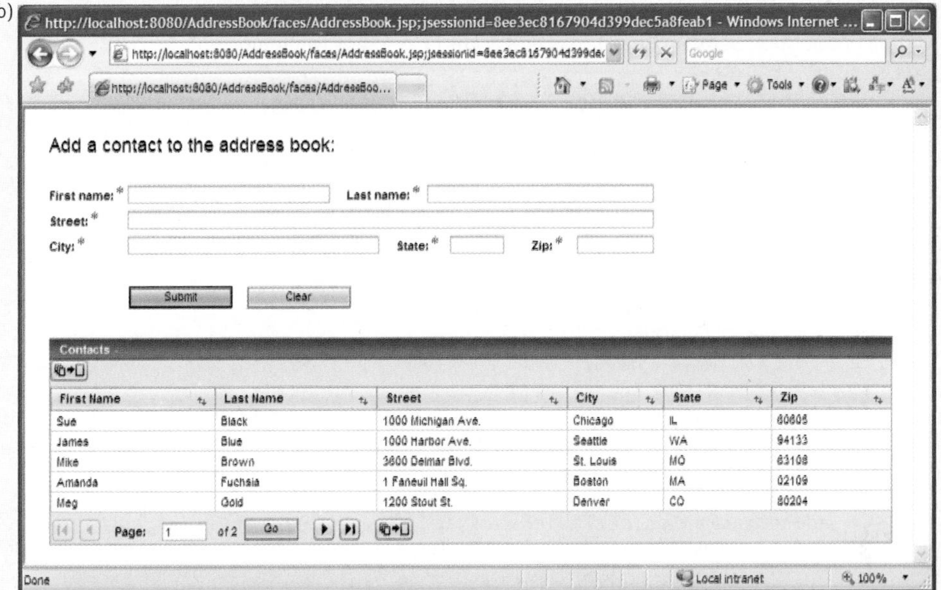

Fig. 27.6 | `AddressBook` JSP with an add form and a **Table** JSF component (Part 5 of 5.)

Lines 21–75 contain the JSF components for the form that gathers user input. Lines 80–138 define the **Table** element (`webuijsf:table`) that displays address information from the database. JSF **Table**s may have multiple groups of rows displaying different data. This **Table** has a single `webuijsf:tableRowGroup` with a start tag in lines 85–89. The row group's `sourceData` attribute is bound to our `addressesDataProvider` and given the variable name `currentRow`. The row group also defines the **Table**'s columns. Each `webuijsf:tableColumn` element (e.g., lines 90–98) contains a `webuijsf:staticText` element with its `text` attribute bound to a column in the data provider `currentRow`. These `webuijsf:staticText` elements enable the **Table** to display each row's data.

Session Bean for the **AddressBook** *Application*

Figure 27.7 displays the `SessionBean1.java` file generated by Netbeans for the `AddressBook` application. The `CachedRowSet` that the **Table** component's data provider uses to access the `AddressBook` database is a property of this class (lines 31–41).

```
1  // Fig. 27.7: SessionBean1.java
2  // Session bean that initializes the data source for the
3  // AddressBook database.
4  package addressbook;
5
6  import com.sun.rave.web.ui.appbase.AbstractSessionBean;
7  import com.sun.sql.rowset.CachedRowSetXImpl;
8  import javax.faces.FacesException;
```

Fig. 27.7 | Session Bean that initializes the data source for the `AddressBook` database. (Part 1 of 2.)

```
9
10  public class SessionBean1 extends AbstractSessionBean
11  {
12     private int __placeholder;
13
14     private void _init() throws Exception
15     {
16        addressesRowSet.setDataSourceName(
17           "java:comp/env/jdbc/dataSource" );
18        addressesRowSet.setCommand(
19           "SELECT ALL IW3HTP4.ADDRESSES.FIRSTNAME, \n" +
20           "IW3HTP4.ADDRESSES.LASTNAME, \n" +
21           "IW3HTP4.ADDRESSES.STREET, \n" +
22           "IW3HTP4.ADDRESSES.CITY, \n" +
23           "IW3HTP4.ADDRESSES.STATE, \n" +
24           "IW3HTP4.ADDRESSES.ZIP \n" +
25           "FROM IW3HTP4.ADDRESSES\n" +
26           "ORDER BY IW3HTP4.ADDRESSES.LASTNAME ASC, \n" +
27           "IW3HTP4.ADDRESSES.FIRSTNAME ASC " );
28        addressesRowSet.setTableName( "ADDRESSES" );
29     } // end method _init
30
31     private CachedRowSetXImpl addressesRowSet = new CachedRowSetXImpl();
32
33     public CachedRowSetXImpl getAddressesRowSet()
34     {
35        return addressesRowSet;
36     }
37
38     public void setAddressesRowSet( CachedRowSetXImpl crsxi )
39     {
40        this.addressesRowSet = crsxi;
41     }
42
43     // To save space, we omitted the code in lines 42-78. The complete
44     // source code is provided with this chapter's examples.
79  } // end class SessionBean1
```

Fig. 27.7 | Session Bean that initializes the data source for the `AddressBook` database. (Part 2 of 2.)

The `_init` method (lines 14–29) configures `addressesRowSet` to interact with the `AddressBook` database (lines 16–28). Lines 16–17 connect the row set to the database. Lines 18–27 set `addressesRowSet`'s SQL command to the query configured in Fig. 27.5. Line 28 sets the `RowSet`'s table name.

27.2.2 Modifying the Page Bean File for the AddressBook Application

After building the web page and configuring the components used in this example, double click the **Submit** button to create an action event handler for this button in the page bean file. The code to insert a contact into the database will be placed in this method. The page bean with the completed event handler is shown in Fig. 27.8 below.

```java
// Fig. 27.8: AddressBook.java
// Page bean for AddressBook.jsp.
package addressbook;

import com.sun.data.provider.RowKey;
import com.sun.data.provider.impl.CachedRowSetDataProvider;
import com.sun.rave.web.ui.appbase.AbstractPageBean;
import com.sun.webui.jsf.component.Body;
import com.sun.webui.jsf.component.Button;
import com.sun.webui.jsf.component.Form;
import com.sun.webui.jsf.component.Head;
import com.sun.webui.jsf.component.Html;
import com.sun.webui.jsf.component.Label;
import com.sun.webui.jsf.component.Link;
import com.sun.webui.jsf.component.MessageGroup;
import com.sun.webui.jsf.component.Page;
import com.sun.webui.jsf.component.StaticText;
import com.sun.webui.jsf.component.Table;
import com.sun.webui.jsf.component.TableColumn;
import com.sun.webui.jsf.component.TableRowGroup;
import com.sun.webui.jsf.component.TextField;
import com.sun.webui.jsf.model.DefaultTableDataProvider;
import javax.faces.FacesException;

public class AddressBook extends AbstractPageBean
{
   private int __placeholder;

   private void _init() throws Exception
   {
      addressesDataProvider.setCachedRowSet(
         ( javax.sql.rowset.CachedRowSet ) getValue(
            "#{SessionBean1.addressesRowSet}" ) );
      addressesTable.setInternalVirtualForm( true );
   } // end method _init

   // To save space, we omitted the code in lines 37-505. The complete
   // source code is provided with this chapter's examples.

   public void prerender()
   {
      addressesDataProvider.refresh();
   } // end method prerender

   public void destroy()
   {
      addressesDataProvider.close();
   } // end method destroy

   // To save space, we omitted the code in lines 516-530. The complete
   // source code is provided with this chapter's examples.

```

Fig. 27.8 | Page bean for adding a contact to the address book. (Part 1 of 2.)

```
531     // action handler that adds a contact to the AddressBook database
532     // when the user clicks Submit
533     public String submitButton_action()
534     {
535        if ( addressesDataProvider.canAppendRow() )
536        {
537           try
538           {
539              RowKey rk = addressesDataProvider.appendRow();
540              addressesDataProvider.setCursorRow( rk );
541
542              addressesDataProvider.setValue( "ADDRESSES.FIRSTNAME",
543                 fnameTextField.getValue() );
544              addressesDataProvider.setValue( "ADDRESSES.LASTNAME",
545                 lnameTextField.getValue() );
546              addressesDataProvider.setValue( "ADDRESSES.STREET",
547                 streetTextField.getValue() );
548              addressesDataProvider.setValue( "ADDRESSES.CITY",
549                 cityTextField.getValue() );
550              addressesDataProvider.setValue( "ADDRESSES.STATE",
551                 stateTextField.getValue() );
552              addressesDataProvider.setValue( "ADDRESSES.ZIP",
553                 zipTextField.getValue() );
554              addressesDataProvider.commitChanges();
555
556              // reset text fields
557              lnameTextField.setValue( "" );
558              fnameTextField.setValue( "" );
559              streetTextField.setValue( "" );
560              cityTextField.setValue( "" );
561              stateTextField.setValue( "" );
562              zipTextField.setValue( "" );
563           } // end try
564           catch ( Exception ex )
565           {
566              error( "The address book was not updated.  " +
567                 ex.getMessage() );
568           } // end catch
569        } // end if
570
571        return null;
572     } // end method submitButton_action
573  } // end class AddressBook
```

Fig. 27.8 | Page bean for adding a contact to the address book. (Part 2 of 2.)

Lines 533–572 contain the event-handling code for the **Submit** button. Line 535 determines whether a new row can be appended to the data provider. If so, a new row is appended at line 539. Every row in a `CachedRowSetDataProvider` has its own key; method **appendRow** returns the key for the new row. Line 540 sets the data provider's cursor to the new row, so that any changes we make to the data provider affect that row. Lines 542–553 set each of the row's columns to the values entered by the user in the corresponding **Text Fields**. Line 554 stores the new contact by calling method `commitChanges` of class `CachedRowSetDataProvider` to insert the new row into the `AddressBook` database.

Lines 557–562 clear the form's **Text Fields**. If these lines are omitted, the fields will retain their current values after the database is updated and the page reloads. Also, the **Clear** button will not work properly if the **Text Fields** are not cleared. Rather than emptying the **Text Fields**, it resets them to the values they held the last time the form was submitted.

Lines 564–568 catch any exceptions that might occur while updating the `AddressBook` database. Lines 566–567 display a message indicating that the database was not updated as well as the exception's error message in the page's `MessageGroup` component.

In method `prerender`, line 508 calls `CachedRowSetDataProvider` method `refresh`. This re-executes the wrapped `CachedRowSet`'s SQL statement and re-sorts the **Table**'s rows so that the new row is displayed in the proper order. If you do not call `refresh`, the new address is displayed at the end of the **Table** (since we appended the new row to the end of the data provider). The IDE automatically generated code to free resources used by the data provider (line 513) in the `destroy` method.

27.3 Ajax-Enabled JSF Components

The Java BluePrints Ajax component library provides Ajax-enabled JSF components. These components rely on Ajax technology to deliver the feel and responsiveness of a desktop application over the web. Figure 27.9 summarizes the current set of components that you can download and use with Netbeans. We demonstrate the **AutoComplete Text Field** and **Map Viewer** components in the next two sections.

Component	Description
AutoComplete Text Field	Makes Ajax requests to display a list of suggestions as the user types in the text field.
Buy Now Button	Initiates a transaction through the PayPal website.
Map Viewer	Uses the Google Maps API to display a map that pans, zooms, and can display markers for locations of interest.
Popup Calendar	Provides a calendar that enables a user to scroll between months and years. Fills a **Text Field** with a formatted date when the user selects a day.
Progress Bar	Visually displays the progress of a long-running operation. Uses a programmer-supplied calculation to determine the progress percentage.
Rating	Provides a customizable five-star rating bar that can display messages as the user moves the mouse over the ratings.
Rich Textarea Editor	Provides an editable text area that allows the user to format text with fonts, colors, hyperlinks and backgrounds.
Select Value Text Field	Displays a list of suggestions in a drop-down list as the user types, similar to the **AutoComplete Text Field**.

Fig. 27.9 | Java BluePrints component library's Ajax-enabled components.

Downloading the Java BluePrints Ajax-Enabled Components

To use the Java BluePrints Ajax-enabled components in Netbeans, you must download and import them. The IDE provides a wizard for installing this group of components (Internet access is required). To access it, choose **Tools > Update Center** to display the **Update Center Wizard** dialog. Click **Next >** to search for available updates. In the **Available Updates and New Modules** area of the dialog, locate and select **BluePrints AJAX Components** then click the **Add >** button to add them to the list of items you'd like to install. Click **Next >** and follow the prompts to accept the terms of use and download the components. When the download completes, click **Next >** then click **Finish**. Click **OK** to restart the IDE.

Importing the Java BluePrints Ajax-Enabled Components into the Netbeans Palette

Next, you must import the components into the **Palette**. Select **Tools > Component Library Manager**, then click **Import...**. Click **Browse...** in the **Component Library Manager** dialog that appears. Select the `ui.complib` file and click **Open**. Click **OK** to import both the **BluePrints AJAX Components** and the **BluePrints AJAX Support Beans**. Close the **Component Library Manager** to return to the IDE.

To see the new components in the **Palette**, you must add the **BluePrints AJAX Components** library to your visual web application. To do so, make sure your application's node is expanded in the **Projects** tab. Right click the **Component Libraries** node and select **Add Component Library**. In the **Add Component Library** dialog box, select the **BluePrints AJAX Components library** and click **Add Component Library**. You should now see two new nodes in the **Palette**. The first, **BluePrints AJAX Components**, provides the eight components listed in Fig. 27.9. The second, **BluePrints AJAX Support Beans**, includes components that support the Ajax components. You can now build high-performance Ajax web applications by dragging, dropping and configuring the component's properties, just as you do with other components in the **Palette**.

27.4 AutoComplete Text Field and Virtual Forms

We demonstrate the **AutoComplete Text Field** component from the BluePrints catalog by modifying the form in our `AddressBook` application. The **AutoComplete Text Field** provides a list of suggestions as the user types. It obtains the suggestions from a data source, such as a database or web service. Eventually, the new form will allow users to search the address book by last name, then first name. If the user selects a contact, the application will display the contact's name and address on a map of the neighborhood. We build this form in two stages. First, we'll add the **AutoComplete Text Field** that will display suggestions as the user types a contact's last name. Then we'll add the search functionality and map display in the next step.

Adding Search Components to the `AddressBook.jsp` *Page*

Using the `AddressBook` application from Section 27.2, drop a **Static Text** component named `searchHeader` below `addressesTable`. Change its text to `"Search the address book by last name:"` and change its font size to `18px`. Now drag an **AutoComplete Text Field** component to the page and name it `nameAutoComplete`. Set this field's `required` property to `true`. Add a **Label** named `nameSearchLabel` containing the text `"Last name:"` to the left of the **AutoComplete Text Field**. Finally, add a button called `lookUpButton` with the text `Look Up` to the right of the **AutoComplete Text Field**.

27.4.1 Configuring Virtual Forms

Virtual forms are used when you would like a button to submit a subset of the page's input fields to the server. Recall that the **Table**'s internal virtual forms were enabled so that clicking the pagination buttons would not submit any of the data in the **Text Field**s used to add a contact to the `AddressBook` database. Virtual forms are particularly useful for displaying multiple forms on the same page. They allow you to specify a submitter component and one or more participant components for a form. When the virtual form's submitter component is clicked, only the values of its participant components will be submitted to the server. We use virtual forms in our `AddressBook` application to separate the form for adding a contact to the `AddressBook` database from the form for searching the database.

To add virtual forms to the page, right click the **Submit** button on the upper form and choose **Configure Virtual Forms...** from the popup menu to display the **Configure Virtual Forms** dialog. Click **New** to add a virtual form, then click in the **Name** column and change the new form's name to `addForm`. Double click the **Submit** column and change the option to **Yes** to indicate that this button should be used to submit the `addForm` virtual form. Click **OK** to exit the dialog. Next, select all the **Text Field**s used to enter a contact's information in the upper form. You can do this by holding the *Ctrl* key while you click each **Text Field**. Right click one of the selected **Text Field**s and choose **Configure Virtual Forms...**. In the **Participate** column of the `addForm`, change the option to **Yes** to indicate that the values in these **Text Field**s should be submitted to the server when the form is submitted. Click **OK** to exit.

Repeat the process described above to create a second virtual form named `searchForm` for the lower form. Figure 27.10 shows the **Configure Virtual Forms** dialog after both virtual forms have been added. The **Look Up** `Button` should submit the `searchForm`, and `nameAutoComplete` should participate in the `searchForm`. Next, return to **Design** mode and click the **Show Virtual Forms** button ( ) at the top of the Visual Designer panel to display a legend of the virtual forms on the page. Your virtual forms should be configured as in Fig. 27.11. The **Text Field**s outlined in blue participate in the virtual form `addForm`. Those outlined in green participate in the virtual form `searchForm`. The components outlined with a dashed line submit their respective forms. A color key is provided at the bottom right of the **Design** area so that you know which components belong to each virtual form.

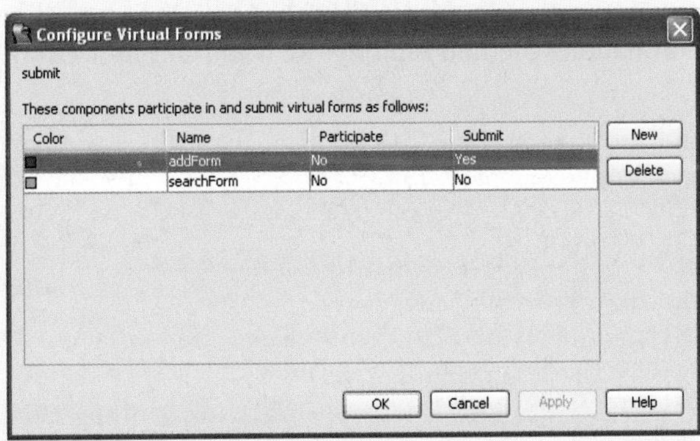

Fig. 27.10 | **Configure Virtual Forms** dialog.

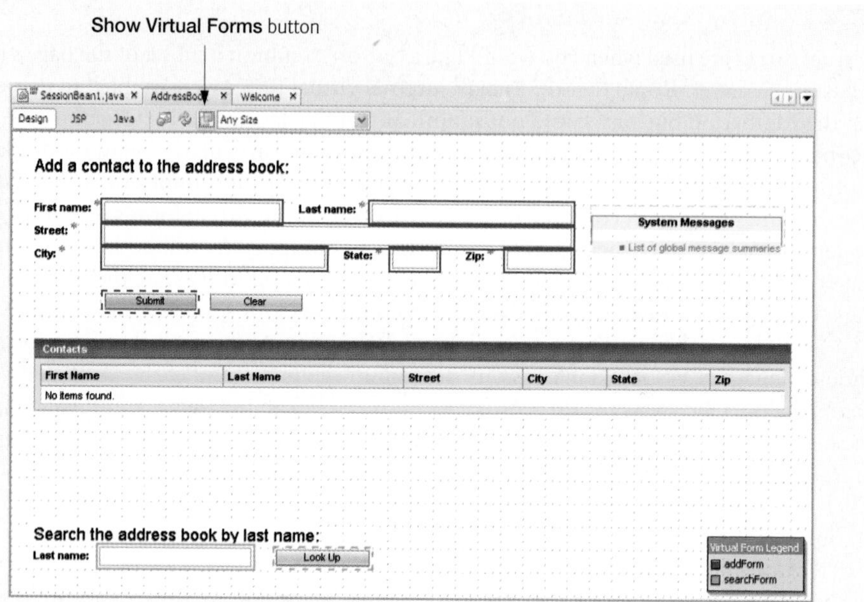

Fig. 27.11 | Virtual forms legend.

27.4.2 JSP File with Virtual Forms and an AutoComplete Text Field

Figure 27.12 presents the JSP file generated by Netbeans for this stage of the `AddressBook` application. A new tag library is specified in the root element (`xmlns:bp="http://java.sun.com/blueprints/ui/14"`; line 5). This is the BluePrints catalog library that provides Ajax-enabled components such as the **AutoComplete Text Field** component. We focus only on the new features of this JSP.

Lines 22–25 configure the virtual forms for this page. Lines 147–151 define the **AutoComplete Text Field** component. This component's `completionMethod` attribute is bound to the page bean's `nameAutoComplete_complete` method (discussed in Section 27.4.3), which provides the list of options the **AutoComplete Text Field** component should suggest. To create this method, right click the `nameAutoComplete` component in **Design** view and select **Edit Event Handler > complete.** Notice that the **Look Up** button (lines 155–157) does not specify an action-handler method binding; we'll add this in Section 27.5.

```
1  <?xml version="1.0" encoding="UTF-8"?>
2  <!-- Fig. 27.12: AddressBook.jsp -->
3  <!-- AddressBook JSP with an add form and a Table JSF component. -->
4  <jsp:root version="1.2"
5     xmlns:bp="http://java.sun.com/blueprints/ui/14"
6     xmlns:f="http://java.sun.com/jsf/core"
7     xmlns:h="http://java.sun.com/jsf/html"
8     xmlns:jsp="http://java.sun.com/JSP/Page"
9     xmlns:webuijsf="http://www.sun.com/webui/webuijsf">
```

Fig. 27.12 | `AddressBook` JSP with an **AutoComplete Text Field** component. (Part 1 of 5.)

```
<jsp:directive.page contentType="text/html;charset=UTF-8"
   pageEncoding="UTF-8"/>
<f:view>
<webuijsf:page binding="#{AddressBook.page1}" id="page1">
   <webuijsf:html binding="#{AddressBook.html1}" id="html1">
      <webuijsf:head binding="#{AddressBook.head1}" id="head1">
         <webuijsf:link binding="#{AddressBook.link1}" id="link1"
            url="/resources/stylesheet.css"/>
      </webuijsf:head>
      <webuijsf:body binding="#{AddressBook.body1}" id="body1"
         style="-rave-layout: grid">
         <webuijsf:form binding="#{AddressBook.form1}" id="form1"
            virtualFormsConfig="addForm | zipTextField lnameTextField
               fnameTextField streetTextField cityTextField
               stateTextField | submitButton , searchForm |
               nameAutoComplete | lookUpButton">
            <webuijsf:staticText binding="#{AddressBook.staticText1}"
               id="staticText1" style="font-size: 18px; left: 24px;
               top: 24px; position: absolute"
               text="Add a contact to the address book:"/>
            <webuijsf:label binding="#{AddressBook.fnameLabel}"
               for="fnameTextField" id="fnameLabel" style="position:
               absolute; left: 24px; top: 72px" text="First name:"/>
            <webuijsf:textField binding="#{AddressBook.fnameTextField}"
               id="fnameTextField" maxLength="30" required="true"
               style="left: 100px; top: 72px; position: absolute;
               width: 192px"/>
            <webuijsf:label binding="#{AddressBook.lnameLabel}"
               for="lnameTextField" id="lnameLabel" style="left: 312px;
               top: 72px; position: absolute" text="Last name:"/>
            <webuijsf:textField binding="#{AddressBook.lnameTextField}"
               id="lnameTextField" maxLength="30" required="true"
               style="left: 390px; top: 72px; position: absolute;
               width: 214px"/>
            <webuijsf:label binding="#{AddressBook.streetLabel}"
               for="streetTextField" id="streetLabel" style="position:
               absolute; left: 24px; top: 96px" text="Street:"/>
            <webuijsf:textField binding=
               "#{AddressBook.streetTextField}" id="streetTextField"
               maxLength="150" required="true" style="left: 100px;
               top: 96px; position: absolute; width: 504px"/>
            <webuijsf:label binding="#{AddressBook.cityLabel}"
               for="cityTextField" id="cityLabel" style="left: 24px;
               top: 120px; position: absolute" text="City:"/>
            <webuijsf:textField binding="#{AddressBook.cityTextField}"
               id="cityTextField" maxLength="30" required="true"
               style="left: 100px; top: 120px; position: absolute;
               width: 240px"/>
            <webuijsf:label binding="#{AddressBook.stateLabel}"
               for="stateTextField" id="stateLabel" style="left: 360px;
               top: 120px; position: absolute" text="State:"/>
```

Fig. 27.12 | AddressBook JSP with an **AutoComplete Text Field** component. (Part 2 of 5.)

```
            <webuijsf:textField binding="#{AddressBook.stateTextField}"
               id="stateTextField" maxLength="2" required="true"
               style="left: 412px; top: 120px; position: absolute;
               width: 48px"/>
            <webuijsf:label binding="#{AddressBook.zipLabel}"
               for="zipTextField" id="zipLabel" style="left: 490px;
               top: 120px; position: absolute" text="Zip:"/>
            <webuijsf:textField binding="#{AddressBook.zipTextField}"
               id="zipTextField" maxLength="5" required="true"
               style="left: 534px; top: 120px; position: absolute;
               width: 70px"/>
            <webuijsf:button actionExpression=
               "#{AddressBook.submitButton_action}" binding=
               "#{AddressBook.submitButton}" id="submitButton" primary=
               "true" style="left: 100px; top: 168px; position:
               absolute; width: 100px" text="Submit"/>
            <webuijsf:button binding="#{AddressBook.clearButton}"
               id="clearButton" reset="true" style="left: 215px; top:
               168px; position: absolute; width: 100px" text="Clear"/>
            <webuijsf:messageGroup binding=
               "#{AddressBook.messageGroup1}" id="messageGroup1"
               showGlobalOnly="true" style="left: 624px; top: 72px;
               position: absolute"/>
            <webuijsf:table augmentTitle="false" binding=
               "#{AddressBook.addressesTable}" id="addressesTable"
               paginateButton="true" paginationControls="true"
               style="left: 24px; top: 216px; position: absolute"
               title="Contacts" width="816">
               <webuijsf:tableRowGroup binding=
                  "#{AddressBook.tableRowGroup1}" id="tableRowGroup1"
                  rows="5" sourceData=
                  "#{AddressBook.addressesDataProvider}"
                  sourceVar="currentRow">
                  <webuijsf:tableColumn binding=
                     "#{AddressBook.fnameColumn}" headerText=
                     "First Name" id="fnameColumn"
                     sort="ADDRESSES.FIRSTNAME">
                     <webuijsf:staticText binding=
                     "#{AddressBook.staticText2}" id="staticText2"
                     text="#{currentRow.value[
                     'ADDRESSES.FIRSTNAME']}"/>
                  </webuijsf:tableColumn>
                  <webuijsf:tableColumn binding=
                     "#{AddressBook.lnameColumn}"
                     headerText="Last Name" id="lnameColumn"
                     sort="ADDRESSES.LASTNAME">
                     <webuijsf:staticText binding=
                        "#{AddressBook.staticText3}" id="staticText3"
                        text="#{currentRow.value[
                        'ADDRESSES.LASTNAME']}"/>
                  </webuijsf:tableColumn>
```

Fig. 27.12 | AddressBook JSP with an **AutoComplete Text Field** component. (Part 3 of 5.)

```
                  <webuijsf:tableColumn binding=
                     "#{AddressBook.streetColumn}" headerText="Street"
                     id="streetColumn" sort="ADDRESSES.STREET">
                     <webuijsf:staticText binding=
                        "#{AddressBook.staticText4}" id="staticText4"
                        text="#{currentRow.value[
                        'ADDRESSES.STREET']}"/>
                  </webuijsf:tableColumn>
                  <webuijsf:tableColumn binding=
                     "#{AddressBook.cityColumn}" headerText="City"
                     id="cityColumn" sort="ADDRESSES.CITY">
                     <webuijsf:staticText binding=
                        "#{AddressBook.staticText5}" id="staticText5"
                        text="#{currentRow.value['ADDRESSES.CITY']}"/>
                  </webuijsf:tableColumn>
                  <webuijsf:tableColumn binding=
                     "#{AddressBook.stateColumn}" headerText="State"
                     id="stateColumn" sort="ADDRESSES.STATE">
                     <webuijsf:staticText binding=
                        "#{AddressBook.staticText6}" id="staticText6"
                        text="#{currentRow.value['ADDRESSES.STATE']}"/>
                  </webuijsf:tableColumn>
                  <webuijsf:tableColumn binding=
                     "#{AddressBook.zipColumn}" headerText="Zip"
                     id="zipColumn" sort="ADDRESSES.ZIP" width="106">
                     <webuijsf:staticText binding=
                        "#{AddressBook.staticText7}" id="staticText7"
                        text="#{currentRow.value['ADDRESSES.ZIP']}"/>
                  </webuijsf:tableColumn>
               </webuijsf:tableRowGroup>
            </webuijsf:table>
            <webuijsf:staticText binding="#{AddressBook.searchHeader}"
               id="searchHeader" style="font-size: 18px; left: 24px;
               top: 420px; position: absolute"
               text="Search the address book by last name:"/>
            <bp:autoComplete binding="#{AddressBook.nameAutoComplete}"
               completionMethod=
               "#{AddressBook.nameAutoComplete_complete}"
               id="nameAutoComplete"
               style="left: 96px; top: 444px; position: absolute"/>
            <webuijsf:label binding="#{AddressBook.label1}"
               for="nameAutoComplete" id="label1" style="left: 24px;
               top: 447px; position: absolute" text="Last name:"/>
            <webuijsf:button binding="#{AddressBook.lookUpButton}"
               id="lookUpButton" style="left: 288px; top: 446px;
               position: absolute; width: 100px" text="Look Up"/>
         </webuijsf:form>
      </webuijsf:body>
   </webuijsf:html>
  </webuijsf:page>
 </f:view>
</jsp:root>
```

Fig. 27.12 | AddressBook JSP with an **AutoComplete Text Field** component. (Part 4 of 5.)

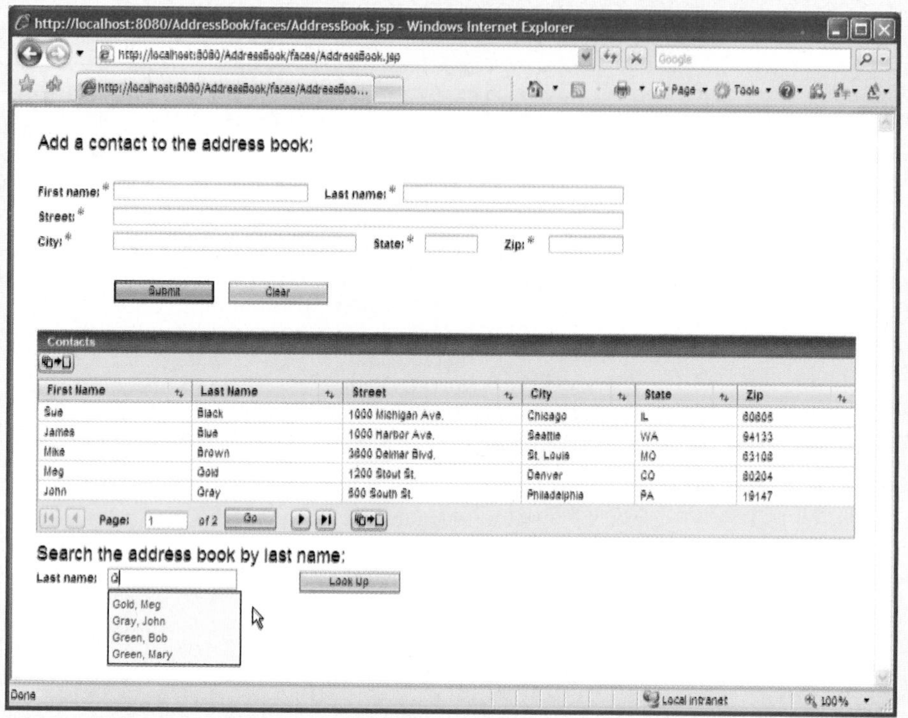

Fig. 27.12 | AddressBook JSP with an **AutoComplete Text Field** component. (Part 5 of 5.)

27.4.3 Providing Suggestions for an AutoComplete Text Field

Figure 27.13 displays the page bean file for the JSP in Fig. 27.12. It includes the method `nameAutoComplete_complete`, which provides the functionality for the **AutoComplete Text Field**. Otherwise, this page bean is identical to the one in Fig. 27.8.

```
// Fig. 27.13: AddressBook.java
// Page bean for AddressBook.jsp.
package addressbook;

import com.sun.data.provider.RowKey;
import com.sun.data.provider.impl.CachedRowSetDataProvider;
import com.sun.j2ee.blueprints.ui.autocomplete.AutoCompleteComponent;
import com.sun.j2ee.blueprints.ui.autocomplete.CompletionResult;
import com.sun.rave.web.ui.appbase.AbstractPageBean;
import com.sun.webui.jsf.component.Body;
import com.sun.webui.jsf.component.Button;
import com.sun.webui.jsf.component.Form;
import com.sun.webui.jsf.component.Head;
import com.sun.webui.jsf.component.Html;
import com.sun.webui.jsf.component.Label;
```

Fig. 27.13 | Page bean that suggests names in the **AutoComplete Text Field**. (Part 1 of 3.)

```
import com.sun.webui.jsf.component.Link;
import com.sun.webui.jsf.component.MessageGroup;
import com.sun.webui.jsf.component.Page;
import com.sun.webui.jsf.component.StaticText;
import com.sun.webui.jsf.component.Table;
import com.sun.webui.jsf.component.TableColumn;
import com.sun.webui.jsf.component.TableRowGroup;
import com.sun.webui.jsf.component.TextField;
import com.sun.webui.jsf.model.DefaultTableDataProvider;
import javax.faces.FacesException;
import javax.faces.context.FacesContext;

public class AddressBook extends AbstractPageBean
{
   // To save space, we omitted the code in lines 30-625. The complete
   // source code is provided with this chapter's examples.

   // action handler for the autocomplete box that fetches names
   // from the address book whose prefixes match the letters typed so far
   // and displays them in a suggestion list.
   public void nameAutoComplete_complete(
      FacesContext context, String prefix, CompletionResult result )
   {
      try
      {
         boolean hasNext = addressesDataProvider.cursorFirst();

         while ( hasNext )
         {
            // get a name from the database
            String name =
               (String) addressesDataProvider.getValue(
               "ADDRESSES.LASTNAME" ) + ", " +
               (String) addressesDataProvider.getValue(
               "ADDRESSES.FIRSTNAME" ) ;

            // if the name in the database starts with the prefix,
            // add it to the list of suggestions
            if ( name.toLowerCase().startsWith( prefix.toLowerCase() ) )
            {
               result.addItem( name );
            } // end if
            else
            {
               // terminate the loop if the rest of the names are
               // alphabetically less than the prefix
               if ( prefix.compareTo( name ) < 0 )
               {
                  break;
               } // end if
            } // end else

```

Fig. 27.13 | Page bean that suggests names in the **AutoComplete Text Field**. (Part 2 of 3.)

```
661                // move cursor to next row of database
662                hasNext = addressesDataProvider.cursorNext();
663             } // end while
664          } // end try
665          catch ( Exception ex )
666          {
667             result.addItem( "Exception getting matching names." );
668          } // end catch
669       } // end method nameAutoComplete_complete
670    } // end class AddressBook
```

Fig. 27.13 | Page bean that suggests names in the **AutoComplete Text Field**. (Part 3 of 3.)

Method `nameAutoComplete_complete` (lines 629–669) is invoked after every keystroke in the **AutoComplete Text Field** to update the list of suggestions based on the text the user has typed so far. The method receives a string (`prefix`) containing the text the user has entered and a `CompletionResult` object (`result`) that is used to display suggestions to the user. The method loops through the rows of the `addressesDataProvider`, retrieves the name from each row, checks whether the name begins with the letters typed so far and, if so, adds the name to `result`. Line 634 sets the cursor to the first row in the data provider. Line 636 determines whether there are more rows in the data provider. If so, lines 639–643 retrieve the last name and first name from the current row and create a `String` in the format *last name, first name*. Line 647 compares the lowercase versions of `name` and `prefix` to determine whether the `name` starts with the characters typed so far. If so, the name is a match and line 649 adds it to `result`.

Recall that the data provider wraps a `CachedRowSet` object that contains a SQL query which returns the rows in the database sorted by last name, then first name. This allows us to stop iterating through the data provider once we reach a row whose name comes alphabetically after the text entered by the user—names in the rows beyond this will all be alphabetically greater and thus are not potential matches. If the `name` does not match the text entered so far, line 655 tests whether the current name is alphabetically greater than the `prefix`. If so, line 657 terminates the loop.

Performance Tip 27.1

When using database columns to provide suggestions in an **AutoComplete Text Field**, *sorting the columns eliminates the need to check every row in the database for potential matches. This significantly improves performance when dealing with a large database.*

If the name is neither a match nor alphabetically greater than `prefix`, then line 662 moves the cursor to the next row in the data provider. If there is another row, the loop iterates again, checking whether the name in the next row matches the `prefix` and should be added to `results`.

Lines 665–668 catch any exceptions generated while searching the database. Line 667 adds text to the suggestion box indicating the error to the user.

27.5 Google Maps Map Viewer Component

We now complete the `AddressBook` application by adding functionality to the **Look Up Button**. When the user clicks this **Button**, the name in the **AutoComplete Text Field** is used to search the AddressBook database. We also add a **Map Viewer** Ajax-enabled JSF component to the page to display a map of the area for the address. A **Map Viewer** uses the Google Maps API web service to find and display maps. (The details of web services are covered in Chapter 28.) In this example, using the Google Maps API is analogous to making ordinary method calls on a **Map Viewer** object and its supporting bean in the page bean file. When a contact is found, we display a map of the neighborhood with a **Map Marker** that points to the location and indicates the contact's name and address.

27.5.1 Obtaining a Google Maps API Key

To use the **Map Viewer** component, you must have an account with Google. Visit the site `https://www.google.com/accounts/ManageAccount` to register for a free account if you do not have one. Once you have logged in to your account, you must obtain a key to use the Google Maps API from `www.google.com/apis/maps`. The key you receive will be specific to this web application and will limit the number of maps the application can display per day. When you sign up for the key, you will be asked to enter the URL for the application that will be using the Google Maps API. If you are deploying the application only on Sun Java System Application Server, enter `http://localhost:8080/` as the URL.

After you accept Google's terms and conditions, you'll be redirected to a page containing your new Google Maps API key. Save this key in a text file in a convenient location for future reference.

27.5.2 Adding a Map Viewer Component to a Page

Now that you have a key to use the Google Maps API, you are ready to complete the `AddressBook` application. With `AddressBook.jsp` open in **Design** mode, add a **Map Viewer** component named `mapViewer` below the `nameAutoComplete`. In the **Properties** window, set the **Map Viewer**'s `key` property to the key you obtained for accessing the Google Maps API. Set the `rendered` property to `false` so that the map will not be displayed when the user has not yet searched for an address. Set the `zoomLevel` property to `1 (In)` so the user can see the street names on the map.

Drop a **Map Marker** (named `mapMarker`) from the **BluePrints AJAX Support Beans** section of the **Palette** anywhere on the page. This component (which is not visible in **Design** view) marks the contact's location on the map. You must bind the marker to the map so that the marker will display on the map. To do so, right click the **Map Viewer** in the **Outline** tab and choose **Property Bindings...** to display the **Property Bindings** dialog. Select `info` from the **Select bindable property** column of the dialog, then select `mapMarker` from the **Select binding target** column. Click **Apply**, then **Close**.

Finally, drop a **Geocoding Service Object** (named `geoCoder`) from the **BluePrints AJAX Support Beans** section of the **Palette** anywhere on the page. This object (which is not visible in **Design** view) converts street addresses into latitudes and longitudes that the **Map Viewer** component uses to display an appropriate map.

Adding a Data Provider to the Page

To complete this application, you need a second data provider to search the `AddressBook` database based on the first and last name entered in the **AutoComplete Text Field**. We want to create a new data source rather than reuse the existing one, because the query to search for contacts is different from the query to display all the contacts. On the **Runtime** tab, expand the **Databases** node, the **AddressBook** database's node and its **Tables** node to reveal the **Addresses** table. Drag the **Addresses** table onto the page to create the new data provider. Select the new data provider in the **Navigator** tab and change its `id` to `addressesSearchDataProvider`. In the **Outline** tab, a new node named `addressesRowSet1` has been added to the `SessionBean1` node. Change the `id` of `addressesRowSet1` to `addressesSearchRowSet`.

Double click the `addressesSearchRowSet` node to edit the SQL statement for this `RowSet`. Since we will use this row set to search the database for a given last and first name, we need to add search parameters to the `SELECT` statement the `RowSet` will execute. To do this, enter the text `"= ?"` in the **Criteria** column of both the first and last name rows in the SQL statement editor table. The number `1` should appear in the **Order** column for first name and `2` should appear for last name. Notice that the lines

```
WHERE JHTP7.ADDRESSES.FIRSTNAME = ?
   AND JHTP7.ADDRESSES.LASTNAME = ?
```

have been added to the SQL statement. This indicates that the `RowSet` now executes a parameterized SQL statement. The parameters can be set programmatically, with the first name as the first parameter and the last name as the second.

27.5.3 JSP File with a Map Viewer Component

Figure 27.14 presents the JSP file for the completed address-book application. It is nearly identical to the JSP for the previous two versions of this application. The new feature is the **Map Viewer** component (and its supporting components) used to display a map with the contact's location. We discuss only the new elements of this file. [*Note:* This code will not run until you have specified your own Google Maps key in lines 165–166. You can paste your key into the **Map Viewer** component's `key` property in the **Properties** window.]

Lines 162–168 define the `mapViewer` component that displays a map of the area surrounding the address. The component's `center` attribute is bound to the page bean property `mapViewer_center`. This property is manipulated in the page bean file to center the map on the desired address.

```
1  <?xml version="1.0" encoding="UTF-8"?>
2  <!-- Fig. 27.14: AddressBook.jsp -->
3  <!-- AddressBook JSP with an add form and a Table JSF component. -->
4
5  <jsp:root version="1.2"
6     xmlns:bp="http://java.sun.com/blueprints/ui/14"
7     xmlns:f="http://java.sun.com/jsf/core"
8     xmlns:h="http://java.sun.com/jsf/html"
9     xmlns:jsp="http://java.sun.com/JSP/Page"
10    xmlns:webuijsf="http://www.sun.com/webui/webuijsf">
11    <jsp:directive.page contentType="text/html;charset=UTF-8"
12       pageEncoding="UTF-8"/>
13    <f:view>
14    <webuijsf:page binding="#{AddressBook.page1}" id="page1">
15       <webuijsf:html binding="#{AddressBook.html1}" id="html1">
```

Fig. 27.14 | `AddressBook` JSP with a **Map Viewer** component. (Part 1 of 5.)

```
        <webuijsf:head binding="#{AddressBook.head1}" id="head1">
          <webuijsf:link binding="#{AddressBook.link1}" id="link1"
            url="/resources/stylesheet.css"/>
        </webuijsf:head>
        <webuijsf:body binding="#{AddressBook.body1}" id="body1"
           style="-rave-layout: grid">
           <webuijsf:form binding="#{AddressBook.form1}" id="form1"
              virtualFormsConfig="addForm | zipTextField lnameTextField
              fnameTextField streetTextField cityTextField stateTextField
              | submitButton , searchForm | nameAutoComplete |
              lookUpButton">
              <webuijsf:staticText binding=
                 "#{AddressBook.staticText1}" id="staticText1" style=
                 "font-size: 18px; left: 24px; top: 24px; position:
                 absolute" text="Add a contact to the address book:"/>
              <webuijsf:label binding="#{AddressBook.fnameLabel}"
                 for="fnameTextField" id="fnameLabel" style="position:
                 absolute; left: 24px; top: 72px" text="First name:"/>
              <webuijsf:textField binding="#{AddressBook.fnameTextField}"
                 id="fnameTextField" maxLength="30" required="true"
                 style="left: 100px; top: 72px; position: absolute;
                 width: 192px"/>
              <webuijsf:label binding="#{AddressBook.lnameLabel}"
                 for="lnameTextField" id="lnameLabel" style="left: 312px;
                 top: 72px; position: absolute" text="Last name:"/>
              <webuijsf:textField binding="#{AddressBook.lnameTextField}"
                 id="lnameTextField" maxLength="30" required="true"
                 style="left: 390px; top: 72px; position: absolute;
                 width: 214px"/>
              <webuijsf:label binding="#{AddressBook.streetLabel}"
                 for="streetTextField" id="streetLabel" style="position:
                 absolute; left: 24px; top: 96px" text="Street:"/>
              <webuijsf:textField binding=
                 "#{AddressBook.streetTextField}" id="streetTextField"
                 maxLength="150" required="true" style="left: 100px;
                 top: 96px; position: absolute; width: 504px"/>
              <webuijsf:label binding="#{AddressBook.cityLabel}"
                 for="cityTextField" id="cityLabel" style="left: 24px;
                 top: 120px; position: absolute" text="City:"/>
              <webuijsf:textField binding="#{AddressBook.cityTextField}"
                 id="cityTextField" maxLength="30" required="true"
                 style="left: 100px; top: 120px; position: absolute;
                 width: 240px"/>
              <webuijsf:label binding="#{AddressBook.stateLabel}"
                 for="stateTextField" id="stateLabel"
                 style="left: 360px; top: 120px; position: absolute"
                 text="State:"/>
              <webuijsf:textField binding="#{AddressBook.stateTextField}"
                 id="stateTextField" maxLength="2" required="true"
                 style="left: 412px; top: 120px; position: absolute;
                 width: 48px"/>
              <webuijsf:label binding="#{AddressBook.zipLabel}"
                 for="zipTextField" id="zipLabel" style="left: 490px;
```

Fig. 27.14 | AddressBook JSP with a **Map Viewer** component. (Part 2 of 5.)

```
            top: 120px; position: absolute" text="Zip:"/>
        <webuijsf:textField binding="#{AddressBook.zipTextField}"
            id="zipTextField" maxLength="5" required="true"
            style="left: 534px; top: 120px; position: absolute;
            width: 70px"/>
        <webuijsf:button actionExpression=
            "#{AddressBook.submitButton_action}" binding=
            "#{AddressBook.submitButton}" id="submitButton"
            primary="true" style="left: 100px; top: 168px; position:
            absolute; width: 100px" text="Submit"/>
        <webuijsf:button binding="#{AddressBook.clearButton}"
            id="clearButton" reset="true" style="left: 215px; top:
            168px; position: absolute; width: 100px" text="Clear"/>
        <webuijsf:messageGroup binding=
            "#{AddressBook.messageGroup1}" id="messageGroup1"
            showGlobalOnly="true" style="left: 624px; top: 72px;
            position: absolute"/>
        <webuijsf:table augmentTitle="false" binding=
            "#{AddressBook.addressesTable}" id="addressesTable"
            paginateButton="true" paginationControls="true"
            style="left: 24px; top: 216px; position: absolute"
            title="Contacts" width="816">
            <webuijsf:tableRowGroup binding=
                "#{AddressBook.tableRowGroup1}" id="tableRowGroup1"
                rows="5" sourceData=
                "#{AddressBook.addressesDataProvider}"
                sourceVar="currentRow">
                <webuijsf:tableColumn binding=
                    "#{AddressBook.fnameColumn}"
                    headerText="First Name" id="fnameColumn"
                    sort="ADDRESSES.FIRSTNAME">
                    <webuijsf:staticText binding=
                        "#{AddressBook.staticText2}" id="staticText2"
                        text="#{currentRow.value[
                        'ADDRESSES.FIRSTNAME']}"/>
                </webuijsf:tableColumn>
                <webuijsf:tableColumn binding=
                    "#{AddressBook.lnameColumn}"
                    headerText="Last Name" id="lnameColumn"
                    sort="ADDRESSES.LASTNAME">
                    <webuijsf:staticText binding=
                        "#{AddressBook.staticText3}" id="staticText3"
                        text="#{currentRow.value[
                        'ADDRESSES.LASTNAME']}"/>
                </webuijsf:tableColumn>
                <webuijsf:tableColumn binding=
                    "#{AddressBook.streetColumn}" headerText="Street"
                    id="streetColumn" sort="ADDRESSES.STREET">
                    <webuijsf:staticText binding=
                        "#{AddressBook.staticText4}" id="staticText4"
                        text="#{currentRow.value[
                        'ADDRESSES.STREET']}"/>
                </webuijsf:tableColumn>
```

Fig. 27.14 | AddressBook JSP with a **Map Viewer** component. (Part 3 of 5.)

```
              <webuijsf:tableColumn binding=
                "#{AddressBook.cityColumn}" headerText="City"
                id="cityColumn" sort="ADDRESSES.CITY">
                <webuijsf:staticText binding=
                  "#{AddressBook.staticText5}" id="staticText5"
                  text="#{currentRow.value['ADDRESSES.CITY']}"/>
              </webuijsf:tableColumn>
              <webuijsf:tableColumn binding=
                "#{AddressBook.stateColumn}" headerText="State"
                id="stateColumn" sort="ADDRESSES.STATE">
                <webuijsf:staticText binding=
                  "#{AddressBook.staticText6}" id="staticText6"
                  text="#{currentRow.value['ADDRESSES.STATE']}"/>
              </webuijsf:tableColumn>
              <webuijsf:tableColumn binding=
                "#{AddressBook.zipColumn}" headerText="Zip"
                id="zipColumn" sort="ADDRESSES.ZIP" width="106">
                <webuijsf:staticText binding=
                  "#{AddressBook.staticText7}" id="staticText7"
                  text="#{currentRow.value['ADDRESSES.ZIP']}"/>
              </webuijsf:tableColumn>
            </webuijsf:tableRowGroup>
          </webuijsf:table>
          <webuijsf:staticText binding="#{AddressBook.searchHeader}"
            id="searchHeader" style="font-size: 18px; left: 24px;
            top: 420px; position: absolute"
            text="Search the address book by last name:"/>
          <bp:autoComplete binding=
            "#{AddressBook.nameAutoComplete}" completionMethod=
            "#{AddressBook.nameAutoComplete_complete}"
            id="nameAutoComplete"
            style="left: 96px; top: 444px; position: absolute"/>
          <webuijsf:label binding="#{AddressBook.label1}"
            for="nameAutoComplete" id="label1" style="left: 24px;
            top: 447px; position: absolute" text="Last name:"/>
          <webuijsf:button actionExpression=
            "#{AddressBook.lookUpButton_action}"
            binding="#{AddressBook.lookUpButton}" id="lookUpButton"
            style="left: 288px; top: 446px; position: absolute;
            width: 100px" text="Look Up"/>
          <bp:mapViewer binding="#{AddressBook.mapViewer}"
            center="#{AddressBook.mapViewer_center}"
            id="mapViewer" info="#{AddressBook.mapMarker}"
            key="XXXXXXXXXXXXXXXXXXXXXXXXXXXXXXXXXXXXXXXXXXXXXXXXX
            XXXXXXXXXXXXXXXXXXXXXXXXXXXXXXXXXXXXXXX"
            style="height: 550px; left: 24px; top: 480px;
            position: absolute; width: 814px" zoomLevel="4"/>
        </webuijsf:form>
      </webuijsf:body>
    </webuijsf:html>
  </webuijsf:page>
  </f:view>
</jsp:root>
```

Fig. 27.14 | AddressBook JSP with a **Map Viewer** component. (Part 4 of 5.)

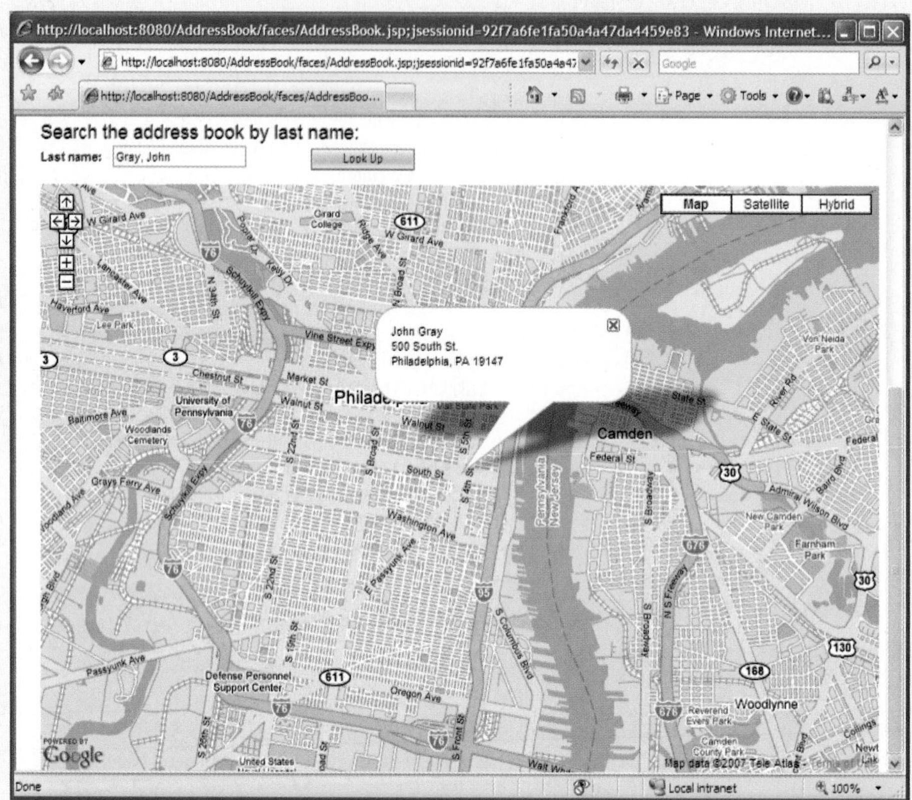

Fig. 27.14 | AddressBook JSP with a **Map Viewer** component. (Part 5 of 5.)

The **Look Up** Button's action attribute is now bound to method `lookUpButton_action` in the page bean (lines 157–158). This action handler searches the AddressBook database for the name entered in the **AutoComplete Text Field** and displays the contact's name and address on a map of the contact's location. We discuss this method in Section 27.5.4.

27.5.4 Page Bean That Displays a Map in the Map Viewer Component

Figure 27.15 presents the page bean for the completed AddressBook application. Most of this file is identical to the page beans for the first two versions of this application. We discuss only the new action-handler method, `lookUpButton_action`.

```
// Fig. 27.15: AddressBook.java
// Page bean for AddressBook.jsp.
package addressbook;

import com.sun.data.provider.RowKey;
import com.sun.data.provider.impl.CachedRowSetDataProvider;
```

Fig. 27.15 | Page bean that gets a map to display in the **Map Viewer** component. (Part 1 of 3.)

```java
import com.sun.j2ee.blueprints.ui.autocomplete.AutoCompleteComponent;
import com.sun.j2ee.blueprints.ui.autocomplete.CompletionResult;
import com.sun.j2ee.blueprints.ui.geocoder.GeoCoder;
import com.sun.j2ee.blueprints.ui.geocoder.GeoPoint;
import com.sun.j2ee.blueprints.ui.mapviewer.MapComponent;
import com.sun.j2ee.blueprints.ui.mapviewer.MapMarker;
import com.sun.j2ee.blueprints.ui.mapviewer.MapPoint;
import com.sun.rave.web.ui.appbase.AbstractPageBean;
import com.sun.webui.jsf.component.Body;
import com.sun.webui.jsf.component.Button;
import com.sun.webui.jsf.component.Form;
import com.sun.webui.jsf.component.Head;
import com.sun.webui.jsf.component.Html;
import com.sun.webui.jsf.component.Label;
import com.sun.webui.jsf.component.Link;
import com.sun.webui.jsf.component.MessageGroup;
import com.sun.webui.jsf.component.Page;
import com.sun.webui.jsf.component.StaticText;
import com.sun.webui.jsf.component.Table;
import com.sun.webui.jsf.component.TableColumn;
import com.sun.webui.jsf.component.TableRowGroup;
import com.sun.webui.jsf.component.TextField;
import javax.faces.FacesException;
import javax.faces.context.FacesContext;

public class AddressBook extends AbstractPageBean
{
   private int __placeholder;

   private void _init() throws Exception
   {
      addressesDataProvider.setCachedRowSet(
         ( javax.sql.rowset.CachedRowSet ) getValue(
         "#{SessionBean1.addressesRowSet}" ) );
      addressesTable.setInternalVirtualForm( true );
      mapViewer.setRendered( false );
      addressesSearchDataProvider.setCachedRowSet(
         ( javax.sql.rowset.CachedRowSet ) getValue(
         "#{SessionBean1.addressesSearchRowSet}" ) );
   } // end method _init

   // To save space, we omitted the code in lines 48-741. The complete
   // source code is provided with this chapter's examples.

   // action handler for the lookUpButton that searches the address book
   // database and displays the requested address on a corresponding map.
   public String lookUpButton_action()
   {
      // split text in autocomplete field into first and last name
      String name = String.valueOf( nameAutoComplete.getValue() );
      int splitIndex = name.indexOf( "," );
      String lname = name.substring( 0, splitIndex );
      String fname = name.substring( splitIndex + 2 );
```

Fig. 27.15 | Page bean that gets a map to display in the **Map Viewer** component. (Part 2 of 3.)

```

      try
      {
         // set the parameters for the addressesSearchDataProvider
         addressesSearchDataProvider.getCachedRowSet().setObject(
            1, fname );
         addressesSearchDataProvider.getCachedRowSet().setObject(
            2, lname );
         addressesSearchDataProvider.refresh();
         String street = (String) addressesSearchDataProvider.getValue(
            "ADDRESSES.STREET" );
         String city = (String) addressesSearchDataProvider.getValue(
            "ADDRESSES.CITY" );
         String state = (String) addressesSearchDataProvider.getValue(
            "ADDRESSES.STATE" );
         String zip =  (String) addressesSearchDataProvider.getValue(
            "ADDRESSES.ZIP" );

         // format the address for Google Maps
         String googleAddress = street + ", " + city + ", " + state +
            " " + zip;

         // get the geopoints for the address
         GeoPoint points[] = geoCoder.geoCode( googleAddress );

         // if Google Maps cannot find the address
         if ( points == null )
         {
            error( "Map for " + googleAddress + " could not be found" );
            mapViewer.setRendered( false ); // hide map
            return null;
         } // end if

         // center the map for the given address
         mapViewer_center.setLatitude( points[0].getLatitude() );
         mapViewer_center.setLongitude( points[0].getLongitude() );

         // create a marker for the address and set its display text
         mapMarker.setLatitude( points[0].getLatitude() );
         mapMarker.setLongitude( points[0].getLongitude() );
         mapMarker.setMarkup(  fname + " " + lname + "<br/>" + street +
            "<br/>" + city + ", " + state + " " + zip );

         mapViewer.setRendered( true ); // show map
      } // end try
      catch ( Exception e )
      {
         error( "Error processing search. " + e.getMessage() );
      } // end catch

      return null;
   } // end method lookUpButton_action
} // end class AddressBook
```

Fig. 27.15 | Page bean that gets a map to display in the **Map Viewer** component. (Part 3 of 3.)

Method `lookUpButton_action` (lines 744–802) is invoked when the user clicks the **Look Up** button in the lower form on the page. Lines 747–750 retrieve the name from the **AutoComplete Text Field** and split it into `Strings` for the first and last name. Lines 755–758 obtain the `addressesSearchDataProvider`'s `CachedRowSet`, then use its method `setObject` to set the parameters for the query to the first and last name. The `setObject` method replaces a parameter in the SQL query with a specified string. Line 759 refreshes the data provider, which executes the wrapped `RowSet`'s query with the new parameters. The result set now contains only rows that match the first and last name from the **AutoComplete Text Field**. Lines 760–767 fetch the street address, city, state and zip code for this contact from the database. Note that in this example, we assume there are not multiple entries in the address book for the same first and last name, as we fetch only the address information for the first row in the data provider. Any additional rows that match the first and last name are ignored.

Lines 770–771 format the address as a `String` for use with the Google Maps API. Line 774 calls the **Geocoding Service Object**'s `geoCode` method with the address as an argument. This method returns an array of `GeoPoint` objects representing locations that match the address parameter. `GeoPoint` objects provide the latitude and longitude of a given location. We supply a complete address with a street, city, state and zip code as an argument to `geoCode`, so the returned array will contain just one `GeoPoint` object. Line 777 determines whether the array of `GeoPoint` objects is `null`. If so, the address could not be found, and lines 779–781 display a message in the **Message Group** informing the user of the search error, hide the **Map Viewer** and return `null` to terminate the processing.

Lines 785–786 set the latitude and longitude of the **Map Viewer**'s center to those of the `GeoPoint` that represents the selected address. Lines 789–792 set the **Map Marker**'s latitude and longitude, and set the text to display on the marker. Line 794 displays the recentered map containing the **Map Marker** that indicates the contact's location.

Lines 796–799 catch any exceptions generated throughout the method body and display an error message in the **Message Group**. If the user has simply selected a name from the list of selections in the **AutoComplete Text Field**, there will be no errors in searching the database, as the name is guaranteed to be in the proper *last name, first name* format and included in the `AddressBook` database. We did not include any special error-handling code for cases in which the user types a name that cannot be found in the `AddressBook` or for improperly formatted names.

27.6 Wrap-Up

In this chapter, we presented a three-part case study on building a web application that interacts with a database and provides rich user interaction using Ajax-enabled JSF components. We first showed how to build an `AddressBook` application that allows a user to add addresses to the `AddressBook` and browse its contents. Through this example, you learned how to insert user input into a Java DB database and how to display the contents of a database on a web page using a **Table** JSF component.

You learned how to download and import the Java BluePrints Ajax-enabled component library. We then extended the `AddressBook` application to include an **AutoComplete Text Field** component. We showed how to use a database to display suggestions in the **AutoComplete Text Field**. You also learned how to use virtual forms to submit subsets of a form's input components to the server for processing.

Finally, we completed the third part of the `AddressBook` application by adding functionality to the search form. You learned how to use a **Map Viewer**, a **Map Marker** and a **Geocoding Service Object** from the Java BluePrints Ajax-enabled component library to display a Google map that shows a contact's location.

27.7 Web Resources

Our Java Resource Centers focus on the enormous amount of free Java content available online. We currently provide six Java-related Resource Centers:

```
www.deitel.com/java/
www.deitel.com/JavaCertification/
www.deitel.com/JavaDesignPatterns/
www.deitel.com/JavaEE5/
www.deitel.com/JavaFX/
www.deitel.com/JavaSE6Mustang/
```

You can view our complete list of Resource Centers at

```
www.deitel.com/ResourceCenters.html
```

Summary

Section 27.2 Accessing Databases in Web Applications

- Many web applications access databases to store and retrieve persistent data. In this section, we build a web application that uses a Java DB database to store contacts in the address book and display contacts from the address book on a web page.
- The **Table** component formats and displays data from database tables.
- Change the **Table**'s `title` property to specify the text displayed at the top of the **Table**.
- To create a database, select **Tools > Java DB Database > Create Java DB Database....** Next, enter the name of the database to create a username and a password, then click **OK** to create the database.
- You can use the **Runtime** tab (to the right of the **Projects** and **Files** tabs) to create tables and to execute SQL statements that populate the database with data. To do so, click the **Runtime** tab and expand the **Databases** node.
- Netbeans must be connected to the database to execute SQL statements. If it is not, the icon appears next to the database's URL. In this case, right click the icon and click **Connect....** Once connected, the icon changes to .
- To add a table to the database using SQL, expand the database's node, right click the **Tables** node and select **Execute Command...** to open a **SQL Command** editor in Netbeans. Paste the SQL code into the **SQL Command** editor in Netbeans. Then, highlight all the SQL commands, right click inside the **SQL Command** editor and select **Run Selection.**
- To configure a **Table** component to display a table's data, simply drag the database table from the **Servers** tab and drop it on the **Table** component to create the binding.
- To select specific columns to display, right click the **Table** component and select **Bind to Data** to display the **Bind to Data** dialog containing the list of the columns in the database table. The items under the **Selected** heading will be displayed in the **Table**. To remove a column, select it and click the < button.

- By default, the **Table** uses the database table's column names in all uppercase letters as headings. To change these headings, select a column and edit its `headerText` property in the **Properties** window. To select a column, click the column's name in the **Design** mode.
- Clicking the checkbox next to the table's `paginationControls` property in the **Properties** window configures this **Table** for automatic pagination. This adds buttons to the bottom of the **Table** for moving forward and backward between groups of contacts. You may use the **Table Layout** dialog's **Options** tab to select the number of rows to display at a time. To view this tab, right click the **Table**, select **Table Layout...**, then click the **Options** tab.
- Virtual forms allow subsets of a form's input components to be submitted to the server. Setting the `internalVirtualForm` property prevents the pagination control buttons on the **Table** from submitting other form components every time the user wishes to view the next group of records from the database.
- A `CachedRowSetDataProvider` provides a scrollable `RowSet` that can be bound to a **Table** component to display the `RowSet`'s data.
- Every row in a `CachedRowSetDataProvider` has its own key; method `appendRow`, which adds a new row to the `CachedRowSet`, returns the key for the new row.
- Method `commitChanges` of class `CachedRowSetDataProvider` applies any changes to the `CachedRowSet` to the database.
- `CachedRowSetDataProvider` method `refresh` re-executes the wrapped `CachedRowSet`'s SQL.

Section 27.3 Ajax-Enabled JSF Components

- The Java BluePrints Ajax component library provides Ajax-enabled JSF components.
- To use the Java BluePrints Ajax-enabled components in Netbeans, you must download and import them. The IDE provides a wizard for installing this group of components (Internet access is required). To access it, choose **Tools > Update Center** to display the **Update Center Wizard** dialog. Click **Next >** to search for available updates. In the **Available Updates and New Modules** area of the dialog, locate and select **BluePrints AJAX Components**, then click the **Add >** button to add them to the list of items you'd like to install. Click **Next >** and follow the prompts to accept the terms of use and download the components. When the download completes, click **Next >**, then click **Finish**. Click **OK** to restart the IDE.
- You must import the components into the **Palette**. Select **Tools > Component Library Manager**, then click **Import...**. Click **Browse...** in the **Component Library Manager** dialog that appears. Select the `ui.complib` file and click **Open**. Click **OK** to import both the **BluePrints AJAX Components** and the **BluePrints AJAX Support Beans**. Close the **Component Library Manager** to return to the IDE.
- To see the new components in the **Palette**, you must add the **BluePrints AJAX Components** library to your visual web application. To do so, make sure your application's node is expanded in the **Projects** tab. Right click the **Component Libraries** node and select **Add Component Library**. In the **Add Component Library** dialog box, select the **BluePrints AJAX Components library** and click **Add Component Library**.

Section 27.4 **AutoComplete Text Field** *and Virtual Forms*

- The **AutoComplete Text Field** provides a list of suggestions from a data source (such as a database or web service) as the user types.
- Virtual forms are used when you would like a button to submit a subset of the page's input fields to the server.
- Virtual forms enable you to display multiple forms on the same page. They allow you to specify a submitter and one or more participants for each form. When the virtual form's submitter component is clicked, only the values of its participant components will be submitted to the server.

- To add virtual forms to a page, right click the submitter component on the form and choose **Configure Virtual Forms...** from the pop-up menu to display the **Configure Virtual Forms** dialog. Click **New** to add a virtual form, then click in the **Name** column and specify the new form's name. Double click the **Submit** column and change the option to **Yes** to indicate that this button should be used to submit the virtual form. Click **OK** to exit the dialog. Next, select all the input components that will participate in the virtual form. Right click one of the selected components and choose **Configure Virtual Forms...**. In the **Participate** column of the appropriate virtual form, change the option to **Yes** to indicate that the values in these components should be submitted to the server when the form is submitted.
- To see the virtual forms in the **Design** mode, click the **Show Virtual Forms** button ( ) at the top of the Visual Designer panel to display a legend of the virtual forms on the page.
- An **AutoComplete Text Field** component's `completionMethod` attribute is bound to a page bean's `complete` event handler. To create this method, right click the **AutoComplete Text Field** component in **Design** view and select **Edit Event Handler > complete.**
- The `complete` event handler is invoked after every keystroke in an **AutoComplete Text Field** to update the list of suggestions based on the text the user has typed so far. The method receives a string containing the text the user has entered and a `CompletionResult` object that is used to display suggestions to the user.

Section 27.5 Google Maps **Map Viewer** *Component*

- A **Map Viewer** Ajax-enabled JSF component uses the Google Maps API web service to find and display maps. A **Map Marker** points to a location on a map.
- To use the **Map Viewer** component, you must have an account with Google. Register for a free account at `https://www.google.com/accounts/ManageAccount`. You must obtain a key to use the Google Maps API from `www.google.com/apis/maps`. The key you receive will be specific to your web application and will limit the number of maps the application can display per day. When you sign up for the key, you will be asked to enter the URL for the application that will be using the Google Maps API.
- To use a **Map Viewer**, set its `key` property to the Google Maps API key you obtained.
- A **Map Marker** (from the **BluePrints AJAX Support Beans** section of the **Palette**) marks a location on a map. You must bind the marker to the map so that the marker will display on the map. To do so, right click the **Map Viewer** in **Design** mode component and choose **Property Bindings...** to display the **Property Bindings** dialog. Select `info` from the **Select bindable property** column of the dialog, then select the **Map Marker** from the **Select binding target** column. Click **Apply**, then **Close.**
- A **Geocoding Service Object** (from the **BluePrints AJAX Support Beans** section of the **Palette**) converts street addresses into latitudes and longitudes that the **Map Viewer** component uses to display an appropriate map.
- The **Map Viewer**'s `center` attribute is bound to the page bean property `mapViewer_center`. This property is manipulated in the page bean file to center the map on the desired address.
- The **Geocoding Service Object**'s `geoCode` method receives an address as an argument and returns an array of `GeoPoint` objects representing locations that match the address parameter. `GeoPoint` objects provide the latitude and longitude of a given location.

Terminology

Ajax
Ajax-enabled JSF components
AutoComplete Text Field JSF component
binding a JSF **Table** to a database table
bundled database server
Button JSF component
Buy Now Button JSF component
`CachedRowSet` interface

CachedRowSetDataProvider class
commitChanges method of classCachedRowSet-DataProvider
data provider
event-processing life cycle
Geocoding Service Object
geoCode method of a Geocoding Service Object
Google Maps
Google Maps API
Java BluePrints
Java BluePrints Ajax component library
Java DB
JavaServer Faces (JSF)
JSF element
Map Marker JSF component
Map Viewer JSF component
Message Group JSF component
participant component in a virtual form
Popup Calendar JSF component
primary property of a JSF Button
Progress Bar JSF component
Rating JSF component
refresh method of classCachedRowSetDataProvider
reset property of a JSF Button
Rich Textarea Editor JSF component
Select Value Text Field JSF component
submitter component in a virtual form
Table JSF component
virtual form
webuijsf:staticText JSF element
webuijsf:table JSF element
webuijsf:tableRowGroup JSF element

Self-Review Exercises

27.1 State whether each of the following is *true* or *false*. If *false*, explain why.

a) The **Table** JSF component allows you to lay out other components and text in tabular format.
b) Virtual forms allow multiple forms, each with its own submitter component and participant components, to be displayed on the same web page.
c) A CachedRowSetDataProvider is stored in the SessionBean and executes SQL queries to provide Table components with data to display.
d) The complete event handler for an **AutoComplete Text Field** is called after every keystroke in the text field to provide a list of suggestions based on what has already been typed.
e) A data provider automatically re-executes its SQL command to provide updated database information at every page refresh.
f) To recenter a **Map Viewer** component, you must set the longitude and latitude of the map's center.

27.2 Fill in the blanks in each of the following statements.

a) Method ________ of class ________ updates a database to reflect any changes made in the database's data provider.
b) A(n) ________ is a supporting component used to translate addresses into latitudes and longitudes for display in a **Map Viewer** component.
c) A virtual form specifies that certain JSF components are ________ whose data will be submitted when the submitter component is clicked.
d) Ajax components for JSF such as the **AutoComplete Text Field** and **Map Viewer** are provided by the ________.

Answers to Self-Review Exercises

27.1 a) False. Table components are used to display data from databases. b) True. c) False. The CachedRowSetDataProvider is a property of the page bean. It wraps a CachedRowSet, which is stored in the SessionBean and executes SQL queries. d) True. e) False. You must call method refresh on the data provider to re-execute the SQL command. f) True.

27.2 a) `commitChanges`, `CachedRowSetDataProvider`. b) **Geocoding Service Object**. c) participants. d) Java BluePrints Ajax component library.

Exercises

27.3 *(Guestbook Application)* Create a JSF web page that allows users to sign and view a guestbook. Use the `Guestbook` database (provided in the examples directory for this chapter) to store guestbook entries. The `Guestbook` database has a single table, `Messages`, which has four columns: `date`, `name`, `email` and `message`. The database already contains a few sample entries. On the web page, provide **Text Field**s for the user's name and e-mail address and a **Text Area** for the message. Add a **Submit Button** and a **Table** component and configure the **Table** to display guestbook entries. Use the **Submit Button**'s action-handler method to insert a new row containing the user's input and today's date into the `Guestbook` database.

27.4 *(`AddressBook` Application Modification)* Modify the `AddressBook` application so that users enter searches in the **AutoComplete Text Field** in the format *first name last name*. You will need to add a new data provider (or modify the existing one) to sort the rows in the `AddressBook` database by first name, then last name.

27.5 *(Map Search Application)* Create a JSF web page that allows users to obtain a map of any address. Recall that a search for a location using the Google Maps API returns an array of `GeoPoint` objects. Search for locations a user enters in a **Text Field** and display a map of the first location in the resulting `GeoPoint` array. To handle multiple search results, display all results in a **Listbox** component. You can obtain a string representation of each result by invoking method `toString` on a `GeoPoint` object. Add a **Button** that allows users to select a result from the **Listbox** and displays a map for that result with a **Map Marker** showing the location on the map. Finally, use a **Message Group** to display messages regarding search errors. In case of an error, and when the page loads for the first time, recenter the map on a default location of your choosing.

28

Web Services

A client is to me a mere unit, a factor in a problem.
—Sir Arthur Conan Doyle

They also serve who only stand and wait.
—John Milton

...if the simplest things of nature have a message that you understand, rejoice, for your soul is alive.
—Eleonora Duse

Protocol is everything
—Francoise Giuliani

OBJECTIVES

In this chapter you will learn:

- What a web service is.
- How to publish and consume Java web services in Netbeans.
- The elements that comprise web services, such as service descriptions and classes that implement web services.
- How to create client desktop and web applications that invoke web service methods.
- The important part that XML and the Simple Object Access Protocol (SOAP) play in enabling web services.
- How to use session tracking in web services to maintain client state information.
- How to connect to databases from web services.
- How to pass objects of user-defined types to and return them from a web service.
- How to build a REST-based web service in ASP.NET.

Outline

28.1 Introduction

This chapter introduces web services, which promote software portability and reusability in applications that operate over the Internet. A **web service** is a software component stored on one computer that can be accessed via method calls by an application (or other software component) on another computer over a network. Web services communicate using such technologies as XML and HTTP. Several Java APIs facilitate web services. In this chapter, we'll be dealing with Java APIs that are based on the **Simple Object Access Protocol (SOAP)**—an XML-based protocol that allows web services and clients to communicate, even if the client and the web service are written in different languages. There are other web services technologies, such as Representational State Transfer (REST), which we cover in the contect of ASP.NET web services in Section 28.9. For information on web services, see the web resources in Section 28.11 and visit our Web Services Resource Center at `www.deitel.com/WebServices`.The Web Services Resource Center includes information on designing and implementing web services in many languages, and information about web services offered by companies such as Google, Amazon and eBay. You'll also find many additional tools for publishing and consuming web services. [*Note:* This chapter assumes that you know Java for Sections 28.2–28.8. To learn more about Java, check out *Java How to Program, Seventh Edition*, or visit our Java Resource Centers at `www.deitel.com/ResourceCenters.html`. For Section 28.9, the chapter assumes you know Visual Basic and ASP.NET. To learn more about Visual Basic and ASP.NET, check out our book *Visual Basic 2005 How to Program, Third Edition* or visit our Visual Basic Resource Center (`www.deitel.com/visualbasic/`) and our ASP.NET Resource Center (`www.deitel.com/aspdotnet/`).]

Web services have important implications for **business-to-business (B2B) transactions**. They enable businesses to conduct transactions via standardized, widely available web services rather than relying on proprietary applications. Web services and SOAP are platform and language independent, so companies can collaborate via web services without worrying about the compatibility of their hardware, software and communications technologies. Companies such as Amazon, Google, eBay, PayPal and many others are using web services to their advantage by making their server-side applications available to partners via web services.

By purchasing web services and using extensive free web services that are relevant to their businesses, companies can spend less time developing new applications and can create innovative new applications. E-businesses can use web services to provide their customers with enhanced shopping experiences. Consider an online music store. The store's website links to information about various CDs, enabling users to purchase the CDs, to learn about the artists, to find more titles by those artists, to find other artists' music they may enjoy, and more. Another company that sells concert tickets provides a web service that displays upcoming concert dates for various artists and allows users to buy tickets. By consuming the concert-ticket web service on its site, the online music store can provide an additional service to its customers, increase its site traffic and perhaps earn a commission on concert-ticket sales. The company that sells concert tickets also benefits from the business relationship by selling more tickets and possibly by receiving revenue from the online music store for the use of the web service.

Any Java programmer with a knowledge of web services can write applications that can "consume" web services. The resulting applications would call web service methods of objects running on servers that could be thousands of miles away. To learn more about Java web services read the Java Technology and Web Services Overview at `java.sun.com/webservices/overview.html`.

Netbeans

Netbeans—developed by Sun—is one of the many tools that enable programmers to "publish" and/or "consume" web services. We demonstrate how to use Netbeans to implement web services and invoke them from client applications. For each example, we provide the web service's code, then present a client application that uses the web service. Our first examples build web services and client applications in Netbeans. Then we demonstrate web services that use more sophisticated features, such as manipulating databases with JDBC and manipulating class objects. For information on downloading and installing the Netbeans 5.5.1 IDE, its Visual Web Pack and the Sun Java System Application Server (SJSAS), see Section 26.1.

28.2 Java Web Services Basics

A web service normally resides on a server. The application (i.e., the client) that accesses the web service sends a method call over a network to the remote machine, which processes the call and returns a response over the network to the application. This kind of distributed computing is beneficial in many applications. For example, a client application without direct access to a database on a remote server might be able to retrieve the data via a web service. Similarly, an application lacking the processing power to perform specific computations could use a web service to take advantage of another system's superior resources.

In Java, a web service is implemented as a class. In previous chapters, all the pieces of an application resided on one machine. The class that represents the web service resides on a server—it's not part of the client application.

Making a web service available to receive client requests is known as publishing a web service; using a web service from a client application is known as consuming a web service. An application that consumes a web service consists of two parts—an object of a proxy class for interacting with the web service and a client application that consumes the web service by invoking methods on the object of the proxy class. The client code invokes methods on the proxy object, which handles the details of communicating with the web service (such as passing method arguments to the web service and receiving return values from the web service) on the client's behalf. This communication can occur over a local network, over the Internet or even with a web service on the same computer. The web service performs the corresponding task and returns the results to the proxy object, which then returns the results to the client code. Figure 28.1 depicts the interactions among the client code, the proxy class and the web service. As you'll soon see, Netbeans creates these proxy classes for you in your client applications.

Requests to and responses from web services created with JAX-WS 2.0 (one of many different web service frameworks) are typically transmitted via SOAP. Any client capable of generating and processing SOAP messages can interact with a web service, regardless of the language in which the web service is written. We discuss SOAP in Section 28.5.

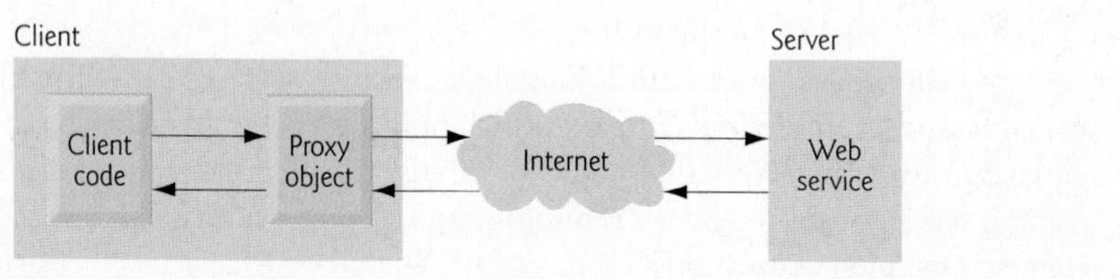

Fig. 28.1 | Interaction between a web service client and a web service.

28.3 Creating, Publishing, Testing and Describing a Web Service

The following subsections demonstrate how to create, publish and test a `HugeInteger` web service that performs calculations with positive integers up to 100 digits long (maintained as arrays of digits). Such integers are much larger than Java's integral primitive types can represent. The `HugeInteger` web service provides methods that take two "huge integers" (represented as `Strings`) and determine their sum, their difference, which is larger, which is smaller or whether the two numbers are equal. These methods will be services available to other applications via the web—hence the term web services.

28.3.1 Creating a Web Application Project and Adding a Web Service Class in Netbeans

When you create a web service in Netbeans, you focus on the web service's logic and let the IDE handle the web service's infrastructure. To create a web service in Netbeans, you first create a **Web Application** project. Netbeans uses this project type for web services that are invoked by other applications.

Creating a **Web Application** *Project in Netbeans*

To create a web application, perform the following steps:

1. Select **File > New Project** to open the **New Project** dialog.
2. Select **Web** from the dialog's **Categories** list, then select **Web Application** from the **Projects** list. Click **Next >**.
3. Specify the name of your project (`HugeInteger`) in the **Project Name** field and specify where you'd like to store the project in the **Project Location** field. You can click the **Browse** button to select the location.
4. Select **Sun Java System Application Server 9** from the **Server** drop-down list.
5. Select **Java EE 5** from the **J2EE Version** drop-down list.
6. Click **Finish** to dismiss the **New Project** dialog.

This creates a web application that will run in a web browser, similar to the **Visual Web Application** projects used in Chapters 26 and 27. Netbeans generates additional files to support the web application. This chapter discusses only the web-service-specific files.

Adding a Web Service Class to a **Web Application** *Project*

Perform the following steps to add a web service class to the project:

1. In the **Projects** tab in Netbeans, right click the **HugeInteger** project's node and select **New > Web Service...** to open the **New Web Service** dialog.
2. Specify `HugeInteger` in the **Web Service Name** field.
3. Specify `com.deitel.iw3htp4.ch28.hugeinteger` in the **Package** field.
4. Click **Finish** to dismiss the **New Web Service** dialog.

The IDE generates a sample web service class with the name you specified in *Step 2*. You can find this class in the **Projects** tab under the **Web Services** node. In this class, you'll define the methods that your web service makes available to client applications. When you eventually build your application, the IDE will generate other supporting files (which we'll discuss shortly) for your web service.

28.3.2 Defining the HugeInteger Web Service in Netbeans

Figure 28.2 contains the `HugeInteger` web service's code. You can implement this code yourself in the `HugeInteger.java` file created in Section 28.3.1, or you can simply replace the code in `HugeInteger.java` with a copy of our code from this example's folder. You can find this file in the project's `src\java\com\deitel\iw3htp4\ch28\hugeinteger` folder. The book's examples can be downloaded from `www.deitel.com/books/iw3htp4/`.

```
// Fig. 28.2: HugeInteger.java
// HugeInteger web service that performs operations on large integers.
package com.deitel.iw3htp4.ch28.hugeinteger;

import javax.jws.WebService; // program uses the annotation @WebService
import javax.jws.WebMethod; // program uses the annotation @WebMethod
import javax.jws.WebParam; // program uses the annotation @WebParam

@WebService( // annotates the class as a web service
   name = "HugeInteger", // sets class name
   serviceName = "HugeIntegerService" ) // sets the service name
public class HugeInteger
{
   private final static int MAXIMUM = 100; // maximum number of digits
   public int[] number = new int[ MAXIMUM ]; // stores the huge integer

   // returns a String representation of a HugeInteger
   public String toString()
   {
      String value = "";

      // convert HugeInteger to a String
      for ( int digit : number )
         value = digit + value; // places next digit at beginning of value

      // locate position of first non-zero digit
      int length = value.length();
      int position = -1;

      for ( int i = 0; i < length; i++ )
      {
         if ( value.charAt( i ) != '0' )
         {
            position = i; // first non-zero digit
            break;
         }
      } // end for

      return ( position != -1 ? value.substring( position ) : "0" );
   } // end method toString

   // creates a HugeInteger from a String
   public static HugeInteger parseHugeInteger( String s )
   {
      HugeInteger temp = new HugeInteger();
      int size = s.length();

      for ( int i = 0; i < size; i++ )
         temp.number[ i ] = s.charAt( size - i - 1 ) - '0';
```

Fig. 28.2 | `HugeInteger` web service that performs operations on large integers. (Part 1 of 3.)

```

      return temp;
   } // end method parseHugeInteger

   // WebMethod that adds huge integers represented by String arguments
   @WebMethod( operationName = "add" )
   public String add( @WebParam( name = "first" ) String first,
      @WebParam( name = "second" ) String second )
   {
      int carry = 0; // the value to be carried
      HugeInteger operand1 = HugeInteger.parseHugeInteger( first );
      HugeInteger operand2 = HugeInteger.parseHugeInteger( second );
      HugeInteger result = new HugeInteger(); // stores addition result

      // perform addition on each digit
      for ( int i = 0; i < MAXIMUM; i++ )
      {
         // add corresponding digits in each number and the carried value;
         // store result in the corresponding column of HugeInteger result
         result.number[ i ] =
            ( operand1.number[ i ] + operand2.number[ i ] + carry ) % 10;

         // set carry for next column
         carry =
            ( operand1.number[ i ] + operand2.number[ i ] + carry ) / 10;
      } // end for

      return result.toString();
   } // end WebMethod add

   // WebMethod that subtracts integers represented by String arguments
   @WebMethod( operationName = "subtract" )
   public String subtract( @WebParam( name = "first" ) String first,
      @WebParam( name = "second" ) String second )
   {
      HugeInteger operand1 = HugeInteger.parseHugeInteger( first );
      HugeInteger operand2 = HugeInteger.parseHugeInteger( second );
      HugeInteger result = new HugeInteger(); // stores difference

      // subtract bottom digit from top digit
      for ( int i = 0; i < MAXIMUM; i++ )
      {
         // if the digit in operand1 is smaller than the corresponding
         // digit in operand2, borrow from the next digit
         if ( operand1.number[ i ] < operand2.number[ i ] )
            operand1.borrow( i );

         // subtract digits
         result.number[ i ] = operand1.number[ i ] - operand2.number[ i ];
      } // end for

      return result.toString();
   } // end WebMethod subtract
```

Fig. 28.2 | HugeInteger web service that performs operations on large integers. (Part 2 of 3.)

```
103
104    // borrow 1 from next digit
105    private void borrow( int place )
106    {
107       if ( place >= MAXIMUM )
108          throw new IndexOutOfBoundsException();
109       else if ( number[ place + 1 ] == 0 ) // if next digit is zero
110          borrow( place + 1 ); // borrow from next digit
111
112       number[ place ] += 10; // add 10 to the borrowing digit
113       --number[ place + 1 ]; // subtract one from the digit to the left
114    } // end method borrow
115
116    // WebMethod that returns true if first integer is greater than second
117    @WebMethod( operationName = "bigger" )
118    public boolean bigger( @WebParam( name = "first" ) String first,
119       @WebParam( name = "second" ) String second )
120    {
121       try // try subtracting first from second
122       {
123          String difference = subtract( first, second );
124          return !difference.matches( "^[0]+$" );
125       } // end try
126       catch ( IndexOutOfBoundsException e ) // first is less than second
127       {
128          return false;
129       } // end catch
130    } // end WebMethod bigger
131
132    // WebMethod that returns true if the first integer is less than second
133    @WebMethod( operationName = "smaller" )
134    public boolean smaller( @WebParam( name = "first" ) String first,
135       @WebParam( name = "second" ) String second )
136    {
137       return bigger( second, first );
138    } // end WebMethod smaller
139
140    // WebMethod that returns true if the first integer equals the second
141    @WebMethod( operationName = "equals" )
142    public boolean equals( @WebParam( name = "first" ) String first,
143       @WebParam( name = "second" ) String second )
144    {
145       return !( bigger( first, second ) || smaller( first, second ) );
146    } // end WebMethod equals
147 } // end class HugeInteger
```

Fig. 28.2 | HugeInteger web service that performs operations on large integers. (Part 3 of 3.)

Lines 5–7 import the annotations used in this example. By default, each new web service class created with the JAX-WS APIs is a **POJO (plain old Java object)**, meaning that—unlike prior Java web service APIs—you do not need to extend a class or implement an interface to create a web service. When you compile a class that uses these JAX-WS 2.0 annotations, the compiler creates all the **server-side artifacts** that support the web service—that is, the compiled code framework that allows the web service to wait for client requests and respond to those requests once the service is deployed on an application server. Popular application servers that support Java web services include the Sun Java System Application Server (`www.sun.com/software/products/appsrvr/index.xml`), GlassFish (`glassfish.dev.java.net`), Apache Tomcat (`tomcat.apache.org`), BEA Weblogic Server (`www.bea.com`) and JBoss Application Server (`www.jboss.org/products/jbossas`). We use Sun Java System Application Server in this chapter.

Lines 9–11 contain a `@WebService` annotation (imported at line 5) with properties `name` and `serviceName`. The **`@WebService` annotation** indicates that class `HugeInteger` implements a web service. The annotation is followed by a set of parentheses containing optional elements. The annotation's **`name` element** (line 10) specifies the name of the proxy class that will be generated for the client. The annotation's **`serviceName` element** (line 11) specifies the name of the class that the client uses to obtain an object of the proxy class. [*Note:* If the `serviceName` element is not specified, the web service's name is assumed to be the class name followed by the word `Service`.] Netbeans places the `@WebService` annotation at the beginning of each new web service class you create. You can then add the `name` and `serviceName` properties in the parentheses following the annotation.

Line 14 declares the constant `MAXIMUM` that specifies the maximum number of digits for a `HugeInteger` (i.e., 100 in this example). Line 15 creates the array that stores the digits in a huge integer. Lines 18–40 declare method `toString`, which returns a `String` representation of a `HugeInteger` without any leading 0s. Lines 43–52 declare `static` method `parseHugeInteger`, which converts a `String` into a `HugeInteger`. The web service's methods `add`, `subtract`, `bigger`, `smaller` and `equals` use `parseHugeInteger` to convert their `String` arguments to `HugeInteger`s for processing.

`HugeInteger` methods `add`, `subtract`, `bigger`, `smaller` and `equals` are tagged with the **`@WebMethod` annotation** (lines 55, 81, 117, 133 and 141) to indicate that they can be called remotely. Any methods that are not tagged with `@WebMethod` are not accessible to clients that consume the web service. Such methods are typically utility methods within the web service class. Note that the `@WebMethod` annotations each use the **`operationName`** element to specify the method name that is exposed to the web service's client.

Common Programming Error 28.1

Failing to expose a method as a web method by declaring it with the `@WebMethod` annotation prevents clients of the web service from accessing the method.

Common Programming Error 28.2

Methods with the `@WebMethod` annotation cannot be `static`. An object of the web service class must exist for a client to access the service's web methods.

Each web method in class `HugeInteger` specifies parameters that are annotated with the **`@WebParam` annotation** (e.g., lines 56–57 of method `add`). The optional `@WebParam` element **`name`** indicates the parameter name that is exposed to the web service's clients.

Lines 55–78 and 81–102 declare `HugeInteger` web methods `add` and `subtract`. We assume for simplicity that `add` does not result in overflow (i.e., the result will be 100 digits or fewer) and that `subtract`'s first argument will always be larger than the second. The `subtract` method calls method `borrow` (lines 105–114) when it is necessary to borrow 1 from the next digit to the left in the first argument—that is, when a particular digit in the left operand is smaller than the corresponding digit in the right operand. Method `borrow` adds 10 to the appropriate digit and subtracts 1 from the next digit to the left. This utility method is not intended to be called remotely, so it is not tagged with `@WebMethod`.

Lines 117–130 declare `HugeInteger` web method `bigger`. Line 123 invokes method `subtract` to calculate the difference between the numbers. If the first number is less than the second, this results in an exception. In this case, `bigger` returns `false`. If `subtract` does not throw an exception, then line 124 returns the result of the expression

```
!difference.matches( "^[0]+$" )
```

This expression calls `String` method `matches` to determine whether the `String difference` matches the regular expression `"^[0]+$"`, which determines if the `String` consists only of one or more `0`s. The symbols `^` and `$` indicate that `matches` should return `true` only if the entire `String difference` matches the regular expression. We then use the logical negation operator (`!`) to return the opposite `boolean` value. Thus, if the numbers are equal (i.e., their difference is 0), the preceding expression returns `false`—the first number is not greater than the second. Otherwise, the expression returns `true`.

Lines 133–146 declare methods `smaller` and `equals`. Method `smaller` returns the result of invoking method `bigger` (line 137) with the arguments reversed—if `first` is less than `second`, then `second` is greater than `first`. Method `equals` invokes methods `bigger` and `smaller` (line 145). If either `bigger` or `smaller` returns `true`, line 145 returns `false`, because the numbers are not equal. If both methods return `false`, the numbers are equal and line 145 returns `true`.

28.3.3 Publishing the HugeInteger Web Service from Netbeans

Now that we've created the `HugeInteger` web service class, we'll use Netbeans to build and publish (i.e., deploy) the web service so that clients can consume its services. Netbeans handles all the details of building and deploying a web service for you. This includes creating the framework required to support the web service. Right click the project name (`HugeInteger`) in the Netbeans **Projects** tab to display the pop-up menu shown in Fig. 28.3. To determine if there are any compilation errors in your project, select the **Build Project** option. When the project compiles successfully, you can select **Deploy Project** to deploy the project to the server you selected when you set up the web application in Section 28.3.1. If the code in the project has changed since the last build, selecting **Deploy Project** also builds the project. Selecting **Run Project** executes the web application. If the web application was not previously built or deployed, this option performs these tasks first. Note that both the **Deploy Project** and **Run Project** options also start the application server (in our case Sun Java System Application Server) if it is not already running. To ensure that all source-code files in a project are recompiled during the next build operation, you can use the **Clean Project** or **Clean and Build Project** options. If you have not already done so, select **Deploy Project** now.

28.3.4 Testing the HugeInteger Web Service with Sun Java System Application Server's Tester Web page

The next step is to test the `HugeInteger` web service. We previously selected the Sun Java System Application Server to execute this web application. This server can dynamically

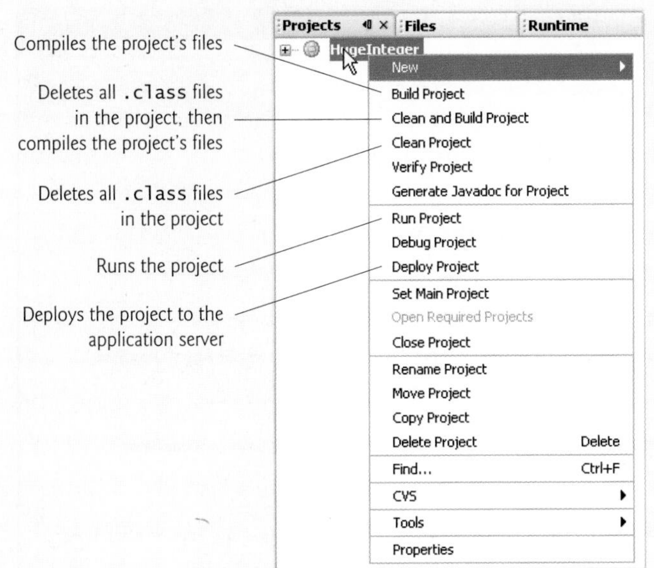

Fig. 28.3 | Pop-up menu that appears when you right click a project name in the Netbeans **Projects** tab.

create a web page for testing a web service's methods from a web browser. To enable this capability:

1. Right click the project name (`HugeInteger`) in the Netbeans **Projects** tab and select **Properties** from the pop-up menu to display the **Project Properties** dialog.
2. Click **Run** under **Categories** to display the options for running the project.
3. In the **Relative URL** field, type `/HugeIntegerService?Tester`.
4. Click **OK** to dismiss the **Project Properties** dialog.

The **Relative URL** field specifies what should happen when the web application executes. If this field is empty, then the web application's default JSP displays when you run the project. When you specify `/HugeIntegerService?Tester` in this field, then run the project, Sun Java System Application Server builds the `Tester` web page and loads it into your web browser. Figure 28.4 shows the `Tester` web page for the `HugeInteger` web service. Once you've deployed the web service, you can also type the URL

```
http://localhost:8080/HugeInteger/HugeIntegerService?Tester
```

in your web browser to view the `Tester` web page. Note that `HugeIntegerService` is the name (specified in line 11 of Fig. 28.2) that clients, including the `Tester` web page, use to access the web service.

To test `HugeInteger`'s web methods, type two positive integers into the text fields to the right of a particular method's button, then click the button to invoke the web method and see the result. Figure 28.5 shows the results of invoking `HugeInteger`'s `add` method with the values `99999999999999999` and `1`. Note that the number `99999999999999999` is larger than primitive type `long` can represent.

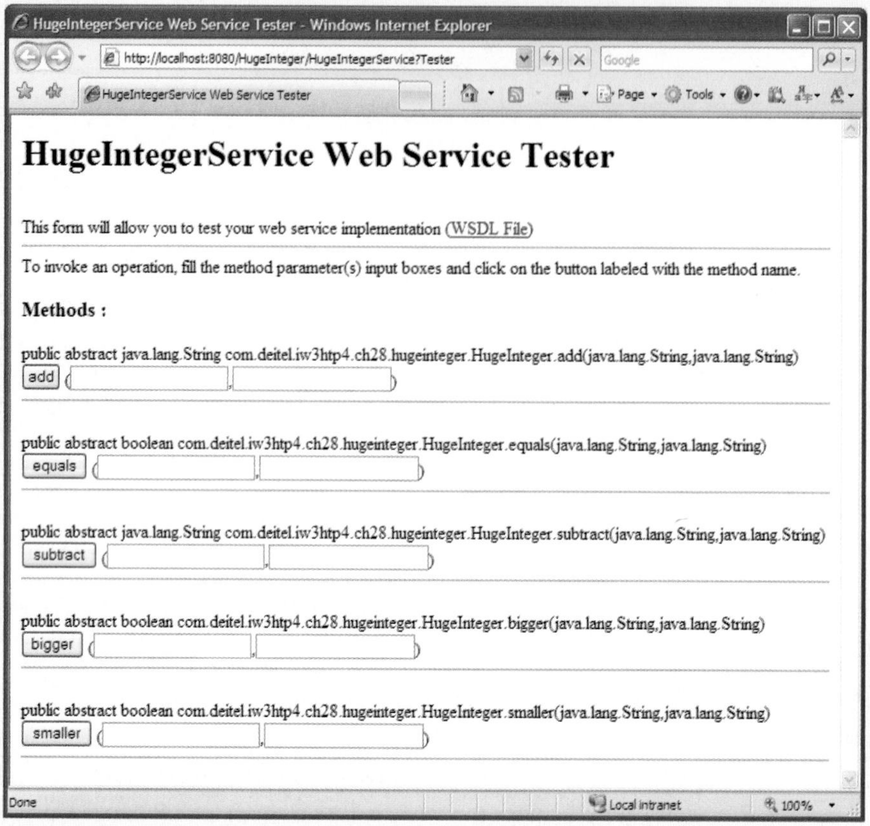

Fig. 28.4 | `Tester` web page created by Sun Java System Application Server for the `HugeInteger` web service.

Note that you can access the web service only when the application server is running. If Netbeans launches the application server for you, it will automatically shut it down when you close Netbeans. To keep the application server up and running, you can launch it independently of Netbeans before you deploy or run web applications in Netbeans. For Sun Java System Application Server running on Windows, you can do this by selecting

a) Invoking the `HugeInteger` web service's `add` method.

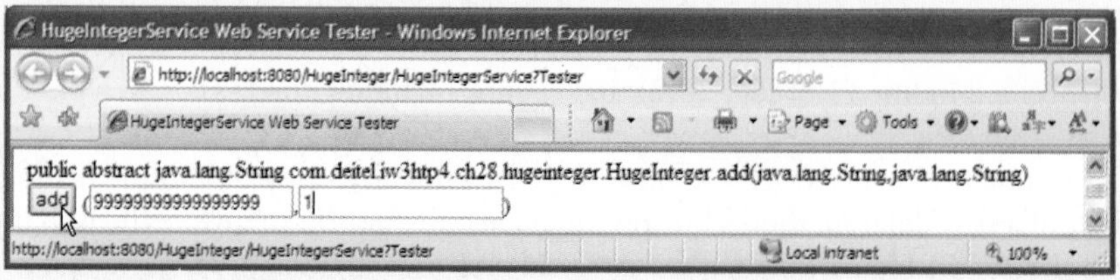

Fig. 28.5 | Testing `HugeInteger`'s `add` method. (Part 1 of 2.)

b) Results of calling the `HugeInteger` web service's `add` method with `"99999999999999999"` and `"1"`

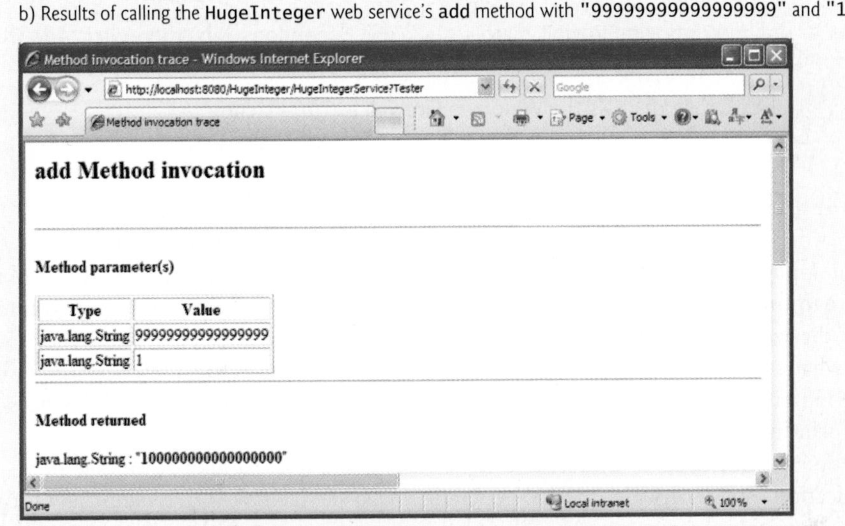

Fig. 28.5 | Testing `HugeInteger`'s `add` method. (Part 2 of 2.)

Start > All Programs > Sun Microsystems > Application Server PE 9 > Start Default Server. To shut down the application server, you can select the **Stop Default Server** option from the same location.

Testing the `HugeInteger` *Web Service from Another Computer*

If your computer is connected to a network and allows HTTP requests, then you can test the web service from another computer on the network by typing the following URL (where *host* is the hostname or IP address of the computer on which the web service is deployed) into a browser on another computer:

```
http://host:8080/HugeInteger/HugeIntegerService?Tester
```

Note to Windows XP Service Pack 2 and Windows Vista Users

For security reasons, computers running Windows XP Service Pack 2 or Windows Vista do not allow HTTP requests from other computers by default. If you wish to allow other computers to connect to your computer using HTTP, perform the following steps on Windows XP SP2:

1. Select **Start > Control Panel** to open your system's **Control Panel** window, then double click **Windows Firewall** to view the **Windows Firewall** settings dialog.
2. In the **Windows Firewall** dialog, click the **Exceptions** tab, then click **Add Port...** and add port 8080 with the name SJSAS.
3. Click **OK** to dismiss the **Windows Firewall** settings dialog.

To allow other computers to connect to your Windows Vista computer using HTTP, perform the following steps:

1. Open the **Control Panel**, switch to **Classic View** and double click **Windows Firewall** to open the **Windows Firewall** dialog.

2. In the **Windows Firewall** dialog click the **Change Settings...** link.
3. In the **Windows Firewall** dialog, click the **Exceptions** tab, then click **Add Port...** and add port 8080 with the name SJSAS.
4. Click **OK** to dismiss the **Windows Firewall** settings dialog.

28.3.5 Describing a Web Service with the Web Service Description Language (WSDL)

Once you implement a web service, compile it and deploy it on an application server, a client application can consume the web service. To do so, however, the client must know where to find the web service and must be provided with a description of how to interact with the web service—that is, what methods are available, what parameters they expect and what each method returns. For this purpose, JAX-WS uses the Web Service Description Language (WSDL)—a standard XML vocabulary for describing web services in a platform-independent manner.

You do not need to understand the details of WSDL to take advantage of it—the application server software (SJSAS) generates a web service's WSDL dynamically for you, and client tools can parse the WSDL to help create the client-side proxy class that a client uses to access the web service. Since the WSDL is created dynamically, clients always receive a deployed web service's most up-to-date description. To view the WSDL for the `HugeInteger` web service (Fig. 28.6), enter the following URL in your browser:

```
http://localhost:8080/HugeInteger/HugeIntegerService?WSDL
```

or click the **WSDL File** link in the `Tester` web page (shown in Fig. 28.4).

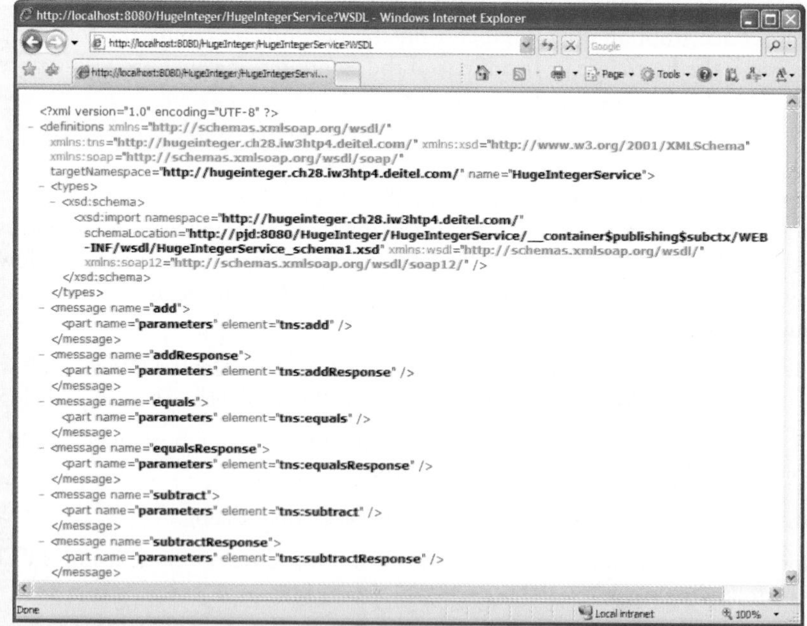

Fig. 28.6 | A portion of the `.wsdl` file for the `HugeInteger` web service.

Accessing the **HugeInteger** *Web Service's WSDL from Another Computer*

Eventually, you'll want clients on other computers to use your web service. Such clients need access to the web service's WSDL, which they would access with the following URL:

```
http://host:8080/HugeInteger/HugeIntegerService?WSDL
```

where *host* is the hostname or IP address of the computer on which the web service is deployed. As we discussed in Section 28.3.4, this will work only if your computer allows HTTP connections from other computers—as is the case for publicly accessible web and application servers.

28.4 Consuming a Web Service

Now that we've defined and deployed our web service, we can consume it from a client application. A web service client can be any type of application or even another web service. You enable a client application to consume a web service by adding a web service reference to the application. This process defines the proxy class that allows the client to access the web service.

28.4.1 Creating a Client in Netbeans to Consume the HugeInteger Web Service

In this section, you'll use Netbeans to create a client Java desktop GUI application, then you'll add a web service reference to the project so the client can access the web service. When you add the web service reference, the IDE creates and compiles the client-side artifacts—the framework of Java code that supports the client-side proxy class. The client then calls methods on an object of the proxy class, which uses the rest of the artifacts to interact with the web service.

Creating a Desktop Application Project in Netbeans

Before performing the steps in this section, ensure that the `HugeInteger` web service has been deployed and that the Sun Java System Application Server is running (see Section 28.3.3). Perform the following steps to create a client Java desktop application in Netbeans:

1. Select **File > New Project...** to open the **New Project** dialog.
2. Select **General** from the **Categories** list and **Java Application** from the **Projects** list, then click **Next >**.
3. Specify the name `UsingHugeInteger` in the **Project Name** field and uncheck the **Create Main Class** checkbox. In a moment, you'll add a subclass of `JFrame` that contains a `main` method.
4. Click **Finish** to create the project.

Adding a Web Service Reference to an Application

Next, you'll add a web service reference to your application so that it can interact with the `HugeInteger` web service. To add a web service reference, perform the following steps.

1. Right click the project name (`UsingHugeInteger`) in the Netbeans **Projects** tab.
2. Select **New > Web Service Client...** from the pop-up menu to display the **New Web Service Client** dialog (Fig. 28.7).

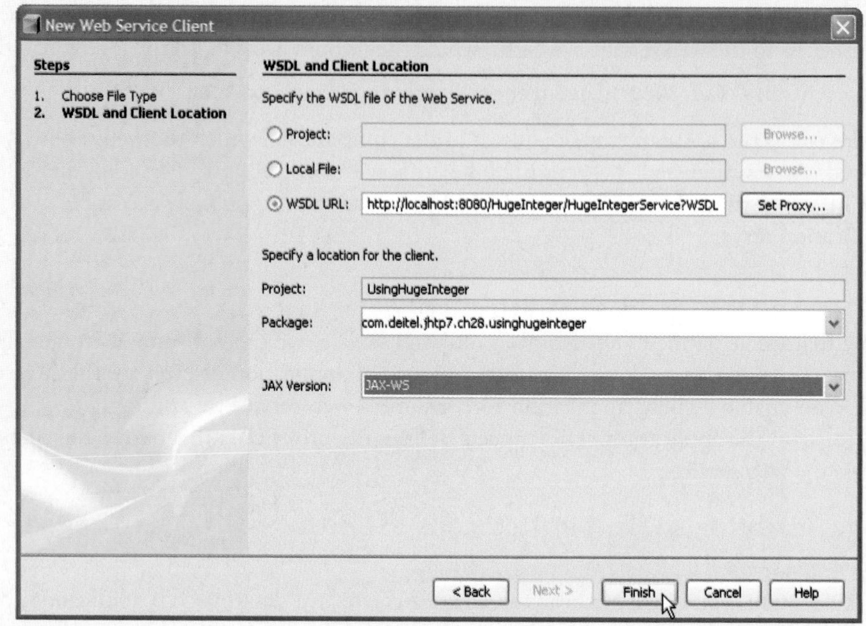

Fig. 28.7 | **New Web Service Client** dialog.

3. In the **WSDL URL** field, specify the URL `http://localhost:8080/HugeInteger/HugeIntegerService?WSDL` (Fig. 28.7). This URL tells the IDE where to find the web service's WSDL description. [*Note:* If the Sun Java System Application Server is located on a different computer, replace `localhost` with the hostname or IP address of that computer.] The IDE uses this WSDL description to generate the client-side artifacts that compose and support the proxy. Note that the **New Web Service Client** dialog enables you to search for web services in several locations. Many companies simply distribute the exact WSDL URLs for their web services, which you can place in the **WSDL URL** field.
4. In the **Package** field, specify `com.deitel.iw3htp4.ch28.usinghugeinteger` as the package name.
5. Click **Finish** to dismiss the **New Web Service Client** dialog.

In the Netbeans **Projects** tab, the `UsingHugeInteger` project now contains a `Web Service References` folder with the `HugeInteger` web service's proxy (Fig. 28.8). Note that the proxy's name is listed as `HugeIntegerService`, as we specified in line 11 of Fig. 28.2.

When you specify the web service you want to consume, Netbeans accesses the web service's WSDL information and copies it into a file in your project (named `HugeIntegerService.wsdl` in this example). You can view this file from the Netbeans **Files** tab by expanding the nodes in the `UsingHugeInteger` project's `xml-resources` folder as shown in Fig. 28.9. If the web service changes, the client-side artifacts and the client's copy of the WSDL file can be regenerated by right clicking the `HugeIntegerService` node shown in Fig. 28.8 and selecting **Refresh Client**.

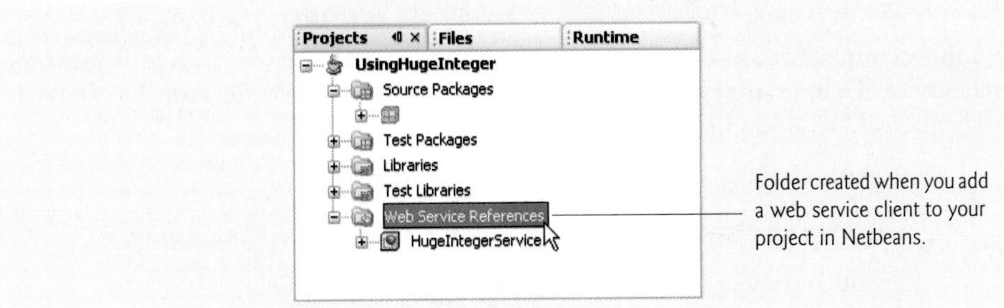

Fig. 28.8 | Netbeans **Project** tab after adding a web service reference to the project.

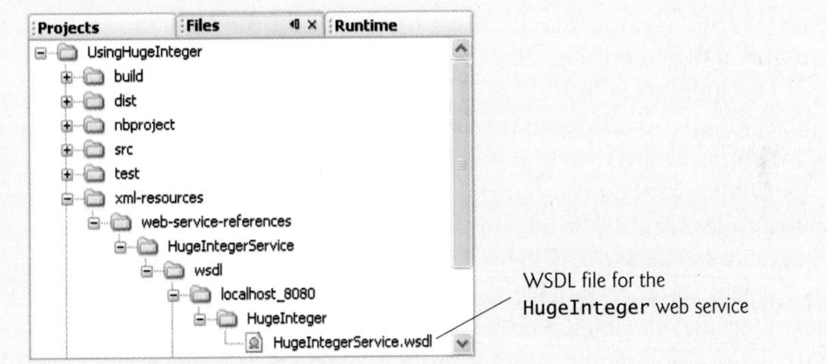

Fig. 28.9 | Locating the `HugeIntegerService.wsdl` file in the Netbeans **Files** tab.

You can view the IDE-generated client-side artifacts by selecting the Netbeans **Files** tab and expanding the `UsingHugeInteger` project's **build** folder as shown in Fig. 28.10.

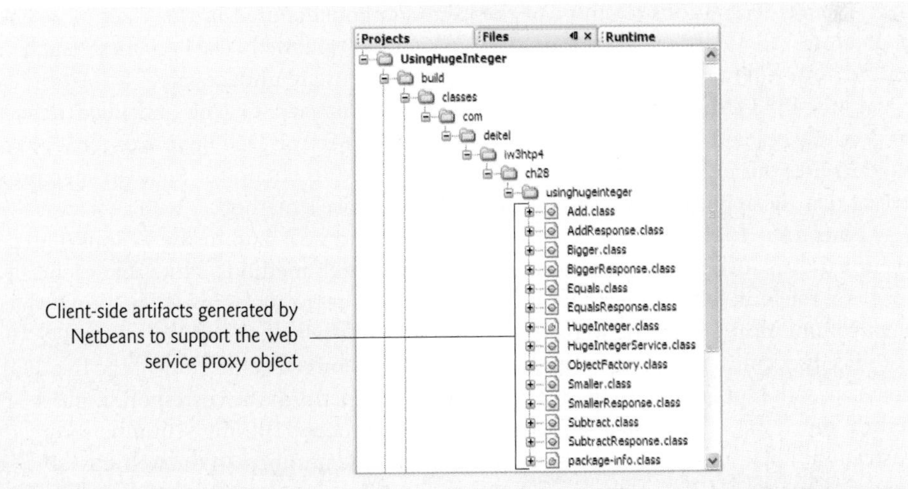

Fig. 28.10 | Viewing the `HugeInteger` web service's client-side artifacts generated by Netbeans.

28.4.2 Consuming the HugeInteger Web Service

For this example, we use a GUI application to interact with the web service `HugeInteger` web service. To build the client application's GUI, you must first add a subclass of `JFrame` to the project. To do so, perform the following steps:

1. Right click the project name in the Netbeans **Project** tab.
2. Select **New > JFrame Form...** to display the **New JFrame Form** dialog.
3. Specify `UsingHugeIntegerJFrame` in the **Class Name** field.
4. Specify `com.deitel.iw3htp4.ch28.hugeintegerclient` in the **Package** field.
5. Click **Finish** to close the **New JFrame Form** dialog.

Next, use the Netbeans GUI design tools to build the GUI shown in the sample screen captures at the end of Fig. 28.11.

The application in Fig. 28.11 uses the `HugeInteger` web service to perform computations with positive integers up to `100` digits long. To save space, we do not show the Netbeans autogenerated `initComponents` method, which contains the code that builds the GUI components, positions them and registers their event handlers. To view the complete source code, open the `UsingHugeIntegerJFrame.java` file in this example's folder under `src\java\com\deitel\iw3htp4\ch28\hugeintegerclient`. Netbeans places the GUI component instance-variable declarations at the end of the class (lines 326–335). Java allows instance variables to be declared anywhere in a class's body as long as they are placed outside the class's methods. We continue to declare our own instance variables at the top of the class.

Lines 6–7 import the classes `HugeInteger` and `HugeIntegerService` that enable the client application to interact with the web service. We include these `import` declarations only for documentation purposes here. These classes are in the same package as `UsingHugeIntegerJFrame`, so these `import` declarations are not necessary. Notice that we do not have `import` declarations for most of the GUI components used in this example. When you create a GUI in Netbeans, it uses fully qualified class names (such as `javax.swing.JFrame` in line 11), so `import` declarations are unnecessary.

Lines 13–14 declare the variables of type `HugeIntegerService` and `HugeInteger`, respectively. Line 24 in the constructor creates an object of type `HugeIntegerService`. Line 25 uses this object's `getHugeIntegerPort` method to obtain the `HugeInteger` proxy object that the application uses to invoke the web service's method.

Lines 165–166, 189–190, 213–214, 240–241 and 267–268 in the various `JButton` event handlers invoke the `HugeInteger` web service's web methods. Note that each call is made on the local proxy object that is referenced by `hugeIntegerProxy`. The proxy object then communicates with the web service on the client's behalf.

The user enters two integers, each up to 100 digits long. Clicking any of the five `JButton`s causes the application to invoke a web method to perform the corresponding task and return the result. Our client application cannot process 100-digit numbers directly. Instead the client passes `String` representations of these numbers to the web service's web methods, which perform tasks for the client. The client application then uses the return value of each operation to display an appropriate message.

```
// Fig. 28.11: UsingHugeIntegerJFrame.java
// Client desktop application for the HugeInteger web service.
package com.deitel.iw3htp4.ch28.hugeintegerclient;

// import classes for accessing HugeInteger web service's proxy
import com.deitel.iw3htp4.ch28.hugeintegerclient.HugeInteger;
import com.deitel.iw3htp4.ch28.hugeintegerclient.HugeIntegerServic

import javax.swing.JOptionPane; // used to display errors to the user

public class UsingHugeIntegerJFrame extends javax.swing.JFrame
{
   private HugeIntegerService hugeIntegerService; // used to obtain proxy
   private HugeInteger hugeIntegerProxy; // used to access the web service

   // no-argument constructor
   public UsingHugeIntegerJFrame()
   {
      initComponents();

      try
      {
         // create the objects for accessing the HugeInteger web service
         hugeIntegerService = new HugeIntegerService();
         hugeIntegerProxy = hugeIntegerService.getHugeIntegerPort();
      }
      catch ( Exception exception )
      {
         exception.printStackTrace();
      }
   } // end UsingHugeIntegerJFrame constructor

   // The initComponents method is autogenerated by Netbeans and is called
   // from the constructor to initialize the GUI. This method is not shown
   // here to save space. Open UsingHugeIntegerJFrame.java in this
   // example's folder to view the complete generated code (lines 37-153).

   // invokes HugeInteger web service's add method to add HugeIntegers
   private void addJButtonActionPerformed(
      java.awt.event.ActionEvent evt )
   {
      String firstNumber = firstJTextField.getText();
      String secondNumber = secondJTextField.getText();

      if ( isValid( firstNumber ) && isValid( secondNumber ) )
      {
         try
         {
            resultsJTextArea.setText(
               hugeIntegerProxy.add( firstNumber, secondNumber ) );
         } // end try
         catch ( Exception e )
         {
```

Fig. 28.11 | Client desktop application for the `HugeInteger` web service. (Part 1 of 6.)

```
            JOptionPane.showMessageDialog( this, e.toString(),
               "Add method failed", JOptionPane.ERROR_MESSAGE );
            e.printStackTrace();
         } // end catch
      } // end if
   } // end method addJButtonActionPerformed

   // invokes HugeInteger web service's subtract method to subtract the
   // second HugeInteger from the first
   private void subtractJButtonActionPerformed(
      java.awt.event.ActionEvent evt )
   {
      String firstNumber = firstJTextField.getText();
      String secondNumber = secondJTextField.getText();

      if ( isValid( firstNumber ) && isValid( secondNumber ) )
      {
         try
         {
            resultsJTextArea.setText(
               hugeIntegerProxy.subtract( firstNumber, secondNumber ) );
         } // end try
         catch ( Exception e )
         {
            JOptionPane.showMessageDialog( this, e.toString(),
               "Subtract method failed", JOptionPane.ERROR_MESSAGE );
            e.printStackTrace();
         } // end catch
      } // end if
   } // end method subtractJButtonActionPerformed

   // invokes HugeInteger web service's bigger method to determine whether
   // the first HugeInteger is greater than the second
   private void biggerJButtonActionPerformed(
      java.awt.event.ActionEvent evt )
   {
      String firstNumber = firstJTextField.getText();
      String secondNumber = secondJTextField.getText();

      if ( isValid( firstNumber ) && isValid( secondNumber ) )
      {
         try
         {
            boolean result =
               hugeIntegerProxy.bigger( firstNumber, secondNumber );
            resultsJTextArea.setText( String.format( "%s %s %s %s",
               firstNumber, ( result ? "is" : "is not" ), "greater than",
               secondNumber ) );
         } // end try
         catch ( Exception e )
         {
            JOptionPane.showMessageDialog( this, e.toString(),
               "Bigger method failed", JOptionPane.ERROR_MESSAGE );
```

Fig. 28.11 | Client desktop application for the HugeInteger web service. (Part 2 of 6.)

```
            e.printStackTrace();
         } // end catch
      } // end if
   } // end method biggerJButtonActionPerformed

   // invokes HugeInteger web service's smaller method to determine
   // whether the first HugeInteger is less than the second
   private void smallerJButtonActionPerformed(
      java.awt.event.ActionEvent evt )
   {
      String firstNumber = firstJTextField.getText();
      String secondNumber = secondJTextField.getText();

      if ( isValid( firstNumber ) && isValid( secondNumber ) )
      {
         try
         {
            boolean result =
               hugeIntegerProxy.smaller( firstNumber, secondNumber );
            resultsJTextArea.setText( String.format( "%s %s %s %s",
               firstNumber, ( result ? "is" : "is not" ), "less than",
               secondNumber ) );
         } // end try
         catch ( Exception e )
         {
            JOptionPane.showMessageDialog( this, e.toString(),
               "Smaller method failed", JOptionPane.ERROR_MESSAGE );
            e.printStackTrace();
         } // end catch
      } // end if
   } // end method smallerJButtonActionPerformed

   // invokes HugeInteger web service's equals method to determine whether
   // the first HugeInteger is equal to the second
   private void equalsJButtonActionPerformed(
      java.awt.event.ActionEvent evt )
   {
      String firstNumber = firstJTextField.getText();
      String secondNumber = secondJTextField.getText();

      if ( isValid( firstNumber ) && isValid( secondNumber ) )
      {
         try
         {
            boolean result =
               hugeIntegerProxy.equals( firstNumber, secondNumber );
            resultsJTextArea.setText( String.format( "%s %s %s %s",
               firstNumber, ( result ? "is" : "is not" ), "equal to",
               secondNumber ) );
         } // end try
         catch ( Exception e )
         {
```

Fig. 28.11 | Client desktop application for the `HugeInteger` web service. (Part 3 of 6.)

```
            JOptionPane.showMessageDialog( this, e.toString(),
               "Equals method failed", JOptionPane.ERROR_MESSAGE );
            e.printStackTrace();
         } // end catch
      } // end if
   } // end method equalsJButtonActionPerformed

   // checks the size of a String to ensure that it is not too big
   // to be used as a HugeInteger; ensure only digits in String
   private boolean isValid( String number )
   {
      // check String's length
      if ( number.length() > 100 )
      {
         JOptionPane.showMessageDialog( this,
            "HugeIntegers must be <= 100 digits.", "HugeInteger Overflow",
            JOptionPane.ERROR_MESSAGE );
         return false;
      } // end if

      // look for nondigit characters in String
      for ( char c : number.toCharArray() )
      {
         if ( !Character.isDigit( c ) )
         {
            JOptionPane.showMessageDialog( this,
               "There are nondigits in the String",
               "HugeInteger Contains Nondigit Characters",
               JOptionPane.ERROR_MESSAGE );
            return false;
         } // end if
      } // end for

      return true; // number can be used as a HugeInteger
   } // end method validate

   // main method begins execution
   public static void main( String args[] )
   {
      java.awt.EventQueue.invokeLater(
         new Runnable()
         {
            public void run()
            {
               new UsingHugeIntegerJFrame().setVisible( true );
            } // end method run
         } // end anonymous inner class
      ); // end call to java.awt.EventQueue.invokeLater
   } // end method main

   // Variables declaration - do not modify
   private javax.swing.JButton addJButton;
```

Fig. 28.11 | Client desktop application for the HugeInteger web service. (Part 4 of 6.)

```
    private javax.swing.JButton biggerJButton;
    private javax.swing.JLabel directionsJLabel;
    private javax.swing.JButton equalsJButton;
    private javax.swing.JTextField firstJTextField;
    private javax.swing.JScrollPane resultsJScrollPane;
    private javax.swing.JTextArea resultsJTextArea;
    private javax.swing.JTextField secondJTextField;
    private javax.swing.JButton smallerJButton;
    private javax.swing.JButton subtractJButton;
    // End of variables declaration
} // end class UsingHugeIntegerJFrame
```

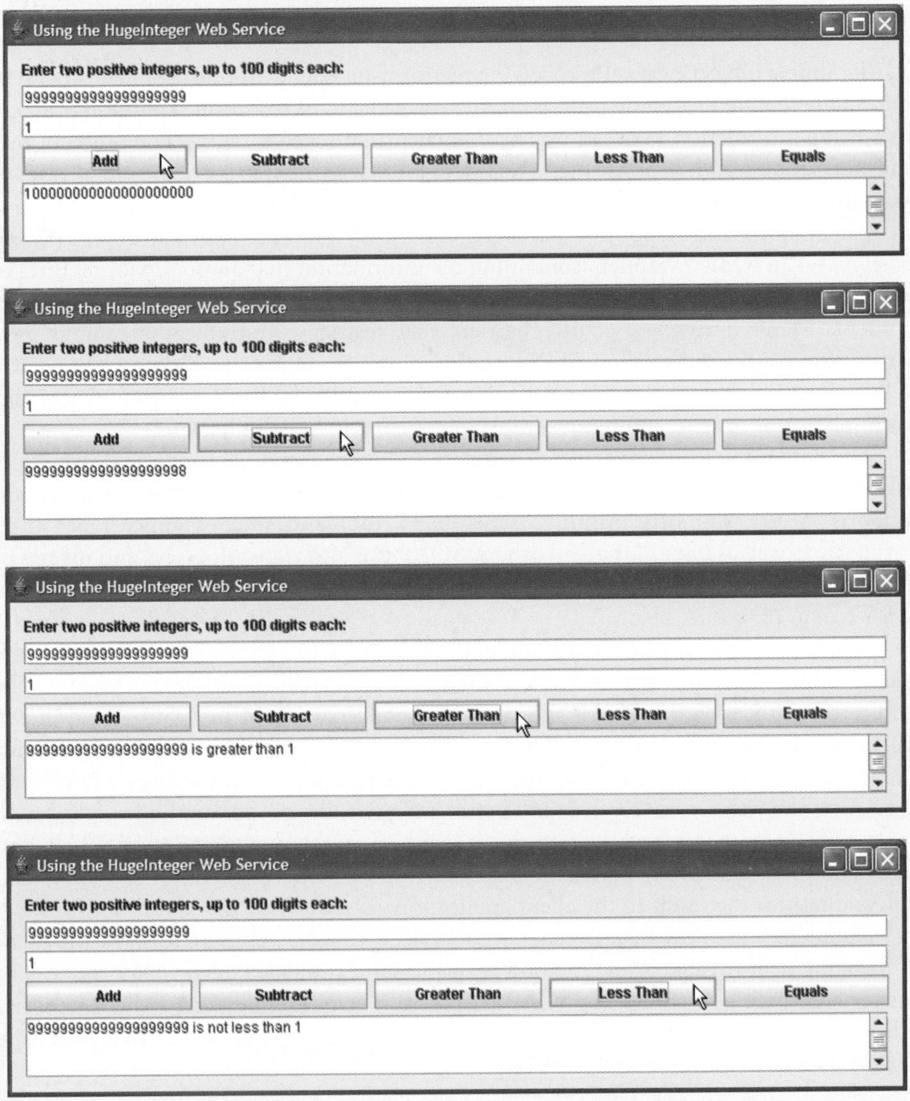

Fig. 28.11 | Client desktop application for the `HugeInteger` web service. (Part 5 of 6.)

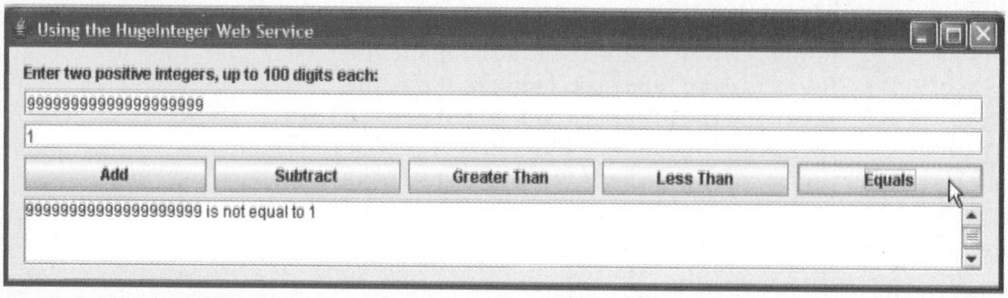

Fig. 28.11 | Client desktop application for the `HugeInteger` web service. (Part 6 of 6.)

28.5 SOAP

SOAP (Simple Object Access Protocol) is a platform-independent protocol that uses XML to facilitate remote procedure calls, typically over HTTP. SOAP is one common protocol for passing information between web service clients and web services. The protocol that transmits request-and-response messages is also known as the web service's **wire format** or **wire protocol**, because it defines how information is sent "along the wire."

Each request and response is packaged in a **SOAP message** (also known as a **SOAP envelope**)—an XML "wrapper" containing the information that a web service requires to process the message. SOAP messages are written in XML so that they are platform independent. Many **firewalls**—security barriers that restrict communication among networks—are configured to allow HTTP traffic to pass through so that clients can browse websites on web servers behind firewalls. Thus, XML and HTTP enable computers on different platforms to send and receive SOAP messages with few limitations.

The wire format used to transmit requests and responses must support all data types passed between the applications. Web services also use SOAP for the many data types it supports. SOAP supports primitive types (e.g., `int`) and their wrapper types (e.g., `Integer`), as well as `Date`, `Time` and others. SOAP can also transmit arrays and objects of user-defined types (as you'll see in Section 28.8). For more SOAP information, visit `www.w3.org/TR/soap/`.

When a program invokes a web method, the request and all relevant information are packaged in a SOAP message and sent to the server on which the web service resides. The web service processes the SOAP message's contents (contained in a SOAP envelope), which specify the method that the client wishes to invoke and the method's arguments. This process of interpreting a SOAP message's contents is known as **parsing a SOAP message**. After the web service receives and parses a request, the proper method is called with any specified arguments, and the response is sent back to the client in another SOAP message. The client-side proxy parses the response, which contains the result of the method call, and returns the result to the client application.

Figure 28.5 used the `HugeInteger` web service's `Tester` web page to show the result of invoking `HugeInteger`'s `add` method with the values `99999999999999999` and `1`. The `Tester` web page also shows the SOAP request and response messages (which were not previously shown). Figure 28.12 shows the SOAP messages in the `Tester` web page from Fig. 28.5 after the calculation. In the request message from Fig. 28.12, the text

```
<ns1:add>
<first>99999999999999999</first>
```

```
<second>1</second>
</ns1:add>
```

specifies the method to call (add), the method's arguments (first and second) and the arguments' values (99999999999999999 and 1). Similarly, the text

```
<ns1:addResponse>
<return>100000000000000000</return>
</ns1:addResponse>
```

from the response message in Fig. 28.12 specifies the return value of method add.

As with the WSDL for a web service, the SOAP messages are generated for you automatically, so you don't need to understand the details of SOAP or XML to take advantage of it when publishing and consuming web services.

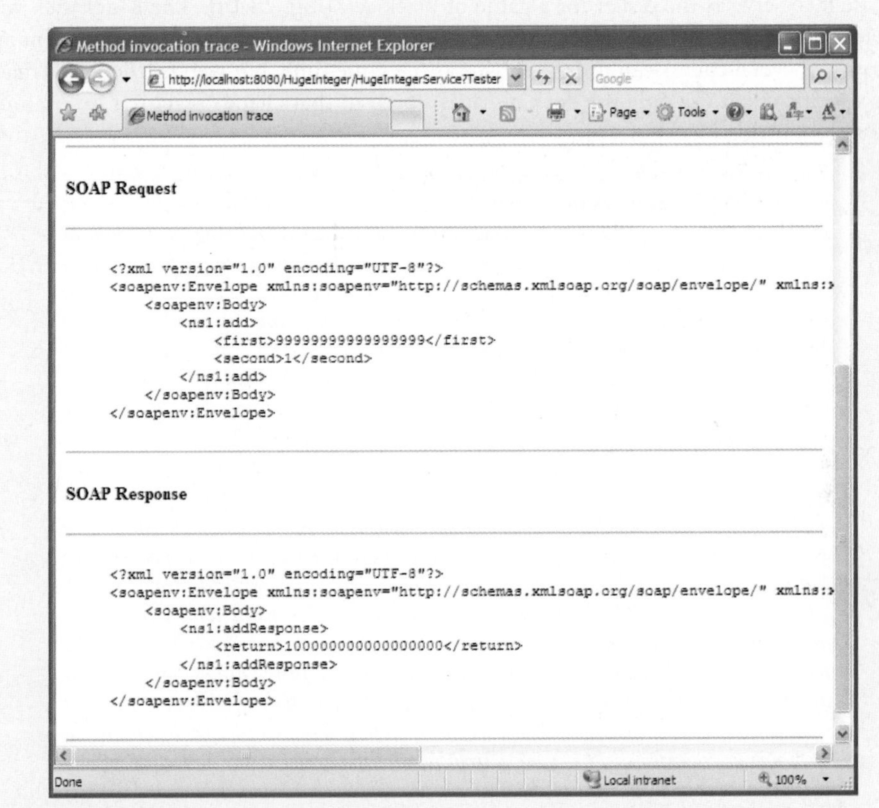

Fig. 28.12 | SOAP messages for the HugeInteger web service's add method as shown by the Sun Java System Application Server's Tester web page.

28.6 Session Tracking in Web Services

Section 26.5 described the advantages of using session tracking to maintain client state information so you can personalize the users' browsing experiences. Now we'll incorporate session tracking into a web service. Suppose a client application needs to call several methods from the same web service, possibly several times each. In such a case, it can be beneficial for the web service to maintain state information for the client, thus eliminating the need for client information to be passed between the client and the web service multiple times. For example, a web service that provides local restaurant reviews could store the client user's street address during the initial request, then use it to return personalized, localized results in subsequent requests. Storing session information also enables a web service to distinguish between clients.

28.6.1 Creating a `Blackjack` Web Service

Our next example is a web service that assists you in developing a blackjack card game. The `Blackjack` web service (Fig. 28.13) provides web methods to shuffle a deck of cards, deal a card from the deck and evaluate a hand of cards. After presenting the web service, we use it to serve as the dealer for a game of blackjack (Fig. 28.14). The `Blackjack` web service uses an `HttpSession` object to maintain a unique deck of cards for each client application. Several clients can use the service at the same time, but web method calls made by a specific client use only the deck of cards stored in that client's session. Our example uses the following blackjack rules:

> *Two cards each are dealt to the dealer and the player. The player's cards are dealt face up. Only the first of the dealer's cards is dealt face up. Each card has a value. A card numbered 2 through 10 is worth its face value. Jacks, queens and kings each count as 10. Aces can count as 1 or 11—whichever value is more beneficial to the player (as we will soon see). If the sum of the player's two initial cards is 21 (i.e., the player was dealt a card valued at 10 and an ace, which counts as 11 in this situation), the player has "blackjack" and immediately wins the game—if the dealer does not also have blackjack (which would result in a "push"—i.e., a tie). Otherwise, the player can begin taking additional cards one at a time. These cards are dealt face up, and the player decides when to stop taking cards. If the player "busts" (i.e., the sum of the player's cards exceeds 21), the game is over, and the player loses. When the player is satisfied with the current set of cards, the player "stands" (i.e., stops taking cards), and the dealer's hidden card is revealed. If the dealer's total is 16 or less, the dealer must take another card; otherwise, the dealer must stand. The dealer must continue taking cards until the sum of the dealer's cards is greater than or equal to 17. If the dealer exceeds 21, the player wins. Otherwise, the hand with the higher point total wins. If the dealer and the player have the same point total, the game is a "push," and no one wins. Note that the value of an ace for a dealer depends on the dealer's other card(s) and the casino's house rules. A dealer typically must hit for totals of 16 or less and must stand for totals of 17 or more. However, for a "soft 17"—a hand with a total of 17 with one ace counted as 11—some casinos require the dealer to hit and some require the dealer to stand (we require the dealer to stand). Such a hand is known as a "soft 17" because taking another card cannot bust the hand.*

The web service (Fig. 28.13) stores each card as a `String` consisting of a number, `1`–`13`, representing the card's face (ace through king, respectively), followed by a space and a digit, `0`–`3`, representing the card's suit (hearts, diamonds, clubs or spades, respectively). For example, the jack of clubs is represented as `"11 2"`, and the two of hearts is represented as `"2 0"`. To create and deploy this web service, follow the steps presented in Sections 28.3.2–28.3.3 for the `HugeInteger` service.

```
// Fig. 28.13: Blackjack.java
// Blackjack web service that deals cards and evaluates hands
package com.deitel.iw3htp4.ch28.blackjack;

import java.util.ArrayList;
import java.util.Random;
import javax.annotation.Resource;
import javax.jws.WebService;
import javax.jws.WebMethod;
import javax.jws.WebParam;
import javax.servlet.http.HttpSession;
import javax.servlet.http.HttpServletRequest;
import javax.xml.ws.WebServiceContext;
import javax.xml.ws.handler.MessageContext;

@WebService( name = "Blackjack", serviceName = "BlackjackService" )
public class Blackjack
{
   // use @Resource to create a WebServiceContext for session tracking
   private @Resource WebServiceContext webServiceContext;
   private MessageContext messageContext; // used in session tracking
   private HttpSession session; // stores attributes of the session

   // deal one card
   @WebMethod( operationName = "dealCard" )
   public String dealCard()
   {
      String card = "";

      ArrayList< String > deck =
         ( ArrayList< String > ) session.getAttribute( "deck" );

      card = deck.get( 0 ); // get top card of deck
      deck.remove( 0 ); // remove top card of deck

      return card;
   } // end WebMethod dealCard

   // shuffle the deck
   @WebMethod( operationName = "shuffle" )
   public void shuffle()
   {
      // obtain the HttpSession object to store deck for current client
      messageContext = webServiceContext.getMessageContext();
      session = ( ( HttpServletRequest ) messageContext.get(
         MessageContext.SERVLET_REQUEST ) ).getSession();

      // populate deck of cards
      ArrayList< String > deck = new ArrayList< String >();

      for ( int face = 1; face <= 13; face++ ) // loop through faces
         for ( int suit = 0; suit <= 3; suit++ ) // loop through suits
            deck.add( face + " " + suit ); // add each card to deck
```

Fig. 28.13 | Blackjack web service that deals cards and evaluates hands. (Part 1 of 3.)

```

      String tempCard; // holds card temporarily during swapping
      Random randomObject = new Random(); // generates random numbers
      int index; // index of randomly selected card

      for ( int i = 0; i < deck.size() ; i++ ) // shuffle
      {
         index = randomObject.nextInt( deck.size() - 1 );

         // swap card at position i with randomly selected card
         tempCard = deck.get( i );
         deck.set( i, deck.get( index ) );
         deck.set( index, tempCard );
      } // end for

      // add this deck to user's session
      session.setAttribute( "deck", deck );
   } // end WebMethod shuffle

   // determine a hand's value
   @WebMethod( operationName = "getHandValue" )
   public int getHandValue( @WebParam( name = "hand" ) String hand )
   {
      // split hand into cards
      String[] cards = hand.split( "\t" );
      int total = 0; // total value of cards in hand
      int face; // face of current card
      int aceCount = 0; // number of aces in hand

      for ( int i = 0; i < cards.length; i++ )
      {
         // parse string and get first int in String
         face = Integer.parseInt(
            cards[ i ].substring( 0, cards[ i ].indexOf( " " ) ) );

         switch ( face )
         {
            case 1: // if ace, increment aceCount
               ++aceCount;
               break;
            case 11: // jack
            case 12: // queen
            case 13: // king
               total += 10;
               break;
            default: // otherwise, add face
               total += face;
               break;
         } // end switch
      } // end for

```

Fig. 28.13 | `Blackjack` web service that deals cards and evaluates hands. (Part 2 of 3.)

```
105          // calculate optimal use of aces
106          if ( aceCount > 0 )
107          {
108             // if possible, count one ace as 11
109             if ( total + 11 + aceCount - 1 <= 21 )
110                total += 11 + aceCount - 1;
111             else // otherwise, count all aces as 1
112                total += aceCount;
113          } // end if
114
115          return total;
116       } // end WebMethod getHandValue
117    } // end class Blackjack
```

Fig. 28.13 | `Blackjack` web service that deals cards and evaluates hands. (Part 3 of 3.)

Session Tracking in Web Services

The `Blackjack` web service client first calls method `shuffle` (lines 40–71) to shuffle the deck of cards. This method also places the deck of cards into an `HttpSession` object that is specific to the client that called `shuffle`. To use session tracking in a Web service, you must include code for the resources that maintain the session state information. In the past, you had to write the sometimes tedious code to create these resources. JAX-WS, however, handles this for you via the **`@Resource` annotation**. This annotation enables tools like Netbeans to "inject" complex support code into your class, thus allowing you to focus on your business logic rather than the support code. The concept of using annotations to add code that supports your classes is known as **dependency injection**. Annotations like `@WebService`, `@WebMethod` and `@WebParam` also perform dependency injection.

Line 20 injects a `WebServiceContext` object into your class. A **`WebServiceContext`** object enables a web service to access and maintain information for a specific request, such as session state. As you look through the code in Fig. 28.13, you'll notice that we never create the `WebServiceContext` object. All of the code necessary to create it is injected into the class by the `@Resource` annotation. Line 21 declares a variable of interface type **`MessageContext`** that the web service will use to obtain an `HttpSession` object for the current client. Line 22 declares the `HttpSession` variable that the web service will use to manipulate the session state information.

Line 44 in method `shuffle` uses the `WebServiceContext` object that was injected in line 20 to obtain a `MessageContext` object. Lines 45–46 then use the `MessageContext` object's `get` method to obtain the `HttpSession` object for the current client. Method `get` receives a constant indicating what to get from the `MessageContext`. In this case, the constant `MessageContext.SERVLET_REQUEST` indicates that we'd like to get the `HttpServletRequest` object for the current client. We then call method `getSession` to get the `HttpSession` object from the `HttpServletRequest` object.

Lines 49–70 generate an `ArrayList` representing a deck of cards, shuffle the deck and store the deck in the client's `session` object. Lines 51–53 use nested loops to generate `Strings` in the form "*face suit*" to represent each possible card in the deck. Lines 59–67 shuffle the deck by swapping each card with another card selected at random. Line 70 inserts the `ArrayList` in the `session` object to maintain the deck between method calls from a particular client.

Lines 25–37 define method dealCard as a web method. Lines 30–31 use the session object to obtain the "deck" session attribute that was stored in line 70 of method shuffle. Method getAttribute takes as a parameter a String that identifies the Object to obtain from the session state. The HttpSession can store many Objects, provided that each has a unique identifier. Note that method shuffle must be called before method dealCard is called the first time for a client—otherwise, an exception occurs at line 33 because getAttribute returns null at lines 30–31. After obtaining the user's deck, dealCard gets the top card from the deck (line 33), removes it from the deck (line 34) and returns the card's value as a String (line 36). Without using session tracking, the deck of cards would need to be passed back and forth with each method call. Session tracking makes the dealCard method easy to call (it requires no arguments) and eliminates the overhead of sending the deck over the network multiple times.

Method getHandValue (lines 74–116) determines the total value of the cards in a hand by trying to attain the highest score possible without going over 21. Recall that an ace can be counted as either 1 or 11, and all face cards count as 10. This method does not use the session object because the deck of cards is not used in this method.

As you'll soon see, the client application maintains a hand of cards as a String in which each card is separated by a tab character. Line 78 tokenizes the hand of cards (represented by hand) into individual cards by calling String method split and passing to it a String containing the delimiter characters (in this case, just a tab). Method split uses the delimiter characters to separate tokens in the String. Lines 83–103 count the value of each card. Lines 86–87 retrieve the first integer—the face—and use that value in the switch statement (lines 89–102). If the card is an ace, the method increments variable aceCount. We discuss how this variable is used shortly. If the card is an 11, 12 or 13 (jack, queen or king), the method adds 10 to the total value of the hand (line 97). If the card is anything else, the method increases the total by that value (line 100).

Because an ace can have either of two values, additional logic is required to process aces. Lines 106–113 of method getHandValue process the aces after all the other cards. If a hand contains several aces, only one ace can be counted as 11. The condition in line 109 determines whether counting one ace as 11 and the rest as 1 will result in a total that does not exceed 21. If this is possible, line 110 adjusts the total accordingly. Otherwise, line 112 adjusts the total, counting each ace as 1.

Method getHandValue maximizes the value of the current cards without exceeding 21. Imagine, for example, that the dealer has a 7 and receives an ace. The new total could be either 8 or 18. However, getHandValue always maximizes the value of the cards without going over 21, so the new total is 18.

28.6.2 Consuming the Blackjack Web Service

The blackjack application in Fig. 28.14 keeps track of the player's and dealer's cards, and the web service tracks the cards that have been dealt. The constructor (lines 34–83) sets up the GUI (line 36), changes the window's background color (line 40) and creates the Blackjack web service's proxy object (lines 46–47). In the GUI, each player has 11 JLabels—the maximum number of cards that can be dealt without automatically exceeding 21 (i.e., four aces, four twos and three threes). These JLabels are placed in an ArrayList of JLabels, (lines 59–82), so we can index the ArrayList during the game to determine the JLabel that will display a particular card image.

With JAX-WS 2.0, the client application must indicate whether it wants to allow the web service to maintain session information. Lines 50–51 in the constructor perform this task. We first cast the proxy object to interface type `BindingProvider`. A **`BindingProvider`** enables the client to manipulate the request information that will be sent to the server. This information is stored in an object that implements interface **`RequestContext`**. The `BindingProvider` and `RequestContext` are part of the framework that is created by the IDE when you add a web service client to the application. Next, lines 50–51 invoke the `BindingProvider`'s **`getRequestContext` method** to obtain the `RequestContext` object. Then the `RequestContext`'s **`put` method** is called to set the property `BindingProvider.SESSION_MAINTAIN_PROPERTY` to `true`, which enables session tracking from the client side so that the web service knows which client is invoking the service's web methods.

```
1  // Fig. 28.14: BlackjackGameJFrame.java
2  // Blackjack game that uses the Blackjack Web Service
3  package com.deitel.iw3htp4.ch28.blackjackclient;
4
5  import java.awt.Color;
6  import java.util.ArrayList;
7  import javax.swing.ImageIcon;
8  import javax.swing.JLabel;
9  import javax.swing.JOptionPane;
10 import javax.xml.ws.BindingProvider;
11 import com.deitel.iw3htp4.ch28.blackjackclient.Blackjack;
12 import com.deitel.iw3htp4.ch28.blackjackclient.BlackjackService;
13
14 public class BlackjackGameJFrame extends javax.swing.JFrame
15 {
16    private String playerCards;
17    private String dealerCards;
18    private ArrayList< JLabel > cardboxes; // list of card image JLabels
19    private int currentPlayerCard; // player's current card number
20    private int currentDealerCard; // blackjackProxy's current card number
21    private BlackjackService blackjackService; // used to obtain proxy
22    private Blackjack blackjackProxy; // used to access the web service
23
24    // enumeration of game states
25    private enum GameStatus
26    {
27       PUSH, // game ends in a tie
28       LOSE, // player loses
29       WIN, // player wins
30       BLACKJACK // player has blackjack
31    } // end enum GameStatus
32
33    // no-argument constructor
34    public BlackjackGameJFrame()
35    {
36       initComponents();
37
```

Fig. 28.14 | Blackjack game that uses the `Blackjack` web service. (Part 1 of 10.)

```
      // due to a bug in Netbeans, we must change the JFrame's background
      // color here rather than in the designer
      getContentPane().setBackground( new Color( 0, 180, 0 ) );

      // initialize the blackjack proxy
      try
      {
         // create the objects for accessing the Blackjack web service
         blackjackService = new BlackjackService();
         blackjackProxy = blackjackService.getBlackjackPort();

         // enable session tracking
         ( ( BindingProvider ) blackjackProxy ).getRequestContext().put(
            BindingProvider.SESSION_MAINTAIN_PROPERTY, true );
      } // end try
      catch ( Exception e )
      {
         e.printStackTrace();
      } // end catch

      // add JLabels to cardBoxes ArrayList for programmatic manipulation
      cardboxes = new ArrayList< JLabel >();

      cardboxes.add( 0, dealerCard1JLabel );
      cardboxes.add( dealerCard2JLabel );
      cardboxes.add( dealerCard3JLabel );
      cardboxes.add( dealerCard4JLabel );
      cardboxes.add( dealerCard5JLabel );
      cardboxes.add( dealerCard6JLabel );
      cardboxes.add( dealerCard7JLabel );
      cardboxes.add( dealerCard8JLabel );
      cardboxes.add( dealerCard9JLabel );
      cardboxes.add( dealerCard10JLabel );
      cardboxes.add( dealerCard11JLabel );
      cardboxes.add( playerCard1JLabel );
      cardboxes.add( playerCard2JLabel );
      cardboxes.add( playerCard3JLabel );
      cardboxes.add( playerCard4JLabel );
      cardboxes.add( playerCard5JLabel );
      cardboxes.add( playerCard6JLabel );
      cardboxes.add( playerCard7JLabel );
      cardboxes.add( playerCard8JLabel );
      cardboxes.add( playerCard9JLabel );
      cardboxes.add( playerCard10JLabel );
      cardboxes.add( playerCard11JLabel );
   } // end no-argument constructor

   // play the dealer's hand
   private void dealerPlay()
   {
      try
      {
```

Fig. 28.14 | Blackjack game that uses the `Blackjack` web service. (Part 2 of 10.)

```
         // while the value of the dealer's hand is below 17
         // the dealer must continue to take cards
         String[] cards = dealerCards.split( "\t" );

         // display dealer's cards
         for ( int i = 0; i < cards.length; i++ )
            displayCard( i, cards[ i ]);

         while ( blackjackProxy.getHandValue( dealerCards ) < 17 )
         {
            String newCard = blackjackProxy.dealCard();
            dealerCards += "\t" + newCard; // deal new card
            displayCard( currentDealerCard, newCard );
            ++currentDealerCard;
            JOptionPane.showMessageDialog( this, "Dealer takes a card",
               "Dealer's turn", JOptionPane.PLAIN_MESSAGE );
         } // end while

         int dealersTotal = blackjackProxy.getHandValue( dealerCards );
         int playersTotal = blackjackProxy.getHandValue( playerCards );

         // if dealer busted, player wins
         if ( dealersTotal > 21 )
         {
            gameOver( GameStatus.WIN );
            return;
         } // end if

         // if dealer and player are below 21
         // higher score wins, equal scores is a push
         if ( dealersTotal > playersTotal )
            gameOver( GameStatus.LOSE );
         else if ( dealersTotal < playersTotal )
            gameOver( GameStatus.WIN );
         else
            gameOver( GameStatus.PUSH );
      } // end try
      catch ( Exception e )
      {
         e.printStackTrace();
      } // end catch
   } // end method dealerPlay

   // displays the card represented by cardValue in specified JLabel
   public void displayCard( int card, String cardValue )
   {
      try
      {
         // retrieve correct JLabel from cardBoxes
         JLabel displayLabel = cardboxes.get( card );

```

Fig. 28.14 | Blackjack game that uses the `Blackjack` web service. (Part 3 of 10.)

```
         // if string representing card is empty, display back of card
         if ( cardValue.equals( "" ) )
         {
             displayLabel.setIcon( new ImageIcon( getClass().getResource(
                "/com/deitel/iw3htp4/ch28/blackjackclient/" +
                "blackjack_images/cardback.png" ) ) ) ;
             return;
         } // end if

         // retrieve the face value of the card
         String face = cardValue.substring( 0, cardValue.indexOf( " " ) );

         // retrieve the suit of the card
         String suit =
            cardValue.substring( cardValue. indexOf( " " ) + 1 );

         char suitLetter; // suit letter used to form image file

         switch ( Integer.parseInt( suit ) )
         {
            case 0: // hearts
               suitLetter = 'h';
               break;
            case 1: // diamonds
               suitLetter = 'd';
               break;
            case 2: // clubs
               suitLetter = 'c';
               break;
            default: // spades
               suitLetter = 's';
               break;
         } // end switch

         // set image for displayLabel
         displayLabel.setIcon( new ImageIcon( getClass().getResource(
            "/com/deitel/iw3htp4/ch28/blackjackclient/blackjack_images/" +
            face + suitLetter + ".png" ) ) );
      } // end try
      catch ( Exception e )
      {
         e.printStackTrace();
      } // end catch
   } // end method displayCard

   // displays all player cards and shows appropriate message
   public void gameOver( GameStatus winner )
   {
      String[] cards = dealerCards.split( "\t" );

      // display blackjackProxy's cards
      for ( int i = 0; i < cards.length; i++ )
         displayCard( i, cards[ i ]);
```

Fig. 28.14 | Blackjack game that uses the `Blackjack` web service. (Part 4 of 10.)

```

      // display appropriate status image
      if ( winner == GameStatus.WIN )
         statusJLabel.setText( "You win!" );
      else if ( winner == GameStatus.LOSE )
         statusJLabel.setText( "You lose." );
      else if ( winner == GameStatus.PUSH )
         statusJLabel.setText( "It's a push." );
      else // blackjack
         statusJLabel.setText( "Blackjack!" );

      // display final scores
      int dealersTotal = blackjackProxy.getHandValue( dealerCards );
      int playersTotal = blackjackProxy.getHandValue( playerCards );
      dealerTotalJLabel.setText( "Dealer: " +  dealersTotal );
      playerTotalJLabel.setText( "Player: " + playersTotal );

      // reset for new game
      standJButton.setEnabled( false );
      hitJButton.setEnabled( false );
      dealJButton.setEnabled( true );
   } // end method gameOver

   // The initComponents method is autogenerated by Netbeans and is called
   // from the constructor to initialize the GUI. This method is not shown
   // here to save space. Open BlackjackGameJFrame.java in this
   // example's folder to view the complete generated code (lines 221-531)

   // handles standJButton click
   private void standJButtonActionPerformed(
      java.awt.event.ActionEvent evt )
   {
      standJButton.setEnabled( false );
      hitJButton.setEnabled( false );
      dealJButton.setEnabled( true );
      dealerPlay();
   } // end method standJButtonActionPerformed

   // handles hitJButton click
   private void hitJButtonActionPerformed(
      java.awt.event.ActionEvent evt )
   {
      // get player another card
      String card = blackjackProxy.dealCard(); // deal new card
      playerCards += "\t" + card; // add card to hand

      // update GUI to display new card
      displayCard( currentPlayerCard, card );
      ++currentPlayerCard;

      // determine new value of player's hand
      int total = blackjackProxy.getHandValue( playerCards );

```

Fig. 28.14 | Blackjack game that uses the `Blackjack` web service. (Part 5 of 10.)

```
         if ( total > 21 ) // player busts
            gameOver( GameStatus.LOSE );
         if ( total == 21 ) // player cannot take any more cards
         {
            hitJButton.setEnabled( false );
            dealerPlay();
         } // end if
      } // end method hitJButtonActionPerformed

      // handles dealJButton click
      private void dealJButtonActionPerformed(
         java.awt.event.ActionEvent evt )
      {
         String card; // stores a card temporarily until it's added to a hand

         // clear card images
         for ( int i = 0; i < cardboxes.size(); i++ )
            cardboxes.get( i ).setIcon( null );

         statusJLabel.setText( "" );
         dealerTotalJLabel.setText( "" );
         playerTotalJLabel.setText( "" );

         // create a new, shuffled deck on remote machine
         blackjackProxy.shuffle();

         // deal two cards to player
         playerCards = blackjackProxy.dealCard(); // add first card to hand
         displayCard( 11, playerCards ); // display first card
         card = blackjackProxy.dealCard(); // deal second card
         displayCard( 12, card ); // display second card
         playerCards += "\t" + card; // add second card to hand

         // deal two cards to blackjackProxy, but only show first
         dealerCards = blackjackProxy.dealCard(); // add first card to hand
         displayCard( 0, dealerCards ); // display first card
         card = blackjackProxy.dealCard(); // deal second card
         displayCard( 1, "" ); // display back of card
         dealerCards += "\t" + card; // add second card to hand

         standJButton.setEnabled( true );
         hitJButton.setEnabled( true );
         dealJButton.setEnabled( false );

         // determine the value of the two hands
         int dealersTotal = blackjackProxy.getHandValue( dealerCards );
         int playersTotal = blackjackProxy.getHandValue( playerCards );

         // if hands both equal 21, it is a push
         if ( playersTotal == dealersTotal && playersTotal == 21 )
            gameOver( GameStatus.PUSH );
         else if ( dealersTotal == 21 ) // blackjackProxy has blackjack
            gameOver( GameStatus.LOSE );
```

Fig. 28.14 | Blackjack game that uses the `Blackjack` web service. (Part 6 of 10.)

```
      else if ( playersTotal == 21 ) // blackjack
         gameOver( GameStatus.BLACKJACK );

      // next card for blackjackProxy has index 2
      currentDealerCard = 2;

      // next card for player has index 13
      currentPlayerCard = 13;
   } // end method dealJButtonActionPerformed

   // begins application execution
   public static void main( String args[] )
   {
      java.awt.EventQueue.invokeLater(
         new Runnable()
         {
            public void run()
            {
               new BlackjackGameJFrame().setVisible(true);
            }
         }
      ); // end call to java.awt.EventQueue.invokeLater
   } // end method main

   // Variables declaration - do not modify
   private javax.swing.JButton dealJButton;
   private javax.swing.JLabel dealerCard10JLabel;
   private javax.swing.JLabel dealerCard11JLabel;
   private javax.swing.JLabel dealerCard1JLabel;
   private javax.swing.JLabel dealerCard2JLabel;
   private javax.swing.JLabel dealerCard3JLabel;
   private javax.swing.JLabel dealerCard4JLabel;
   private javax.swing.JLabel dealerCard5JLabel;
   private javax.swing.JLabel dealerCard6JLabel;
   private javax.swing.JLabel dealerCard7JLabel;
   private javax.swing.JLabel dealerCard8JLabel;
   private javax.swing.JLabel dealerCard9JLabel;
   private javax.swing.JLabel dealerJLabel;
   private javax.swing.JLabel dealerTotalJLabel;
   private javax.swing.JButton hitJButton;
   private javax.swing.JLabel playerCard10JLabel;
   private javax.swing.JLabel playerCard11JLabel;
   private javax.swing.JLabel playerCard1JLabel;
   private javax.swing.JLabel playerCard2JLabel;
   private javax.swing.JLabel playerCard3JLabel;
   private javax.swing.JLabel playerCard4JLabel;
   private javax.swing.JLabel playerCard5JLabel;
   private javax.swing.JLabel playerCard6JLabel;
   private javax.swing.JLabel playerCard7JLabel;
   private javax.swing.JLabel playerCard8JLabel;
   private javax.swing.JLabel playerCard9JLabel;
   private javax.swing.JLabel playerJLabel;
   private javax.swing.JLabel playerTotalJLabel;
```

Fig. 28.14 | Blackjack game that uses the `Blackjack` web service. (Part 7 of 10.)

```
    private javax.swing.JButton standJButton;
    private javax.swing.JLabel statusJLabel;
    // End of variables declaration
} // end class BlackjackGameJFrame
```

a) Dealer and player hands after the user clicks the **Deal** `JButton`.

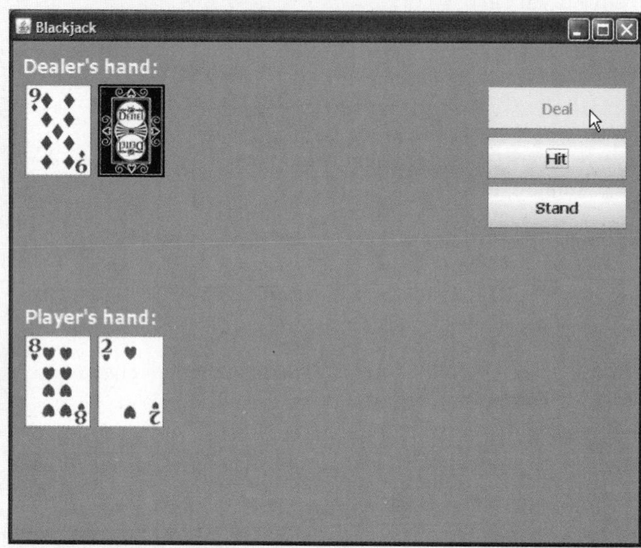

b) Dealer and player hands after the user clicks **Hit** twice, then clicks **Stand**. In this case, the player wins.

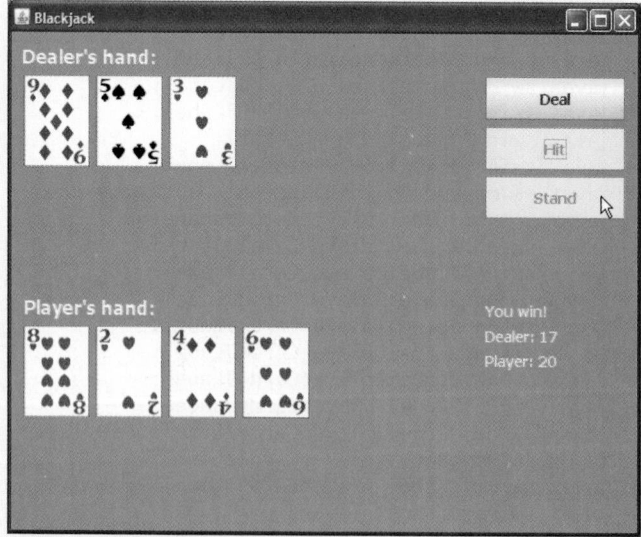

Fig. 28.14 | Blackjack game that uses the `Blackjack` web service. (Part 8 of 10.)

c) Dealer and player hands after the user clicks **Stand** based on the initial hand. In this case, the player loses.

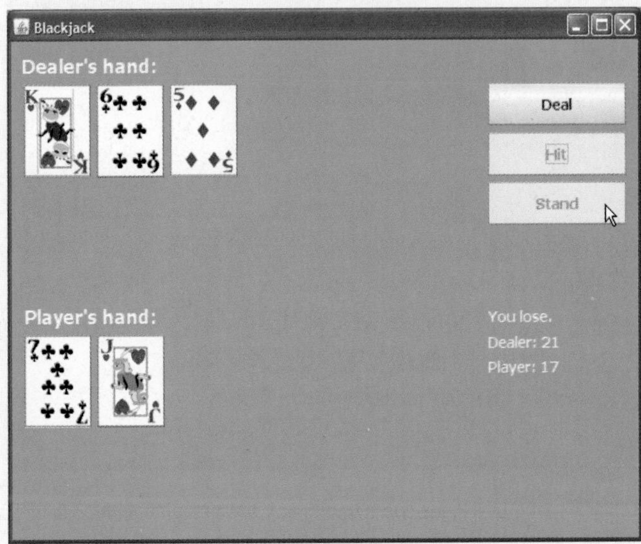

d) Dealer and player hands after the user is dealt blackjack.

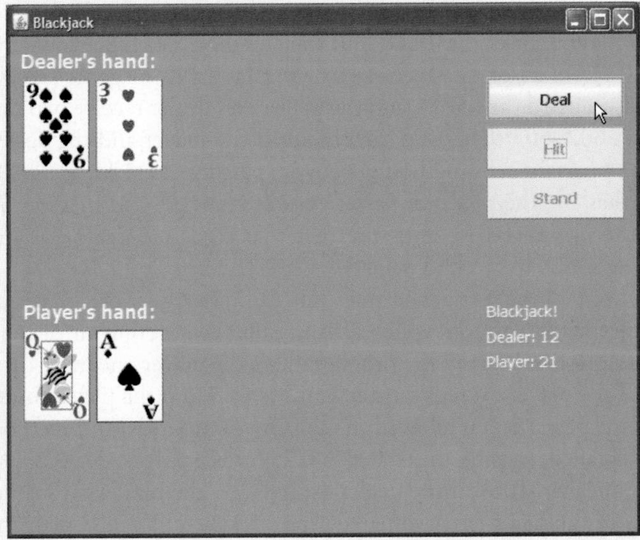

Fig. 28.14 | Blackjack game that uses the `Blackjack` web service. (Part 9 of 10.)

e) Dealer and player hands after the dealer is dealt blackjack.

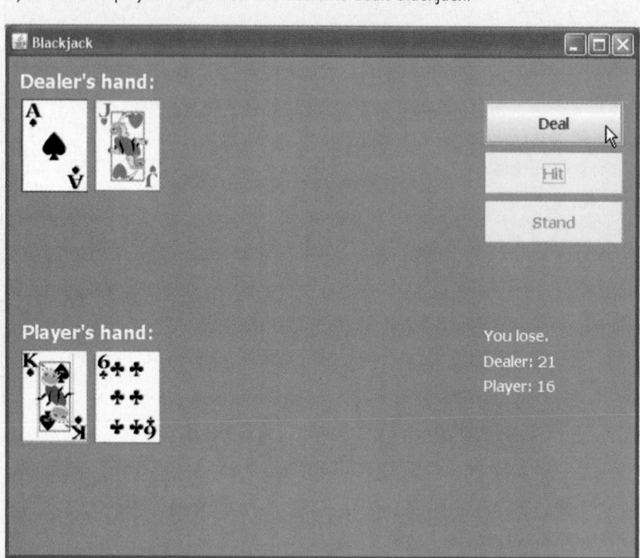

Fig. 28.14 | Blackjack game that uses the `Blackjack` web service. (Part 10 of 10.)

Method `gameOver` (lines 187–215) displays all the dealer's cards, shows the appropriate message in `statusJLabel` and displays the final point totals of both the dealer and the player. Method `gameOver` receives as an argument a member of the `GameStatus` enumeration (defined in lines 25–31). The enumeration represents whether the player tied, lost or won the game; its four members are `PUSH`, `LOSE`, `WIN` and `BLACKJACK`.

When the player clicks the **Deal** `JButton`, method `dealJButtonActionPerformed` (lines 567–618) clears all of the `JLabels` that display cards or game status information. Next, the deck is shuffled (line 581), and the player and dealer receive two cards each (lines 584–595). Lines 602–603 then total each hand. If the player and the dealer both obtain scores of 21, the program calls method `gameOver`, passing `GameStatus.PUSH` (line 607). If only the dealer has 21, the program passes `GameStatus.LOSE` to method `gameOver` (line 609). If only the player has 21 after the first two cards are dealt, the program passes `GameStatus.BLACKJACK` to method `gameOver` (line 611).

If `dealJButtonActionPerformed` does not call `gameOver`, the player can take more cards by clicking the **Hit** `JButton`, which calls `hitJButtonActionPerformed` in lines 543–564. Each time a player clicks **Hit**, the program deals the player one more card and displays it in the GUI. If the player exceeds 21, the game is over and the player loses. If the player has exactly 21, the player is not allowed to take any more cards, and method `dealerPlay` (lines 86–131) is called, causing the dealer to take cards until the dealer's hand has a value of 17 or more (lines 98–106). If the dealer exceeds 21, the player wins (line 114); otherwise, the values of the hands are compared, and `gameOver` is called with the appropriate argument (lines 120–125).

Clicking the **Stand** `JButton` indicates that a player does not want to be dealt another card. Method `standJButtonActionPerformed` (lines 533–540) disables the **Hit** and **Stand** buttons, enables the **Deal** button, then calls method `dealerPlay`.

Method `displayCard` (lines 134–184) updates the GUI to display a newly dealt card. The method takes as arguments an integer index for the `JLabel` in the `ArrayList` that must have its image set and a `String` representing the card. An empty `String` indicates that we wish to display the card face down. If method `displayCard` receives a `String` that's not empty, the program extracts the face and suit from the `String` and uses this information to display the correct image. The `switch` statement (lines 159–173) converts the number representing the suit to an integer and assigns the appropriate character to `suitLetter` (`h` for hearts, `d` for diamonds, `c` for clubs and `s` for spades). The character in `suitLetter` is used to complete the image's filename (lines 176–178).

In this example, you learned how to set up a web service to support session handling so that you could keep track of each client's session state. You also learned how to indicate from a desktop client application that it wishes to take part in session tracking. You'll now learn how to access a database from a web service and how to consume a web service from a client web application.

28.7 Consuming a Database-Driven Web Service from a Web Application

Our prior examples accessed web services from desktop applications created in Netbeans. However, we can just as easily use them in web applications created with Netbeans. In fact, because web-based businesses are becoming increasingly prevalent, it is common for web applications to consume web services. In this section, we present an airline reservation web service that receives information regarding the type of seat a customer wishes to reserve and makes a reservation if such a seat is available. Later in the section, we present a web application that allows a customer to specify a reservation request, then uses the airline reservation web service to attempt to execute the request.

28.7.1 Configuring Java DB in Netbeans and Creating the `Reservation` Database

In this example, our web service uses a `Reservation` database containing a single table named `Seats` to locate a seat matching a client's request. To build the `Reservation` database, review the steps presented in Section 27.2.1 for building the `AddressBook` database. This chapters examples directory contains a SQL script to build the `Seats` table and populate it with sample data. The sample data is shown in Fig. 28.15.

Number	Location	Class	Taken
1	Aisle	Economy	0
2	Aisle	Economy	0
3	Aisle	First	0
4	Middle	Economy	0
5	Middle	Economy	0

Fig. 28.15 | `Seats` table's data. (Part 1 of 2.)

Number	Location	Class	Taken
6	Middle	First	0
7	Window	Economy	0
8	Window	Economy	0
9	Window	First	0
10	Window	First	0

Fig. 28.15 | Seats table's data. (Part 2 of 2.)

Creating the Reservation Web Service

You can now create a web service that uses the `Reservation` database (Fig. 28.16). The airline reservation web service has a single web method—`reserve` (lines 26–78)—which searches the `Seats` table to locate a seat matching a user's request. The method takes two arguments—a `String` representing the desired seat type (i.e., `"Window"`, `"Middle"` or `"Aisle"`) and a `String` representing the desired class type (i.e., `"Economy"` or `"First"`). If it finds an appropriate seat, method `reserve` updates the database to make the reservation and returns `true`; otherwise, no reservation is made, and the method returns `false`. Note that the statements at lines 34–39 and lines 44–48 that query and update the database use objects of JDBC types `ResultSet` and `PreparedStatement`.

Software Engineering Observation 28.1

Using `PreparedStatements` to create SQL statements is highly recommended to secure against so-called SQL injection attacks in which executable code is inserted SQL code. The site `www.owasp.org/index.php/Preventing_SQL_Injection_in_Java` provides a summary of SQL injection attacks and ways to mitigate against them..

Our database contains four columns—the seat number (i.e., `1`–`10`), the seat type (i.e., `Window`, `Middle` or `Aisle`), the class type (i.e., `Economy` or `First`) and a column containing either `1` (true) or `0` (false) to indicate whether the seat is taken. Lines 34–39 retrieve the seat numbers of any available seats matching the requested seat and class type. This statement fills the `resultSet` with the results of the query

```
SELECT "NUMBER"
FROM "SEATS"
WHERE ("TAKEN" = 0) AND ("TYPE" = type) AND ("CLASS" = class)
```

The parameters *type* and *class* in the query are replaced with values of method `reserve`'s `seatType` and `classType` parameters. When you use the Netbeans tools to create a database table and its columns, the Netbeans tools automatically place the table and column names in double quotes. For this reason, you must place the table and column names in double quotes in the SQL statements that interact with the `Reservation` database.

If `resultSet` is not empty (i.e., at least one seat is available that matches the selected criteria), the condition in line 42 is `true` and the web service reserves the first matching seat number. Recall that `ResultSet` method `next` returns `true` if a nonempty row exists, and positions the cursor on that row. We obtain the seat number (line 44) by accessing `resultSet`'s first column (i.e., `resultSet.getInt(1)`—the first column in the row). Then lines 45–48 configure a `PreparedStatement` and execute the SQL:

```
UPDATE "SEATS"
SET "TAKEN" = 1
WHERE ("NUMBER" = number)
```

which marks the seat as taken in the database. The parameter *number* is replaced with the value of `seat`. Method `reserve` returns `true` (line 49) to indicate that the reservation was successful. If there are no matching seats, or if an exception occurred, method `reserve` returns `false` (lines 52, 57, 62 and 75) to indicate that no seats matched the user's request.

```
1  // Fig. 28.16: Reservation.java
2  // Airline reservation web service.
3  package com.deitel.iw3htp4.ch28.reservation;
4
5  import java.sql.Connection;
6  import java.sql.PreparedStatement;
7  import java.sql.DriverManager;
8  import java.sql.ResultSet;
9  import java.sql.SQLException;
10 import javax.jws.WebService;
11 import javax.jws.WebMethod;
12 import javax.jws.WebParam;
13
14 @WebService( name = "Reservation", serviceName = "ReservationService" )
15 public class Reservation
16 {
17    private static final String DATABASE_URL =
18       "jdbc:derby://localhost:1527/Reservation";
19    private static final String USERNAME = "iw3htp4";
20    private static final String PASSWORD = "iw3htp4";
21    private Connection connection;
22    private PreparedStatement lookupSeat;
23    private PreparedStatement reserveSeat;
24
25    // a WebMethod that can reserve a seat
26    @WebMethod( operationName = "reserve" )
27    public boolean reserve( @WebParam( name = "seatType" ) String seatType,
28       @WebParam( name = "classType" ) String classType )
29    {
30       try
31       {
32          connection = DriverManager.getConnection(
33             DATABASE_URL, USERNAME, PASSWORD );
34          lookupSeat = connection.prepareStatement(
35             "SELECT \"NUMBER\" FROM \"SEATS\" WHERE (\"TAKEN\" = 0) " +
36             "AND (\"LOCATION\" = ?) AND (\"CLASS\" = ?)" );
37          lookupSeat.setString( 1, seatType );
38          lookupSeat.setString( 2, classType );
39          ResultSet resultSet = lookupSeat.executeQuery();
```

Fig. 28.16 | Airline reservation web service. (Part 1 of 2.)

```

         // if requested seat is available, reserve it
         if ( resultSet.next() )
         {
            int seat = resultSet.getInt( 1 );
            reserveSeat = connection.prepareStatement(
               "UPDATE \"SEATS\" SET \"TAKEN\"=1 WHERE \"NUMBER\"=?" );
            reserveSeat.setInt( 1, seat );
            reserveSeat.executeUpdate();
            return true;
         } // end if

         return false;
      } // end try
      catch ( SQLException e )
      {
         e.printStackTrace();
         return false;
      } // end catch
      catch ( Exception e )
      {
         e.printStackTrace();
         return false;
      } // end catch
      finally
      {
         try
         {
            lookupSeat.close();
            reserveSeat.close();
            connection.close();
         } // end try
         catch ( Exception e )
         {
            e.printStackTrace();
            return false;
         } // end catch
      } // end finally
   } // end WebMethod reserve
} // end class Reservation
```

Fig. 28.16 | Airline reservation web service. (Part 2 of 2.)

28.7.2 Creating a Web Application to Interact with the Reservation Web Service

This section presents a `ReservationClient` web application that consumes the `Reservation` web service. The application allows users to select seats based on class (`"Economy"` or `"First"`) and location (`"Aisle"`, `"Middle"` or `"Window"`), then submit their requests to the airline reservation web service. If the database request is not successful, the application instructs the user to modify the request and try again. The application presented here was built using the techniques presented in Chapters 26–27. We assume that you've already read those chapters, and thus know how to build a web application's GUI, create event handlers and add properties to a web application's session bean (Section 27.2.1).

Reserve.jsp

`Reserve.jsp` (Fig. 28.17) defines two `DropDownLists` and a `Button`. The `seatTypeDropDown` (lines 26–31) displays all the seat types from which users can select. The `classTypeDropDownList` (lines 32–37) provides choices for the class type. Users click the `reserveButton` (lines 38–42) to submit requests after making selections from the `DropDownLists`. The page also defines three `Labels`—`instructionLabel` (lines 22–25) to display instructions, `errorLabel` (lines 43–47) to display an appropriate message if no seat matching the user's selection is available and `successLabel` (lines 48–51) to indicate a successful reservation. The page bean file (Fig. 28.18) attaches event handlers to `seatTypeDropDown`, `classTypeDropDown` and `reserveButton`.

```
1  <?xml version="1.0" encoding="UTF-8"?>
2
3  <!-- Fig. 28.17 Reserve.jsp -->
4  <!-- JSP that allows a user to select a seat -->
5  <jsp:root version="1.2"
6     xmlns:f="http://java.sun.com/jsf/core"
7     xmlns:h="http://java.sun.com/jsf/html"
8     xmlns:jsp="http://java.sun.com/JSP/Page"
9     xmlns:webuijsf="http://www.sun.com/webui/webuijsf">
10    <jsp:directive.page contentType="text/html;charset=UTF-8"
11       pageEncoding="UTF-8"/>
12    <f:view>
13    <webuijsf:page binding="#{Reserve.page1}" id="page1">
14       <webuijsf:html binding="#{Reserve.html1}" id="html1">
15          <webuijsf:head binding="#{Reserve.head1}" id="head1">
16             <webuijsf:link binding="#{Reserve.link1}" id="link1"
17                url="/resources/stylesheet.css"/>
18          </webuijsf:head>
19          <webuijsf:body binding="#{Reserve.body1}" id="body1"
20             style="-rave-layout: grid">
21             <webuijsf:form binding="#{Reserve.form1}" id="form1">
22                <webuijsf:label binding="#{Reserve.instructionLabel}"
23                   id="instructionLabel" style="left: 24px; top: 24px;
24                   position: absolute" text="Please select the seat type
25                   and class to reserve:"/>
26                <webuijsf:dropDown binding="#{Reserve.seatTypeDropDown}"
27                   id="seatTypeDropDown" items=
28                   "#{Reserve.seatTypeDropDownDefaultOptions.options}"
29                   style="left: 310px; top: 21px; position: absolute"
30                   valueChangeListenerExpression=
31                   "#{Reserve.seatTypeDropDown_processValueChange}"/>
32                <webuijsf:dropDown binding="#{Reserve.classTypeDropDown}"
33                   id="classTypeDropDown" items=
34                   "#{Reserve.classTypeDropDownDefaultOptions.options}"
35                   style="left: 385px; top: 21px; position: absolute"
36                   valueChangeListenerExpression=
37                   "#{Reserve.classTypeDropDown_processValueChange}"/>
```

Fig. 28.17 | JSP that allows a user to select a seat. (Part 1 of 3.)

```
                <webuijsf:button actionExpression=
                    "#{Reserve.reserveButton_action}" binding=
                    "#{Reserve.reserveButton}" id="reserveButton" style=
                    "height: 20px; left: 460px; top: 21px; position:
                    absolute; width: 100px" text="Reserve"/>
                <webuijsf:label binding="#{Reserve.errorLabel}"
                    id="errorLabel" rendered="false" style="color: red;
                    left: 24px; top: 48px; position: absolute" text="This
                    type of seat is not available. Please modify your
                    request and try again."/>
                <webuijsf:label binding="#{Reserve.successLabel}"
                    id="successLabel" rendered="false" style="left: 24px;
                    top: 24px; position: absolute"
                    text="Your reservation has been made. Thank you!"/>
            </webuijsf:form>
        </webuijsf:body>
    </webuijsf:html>
</webuijsf:page>
</f:view>
</jsp:root>
```

a) Selecting a seat:

b) Seat reserved successfully:

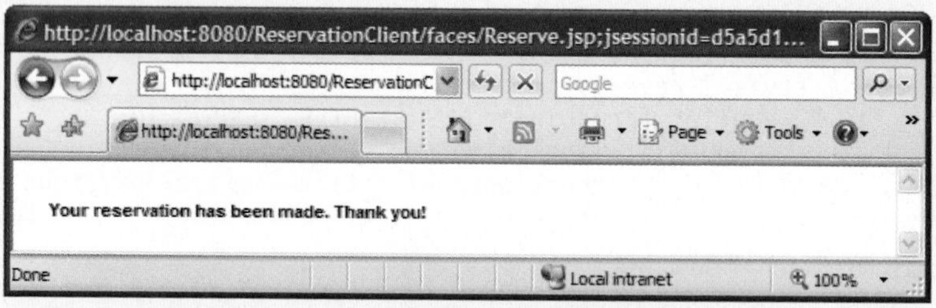

c) Attempting to reserve another window seat in economy when there are no such seats available:

Fig. 28.17 | JSP that allows a user to select a seat. (Part 2 of 3.)

d) No seats match the requested seat type and class:

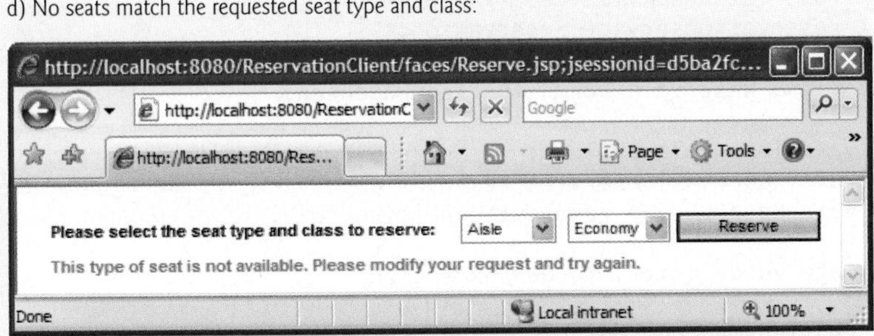

Fig. 28.17 | JSP that allows a user to select a seat. (Part 3 of 3.)

Reserve.java

Figure 28.18 contains the page bean code that provides the logic for `Reserve.jsp`. As discussed in Section 26.5.2, the class that represents the page's bean extends `AbstractPageBean`. When the user selects a value in one of the `DropDownLists`, the corresponding event handler—`classTypeDropDown_processValueChange` (lines 262–267) or `seatTypeDropDown_processValueChange` (lines 270–275)—is called to set the session properties `seatType` and `classType`, which we added to the web application's session bean. The values of these properties are used as the arguments in the call to the web service's `reserve` method. When the user clicks **Reserve** in the JSP, the event handler `reserveButton_action` (lines 278–311) executes. Lines 282–284 use the proxy object (created in lines 38–39) to invoke the web service's `reserve` method, passing the selected seat type and class type as arguments. If `reserve` returns `true`, lines 288–293 hide the GUI components in the JSP and display the `successLabel` (line 292) to thank the user for making a reservation; otherwise, lines 297–302 ensure that the GUI components remain displayed and display the `errorLabel` (line 302) to notify the user that the requested seat type is not available and instruct the user to try again.

```
1  // Fig. 28.18: Reserve.java
2  // Page scope backing bean class for seat reservation client
3  package com.deitel.iw3htp4.ch28.reservationclient;
4
5  import com.sun.rave.web.ui.appbase.AbstractPageBean;
6  import com.sun.webui.jsf.component.Body;
7  import com.sun.webui.jsf.component.Button;
8  import com.sun.webui.jsf.component.DropDown;
9  import com.sun.webui.jsf.component.Form;
10 import com.sun.webui.jsf.component.Head;
11 import com.sun.webui.jsf.component.Html;
12 import com.sun.webui.jsf.component.Label;
13 import com.sun.webui.jsf.component.Link;
14 import com.sun.webui.jsf.component.Page;
15 import com.sun.webui.jsf.model.SingleSelectOptionsList;
16 import javax.faces.FacesException;
17 import javax.faces.event.ValueChangeEvent;
```

Fig. 28.18 | Page scope backing bean class for seat reservation client. (Part 1 of 3.)

```
import reservationservice.ReservationService;
import reservationservice.Reservation;

public class Reserve extends AbstractPageBean
{
   private int __placeholder;
   private ReservationService reservationService; // reference to service
   private Reservation reservationServiceProxy; // reference to proxy

   private void _init() throws Exception
   {
      seatTypeDropDownDefaultOptions.setOptions(
         new com.sun.webui.jsf.model.Option[] {
            new com.sun.webui.jsf.model.Option( "Aisle", "Aisle" ),
            new com.sun.webui.jsf.model.Option( "Middle", "Middle" ),
            new com.sun.webui.jsf.model.Option( "Window", "Window" ) } );
      classTypeDropDownDefaultOptions.setOptions(
         new com.sun.webui.jsf.model.Option[] {
            new com.sun.webui.jsf.model.Option( "Economy", "Economy" ),
            new com.sun.webui.jsf.model.Option( "First", "First" ) } );
      reservationService = new ReservationService();
      reservationServiceProxy = reservationService.getReservationPort();
   } // end method

   // Lines 42-260 of the autogenerated code have been removed to save
   // space. The complete code is available in this example's folder.

   // store selected class in session bean
   public void classTypeDropDown_processValueChange(
      ValueChangeEvent event )
   {
      getSessionBean1().setClassType(
         ( String ) classTypeDropDown.getSelected() );
   } // end method classTypeDropDown_processValueChange

   // store selected seat type in session bean
   public void seatTypeDropDown_processValueChange(
      ValueChangeEvent event )
   {
      getSessionBean1().setSeatType(
         ( String ) seatTypeDropDown.getSelected() );
   } // end method seatTypeDropDown_processValueChange

   // invoke the web service when the user clicks Reserve button
   public String reserveButton_action()
   {
      try
      {
         boolean reserved = reservationServiceProxy.reserve(
            getSessionBean1().getSeatType(),
            getSessionBean1().getClassType() );

```

Fig. 28.18 | Page scope backing bean class for seat reservation client. (Part 2 of 3.)

```
         if ( reserved ) // display successLabel; hide all others
         {
            instructionLabel.setRendered( false );
            seatTypeDropDown.setRendered( false );
            classTypeDropDown.setRendered( false );
            reserveButton.setRendered( false );
            successLabel.setRendered( true );
            errorLabel.setRendered( false );
         } // end if
         else // display all but successLabel
         {
            instructionLabel.setRendered( true );
            seatTypeDropDown.setRendered( true );
            classTypeDropDown.setRendered( true );
            reserveButton.setRendered( true );
            successLabel.setRendered( false );
            errorLabel.setRendered( true );
         } // end else
      } // end try
      catch ( Exception e )
      {
         e.printStackTrace();
      } // end catch

      return null;
   } // end method reserveButton_action
} // end class Reserve
```

Fig. 28.18 | Page scope backing bean class for seat reservation client. (Part 3 of 3.)

28.8 Passing an Object of a User-Defined Type to a Web Service

The web methods we've demonstrated so far each receive and return only primitive values or `Strings`. Web services also can receive and return objects of user-defined types—known as custom types. This section presents an `EquationGenerator` web service that generates random arithmetic questions of type `Equation`. The client is a math-tutoring desktop application in which the user selects the type of mathematical question to attempt (addition, subtraction or multiplication) and the skill level of the user—level 1 uses one-digit numbers in each question, level 2 uses two-digit numbers and level 3 uses three-digit numbers. The client passes this information to the web service, which then generates an `Equation` consisting of random numbers with the proper number of digits. The client application receives the `Equation`, displays the sample question to the user in a Java application, allows the user to provide an answer and checks the answer to determine whether it is correct.

Serialization of User-Defined Types

We mentioned earlier that all types passed to and from SOAP web services must be supported by SOAP. How, then, can SOAP support a type that is not even created yet? Custom types that are sent to or from a web service are serialized into XML format. This process is referred to as XML serialization. The process of serializing objects to XML and deserializing objects from XML is handled for you automatically.

Requirements for User-Defined Types Used with Web Methods

A class that is used to specify parameter or return types in web methods must meet several requirements:

1. It must provide a `public` default or no-argument constructor. When a web service or web service consumer receives an XML serialized object, the JAX-WS 2.0 Framework must be able to call this constructor when deserializing the object (i.e., converting it from XML back to a Java object).
2. Instance variables that should be serialized in XML format must have `public` *set* and *get* methods to access the `private` instance variables (recommended), or the instance variables must be declared `public` (not recommended).
3. Non-`public` instance variables that should be serialized must provide both *set* and *get* methods (even if they have empty bodies); otherwise, they are not serialized.

Any instance variable that is not serialized simply receives its default value (or the value provided by the no-argument constructor) when an object of the class is deserialized.

Common Programming Error 28.3

A runtime error occurs if an attempt is made to deserialize an object of a class that does not have a default or no-argument constructor.

Defining Class `Equation`

Figure 28.19 defines class `Equation`. Lines 18–31 define a constructor that takes three arguments—two `int`s representing the left and right operands and a `String` that represents the arithmetic operation to perform. The constructor sets the `leftOperand`, `rightOperand` and `operationType` instance variables, then calculates the appropriate result. The no-argument constructor (lines 13–16) calls the three-argument constructor (lines 18–31) and passes default values. We do not use the no-argument constructor explicitly, but the XML serialization mechanism uses it when objects of this class are deserialized. Because we provide a constructor with parameters, we must explicitly define the no-argument constructor in this class so that objects of the class can be passed to or returned from web methods.

```
1  // Fig. 28.19: Equation.java
2  // Class Equation that contains information about an equation
3  package com.deitel.iw3htp4.generator;
4
5  public class Equation
6  {
7     private int leftOperand;
8     private int rightOperand;
9     private int resultValue;
10    private String operationType;
11
12    // required no-argument constructor
13    public Equation()
14    {
```

Fig. 28.19 | Class `Equation` that stores information about an equation. (Part 1 of 3.)

```
      this( 0, 0, "+" );
   } // end no-argument constructor

   public Equation( int leftValue, int rightValue, String type )
   {
      leftOperand = leftValue;
      rightOperand = rightValue;
      operationType = type;

      //determine resultValue
      if ( operationType.equals( "+" ) ) // addition
         resultValue = leftOperand + rightOperand;
      else if ( operationType.equals( "-" ) ) // subtraction
         resultValue = leftOperand - rightOperand;
      else // multiplication
         resultValue = leftOperand * rightOperand;
   } // end three argument constructor

   // method that overrides Object.toString()
   public String toString()
   {
      return leftOperand + " " + operationType + " " +
         rightOperand + " = " + resultValue;
   } // end method toString

   // returns the left hand side of the equation as a String
   public String getLeftHandSide()
   {
      return leftOperand + " " + operationType + " " + rightOperand;
   } // end method getLeftHandSide

   // returns the right hand side of the equation as a String
   public String getRightHandSide()
   {
      return "" + resultValue;
   } // end method getRightHandSide

   // gets the leftOperand
   public int getLeftOperand()
   {
      return leftOperand;
   } // end method getLeftOperand

   // gets the rightOperand
   public int getRightOperand()
   {
      return rightOperand;
   } // end method getRightOperand

   // gets the resultValue
   public int getReturnValue()
   {
```

Fig. 28.19 | Class `Equation` that stores information about an equation. (Part 2 of 3.)

```
67          return resultValue;
68       } // end method getResultValue
69
70       // gets the operationType
71       public String getOperationType()
72       {
73          return operationType;
74       } // end method getOperationType
75
76       // required setter
77       public void setLeftHandSide( String value )
78       {
79          // empty body
80       } // end setLeftHandSide
81
82       // required setter
83       public void setRightHandSide( String value )
84       {
85          // empty body
86       } // end setRightHandSide
87
88       // required setter
89       public void setLeftOperand( int value )
90       {
91          // empty body
92       } // end method setLeftOperand
93
94       // required setter
95       public void setRightOperand( int value )
96       {
97          // empty body
98       } // end method setRightOperand
99
100      // required setter
101      public void setReturnValue( int value )
102      {
103         // empty body
104      } // end method setResultOperand
105
106      // required setter
107      public void setOperationType( String value )
108      {
109         // empty body
110      } // end method setOperationType
111   } // end class Equation
```

Fig. 28.19 | Class `Equation` that stores information about an equation. (Part 3 of 3.)

Class `Equation` defines methods `getLeftHandSide` and `setLeftHandSide` (lines 41–44 and 77–80); `getRightHandSide` and `setRightHandSide` (lines 47–50 and 83–86); `getLeftOperand` and `setLeftOperand` (lines 53–56 and 89–92); `getRightOperand` and `setRightOperand` (lines 59–62 and 95–98); `getReturnValue` and `setReturnValue` (lines 65–68 and 101–104); and `getOperationType` and `setOperationType` (lines 71–74 and

107–110). The client of the web service does not need to modify the values of the instance variables. However, recall that a property can be serialized only if it has both a *get* and a *set* accessor, or if it is `public`. So we provided *set* methods with empty bodies for each of the class's instance variables. Method `getLeftHandSide` (lines 41–44) returns a `String` representing everything to the left of the equals (=) sign in the equation, and `getRightHandSide` (lines 47–50) returns a `String` representing everything to the right of the equals (=) sign. Method `getLeftOperand` (lines 53–56) returns the integer to the left of the operator, and `getRightOperand` (lines 59–62) returns the integer to the right of the operator. Method `getResultValue` (lines 65–68) returns the solution to the equation, and `getOperationType` (lines 71–74) returns the operator in the equation. The client in this example does not use the `rightHandSide` property, but we included it so future clients can use it.

Creating the `EquationGenerator` *Web Service*

Figure 28.20 presents the `EquationGenerator` web service, which creates random, customized `Equations`. This web service contains only method `generateEquation` (lines 18–31), which takes two parameters—the mathematical operation (one of "+", "-" or "*") and an `int` representing the difficulty level (1–3).

```
1  // Fig. 28.20: Generator.java
2  // Web service that generates random equations
3  package com.deitel.iw3htp4.ch28.equationgenerator;
4
5  import java.util.Random;
6  import javax.jws.WebService;
7  import javax.jws.WebMethod;
8  import javax.jws.WebParam;
9
10 @WebService( name = "EquationGenerator",
11    serviceName = "EquationGeneratorService" )
12 public class EquationGenerator
13 {
14    private int minimum;
15    private int maximum;
16
17    // generates a math equation and returns it as an Equation object
18    @WebMethod( operationName = "generateEquation" )
19    public Equation generateEquation(
20       @WebParam( name = "operation" ) String operation,
21       @WebParam( name = "difficulty" ) int difficulty )
22    {
23       minimum = ( int ) Math.pow( 10, difficulty - 1 );
24       maximum = ( int ) Math.pow( 10, difficulty );
25
26       Random randomObject = new Random();
27
28       return new Equation(
29          randomObject.nextInt( maximum - minimum ) + minimum,
30          randomObject.nextInt( maximum - minimum ) + minimum, operation );
31    } // end method generateEquation
32 } // end class EquationGenerator
```

Fig. 28.20 | Web service that generates random equations.

Testing the **`EquationGenerator`** *Web Service*

Figure 28.21 shows the result of testing the `EquationGenerator` service with the `Tester` web page. In *Part b* of the figure, note that the web method's return value is XML encoded. However, this example differs from previous ones in that the XML specifies the values for all the data of the returned XML serialized object returned. The proxy class receives this return value and deserializes it into an object of class `Equation`, then passes it to the client.

Note that an `Equation` object is *not* being passed between the web service and the client. Rather, the information in the object is being sent as XML-encoded data. Clients created using Java will take the information and create a new `Equation` object. Clients created on other platforms, however, may use the information differently. Readers creating clients on other platforms should check the web services documentation for the specific platform they are using, to see how their clients may process custom types.

Details of the **`EquationGenerator`** *Web Service*

Let's examine web method `generateEquation` more closely. Lines 23–24 of Fig. 28.20 define the upper and lower bounds of the random numbers that the method uses to generate an `Equation`. To set these limits, the program first calls `static` method `pow` of class `Math`—this method raises its first argument to the power of its second argument. Variable `minimum`'s value is determined by raising `10` to a power one less than `difficulty` (line 23). This calculates the smallest number with `difficulty` digits. If `difficulty` is `1`, `minimum` is `1`; if `difficulty` is `2`, `minimum` is `10`; and if `difficulty` is `3`, `minimum` is `100`. To calculate the value of `maximum` (the upper bound for numbers used to form an `Equation`), the program raises `10` to the power of the specified `difficulty` argument (line 24). If `difficulty` is `1`, `maximum` is `10`; if `difficulty` is `2`, `maximum` is `100`; and if `difficulty` is `3`, `maximum` is `1000`.

Lines 28–30 create and return a new `Equation` object consisting of two random numbers and the `String` `operation` received by `generateEquation`. `Random` method `nextInt` returns an `int` that is less than the specified upper bound. `generateEquation` generates operand values that are greater than or equal to `minimum` but less than `maximum` (i.e., a number with `difficulty` number of digits).

a) Using the `EquationGenerator` web service's `Tester` web page to generate an `Equation`.

Fig. 28.21 | Testing a web method that returns an XML serialized `Equation` object. (Part 1 of 2.)

b) Result of generating an `Equation`.

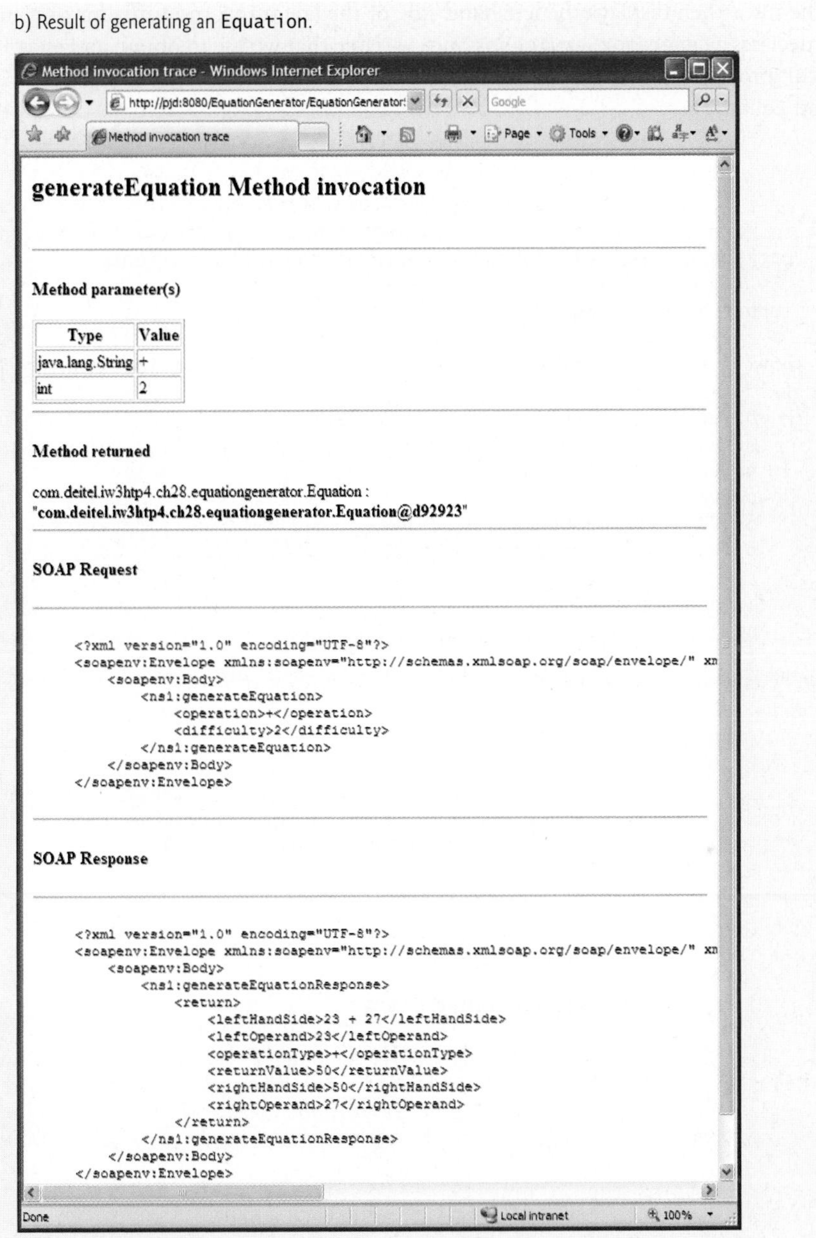

Fig. 28.21 | Testing a web method that returns an XML serialized `Equation` object. (Part 2 of 2.)

Consuming the `EquationGenerator` *Web Service*

The **Math Tutor** application (Fig. 28.22) uses the `EquationGenerator` web service. The application calls the web service's `generateEquation` method to create an `Equation` object.

The tutor then displays the left-hand side of the `Equation` and waits for user input. Line 9 declares a `GeneratorService` instance variable that we use to obtain an `EquationGenerator` proxy object. Lines 10–11 declare instance variables of types `EquationGenerator` and `Equation`.

```
1  // Fig. 28.22: EquationGeneratorClientJFrame.java
2  // Math tutoring program using web services to generate equations
3  package com.deitel.iw3htp4.ch28.equationgeneratorclient;
4
5  import javax.swing.JOptionPane;
6
7  public class EquationGeneratorClientJFrame extends javax.swing.JFrame
8  {
9     private EquationGeneratorService service; // used to obtain proxy
10    private EquationGenerator proxy; // used to access the web service
11    private Equation equation; // represents an equation
12    private int answer; // the user's answer to the question
13    private String operation = "+"; // mathematical operation +, - or *
14    private int difficulty = 1; // 1, 2 or 3 digits in each number
15
16    // no-argument constructor
17    public EquationGeneratorClientJFrame()
18    {
19       initComponents();
20
21       try
22       {
23          // create the objects for accessing the EquationGenerator service
24          service = new EquationGeneratorService();
25          proxy = service.getEquationGeneratorPort();
26       } // end try
27       catch ( Exception ex )
28       {
29          ex.printStackTrace();
30       } // end catch
31    } // end no-argument constructors
32
33    // The initComponents method is autogenerated by Netbeans and is called
34    // from the constructor to initialize the GUI. This method is not shown
35    // here to save space. Open EquationGeneratorClientJFrame.java in this
36    // example's folder to view the complete generated code (lines 37-156).
37
38    // obtains the difficulty level selected by the user
39    private void levelJComboBoxItemStateChanged(
40       java.awt.event.ItemEvent evt )
41    {
42       // indices start at 0, so add 1 to get the difficulty level
43       difficulty = levelJComboBox.getSelectedIndex() + 1;
44    } // end method levelJComboBoxItemStateChanged
45
```

Fig. 28.22 | Math tutoring application. (Part 1 of 4.)

```
   // obtains the mathematical operation selected by the user
   private void operationJComboBoxItemStateChanged(
      java.awt.event.ItemEvent evt )
   {
      String item = ( String ) operationJComboBox.getSelectedItem();

      if ( item.equals( "Addition" ) )
         operation = "+"; // user selected addition
      else if ( item.equals( "Subtraction" ) )
         operation = "-"; // user selected subtraction
      else
         operation = "*"; // user selected multiplication
   } // end method operationJComboBoxItemStateChanged

   // checks the user's answer
   private void checkAnswerJButtonActionPerformed(
      java.awt.event.ActionEvent evt )
   {
      if ( answerJTextField.getText().equals( "" ) )
      {
         JOptionPane.showMessageDialog(
            this, "Please enter your answer." );
      } // end if

      int userAnswer = Integer.parseInt( answerJTextField.getText() );

      if ( userAnswer == answer )
      {
         equationJLabel.setText( "" );
         answerJTextField.setText( "" );
         checkAnswerJButton.setEnabled( false );
         JOptionPane.showMessageDialog( this, "Correct! Good Job!",
            "Correct", JOptionPane.PLAIN_MESSAGE );
      } // end if
      else
      {
         JOptionPane.showMessageDialog( this, "Incorrect. Try again.",
            "Incorrect", JOptionPane.PLAIN_MESSAGE );
      } // end else
   } // end method checkAnswerJButtonActionPerformed

   // generates a new Equation based on user's selections
   private void generateJButtonActionPerformed(
      java.awt.event.ActionEvent evt )
   {
      try
      {
         equation = proxy.generateEquation( operation, difficulty );
         answer = equation.getReturnValue();
         equationJLabel.setText( equation.getLeftHandSide() + " =" );
         checkAnswerJButton.setEnabled( true );
      } // end try
```

Fig. 28.22 | Math tutoring application. (Part 2 of 4.)

```
      catch ( Exception e )
      {
         e.printStackTrace();
      } // end catch
   } // end method generateJButtonActionPerformed

   // begins program execution
   public static void main( String args[] )
   {
      java.awt.EventQueue.invokeLater(
         new Runnable()
         {
            public void run()
            {
               new EquationGeneratorClientJFrame().setVisible( true );
            } // end method run
         } // end anonymous inner class
      ); // end call to java.awt.EventQueue.invokeLater
   } // end method main

   // Variables declaration - do not modify
   private javax.swing.JLabel answerJLabel;
   private javax.swing.JTextField answerJTextField;
   private javax.swing.JButton checkAnswerJButton;
   private javax.swing.JLabel equationJLabel;
   private javax.swing.JButton generateJButton;
   private javax.swing.JComboBox levelJComboBox;
   private javax.swing.JLabel levelJLabel;
   private javax.swing.JComboBox operationJComboBox;
   private javax.swing.JLabel operationJLabel;
   private javax.swing.JLabel questionJLabel;
   // End of variables declaration
} // end class EquationGeneratorClientJFrame
```

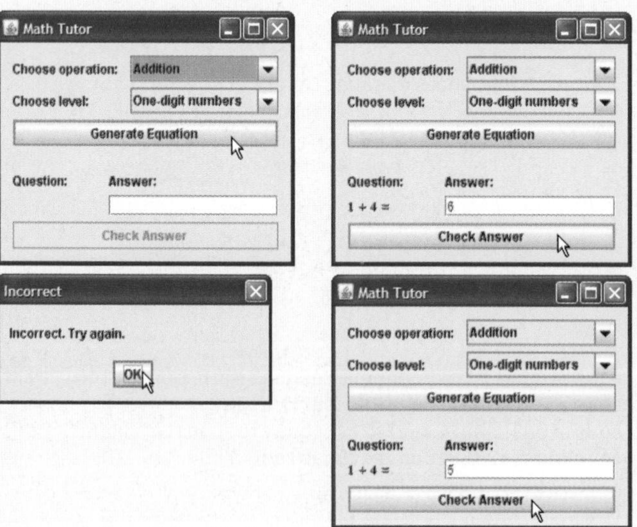

Fig. 28.22 | Math tutoring application. (Part 3 of 4.)

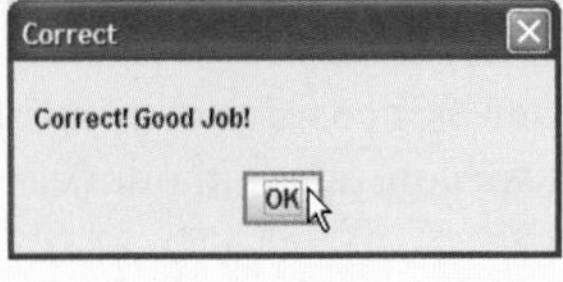

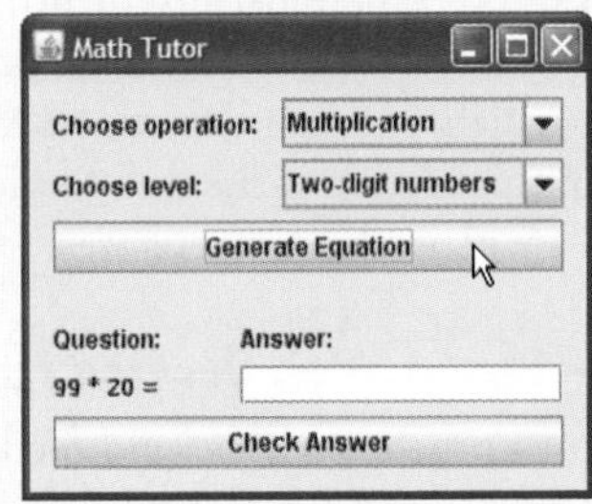

Fig. 28.22 | Math tutoring application. (Part 4 of 4.)

After displaying an equation, the application waits for the user to enter an answer. The default setting for the difficulty level is **One-digit numbers**, but the user can change this by choosing a level from the **Choose level** `JComboBox`. Clicking any of the levels invokes `levelJComboBoxItemStateChanged` (lines 158–163), which sets the variable `difficulty` to the level selected by the user. Although the default setting for the question type is **Addition**, the user also can change this by selecting an operation from the **Choose operation** `JComboBox`. Doing so invokes `operationJComboBoxItemStateChanged` (lines 166–177), which sets the `String operation` to the appropriate mathematical symbol.

When the user clicks the **Generate Equation** `JButton`, method `generateButton-ActionPerformed` (lines 207–221) invokes the `EquationGenerator` web service's `generateEquation` (line 212) method. After receiving an `Equation` object from the web service, the handler displays the left-hand side of the equation in `equationJLabel` (line 214) and enables the `checkAnswerJButton` so that the user can submit an answer. When the user clicks the **Check Answer** `JButton`, method `checkAnswerJButtonActionPerformed` (lines 180–204) determines whether the user provided the correct answer.

28.9 REST-Based Web Services in ASP.NET

[*Note:* This section assumes you already know ASP.NET (Chapter 25).] In this section, we discuss how to build ASP.NET REST-based web services. Representational State Transfer (REST) (originally proposed in Roy Thomas Fielding's doctoral dissertation[1]) refers to an architectural style for implementing web services. Though REST is not a standard, RESTful web services are implemented using web standards, such as HTTP, XML and JSON. Each operation in a RESTful web service is easily identified by a unique URL. So, when the server receives a request, it immediately knows what operation to perform. Such web services can be invoked from a program or directly from a web browser by entering the URL in the browser's address field. In some cases, the results of a particular operation may be cached locally by the browser. This can make subsequent requests for the same operation faster by loading the result directly from the browser's cache.[2] Many Web 2.0 web services provide RESTful interfaces.[3]

1. Fielding, R. T. "Architectural Styles and the Design of Network-based Software Architectures." `<http://www.ics.uci.edu/~fielding/pubs/dissertation/top.htm>`.
2. Costello, R. "REST Tutorial." *xFront*, 26 June 2002 `<http://www.xfront.com/REST.html>`.
3. Richardson, L. and S. Ruby. *RESTful Web Services.* O'Reilly, 2007.

We use ASP.NET here because it provides a simple way to build REST-based web services. We take advantage of the tools provided in Microsoft's Visual Web Developer 2005 Express, which you can download from `msdn.microsoft.com/vstudio/express`. The example in this section is the web service that we consumed in our `Calendar` application from Fig. 15.11 in the Ajax chapter.

28.9.1 REST-Based Web Service Functionality

Figure 28.23 presents the code-behind file for the `CalendarSevice` web service that you'll build in Section 28.9.2. When creating a web service in Visual Web Developer, you work almost exclusively in the code-behind file. This web service is designed to give the client access to a database of events. A client can access all events that occur on a specific day using the `getItemsByDate` method or request a specific event using the `getItemById` method. In addition, the client can modify an event by calling the `Save` method.

```
' Fig. 28.23 CalendarService.vb
' REST-based event web service.
Imports System.Web
Imports System.Web.Services
Imports System.Web.Services.Protocols
Imports System.Data ' Used to access a database
Imports System.Web.Script.Serialization ' Used to return JSON

<WebService(Namespace:="http://www.deitel.com/")> _
<WebServiceBinding(ConformsTo:=WsiProfiles.BasicProfile1_1)> _
<Global.Microsoft.VisualBasic.CompilerServices.DesignerGenerated()> _
Public Class CalendarService
   Inherits System.Web.Services.WebService

   ' variables used to access the database
   Private calendarDataSet As New CalendarDataSet()
   Private eventsTableAdapter As _
      New CalendarDataSetTableAdapters.EventsTableAdapter()

   ' retrieve the event from the database given an id
   <WebMethod(Description:="Gets a list of events for a given id.")> _
   Public Sub getItemById(ByVal id As Integer)
      ' set up the data set
      eventsTableAdapter.FillById(calendarDataSet.Events, id)

      ' insert the data into an Item object.
      Dim identification As String = calendarDataSet.Events(0).ID
      Dim description As String = calendarDataSet.Events(0).Description
      Dim itemObject As New Item(identification, description)

      ' convert the data to JSON and send it back to the client
      Dim serializer As JavaScriptSerializer = New JavaScriptSerializer()
      Dim response As String = serializer.Serialize(itemObject)
      HttpContext.Current.Response.Write(response) ' send to client
   End Sub ' getItemById

```

Fig. 28.23 | REST-based event web service. (Part 1 of 2.)

```
37      ' retrieve the list of events that occur on a specific date
38      <WebMethod(Description:="Gets a list of events for a given date.")> _
39      Public Sub getItemsByDate(ByVal eventDate As String)
40         eventsTableAdapter.FillByDate(calendarDataSet.Events, eventDate)
41         Dim identification As String ' string used to store the id
42         Dim description As String ' string used to store the description
43         Dim eventRow As DataRow ' used to iterate over the DataSet
44         Dim length As Integer = calendarDataSet.Events.Rows.Count
45         Dim itemObject As = New Item(0 To length - 1) {} ' initialize array
46         Dim count As Integer = 0
47
48         ' insert the data into an array of Item objects
49         For Each eventRow In calendarDataSet.Events.Rows
50            identification = eventRow.Item("ID")
51            description = eventRow.Item("Description")
52            itemObject(count) = New Item(identification, description)
53            count += 1
54         Next
55
56         ' convert the data to JSON and send it back to the client
57         Dim serializer As New JavaScriptSerializer()
58         Dim response As String = serializer.Serialize(itemObject)
59         HttpContext.Current.Response.Write(response)
60      End Sub ' getItemsByDate
61
62      ' modify the description of the event with the given id
63      <WebMethod(Description:="Updates an event's description.")> _
64      Public Sub Save(ByVal id As String, ByVal descr As String)
65         eventsTableAdapter.UpdateDescription(descr, id)
66         getItemById(id)
67      End Sub ' Save
68   End Class ' CalendarService
```

Fig. 28.23 | REST-based event web service. (Part 2 of 2.)

Lines 3–7 import all the necessary libraries for b. Lines 3–5 are generated by Visual Web Developer for every web service. Line 6 enables us to use capabilities for interacting with databases. Line 7 imports the `System.Web.Script.Serialization` namespace, which provides tools to convert .NET objects into JSON strings.

Line 9 contains a **`WebService`** attribute. Attaching this attribute to a web service class indicates that the class implements a web service and allows you to specify the web service's namespace. We specify `http://www.deitel.com` as the web service's namespace using the `WebService` attribute's **`Namespace`** property.

Visual Web Developer places line 10 in all newly created web services. This line indicates that the web service conforms to the **Basic Profile 1.1** (**BP 1.1**) developed by the **Web Services Interoperability Organization** (**WS-I**), a group dedicated to promoting interoperability among web services developed on different platforms with different programming languages. BP 1.1 is a document that defines best practices for various aspects of web service creation and consumption (`www.WS-I.org`). Setting the **`WebServiceBinding`** attribute's **`ConformsTo`** property to **`WsiProfiles.BasicProfile1_1`** instructs Visual Web Developer to perform its "behind-the-scenes" work, such as generating WSDL file and the ASMX file (which provides access to the web service) in conformance with the guidelines laid out in BP 1.1. For more information on web services interoperability and the Basic Profile 1.1, visit the WS-I web site at www.ws-i.org.

By default, each new web service class created in Visual Web Developer inherits from class System.Web.Services.WebService (line 13). Although a web service need not do this, class WebService provides members that are useful in determining information about the client and the web service itself. All methods in class CalendarService are tagged with the **WebMethod attribute** (lines 21, 38 and 63), which exposes a method so that it can be called remotely (similar to Java's @WebMethod annotation that you learned earlier in this chapter).

Accessing the Database

Lines 16–18 create the calendarDataSet and eventsTableAdapter objects that are used to access the database. The classes CalendarDataSet and CalendarDataSetTableAdapter.EventsTableAdapter are created for you when you use Visual Web Developer's **DataSet Designer** to add a DataSet to a project. Section 28.9.3 discusses the steps for this.

Our database has one table called Events containing three columns—the numeric ID of an event, the Date on which the event occurs and the event's Description. Line 24 calls the method FillById, which fills the calendarDataSet with results of the query

```
SELECT    ID, Description
FROM      Events
WHERE     (ID = @id)
```

The parameter @id is replaced with the id that was passed from the client, which we pass as an argument to the FillById method. Lines 27–29 store the results of the query in the variable of class Item, which will be defined shortly. An Item object stores the id and the description of an event. The id and description are obtained by accessing the ID and Description values of the first row of the calendarDataSet.

Line 40 calls the method FillByDate which fills the CalendarDataSet with results of the query

```
SELECT   ID, Description
FROM     Events
WHERE    (Date = @date)
```

The parameter @date is replaced with the eventDate that was passed from the client, which we pass as an argument to the FillByDate method. Lines 49–54 iterate over the rows in the calendarDataSet and store the ID and Description values in an array of Items.

Line 65 calls method UpdateDescription which modifies the database with the UPDATE statement.

```
UPDATE   Events
SET      Description = @descr
WHERE    (ID = @id)
```

The parameters @descr and @id are replaced with arguments passed from the client to the updateDescription method.

Responses Formatted as JSON

The web service uses JSON (discussed in Section 15.7) to pass data to the client. To return JSON data, we must first create a class to define objects which will be converted into JSON format. Figure 28.24 defines a simple `Item` class that contains `Description` and `ID` members, and two constructors. The `Description` and `ID` are declared as `Public` members so that `Item` objects can be properly converted to JSON.

Common Programming Error 28.4

Properties and instance variables that are not public will not be serialized as part of an object's JSON representation.

After the `Item` objects have been created and initialized with data from the database, lines 33 and 58 in Fig. 28.23 use the `JavaScriptSerializer`'s `Serialize` method to con-

```
' Fig. 28.24 Item.vb
' A simple class to create objects to be converted into JSON format.
Imports Microsoft.VisualBasic
Public Class Item
   Private descriptionValue As String ' the item's description
   Private idValue As String ' the item's id

   ' Default constructor
   Public Sub New()
   End Sub 'New

   ' constructor that initializes id and description
   Public Sub New(ByVal ident As String, ByVal descr As String)
      id = ident
      description = descr
   End Sub 'New

   ' property that encapsulates the description
   Public Property description() As String
      Get
         Return descriptionValue
      End Get
      Set(ByVal value As String)
         descriptionValue = value
      End Set
   End Property ' description

   ' Property that encapsulates the id
   Public Property id() As String
      Get
         Return idValue
      End Get
      Set(ByVal value As String)
         idValue = value
      End Set
   End Property ' id.
End Class ' Item
```

Fig. 28.24 | A simple class to create objects to be converted into JSON format.

vert the objects into JSON strings. Then, lines 34 and 59 obtain a response object for the current client, using the `Current` property of the `HttpContext` object. Then we use this object to write the newly constructed JSON string as part of the response attribute, initiating the server response to the Ajax application in Fig. 15.11. To learn more about JSON visit our JSON Resource Center at `www.deitel.com/JSON`.

28.9.2 Creating an ASP.NET REST-Based Web Service

We now show you how to create the `CalendarService` web service in Visual Web Developer. In the following steps, you'll create an **ASP.NET Web Service** project that executes on your computer's local IIS web server. Note that when you run this web service on your local computer the Ajax application from Fig. 15.11 can interact with the service only if it is served from your local computer. We discuss this at the end of this section. To create the `CalendarService` web service in Visual Web Developer, perform the following steps:

Step 1: Creating the Project

To begin, use Visual Web Developer create a project of type **ASP.NET Web Service.** Select **File > New Web Site...** to display the **New Web Site** dialog (Fig. 28.25). Select **ASP.NET Web Service** in the **Templates** pane. Select **HTTP** from the **Location** drop-down list to indicate that the files should be placed on a web server. By default, Visual Web Developer indicates that it will place the files on the local machine's IIS web server in a virtual directory named `WebSite` (`http://localhost/WebSite`). Replace the name `WebSite` with `CalendarService` for this example. Next, select **Visual Basic** from the **Language** drop-down list to indicate that you will use Visual Basic to build this web service.

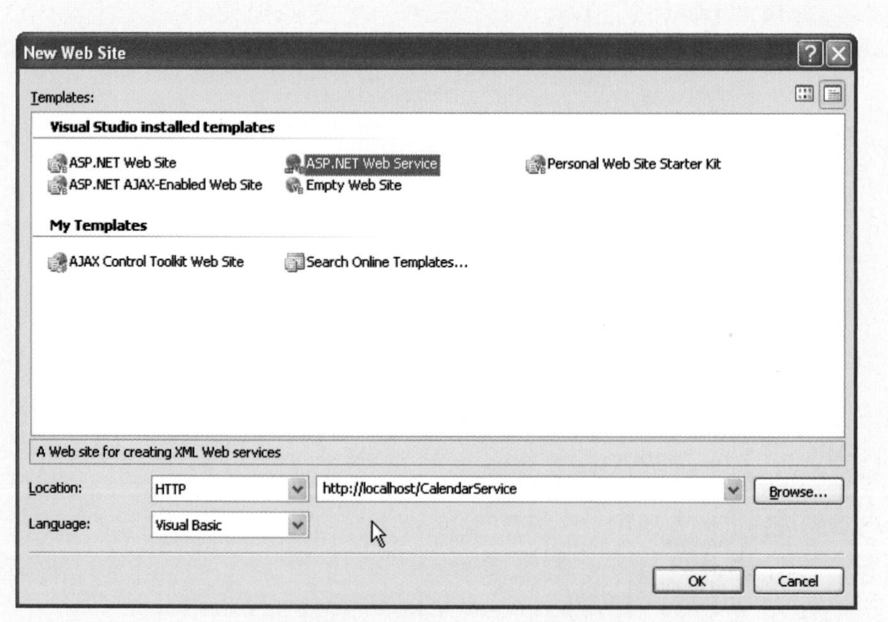

Fig. 28.25 | Creating an **ASP.NET Web Service** in Visual Web Developer

Step 2: Examining the Newly Created Project

After you create the project, you should see the code-behind file `Service.vb`, which contains code for a simple web service (Fig. 28.26). If the code-behind file is not open, it can be opened by double clicking the file in the **App_Code** directory from the **Solution Explorer**. Visual Web Developer includes three `Imports` statements that are helpful for developing web services (lines 1–3). By default, a new code-behind file defines a class named `Service` that is marked with the `WebService` and `WebServiceBinding` attributes (lines 5–6). The class contains a sample web method named `HelloWorld` (lines 11–14). This method is a placeholder that you will replace with your own method(s).

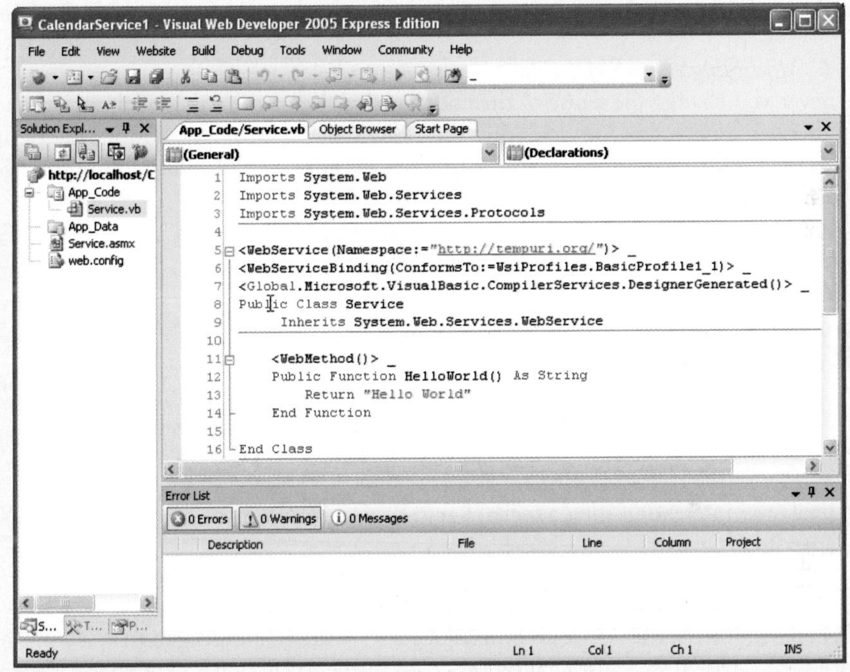

Fig. 28.26 | Code view of a web service.

Step 3: Modifying and Renaming the Code-Behind File

To create the `CalendarService` web service developed in this section, modify `Service.vb` by replacing the sample code provided by Visual Web Developer with the code from the `CalendarService` code-behind file (Fig. 28.23). Then rename the file `CalendarService.vb` (by right clicking the file in the **Solution Explorer** and choosing **Rename**). This code is provided in the examples directory for this chapter. You can download the examples from `www.deitel.com/books/iw3htp4/`.

Step 4 Creating an `Item` Class

Select **File > New File...** to display the **Add New Item** dialog. Select **Class** in the **Templates** pane and change the name of the file to `Item.vb`. Then paste the code for `Item.vb` (Fig. 28.24) into the file.

Step 5: Examining the ASMX File

The **Solution Explorer** lists a `Service.asmx` file in addition to the code-behind file. A web service's ASMX page, when accessed through a web browser, displays information about the web service's methods and provides access to the web service's WSDL information. However, if you open the ASMX file on disk, you will see that it actually contains only

```
<%@ WebService Language="vb" CodeBehind="~/App_Code/Service.vb"
Class="Service" %>
```

to indicate the programming language in which the web service's code-behind file is written, the code-behind file's location and the class that defines the web service. When you request the ASMX page through IIS, ASP.NET uses this information to generate the content displayed in the web browser (i.e., the list of web methods and their descriptions).

Step 6: Modifying the ASMX File

Whenever you change the name of the code-behind file or the name of the class that defines the web service, you must modify the ASMX file accordingly. Thus, after defining class `CalendarService` in the code-behind file `CalendarService.vb`, modify the ASMX file to contain the lines

```
<%@ WebService Language="vb" CodeBehind=
"~/App_Code/CalendarService.vb" Class="CalendarService" %>
```

Error-Prevention Tip 28.1

Update the web service's ASMX file appropriately whenever the name of a web service's code-behind file or the class name changes. Visual Web Developer creates the ASMX file, but does not automatically update it when you make changes to other files in the project.

Step 7: Renaming the ASMX File

The final step in creating the `CalendarService` web service is to rename the ASMX file `CalendarService.asmx`.

Step 8: Changing the `Web.Config` File to allow REST requests.

By default ASP.NET web services communicate with the client using SOAP. To make this service REST-based, we must change `web.config` file to allow REST requests. Open the `web.config` file from the **Solution Explorer** and paste the following code as a new element in the `system.web` element.

```
<webServices>
   <protocols>
      <add name="HttpGet"/>
      <add name="HttpPost"/>
   </protocols>
</webServices>
```

Step 9: Adding the `System.Web.Extensions` Reference

The `JavaScriptSerializer` class that we use to generate JSON strings, is part of the Ajax Extensions package. You can find information on installing and downloading ASP.NET Ajax in Section 25.9. After you have installed ASP.NET Ajax, right click the project name in the solution explorer and select **Add Reference...** to display the **Add Reference** window. Select `System.Web.Extensions` from the **.NET** tab and click **OK**.

28.9.3 Adding Data Components to a Web Service

Next, you'll use Visual Web Developer's tools to configure a `DataSet` that allows our Web service to interact with the `Calendar.mdf` SQL Server 2005 Express database file. You can download `Calendar.mdf` with the rest of the code for this example at `www.deitel.com/books/iw3htp4`. You'll add a new `DataSet` to the project, then configure the `DataSet`'s `TableAdapter` using the **TableAdapter Configuration Wizard**. The wizard allows you to select the data source (`Calendar.mdf`) and to create the SQL statements necessary to support the database operations discussed in Fig. 28.23's description.

Step 1: Adding a **`DataSet`** *to the Project*

Add a `DataSet` named `CalendarDataSet` to the project. Right click the **App_Code** folder in the **Solution Explorer** and select **Add New Item...** from the pop-up menu. In the **Add New Item** dialog, select **DataSet**, specify `CalendarDataSet.xsd` in the **Name** field and click **Add**. This displays the `CalendarDataSet` in design view and opens the **TableAdapter Configuration Wizard**. When you add a `DataSet` to a project, the IDE creates appropriate `TableAdapter` classes for interacting with the database tables.

Step 2: Selecting the Data Source and Creating a Connection

You'll use the **TableAdapter Configuration Wizard** in the next several steps to configure a `TableAdapter` for manipulating the `Events` table in the `Calendar.mdf` database. Now, you must select the database. In the **TableAdapter Configuration Wizard**, click the **New Connection...** button to display the **Add Connection** dialog. In this dialog, specify **Microsoft SQL Server Database File** as the **Data source**, then click the **Browse...** button to display the **Select SQL Server Database File** dialog. Locate `Calendar.mdf` on your computer, select it and click the **Open** button to return to the **Add Connection** dialog. Click the **Test Connection** button to test the database connection, then click **OK** to return to the **TableAdapter Configuration Wizard**. Click **Next >**, then click **Yes** when you are asked whether you would like to add the file to your project and modify the connection. Click **Next >** to save the connection string in the application configuration file.

Step 3: Opening the **Query Builder** *and Adding the* **`Events`** *Table from* **`Calendar.mdf`**

You must specify how the `TableAdapter` will access the database. In this example, you'll use SQL statements, so choose **Use SQL Statements**, then click **Next >**. Click **Query Builder...** to display the **Query Builder** and **Add Table** dialogs. Before building a SQL query, you must specify the table(s) to use in the query. The `Calendar.mdf` database contains only one table, named `Events`. Select this table from the **Tables** tab and click **Add**. Click **Close** to close the **Add Table** dialog.

Step 4: Configuring a **SELECT** *Query to Obtain a Specific Event*

Now let's create a query which selects an event with a particular `ID`. Select **ID** and **Description** from the **Events** table at the top of the **Query Builder** dialog. Next, specify the criteria for selecting seats. In the **Filter** column of the **ID** row specify `=@id` to indicate that this filter value also will be specified as a method argument. The **Query Builder** dialog should now appear as shown in Fig. 28.27. Click **OK** to close the **Query Builder** dialog. Click **Next >** to choose the names of the methods to generate. Name the `Fill` method `FillById`. Click the **Finish** button to generate this method.

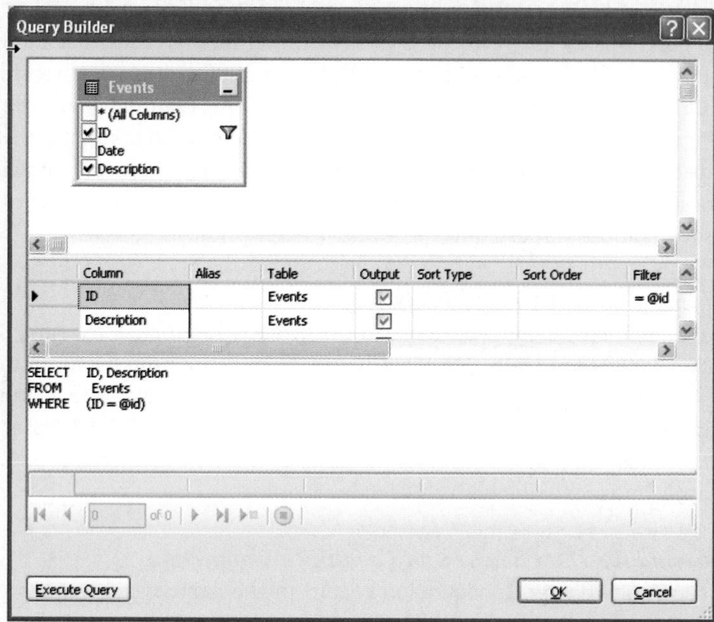

Fig. 28.27 | **QueryBuilder** dialog specifying a `SELECT` query that selects an event with a specific ID.

Step 5: Adding Another Query to the `EventsTableAdapter` *for the* `CalendarDataSet`

Now, you'll create an `UPDATE` query that modifies a description of a specific event. In the design area for the `CalendarDataSet`, click **EventsTableAdapter** to select it, then right click it and select **Add Query...** to display the **TableAdapter Query Configuration Wizard**. Select **Use SQL Statements** and click **Next >**. Select **Update** as the query type and click **Next >**. Clear the text field and click **Query Builder...** to display the **Query Builder** and **Add Table** dialogs. Then add the `Events` table as you did in *Step 3* and click **Close** to return to the **Query Builder** dialog.

Step 6: Configuring an `UPDATE` *Statement to Modify a Description of a Specific Event*

In the **Query Builder** dialog, select the **Description** column from the **Events** table at the top of the dialog. In the middle of the dialog, place the `@descr` in the **New Value** column for the **Description** row to indicate that the new description will be specified as an argument to the method that implements this query. In the row below **Description**, select **ID** and specify `@id` as the **Filter** value to indicate that the `ID` will be specified as an argument to the method that implements this query. The **Query Builder** dialog should now appear as shown in Fig. 28.28. Click **OK** to return to the **TableAdapter Query Configuration Wizard**. Then click **Next >** to choose the name of the update method. Name the method `UpdateDescription`, then click **Finish** to close the **TableAdapter Query Configuration Wizard**.

Step 7: Adding a `getItemsByDate` *Query*

Using similar techniques to *Steps 5–6*, add a query that selects all events that have a specified date. Name the query `FillByDate`.

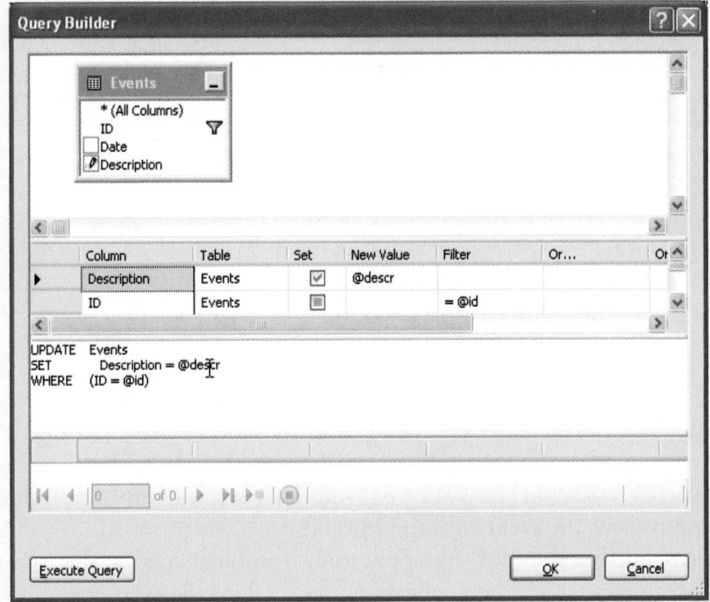

Fig. 28.28 | **QueryBuilder** specifying an UPDATE statement used to modify a description.

Step 8: Testing the Web Service

At this point, you can use the `CalendarService.asmx` page to test the web service's methods. To do so, select **Start Without Debugging** from the **Debug** menu. Figure 28.29 shows the test page that is displayed for this web service when you run the web service application.

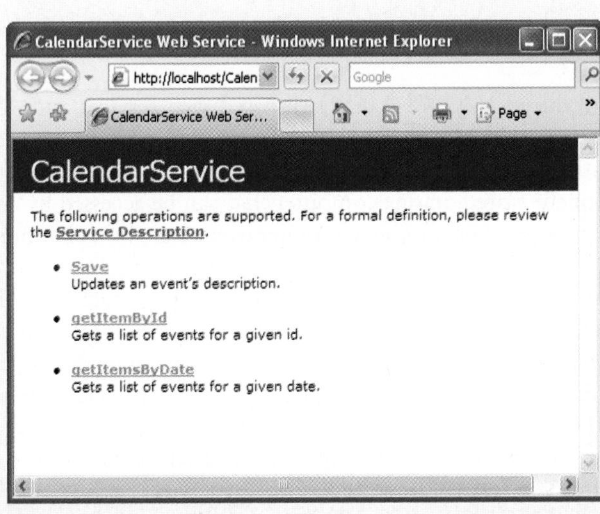

Fig. 28.29 | The test page for the `CalendarService` web service. (Part 1 of 2.)

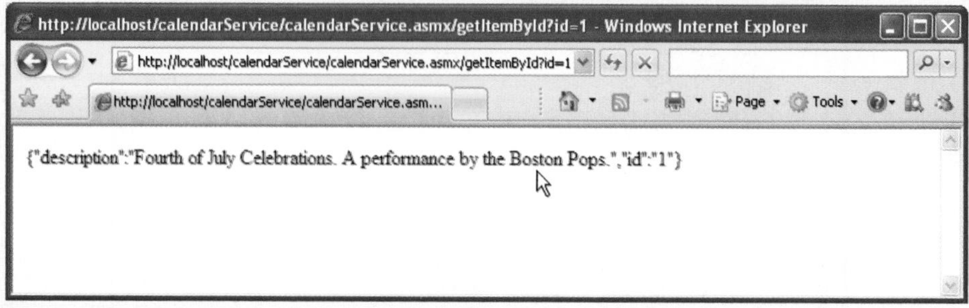

Fig. 28.29 | The test page for the `CalendarService` web service. (Part 2 of 2.)

Calling a REST-based web service is simpler than calling SOAP web services demonstrated earlier. Fig. 28.29 shows that you can invoke the web service directly from your browser. For example, if you type the URL `http://localhost/calendarService/calendarService.asmx/getItemById?id=1` the browser will invoke the method `getItemById` and retrieve the event with the `id` value `1`.

The client side interface for this application is implemented in the Ajax chapter, in Fig 15.11. Because our Calendar application uses the Dojo Toolkit, you must have Dojo installed on your computer. Download Dojo 0.4.3 from `dojotoolkit.org/downloads`, extract the Dojo directory and rename it to `dojo043`. Then place the `CalendarService` folder that contains your web service, the `dojo043` folder that contains the Dojo toolkit and the `Calendar.html` file in the same directory in the root directory of your web server.

Run the web service and direct your browser to the location of the `Calendar.html` file. We populated the database only with events for July 2007, so the calendar is coded to always display July 2007 when the application is loaded. To test whether the web service works click a few dates like the fourth of July, the sixth of July or the twentieth of July for which events exist in the Calendar database

28.10 Wrap-Up

This chapter introduced JAX-WS 2.0 SOAP-based web services and ASP.NET REST-based web services. You learned that web services promote software portability and reusability in applications that operate over the Internet. You also learned that a web service is a software component stored on one computer that can be accessed by an application (or other software component) on another computer over a network, communicating via such technologies as XML, SOAP and HTTP. We discussed several benefits of this kind of distributed computing—e.g., clients can access data on remote machines, clients lacking the processing power to perform specific computations can leverage remote machines' resources and entirely new types of innovative applications can be developed.

We explained how Netbeans and the JAX-WS 2.0 APIs facilitate the creation and consumption of JAX-WS web services. We showed how to set up projects and files in these tools and how the tools manage the web service infrastructure necessary to support the web services you create. You learned how to define web services and web methods, as well as how to consume them both from Java desktop applications and from web applications created in Netbeans. After explaining the mechanics of web services with our `HugeInteger` example, we demonstrated more sophisticated web services that use session tracking in both the server side and the client side, and web services that access databases using JDBC. We also explained XML serialization and showed how to pass objects of user-defined types to web services and return them from web services. Finally, we discussed how to build a REST-based web service in ASP.NET with Microsoft's Visual Web Developer Express.

28.11 Web Resources

`www.deitel.com/WebServices/`
Visit our Web Services Resource Center for information on designing and implementing web services in many languages, and information about web services offered by companies such as Google, Amazon and eBay. You'll also find many additional Java tools for publishing and consuming web services.

`www.deitel.com/java/`
`www.deitel.com/JavaSE6Mustang/`
`www.deitel.com/JavaEE5/`
`www.deitel.com/JavaCertification/`
`www.deitel.com/JavaDesignPatterns/`
Our Java Resource Centers provide Java-specific information, such as books, papers, articles, journals, websites and blogs that cover a broad range of Java topics (including Java web services).

`www.deitel.com/ResourceCenters.html`
Check out our growing list of Resource Centers on programming, Web 2.0, software and other interesting topics.

`java.sun.com/webservices/jaxws/index.jsp`
The official site for the Sun Java API for XML Web Services (JAX-WS). Includes the API, documentation, tutorials and other useful links.

`www.webservices.org`
Provides industry-related news, articles and resources for web services.

`www-130.ibm.com/developerworks/webservices`
IBM's site for service-oriented architecture (SOA) and web services includes articles, downloads, demos and discussion forums regarding web services technology.

`www.w3.org/TR/wsdl`
Provides extensive documentation on WSDL, including a thorough discussion of web services and related technologies such as XML, SOAP, HTTP and MIME types in the context of WSDL.

`www.w3.org/TR/soap`
Provides extensive documentation on SOAP messages, using SOAP with HTTP and SOAP security issues.

`www.ws-i.org`
The Web Services Interoperability Organization's website provides detailed information regarding building web services based on standards that promote interoperability and true platform independence.

`webservices.xml.com/security`
Articles about web services security and standard security protocols.

REST-Based Web Services

`en.wikipedia.org/wiki/REST`
Wikipedia resource explaining Representational State Transfer (REST).

`www.xfront.com/REST-Web-Services.html`
Article entitled "Building Web Services the REST Way."

`www.ics.uci.edu/~fielding/pubs/dissertation/rest_arch_style.htm`
The dissertation that originally proposed the concept of REST-based services.

`rest.blueoxen.net/cgi-bin/wiki.pl?ShortSummaryOfRest`
A short introduction to REST.

`www.prescod.net/rest`
Links to many REST resources.

Summary

Section 28.1 Introduction

- A web service is a software component stored on one computer that can be accessed via method calls by an application (or other software component) on another computer over a network.
- Web services communicate using such technologies as XML and HTTP.
- The Simple Object Access Protocol (SOAP) is an XML-based protocol that allows web services and clients to communicate in a platform-independent manner.
- Web services enable businesses to conduct transactions via standardized, widely available web services rather than relying on proprietary applications.
- Companies such as Amazon, Google, eBay, PayPal and many others are using web services to their advantage by making their server-side applications available to partners via web services.
- By purchasing web services and using extensive free web services, companies can spend less time developing new applications and can create innovative new applications.
- Netbeans is one of the many tools that enable programmers to "publish" and/or "consume" web services.

Section 28.2 Java Web Services Basics

- The computer on which a web service resides is referred to as a remote machine or server. A client application that accesses a web service sends a method call over a network to the remote machine, which processes the call and returns a response over the network to the application.
- In Java, a web service is implemented as a class. The class that represents the web service resides on a server—it's not part of the client application.
- Making a web service available to receive client requests is known as publishing a web service; using a web service from a client application is known as consuming a web service.
- An application that consumes a web service consists of two parts—an object of a proxy class for interacting with the web service and a client application that consumes the web service by invoking methods on the proxy object. The proxy object handles the details of communicating with the web service on the client's behalf.
- Requests to and responses from web services created with JAX-WS 2.0 are typically transmitted via SOAP. Any client capable of generating and processing SOAP messages can interact with a web service, regardless of the language in which the web service is written.

Section 28.3.1 Creating a Web Application Project and Adding a Web Service Class in Netbeans

- When you create a web service in Netbeans, you focus on the logic of the web service and let the IDE handle the web service's infrastructure.
- To create a web service in Netbeans, you first create a project of type **Web Application**. Netbeans uses this project type for web applications that execute in browser-based clients and for web services that are invoked by other applications.

- When you create a **Web Application** in Netbeans, the IDE generates additional files that support the web application.

Section 28.3.2 Defining the `HugeInteger` Web Service in Netbeans

- By default, each new web service class created with the JAX-WS APIs is a POJO (plain old Java object)—you do not need to extend a class or implement an interface to create a web service.
- When you compile a class that uses these JAX-WS 2.0 annotations, the compiler creates the compiled code framework that allows the web service to wait for and respond to client requests.
- The `@WebService` annotation indicates that a class represents a web service. Optional element `name` specifies the name of the proxy class that will be generated for the client. Optional element `serviceName` specifies the name of the class that the client uses to obtain a proxy object.
- Netbeans places the `@WebService` annotation at the beginning of each new web service class you create. You can add the optional `name` and `serviceName` elements in the annotation's parentheses.
- Methods that are tagged with the `@WebMethod` annotation can be called remotely.
- Methods that are not tagged with `@WebMethod` are not accessible to clients that consume the web service. Such methods are typically utility methods within the web service class.
- The `@WebMethod` annotation has an optional `operationName` element to specify the method name that is exposed to the web service's client.
- Parameters of web methods are annotated with the `@WebParam` annotation. The optional element `name` indicates the parameter name that is exposed to the web service's clients.

Section 28.3.3 Publishing the `HugeInteger` Web Service from Netbeans

- Netbeans handles all the details of building and deploying a web service for you. This includes creating the framework required to support the web service.
- To determine if there are any compilation errors in your project, right click the project name in the Netbeans **Projects** tab, then select the **Build Project** option.
- Select **Deploy Project** to deploy the project to the server you selected during application setup.
- Select **Run Project** to execute the web application.
- Both the **Deploy Project** and **Run Project** options also build the project if it has changed and start the application server if it is not already running.
- To ensure that all source-code files in a project are recompiled during the next build operation, you can use the **Clean Project** or **Clean and Build Project** options.

Section 28.3.4 Testing the `HugeInteger` Web Service with Sun Java System Application Server's `Tester` Web Page

- Sun Java System Application Server can dynamically create a `Tester` web page for testing a web service's methods from a web browser. You can enable this feature via the project's **Run** options.
- To display the `Tester` web page, run the web application from Netbeans or type the URL of the web service in the browser's address field followed by `?Tester`.
- A client can access a web service only when the application server is running. If Netbeans launches the application server for you, the server will shut down when you close Netbeans. To keep the application server up and running, you can launch it independently of Netbeans.

Section 28.3.5 Describing a Web Service with the Web Service Description Language (WSDL)

- To consume a web service, a client must know where to find the web service and must be provided with the web service's description.

- JAX-WS uses the Web Service Description Language (WSDL)—a standard XML vocabulary for describing web services in a platform-independent manner.
- You do not need to understand WSDL to take advantage of it—the server generates a web service's WSDL dynamically for you, and client tools can parse the WSDL to help create the client-side proxy class that a client uses to access the web service.
- Since the WSDL is created dynamically, clients always receive a deployed web service's most up-to-date description.
- To view the WSDL for a web service, type its URL in the browser's address field followed by `?WSDL` or click the **WSDL File** link in the Sun Java System Application Server's `Tester` web page.

Section 28.4 Consuming a Web Service

- A web service client can be any type of application or even another web service.
- In Netbeans, you enable a client application to consume a web service by adding a web service reference to the application, which defines the client-side proxy class.

Section 28.4.1 Creating a Client in Netbeans to Consume the `HugeInteger` *Web Service*

- When you add a web service reference, the IDE creates and compiles the client-side artifacts—the framework of Java code that supports the client-side proxy class.
- The client calls methods on a proxy object, which uses the client-side artifacts to interact with the web service.
- To add a web service reference, right click the client project name in the Netbeans **Projects** tab, then select **New > Web Service Client…**. In the dialog's **WSDL URL** field, specify the URL of the web service's WSDL.
- Netbeans uses the WSDL description to generate the client-side proxy class and artifacts.
- When you specify the web service you want to consume, Netbeans copies the web service's WSDL into a file in your project. You can view this file from the Netbeans **Files** tab by expanding the nodes in the project's `xml-resources` folder.
- The client-side artifacts and the client's copy of the WSDL file can be regenerated by right clicking the web service's node in the Netbeans **Projects** tab and selecting **Refresh Client**.
- You can view the IDE-generated client-side artifacts by selecting the Netbeans **Files** tab and expanding the project's `build` folder.

Section 28.5 SOAP

- SOAP is a commonly used, platform-independent, XML-based protocol that facilitates remote procedure calls, typically over HTTP.
- The protocol that transmits request-and-response messages is also known as the web service's wire format or wire protocol, because it defines how information is sent "along the wire."
- Each request and response is packaged in a SOAP message (also known as a SOAP envelope) containing the information that a web service requires to process the message.
- The wire format used to transmit requests and responses must support all types passed between the applications. SOAP supports primitive types and their wrapper types, as well as `Date`, `Time` and others. SOAP can also transmit arrays and objects of user-defined types.
- When a program invokes a web method, the request and all relevant information are packaged in a SOAP message and sent to the server on which the web service resides. The web service processes the SOAP message's contents, which specify the method to invoke and its arguments. After the web service receives and parses a request, the proper method is called, and the response is sent

back to the client in another SOAP message. The client-side proxy parses the response, which contains the result of the method call, and returns the result to the client application.

- The SOAP messages are generated for you automatically. So you don't need to understand the details of SOAP or XML to take advantage of it when publishing and consuming web services.

Section 28.6 Session Tracking in Web Services

- Storing session information also enables a web service to distinguish between clients and eliminates the need to pass client information between the client and the web service multiple times.

Section 28.6.1 Creating a `Blackjack` Web Service

- To use session tracking in a web service, you must include code for the resources that maintain the session state information. In the past, you had to write the sometimes tedious code to create these resources. JAX-WS, however, handles this for you via the `@Resource` annotation. This annotation enables tools like Netbeans to "inject" complex support code into your class, thus allowing you to focus on your business logic rather than the support code.
- Using annotations to add code that supports your classes is known as dependency injection. Annotations like `@WebService`, `@WebMethod` and `@WebParam` also perform dependency injection.
- A `WebServiceContext` object enables a web service to access and maintain information for a specific request, such as session state. The code that creates a `WebServiceContext` object is injected into the class by an `@Resource` annotation.
- The `WebServiceContext` object is used to obtain a `MessageContext` object. A web service uses a `MessageContext` to obtain an `HttpSession` object for the current client.
- The `MessageContext` object's `get` method is used to obtain the `HttpSession` object for the current client. Method `get` receives a constant indicating what to get from the `MessageContext`. The constant `MessageContext.SERVLET_REQUEST` indicates that we'd like to get the `HttpServletRequest` object for the current client. We then call method `getSession` to get the `HttpSession` object from the `HttpServletRequest` object.
- `HttpSession` method `getAttribute` receives a `String` that identifies the `Object` to obtain from the session state.

Section 28.6.2 Consuming the `Blackjack` Web Service

- In the JAX-WS 2.0 framework, the client must indicate whether it wants to allow the web service to maintain session information. To do this, first cast the proxy object to interface type `BindingProvider`. A `BindingProvider` enables the client to manipulate the request information that will be sent to the server. This information is stored in an object that implements interface `RequestContext`. The `BindingProvider` and `RequestContext` are part of the framework that is created by the IDE when you add a web service client to the application.
- Next, invoke the `BindingProvider`'s `getRequestContext` method to obtain the `RequestContext` object. Then call the `RequestContext`'s `put` method to set the property `BindingProvider.SESSION_MAINTAIN_PROPERTY` to `true`, which enables session tracking from the client side so that the web service knows which client is invoking the service's web methods.

Section 28.8 Passing an Object of a User-Defined Type to a Web Service

- Web services can receive and return objects of user-defined types—known as custom types.
- Custom types that are sent to or from a web service using SOAP are serialized into XML format. This process is referred to as XML serialization and is handled for you automatically.
- A class that is used to specify parameter or return types in web methods must provide a `public` default or no-argument constructor. Also, any instance variables that should be serialized must have `public` *set* and *get* methods or the instance variables must be declared `public`.

- Any instance variable that is not serialized simply receives its default value (or the value provided by the no-argument constructor) when an object of the class is deserialized.

Terminology

`AbstractPageBean` class
adding a web service reference to a project in Netbeans
Apache Tomcat server
application server
B2B (business-to-business) transactions
BEA Weblogic Server
`BindingProvider` interface
Build Project option in Netbeans
business-to-business (B2B) transactions
Clean and Build Project option in Netbeans
Clean Project option in Netbeans
client-side artifacts
consume a web service
custom type
dependency injection
Deploy Project option in Netbeans
deploy a web service
`get` method of interface `MessageContext`
`getRequestContext` method of interface `BindingProvider`
GlassFish server
JAX-WS 2.0
JBoss Application Server
`MessageContext` interface
Netbeans 5.5 IDE
New Project dialog in Netbeans
New Web Service Client dialog in Netbeans
New Web Service dialog in Netbeans
parse a SOAP message
POJO (plain old Java object)
Project Properties dialog in Netbeans
proxy class for a web service
proxy object handles the details of communicating with the web service
publish a web service
`put` method of interface `RequestContext`
remote machine
Representational State Transfer (REST)
`RequestContext` interface
`@Resource` annotation
REST (Representational State Transfer)
Run Project option in Netbeans
server-side artifacts
session tracking in web services
SOAP envelope
SOAP message
SOAP (Simple Object Access Protocol)
Sun Java System Application Server
Sun Java System Application Server `Tester` web page
test a web service
Web Application project in Netbeans
Web Service Description Language (WSDL)
web service reference
Web Services Interoperability Organization (WS-I)
`@WebMethod` annotation
`@WebMethod` annotation `operationName` element
`@WebParam` annotation
`@WebParam` annotation `name` element
`@WebService` annotation
`@WebService` annotation `name` element
`@WebService` annotation `serviceName` element
`WebServiceContext` interface
wire format
wire protocol
WS-I Basic Profile 1.1 (BP 1.1)
XML serialization

Self-Review Exercises

28.1 State whether each of the following is *true* or *false*. If *false*, explain why.

a) All methods of a web service class can be invoked by clients of that web service.
b) When consuming a web service in a client application created in Netbeans, you must create the proxy class that enables the client to communicate with the web service.
c) A proxy class communicating with a web service normally uses SOAP to send and receive messages.
d) Session tracking is automatically enabled in a client of a web service.
e) Web methods cannot be declared `static`.

f) A user-defined type used in a web service must define both *get* and *set* methods for any property that will be serialized.
g) RESTful web services are implemented using web standards, such as HTTP, XML and JSON.

28.2 Fill in the blanks for each of the following statements:
a) When messages are sent between an application and a web service using SOAP, each message is placed in a(n) ________.
b) ________ refers to an architectural style for implementing web services.
c) A web service in Java is a(n) ________—it does not need to implement any interfaces or extend any classes.
d) Web service requests are typically transported over the Internet via the ________ protocol.
e) To set the exposed name of a web method, use the ________ element of the `@WebMethod` annotation.
f) ________ transforms an object into a format that can be sent between a web service and a client.

Answers to Self-Review Exercises

28.1 a) False. Only methods declared with the `@WebMethod` annotation can be invoked by a web service's clients. b) False. The proxy class is created by Netbeans when you add a web service client to the application. c) True. d) False. In the JAX-WS 2.0 framework, the client must indicate whether it wants to allow the web service to maintain session information. First, you must cast the proxy object to interface type `BindingProvider`, then use the `BindingProvider`'s `getRequestContext` method to obtain the `RequestContext` object. Finally, you must use the `RequestContext`'s `put` method to set the property `BindingProvider.SESSION_MAINTAIN_PROPERTY` to `true`. e) True. f) False. You may also declare an instance variable as `public`. g) true.

28.2 a) SOAP message or SOAP envelope. b) Representational State Transfer (REST). c) POJO (plain old Java object) d) HTTP. e) `operationName`. f) XML serialization.

Exercises

28.3 *(Phone Book Web Service)* Create a web service that stores phone book entries in the database `PhoneBookDB` and a web client application that consumes this service. Use the steps in Section 28.7.1 to create the `PhoneBook` database. The database should contain one table—`PhoneBook`—with three columns—`LastName`, `FirstName` and `PhoneNumber`—each of type `VARCHAR`. The `LastName` and `FirstName` columns should store up to 30 characters. The `PhoneNumber` column should support phone numbers of the form `(800) 555-1212` that contain 14 characters.

Give the client user the capability to enter a new contact (web method `addEntry`) and to find contacts by last name (web method `getEntries`). Pass only `String`s as arguments to the web service. The `getEntries` web method should return an array of `String`s that contains the matching phone book entries. Each `String` in the array should consist of the last name, first name and phone number for one phone book entry. These values should be separated by commas.

The `SELECT` query that will find a `PhoneBook` entry by last name should be:

```
SELECT LastName, FirstName, PhoneNumber
FROM PhoneBook
WHERE (LastName = LastName)
```

The `INSERT` statement that inserts a new entry into the `PhoneBook` database should be:

```
INSERT INTO PhoneBook (LastName, FirstName, PhoneNumber)
VALUES (LastName, FirstName, PhoneNumber)
```

28.4 *(Phone Book Web Service Modification)* Modify Exercise 28.3 so that it uses a class named `PhoneBookEntry` to represent a row in the database. The client application should provide objects of type `PhoneBookEntry` to the web service when adding contacts and should receive objects of type `PhoneBookEntry` when searching for contacts.

28.5 *(Blackjack Web Service Modification)* Modify the blackjack web service example in Section 28.6 to include class `Card`. Modify web method `dealCard` so that it returns an object of type `Card` and modify web method `getHandValue` so that it receives an array of `Card` objects from the client. Also modify the client application to keep track of what cards have been dealt by using `ArrayLists` of `Card` objects. The proxy class created by Netbeans will treat a web method's array parameter as a `List`, so you can pass these `ArrayLists` of `Card` objects directly to the `getHandValue` method. Your `Card` class should include *set* and *get* methods for the face and suit of the card.

5 PART

Appendices

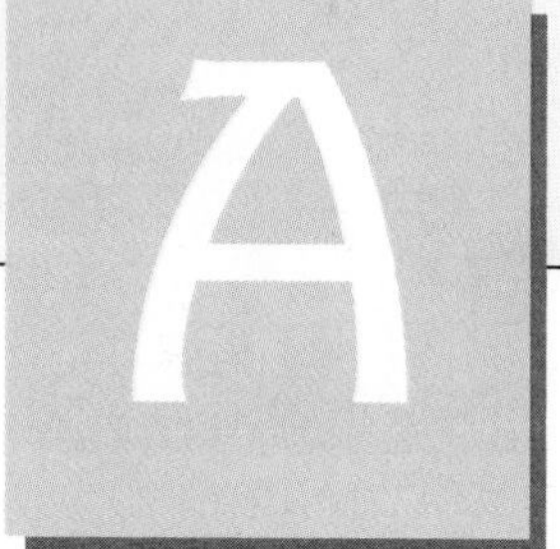

XHTML Special Characters

The table of Fig. A.1 shows many commonly used XHTML special characters—called **character entity references** by the World Wide Web Consortium. For a complete list of character entity references, see the site `www.w3.org/TR/REC-html40/sgml/entities.html`.

Character	XHTML encoding	Character	XHTML encoding
non-breaking space		ê	ê
§	§	ì	ì
©	©	í	í
®	®	î	î
π	¼	ñ	ñ
∫	½	ò	ò
Ω	¾	ó	ó
à	à	ô	ô
á	á	õ	õ
â	â	÷	÷
ã	ã	ù	ù
å	å	ú	ú
ç	ç	û	û
è	è	•	•
é	é	™	™

Fig. A.1 | XHTML special characters.

B

XHTML Colors

Colors may be specified by using a standard name (such as aqua) or a hexadecimal RGB value (such as #00FFFF for aqua). Of the six hexadecimal digits in an RGB value, the first two represent the amount of red in the color, the middle two represent the amount of green in the color, and the last two represent the amount of blue in the color. For example, black is the absence of color and is defined by #000000, whereas white is the maximum amount of red, green and blue and is defined by #FFFFFF. Pure red is #FF0000, pure green (which the standard calls lime) is #00FF00 and pure blue is #00FFFF. Note that green in the standard is defined as #008000. Figure B.1 contains the XHTML standard color set. Figure B.2 contains the XHTML extended color set.

Color name	Value	Color name	Value
aqua	#00FFFF	navy	#000080
black	#000000	olive	#808000
blue	#0000FF	purple	#800080
fuchsia	#FF00FF	red	#FF0000
gray	#808080	silver	#C0C0C0
green	#008000	teal	#008080
lime	#00FF00	yellow	#FFFF00
maroon	#800000	white	#FFFFFF

Fig. B.1 | XHTML standard colors and hexadecimal RGB values.

Color name	Value	Color name	Value
aliceblue	#F0F8FF	dodgerblue	#1E90FF
antiquewhite	#FAEBD7	firebrick	#B22222
aquamarine	#7FFFD4	floralwhite	#FFFAF0
azure	#F0FFFF	forestgreen	#228B22
beige	#F5F5DC	gainsboro	#DCDCDC
bisque	#FFE4C4	ghostwhite	#F8F8FF
blanchedalmond	#FFEBCD	gold	#FFD700
blueviolet	#8A2BE2	goldenrod	#DAA520
brown	#A52A2A	greenyellow	#ADFF2F
burlywood	#DEB887	honeydew	#F0FFF0
cadetblue	#5F9EA0	hotpink	#FF69B4
chartreuse	#7FFF00	indianred	#CD5C5C
chocolate	#D2691E	indigo	#4B0082
coral	#FF7F50	ivory	#FFFFF0
cornflowerblue	#6495ED	khaki	#F0E68C
cornsilk	#FFF8DC	lavender	#E6E6FA
crimson	#DC143C	lavenderblush	#FFF0F5
cyan	#00FFFF	lawngreen	#7CFC00
darkblue	#00008B	lemonchiffon	#FFFACD
darkcyan	#008B8B	lightblue	#ADD8E6
darkgoldenrod	#B8860B	lightcoral	#F08080
darkgray	#A9A9A9	lightcyan	#E0FFFF
darkgreen	#006400	lightgoldenrodyellow	#FAFAD2
darkkhaki	#BDB76B	lightgreen	#90EE90
darkmagenta	#8B008B	lightgrey	#D3D3D3
darkolivegreen	#556B2F	lightpink	#FFB6C1
darkorange	#FF8C00	lightsalmon	#FFA07A
darkorchid	#9932CC	lightseagreen	#20B2AA
darkred	#8B0000	lightskyblue	#87CEFA
darksalmon	#E9967A	lightslategray	#778899
darkseagreen	#8FBC8F	lightsteelblue	#B0C4DE
darkslateblue	#483D8B	lightyellow	#FFFFE0
darkslategray	#2F4F4F	limegreen	#32CD32
darkturquoise	#00CED1	linen	#FAF0E6
darkviolet	#9400D3	magenta	#FF00FF
deeppink	#FF1493	mediumaquamarine	#66CDAA
deepskyblue	#00BFFF	mediumblue	#0000CD
dimgray	#696969	mediumorchid	#BA55D3

Fig. B.2 | XHTML extended colors and hexadecimal RGB values. (Part 1 of 2.)

Color name	Value	Color name	Value
mediumpurple	#9370DB	plum	#DDA0DD
mediumseagreen	#3CB371	powderblue	#B0E0E6
mediumslateblue	#7B68EE	rosybrown	#BC8F8F
mediumspringgreen	#00FA9A	royalblue	#4169E1
mediumturquoise	#48D1CC	saddlebrown	#8B4513
mediumvioletred	#C71585	salmon	#FA8072
midnightblue	#191970	sandybrown	#F4A460
mintcream	#F5FFFA	seagreen	#2E8B57
mistyrose	#FFE4E1	seashell	#FFF5EE
moccasin	#FFE4B5	sienna	#A0522D
navajowhite	#FFDEAD	skyblue	#87CEEB
oldlace	#FDF5E6	slateblue	#6A5ACD
olivedrab	#6B8E23	slategray	#708090
orange	#FFA500	snow	#FFFAFA
orangered	#FF4500	springgreen	#00FF7F
orchid	#DA70D6	steelblue	#4682B4
palegoldenrod	#EEE8AA	tan	#D2B48C
palegreen	#98FB98	thistle	#D8BFD8
paleturquoise	#AFEEEE	tomato	#FF6347
palevioletred	#DB7093	turquoise	#40E0D0
papayawhip	#FFEFD5	violet	#EE82EE
peachpuff	#FFDAB9	wheat	#F5DEB3
peru	#CD853F	whitesmoke	#F5F5F5
pink	#FFC0CB	yellowgreen	#9ACD32

Fig. B.2 | XHTML extended colors and hexadecimal RGB values. (Part 2 of 2.)

JavaScript Operator Precedence Chart

This appendix contains the operator precedence chart for JavaScript/ECMAScript (Fig. C.1). The operators are shown in decreasing order of precedence from top to bottom.

Operator	Type	Associativity
`.`	member access	left to right
`[]`	array indexing	
`()`	function calls	
`++`	increment	right to left
`--`	decrement	
`-`	unary minus	
`~`	bitwise complement	
`!`	logical NOT	
`delete`	deletes an array element or object property	
`new`	creates a new object	
`typeof`	returns the data type of its argument	
`void`	prevents an expression from returning a value	
`*`	multiplication	left to right
`/`	division	
`%`	modulus	

Fig. C.1 | JavaScript/ECMAScript operator precedence and associativity. (Part 1 of 2.)

Operator	Type	Associativity
+	addition	left to right
-	subtraction	
+	string concatenation	
<<	left shift	left to right
>>	right shift with sign extension	
>>>	right shift with zero extension	
<	less than	left to right
<=	less than or equal	
>	greater than	
>=	greater than or equal	
instanceof	type comparison	
==	equality	left to right
!=	inequality	
===	identity	
!==	nonidentity	
&	bitwise AND	left to right
^	bitwise XOR	left to right
|	bitwise OR	left to right
&&	logical AND	left to right
||	logical OR	left to right
?:	conditional	right to left
=	assignment	right to left
+=	addition assignment	
-=	subtraction assignment	
*=	multiplication assignment	
/=	division assignment	
%=	modulus assignment	
&=	bitwise AND assignment	
^=	bitwise exclusive OR assignment	
|=	bitwise inclusive OR assignment	
<<=	bitwise left shift assignment	
>>=	bitwise right shift with sign extension assignment	
>>>=	bitwise right shift with zero extension assignment	

Fig. C.1 | JavaScript/ECMAScript operator precedence and associativity. (Part 2 of 2.)

ASCII Character Set

In Fig. D.1, the digits at the left of the table are the left digits of the decimal equivalent (0–127) of the character code, and the digits at the top of the table are the right digits of the character code—e.g., the character code for “F” is 70, and the character code for “&” is 38.

Most users of this book are interested in the ASCII character set used to represent English characters on many computers. The ASCII character set is a subset of the Unicode character set used by scripting languages to represent characters from most of the world's languages. For more information on the Unicode character set, see Appendix F.

ASCII character set

	0	1	2	3	4	5	6	7	8	9
0	nul	soh	stx	etx	eot	enq	ack	bel	bs	ht
1	nl	vt	ff	cr	so	si	dle	dc1	dc2	dc3
2	dc4	nak	syn	etb	can	em	sub	esc	fs	gs
3	rs	us	sp	!	"	#	$	%	&	‘
4	(	)	*	+	,	-	.	/	0	1
5	2	3	4	5	6	7	8	9	:	;
6	<	=	>	?	@	A	B	C	D	E
7	F	G	H	I	J	K	L	M	N	O
8	P	Q	R	S	T	U	V	W	X	Y
9	Z	[	\	]	^	_	’	a	b	c
10	d	e	f	g	h	i	j	k	l	m
11	n	o	p	q	r	s	t	u	v	w
12	x	y	z	{	|	}	~	del		

Fig. D.1 | ASCII character set.

Here are only numbers ratified.
—William Shakespeare

Nature has some sort of arithmetic-geometrical coordinate system, because nature has all kinds of models. What we experience of nature is in models, and all of nature's models are so beautiful.

It struck me that nature's system must be a real beauty, because in chemistry we find that the associations are always in beautiful whole numbers—there are no fractions.
—Richard Buckminster Fuller

Number Systems

OBJECTIVES

In this chapter you will learn:

- To understand basic number systems concepts such as base, positional value and symbol value.
- How to work with numbers represented in the binary, octal and hexadecimal number systems
- To abbreviate binary numbers as octal numbers or hexadecimal numbers.
- To convert octal numbers and hexadecimal numbers to binary numbers.
- To convert back and forth between decimal numbers and their binary, octal and hexadecimal equivalents.
- To understand binary arithmetic, and how negative binary numbers are represented using two's complement notation.

Outline

E.1 Introduction

In this appendix, we introduce the key number systems that JavaScript programmers use, especially when they are working on software projects that require close interaction with "machine-level" hardware. Projects like this include operating systems, computer networking software, compilers, database systems and applications requiring high performance.

When we write an integer such as 227 or –63 in a JavaScript program, the number is assumed to be in the decimal (base 10) number system. The digits in the decimal number system are 0, 1, 2, 3, 4, 5, 6, 7, 8 and 9. The lowest digit is 0 and the highest digit is 9—one less than the base of 10. Internally, computers use the binary (base 2) number system. The binary number system has only two digits, namely 0 and 1. Its lowest digit is 0 and its highest digit is 1—one less than the base of 2.

As we will see, binary numbers tend to be much longer than their decimal equivalents. Programmers who work in assembly languages that enable them to reach down to the "machine level" find it cumbersome to work with binary numbers. So two other number systems—the octal number system (base 8) and the hexadecimal number system (base 16)—are popular, primarily because they can easily be converted to and from binary (as we will see later) and represent these numbers in fewer digits.

In the octal number system, the digits range from 0 to 7. Because both the binary number system and the octal number system have fewer digits than the decimal number system, their digits are the same as the corresponding digits in decimal.

The hexadecimal number system poses a problem because it requires sixteen digits—a lowest digit of 0 and a highest digit with a value equivalent to decimal 15 (one less than the base of 16). By convention, we use the letters A through F to represent the hexadecimal digits corresponding to decimal values 10 through 15. Thus, in hexadecimal we can have numbers like 876 consisting solely of decimal-like digits, numbers like 8A55F consisting of digits and letters, and numbers like FFE consisting solely of letters. Occasionally, a hexadecimal number spells a common word such as FACE or FEED—this can appear strange to programmers accustomed to working with decimal numbers.

Each of these number systems uses positional notation—each position in which a digit is written has a different positional value. For example, in the decimal number 937 (the 9, the 3, and the 7 are referred to as symbol values), we say that the 7 is written in the ones position, the 3 is written in the tens position, and the 9 is written in the hundreds position. Notice that each of these positions is a power of the base (base 10), and that these powers begin at 0 and increase by 1 as we move left in the number. Figures E.1–E.3 compare the binary, octal, decimal and hexadecimal number systems.

Binary digit	Octal digit	Decimal digit	Hexadecimal digit
0	0	0	0
1	1	1	1
	2	2	2
	3	3	3
	4	4	4
	5	5	5
	6	6	6
	7	7	7
		8	8
		9	9
			A (decimal value of 10)
			B (decimal value of 11)
			C (decimal value of 12)
			D (decimal value of 13)
			E (decimal value of 14)
			F (decimal value of 15)

Fig. E.1 | Digits of the binary, octal, decimal and hexadecimal number systems.

Attribute	Binary	Octal	Decimal	Hexadecimal
Base	2	8	10	16
Lowest digit	0	0	0	0
Highest digit	1	7	9	F

Fig. E.2 | Comparing the binary, octal, decimal and hexadecimal number systems.

Positional values in the decimal number system			
Decimal digit	9	3	7
Position name	Hundreds	Tens	Ones
Positional value	100	10	1
Positional value as a power of the base (10)	10^2	10^1	10^0

Fig. E.3 | Positional values in the decimal number system.

For longer decimal numbers, the next positions to the left would be the thousands position (10 to the 3rd power), the ten-thousands position (10 to the 4th power), the hundred-thousands position (10 to the 5th power), the millions position (10 to the 6th power), the ten-millions position (10 to the 7th power) and so on.

In the binary number 101, we say that the rightmost 1 is written in the ones position, the 0 is written in the twos position and the leftmost 1 is written in the fours position. Notice that each of these positions is a power of the base (base 2), and that these powers begin at 0 and increase by 1 as we move left in the number (Fig. E.4).

For longer binary numbers, the next positions to the left would be the eights position (2 to the 3rd power), the sixteens position (2 to the 4th power), the thirty-twos position (2 to the 5th power), the sixty-fours position (2 to the 6th power) and so on.

In the octal number 425, we say that the 5 is written in the ones position, the 2 is written in the eights position, and the 4 is written in the sixty-fours position. Notice that each of these positions is a power of the base (base 8), and that these powers begin at 0 and increase by 1 as we move left in the number (Fig. E.5).

For longer octal numbers, the next positions to the left would be the five-hundred-and-twelves position (8 to the 3rd power), the four-thousand-and-ninety-sixes position (8 to the 4th power), the thirty-two-thousand-seven-hundred-and-sixty eights position (8 to the 5th power) and so on.

Positional values in the binary number system			
Binary digit	1	0	1
Position name	Fours	Twos	Ones
Positional value	4	2	1
Positional value as a power of the base (2)	2^2	2^1	2^0

Fig. E.4 | Positional values in the binary number system.

Positional values in the octal number system			
Decimal digit	4	2	5
Position name	Sixty-fours	Eights	Ones
Positional value	64	8	1
Positional value as a power of the base (8)	8^2	8^1	8^0

Fig. E.5 | Positional values in the octal number system.

In the hexadecimal number 3DA, we say that the A is written in the ones position, the D is written in the sixteens position and the 3 is written in the two-hundred-and-fifty-sixes position. Notice that each of these positions is a power of the base (base 16), and that these powers begin at 0 and increase by 1 as we move left in the number (Fig. E.6).

For longer hexadecimal numbers, the next positions to the left would be the four-thousand-and-ninety-sixes position (16 to the 3rd power), the sixty-five-thousand-five-hundred-and-thirty-sixes position (16 to the 4th power) and so on.

Positional values in the hexadecimal number system			
Decimal digit	3	D	A
Position name	Two-hundred-and-fifty-sixes	Sixteens	Ones
Positional value	256	16	1
Positional value as a power of the base (16)	16^2	16^1	16^0

Fig. E.6 | Positional values in the hexadecimal number system.

E.2 Abbreviating Binary Numbers as Octal and Hexadecimal Numbers

The main use for octal and hexadecimal numbers in computing is for abbreviating lengthy binary representations. Figure E.7 highlights the fact that lengthy binary numbers can be expressed concisely in number systems with bases higher than two.

A particularly important relationship that both the octal number system and the hexadecimal number system have to the binary system is that the bases of octal and hexadecimal (8 and 16, respectively) are powers of the base of the binary number system (base 2). Consider the following 12-digit binary number and its octal and hexadecimal equivalents. See if you can determine how this relationship makes it convenient to abbreviate binary numbers in octal or hexadecimal. The answer follows the numbers.

Binary number	Octal equivalent	Hexadecimal equivalent
100011010001	4321	8D1

To see how the binary number converts easily to octal, simply break the 12-digit binary number into groups of three consecutive bits each (note that $8 = 2^3$), and write those groups over the corresponding digits of the octal number as follows:

```
100   011   010   001
4     3     2     1
```

Notice that the octal digit you have written under each group of three bits corresponds precisely to the octal equivalent of that 3-digit binary number as shown in Fig. E.7.

Decimal number	Binary representation	Octal representation	Hexadecimal representation
0	0	0	0
1	1	1	1
2	10	2	2
3	11	3	3
4	100	4	4
5	101	5	5
6	110	6	6
7	111	7	7
8	1000	10	8
9	1001	11	9
10	1010	12	A
11	1011	13	B
12	1100	14	C
13	1101	15	D
14	1110	16	E
15	1111	17	F
16	10000	20	10

Fig. E.7 | Decimal, binary, octal and hexadecimal equivalents.

The same kind of relationship may be observed in converting numbers from binary to hexadecimal. In particular, break the 12-digit binary number into groups of four consecutive bits each (note that $16 = 2^4$) and write those groups over the corresponding digits of the hexadecimal number as follows:

```
1000   1101   0001
8      D      1
```

Notice that the hexadecimal digit you wrote under each group of four bits corresponds precisely to the hexadecimal equivalent of that 4-digit binary number as shown in Fig. E.7.

E.3 Converting Octal and Hexadecimal Numbers to Binary Numbers

In the previous section, we saw how to convert binary numbers to their octal and hexadecimal equivalents by forming groups of binary digits and simply rewriting these groups as their equivalent octal digit values or hexadecimal digit values. This process may be used in reverse to produce the binary equivalent of a given octal or hexadecimal number.

For example, the octal number 653 is converted to binary simply by writing the 6 as its 3-digit binary equivalent 110, the 5 as its 3-digit binary equivalent 101 and the 3 as its 3-digit binary equivalent 011 to form the 9-digit binary number 110101011.

The hexadecimal number FAD5 is converted to binary simply by writing the F as its 4-digit binary equivalent 1111, the A as its 4-digit binary equivalent 1010, the D as its 4-

digit binary equivalent 1101 and the 5 as its 4-digit binary equivalent 0101 to form the 16-digit 1111101011010101.

E.4 Converting from Binary, Octal or Hexadecimal to Decimal

Because we are accustomed to working in decimal, it is often convenient to convert a binary, octal or hexadecimal number to decimal to get a sense of what the number is "really" worth. Our diagrams in Section E.1 express the positional values in decimal. To convert a number to decimal from another base, multiply the decimal equivalent of each digit by its positional value, and sum these products. For example, the binary number 110101 is converted to decimal 53 as shown in Fig. E.8.

To convert octal 7614 to decimal 3980, we use the same technique, this time using appropriate octal positional values as shown in Fig. E.9.

To convert hexadecimal AD3B to decimal 44347, we use the same technique, this time using appropriate hexadecimal positional values as shown in Fig. E.10.

Converting a binary number to decimal						
Positional values:	32	16	8	4	2	1
Symbol values:	1	1	0	1	0	1
Products:	1*32=32	1*16=16	0*8=0	1*4=4	0*2=0	1*1=1
Sum:	= 32 + 16 + 0 + 4 + 0 + 1 = 53					

Fig. E.8 | Converting a binary number to decimal.

Converting an octal number to decimal				
Positional values:	512	64	8	1
Symbol values:	7	6	1	4
Products	7*512=3584	6*64=384	1*8=8	4*1=4
Sum:	= 3584 + 384 + 8 + 4 = 3980			

Fig. E.9 | Converting an octal number to decimal.

Converting a hexadecimal number to decimal				
Positional values:	4096	256	16	1
Symbol values:	A	D	3	B
Products	A*4096=40960	D*256=3328	3*16=48	B*1=11
Sum:	= 40960 + 3328 + 48 + 11 = 44347			

Fig. E.10 | Converting a hexadecimal number to decimal.

E.5 Converting from Decimal to Binary, Octal or Hexadecimal

The conversions of the previous section follow naturally from the positional notation conventions. Converting from decimal to binary, octal or hexadecimal also follows these conventions.

Suppose we wish to convert decimal 57 to binary. We begin by writing the positional values of the columns right to left until we reach a column whose positional value is greater than the decimal number. We do not need that column, so we discard it. Thus, we first write:

```
Positional values:  64    32    16    8    4    2    1
```

Then we discard the column with positional value 64 leaving:

```
Positional values:        32    16    8    4    2    1
```

Next we work from the leftmost column to the right. We divide 32 into 57 and observe that there is one 32 in 57 with a remainder of 25, so we write 1 in the 32 column. We divide 16 into 25 and observe that there is one 16 in 25 with a remainder of 9 and write 1 in the 16 column. We divide 8 into 9 and observe that there is one 8 in 9 with a remainder of 1. The next two columns each produce quotients of zero when their positional values are divided into 1 so we write 0s in the 4 and 2 columns. Finally, 1 into 1 is 1 so we write 1 in the 1 column. This yields:

```
Positional values: 32  16   8   4   2   1
Symbol values:      1   1   1   0   0   1
```

and thus decimal 57 is equivalent to binary 111001.

To convert decimal 103 to octal, we begin by writing the positional values of the columns until we reach a column whose positional value is greater than the decimal number. We do not need that column, so we discard it. Thus, we first write:

```
Positional values:    512     64    8    1
```

Then we discard the column with positional value 512, yielding:

```
Positional values:            64    8    1
```

Next we work from the leftmost column to the right. We divide 64 into 103 and observe that there is one 64 in 103 with a remainder of 39, so we write 1 in the 64 column. We divide 8 into 39 and observe that there are four 8s in 39 with a remainder of 7 and write 4 in the 8 column. Finally, we divide 1 into 7 and observe that there are seven 1s in 7 with no remainder so we write 7 in the 1 column. This yields:

```
Positional values: 64    8    1
Symbol values:      1    4    7
```

and thus decimal 103 is equivalent to octal 147.

To convert decimal 375 to hexadecimal, we begin by writing the positional values of the columns until we reach a column whose positional value is greater than the decimal number. We do not need that column, so we discard it. Thus, we first write:

```
Positional values: 4096   256   16   1
```

Then we discard the column with positional value 4096, yielding:

```
Positional values:  256    16    1
```

Next we work from the leftmost column to the right. We divide 256 into 375 and observe that there is one 256 in 375 with a remainder of 119, so we write 1 in the 256 column. We divide 16 into 119 and observe that there are seven 16s in 119 with a remainder of 7 and write 7 in the 16 column. Finally, we divide 1 into 7 and observe that there are seven 1s in 7 with no remainder so we write 7 in the 1 column. This yields:

```
Positional values:  256    16    1
Symbol values:        1     7    7
```

and thus decimal 375 is equivalent to hexadecimal 177.

In general, to convert between two non-decimal bases, we can use the techniques shown above to convert from the original base to decimal, then from decimal to the desired base. When converting between octal and hexadecimal numbers, it is easiest to use binary as the intermediate base.

E.6 Negative Binary Numbers: Two's Complement Notation

The discussion in this appendix has been focussed on positive numbers. In this section, we explain how computers represent negative numbers using two's complement notation. First we explain how the two's complement of a binary number is formed, and then we show why it represents the negative value of the given binary number.

Consider a machine with 32-bit integers. Suppose

```
var value = 13;
```

The 32-bit representation of `value` is

```
00000000 00000000 00000000 00001101
```

To form the negative of `value` we first form its **one's complement** by applying JavaScript's bitwise complement operator (~):

```
onesComplementOfValue = ~value;
```

Internally, `~value` is now `value` with each of its bits reversed—ones become zeros and zeros become ones as follows:

```
value:
00000000 00000000 00000000 00001101

~value (i.e., value's ones complement):
11111111 11111111 11111111 11110010
```

To form the two's complement of `value` we simply add 1 to `value`'s one's complement. Thus

```
Two's complement of value:
11111111 11111111 11111111 11110011
```

Now if this is in fact equal to –13, we should be able to add it to binary 13 and obtain a result of 0. Let us try this:

```
 00000000 00000000 00000000 00001101
+11111111 11111111 11111111 11110011
------------------------------------
 00000000 00000000 00000000 00000000
```

The carry bit coming out of the leftmost column is ignored (because it is outside the range of our 32-bit integer), so we indeed get zero as a result. If we add the one's complement of a number to the original number, the result would be all 1s. The key to getting a result of all zeros is that the twos complement is 1 more than the one's complement. The addition of 1 causes each column to add to 0 with a carry of 1. The carry keeps moving leftward until it is discarded from the leftmost bit, and hence the resulting number is all zeros.

Computers actually perform a subtraction such as

```
x = a - value;
```

by adding the two's complement of `value` to `a` as follows:

```
x = a + (~value + 1);
```

Suppose `a` is 27 and `value` is 13 as before. If the two's complement of `value` is actually the negative of `value`, then adding the two's complement of `value` to `a` should produce the result 14. Let us try this:

```
a (i.e., 27)         00000000 00000000 00000000 00011011
+(~value + 1)       +11111111 11111111 11111111 11110011
                    ------------------------------------
                     00000000 00000000 00000000 00001110
```

which is indeed equal to 14.

Summary

Section E.1 Introduction

- When we write an integer such as 19 or 227 or –63 in a JavaScript program, the number is automatically assumed to be in the decimal (base 10) number system. The digits in the decimal number system are 0, 1, 2, 3, 4, 5, 6, 7, 8, and 9. The lowest digit is 0 and the highest digit is 9—one less than the base of 10.
- Internally, computers use the binary (base 2) number system. The binary number system has only two digits, namely 0 and 1. Its lowest digit is 0 and its highest digit is 1—one less than the base of 2.
- The octal number system (base 8) and the hexadecimal number system (base 16) are popular primarily because they can easily be converted to and from binary and represent these numbers in fewer digits.
- The digits of the octal number system range from 0 to 7.
- The hexadecimal number system poses a problem because it requires sixteen digits—a lowest digit of 0 and a highest digit with a value equivalent to decimal 15 (one less than the base of 16). By convention, we use the letters A through F to represent the hexadecimal digits corresponding to decimal values 10 through 15.
- Each number system uses positional notation—each position in which a digit is written has a different positional value.

Section E.2 Abbreviating Binary Numbers as Octal and Hexadecimal Numbers

- A particularly important relationship that both the octal number system and the hexadecimal number system have to the binary system is that the bases of octal and hexadecimal (8 and 16 respectively) are powers of the base of the binary number system (base 2).

Section E.3 Converting Octal and Hexadecimal Numbers to Binary Numbers

- To convert an octal number to a binary number, simply replace each octal digit with its three-digit binary equivalent.
- To convert a hexadecimal number to a binary number, simply replace each hexadecimal digit with its four-digit binary equivalent.

Section E.4 Converting from Binary, Octal or Hexadecimal to Decimal

- Because we are accustomed to working in decimal, it is convenient to convert a binary, octal or hexadecimal number to decimal to get a sense of the number's "real" worth.
- To convert a number to decimal from another base, multiply the decimal equivalent of each digit by its positional value, and sum these products.

Section E.5 Converting from Decimal to Binary, Octal or Hexadecimal

- To convert a number from decimal to another base, write out the base's positional values up to the largest one that is not greater than the number. Then, starting with the leftmost position, write down how many times the positional value can fit into the number, then repeat the process with the remainder of the number in the next position to the right until you're left with no remainder.

Section E.6 Negative Binary Numbers: Two's Complement Notation

- Computers represent negative numbers using two's complement notation.
- To form the negative of a value in binary, first form its one's complement by applying JavaScript's bitwise complement operator (~). This reverses the bits of the value. To form the two's complement of a value, simply add one to the value's one's complement.

Terminology

base
base 2 number system
base 8 number system
base 10 number system
base 16 number system
binary number system
bitwise complement operator (~)
conversions
decimal number system
digit
hexadecimal number system
negative value
octal number system
one's complement notation
positional notation
positional value
symbol value
two's complement notation

Self-Review Exercises

E.1 The bases of the decimal, binary, octal, and hexadecimal number systems are _______, _______, _______ and _______, respectively.

E.2 In general, the decimal, octal and hexadecimal representations of a given binary number contain (more/fewer) digits than the binary number contains.

E.3 (True/False) A popular reason for using the decimal number system is that it forms a convenient notation for abbreviating binary numbers simply by substituting one decimal digit per group of four binary bits.

E.4 The (octal / hexadecimal / decimal) representation of a large binary value is the most concise (of the given alternatives).

E.5 (True/False) The highest digit in any base is one more than the base.

E.6 (True/False) The lowest digit in any base is one less than the base.

E.7 The positional value of the rightmost digit of any number in either binary, octal, decimal or hexadecimal is always __________.

E.8 The positional value of the digit to the left of the rightmost digit of any number in binary, octal, decimal or hexadecimal is always equal to __________.

E.9 Fill in the missing values in this chart of positional values for the rightmost four positions in each of the indicated number systems:

decimal	1000	100	10	1
hexadecimal	...	256	...	...
binary	...	...	...	...
octal	512	...	8	...

E.10 Convert binary 110101011000 to octal and to hexadecimal.

E.11 Convert hexadecimal FACE to binary.

E.12 Convert octal 7316 to binary.

E.13 Convert hexadecimal 4FEC to octal. [*Hint:* First convert 4FEC to binary then convert that binary number to octal.]

E.14 Convert binary 1101110 to decimal.

E.15 Convert octal 317 to decimal.

E.16 Convert hexadecimal EFD4 to decimal.

E.17 Convert decimal 177 to binary, to octal and to hexadecimal.

E.18 Show the binary representation of decimal 417. Then show the one's complement of 417 and the two's complement of 417.

E.19 What is the result when a number and its two's complement are added to each other?

Answers to Self-Review Exercises

E.1 10, 2, 8, 16.

E.2 Fewer.

E.3 False.

E.4 Hexadecimal.

E.5 False. The highest digit in any base is one less than the base.

E.6 False. The lowest digit in any base is zero.

E.7 1 (the base raised to the zero power).

E.8 The base of the number system.

E.9 Fill in the missing values in this chart of positional values for the rightmost four positions in each of the indicated number systems:

decimal	1000	100	10	1
hexadecimal	4096	256	16	1
binary	8	4	2	1
octal	512	64	8	1

E.10 Octal 6530; Hexadecimal D58.

E.11 Binary 1111 1010 1100 1110.

E.12 Binary 111 011 001 110.

E.13 Binary 0 100 111 111 101 100; Octal 47754.

E.14 Decimal 2+4+8+32+64=110.

E.15 Decimal 7+1*8+3*64=7+8+192=207.

E.16 Decimal 4+13*16+15*256+14*4096=61396.

E.17 Decimal 177
to binary:

```
256 128 64 32 16 8 4 2 1
128 64 32 16 8 4 2 1
(1*128)+(0*64)+(1*32)+(1*16)+(0*8)+(0*4)+(0*2)+(1*1)
10110001
```

to octal:

```
512 64 8 1
64 8 1
(2*64)+(6*8)+(1*1)
261
```

to hexadecimal:

```
256 16 1
16 1
(11*16)+(1*1)
(B*16)+(1*1)
B1
```

E.18 Binary:

```
512 256 128 64 32 16 8 4 2 1
256 128 64 32 16 8 4 2 1
(1*256)+(1*128)+(0*64)+(1*32)+(0*16)+(0*8)+(0*4)+(0*2)+
(1*1)
110100001
```

One's complement: 001011110
Two's complement: 001011111
Check: Original binary number + its two's complement

```
 110100001
+001011111
----------
 000000000
```

E.19 Zero.

Exercises

E.20 Some people argue that many of our calculations would be easier in the base 12 number system because 12 is divisible by so many more numbers than 10 (for base 10). What is the lowest digit in base 12? What might the highest symbol for the digit in base 12 be? What are the positional values of the rightmost four positions of any number in the base 12 number system?

E.21 How is the highest symbol value in the number systems we discussed related to the positional value of the first digit to the left of the rightmost digit of any number in these number systems?

E.22 Complete the following chart of positional values for the rightmost four positions in each of the indicated number systems:

decimal	1000	100	10	1
base 6	...	...	6	...
base 13	...	169	...	...
base 3	27	...	...	...

E.23 Convert binary 100101111010 to octal and to hexadecimal.

E.24 Convert hexadecimal 3A7D to binary.

E.25 Convert hexadecimal 765F to octal. [*Hint:* First convert 765F to binary, then convert that binary number to octal.]

E.26 Convert binary 1011110 to decimal.

E.27 Convert octal 426 to decimal.

E.28 Convert hexadecimal FFFF to decimal.

E.29 Convert decimal 299 to binary, to octal, and to hexadecimal.

E.30 Show the binary representation of decimal 779. Then show the one's complement of 779, and the two's complement of 779.

E.31 What is the result when the two's complement of a number is added to itself?

E.32 Show the two's complement of integer value –1 on a machine with 32-bit integers.

F

Unicode®

OBJECTIVES

In this chapter you will learn:

- To become familiar with Unicode.
- The mission of the Unicode Consortium
- The design basis of Unicode.
- The three Unicode encoding forms: UTF-8, UTF-16 and UTF-32.
- Characters and glyphs.
- The advantages and disadvantages of using Unicode.
- A brief tour of the Unicode Consortium's website.

Outline

F.1 Introduction

The use of inconsistent character encodings (i.e., numeric values associated with characters) when developing global software products causes serious problems because computers process information using numbers. For instance, the character "a" is converted to a numeric value so that a computer can manipulate that piece of data. Many countries and corporations have developed their own encoding systems that are incompatible with the encoding systems of other countries and corporations. For example, the Microsoft Windows operating system assigns the value 0xC0 to the character "A with a grave accent" while the Apple Macintosh operating system assigns that same value to an upside-down question mark. This results in the misrepresentation and possible corruption of data because data is not processed as intended.

In the absence of a widely implemented universal character encoding standard, global software developers had to localize their products extensively before distribution. Localization includes the language translation and cultural adaptation of content. The process of localization usually includes significant modifications to the source code (such as the conversion of numeric values and the underlying assumptions made by programmers), which results in increased costs and delays releasing the software. For example, some English-speaking programmers might design global software products assuming that a single character can be represented by one byte. However, when those products are localized for Asian markets, the programmer's assumptions are no longer valid, thus the majority, if not the entirety, of the code needs to be rewritten. Localization is necessary with each release of a version. By the time a software product is localized for a particular market, a newer version, which needs to be localized as well, may be ready for distribution. As a result, it is cumbersome and costly to produce and distribute global software products in a market where there is no universal character encoding standard.

In response to this situation, the Unicode Standard, an encoding standard that facilitates the production and distribution of software, was created. The Unicode Standard outlines a specification to produce consistent encoding of the world's characters and symbols. Software products which handle text encoded in the Unicode Standard need to be localized, but the localization process is simpler and more efficient because the numeric values need not be converted and the assumptions made by programmers about the character encoding are universal. The Unicode Standard is maintained by a non-profit organization called the Unicode Consortium, whose members include Apple, IBM, Microsoft, Oracle, Sun Microsystems, Sybase and many others.

When the Consortium envisioned and developed the Unicode Standard, they wanted an encoding system that was **universal**, **efficient**, **uniform** and **unambiguous**. A universal encoding system encompasses all commonly used characters. An efficient encoding system allows text files to be parsed easily. A uniform encoding system assigns fixed values to all characters. An unambiguous encoding system represents a given character in a consistent manner. These four terms are referred to as the Unicode Standard **design basis**.

F.2 Unicode Transformation Formats

Although Unicode incorporates the limited ASCII **character set** (i.e., a collection of characters), it encompasses a more comprehensive character set. In ASCII each character is represented by a byte containing 0s and 1s. One byte is capable of storing the binary numbers from 0 to 255. Each character is assigned a number between 0 and 255, thus ASCII-based systems can support only 256 characters, a tiny fraction of the world's characters. Unicode extends the ASCII character set by encoding the vast majority of the world's characters. The Unicode Standard encodes all of those characters in a uniform numerical space from 0 to 10FFFF hexadecimal. An implementation will express these numbers in one of several transformation formats, choosing the one that best fits the particular application at hand.

Three such formats are in use, called **UTF-8**, **UTF-16** and **UTF-32**, depending on the size of the units—in **bits**—being used. UTF-8, a variable width encoding form, requires one to four bytes to express each Unicode character. UTF-8 data consists of 8-bit bytes (sequences of one, two, three or four bytes depending on the character being encoded) and is well suited for ASCII-based systems when there is a predominance of one-byte characters (ASCII represents characters as one-byte). Currently, UTF-8 is widely implemented in UNIX systems and in databases.

The variable width UTF-16 encoding form expresses Unicode characters in units of 16 bits (i.e., as two adjacent bytes, or a short integer in many machines). Most characters of Unicode are expressed in a single 16-bit unit. However, characters with values above FFFF hexadecimal are expressed with an ordered pair of 16-bit units called **surrogates**. Surrogates are 16-bit integers in the range D800 through DFFF, which are used solely for the purpose of "escaping" into higher numbered characters. Approximately one million characters can be expressed in this manner. Although a surrogate pair requires 32 bits to represent characters, it is space-efficient to use these 16-bit units. Surrogates are rare characters in current implementations. Many string-handling implementations are written in terms of UTF-16. [*Note:* Details and sample-code for UTF-16 handling are available on the Unicode Consortium website at `www.unicode.org`.]

Implementations that require significant use of rare characters or entire scripts encoded above FFFF hexadecimal, should use UTF-32, a 32-bit, fixed-width encoding form that usually requires twice as much memory as UTF-16 encoded characters. The major advantage of the fixed-width UTF-32 encoding form is that it uniformly expresses all characters, so it is easy to handle in arrays.

There are few guidelines that state when to use a particular encoding form. The best encoding form to use depends on computer systems and business protocols, not on the data itself. Typically, the UTF-8 encoding form should be used where computer systems and business protocols require data to be handled in 8-bit units, particularly in legacy systems being upgraded because it often simplifies changes to existing programs. For this reason, UTF-8 has become the encoding form of choice on the Internet. Likewise, UTF-

16 is the encoding form of choice on Microsoft Windows applications. UTF-32 is likely to become more widely used in the future as more characters are encoded with values above FFFF hexadecimal. Also, UTF-32 requires less sophisticated handling than UTF-16 in the presence of surrogate pairs. Figure F.1 shows the different ways in which the three encoding forms handle character encoding.

Character	UTF-8	UTF-16	UTF-32
LATIN CAPITAL LETTER A	0x41	0x0041	0x00000041
GREEK CAPITAL LETTER ALPHA	0xCD 0x91	0x0391	0x00000391
CJK UNIFIED IDEOGRAPH-4E95	0xE4 0xBA 0x95	0x4E95	0x00004E95
OLD ITALIC LETTER A	0xF0 0x80 0x83 0x80	0xDC00 0xDF00	0x00010300

Fig. F.1 | Correlation between the three encoding forms.

F.3 Characters and Glyphs

The Unicode Standard consists of **characters**, written components (i.e., alphabetic letters, numerals, punctuation marks, accent marks, etc.) that can be represented by numeric values. Examples of characters include: U+0041 LATIN CAPITAL LETTER A. In the first character representation, U+*yyyy* is a **code value**, in which U+ refers to Unicode code values, as opposed to other hexadecimal values. The *yyyy* represents a four-digit hexadecimal number of an encoded character. Code values are bit combinations that represent encoded characters. Characters are represented using **glyphs**, various shapes, fonts and sizes for displaying characters. There are no code values for glyphs in the Unicode Standard. Examples of glyphs are shown in Fig. F.2.

The Unicode Standard encompasses the alphabets, ideographs, syllabaries, punctuation marks, **diacritics**, mathematical operators, etc. that comprise the written languages and scripts of the world. A diacritic is a special mark added to a character to distinguish it from another letter or to indicate an accent (e.g., in Spanish, the tilde "~" above the character "n"). Currently, Unicode provides code values for 94,140 character representations, with more than 880,000 code values reserved for future expansion.

Fig. F.2 | Various glyphs of the character A.

F.4 Advantages/Disadvantages of Unicode

The Unicode Standard has several significant advantages that promote its use. One is the impact it has on the performance of the international economy. Unicode standardizes the characters for the world's writing systems to a uniform model that promotes transferring and sharing data. Programs developed using such a schema maintain their accuracy because each character has a single definition (i.e., *a* is always U+0061, *%* is always U+0025). This enables corporations to manage the high demands of international markets by processing different writing systems at the same time. Also, all characters can be managed in an identical manner, thus avoiding any confusion caused by different character code architectures. Moreover, managing data in a consistent manner eliminates data corruption, because data can be sorted, searched and manipulated using a consistent process.

Another advantage of the Unicode Standard is portability (i.e., the ability to execute software on disparate computers or with disparate operating systems). Most operating systems, databases, programming languages and web browsers currently support, or are planning to support, Unicode.

A disadvantage of the Unicode Standard is the amount of memory required by UTF-16 and UTF-32. ASCII character sets are 8 bits in length, so they require less storage than the default 16-bit Unicode character set. However, the double-byte character set (DBCS) and the multi-byte character set (MBCS) that encode Asian characters (ideographs) require two to four bytes, respectively. In such instances, the UTF-16 or the UTF-32 encoding forms may be used with little hindrance on memory and performance.

Another disadvantage of Unicode is that although it includes more characters than any other character set in common use, it does not yet encode all of the world's written characters. One additional disadvantage of the Unicode Standard is that UTF-8 and UTF-16 are variable width encoding forms, so characters occupy different amounts of memory.

F.5 Unicode Consortium's Website

If you would like to learn more about the Unicode Standard, visit `www.unicode.org`. This site provides a wealth of information about the Unicode Standard. Currently, the home page is organized into various sections: **New to Unicode?**, **General Information**, **The Consortium**, **The Unicode Standard**, **Key Specifications**, **Technical Publications**, **Work in Progress** and **For Members Only**.

The **New to Unicode?** section consists of four subsections: **What is Unicode?**, **How to Use this Site**, **FAQ**, and **Glossary of Unicode Terms**. The first subsection provides a technical introduction to Unicode by describing design principles, character interpretations and assignments, text processing and Unicode conformance. This subsection is recommended reading for anyone new to Unicode. Also, this subsection provides a list of related links that provide the reader with additional information about Unicode. The **How to Use this Site** subsection contains information about using and navigating the site as well hyperlinks to additional resources. The **FAQ** contains a list of frequently asked questions and their answers, and the **Glossary of Unicode Terms** contains definitions of several terms used in *The Unicode Standard, Version 5.0*.

The **General Information** section contains six subsections: **Where is my Character?**, **Display Problems?**, **Useful Resources**, **Unicode Enabled Products**, **Mail Lists** and **Subset of the Unicode website in French**. The main areas covered in this section include a link to the Unicode code charts (a complete listing of code values) assembled by the Unicode Consortium as well as a detailed outline on how to locate an encoded character in the code chart. Also, the section contains advice on how to configure different operating systems and web browsers so that the Unicode characters can be viewed properly. Moreover, from this section, the user can navigate to other sites that provide information on various topics such as, fonts, linguistics and other standards such as the *Chinese GB 18030 Encoding Standard*.

The Consortium section consists of eight subsections: **Who we are**, **Our Members**, **How to Join**, **Conferences**, **Job Postings**, **Press Info**, **Policies & Positions** and **Contact Us**. This section provides a list of the current Unicode Consortium members as well as information on how to become a member. Privileges for each member type—*full*, *institutional*, *supporting*, *associate*, *individual* and *liaison*—and the fees assessed to each member are listed here.

The Unicode Standard section consists of five subsections: **Start Here**, **Latest Version**, **Code Charts**, **Unicode Character Database**, and **Unihan Database**. This section describes the updates applied to the latest version of the Unicode Standard as well as categorizing all defined encoding. The user can learn how the latest version has been modified to encompass more features and capabilities. For instance, one enhancement of Version 5.0 is that it contains additional encoded characters.

The **Key Specifications** section consists of six subsections: **Unicode Collation (UCA)**, **Bidirectional Algorithm (Bidi)**, **Normalization (NFC, NFD, ...) Locale Data (CLDR)**, **Script Codes (ISO 15924)**, and **Security Considerations**. This section links to reports that provide the specifications for how to compare two Unicode strings, how to position characters that flow from right to left, and normalized forms of Unicode text, as well as links to download a data repository for software internationalization and localization, and a summary of security considerations.

The **Technical Publications** section consists of five subsections: **Technical Reports & Standards**, **Technical Notes**, **Online Data Tables**, **The Unicode Guide** and **Updates & Errata**. This section provides several technical documents that describe standards, contain conversion tables and list related standards organizations.

The **Work in Progress** section consists of eight subsections: **Calendar of Meetings**, **Proposals for Public Review**, **Unicode Techical Committee**, **UTC Meeting Minutes**, **Proposed Characters**, **Submitting Proposals**, **CLDR Technical Committee** and **UDHR in Unicode**. This section presents the user with a catalog of characters being considered for inclusion. If users determine that a character has been overlooked, then they can submit a written proposal for the inclusion of that character. The **Submitting Proposals** subsection contains strict guidelines that must be adhered to when submitting written proposals, and the **Unicode Technical Committee Minutes** subsection provides links to to all of the preliminary minutes of the meetings of the Unicode Technical Committee.

The **For Members** section consists of two subsections: **Member Resources** and **Working Documents**. These subsections are password protected—only consortium members can access these links.

F.6 Using Unicode

The primary use of the Unicode Standard is the Internet—it has become the default encoding system for XML and any language derived from XML such as XHTML. Figure F.3 marks up (as XML) the text "Welcome to Unicode!" in ten different languages: English, French, German, Japanese, Kannada (India), Portuguese, Russian, Spanish, Telugu (India) and Traditional Chinese. [*Note:* The Unicode Consortium's website contains a link to code charts that lists the 16-bit Unicode code values.]

Line 1 of the document specifies the XML declaration that contains the Unicode `encoding` used. A UTF-8 `encoding` indicates that the document conforms to the form of

Unicode that uses sequences of one to four bytes. [*Note:* This document uses XML **entity references** to represent characters. Also, UTF-16 and UTF-32 have yet to be supported by Internet Explorer 5.5 and Netscape Communicator 6.] Line 6 defines the root element, `UnicodeEncodings`, which contains all other elements (e.g., `WelcomeNote`) in the document. The first `WelcomeNote` element (lines 9–15) contains the entity references for the English text. The **Code Charts** page on the Unicode Consortium website contains the code values for the **Basic Latin** **block** (or category), which includes the English alphabet. The entity reference on line 10 equates to "Welcome" in basic text. When marking up Unicode characters in XML (or XHTML), the entity reference &#x*yyyy*; is used, where *yyyy* represents the hexadecimal Unicode encoding. For example, the letter "W" (in "Welcome") is denoted by `W`. Lines 11 and 13 contain the entity reference for the *space* character. The entity reference for the word "to" is on line 12 and the word "Unicode" is on line 14. "Unicode" is not encoded because it is a registered trademark and has no equivalent translation in most languages. Line 14 also contains the `!` notation for the exclamation mark (`!`).

```
1   <?xml version = "1.0" encoding = "UTF-8"?>
2
3   <!-- Fig. F.3: Unicode.xml -->
4   <!-- Unicode encoding for ten different languages -->
5
6   <UnicodeEncodings>
7
8      <!-- English -->
9      <WelcomeNote>
10        &#x0057;&#x0065;&#x006C;&#x0063;&#x006F;&#x006D;&#x0065;
11        &#x0020;
12        &#x0074;&#x006F;
13        &#x0020;
14        Unicode&#x0021;
15     </WelcomeNote>
16
17     <!-- French -->
18     <WelcomeNote>
19        &#x0042;&#x0069;&#x0065;&#x006E;&#x0076;&#x0065;&#x006E;&#x0075;
20        &#x0065;
21        &#x0020;
22        &#x0061;&#x0075;
23        &#x0020;
24        Unicode&#x0021;
25     </WelcomeNote>
26
27     <!-- German -->
28     <WelcomeNote>
29        &#x0057;&#x0069;&#x006C;&#x006B;&#x006F;&#x006D;&#x006D;&#x0065;
30        &#x006E;
31        &#x0020;
32        &#x007A;&#x0075;
33        &#x0020;
34        Unicode&#x0021;
35     </WelcomeNote>
```

Fig. F.3 | XML document using Unicode encoding (Part 1 of 3.).

```

   <!-- Japanese -->
   <WelcomeNote>
      Unicode
      &#x3078;&#x3087;&#x3045;&#x3053;&#x305D;&#x0021;
   </WelcomeNote>

   <!-- Kannada -->
   <WelcomeNote>
      &#x0CB8;&#x0CC1;&#x0CB8;&#x0CCD;&#x0CB5;&#x0C97;&#x0CA4;
      &#x0020;
      Unicode&#x0021;
   </WelcomeNote>

   <!-- Portuguese -->
   <WelcomeNote>
      &#x0053;&#x00E9;&#x006A;&#x0061;
      &#x0020;
      &#x0042;&#x0065;&#x006D;&#x0076;&#x0069;&#x006E;&#x0064;&#x006F;
      &#x0020;
      Unicode&#x0021;
   </WelcomeNote>

   <!-- Russian -->
   <WelcomeNote>
      &#x0414;&#x043E;&#x0431;&#x0440;&#x043E;
      &#x0020;
      &#x043F;&#x043E;&#x0436;&#x0430;&#x043B;&#x043E;&#x0432;&#x0430;
      &#x0442;&#x044A;
      &#x0020;
      &#x0432;
      &#x0020;
      Unicode&#x0021;
   </WelcomeNote>

   <!-- Spanish -->
   <WelcomeNote>
      &#x0042;&#x0069;&#x0065;&#x006E;&#x0076;&#x0065;&#x006E;&#x0069;
      &#x0064;&#x0061;
      &#x0020;
      &#x0061;
      &#x0020;
      Unicode&#x0021;
   </WelcomeNote>

   <!-- Telugu -->
   <WelcomeNote>
      &#x0C38;&#x0C41;&#x0C38;&#x0C3E;&#x0C35;&#x0C17;&#x0C24;&#x0C02;
      &#x0020;
      Unicode&#x0021;
   </WelcomeNote>

```

Fig. F.3 | XML document using Unicode encoding (Part 2 of 3.).

```
88    <!-- Traditional Chinese -->
89    <WelcomeNote>
90       &#x6B22;&#x8FCE;
91       &#x4F7F;&#x7528;
92       &#x0020;
93       Unicode&#x0021;
94    </WelcomeNote>
95
96 </UnicodeEncodings>
```

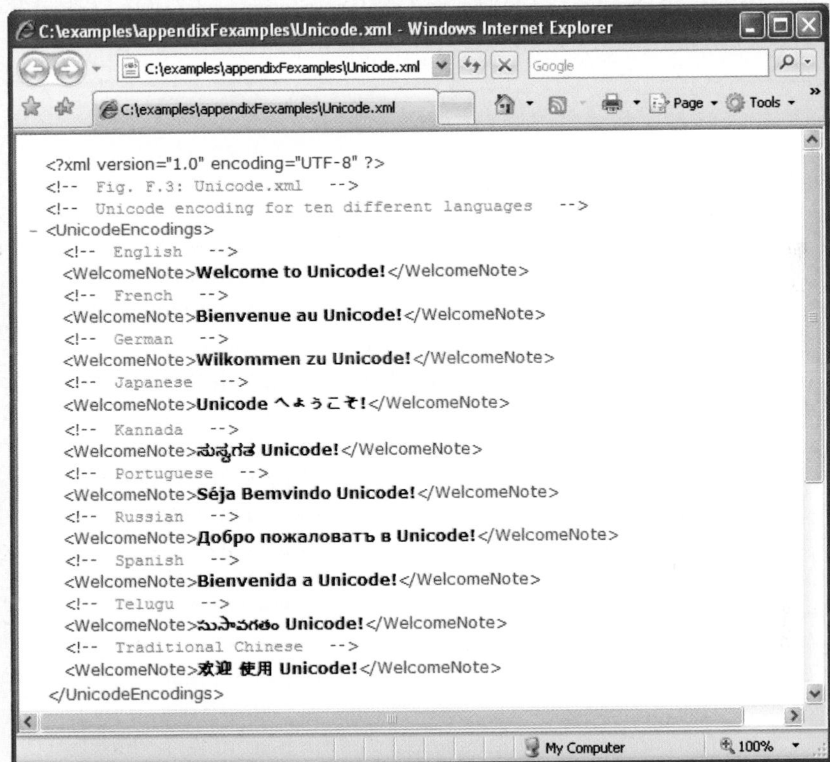

Fig. F.3 | XML document using Unicode encoding (Part 3 of 3.).

The remaining `WelcomeNote` elements (lines 18–94) contain the entity references for the other nine languages. The code values used for the French, German, Portuguese and Spanish text are located in the **Basic Latin** block, the code values used for the Traditional Chinese text are located in the **CJK Unified Ideographs** block, the code values used for the Russian text are located in the **Cyrillic** block, the code values used for the Japanese text are located in the **Hiragana** block, and the code values used for the Kannada and Telugu texts are located in their respective blocks.

To render Asian characters in a web browser, the proper language files must be installed. For Windows XP and Vista, directions for ensuring that you have the proper language support can be obtained from the Microsoft website at `www.microsoft.com`. For additional assistance, visit `www.unicode.org/help/display_problems.html`.

F.7 Character Ranges

The Unicode Standard assigns code values, which range from 0000 (**Basic Latin**) to E007F (**Tags**), to the written characters of the world. Currently, there are code values for 94,140 characters. To simplify the search for a character and its associated code value, the Unicode Standard generally groups code values by **script** and function (i.e., Latin characters are grouped in a block, mathematical operators are grouped in another block, etc.). As a rule, a script is a single writing system that is used for multiple languages (e.g., the Latin script is used for English, French, Spanish, etc.). The **Code Charts** page on the Unicode Consortium website lists all the defined blocks and their respective code values. Figure F.4 lists some blocks (scripts) from the website and their range of code values.

Script	Range of Code Values
Arabic	U+0600–U+06FF
Basic Latin	U+0000–U+007F
Bengali (India)	U+0980–U+09FF
Cherokee (Native America)	U+13A0–U+13FF
CJK Unified Ideographs (East Asia)	U+4E00–U+9FBF
Cyrillic (Russia and Eastern Europe)	U+0400–U+04FF
Ethiopic	U+1200–U+137F
Greek	U+0370–U+03FF
Hangul Jamo (Korea)	U+1100–U+11FF
Hebrew	U+0590–U+05FF
Hiragana (Japan)	U+3040–U+309F
Khmer (Cambodia)	U+1780–U+17FF
Lao (Laos)	U+0E80–U+0EFF
Mongolian	U+1800–U+18AF
Myanmar	U+1000–U+109F
Ogham (Ireland)	U+1680–U+169F
Runic (Germany and Scandinavia)	U+16A0–U+16FF
Sinhala (Sri Lanka)	U+0D80–U+0DFF
Telugu (India)	U+0C00–U+0C7F
Thai	U+0E00–U+0E7F

Fig. F.4 | Some character ranges.

Summary

Section F.1 Introduction

- Before Unicode, software developers were plagued by the use of inconsistent character encoding (i.e., numeric values for characters). Most countries and organizations had their own encoding systems, which were incompatible. A good example is the individual encoding systems on the Windows and Macintosh platforms.

- Computers process data by converting characters to numeric values. For instance, the character "a" is converted to a numeric value so that a computer can manipulate that piece of data.
- Without Unicode, localization of global software requires significant modifications to the source code, which results in increased cost and in delays releasing the product.
- Localization is necessary with each release of a version. By the time a software product is localized for a particular market, a newer version, which needs to be localized as well, is ready for distribution. As a result, it is cumbersome and costly to produce and distribute global software products in a market where there is no universal character encoding standard.
- The Unicode Consortium developed the Unicode Standard in response to the serious problems created by multiple character encodings and the use of those encodings.
- The Unicode Standard facilitates the production and distribution of localized software. It outlines a specification for the consistent encoding of the world's characters and symbols.
- Software products which handle text encoded in Unicode need to be localized, but the localization process is simpler and more efficient because the numeric values need not be converted.
- The Unicode Standard is designed to be universal, efficient, uniform and unambiguous.
- A universal encoding system encompasses all commonly used characters; an efficient encoding system parses text files easily; a uniform encoding system assigns fixed values to all characters; and an unambiguous encoding system represents the same character for any given value.

Section F.2 Unicode Transformation Formats

- Unicode extends the limited ASCII character set to include all the major characters of the world.
- Unicode makes use of three Unicode Transformation Formats (UTF): UTF-8, UTF-16 and UTF-32, each of which may be appropriate for use in different contexts.
- UTF-8 data consists of 8-bit bytes (sequences of one, two, three or four bytes depending on the character being encoded) and is well suited for ASCII-based systems when there is a predominance of one-byte characters (ASCII represents characters as one-byte).
- UTF-8 is a variable width encoding form that is more compact for text involving mostly Latin characters and ASCII punctuation.
- UTF-16 is the default encoding form of the Unicode Standard. It is a variable width encoding form that uses 16-bit code units instead of bytes. Most characters are represented by a single unit, but some characters require surrogate pairs.
- Surrogates are 16-bit integers in the range D800 through DFFF, which are used solely for the purpose of "escaping" into higher numbered characters.
- Without surrogate pairs, the UTF-16 encoding form can only encompass 65,000 characters, but with the surrogate pairs, this is expanded to include over a million characters.
- UTF-32 is a 32-bit encoding form. The major advantage of the fixed-width encoding form is that it uniformly expresses all characters, so that they are easy to handle in arrays and so forth.

Section F.3 Characters and Glyphs

- The Unicode Standard consists of characters. A character is any written component that can be represented by a numeric value.
- Characters are represented using glyphs, various shapes, fonts and sizes for displaying characters.
- Code values are bit combinations that represent encoded characters. The Unicode notation for a code value is U+*yyyy* in which U+ refers to the Unicode code values, as opposed to other hexadecimal values. The *yyyy* represents a four-digit hexadecimal number.
- Currently, the Unicode Standard provides code values for 94,140 character representations.

Section F.4 Advantages/Disadvantages of Unicode

- An advantage of the Unicode Standard is its impact on the overall performance of the international economy. Applications that conform to an encoding standard can be processed easily by computers anywhere.
- Another advantage of the Unicode Standard is its portability. Applications written in Unicode can be easily transferred to different operating systems, databases, web browsers, etc. Most companies currently support, or are planning to support, Unicode.

Section F.5 Unicode Consortium's Website

- To obtain more information about the Unicode Standard and the Unicode Consortium, visit `www.unicode.org`. It contains a link to the code charts, which contain the 16-bit code values for the currently encoded characters.

Section F.6 Using Unicode

- The Unicode Standard has become the default encoding system for XML and any language derived from XML, such as XHTML.
- When marking up XML-derived documents, the entity reference `&#x`*yyyy*`;` is used, where *yyyy* represents the hexadecimal code value.

Section F.7 Character Ranges

- To simplify the search for a character and its associated code value, the Unicode Standard generally groups code values by script and function. As a rule, a script is a single writing system that is used for multiple languages.
- The **Code Charts** page on the Unicode Consortium website lists all the defined blocks and their respective code values.

Terminology

`&#x`*yyyy*`;` notation
ASCII
block
character
character set
code value
diacritic
double-byte character set (DBCS)
efficient (Unicode design basis)
encode
entity reference
glyph
hexadecimal notation
localization
multi-byte character set (MBCS)
portability
script
surrogate
symbol
unambiguous (Unicode design basis)
Unicode Consortium
Unicode design basis
Unicode Standard
Unicode Transformation Format (UTF)
uniform (Unicode design basis)
universal (Unicode design basis)
UTF-8
UTF-16
UTF-32

Self-Review Exercises

F.1 Fill in the blanks in each of the following.

a) Global software developers had to _______ their products to a specific market before distribution.

b) The Unicode Standard is a(n) _______ standard that facilitates the uniform production and distribution of software products.

c) The design principles of Unicode are: ________, ________, ________ and ________.
d) Software that can execute on different operating systems is said to be ________.
e) Unicode incorporates the limited ________ character set .

F.2 State whether each of the following is *true* or *false*. If *false*, explain why.
a) The Unicode Standard encompasses all the world's characters.
b) A Unicode code value is represented as U+*yyyy*, where *yyyy* represents a number in binary notation.
c) A diacritic is a character with a special mark that emphasizes an accent.
d) Unicode is portable.
e) When designing XHTML and XML documents, the entity reference is denoted by `#U+yyyy`.

Answers to Self-Review Exercises

F.1 a) localize. b) encoding. c) universal, efficient, uniform, unambiguous. d) portable. e) ASCII.

F.2 a) False. It encompasses the majority of the world's characters. b) False. The *yyyy* represents a hexadecimal number. c) False. A diacritic is a special mark added to a character to distinguish it from another letter or to indicate an accent. d) True. e) False. The entity reference is denoted by `&#xyyyy`.

Exercises

F.3 Navigate to the Unicode Consortium website (`www.unicode.org`) and write the hexadecimal code values for the following characters. In which block are they located?
a) Latin letter "Z."
b) Latin letter "n" with the "tilde (~)."
c) Greek letter "delta."
d) Mathematical operator "less than or equal to."
e) Punctuation symbol "open quote (")."

F.4 Describe the Unicode Standard design basis.

F.5 Define the following terms:
a) code value.
b) surrogates.
c) Unicode Standard.
d) UTF-8.
e) UTF-16.
f) UTF-32.

F.6 Describe a scenario where it is optimal to store your data in UTF-16 format.

F.7 Using the Unicode Standard code values, create an XML document that prints your first and last name. The documents should contain the tags `<Uppercase>` and `<Lowercase>` that encode your name in uppercase and lowercase letters, respectively. If you know other writing systems, print your first and last name in those as well. Use a web browser to render the document.

F.8 Write a JavaScript program that prints "Welcome to Unicode!" in English, French, German, Japanese, Kannada, Portuguese, Russian, Spanish, Telugu and Traditional Chinese. Use the code values provided in Fig. F.3. In JavaScript, a code value is represented through an escape sequence `\u`*yyyy*, where *yyyy* is a four-digit hexadecimal number. Call `document.write` to render the text in a web browser.

Index

Symbols

Numerics

A

B

C

G

J

M

Q

R

S

T

U

V

Z

The DEITEL® Suite of Products...

HOW TO PROGRAM BOOKS

C++ How to Program Sixth Edition

BOOK / CD-ROM

©2008, 1400 pp., paper (0-13-615250-3)

The complete authoritative DEITEL® *LIVE-CODE* introduction to programming with C++! The Sixth Edition takes an easy-to-follow, carefully developed early classes and objects approach to programming in C++. The text includes comprehensive coverage of the fundamentals of object-oriented programming in C++. It includes an optional automated teller machine (ATM) case study that teaches the fundamentals of software engineering and object-oriented design with the UML 2.0 in Chapters 1-7, 9 and 13. Additional integrated case studies appear throughout the text, including the `Time` class (Chapter 9), the `Employee` class (Chapters 12 and 13) and the `GradeBook` class (Chapters 3-7). This new edition includes a chapter on C++ game programming with the OGRE and OpenAL libraries, and a chapter on the Boost C++ Libraries, Technical Report 1 (TR1) and the forthcoming C++0X standard.

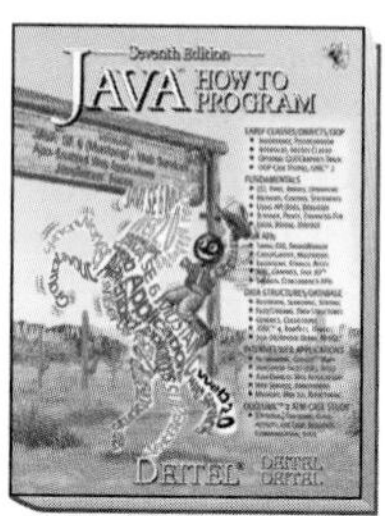

Java™ How to Program Seventh Edition

BOOK / CD-ROM

©2007, 1596 pp., paper (0-13-222220-5)

The complete authoritative DEITEL® *LIVE-CODE* introduction to programming with the new Java™ Standard Edition 6! *Java How to Program, Seventh Edition* is up-to-date with Java™ SE 6 and includes comprehensive coverage of the fundamentals of object-oriented programming in Java; an early classes and objects approach; and an optional automated teller machine (ATM) case study that teaches the fundamentals of software engineering and object oriented design with the UML 2.0 in Chapters 1-8 and 10. Additional integrated case studies appear throughout the text, including GUI and graphics (Chapters 3-12), the `Time` class (Chapter 8), the `Employee` class (Chapters 9 and 10) and the `GradeBook` class (Chapters 3-8). New topics covered include Java Desktop Integration Components, Ajax Web application development with JavaServer Faces, web services and more.

Small C++ How to Program Fifth Edition

BOOK / CD-ROM

©2005, 773 pp., paper (0-13-185758-4)

Based on chapters 1-13 (except the optional OOD/UML case study) and appendices of *C++ How to Program, Fifth Edition, Small C++* features a new early classes and objects approach and comprehensive coverage of the fundamentals of object-oriented programming in C++. Key topics include applications, variables, memory concepts, data types, control statements, functions, arrays, pointers and strings, inheritance and polymorphism.

Now available for both *C++ How to Program, 6/e* and *Small C++ How to Program, 5/e:* C++ Web-based *Cyber Classroom* included with the purchase of a new textbook. The *Cyber Classroom* includes a complete e-book, audio walkthroughs of the code examples, a Lab Manual and selected student solutions. See the *Cyber Classroom* section of this advertorial for more information.

Small Java™ How to Program Sixth Edition

BOOK / CD-ROM

©2005, 540 pp., paper (0-13-148660-8)

Based on chapters 1-10 of *Java™ How to Program, Sixth Edition* (not Seventh), *Small Java* is for use with J2SE™ 5.0, features an early classes and objects approach and comprehensive coverage of the fundamentals of object-oriented programming in Java. Key topics include applications, variables, data types, control statements, methods, arrays, object-based programming, inheritance and polymorphism.

Now available for both *Java How to Program, 7/e* and *Small Java How to Program, 6/e:* Java Web-based *Cyber Classroom* included with the purchase of a new textbook. The *Cyber Classroom* includes a complete e-book, audio walkthroughs of the code examples, a Lab Manual and selected student solutions. See the *Cyber Classroom* section of this advertorial for more information.

Sign up now for the FREE ***DEITEL® Buzz Online*** newsletter at:
`www.deitel.com/newsletter/subscribe.html`

Visual Basic® 2005 How to Program Third Edition

BOOK / CD-ROM

©2006, 1513 pp., paper (0-13-186900-0)

The complete authoritative DEITEL® *LIVE-CODE* introduction to Visual Basic programming. *Visual Basic® 2005 How to Program, Third Edition* is up-to-date with Microsoft's Visual Basic 2005. The text includes comprehensive coverage of the fundamentals of object-oriented programming in Visual Basic including a new early classes and objects approach and a new optional automated teller machine (ATM) case study that teaches the fundamentals of software engineering and object-oriented design with the UML 2.0 in Chapters 1, 3–9 and 11. Additional integrated case studies appear throughout the text, including the `Time` class (Chapter 9), the `Employee` class (Chapters 10 and 11) and the `Gradebook` class (Chapters 4–9). This book also includes discussions of more advanced topics such as XML, ASP.NET, ADO.NET and Web services. New Visual Basic 2005 topics covered include partial classes, generics, the My namespace and Visual Studio's updated debugger features.

Visual C++ .NET® How To Program

BOOK / CD-ROM

©2004, 1319 pp., paper (0-13-437377-4)

Written by the authors of the world's best-selling introductory/intermediate C and C++ textbooks, this comprehensive book thoroughly examines Visual C++® .NET 2003. *Visual C++® .NET How to Program* begins with a strong foundation in the introductory and intermediate programming principles students will need in industry, including fundamental topics such as arrays, functions and control statements. Readers learn the concepts of object-oriented programming, then the text explores such essential topics as networking, databases, XML and multimedia. Graphical user interfaces are also extensively covered, giving students the tools to build compelling and fully interactive programs using the "drag-and-drop" techniques provided by Visual Studio .NET 2003.

Visual C#® 2005 How to Program Second Edition

BOOK / CD-ROM

©2006, 1591 pp., paper (0-13-152523-9)

The complete authoritative DEITEL® *LIVE-CODE* introduction to C# programming. *Visual C#® 2005 How to Program, Second Edition* is up-to-date with Microsoft's Visual C# 2005. The text includes comprehensive coverage of the fundamentals of object-oriented programming in C#, including a new early classes and objects approach and a new optional automated teller machine (ATM) case study that teaches the fundamentals of software engineering and object-oriented design with the UML 2.0 in Chapters 1, 3–9 and 11. Additional integrated case studies appear throughout the text, including the `Time` class (Chapter 9), the `Employee` class (Chapters 10 and 11) and the `Gradebook` class (Chapters 4–9). This book also includes discussions of more advanced topics such as XML, ASP.NET, ADO.NET and Web services. New Visual C# 2005 topics covered include partial classes, generics, the My namespace, .NET remoting and Visual Studio's updated debugger features.

C How to Program Fifth Edition

BOOK / CD-ROM

©2007, 1130 pp., paper (0-13-240416-8)

C How to Program, Fifth Edition—the world's best-selling C text—is designed for introductory through intermediate courses and programming languages survey courses. This comprehensive text is aimed at readers with little or no programming experience through intermediate audiences. Highly practical in approach, it introduces fundamental notions of structured programming and software engineering and gets up to speed quickly. The Fifth Edition features new chapters on the C99 standard and an introduction to game programming with the Allegro C Library.

www.deitel.com www.prenhall.com/deitel

Check out our Resource Centers at www.deitel.com/resourcecenters.html

Advanced Java™ 2 Platform How to Program

BOOK / CD-ROM

©2002, 1811 pp., paper (0-13-089560-1)

Expanding on the world's best-selling Java textbook—*Java™ How to Program*—*Advanced Java™ 2 Platform How To Program* presents advanced Java topics for developing sophisticated, user-friendly GUIs; significant, scalable enterprise applications; wireless applications and distributed systems. Primarily based on Java 2 Enterprise Edition (J2EE) 1.2.1, this textbook integrates technologies such as XML, JavaBeans, security, JDBC™, JavaServer Pages (JSP™), servlets, Remote Method Invocation (RMI), Enterprise JavaBeans™ (EJB), design patterns, Swing, J2ME™, Java 2D and 3D, XML, design patterns, CORBA, Jini™, JavaSpaces™, Jiro™, Java Management Extensions (JMX) and Peer-to-Peer networking with an introduction to JXTA.

Internet & World Wide Web How to Program Fourth Edition

BOOK / CD-ROM

©2008, 1500 pp., paper (0-13-175242-1)

This book introduces students with little or no programming experience to the exciting world of Web-based applications. It has been substantially reworked to reflect today's Web 2.0 rich Internet application-development methodologies. The book teaches the skills and tools for creating dynamic Web applications. Topics include introductory programming principles, markup languages (XHTML/XML), scripting languages (JavaScript, PHP and Ruby/Ruby on Rails), Ajax, web services, web servers (IIS/Apache), relational databases (MySQL/SQL Server 2005 Express/Apache Derby/Java DB), ASP .NET 2.0 and JavaServer™ Faces (JSF). You'll build Ajax-enabled rich Internet applications (RIAs)—using Ajax frameworks, Adobe® Flex™ and Microsoft® Silverlight—with the look-and-feel of desktop applications. The Dive Into® Web 2.0 chapter exposes readers to many other topics associated with Web 2.0 applications and businesses. After mastering the material in this book, students will be well prepared to build real-world, industrial-strength, Web-based applications.

"As always, I am impressed with the Deitel organization and its books. I love teaching from them not only because the content is so sound, but also because of the competent and timely expertise and support provided."
— Robert A. Long, Indiana University

Python How to Program

BOOK / CD-ROM

©2002, 1376 pp., paper (0-13-092361-3)

This exciting textbook provides a comprehensive introduction to Python—a powerful object-oriented programming language with clear syntax and the ability to bring together various technologies quickly and easily. This book covers introductory programming techniques and more advanced topics such as graphical user interfaces, databases, wireless Internet programming, networking, security, process management, multithreading, XHTML, CSS, PSP and multimedia. Readers will learn principles that are applicable to both systems development and Web programming.

XML How to Program

BOOK / CD-ROM

©2001, 934 pp., paper (0-13-028417-3)

This book is a comprehensive guide to programming in XML. It teaches how to use XML to create customized tags and includes chapters that address markup languages for science and technology, multimedia, commerce and many other fields. Concise introductions to Java, JavaServer Pages, VBScript, Active Server Pages and Perl/CGI provide readers with the essentials of these programming languages and server-side development technologies to enable them to work effectively with XML. The book also covers topics such as XSL, DOM™, SAX, a real-world e-commerce case study and a complete chapter on Web accessibility that addresses Voice XML. Other topics covered include XHTML, CSS, DTD, schema, parsers, XPath, XLink, namespaces, XBase, XInclude, XPointer, XSLT, XSL Formatting Objects, JavaServer Pages, XForms, topic maps, X3D, MathML, OpenMath, CML, BML, CDF, RDF, SVG, Cocoon, WML, XBRL and BizTalk™ and SOAP™ Web resources.

Perl How to Program

©2001, 1057 pp., paper (0-13-028418-1)

This comprehensive guide to Perl programming emphasizes the use of the Common Gateway Interface (CGI) with Perl to create powerful, dynamic multi-tier Web-based client/server applications. The book begins with a clear and careful introduction to programming concepts at a level suitable for beginners, and proceeds through advanced topics such as references and complex data structures. Key Perl topics such as regular expressions and string manipulation are covered in detail. The authors address important and topical issues such as object-oriented programming, the Perl database interface (DBI), graphics and security. Also included is a treatment of XML, a bonus chapter introducing the Python programming language, supplemental material on career resources and a complete chapter on Web accessibility.

e-Business & e-Commerce How to Program

BOOK / CD-ROM

©2001, 1254 pp., paper (0-13-028419-X)

This book explores programming technologies for developing Web-based e-business and e-commerce solutions, and covers e-business and e-commerce models and business issues. Readers learn a full range of options, from "build-your-own" to turnkey solutions. The book examines scores of the top e-businesses (examples include Amazon, eBay, Priceline, Travelocity, etc.), explaining the technical details of building successful e-business and e-commerce sites and their underlying business premises. Learn how to implement the dominant e-commerce models—shopping carts, auctions, name-your-own-price, comparison shopping and bots/intelligent agents—by using markup languages (HTML, Dynamic HTML and XML), scripting languages (JavaScript, VBScript and Perl), server-side technologies (Active Server Pages and Perl/CGI) and database (SQL and ADO), security and online payment technologies.

"In my courses, I've read several Deitel books. I really enjoy reading and learning from them because they're written in a fashion that's very easy to follow. It's almost like someone is speaking to you, and you don't get lost in a lot of unnecessarily complicated paragraphs. There are sections that have some humor and the real world examples they use help you understand why some things that are good in theory don't work as well in practice. I think Paul and Harvey Deitel have done an amazing job researching the latest technologies and then presenting them in a very understandable way. Whenever I take a new class and find out that we are to use a Deitel book, I'm very happy about that because they're my favorite. I know I can rely upon the book to explain the subject clearly."

— Christine Spencer, Graduate of MIT

www.deitel.com www.prenhall.com/deitel

Check out our Resource Centers at www.deitel.com/resourcecenters.html

For ordering information,
visit us on the Web at www.prenhall.com.

INTERNATIONAL ORDERING INFORMATION

CANADA:
Pearson Education Canada
26 Prince Andrew Place
PO Box 580
Don Mills, Ontario M3C 2T8 Canada
Tel.: 416-925-2249; Fax: 416-925-0068
e-mail: phcinfo.pubcanada@pearsoned.com

EUROPE, MIDDLE EAST, AND AFRICA:
Pearson Education
Edinburgh Gate
Harlow, Essex CM20 2JE UK
Tel: 01279 623928; Fax: 01279 414130
e-mail: enq.orders@pearsoned-ema.com

BENELUX REGION:
Pearson Education
Concertgebouwplein 25
1071 LM Amsterdam
The Netherlands
Tel: 31 20 5755 800; Fax: 31 20 664 5334
e-mail: amsterdam@pearsoned-ema.com

ASIA:
Pearson Education Asia Pte. Ltd.
23/25 First Lok Yang Road
Jurong, 629733 Singapore
Tel: 65 476 4688; Fax: 65 378 0370

JAPAN:
Pearson Education Japan
Ogikubo TM Bldg. 6F. 5-26-13 Ogikubo
Suginami-ku, Tokyo 167-0051 Japan
Tel: 81 3 3365 9001; Fax: 81 3 3365 9009

INDIA:
Pearson Education
Indian Branch
482 FIE, Patparganj
Delhi – 110092 India
Tel: 91 11 2059850 & 2059851
Fax: 91 11 2059852

AUSTRALIA:
Pearson Education Australia
Unit 4, Level 2, 14 Aquatic Drive
Frenchs Forest, NSW 2086, Australia
Tel: 61 2 9454 2200; Fax: 61 2 9453 0089
e-mail: marketing@pearsoned.com.au

NEW ZEALAND/FIJI:
Pearson Education
46 Hillside Road
Auckland 10, New Zealand
Tel: 649 444 4968; Fax: 649 444 4957
E-mail: sales@pearsoned.co.nz

SOUTH AFRICA:
Maskew Miller Longman
Central Park Block H
16th Street Midrand 1685
South Africa
Tel: 27 21 686 6356; Fax: 27 21 686 4590

LATIN AMERICA:
Pearson Education Latin America
Attn: Tina Sheldon
1 Lake Street
Upper Saddle River, NJ 07458

MULTIMEDIA CYBER CLASSROOMS

Premium content available with *Java™ How to Program, Seventh Edition* and *C++ How to Program, Sixth Edition!*

Java How to Program, 7/e and *C++ How to Program, 6/e* are now available with 12-month access to the Web-based *Multimedia Cyber Classroom* for students who purchase new copies of these books! The *Cyber Classroom* is an interactive, multimedia, tutorial version of DEITEL textbooks. *Cyber Classrooms* are a great value, giving students additional hands-on experience and study aids.

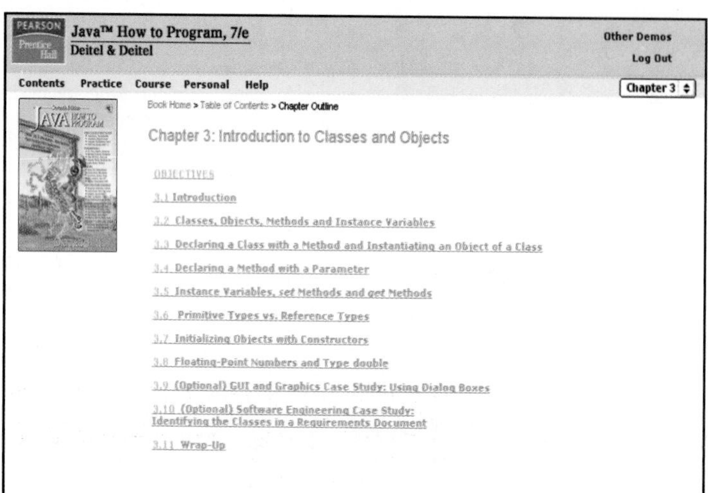

DEITEL® Multimedia Cyber Classrooms *feature an e-book with the complete text of their corresponding* How to Program *titles.*

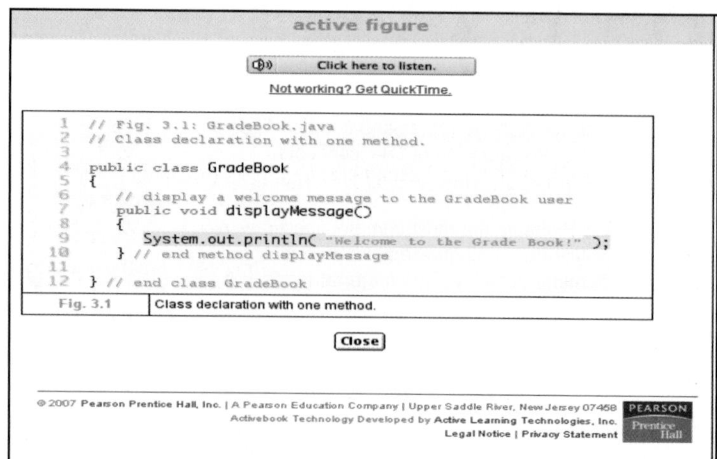

Unique audio "walkthroughs" of code examples reinforce key concepts.

Sign up now for the FREE ***DEITEL® Buzz Online*** newsletter at:
www.deitel.com/newsletter/subscribe.html